Research Methods for Business Students

Visit the *Research Methods for Business Students*, 6th edition, Companion Website at **www.pearsoned.co.uk/saunders** to find valuable **student** learning material including:

- Multiple-choice questions to test your learning
- Tutorials and datasets for Excel, NVivo and SPSS
- Updated research datasets to practise with
- Updated additional case studies with accompanying questions
- Smarter Online Searching Guide – how to make the most of the Internet in your research
- Online glossary

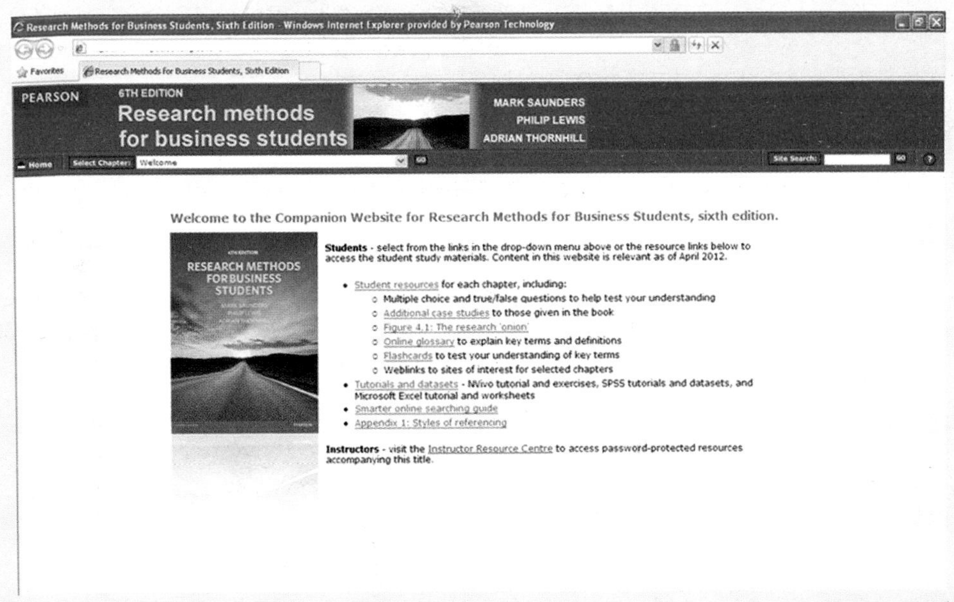

At Pearson, we take learning personally. Our courses and resources are available as books, online and via multi-lingual packages, helping people learn whatever, wherever and however they choose.

We work with leading authors to develop the strongest learning experiences, bringing cutting-edge thinking and best learning practice to a global market. We craft our print and digital resources to do more to help learners not only understand their content, but to see it in action and apply what they learn, whether studying or at work.

Pearson is the world's leading learning company. Our portfolio includes Penguin, Dorling Kindersley, the Financial Times and our educational business, Pearson International. We are also a leading provider of electronic learning programmes and of test development, processing and scoring services to educational institutions, corporations and professional bodies around the world.

Every day our work helps learning flourish, and wherever learning flourishes, so do people.

To learn more please visit us at: **www.pearson.com/uk**

Research Methods for Business Students

Sixth edition

Mark Saunders
Philip Lewis
Adrian Thornhill

PEARSON

Harlow, England • London • New York • Boston • San Francisco • Toronto • Sydney • Auckland • Singapore • Hong Kong
Tokyo • Seoul • Taipei • New Delhi • Cape Town • São Paulo • Mexico City • Madrid • Amsterdam • Munich • Paris • Milan

Pearson Education Limited
Edinburgh Gate
Harlow
Essex CM20 2JE
England
and Associated Companies throughout the world

Visit us on the World Wide Web at:

www.pearson.com/uk

First published under the Pitman Publishing imprint in 1997
Second edition 2000
Third edition 2003
Fourth edition 2007
Fifth edition 2009
Sixth edition 2012

ISBN: 978-0-273-75075-8

British Library Cataloguing-in-Publication Data
A catalogue record for this book is available from the British Library

Library of Congress Cataloging-in-Publication Data
Saunders, Mark, 1959–
Research methods for business students / Mark Saunders, Philip Lewis, Adrian Thornhill. — 6th ed.
p. cm.
Includes bibliographical references and index.
ISBN 978-0-273-75075-8
1. Business—Research. 2. Business—Research—Data processing. I. Lewis, Philip, 1945–
II. Thornhill, Adrian. III. Title.
HD30.4.S28 2012
650.072—dc23

2011050137

12 11 10 9 8 7 6 5 4 3 2
15 14 13

Typeset in 9.5/12.5 ITC Slimbach Std. by 73

Printed and bound by L.E.G.O. S.p.A., Italy

The publisher's policy is to use paper manufactured from sustainable forests

Brief contents

How to use this book xvii
Guided tour xxii
Preface xxv
Contributors xxvii
Publisher's acknowledgements xxix

1 Business and management research, reflective diaries and the purpose of this book 2
2 Formulating and clarifying the research topic 26
3 Critically reviewing the literature 70
4 Understanding research philosophies and approaches 126
5 Formulating the research design 158
6 Negotiating access and research ethics 208
7 Selecting samples 258
8 Using secondary data 304
9 Collecting primary data through observation 340
10 Collecting primary data using semi-structured, in-depth and group interviews 372
11 Collecting primary data using questionnaires 416
12 Analysing quantitative data 472
13 Analysing qualitative data 544
14 Writing and presenting your project report 594

Bibliography 632
Appendices 644
Glossary 665
Index 685

Contents

How to use this book xvii
Guided tour xxii
Preface xxv
Contributors xxvii
Publisher's acknowledgements xxix

1 Business and management research, reflective diaries and the purpose of this book 2

Mark Saunders Philip Lewis and Adrian Thornhill

Learning outcomes 2
1.1 Introduction 2
1.2 The nature of research 4
1.3 Business and management research 6
1.4 The research process 12
1.5 Keeping a reflective diary or research notebook 13
1.6 The purpose and structure of this book 15
1.7 Summary 19
Self-check questions 19
Review and discussion questions 19
Progressing your research project: starting your reflective diary or notebook 20
References 20
Further reading 21
Case 1: Reporting evidence from business and management research 22
Mark Learmonth
Self-check answers 24

2 Formulating and clarifying the research topic 26

Mark Saunders Philip Lewis and Adrian Thornhill

	Learning outcomes	26
2.1	Introduction	26
2.2	Attributes of a good research topic	28
2.3	Generating and refining research ideas	30
2.4	Turning research ideas into research projects	40
2.5	Writing your research proposal	50
2.6	Summary	59
	Self-check questions	60
	Review and discussion questions	60
	Progressing your research project: from research ideas to a research proposal	61
	References	61
	Further reading	63
	Case 2: Self-service technology: does co-production harm value co-creation? *Toni Hilton*	**63**
	Self-check answers	67

3 Critically reviewing the literature 70

Mark Saunders Philip Lewis and Adrian Thornhill

	Learning outcomes	70
3.1	Introduction	70
3.2	The critical review	73
3.3	Literature sources available	82
3.4	Planning your literature search strategy	90
3.5	Conducting your literature search	97
3.6	Obtaining and evaluating the literature	105
3.7	Recording the literature	108
3.8	Using Systematic Review	112
3.9	Plagiarism	113
3.10	Summary	115
	Self-check questions	115
	Review and discussion questions	117
	Progressing your research project: critically reviewing the literature	117
	References	117

	Further reading	119
	Case 3: Individual workplace performance: systematically reviewed	**119**
	Céline Rojon	
	Self-check answers	123
4	**Understanding research philosophies and approaches**	**126**
	Mark Saunders Philip Lewis and Adrian Thornhill	
	Learning outcomes	126
4.1	Introduction	126
4.2	Understanding your research philosophy	127
4.3	Research approaches	143
4.4	Summary	149
	Self-check questions	150
	Review and discussion questions	150
	Progressing your research project: diagnose your research philosophy	151
	References	152
	Further reading	153
	Case 4: Organisational learning in an English regional theatre	**153**
	Dawn Langley and Paul Tosey	
	Self-check answers	156
5	**Formulating the research design**	**158**
	Mark Saunders Philip Lewis and Adrian Thornhill	
	Learning outcomes	158
5.1	Introduction	158
5.2	Choice and coherence in research design	159
5.3	Choosing a quantitative, qualitative or multiple methods research design	161
5.4	Recognising the nature of your research design	170
5.5	Choosing a research strategy or strategies	173
5.6	Choosing a time horizon	190
5.7	Establishing the ethics of the research design	191

5.8 Establishing the quality of the research design 191
5.9 Taking into account your role as researcher 195
5.10 Summary 196
Self-check questions 197
Review and discussion questions 198
Progressing your research project: deciding on your research design 198
References 199
Further reading 201
Case 5: Sangita's career **202**
Mark Saunders Philip Lewis and Adrian Thornhill
Ongoing case: Researching emotional labour **204**
Part 1: Some reading and a possible research design? **204**
Karen Handley and Lindsay Williams
Self-check answers 206

6 Negotiating access and research ethics 208

Mark Saunders Philip Lewis and Adrian Thornhill

Learning outcomes 208
6.1 Introduction 208
6.2 Issues associated with gaining traditional access 210
6.3 Issues associated with Internet-mediated access 214
6.4 Strategies to gain access 216
6.5 Research ethics and why you should act ethically 226
6.6 Ethical issues at specific stages of the research process 236
6.7 An introduction to the principles of data protection and data management 247
6.8 Summary 249
Self-check questions 250
Review and discussion questions 250
Progressing your research project: negotiating access and addressing ethical issues 251
References 251
Further reading 253
Case 6: The impact of colour on children's brand choices **253**
Zoe Jowers
Self-check answers 255

7 Selecting samples 258

Mark Saunders Philip Lewis and Adrian Thornhill

	Learning outcomes	258
7.1	Introduction	258
7.2	Probability sampling	262
7.3	Non-probability sampling	281
7.4	Summary	291
	Self-check questions	292
	Review and discussion questions	294
	Progressing your research project: using sampling as part of your research	295
	References	295
	Further reading	296
	Case 7: Comparing UK and French perceptions and expectations of online supermarket shopping *Marie Ashwin and Alan Hirst*	**297**
	Self-check answers	300

8 Using secondary data 304

Mark Saunders Philip Lewis and Adrian Thornhill

	Learning outcomes	304
8.1	Introduction	304
8.2	Types of secondary data and uses in research	307
8.3	Locating secondary data	314
8.4	Advantages and disadvantages of secondary data	317
8.5	Evaluating secondary data sources	321
8.6	Summary	331
	Self-check questions	331
	Review and discussion questions	332
	Progressing your research project: assessing the suitability of secondary data for your research	332
	References	333
	Further reading	334
	Case 8: Trust repair in a major finance company *Graham Dietz*	**335**
	Ongoing case: Researching emotional labour	**337**

Part 2: Permission to collect data is unlikely, so what about secondary data? **337**
Karen Handley and Lindsay Williams
Self-check answers 338

9 Collecting primary data through observation 340
Mark Saunders Philip Lewis and Adrian Thornhill

Learning outcomes 340
9.1 Introduction 340
9.2 Participant observation 342
9.3 Structured observation 355
9.4 Summary 362
Self-check questions 363
Review and discussion questions 364
Progressing your research project: deciding on the appropriateness of observation 364
References 364
Further reading 365
Case 9: Strategy options in a mature market **366**
Hester Nienaber
Self-check answers 369

10 Collecting primary data using semi-structured, in-depth and group interviews 372
Mark Saunders Philip Lewis and Adrian Thornhill

Learning outcomes 372
10.1 Introduction 372
10.2 Types of interview and their link to the purpose of research and research strategy 374
10.3 When to use semi-structured and in-depth interviews 378
10.4 Data quality issues associated with semi-structured and in-depth interviews 380
10.5 Preparing for semi-structured or in-depth interviews 384
10.6 Conducting semi-structured or in-depth interviews 388

10.7 Managing logistical and resource issues 398
10.8 Group interviews and focus groups 400
10.9 Telephone, Internet- and intranet-mediated interviews 404
10.10 Summary 408
Self-check questions 408
Review and discussion questions 409
Progressing your research project: using semi-structured or in-depth interviews in your research 410
References 410
Further reading 411
Case 10: Organisations in a flash? 412
Samantha Warren
Self-check answers 414

11 Collecting primary data using questionnaires 416

Mark Saunders Philip Lewis and Adrian Thornhill

Learning outcomes 416
11.1 Introduction 416
11.2 An overview of questionnaires 419
11.3 Deciding what data need to be collected 423
11.4 Designing the questionnaire 428
11.5 Delivering and collecting the questionnaire 452
11.6 Summary 458
Self-check questions 459
Review and discussion questions 461
Progressing your research project: using questionnaires in your research 461
References 462
Further reading 463
Case 11: A quantitative evaluation of students' desire for self employment 464
Victoria Harte and Jim Stewart
Self-check answers 467

12 Analysing quantitative data 472

Mark Saunders, Philip Lewis, Adrian Thornhill and Catherine Wang

	Learning outcomes	472
12.1	Introduction	472
12.2	Preparing, inputting and checking data	474
12.3	Exploring and presenting data	487
12.4	Describing data using statistics	502
12.5	Examining relationships, differences and trends using statistics	508
12.6	Summary	529
	Self-check questions	530
	Review and discussion questions	532
	Progressing your research project: analysing your data quantitatively	532
	References	533
	Further reading	534
	Case 12: Food miles, carbon footprints and supply chains *David Oglethorpe*	**535**
	Self-check answers	541

13 Analysing qualitative data 544

Mark Saunders Philip Lewis and Adrian Thornhill

	Learning outcomes	544
13.1	Introduction	544
13.2	Qualitative data	546
13.3	Deciding on your approach to analysis	548
13.4	Preparing your data for analysis	550
13.5	Aids to help your analysis	553
13.6	Generic approaches to analysis	556
13.7	Specific approaches to analysis: inductive procedures	566
13.8	Specific approaches to analysis: deductive procedures	578
13.9	Using CAQDAS	581
13.10	Summary	583
	Self-check questions	584
	Review and discussion questions	584
	Progressing your research project: analysing your data qualitatively	585

References 585
Further reading 587
Case 13: Creating environmentally friendly office spaces 587
Catherine Cassell and Bill Lee
Ongoing case: Researching emotional labour 589
Part 3: A revised research question, a variety of secondary data, but what about the analysis? 589
Karen Handley and Lindsay Williams
Self-check answers 591

14 Writing and presenting your project report 594

Mark Saunders Philip Lewis and Adrian Thornhill

Learning outcomes 594
14.1 Introduction 594
14.2 Getting started with writing 596
14.3 Structuring your project report 600
14.4 Organising the project report's content 610
14.5 Developing an appropriate writing style 614
14.6 Meeting the assessment criteria 619
14.7 Oral presentation of the report 620
14.8 Summary 624
Self-check questions 624
Review and discussion questions 625
Progressing your research project: writing your project report 625
References 625
Further reading 626
Case 14: Clare's research project presentation 627
Lindy Blair
Self-check answers 630

Bibliography 632

Appendices

1	Systems of referencing	644
2	Calculating the minimum sample size	659
3	Random sampling numbers	661
4	Guidelines for non-discriminatory language	662

Glossary 665

Index 685

Supporting resources

Visit **www.pearsoned.co.uk/saunders** to find valuable online resources:

Companion Website for students

- Multiple-choice questions to test your learning
- Tutorials and datasets for Excel, NVivo and SPSS
- Updated research datasets to practise with
- Updated additional case studies with accompanying questions
- Smarter Online Searching Guide — how to make the most of the Internet in your research
- Online glossary

For instructors

- Complete, downloadable Instructor's Manual
- PowerPoint slides that can be downloaded and used for presentations

Also: The regularly maintained Companion Website provides the following features:

- Search tool to help locate specific items of content
- E-mail results and profile tools to send results of quizzes to instructors
- Online help and support to assist with website usage and troubleshooting

For more information please contact your local Pearson Education sales representative or visit www.pearsoned.co.uk/saunders

How to use this book

This book is written with a progressive logic, which means that terms and concepts are defined when they are first introduced. One implication of this is that it is sensible for you to start at the beginning and to work your way through the text, various boxes, self-check questions, review and discussion questions, case studies and case study questions. You can do this in a variety of ways depending on your reasons for using this book. However, this approach may not necessarily be suitable for your purposes, and you may wish to read the chapters in a different order or just dip into particular sections of the book. If this is true for you then you will probably need to use the glossary to check that you understand some of the terms and concepts used in the chapters you read. Suggestions for three of the more common ways in which you might wish to use this book are given below.

As part of a research methods course or for self-study for your research project

If you are using this book as part of a research methods course the order in which you read the chapters is likely to be prescribed by your tutors and dependent upon their perceptions of your needs. Conversely, if you are pursuing a course of self-study for your research project, dissertation or consultancy report, the order in which you read the chapters is your own choice. However, whichever of these you are, we would argue that the order in which you read the chapters is dependent upon your recent academic experience.

For many students, such as those taking an undergraduate degree in business or management, the research methods course and associated project, dissertation or consultancy report comes in either the second or the final year of study. In such situations it is probable that you will follow the chapter order quite closely (see Figure P.1). Groups of chapters within which we believe you can switch the order without affecting the logic of the flow too much are shown on the same level in this diagram and are:

- those chapters associated with data collection (Chapters 8, 9, 10 and 11);
- those associated with data analysis (Chapters 12 and 13).

Within the book we emphasise the importance of beginning to write early on in the research process as a way of clarifying your thoughts. In Chapter 1 we encourage you to keep a reflective diary or notebook throughout the research process so it is helpful to read this chapter early on. We recommend you also read the sections in Chapter 14 on writing prior to starting to draft your critical review of the literature (Chapter 3).

Alternatively, you may be returning to academic study after a gap of some years, to take a full-time or part-time course such as a Master of Business Administration, a Master of Arts or a Master of Science with a Business and Management focus. Many students in such situations need to refresh their study skills early in their programme, particularly those associated with critical reading of academic literature and academic writing. If you

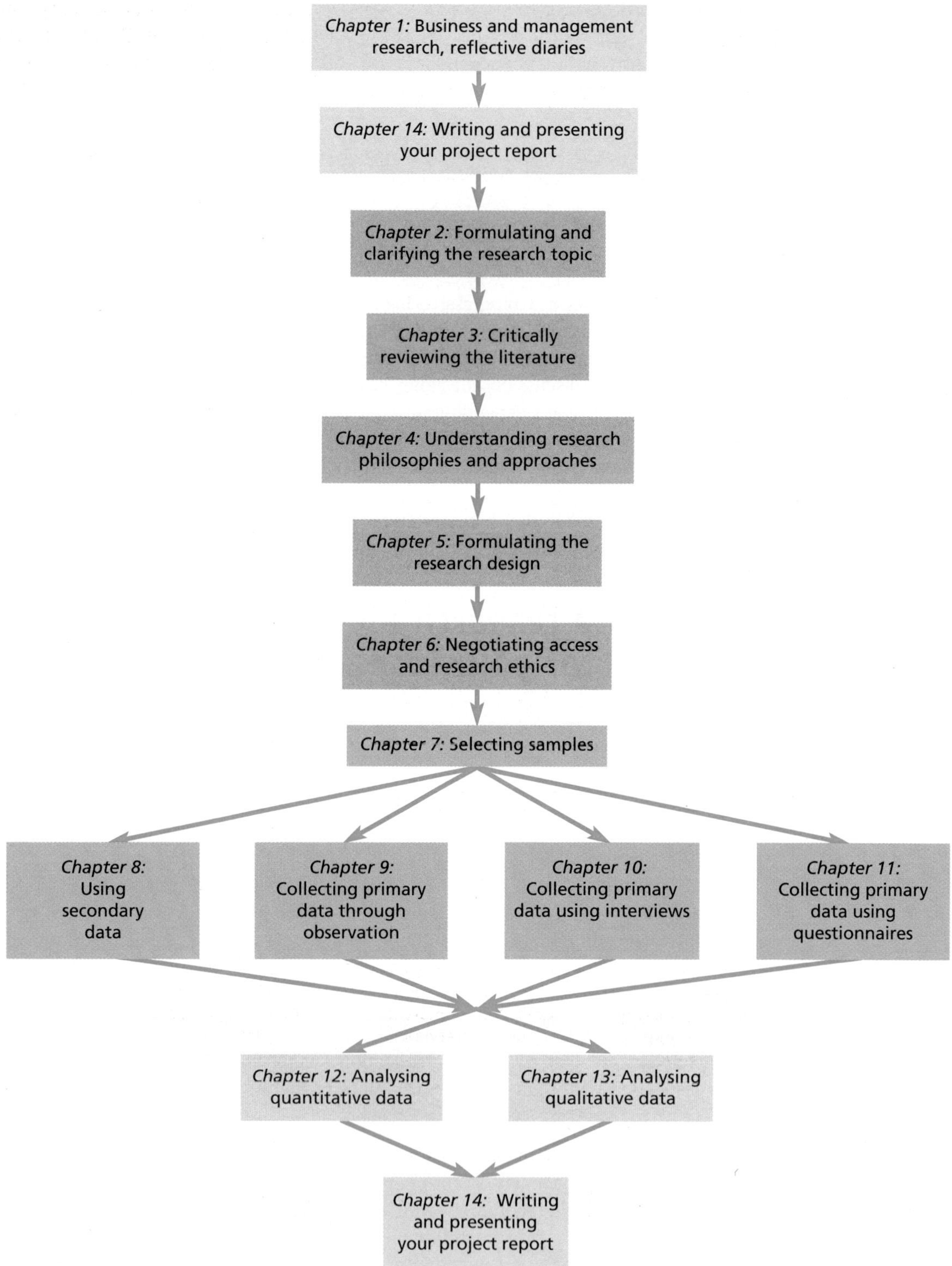

Figure P.1 Using this book in your second or final year of study

feel the need to do this, you may wish to start with those chapters that support you in developing and refining these skills (Chapters 3 and 14), followed by Chapter 8, which introduces you to the range of secondary data sources available that might be of use for other assignments (Figure P.2). Once again, groups of chapters within which we believe

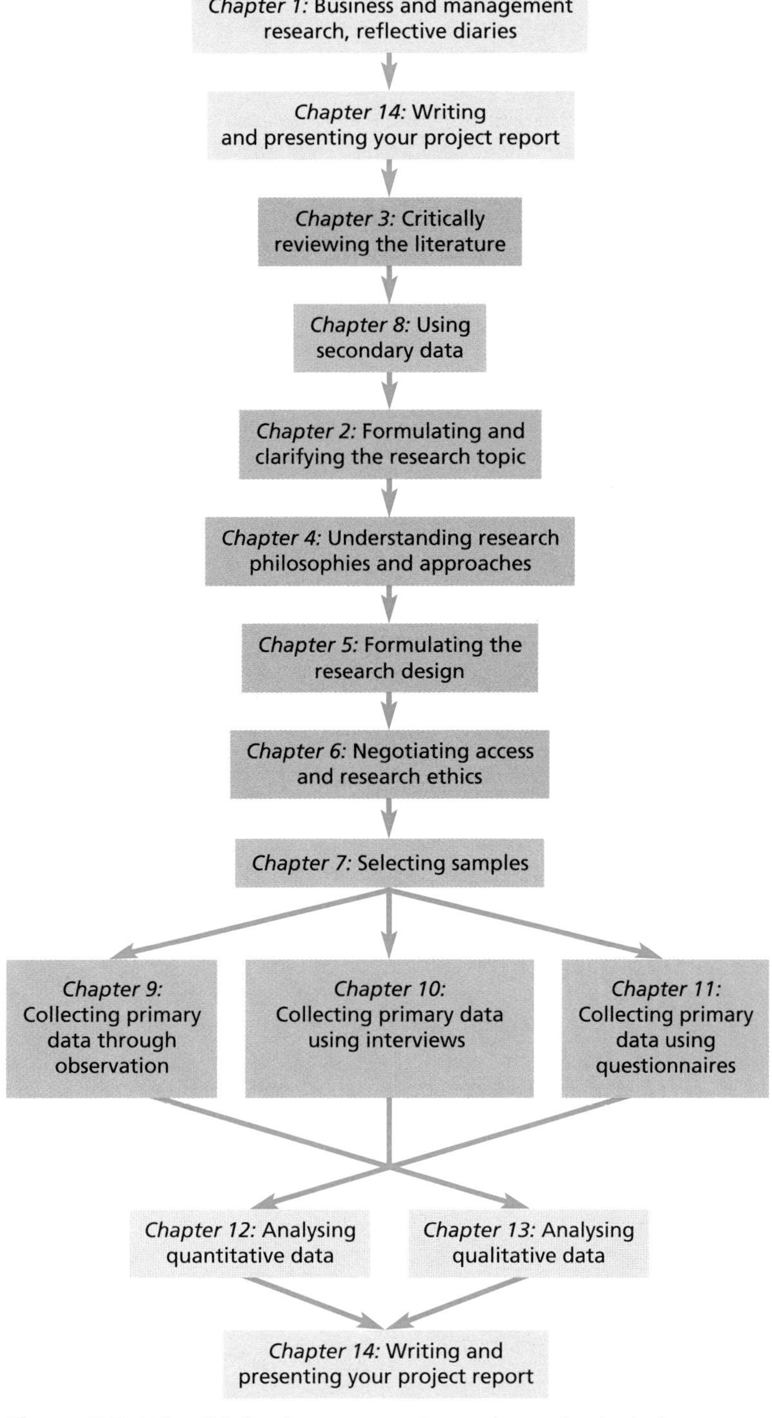

Figure P.2 Using this book as a new returner to academic study

you can switch the order without affecting the logic of the flow too much are shown on the same level in the diagram and are:

- those chapters associated with primary data collection (Chapters 9, 10 and 11);
- those associated with data analysis (Chapters 12 and 13).

In addition, we would recommend that you reread Chapter 14 prior to starting to write your project report, dissertation or consultancy report; or if you need to undertake a presentation.

Whichever order you choose to read the chapters in, we would recommend that you attempt all the self-check questions, review and discussion questions and those questions associated with the case studies. Your answers to the self-check questions can be self-assessed using the answers at the end of each chapter. However, we hope that you will actually have a go at each question prior to reading the answer! If you need further information on an idea or a technique, then first look at the references in the further reading section.

At the end of each chapter, the section headed 'Progressing your research project' lists a number of tasks. Such tasks might involve you in just planning a research project or, alternatively, designing and administering a questionnaire of your own. They all include making an entry in your reflective diary or notebook. When completed, these tasks will provide a useful aide-memoire for assessed work (including a reflective essay or learning log) and can be used as the basis for the first draft of your project report. It is worth pointing out here that many consultancy reports for organisations do not require you to include a review of the academic literature.

As a guide through the research process

If you are intending to use this book to guide you through the research process for a research project you are undertaking, such as your dissertation, we recommend that you read the entire book quickly before starting your research. In that way you will have a good overview of the entire process, including the range of techniques available, and will be better able to plan your work.

After you have read the book once, we suggest that you reread Section 1.5 on keeping a reflective diary or notebook and Sections 14.5–14.6 on writing first. Then work your way through the book again following the chapter order. This time you should attempt the self-check questions, review and discussion questions and those questions associated with each case study to ensure that you have understood the material contained in each chapter prior to applying it to your own research project. Your responses to self-check questions can be assessed using the answers at the end of each chapter.

If you are still unsure as to whether particular techniques, procedures or ideas are relevant, then pay special attention to the 'focus on student research', 'focus on management research' and 'focus on research in the news' boxes. 'Focus on student research' boxes are based on actual students' experiences and illustrate how an issue has been addressed or a technique or procedure used in a student's research project. 'Focus on management research' boxes discuss recent research articles in established refereed academic journals, allowing you to see how research is undertaken successfully. These articles are easily accessible via the main online business and management databases. 'Focus on research in the news' boxes provide topical news stories of how particular research techniques, procedures and ideas are used in the business world. You can also look in the 'further reading' for other examples of research where these have been used. If you need further information on an idea, technique or procedure then, again, start with the references in the further reading section.

Material in some of the chapters is likely to prove less relevant to some research topics than others. However, you should beware of choosing techniques because you are happy with them, if they are inappropriate. Completion of the tasks in the section headed 'Progressing your research project' at the end of Chapters 2–13 will enable you to generate all the material that you will need to include in your research project, dissertation or consultancy report. This will also help you to focus on the techniques and ideas that are most appropriate to your research. When you have completed these tasks for Chapter 14 you will have written your research project, dissertation or consultancy report.

As a reference source

It may be that you wish to use this book now or subsequently as a reference source. If this is the case, an extensive index will point you to the appropriate page or pages. Often you will find a 'checklist' box within these pages. 'Checklist' boxes are designed to provide you with further guidance on the particular topic. You will also find the contents pages and the glossary useful reference sources, the latter defining nearly 600 research terms. In addition, we have tried to help you to use the book in this way by including cross-references between sections in chapters as appropriate. Do follow these up as necessary. If you need further information on an idea or a technique then begin by consulting the references in the further reading section. Wherever possible we have tried to reference books that are in print and readily available in university libraries.

Guided tour

Chapter 5

Formulating the research design

Learning outcomes

By the end of this chapter you should be able to:

- understand the importance of your decisions when designing research and the need to achieve methodological coherence throughout your own research design;
- explain the differences between quantitative, qualitative and multiple methods research designs and choose between these to design your own research;
- explain the differences between exploratory, descriptive and explanatory research to understand the nature of your own research;
- identify the main research strategies and choose from amongst these to achieve coherence throughout your research design;
- consider the implications of the time frames required for different research designs when designing your own research;
- consider some of the main ethical issues implied by your research design;
- identify some of the issues that affect the quality of research and consider these when designing your own research;
- consider the constraints of your role as researcher when designing your own research.

5.1 Introduction

In Chapter 4 we introduced the research onion as a way of depicting the issues underlying your choice of data collection method or methods and peeled away the outer two layers – research philosophies and research approaches. In this chapter we uncover the next three layers: methodological choice, research strategy or strategies and choosing the time horizon for your research. As we saw in Chapter 4, the way you answer your research question will be influenced by your research philosophy and approach to theory. Your research philosophy and research approach, whether this is deliberate or by default, will subsequently influence your selections shown in the next three layers of the research onion. These three layers can be thought of as focusing on the process of research design, which is the way you turn your research question into a research project. The key to these selections will be to achieve coherence all the way through your research design.

158

5.2 Choice and coherence in research design

Your **research design** is the general plan of how you will go about answering your research question(s) (the importance of clearly defining the research question cannot be overemphasised). It will contain clear objectives derived from your research question(s), specify the sources from which you intend to collect data, how you propose to collect and analyse these, discuss ethical issues and the constraints you will inevitably encounter (e.g. access to data,

Ridenour and Newman (2008) stress the importance of coherence in research design and represent the research process as an interactive continuum. The cover shots of recent editions of this book have indicated that the research process is like a journey – a journey along a road with you as the driver of the vehicle (two wheels or four, whichever you prefer!). Like many such journeys, there is generally a choice of roads to travel along. When you are thinking about setting out on a new journey of some distance, you will probably find a road map and look at the options to get to your destination. A number of factors may influence your decision about which route to take, including speed, time, cost and your preference between taking the shortest route or staying on the motorway network and main roads. The route you plan is likely to be as coherent as you can work out from the map in front of you given your travel criteria. As you actually undertake your journey you will find yourself interacting with the reality of your planned route. Some parts of the journey will go according to plan; other parts may not and you may need to alter your route. You may change your route because a better option presents itself as you travel along. In many ways, designing research is like planning a journey. Formulating the most appropriate way to address your research question is similar to planning the route to your destination, your research objectives are a little like your planning criteria, the need for coherence is the same in each situation and the journey itself, like the research process, will necessarily prove to be an interactive experience.

Looking at a possible route from the top of St Paul's Cathedral, London!
Source: © Jan Thornhill 2011

159

Chapter openers provide a clear and concise introduction to the topics to be covered, together with a list of **Learning outcomes** that you should have achieved by the end of the chapter.

Chapter 11 Collecting primary data using questionnaires

Box 11.3 Focus on student research

Opinion, behaviour and attribute questions

Sally was asked by her employer to undertake an anonymous survey of financial advisers' ethical values. In particular, her employer was interested in the advice given to clients. After some deliberation she came up with three questions that addressed the issue of putting clients' interests before their own:

2 How do you feel about the following statement? 'Financial advisors should place their clients' interest before their own.'

	strongly agree	❑
	mildly agree	❑
(please tick the appropriate box)	neither agree or disagree	❑
	mildly disagree	❑
	strongly disagree	❑

3 In general, do financial advisors place their clients' interests before their own?

	always yes	❑
	usually yes	❑
(please tick the appropriate box)	sometimes yes	❑
	seldom yes	❑
	never yes	❑

4 How often do you place your clients' interests before your own?

	81–100% of my time	❑
	61–80% of my time	❑
(please tick the appropriate box)	41–60% of my time	❑
	21–40% of my time	❑
	0–20% of my time	❑

Sally's choice of question or questions to include in her questionnaire was dependent on whether she needed to collect data on financial advisors' opinions or behaviours. She designed question 2 to collect data on respondents' opinions about financial advisors placing their clients' interest before their own. This question asks respondents how they feel. In contrast, question 3 asks respondents whether financial advisors in general place their clients' interests before their own. It is therefore concerned with their individual beliefs regarding how financial advisors act. Question 4 focuses on how often the respondents actually place their clients' interests before their own. Unlike the previous questions, it is concerned with their actual behaviour rather than their opinion.

To answer her research questions and to meet her objectives Sally also needed to collect data to explore how ethical values differed between subgroupings of financial advisors. One theory she had was that ethical values were related to age. To test this she needed to collect data on the attribute age. After some deliberation she came up with question 5:

5 How old are you?

	Less than 30 years	❑
	30 to less than 40 years	❑
(please tick the appropriate box)	40 to less than 50 years	❑
	50 to less than 60 years	❑
	60 years or over	❑

426

Chapter 11 Collecting primary data using questionnaires

Case 11
A quantitative evaluation of students' desire for self-employment

Thomas is a part-time master's student who has been successfully self-employed for the last six years in the web technologies industry. As a consequence of his current employment status and area of expertise, he has chosen to research the impact of enterprise modules on undergraduate students at his university. He is interested in seeing whether there has been an increase over the past 10 years in students considering self-employment after their studies, particularly in the high-technology industries. Furthermore, as he is an expert in technology he wishes to put his skills to use in obtaining his data.

Source: Shutterstock.com/Eimantas Buzas

Thomas began his research project with a comprehensive search and review of the literature. He broke down his search into three main areas: research methods, enterprise education and technologically oriented students. Following his review of the literature on research methods, Thomas felt his world view was most closely related to an objectivist paradigm within a positivist philosophy. Thomas used his review of enterprise education literature to develop his research aims and form four hypotheses to test. These were:

H1: Students' desires to enter self-employment following graduation are greater compared with 10 years ago

H2: More female students are considering self-employment following graduation compared with 10 years ago

H3: More students wish become self-employed in the technology industry following graduation compared with 10 years ago

H4: Students who take at least one enterprise module are more likely to wish to enter self-employment following graduation than those who do not

Thomas decided that the way forward for his research was to use an online questionnaire delivered via an email with a weblink, as opposed to paper completion. His reasons for this were twofold:

- literature had highlighted that students were now more technologically orientated than in the past (Greenlaw and Welty-Brown 2009; Oblinger 2003) and so, he assumed, would be willing to complete his online questionnaire;

464

Practical illustrations bring to life some of the issues and challenges you will encounter during your course and beyond. These include short **Focus on student research** and longer **Cases**.

Generating and refining research ideas

Box 2.7 Focus on management research

The rare case of a reported preliminary inquiry

There are few reports in journal articles of the preliminary inquiries that researchers undertake. Generally the 'methods' section of a journal article only describes the research methodology and techniques used in the actual study. This is probably due to word limits and the presentation of research as an unproblematic process. However, in many studies there may not be a well-defined theoretical base from which to commence the research. There may instead be several possible theoretical strands that might be useful for the proposed study, which need to be explored first. Researchers may need to search for and familiarise themselves with theoretical strands that were previously unknown to them. These possibilities are likely to be the case where the proposed research seeks to explore a new area.

An excellent example describing the way a group of researchers undertook a preliminary inquiry is found in Elsbach et al. (2010). Their study, published in *Human Relations*, examines 'how passive "face time" (i.e. the amount of time one is passively observed without interaction) affects how one is perceived at work' (Elsbach et al. 2010: 735). For example, it is likely to be important for new employees to create an impression of being a diligent worker, without the observer knowing exactly what the person being observed is actually doing. Being seen is what Elsbach and colleagues call 'expected face time'. Positive impressions may be created by being seen in the right places (e.g. at one's desk, in meetings, taking part in events) rather than being based on actual performance. There is also 'extracurricular face time', where the impression an employee creates is also shaped by his or her involvement outside work.

Elsbach et al. identified this as a research idea that had not been investigated previously. They thought that this was surprising because of the increasing numbers of employees who spend much time working away from their work base, as well as the existence of anecdotal evidence indicating that remote workers may feel anxious about their lack of face time.

They conducted a preliminary inquiry that commenced with the collection of anecdotal evidence which suggested that passive face time was linked to the creation of positive impressions of employees in professional jobs. This anecdotal evidence was gleaned from newspaper articles, business magazines and books. In order to understand this relationship further they located two strands of theoretical literature which offered them 'clues' about 'how and why passive face time affects perceptions of employees who display it' (Elsbach et al. 2010: 739). These two strands of literature related to research on organisational citizenship behaviour and research on trait inferences. While these strands of literature had not been designed to focus on passive face time, they lent some support to the idea that being seen in the workplace was likely to lead observers to infer positive attributes about those being observed.

This preliminary inquiry led Elsbach and colleagues to identify that this was an area worth researching to close the gap in our understanding of this phenomenon. They devised a research question – 'How do observers perceive displayers of passive face time in professional work contexts?' – as a result of their preliminary inquiry, which led to a substantive research project composed of two stages. The first of these, called 'Study 1', involved an exploratory stage that used semi-structured interviews which were analysed inductively using the principles of Grounded Theory (see Chapters 4 and 5). The second of these, called 'Study 2', involved an experimental design (see Chapter 5) to test the 'proposed effects of passive face time' (Elsbach et al. 2010: 748).

This published study by Elsbach et al. is rare in terms of describing how their preliminary inquiry helped to establish the need for a substantive research study and the definition of that study. As such, this article may be seen as a model example of the process of a research project from conception to execution.

39

Chapter 4 Understanding research philosophies and approaches

Box 4.5 Focus on research in the news FT

Crop science: global food presents opportunity to reap a profit

The world already does a pretty miserable job of providing adequate food for vast swathes of its 7bn-strong population. With that number set to rise to close to 9bn by 2050, the issue of food security – ensuring people have access to an adequate supply of safe, nutritious and affordable food – is perhaps the most pressing facing crop scientists. 'Global food security ultimately depends on growing enough crops', says Professor Janet Allen, director of research at the Biotechnology and Biological Sciences Research Council (BBSRC), the UK's funding agency for biosciences. For crop scientists, that means selecting crop traits and production systems that can increase yields and reduce losses to pests and diseases.

But population growth is not the only challenge they face in their search for better, more hardy and more abundant crops. Climate change, too, is a big concern, with its potential to bring droughts and floods, new pests and diseases, and geopolitical conflict for resources and raw materials. Even if global food production can keep pace with population growth – and that is a big if – it is unlikely to be enough to accommodate serious weather-related disruptions in supply.

Addressing the productivity gap represents a significant business opportunity for the life sciences companies that lead the market in crop protection: Monsanto, Syngenta, Bayer, Dow and DuPont. These companies are already active and vocal participants in the global food security debate, but recognise that new business models are required to address new audiences in the developing world – and, perhaps, to overcome public resistance to big companies profiting from world hunger.

'Growers are our customers and our aim is to put them at the heart of our technology. That's just as true of smallholders in developing countries as it is of wealthier customers,' argues Kavita Prakash-Mani, head of food security agenda at Syngenta. An increasing share of Syngenta's profits, she says, comes from the developing world, particularly Asia-Pacific and Latin America, but also Africa. 'Farmers everywhere should be able to enjoy a choice of solutions to help them feed their families and communities, ones that are developed specifically to suit their growing conditions and their pockets.' Syngenta, for example, is working alongside its non-profit arm, the Syngenta Foundation for Sustainable Agriculture, and the International Maize and Wheat Improvement Centre (Cimmyt), another non-profit organisation based in Mexico, to develop drought-tolerant maize for smallholder farmers in Asia who lack access to irrigation. Drought-tolerant African maize developed by Cimmyt will be crossed with Syngenta varieties bred for Asia, applying Syngenta's genetic mapping technology to speed up the identification of the best varieties for the region in a project set to last five years.

But the application of GM technology to crops intended for the developing world – and, indeed, elsewhere – remains deeply controversial. For example, ActionAid, a development charity, fiercely opposes it, contending that market domination of GM technology by a handful of multinationals gives them unfair control over farmers' choices of seeds and the chemicals to go with them. 'It's a question of making poor people reliant on external inputs to succeed in feeding their families', argues Ruchi Tripathi, ActionAid's head of food rights. 'Once farmers are on a chemical treadmill, they find it hard to get off.' Instead, the charity favours an approach based on knowledge development, seed conservation and the establishment of gene banks for non-GM plant breeding, she says. The fact remains, however, that developing countries are planting GM crops at a more rapid rate than rich countries. According to the International Service for the Acquisition of Agri-biotech Applications, an industry body, Brazil has added some 10m hectares since 2008 and has overtaken Argentina as the second-biggest grower (after the US) of GM crops. India, meanwhile, increased land area given over to GM crops by 10 per cent in 2010. The most popular crop is soya, while the most common modification is tolerance to herbicides.

138

Explore recent articles and up-to-date issues in research practice through the **Focus on management research** and **Research in the news** features.

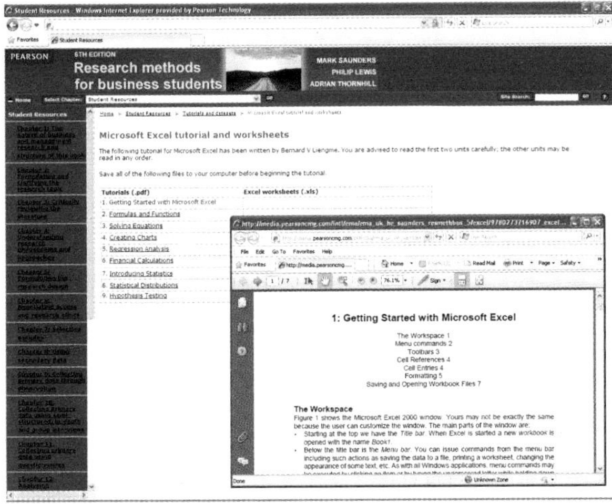

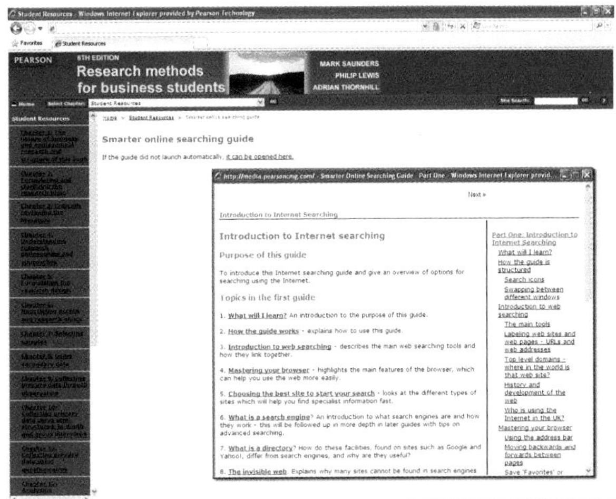

Save time and improve your research results by using the **Tutorials** on Excel, NVivo and SPSS, and the **Smarter Online Searching Guide**. Both of these valuable resources are accessible at **www.pearsoned.co.uk/saunders**.

Conducting semi-structured or in-depth interviews

Box 10.14 Checklist

To help you conduct your semi-structured or in-depth interview

Appearance at the interview

- ✔ How will your appearance at the interview affect the willingness of the interviewee to share data?

Opening the interview

- ✔ How will you commence the interview to gain the confidence of your interviewee?
- ✔ What will you tell your interviewee about yourself, the purpose of your research, its funding and your progress?
- ✔ What concerns, or need for clarification, may your interviewee have?
- ✔ How will you seek to overcome these concerns or provide this clarification?
- ✔ In particular, how do you intend to use the data to which you are given access, ensuring, where appropriate, its confidentiality and your interviewee's anonymity?
- ✔ What will you tell your interviewee about their right not to answer particular questions and to end the interview should they wish?
- ✔ How do you wish to conduct (or structure) the interview?

Asking questions and behaviour during the interview

- ✔ How will you use appropriate language and tone of voice, and avoid jargon when asking questions or discussing themes?
- ✔ How will you word open questions appropriately to obtain relevant data?
- ✔ How will you word probing questions to build on, clarify or explain your interviewee's responses?
- ✔ How will you avoid asking leading questions that may introduce forms of bias?
- ✔ Have you devised an appropriate order for your questions to avoid asking sensitive questions too early where this may introduce interviewee bias?
- ✔ How will you maintain a check on the interview themes that you intend to cover and to steer the discussion where appropriate to raise and explore these aspects?
- ✔ How will you avoid overzealously asking questions and pressing your interviewee for a response where it should be clear that they do not wish to provide one?
- ✔ How will you avoid projecting your own views or feelings through your actions or comments?
- ✔ How might you identify actions and comments made by your interviewee that indicate an aspect of the discussion that should be explored in order to reveal the reason for the response?
- ✔ How will you listen attentively and demonstrate this to your interviewee?
- ✔ How will you summarise and test your understanding of the data that are shared with you in order to ensure accuracy in your interpretation?
- ✔ Where appropriate, how will you deal with difficult participants whilst remaining polite?

Recording data during the interview

- ✔ How would you like to record the data that are revealed to you during the interview? Where this involves using an audio recorder, have you raised this as a request and provided a reason why it would help you to use this technique?
- ✔ How will you allow your interviewee to maintain control over the use of an audio recorder, where used, where they may wish to exercise this?
- ✔ Have you practised to ensure you can carry out a number of tasks at the same time, including listening, note taking and identifying where you need to probe further?

Closing the interview

- ✔ How do you plan to draw the interview to a close within the agreed time limit and to thank the interviewee for their time and the data they have shared with you?

397

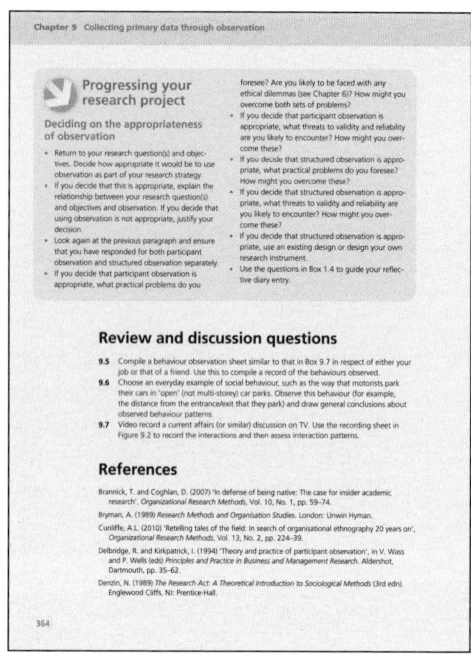

Chapter 9 Collecting primary data through observation

Progressing your research project

Deciding on the appropriateness of observation

- Return to your research question(s) and objectives. Decide how appropriate it would be to use observation as part of your research strategy.
- If you decide that this is appropriate, explain the relationship between your research question(s) and objectives and observation. If you decide that using observation is not appropriate, justify your decision.
- Look again at the previous paragraph and ensure that you have responded for both participant observation and structured observation separately.
- If you decide that participant observation is appropriate, what practical problems do you foresee? Are you likely to be faced with any ethical dilemmas (see Chapter 6)? How might you overcome both sets of problems?
- If you decide that participant observation is appropriate, what threats to validity and reliability are you likely to encounter? How might you overcome these?
- If you decide that structured observation is appropriate, what practical problems do you foresee? How might you overcome these?
- If you decide that structured observation is appropriate, what threats to validity and reliability are you likely to encounter? How might you overcome these?
- If you decide that structured observation is appropriate, use an existing design or design your own research instrument.
- Use the questions in Box 1.4 to guide your reflective diary entry.

Review and discussion questions

9.5 Compile a behaviour observation sheet similar to that in Box 9.7 in respect of either your job or that of a friend. Use this to compile a record of the behaviours observed.

9.6 Choose an everyday example of social behaviour, such as the way that motorists park their cars in 'open' (not multi-storey) car parks. Observe this behaviour (for example, the distance from the entrance/exit that they park) and draw general conclusions about observed behaviour patterns.

9.7 Video record a current affairs (or similar) discussion on TV. Use the recording sheet in Figure 9.2 to record the interactions and then assess interaction patterns.

References

Brannick, T. and Coghlan, D. (2007) 'In defense of being native: The case for insider academic research', *Organizational Research Methods*, Vol. 10, No. 1, pp. 59–74.

Bryman, A. (1989) *Research Methods and Organisation Studies*. London: Unwin Hyman.

Cunliffe, A.L. (2010) 'Retelling tales of the field: In search of organisational ethnography 20 years on', *Organizational Research Methods*, Vol. 13, No. 2, pp. 224–39.

Delbridge, R. and Kirkpatrick, I. (1994) 'Theory and practice of participant observation', in V. Wass and P. Wells (eds) *Principles and Practice in Business and Management Research*. Aldershot, Dartmouth, pp. 35–62.

Denzin, N. (1989) *The Research Act: A Theoretical Introduction to Sociological Methods* (3rd edn). Englewood Cliffs, NJ: Prentice-Hall.

364

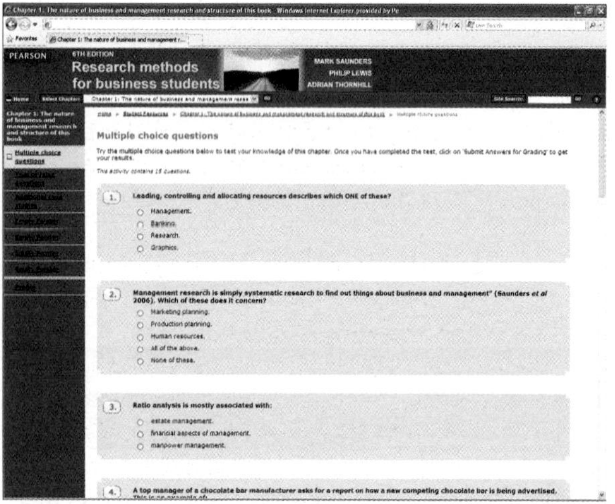

You will be given lots of opportunities to review your progress! Every chapter includes handy **Checklists**, tips on **Progressing your research project**, as well as Self-check questions (at the end of the chapter). There are additional interactive **Multiple choice questions** on the Companion Website.

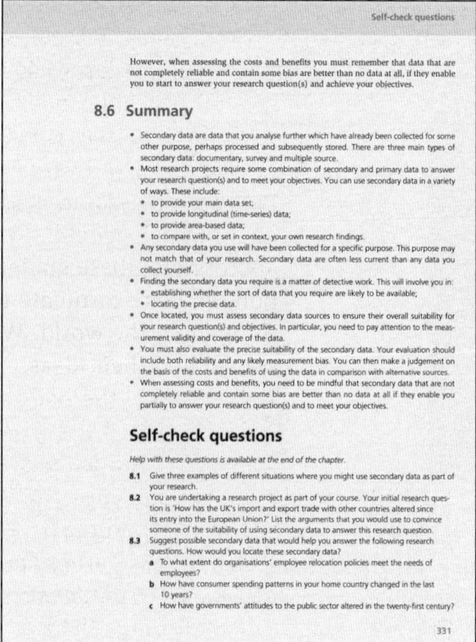

Self-check questions

However, when assessing the costs and benefits you must remember that data that are not completely reliable and contain some bias are better than no data at all, if they enable you to start to answer your research question(s) and achieve your objectives.

8.6 Summary

- Secondary data are data that you analyse further which have already been collected for some other purpose, perhaps processed and subsequently stored. There are three main types of secondary data: documentary, survey and multiple source.
- Most research projects require some combination of secondary and primary data to answer your research question(s) and to meet your objectives. You can use secondary data in a variety of ways. These include:
  - to provide your main data set;
  - to provide longitudinal (time-series) data;
  - to provide area-based data;
  - to compare with, or set in context, your own research findings.
- Any secondary data you use will have been collected for a specific purpose. This purpose may not match that of your research. Secondary data are often less current than any data you collect yourself.
- Finding the secondary data you require is a matter of detective work. This will involve you in:
  - establishing whether the sort of data that you require are likely to be available;
  - locating the precise data.
- Once located, you must assess secondary data sources to ensure their overall suitability for your research question(s) and objectives. In particular, you need to pay attention to the measurement validity and coverage of the data.
- You must also evaluate the precise suitability of the secondary data. Your evaluation should include both reliability and any likely measurement bias. You can then make a judgement on the basis of the costs and benefits of using the data in comparison with alternative sources.
- When assessing costs and benefits, you need to be mindful that secondary data that are not completely reliable and contain some bias are better than no data at all if they enable you partially to answer your research question(s) and to meet your objectives.

Self-check questions

Help with these questions is available at the end of the chapter.

8.1 Give three examples of different situations where you might use secondary data as part of your research.

8.2 You are undertaking a research project as part of your course. Your initial research question is 'How has the UK's import and export trade with other countries altered since its entry into the European Union?' List the arguments that you would use to convince someone of the suitability of using secondary data to answer this research question.

8.3 Suggest possible secondary data that would help you answer the following research questions. How would you locate these secondary data?

- **a** To what extent do organisations' employee relocation policies meet the needs of employees?
- **b** How have consumer spending patterns in your home country changed in the last 10 years?
- **c** How have governments' attitudes to the public sector altered in the twenty-first century?

331

A **Summary, Self-check questions** and **Review and discussion questions**, and recommended **Further reading** at the end of each chapter enable you to reflect upon key points and pursue topics in more depth.

Preface

In writing the sixth edition of *Research Methods for Business Students* we have responded to the many comments we have received regarding previous editions. In particular, this has led us to revise Chapter 1 to include a new section on keeping a reflective diary or notebook, Chapter 3 to include a section on systematic review of the literature, Chapter 4 to incorporate abductive approaches, Chapter 5 in relation particularly to research strategies and recent developments in multiple methods, Chapter 6 to include a section on Internet-mediated access, Chapter 8 to reflect the use of the Internet as a major source of secondary data, Chapter 13 including restructuring and incorporating analytical procedures that link to the qualitative strategies discussed in Chapter 5 and to further develop the Glossary which now includes nearly 600 research-related terms. The new case studies at the end of each chapter and, for this edition, the longer ongoing case study at the end of Chapters 5, 8 and 13 have been developed with colleagues, providing up-to-date scenarios through which to illustrate issues associated with undertaking research. In our revisions we have fully integrated the use of the Internet in business and management research. As part of this we have taken the opportunity to check and revise the tables of Internet addresses fully and to take account of the latest research associated with the use of email, Internet chat rooms in interviewing (Chapter 10) and Internet- and intranet-mediated questionnaires (Chapter 11).

As in previous editions, we have taken a predominantly non-software-specific approach in our discussion of methods. By doing this, we have been able to focus on the general principles needed to utilise a range of analysis software and the Internet effectively for research. However, recognising that many students have access to sophisticated data-analysis software and may need help in developing these skills, we continue to provide access to up-to-date 'teach yourself' guides to IBM SPSS Statistics™, Excel™, NVivo™ and Internet searching via the book's website (www.pearsoned.co.uk/saunders). Where appropriate, these guides are provided with data sets. In the preparation of the sixth edition we were fortunate to receive considerable feedback from colleagues in universities throughout the world. We are extremely grateful to all the reviewers who gave their time and shared their ideas.

Inevitably, the body of knowledge of research methods has developed further since 2009, and we have revised the chapters accordingly. Our experiences of teaching and supervising students and working through the methods in classes have suggested alternative approaches and the need to provide additional material. Consequently, we have taken the opportunity to update and refine existing worked examples and develop new ones where appropriate. However, the basic structure remains much the same as the previous five editions.

Other minor changes and updating have been made throughout. Needless to say, any errors of omission and commission are our responsibility.

As with previous editions, much of our updating has been guided by comments from students and colleagues, to whom we are most grateful. We should like to thank students from University of Surrey, Oxford Brookes University, Northumbria University and on the Research Methods Summer Schools for their comments on all of the chapters. Colleagues in both our own and other universities have continued to provide helpful comments and advice. We are particularly grateful to Hesham Al-Sabbahy (University of Surrey), Levent Altinay (Oxford Brookes University), Andrew Armitage (Anglia Ruskin University), Frank Bezzina (University of Malta), Murray Clark (Sheffield Hallam University), Yvonne Moogan (Kaplan Business School, London), Trevor Morrow (University of Ulster), Angela Roper (University of Surrey), Richard Slack (Northumbria University) and John Venable (Curtin University). We also thank Nigel Petts (Northumbria University) for his support regarding NVivo and, in particular, for developing the Guide to NVivo 9. Colleagues and friends again deserve thanks for their assistance in providing examples of research across the spectrum of business and management, co-authoring chapters, writing case studies and in reviewing parts of this book, Marie Ashwin (Ecole de Management de Normandie), Lindy Blair (University of Surrey), Catherine Cassell (University of Manchester), Graham Dietz (Durham University), Karen Handley (Oxford Brookes University), Victoria Harte (Leeds Metropolitan University), Toni Hilton (University of Westminster), Alan Hirst (London South Bank University), Zoe Jowers (Liverpool John Moores University), Dawn Langley (Alchemy Research and Consulting), Mark Learmonth (Durham University), Bill Lee (Keele University), Hester Nienaber (University of South Africa), David Oglethorpe (Northumbria University), Céline Rojon (University of Surrey), Jim Stewart (Leeds Metropolitan University), Paul Tosey (University of Surrey), Catherine Wang (Royal Holloway, University of London), Samantha Warren (Essex University) and Lindsay Williams (Oxford Brookes University).

The contributions of Lynette Bailey, Darren Bolton and Martin Jenkins to Chapters 3 and 8 and of Andrew Guppy to Chapter 12 in early editions of this book are gratefully acknowledged.

We would also like to thank all of the staff at Pearson Education (both past and present) who supported us through the process of writing the sixth edition. Our thanks go, in particular, to Rufus Curnow, our present commissioning editor, and Matthew Walker, our previous commissioning editor for their support and enthusiasm throughout the process. We would also like to express our thanks to Carole Drummond as desk editor and Joan Dale Lace as copy-editor.

Once again, our thanks are due to Jane, Jenny, Jan, Jemma, Ben, Andrew and Katie, who still allow us the time to absent ourselves to think and write.

MNKS
PL
AT
September 2011

Contributors

Mark N.K. Saunders, BA, MSc, PGCE, PhD, Chartered FCIPD, is Professor in Business Research Methods and Director of Postgraduate Research Programmes at the Surrey Business School, University of Surrey. For the past six years he has been a visiting professor at Newcastle Business School (Northumbria University) and also holds a visiting professorship at the University of Worcester. He was formerly Professor of Business Research Methods and Assistant Dean (Director of Research and Doctoral Programmes) at Oxford Brookes University Business School. He teaches research methods to master's and doctoral students as well as supervising master's dissertations and research degrees. Mark has published articles on research methods, trust and organisational justice perspectives on the management of change and service quality. He is co-author with Phil and Adrian of *Employee Relations: Understanding the Employment Relationship*, with Phil, Adrian, Mike Millmore and Trevor Morrow of *Strategic Human Resource Management* and with Adrian, Phil and Mike Millmore of *Managing Change: A Human Resource Strategy Approach*, all published by Financial Times Prentice Hall. He is lead editor of *Organizational Trust: A Cultural Perspective*. He has also written two books on business statistics, the most recent being *Statistics: What You Need to Know*, co-authored with Reva Berman-Brown. He continues to undertake consultancy in the public, private and not-for-profit sectors. Prior to becoming an academic, he had a variety of research jobs in the public sector.

Philip Lewis, BA, PhD, MSc, Chartered MCIPD, PGDipM, Cert Ed, began his career in HR as a training adviser with the Distributive Industry Training Board. He then taught HRM and research methods in three UK universities. He studied part-time for degrees with the Open University and the University of Bath, from which he gained an MSc in industrial relations and a PhD for his research on performance pay in retail financial services. He is co-author with Adrian and Mark of *Employee Relations: Understanding the Employment Relationship* and *Managing Change: A Human Resource Strategy Approach*, with Mark, Adrian, Mike Millmore and Trevor Morrow of *Strategic Human Resource Management* and with Adrian, Mark and Mike Millmore of *Managing Change: A Human Resource Strategy Approach*, all published by Financial Times Prentice Hall. He has undertaken consultancy in both public and private sectors.

Adrian Thornhill, BA, PhD, PGCE, Chartered FCIPD. Prior to his career as a university lecturer and Head of Department, he worked as an industrial relations researcher and in training and vocational education. He has also undertaken consultancy and training for a range of private and public sector organisations. He has taught a range of subjects including HRM, the management of change and research methods to undergraduate, postgraduate and professional students. He has experience of supervising undergraduate and postgraduate dissertations, professional management projects and research degrees. Adrian has published a number of articles principally associated with employee and justice perspectives related to managing change and the management of organisational downsizing and redundancy. He is co-author with Phil and Mark of *Employee Relations: Understanding the Employment Relationship*, with Phil, Mark, Mike Millmore and Trevor Morrow of *Strategic*

Human Resource Management and with Phil, Mark and Mike Millmore of *Managing Change: A Human Resource Strategy Approach*, all published by Financial Times Prentice Hall. He has also co-authored a book on downsizing and redundancy.

Professor Marie Ashwin is Professor of Marketing and Management at the Ecole de Management de Normandie, Caen, France.

Lindy Blair is Senior Professional Training Tutor in the Faculty of Business, Economics and Law at the University of Surrey.

Professor Catherine Cassell is Professor of Organisational Psychology and Head of the People, Management and Organisations Division at Manchester Business School, the University of Manchester.

Dr Graham Dietz is a Senior Lecturer in Human Resource Management at Durham Business School, Durham University.

Dr Karen Handley is a Reader in Organisational Behaviour at Oxford Brookes University Business School.

Victoria Harte is Research Officer in the Human Resource Development and Leadership Research Unit in the Faculty of Business and Law at Leeds Business School, Leeds Metropolitan University.

Dr Toni Hilton is Associate Dean Research and Knowledge Transfer at Westminster Business School, University of Westminster.

Dr Alan Hirst is a Senior Lecturer in International Marketing in the Faculty of Business at London South Bank University.

Zoe Jowers is a Senior Lecturer in Marketing at the Liverpool Business School, Liverpool John Moores University.

Dr Dawn Langley is an independent researcher and Director of Alchemy Research and Consulting.

Professor Mark Learmonth is Professor of Organization Studies at Durham Business School, Durham University.

Professor Bill Lee is Head of Accounting at Keele Management School, Keele University.

Dr Hester Nienaber is an Associate Professor in Strategy at the University of South Africa's Department of Business Management.

Professor David Oglethorpe is Professor of Logistics and Supply Chain Management at Newcastle Business School, Northumbria University.

Céline Rojon is a postgraduate research student in the University of Surrey Business School and the School of Psychology.

Professor Jim Stewart is Director of the Human Resource Development and Leadership Research Unit and of DBA Programmes in the Faculty of Business and Law at Leeds Business School, Leeds Metropolitan University.

Dr Paul Tosey is a Senior Lecturer in Management at the University of Surrey Business School.

Professor Catherine L. Wang is Professor of Entrepreneurship and Innovation at the School of Management, Royal Holloway, University of London.

Professor Samantha Warren is Professor of Management at Essex Business School, University of Essex.

Lindsay Williams is Principal Lecturer at Oxford Brookes University Business School.

Publisher's acknowledgements

Reviewers

We would like to express thanks to the reviewers who have been involved in the development of the fifth edition of this book. We are grateful for their insight and helpful recommendations.

We are grateful to the following for permission to reproduce copyright material:

Figures

Figure 3.6 from EndNote® Screenshot © copyright 2011 Thomson Reuters; Figure on p. 102 from EBSCOhost screenshot; Figure 4.2 adapted from *Sociological Paradigms and Organisational Analysis*, Heinemann (Burrell, G. and Morgan, G. 1982) © Ashgate Publishing Ltd; Figure on p. 259 from iTunes silhouette poster, with permission of Lee J. Razalan, Media Arts Lab, and Matthew Welch, © Apple Inc. Used with permission. All rights reserved. Apple® and the Apple logo are registered trademarks of Apple Inc.; Figure 9.2 from *Management and Organisational Behaviour*, 9th ed., Financial Times Prentice Hall (L.J. Mullins, 2010) p. 352; Figure on p. 417 from Morrison Bowmore Distillers Ltd; Figure 12.2 adapted from Eurostat (2011) Environment and Energy Statistics © European Communities, 1995–2010; Figure 12.3 from Eurostat (2011) Environmental and Energy Statistics © European Communities, 1995–2010; Figure 14.2 adapted from *Management Projects: Design, Research and Presentation*, Chapman and Hall (P. Raimond, 1993) p. 175, Reproduced with permission of Cengage Learning EMEA Ltd.

Screenshots

Screenshot on p. 102 from EBSCOhost screenshot; screenshot on p. 106 from UK 'Managers' conceptions of employee training and development' (abstract), *Journal of European Industrial Training*, 34 (7), pp. 609–30 (A. McDowall and M.K. Saunders, 2010), http://www.emeraldinsight.com/journals.htm?articleid=1881302&; screenshots on p. 292, p. 309 from email screenshot, Microsoft product screenshot(s) reprinted with permission from Microsoft Corporation; screenshots on pp. 292, 309 from email screenshot, Microsoft product screenshot(s) reprinted with permission from Microsoft Corporation; screenshot on p. 324 from Facebook – Morgan Motor Company (2011); screenshot on p. 327 from Eurostat screenshots (2011) © European Communities, 1995–2010; screenshot on p. 328 from Eurostat (2011) © European Communities, 1995–2010; screenshots on p. 440, p. 443 from question layout created by SurveyMonkey.com, LLC (2011) Palo Alto, California; author/owner: Ryan Finley, reproduced with permission, author/owner: Ryan Finley; screenshot on p. 465 from Hotmail screenshot, Microsoft product screenshot(s) reprinted with permission from Microsoft Corporation; screenshots on pp. 478, 481, 484, 496, 497, 511, 515, 516, 522, 526, 526, 531 from SPSS Screenshot, reprint courtesy of International Business Machines Corporation, © SPSS, Inc., an IBM Company. SPSS was acquired by IBM in October 2009; screenshots on pp. 480, 507, 518 from MS Excel screenshot, Microsoft product screenshot(s) reprinted with permission from Microsoft Corporation; screenshot on p. 566 from WordStat screenshot; screenshot on p. 570 from CAQDAS package NVivo™, reproduced by permission of Dr C. Silver and Mrs A. Lewins.

Slides

Slides on pp. 621, 622, from Powerpoint slide, Microsoft product screenshot(s) reprinted with permission from Microsoft Corporation

Tables

Table on p. 661 from *Quantatative Approaches in Business Studies*, 8th ed., Pearson Education Ltd (C. Morris 2012); Table 4.1 adapted from Language and the BSA: Sex and Gender, pp. 35–6, http://www.britsoc.co.uk/equality/; Table A4.1 adapted from 'Guidelines for the use of non-sexist language', *The Psychologist*, 1(2), pp. 53–4 (1988); Table A4.2 adapted from Language and the BSA: Non-disablist, pp. 35–6, http://www.britsoc.co.uk/equality; Table 1.1 adapted from Re-aligning the stakeholders in management research: Lessons from industrial, work and organizational psychology, *British Journal of Management*, 12 (special), pp. 41–8 (G.P. Hodgkinson, P. Herriot, and N. Anderson, 2001); Table 1.2 adapted from *Challenges and Controversies in Management Research*, Routledge (B. Lee and C. Cassell (eds), 2011) pp. 243–57; Table 7.3 from *Quantatative Approaches in Business Studies*, 8th ed., Pearson Education Ltd (C. Morris, 2012) App 3; Table 9.1 adapted from *Principles and Practice in Business and Management Research*, Dartmouth (V. Wass and P. Wells (eds), 1994) pp. 35–62, reproduced by permission of Professor Ian Kirkpatrick and Professor Rick Delbridge; Table 10.2 adapted from *Essential Guide to Qualitative Methods in Organizational Research*, Sage Publications (G. Symon and C. Cassell (eds) 2004) pp. 18–19; Table 11.3 adapted from *Management Research Methods*, Cambridge University Press (P. Tharenou, R. Donohue, and B. Cooper, 2007) © Phyllis Tharenou, Ross Donohue, Brian Cooper 2007, reproduced with permission of the authors and the publisher; Table 11.4 adapted from *International and Cross-cultural Management Research*, Sage Publications (J.C. Usunier, 1998) pp. 51–2; Table 13.4 after *Choosing a CAQDAS Package: A Working Paper*, 6th ed., CAQDAS Networking Project (A. Lewins and C. Silver, 2009), reproduced by permission of Dr C. Silver and Mrs A. Lewins; Table 14.1 adapted from *How to Write and Publish a Scientific Paper*, 5th ed., Oryx Press (R. Day, 1998) copyright © 1998 by Robert A. Day and Barbara Gastel. Reproduced with permission of ABC-CLIO, LLC.

Text

Box 3.17 from Plagiarism – University of Leeds Guide, http://www.lts.leeds.ac.uk/plagiarism/penalties.php?PHPSESSID=4582f0d02aa8927c671b34ddb8c4f459; newspaper headline on p. 435 from Masthead, *The Independent;* Newspaper headline on p. 435 from Masthead, *The Daily Telegraph*, copyright © Telegraph Media Group Limited; newspaper headline on p. 435 from Masthead, *The Guardian;* Newspaper headline on

p. 435 from Masthead, *Daily Star and Daily Express;* newspaper headline on p. 435 from Masthead, *Daily Mirror*, reproduced by permission of Mirrorpix; newspaper headline on p. 435 from Masthead, *Daily Mail;* newspaper headline on p. 435 from Masthead, *The Times and The Sun;* Box 14.6 from 'The management of post merger cultural integration: implications from the hotel industry', *Services Industries Journal*, 29(10), pp. 1359–75 (M.N.K. Saunders, L. Altinay and K. Riordan, 2009), http://www.tandfonline.com/doi/abs/10.1080/02642060903026213

The Financial Times

Box 1.1 from 'Business slow to assess Olympics impact,' *The Financial Times*, 25/06/2011 (V. Kortekaas), copyright © The Financial Times Ltd; Box 1.2 adapted from Academia strives for relevance, *The Financial Times*, 25/04/2011 (B. Schiller), copyright © The Financial Times Ltd.; Box 3.6 adapted from 'Lenders wary of high growth business', *Financial Times*, 18/03/2011 (B. Groom); Box 3.9 adapted from 'Fact and friction', *Financial Times*, 01/01/2011 (R. Waters); Box 4.3 from 'Suits and cars and rock 'n' roll', *Financial Times*, 20/05/2011 (R. Shrimsley); Box 4.5 from 'Crop science: global food presents opportunity to reap a profit', *Financial Times*, 27/06/2011 (J. Twentyman); Box 7.1 adapted from 'More top graduates chase fewer jobs', *Financial Times*, 18/01/2011 (C. Cook); Box 8.4 from 'University fees system mystery to many', *Financial Times*, 27/06/2011 (C. Cook); Box 8.8 from Builders reject ONS sector data, *Financial Times*, 08/05/2011 (E. Hammond and N. Cohen); Box 9.8 from' Online advertising: it is hard to tell if the ads work', *Financial Times*, 15/03/2011 (D. Gelles); Box 10.1 from 'Users' trust of online news rises', *Financial Times*, 18/05/2010 (T. Bradshaw); Newspaper headline on p. 435 from Masthead, *Financial Times;* Box 11.5 from 'Builders reject ONS sector data', *Financial Times*, 8/5/2011 (E. Hammond and N. Cohen); Box 12.9 from International Coffee Organisation, Associacao Brasileira de CO; Bloomberg; Box 12.21 from 'Resource stocks set to skew FTSE 100', *Financial Times*, 06/05/2011 (N. Hume); Box 13.1 from 'Rank sets out to discover home truths', *Financial Times*, 07/02/2011 (R. Jacons); Box 14.9 from 'Green jobs boost for the UK', *Financial Times*, 14/04/2011 (S. Kiran).

Picture credits

The publisher would like to thank the following for their kind permission to reproduce their photographs:

Alamy Images: David J. Green – Lifestyle 2 (p. 590), David R. Frazier Photolibrary Inc. (p. 337), Ellen Issacs (p. 27), Gavin Hellier (p. 335), Marshall Ikonography (p. 545), Jaak Nilson (p. 588), Justin Kase (p. 22); **Corbis:** ER productions/Blend Images (p. 627); **Getty Images:** (pp. 373, 412), Bloomberg (p. 297); **Mary Evans Picture Library:** (p. 209); **Pearson Education Ltd:** Rob Judges (p. 119); Pearson Education/Photodisc/Kevin Peterson (p. 202); **Press Association Images:** Jacquelyn Martin (p. 341); **Shutterstock.com:** Adrian Reynolds (p. 537), Dmitriy Shironosov (p. 254), Eimantas Buzas (p. 464), F. Chi (p. 153), max blain (p. 537), Paul Prescott (p. 473), Tom Hirtreiter (p. 204)

Every effort has been made to trace the copyright holders and we apologise in advance for any unintentional omissions. We would be pleased to insert the appropriate acknowledgement in any subsequent edition of this publication.

Chapter 1

Business and management research, reflective diaries and the purpose of this book

Learning outcomes

By the end of this chapter you should:

- be able to outline the purpose and distinct focus of business and management research;
- be able to place your research project on a basic–applied research continuum according to its purpose and context;
- understand the utility and importance of keeping a reflective diary;
- understand the stages you will need to complete (and revisit) as part of your research process;
- have an overview of this book's purpose, structure and features;
- be aware of some of the ways you can use this book.

1.1 Introduction

This book is designed to help you to undertake your research project, whether you are an undergraduate or postgraduate student of business and management or a manager. It provides a clear guide on how to undertake research as well as highlighting the realities of undertaking research, including the more common pitfalls. The book is written as an introductory text to provide you with a guide to the research process and with the necessary knowledge and skills to undertake a piece of research from thinking of a research topic to writing your project report. As such, you will find it useful as a manual or handbook on how to tackle your research project.

After reading the book you will have been introduced to and explored a range of approaches, strategies, techniques and procedures with which you could tackle your research project. Of equal importance, you will know that there is no one best way for undertaking all research. Rather you will be aware of the choice you will have to make and how this choice will impact upon what you can find out. This means you will be able to make an informed choice about the approaches, strategies, techniques and procedures that are most suitable to your own research project and be able to justify this choice. In reading the book you will have been introduced to the wealth of data that can be obtained via the Internet, techniques for collecting your own data and procedures for analysing different types of data, have had a chance to practise them, and be able to select and justify which to use. When selecting and using these

techniques procedures you will be aware of the contribution that the appropriate use of information technology can make to your research.

However, a word of caution before you continue. In your study, you will inevitably read a wide range of books and articles. In many of these the terms 'research method' and 'research methodology' will be used interchangeably, perhaps just using methodology as a more verbose way of saying method. In this book we have been more precise in our use of these terms.

The Post-it® note is one of the best known and most widely used office products in the world. Yet, despite the discovery of the repositionable adhesive that made the Post-it® note possible in 1968, it was not until 1980 that the product was introduced to the market (Post-it 2011). In the 1960s 3M research scientist Spence Silver was looking for ways to improve the adhesive used in tapes. However, he discovered something quite different from what he was looking for, an adhesive that did not stick strongly when coated onto the back of tapes! What was unclear was how it might be used. Over the next five years he demonstrated and talked about his new adhesive to people working within the company.

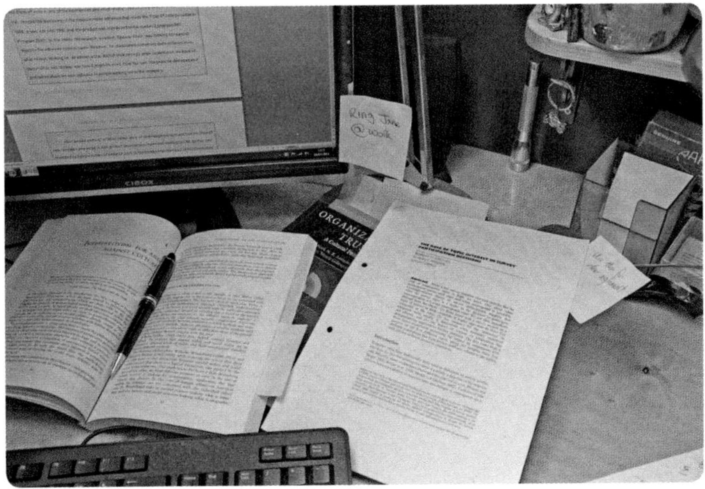

Post-it® notes in use
Source: © Mark Saunders 2011

Most people working for 3M know the story of what happened next and how the Post-it® note concept came about. A new product development researcher working for 3M, Art Fry, was frustrated by how the scraps of paper he used as bookmarks kept falling out of his church choir hymn book. He realised that Silver's adhesive would mean his bookmarks would not fall out. Soon afterwards the Post-it® note concept was developed and market research undertaken. This was extremely difficult as the product was revolutionary and was, in effect, designed to replace pieces of torn scrap paper! However, despite some initial scepticism within the company, Post-it® notes were launched in 1980. One year after their launch, they were named 3M's outstanding new product.

Whilst your research project will be within the business and management discipline rather than natural science (such as developing a new adhesive), our introductory example still offers a number of insights into the nature of research and in particular the business and management research you will be undertaking. In particular, it highlights that when undertaking research we should be open to finding the unexpected and how sometimes the applicability of our research findings may not be immediately obvious. It also emphasises the importance of discussing your ideas with other people.

Throughout the book we use the term **methods** to refer to techniques and procedures used to obtain and analyse data. This, therefore, includes questionnaires, observation and interviews as well as both quantitative (statistical) and qualitative (non-statistical) analysis techniques and, as you have probably gathered from the title, is the main focus of this book. In contrast, the term **methodology** refers to the theory of how research should be undertaken. We believe it is important that you have some understanding of this so that you can make an informed choice about your research. For this reason, we also discuss a range of philosophical assumptions upon which research can be based and the implications of these for the method or methods adopted.

1.2 The nature of research

When listening to the radio, watching the television or reading a daily newspaper it is difficult to avoid the term 'research'. The results of 'research' are all around us. A debate about the findings of a recent poll of people's opinions inevitably includes a discussion of 'research', normally referring to the way in which the data were collected. Politicians often justify their policy decisions on the basis of 'research'. Newspapers report the findings of research companies' surveys (Box 1.1). Documentary programmes tell us about 'research findings', and advertisers may highlight the 'results of research' to encourage you to buy a particular product or brand. However, we believe that what these examples really emphasise is the wide range of meanings given to the term 'research' in everyday speech.

Walliman (2011) argues that many of these everyday uses of the term 'research' are not research in the true meaning of the word. As part of this, he highlights ways in which the term is used wrongly:

- just collecting facts or information with no clear purpose;
- reassembling and reordering facts or information without interpretation;
- as an esoteric activity with no or little relevance to everyday life;
- as a term to get your product or idea noticed and respected.

The first of these highlights the fact that, although research often involves the collection of information, it is more than just reading a few books or articles, talking to a few people or asking people questions. While collecting data may be part of the research process, if it is not undertaken in a systematic way, on its own and, in particular, without a clear purpose, it will not be seen as research. The second of these is commonplace in many reports. Data are collected, perhaps from a variety of different sources, and then assembled in a single document with the sources of these data listed. However, there is no interpretation of the data collected. Again, while the assembly of data from a variety of sources may be part of the process of research, without interpretation it is not research. The third emphasises how despite research often appearing abstract, it influences our daily lives and creates our understanding of the world. Finally, the term 'research' can be used to get an idea or product noticed by people and to suggest that people should have confidence in it. In such instances, when you ask for details of the research process, these are either unclear or not forthcoming.

Based upon this brief discussion we can already see that research has a number of characteristics:

- Data are collected systematically.
- Data are interpreted systematically.
- There is a clear purpose: to find things out.

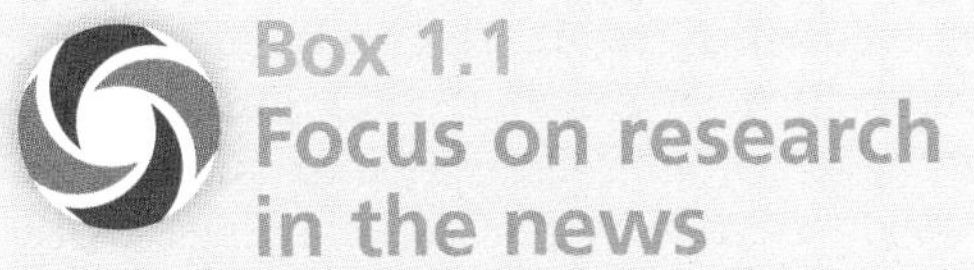

Box 1.1
Focus on research
in the news

FT

Business slow to assess Olympics impact

According to a survey, with just over a year to go until the games more than half of Britain's large businesses have yet to assess the impact the Olympics will have on their operations. Research by Deloitte, the professional services group, showed that 53 per cent of UK businesses have not examined the challenges and opportunities of hosting the world's largest sporting event.

Heather Hancock, lead London 2012 partner at Deloitte, said businesses needed to recognise that the Olympic Games is an immovable deadline and 'time is starting to run out'. Rick Cudworth, head of business continuity and resilience at the consultancy, said any excuses for not starting to plan yet – because of a lack of information, for example – were 'disappearing'. Companies are becoming more aware of the potentially disruptive effects of the games – on issues from transport to supply chain concerns – with some 42 per cent having assessed the ramifications, compared with 15 per cent in October last year. But Mr Cudworth said businesses were still not 'doing enough early enough'. It typically takes at least 12 months for companies to be 'thoroughly prepared' for the knock-on effects of an event of this magnitude, he said. Companies that fail to do so could fall short on key supplies, such as hotel vacancies. Mr Cudworth said even small changes, such as encouraging staff to cycle to work, took time because this also required companies to provide shower facilities and a place to store bicycles.

Lack of available staff was cited as the biggest concern for companies surveyed, with 43 per cent saying they thought it could cause the most disruption to their operations. Security was second at 37 per cent. Despite Transport for London's warning that the games will have 'some form of transport impact' for about 100 days, only 35 per cent of respondents, and 32 per cent in London, thought it posed the greatest risk of disruption to them. Mr Cudworth said companies should track staff holiday levels and absences, and their intentions during the games, adding, '[companies need to] make sure your policies, your plans, your staff intentions, match your ability to maintain business throughout the periods of the day you need to operate'. Only 18 per cent of businesses surveyed – and 15 per cent in London – said potential disruptions to the supply chain were a key risk to their operations, a level Mr Cudworth described as unrealistic.

The survey also revealed a 'relatively widespread' trend among businesses of a lack of involvement in planning by senior leadership. 'If I have a fear it is that for some businesses, [planning for the Olympics] is still an underground movement, so it's operating somewhat below the senior executive level,' said Mr Cudworth. Twelve per cent of senior business leaders said they did not intend to assess the impact the Olympics would have on their businesses. Mr Cudworth said executive involvement would produce more 'appropriate and proportionate' plans to operate during the games and he urged executives not to leave planning 'to be run under the covers'.

Mark Prisk, minister for business and enterprise, said: 'Frustrating events like late running transport, sickness, supplier delays, computer crashes, accidents and fraud can cause nuisance or disruption but if something similar happened during London 2012 the impact could prevent you from conducting business and damage your reputation.'

Source: Article by Vanessa Kortekaas, *Financial Times*, 25 June 2011.

We can therefore define **research** as something that people undertake in order to find out things in a systematic way, thereby increasing their knowledge. Two phrases are important in this definition: 'systematic way' and 'to find out things'. 'Systematic' suggests that research is based on logical relationships and not just beliefs (Ghauri and Grønhaug 2010). As part of this, your research will involve an explanation of the method or methods used to collect the data, will argue why the results obtained are meaningful and will explain any limitations that are associated with them. 'To find out things' suggests there are a multiplicity of possible purposes for your research. It is therefore an activity which means it has to be finished at some time to be of use (Becker 1998). This will undoubtedly be true for your research project, which will have a specific deadline. Purposes may include describing, explaining, understanding, criticising and analysing (Ghauri and Grønhaug 2010). However, it also suggests that you have a clear purpose or set of 'things' that you want to find out, such as the answer to a question or number of questions.

1.3 Business and management research

Using our earlier definition of research we can define business and management research as undertaking systematic research to find out things about business and management.

Easterby-Smith et al. (2008) argue that four things combine to make business and management a distinctive focus for research:

- The way in which managers (and researchers) draw on knowledge developed by other disciplines.
- The fact that managers tend to be powerful and busy people. Therefore, they are unlikely to allow research access unless they can see personal or commercial advantages.
- The fact that managers are educated. Many now have undergraduate and postgraduate degrees and, as such, tend often to be as well educated as those conducting research about them.
- The requirement for the research to have some practical consequence. This means it either needs to contain the potential for taking some form of action or needs to take account of the practical consequences of the findings.

Ongoing debate within journals has explored the nature and purpose of business and management research, its relevance as well as the purpose and future status of business schools where much of this research is located (Cassell and Lee 2011). These debates have, at times, been reflected in the media (Box 1.2). One feature, which has

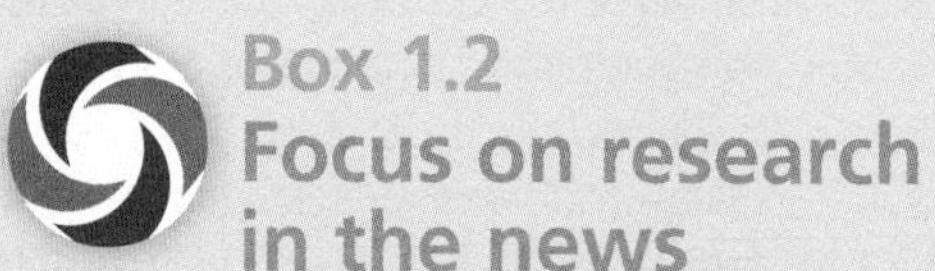

Box 1.2 Focus on research in the news

FT

Academia strives for relevance

Are business schools relevant? Given the expansion of management education in recent years, the question may seem moot. But, with critics continuing to query the real-world value of research and teaching, relevance has remained an issue for school administrators.

This month, David Willetts, the UK universities minister, criticised business schools for focusing on peer-reviewed research at the expense of applied studies. 'I am very aware we have inherited a structure of rewarding research excellence in particular that can have a very damaging practical effect on the work of a business school,' he said. British academics, he added, should concentrate more on teaching rather than publishing research in US journals. 'We have created a system in which research has much greater incentives and rewards than teaching, which I think is very bad for our universities.' Though it is rare for a minister to question the role of business schools, the comments were familiar to deans and other academic staff. Dan LeClair, senior vice president at the Association to Advance Collegiate Schools of Business (AACSB), which accredits more than 500 institutions worldwide, says deans are under more pressure than ever to justify what they do. 'The deans have been telling us that major donors are asking tough questions like "you have all these faculty members who you are very proud of, but can you tell me how this research has made a difference?"', he says. 'It's also the alumni and even the provosts and presidents of the institutions. They are all asking schools to not only describe what they are trying to achieve, but also to demonstrate it.'

Business schools are frequently criticised for overemphasising academic rigour over relevance to practice. And many believe the structures of the business school world feed the tendency: that promotion is based on articles few managers read; and that accreditation bodies and rankings providers count journal entries, and citations, to assess worthiness. Mr LeClair says the Florida-based AACSB has sometimes encouraged research that is 'narrow and theoretical and more mathematical' because it is easier to quantify. 'By focusing on that, it takes some of the uncertainty away about whether a school is accreditable. It gives us something to count. Applied research is more difficult to measure.'

Following a 2008 report calling for schools to have greater contact with business, the AACSB has been studying how to measure the impact of 'faculty intellectual contributions on targeted audiences'. Ten schools are taking part in a study where they self-assess their work against five criteria – each taken from mission statements. Saint Joseph's University in Philadelphia, for example, is assessing whether it meets the needs of 'key industries and strategic niches', contributes to the practice of management and teaching and upholds its Jesuit values. Although the exercise is not finished, Mr LeClair said it has helped to develop measures for impact in areas such as executive education and the work of research centres. In future, it may be possible to assess how customised teaching programmes, for example, help companies reach their objectives. Other schools are framing similar exercises. The Erasmus Research Institute of Management (ERIM) in Rotterdam is introducing a 'dual impact' system where it measures both academic influence (through journal articles and citations) and managerial relevance (consultancy requests and advisory board memberships). ERIM is also beginning to collect 'stakeholder' data from government agencies and even the general public. Scientific director Ale Smidts estimates that ERIM faculty are now appraised 80 per cent by standard academic criteria and 20 per cent by managerial relevance. He notes the influence of the national funding agency, the Netherlands Organisation of Scientific Research. 'It used to be that you only had to focus on originality and rigour, and if you had a relevant aspect it counted as a plus. Now it [relevance] is more of a necessity. If you can't show relevance, you get a negative on that aspect,' he says.

Robin Wensley, director of the UK's Advanced Institute of Management and professor of policy and marketing at Warwick Business School, says it is vital that academics become 'more engaged' with business, seeing businesspeople as 'knowledgeable actors in situations, as much as thinking we have all the answers'. He is also in favour of changing incentive structures to promote more relevant research. But he cautions against academics becoming the 'the same people' as the subjects they are trying to analyse.

Mr LeClair stresses that the AASCB's relevance initiative is designed for schools to meet their own criteria for relevance, rather than a general standard. And Esade dean Professor Alfons Sauquet argues that it is vital for schools to have a mixture of practice-focused and more theoretically minded staff. 'As deans we cannot fall too much into either camp. If we follow the business side position we would end up as consultants. If we followed just the academic research, we would be ivory tower people. I think we have to play both roles, and that's the tricky thing.'

Source: Adapted from 'Academia strives for relevance', Ben Schiller, *Financial Times*, 25 April 2011.

gained considerable support, is the transdisciplinary nature of such research. While this has similarities to Easterby-Smith et al.'s (2008) point regarding the use of knowledge from other disciplines, it also emphasises that the research 'cannot be reduced to any sum of parts framed in terms of contributions to associated disciplines' (Tranfield and Starkey 1998: 352). In other words, using knowledge from a range of disciplines enables management research to gain new insights that cannot be obtained through all of these disciplines separately. Another feature of management research highlighted in the debate is a belief that it should be able to develop ideas and relate them to practice. In particular, that research should complete a virtuous circle of theory and practice (Tranfield and Starkey 1998) through which research on managerial practice informs practically derived theory. This in turn becomes a blueprint for managerial practice, thereby increasing the stock of relevant and practical management knowledge. Thus, business and management research needs to engage with both the world of theory and the world of practice. Consequently, the problems addressed should grow out of interaction between these two worlds rather than either on their own.

An article by Hodgkinson et al. (2001) offers a useful four-fold taxonomy for considering rigour and relevance in relation to managerial knowledge. Using the dimensions of theoretical and methodological rigour and of practical relevance they identify four quadrants (see Table 1.1). Hodgkinson et al. argue that pedantic science is characterised by a focus on increasing methodological rigour at the expense of results that are relevant and can sometimes be found in refereed academic journals. In contrast, popularist science is characterised by a focus on relevance and usefulness whilst neglecting theoretical and methodological rigour, examples being found in some books targeted at practising managers. Consequently, whilst findings might be useful to managers, the research upon which they are based is unlikely to be valid or reliable. Puerile science both lacks methodological rigour and is of limited practical relevance and, although unlikely to be found in refereed academic journals, can be found in other media. Finally, pragmatic science is both theoretically and methodologically rigorous and relevant.

In the past decade debate about the nature of management research has focused on how it can meet the *double hurdle* of being both theoretically and methodologically rigorous, while at the same time embracing the world of practice and being of practical relevance (Hodgkinson et al. 2001; Wensley 2011). Much of this debate has centred around the work by Gibbons et al. (1994) on the production of knowledge and, in particular, the concepts of Mode 1 and Mode 2 knowledge creation. **Mode 1** knowledge creation emphasises research in which the questions are set and solved by academic interests, emphasising a fundamental rather than applied nature, where there is little if any focus on utilisation of the research by practitioners. In contrast, **Mode 2** emphasises a context

Table 1.1 A taxonomy for considering the 'relevance gap' in relation to managerial knowledge

Theoretical and methodological rigour	Practical relevance	Quadrant
Higher	Lower	Pedantic science
Lower	Higher	Popularist science
Lower	Lower	Puerile science
Higher	Higher	Pragmatic science

Source: Developed from Hodgkinson et al. (2001)

for research governed by the world of practice, highlighting the importance of collaboration both with and between practitioners (Starkey and Madan 2001) and the need for the production of practical relevant knowledge. Based upon this, Starkey and Madan (2001) observe that research within the Mode 2 approach offers a way of bringing the supply side of knowledge represented by universities together with the demand side represented by businesses and overcoming the double hurdle.

Drawing upon these debates, it could be argued that business and management research not only needs to provide findings that advance knowledge and understanding, it also needs to address business issues and practical managerial problems. However, this would negate the observation that Mode 2 practices develop from Mode 1. It might also result in business and management research that did not have obvious commercial benefit not being pursued. This, Huff and Huff (2001) argue, could jeopardise future knowledge creation as research that is currently not valued commercially might have value in the future. Building upon these ideas, Huff and Huff, rather like Fukami (2007) who found a third road in addition to the two academic career roads of research and teaching, highlight a further form of knowledge production: Mode 3. **Mode 3** knowledge production focuses on an appreciation of the human condition as it is and as it might become, its purpose being to 'assure survival and promote the common good at various levels of social aggregation' (Huff and Huff 2001: 53). This emphasises the importance of broader issues of human relevance of research. Consequently, in addition to research that satisfies your intellectual curiosity for its own sake, the findings of business and management research might also contain practical implications, and these findings may have societal consequences far broader and complex than perhaps envisaged by Mode 2. This, Syed et al. (2010) argue, is particularly important now given the major concerns about the behaviour of organisations and their impacts on society and the environment:

- breaches of legitimacy and trust such as Enron and some UK members of parliament;
- human rights violations and collaboration with repressive regimes such as by some energy companies;
- power of multinational corporations, a number having greater economic and political influence than some governments;
- reluctance to accept the reality and consequences of global warming.

Tranfield and Denyer (2004) draw attention to concerns resulting from the separation of knowledge producers from knowledge users. This has introduced a schism, or what Starkey and Madan (2001) call the 'relevance gap', which has been the subject of considerable debate for more than a decade. Rousseau (2006) has drawn attention to ways of closing what she terms the prevailing 'research–practice gap' – the failure of organisations and managers to base practices on the best available evidence. She extols the virtues of 'evidence-based management' which derives principles from research evidence and translates them into practices that solve organisational problems. Research findings do not appear to have transferred well to the workplace. Instead of a scientific understanding of human behaviour and organisations, managers, including those with MBAs, continue to rely largely on personal experience, to the exclusion of more systematic knowledge. This has been discussed in articles and entire special issues of journals including the *Journal of Management Studies* (2009, volume 46, number 3) and the *British Journal of Management* (2010, volume 21, supplement) as well as in volumes such as Cassell and Lee's (2011) *Challenges and Controversies in Management Research*. Within these debates some maintain that the gap between rigour and relevance is fundamentally unbridgeable because management researchers and the researched inhabit different worlds, are engaged in different activities and have different research orientations, whilst others disagree. Hodgkinson and Rousseau (2009), for example, argue that

Table 1.2 Practitioner and management researcher orientations

Management researcher		Practitioner
Basic understanding	**Focus of interest**	Useable knowledge
General enlightenment		Instrumental
Theoretical explanation		Practical problem solutions
'Why' knowledge		'How to' knowledge
Substantive theory building		Local theory-in-use
Theoretical and methodological rigour	**Methodological imperative**	Timeliness
Academic publication	**Key outcome**	Actionable results with practice impact
Disdain of practitioner	**Views of other**	Deprecate or ignore
Desire to make a difference to practice		Belief research can provide relevant fresh insights to managers' problems

Source: Developed from Saunders (2011)

the research–practice gap is due to more than differences in style and language, and that management researchers can generate knowledge that is both socially useful and academically rigorous.

Not surprisingly, many managers and academics perceive the gap between research undertaken by academics and the practice of management as a problem. Saunders (2011) categorises these as differences between academics and practitioners' orientations in relation to their foci of interest, methodological imperatives, the key outcomes, and how each views the other. These we summarise in Table 1.2, the contrasting orientations indicating where tensions may occur.

However, perhaps the most telling comment on the so-called 'relevance gap' is from Tranfield and Denyer (2004: 13), who assert that ignoring such a gap would be 'unthinkable in other professional fields, such as medicine or engineering, where a national scandal would ensue if science base and practice were not inextricably and necessarily interlinked'. This links to the idea of conceptualising management as a design science rather than a social science. From the design science perspective, the main purpose of academic management research is therefore only to develop valid knowledge to support organisational problem solving (Box 1.3). Whilst many researchers would probably agree that the mission of management research, like other social sciences, is description, explanation and prediction, taking a design science mission therefore focuses upon solution-orientated research to develop valid knowledge which supports practitioners in solving business problems (Van Aken 2005).

Within the boundaries of advancing knowledge, addressing business issues, solving managerial problems and promoting the common good, the purpose and the context of your research project can differ considerably. For some research projects your purpose may be to understand and explain the impact of something, such as a particular policy. You may undertake this research within an individual organisation and suggest appropriate action on the basis of your findings. For other research projects you may wish to explore the ways in which various organisations do things differently. In such projects

Box 1.3 Focus on management research

Management research as design science?

An article by Pandza and Thorpe (2010) in the *British Journal of Management* considers the notion of management as a design science and whether it offers a genuine alternative to management as a social science. Within this they argue that if the design science notion represents the production and verification of problem-solving methods and technological rules to guide planned interventions in organisations then it does offer something different to management. However, they also comment that, if this is the case, it is only applicable in some situations and so represents an umbrella term for some methodologies.

Pandza and Thorpe believe that management practice is characterised by a wide variety of organisational phenomena which are often ambiguous and not suited to prescriptive (rule-like) explanations offered by design science. They argue that researchers are better at explaining such phenomena rather than rigorously guiding them. They conclude (2010: 183): 'There needs to be, in our view, balance between the domains of explanation and application. We recognize this is difficult to achieve simultaneously, since the study of management is the study of practice – not a practical science.'

your purpose may be to discover and understand better the underlying processes in a wider context, thereby providing greater understanding for practitioners. For yet other research projects you may wish to place an in-depth investigation of an organisation within the context of a wider understanding of the processes that are operating.

Despite this variety, we believe that all business and management research projects can be placed on a continuum (Figure 1.1) according to their purpose and context. At

Basic research ⟵	⟶ **Applied research**
Purpose:	***Purpose:***
• expand knowledge of processes of business and management	• improve understanding of particular business or management problem
• results in universal principles relating to the process and its relationship to outcomes	• results in solution to problem
	• new knowledge limited to problem
• findings of significance and value to society in general	• findings of practical relevance and value to manager(s) in organisation(s)
Context:	***Context:***
• undertaken by people based in universities	• undertaken by people based in a variety of settings including organisations and universities
• choice of topic and objectives determined by the researcher	• objectives negotiated with originator
• flexible time scales	• tight time scales

Figure 1.1 Basic and applied research
Sources: Authors' experience; Easterby-Smith et al. (2008), Hedrick et al. (1993)

one extreme of the continuum is research that is undertaken purely to understand the processes of business and management and their outcomes. Such research is undertaken largely in universities and largely as the result of an academic agenda. Its key consumer is the academic community, with relatively little attention being given to its practical applications. This is often termed **basic**, **fundamental** or **pure research**. Given our earlier discussion, it is unlikely that Mode 2 and Mode 3 business and management research would fulfil the criterion of being undertaken 'purely to understand' due to at least some consideration being given to the practical consequences of what has been found out. Through considering the practical consequences, the research would start to move towards the other end of the continuum (Figure 1.1). At this end is research that is of direct and immediate relevance to managers, addresses issues that they see as important, and is presented in ways that they understand and can act on. This is termed **applied research**. In our view applied research can be very similar to consultancy, particularly when the latter is conducted in a thorough manner.

Wherever your research project lies on this basic–applied continuum, and for each of the orientations in Table 1.2, we believe that you should undertake your research with rigour. To do this you will need to pay careful attention to the entire research process.

Inevitably, your own beliefs and feelings will impact upon your research. Although you might feel that your research will be value neutral (we will discuss this in greater detail later, particularly in Chapter 4), it is unlikely that you will stop your own beliefs and feelings influencing your research. Your choice of what to research is also likely to be influenced by topics that excite you, and the way you collect and analyse your data by the skills you have or are able to develop. Similarly, as hinted by 'timeliness' in Table 1.2, in Chapter 2 we discuss practical considerations such as access to data and the time and resources you have available, which will also impact upon your research process.

1.4 The research process

Most research textbooks represent research as a multi-stage process that you must follow in order to undertake and complete your research project. The precise number of stages varies, but they usually include formulating and clarifying a topic, reviewing the literature, designing the research, collecting data, analysing data and writing up. In the majority of these the research process, although presented with rationalised examples, is described as a series of stages through which you must pass. Articles you have read may also suggest that the research process is rational and straightforward. Unfortunately this is very rarely true, and the reality is considerably messier, with what initially appear as great ideas sometimes having little or no relevance. While research is often depicted as moving through each of the stages outlined above, one after the other, this is unlikely to be the case. In reality some stages will overlap and you will probably revisit each stage more than once. Each time you revisit a stage you will need to reflect on the associated issues and refine your ideas. In addition, as highlighted by some textbooks, you will need to consider ethical and access issues during the process.

This textbook also presents the research process as a series of linked stages and gives the appearance of being organised in a linear manner. However, as you use the book you will see that we have recognised the concurrent and iterative nature of the research process you will follow in the examples of research by well-known academic researchers, student research, how research is reported in the news and case studies as well as our extensive use of cross-referencing. As part of this process, we believe it is vital that you spend time formulating and clarifying your research topic. This we believe should be expressed as one or more research questions that your research must answer, accompanied by a set of objectives that your research must address. However, we would also stress the need to reflect on your ideas continually and revise both these and the way in which you intend to progress your research.

We believe that writing is an intrinsic part of developing your ideas and understanding your research. Indeed, we and our students have found that it is not until we write our ideas in prose on the computer screen that we discover where our arguments need further clarification. Often this will involve revisiting stages (including research question(s) and objectives) and working through them again. There is also a need to plan ahead, thereby ensuring that the necessary preliminary work for later stages has been undertaken. This is emphasised by Figure 1.2, which also provides a schematic index to the remaining chapters of the book. Within this flow chart (Figure 1.2) the stages you will need to complete as part of your research project are emphasised in the centre of the chart. However, be warned: the process is far messier than a brief glance at Figure 1.2 suggests!

1.5 Keeping a reflective diary or research notebook

You will notice in Figure 1.2 on p. 14 that we included a series of arrows labelled 'reflection and revision' During your research project you will find it helpful to keep a separate **reflective diary** in which you note down what has happened and the lessons you have learnt both from things that have gone well and things that have not gone so well during the research process. Some researchers incorporate their reflective diary into a **research notebook** in which they record chronologically other aspects of their research project such as useful articles they have read, notes of discussions with their project supervisor and other interesting conversations alongside their emergent thoughts about all aspects of their research. We have also found this helpful.

You will almost certainly remember from your earlier studies the work of Kolb and of Honey and Mumford on the learning cycle (Marchington and Wilkinson 2008). This views the learning process as going through a four-stage cycle of:

1 concrete experience;
2 observation and reflection in relation to the experience;
3 forming abstract concepts and generalisations from these observations and reflections;
4 testing these concepts and generalisations in new situations.

The learning cycle emphasises that for learning to happen you need to pass through the complete cycle, as without reflection there will be no learning from experience. Such reflection is the process of stopping and thinking about a concrete experience that has happened or is happening, and the subsequent forming of concepts and generalisations; so you can apply what you have learnt from your experiences to new situations.

Given the benefits to learning, it is not surprising that many universities require students to write a reflective essay or a reflective practice statement as part of the assessment for their research project. In order to do this well, and more importantly to enhance your learning during the research process, we recommend that you keep a reflective diary or notebook (sometimes called a learning log or learning journal) in which you make entries at regular intervals regarding what has gone well, what has gone less well, what you have learnt from each experience and how you will apply this learning in the future. Indeed, as you read on you will find that we ask you to do this at the end of each chapter in the section 'Progressing your research project'! Questions our students have found helpful to guide them when making their diary entries are listed as a checklist in

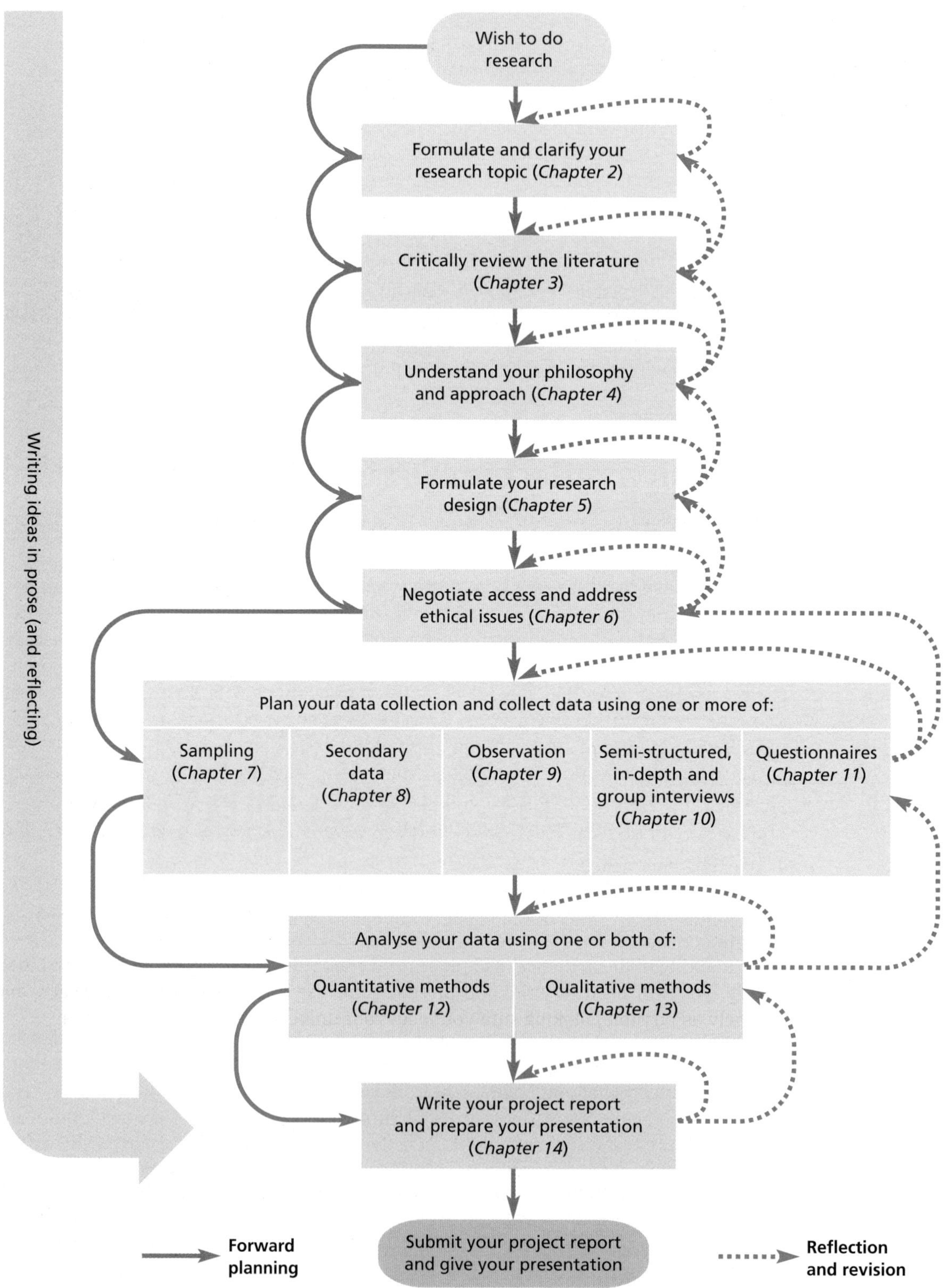

Figure 1.2 The research process
Source: © Mark Saunders, Philip Lewis and Adrian Thornhill 2011

Box 1.4 Checklist of questions to ask yourself when making reflective diary entries

- ✔ What has gone well in relation to each experience?
  - Why has it gone well?
- ✔ What has not gone so well in relation to each experience?
  - Why has it not gone so well?
- ✔ What adjustments will/did I make to my ongoing research following my reflection?
  - Why will/did I make these adjustments?
- ✔ (Looking back) how could I have improved on these adjustments?
  - Why?
- ✔ What have I learnt in relation to each experience?
- ✔ How will I apply what I have learnt from each experience to new situations?

Box 1.4. Be warned, many students forget to make entries in their reflective diaries regularly; this makes writing a good reflective essay difficult as much of the learning will have been forgotten!

1.6 The purpose and structure of this book

The purpose

As we stated earlier (Section 1.1), the overriding purpose of this book is to help you to undertake research. This means that early on in your research project you will need to be clear about what you are doing, why you are doing it, and the associated implications of what you are seeking to do. You will also need to ensure that you can show how your ideas relate to research that has already been undertaken in your topic area and that you have a clear research design and have thought about how you will collect and analyse your data. As part of this you will need to consider the validity and reliability of the data you intend to use, along with associated ethical and access issues. The appropriateness and suitability of the analytical techniques you choose to use will be of equal importance. Finally, you will need to write and present your research project report as clearly and precisely as possible, making sure you meet your university's assessment criteria.

The structure of each chapter

Each of the subsequent chapters deals with part of the research process outlined in Figure 1.2. The ideas, methods and techniques are discussed using as little jargon as possible. Where appropriate you will find summaries of these, using tables, checklists or diagrams. When new terms are introduced for the first time they are shown in **bold**, and a definition or explanation follows shortly afterwards. They are also listed with a brief definition in the glossary. The use of the Internet and application of appropriate information technology is considered in most instances as an integral part of the text. Discussion of information technology is not software specific but is concerned with general principles. However, we recognise that you may wish to find out more about how to use data analysis software packages and so have included tutorials for the quantitative data analysis software IBM SPSS Statistics, the spreadsheet Excel™ and the qualitative data analysis software NVivo™ (with practice data sets) on this book's companion website. These will enable you to utilise whatever software you have available most effectively. We have also included the Smarter Online Searching Guide to help you with your Internet searches. Chapters have been cross-referenced as appropriate, and an index is provided to help you to find your way around the book.

Included within the text of each subsequent chapter is a series of boxes which are called *Focus on student research*. These reflect actual research projects, undertaken by students, in which points made in the text are illustrated. In many instances these examples illustrate possible pitfalls you may come across while undertaking your research. Further illustrations are provided by *Focus on management research* and *Focus on research in the news* boxes. *Focus on management research* boxes (such as Box 1.3) discuss recent research in business and management. These are normally derived from refereed academic journal articles and you are likely to be able to download the actual articles from online databases at your university. *Focus on research in the news* boxes, two of which you will have already read (Boxes 1.1 and Box 1.2), provide topical newspaper articles that illustrate pertinent research-related issues. All these will help you to understand the technique or idea and to assess its suitability or appropriateness for your research. Where a pitfall has been illustrated, it will, it is hoped, help you to avoid making the same mistake. There is also a series of boxed *Checklists* (such as Box 1.4) to provide you with further focused guidance for your own research. At the end of each chapter there is a *Summary* of key points, which you may look at before and after reading the chapter to ensure that you have digested the main points.

To enable you to check that you have understood the chapter a series of *Self-check questions* is included at the end. These can be answered without recourse to other (external) resources. *Answers* are provided to all these self-check questions at the end of each chapter. Self-check questions are followed by *Review and discussion questions*. These suggest a variety of activities you can undertake to help you further develop your knowledge and understanding of the material in the chapter, often involving discussion with a friend. Self-test multiple choice questions are available on this book's companion website. Each chapter also includes a section towards the end headed *Progressing your research project*. This contains a series of questions that will help you to consider the implications of the material covered by the chapter for your research project. Answering the questions in the section *Progressing your research project* for each chapter will enable you to generate all the material that you will need to include in your project report and, where required, your reflective statement. Each chapter's questions involve you in undertaking activities that are more complex than self-check questions, such as a library-based literature search or designing and piloting a questionnaire. They are designed to help you to focus on the techniques that are most appropriate to your research. However, as emphasised by Figure 1.2, you will almost certainly need to revisit and revise your answers as your research progresses.

Each chapter is also accompanied by References, Further reading and a Case study. Further reading is included for two distinct reasons:

- to direct you to other work on the ideas contained within the chapter;
- to direct you to further examples of research where the ideas contained in the chapter have been used.

The main reasons for our choice of further reading are therefore indicated.

The new case studies towards the end of every chapter are drawn from a variety of business and management research scenarios and have been based on the case study's authors' and students' experiences when undertaking a research project. In addition there is an ongoing case study which starts at the end of Chapter 5, continues at the end of Chapter 8, and finishes at the end of Chapter 13. All case studies have been written to highlight real issues that occur when undertaking business and management research. To help to focus your thoughts or discussion on some of the pertinent issues, each case is followed by evaluative questions. Further case studies relating to each chapter are available from the book's companion website. This provides hyperlinks to over 50 additional case studies.

An outline of the chapters

The book is organised in the following way.

Chapter 2 is written to assist you in the generation of ideas, which will help you to choose a suitable research topic, and offers advice on what makes a good research topic. If you have already been given a research topic, perhaps by an organisation or tutor, you will need to refine it into one that is feasible, and should still therefore read this chapter. After your idea has been generated and refined, the chapter discusses how to turn this idea into a clear research question(s) and objectives. (Research questions and objectives are referred to throughout the book.) Finally, the chapter provides advice on how to write your research proposal.

The importance of the critical literature review to your research is discussed in Chapter 3. This chapter outlines what a critical review needs to include and the range of primary, secondary and tertiary literature sources available. The chapter explains the purpose of reviewing the literature, discusses a range of search strategies, and contains advice on how to plan and undertake your search and to write your review. The processes of identifying key words and searching using online databases and the Internet are outlined. It also offers advice on how to record items and to evaluate their relevance.

Chapter 4 addresses the issue of understanding different research philosophies, including positivism, realism, interpretivism and pragmatism. Within this the functionalist, interpretive, radical humanist and radical structuralist paradigms are discussed. Deductive, inductive and abductive approaches to research are also considered. In this chapter we challenge you to think about your own values and how you view the world and the impact this will have on the way you undertake your research.

These ideas are developed further in Chapter 5, which explores formulating your research design. As part of this, the methodological choice of quantitative, qualitative or multiple methods is considered. A variety of research strategies are explored and longitudinal and cross-sectional time horizons discussed. Consideration is given to the implications of design choice for the credibility of your research findings and conclusions.

Chapter 6 explores issues related to gaining access and to research ethics. It offers advice on how to gain access both to organisations and to individuals using both traditional and Internet-mediated strategies. Potential ethical issues are discussed in relation to each stage of the research process and different data collection methods. Issues of data protection are also introduced.

A range of the probability and non-probability sampling techniques available for use in your research is explained in Chapter 7. The chapter considers why sampling is necessary, and looks at issues of sample size and likely response rates for both probability and non-probability samples. Advice on how to relate your choice of sampling techniques to your research topic is given, and techniques for assessing the representativeness of those who respond are discussed.

Chapters 8, 9, 10 and 11 are concerned with different methods of obtaining data. The use of secondary data is discussed in Chapter 8. This chapter introduces the variety of data that are likely to be available, and suggests ways in which they can be used.

Advantages and disadvantages of secondary data are discussed, and a range of techniques for locating these data is suggested. Chapter 8 provides an indication of the myriad of sources available via the Internet and also offers advice on how to evaluate the suitability of secondary data for your research.

In contrast, Chapter 9 is concerned with collecting primary data through observation. The chapter examines two types of observation: participant observation and structured observation. Practical advice on using each is offered, and particular attention is given to ensuring that the data you obtain are both valid and reliable.

Chapter 10 is also concerned with collecting primary data, this time using semi-structured, in-depth and group interviews. The appropriateness of using these interviews in relation to your research strategy is discussed. Advice on how to undertake such interviews is offered, including the conduct of focus groups, Internet-mediated (including online) and telephone interviews. Particular attention is given to ensuring that the data collected are both reliable and valid.

Chapter 11 is the final chapter concerned with collecting data. It introduces you to the use of both self-administered and interviewer-administered questionnaires, and explores their advantages and disadvantages. Practical advice is offered on the process of designing, piloting and administering Internet-mediated, postal, delivery and collection, and telephone questionnaires to enhance their response rates. Particular attention is again given to ensuring that the data collected are both reliable and valid.

Analysis of data is covered in Chapters 12 and 13. Chapter 12 outlines and illustrates the main issues that you need to consider when preparing data for quantitative analysis and when analysing these data by computer. Different types of data are defined and advice is given on how to create a data matrix and to code data. Practical advice is also offered on the analysis of these data using computer-based analysis software. The most appropriate diagrams to explore and illustrate data are discussed and suggestions are made about the most appropriate statistics to use to describe data, to explore relationships and to examine trends.

Chapter 13 outlines and discusses the main approaches available to you to analyse data qualitatively both manually and using computer-aided qualitative data analysis software (**CAQDAS**). The nature of qualitative data and issues associated with transcription are discussed. The use of deductively based and inductively based analytical approaches is discussed and different types of procedures are outlined to analyse your qualitative data. A number of aids that will help you to analyse these data and record your ideas about progressing your research are also discussed.

Chapter 14 helps you with the structure, content and style of your final project report and any associated oral and poster presentations. Above all, and as illustrated by Figure 1.2, it encourages you to see writing as an intrinsic part of the research process that should not be left until everything else is completed.

Appendices and glossary

This book contains four appendices designed to support you at different stages of your research project. In the early stages, as you begin to read, you will need to keep a reference of what you have read using a recognised system, the most frequently used of which are detailed in Appendix 1. When selecting your sample you may need to calculate the minimum sample size required and use random sampling numbers (Appendices 2 and 3). Finally, when designing your data collection tools and writing your project report you will need to ensure that the language you use is non-discriminatory. Guidelines for these are given in Appendix 4. A separate glossary of nearly 600 research-methods-related terms is also included for quick reference.

1.7 Summary

- This book is designed to help you to undertake a research project whether you are an undergraduate or postgraduate student of business and management or a manager. It is designed as an introductory text and will guide you through the entire research process.
- Business and management research involves undertaking systematic research to find out things. It is transdisciplinary, and engages with both theory and practice.
- All business and management research projects can be placed on a basic–applied continuum according to their purpose and context.
- Wherever your research project lies on this continuum, you should undertake your research with rigour. To do this you will need to pay careful attention to the entire research process.
- In order to enhance your learning during your research we recommend you keep a reflective diary or notebook.
- In this book, research is represented as a multi-stage process; however, this process is rarely straightforward and will involve both reflecting on and revising stages already undertaken and forward planning.
- The text of each chapter is supported through a series of boxed examples. These include, focus on student research and focus on research in the news. In addition, there are checklists, self-check questions and review and discussion questions, an assignment and a case study with questions. Answers to all self-check questions are at the end of the appropriate chapter.
- Answering the questions in the section 'Progressing your research project' for Chapters 2–13 will enable you to generate all the material that you will need to include in your project report and reflect on what you have learnt. When you have also answered the questions in this section for Chapter 14, you will have written your research report.

Self-check questions

Help with these questions is available at the end of the chapter.

1.1 Outline the features that can make business and management research distinctive from research in other disciplines.

1.2 What are the key differences between basic and applied research (and consultancy)?

1.3 Examine Figure 1.2 What does this suggest about the need to plan and to reflect on and revise your ideas?

Review and discussion questions

1.4 Agree with a friend to each read a different quality newspaper. Make a note of at least 10 articles in your newspaper that mention the word 'research'. Now examine the articles one at a time. As you examine each article, does the reference to research:

- refer to the collection of facts or information with no clear purpose?
- refer to the reassembling and reordering of facts or information without interpretation?
- provide a means of getting the reader to respect what is being written?
- refer to the systematic collection and interpretation of data with a clear purpose?

Discuss your answers with your friend.

1.5 Revisit Table 1.2 and look at the differences in management researcher and practitioner orientations for foci of interest, methodological imperatives, key outcomes and how each views the other. For each of the continua implied by this table, where would you place yourself? To what extent do you believe that business and management research should meet the practitioner requirements? Give reasons for your answer.

Progressing your research project

Starting your reflective diary or notebook

- Find out if your university requires you to write a reflective practice statement, learning journal or keep a reflective diary or research notebook as part of your research project or research methods module.
- If the answer is 'yes', look carefully at what is required by the assessment criteria and ensure that your reflective diary or research notebook entries will enable you to meet fully the assessment criteria. When doing this, amend the questions in Box 1.4 to guide your reflective entries as necessary.
- If the answer is 'no', we still believe it will be beneficial to your learning for your research project or research methods module if you keep a reflective diary or research notebook on a regular basis. Please use the questions in Box 1.4 to guide your reflective entries at the end of each chapter.

References

Becker, H.S. (1998) *Tricks of the Trade: How to Think about Your Research While You're Are Doing It*. Chicago, IL: University of Chicago Press.

Cassell, C. and Lee, B. (eds) (2011) *Challenges and Controversies in Management Research*. New York: Routledge.

Cassell, C. and Lee, B. (2011) 'Introduction: Key debates, challenges and controversies in management research', in C. Cassell and B. Lee (eds) *Challenges and Controversies in Management Research*. New York: Routledge, pp. 1–16.

Easterby-Smith, M., Thorpe, R., Jackson, P. and Lowe, A. (2008) *Management Research* (3rd edn). London: Sage.

Fukami, C. (2007) 'The third road', *Journal of Management Education*, Vol. 31, pp. 358–64.

Ghauri, P. and Grønhaug, K. (2010) *Research Methods in Business Studies: A Practical Guide* (4th edn). Harlow: FT Prentice Hall.

Gibbons, M.L., Limoges, H., Nowotny, S., Schwartman, P., Scott, P. and Trow, M. (1994) *The New Production of Knowledge: The Dynamics of Science and Research in Contemporary Societies*. London: Sage.

Hedrick, T.E., Bickmann, L. and Rog, D.J. (1993) *Applied Research Design*. Newbury Park, CA: Sage.

Hodgkinson, G.P., Herriot, P. and Anderson, N. (2001) 'Re-aligning the stakeholders in management research: Lessons from industrial, work and organizational psychology', *British Journal of Management*, Vol. 12, Special Issue, pp. 41–8.

Hodgkinson, G.P. and Rousseau, D. (2009) 'Bridging the rigour–relevance gap in management research. It's already happening!', *Journal of Management Studies*, Vol. 46, No. 3, pp. 534–46.

Huff, A.S. and Huff, J.O. (2001) 'Re-focusing the business school agenda', *British Journal of Management*, Vol. 12, Special Issue, pp. 49–54.

Marchington, M. and Wilkinson, A. (2008) *Human Resource Management at Work* (4th edn). London: Chartered Institute of Personnel and Development.

Pandza, K. and Thorpe, R. (2010) 'Management as design, but what kind of design? An appraisal of the design science analogy for management', *British Journal of Management,* Vol. 21, No. 2, pp. 171–86.

Post-it (2011) *Post-it history and facts*. Available at http://solutions.3m.co.uk/wps/portal/3M/en_GB/Post-Its/Post-It/Solutions/History/ [Accessed 15 July 2011].

Rouseau, D. (2006). 'Is there such a thing as "Evidence-Based Management"?', *Academy of Management Review,* Vol. 31, No. 2, pp. 256–69.

Saunders, M.N.K. (2011) 'The management researcher as practitioner', in B. Lee and C. Cassell (eds) *Challenges and Controversies in Management Research.* New York: Routledge, pp. 243–57.

Starkey, K. and Madan, P. (2001) 'Bridging the relevance gap: Aligning stakeholders in the future of management research', *British Journal of Management*, Vol. 12, Special Issue, pp. 3–26.

Syed, J., Mingers, J. and Murray, P.A. (2010) 'Beyond rigour and relevance: A critical realist approach to business education', *Management Learning*, Vol. 41, No. 1, pp. 71–85.

Tranfield, D. and Denyer, D. (2004) 'Linking theory to practice: A grand challenge for management research in the 21st century?', *Organization Management Journal*, Vol. 1, No. 1, pp. 10–14.

Tranfield, D. and Starkey, K. (1998) 'The nature, social organization and promotion of management research: Towards policy', *British Journal of Management*, Vol. 9, pp. 341–53.

Van Aken, J.E. (2005) 'Management research as a design science: Articulating the research products of Mode 2 knowledge production in management', *British Journal of Management*, Vol. 16, No.1, pp. 19–36.

Walliman, N. (2011) *Your Research Project: A Step by Step Guide for the First-Time Researcher* (3rd edn). London: Sage.

Wensley, R. (2011) 'Seeking relevance in management research', in C. Cassell and B. Lee (eds) *Challenges and Controversies in Management Research.* New York: Routledge, pp. 258–74.

Further reading

Cassell, C. and Lee, B. (eds) (2011) *Challenges and Controversies in Management Research.* New York: Routledge. This edited volume consists of a series of chapters looking at the key challenges and controversies facing business and management research at the start of the twenty-first century. The opening chapter includes a useful overview of the rest of the book and will enable you to easily follow up those aspects that you feel are most pertinent.

Easterby-Smith, M., Thorpe, R., Jackson, P. and Lowe, A. (2008) *Management Research* (3rd edn). London: Sage. Chapter 1 provides a very clear and readable introduction to management research and how it is distinct from other forms of research.

Salmon, P. (2003) 'How do we recognise good research?', *The Psychologist*, Vol. 16, No. 1, pp. 24–7. This short article looks at how we can evaluate research in general looking at rigour of method and 'fit' with what is being studied, clarity and coherence of what has been undertaken and its utility.

Starkey, K. and Madan, P. (2001) 'Bridging the relevance gap: Aligning stakeholders in the future of management research', *British Journal of Management*, Vol. 12, Special Issue, pp. 3–26. This article argues the need for relevant management research within a Mode 2 framework, emphasising a need for research partnership.

Case 1

Reporting evidence from business and management research

Katie is working in her local NHS hospital on a six-month internship. During her time there, the hospital plans the introduction of what they call a 'Leadership at all Levels' programme. All staff are to be encouraged to act as leaders, and Katie is asked to write a report for her manager setting out the best way to ensure that the aims of the programme actually happen. Her manager makes a special point of telling Katie that the hospital wants to make its introduction 'evidence-based'. This means, he explains, that he would like her report to set out the scientific evidence about what works in these kinds of initiatives. Katie agrees to do the report, and she thinks it may also be suitable as the research project for her degree.

Source: Alamy Images/Justin Kase

'Where do you start with a project like this?' Katie wonders. 'Well', she thinks, 'I may as well type "leadership at all levels" into Google!' On the day she does this, the entry at the very top of the list takes her straight to 'Leadership at all levels: Leading public sector organisations in an age of austerity'. The title page says it is a 'research paper' and it is published by the prestigious firm of management consultants, Deloitte (Deloitte 2010). She reads it all carefully. While the report is very enthusiastic about leadership as a general idea for improving public services, she is surprised to see that it contains very few concrete details. Although it is 16 pages long, there is nothing specifically about what leadership is, nothing about how 'leadership at all levels' is actually going to happen; no academic research at all, as far as she can see. In fact, the more she thinks about it, the more she feels its recommendations are vague with little justification. For instance, among a list of bullet-points on page 12, it recommends that top public sector leaders ask themselves questions like:

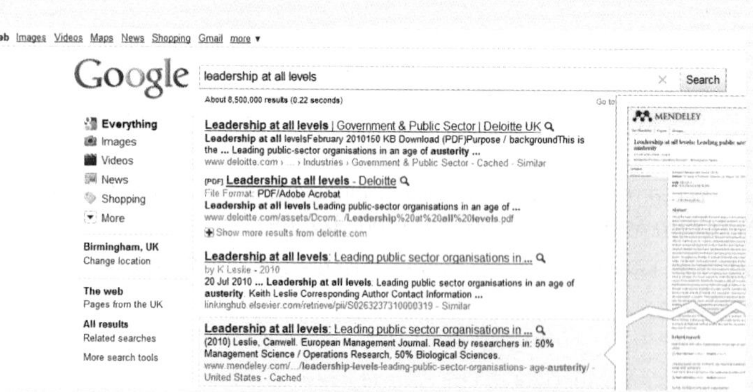

- Do you have a senior team that is ready for change and is working collectively to enable it?
- Can you articulate a brief, compelling message of change, framed appropriately to connect with your staff?

'But how could chief executives really know whether their answers to such questions were correct?' Katie ponders. She feels chief executives are likely to have a vested interest in making their answers fit with what they already believe to be the case. Even if they can put their managerial interests aside, she thinks that the questions arising from the bullet point list such as 'how "ready for change" is my team?' or 'how "compelling [a] message" might I be delivering to staff?' are never going to be things that can be measured with any degree of objectivity. They are quite different from the kind of medical questions a hospital generally deals with; such as: 'what is this patient's body-mass index and blood pressure?' 'So', Katie thinks, 'Deloitte's is probably not the kind of scientific evidence my manager had in mind when he asked me for an evidence-based report!'

She decides to look instead at academic journals, thinking that they might be a better place to look for scientific evidence than the World Wide Web. But she soon finds it a rather daunting task. Not only is there an almost overwhelming number of potentially relevant research papers, when she starts reading them she gets very confused. Not primarily because she doesn't understand them (though because of the language that can sometimes be a problem!) Still, her confusion is more down to the fact that many of the articles apparently contradict one another – even within the same journal. What is worse, their disagreements are often over fundamentals, rather than over details. For example, in the journal *Human Relations*, while Schippers et al. (2008: 1593) think that transformational leadership is key to the 'adoption of a shared vision by the team', Harding et al. (2011:1) claim 'that leaders evoke a homoerotic desire in followers such that followers are seduced into achieving organizational goals'.

After a few weeks of reading this evidence, Katie starts to think that she has been asked to do something that misunderstands the nature of scientific evidence – at least that of business and management studies. Her manager appears to have assumed that 'the evidence' will all point in the same direction. But Katie has discovered that in the case of leadership, 'the evidence' cannot even agree what leadership is, or whether it is a good or a bad thing for managers to adopt – never mind the best way to get all staff to become leaders. Authors disagree so much – and so fundamentally – that she finds it impossible to extract 'best practice'.

Unfortunately, Katie did say she would write the report. It occurs to her that she could just mention those articles that imply leadership is a good thing, and that detail ways of involving staff in it. She thinks that's really what her manager would like. After all, it's already been announced across the hospital that a Leadership at all Levels programme is going to happen, and her report would still enable him to tell people that what he was doing was 'evidence-based'. After some soul-searching she decides to write this partial and somewhat misleading report (recognising she will need a good reference from him if she wants to get a job). But all her other reading won't go to waste – at least she can include it in her research project for university!

References

Deloitte (2010) Leadership at all levels: Leading public sector organisations in an age of austerity. Available at www.deloitte.com/assets/Dcom-UnitedKingdom/Local%20Assets/Documents/Industries/GPS/UK_GPS_Leadership_at_all_levels.pdf [Accessed 24 March 2011].

Harding, N., Lee, H., Ford, J. and Learmonth, M. (2011) 'Leadership and charisma: A desire that cannot speak its name?', *Human Relations*, Vol. 64, No. 7, pp. 927–49

Schippers, M.C., Den Hartog, D.N., Koopman, P.L. and van Knippenberg, P. (2008) 'The role of transformational leadership in enhancing team reflexivity', *Human Relations,* Vol. 61, No. 11, pp. 1593–1616.

Questions

1 If Katie is correct, and evidence doesn't necessarily tell managers the best way to take action, do we still need evidence?

2 Can Katie's decision to submit a report she thinks is misleading be justified on ethical grounds?

3 In what ways are the kinds of research projects that most managers want to read likely to be different from the kinds of research projects that get high marks at university?

An additional case study relating to material covered in this chapter is available via the book's companion website: **www.pearsoned.co.uk/saunders**.

It is:

Isabelle's research dilemma.

Self-check answers

1.1 The features you outline are likely to include:

- the transdisciplinary nature of business and management research;
- the development of ideas that are related to practice and in particular the requirement for the research to have some practical consequence;
- the need for research to complete the virtuous circle of theory and practice;
- addressing problems that grow out of the interaction between the worlds of theory and practice.

1.2 The key differences between basic and applied research relate to both the purpose and the context in which it is undertaken. They are summarised in Figure 1.1.

1.3 Figure 1.2 emphasises the importance of planning during your research project. Forward planning needs to occur at all stages up to submission. In addition, you will need to reflect on and to revise your work throughout the life of the research project. This reflection needs to have a wide focus. You should both consider the stage you have reached and revisit earlier stages and work through them again. Reflection may also lead you to amend your research plan. This should be expected, although large amendments in the later stages of your research project are unlikely.

Get ahead using resources on the companion website at:
www.pearsoned.co.uk/saunders

- Improve your IBM SPSS Statistics and NVivo research analysis with practice tutorials.
- Save time researching on the Internet with the Smarter Online Searching Guide.
- Test your progress using self-assessment questions.
- Follow live links to useful websites.

Chapter 2

Formulating and clarifying the research topic

Learning outcomes

By the end of this chapter you should be able to:

- identify the attributes of a good research topic;
- generate ideas and explore sources that will help you to choose a suitable research topic;
- refine your ideas to clarify your research topic;
- turn research ideas into a research project that has a clear research question(s) and objectives;
- draft a written research proposal.

2.1 Introduction

Many students think that choosing their research topic is the most exciting part of their course. After all, this is something that they get to decide for themselves rather than having to complete a task decided by their tutors. We will stress in this chapter that it is important to choose something that will sustain your interest throughout the months that you will need to complete it. You may even decide to do some research on something that forms part of your leisure activities!

Before you start your research you need to have at least some idea of what you want to do. This is probably the most difficult, and yet the most important, part of your research project. Up until now most of your studies have been concerned with answering questions that other people have set. This chapter is concerned with how to formulate and clarify your research topic, research question and related objectives. Without being clear about what you are going to research it is difficult to plan how you are going to research it. This reminds us of a favourite quote in *Alice's Adventures in Wonderland*. This is part of Alice's conversation with the Cheshire Cat. In this Alice asks the Cat (Carroll 1989: 63–4):

> 'Would you tell me, please, which way I ought to walk from here?'
> 'That depends a good deal on where you want to get to', said the Cat.
> 'I don't much care where', said Alice.
> 'Then it doesn't matter which way you walk', said the Cat.

Formulating and clarifying the research topic is the starting point of your research project (Ghauri and Grønhaug 2010; Smith and Dainty 1991). Once you are clear about this, you will

be able to choose the most appropriate research strategy and data collection and analysis techniques. The formulating and clarifying process is time-consuming and will probably take you up blind alleys (Saunders and Lewis 1997). However, without spending time on this stage you are far less likely to achieve a successful project (Raimond 1993).

In the initial stages of the formulating and clarifying process you will be generating and refining research ideas (Section 2.3). It may be that you have already been given a research idea, perhaps by an organisation or tutor. Even if this has happened you will still need to refine the idea into one that is feasible. Once you have done this you will need to turn the idea into research questions and objectives (Section 2.4) and to write the research proposal for your project (Section 2.5).

Research has found that shopping may prolong your life. This is the physical type, not the one where you switch on your computer and surf the Internet. For those who raise a sceptical eyebrow at such a thought, perhaps you should remember this the next time you go shopping in an unbearably crowded retail centre and the experience begins to drain your energy! Men were found to benefit more than women from shopping every day.

Source: Alamy Images/Ellen Issacs

Ageing and shopping was the research topic chosen by a group of researchers in Taiwan. The variables in which they were interested were shopping frequency and health. To conduct this study, they designed a longitudinal research project based on a representative sample of 1841 Taiwanese people aged over 65 who lived independently. Data were collected on a range of factors including age, socioeconomic status, health, physical and cognitive wellbeing as well as shopping behaviours. Data were linked to mortality records between 1999 and 2008. After other variables were controlled for, the researchers found a statistically significant relationship between shopping frequency and life expectancy. Older people who went shopping every day were found to have a 27 per cent lower risk of death compared with those who went shopping least frequently. Men had a 28 per cent lower risk and women a 23 per cent lower risk (BBC 2011; Chang et al. 2011).

They explained this relationship by the potential for wellbeing that shopping may promote. Shopping involves sustainable physical activity and social interaction. It can be pleasurable and may promote psychological wellbeing and satisfaction. The relationship between shopping frequency and life expectancy lead Chang et al. to claim that, 'Shopping behaviour favourably predicts survival.'

This research may give a whole new meaning to the expression, 'shop till you drop'. Time to go and find where you left your 'lifetime' shopping bags. . . .

However, before you start the formulating and clarifying process we believe that you need to understand what makes a good research topic. For this reason we begin this chapter with a discussion of the attributes required for a good research topic.

2.2 Attributes of a good research topic

The attributes of a business and management research topic do not vary a great deal between universities (Raimond 1993), although there will be differences in the emphasis placed on these attributes. If you are undertaking your research project as part of a course of study then the most important attribute will be that it meets the examining body's requirements and, in particular, that it is at the correct level. This means that you must choose your topic with care. For example, some universities require students to collect their own data as part of their research project, whereas others allow them to base their project on data that have already been collected. Alternatively, some ask you to undertake an organisation-based piece of applied research, whilst others simply say that it must be within the subject matter of your course or programme. You therefore need to check the assessment criteria for your project and ensure that your choice of topic will enable you to meet these criteria. If you are unsure, you should discuss any uncertainties with your project tutor.

In addition, your research topic must be something you are capable of undertaking and one that excites your imagination. Capability can be considered in a variety of ways. At the personal level you need to feel comfortable that you have, or can develop, the skills that will be required to research the topic. We hope that you will develop your research skills as part of undertaking your project. However, some skills, for example learning a new foreign language, may be impossible to acquire in the time you have available. As well as having the necessary skills we believe that you also need to have a genuine interest in the topic. Most research projects are undertaken over at least a four-month period. A topic in which you are only vaguely interested at the start is likely to become a topic in which you have no interest and with which you will fail to produce your best work.

Your ability to find the financial and time resources to undertake research on the topic will also affect your capability. This relates to the concept of feasibility, which we also discuss in Chapter 6 (see Section 6.2). Some topics are unlikely to be possible to complete in the time allowed by your course of study. This may be because they require you to measure the impact of an intervention over a long time period (Box 2.1). Similarly, topics that are likely to require you to travel widely or need expensive equipment should also be disregarded unless financial resources permit.

Capability also means you must be reasonably certain of gaining access to any data you might need to collect. Many people start with ideas where access to data will prove difficult. Certain, more sensitive topics, such as financial performance or decision making by senior managers, are potentially fascinating. However, they may present considerable access problems. You should therefore, discuss this with your project tutor after reading Chapter 6.

It is important that the issues within your research are capable of being linked to academic theory. Initially, theory may be based just on the reading you have undertaken as part of your study to date. However, as part of your assessment criteria you are almost certain to be asked to set your topic in context (Sections 2.4 and 3.2). As a consequence you will need to have knowledge of the literature and to undertake further reading as part of defining your research questions and objectives (Section 2.4).

Box 2.1 Focus on student research

Turning ideas into a viable project

Zaynab was not short of ideas for her research. But she was much less sure about how to turn her topic of interest into a question that could be answered for her research project. Her tutors emphasised that thinking of topics was relatively easy compared to turning them into viable research projects.

Having explored various websites and looked at relevant publications in the library, she drew up a plan of action which she was sure would give her the material necessary to write her research proposal.

Charting ideas

At the start her project, Zaynab got a huge sheet of paper to make a mind map of all of her ideas, questions, associations, sources and leads. She marked her most compelling thoughts in red. Then she marked the main links to those ideas in red too. She was careful not to throw out her weaker or isolated thoughts. She felt this mind map would help her know the place of all her thoughts. She thought that she could make another mind map later in the project if she felt there was too much information.

Recording questions

Next Zaynab recorded who had originally asked a potential research question and left a space by each to record possible answers or places to look for answers. Then she highlighted the questions that she found most exciting; the ones that really grabbed her attention. She thought that recording all of these questions would encourage her to develop her own ideas. She also recorded her own thoughts as a further set of questions that were designed as prompts to help her to be clear about what she needed to do to progress her research ideas.

Blogging it

Zaynab was a keen blogger so she posted summaries of her ideas and questions on a weblog. She asked site visitors to suggest further reading, new research methods or for possible answers to her questions. She received 20 posts which she used to help turn her favourite idea into a question that could be answered for her research project.

Thinking about applying findings

Zaynab knew that she would be expected to comment on the practical implications of her findings when writing up her research. Therefore, an important part of her action plan was to ask herself what would be the implications for practice for the various outcomes that might be expected.

Most project tutors will argue that one of the attributes of a good topic is clearly defined research questions and objectives (Section 2.4). These will, along with a good knowledge of the literature, enable you to assess the extent to which your research is likely to provide new insights into the topic. Many students believe this is going to be difficult. Fortunately there are numerous ways in which such insight can be defined as new (see Sections 2.3 and 2.4).

If you have already been given a research idea (perhaps by an organisation) you will need to ensure that your questions and objectives relate clearly to the idea. It is also important that your topic will have **symmetry of potential outcomes**: that is, your results will be of similar value whatever you find out (Gill and Johnson 2010). Without this symmetry you may spend a considerable amount of time researching your topic only to find an answer of little importance. Whatever the outcome, you need to ensure you have the scope to write an interesting project report.

Finally, it may be important to consider your future aspirations. If you wish to obtain employment or pursue a career in a particular subject area, it is sensible to use this opportunity to start to develop some expertise in it.

Box 2.2
Checklist

Attributes of a good research topic

Capability: is it feasible?

✔ Is the topic something with which you are really fascinated?
✔ Do you have, or can you develop within the project time frame, the necessary research skills to undertake the topic?
✔ Is the research topic achievable within the available time?
✔ Will the topic still be current when you finish your project?
✔ Is the topic achievable within the financial resources that are likely to be available?
✔ Are you reasonably certain of being able to gain access to data you are likely to require for this topic?

Appropriateness: is it worthwhile?

✔ Does the topic fit the specifications and meet the standards set by the examining institution?
✔ Does your topic contain issues that have a clear link to theory?
✔ Are you able to state your research question(s) and objectives clearly?
✔ Will your proposed research be able to provide fresh insights into this topic?
✔ Does your topic relate clearly to the idea you have been given (perhaps by an organisation)?
✔ Are the findings for this topic likely to be symmetrical: that is, of similar value whatever the outcome?
✔ Does the topic match your career goals?

It is almost inevitable that the extent to which the attributes we have discussed apply to your research topic will depend on your topic and the reasons why you are undertaking the research. However, most will apply. For this reason it is important that you check and continue to check any potential research topic against the summary checklist contained in Box 2.2.

2.3 Generating and refining research ideas

Some business and management students are expected both to generate and to refine their own research ideas. Others, particularly those on professional and post-experience courses, are provided with a research idea by an organisation or their university. In the initial stages of their research they are expected to refine this to a clear and feasible idea that meets the requirements of the examining organisation. If you have already been given a research idea we believe you will still find it useful to read the next subsection, which deals with generating research ideas. Many of the techniques which can be used for generating research ideas can also be used for the refining process.

Generating research ideas

If you have not been given an initial **research idea** there is a range of techniques that can be used to find and select a topic that you would like to research. They can be thought of as those that are predominantly **rational thinking** and those that involve more **creative thinking** (Table 2.1). The precise techniques that you choose to use and the order in which you use them are entirely up to you. However, like Raimond (1993), we believe you should use both rational and creative techniques, choosing those that you believe are going to be of most use to you and which you will enjoy using. By using one or more

Table 2.1 More frequently used techniques for generating and refining research ideas

Rational thinking	Creative thinking
Examining your own strengths and interests	Keeping a notebook of your ideas
Examining staff research interests	Exploring personal preferences using past projects
Looking at past project titles	Exploring relevance to business using the literature
Discussion	Relevance trees
Searching the literature	Brainstorming
Scanning the media	

creative techniques you are more likely to ensure that your heart as well as your head is in your research project. In our experience, it is usually better to use a variety of techniques. In order to do this you will need to have some understanding of the techniques and the ways in which they work. We therefore outline the techniques in Table 2.1 and subsequently discuss possible ways they might be used to generate research ideas. These techniques will generate one of two outcomes:

- one or more possible project ideas that you might undertake;
- few ideas that relate to your interests. In this case you may want to revise the area in which you are interested, either by choosing another area or by refining and perhaps narrowing or widening your original area of interest.

In either instance we suggest that you make some notes and arrange to talk to your project tutor.

Examining your own strengths and interests

It is important that you choose a topic in which you are likely to do well and, if possible, already have some academic knowledge. One way of doing this is to look at those assignments for which you have received good grades. For most of these assignments they are also likely to be the topics in which you were interested (Box 2.1). They will provide you with an area in which to search and find a research idea. In addition, you may, as part of your reading, be able to focus more precisely on the sort of ideas about which you wish to conduct your research.

As noted in Section 2.1, there is the need to think about your future. If you plan to work in financial management it would be sensible to choose a research project in the financial management field. One part of your course that will inevitably be discussed at any job interview is your research project. A project in the same field will provide you with the opportunity to display clearly your depth of knowledge and your enthusiasm.

Examining staff research interests

You may follow the links within your institution's website to the profile pages of academic staff. These pages are likely to display information about their teaching and research interests. You may be able to use this as a funnel to help you to explore and generate research ideas in which you would be interested for your own project. In very many cases, these pages will provide you with the overall subject area taught by each member of staff (e.g. accounting, international management, marketing, strategic management). These pages are also likely to list the particular research interests of each member of staff within her or his subject area (e.g. regulation of accounting standards, transnational management, pricing and price promotions, organisational learning). In many cases, a member of staff will offer a short commentary on her or his research interests which will provide more specific details. Lists of publications and conference papers with direct links to online copies may be included. These will provide even more detail about the exact nature of the research interests of a member of staff. Working through this information may allow you to generate ideas for your own research and guide you to some initial reading to test this interest.

Looking at past project titles

Many of our students have found looking at past projects a useful way of generating research ideas. For undergraduate and taught master's degrees these are often called **dissertations**. For research degrees they are termed **theses**. A common way of doing this is to scan your university's list of past project titles for anything that captures your imagination. Titles that look interesting or which grab your attention should be noted down, as should any thoughts you have about the title in relation to your own research idea. In this process the fact that the title is poorly worded or the project report received a low mark is immaterial. What matters is the fact that you have found a topic that interests you. Based on this you can think of new ideas in the same general area that will enable you to provide fresh insights.

Scanning actual research projects may also produce research ideas. However, you need to beware. The fact that a project is in your library is no guarantee of the quality of the arguments and observations it contains. In many universities all projects are placed in the library whether they are bare passes or distinctions.

Discussion

Colleagues, friends and university tutors are all good sources of possible project ideas. Often project tutors will have ideas for possible student projects, which they will be pleased to discuss with you. In addition, ideas can be obtained by talking to practitioners and professional groups. It is important that as well as discussing possible ideas you also make a note of them. What seemed like a good idea in the coffee shop may not be remembered quite so clearly after the following lecture!

Searching the literature

As part of your discussions, relevant literature may also be suggested. Sharp et al. (2002) discuss types of literature that are of particular use for generating research ideas. These include:

- articles in academic and professional journals;
- reports;
- books.

Of particular use are academic **review articles**. These articles contain a considered review of the state of knowledge in a particular topic area and are therefore likely to contain a wealth of ideas about that area (see Box 2.3). These ideas will act as pointers towards aspects where further research needs to be undertaken. In addition, you can browse recent publications, in particular journals, for possible research ideas (Section 3.5). For many subject areas your project tutor will be able to suggest possible recent review articles, or articles that contain recommendations for further research. Reports may also be of use. The most recently published are usually up to date and, again, often contain recommendations that may form the basis of your research idea. Books by contrast may be less up to date than other written sources. They do, however, often contain a good overview of research that has been undertaken, which may suggest ideas to you.

Box 2.3 Focus on management research

Research ideas in organisational behaviour

Morrison (2010) undertook a review of recent research topics in organisational behaviour (OB). Her study identified topics in OB-focused manuscripts submitted for consideration for publication in the *Academy of Management Journal* (AMJ) during the first two years of her term as an associate editor and also topics in OB papers actually published in the first decade of this century.

In the first category, she identified the 10 most frequent topics in OB submissions to the AMJ in 2007 to 2009. These were: 'groups/teams', 'leadership', 'diversity', 'turnover', 'work-related attitudes and behaviours', 'incentives/motivation', 'attitudes/beliefs', 'emotions/mood', 'organisational citizenship behaviour' and 'cognition/perception' (Morrison 2010: 934).

In the second category, she identified the five most frequent topics in published OB articles: 'team processes/performance'; 'job performance'; 'organisational citizenship behaviour'; 'leadership'; 'job attitudes' (Morrison 2010: 933). Morrison also identified two further categories of topics that occurred in published OB articles less often and more rarely. Topics occurring less often were: 'goals', 'turnover', 'stress', 'careers' and 'career transitions' (Morrison 2010: 933). Topics occurring more rarely were: 'conflict', 'power or influence', 'organisational climate', 'personality', 'cultural differences or values', 'counterproductive behaviour', 'communication and motivation' (Morrison 2010: 933).

Morrison (2010: 933) also usefully suggested a further list of research topics that she recognised as being 'underrepresented, at least relative to my perception of the prevalence of those topics in the OB literature more generally'. These were: 'creativity, diversity, social exchange/psychological contracts and justice/fairness' (Morrison 2010: 933).

If you are interested in conducting your research in the area of OB you should read Morrison's article. You may be able to examine the topics she highlights to generate your own research ideas. You may be interested to explore the relationship between two, or perhaps three, of these concepts within the context of a particular organisation. For example, you may be interested in the relationship between leadership and team working, or team working and motivation, or communication, attitudes and justice, or other possible relationships between these variables. You could then develop this through identifying terms to search online databases to locate relevant literature and refine your research idea.

Searching for publications is only possible when you have at least some idea of the area in which you wish to undertake your research. One way of obtaining this is to re-examine your lecture notes and course textbooks and to note those subjects that appear most interesting (discussed earlier in this section) and the names of relevant authors. This will give you a basis on which to undertake a **preliminary search** (using techniques outlined in Section 3.4 and 3.5). When the articles, reports and other items have been obtained it is often helpful to look for unfounded assertions and statements on the absence of research (Raimond 1993), as these are likely to contain ideas that will enable you to provide fresh insights.

Scanning the media

Keeping up to date with items in the news can be a very rich source of ideas. The stories which occur every day in the 'broadsheet' or 'compact' newspapers, in both online and traditional print versions, may provide ideas which relate directly to the item (e.g. the extent to which items sold by supermarkets contravene the principles of 'green consumerism' by involving excessive 'food miles' in order import them). Please note however that some of these online media are only available by subscription. The stories in these media may also suggest other ideas which flow from the central story (e.g. the degree to which a company uses its claimed environmental credentials as part of its marketing campaign).

Keeping a notebook of ideas

One of the more creative techniques that we all use is to keep a **notebook of ideas**. All this involves is simply noting down any interesting research ideas as you think of them and, of equal importance, what sparked off your thought. You can then pursue the idea using more rational thinking techniques later. Mark keeps a notebook by his bed so he can jot down any flashes of inspiration that occur to him in the middle of the night!

Exploring personal preferences using past projects

Another way of generating possible project ideas is to explore your personal preferences using past project reports from your university. To do this Raimond (1993) suggests that you:

1 Select six projects that you like.
2 For each of these six projects, note down your first thoughts in response to three questions (if responses for different projects are the same this does not matter):
  a What appeals to you about the project?
  b What is good about the project?
  c Why is the project good?
3 Select three projects that you do not like.
4 For each of these three projects, note down your first thoughts in response to three questions (if responses for different projects are the same, or cannot be clearly expressed, this does not matter; note them down anyway):
  a What do you dislike about the project?
  b What is bad about the project?
  c Why is the project bad?

You now have a list of what you consider to be excellent and what you consider to be poor in projects. This will not be the same as a list generated by anyone else. It is also very unlikely to match the attributes of a good research project (Box 2.2). However, by examining this list you will begin to understand those project characteristics that are important to you and with which you feel comfortable. Of equal importance is that you will have identified those that you are uncomfortable with and should avoid. These can be used as the parameters against which to evaluate possible research ideas.

Exploring relevance to business using the literature

There has been a debate running in the pages of the *Financial Times* over recent years about the relevance of business research for managers (see Box 2.4). This debate raises a number of issues for business research in general as well as opportunities for you, as you seek to generate research ideas.

In reality, business and management journals range from those with a more applied focus through to those that are more esoteric. Even more esoteric journal articles will still contain a wealth of ideas. Part of the issue of relevance may be the style of writing. The language codes of academics and managers are likely to vary: 'academic speak' may not be the same as 'management speak'! However Yip (see Box 2.4) believes that the issue of relevance is also related to different methodological preferences.

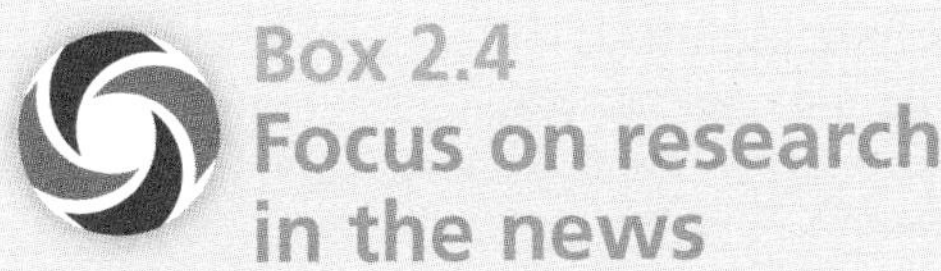

Box 2.4
Focus on research in the news

How relevant is business research to managers?

In 2008, Michael Skapinker, an assistant editor and columnist at the *Financial Times* (FT), wrote an article pointing out that whilst professions such as lawyers, medical practitioners and engineers read the journals published by law schools, medical schools and engineering schools, the same relationship does not exist between managers and journals produced by business schools (Skapinker 2008).

In October 2010, Jordi Canals, dean of Lese Business School, wrote in the FT: 'Business Schools became relevant because they developed knowledge about the main areas of management. But as some schools became more interested in promoting research similar to other disciplines (economics etc.), some research output became increasingly irrelevant to management practice' (Canals 2010).

This debate seems to have developed some momentum in early 2011. Freek Vermeulen, associate professor of Strategic and International Management at the London Business School (LBS), commented that, 'There is a great divide in business schools . . . between research and teaching. There is little relation between them . . . The consequences of this divide are grave. First of all for research: because none of this research is really intended to be used in the classroom, or to be communicated to managers in some other form . . . The goal is publication in a prestigious academic journal' (Vermeulen 2011). He then went on to develop the consequences, as he saw them, for teaching.

About the same time Michael Skapinker returned to the debate with another article, entitled 'Why business still ignores business schools' (Skapinker 2011). These contributions raised comment from academics in the Letters pages of the FT. Timothy Devinney, professor of Strategy at the University of Technology, Sidney in Australia, wrote, 'While I am slightly amenable to Freek Vermeulen's argument, it is simplistic. The reality is that our research does inform our teaching, but does so subtly . . . Where research gets into teaching is through the teacher who translates ideas rather than regurgitates them' (Devinney 2011).

As a final contribution to this on-going debate we cite George Yip, who has taught at a number of universities: LBS, Cambridge, UCLA, Harvard, Erasmus and Ceibs, Shanghai (Bradshaw 2011). Yip wrote: 'Even when business academics can gather data and conduct research on business topics, they face the additional challenge that the great majority of their findings – predictions about what will happen on average – is generally not what managers can use.

'Managers are far more interested in pattern recognition. Does this configuration of external circumstances mesh with my particular configuration of strategies and actions to produce a successful outcome for my company? That is why managers much prefer to read managerial articles in managerial journals that are based on in-depth case studies where there are more variables than observations, rather than large samples statistical studies with many more observations than variables.

'This preference of the managerial audience for case-based evidence raises the challenging requirement for top business schools to conduct research with two types of methodology . . . to gather and test large sample quantitative data and to gather in-depth case studies . . . I am not saying that all, or even most, business researchers must conduct immediately relevant research. The same researchers can make the conversion to relevance at a later date; other academic researchers can make the conversion; or practitioners . . . can make the conversion. In the meantime, with rework and added case examples some academic research can be made readable for managers.' (Yip 2011).

Articles may be based on abstract ideas or on empirical studies. By abstract ideas in this context, we mean work based on conceptual thinking rather than on data. In contrast, empirical studies will be based on collected and analysed data. Both of these may be potentially useful for you as you seek to generate research ideas. Even esoteric, conceptual pieces may contain ideas that you may be able to translate, make operational and test in practice in a given setting, such as a particular organisation, albeit using a simpler methodology to any used in the published study (see Box 2.4).

Articles based on empirical studies may also provide you with research ideas. A published empirical study may have been undertaken as a case study. It may have been based in a particular sector or industry, and it may have been based in a particular organisation or type of organisation. Reading it may lead you to think that you could undertake a similar study, albeit possibly scaled down, in a different type of organisation, in a different industry or sector.

Picking up on Yip's point in Box 2.4, there may be scope for you to undertake a case study that seeks to apply the findings from a large sample statistical study to a particular organisational context or type of organisation. This will allow you to test the applicability of these previous findings and to convert them into a relevant and accessible form for a particular context.

Creatively approaching the literature to convert existing work into a relevant and specifically applied study, in the ways described above, may provide you with a rich and valuable research idea.

Relevance trees

Relevance trees may also prove useful in generating research topics. In this instance, their use is similar to that of mind mapping (Buzan 2011), in which you start with a broad concept from which you generate further (usually more specific) topics. Each of these topics forms a separate branch from which you can generate further, more detailed sub-branches. As you proceed down the sub-branches more ideas are generated and recorded. These can then be examined and a number selected and combined to provide a research idea (Sharp et al. 2002). This technique is discussed in more detail in Section 3.4 (see in particular, Box 3.11).

Brainstorming

The technique of **brainstorming** (Box 2.5), taught as a problem-solving technique on many business and management courses, can also be used to generate and refine research ideas. It is best undertaken with a group of people, although you can brainstorm on your own. Brainstorming involves a number of stages:

1 *Defining the problem*. This will focus on the sorts of ideas you are interested in – as precisely as possible. In the early stages of formulating a topic this may be as vague as, 'I am interested in marketing but don't know what to do for my research topic'.
2 *Asking for suggestions*. These will relate to the problem.
3 *Recording suggestions*. As you record these you will need to observe the following rules:
   - No suggestion should be criticised or evaluated in any way before all ideas have been considered.
   - All suggestions, however wild, should be recorded and considered.
   - As many suggestions as possible should be recorded.
4 *Reviewing suggestions*. You will seek to explore what is meant by each as you review these.
5 *Analysing suggestions*. Work through the list of ideas and decide which appeal to you most as research ideas and why.

Box 2.5 Focus on student research

Brainstorming

George's main interest was football. When he finished university he wanted to work in marketing, preferably for a sports goods manufacturer. He had examined his own strengths and discovered that his best marks were in marketing. He wanted to do his research project on some aspect of marketing, preferably linked to football, but had no real research idea. He asked three friends, all taking business studies degrees, to help him brainstorm the problem.

George began by explaining the problem in some detail. At first the suggestions emerged slowly. He noted them down on the whiteboard. Soon the board was covered with suggestions. George counted these and discovered there were over 100.

Reviewing individual suggestions produced nothing that any of the group felt to be of sufficient merit for a research project. However, one of George's friends pointed out that combining the suggestions of Premier League football, television rights and sponsorship might provide an idea which satisfied the assessment requirements of the project.

They discussed the suggestion further, and George noted the research idea as 'something about how confining the rights to show live Premiership football to paid-for satellite TV channels would impact upon the sale of Premiership club-specific merchandise'.

George arranged to see his project tutor to discuss how to refine the idea they had just generated.

Refining research ideas

The Delphi technique

An additional approach that our students have found particularly useful in refining their research ideas is the **Delphi technique** (Box 2.6). This involves using a group of people who are either involved or interested in the research idea to generate and choose a more specific research idea (Robson 2011). To use this technique you need:

1. to brief the members of the group about the research idea (they can make notes if they wish);
2. at the end of the briefing to encourage group members to seek clarification and more information as appropriate;
3. to ask each member of the group, including the originator of the research idea, to generate independently up to three specific research ideas based on the idea that has been described (they can also be asked to provide a justification for their specific ideas);
4. to collect the research ideas in an unedited and non-attributable form and to distribute them to all members of the group;
5. a second cycle of the process (steps 2 to 4) in which individuals comment on the research ideas and revise their own contributions in the light of what others have said;
6. subsequent cycles of the process until a consensus is reached. These either follow a similar pattern (steps 2 to 4) or use discussion, voting or some other method.

This process works well, not least because people enjoy trying to help one another. In addition, it is very useful in moulding groups into a cohesive whole.

The preliminary inquiry

It is often necessary to refine your research idea in order to turn it into a research question and then into your research project. This process is called the **preliminary inquiry**

Box 2.6 Focus on student research

Using a Delphi Group

Tim explained to the group that his research idea was concerned with understanding the decision-making processes associated with mortgage applications and loan advances. His briefing to the three other group members, and the questions that they asked him, considered aspects such as:

- the influences on a potential first-time buyer to approach a specific financial institution;
- the influence on decision making of face-to-face contact between potential borrowers and potential lenders.

The group then moved on to generate a number of more specific research ideas, among which were the following:

- the factors that influenced potential first-time house purchasers to deal with particular financial institutions;
- the effect of interpersonal contact on mortgage decisions;
- the qualities that potential applicants look for in mortgage advisers.

These were considered and commented on by all the group members. At the end of the second cycle Tim had, with the other students' agreement, refined his research idea to:

- the way in which a range of factors influenced potential first-time buyers' choice of lending institution.

He now needed to pursue these ideas by undertaking a preliminary search of the literature.

or initial inquiry. This is likely to involve searching for and evaluating relevant literature and other related sources (see Box 2.7 for a rare reported example of this in the literature). This may lead to the first iteration of your critical literature review, or help to inform it (see Figure 3.1 later).

For some researchers this process may also include informal discussions with people who have personal experience of and knowledge about your research ideas. It may also involve **shadowing** employees that are likely to be important in your research and who may therefore be able to provide some initial insights. If you are planning on undertaking your research within an organisation it is also important to gain a good understanding of your host organisation (McDonald 2005). However, whatever techniques you use, the underlying purpose is to gain a greater understanding so that your research question can be refined, perhaps by also revisiting some of the techniques we discussed earlier in this section.

At this stage you will need to test your research ideas against the checklist in Box 2.2 and where necessary change them. It may be that after a preliminary inquiry, or discussing your ideas with colleagues, you decide that the research idea is no longer feasible in the form in which you first envisaged it. If this is the case, do not be too downhearted. It is far better to revise your research ideas at this stage than to have to do it later, when you have undertaken far more work.

Integrating ideas

The integration of ideas from these techniques is essential if your research is to have a clear direction and not contain a mismatch between objectives and your final project report. Jankowicz (2005: 34–6) suggests an integrative process that our students have found most useful. This he terms 'working up and narrowing down'. It involves classifying each research idea first into its area, then its field, and finally the precise aspect

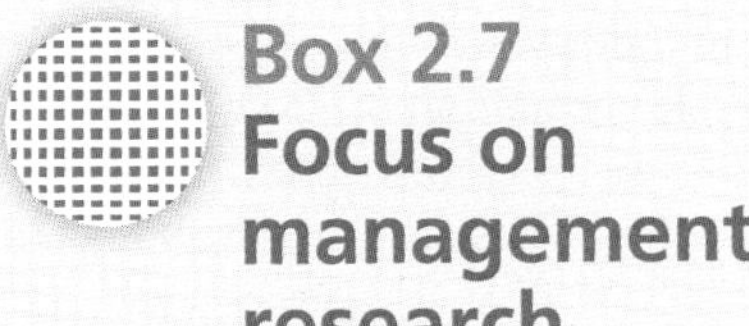

Box 2.7 Focus on management research

The rare case of a reported preliminary inquiry

There are few reports in journal articles of the preliminary inquiries that researchers undertake. Generally the 'methods' section of a journal article only describes the research methodology and techniques used in the actual study. This is probably due to word limits and the presentation of research as an unproblematic process. However, in many studies there may not be a well-defined theoretical base from which to commence the research. There may instead be several possible theoretical strands that might be useful for the proposed study, which need to be explored first. Researchers may need to search for and familiarise themselves with theoretical strands that were previously unknown to them. These possibilities are likely to be the case where the proposed research seeks to explore a new area.

An excellent example describing the way a group of researchers undertook a preliminary inquiry is found in Elsbach et al. (2010). Their study, published in *Human Relations*, examines 'how passive "face time" (i.e. the amount of time one is passively observed without interaction) affects how one is perceived at work' (Elsbach et al. 2010: 735). For example, it is likely to be important for new employees to create an impression of being a diligent worker, without the observer knowing exactly what the person being observed is actually doing. Being seen is what Elsbach and colleagues call 'expected face time'. Positive impressions may be created by being seen in the right places (e.g. at one's desk, in meetings, taking part in events) rather than being based on actual performance. There is also 'extracurricular face time', where the impression an employee creates is also shaped by his or her involvement outside work.

Elsbach et al. identified this as a research idea that had not been investigated previously. They thought that this was surprising because of the increasing numbers of employees who spend much time working away from their work base, as well as the existence of anecdotal evidence indicating that remote workers may feel anxious about their lack of face time.

They conducted a preliminary inquiry that commenced with the collection of anecdotal evidence which suggested that passive face time was linked to the creation of positive impressions of employees in professional jobs. This anecdotal evidence was gleaned from newspaper articles, business magazines and books. In order to understand this relationship further they located two strands of theoretical literature which offered them 'clues' about 'how and why passive face time affects perceptions of employees who display it' (Elsbach et al. 2010: 739). These two strands of literature related to research on organisational citizenship behaviour and research on trait inferences. While these strands of literature had not been designed to focus on passive face time, they lent some support to the idea that being seen in the workplace was likely to lead observers to infer positive attributes about those being observed.

This preliminary inquiry led Elsbach and colleagues to identify that this was an area worth researching to close the gap in our understanding of this phenomenon. They devised a research question – 'How do observers perceive displayers of passive face time in professional work contexts?' – as a result of their preliminary inquiry, which led to a substantive research project composed of two stages. The first of these, called 'Study 1', involved an exploratory stage that used semi-structured interviews which were analysed inductively using the principles of Grounded Theory (see Chapters 4 and 5). The second of these, called 'Study 2', involved an experimental design (see Chapter 5) to test the 'proposed effects of passive face time' (Elsbach et al. 2010: 748).

This published study by Elsbach et al. is rare in terms of describing how their preliminary inquiry helped to establish the need for a substantive research study and the definition of that study. As such, this article may be seen as a model example of the process of a research project from conception to execution.

in which you are interested. These represent an increasingly detailed description of the research idea. Thus your initial area, based on examining your coursework, might be accountancy. After browsing some recent journals and discussion with colleagues this becomes more focused on the field of financial accounting methods. With further reading, the use of the Delphi technique and discussion with your project tutor you decide to focus on the aspect of activity-based costing.

You will know when the process of generating and refining ideas is complete as you will be able to say, 'I'd like to do some research on . . .'. Obviously there will still be a big gap between this and the point when you are ready to start serious work on your research. Sections 2.4 and 2.5 will ensure that you are ready to bridge that gap.

Refining topics given by your employing organisation

If, as a part-time student, your manager gives you a topic, this may present particular problems. It may be something in which you are not particularly interested. In this case you will have to weigh the advantage of doing something useful to the organisation against the disadvantage of a potential lack of personal motivation. You therefore need to achieve a balance. Often the research project your manager wishes you to undertake is larger than is appropriate for your course. In such cases, it may be possible to complete both by isolating an element of the larger organisational project that you find interesting and treating this as the project for your course.

One of our students was asked to do a preliminary investigation of the strengths and weaknesses of her organisation's pay system and then to recommend consultants to design and implement a new system. She was not particularly interested in this project. However, she was considering becoming a freelance personnel consultant. Therefore, for her research project she decided to study the decision-making process in relation to the appointment of personnel consultants. Her organisation's decision on which consultant to appoint, and why this decision was taken, proved to be a useful case study against which to compare management decision-making theory.

In this event you would write a larger report for your organisation and a part of it for your project report. Section 14.4 offers some guidance on writing two separate reports for different audiences.

Other problems may involve your political relationships in the organisation. For example, there will be those keen to commission a project which justifies their particular policy position and see you as a useful pawn in advancing their political interests. It is important to have a clear stance with regard to what you want to do, and your personal objectives, and to stick to this.

Finally, perhaps the biggest potential problem may be one of your own making: to promise to deliver research outcomes to your employer and not do so.

2.4 Turning research ideas into research projects

Writing research questions

Much is made in this book of the importance of defining clear research questions at the beginning of the research process. The importance of this cannot be overemphasised. One of the key criteria of your research success will be whether you have developed a set of clear conclusions from the data you have collected. The extent to which you can do that will be determined largely by the clarity with which you have posed your research questions (Box 2.8).

Box 2.8 Focus on student research

Defining the research question

Imran was studying for a BA in Business Studies and undertaking his placement year in an advanced consumer electronics company. When he first joined the company he was surprised to note that the company's business strategy, which was announced in the company newsletter, seemed to be inconsistent with what Imran knew of the product market.

Imran had become particularly interested in corporate strategy in his degree. He was familiar with some of the literature which suggested that corporate strategy should be linked to the general external environment in which the organisation operated. He wanted to do some research on corporate strategy in his organisation for his degree dissertation.

After talking this over with his project tutor, Imran decided on the following research question: 'Why does [organisation's name]'s corporate strategy not seem to reflect the major factors in the external operating environment?'

Defining research questions, rather like generating research ideas (Section 2.3), is not a straightforward matter. It is important that the question is sufficiently involved to generate the sort of project that is consistent with the standards expected of you (Box 2.2). A question that only prompts a descriptive answer – for example, 'What is the proportion of graduates entering the civil service who attended the pre-1992 UK universities?' – is far easier to answer than: 'Why are graduates from pre-1992 UK universities more likely to enter the civil service than graduates from other universities?'

Questions may be divided into ones that are descriptive, evaluative and/or explanatory. A question that commences with 'What', 'When', 'Where', 'Who' or 'How' will lead to an answer that will be at least partly descriptive. Questions that seek explanations will either commence with 'Why' or contain this word within the question. For example, a question may ask customers what they think about a new product and why they like or dislike it.

Many research questions commence with 'What' or 'How' but go beyond seeking a descriptive answer. There is a clear distinction between asking, 'How much did the marketing campaign for the new range of products cost?' and 'How effective was the marketing campaign for the new range of products?' The first question, 'How much . . .?', will only reveal a descriptive answer. The second question, 'How effective . . . ?', is designed to be evaluative as well as descriptive. In order to make sure that this question is evaluative it will be necessary to identify a set of evaluation criteria within the research objectives that are devised to operationalise this question (Box 2.9). There is a role for research that evaluates as well develops explanations in business and management. Another way of wording this type of question might be, 'To what extent was the marketing campaign effective and why?' There is further consideration of the relationship between 'what', 'how' and 'why' questions later in this section.

While some questions may be too simple, it is perhaps more likely that you might fall into the trap of asking research questions that are too difficult. The question cited above, 'Why are graduates from pre-1992 UK universities more likely to enter the civil service than graduates from other universities?', is a case in point. It would probably be very difficult to gain sufficient access to the inner portals of the civil service to get a good grasp of the subtle 'unofficial' processes that go on at staff selection which may favour one type of candidate over another. Over-reaching yourself in the definition of research questions is a danger.

Box 2.9 Focus on student research

Writing a set of research objectives

Tom was a part-time student who worked for a large power and gas company employing several thousand employees across many different sites. Tom had been undertaking an employment-related project on employee engagement and had decided to focus his university research project on employee communication. His employing organisation had been refocusing its employee communication away from traditional methods towards Internet- and intranet-based channels. Tom had noted the following comment in the CIPD Research Insight (2010: 14): 'The measurement of communication does not appear in HR research or literature very often and yet measurement is essential to evaluate, guide and direct communication initiatives and investments.'

Following a process of generating and refining ideas for research Tom decided that he would like to explore the effectiveness of employee communication developments in his employing organisation. This idea had been approved by the internal communication management team and he was informed that his request for access to managers would be supported.

Tom refined his research question until he was satisfied with it: 'How effective are Internet and intranet channels as a means to communicate with employees in [company name]?' He and his project tutor felt that the scope of this research question was 'just about right'. They felt it was 'doable' and that it focused on an issue that was important and relevant for the business.

Tom's project tutor asked Tom to draw up a set of interconnected research objectives that would operationalise his research and provide a set of evaluation criteria to enable him to address his 'how effective . . .' type of question. Tom came up with the following set of research objectives. Objective 2 allowed Tom to identify the company's objectives for each channel and objectives 3–6 allowed Tom to measure and then compare channels in order to draw conclusions about 'how effective' they were.

1 To identify each Internet and intranet channel of employee communication used in the company;
2 To describe the company's objectives for each channel (e.g. conveying news about the business, facilitating communication across the company, announcing results and targets, bringing about behavioural change);
3 To identify and explore specific examples of how each channel has been beneficial or influential;
4 To identify and explore specific examples where each channel has not been beneficial or influential;
5 To determine a measure of effectiveness for each channel that shows whether and how the channel had met, exceeded or failed to meet the objectives set for it;
6 To compare measures of effectiveness across channels related to different organisational objectives;
7 To make recommendations about each channel's future use and fitness for purpose.

Clough and Nutbrown (2002) use what they call the **'Goldilocks test'** to decide if research questions are either 'too big', 'too small', 'too hot' or 'just right'. Those that are too big probably need significant research funding because they demand too many resources. Questions that are too small are likely to be of insufficient substance, while those that are too 'hot' may be so because of sensitivities that might be aroused as a result of doing the research. This may be because of the timing of the research or the many other reasons that could upset key people who have a role to play, either directly or indirectly, in the research context. Research questions that are 'just right', note Clough and Nutbrown (2002: 34), are those that are 'just right for investigation at *this* time, by *this* researcher in *this* setting'.

The pitfall you must avoid at all costs is asking research questions that will not generate new insights (Box 2.2). This raises the question of the extent to which you have consulted the relevant literature. It is perfectly legitimate to replicate research because

Table 2.2 Examples of research ideas and resulting general focus research questions

Research idea	Research questions
Advertising and share prices	How does the running of a TV advertising campaign designed to boost the image of a company affect its share price?
Job recruitment via the Internet	How effective is recruiting for new staff via the Internet in comparison with traditional methods?
The use of aromas as a marketing device	In what ways does the use of specific aromas in supermarkets affect buyer behaviour?
The use of Internet banking	What effect has the growth of Internet banking had upon the uses customers make of branch facilities and why?

you have a genuine concern about its applicability to your research setting (for example, your organisation). However, it certainly is not legitimate to display your ignorance of the literature.

McNiff and Whitehead (2000) make the point that the research question may not emerge until the research process has started and is therefore part of the process of 'progressive illumination'. They note that this is particularly likely to be the case in practitioner-led action research (see Sections 4.3 and 5.5).

It is often a useful starting point in the writing of research questions to begin with one **research question** that flows from your research idea. This may lead to several more detailed questions or the definition of research objectives. Table 2.2 has some examples of general focus research questions.

In order to clarify the research question, Clough and Nutbrown (2002) talk of the Russian doll principle. This means taking the research idea and 'breaking down the research questions from the original statement to something which strips away the complication of layers and obscurities until the very essence – the heart – of the question can be expressed . . . just as the Russian doll is taken apart to reveal a tiny doll at the centre' (Clough and Nutbrown 2002: 34).

Writing your research questions will be, in most cases, your individual concern but it is useful to get other people to help. An obvious source of guidance is your project tutor. Consulting your project tutor will avoid the pitfalls of the questions that are too easy or too difficult or have been answered before. Discussing your area of interest with your project tutor will lead to your research questions becoming much clearer.

Prior to discussion with your project tutor you may wish to conduct a brainstorming session with your peers or use the Delphi technique (Section 2.3). Your research questions may flow from your initial examination of the relevant literature. As outlined in Section 2.3, journal articles reporting primary research will often end with a conclusion that includes the consideration by the author of the implications for future research of the work in the article. This may be phrased in the form of research questions. However, even if it is not, it may suggest possible research questions to you.

Writing research objectives

Your research question may be used to generate more detailed investigative questions, or you may use it as a base from which to write a set of **research objectives**. Objectives are more generally acceptable to the research community as evidence of the researcher's clear sense of purpose and direction. Once you have devised your research question, we believe that research objectives are likely to lead to greater specificity than using

Table 2.3 Criteria to devise useful research objectives

Criterion	Purpose
Transparency (What does it mean?)	The meaning of the research objective is clear and unambiguous
Specificity (What I am going to do?)	The purpose of the research objective is clear and easily understood, as are the actions required to fulfil it
Relevancy (Why I am going to do this)	The research objective's link to the research question and wider research project is clear
Interconnectivity (How will it help to complete the research project?)	Taken together as a set, the research objectives illustrate the steps in the research process from its start to its conclusion, without leaving any gaps. In this way, the research objectives form a coherent whole
Answerability (Will this be possible?) (Where shall I obtain data?)	The intended outcome of the research objective is achievable. Where this relates to data, the nature of the data required will be clear or at least implied
Measurability (When will it be done?)	The intended product of the research objective will be evident when it has been achieved

investigative questions. It may be that either is satisfactory. Do check whether your examining body has a preference.

Your research question allows you to say what the issue or problem is that you wish to study. Research objectives allow you to **operationalise** your question – that is, to state the steps you intend to take to answer it. A similar way of thinking about the difference between questions and objectives is related to 'what' and 'how'. Research questions express 'what' your research is about. Research objectives express 'how' you intend to structure the research process to answer your question. In this way, research objectives can be seen to complement a research question, through providing the means to operationalise it. They provide a key step to transform your research question into your research project.

Writing useful research objectives requires you to fulfil a number of fit-for-purpose criteria. Table 2.3 sets out criteria to help you devise research objectives to operationalise your research question. Each of these criteria is also rephrased as a question, which you can use as a checklist to evaluate your own draft research objectives. Box 2.9 provides an example set of objectives at the stage when a student's research question was being developed into a sequence of research objectives.

The importance of theory in writing research questions and objectives

Section 4.3 outlines the role of theory in helping you to decide your approach to research design. However, your consideration of theory should begin earlier than this. It should inform your research questions and research objectives.

To help you to think about this, we may ask four questions that relate to the role of theory. What is theory? Why is theory important? How is theory developed? What types of theoretical contribution might be made? These questions lead into the discussion in Section 4.3

What is theory?

To address the question 'what is theory?' we use the influential work of Whetten (1989). Whetten identified that theory is composed of four elements, related to 'what', 'how', 'why' and a fourth group of 'who', 'where' and 'when'. The first of these may be summarised as: what are the variables or concepts that the theory examines? For example, in Box 2.9, the variables in Tom's research question are communication channels and employees (their awareness and behaviours).

The second element may be summarised as: how are these variables or concepts related? Tom's research question was designed to examine the relationship between communication channels and employees. A key aspect here is **causality**. Theory is concerned with cause and effect. In Tom's research, Tom was interested to explore how each communication channel influenced employees' levels of awareness and behaviour. In other words, does the use of a particular channel cause an effect on employees' levels of awareness and behaviour.

The third element may be summarised as: why are these variables or concepts related? This is the critical element in a theory because it explains the nature of the relationship between the variables or concepts. According to Whetten, 'what' and 'how' are descriptive; it is 'why' that explains the relationship. This point is worth developing, as you may be asking, 'what is the difference between "how" and "why" in this context?' In the case of Tom's research, Tom found that his data suggested some channels were better at communicating 'top-down' news, whereas other channels were better at facilitating communication across the company. His data helped him to recognise relationships that he could describe. However, Tom needed to analyse his data further (and where necessary to extend its collection) to answer the question, 'why do these relationships exist in my data?'

To summarise so far, good theory must not only include 'what' and 'how' elements to identify underpinning variables and describe the nature of their relationship (cause and effect); it must also use **logical reasoning** to explain why the relationship exists. 'Logical' because you will be looking for good reasons to explain 'why' and 'reasoning' because your use of logic will be based on what you already know, related to the 'what' and 'how'. Once a valid explanation has been developed, the theory may be used not only to explain why the relationship exists but also to make predictions about new outcomes if the variables on which the theory is based are manipulated (or changed). In the case of Tom's research, his theory may be used to predict that increasing investment in an effective communication channel will lead to improvements in employee awareness. Conversely, it may be used to predict that withdrawing investment in this channel will be a false cost saving.

While good theory has the power to explain and predict, it may also be subject to limitations. The scope of many theories will be limited by one or more constraints. The fourth group of elements that Whetten identified may therefore be summarised as: who does this theory apply to; where does this theory apply; when does this theory apply? In the case of Tom's research, Tom recognised that some of his theoretical conclusions applied to engineering staff but not to administrative staff. Other conclusions applied to head office employees but not to regional employees. He also recognised that as some communication channels continued to develop, his conclusions about those would need to be re-evaluated in the future.

In this way, the explanations of the cause-and-effect relationships between variables in a theory may be contextual and time limited, indicating constraints to their generalisability. Another important contribution that addresses the question 'what is theory?' starts from the opposite perspective by discussing 'What theory is not?' (Sutton and Staw 1995). This is a helpful contribution to our understanding and provides a complementary approach to that of Whetten (1989) (see Box 2.10).

Box 2.10 Focus on management research

Clarifying what theory is not

Sutton and Staw (1995) make a helpful contribution to the question 'What is theory?' by defining what it is not. In their view theory is not:

1. *References.* Listing references to existing theories and mentioning the names of such theories may look impressive. However, alluding to the theory developed by other researchers may only provide a smokescreen. Instead researchers need to identify the concepts, casual relationships and logical explanations that they are using from previous theoretical work in relation to their own work.
2. *Data.* Data are important to be able to confirm, revise or overturn existing theory and to be able to develop new theory. However, data are used to describe the relationships or patterns that are revealed from their collection and analysis. Description by itself does not equal theory. Theory also requires logical explanations to discuss why such relationships or patterns were revealed, or why they might be expected to be revealed when testing existing theory (see Section 4.3).
3. *Lists of variables.* Variables are important in the process of theory development but simply presenting or listing these by themselves does not represent a theory.
4. *Diagrams.* Diagrams are often helpful to show observed or expected casual relationships and how different relationships are related or how they are expected to be related. However, by themselves diagrams or figures are not theory. Sutton and Staw (1995: 376) state: 'Good theory is often representational and verbal.' They say that clear explanations can be represented graphically but that, to be able to develop a rich theoretical understanding, these will also require written discussion to explain why these relationships exist.
5. *Hypotheses or predictions.* In a similar manner to point 3 above, hypotheses are an important part of the process of developing and testing theory in particular theoretical approaches (see Experiment in Section 5.5), but they do not constitute a theory by themselves.

You are likely to use research questions rather than hypotheses in your research design and we would add to point 5 that the propositions or concepts that inform your research questions are also not theory by themselves.

Why is theory important?

There is probably no word that is more misused and misunderstood in education than the word 'theory'. It is thought that material included in textbooks is 'theory', whereas what is happening in the 'real world' is practice. Students who saw earlier editions of this book remarked that they were pleased that the book was not too 'theoretical'. What they meant was that the book concentrated on giving lots of practical advice. Yet the book is full of theory. Advising you to carry out research in a particular way (variable A) is based on the theory that this will yield effective results (variable B). This is the cause-and-effect relationship referred to in the definition of theory developed above and is very much the view of Kelly (1955). Kelly argues that the individual who attempts to solve the daily problems which we all face goes about this activity in much the same way as the scientist. Both continuously make and test hypotheses and revise their concepts accordingly. Both organise their results into what are called schemata and then into a system of broader schemata which are called theories. Kelly asserts that we need such schemata and theories in order to make sense of the complexity of the world in which we live. Without these organising frameworks we would be overwhelmed by the unconnected detail we would have to recall.

Implicitly each of us uses theory in our lives and in the jobs that we undertake. For example, the marketing manager believes that the use of loyalty cards in the supermarket chain for which he or she works makes customers less likely to shop regularly at a competitor supermarket. This is a theory even through the marketing manager would probably not recognise it as such. He or she is still less likely to refer to it as a theory, particularly in the company of fellow managers. Many managers are very dismissive of any talk that smacks of 'theory'. It is thought of as something that is all very well to learn about at business school but which bears little relation to what goes on in everyday organisational life. Yet the loyalty card example shows that it has everything to do with what goes on in everyday organisational life. By introducing loyalty cards (variable A), the retailing company is attempting to influence the behaviour of customers (variable B). As every supermarket chain introduces their own loyalty card, the marketing manager's personal theory that this encourages loyalty may begin to seem inadequate when confronted by a range of other complementary and innovative strategies to encourage customers to switch where they shop.

The use of a loyalty card may become just one variable among many as supermarkets compete by offering extra loyalty card bonus points on particular goods, double or treble points if customers spend over a certain amount, the opportunity to redeem the value from accumulated bonus points against a range of discounted offers and so on. In this case, research will provide the marketing manager with a much greater understanding of the effectiveness of the strategies used within her or his supermarket chain. The data collected will allow theoretical explanations to be developed based on causal relationships that may then be used to predict which of these strategies is more effective. It may also indicate that different strategies will be effective in different locations and perhaps that specific strategies are more effective at particular times of the year, or that specific strategies should be targeted at particular socioeconomic groups. The ability to make these predictions potentially allows the supermarket chain to compete more effectively against its rivals. Valid theoretical explanations may lead to predictions that offer the supermarket chain increased opportunities for influence and control and the possibility of increasing market share.

If theory is so rooted in our everyday lives it is something that we need not be apprehensive about. If it is implicit in all of our decisions and actions then recognising its importance means making it explicit. In research, the importance of theory must be recognised: therefore it must be made explicit.

How is theory developed and how does this inform your research question and research objectives?

So far we have defined the elements of theory and discussed the need to recognise it in your research, even as you start to plan this. You may ask, 'why is it important for me to recognise theory at this early stage, when writing my research question and research objectives?' Apart from its capacity to inform your research ideas (discussed earlier), the answer to this relates to the way theory may also inform your research question and how theory is developed.

Just as literature and the theory contained within it may provide you with research ideas, theory may also inform your research question. Theory may provide you with an idea for a research question and a set of variables or concepts that you then test to determine whether, how and why they are related in the context of your own research (see Box 2.11). In 1945, Kurt Lewin used the expression 'nothing is as practical as a good theory' (1945: 129). Van de Ven (1989) utilised Lewin's expression to illustrate that good theory always indicates important questions for further research.

Box 2.11 Focus on student research

Writing a research question based on theory

Justine was a final-year marketing undergraduate who was interested in the theory of cognitive dissonance (Festinger 1957). She wanted to apply this to consumer purchasing decision making in the snack foods industry (e.g. buying potato crisps) in the light of the adverse publicity that the consumption of such foods has as a result of 'healthy eating' campaigns.

Justine applied Festinger's theory by arguing in her research project proposal that a consumer who learns that eating too many snacks is bad for her health will experience dissonance, because the knowledge that eating too much snack food is bad for her health will be dissonant with the cognition that she continues to eat too many snacks. She can reduce the dissonance by changing her behaviour, i.e., she could stop eating so many snacks. (This would be consonant with the cognition that eating too many snacks is bad for her health.) Alternatively, she could reduce dissonance by changing her cognition about the effect of snack over-eating on health and persuade herself that does not have a harmful effect on health. She would look for positive effects of eating snacks, for example by believing that it is an important source of enjoyment which outweighs any harmful effects. Alternatively, she might persuade herself that the risk to health from snack over-eating is negligible compared with the danger of car accidents (reducing the importance of the dissonant cognition).

Justine's research question was, 'To what extent does adverse "healthy eating" campaign publicity affect the consumer's decision to purchase snack foods and why?'

Research questions may also be inspired by sources other than existing theory. Kilduff (2006) suggests that an important inspiration for research flows from your involvement with issues in which you are personally interested. Even in this case, however, theory will allow you to familiarise yourself with your area of interest and may help you to draft your research question.

How theory is developed also provides a crucial reason for recognising relevant theory when writing your research question and objectives. Your research project will be designed to test a theory or to develop a theory. Where you wish to adopt a clear theoretical position that you will test though the collection of data, your research project will be theory driven and you will be using a **deductive approach**. Where you wish to explore a topic and develop a theoretical explanation as the data are collected and analysed, your research project will be data driven and you will be adopting an **inductive approach**.

We discuss theory development in much greater detail in Section 4.3, but it is useful to introduce this fundamental difference in the way theory is developed to be able to show why you need to think about this when drafting your research question and research objectives. A deductive approach will require you identify a clear theoretical position when you draft the research question that you will then test. This is the approach we outlined above (see Box 2.11). An inductive approach does not rely on identifying an existing theoretical position but it is likely that if you adopt this approach you will still need to familiarise yourself with theory in your chosen subject area before you draft your research question. Using an inductive approach does not mean disregarding theory as you formulate your research question and objectives. An inductive approach is intended to allow meanings to emerge from data as you collect them in order to identify patterns and relationships to build a theory, but it does not prevent you from using existing theory to formulate your research question and even to identify concepts that you wish to explore in the research process (see Section 4.3). In this way, all researchers are likely to commence their research with knowledge of relevant literature and the theory it contains.

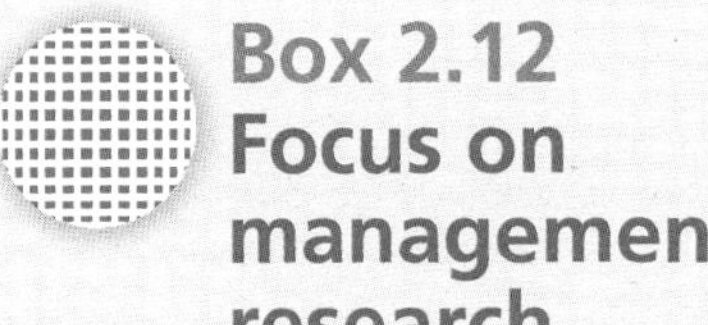

Box 2.12 Focus on management research

Thanks for the description; I'd like some more explanation please!

Mackenzie (2000a, 2000b) argues that research using opinion surveys leads to ambiguous conclusions if these only ask questions about what respondents believe rather than asking other questions that reveal why they hold those beliefs. For example, an opinion survey in a workplace may include the statement, 'I am satisfied with my overall compensation'. Respondents will typically be asked to respond by ticking a box which indicates whether they strongly agree, agree, disagree or strongly disagree. The data produced will be very useful in analytical terms, since they will provide an organisation-wide measure of satisfaction and allow comparisons to be made across and between departments, occupations, grades, genders and locations, etc. However, when it comes to developing conclusions and recommendations, other data will be required that explain why these beliefs are held. For example, why might 65 per cent agree with the statement, 'I am provided with the necessary training to do my job well'. Perhaps more importantly, why might 35 per cent be disagreeing? Other data related to the context of the workplace and to the implementation of organisational processes (e.g. related to pay and to training in our examples) will be required to understand why respondents hold the views that they do.

Without such data, meaningful explanations can only be guessed. For you to be able to develop a theoretical explanation you will need not only 'what'-type data but also 'why'-type data. 'What'-type data are referred to as descriptive research. Whilst these are essential for analytical purposes, you will also need to develop explanatory research to be able to build and test theory.

There is a third relationship between theory and your research question that is important to recognise when drafting your research question. In our discussion of theory we recognised that it is crucial to be able to explain how variables or concepts are related and why they are related. Research questions may therefore play a crucial role in encouraging research that is designed to produce theoretical explanations, no matter how limited these explanations might be (see the following subsection). A question that only encourages a descriptive outcome will not lead to a theoretical explanation. For example, compare the following questions. 'How satisfied are employees with recent changes in the department's business strategy?' 'What are the implications of recent changes in the department's business strategy for employee satisfaction and why?' The first question is written to produce a descriptive outcome. The second question has the potential to explore and test relationships and to arrive at theoretical explanations to explain why these might exist (see Box 2.12).

What types of theoretical contribution might be made?

This discussion of theory has probably left you asking, 'what does this mean for me?' While you will be expected to produce a theoretical explanation, you will not be expected to develop a momentous theory that leads to a new way of thinking about management! Not all theoretical contributions are the same and it is reassuring to look at the threefold typology of theories shown in Figure 2.1

'Grand theories' are usually thought to be the province of the natural scientists (e.g. Newton's theory of gravity, Darwin's theory of evolution or Einstein's theory of relativity). These may be contrasted with 'middle-range theories', which lack the capacity to change the way in which we think about the world but are nonetheless of significance. Some of the theories of human motivation well known to managers would be in

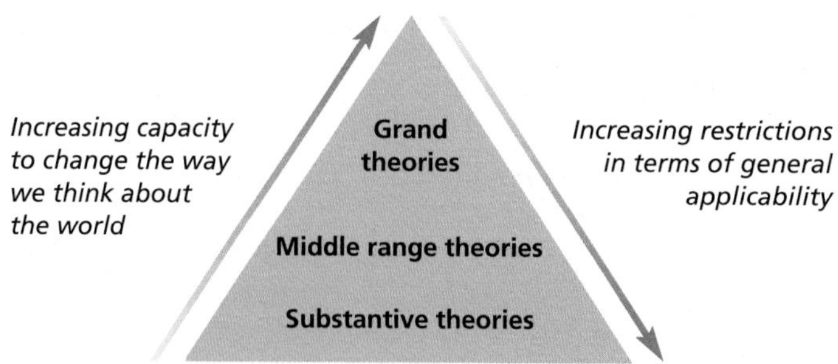

Figure 2.1 Grand, middle-range and substantive theories

this category. However, most of us are concerned with 'substantive theories' that are restricted to a particular time, research setting, group or population or problem.

For example, studying the implications of a cost-saving strategy in a particular organisation would be an example of a substantive theory. Restricted they may be, but a host of 'substantive theories' that present similar propositions may lead to 'middle-range theories'. By developing 'substantive theories', however modest, we are doing our bit as researchers to enhance our understanding of the world about us. A grand claim, but a valid one!

2.5 Writing your research proposal

The **research proposal**, occasionally referred to as a protocol or outline, is a structured plan of your proposed research project. In this section we discuss why it is necessary and how it may be structured, but it is important to recognise that a competent research proposal needs to draw on material discussed in subsequent chapters. Before you can write your research proposal you will need to be aware of available literature and appropriate theory (Section 2.4 and Chapter 3), the research philosophy and approach that you wish to use (Chapter 4), your research design including methodological choice, research strategy and time frame (Chapter 5), access and ethical issues (Chapter 6), sample selection (Chapter 7), data collection methods and data analysis techniques (Chapters 8–13).

Why is a research proposal necessary?

Creating a clear specification to guide your research project

Your research project is likely to be a large element in your course. It is also student driven. You will be responsible for conceiving, conducting and concluding this project and creating a dissertation, thesis or report. Apart from applying your research methods training and the advice you receive from your project tutor, it will be your piece of work. From this perspective, developing a research proposal offers you the opportunity to think carefully about your research project (see Table 2.4).

We do not suggest that you use these questions to provide headings under which you write responses, but we feel that they should be helpful as a guide and as a checklist against which to evaluate your research proposal before submitting it to your tutor. A well-thought-out and well-written research proposal has the potential to provide you with a clear specification of the what, why, how, when and where of your research project.

Table 2.4 Key questions to guide and evaluate a research proposal

- What am I going to do?
- Why am I doing this?
- Why is it worth doing?
- How does it relate to what has been done before in my subject area?
- Which theory or theories will inform what I am doing and how will I use it or them?
- What is my research question and what are my research objectives?
- How shall I conduct my research?
- What is my research design?
- What type of data do I need?
- Who and where are my intended participants?
- How will I gain access?
- How shall I select them?
- How will I collect my data?
- How will I analyse my data and use this to develop theoretical explanations?
- What data quality issues might I encounter?
- How will I seek to overcome these?
- What ethical issues might I encounter at each stage of my research?
- How will I overcome these?

Producing a research proposal is demanding: thinking through what you wish to do and why, identifying and synthesising literature and then envisaging all of the stages of your research will be time-consuming, as will the necessary revisions to create a coherent and clearly written proposal. However, the effort is likely to prove to be very worthwhile. As you juggle several activities during the period of your research project, there may be occasions when you pick up your research proposal and feel glad that you spent so much time producing a clear specification to guide your project through its various stages.

Meeting the requirements of those who approve and assess your project

It is likely that your research proposal will be assessed before you are allowed to carry on with your proposed research project. A proportion of the overall marks available for your project report may be set aside to assess the research proposal. Alternatively, a research proposal may be subject to approval before you are permitted to proceed with your research project. In either case, it will be necessary to pass a certain standard before being allowed to progress. There are potentially a number of different criteria that may be used to assess a research proposal. These may include criteria that are specific to each of the components of the proposal, which we describe below. Part of the assessment and approval process may also centre on criteria that focus on more general concerns. We discuss three such criteria that are likely to be used to assess your research proposal: coherence, ethical clearance and feasibility.

Coherence

A research project is a complex and time-consuming activity. As we indicated above, you are likely to benefit from creating a clear specification to guide your research project. Your project tutor and any other assessor will be looking for evidence of coherence and lucidity in the way you have written your research proposal, to demonstrate that it will be fit for purpose and able to direct your research activity.

Ethical clearance

Part of the approval process for your research proposal may involve it being considered and approved by a research ethics committee. Your university's code of ethical practice is likely to require all research involving human participants to be considered and approved, especially where research involves young or vulnerable participants. It may also be necessary to state how data will be stored, whether they will be kept subsequently and under what conditions, in order to ensure the continuing anonymity of the participants and confidentiality of their data. Section 6.5 discusses ethical issues related to the design stage of a research project. You will need to be aware of and abide by the ethical requirements of your institution. These requirements will add to the time that you will need to allow for the planning stage of your research project. As a professional student you may also need to be aware of and abide by the ethical requirements of your professional institute.

Feasibility

You may have devised a coherent and well-structured research proposal that would create much interest but it may not be possible to achieve, or sensible to contemplate. Feasibility is a multifaceted criterion that your assessors will be concerned about. Your proposal may not be possible to achieve in the time available to undertake the research project and produce your dissertation or management report. It may be that data collection would not be possible because you would not be able to gain access to participants, or it might not be practical and your tutor will tell you so! The proposal may require resources that are not available, finance commitments that are unaffordable or skills that you have not developed and would not be able to do so in the timescale of the project.

It is always helpful to discuss your research proposal with a tutor. Where there are concerns about any of the issues just considered, it will be possible to discuss these to work out how the proposed research may be amended. For example, in relation to feasibility something more modest in scope may be discussed. Your task will then be to amend initial ideas and convince your tutor that the proposed research is achievable within the time and other resources available.

Ensuring that your research project isn't based on preconceived ideas

Your research project offers a valuable way to learn the skills involved in this activity. These skills are transferable to many other situations including the world of work. It is about process as well as outcome. Concerns about feasibility (related to overenthusiasm) lie at one end of a continuum, at other end of which lies a very occasional concern about sincerity. Do not be like the student who came to Phil to talk over a research proposal and said, 'Of course, I know what the answer will be'. When asked to explain the purpose of doing the research if he already knew the answer, he became rather defensive and eventually looked for another supervisor and, probably, another topic.

Approval of your research proposal implies that it is satisfactory. While this is no guarantee of subsequent success, it will reassure you to know that you have started your research journey with an appropriate destination and journey plan. It will be for you to ensure that you do not get lost!

How may your research project be structured?

Perhaps the first comment to make is that there are potentially different ways to structure your research proposal. Different research traditions (see Chapter 5) may lead to different

Box 2.13 Focus on student research

Devising research proposal titles

Imran (see Box 2.8) reworded his research question into the following title for his research proposal:

> 'Reasons for mismatch between corporate strategy and the external environment.'

Tom (see Box 2.9) devised this title for his research proposal:

> 'The effectiveness of Internet and intranet channels for employee communication.'

Justine (see Box 2.11) used her research question to develop this title for her proposal:

> 'The effect of healthy eating publicity on snack foods purchasing decisions.'

ways of structuring your proposal and, later on, your project report (see Chapter 14). We describe what may be thought of as the standard approach to structuring your research proposal. You will need to make yourself aware if there is any variation to this in your institution's or faculty's requirements. Whichever structure you are required to adopt, this will be driven by and focused on your research question and research objectives, and you will need to ensure that you produce a coherent proposal.

Title

The title should simply and concisely summarise the research question. It should avoid unnecessary phrases such as, 'A study to explore . . .' Instead it should reflect the concepts or variables in your research (see Box 2.13). If your research question changes, this will naturally lead to a change to your title.

Background

This section has a number of related functions. It needs to introduce the reader to the research issue or problem. This addresses the question, 'what am I going to do?' You also need to provide a rationale for your proposed research and to justify this. This may be composed of two elements, one relating to you and the other relating to the value of the work. Your reader will be looking for some evidence that this is a topic in which you have sufficient interest to sustain the effort that will be required from you over the period of the research project. This may relate to the need to tackle a problem, to your intellectual curiosity, or to your intended career direction. It relates to the question, 'why am I going to do this?' The rationale will also need to address the question, 'why is it worth doing?' This will relate to one of the following types of justification: the application of a theory to a particular context (such as within an organisation); the development of a theory within a research setting; testing a theory within a given context. Your research may propose other such justifications depending on its nature.

This leads to another function of this section: to demonstrate 'how my research relates to what has been done before in this subject area'. In achieving this you will show your knowledge of relevant literature and clarify where your proposal fits into the debate in this literature (see Section 3.2). You will also be able to begin to show 'which theory or theories will inform what I am doing and how I will use it or them'. The intention will be not to write a detailed review of the literature but rather to provide an overview of key literature sources from which you will draw and the theory or theories within them. This will not be the same as the critical literature review (Section 3.2) that you will present in your final project report but the start of the process that leads to it.

Research questions and objectives

The Background section should lead logically into a statement of your research question(s) and research objectives. These should leave the reader in no doubt about what your research seeks to achieve. Be careful here to ensure that your objectives are precisely written and will lead to observable outcomes (see Box 2.9).

Method

The Background and Method will be the longest sections of your proposal. The Method is designed to address the general question, 'how shall I conduct my research?' The Method may be divided into subsections that deal with research design, participants, techniques and procedures, and ethical considerations. This final element may need to be dealt with in a discrete section of your research proposal.

Research design is discussed in Chapter 5. It involves you making a number of decisions about, 'what is my research design?' You will need to make a methodological choice between a quantitative, qualitative or multiple methods design. You will also need to select one or more research strategies (e.g. an experiment, a case study, a survey or a Grounded Theory strategy etc.) and determine an appropriate time frame for your project depending on the nature of your research. You will need to describe each of these and justify your choice by the way these elements fit together to form a coherent whole.

How you design your research will affect the type of data you require, where you intend to locate them and from whom you will collect them. Your data may be collected from human participants, or they may be secondary data (see Chapter 8) such as from archival research (see Section 5.5) or a combination of these. You will therefore need to address the question, 'what type of data do I need?' If you are using secondary data you will need to explain what these are, where they are located, any issues related to access and justify this choice. If you intend to collect data from human participants, you will need to answer, 'who and where are my intended participants?' You may be intending to conduct research in a single organisation or across a number of organisations. You will need to explain and justify the nature of the organisation or organisations and possibly the sector or sectors within which it operates (or they operate). Your intended participants may be located within a specific part of an organisation or be drawn from across it. You will need to explain and justify this.

You will also need to explain the nature of your research population and why you chose it. For example, they may either be entrepreneurs, managerial employees, non-managerial employees, a particular occupational group, trade union officials, or some combination of these. Where you need to select a sample from within a research population you will need to address the question, 'how shall I select them?' Chapter 7 discusses types of probability and non-probability sampling and you will need to describe and justify your sampling technique and sample size.

You will also need to describe the data collection and analysis techniques you intend to use by answering the questions, 'how will I collect my data?' and 'how will I analyse it and use this to develop theoretical explanations?' Data collection techniques include examination of secondary data, questionnaires, interviews and observation (see Chapters 8–11). You will not need to explain the precise details of the technique you intend to use, such as including a copy of your questionnaire, interview questions or the content of an observation schedule but you will need to describe how you will use them. For example, if you are using interviews what type will you use, how many will you conduct, with what type of participant, their intended duration, how you will record the data (e.g. note taking and/or audio-recording). You will also need to describe, albeit briefly, how you intend to analyse each type of data that you collect.

It will also be important to discuss ethical considerations so that you anticipate these and demonstrate to your tutor and ethics committee that your research design and proposal has been formulated to minimise ethical concerns and avoid unethical practice. This will be essential where you are dealing with human participants, and sometimes even with secondary data collected from human participants. There may be a reduced need for some of you undertaking certain types of research (e.g. where this is based on macro-level, completely anonymised data) but in nearly all cases this requirement is very likely to mean that business and management researchers need to be sensitive to ethical concerns.

Timescale

This will help you and your reader to decide on the viability of your research proposal. It will be helpful if you divide your research plan into stages. This will give you a clear idea as to what is possible in the given timescale. Experience has shown that however well the researcher's time is organised the whole process seems to take longer than anticipated (Box 2.14).

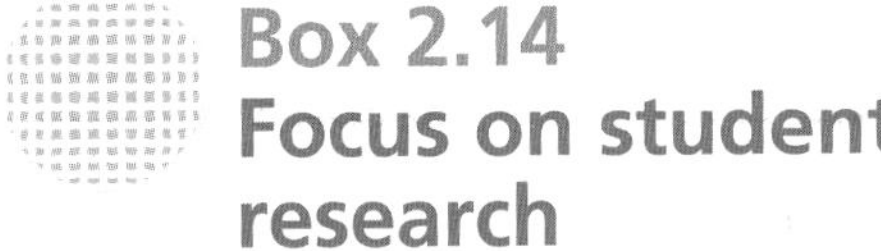

Box 2.14 Focus on student research

Louisa's research timescale

As part of the final year of her undergraduate business studies degree, Louisa had to undertake an 8000–10,000 word research project. In order to assist her with her time management, she discussed the following 'To-Do List', developed using Microsoft Outlook's project planning tool 'Tasks', with her tutor.

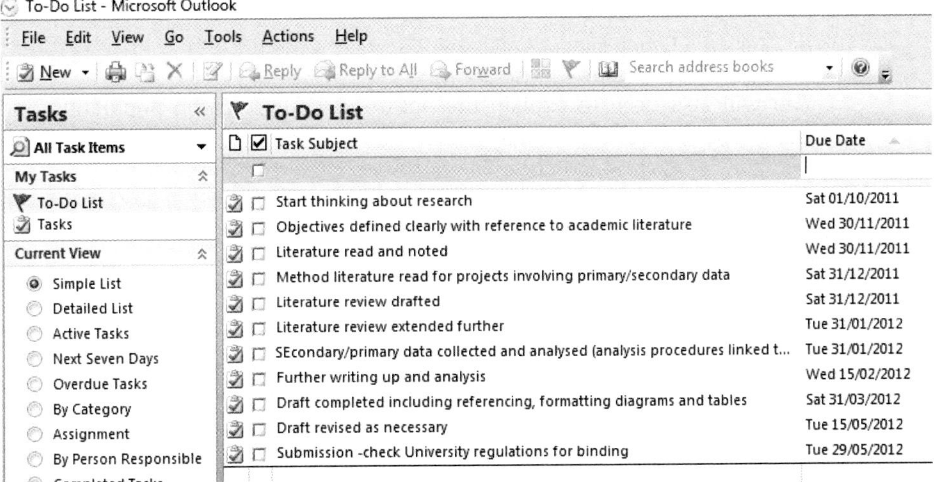

As part of this section of their proposal, many researchers find it useful to produce a schedule for their research using a Gantt chart. Developed by Henry Gantt in 1917, this provides a simple visual representation of the tasks or activities that make up your research project, each being plotted against a timeline. The time we estimate each task will take is represented by the length of an associated horizontal bar, whilst the task's start and finish times are represented by its position on the timeline. Box 2.15 includes a Gantt chart for a student's research project. As we can see from the

Box 2.15 Focus on student research

A student research proposal

Jian was a student from China. Jian was interested in the applicability of theory relating to organisational citizenship behaviours to Chinese workers. An abbreviated version of Jian's research proposal follows. Whilst this is not perfect, it provides an idea of what may be expected.

Title

The applicability of organisational citizenship behaviour theory to a Chinese organisation.

Background

The early definition of organisational citizenship behaviour (OCB) viewed this as discretionary behaviour on the part of employees that was not recognised through the reward system (Organ 1988; Organ et al. 2006). This was contested and led to OCB being defined as 'performance that supports the social and psychological environment' within which work occurs (Organ 1997: 95). It has been adopted by researchers such as Bolino et al. (2002) to indicate situations where employees work beyond contractual requirements to support one another, to subordinate individual interests to organisational ones and to demonstrate organisational commitment. In this way organisational citizenship behaviours may contribute to organisational performance and potentially offer a source of competitive advantage.

Previous studies have demonstrated that theories relating to organisational justice and the psychological contract are positively correlated to OCB and may be amongst the antecedents of OCB (Farh et al. 1997; Hui et al. 2004). OCB is both complex and contested and studies may reflect the cultural context within which they are conducted (Choi 2009). I have therefore become interested to find out whether theories that I have learnt about that are based on research conducted within a particular cultural context may be applied to other national contexts, or whether a different theoretical approach may be required to explain work relationships and potential causes of competitive advantage.

The applicability of these concepts to other cultural settings therefore requires further research. There are cultural and institutional differences that question the cross-cultural and cross-national applicability of these concepts. These include psychological, social and national differences that affect the nature of employment relationships between countries (Hui et al. 2004). This study therefore uses initial research by Farh et al. (1997) to examine how applicable these concepts may be in the context of a Chinese organisation.

Research question and research objectives

The research question is:

To what extent are organisational citizenship behaviour theory, organisational justice theory and psychological contract theory applicable to Chinese organisations and why?

The research objectives are:

1 To identify suitable measurement scales for each theory, to use in the case study Chinese organisation.
2 To examine the relationship in the case study organisation between findings from the organisational justice scale and findings from the organisational citizenship behaviour scale.
3 To examine the relationship in the case study organisation between findings from the psychological contract scale and findings from the organisational citizenship behaviour scale.
4 To examine the relationship between findings in the case study organisation from the organisational

citizenship behaviour scale and findings in other national contexts from organisational citizenship behaviour research.

5 To draw conclusions from the relationships observed in objectives 2, 3 and 4, to evaluate the applicability of these concepts in a Chinese organisation.

Method

Research design

This research is designed to test the applicability of these theories in a case study, Chinese organisation. The research will use a survey strategy incorporating existing scales from published, peer-reviewed, high-quality academic journals. The research will be cross-sectional in nature.

Participants

The intended participants in this study work for [company name] in China. Its management have formally agreed to grant me access to a representative sample of employees drawn from the different grades and occupations and between males and females employed within the organisation [email attached]. I am currently in correspondence with the manager of the human resource department to finalise a stratified random sample to represent the characteristics of the organisation's workforce. It is envisaged that the sample size will be 200 employees.

Techniques

The scales for organisational citizenship behaviour, organisational justice and the psychological contract will be incorporated into a questionnaire that will also collect data about respondents' demographic characteristics. This questionnaire will be administered in Chinese. It will be checked for accuracy of translation and pilot tested by some of my fellow students. Amendments will be made where necessary. It will then be administered in paper form. My data will be analysed quantitatively using IBM SPSS statistics. A range of statistical techniques will be used to analyse these data and the results from these will be used to identify relationships between the concepts identified in the research objectives and to allow comparison with previously published research.

Ethical considerations and procedures

I will compose a letter to be sent to members of the sample that informs them about who I am and the purpose of my research project, and to assure them that their responses to each of the questionnaire items will only be seen and used by me. Respondents will not be asked for their name on the questionnaire. The questionnaire will only ask for limited personal data about each participant [for example, whether they are male or female as previous research has found this to be a significant factor in the applicability of organisational justice and organisational citizenship behaviours in a Chinese context (Farh et al. 1997)].

Completed questionnaires will be posted into a sealed container that will be returned to me to ensure respondent confidentiality and the anonymity of the data that they provide. These questionnaires will be given an anonymous code and the data they contain entered into a spreadsheet by me. Once data input has been checked carefully to ensure accuracy they will be shredded by me.

Ensuring confidentiality and anonymity should mean that no harm should result from participating in this survey. Part of my covering letter will state that participation is entirely voluntary and if an intended participant does not wish to take part, they are not under any obligation to do so. Another matching employee will be sent a copy of my letter and asked if they would like to receive a copy of my questionnaire. If he or she is willing to complete the questionnaire, he or she will be informed to post it personally into the sealed container.

Timescale (please see Gantt chart)

KEY DATES:

1 Nov Submit proposal to tutor
20 Jan Begin data collection
1 March Complete data collection
20 April Complete draft and hand to tutor
30 May Submission

Resources

As outlined above, data access has been negotiated in a case study organisation.

I will be responsible for producing and copying the questionnaire. I will pay for the cost of posting these to China. I also have access to IBM SPSS statistics and am competent in the analytical techniques required to analyse the data and interpret this analysis. The company has kindly agreed to pay the costs of returning the completed questionnaires to me. Once I have received

Box 2.15 Focus on student research *(continued)*

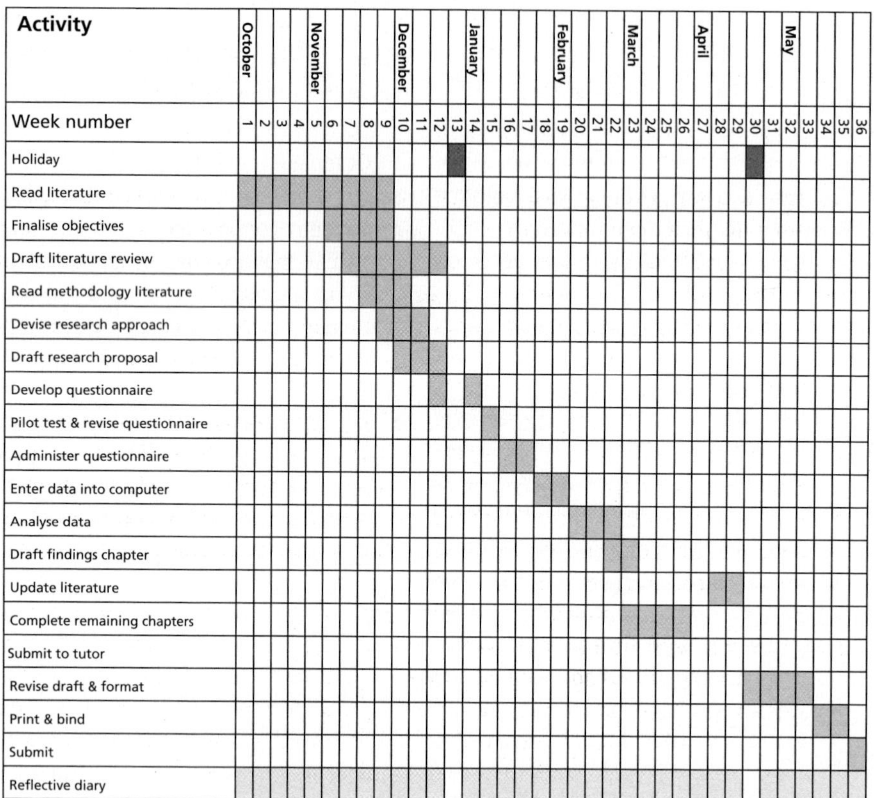

these questionnaires I will be responsible for inputting the data into the software to analyse it. There should not be any other resource requirements in order to be able to undertake this research project.

References

Bolino, M.C., Turnley, W.H. and Bloodgood, J.M. (2002) 'Citizenship behaviour and the creation of social capital in organizations', *Academy of Management Review*, Vol. 27, No. 4, pp. 505–22.

Choi, J.N. (2009) 'Collective dynamics of citizenship behaviour: What group characteristics promote group-level helping?', *Journal of Management Studies*, Vol. 46, No. 8, pp. 1396–1420.

Farh, J.L., Earley, P.C. and Lin, S.C. (1997) 'Impetus for action: A cultural analysis of justice and organizational citizenship behaviour in Chinese society', *Administrative Science Quarterly*, Vol. 42, No. 3, pp. 421–44.

Hui, C., Lee, C. and Rousseau, D.M. (2004) 'Psychological contract and organizational citizenship behaviour in China: Generalizability and Instrumentality', *Journal of Applied Psychology*, Vol. 89, No. 2, pp. 311–21.

Organ, D.W. (1988) *Organizational Citizenship Behaviour: The Good Soldier Syndrome*. Lexington, MA: Lexington Books.

Organ, D.W. (1997) 'Organizational citizenship behaviour: It's construct cleanup time', *Human Performance*, Vol. 10, No. 2, pp. 85–97.

Organ, D.W., Podsakoff, P.M. and MacKenzie, S.B. (2006) *Organizational Citizenship Behaviour: Its Nature, Antecedents, and Consequences*. Thousand Oaks, CA: Sage.

first bar on this chart, the student has decided to schedule in two weeks of holiday. The first of these occurs over the Christmas and New Year period, and the second occurs while her tutor is reading a draft copy of the completed project in April. We can also see from the second and fourth bar that, like many of our students, she intends to begin to draft her literature review while she is still reading new articles and books. However, she has also recognised that some activities must be undertaken sequentially. For example, bars 9 and 10 highlight that before she can administer her questionnaire (bar 10) she must complete all the revisions highlighted as necessary by the pilot testing (bar 9). Finally this student has noted that her project assessment criteria include a reflective essay and has decided to keep a reflective diary throughout the research project (bar 20).

Resources

This is another facet of feasibility (Box 2.2 and also our earlier discussion in this section). Including this discussion in your research proposal will allow you and your tutor to assess whether what you are proposing can be resourced. Resource considerations may be categorised as finance, data access and equipment.

Conducting research costs money. This may be for travel, subsistence, help with data analysis, or postage for questionnaires. Think through the expenses involved and ensure that you can meet them.

Assessors of your proposal will need to be convinced that you have access to the data you need to conduct your research (Sections 6.2 and 6.3). This may be unproblematic if you are carrying out research in your own organisation. Many academic committees wish to see written approval from host organisations in which researchers are planning to conduct research. You will also need to convince your reader of the likely response rate to any questionnaire that you send.

It is surprising how many research proposals have ambitious plans for large-scale data collection with no thought given to how the data will be analysed. It is important that you convince the reader of your proposal that you have access to the necessary computer software to analyse your data. Moreover, it will be necessary for you to demonstrate that you have either the necessary skills to perform the analysis or can learn the skills in an appropriate time, or you have access to help.

References

It is not necessary to try to impress your proposal reader with an enormous list of references. A few key literature sources to which you have referred in the background section and which relate to the previous work and theory that directly informs your own proposal should be all that is necessary.

An example of a student research proposal is shown in Box 2.15.

2.6 Summary

- The process of formulating and clarifying your research topic is a key part of your research project.
- Attributes of a good research topic do not vary a great deal between universities. The most important of these is that your research topic will meet the requirements of the examining body.
- Generating and refining research ideas makes use of a variety of techniques. It is important that you use a variety of techniques, including those involving rational thinking and those involving creative thinking.

- Further refinement of research ideas may be achieved through using the Delphi technique, conducting a preliminary inquiry and integrating ideas by working these up and narrowing them down.
- A clearly defined research question expresses what your research is about and will become the focal point of your research project.
- Well-formulated research objectives operationalise how you intend to conduct your research by providing a set of coherent and connected steps to answer your research question.
- It will be important to use academic theory to inform your research topic irrespective of the approach you will use to conduct your research project.
- A research proposal is a structured plan of your proposed research project.
- A well-thought-out and well-written research proposal has the potential to provide you with a clear specification of the what, why, how, when and where of your research project.

Self-check questions

Help with these questions is available at the end of the chapter.

2.1 For the workplace project for her professional course, Karen had decided to undertake a study of the effectiveness of the joint consultative committee in her NHS Trust. Her title was 'An evaluation of the effectiveness of the Joint Consultative Committee in Anyshire's Hospitals NHS Foundation Trust'. Draft some objectives which Karen may adopt to complement her title.

2.2 You have decided to search the literature to 'try to come up with some research ideas in the area of Operations Management'. How will you go about this?

2.3 A colleague of yours wishes to generate a research idea in the area of accounting. He has examined his own strengths and interests on the basis of his assignments and has read some review articles, but has failed to find an idea about which he is excited. He comes and asks you for advice. Suggest two techniques that your colleague could use, and justify your choice.

2.4 You are interested in doing some research on the interface between business organisations and schools. Write three research questions that may be appropriate.

2.5 How may the formulation of an initial substantive theory help in the development of a research proposal?

2.6 How would you demonstrate the influence of relevant theory in your research proposal?

Review and discussion questions

2.7 Together with your colleagues, decide on the extent to which a set of research ideas constitute a 'good research topic' according to the checklist in Box 2.2. The set of topics you choose may be past ones obtained from your tutor that relate to your course. Alternatively, they may be those which have been written by you and your colleagues as preparation for your project(s).

2.8 Look through several of the academic journals which relate to your subject area. Choose an article which is based upon primary research. Assuming that the research question and objectives are not made explicit, infer from the content of the article what the research question and objectives may have been.

2.9 Watch the news on television. Most bulletins will contain stories on research which has been carried out to report the current state of affairs in a particular field. Spend some time investigating news sites on the Internet (e.g. http://www.news.google.com) in order to learn more about the research which relates to the news story. Study the story carefully and decide what further questions the report raises. Use this as the basis to draft an outline proposal to seek answers to one (or more) of these questions.

Progressing your research project

From research ideas to a research proposal

- If you have not been given a research idea, consider the techniques available for generating and refining research ideas. Choose a selection of those with which you feel most comfortable, making sure to include both rational and creative thinking techniques. Use these to try to generate a research idea or ideas. Once you have got some research ideas, or if you have been unable to find an idea, talk to your project tutor.
- Evaluate your research ideas against the checklist of attributes of a good research project (Box 2.2).
- Refine your research ideas using a selection of the techniques available for generating and refining research ideas. Re-evaluate your research ideas against the checklist of attributes of a good research project (Box 2.2). Remember that it is better to revise (and in some situations to discard) ideas that do not appear to be feasible at this stage. Integrate your ideas using the process of working up and narrowing down to form one research idea.
- Use your research idea to write a research question. Where possible this should be a 'how?' or a 'why?' rather than a 'what?' question.
- Use this research question to write a set of connected research objectives.
- Write your research proposal making sure it includes a clear title and sections on:
  - the background to your research;
  - your research questions and research objectives;
  - the method you intend to use including research design, participants (data), techniques, and ethical considerations and procedures;
  - the timescale for your research;
  - the resources you require;
  - references to any literature to which you have referred.
- Use the questions in Box 1.4 to guide your reflective diary entry.

References

BBC (2011) *Shopping 'may improve health'*. Available at www.bbc.co.uk/news/health-12990071 [Accessed 7 April 2011].

Bradshaw, D. (2011) 'Rotterdam dean eyes China', *Financial Times*, 11 March. Available at www.ft.com/ [Accessed 17 March 2011].

Buzan, T. (2011) *Buzan's Study Skills: Mind Maps, Memory Techniques, Speed Reading and More*. London: BBC.

Canals, J. (2010) 'Crisis offers a chance to reflect on strategy', *Financial Times*, 17 October. Available at www.ft.com/ [Accessed 17 March 2011].

Carroll, L. (1989) *Alice's Adventures in Wonderland*. London: Hutchinson.

Chang, Y.H., Chen, R.C.Y., Wahlqvist, M.L. and Lee, M.S. (2011) 'Frequent shopping by men and women increases survival in the older Taiwanese population', *Journal of Epidemiology and Community Health Online*, 6 April. Available at http://jech.bmj.com/ [Accessed 7 April 2011].

CIPD (2010) *Research Insight: Harnessing the Power of Employee Communication*. London: Chartered Institute of Personnel and Development.

Clough, P. and Nutbrown, C. (2002) *A Student's Guide to Methodology*. London: Sage.

Devinney, T. (2011) 'Research generates better business scholarship', *Financial Times*, 31 January. Available at www.ft.com/ [Accessed 17 March 2011].

Elsbach, K.D., Cable, D.M. and Sherman, J.W. (2010) 'How passive "face time" affects perceptions of employees: Evidence of spontaneous trait inference', *Human Relations*, Vol. 63, No. 6, pp. 735–60.

Festinger, L. (1957) *A Theory of Cognitive Dissonance*. Stanford, CA: Stanford University Press.

Ghauri, P. and Grønhaug, K. (2010) *Research Methods in Business Studies* (4th edn). Harlow: Financial Times Prentice Hall.

Gill, J. and Johnson, P. (2010) *Research Methods for Managers* (4th edn). London: Sage.

Jankowicz, A.D. (2005) *Business Research Projects* (4th edn). London: Thomson Learning.

Kelly, G.A. (1955) *The Psychology of Personal Constructs*. New York: Norton.

Kilduff, M. (2006) 'Editors comments: Publishing theory', *Academy of Management Review*, Vol. 31, No. 2, pp. 252–5.

Lewin, K. (1945) 'The Research Center for Group Dynamics at Massachusetts Institute of Technology', *Sociometry*, Vol. 8, No. 2, pp. 126–36.

Mackenzie, K.D. (2000a) 'Knobby analyses of knobless survey items, part I: The approach', *International Journal of Organizational Analysis*, Vol. 8, No. 2, pp. 131–54.

Mackenzie, K.D. (2000b) 'Knobby analyses of knobless survey items, part II: An application', *International Journal of Organizational Analysis*, Vol. 8, No. 3, pp. 238–61.

McDonald, S. (2005) 'Studying actions in context: A qualitative shadowing method for organisational research', *Qualitative Research*, Vol. 5, No. 4, pp. 455–73.

McNiff, J. with Whitehead, J. (2000) *Action Research in Organizations*. London: Routledge.

Morrison, E. (2010) 'OB in *AMJ*: What is hot and what is not?', *Academy of Management Journal*, Vol. 53, No. 5, pp. 932–36.

Raimond, P. (1993) *Management Projects*. London: Chapman & Hall.

Robson, C. (2011) *Real World Research: A Resource for Users of Social Research Methods in Applied Settings* (3rd edn). Chichester: John Wiley.

Saunders, M.N.K. and Lewis, P. (1997) 'Great ideas and blind alleys? A review of the literature on starting research', *Management Learning*, Vol. 28, No. 3, pp. 283–99.

Sharp, J., Peters, J. and Howard, K. (2002) *The Management of a Student Research Project* (3rd edn). Aldershot: Gower.

Skapinker, M. (2008) 'Why business ignores business schools', *Financial Times*, 7 January. Available at www.ft.com/ [Accessed 17 March 2011].

Skapinker, M. (2011) 'Why business still ignores business schools', *Financial Times*, 24 January. Available at www.ft.com/ [Accessed 17 March 2011].

Smith, N.C. and Dainty, P. (1991) *The Management Research Handbook*. London: Routledge.

Sutton, R. and Staw, B. (1995) 'What theory is not', *Administrative Science Quarterly*, Vol. 40, No. 3, pp. 371–84.

Van de Ven, A.H. (1989) 'Nothing is quite so practical as a good theory', *Academy of Management Review*, Vol. 14, No. 4, pp. 486–9.

Vermeulen, F. (2011) 'Popular fads replace relevant teaching', *Financial Times*, 24 January. Available at www.ft.com/[Accessed 17 March 2011].

Whetten, D. (1989) 'What constitutes a theoretical contribution?', *Academy of Management Review*, Vol. 14, No. 4, pp. 490–95.

Yip, G. (2011) 'Business research needs to be more relevant for managers', *Financial Times*, 14 February. Available at www.ft.com/[Accessed 17 March 2011].

Further reading

Robson, C. (2011) *Real World Research: A Resource for Users of Social Research Methods in Applied Settings* (3rd edn). Chichester: John Wiley. Chapter 3 covers similar ground to this chapter, providing helpful advice on generating research ideas, developing research questions and the role of theory in your research.

Gill, J. and Johnson, P. (2010) *Research Methods for Managers* (4th edn). London: Sage. The initial part of Chapter 2 contains a helpful discussion on the characteristics of a research topic and ways of generating research topics, while the initial part of Chapter 3 contains a useful discussion of the role of theory in research.

Sutton, R. and Staw, B. (1995) 'What theory is not', *Administrative Science Quarterly*, Vol. 40, No. 3, pp. 371–84. This is a helpful article to read to gain some insights into the role of theory if you find this aspect daunting. In telling us what theory is not, they provide a very helpful discussion about what it is by referring to their own experiences. They also go further than this and evaluate the role of theory.

Van Maanen, J. Sorensen, J.B. and Mitchell, T.R. (2007) 'The interplay between theory and method', *Academy of Management Review*, Vol. 32, No. 4, pp. 1145–54. We haven't referenced this article in this particular chapter but it provides an extension to some of the material in Section 2.4 and a link to some of our discussion later on, notably to Chapters 4 and 5, and to some material in later, methods, chapters. Van Maanen et al. provide a thoughtful discussion of the relationship between theory and methods and the primacy of theory versus the primacy of data.

Case 2
Self-service technology: does co-production harm value co-creation?

George was in his final year of an MSc Marketing degree. He had booked a meeting with his project tutor in the expectation that having a deadline would concentrate his efforts on identifying a suitable research project. He now had 10 days to prepare for the meeting and was still searching for inspiration.

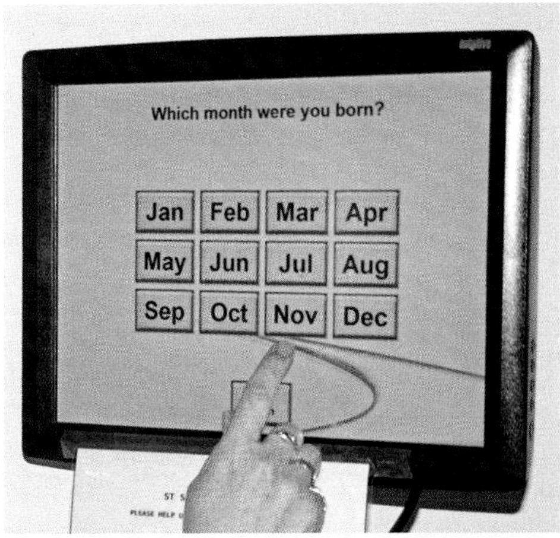

'Arrive me' touch screen at a Doctor's surgery
Source: © Mark Saunders 2011

George wanted to research something that was relevant to him so he listed out the activities he engaged in as a customer or consumer. He was struck by the fact that most of his activities involved services rather than product marketing: shopping, banking, dining, broadband and travelling. George remembered that one of the differences between product and services marketing that had been stressed by his lecturers was the important role of people, especially the service employees, and the face-to-face experiences they provided. Thinking more deeply about the way in which he experienced most of the services he had listed, George realised that there was a lack of people, particularly service employees, involved in his experiences. This mismatch between what he had learned so far and his own experiences took him by surprise, so he decided to see what his friends thought.

Over the next few days George spent a lot of time asking other people about their experiences of services, writing them down in his notebook. George also added notes about his own experiences now that he was looking at them afresh. He concluded that there was indeed a gap between what he had been taught in his lectures, his reading on the subject and the way in which he and his friends experienced services today. George decided that this was probably interesting enough to him to form the basis of his research project.

George remembered that he needed to read around the topic to find out what had already been written, and to ensure that much of this reading was in academic journals because that is where current thinking is more likely to be found. George enlisted the help of a librarian as he did not feel confident to use the search engines within the business and management databases. She encouraged him to think of words that might bring up relevant articles. After several false starts George stumbled on 'self-service', 'self-service technologies', the abbreviation 'SST' and 'Technology-based self-service' often abbreviated to 'TBSS'. These key words resulted in a number of interesting articles that seemed relevant.

Many of the articles seemed to deal with the technology systems and how easy or difficult they were to follow. Others dealt with the security aspects or customer satisfaction (Meuter et al. 2000) while another article talked about the need to incorporate a sense of 'fun' to encourage customers to use the SST (Curran and Meuter 2007). George realised that he needed to do some serious thinking to come up with a practical project.

Reviewing the notes he had made when talking to his friends and considering his own SST experiences, George realised that SSTs were everywhere. Some are 'in situ': self-scanning in shops or ticket machines at the train station and self-check-ins at airports. Then there were all the services that could be accessed via the Internet including banking and travelling. A friend had even mentioned an 'arrive me' touchscreen at the doctor's surgery. His father had done his tax return online and his grandfather, who had just had his 70th birthday, had renewed his driving licence online – so SST experiences are not confined to the young!

The day before the meeting with his project tutor, George attended a seminar for the Contemporary Issues in Marketing module entitled: 'Service-dominant logic'. He read the two articles prescribed for the seminar, both by Vargo and Lusch (2004, 2008), and felt that much of what he had heard and read was relevant to self-service technologies. Service-dominant logic talks about 'co-creating value' and it seemed to George that customers using SST were co-creating the services they received. He also noted that Vargo and Lusch suggest that the knowledge, skills and effort (operant resources) are the basis for competitive advantage and what that might mean for consumer experiences if SSTs substitute customer resources for employee resources (Hilton 2008).

George made a list for the meeting with his project tutor:

- Self-service technologies: everywhere and for everyone.
- Service-dominant logic framework.
- Co-creating value.
- Operant resources being the basis for competitive advantage.
- Does SST facilitate co-creation?
- Are companies relying too much on the operant resources of their customers to gain a competitive advantage when using SST?

Although the project tutor was very supportive of George's initial ideas, saying that it was very topical and had lots of potential, it was clear that he still had a lot of work to do before he could put his proposal together. George still needed to determine a research question, a clear aim for his research and research objectives. George's project tutor also drew his attention to the descriptive nature of the two questions he had identified and reaffirmed the need for research questions to have an explanatory dimension in order to generate new insights. During the meeting they discussed service-dominant logic and the emphasis on co-creation of value. George was asked to consider whether customers were co-creating value or co-producing the service and what the difference might be. That had not occurred to George. He had assumed the two words meant the same thing and realised he had to read more thoroughly to become familiar with the terminology being used. George was also not able to answer any of the project tutor's questions about the research design at the meeting. He did not know what data he needed to collect, from whom, or how he would go about it. George began to realise that defining terms and words is critical when framing the research question and planning the research project.

His project tutor reminded him that, realistically, he would only have two months to collect his data because he had to also allow time for data analysis, writing his draft project report, submitting the draft for project tutor feedback and preparing the final submission. His research design had to be achievable within the time constraints. He needed to think about how easy it would be to get access to the people from whom he needed to collect data for his research. They had discussed the fact that SST changed the role of the service employee as well as the customer and that might be an interesting angle to pursue. However, George did not think he could get access to an organisation in the time allowed. He felt that might be more of an HRM (Human Resource Management) or Organisational Studies project and not draw as heavily upon marketing literature as he needed to do for his degree. George also had to consider the costs involved in collecting any data.

Then George came across a weblink to an article by Hilton (2011) about self-service technology, co-production and co-creation that helped him to narrow down his ideas: www.mycustomer.com/topic/customer-experience/does-self-service-technology-mean-co-production-harming-co-creation/119301. Reading this article, George became aware of the different ways in which he evaluated his own SST experiences. He found great value in online banking because it was 'open' 24/7 and he had more control over his banking arrangements than he would have if he had to deal with branch employees. However, he did not get a lot of value from the self-scanning in the supermarket because he invariably needed an employee to help him with some aspect of it, which was very frustrating. George wanted to know how other consumers evaluated their experiences, to see whether the value they received was commensurate with the effort they were contributing to the production of the services and, to explore what characteristics of people or the SST led different people to different valuations. He also found an article by Stephen Brown (2007) calling for empirical testing to build knowledge of how consumers participate in or make sense of any role they play in 'co-creating value'. These articles led George to begin to narrow his research aim to understanding more about the influence that increasing the customer co-production role might have on the evaluation of the value that is co-created. Bearing in mind the need to adopt an explanatory perspective, George's title became: 'Self-service technology: To what extent does co-production harm value co-creation and why?' He summarised his initial ideas as a simple relevance tree (Figure 2.2).

Next George thought about the people he could access most easily and decided that they would be his peer group of university students. George realised that he did not know enough about what might constitute co-production, co-creation or value to develop a survey or measurement instrument: what behaviours, outcomes or attitudes would he measure? This exploratory study would have to focus on understanding the phenomena that constitute co-production and value. He felt qualitative methods would be more appropriate than quantitative methods. George then found an article by Baron et al. (2010) which calls for the use of more interpretive research approaches that encourage consumers to reflect upon their experiences when researching the application of service-dominant logic to marketing practice. This confirmed George's decision to adopt qualitative methods. George realised that he had now narrowed down the area for his literature review to something manageable: co-production, co-creation and value. He had also managed to align his project to an emerging area of theory

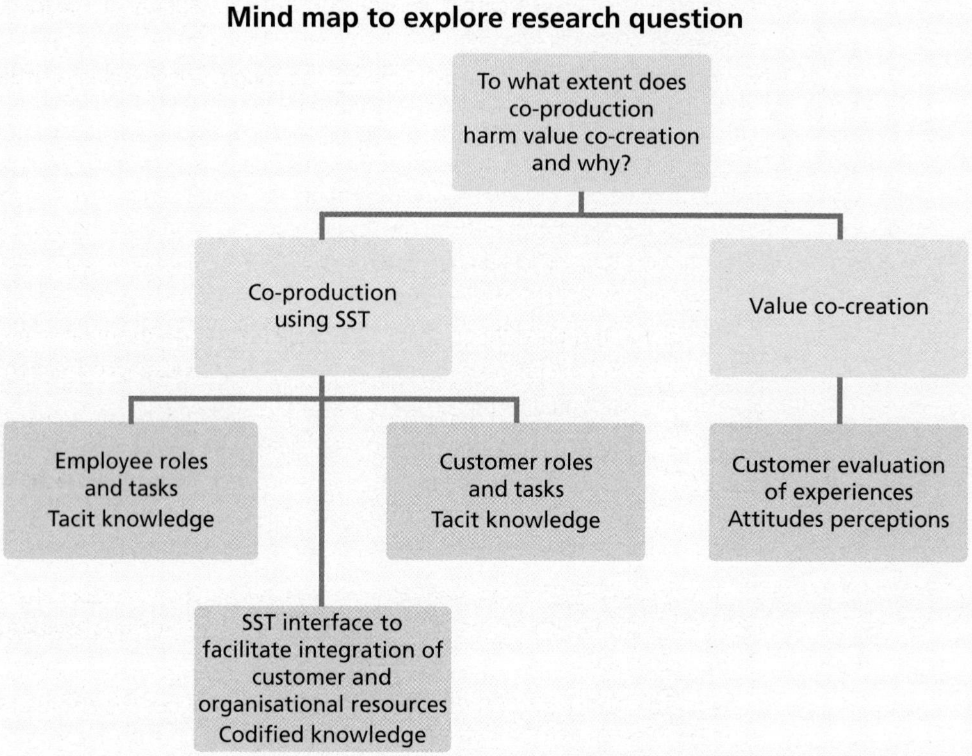

Mind map to explore research question

Figure 2.2 Relevance tree of self-service technology and value co-creation

development (service-dominant logic) and a growing area of marketing practice. This he felt was a topical project that had the potential to be useful to both academics and practitioners.

References

Baron, S., Patterson, A., Warnaby, G. and Harris, K. (2010) 'Service-dominant logic: Marketing research implications and opportunities', *Journal of Customer Behaviour*, Vol. 9, No. 3, pp. 253–64.

Brown, S. (2007) 'Are we nearly there yet? On the retro-dominant logic of marketing', *Marketing Theory*, Vol. 7, No. 3, pp. 291–300.

Curran, J.M. and Meuter, M.L. (2007) 'Encouraging existing customers to switch to self-service technologies: Put a little fun in their lives', *Journal of Marketing Theory and Practice*, Vol. 15, No. 4, pp. 283–98.

Hilton, T. (2008) 'Leveraging operant resources of consumers: Improving consumer experiences or productivity?', *The Marketing Review*, Vol. 8, No. 4, pp. 359–66.

Hilton, T. (2011) 'Self-service technology: How co-production could be harming co-creation'. Available at www.mycustomer.com/topic/customer-experience/does-self-service-technology-mean-co-production-harming-co-creation/119301 [Accessed 31 January 2011].

Meuter, M.L., Ostrom, A.L., Roundtree, R.I. and Bitner, M.J. (2000) 'Self-service technologies: Understanding customer satisfaction with technology-based service encounters', *Journal of Marketing*, Vol. 64 (July), pp. 50–64.

Vargo, S.L. and Lusch, R.F. (2004) 'Evolving to a new dominant logic for marketing', *Journal of Marketing*, Vol. 68, No. 1, pp. 1–17.

Vargo, S.L. and Lusch, R.F. (2008) 'Service-dominant logic: Continuing the evolution', *Journal of the Academy of Marketing Science*, Vol. 36, pp. 1–10.

Questions

1 **a** Why is it important that George's research draws upon existing theory?
  b At what point in the process should he identify a relevant model, theory or framework to guide his work?

2 George has identified the need for qualitative rather than quantitative methods in order to understand the phenomena that constitute co-production, co-creation and value. What ways of collecting data might he consider using and why?

3 George plans to collect his data from his fellow university students.
  a Is this a good idea?
  b What issues should George consider before commencing and why?

Additional case studies relating to material covered in this chapter are available via the book's companion website: **www.pearsoned.co.uk/saunders**. They are:

- The use of internal and word of mouth recruitment methods.
- Strategic issues in the brewing industry.
- Catherine Chang and women in management.
- Media climate change reporting and environmetnal disclosure patterns in the low-cost airline industry in the twenty-first century.

Self-check answers

2.1 These may include:
- To identify the management and trade union objectives for the Joint Consultative Committee and use this to establish suitable effectiveness criteria.
- To review key literature on the use of joint consultative committees.
- To carry out primary research in the organisation to measure the effectiveness of the Joint Consultative Committee.
- To identify the strengths and weaknesses of the Joint Consultative Committee.
- To make recommendations for action to ensure the effective function of the Joint Consultative Committee.

2.2 One starting point would be to ask your project tutor for suggestions of possible recent review articles or articles containing recommendations for further work that he or she has read. Another would be to browse recent editions of operations management journals such as the *International Journal of Operations and Production Management* for possible research ideas. These would include both statements of the absence of research and unfounded assertions. Recent reports held in your library or on the Internet may also be of use here. You could also scan one or two recently published operations management textbooks for overviews of research that has been undertaken.

2.3 From the description given, it would appear that your colleague has considered only rational thinking techniques. It would therefore seem sensible to suggest two creative

thinking techniques, as these would hopefully generate an idea that would appeal to him. One technique that you could suggest is brainstorming, perhaps emphasising the need to do it with other colleagues. Exploring past projects in the accountancy area would be another possibility. You might also suggest that he keeps a notebook of ideas.

2.4 Your answer will probably differ from that below. However, the sorts of things you could be considering include:

- How do business organisations benefit from their liaison with schools?
- Why do business organisations undertake school liaison activities?
- To what extent do business organisations receive value for money in their school liaison activities?

2.5 Let us go back to the example used in the chapter of the supermarket marketing manager who theorises that the introduction of a loyalty card will mean that regular customers are less likely to shop at competitor supermarkets. This could be the research proposal's starting point, i.e., a hypothesis that the introduction of a loyalty card will mean that regular customers are less likely to shop at competitor supermarkets. This prompts thoughts about the possible use of literature in the proposal and the research project itself. This literature could have at least two strands. First, a practical strand which looks at the research evidence which lends credence to the hypothesis. Second, a more abstract strand that studies human consumer behaviour and looks at the cognitive processes which affect consumer purchasing decisions.

This ensures that the proposal and resultant research project are both theory driven and also ensures that relevant theory is covered in the literature.

2.6 Try including a subsection in the background section that is headed 'How the previous published research has informed my research questions and objectives'. Then show how, say, a gap in the previous research that is there because nobody has pursued a particular approach before has led to you filling that gap.

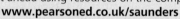

Get ahead using resources on the companion website at:
www.pearsoned.co.uk/saunders

- Improve your IBM SPSS Statistics and NVivo research analysis with practice tutorials.
- Save time researching on the Internet with the Smarter Online Searching Guide.

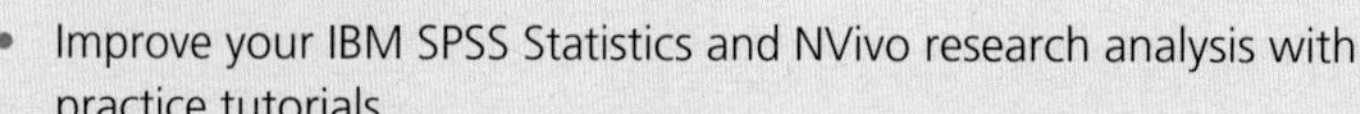

- Test your progress using self-assessment questions.
- Follow live links to useful websites.

Chapter 3

Critically reviewing the literature

Learning outcomes

By the end of this chapter you should:

- understand the importance and purpose of the critical literature review to your research project;
- be able to adopt a critical perspective in your reading;
- know what you need to include when writing your critical review;
- be aware of the range of primary, secondary and tertiary literature sources available;
- be able to identify search terms and to undertake online literature searches;
- be able to evaluate the relevance, value and sufficiency of the literature found;
- be able to reference the literature found accurately;
- understand what is meant by plagiarism;
- be able to apply the knowledge, skills and understanding gained to your own research project.

3.1 Introduction

As part of your studies, you have almost certainly been asked by your tutors to 'review the literature', 'write a literature review' or 'critically review the literature' on a given topic. You may be like many students and have grown to fear the literature review, not because of the associated reading but because of the requirement both to make reasoned judgements about the value of each piece of work and to organise ideas and findings of value into a review. It is these two processes in particular that many find both difficult and time-consuming.

Two major reasons exist for reviewing the literature (Sharp et al. 2002). The first, the preliminary search that helps you to generate and refine your research ideas, has already been discussed in Section 2.3. The second, often referred to as the **critical review** or **critical literature review**, is part of your research project proper. Most research textbooks, as well as your project tutor, will argue that this critical review of the literature is necessary. Although you may feel that you already have a reasonable knowledge of your research area, we believe that reviewing

the literature critically is essential. Project assessment criteria usually require you to demonstrate awareness of the current state of knowledge in your subject, its limitations and how your research fits in this wider context (Gill and Johnson 2010). As Jankowicz (2005) emphasises, your research is not done in a vacuum and should not reinvent the wheel! This means you have to discuss what has been published and is relevant to your research topic critically.

The significance of your research and what you find out will inevitably be judged in relation to other people's research and their findings. You therefore need to show you understand your field and its key theories, concepts and ideas, as well as the major issues and debates about your topic (Denyer and Tranfield 2009). In doing this you are establishing what research

Recently, we were discussing the difficulties students have when writing their literature reviews for their research projects. Mark summarised what he felt we and fellow project tutors were saying:

> So what happens sometimes is . . . a student comes to see their project tutor having obviously done a great deal of work. The student presents the tutor with what they say is the finished literature review. Yet the purpose of their review is unclear. It is little more than a summary of the articles and books read, each article or book being given one paragraph. Some students have arranged these paragraphs alphabetically in author order, others have arranged them in chronological order. None have linked or juxtaposed the ideas. Their literature reviews look more like adjacent pages from a catalogue rather than a critical review. Just like the items on these pages, each article or book has some similarities in terms of subject matter and so are grouped together. As in the catalogue, the reasons for these groupings are not made explicit. In addition, like the summary descriptions of items on the pages of a home shopping catalogue, each book or article is accorded equal status rather than the amount written reflecting its value to the student's research project.

He concluded: 'Whilst such an approach obviously makes good sense for a shopping catalogue, it does not work for the critical review of the literature. We obviously need to explain better what we mean by a critical review of the literature to our students.'

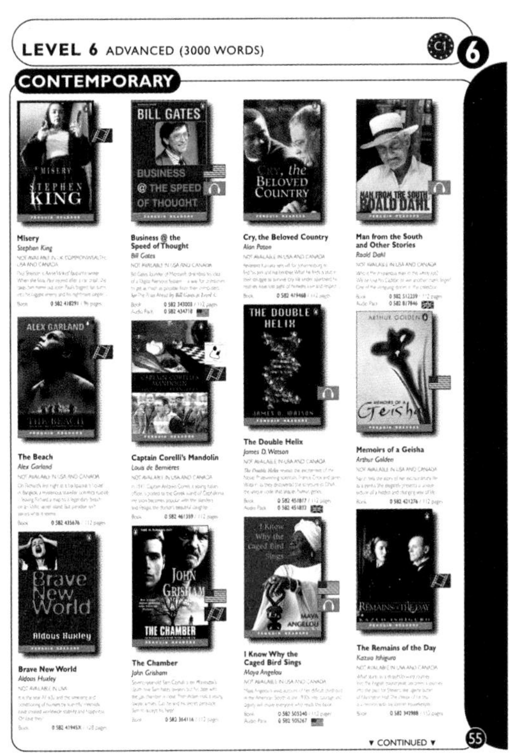

A page from a book catalogue
Source: Pearson Education Ltd

has been published in your chosen area and, if possible, identifying any other research that might currently be in progress. Although the literature you read will enhance your subject knowledge and help you to clarify your research question(s) further, only those that are relevant to your research will be included in your review. This process is called 'critically reviewing the literature'.

For most research projects, your literature search will be an early activity. Despite this early start, it is usually necessary to continue searching throughout your project's life. The process can be likened to an upward spiral, culminating in the final draft of your written critical literature review (Figure 3.1). Traditionally, in the initial stage of your literature review you will start to define the parameters to your research question(s) and objectives (Section 3.4). After generating search terms and conducting your first search (Section 3.5), you will have a list of references to authors who have published on these subjects. Once these have been obtained, you can read and evaluate them (Section 3.6), record the ideas (Section 3.7) and start drafting your review, fully acknowledging the sources. By doing this you will avoid charges of plagiarism and associated penalties (Section 3.9).

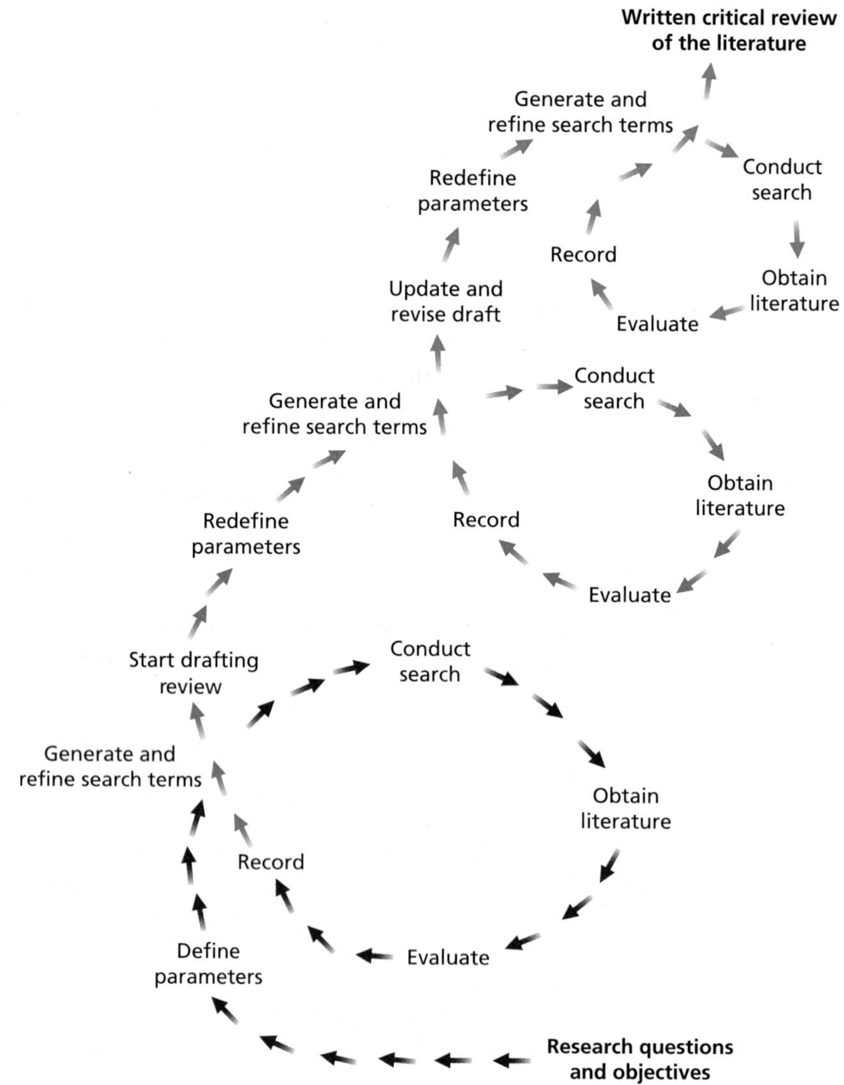

Figure 3.1 The literature review process

After the initial search, you will be able to redefine your parameters more precisely and undertake further searches, keeping in mind your research question(s) and objectives. As your thoughts develop, each later search will be focused more precisely on material that is likely to be relevant. At the same time, you will probably also refine your research question(s) and objectives in the light of your reading (Section 2.4).

Alternatively, you may decide that rather than undertaking a traditional literature review, your review will be a self-contained project to explore a clearly defined research question. In such situations, particularly where questions are derived from organisational practice or policy problems, business and management researchers are increasingly adopting the Systematic Review methodology to critically review the literature. We discuss this in more detail in Section 3.8.

Unlike some academic disciplines, business and management research makes use of a wide range of literature. While your review is likely to include specific business disciplines such as finance, marketing and human resource management, it is also likely to include other disciplines. Those most frequently consulted by our students include economics, psychology, sociology and geography. Given this, and the importance of the review to your research, it is vital for you to be aware of what a critical literature review is and the range of literature available before you start the reviewing process. For these reasons, we start this chapter by outlining the purpose of your critical review of the literature, its content and what we mean by 'critical' (Section 3.2) and then discussing the literature resources available (Section 3.3).

3.2 The critical review

Your critical literature review should be a constructively critical analysis that develops a clear argument about what the published literature indicates is known and not known about your research question (Wallace and Wray 2011). This means your literature review is not just a series of book and journal article reviews describing and summarising what each is about. Rather, you will need to assess what is significant to your research and, on this basis, decide whether or not to include it. If you think the concepts, theories, arguments or empirical research findings reported and discussed in an article are unclear, biased or inconsistent with other work and need to be researched further, you will need to justify why. This is not easy and requires careful thought. However, by doing this you will be able to provide a reasonably detailed, constructively critical analysis of the key literature that relates to your research question. Within this you will need to include both theoretical research and empirical research that supports and research that opposes your ideas.

The purpose of the critical review

Reviewing the literature critically will provide the foundation on which your research is built. As you will have gathered from the introduction, it will help you to develop a good understanding and insight into relevant previous research and the trends that have emerged. You would not expect a scientific researcher inquiring into the causes of cot death to start his or her research without first reading about the findings of other cot death research. Likewise, you should not expect to start your research without first reading what other researchers in your area have already found out.

The precise purpose of your reading of the literature will depend on the approach you are intending to use in your research. For some research projects you will use the literature to help you to identify theories and ideas that you will test using data. This is known as a **deductive approach** (Section 4.3) in which you develop a theoretical or conceptual framework which you subsequently test using data. For other research projects you will be planning to explore your data and to develop theories from them that you will subsequently relate to the literature in subsequent discussion. This is known as an **inductive approach** (Section 4.3) and, although your research still has a clearly defined purpose with research question(s) and objectives, you do not start with any predetermined theories or conceptual frameworks. We believe such an approach cannot be taken without a competent knowledge of your subject area. Cresswell (2007) highlights three ways in which you are likely to use the literature. Firstly, you can use it to frame your research question in the initial stages of your research such as when you draft your research proposal (Section 2.5). Secondly, you will use it to provide the context and theoretical framework for your research and, finally, to help place your research findings within the wider body of knowledge. As you discuss your findings in relation to the literature reviewed, you will be able to highlight both similarities and differences.

It is, however, impossible to review every single piece of the literature before collecting your data. The purpose of your literature review is not to provide a summary of everything that has been written on your research topic, but to review the most relevant and significant research on your topic. If your analysis is effective, new findings and theories will emerge that neither you nor anyone else has thought about (Corbin and Strauss 2008). Despite this, when you write your critical review you will need to show how your findings and the theories you have developed or are using relate to the research that has gone before. This will help you demonstrate you are familiar with what is already known about your research topic.

Your review also has a number of other purposes. Many of these have been highlighted by Gall et al. (2006) in their book for students undertaking educational research and are, we believe, of equal relevance to business and management researchers:

- to help you to refine your research question(s) and objectives further;
- to highlight research possibilities that have been overlooked implicitly in research to date;
- to discover explicit recommendations for further research. These can provide you with a superb justification for your own research question(s) and objectives;
- to help you to avoid simply repeating work that has been done already;
- to sample current opinions in newspapers, professional and trade journals, thereby gaining insights into the aspects of your research question(s) and objectives that are considered newsworthy and relevant (Section 2.3);
- to discover and provide an insight into research approaches (Section 4.3), strategies (Section 5.5) and techniques that may be appropriate to your own research question(s) and objectives.

Adopting critical perspective in your reading

Harvard College Library (2006) provides its students with a useful checklist of skills to be practised for effective reading. These skills include:

Previewing, which is looking around the text before you start reading in order to establish precisely its purpose and how it may inform your literature search;
Annotating: that is, conducting a dialogue with yourself, the author and the issues and ideas at stake (Box 3.1).
Summarising: the best way to determine that you've really got the point is to be able to state it in your own words. Outlining the argument of a text is a version of annotating, and can be done quite informally in the margins of the text.
Comparing and contrasting: ask yourself how your thinking has been altered by this reading or how has it affected your response to the issues and themes in your research?

Box 3.1 Checklist

Annotating your critical reading. Advice on how to read in a 'thinking-intensive' way

- ✔ First of all, throw away the highlighter in favour of a pen or pencil. Highlighting can actually distract from the business of learning and dilute your comprehension. It only seems like an active reading strategy; in actual fact, it can lull you into a dangerous passivity.
- ✔ Mark up the margins of your text with words: ideas that occur to you, notes about things that seem important to you, reminders of how issues in a text may connect with your research questions and objectives. If you are reading a pdf copy on screen, use the 'sticky notes' feature of Adobe Reader®. This kind of interaction keeps you conscious of the reason you are reading. Throughout your research these annotations will be useful memory triggers.
- ✔ Develop your own symbol system: asterisk a key idea, for example, or use an exclamation point for the surprising, absurd, bizarre etc. Like your margin words, your hieroglyphs can help you reconstruct the important observations that you made at an earlier time. And they will be indispensable when you return to a text later in the term, in search of a particular passage that you may want to include in your project report.
- ✔ Get in the habit of hearing yourself ask questions – 'what does this mean?'; 'why is he or she drawing that conclusion?' Write the questions down (in your margins, at the beginning or end of the reading, in a notebook, or elsewhere). They are reminders of the unfinished business you still have with a text: to come to terms with on your own, once you've had a chance to digest the material further, or have done further reading.

The Harvard College Library advice suggests that you should get in the habit of hearing yourself ask questions of your reading. Wallace and Wray (2011) recommend the use of **review questions**. These are specific questions you ask of the reading, which will be linked either directly or indirectly to your research question. So you may, for example, address a piece of reading with the view to it answering the question: 'What does research suggest are the main reasons why customers are likely to change car insurance provider?'

The word 'critical' has appeared in this chapter a number of times so far. It is vital in your reading of the literature that a critical stance should be taken. So what is meant by critical reading? Wallace and Wray (2011: 9) sum this up rather succinctly by saying that 'the lengthy list of critical skills (required for critical reading) boil down to just two: the capacity to evaluate what you read and the capacity to relate what you read to other information'.

More specifically Wallace and Wray (2011) advocate the use of five critical questions to employ in critical reading. These are:

1. Why am I reading this? (The authors argue that this is where the review question is particularly valuable. It acts as a focusing device and ensures that you stick to the purpose of the reading and do not get sidetracked too much by the author's agenda.)
2. What is the author trying to do in writing this? (The answer to this may assist you in deciding how valuable the writing may be for your purposes.)
3. What is the writer saying that is relevant to what I want to find out?
4. How convincing is what the author is saying? (In particular, is the argument based on a conclusion which is justified by the evidence?)
5. What use can I make of the reading?

The content of the critical review

As you begin to find, read and evaluate the literature, you will need to think how to combine the academic theories and ideas about which you are reading to form the critical review that will appear in your project report. Your review will need to evaluate the research that has already been undertaken in the area of your research project, show and explain the relationships between published research findings and reference the literature in which they were reported (Appendix 1). It will draw out the key points and trends (recognising any omissions and bias) and present them in a logical way which also shows the relationship to your own research. In doing this you will provide readers of your project report with the necessary background knowledge to your research question(s) and objectives and establish the boundaries of your own research. Your review will also enable the readers to see your ideas against the background of previous published research in the area. This does not necessarily mean that your ideas must extend, follow or approve those set out in the literature. You may be highly critical of the earlier research reported in the literature and seek to question or revise it through your own research. However, if you wish to do this you must still review this literature, explain clearly why you consider it may require revision and justify your own ideas through clear argument and with reference to the literature.

In considering the content of your critical review, you will therefore need:

- to include the key academic theories within your chosen area of research that are pertinent to or contextualise your research question;
- to demonstrate that your knowledge of your chosen area is up to date;
- through clear complete referencing, enable those reading your project report to find the original publications which you cite.

The content of your critical review can be evaluated using the checklist in Box 3.2.

What is really meant by being 'critical' about the content

Within the context of your course you have probably already been asked to take a critical approach for previous assignments. However, it is worth considering what we mean by critical within the context of your literature review. Mingers (2000: 225–6) argues

Box 3.2 Checklist

Evaluating the content of your critical literature review

✔ Have you ensured that the literature covered relates clearly to your research question and objectives?

✔ Have you covered the most relevant and significant theories of recognised experts in the area?

✔ Have you covered the most relevant and significant literature or at least a representative sample?

✔ Have you included up-to-date relevant literature?

✔ Have you referenced all the literature used in the format prescribed in the assessment criteria?

that there are four aspects of a critical approach that should be fostered by management education:

- critique of rhetoric;
- critique of tradition;
- critique of authority;
- critique of objectivity.

The first of these, the 'critique of rhetoric', means appraising or evaluating a problem with effective use of language. In the context of your critical literature review, this emphasises the need for you, as the reviewer, to use your skills to make reasoned judgements and to argue effectively in writing. The other three aspects Mingers identifies also have implications for being critical when reading and writing about the work of others. This includes using other literature sources to question, where justification exists to do so, the conventional wisdom, the 'critique of tradition' and the dominant view portrayed in the literature you are reading, the 'critique of authority'. Finally, it is likely also to include recognising in your review that the knowledge and information you are discussing are not value free, the 'critique of objectivity'.

Being critical in reviewing the literature is, therefore, a combination of your skills and the attitude with which you read. In critically reviewing the literature, you need to read the literature about your research topic with some scepticism and be willing to question what you read. This means you need to be constantly considering and justifying your own critical stance with clear arguments and references to the literature rather than just giving your own opinion. You will have to read widely on your research topic and have a good understanding of the literature. Critically reviewing the literature for your research project, therefore, requires you to have gained topic-based background knowledge, understanding, the ability to reflect upon and to analyse the literature and, based on this, to make reasoned judgements that are argued effectively. When you use these skills to review the literature, the term 'critical' refers to the judgement you exercise. It therefore describes the process of providing a detailed and justified analysis of, and commentary on, the merits and faults of the key literature within your chosen area. This means that, for your review to be critical, you will need to have shown critical judgement.

Part of this judgement will inevitably mean being able to identify the most relevant and significant theories and recognised experts highlighted in Box 3.3. For some research topics there will be a pre-exisiting, clearly developed theoretical base. For others you will need to integrate a number of different theoretical strands to develop your understanding. Dees (2003) suggests that this means you should:

- refer to and assess research by recognised experts in your chosen area;
- consider and discuss research that supports and research that opposes your ideas;
- make reasoned judgements regarding the value of others' research, showing clearly how it relates to your research;
- justify your arguments with valid evidence in a logical manner;
- distinguish clearly between fact and opinion.

These points are developed in Box 3.3, which contains a checklist to evaluate the extent to which your literature review is critical. The more questions to which you can answer 'yes', the more likely your review will be critical!

The structure of the critical review

The **literature review** that you write for your project report should be a description and critical analysis of what other authors have written. When drafting your review you

Box 3.3 Checklist

Evaluating whether your literature review is critical

- ✔ Have you contextualised your own research showing how your research question relates to previous research reviewed?
- ✔ Have you assessed the strengths and weaknesses of the previous research reviewed?
- ✔ Have you been objective in your discussion and assessment of other people's research?
- ✔ Have you included references to research that is counter to, as well as supports, your own opinions?
- ✔ Have you distinguished clearly between facts and opinions?
- ✔ Have you made reasoned judgements about the value and relevance of others' research to your own?
- ✔ Have you justified clearly your own ideas?
- ✔ Have you highlighted those areas where new research (yours!) is needed to provide fresh insights and taken these into account in your arguments? In particular:
  - where there are inconsistencies in current knowledge and understanding?
  - where there are omissions or bias in published research?
  - where research findings need to be tested further?
  - where evidence is lacking, inconclusive, contradictory or limited?
- ✔ Have you justified your arguments by referencing correctly published research?

therefore need to focus on your research question(s) and objectives. One way of helping you to focus is to think of your literature review as discussing how far existing published research goes in answering your research question(s). The shortfall in the literature will be addressed, at least partially, in the remainder of your project report – unless your entire research project is a literature review! Another way of helping you to focus is to ask yourself how your review relates to your objectives. If it does not, or does so only partially, there is a need for a clearer focus on your objectives. The precise structure of the critical review is usually your choice, although you should check, as it may be specified in the assessment criteria. Three common structures are:

- a single chapter;
- a series of chapters (for example in a larger research project);
- occurring throughout the project report as you tackle various issues (for example where your research project is conducted inductively).

In all project reports, you should return to the key issues from the literature in your discussion and conclusions (Section 14.3).

Within your critical review, you will need to juxtapose different authors' ideas and form your own opinions and conclusions based on these. Although you will not be able to start writing until you have undertaken some reading, we recommend that you start drafting your review early (Figure 3.1). What you write can then be updated and revised as you read more.

A common mistake with critical literature reviews, highlighted at the start of this chapter, is that they become uncritical listings of previous research. Often they are little more than annotated bibliographies (Hart 1998), individual items being selected because they fit with what the researcher is proposing (Greenhalgh 1997). As we highlighted in the introduction, they just describe what each author has written, one author after another (vertical arrows in Figure 3.2). It is much easier to be critical (and more interesting to read) if you take a thematic approach comparing and, where necessary, contrasting

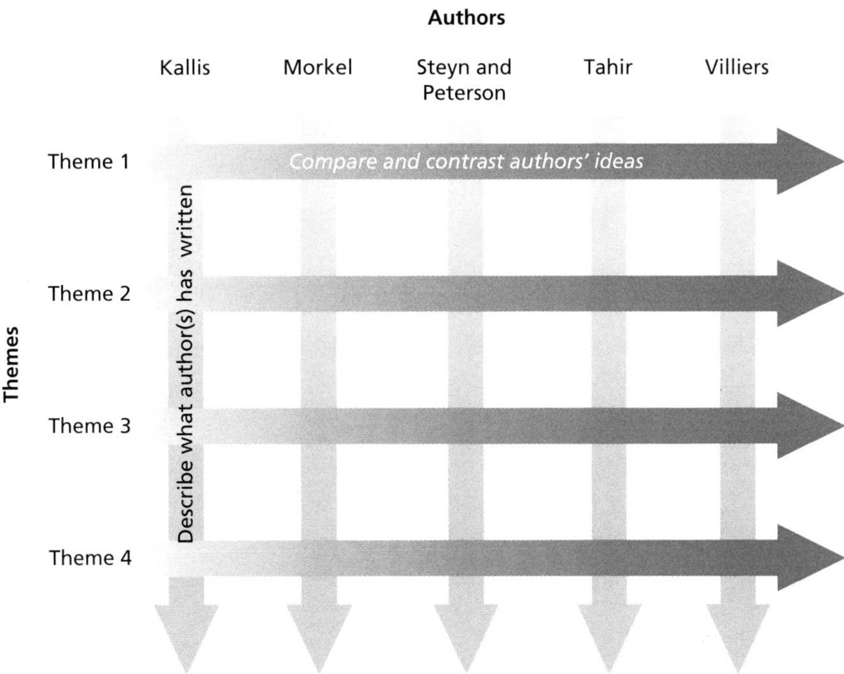

Figure 3.2 Literature review structures

those authors who discuss each theme (horizontal arrows in Figure 3.2). Although there is no single structure that your critical review should take, our students have found it useful to think of the review as a funnel in which you:

1 start at a more general level before narrowing down to your specific research question(s) and objectives;
2 provide a brief overview of key ideas and themes;
3 summarise, compare and contrast the research of the key authors;
4 narrow down to highlight previous research work most relevant to your own research;
5 provide a detailed account of the findings of this research and show how they are related;
6 highlight those aspects where your own research will provide fresh insights;
7 lead the reader into subsequent sections of your project report, which explore these issues.

In order to improve the transparency of your review process, you should explain precisely how you searched for selected the literature you have included in your review, outlining your choice of search terms and of databases used (Tranfield et al. 2003). This is essential if you are using the Systematic Review methodology (Section 3.8). Within the 'funnel' we have just proposed, this can be thought of as step 0! This is discussed in more detail in Sections 3.4 and 3.5.

Whichever way you structure your review you must demonstrate that you have read, understood and evaluated the items you have located. The key to writing a critical literature review is therefore to link the different ideas you find in the literature to form a coherent and cohesive argument, which sets in context and justifies your research. Obviously, it should relate to your research question and objectives. It should show a clear link from these as well as a clear link to the empirical work that will follow. Box 3.4 provides a checklist to help you ensure that the structure of your literature review supports this. Subsequent parts of your project report (Section 14.3) must follow on from this.

Box 3.4 Checklist

Evaluating the structure of your literature review

- ✔ Does your literature review have a clear title which describes the focus of your research rather than just saying 'literature review'?
- ✔ Have you explained precisely how you searched the literature, and the criteria used to select those studies included?
- ✔ Does your review start at a more general level before narrowing down?
- ✔ Is your literature review organised thematically around the ideas contained in the research being reviewed rather than the researchers?
- ✔ Are your arguments coherent and cohesive – do your ideas link in a way that will be logical to your reader?
- ✔ Have you used subheadings within the literature review to help guide your reader?
- ✔ Does the way you have structured your literature review draw your reader's attention to those issues which are going to be the focus of your research, in particular your objectives?
- ✔ Does your literature review lead your reader into subsequent sections of your project report?

Box 3.5 Focus on management research

Structure of the literature review

An article published by Mark Saunders, Levent Altinay and Katharine Riordan in the *Service Industries Journal* (Saunders et al. 2009: 1360–62) includes a review of the literature on the influence of culture in mergers and acquisitions (M&A). The following extract is taken from this review. Although your literature review will be longer than this, the extract illustrates:

- the overall structure of starting at a more general level before narrowing down;
- the provision of a brief overview of the key ideas;
- the linking of ideas;
- narrowing down to highlight that work which is most relevant to the research reported.

In their paper, Saunders et al. subsequently focus on those aspects of culture that need to be considered in relation to mergers and acquisitions before introducing their empirical research conducted in the hospitality industry:

> Academic interest in M&As has a long history, the importance of the management of the transition process and of the working relationship between merging organisations being first recognised in the 1960s (Kitching, 1967). However, it was not until the late 1980s that research began to focus on the human dynamics and people management issues (Cartwright & Cooper, 1990). This highlighted the importance of organisational cultures in relation to their influences on managerial styles and behaviours prior to the merger and during the subsequent integration period for both the organisation and its employees. Although the impact of M&As has subsequently been explored widely in relation to employee behaviours considering as part of this the influence of organisational cultures; this has rarely considered both acquired and acquiring employees or their emotional responses.
>
> Schraeder and Self (2003) cite organisational culture as the 'make or break factor' in M&As, their claims being supported by others who see culture as the catalyst to successful integration (Lakomski, 2001;

Carleton & Lineberry, 2004; Styhre et al., 2006). A study by Watson Wyatt Worldwide (1998) questioned 190 Chief Executive Officers and Chief Finance Officers involved in global acquisitions. They found that, whilst cultural incompatibility was consistently rated as the greatest barrier to post-merger integration, research into these organisations' cultures was least likely to be included in the due diligence process. Some authors argue that cultural due diligence is critical at the outset of the deal; providing a diagnostic to ascertain the degree of cultural compatibility between organisations through a cultural audit (Cartwright & Cooper, 1993; Lindblom & Koch, 2002). Others maintain that the focus given to the integration of the two cultures post-merger is the determinant of success (Carleton & Lineberry, 2004) arguing that successful integration is possible even between highly diverse cultures (Salama et al. 2003). However, it is worth noting that evaluating the degree of cultural compatibility between the organisations requires a thorough understanding of their cultures and this is not a simple straightforward process.

Before continuing with our discussion, it is important to establish what we mean by organisational culture. Although the majority of researchers see organisational culture as an objective entity, two distinct approaches are evident. The first of these consider culture as something an organisation *is* rather than a variable that can be manipulated by managers. Consequently all an organisation's features and behaviours including its systems, procedures, policies and processes are part of its culture (Meek, 1992; Pacanowsky & O'Dennell-Trujillo, 1982). The alternative approach, which we adopt in this paper, is to consider culture as a variable that an organisation *has* (Schein, 2004); thereby implying it is possible for an organisation to manage at least some aspects of its own culture. We therefore use organisational culture to collectively refer to a particular pattern of beliefs, values and behaviours that will have proven valid and useful for that organisational group, and will therefore have been shared with new group members (Schein, 2004). Inevitably this will not exist in a vacuum. Rather it is affected by what Schneider and Barsoux (2003, p. 51) term other 'interacting spheres of culture' such as national, industry, functional and professional cultures.

It therefore follows that after M&A activity, an organisation's culture may need to adapt if the beliefs, values and behaviours no longer work or when the external environment necessitates different responses. Within such adaptations there may be different organisational subcultures owing to the influence of different cultural spheres as well as political, economic, technical and social factors. All of these will impact upon each other and the overall culture of the organisation, this being most visible through a series of artefacts which have symbolic value to employees. These artefacts can be thought of as a cultural web of stories, symbols, power structures, organisational structures, control systems, rituals and routines (Johnson & Scholes, 2008), which can be managed to influence the culture.

M&A activities clearly involve employees. This places considerable emphasis on the way an organisation manages people during the merger and in the subsequent integration period. Cartwright and Cooper (1995) identified four core HRM practices that could contribute significantly to successful integration, namely: management of cultural differences, motivation of employees, retention of employees and setting the long term vision. Such success has been argued to be dependent upon associated HR interventions (Badrtalei & Bates, 2007; Birkinshaw et al., 2000). For example, Lodorfos and Boateng (2006) found that the communication was critical in developing trust among the employees of the organisations involved in M&A leading to successful integration. In contrast, credibility could be lost if promises were made and later reneged (Appelbaum et al., 2000).

Box 3.5 Focus on management research (*continued*)

Increased frequency of honest and consistent communication was found to lead to the reduction of fear (Appelbaum et al., 2000), to the creation of a climate of trust between employees and management and retention of employees. Where leaders acted as cultural role models in post-merger acculturation (Feldman & Spratt, 1999) their changed personal behaviours were argued to actively demonstrate the new changed culture and the long term vision (Schein, 2004).

Elsass and Veiga (1994) propose four archetypal modes of acculturation in M&As based on the need for integration and the extent to which each organisation desires to maintain its original cultural identity, namely: deculturation, assimilation, separation and acculturative tension. Deculturation occurs when the acquiring organisation does not attempt to impose its culture and the acquired organisation has no desire to maintain a separate culture, resulting in employees not being heavily influenced by either culture. In the case of assimilation, one organisation adopts the culture of the other, relinquishing its prior cultural identity. Separation involves both organisations actively preserving their cultural identity, whilst acculturative attention occurs when forces for organisational integration and for cultural differentiation are strong, resulting in both organisations' employees experiencing high levels of stress and tension.

Source: Saunders, M.N.K., Altinay, L. and Riordan, K. (2009).

3.3 Literature sources available

An overview

The literature sources available to help you to develop a good understanding of, and insight into, previous research can be divided into three categories: primary (published and unpublished), secondary and tertiary (Figure 3.3). In reality these categories often overlap: for example, primary literature sources, including conference proceedings, can appear in journals, and some books contain indexes to primary and secondary literature.

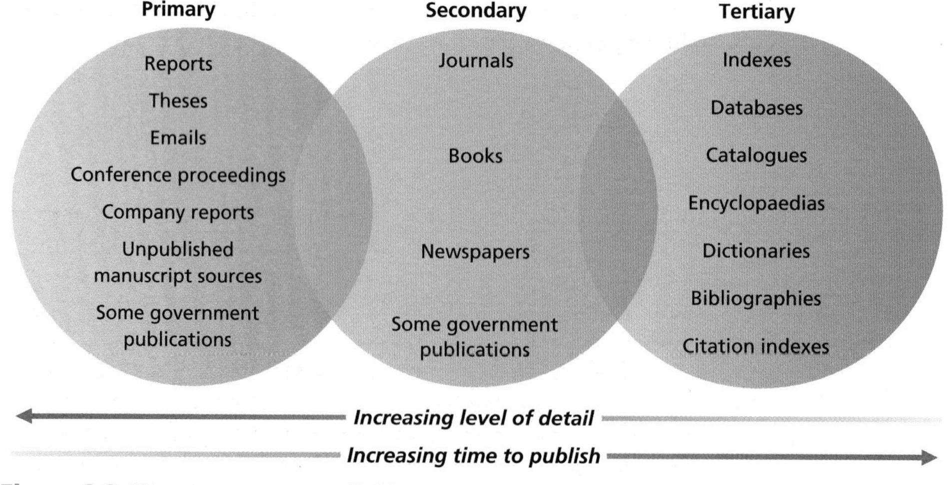

Figure 3.3 Literature sources available

The different categories of literature resources represent the flow of information from the original source. Often as information flows from primary to secondary to tertiary sources it becomes less detailed and authoritative but more easily accessible. Recognising this information flow helps you to identify the most appropriate sources of literature for your needs. Some research projects may access only secondary literature sources whereas others will necessitate the use of primary sources.

The nature of this information flow was typical of traditional printed publications. However, the Internet has changed this situation, providing a more direct means of both publishing and accessing information. Alongside this, 'freedom of information' legislation in many countries means that what was traditionally 'grey literature', such as some government's publications, is increasingly being made available via the Internet. Although many academic publications still exhibit this information flow, increasingly journal articles are either published by the journal online in advance of the print copy or only via the Internet.

Figure 3.3 also illustrates the reduced currency of secondary literature sources, which are utilising information already published in primary sources. Because of the time taken to publish, the information in these sources can be dated. Your literature review should include current thinking as far as possible, so the limitations of such sources must be recognised.

Primary literature sources are the first occurrence of a piece of work. They include published sources such as reports and some central and local government publications such as White Papers and planning documents. They also include unpublished manuscript sources such as letters, memos and committee minutes that may be analysed as data in their own right (Section 8.2). It is because primary literature sources can be difficult to trace that they are sometimes referred to as **grey literature**.

Secondary literature sources such as books and journals are the subsequent publication of primary literature. These publications are aimed at a wider audience. They are easier to locate than primary literature as they are better covered by the tertiary literature.

Tertiary literature sources, also called 'search tools', are designed either to help to locate primary and secondary literature or to introduce a topic. They therefore include online databases and indexes as well as encyclopaedias and bibliographies.

Your use of these sources will depend on your research question(s) and objectives, the need for secondary data to answer them (Section 8.3) and the time available. For some research projects you may use only tertiary and secondary literature; for others you may need to locate primary literature as well. Most research projects will make the greatest use of secondary literature, and so it is this we consider first, followed by the primary literature. Tertiary literature sources are not discussed until Section 3.5, as their major use is in conducting a literature search.

Secondary literature sources

The number of secondary literature sources available to you is expanding rapidly as new resources are developed and made available via the Internet. Your university's librarians are likely to be aware of a wide range of secondary literature in business and management that can be accessed principally from your library's web pages, and will keep themselves up to date with new resources. In addition you may wish to visit your country's national library.

The main secondary literature sources that you are likely to use, along with those primary sources most frequently used for a literature review, are outlined in Table 3.1. The most important when placing your ideas in the context of earlier research are refereed academic journals. Books are, however, likely to be more important than professional and trade journals in this context.

Table 3.1 Main secondary and primary literature sources

Source	Content	Use for the literature review	Coverage by abstracts and indexes (tertiary sources)	Likely availability
Refereed (peer reviewed) academic journal	Detailed reports of research. Written by experts and evaluated by other experts to assess quality and suitability for publication. Rigorous attention paid to detail and verification	Most useful of all	Well covered. In addition, content pages often available for searching via publishers' websites	Majority accessible via the Internet through various subscription services. Those not available can usually be obtained using inter-library loans. Professional organisations may also provide access to their journals via their own web pages
Non-refereed academic journal	May contain detailed reports of research. Selected by editor or editorial board with subject knowledge	Varies considerably. Beware of bias	Reasonably well covered. In addition, content pages often available for searching via publishers' websites	Majority accessible via the Internet through various subscription services. Those not available can usually be obtained using inter-library loans
Professional journals	Mix of news items and practical detailed accounts. Sometimes include summaries of research	Insights into practice but use with caution	Increasingly well covered by online databases. In addition, content pages often available for searching via professional associations' websites	Majority accessible via the Internet through various subscription services. Those available can usually be obtained using inter-library loans. Professional associations may also provide access to their journals via their own web pages
Trade journals/ magazines	Mix of news items and practical detailed accounts	Insights into practice but use with caution	Content pages often available for searching via professional associations' websites	Not as widely available in university libraries as academic and refereed journals. Most trade associations will have an associated website

Source	Content	Use for the literature review	Coverage by abstracts and indexes (tertiary sources)	Likely availability
Books	Written for specific audiences. Usually in an ordered and relatively accessible format. Often draw on wide range of sources	Particularly useful for an overview and to find recognised experts	Well covered by abstracts and indexes. Searches can be undertaken on remote university OPACs* via the Internet	Widely available. Those not available locally can be obtained using inter-library loans
Newspapers	Written for a particular market segment. Filtered dependent on events. May be written from particular viewpoint	Good for topical developments. Beware of possible bias in reporting and coverage	National newspapers reasonably well covered by specialised databases	Recent paper copies of home nation 'quality' newspapers kept as reference in most university libraries. Internet access to stories, often with additional information on the websites, for most national and international 'quality' newspapers increasingly via subscription services
Conference proceedings	Selected papers presented at a conference	Can be very useful if on same theme as research	Depends on conference, although often limited. Specialist indexes sometimes available, such as 'Index to conference proceedings'	Not widely held by university libraries. Can be difficult to find unless online
Reports	Topic specific. Written by academics and organisations. Those from established organisations often of high quality	Very useful, when matches your topic	Poor compared with most secondary sources, although some specialised indexes exist	Not widely held by university libraries. Increasingly available via the Internet. May be possible to obtain others using inter-library loans
Theses	Often most up-to-date research but very specific	Good for PhD and MPhil research degrees, otherwise less useful	Covered by Indices of theses	Still usually obtained using inter-library loans, although starting to be available electronically. May only be one hard (paper) copy

*OPAC, Online Public Access Catalogue.

Source: © Mark Saunders, Philip Lewis and Adrian Thornhill 2011

Journals

Journals are also known as 'periodicals', 'serials' and 'magazines', and are published on a regular basis. While many are still produced in printed form, virtually all can now be accessed online using tertiary literature sources, in particular full text online databases. Journals are a vital literature source for any research. The articles are easily accessible, although online access is usually restricted to members of the university (Table 3.1). Trade and some professional journals may be covered only partially by the tertiary literature (Table 3.2). You therefore need to browse these journals regularly to be sure of finding useful items. Although these are increasingly available online, they are often only available to subscribers. For many academic journals you can receive email 'alerts' of the table of contents (TOC). TOCs can also be browsed online and downloaded through tertiary literature sources such as ticTOCs and the British Library's ZETOC database (Table 3.2 and Section 3.5).

Many universities now expect their academics to deposit digital full text copies of their publications, particularly journal articles, in an open access resource. Providing you know the author and their university, you can often access their publications through these resources free of charge. This is particularly useful if your university does not subscribe to the online database of full text articles in which their publications are stored.

Articles in **refereed academic journals** (such as the *Journal of Management Studies* and the *Academy of Management Review*) are evaluated by academic peers prior to publication, to assess their quality and suitability. They are usually written by recognised experts in the field. There will usually be detailed footnotes; an extensive list of references; rigorous attention to detail; and verification of information. Such articles are written for a narrower audience of scholars with a particular interest in the field. The language used may be technical or highly specialised as a prior knowledge of the topic will be assumed. Prior to being accepted for publication, articles usually undergo several serious revisions, based on the referees' comments, before they actually appear in print.

These are usually the most useful for research projects as they will contain detailed reports of relevant earlier research. Not all academic journals are refereed. Most *non-refereed academic journals* will have an editor and possibly an editorial board with subject knowledge to select articles. The relevance and usefulness of such journals varies considerably, and occasionally you may need to be wary of possible bias (Section 3.6).

Professional journals (such as *People Management*) are produced for their members by organisations such as the Chartered Institute of Personnel and Development (CIPD), the Association of Chartered Certified Accountants (ACCA) and the American Marketing Association (AMA). They contain a mix of news-related items and articles that are more detailed. However, you need to exercise caution, as articles can be biased towards their author's or the organisation's views. Articles are often of a more practical nature and more closely related to professional needs than those in academic journals. Some organisations will also produce newsletters or current awareness publications that you may find useful for up-to-date information. Some professional organisations now give access to selected articles in their journals via their web pages, although these may be only accessible to members (see Table 8.1 and Section 3.5). **Trade journals** fulfil a similar function to professional journals. They are published by trade organisations or aimed at particular industries or trades such as catering or mining. Often they focus on new products or services and news items. They rarely contain articles based on empirical research, although some provide summaries of research. You should therefore use these with considerable caution for your research project.

Table 3.2 Online tertiary literature sources and their coverage

Name	Coverage
ABI/INFORM Complete (also referred to as ProQuest ABI/INFORM Complete)	Database covering over 5400 journals, covering key business disciplines over 80 per cent in full text. Includes wide range of trade and professional titles. Covers additional subjects such as engineering, law and medicine
Blackwell Reference Online	Blackwell Encyclopedia of Management, Blackwell 'handbooks' and 'Companions' in Management
British National Bibliography (BNB)	Bibliographic information for books and serials (journals) deposited at the British Library by UK and Irish publishers since 1950
British Library Integrated Catalogue	British Library catalogues including reference collections and document supply collections (books, journals, reports, conferences, theses)
British Newspapers 1600–1900	Cross-searchable interface to full-text British Newspapers
Business Insights	Database including reports on a wide range of sectors including retail, pharmaceuticals, energy, finance, health care and technology. Some UK/Europe focus
Business Source Complete (also referred to as EBSCO)	Database including full-text articles from over 2900 management, business, economics and information technology journals, mainly since 1990s. Contains a wide range of trade and professional titles. Gives access to *Datamonitor* (see below)
Datamonitor	Database of company profiles for world's 10,000 largest companies, Industry profiles for various industries (see also *Business Source Complete* above)
Emerald Management eJournals	Database providing access to over 160 full-text journals and reviews from 300 management journals
Global Books in Print	English language bibliographic information for books in print from most of the world
Hospitality and Tourism Index	Bibliographic database covering English language hospitality and tourism journals and trade magazines. Some full-text links. Coverage since early 1960s
Index to Conference Proceedings	Database containing proceedings of all significant conferences held worldwide (over 450,000 at time of writing). Available via the website as part of the Document Supply Conference File from the British Library Integrated Catalogue
Index to Theses	A comprehensive listing of theses with abstracts accepted for higher degrees by universities in Great Britain and Ireland since 1716
IngentaConnect	Details of articles from over 28,000 publications, some of which are available on subscription. Pay-per-view access available. Updated daily
ISI Web of Knowledge	Includes access to a wide range of services, including citation indexes for social sciences and for arts and humanities
JSTOR	Database containing full-text journals, most going back to first issue (in some cases going back to the eighteenth or nineteenth century). Covers sciences, social sciences and arts and humanities. Most recent years usually not available
Key Note Reports	Database containing over 1600 market reports covering a range of sectors
Mintel Reports	Database containing detailed market research reports on wide range of sectors
Nexis	Database of full text of UK national and regional newspapers. Some international coverage and company data

(continued)

Table 3.2 (*continued*)

Name	Coverage
Regional Business News	Database of full text of United States business journals, newspapers and newswires. Updated daily
Research Index	Indexes articles and news items of financial interest that appear in the UK national newspapers, professional and trade journals (updated frequently)
Sage Premier	Database of full text of over 480 Sage journals including business, humanities, social sciences and research methods since 1999
Science Direct	Database of full text of over 1600 Elsevier journals including social sciences
Social Science Citation Index	Access to current and retrospective bibliographic information, author abstracts, and cited references found in over 1700 social sciences journals covering more than 50 disciplines. Also covers items from approximately 3300 of the world's leading science and technology journals
ticTOCs	Service to export selected journal tables of contents (TOCs) from over 400 publishers
Times Digital Archive 1785–1985	Database containing complete digital editions (including photographs, illustrations and advertisements) from *The Times* national newspaper (UK)
Web of Science Proceedings	Index to published literature of most significant conferences, symposia, seminars, colloquia and conventions in a wide range of disciplines since 1990
Wiley Online	Database of 1100 full-text journals including business and law
Wilson Business Periodicals Index	Indexes English language business periodicals (articles and book reviews). North American focus. Selection for indexing is by subscriber preference and has altered over time (since 1959)
ZETOC	British Library's index of journals and conference proceedings tables of contents (TOCs). Allows setting up of email alerts of selected journal contents pages

Books

Books and monographs are written for specific audiences. Some are aimed at the academic market, with a theoretical slant. Others, aimed at practising professionals, may be more applied in their content. The material in books is usually presented in a more ordered and accessible manner than in journals, pulling together a wider range of topics. They are, therefore, particularly useful as introductory sources to help clarify your research question(s) and objectives or the research methods you intend to use. Most academic textbooks, like this one, are supported by web pages providing additional information. However, books may contain out-of-date material even by the time they are published.

Newspapers

Newspapers are a good source of topical events, developments within business and government, as well as recent statistical information such as share prices. They also sometimes review recent research reports (Box 3.6). The main 'quality' newspapers have websites carrying the main stories and supporting information. Back copies starting in the early 1990s are available on CD-ROM or online via a full-text subscription service, such as *Nexis* (Table 3.2). Current editions of newspapers can nearly always be found via the Internet, although increasingly there is a charge for access. Items in earlier issues

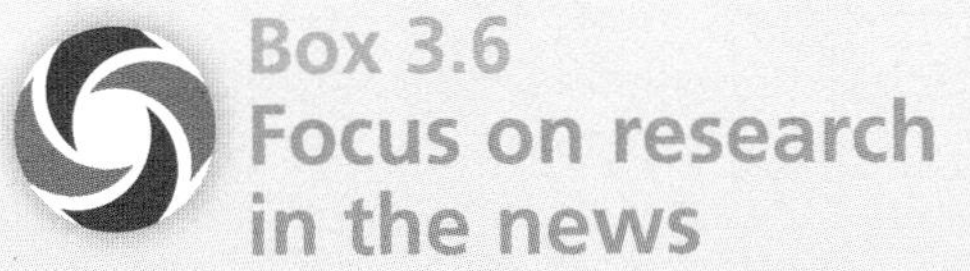

Box 3.6
Focus on research in the news

FT

Lenders wary of high-growth business

Banks are failing to back many of the high-growth companies that the UK will rely on to create hundreds of thousands of jobs over the next few years, according to research. It suggests the credit-scoring systems that banks use to make lending decisions exaggerate the riskiness of such businesses, sometimes known as 'gazelles'.

The findings, in a report by the National Endowment for Science, Technology and the Arts, have potentially serious implications for jobs growth and suggest banks may be missing out on opportunities for profitable lending. Fast-growth companies have a greater need for capital, but greater difficulty in accessing finance than slower-growth businesses, the report says. The research is likely to be seized on by the government, which has embraced Nesta's earlier research finding that just 6 per cent of companies generated 54 per cent of the new jobs created by existing businesses between 2002 and 2008. It has now updated that research and found these businesses performed strongly during the recession. In 2007–10, 7 per cent of businesses generated 49 per cent of new jobs created by companies with 10 or more employees. The fast growers tend to be at least five years old and are spread widely across all sectors. Innovations in services, processes and business models are as important as new technology.

Its most controversial finding gives weight to complaints from expanding companies that banks do not understand them. Nesta used Experian's credit rating system – equivalent to banks' internal systems – and found that high-growth companies were judged less creditworthy than other businesses, even though they had lower insolvency rates.

'It appears that these bank ratings are over-penalising riskier high-growth firms. It's particularly worrying when you combine that with the fact that risk capital is also harder to find,' said Stian Westlake, Nesta's research director. He urged banks to do extra due diligence and look at wider characteristics when assessing lending requests from fast-growth businesses. Nesta also wants the government to do more to encourage venture capital via public–private funds. It calls on ministers to remove barriers to innovation, such as tackling blockages in the planning system and ensuring companies can import highly skilled migrant staff despite the immigration cap. Nesta also wants improved networks between business and universities and better government procurement to encourage innovation.

Source of extract: Groom, B. (2011) 'Lenders wary of high growth business', *Financial Times*, 18 March. Available at www.ft.com/cms/s/0/3bc112bc-50cf-11e0-9227-00144feab49a.html#ixzz1Gx1ZWX1q [Accessed 20 March 2011].

are more difficult to access and often only include text. An exception is the *Times Digital Archive 1785–1985* (Table 3.2) of *The Times* newspaper. You need to be careful, as newspapers may contain bias in their coverage, be it political, geographical or personal. Reporting can also be inaccurate, and you may not pick up any subsequent amendments. In addition, the news presented is filtered depending on events at the time, with priority given to more headline-grabbing stories (Stewart and Kamins 1993).

Primary literature sources

Primary literature sources are becoming easier to locate, as they are made available via the Internet (Table 3.1). The most accessible and those most likely to be of use in showing how your research relates to that of other people, are reports, conference proceedings and theses.

Reports

Reports include market research reports such as those produced by Mintel and Keynote, government reports and academic reports. Even if you are able to locate these, you may find it difficult to gain access to them because they are not as widely available as books (Section 8.4). Reports are not well indexed in the tertiary literature, and you will need to rely on specific search tools such as the *British National Bibliography for Report Literature* and the British Library Public Catalogue (see Table 3.2).

Freedom of information legislation by many governments now means far more information is available via the web, for example the European Union's (EU) European Commission website and the Commission's Statistics website Eurostat. These and other governmental websites are listed in Table 8.2. European 'grey literature', including reports, conference proceedings, and discussion and policy papers, has been covered since 1980 by OpenSIGLE (Open System for Information on Grey Literature in Europe) and is available online via the Internet.

Conference proceedings

Conference proceedings, sometimes referred to as symposia, are often published as unique titles within journals or as books. Most conferences will have a theme that is very specific, but some have a wide-ranging overview. Proceedings are not well indexed by tertiary literature so, as with reports, you may have to rely on specific search tools such as the *Index to Conference Proceedings* and the *British Library Integrated Catalogue* (Table 3.2) as well as general search engines such as Google or Bing. If you do locate and are able to obtain the proceedings for a conference on the theme of your research, you will have a wealth of relevant information. Many conferences have associated web pages providing abstracts and occasionally the full papers presented at the conference.

Theses

Theses are unique and so for a major research project can be a good source of detailed information; they will also be a good source of further references. Unfortunately, they can be difficult to locate and, when found, difficult to access as there may be only one copy at the awarding institution. Specific search tools are available, such as *Index to Theses* (see Table 3.2). Only research degrees such as PhD and MPhil are covered well by these tertiary resources. Research undertaken as part of a taught masters degree is not covered as systematically.

3.4 Planning your literature search strategy

It is important that you plan this search carefully to ensure that you locate relevant and up-to-date literature. This will enable you to establish what research has previously been published in your area and to relate your own research to it. All our students have found their literature search a time-consuming process, which takes far longer than expected. Fortunately, time spent planning will be repaid in time saved when searching the literature. As you start to plan your search, you need to beware of information overload! One of the easiest ways to avoid this is to start the main search for your critical review with clearly defined research question(s), objectives and outline proposal (Sections 2.4 and 2.5). Before commencing your literature search, we suggest that you undertake further planning by writing down your search strategy and, if possible, discussing it with your project tutor. This should include:

- the parameters of your search;
- the search terms and phrases you intend to use;
- the online databases and search engines you intend to use;
- the criteria you intend to use to select the relevant and useful studies from all the items you find.

Whilst it is inevitable that your search strategy will be refined as your literature search progresses, we believe that such a planned approach is important as it forces you to think carefully about your research strategy and justify, at least to yourself, why you are doing what you are doing.

Defining the parameters of your search

For most research questions and objectives you will have a good idea of which subject matter is going to be relevant. You will, however, be less clear about the parameters within which you need to search. In particular, you need to be clear about the following (derived from Bell 2010):

- language of publication (e.g. English);
- subject area (e.g. accountancy);
- business sector (e.g. manufacturing);
- geographical area (e.g. Europe);
- publication period (e.g. the last 10 years);
- literature type (e.g. refereed journals and books).

One way of starting to firm up these parameters is to re-examine your lecture notes and course textbooks in the area of your research question. While re-examining these, we suggest you make a note of subjects that appear most pertinent to your research question and the names of relevant authors. These will be helpful when generating possible search terms and phrases later.

For example, if your research was on the benefits of cause-related marketing to charities you might identify the subject area as marketing and charities. Implicit in this is the need to think broadly. A frequent comment we hear from students who have attempted a literature search is 'there's nothing written on my research topic'. This is usually because they have identified one or more of their parameters too narrowly (or chosen their search terms poorly, Section 3.5). We therefore recommend that if you encounter this problem you broaden one or more of your parameters to include material that your narrower search would not have located (Box 3.7).

Generating your search terms

It is important at this stage to read both articles by key authors and recent review articles in the area of your research. This will help you to define your subject matter and to suggest appropriate search terms and phrases. Recent review articles in your research area are often helpful here as they discuss the current state of research for a particular topic and can help you to refine your search terms. In addition, they will probably contain references to other work that is pertinent to your research question(s) and objectives

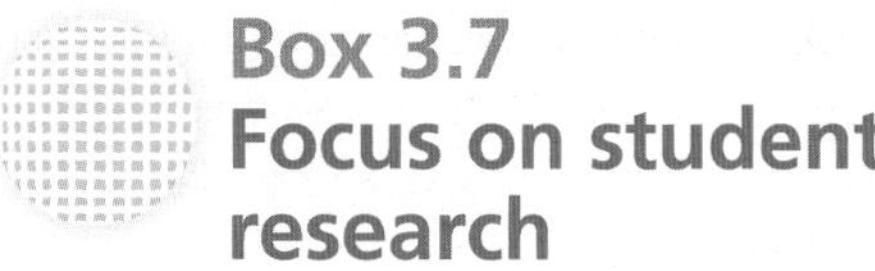

Box 3.7 Focus on student research

Defining parameters for a research question

Simon's research question was 'How have green issues influenced the way in which manufacturers advertise cars?' To be certain of finding material, he defined search terms for each parameter in narrow and, in most instances, broader terms:

Parameter	Narrow	Broader
Language of publication	UK English (e.g. car)	UK and USA English (e.g. car and automobile)
Subject area	Green issues	Environmental issues
	Motor industry	Manufacturing
	Advertising	Marketing
Business sector	Motor industry	Manufacturing
Geographical area	UK	Europe and North America
Publication period	Last 5 years	Last 15 years
Literature type	Refereed journals and books	Journals and books

(Box 3.8). If you are unsure about review articles, your project tutor should be able to point you in the right direction. Another potentially useful source of references is dissertations and theses in your university's library.

After rereading your lecture notes and textbooks and undertaking this limited reading you will have a list of subjects that appear relevant to your research project. You now need to define precisely what is relevant to your research in terms of search terms.

The identification of search terms is the most important part of planning your search for relevant literature (Bell 2010). **Search terms** are the basic terms that describe your research question(s) and objectives, and will be used to search the tertiary literature. Search terms (which can include authors' family names identified in the examination of your lecture notes and course textbooks) can be identified using one or a number of different techniques in combination. Those found most useful by our students include:

Discussion

We believe you should be taking every opportunity to discuss your research. In discussing your work with others, whether face to face, by facebook or by email, you will be sharing your ideas, getting feedback and obtaining new ideas and approaches. This process will help you to refine and clarify your topic.

Initial reading, dictionaries, encyclopaedias, handbooks and thesauruses

To produce the most relevant search terms you may need to build on your brainstorming session with support materials such as dictionaries, encyclopedias, handbooks and thesauruses, both general and subject specific. These are also good starting points for

Box 3.8 Focus on management research

Identifying areas of convergence, divergence and research gaps

In a recent article in the *International Journal of Management Reviews*, Meier (2011) develops an integrative framework which he uses to organise empirical research on knowledge management in strategic alliances. Based on this he identifies areas of convergence, divergence and knowledge gaps.

Meier's article is divided into four substantive sections:

- The framework of knowledge management in strategic alliances.
- The methods used to search the literature.
- An overview of empirical evidence on knowledge management in strategic alliances.
- A discussion outlining the key findings and possible future research directions.

The process used to search the literature followed the Systematic Review methodology (see also Section 3.8). This involved:

1 Generating an initial list of 25 keywords based on Meier's prior experience, which were combined using Boolean operators to create search strings and discussed with a review panel of experts.

2 Identifying 83 high-quality peer-reviewed journals and subsequently searching their abstracts and titles using either the online databases *Business Source Complete* and *Science Direct* or, where this was not possible, manually.

3 Evaluating the title and abstract of the 365 articles retrieved against clear inclusion/exclusion criteria to establish their suitability, resulting in 71 relevant articles.

4 Using the reference lists from the 10 most frequently cited articles to identify further references. These further 684 articles were subject to the same inclusion/exclusion criteria, resulting in an additional 10 relevant articles.

The majority of these articles focused on how alliance partners characteristics, their interactions and the actions they take to manage knowledge can influence knowledge transfer. Few empirically examined the way in which knowledge was created and applied in alliances.

Based on his review Meier produced a table summarising the research findings to date and highlighting 13 clear research gaps in the literature. Some of those he highlighted were due to a lack of longitudinal studies. These included research questions such as 'How "learning races" destabilize a relationship (Inkpen and Beamish 1997), how different types of trust develop in alliances, and how firms reduce knowledge ambiguity' (Meier 2011: 19).

Source: Developed from Meier (2011)

new topics with which you may be unfamiliar and for related subject areas. Initial reading, particularly of recent review articles, may also be of help here. Project tutors, colleagues and librarians can also be useful sources of ideas.

It is also possible to obtain definitions via the Internet. The online search engine Google offers a 'define' search option (by typing 'Define:[enter term]') that provides links to websites providing definitions. Definitions are also offered in free online encyclopaedias such as Wikipedia (Box 3.9). These are often available in multiple languages and, although anyone is allowed to edit the entries, inappropriate changes are usually removed quickly. Whilst articles tend to become more comprehensive and balanced as contributors add to and revise them, recent articles in particular may contain misinformation or unencyclopaedic content (Wikipedia 2011). However, whilst these websites may be useful for a quick reference or in helping to define keywords, your university will almost certainly expect you to justify the definitions in your research project using refereed journal articles or textbooks.

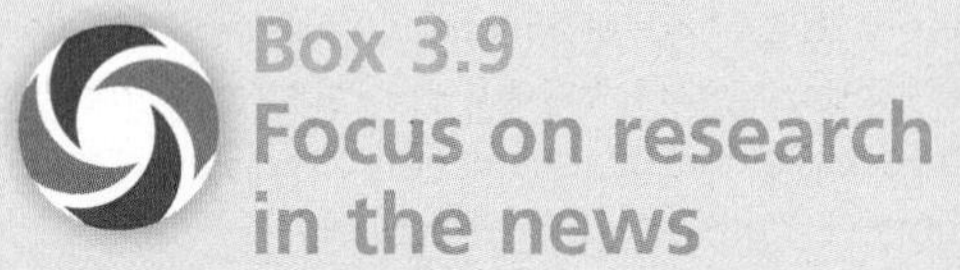

FT

Fact and friction

It is one of the great paradoxes of the Internet: an essentially open medium has created deeply entrenched information powers. Within a remarkably short time, companies such Google, YouTube and Facebook have come to dominate the business of search, user-generated video and social networking – even though barriers to entry in theory remain low.

Among the members of this emerging online oligopoly, none is more intriguing than Wikipedia. An outlandish experiment in communitarian action when it was launched in 2001, the user-generated encyclopaedia has become the world's fifth most visited website and the first reference source for schoolchildren and adults alike – even if most swear a half-hearted oath to double-check anything they read there.

Yet in spite – or perhaps because – of its success, Wikipedia is proving slow to adapt. Even relatively simple ideas aimed at reinforcing its basic quality and reliability have turned out to be hard to push through.

Take a plan to improve the English-language version, the most extensive with more than 3 million articles, by subjecting changes proposed by newcomers to approval by more experienced editors and flagging up any revisions. A minor but highly symbolic innovation, this idea was introduced in the German version more than 18 months ago but its appearance in English has been delayed by disagreements over how it should work. A more limited set of changes is now set for early this year, Wikipedia says.

With this service still less than a decade old and its evolution hard to predict, Wikipedia's entrenched position raises uncomfortable questions. Wikipedians dispute recent claims by a Spanish academic, for example, that the ranks of active editors are declining, but concede that the site's English version is undergoing an important transition. Sue Gardner, executive director of the Wikimedia Foundation, the charity that oversees the running of Wikipedia, says external data show that the editing ranks 'started to stagnate' in 2006, though she adds that it is not clear yet what this portends for the service.

Critics are more forthright. With editor numbers no longer growing in spite of an increase in articles, it will be harder to monitor quality – and vested interests could find it easier to make alterations that reflect their own views, warns Andrew Lih of the University of Southern California and author of *The Wikipedia Revolution*. 'My biggest fear is a slow leakage of the truth, which might not easily be detected.'

Any critique of Wikipedia's fundamental quality has to begin with an acknowledgement: in the field of supposedly objective reference information, there are no absolutes.

'How many publications in human history can you trust?', asks Craig Newmark, founder of Craigslist, the online classified advertising service, and a Wikimedia Foundation adviser. 'All have been subject to some disinformation that has been put in there by the powerful; disinformation has been a normal part of human reality forever.' Idealists such as Mr Newmark argue that, freed from the inherent flaws of publications dominated by a narrow range of interests, Wikipedia could become 'more reliable than anything we've ever seen'.

Yet even optimists such as he agree with the more sceptical observers on this: that, in terms of reliability and service, Wikipedia still has a long way to go. That makes the foot-dragging over flagged revisions look like a bad omen. It points to a fundamental tension at the heart of Wikipedia that has stalled its development. Founded on an ideal of complete openness, any adjustment that seems to favour one group of contributors over another can seem like a betrayal of the principle.

'They're sending out a message, even if in a quiet way, that some editors are more important than others,' says Matt Curinga, a software programmer and occasional contributor who is working on a doctorate on services such as Wikipedia.

While technical considerations have contributed to the delay, 'the majority of people didn't like the idea', adds Mr Lih. 'I'm certainly not sure that the English-language Wikipedia, with its free-wheeling culture, is ready for that yet.'

If even a modest idea such as this – aimed mainly at preventing vandalism to articles by casual visitors – can be stalled, it does not bode well for more important changes that will be needed in the future, adds Mr Sanger.

There are two potential longer-term approaches to boosting the site's accuracy and reliability. The first, favoured by the powers that be, involves refinements to mechanisms that enable self-policing. With the right processes, the interaction of the crowd will produce the best results, suggests Mr Wales. Quality 'emerges from lots of participation', he says. 'It's just giving the people who are participating the tools they need.'

In future, adds Mr Newmark, it may be necessary to track the identity of editors, or find ways to measure their reputations, then rank their work – ideas that seem anathema in the present culture. When it comes to trying to distinguish good editors from bad, 'we don't have good, consistent measures, which is a problem for us', says Ms Gardner.

A related push involves helping readers to distinguish the reliable from the unreliable. The problem is not necessarily that the average quality of articles is low, rather that there is no way to tell which can truly be relied on. Little effort has so far been put into analysing overall quality – a situation about which Mr Wales expresses frustration – let alone the quality of individual articles or the editors who compose or revise them.

Nor do the search engines that generate so much of Wikipedia's audience attempt to discriminate between reliable and less reliable articles. Some 60–70 per cent of the site's traffic comes from search engines, says Mr Wales, and the fact that it appears at, or close to, the top of many search results is a big source of its success.

One potential approach is to use internal clues in Wikipedia itself to make educated guesses about which information is most reliable. For example, Google could analyse the records of individual editors, says Marissa Mayer, Google's head of search products. That information could be used to rank articles in its search index.

Yet she says Google has no plans to do that, which means reliable and suspect articles alike will continue to figure prominently in search results.

Wikipedia is testing its own tools for helping readers assess quality. For example, an experiment at the University of California at Santa Cruz colour-codes different segments of text in articles based on how long they have remained unedited, on the assumption that the most reliable parts remain untouched the longest. Wikipedia also plans this year to add a 'rate this article' option to help guide readers.

The second potential approach to boosting quality is more fundamental and raises deeper questions about the direction of the site. 'What they really need is some sort of rating or approval process that engages actual experts,' says Mr Sanger.

The idea that experts should have a superior status is a taboo, guaranteed to provoke a strong backlash. For a site – Wikipedia prefers 'community' – founded on ideas of radical egalitarianism, it smacks of revisionism. Yet even some enthusiastic supporters say there is no alternative in the long term. 'You need experts balanced by citizens, and vice versa,' says Mr Newmark.

Informally, Wikipedia is already trying to draw in more experts. To overcome the strong resistance of many in academia, Ms Gardner says the foundation has been encouraging academics to contribute more. She quotes with approval experiments in which professors have set their students projects to improve certain articles.

Yet that may have a lasting impact only if the work of experts is clearly accorded a higher standing. 'Ultimately, that's what has to be done – I just don't think they'll do it,' says Mr Sanger.

While this struggle over the soul of the Internet's most successful experiment in user participation rages, the watchword for visitors to Wikipedia will remain the same: *caveat lector* – or, as the site itself helpfully translates, 'Let the reader beware'.

Source of extract: Waters, R. (2011). 'Fact or friction', *Financial Times*, 18 March. Available at www.ft.com/cms/s/0/8c751538-f73d-11de-9fb5-00144feab49a.html#ixzz1GxFAGkM9 [Accessed 20 March 2011].

Box 3.10 Focus on student research

Generating search terms

Han's research question was 'How do the actual management requirements of a school pupil record administration system differ from those suggested by the literature?' She brainstormed this question with her peer group, all of whom were teachers in Hong Kong. The resulting list included the following search terms and phrases:

> schools, pupil records, administration, user requirements, computer, management information system, access, legislation, information, database, security, UK, Hong Kong, theories

The group evaluated these and others. As a result, the following search terms (and phrases) were selected:

> pupil records, management information system, computer, database, user requirement

Online dictionaries and encyclopaedias were used subsequently to add to the choice of search terms:

> student record, MIS, security

Han made a note of these prior to using them in combination to search the tertiary literature sources.

Brainstorming

Brainstorming has already been outlined as a technique for helping you to develop your research question (Section 2.3). However, it is also helpful for generating search terms. Either individually or as part of a group, you write down all the words and short phrases that come to mind on your research topic (Box 3.10). These are then evaluated and search terms (and phrases) selected.

Relevance trees

Relevance trees provide a useful method of bringing some form of structure to your literature search and of guiding your search process (Sharp et al. 2002). They look similar to an organisation chart and are a hierarchical 'graph-like' arrangement of headings and subheadings (Box 3.11). These headings and subheadings describe your research question(s) and objectives and may be terms (including authors' names) with which you can search. Relevance trees are often constructed after brainstorming. They enable you to decide, either with help or on your own (Jankowicz 2005):

- which search terms are directly relevant to your research question(s) and objectives;
- which areas you will search first and which your search will use later;
- which areas are more important – these tend to have more branches.

To construct a relevance tree:

1. Start with your research question or an objective at the top level.
2. Identify two or more subject areas that you think are important.
3. Further subdivide each major subject area into sub-areas that you think are of relevance.
4. Further divide the sub-areas into more precise sub-areas that you think are of relevance.
5. Identify those areas that you need to search immediately and those that you particularly need to focus on. Your project tutor will be of particular help here.
6. As your reading and reviewing progress, add new areas to your relevance tree.

Box 3.11 Focus on student research

Using a relevance tree

Sadie's research question was 'Is there a link between benchmarking and Total Quality Management?' After brainstorming her question, she decided to construct a relevance tree using the search terms and phrases that had been generated.

Using her relevance tree Sadie identified those areas that she needed to search immediately (underlined) and those that she particularly needed to focus on (starred*):

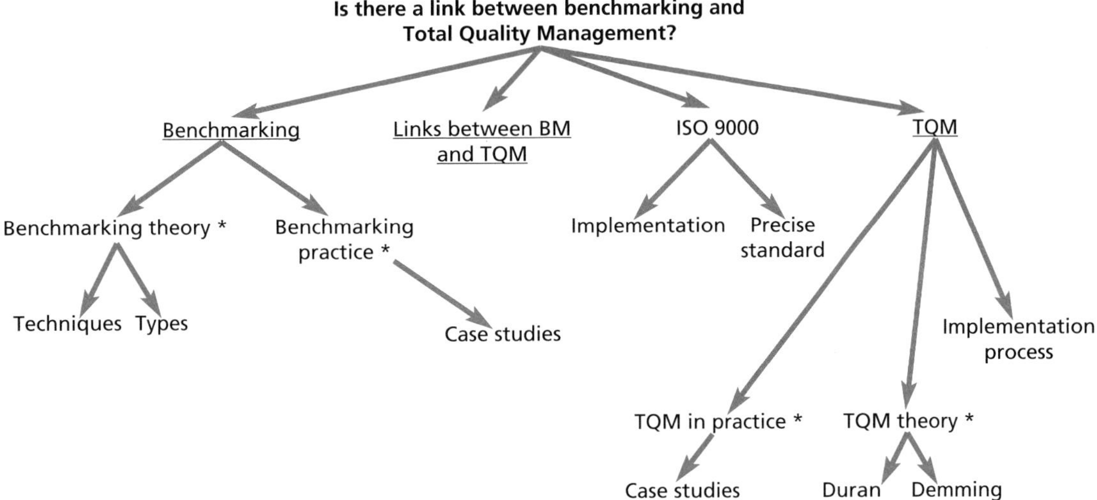

Computer software to help generate relevance trees, such as Inspiration (2011) and MindGenius (2011), is also increasingly available in universities. Using such software also allows you to attach notes to your relevance tree and can help generate an initial structure for your literature review.

3.5 Conducting your literature search

Your literature search will probably be conducted using a variety of approaches:

- searching using tertiary literature sources, in particular online databases;
- obtaining relevant literature (Section 3.6) referenced in books and journal articles you have already read;
- scanning and browsing secondary literature in your library;
- general Internet searching.

Eventually it is likely you will be using a variety of these in combination. However, we suggest that you start your search by obtaining relevant literature that has been referenced in books and articles you have already read. Although books are unlikely to give adequate up-to-date coverage of your research question, they provide a useful starting point and usually contain some references to further reading. Reading these will enable you to refine your research question(s), objectives and the associated search terms prior to searching using tertiary literature sources. It will also help you to see more clearly how your research relates to previous research, and will provide fresh insights.

Tertiary literature sources

It is very tempting with easy access to the Internet to start your literature search with an general search engine such as Bing or Google. Whilst this can retrieve some useful information it must be treated with care. Your project report is expected to be an academic piece of work and hence must use academic sources. Therefore it is essential that you use tertiary sources which provide access to academic literature. These consist of three types of online databases and are listed in order of likely importance to your search:

Full text online databases that index and provide a summary of articles from a range of journals (and sometimes books, chapters from books, reports, theses and conferences), as well as the full text of articles.

Abstracts that only include an index and a summary of articles from a range of journals (and sometimes books, chapters from books, reports, theses and conferences), hence the name abstract.

Indexes that, as the name suggest, only index articles from a range of journals (and sometimes books, chapters from books, reports, theses and conferences).

Within all of these, the information provided will be sufficient to locate the item – for example, for journal articles:

- author or authors of the article;
- date of publication;
- title of the article;
- title of the journal;
- volume and part number of the journal issue;
- page numbers of the article.

Most index searches will be undertaken to find articles using key words selected from a pre-specified list or the author's name. Occasionally you may wish to search by finding those authors who have referenced (cited) an article after it has been published. A citation index enables you to do this as it lists by author the other authors who have cited that author's works subsequent to their publication. In contrast, the abstract can be useful in helping you to assess the content and relevance of an article to your research before obtaining a copy. You should beware of using abstracts, as a substitute for the full article, as a source of information for your research. They contain only a summary of the article and are likely to exclude much of relevance. Full-text databases usually allow both the searching and retrieval of the full text, principally of journal articles; the articles being retrieved in portable document file (pdf) format. These are read using software such as an Adobe Reader, which can be downloaded free of charge.

Your access to the majority of online databases will be paid for by a subscription from your university. There are, however, some pay-as-you-use online databases, where the cost of the search is passed on to the user. Online databases provide a wealth of information. Whilst many online databases are intuitive to use, it is still advisable to obtain a librarian's help or to attend a training session prior to your search to find out about the specific features available. It is also vital that you plan and prepare your search in advance so your time is not wasted. For virtually all online databases, password protected access is now possible from anywhere via the Internet. An additional source of information via the Internet, which our students have found useful, is publishers' web pages. These often include journals' content pages (see Table 3.4).

Virtually all university library OPACs (online public access catalogues) are now accessible via the Internet (see Table 3.5). These provide a very useful means of locating resources. If you identify useful collections of books and journals, it is possible to make use of other university libraries in the vacations. Within the UK, the SCONUL Vacation

Access Scheme gives details of access policies of the libraries in UK higher-education institutions.[1] Some of the largest research libraries in the UK and Ireland (including the British Library, Oxford and Cambridge Universities and the National Libraries of Scotland and Wales) have also made their catalogues available online. These can be accessed through COPAC, the National Academic and Specialist Library Catalogue.[2]

To ensure maximum coverage in your search, you need to use all appropriate online databases. One mistake many people make is to restrict their searches to one or two business and management tertiary sources rather than to use a variety. The coverage of each online database differs both geographically and in type of journal (Section 3.3). In addition, a database may state that it indexes a particular journal yet may do so only selectively. This emphasises the importance of using a range of databases to ensure a wide coverage of available literature. Some of those more frequently used are outlined in Table 3.2. However, new databases are being developed all the time so it is worth asking a librarian for advice.

Searching using online (tertiary literature) databases

Once your search terms have been identified, searching using tertiary literature is a relatively straightforward process. You need to:

1 make a list of the search terms that describe your research question(s) and objectives;
2 search appropriate online databases;
3 note precise details, including the search strings used, of the actual searches you have undertaken for each database;
4 note the full reference of each item found; this can normally be done by cutting and pasting the references or importing them into software for managing bibliographies, such as Endnote® or Reference Manager®.
5 Wherever possible download the article in pdf format and save it on your USB mass storage device using the author, date and a brief description as a filename. This will help you locate it later. For example, an article by Mark on the use of web questionnaires might be saved using the filename: Saunders[2012]web_questionnaire.pdf.

Tranfield et al. (2003) emphasise the importance of reporting your literature search strategy in sufficient detail to ensure that your search could be replicated (Box 3.13).

Box 3.12 Checklist

Minimising problems with your search terms

- ✔ Is the spelling incorrect? Behaviour is spelt with a 'u' in the UK but without in the USA.
- ✔ Is the language incorrect? Chemists in the UK but drug stores in the USA.
- ✔ Are you using incorrect terminology? In recent years some terms have been replaced by others, such as 'redundancy' being replaced by 'downsizing'.
- ✔ Are you using recognised acronyms and abbreviations? For example, UK for United Kingdom or BA instead of British Airways.
- ✔ Are you avoiding jargon and using accepted terminology? For example, downsizing rather than redundancy.
- ✔ Are you avoiding words that are not in the controlled index language?

[1]Details of these can be found on the Internet at: www.sconul.ac.uk/use_lib/vacation.html.

[2]The Internet address for COPAC is http://copac.ac.uk.

Your review will be based on the subset of those items found which you consider are relevant.

Most online databases now allow full-text searches using natural language where you decide on the word or phrase combinations for search terms. This means, for example, you can search the complete text of an article using your search terms. However, some databases rely on or also offer the option to search using a **controlled index language** of pre-selected terms and phrases or 'descriptors'. These can include specified subject words, author names and journal titles. If your search terms do not match those in the controlled index language, your search will be unsuccessful. In such a situation, you therefore need to check your search terms with the 'index' or 'browse' option prior to searching. This is especially useful to establish how an author is indexed or whether hyphens should be used when entering specific terms. Despite using these tools, your searches may still be unsuccessful. The most frequent causes of failure are summarised in Box 3.12 as a checklist.

Searches normally use a combination of search terms linked using **Boolean logic**. These are known as **search strings** and enable you to combine, limit or widen the variety of items found using 'link terms' (Table 3.3). Boolean logic can also be used to construct search strings using dates, journal titles and names of organisations or people. Initially it may be useful to limit your search to peer-reviewed journal articles for which the full text is available. It may also be valuable to narrow your search to specific years, especially if you are finding a wealth of items and need to concentrate on the most up to date. By contrast, searching by author allows you to broaden your search to find other work by known researchers in your area.

There are, however, problems with searching the full text. In particular, the context of a search term may be inappropriate, leading to retrieval of numerous irrelevant articles and information overload. Fortunately, you can also search one or more specified fields in the database such as the abstract, author or title. Usually searching the abstract results in fewer irrelevant articles although, inevitably, you may not find some relevant ones either! Specifying other fields, for example the abstract, will be useful if you wish to find articles by a key author in your subject area.

Table 3.3 Common link terms that use Boolean logic

Link term	Purpose	Example	Outcome
AND	Narrows search	Recruitment AND interviewing AND skills	Only articles containing all three search terms selected
OR	Widens search	Recruitment OR selection	Articles with at least one search term selected
NOT	Excludes terms from search	Recruitment NOT selection	Selects articles containing the search term 'recruitment' that do not contain the search term 'selection'
*(truncation)	Uses word stems to pick up different word forms	Motivat*	Selects articles with: motivate, motivation, motivating
? (wild card)	Picks up different spellings	behavio?r	Selects articles with: behavior, behaviour

Scanning and browsing

Any search will find only some of the relevant literature. You will therefore also need to scan and browse the literature. New publications such as journals are unlikely to be indexed immediately in tertiary literature, so you will need to browse these publications to gain an idea of their content. In contrast, scanning will involve you going through individual items such as a journal article to pick out points that relate to your own research. It is particularly important that you browse and scan trade and professional journals, as these are less likely to be covered by the tertiary literature.

To make browsing and scanning easier you should:

- identify when those journals that are the most relevant are published and, where possible, ensure you receive email 'alerts' of their tables of contents (TOCs);
- identify those professional journals that are most relevant and regularly browse them;
- browse new book displays in libraries;
- scan new book reviews in journals and newspapers;
- scan publishers' new book catalogues where available;
- discuss your research with your project tutor and librarians, who may be aware of other relevant literature.

Publishers make their current book catalogues available on the Internet, and these can be accessed either directly or through the publishers' catalogues' home pages. In addition, websites of bookshops such as Amazon, Blackwell and the Internet Book Shop provide access to catalogues of books in print. These can usually be searched by author, title and subject, and may have reviews attached (Table 3.4). Some bookseller websites (and Google Books) have a facility whereby you can view selected pages from the book. However, as when using electronic indexes and abstracts, it is important that you keep full details of the literature you have scanned and browsed (Box 3.13). As well as enabling you to outline the method you used for your literature review, it will also help prevent you repeating searches you have already undertaken.

Table 3.4 Selected online bookshops

Name	Internet address	Contents
Amazon	www.amazon.co.uk	Searchable database principally of books (UK site)
	www.amazon.com	Searchable database principally of books (USA site)
Abe Books	www.abebooks.co.uk	New, second-hand, rare or out-of-print, through 13,500 independent booksellers
Blackwell	www.blackwell.co.uk	Searchable database principally of books
Internet Book Shop UK	www.ibuk.com	Searchable database principally of books, including second-hand
The Book Depository	www.bookdepository.co.uk/	Searchable database principally of books. Wide variety
The Book Place	www.thebookplace.co.uk	Searchable database principally of books
TSO (The Stationery Office)	www.tsoshop.co.uk	Searchable database of UK books in print. Especially useful for UK government reports

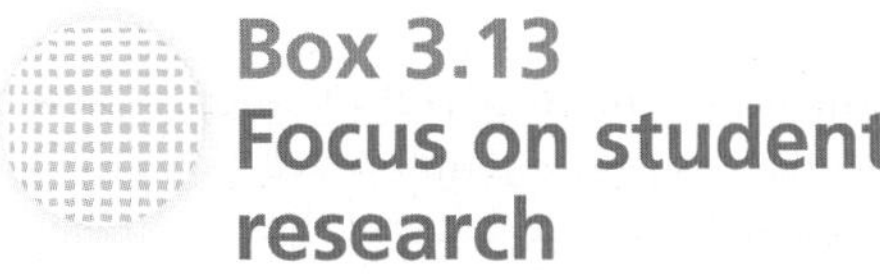

Box 3.13 Focus on student research

Searching using online databases

Matthew described his research project using the search terms 'entrepreneur' and 'finance'. Unfortunately, he encountered problems when carrying out his search using one of the online databases of full text and abstracts for business, management and economics journals to which his university subscribed:

When he entered the search term 'entrepreneur', he retrieved references to over 47,000 items, many of which were in trade magazines. Entering the term 'finance' on its own retrieved even more references, over 880,000!

He was unsure how to combine his search terms into search strings to make his search more specific.

Full-text versions were not available for the many of the most recent items retrieved.

After discussing the problem, the librarian showed Matthew how to use the advanced search option of the online database. Using this, Matthew first searched using the terms 'entrepreneur' AND 'finance' combined as a search string. This still resulted in over 3500 items being highlighted.

He then refined his search further by limiting it to the collection of scholarly (peer-reviewed) journals. This resulted in over 800 items being retrieved. He therefore decided to limit his search to the abstract field rather than the full text. This resulted in 248 items being retrieved.

Matthew made a note of the details of his search:

Database:	Business Source Complete
Collection:	Scholarly (peer reviewed) journals
Dates:	1934 to 2011
Search:	small business AND finance
Fields searched:	Abstract
Date of search:	25 March 2011
Total items retrieved	248

He then copied the references for these items (articles) onto his MP3 player. As Matthew scrolled through these, he noted that some of them had direct links to copies of the full text stored as a pdf file. For many of the others, the librarian informed him that he could access the full text using different online databases. However, he still needed to assess each article's relevance to his research before obtaining full copies.

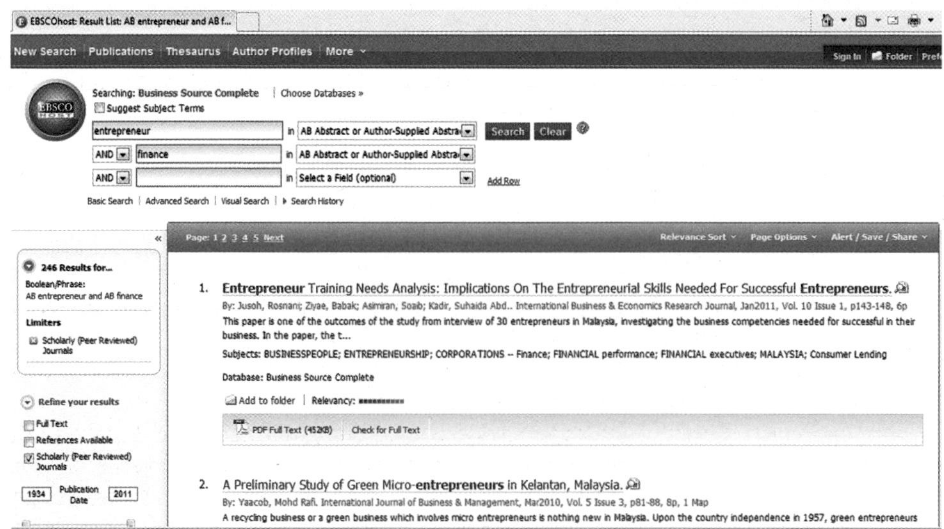

Source: EBSCO Information Services, reproduced with permission.

Searching the Internet

Although the Internet has revolutionised information gathering, including searching for literature, you should beware, as the quality of the material is highly variable. This is emphasised by Clausen (1996: 4), who likens the Internet to:

> . . . a huge vandalized library where someone has destroyed the catalogue and removed the front matter and indexes from most of the books. In addition thousands of unorganized fragments are added daily by a myriad of cranks, sages and persons with time on their hands who launch their unfiltered messages into cyberspace.

When searching the Internet, we recommend you keep full details of the searches you have undertaken, making a note of:

- the search tool used;
- the precise search undertaken;
- the date when the search was undertaken;
- the total number of items retrieved.

Home pages

Addresses of Internet sites or home pages (such as www.surrey.ac.uk) can be the quickest and most direct method of accessing these resources. Addresses can be obtained from many sources, the most frequently used of which are newspaper reviews, articles in journals, librarians and lecturers. Home pages, which can have multiple linked pages and hypertext links whereby pointing and clicking on the screen takes you to another website, are similar to a title or contents page. Although home pages often contain publicity for a company or institution, they are an excellent way of navigating around the Internet, as they bring a selection of Internet site addresses and search tools together (Table 3.5). A problem with going directly to one address is that your search is constrained by other people's ideas. Similarly, hypertext links are limited by other people's ideas and the way they have linked pages.

Search tools

Search tools, often referred to as **search engines**, are probably the most important method of Internet searching for your literature review as they will enable you to locate most current and up-to-date items. Although normally accessed through home pages, each search tool will have its own address (Table 3.5). Search tools can be divided into four distinct categories (Table 3.5):

- general search engines;
- metasearch engines;
- specialised search engines and information gateways;
- subject directories.

Most search engines index every separate document. In contrast, subject directories index only the 'most important' Internet documents. Therefore, if you are using a clear term to search for an unknown vaguely described document, use a search engine. If you are looking for a document about a particular topic, use a subject directory.

General search engines such as Google and Bing normally search parts of the Internet using search terms and Boolean logic (Table 3.3) or a phrase. Each search engine indexes and searches automatically, usually finding a very large number of sites. As people have not evaluated these sites, many are inappropriate or unreliable. As no two general search engines search in precisely the same way, it is advisable (and often necessary) to use more than one. In contrast, metasearch engines allow you to search using a selection of

Table 3.5 Selected Internet search tools and their coverage

Name	Internet address	Comment
General search engines		
Bing	www.bing.com	Access to billions of web pages, can link to facebook
Google	www.google.com	Access to billions of web pages
Google UK	www.google.co.uk	Country-based Google – optimised to show country results
Specialised search engines		
Google Scholar	www.scholar.google.com	Searches scholarly literature allowing you to locate the complete document
UK government	www.direct.gov.uk	Searches central and local government websites and government agencies
Information gateways		
Biz/Ed	www.bized.co.uk	Information service, links economics and business students and teachers and information providers
BUBL subject tree	http://bubl.ac.uk	Links to a vast range of Internet resources by alphabetical subject list or by class (subject) number order
Pinakes	www.hw.ac.uk/libWWW/irn/pinakes/pinakes.html	Links to major information gateways to Internet resources (especially UK based)
Publishers' catalogues homepage	www.lights.ca/publisher/	Searchable links to major publishers' websites, listed alphabetically by country
Subject directories		
About.com	www.about.com	Organised by subjects, offers numerous guides
Google Directory	http://directory.google.com	Organised by topic into categories – wide- ranging
ipl2	www.ipl.org	High-quality site only providing 'information you can trust'
Yahoo!	http://dir.yahoo.com/	Organised by subject, particularly useful for popular and commercial topics
Yellow Pages UK	www.yell.co.uk	Telephone yellow pages with useful links to UK companies' home pages

search engines at the same time, using the same interface. This makes searching easier, and the search can be faster. Unfortunately, it is less easy to control the sites that are retrieved. Consequently, metasearch engines often generate more inappropriate or unreliable sites than general search engines.

Specialised search engines cater for specific subject areas. For example, Google Scholar searches scholarly literature across many disciplines using sources such as articles, theses, books and abstracts from academic publishers, professional bodies, universities and websites, allowing you to locate the complete document. Documents are subsequently ranked on a combination of factors including how often it has been cited, where it was published and by whom it was written. To use specialised search engines it is necessary to define your general subject area prior to your search. Information gateways also require you to define your subject area. Information gateways are often compiled by staff from departments in academic institutions. Although the number of websites obtained is fewer, they can be far more relevant, as each site is evaluated prior to being added to the gateway.

Subject directories are searchable catalogues of sites collected and organised by humans. The sites are categorised into subject areas, and are useful for searching for broad topics. As people normally compile them, their content has been partly censored and evaluated. Consequently, the number of sites retrieved is fewer but they usually provide material that is more appropriate (Table 3.5).

Search tools are becoming more sophisticated all the time. Be careful, their use can be extremely time-consuming. Your search will probably locate a mass of resources, many of which will be irrelevant to you. It is also easy to become sidetracked to more interesting and glossy websites not relevant to your research needs! There are an increasing number of web-based tutorials to help you learn to search the web. One of these, Marketing Insights' *Smarter Online Searching Guide,* is available via this book's web page. This highlights using search tools, including Advanced search in Google and online e-business resources.

Bookmarking

Once you have found a useful Internet site, you can note its address electronically by adding it to your 'favourites' or 'bookmarks', depending on the Internet browser you use. The vast amount of resources available, and the fact that resources, home pages and sites can be added and deleted by their producers, means it is vital to keep a record of the addresses and a note of the date you accessed it (Section 3.7). These will be needed to reference your sources when you write your critical review (Section 3.2). When sufficient sites have been added to your 'favourites' or 'bookmarks', it is possible to arrange them in whatever hierarchical way you wish.

3.6 Obtaining and evaluating the literature

Obtaining the literature

After your initial search of books and journal articles, tertiary literature will provide you with details of what literature is available and where to locate it. The next stage (Figure 3.1) is to obtain these items. To do this you need to:

1 Check your library catalogue to find out whether your library holds the appropriate publication. Remember many libraries now, rather than holding publications such as journals and newspapers in paper form or CD-ROM, provide access via the Internet. Similarly books are increasingly being provided electronically.

2 (For those publications that are held by your library or available via the Internet) note their location and:
   - i find the publication and scan it to discover whether it is likely to be worth reading thoroughly – for articles it is often possible to make a reasonable assessment of their utility using the abstract (Box 3.14); or
   - ii browse other books and journals with similar class marks to see whether they may also be of use.

3 For those items not held by your library, it may be possible to obtain them through Google Books, particularly if they are no longer copyright.

4 (For those items that are not held by your library or available via the Internet) order the item from another library using **inter-library loan**. This is not a free service so make sure you really need it first. Our students have found that, in general, it is only worthwhile to use inter-library loans for articles from refereed journals and books.

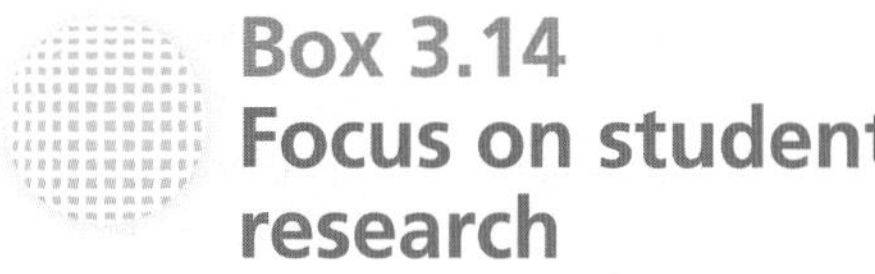

Box 3.14 Focus on student research

Assessing the utility of an article using the abstract

Jana's research project was about the extent managers' use of training and development differed between Eastern and Western European countries. In a search using the Emerald eJournals online database she had found a peer-reviewed article in the *Journal of European Industrial Training* by McDowall and Saunders (2010) that she considered might be useful. She decided to read the abstract online to check:

The abstract confirmed that the **Purpose** of the article included an investigation of how managers responsible for the training and development function conceptualised these activities and the factors

Home TextView Contact Us Site Map Support Register Administrators

Emerald
Research you can use

Login
Welcome: UNIVERSITY OF SURREY
Account info Logout
Search for:
in: All content Go
Advanced search
Marked lists
Browse:
Books & Journals
Bibliographic Databases
Resources:
Product information
Licensing Solutions
For Authors
For Librarians
For Engineers
Research Zone
Learning Zone
Teaching Zone
Support Resources
About Emerald
EmeraldReadingListAssist
Our unique new Teaching Zone service coming soon in 2011 ...

Home > Journal of European Industrial Training > Volume 34 issue 7 > UK managers' conceptions of employee training and development

Journal of European Industrial Training
ISSN: 0309-0590
Online from: 1977
Content: Latest Issue | RSS Latest Issue RSS | Previous Issues
Options: To add Favourites and Table of Contents Alerts please take a Emerald profile

Search in this title: Go

UK managers' conceptions of employee training and development

Document Information:

Title: UK managers' conceptions of employee training and development

Author(s): Almuth McDowall, (Psychology Department, University of Surrey, Guildford, UK), Mark N.K. Saunders, (School of Management, University of Surrey, Guildford, UK)

Citation: Almuth McDowall, Mark N.K. Saunders, (2010) "UK managers' conceptions of employee training and development", Journal of European Industrial Training, Vol. 34 Iss: 7, pp.609 - 630

Keywords: Decision making, Individual development, Managers, Training, Training evaluation

Article type: Research paper

DOI: 10.1108/03090591011070752 (Permanent URL)

Publisher: Emerald Group Publishing Limited

Abstract:

Purpose – The first purpose of this paper is to review the practical and theoretical distinctions between training and development in the organisational psychology and human resource development (HRD) literatures. Then the paper seeks to investigate how managers responsible for the training and development function conceptualise these activities in practice, the factors that guide their decision making, how they evaluate the outcomes and the extent to which they perceive a relationship between training and development.

Design/methodology/approach – Taking a critical realist perspective, 26 interviews were conducted with UK managers and analysed through thematic coding using template analysis.

Findings – Managers' conceptualisations of training and development vary. Formal training is prioritised due to a perceived more tangible demonstrable return on investment. Perceived success in training focuses on improvements to job-related skills, whereas success outcomes for development are more varied and difficult to measure. Managers consider that training and development are more valuable when combined.

Research limitations/implications – There is a need for further process-driven research to understand the interrelationship between training and development and to develop methods that can be used by organisations to evaluate both. This necessitates going beyond methods currently in use and including both qualitative and quantitative measures.

Practical implications – Managers may take a more proactive and directive role in facilitating development than the literature suggests; consequently, their role needs to be considered more actively in HRD learning strategies.

Originality/value – This is one of the first qualitative studies to explore the conceptualisations of managers responsible for training and development, highlighting the inter-relationship between training and development and the factors guiding decisions regarding these activities.

Document Options:
Content access
View HTML
View PDF (130kb)
References
• References (67)
Further reading
• Related items
• Key readings
Marked list
Add to: Session Go
Reprints & permissions
Request

© Emerald Group Publishing Limited | Copyright info | Site Policies

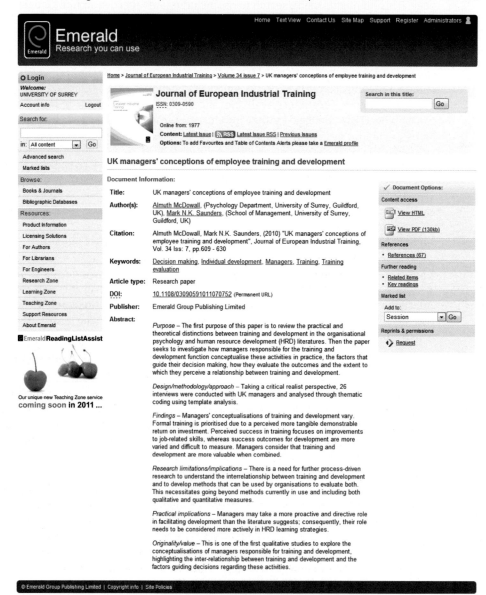

Source: McDowall and Saunders (2010). Copyright © 2010 Emerald Group Publishing (www.emeraldinsight.com/journals.htm?issn=0309-0590&volume=34&issue=7&articleid=1881302&show=abstract). Reproduced by permission of the publisher

which guide their decision making. More details regarding this were given in the **Findings** and **Research limitations/implications** sections of the abstract. The **design/methodology/approach** indicated that the research had been undertaken with UK managers and suggested that the paper might also be helpful regarding ideas about methods for collecting and analysing data.

Based on this information, Jana decided the article was likely to be useful for her research project, so downloaded and saved an electronic copy in pdf format.

5 Alternatively, visit a library where they are held as 'reference only' copies. The British Library in London, for example, has one of the most extensive collection of books, journals, market research reports, trade literature, company annual reports, research reports, doctoral theses and conference proceedings in the world.[3]

Evaluating the literature

Two questions frequently asked by our students are 'How do I know what I'm reading is relevant?' and 'How do I know when I've read enough?' Both of these are concerned with the process of evaluation. They involve defining the scope of your review and assessing the value of the items that you have obtained in helping you to answer your research question(s). Although there are no set ways of approaching these questions, our students have found the following advice helpful.

You should, of course, read all the literature that is closely related to your research question(s) and objectives. The literature that is most likely to cause problems is that which is less closely related (Gall et al. 2006). For some research questions, particularly for new research areas, there is unlikely to be much closely related literature and so you will have to review more broadly. For research questions where research has been going on for some years you may be able to focus on more closely related literature.

Assessing relevance and value

Assessing the relevance of the literature you have collected to your research depends on your research question(s) and objectives. Remember that you are looking for relevance, not critically assessing the ideas contained within. When doing this, it helps to have thought about and made a note of the criteria for inclusion and exclusion prior to assessing each item of literature. In contrast, assessing the value of the literature you have collected is concerned with the quality of the research that has been undertaken. As such it is concerned with issues such as methodological rigour and theory robustness as well as the quality of the reasoning or arguments. For example, you need to beware of managerial autobiographies, where a successful entrepreneur's or managing director's work experiences are presented as the way to achieve business success (Fisher 2010) and articles in trade magazines. The knowledge presented in such books and articles may well be subjective rather than based upon systematic research.

[3]Further details of the business and management collection can be found at www.bl.uk/managementbusiness.

Box 3.15 Checklist

Evaluating the relevance and value of literature to your research

Relevance

- ✔ How recent is the item?
- ✔ Is the item likely to have been superseded?
- ✔ Are the research questions or objectives sufficiently close to your own to make it relevant to your own research (in other words, does the item meet your relevance criteria for inclusion)?
- ✔ Is the context sufficiently different to make it marginal to your research question(s) and objectives (in other words, is the item excluded by your relevance criteria)?
- ✔ Have you seen references to this item (or its author) in other items that were useful?
- ✔ Does the item support or contradict your arguments? For either it will probably be worth reading!

Value

- ✔ Does the item appear to be biased? For example, does it use an illogical argument, emotionally toned words or appear to choose only those cases that support the point being made? Even if it is, it may still be relevant to your critical review!
- ✔ What are the methodological omissions within the work (e.g. sample selection, data collection, data analysis)? Even if there are many it still may be of relevance!
- ✔ Is the precision sufficient? Even if it is imprecise it may be the only item you can find and so still of relevance!
- ✔ Does the item provide guidance for future research?

Sources: Authors' experience; Bell (2010); Fisher (2010); Jankowicz (2005); McNeill (2005)

Box 3.15 provides a checklist to help you in this process.

Remember to make notes about the relevance of each item as you read it and the reasons why you came to your conclusion. You may need to include your evaluation as part of your critical review.

Assessing sufficiency

Your assessment of whether you have read a sufficient amount is even more complex. It is impossible to read everything, as you would never start to write your critical review, let alone your project report. Yet you need to be sure that your critical review discusses what research has already been undertaken and that you have positioned your research project in the wider context, citing the main writers in the field (Section 3.2). One clue that you have achieved this is when further searches provide mainly references to items you have already read. You also need to check what constitutes an acceptable amount of reading, in terms of both quality and quantity, with your project tutor.

3.7 Recording the literature

The literature search, as you will now be aware, is a vital part of your research project, in which you will invest a great deal of time and effort. As you read each item, you need to ask yourself how it contributes to your research question(s) and objectives and to make notes with this focus (Bell 2010). When doing this, many students download and print copies of articles or photocopy or scan pages from books to ensure that they have all the material. We believe that, even if you print or photocopy, you still need to make notes.

The process of note making will help you to think through the ideas in the literature in relation to your research. When making your notes make sure you always use quotation marks and note the page number if you are copying the text exactly. This will ensure you know it is a direct quotation when you begin to write your project report and so help you avoid committing plagiarism (Section 3.9).

In addition to making notes, Sharp et al. (2002) identify three sets of information you need to record. These are:

- bibliographic details;
- brief summary of content;
- supplementary information.

Database software such as Microsoft's Access™ or specialist bibliographic software such as Reference Manager™ or EndNote™ provide a powerful and flexible method for recording the literature. Many search engines, such as Google Scholar, allow references to be exported directly into bibliographic software. Where this is not the case, recording can seem very tedious, but it must be done. We have seen many students frantically repeating searches for items that are crucial to their research because they failed to record all the necessary details in their database of references.

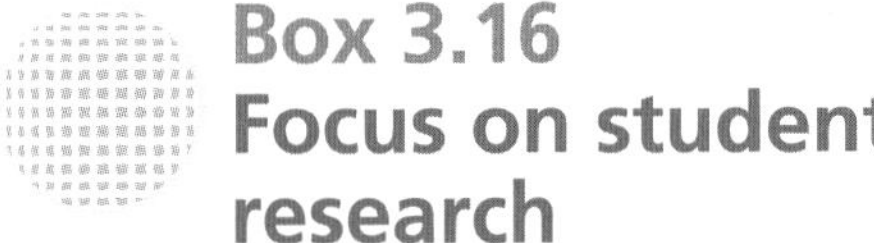

Box 3.16 Focus on student research

Undertaking an Internet search using a general search engine

Ceinwen's research question was reasonably defined, if somewhat broad. She wanted to assess the impact of the 26 December 2004 tsunami on tourism in Thailand. As part of her search strategy she decided, in addition to the academic databases of business and management journals, to search the Internet using a general search engine. Her first search term 'Thailand tsunami' revealed that there were over 33,300,000 sites and displayed the first 10. Of these, although in the broad topic area, none appeared to be relevant as they were not related specifically to the impact of the tsunami on tourism:

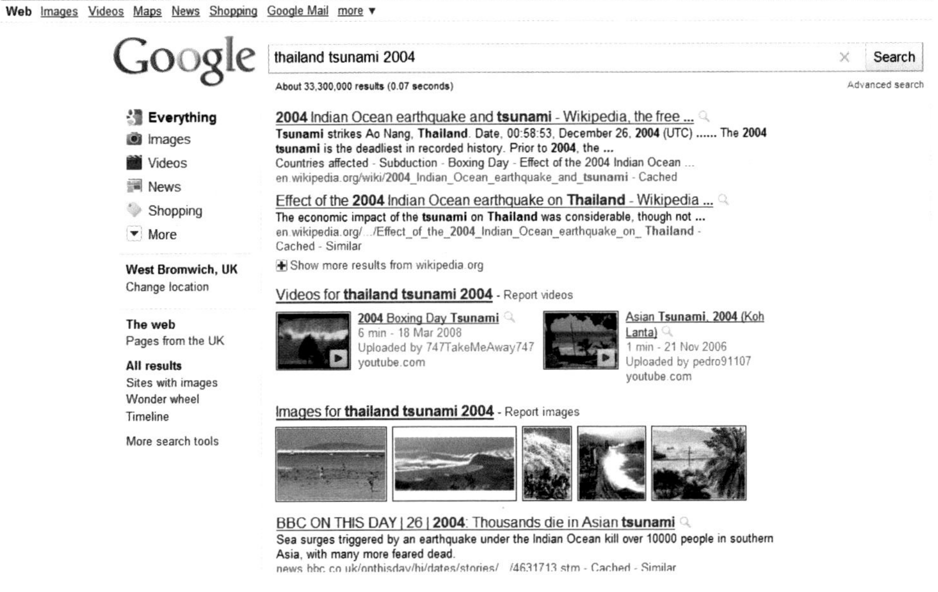

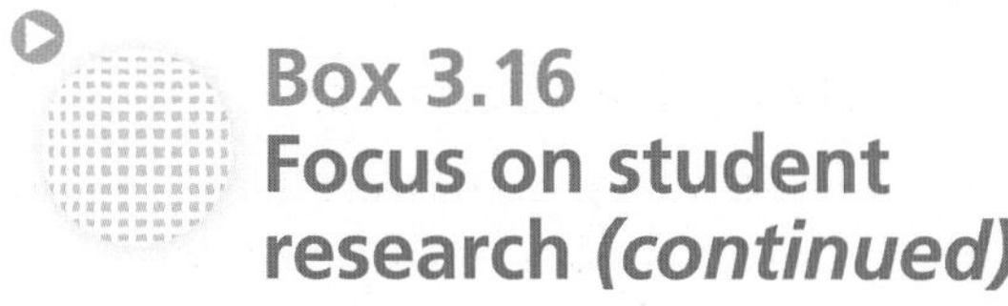

Box 3.16 Focus on student research *(continued)*

She decided to refine her search using the advanced search features of the search engine including the exact wording 'effect on tourism'. Although the search engine still found over 10,400 sites, the content of the first 10 appeared more relevant to her research question:

Ceinwen looked at the second site and found that it was a direct link to a pdf file containing the summary record of the 2009 *Second ASEAN Plus Three Workshop on Healthy Travel and Tourism*. This included a section on risk management post-tsunami in Phuket, Thailand. She downloaded and saved the file on her MP3 player.

She then made a note of the conference name and the academic presenter, and that her full presentation was also likely to be available via the Internet. Noting the academic's name meant she could search for supplementary information such as academic articles written by her, using the university's online databases. Ceinwen then proceeded to look at the next site in the Google list.

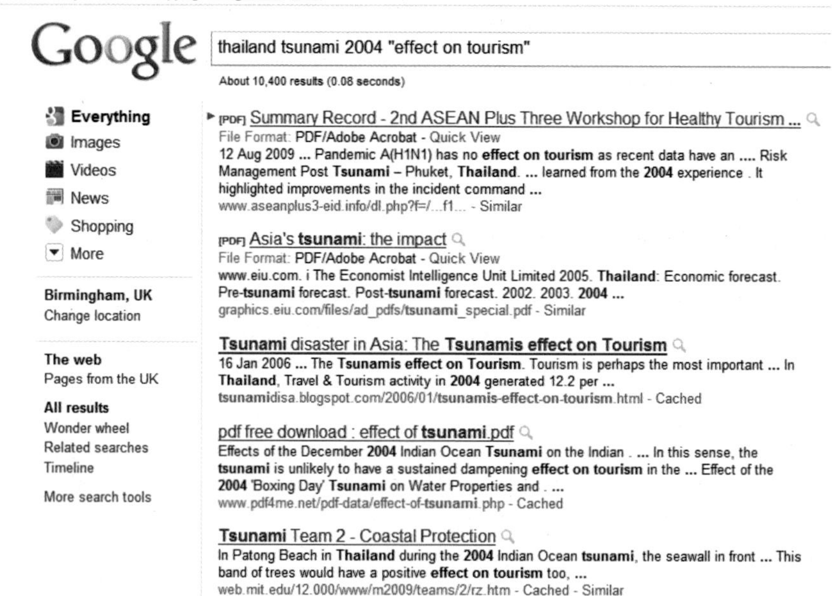

Bibliographic details

For some project reports you will be required to include a **bibliography**. Convention dictates that this should include all the relevant items you consulted for your project, including those not directly referred to in the text. For others, you will be asked to include only a list of **references** for those items referred to directly in the text. The **bibliographic details** contained in both need to be sufficient to enable readers to find the original items. These details are summarised in Table 3.6.

If an item has been taken from an electronic source you need to record as much of the information in Table 3.6 as is available along with details of format (e.g. CD-ROM). If you located the item via the Internet, you need to record the full address of the resource and the date you accessed the information (Appendix 1). This address is often referred to as the URL, the unique resource location or universal/uniform resource locator.

Most universities have a preferred referencing style that you must use in your project report. This will normally be prescribed in your assessment criteria. Three of the most

Table 3.6 Bibliographic details required

Journal	Book	Chapter in an edited book
• Author(s) – family name, first name, initials • Year of publication (in parentheses) • Title of article • Title of journal (italicised) • Volume • Part/issue • Page numbers (preceded by 'p.' for page or 'pp.' for pages)	• Author(s) – family name, first name initials • Year of publication (in parentheses) • Title and subtitle of book (italicised) • Edition (unless first) • Place of publication • Publisher	• Author(s) – family name, first name initials • Year of publication (in parentheses) • Title of chapter • Author(s) of book – family name, first name initials • Title and subtitle of book (italicised) • Edition (unless first) • Place of publication • Publisher • Page numbers of chapter (preceded by 'pp.' for pages)

common styles are the Harvard system (a version of which we have used in this book), the American Psychological Association (APA) System and the Vancouver or footnotes system. Guidelines on using each of these are given in Appendix 1.

Brief summary

A brief summary of the content of each item in your reference database will help you to locate the relevant items and facilitate reference to your notes and photocopies. This can be done by annotating each record with the search terms used, to help locate the item and the abstract. It will also help you to maintain consistency in your searches.

Supplementary information

As well as recording the details discussed earlier, other information may also be worth recording. These items can be anything you feel will be of value. In Table 3.7 we outline those that we have found most useful.

Table 3.7 Supplementary information

Information	Reason
ISBN	The identifier for any book, and useful if the book has to be requested on inter-library loan
Class number (e.g. Dewey decimal)	Useful to locate books in your university's library and as a pointer to finding other books on the same subject
Quotations	Always note useful quotations in full and with the page number of the quote; if possible also take a photocopy or save entire document as a PDF file
Where it was found	Noting where you found the item is useful, especially if it is not in your university library and you could only take notes
The tertiary resource used and the search terms used to locate it	Useful to help identify resources for follow-up searches
Evaluative comments	Your personal notes on the value of the item to your research in relation to your relevance and value criteria
When the item was consulted	Especially important for items found via the Internet as these may disappear without trace
Filename	Useful if you have saved the document as a PDF file

3.8 Using Systematic Review

Systematic Review is a process for reviewing the literature using a comprehensive preplanned strategy to locate existing literature, evaluate the contribution, analyse and synthesise the findings and report the evidence to allow conclusions to be reached about what is known and, also, what is not known (Denyer and Tranfield 2009). Originating in the medical sciences, Systematic Review has been used widely to evaluate specific medical treatments; in the past two decades its importance has been recognised in other disciplines. Within business and management Denyer and Tranfield (2009) have adapted the medical sciences guidance ensuring that the process is transparent, inclusive, explanatory and enables learning. Systematic Reviews usually, although not exclusively, focus on policy or practice questions such as the effectiveness of a particular intervention with an emphasis on informing action. It is therefore not surprising that Petticrew and Roberts (2006) argue that Systematic Review is only suitable for some research projects (Box 3.18), emphasising that it is time-consuming and the need to involve others in the process.

Prior to conducting your Systematic Review, most writers suggest you undertake an exploratory **scoping study** to assess whether or not other Systematic Reviews have already been published and determine the focus of the literature search. Subsequent to this a five-step process in which the each stage is noted precisely is suggested (Denyer and Tranfield 2009):

1 Formulate the review question(s), for example 'What are marketing professionals' understanding and definition of viral marketing?', involving a broad range of expert stakeholders such as potential academic and practitioner users of the review as an advisory group.
2 Locate and generate a comprehensive list of potentially relevant research studies using online database searches, specialist bibliographies, tables of contents and other sources and attempt to track down unpublished research (Section 3.3).
3 Select and evaluate relevant research studies using predetermined explicit inclusion and exclusion (selection) checklists of criteria to assess the relevance of each in relation to the review question(s). These checklists can be developed by undertaking a small number of pilot searches and making a list for reasons for inclusion or exclusion of each article or adapting checklists developed for previous Systematic Reviews, by journals to assess general quality of research or to assess issues of relevance and value

Box 3.18 Checklist

Establishing whether a project may be suitable for Systematic Review

- ✔ Is there uncertainty about the effectiveness of the policy/service/intervention?
- ✔ Is there a need for evidence about the likely effects of a policy/service/intervention?
- ✔ Despite a large amount of research on the topic, do key questions remain unanswered?
- ✔ Is there a need for a general overall picture of the research evidence on the topic to direct future research?
- ✔ Is an accurate picture of past research and associated methods needed to help develop new methods?

(If the answer to one or more of these is 'yes' then the project may be suitable for Systematic Review.)

Source: Developed from Petticrew and Roberts (2006)

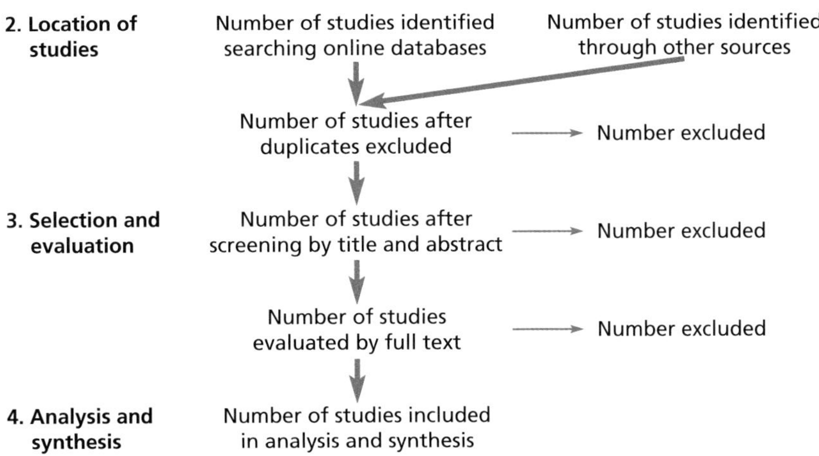

Figure 3.4 Flow diagram for reporting Systematic Review study location, selection and evaluation
Source: Developed from Moher et al., 2009

(Box 3.15). Common criteria include adequate methods, clear data analysis and conclusions derived from findings. Selection and evaluation are usually undertaken:

a Initially by title and abstract;
b For those not excluded by title and abstract, by reading the full text.

4 Analyse and synthesise the relevant research studies by:
   a Breaking down each study into its constituent parts and recording the key points (research question/aim; study context – country, industry sector, organisational setting etc.; method(s) of data collection; sample size, frame and demographics; key findings; relevance to review questions) on a data extraction form;
   b Using the data extraction forms to explore and integrate the studies and answer the specific review questions.
5 Report the results providing:
   a an introductory section that states the problem and review questions;
   b a methodology section that provides precise details of how the review was conducted (search strategy, selection criteria, key points used for the analysis and synthesis) (Sections 3.3 and 3.4);
   c findings and discussion sections that review all the studies (Section 3.2), specifies precisely what is known and what is not known in relation to the review questions.

Many researchers who use Systematic Review are adopting the PRISMA (Preferred Reporting Items for Systematic Reviews and Meta Analyses) checklist (Moher et al. 2009) and flow diagram for reporting and presenting their Systematic Reviews. Using their checklist when presenting your Systematic Review will help ensure the report of your review is clear, allowing others to assess the strengths and weaknesses of the studies you have reviewed. Using a flow diagram (Figure 3.4) allows the number of studies reviewed in stages two and three in the Systematic Review process to be reported clearly.

3.9 Plagiarism

There is no doubt that plagiarism has become an enormous concern in academic institutions in recent years, largely as a result of the ease with which material can be copied from the Internet and passed off as the work of the individual student. It is a serious topic

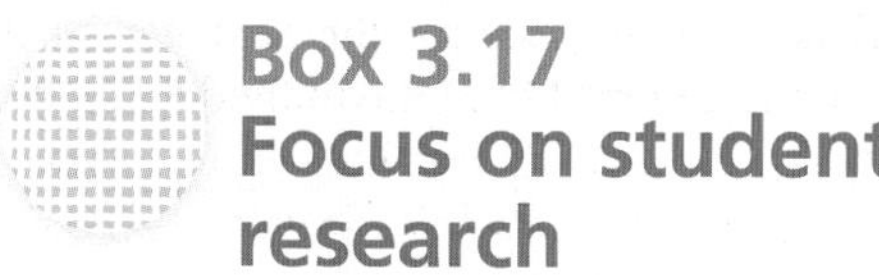

Box 3.17 Focus on student research

Penalties for being found guilty of plagiarism

Overview of the penalties

There is a range of penalties that can be applied in cases of plagiarism. The penalty is chosen either by the School or the Committee on Applications and will depend on the seriousness of the offence and on whether there are any mitigating circumstances. Example penalties are:

- only the sections of the assignment determined not to be plagiarised are marked;
- academic year is failed and must be retaken;
- student is excluded from the university.

The seriousness of the offence is related to issues such as:

- whether the student has committed offences previously;
- the magnitude of the plagiarism;
- the number of marks and the level of the assignment involved.

Source: University of Leeds. Available at www.lts.leeds.ac.uk/plagiarism/penalties.php?PHPSESSID=4582f0d02aa8927c671b34ddb8c4f459

because the consequences of being found guilty of plagiarism can be severe, as the example in Box 3.17 from a UK university shows.

Neville (2010) argues that plagiarism is an issue that runs parallel to a debate with recurring questions about the purpose of higher education in the twenty-first century. He notes that, on the one hand, there is the argument that an insistence on 'correct' referencing is supporting a system and a process of learning that is a legacy of a different time and society. This argument holds that universities are enforcing upon you an arcane practice of referencing that you will probably never use again outside higher education. On the other hand, there is the argument that plagiarism is an attack upon values of ethical, proper, decent behaviour – values consistent with a respect for others. These are ageless societal values that universities should try to maintain.

So what precisely is plagiarism? Quite simply, it is presenting work or ideas as if they are your own when in reality they are the work or ideas of someone else, and failing to acknowledge the original source. Park (2003) lists four common forms of plagiarism which are commonly found in universities. These are:

1. Stealing material from another source and passing it off as your own, for example:
   - buying a paper from a research service, essay bank or term-paper mill (either specially written for the individual or pre-written);
   - copying a whole paper from a source text without proper acknowledgement;
   - submitting another student's work with or without that student's knowledge (e.g. by copying a computer disk);
2. submitting a paper written by someone else (e.g. a peer or relative) and passing it off as your own;
3. copying sections of material from one or more source texts, supplying proper documentation (including the full reference) but leaving out quotation marks, thus giving the impression that the material has been paraphrased rather than directly quoted;
4. paraphrasing material from one or more source texts without supplying appropriate documentation.

It is tempting to think that all cases of plagiarism are a consequence of students either being too idle to pursue their research and writing diligently, or wishing to appear cleverer that they really are. But the fact is that plagiarism is an extremely complex issue and the reasons for it may owe as much to student confusion as wilful negligence. That said, there is little excuse for confusion. All universities have ample guidance for students on the topic of plagiarism and will emphasise that it is the responsibility of the individual student to become aware of the university's regulations surrounding its conduct. In addition, an increasing number of universities ask students to check their own work using plagiarism detection software and submit an electronic copy of their work.

3.10 Summary

- A critical review of the literature is necessary to help you to develop a thorough understanding of, and insight into, previous work that relates to your research question(s) and objectives. Your review will set your research in context by critically discussing and referencing work that has already been undertaken, drawing out key points and presenting them in a logically argued way, and highlighting those areas where you will provide fresh insights. It will lead the reader into subsequent sections of your project report.
- There is no one correct structure for a critical review, although it is helpful to think of it as a funnel in which you start at a more general level prior to narrowing down to your specific research question(s) and objectives.
- Literature sources can be divided into three categories: primary, secondary and tertiary. In reality, these categories often overlap. Your use of these resources will depend on your research question(s) and objectives. Some may use only tertiary and secondary literature. For others, you may need to locate primary literature as well.
- When planning your literature search you need to:
  - have a clearly defined research question(s) and research objectives;
  - define the parameters of your search;
  - generate search terms and phrases;
  - discuss your ideas as widely as possible.
- Techniques to help you in this include brainstorming and relevance trees.
- Your literature search is likely to be undertaken using a variety of approaches in tandem. These will include:
  - searching using tertiary sources and the Internet;
  - following up references in articles you have already read;
  - scanning and browsing secondary literature in your library.
- Don't forget to make precise notes of the search processes you have used and their results.
- Once obtained, the literature must be evaluated for its relevance to your research question(s) and objectives using clearly defined criteria. This must include a consideration of each item's currency. Each item must be read and noted. Bibliographic details, a brief description of the content and appropriate supplementary information should also be recorded.
- For literature reviews focusing on policy or practice questions in particular, you may decide to a use a Systematic Review.
- Care should be taken when writing your literature review not to plagiarise the work of others.

Self-check questions

Help with these questions is available at the end of the chapter.

3.1 The following extract and associated references are taken from the first draft of a critical literature review. The research project was concerned with the impact of direct insurers on the traditional motor insurer.

List the problems with this extract in terms of its:

a content;

b structure.

Jackson (1995) suggests that businesses must be developed from a customer rather than a product perspective. Lindesfarne (1994) demonstrates that direct selling gives the consumer increased control as it is up to them when and if they wish to respond to adverts or direct mail. MacKenzie (1995) comments that free gifts are useful for getting responses to adverts, which is ultimately what all direct insurers need. Bowen (1995) suggests that this type of company can be split into three equally important parts: marketing, insurance and information technology. Motor insurance is particularly price sensitive because of its compulsory nature and its perception by many to have no real 'value' to themselves.

Bowen, I. (1994) 'Short cut to success', *Post Magazine* 2, 26 July.

Jackson, D.R. (1995) 'Prudential's prudent parochialism', *Direct Marketing*, 26–29 April.

Lindisfarne, I. (1995) 'Death of a salesman', *Post Magazine* 15, 30–31 June.

MacKenzie, G. (1995) 'Rise of the freebie', *Post Magazine* 2, 5–6 February.

3.2 Outline the advice you would give a colleague on:

a how to plan her search;

b which literature to search first.

3.3 Brainstorm at least one of the following research questions, either on your own or with a colleague, and list the search terms that you have generated.

How effective are share options as a motivator?

How do the opportunities available to a first-time house buyer through interpersonal discussion influence the process of selecting a financial institution for the purposes of applying for a house purchase loan?

To what extent do new methods of direct selling of financial services pose a threat to existing providers?

3.4 You are having considerable problems with finding relevant material for your research when searching online databases. Suggest possible reasons why this might be so.

3.5 Rewrite the following passage as part of a critical literature review using the Harvard system of referencing:

Social Media is a new form of media that uses the Internet to facilitate conversations[1]. Social Media sources enable consumers to create, edit, contribute and share 'content' [2,3,4]. Drury[2] explains that rather than focus on the 'media', emphasis should be placed on the 'social' element. He argues that users connecting and interacting with each other and sharing content is key to Social Media. Similarly, Mayfield[5] emphasises characteristics such as participation, conversation and community as the defining features of Social Media. Social Media tools range from Blogs, Social Network Sites, Podcasts, Forums, Content Communities and Wikis[5]. The most commonly used Social Media tools include sites such as Facebook, MySpace, Twitter, Flickr, LinkedIn, del.icio.us, YouTube and Wikipedia[3].

[1]Solis, B. and Breakenridge, D. (2009) Putting the public back in Public Relations: How Social is reinventing the ageing business of PR, New Jersey, Pearson.

[2]Drury, G. (2008) 'Social media: Should marketers engage and how can it be done effectively?' *Journal of Direct, Data and Digital Marketing Practice.* Vol. 9, pp. 274–277.

[3]Mangold, W. and Faulds, D. (2009) 'Social media: The new hybrid element of the promotion mix'. *Business Horizons.* Vol. 52. pp. 357–365.

[4]Parise, S., Guinan, P. and Weinberg, G. (2008) *'The secrets of marketing in a web 2.0 world'*. Available at: http://sloanreview.mit.edu/executive-adviser/articles/2008/6/5068/the-secrets-of-marketing-in-a-web-20-world/ (Accessed 27 Mar. 2011).

[5]Mayfield, A. (2008) "What is social media?", *Networks*, V1.4 UPDAT, p.36. Available at: http://www.icrossing.co.uk/fileadmin/uploads/eBooks/What_is_Social_Media_iCrossing_ebook.pdf

Review and discussion questions

3.6 Go to the website of the general search engine Google (www.google.com). Use the different Google services such as 'Google Search', 'Google Scholar' and 'University Search' to search for articles on a topic which you are currently studying as part of your course.

a Make notes regarding the types of items that each of these services finds.

b How do these services differ?

c Which service do you think is likely to prove most useful to your research project?

3.7 Agree with a friend to each review the same article from a refereed academic journal which contains a clear literature review section. Evaluate independently the literature review in your chosen article with regard to its content, critical nature and structure using the checklists in Boxes 3.2, 3.3 and 3.4 respectively. Do not forget to make notes regarding your answers to each of the points raised in the checklists. Discuss your answers with your friend.

3.8 Visit an online database or your university library and obtain a copy of an article that you think will be of use to an assignment you are both currently working on. Use the checklist in Box 3.16 to assess the relevance and value of the article to your assignment.

Progressing your research project

Critically reviewing the literature

- Consider your research question(s) and objectives. Use your lecture notes, course textbooks and relevant review articles to define both narrow and broader parameters of your literature search, considering language, subject area, business sector, geographical area, publication period and literature type.
- Generate search terms using one or a variety of techniques such as reading, brainstorming and relevance trees. Discuss your ideas widely, including with your project tutor and colleagues.
- Start your search using both database and printed tertiary sources to identify relevant secondary literature. Begin with those tertiary sources that abstract and index academic journal articles and books. At the same time, obtain relevant literature that has been referenced in articles you have already read. Do not forget to record your searches systematically and in detail.
- Expand your search via other sources such as the Internet and by browsing and scanning.
- Obtain copies of items, evaluate them systematically and make notes. Remember also to record bibliographic details, a brief description of the content and supplementary information on an index card or in your reference database.
- Start drafting your critical review as early as possible, keeping in mind its purpose and taking care to reference properly and avoid plagiarism.
- Continue to search the literature throughout your research project to ensure that your review remains up to date.
- Use the questions in Box 1.4 to guide your reflective diary entry.

References

Bell, J. (2010) *Doing Your Research Project* (5th edn). Maidenhead: Open University Press.

Clausen, H. (1996) 'Web information quality as seen from libraries', *New Library World*, 97, Vol. No. 1130, pp. 4–8.

Corbin, J. and Strauss, A. (2008) *Basics of Qualitative Research* (3rd edn). Thousand Oaks, CA: Sage.

Cresswell, J.W. (2007) *Qualitative Inquiry and Research Design: Choosing Among Five Approaches.* Thousand Oaks, CA: Sage.

Dees, R. (2003) *Writing the Modern Research Paper* (4th edn). Boston, MA: Allyn and Bacon.

Denyer, D. and Tranfield, D. (2009) 'Producing a Systematic Review', in D.A. Buchanan and A. Bryman (eds) *The Sage Handbook of Organisational Research Methods*. London: Sage, pp. 671–89.

Fisher, C. (2010) *Researching and Writing a Dissertation for Business Students* (3rd edn). Harlow: Financial Times Prentice Hall.

Gall, M.D., Gall, J.P. and Borg, W. (2006) *Educational Research: An Introduction* (8th edn). New York: Longman.

Gill, J. and Johnson, P. (2010) *Research Methods for Managers* (4th edn). London: Sage.

Greenhalgh, T. (1997) 'Papers that summarize other papers (systematic reviews and meta-analyses)', *British Medical Journal*, Vol. 315, pp. 672–5.

Hart, C. (1998) *Doing a Literature Review*. London: Sage.

Harvard College Library (2006) *Interrogating texts: 6 reading habits to develop in your first year at Harvard*. Available at: http://hcl.harvard.edu/research/guides/lamont_handouts/interrogatingtexts.html [Accessed 20 May 2008].

Inspiration (2011) *Inspiration homepage*. Available at www.inspiration.com/Inspiration [Accessed 21 March 2011].

Jankowicz, A.D. (2005) *Business Research Projects* (4th edn). London: Thomson Learning.

McNeill, P. (2005) *Research Methods* (3rd edn). London: Routledge.

Meier, M. (2011) 'Knowledge management in strategic alliances: A review of empirical evidence', *International Journal of Management Reviews*, Vol. 13, pp. 1–23.

MindGenius (2011) *MindGenius homepage*. Available at www.mindgenius.com/home.aspx [Accessed 21 March 2011].

Mingers, J. (2000) 'What is it to be critical? Teaching a critical approach to management undergraduates', *Management Learning*, Vol. 31, No. 2, pp. 219–37.

Moher, D., Liberati, A., Tetzlaff, J. and Altman, D.G. (2009) 'Preferred reporting for systematic reviews and meta-analyses: the PRISMA statement', *British Medical Journal (BMJ)*, No. 338, b2535. Available at www.bmj.com/content/339/bmj.b2535.full?view=long&pmid=19622551 [Accessed 27 March 2011].

Neville, C. (2010) *The Complete Guide to Referencing and Plagiarism* (2nd edn). Maidenhead: Open University Press.

Park, C. (2003) 'In other (people's) words: Plagiarism by university students – literature and lessons', *Assessment and Evaluation in Higher Education*, Vol. 28, No. 5, pp. 471–88.

Petticrew, M. and Roberts, H. (2006) *Systematic Review in the Social Sciences: A Practical Guide*. Malden, MA: Blackwell.

Saunders, M.N.K., Altinay, L. and Riordan, K. (2009) 'The management of post-merger cultural integration: implications from the hotel industry', *Service Industries Journal*, Vol. 29, No. 10, pp. 1359–75.

Sharp, J.A., Peters, J. and Howard, K. (2002) *The Management of a Student Research Project* (3rd edn). Aldershot: Gower.

Stewart, D.W. and Kamins, M.A. (1993) *Secondary Research: Information Sources and Methods* (2nd edn). Newbury Park: CA, Sage.

Tranfield, D., Denyer, D. and Smart, P. (2003) 'Towards a methodology for developing evidence-informed management knowledge by means of systematic review', *British Journal of Management*, Vol. 14, No. 3, pp. 207–22.

Wallace, M. and Wray, A. (2011) *Critical Reading and Writing for Postgraduates* (2nd edn). London: Sage.

Wikipedia (2011) *Wikipedia:About*. Available at http://en.wikipedia.org/wiki/Wikipedia:About [Accessed 20 March 2011].

Further reading

Bell, J. (2010) *Doing Your Research Project* (5th edn). Maidenhead: Open University Press. Chapter 5 provides a good introduction to the process of reviewing the literature. The sections on the critical review are especially helpful.

Neville, C. (2010) *The Complete Guide to Referencing and Plagiarism* (2nd edn). Maidenhead: Open University Press. Chapter 4 is a very helpful guide on what constitutes plagiarism and how it can be avoided. The chapter ends with some useful exercises designed to ensure that the reader does not fall into some common traps.

Sharp, J.A., Peters, J. and Howard, K. (2002) *The Management of a Student Research Project* (3rd edn). Aldershot: Gower. Chapter 4 contains a useful in-depth discussion of the use of relevance trees in your literature search.

Denyer, D. and Tranfield, D. (2009) 'Producing a Systematic Review', in D.A. Buchanan and A. Bryman (eds) *The Sage Handbook of Organizational Research Methods.* London: Sage, pp. 671–89. This chapter provides an excellent introduction to the process of Systematic Review. Although a full Systematic Review as outlined in this chapter may be too time-consuming for your research project, there are many useful points made regarding how to plan your search strategy and explain in your project report how your review was undertaken.

Case 3
Individual workplace performance: systematically reviewed

Emily had completed the first semester of her master's programme in Human Resource Management. She had already passed a number of the assignments, but had not yet given much thought to her research project. She knew, however, that she had to make a start on this.

Source: Rob Judges

A few weeks previously the course lecturers had presented a number of topics that students might consider for their research project. Emily was particularly interested in one of these, which was about individual workplace performance in the finance industry. As her first degree was in Psychology, she felt that this topic would be ideally suited, combining her prior background and interests with what she was learning in her Master's programme – even more so as she'd spent the previous summer holidays working for a financial consultancy. A meeting with the respective project tutor confirmed for Emily that she would like to work on this research project.

Her project tutor suggested she make a start on the research by doing a literature review on individual workplace performance, with a particular focus on the finance industry. Emily knew from her Research Methods module that there were several approaches to reviewing the literature. One type of literature review, the Systematic Review, had stood out for her, because it seemed a structured and comprehensive way of examining the evidence base of a particular topic. Emily discussed the idea of doing a Systematic Review with her tutor, who recommended she read a book chapter by Denyer and Tranfield (2009) on how to produce a Systematic Review in the management sciences, and Petticrew and Roberts' (2006) book about Systematic Reviews in social sciences. He also said she would have to be very careful to keep the review manageable within the time she had available. Emily read the book chapter first, finding it a helpful guide as it clarified the principles underlying Systematic Reviews and explained in more detail the various steps that need to be followed when conducting a Systematic Review. After also reading those sections of Petticrew and Roberts' book she thought most useful for her purposes, Emily felt ready to make a start on her review. She understood that she would initially need to come up with a question her review should address and that she would draw upon expert advice to help formulate this question. This would enable her to undertake a focused and comprehensive search of the literature. Having searched for and found references to potentially relevant publications, she would need to sift through and evaluate these to decide which to use to answer her review question. Emily would then have to record the key points for all these relevant publications, using her notes to write her literature review by answering her review question.

She began by trying to come up with a question her Systematic Review should address – she knew the question had to be clear and specific so that she would be able to answer it for her literature review. Emily had read that review questions should be informed by stakeholders (an expert panel), such as academics who were subject specialists or practitioners. She decided to use her project tutor and one other lecturer from her programme, who also had a research interest in workplace performance, as her stakeholders. She asked them what they meant when talking about individual workplace performance, about areas in the literature they thought under- and over-researched and also about specific questions a literature review could address. Based on their answers, Emily formulated her own review question: 'What is the finance industry's understanding and definition of individual workplace performance?'

Next, Emily needed to find literature that could be used to answer the review question. She discussed her planned search strategy (including search terms and start date of the search) with a subject librarian. Using the EBSCOhost interface, Emily systematically searched two online databases, Business Source Complete and PsycInfo. Setting the start date for her search as 1950, she used the following search strings (Figure 3.5):

perform* OR efficien* OR productiv* OR effective* (string 1)
work* OR job OR individual OR occupation* OR vocation* (string 2)
financ* (string 3)

The database searches produced 2598 potentially relevant publications. Her tutor also suggested that she contact one academic researcher she thought influential in the area of individual workplace performance to check for any further potentially relevant, as yet unpublished work.

Emily imported the references and abstracts for the potentially relevant publications she found into the EndNote reference management software, creating a 'library' (Figure 3.6).

Emily started sifting through the references she'd found to identify publications that looked as if they might address her review question. This was a relatively tedious process, as she had to read each publication's title and abstract before making a decision. Emily found this task quite challenging, because she had to strike a balance between discarding as many irrelevant

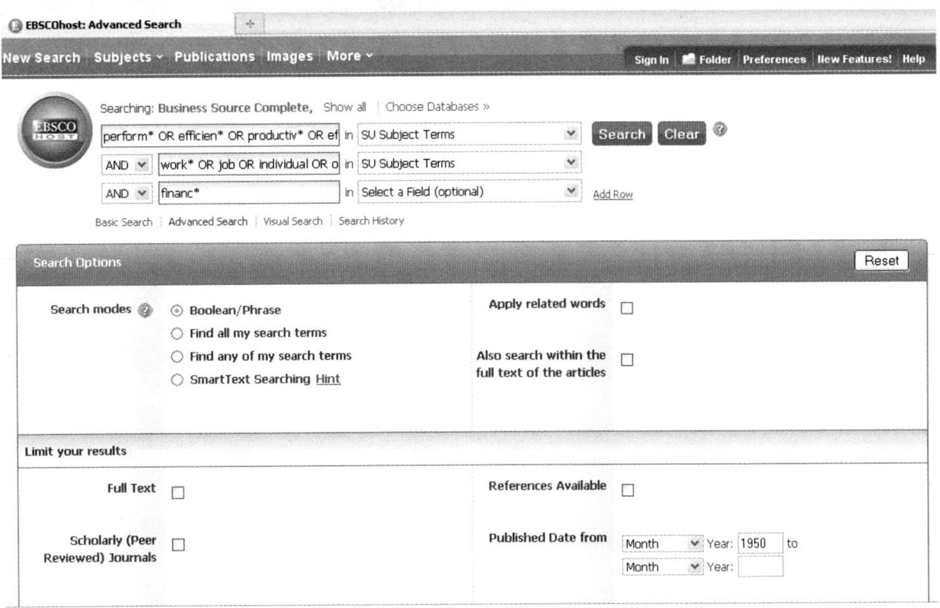

Figure 3.5 Searching using Business Source Complete

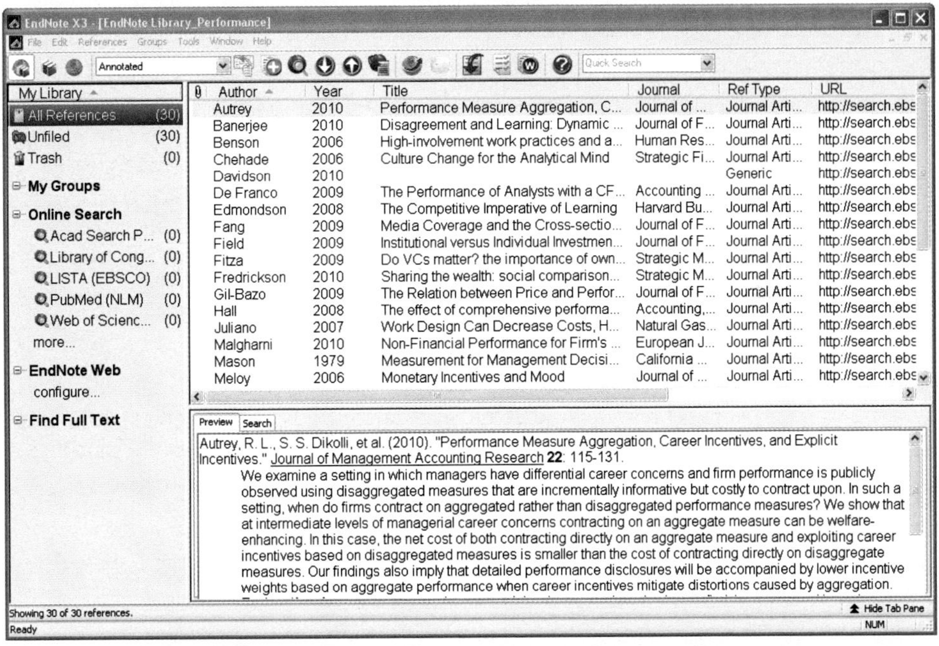

Figure 3.6 EndNote library® screenshot © copyright 2011 Thomson Reuters

publications as possible to make the subsequent review process manageable, whilst also ensuring that no potentially relevant publications were accidentally sifted out. She asked a friend to look through 10 of her references to assess how much he agreed whether or not these publications were potentially relevant. They agreed regarding nine of the references, which made Emily confident that her review question was defined in a sufficiently clear way. Her sifting of references resulted in 126 potentially useful publications that seemed appropriate to answering the review question.

Emily now had to decide on the inclusion and exclusion criteria she would be using to evaluate the quality of these 126 publications. She based the development of her criteria on Petticrew and Roberts' (2006) book chapter on assessing study quality. Upon her tutor's recommendation, she also considered Wallace and Wray's book on critical reading and writing for postgraduates (2011). She decided a publication would be included if:

- the methods were adequate (i.e. do the authors explain clearly what methods of data collection they chose and why?; is a rationale given for the sample selection technique that was employed?);
- the data analysis was clear (i.e. do the authors explain the data analysis they have performed and why?);
- the conclusions were derived from the findings (i.e. do the authors link the conclusions back to the purpose and aims of their research, making it clear what their results mean?).

After applying these inclusion and exclusion criteria Emily had 71 publications to download in pdf format and read. For each of these she noted key points, including the aims/objectives, methods, underlying theory and main findings. She also made a note of what the study said about her review question. Now that she had obtained all the relevant information, Emily could start comparing and relating the publications' findings to one another. Eventually, based on what she had found, she was able to summarise and discuss what was currently known about the understanding and definition of individual workplace performance in the finance industry, what was not known yet and areas for future research. This answered her review question.

When asked by her tutor to reflect on her experience of doing a Systematic Review, Emily said that it took her longer than expected – she had worked hard on it for two months! On the upside, she liked that she'd always been aware of what to do next, the process being clearly structured. She also felt really confident that she now knew what the literature said about the finance industry's understanding of individual workplace performance. Overall, even though she realised she would be constrained by the time remaining for her to undertake her data collection and analysis, Emily was satisfied with her decision to do a Systematic Review rather than a different type of literature review.

References

Denyer, D. and Tranfield, D. (2009) 'Producing a Systematic Review', in D. Buchanan and A. Bryman (eds) *The SAGE Handbook of Organizational Research Methods*. London: Sage.

Petticrew, M. and Roberts, H. (2006) *Systematic Reviews in the Social Sciences. A Practical Guide*. Oxford: Blackwell Publishing.

Wallace, M. and Wray, A. (2011) *Critical Reading and Writing for Postgraduates* (2nd edn). London: Sage.

Questions

1 a Why is it important to apply inclusion and exclusion criteria when deciding which publications to include in a Systematic Review?

  b What other quality criteria might you use?

2 What are the advantages and disadvantages in using an expert panel of stakeholders to assist in determining a review question?

3 Emily has decided to collect her primary data by interviewing human resource managers in the finance sector. How can she use the findings of her Systematic Review to inform her subsequent data collection?

Additional case studies relating to material covered in this chapter are available via the book's companion website: **www.pearsoned.co.uk/saunders**.

They are:

- The development of discount warehouse clubs.
- The problems of valuing intellectual capital.
- National cultures and management styles.
- Complexity theory and emergent change.

Self-check answers

3.1 There are numerous problems with the content and structure of this extract. Some of the more obvious include:

- The content consists of predominantly trade magazines, in particular *Post Magazine*, and there are no references of academic substance. Some of the references to individual authors have discrepancies: for example, was the article by Lindisfarne (or is it Lindesfarne?) published in 1994 or 1995?
- The items referenced are from 1994 and 1995. It is certain that more recent items are available.
- There is no real structure or argument in the extract. The extract is a list of what people have written, with no attempt to critically evaluate or juxtapose the ideas.

3.2 This is a difficult one without knowing her research question! However, you could still advise her on the general principles. Your advice will probably include:

- Define the parameters of the research, considering language, subject area, business sector, geographical area, publication period and literature type. Generate search terms using one or a variety of techniques such as reading, brainstorming or relevance trees. Discuss her ideas as widely as possible, including with her tutor, librarians and you.
- Start the search using tertiary sources to identify relevant secondary literature. She should commence with those tertiary sources that abstract and index academic journal articles and books. At the same time she should obtain relevant literature that has been referenced in articles that she has already read.

3.3 There are no incorrect answers with brainstorming! However, you might like to check your search terms for suitability prior to using them to search an appropriate database. We suggest that you follow the approach outlined in Section 3.5 under 'searching using the tertiary literature'.

3.4 There is a variety of possible reasons, including:

- One or more of the parameters of your search are defined too narrowly.
- The keywords you have chosen do not appear in the controlled index language.
- Your spelling of the search term is incorrect.
- The terminology you are using is incorrect.
- The acronyms you have chosen are not used by databases.
- You are using jargon rather than accepted terminology.

3.5 There are two parts to this answer: rewriting the text and using the Harvard system of referencing. Your text will inevitably differ from the answer given below owing to your personal writing style. Don't worry about this too much as it is discussed in far more detail in Section 14.5. The references should follow the same format.

Social Media is a new form of media that uses the Internet to facilitate conversations (Solis and Breakenridge, 2009). Social Media sources enable consumers to create, edit, contribute and share 'content' (Drury, 2007. Parise et al., 2008. Mangold and Faulds, 2009). Drury (2007) explains that rather than focus on the 'media' aspect, emphasis should be placed on the 'social' element. He argues that users connecting and interacting with each other and sharing content is key to Social Media. Similarly, Mayfield (2008) emphasises characteristics such as participation, conversation and community as the defining features of Social Media. Social Media tools range from Blogs, Social Network Sites, Podcasts, Forums, Content Communities and Wikis (Mayfield, 2008). The most commonly used examples of Social Media tools include sites such as Facebook, Myspace, Twitter, Flickr, LinkedIn, del.icio.us, YouTube and Wikipedia (Mangold and Faulds, 2009).

Drury, G. (2008) 'Social media: Should marketers engage and how can it be done effectively?' *Journal of Direct, Data and Digital Marketing Practice*. Vol. 9, pp. 274–277.

Mangold, W. and Faulds, D. (2009) 'Social media: The new hybrid element of the promotion mix'. *Business Horizons*. Vol. 52, pp. 357–365.

Mayfield, A. (2008) 'What is social media?'. *Networks*. V. 4 UPDAT, p. 36. Available at: http://www.icrossing.co.uk/fileadmin/uploads/eBooks/What_is_Social_Media_iCrossing_ebook.pdf

Parise, S., Guinan, P. and Weinberg, G. (2008) 'The secrets of marketing in a web 2.0 world'. Available at: http://sloanreview.mit.edu/executive-adviser/articles/2008/6/5068/the-secrets-of-marketing-in-a-web-20-world/ (Accessed 27 Mar. 2011).

Solis, B. and Breakenridge, D. (2009) *Putting the public back in Public Relations: How Social is reinventing the ageing business of PR*, New Jersey, Pearson.

Get ahead using resources on the Companion Website at:
www.pearsoned.co.uk/saunders

- Improve your SPSS and NVivo research analysis with practice tutorials.
- Save time researching on the Internet with the Smarter Online Searching Guide.
- Test your progress using self-assessment questions.
- Follow live links to useful websites.

Chapter 4

Understanding research philosophies and approaches

Learning outcomes

By the end of this chapter you should be able to:

- define the key terms ontology, epistemology and axiology and explain their relevance to business research;
- explain the relevance for business research of philosophical perspectives such as positivism, realism, pragmatism and interpretivism;
- understand the main research paradigms which are significant for business research;
- distinguish between deductive, inductive and abductive research approaches;
- state your own epistemological, ontological and axiological positions.

4.1 Introduction

Much of this book is concerned with the way in which you collect data to answer your research question(s). Most people plan their research in relation to a question that needs to be answered or a problem that needs to be solved. They then go on to think about what data they need and the techniques they use to collect them. You are not therefore unusual if early on in your research you consider whether you should, for example, use a questionnaire or undertake interviews. However, how you collect your data belongs in the centre of the research 'onion', by which means we have chosen to depict the issues underlying the choice of data collection techniques and analysis procedures in Figure 4.1. In coming to this central point you need to explain why you made the choice you did so that others can see that your research should be taken seriously (Crotty 1998). Consequently there are important outer layers of the onion that you need to understand and explain rather than just peel and throw away!

This chapter is concerned principally with the outer two of the onion's layers: research philosophies (Section 4.2) and research approaches (Section 4.3). In the next chapter we examine the layers we call methodological choice, strategy and time horizon. The sixth layer, data collection techniques and analysis procedures, is dealt with in Chapters 7–13.

4.2 Understanding your research philosophy

In this first part of the chapter we examine **research philosophy** (Figure 4.1). This overarching term relates to the development of knowledge and the nature of that knowledge. At first reading this sounds rather profound. But the point is that this is precisely what you are doing when embarking on research – developing knowledge in a particular field. The knowledge development you are embarking upon may not be as dramatic as a new theory of human motivation. But even if the purpose has the relatively modest ambition of answering a specific problem in a particular organisation it is, nonetheless, developing new knowledge.

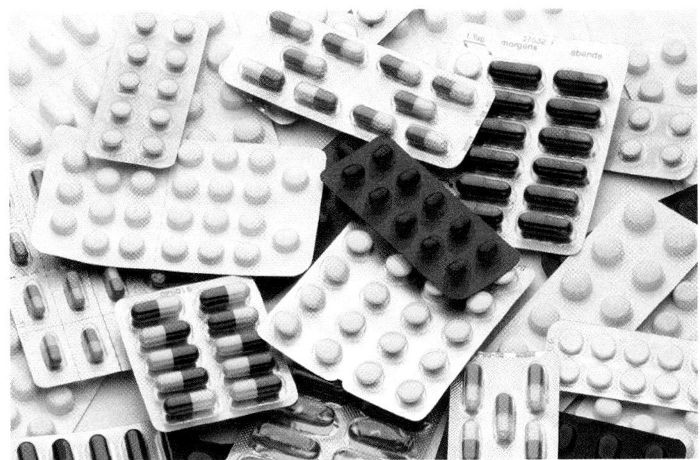

Source: Science Photo Library

Our values can have an important impact on the research we decide to pursue and the way in which we pursue it. This may not lead to any form of discord, but it may mean that some observers accuse us of untoward bias. In 2003 the *British Medical Journal* reported that the leading independent medical journal *The Lancet* had taken the unprecedented step of accusing a major European pharmaceutical company of sponsoring biased research into its new anti-cholesterol drug.

In his editorial in *The Lancet*, Richard Horton, the journal's editor, said the company's tactics 'raise disturbing questions about how drugs enter clinical practice and what measures exist to protect patients from inadequately investigated medicines'. He accused the clinical trials, which investigated the efficacy of the new drug, of including 'weak data', 'adventurous statistics', and 'marketing dressed up as research'. The editorial argued that 'physicians must tell their patients the truth about the drug that compared with competitors, it has an inferior evidence base supporting its safe use'.

In the same edition of *The Lancet* the company issued a furious response. 'Regulators, doctors, and patients as well as my company have been poorly served by your flawed and incorrect editorial', wrote the CEO. He said that he deplored the fact that a respected scientific journal should make such an outrageous critique of a serious, well studied and important medicine.

Source: Dyer (2003: 1005)

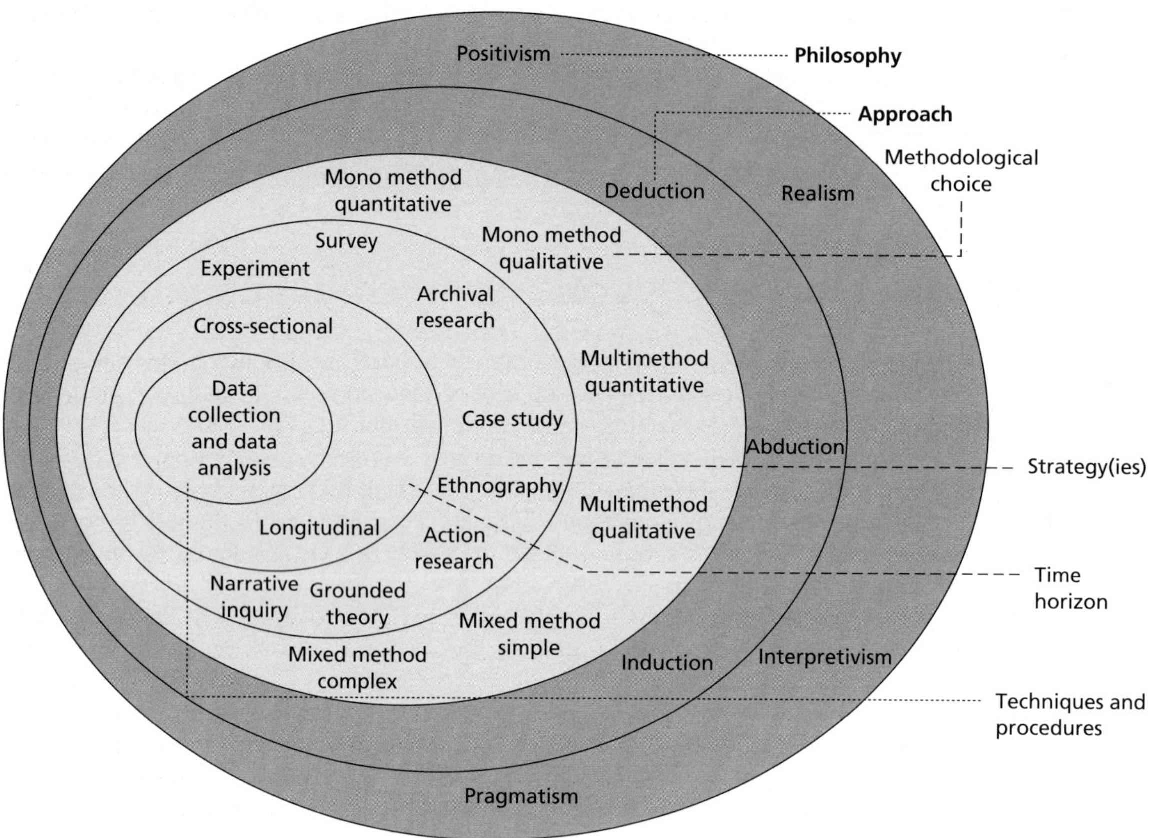

Figure 4.1 The research 'onion'
Source: © Mark Saunders, Philip Lewis and Adrian Thornhill 2011

At every stage in our research we make assumptions. Your assumptions about human knowledge and about the nature of the realities you encounter in your research inevitably shape how you understand your research questions, the methods you use and how you interpret your findings (Crotty 1998). The research philosophy you adopt can be thought of as your assumptions about the way in which you view the world. These assumptions will underpin your research strategy and the methods you choose as part of that strategy. Johnson and Clark (2006) note that as business and management researchers we need to be aware of the philosophical commitments we make through our choice of research strategy since this will have a significant impact not only on what we do but how we understand what it is we are investigating.

In part, the philosophy you adopt will be influenced by practical considerations. However, the main influence is likely to be your particular view of what is acceptable knowledge and the process by which this is developed. A researcher who is concerned with facts, such as the resources needed in a manufacturing process, is likely to have a very different view on the way research should be conducted from a researcher concerned with the feelings and attitudes of the workers towards their managers in that same manufacturing process. Not only will their strategies and methods probably differ considerably, but so will their views on what is important and, perhaps more significantly, what is useful.

In summary, we agree with Johnson and Clark (2006), who argue that the important issue is not so much whether our research should be philosophically informed, but how well we are able to reflect upon our philosophical choices and defend them in relation to the alternatives we could have adopted.

When thinking about philosophies it would be easy to fall into the trap of thinking that one research philosophy is 'better' than another. This would miss the point. They are 'suited' to achieving different things. As always, this depends on the research question(s) you are seeking to answer. Of course, the practical reality is that a particular research question can rarely be answered only within one philosophical domain, as suggested in the 'onion' (Figure 4.1).

You may still be asking, what practical use is an understanding of your philosophical position? Is it as much use as the outer layer on a real onion, which is cast aside, with only the inner layers retained? We think that it is of practical benefit to understand the taken-for-granted assumptions that we all have about the way the world works. Only if we have such an understanding can we examine these assumptions, evaluate their appropriateness and perhaps amend them.

In this discussion we examine two major ways of thinking about research philosophy: ontology and epistemology. Each highlights important differences which will influence the way in which you think about the research process. This is the purpose of this chapter. It is not to offer a shopping list from which you may wish to choose that philosophy or approach that suits you best. It is to enhance your understanding of the ways in which you may approach the study of our particular field of activity. Through this you will be better equipped to explain and justify your own methodological choice, strategy or strategies and data collection techniques.

Having said all this by way of introduction to this section on research philosophies, we start by considering whether you have to adopt a particular philosophical position. Subsequently, we will consider the role of assumptions we make about the way in which the world works; what different philosophies consider to be acceptable knowledge; the role of our own values and research paradigms.

Do you have to adopt one position?

It is unavoidable that the debate on ontology and epistemology which follows has a competitive ring. The debate is often framed in terms of a choice between positivist and interpretivist research philosophies or between quantitative and qualitative methods. However, in recent years there have been suggestions that it is more appropriate for the researcher undertaking a particular study to think of the philosophy adopted as a multidimensional set of continua rather than separate positions (Niglas 2010). Such continua can be seen in the answers to three questions which we consider in more detail in this section (Table 4.1)

Table 4.1 Research philosophy as a multidimensional set of continua

Question (dimension)	Continua		
• What is the **nature of reality**?	external	⇔	socially constructed
	objective	⇔	subjective
• What is considered **acceptable knowledge**?	observable phenomena	⇔	subjective meanings
	law-like generalisations	⇔	details of specifics
• What is the **role of values**?	value free	⇔	value bound

Box 4.1 Focus on management research

Investigating the realities of how things work in organisations

In a recent article in the *Journal of Management Studies,* Watson (2011) outlines and discusses the rationale for undertaking good ethnographic research when investigating the realities of how things work in organisations. Within this he argues that pragmatist realist principles of truth, reality and relevance to practice provide a powerful rationale for focusing on investigating the realities of how things work in organisations using ethnography.

In his article Watson highlights how he has always believed that it is not possible to learn a great deal about what actually happens or how things work in organisations without undertaking intensive research that involves observation or the researcher participating, both of which are essential to ethnography. In developing his argument, Watson (2011: 204) emphasises the importance of the 'relevance to practice' principle of pragmatism stating: 'I felt that there was no real alternative to this if I wanted to contribute in a worthwhile way to the social scientific understanding of how managers manage, how organizational change comes about, how micro politics operate, and how employment relationships are shaped and maintained.'

Even if you accept the argument that philosophy should be thought of as a multidimensional set of continua, you might still consider that choosing your position on each of the continua is somewhat unrealistic in practice. If this is your view then you would be adopting the position of the pragmatist.

Pragmatism

Pragmatism asserts that concepts are only relevant where they support action (Kelemen and Rumens 2008). This means that the most important determinant of your position on each of the continua is the research question – one position may be more appropriate than another for answering a particular question (Table 4.1). Moreover, if the research question does not suggest unambiguously that a particular philosophy should be adopted, this confirms the pragmatist's view that it is perfectly possible to work with different philosophical positions. This reflects a theme which recurs in this book – that multiple methods are often possible, and possibly highly appropriate, within one study (see Section 5.3).

For pragmatists, the importance of the meaning of an idea (or a research finding) are its practical consequences (Box 4.1). Pragmatists recognise that there are many different ways of interpreting the world and undertaking research, that no single point of view can ever give the entire picture and that there maybe multiple realities. This does not mean that pragmatists always use multiple methods, rather they use the method or methods that enable credible, well-founded, reliable and relevant data to be collected that advance the research (Kelemen and Rumens 2008).

Ontology: the nature of reality

Ontology is concerned with nature of reality. This raises questions of the assumptions researchers have about the way the world operates and the commitment to particular views. The two aspects of ontology we describe here both have their devotees among

Box 4.2 Focus on student research

A management exodus at ChemCo

As part of a major organisational change all the managers in the marketing department of the chemical manufacturer ChemCo left the organisation. They were replaced by new managers who were thought to be more in tune with the more commercially aggressive new culture that the organisation was trying to create. The new managers entering the organisation filled the roles of the managers who had left and had essentially the same job duties and procedures as their predecessors.

John wanted to study the role of management in ChemCo and in particular the way in which managers liaised with external stakeholders. He decided to use the new managers in the marketing department as his research 'subjects'.

In his research proposal he outlined briefly his research philosophy. He defined his ontological position as that of the objectivist. His reasoning was that management in ChemCo had a reality that was separate from the managers who inhabit that reality. He pointed to the fact that the formal management structure at ChemCo was largely unchanged from that which was practised by the managers who had left the organisation. The process of management would continue in largely the same way in spite of the change in personnel.

business and management researchers. In addition, both are likely to be accepted as producing valid knowledge by many researchers.

The first aspect of ontology we discuss is **objectivism**. This portrays the position that things, such as social entities, exist as a meaningful reality external to those social actors concerned with their existence (Crotty 1998). The second aspect, **subjectivism**, holds that social phenomena are created through the perceptions and consequent actions of affected social actors.

Objectivism

Objectivism represents the position that social entities exist in reality external to and independent of social actors. An example of this may be management itself (Box 4.2). You may argue that management is an objective entity and decide to adopt an objectivist stance to the study of particular aspects of management in a specific organisation. In order to substantiate your view you would say that the managers in your organisation have job descriptions which prescribe their duties, there are operating procedures to which they are supposed to adhere, they are part of a formal structure which locates them in a hierarchy with people reporting to them and they in turn report to more senior managers. This view emphasises the structural aspects of management and assumes that management is similar in all organisations. Aspects of the structure in which management operates may differ but the essence of the function is very much the same in all organisations. Insofar as management does differ in organisations it is a function of the different objective aspects of management.

Subjectivism

For your approach to the study of management you may prefer to take the view that the objective aspects of management are less important than the way in which the managers themselves attach their own individual meanings to their jobs and the way they think that those jobs should be performed. This approach would be very much more akin to the subjectivist view.

Subjectivism asserts that social phenomena are created from the perceptions and consequent actions of social actors. As social interactions between actors are a continual process, social phenomena are in a constant state of revision. This means it is necessary to study the details of a situation in order to understand what is happening or even the reality occurring behind what is happening. This is often associated with the term constructionism, or **social constructionism**, which views reality as being socially constructed. Social actors, such as the customers you might plan to study for an organisation, may place many different interpretations on the situations in which they find themselves. This means individual customers may perceive different situations in varying ways as a consequence of their own view of the world. This perception is likely to be relativist – that is, related to each customer's relationship to the situation – rather than an absolutist view of the world. Their different interpretations are likely to affect their actions and the nature of their social interaction with others. In this sense, the customers you are studying not only interact with their environment; they also seek to make sense of it through their interpretation of events and the meanings that they draw from these events. In turn, their own actions may be seen by others as being meaningful in the context of these socially constructed interpretations and meanings.

Therefore, in the case of the customers you are studying, it is your role as the researcher to seek to understand the subjective reality of the customers in order to be able to make sense of and understand their motives, actions and intentions in a way that is meaningful (Box 4.3). All this is some way from the position that customer service in an organisation has a reality that is separate from the customers who perceive that reality. The subjectivist view is that customer service is produced through the social interactions between service providers and customers and is continually being revised as a result of this. In other words, at no time is there a definitive entity called 'customer service'. It is constantly changing.

This objectivist–subjectivist debate is somewhat similar to the different ways in which the theoretical and practical approaches to organisational culture have developed in the past 30 years. Objectivists would tend to view the culture of an organisation as something that the organisation 'has'. On the other hand, the subjectivist's view would be that culture is something that the organisation 'is' as a result as a process of continuing social enactment (Millmore et al. 2007). Management theory and practice has leaned towards treating organisational culture as a variable, something that the organisation 'has': something that can be manipulated, changed in order to produce the sort of state desired by managers. The subjectivist viewpoint would be to reject this as too simplistic and argue that culture is something that is created and re-created through a complex array of phenomena which include social interactions and the impact of physical factors such as office layout to which individuals attach certain meanings, rituals and myths. It is the meanings that are attached to these phenomena by social actors within the organisation that need to be understood in order for the culture to be understood. Furthermore, because of the continual creation and re-creation of an organisation's culture it is difficult for it to be isolated, understood and then manipulated. It is however worth noting that in your research it is possible to make use of both objective and subjective lenses.

Epistemology: what is considered acceptable knowledge

Epistemology concerns what constitutes acceptable knowledge in a field of study. The most important distinction is one hinted at the start of Section 4.2 in our example of two researchers' views of what they consider important in the study of the manufacturing

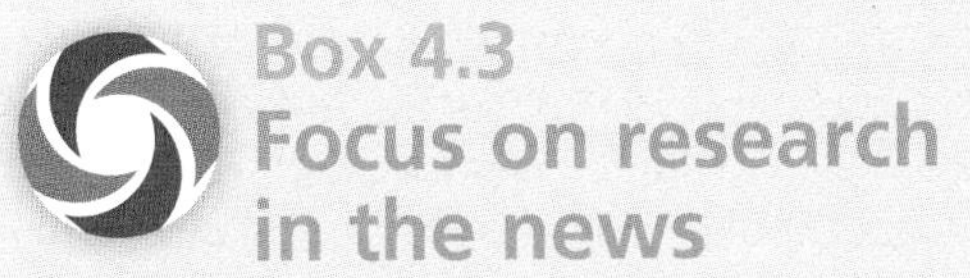

FT

Suits and cars and rock 'n' roll

It was as I glanced around the crowds gathered in the O2 arena for Roger Waters' *The Wall* concert that the realisation hit me: this was perhaps not the young, happening event of the capital. Middle-aged London was out in force. Or rather middle-aged male London. Across the venue one could see the serried ranks of receding hairlines and relaxed-fit jeans. They were paunchy, proud and ready to rock. The car park was full of family saloons and expensive cars. In fact it was as if someone had cloned 12,000 Jeremy Clarksons and put them all in a single venue. So there we were, thousands of older types nodding in unison and resisting the urge to correct the English on 'we don't need no education'. Of course there were some members of the younger generation there, swilling back the lager and being far too raucous; but we all knew they were just trying to look big. I imagine gangs of balding men accosting them in the car park, yelling things like 'Wanna bit of Bovril?' or 'Are you looking at me? I only ask as I'm wearing my reading glasses'.

The whole nostalgia rock phenomenon is a particularly pleasing one for men and women of a certain generation. We don't want to think we are too old to go to gigs, so we've found a class of gigs that are old enough to come to us. We wouldn't be so square as to deride the quality of modern music; much more cred instead to dismiss it as 'derivative' and stick to the original.

A year ago it was The Specials at Hammersmith. This was a particularly big deal for me, as I hadn't been cool enough to see them the first time around. In point of fact it occurred to me, as I stood there in a suit, having rushed straight from work, that I might not be cool enough the second time either. Fortunately lots of other fans had obviously rushed straight from work too. We may not, it's true, have cut it as Rude Boys, but to hell with it, we could certainly be brusque.

There are some who never lost the youthful spirit; guys who pack their tent each year and head off to brave the mud, rain and primal screams of Glastonbury. I've always been rather torn when it comes to Glastonbury. It does look huge fun if you have the generosity of spirit to put up with all the immense discomfort and inconvenience. If only there was a good hotel within walking distance; a nice one, with a decent restaurant and a swimming pool. I also suspect that it's much better once you've been once or twice and know the tricks and pitfalls. This, however, means that you should really only go if you've been before. Everyone should go to Glastonbury, but never for the first time. But now, who needs to? We olds have got a lock on the best venues. Promoters have realised how much more money they can pull in by appealing to the older audience. Why waste money on impoverished students when you can take their parents for a few hundred quid a time? You'll be lucky to get more than beer money out of a teenager, but at the Wall concert you could charge £20 ($32) for a programme.

When we were young, we raged against the machine. We really wanted Bob Dylan's 'The Times They Are A-Changin'' to mean something. Now, we may sing The Who's 'My Generation', but actually we no longer hope we die before we get old. We may have mellowed, but so have the groups. I recall one former hellraiser admitting that where once he'd head out partying after a concert, now he mostly liked to 'get off home'. And this is the latest evolution. Once there was prog rock, then punk rock and now there's smug rock. Smug rockers still know all the words to Public Enemy's 'Fight the Power', but these days the struggle is more likely to take the form of arguing with the Ocado man. Smug rockers may have kids and mortgages and serious jobs but, deep down, we know that we've still got it – it's just that now there's a nice dinner beforehand and a taxi home afterwards.

Rock'n'roll; I tell you: it's wasted on the young.

Source: From 'suits and cars and rock 'n' roll', Robert Shrimsley (2011) *Financial Times*, 20 May.

process. The researcher (the 'resources' researcher) who considers data on resources needed is likely to be more akin to the position of the natural scientist. This may be the position of the operations management specialist who is comfortable with the collection and analysis of 'facts'. For that researcher, reality is represented by objects that are considered to be 'real', such as computers, trucks, machines and actual employees. These objects have a separate existence to that of the researcher and, for that reason, this researcher would argue that the data collected are far less open to bias and therefore more 'objective'. The 'resources' researcher would place much less authority on the data collected by the 'feelings' researcher, who is concerned with the feelings and attitudes of the workers towards their managers in that same manufacturing process. The 'resources' researcher would view the objects studied by the 'feelings' researcher – feelings and attitudes – as social phenomena which have no external reality. Unlike computers, trucks and machines, they would consider that employees' feelings and attitudes cannot be seen, measured or modified. You may argue, of course, that human feelings and attitudes can be, and frequently are, measured. Indeed, the 'resources' researcher may place more authority on such data were they to be presented in the form of a table of statistical data. This would lend the data more objectivity in the view of the 'resources' researcher. But this raises the question of whether those data presented in statistical form are any more deserving of authority than those presented in a narrative, which may be the choice of the 'feelings' researcher.

The 'resources' researcher is embracing what is called the positivist philosophy to the development of knowledge whereas the 'feelings' researcher is adopting the interpretivist philosophy. We deal with both in this subsection on epistemology, as well as the stance of the researcher embracing the realist and interpretivist philosophies.

Positivism

If your research reflects the philosophy of **positivism** then you will probably adopt the philosophical stance of the natural scientist (Table 4.1). You will prefer collecting data about an observable reality and search for regularities and causal relationships in your data to create law-like generalisations like those produced by scientists (Gill and Johnson 2010).

Like the 'resources' researcher earlier, only phenomena that you can observe will lead to the production of credible data. To generate a research strategy to collect these data you may use existing theory to develop hypotheses. These hypotheses will be tested and confirmed, in whole or part, or refuted, leading to the further development of theory which then may be tested by further research. However, this does not mean as a positivist you have to start with existing theory. All natural sciences have developed from an engagement with the world in which data were collected and observations made prior to hypotheses being formulated and tested.

The hypotheses developed, as in Box 4.4, lead to the gathering of facts that provide the basis for subsequent hypothesis testing. Both the examples we have cited so far, that of the 'resources' researcher and student in Box 4.2, will be concerned with facts rather than impressions. Such facts are consistent with the notion of 'observable social reality' similar to that employed by the physical and natural scientists to which we referred to earlier.

Another important component of the positivist approach to research is that the research is undertaken, as far as possible, in a value-free way. At first sight this is a plausible position, particularly when one contrasts the perspective of the 'resources' researcher with the 'feelings' researcher in our earlier example. The 'resources' researcher would claim to be external to the process of data collection in the sense that there is little that

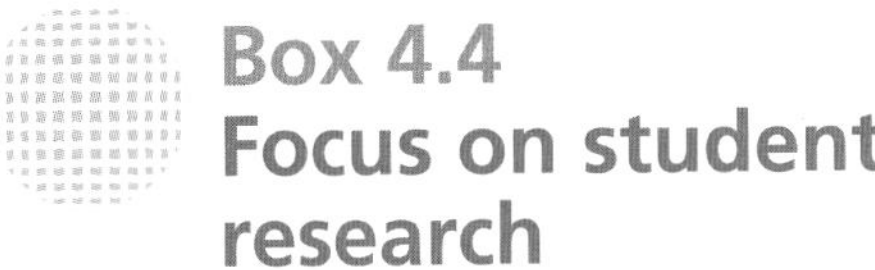

Box 4.4 Focus on student research

The development of hypotheses

Brett was conducting a piece of research for his project on the economic benefits of working from home for software developers. He studied the literature on home working in general and read in detail two past dissertations in his university library that dealt with the same phenomenon, albeit that they did not relate specifically to software developers. As a result of his reading, Brett developed a number of theoretical propositions, each of which contained specific hypotheses. Listed below is that which Brett developed in relation to potential increased costs, which may negate the economic gains of home working.

THEORETICAL PROPOSITION: Increased costs may negate the productivity gains from home working.

Specific hypotheses

1 Increased costs for computer hardware, software and telecommunications equipment will negate the productivity gains from home working.
2 Home workers will require additional support from on-site employees, for example technicians, which will negate the productivity gains from home working.
3 Work displaced to other employees and/or increased supervisory requirements will negate the productivity gains from home working.
4 Reduced face-to-face access by home workers to colleagues will result in lost opportunities to increase efficiencies, which will negate the productivity gains from home working.

can be done to alter the substance of the data collected. The assumption is that 'the researcher is value neutral, although absolutist claims that the outcome is totally objective and unquestionably certain are made rarely (Crotty 1998). Rather, findings are tentative and qualified. To test the hypotheses in Box 4.4, the student would collect data with which he could estimate productivity, costs and supervisory requirements. A 'resources' researcher's claim to do this in a more value-free way is, on the face of it, rather stronger than that of the 'feelings' researcher. It may be argued that the 'feelings' researcher is part of the data collection process. It would be normal for at least part of the process of data collection on the feelings and attitudes of the workers towards their managers for the 'feelings' researcher to interact with those workers socially to collect data. A person-to-person interview, for example, will involve the 'feelings' researcher framing the questions to ask and interpreting the respondent's examples. It is hard to imagine that the 'feelings' researcher would ask every respondent exactly the same question in exactly the same way and interpret every response with computer-like consistency.

You may argue, of course, that excluding our own values as researchers is impossible. Even a researcher adopting a positivist stance exercises choice in the issue to study, the research objectives to pursue and the data to collect. Indeed, it could be argued that the decision to try and adopt a value-free perspective suggests the existence of a certain value position!

It is frequently advocated that the positivist researcher will be likely to use a highly structured methodology in order to facilitate replication (Gill and Johnson 2010). Furthermore, the emphasis will be on quantifiable observations that lend themselves to statistical analysis. However, as you read through this chapter and the next you will note that this may not necessarily be the case since it is perfectly possible to adopt some of the characteristics of positivism in your research, for example hypothesis testing, using data originally collected in in-depth interviews.

Realism

Realism is another philosophical position which relates to scientific enquiry. The essence of **realism** is that what we sense is reality: that objects have an existence independent of the human mind (Table 4.1). The philosophy of realism is that there is a reality quite independent of the mind. In this sense, realism is opposed to idealism, the theory that only the mind and its contents exist (Crotty 1998). Realism is a branch of epistemology which is similar to positivism in that it assumes a scientific approach to the development of knowledge. This assumption underpins the collection of data and the understanding of those data. This meaning (and in particular the relevance of realism for business and management research) becomes clearer when two forms of realism are contrasted.

The first type of realism is direct realism. **Direct realism** says that what you see is what you get: what we experience through our senses portrays the world accurately. The second kind of realism is called **critical realism**. Critical realists argue that what we experience are sensations, the images of the things in the real world, not the things directly. Critical realists point out how often our senses deceive us. For example, when you next watch an international rugby or cricket match on television you are likely to see an advertisement for the sponsor in a prominent position on the actual playing surface. This looks like it is standing upright on the field. However, this is an illusion. It is in fact painted on the grass. So what we really see are sensations, which are representations of what is real.

The direct realist would respond to the critical realist by arguing that what we call illusions are actually due to the fact that we have insufficient information. We do not perceive the world in television images. We move around, move our eyes and ears, use all our senses. In the case of the television advertisement, the complete experience of it would include seeing it from all directions and angles.

A simple way to think about the difference between direct and critical realism is as follows. Critical realism claims that there are two steps to experiencing the world. First, there is the thing itself and the sensations it conveys. Second, there is the mental processing that goes on sometime after that sensation meets our senses. Direct realism says that the first step is enough. To pursue our cricket (or rugby) example, the umpire who is the critical realist would say about his umpiring decisions: 'I give them as I see them!' The umpire who is a direct realist would say 'I give them as they are!'

Business and management research is concerned with the social world in which we live. So you may agree with writers such as Bhaskar (1989) who identify with the epistemology of critical realists. Their argument is that as researchers we will only be able to understand what is going on in the social world if we understand the social structures that have given rise to the phenomena that we are trying to understand. In other words, what we see is only part of the bigger picture. Bhaskar (1989) argues that we can identify what we do not see through the practical and theoretical processes of the social sciences.

Thus, the critical realist's position is that our knowledge of reality is a result of social conditioning (e.g. we know that if the rugby player runs into the advertisement that is standing up he will fall over!) and cannot be understood independently of the social actors involved in the knowledge derivation process (Dobson 2002).

A further important point needs to be made about the distinction between direct and critical realism, both of which are important in relation to the pursuit of business and management research. The first relates the capacity of research to change the world which it studies. The direct realist perspective would suggest the world is relatively unchanging: that it operates, in the business context, at one level (the individual, the group or the organisation). The critical realist, on the other hand, would recognise the importance of multilevel study (e.g. at the level of the individual, the group and the organisation). Each of these levels has the capacity to change the researcher's understanding of that which is being studied. This would be the consequence of the existence of a greater variety of structures, procedures and processes and the capacity that these structures, procedures and processes have to interact with one another. We would therefore argue that the critical realist's position that the social world is constantly changing is much more in line with the purpose of business and management research, which is too often to understand the reason for phenomena as a precursor to recommending change.

Interpretivism

You may be critical of the positivist tradition and argue that the social world of business and management is far too complex to lend itself to theorising by definite 'laws' in the same way as the physical sciences. Those researchers critical of positivism argue that rich insights into this complex world are lost if such complexity is reduced entirely to a series of law-like generalisations. If you sympathise with such a view, your research philosophy is likely to be nearer to that of the interpretivist.

Interpretivism advocates that it is necessary for the researcher to understand differences between humans in our role as social actors (Table 4.1). This emphasises the difference between conducting research among people rather than about objects such as trucks and computers. The term 'social actors' is quite significant here. The metaphor of the theatre suggests that as humans we play a part on the stage of human life. In theatrical productions, actors play a part which they interpret in a particular way (which may be their own or that of the director) and act out their part in accordance with this interpretation. In the same way, we interpret our everyday social roles in accordance with the meaning we give to these roles. In addition, we interpret the social roles of others in accordance with our own set of meanings.

The heritage of this strand of interpretivism comes from two intellectual traditions: **phenomenology** and **symbolic interactionism** (Chapter 9). Phenomenology refers to the way in which we as humans make sense of the world around us. In symbolic interactionism we are in a continual process of interpreting the social world around us in that we interpret the actions of others with whom we interact and this interpretation leads to adjustment of our own meanings and actions.

Crucial to the interpretivist philosophy is that the researcher has to adopt an empathetic stance. The challenge here is to enter the social world of our research subjects and understand their world from their point of view. Some would argue that an interpretivist perspective is highly appropriate in the case of business and management research, particularly in such fields as organisational behaviour, marketing and human resource management. Not only are business situations complex, they are also unique. They are a function of a particular set of circumstances and individuals coming together at a specific time.

What is the role of values?

Axiology is a branch of philosophy that studies judgements about value. Although this may include values we possess in the fields of aesthetics and ethics, it is the process of social enquiry with which we are concerned here. The role that your own values play in all stages of the research process is of great importance if you wish your research results to be credible. This is why we think it is worth noting this important topic here, particularly through the example in Box 4.5.

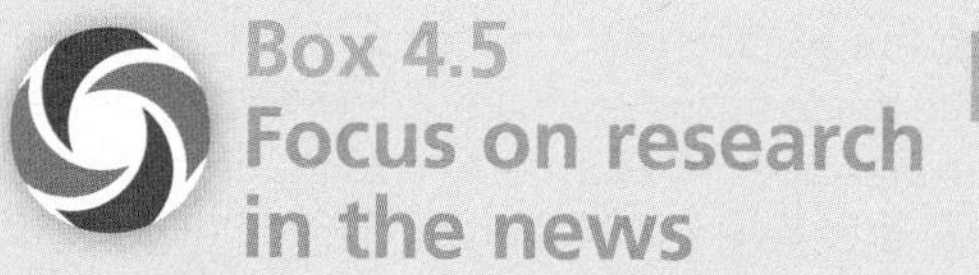

Box 4.5
Focus on research in the news

FT

Crop science: global food presents opportunity to reap a profit

The world already does a pretty miserable job of providing adequate food for vast swathes of its 7bn-strong population. With that number set to rise to close to 9bn by 2050, the issue of food security – ensuring people have access to an adequate supply of safe, nutritious and affordable food – is perhaps the most pressing facing crop scientists. 'Global food security ultimately depends on growing enough crops', says Professor Janet Allen, director of research at the Biotechnology and Biological Sciences Research Council (BBSRC), the UK's funding agency for biosciences. For crop scientists, that means selecting crop traits and production systems that can increase yields and reduce losses to pests and diseases.

But population growth is not the only challenge they face in their search for better, more hardy and more abundant crops. Climate change, too, is a big concern, with its potential to bring droughts and floods, new pests and diseases, and geopolitical conflict for resources and raw materials. Even if global food production can keep pace with population growth – and that is a big if – it is unlikely to be enough to accommodate serious weather-related disruptions in supply.

Addressing the productivity gap represents a significant business opportunity for the life sciences companies that lead the market in crop protection: Monsanto, Syngenta, Bayer, Dow and DuPont. These companies are already active and vocal participants in the global food security debate, but recognise that new business models are required to address new audiences in the developing world – and, perhaps, to overcome public resistance to big companies profiting from world hunger.

'Growers are our customers and our aim is to put them at the heart of our technology. That's just as true of smallholders in developing countries as it is of wealthier customers,' argues Kavita Prakash-Mani, head of food security agenda at Syngenta. An increasing share of Syngenta's profits, she says, comes from the developing world, particularly Asia-Pacific and Latin America, but also Africa. 'Farmers everywhere should be able to enjoy a choice of solutions to help them feed their families and communities, ones that are developed specifically to suit their growing conditions and their pockets.' Syngenta, for example, is working alongside its non-profit arm, the Syngenta Foundation for Sustainable Agriculture, and the International Maize and Wheat Improvement Centre (Cimmyt), another non-profit organisation based in Mexico, to develop drought-tolerant maize for smallholder farmers in Asia who lack access to irrigation. Drought-tolerant African maize developed by Cimmyt will be crossed with Syngenta varieties bred for Asia, applying Syngenta's genetic mapping technology to speed up the identification of the best varieties for the region in a project set to last five years.

But the application of GM technology to crops intended for the developing world – and, indeed, elsewhere – remains deeply controversial. For example, ActionAid, a development charity, fiercely opposes it, contending that market domination of GM technology by a handful of multinationals gives them unfair control over farmers' choices of seeds and the chemicals to go with them. 'It's a question of making poor people reliant on external inputs to succeed in feeding their families', argues Ruchi Tripathi, ActionAid's head of food rights. 'Once farmers are on a chemical treadmill, they find it hard to get off.' Instead, the charity favours an approach based on knowledge development, seed conservation and the establishment of gene banks for non-GM plant breeding, she says. The fact remains, however, that developing countries are planting GM crops at a more rapid rate than rich countries. According to the International Service for the Acquisition of Agri-biotech Applications, an industry body, Brazil has added some 10m hectares since 2008 and has overtaken Argentina as the second-biggest grower (after the US) of GM crops. India, meanwhile, increased land area given over to GM crops by 10 per cent in 2010. The most popular crop is soya, while the most common modification is tolerance to herbicides.

Could the escalating food security issue be helping crop scientists to win support in the war over GM technologies? Perhaps. In the UK, which is subject to EU restrictions on the growing of GM crops, the BBSRC staunchly backs the use of GM as a laboratory tool and promotes research into its potential to 'stabilise and increase food production more radically and more rapidly than is achievable through conventional breeding programmes alone'. Indeed, Professor Sir John Beddington, the UK government's chief scientific adviser, recently argued that moves to block cultivation of GM crops in the developing world can no longer be tolerated on 'ethical or moral grounds'. In remarks made ahead of the January 2011 release of a UK government report on food security, *The Future of Food and Farming*, Prof Beddington argued that crop science, including GM technologies, holds the key to tackling world hunger. 'There will be no silver bullet, but it is very hard to see how it would be remotely sensible to justify not using new technologies such as GM', he says.

Source: From 'Crop science: global food presents opportunity to reap a profit', by Jessica Twentyman (2011) *Financial Times*, 27 June.

Heron (1996) argues that our values are the guiding reason of all human action. He further argues that researchers demonstrate axiological skill by being able to articulate their values as a basis for making judgements about what research they are conducting and how they go about doing it. After all, at all stages in the research process you will be demonstrating your values. The example in Box 4.5 illustrates the relevance of values in how you view a potential research topic. Choosing one topic rather than another suggests that you think one of the topics is more important. Your choice of philosophical approach is a reflection of your values, as is your choice of data collection techniques. For example, to conduct a study where you place great importance on data collected through interview work suggests that you value personal interaction with your respondents more highly than their views expressed through an anonymous questionnaire.

An interesting idea which comes from Heron's (1996) discussion of axiology is the possibility of writing your own statement of personal values in relation to the topic you are studying. This may be more evidently applicable to some research topics than others. Those topics concerned with personal career development, for example, may be obvious candidates for this process: it would be an issue of personal value that it is the responsibility of the individual to take charge of their own career development. In areas of finance, it may be a strongly held value of the researcher that as much information as possible should be available to as many stakeholders as possible.

A statement of values may be of use both to you as the researcher and those parties with whom you have contact in your research. The use to you would be a result of your 'being honest with yourself' about quite what your values are. This would, for example, heighten your awareness of value judgements you are making in drawing conclusions from your data. These value judgements may lead to the drawing of conclusions which may be different from those drawn by researchers with other values. Other relevant parties connected with your research may include any fellow researchers, your supervisor and the university research ethics committee. This latter body may be of particular relevance to thoughts about the role of values in research topic choice and ways of pursuing research. Being clear about your own value position may help you in deciding what is appropriate ethically and arguing your position in the event of queries about decisions you have made. Sections 6.5 to 6.7 go into more detail about research ethics.

Table 4.2 Comparison of four research philosophies in business and management research

	Pragmatism	Positivism	Realism	Interpretivism
Ontology: the researcher's view of the nature of reality or being	External, multiple, view chosen to best enable answering of research question	External, objective and independent of social actors	Is objective. Exists independently of human thoughts and beliefs or knowledge of their existence (realist), but is interpreted through social conditioning (critical realist)	Socially constructed, subjective, may change, multiple
Epistemology: the researcher's view regarding what constitutes acceptable knowledge	Either or both observable phenomena and subjective meanings can provide acceptable knowledge dependent upon the research question. Focus on practical applied research, integrating different perspectives to help interpret the data	Only observable phenomena can provide credible data, facts. Focus on causality and law-like generalisations, reducing phenomena to simplest elements	Observable phenomena provide credible data, facts. Insufficient data means inaccuracies in sensations (direct realism). Alternatively, phenomena create sensations which are open to misinterpretation (critical realism). Focus on explaining within a context or contexts	Subjective meanings and social phenomena. Focus upon the details of situation, a reality behind these details, subjective meanings motivating actions
Axiology: the researcher's view of the role of values in research	Values play a large role in interpreting results, the researcher adopting both objective and subjective points of view	Research is undertaken in a value-free way, the researcher is independent of the data and maintains an objective stance	Research is value laden; the researcher is biased by world views, cultural experiences and upbringing. These will impact on the research	Research is value bound, the researcher is part of what is being researched, cannot be separated and so will be subjective
Data collection techniques most often used	Mixed or multiple method designs, quantitative and qualitative	Highly structured, large samples, measurement, quantitative, but can use qualitative	Methods chosen must fit the subject matter, quantitative or qualitative	Small samples, in-depth investigations, qualitative

Research paradigms

To draw this section on research philosophies together we explore research philosophy further through the concept of research paradigms. Paradigm is a term frequently used in the social sciences, but one which can lead to confusion because it tends to have multiple meanings. The definition we use here is that a **paradigm** is a way of examining social

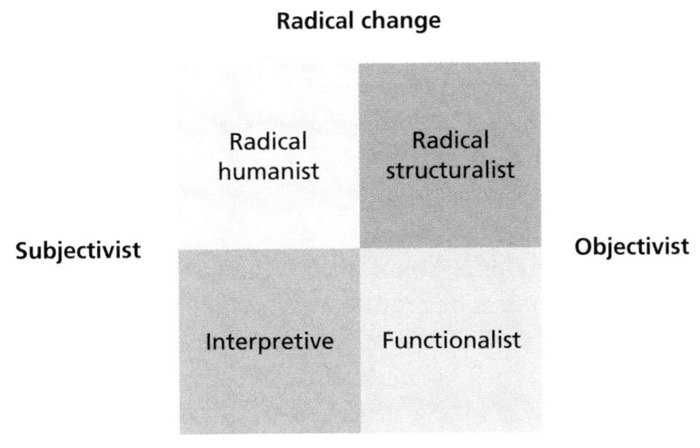

Figure 4.2 Four paradigms for the analysis of social theory

Source: Developed from Burrell and Morgan (1982) *Sociological Paradigms and Organisational Analysis*. Reproduced with permission of Ashgate Publishing Company

phenomena from which particular understandings of these phenomena can be gained and explanations attempted.

In our view the work of Burrell and Morgan (1982) is particularly helpful in summarising and clarifying the epistemologies and ontologies we have covered above. In addition, these writers have offered a fourfold categorisation of social science paradigms that represent the major belief systems of management and business researchers dependent upon their views regarding the ontology of research and the nature of society (Kelemen and Rumens 2008).

Figure 4.2 shows how the four paradigms can be arranged as a matrix corresponding to two conceptual dimensions: subjectivist to objectivist, and radical change to regulation. The first dimension will be familiar to you from our discussion of ontology in the previous section. In relation to the second dimension, **radical change** relates to a judgement about the way organisational affairs should be conducted and suggests ways in which these affairs may be conducted in order to make fundamental changes to the normal order of things. In short, the radical change dimension adopts a critical perspective on organisational life. Regulation is less judgemental and critical. This **regulatory perspective** seeks to explain the way in which organisational affairs are regulated and offer suggestions as to how they may be improved within the framework of the way things are done at present. In other words, the radical change dimension approaches organisational problems from the viewpoint of overturning the existing state of affairs; the regulatory dimension seeks to work within the existing state of affairs.

Burrell and Morgan (1982) note that the purposes of their four paradigms are:

- to help researchers clarify their assumptions about their view of the nature of science and society;
- to offer a useful way of understanding the way in which other researchers approach their work;
- to help researchers plot their own route through their research; to understand where it is possible to go and where they are going.

In the bottom right corner of the quadrant is the **functionalist paradigm**. This is located on the objectivist and regulatory dimensions. Objectivism is the ontological position you are likely to adopt if you are operating with this paradigm. It is regulatory in that you will probably be more concerned with a rational explanation of why a particular organisational problem is occurring and developing a set of recommendations within the structure of the organisation's current management. This is the paradigm within which most business and management research operates. Functionalist theories and models of management, for example business process re-engineering, are often generalised to other contexts; the idea being that they can be used universally providing they are correctly implemented and monitored (Kelemen and Rumens 2008). Perhaps the key assumption you would be making here is that organisations are rational entities, in which rational explanations offer solutions to rational problems. A typical example of a management research project operating within the functionalist paradigm would be an evaluation study of a communication strategy to assess its effectiveness and make recommendations as to how it may be made more effective.

Contained in the bottom left corner of the quadrant is the **interpretive paradigm**. As has been noted, the philosophical position to which this refers (interpretivism) is the way we as humans attempt to make sense of the world around us (Box 4.6). The concern you would have working within this paradigm would be to understand the fundamental meanings attached to organisational life. Far from emphasising rationality, it may be that the principal concern you have here is discovering irrationalities. Concern with studying

Box 4.6 Focus on student research

Researching the emotional effect of psychological contract violation

As an interpretivist Robin believed that reality was socially constructed, subjective and could be perceived in different ways by different people. Whilst reading for her master's programme she had been struck by how many of the research papers she read on the psychological contract, an individual's belief regarding the terms and conditions of a reciprocal agreement between themselves and another, were quantitative, focusing on aggregate findings rather than the details of situations. She considered that these researchers often ignored the individualistic and subjective aspects of contracts as well as individuals' emotional responses. Robin therefore decided her research would be concerned with the emotional effect that employers' psychological contract violation had on employees, and how these emotions impacted upon their attitudes and behaviours. Based on a more thorough review of the literature she developed three objectives:

- To establish how individuals decided their psychological contracts were being violated and their emotions in response to this violation.
- To ascertain the extent to which individuals' attitudes towards their employer changed as a result of these emotions, and whom the target of this shift in attitude was.
- To explore attitude and behavioural consequences of this violation.

Robin argued in her methodology chapter that, as a subjectivist, she was concerned with understanding what her research participants perceived to be the reality of their psychological contract violation as they constructed it. Within her chapter she stated her assumption that every action and reaction was based in a context that was interpreted by the participant as she or he made sense of what had happened. It was her participants' perceptions and their emotional reactions to these perceptions that would then inform their actions. Robin also made clear in the methodology chapter that her research was concerned primarily with finding the meaning and emotions that each participant attached to their violation and their reactions rather than changing the status quo. This she equated with the regulatory perspective. Not surprisingly, Robin stated that her research was conducted within an interpretive paradigm.

an organisation's communication strategy may soon turn to understanding the ways in which the intentions of management become derailed for completely unseen reasons, maybe reasons which are not apparent even to those involved with the strategy. This is likely to take you into the realm of the organisation's politics and the way in which power is used. Your concern here would be to become involved in the organisation's everyday activities in order to understand and explain what is going on, rather than change things (Kelemen and Rumens 2008).

In the top left corner the **radical humanist paradigm** is located within the subjectivist and radical change dimensions. As we said earlier, the radical change dimension adopts a critical perspective on organisational life. It emphasises both its political nature and the consequences that one's words and deeds have upon others (Kelemen and Rumens 2008). As such, working within this paradigm you would be concerned with changing the status quo, or in Burrell and Morgan's (1982: 32) words, 'to articulate ways in which humans can transcend the spiritual bonds and fetters which tie them into existing social patterns and thus realise their full potential'. The ontological perspective you would adopt here, as in the interpretive paradigm, would be subjectivist.

Finally, in the top right corner of the quadrant is the **radical structuralist paradigm**. Here your concern would be to approach your research with a view to achieving fundamental change based upon an analysis of such organisational phenomena as power relationships and patterns of conflict. The radical structuralist paradigm is involved in understanding structural patterns within work organisations such as hierarchies and reporting relationships and the extent to which these may produce dysfunctionalities. It adopts an objectivist perspective because it is concerned with objective entities, unlike the radical humanist ontology, which attempts to understand the meanings of social phenomena from the subjective perspective of participating social actors.

4.3 Research approaches

In Chapter 2 we emphasised that your research project will involve the use of theory. That theory may or may not be made explicit in the design of the research (Chapter 5), although it will usually be made explicit in your presentation of the findings and conclusions. The extent to which you are clear about the theory at the beginning of your research raises an important question concerning the design of your research project. This is often portrayed as two approaches based upon the reasoning you adopt: deductive or inductive. Deductive reasoning occurs when the conclusion is derived logically from a set of premises, the conclusion being true when all the premises are true (Ketokivi and Mantere 2010). For example, our research may concern likely online retail sales of a soon-to-be-launched new games console. We form three premises:

- that online retailers have been allocated limited stock of the new games consoles by the manufacturer;
- that customers' demand for the consoles exceeds supply;
- that online retailers allow customers to pre-order the consoles.

If these premises are true we can deduce that the conclusion that online retailers will have 'sold' their entire allocation of the new games consoles by the release day will also be true.

In contrast in inductive reasoning, there is a gap in the logic argument between the conclusion and the premises observed, the conclusion being 'judged' to be supported by the observations made (Ketokivi and Mantere 2010). Returning to our example of the likely online retail sales of a soon-to-be-launched new games console, we would start with observations about the forthcoming launch. Our observed premises would be:

- that news media are reporting that online retailers are complaining about only being allocated limited stock of the new games consoles by manufacturers;
- that news media are reporting that demand for the consoles will exceed supply;
- that online retailers are allowing customers to pre-order the consoles.

Based on these observations, we have good reason to believe online retailers will have 'sold' their entire allocation of the new games consoles by the release day. However, although our conclusion is supported by our observations, it is not guaranteed. In the past, manufacturers have launched new games consoles which have been commercial failures; how many of us remember Nintendo's 'Virtual Boy' (Snow 2007)?

There is also a third form of reasoning that is just as common in research, abductive reasoning, which begins with a 'surprising fact' being observed (Ketokivi and Mantere 2010). This surprising fact is the conclusion rather than a premise. Based on this conclusion, a set of possible premises is determined that is considered sufficient or nearly sufficient to explain the conclusion. It is reasoned that, if this set of premises was true, then the conclusion would be true as a matter of course. Because the set of premises are sufficient (or nearly sufficient) to generate the conclusion, this provides reason to believe that they are also true. Returning once again to our example of the likely online retail sales of a soon-to-be-launched new games console, a surprising fact (conclusion) might be that online retailers are reported in the news media as stating they will have no remaining stock of a new games console for sale on the day of its release. However, if the online retailers are allowing customers to pre-order the console prior to its release then it would not be surprising if these retailers had already sold their allocation of consoles. Therefore, using abductive reasoning, the possibility that online retailers have no remaining stock on the day of release is reasonable.

Building on these three forms of reasoning, if your research starts with theory, often developed from your reading of the academic literature, and you design a research strategy to test the theory, you are using a **deductive approach** (Table 4.3). Conversely,

Table 4.3 Deduction, induction and abduction: from reason to research

	Deduction	Induction	Abduction
Logic	In a deductive inference, when the premises are true, the conclusion must also be true	In an inductive inference, known premises are used to generate untested conclusions	In an abductive inference, known premises are used to generate testable conclusions
Generalisability	Generalising from the general to the specific	Generalising from the specific to the general	Generalising from the interactions between the specific and the general
Use of data	Data collection is used to evaluate propositions or hypotheses related to an existing theory	Data collection is used to explore a phenomenon, identify themes and patterns and create a conceptual framework	Data collection is used to explore a phenomenon, identify themes and patterns, locate these in a conceptual framework and test this through subsequent data collection and so forth
Theory	Theory falsification or verification	Theory generation and building	Theory generation or modification; incorporating existing theory where appropriate, to build new theory or modify existing theory

if your research starts by collecting data to explore a phenomenon and you generate or build theory (often in the form of a conceptual framework), then you are using an **inductive approach** (Table 4.3). Where you are collecting data to explore a phenomenon, identify themes and explain patterns, to generate a new or modify an existing theory which you subsequently test through additional data collection, you are using an **abductive approach** (Table 4.3).

The next three subsections of this chapter explore the differences and similarities between these three approaches and their implications for your research.

Deduction

As noted earlier, deduction owes much to what we would think of as scientific research. It involves the development of a theory that is then subjected to a rigorous test through a series of propositions. As such, it is the dominant research approach in the natural sciences, where laws present the basis of explanation, allow the anticipation of phenomena, predict their occurrence and therefore permit them to be controlled.

Blaikie (2010) lists six sequential steps through which a deductive research approach will progress:

1. Put forward a tentative idea, a premise, a hypothesis (a testable proposition about the relationship between two or more concepts or variables) or set of hypotheses to form a theory.
2. By using existing literature, or by specifying the conditions under which the theory are expected to hold, deduce a testable proposition or number of propositions.
3. Examine the premises and the logic of the argument that produced them, comparing this argument with existing theories to see if it offers an advance in understanding. If it does, then continue . . .;
4. Test the premises by collecting appropriate data to measure the concepts or variables and analysing it.
5. If the results of the analysis are not consistent with the premises (the tests fail!) the theory is false and must either be rejected, or modified and the process restarted.
6. If the results of the analysis are consistent with the premises then the theory is corroborated.

Deduction possesses several important characteristics. First, there is the search to explain causal relationships between concepts and variables. It may be that you wish to establish the reasons for high employee absenteeism in a retail store. After reading about absence patterns in the academic literature you develop a theory that there is a relationship between absence, the age of workers and length of service. Consequently, you develop a number of hypotheses including one which states that absenteeism is significantly more likely to be prevalent among younger workers and another which states that absenteeism is significantly more likely to be prevalent among workers who have been employed by the organisation for a relatively short period of time. To test this proposition you collect quantitative data. (This is not to say that a deductive approach may not use qualitative data.) It may be that there are important differences in the way work is arranged in different stores: therefore you would need to specify precisely the conditions under which your theory is likely to hold and collect appropriate data within these conditions. By doing this you would help to ensure that any change in absenteeism was a function of worker age and length of service rather than any other aspect of the store, for example the way in which people were managed. Your research would use a highly **structured methodology** to facilitate replication (Gill and Johnson 2010), an important issue to ensure reliability, as we shall emphasise in Section 5.8.

An additional important characteristic of deduction is that concepts need to be **operationalised** in a way that enables facts to be measured, often quantitatively. In our example, one variable that needs to be measured is absenteeism. Just what constitutes absenteeism would have to be strictly defined: an absence for a complete day would probably count, but what about absence for two hours? In addition, what would constitute a 'short period of employment' and 'younger' employees? What is happening here is that the principle of **reductionism** is being followed. This holds that problems as a whole are better understood if they are reduced to the simplest possible elements.

The final characteristic of deduction is **generalisation.** In order to be able to generalise it is necessary to select our sample carefully and for it to be of sufficient size (Section 7.2 and 7.3). In our example above, research at a particular store would allow us only to make inferences about that store; it would be dangerous to predict that worker youth and short length of service lead to absenteeism in all cases. This is discussed in more detail in Section 5.8

Induction

An alternative approach to conducting research on retail store employee absenteeism would be to start by interviewing a sample of the employees and their supervisors about the experience of working at the store. The purpose here would be to get a feel of what was going on, so as to understand better the nature of the problem. Your task then would be to make sense of the interview data you collected through your analysis. The result of this analysis would be the formulation of a theory, often expressed as a conceptual framework. This may be that there is a relationship between absence and the length of time a person has worked for the retail store. Alternatively, you may discover that there are other competing reasons for absence that may or may not be related to worker age or length of service. You may end up with the same theory, but you would have gone about the production of that theory using an inductive approach: theory would follow data rather than vice versa, as with deduction.

We noted earlier that deduction has its origins in research in the natural sciences. However, the emergence of the social sciences in the twentieth century led social science researchers to be wary of deduction. They were critical of an approach that enabled a cause–effect link to be made between particular variables without an understanding of the way in which humans interpreted their social world. Developing such an understanding is, of course, the strength of an inductive approach. In our absenteeism example, if you were adopting an inductive approach you would argue that it is more realistic to treat workers as humans whose attendance behaviour is a consequence of the way in which they perceive their work experience, rather than as if they were unthinking research objects who respond in a mechanistic way to certain circumstances.

Followers of induction would also criticise deduction because of its tendency to construct a rigid methodology that does not permit alternative explanations of what is going on. In that sense, there is an air of finality about the choice of theory and definition of the hypothesis. Alternative theories may be suggested by deduction. However, these would be within the limits set by the highly structured research design. In this respect, a significant characteristic of the absenteeism research design noted above is that of the operationalisation of concepts. As we saw in the absenteeism example, age was precisely defined. However, a less structured approach might reveal alternative explanations of the absenteeism–age relationship denied by a stricter definition of age.

Research using an inductive approach is likely to be particularly concerned with the context in which such events were taking place. Therefore, the study of a small sample of subjects might be more appropriate than a large number as with the deductive approach. As will be seen in Chapter 10, researchers in this tradition are more likely to work with

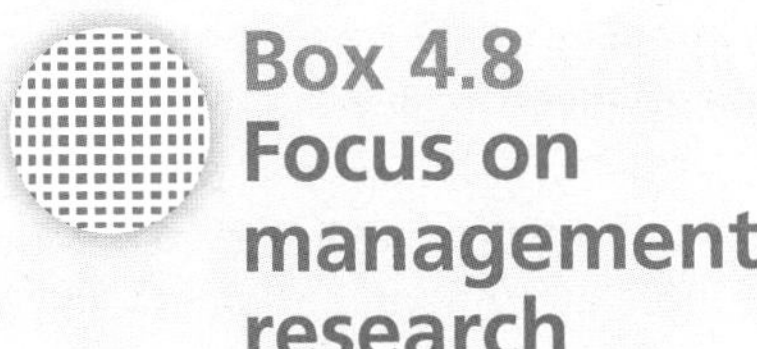

Box 4.8 Focus on management research

Using inductive research

In their paper entitled 'Sustainable entrepreneurship, is entrepreneurial will enough?' Spence, Gherib and Biwolé (2010) analyse 44 cases from Canada, Tunisia and Cameroon to determine the fundamentals of sustainable entrepreneurship in small and medium sized enterprises (SMEs). The overall objective of their research was to analyse and explain SMEs' practices by comparing and contrasting levels of sustainable entrepreneurship in these three countries. They argued that, because the concept of sustainable entrepreneurship was not well defined amongst SMEs in emerging and developing countries, an inductive approach would be most appropriate.

Data were collected using interviews, organisational documents provided by the owner-manager and by examining the SMEs' websites where available. Interviews lasted between one and two hours and were undertaken using a guide comprising of open questions designed to enable an understanding of each SME's level of sustainable entrepreneurship, as well as their business objectives. The questions allowed the interviewer to pursue topics such as the owner-manager's knowledge of sustainability issues, their personal beliefs and a detailed account of their firm's involvement in sustainability.

These data were used subsequently to induce qualitative indicators and develop a typology of sustainable development.

qualitative data and to use a variety of methods to collect these data in order to establish different views of phenomena (Easterby-Smith et al. 2008).

Abduction

Instead of moving from theory to data (as in deduction) or data to theory (as in induction) an abductive approach moves back and forth, in effect combining deduction and induction (Suddaby 2006). This, as we have noted earlier, matches what many business and management researchers actually do. Abduction begins with the observation of a 'surprising fact'; it then works out a plausible theory of how this could have occurred. Van Maanen et al. (2007) note that some plausible theories can account for what is observed better than others and it is these theories that will help uncover more 'surprising facts'. These surprises, they argue, can occur at any stage in the research process, including when writing your project report! Van Maanen et al. also stress that deduction and induction complement abduction as logics for testing plausible theories.

Applying an abductive approach to our research on the reasons for high employee absenteeism in a retail store would mean obtaining data that were sufficiently detailed and rich to allow us to explore the phenomenon and identify and explain themes and patterns regarding employee absenteeism. We would then try and integrate these explanations in an overall conceptual framework, thereby building up a theory of employee absenteeism in a retail store. This we would test using evidence provided by existing data and new data and revise as necessary.

At this stage you may be asking yourself: So what? Why is the choice that I make about my research approach important? Easterby-Smith et al. (2008) suggest three reasons. First, it enables you to take a more informed decision about your research design (Chapter 5), which is more than just the techniques by which data are collected and procedures by which they are analysed. It is the overall configuration of a piece of research involving questions about what kind of evidence is gathered and from where, and how such evidence is interpreted in order to provide good answers to your initial research question.

Second, it will help you to think about those research strategies and methodological choice that will work for you and, crucially, those that will not. For example, if you are particularly interested in understanding why something is happening, rather than being able to describe what is happening, it may be more appropriate to undertake your research inductively rather than deductively.

Third, Easterby-Smith et al. (2008) argue that knowledge of the different research traditions enables you to adapt your research design to cater for constraints. These may be practical, involving, say, limited access to data, or they may arise from a lack of prior knowledge of the subject. You simply may not be in a position to frame a hypothesis because you have insufficient understanding of the topic to do this.

Using research approaches in combination

So far when discussing induction and deduction we have conveyed the impression that there are rigid divisions between deduction and induction. This would be misleading. As we have seen in our discussion of abduction, is it possible to combine deduction and induction within the same piece of research. It is also, in our experience, often advantageous to do so although often one approach or another is dominant.

At this point you may be wondering whether your research will be predominantly deductive, inductive or abductive. The honest answer is, 'it depends'. In particular, it depends on the emphasis of the research (Box 4.9) and the nature of the research topic. A topic on which there is a wealth of literature from which you can define a theoretical framework and a hypothesis lends itself more readily to deduction. With research into a topic that is new, is exciting much debate and on which there is little existing literature, it may be more appropriate to work inductively by generating data and analysing and reflecting upon what theoretical themes the data are suggesting. Alternatively, a topic about which there is a wealth of information in one context but far less in the context in which you are researching may lend itself to an abductive approach enabling you to modify an existing theory.

The time you have available will be an issue. Deductive research can be quicker to complete, albeit that time must be devoted to setting up the study prior to data collection and analysis. Data collection is often based on 'one take'. It is normally possible to predict the time schedules accurately. On the other hand, abductive and, particularly, inductive research can be much more protracted. Often the ideas, based on a much longer period of data collection and analysis, have to emerge gradually. This leads to another important consideration, the extent to which you are prepared to indulge in risk. Deduction can be a lower-risk strategy, although there are risks, such as the non-return of questionnaires. With induction and abduction you have to live with the fear that no useful data patterns and theory will emerge. Finally, there is the question of audience. In our experience, most managers are familiar with deduction and much more likely to put faith in the conclusions emanating from this approach. You may also wish to consider the preferences of the person marking your research report. We all have our preferences about the approach to adopt. You may be wise to establish these before nailing your colours too firmly to one mast.

This last point suggests that not all the decisions about the research approach that you make should always be so practical. Hakim (2000) uses an architectural metaphor to illustrate the choice of approach. She introduces the notion of the researcher's preferred style, which, rather like the architect's, may reflect 'the architect's own preferences and ideas . . . and the stylistic preferences of those who pay for the work and have to live with

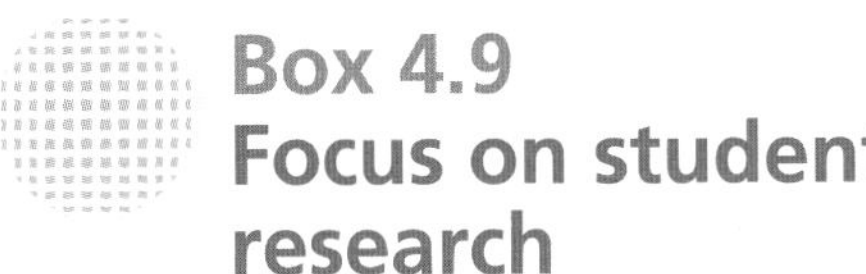

Box 4.9 Focus on student research

Deductive and inductive research

Sadie decided to conduct a research project on violence at work and its effects on the stress levels of staff. She considered the different ways she would approach the work were she to adopt:

- the deductive approach;
- the inductive approach;
- the abductive approach.

If she adopted a deductive approach to her work, she would have to:

1 start with the hypothesis that staff working directly with the public are more likely to experience the threat or reality of violence and resultant stress;
2 decide to research a population in which she would have expected to find evidence of violence, for example, a sizeable social security office;
3 administer a questionnaire to a large sample of staff in order to establish the extent of violence (either actually experienced or threatened) and the levels of stress experienced by them;
4 be particularly careful about how she defined violence;
5 standardise the stress responses of the staff, for example, days off sick or sessions with a counsellor.

If she adopted an inductive approach then she might have decided to interview some staff who had been subjected to violence at work. She might have been interested in their feelings about the events that they had experienced, how they coped with the problems they experienced, and their views about the possible causes of the violence.

If she adopted an abductive approach, she might have developed a conceptual model on the basis of her interview. She might then have used this model to develop a series of hypotheses and designed a questionnaire to collect data with which to test these hypotheses. Based on analyses of these data she might then have refined her conceptual model.

All approaches would have yielded valuable data about this problem (indeed, within this abductive approach, both inductive and deductive approaches were used at different stages). No approach should be thought of as better than the others. They are better at different things. It depends where her research emphasis lies.

the final result' (Hakim 2000: 1). This echoes the feelings of Buchanan et al. (1988: 59), who argue that 'needs, interests and preferences (of the researcher) . . . are typically overlooked but are central to the progress of fieldwork'. However, a note of caution: it is important that your preferences do not lead to you changing the essence of the research question, particularly if it has been given to you by an organisation as a consultancy project.

4.4 Summary

- The term research philosophy relates to the development of knowledge and the nature of that knowledge.
- Your research philosophy contains important assumptions about the way in which you view the world.
- There are three major ways of thinking about research philosophy: epistemology, ontology and axiology. Each contains important differences which will influence the way in which you think about the research process.
- Pragmatism holds that the most important determinant of the epistemology, ontology and axiology adopted is the research question.

- Ontology is a branch of philosophy which is concerned with the nature of social phenomena as entities.
- Objectivism is the ontological position which holds that social entities exist in reality external to social actors whereas the subjectivist view is that social phenomena are created through the perceptions and consequent actions of social actors.
- Epistemology concerns what constitutes acceptable knowledge in a field of study.
- Positivism relates to the philosophical stance of the natural scientist. This entails working with an observable social reality and the end product can be law-like generalisations similar to those in the physical and natural sciences.
- The essence of realism is that what the senses show us is reality, is the truth: that objects have an existence independent of the human mind.
- Interpretivism is an epistemology that advocates that it is necessary for the researcher to understand the differences between humans in our role as social actors.
- Axiology is a branch of philosophy that studies judgements about values.
- Social science paradigms can be used in management and business research to generate fresh insights into real-life issues and problems. The four paradigms explained in the chapter are: functionalist; interpretive; radical humanist; and radical structuralist.
- There are three main research approaches: deduction, induction and abduction. With deduction, a theory and hypothesis (or hypotheses) are developed and a research strategy designed to test the hypothesis. With induction, data are collected and a theory developed as a result of the data analysis. With abduction, data are used to explore a phenomenon, identify themes and explain patterns, to generate a new or modify an existing theory which is subsequently tested, often through additional data collection.

Self-check questions

Help with these questions is available at the end of the chapter.

4.1 You have decided to undertake a project and have defined the main research question as 'What are the opinions of consumers to a 10 per cent reduction in weight, with the price remaining the same, of "Snackers" chocolate bars?' Write a hypothesis that you could test in your project.

4.2 Why may it be argued that the concept of the manager is socially constructed rather than 'real'?

4.3 Why are the radical paradigms relevant in business and management research given that most managers would say that the purpose of organisational investigation is to develop recommendations for action to solve problems without radical change?

4.4 You have chosen to undertake your research project following a deductive approach. What factors may cause you to work inductively, although working deductively is your preferred choice?

Review and discussion questions

4.6 Visit an online database or your university library and obtain a copy of a research-based refereed journal article that you think will be of use to an assignment you are currently working on. Read this article carefully. What research philosophy do you think the author has adopted? Use Section 4.2 to help you develop a clear justification for your answer.

4.7 Think about the last assignment you undertook for your course. In undertaking this assignment, were you predominantly inductive or deductive? Discuss your thoughts with a friend who also undertook this assignment.

4.8 Agree with a friend to watch the same television documentary.
- **a** To what extent is the documentary inductive, deductive or abductive in its use of data?
- **b** Have the documentary makers adopted a positivist, realist, interpretivist or pragmatist philosophy?
- **c** Do not forget to make notes regarding your reasons for your answers to each of these questions and to discuss your answers with your friend.

Progressing your research project

Diagnose your research philosophy

Place indicate your agreement or disagreement with each of these statements. There are no wrong answers.

		Strongly	Agree	Agree slightly	Slightly	Disagree	Disagree strongly
1	For the topic being researched there is one single reality, the task of the researcher is to discover it	❑	❑	❑	❑	❑	❑
2	The reality of the topic being researched exists separately from the researcher	❑	❑	❑	❑	❑	❑
3	Management research is value laden	❑	❑	❑	❑	❑	❑
4	A researcher cannot be separated from what is being researched and so will inevitably be subjective	❑	❑	❑	❑	❑	❑
5	A variety of data collection techniques should be used in research, both quantitative and qualitative	❑	❑	❑	❑	❑	❑
6	The reality of what is being researched exists independently of people's thoughts, beliefs and knowledge of their existence	❑	❑	❑	❑	❑	❑
7	Researchers must remain objective and independent from the phenomena they are studying, ensuring that their own values do not impact on data interpretation	❑	❑	❑	❑	❑	❑
8	Management research should be practical and applied	❑	❑	❑	❑	❑	❑
9	Management research should integrate different perspectives to help interpret the data	❑	❑	❑	❑	❑	❑
10	Management researchers need to employ methods that allow in-depth exploration of the details behind a phenomenon	❑	❑	❑	❑	❑	❑

Now discuss your answers with your colleagues. To guide your discussion you need to think about:

1. What do you consider to be the nature of reality? Why?
2. To what extent do your own values influence your research?Why?
3. What is your relationship with what you research? Why?

Don't forget to also use the questions in Box 1.4 to guide your reflective diary entry.
Developed with help from Judith Thomas and Joanne Duberley.

References

Bhaskar, R. (1989) *Reclaiming Reality: A Critical Introduction to Contemporary Philosophy*. London: Verso.

Blaikie, N. (2010) *Designing Social Research* (2nd edn). Cambridge: Polity.

Buchanan, D., Boddy, D. and McAlman, J. (1988) 'Getting in, getting on, getting out and getting back', in A. Bryman (ed.) *Doing Research in Organisations*. London: Routledge, pp. 53–67.

Burrell, G. and Morgan, G. (1982) *Sociological Paradigms and Organisational Analysis*. London: Heinemann.

Crotty, M. (1998) *The Foundations of Social Research.* London: Sage.

Dobson, P. (2002) 'Critical realism and information systems research: Why bother with philosophy?', *Information Research*, Vol. 7, No. 2. Available at http://informationr.net/ir/7-2/paper124.html [Accessed 11 July 2011].

Dyer, O. (2003) 'Lancet accuses AstraZeneca of sponsoring biased research', *British Medical Journal*, Vol. 327, No. 1, p. 1005.

Easterby-Smith, M., Thorpe, R., Jackson, P. and Lowe, A. (2008) *Management Research* (3rd edn). Sage: London.

Gill, J. and Johnson, P. (2010) *Research Methods for Managers* (4th edn). London: Sage.

Hakim, C. (2000) *Research Design: Successful Designs for Social and Economic Research* (2nd edn). London: Routledge.

Heron, J. (1996) *Co-operative Inquiry: Research into the Human Condition*. London: Sage.

Johnson, P. and Clark, M. (2006) 'Editors' introduction: Mapping the terrain: An overview of business and management research methodologies', in P. Johnson and M. Clark (eds) *Business and Management Research Methodologies.* London: Sage, pp. xxv–lv.

Kelemen, M. and Rumens, N. (2008) *An Introduction to Critical Management Research.* London: Sage.

Ketokivi, M. and Mantere, S. (2010) 'Two strategies for inductive reasoning in organizational research', *Academy of Management Review*, Vol. 35, No. 2, pp. 315–33.

Millmore, M., Lewis, P., Saunders, M., Thornhill, A. and Morrow, T. (2007) *Strategic Human Resource Management*. Harlow: FT Prentice Hall.

Niglas, K. (2010) 'The multidimensional model of research methodology: An integrated set of continua', in A. Tashakkori and C. Teddlie (eds) *The Sage Handbook of Mixed Methods in Social and Behavioural Research*. Thousand Oaks, CA: Sage, pp. 215–36.

Snow, B (2007) *The ten worst-selling games consoles of all time*. Available at www.gamepro.com/article/features/111822/the-10-worst-selling-consoles-of-all-time/ [Accessed 15 July 2011].

Spence, M., Gherib, J.B.B. and Biwolé, V.O. (2011) 'Sustainable development: Is entrepreneurial will enough?', *Journal of Business Ethics,* Vol. 99, No. 3, pp. 335–67.

Suddaby, R. (2006) 'What grounded theory is not', *Academy of Management Journal,* Vol. 49, No. 4, pp. 633–43.

Van Maanen, J., Sørensen, J.B. and Mitchell, T.R. (2007) 'The interplay between theory and method', *Academy of Management Review*, Vol. 32, No. 4, pp. 1145–54.

Watson, T. (2011) 'Ethnography, reality and truth: The vital need for studies of "how things work" in organizations and management', *Journal of Management Studies*, Vol. 48, No. 1, pp. 202–17.

Further reading

Burrell, G. and Morgan, G. (1982) *Sociological Paradigms and Organisational Analysis*. London: Heinemann. This is an excellent book on paradigms which goes into far more detail than space has allowed in this chapter.

Hatch, M.J. and Yanow, D. (2008) 'Methodology by metaphor: Ways of seeing in painting and research', *Organization Studies*, Vol. 29, No. 1, pp. 23–44. A really enjoyable paper which uses the metaphor of paintings by Rembrandt and Pollock to explain differences between realism and interpretivism.

Kelemen, M. and Rumens, N. (2008) *An Introduction to Critical Management Research*. London: Sage. This contains an excellent chapter on pragmatism as well as going into considerable detail on other theoretical perspectives not covered in this chapter including postmodernism, feminism and queer theory.

Kvale, S. and Brinkmann, S. (2009) *InterViews*. Los Angeles, CA: Sage. Chapter 3 provides an accessible discussion of the epistemological issues associated with interviewing.

Case 4
Organisational learning in an English regional theatre

The sound of her pen tapping the desk brought Zoe out of her thoughts and back into the room. She had been musing over the questions that surrounded her research project and whether she would adopt an inductive or deductive approach. She had been warned by her supervisor that finalising her research question might take several attempts and that it would probably have to be reworked a few times as she gained a better understanding of the implications of her research philosophy and formulated her research design.

Source: Schutterstock/F. Chi

Zoe works for a small UK-based training and development consultancy which specialises in the not-for-profit sector and has built a particular niche for itself in working within the cultural industries – museums, galleries, libraries, theatres and so on. She often works with small arts organisations helping them identify and address their learning and development needs. She is used to doing one-to-one development interviews and helping people create their own action plans. She knows this is a sector which does not favour traditional training and has few resources to dedicate to formal training and development programmes. There are 74,640 organisations in the sector, 87 per cent of which employ fewer than 10 people (Creative & Cultural Skills 2008).

She is currently negotiating with one of their larger clients, TheatreCo, an English regional theatre, to undertake her master's degree research project with them. They have recently been through a change process and are working on a new production, which is set in the 'round' (that is, the audience completely surrounds the stage area). This is something they have never attempted before. The theatre has two auditoria, one of 400 seats and one of 150 seats. It shows a mixture of work, some produced in-house and some toured in from other companies. It has a staff complement of 200 people on a mixture of full-time, part-time and casual contracts. Most staff are graduates and are working there because of a passion for the arts and theatre in particular. It receives over half of its income from Arts Council England (the state body responsible for arts funding in England), some funding from the local authority and the rest from its trading activities.

As Zoe sat in on a production meeting the previous week she heard stories of previous productions. She heard a discussion about how to make the new production a multi-sensory event (how the audience might see, hear, smell and feel the production), and witnessed concerns regarding how they would manage it with people contemplating the impact it would have on their particular departments. The Chief Executive, Emma Davis, had talked to Zoe about her interest in how best to develop her team as a whole and that she was keen on Zoe's proposal to look at how people experienced learning across the organisation. Recognising they had recently been through some big challenges, Emma wondered how they might do things better in future. She was also eager to instil an approach that allowed people to work more actively across departments rather than staying in what she described as 'their comfort silos'. This had given Zoe an initial research question: 'how do people in an arts organisation experience learning and how might this be done better in the future?' She recognised this needed further refining, but at least it was a start.

Zoe had studied theatre at university but had found her way subsequently into the training and development field. She had been working in this field for eight years and had decided to go back to university to build her knowledge of management. Initially, she had thought that the research project would be a relatively straightforward proposition; she would do a few interviews, analyse trends and identify some strengths and weaknesses. However, in her heart Zoe knew that would never satisfy her need to understand more about the social world that existed in the theatre and her belief that the way the staff interacted with each other shaped their experiences and understandings. Her conversations with Emma also kept nagging away at her.

Emma had said she was interested in the organisation's culture, the experiences of her staff and she had talked about the need to understand better how they did what they did. She was not interested too much in why things were happening but more about getting a better awareness of what was actually happening. This suggested to Zoe that a positivist philosophy and testing specific hypotheses was unlikely to capture the experiences and feelings that Emma seemed concerned with.

Zoe had been to the theatre on several occasions and she recognised that it was a complex environment. She had seen how the staff members interacted and believed that something important happened amongst the team during the artistic process, although she could not specify what it was at this point. She was not convinced that a questionnaire to employees would deliver the depth of awareness and meaning that Emma was looking for. She was also aware that the people she met at the theatre were keen to tell their stories – stories that clearly had meaning for the different staff members – and these were most likely to be picked up by qualitative methods. Zoe felt this was important as she believed the rich insights these could give her would help her interpret what was happening. Zoe was concerned that her project tutor might not feel this was a valid area of research but was heartened by some recent reading she had been doing on storytelling in organisations (Boje 1991; Gabriel 2000). This suggested 'that a good story itself is theoretical . . . When people tell their stories, they employ analytic techniques to interpret their worlds' (Ellis 2004: 196).

Zoe had worked with the TheatreCo before and was worried that if she worked within an interpretive paradigm her research project might be judged as subjective and biased. She knew other students in her study group were working within a functionalist paradigm but she instinctively felt her project needed something different. Zoe took her concerns back to her project tutor and described how she felt that a positivist philosophy, and adopting a functionalist paradigm and using quantitative methods, was unlikely to take account of the theatre's complexity or address what she thought the Chief Executive was looking for. She had read a bit about using ethnography to gain an in-depth understanding of culture but was not sure how she would draw any useful conclusions from such an apparently open and in-depth approach. Her project tutor agreed that ethnography would allow her to study people in their own environment, as it is concerned with taking a 'cultural perspective' (Patton 2002: 84), but reminded Zoe that she needed to focus on keeping her research project manageable and to make sure she answered her question. She also asked Zoe whether she was intending to adopt an inductive or a deductive approach.

References

Boje, D.M. (1991) 'The storytelling organization: A study of story performance in an office-supply firm', *Administrative Science Quarterly,* Vol. 36, No. 1, pp. 106–126.

Creative & Cultural Skills (2008) *Creative and cultural industry impact and footprint, 2008–9*. Available at www.ccskills.org.uk/Research/Industryresearch/tabid/832/Default.aspx [Accessed 31 January 2011].

Ellis, C. (2004) *The Ethnographic I: A Methodological Novel About Autoethnography*. Walnut Creek, CA: Altamira Press.

Gabriel, Y. (2000) *Storytelling in Organizations: Facts, Fictions, and Fantasies.* Oxford: Oxford University Press.

Patton, M.Q. (2002). *Qualitative Research and Evaluation Methods* (3rd edn). London: Sage Publications.

Questions

1 Why is it important for Zoe to be aware of her values and beliefs as an individual researcher?
2 Why should Zoe have been concerned about her previous relationship with the Theatre she was researching?
3 How might Zoe's interpretivist philosophy and approach impact on how she frames her research question?

Additional case studies relating to material covered in this chapter are available via this book's companion website: **www.pearsoned.co.uk/saunders**. They are:

- Marketing music products alongside emerging digital music channels.
- Consultancy research for a not-for-profit organisation.

Self-check answers

4.1 Probably the most realistic hypothesis here would be 'consumers of "Snackers" chocolate bars did not notice the difference between the current bar and its reduced weight successor'. Doubtless that is what the Snackers' manufacturer would want confirmed!

4.2 Although you can see and touch a manager, you are only seeing and touching another human being. The point is that the role of the manager is a socially constructed concept. What a manager is will differ between different national and organisational cultures and will differ over time. Indeed, the concept of the manager as we generally understand it is a relatively recent human invention, arriving at the same time as the formal organisation in the past couple of hundred years.

4.3 The researcher working in the radical humanist or structuralist paradigms may argue that it is predictable that managers would say that the purpose of organisational investigation is to develop recommendations for action to solve problems without radical change because radical change may involve changing managers! Radicalism implies-root-and-branch investigation and possible change and most of us prefer 'fine-tuning' within the framework of what exists already, particularly if change threatens our vested interests.

4.4 The question implies an either/or choice. But as you work through this chapter and, in particular, the next on deciding your research design, you will see that life is rarely so clear-cut! Perhaps the main factor that would cause you to review the appropriateness of the deductive approach would be that the data you collected might suggest an important hypothesis, which you did not envisage when you framed your research objectives and hypotheses. This may entail going further with the data collection, perhaps by engaging in some qualitative work, which would yield further data to answer the new hypothesis.

Get ahead using resources on the companion website at: **www.pearsoned.co.uk/saunders**

- Improve your IBM SPSS Statistics and NVivo research analysis with practice tutorials.
- Save time researching on the Internet with the Smarter Online Searching Guide.
- Test your progress using self-assessment questions.
- Follow live links to useful websites.

Chapter 5

Formulating the research design

Learning outcomes

By the end of this chapter you should be able to:

- understand the importance of your decisions when designing research and the need to achieve methodological coherence throughout your own research design;
- explain the differences between quantitative, qualitative and multiple methods research designs and choose between these to design your own research;
- explain the differences between exploratory, descriptive and explanatory research to understand the nature of your own research;
- identify the main research strategies and choose from amongst these to achieve coherence throughout your research design;
- consider the implications of the time frames required for different research designs when designing your own research;
- consider some of the main ethical issues implied by your research design;
- identify some of the issues that affect the quality of research and consider these when designing your own research;
- consider the constraints of your role as researcher when designing your own research.

5.1 Introduction

In Chapter 4 we introduced the research onion as a way of depicting the issues underlying your choice of data collection method or methods and peeled away the outer two layers – research philosophies and research approaches. In this chapter we uncover the next three layers: methodological choice, research strategy or strategies and choosing the time horizon for your research. As we saw in Chapter 4, the way you answer your research question will be influenced by your research philosophy and approach to theory. Your research philosophy and research approach, whether this is deliberate or by default, will subsequently influence your selections shown in the next three layers of the research onion. These three layers can be thought of as focusing on the process of research design, which is the way you turn your research question into a

research project. The key to these selections will be to achieve coherence all the way through your research design.

5.2 Choice and coherence in research design

Your **research design** is the general plan of how you will go about answering your research question(s) (the importance of clearly defining the research question cannot be overemphasised). It will contain clear objectives derived from your research question(s), specify the sources from which you intend to collect data, how you propose to collect and analyse these, discuss ethical issues and the constraints you will inevitably encounter (e.g. access to data,

Ridenour and Newman (2008) stress the importance of coherence in research design and represent the research process as an interactive continuum. The cover shots of recent editions of this book have indicated that the research process is like a journey – a journey along a road with you as the driver of the vehicle (two wheels or four, whichever you prefer!). Like many such journeys, there is generally a choice of roads to travel along. When you are thinking about setting out on a new journey of some distance, you will probably find a road map and look at the options to get to your destination. A number of factors may influence your decision about which route to take, including speed, time, cost and your preference between taking the shortest route or staying on the motorway network and main roads. The route you plan is likely to be as coherent as you can work out from the map in front of you given your travel criteria. As you actually undertake your journey you will find yourself interacting with the reality of your planned route. Some parts of the journey will go according to plan; other parts may not and you may need to alter your route. You may change your route because a better option presents itself as you travel along. In many ways, designing research is like planning a journey. Formulating the most appropriate way to address your research question is similar to planning the route to your destination, your research objectives are a little like your planning criteria, the need for coherence is the same in each situation and the journey itself, like the research process, will necessarily prove to be an interactive experience.

Looking at a possible route from the top of St Paul's Cathedral, London!
Source: © Jan Thornhill 2011

time, location and money). Crucially, it should demonstrate that you have thought through the elements of your particular research design. The first methodological choice below is related to whether you follow a single quantitative or qualitative (mono method) or multiple methods research design. Each of these options is likely to call for a different set of elements to achieve coherence in your research design. We return to consider what this involves in Section 5.3. The nature of your research project will also be either exploratory, descriptive, explanatory or a combination of these, and we discuss the role of these in your research design in Section 5.4. Within your research design you will need to use one or more research strategies, to ensure coherence within your research project. We discuss research strategies, their fit to research philosophy and to quantitative, qualitative or multiple methods research methodologies in Section 5.5. Your methodological choice and related strategies will also influence the selection of an appropriate time horizon, and we consider this in Section 5.6. Each research design will lead to potential ethical concerns and it will be important to consider these, in order to minimise or overcome them. We briefly consider ethical issues related to research designs in Section 5.7 before discussing these in greater detail in Sections 6.5 and 6.6. It is also important to establish the quality of your research design, and we discuss the ways in which this may be considered in Section 5.8. Finally, we recognise that practical constraints will affect research design, especially the nature of your own role as researcher, and briefly consider this in Section 5.9.

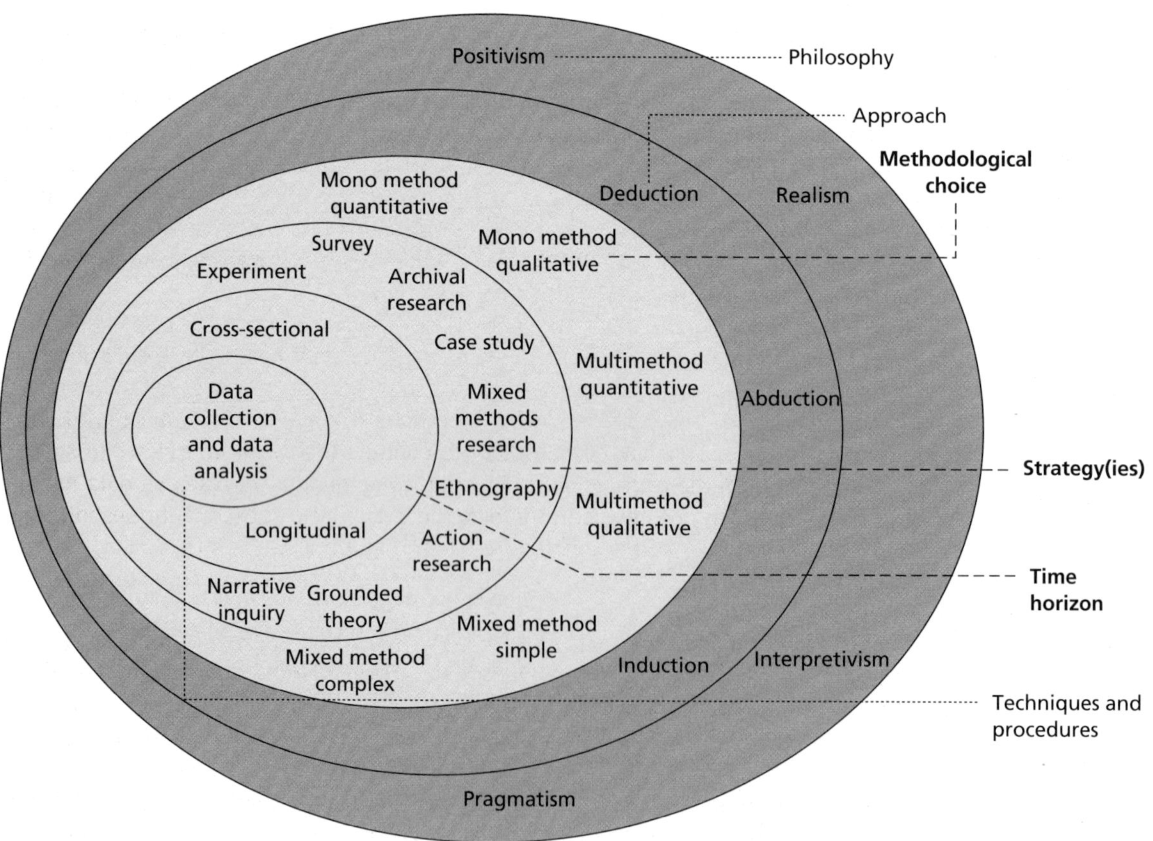

Figure 5.1 The research 'onion'

Source: © Mark Saunders, Philip Lewis and Adrian Thornhill 2011

These aspects of your research design are vital to understand what you wish to achieve and how you intend to do so, even if your design changes subsequently. You are likely to be assessed at this stage of your research project. For example, some universities award a percentage of the overall marks available for undergraduate and postgraduate research projects to the research design. Others will not allow you to proceed without a satisfactory research design. You therefore need to have a clear design with valid reasons for each of your research design decisions. Your justification for each element should be based on the nature of your research question(s) and objectives, show consistency with your research philosophy and demonstrate coherence across your research design.

At this point we make a distinction between design and tactics. Design is concerned with the overall plan for your research; tactics are about the finer details of data collection and analysis – the centre of the research onion. Decisions about tactics will involve you being clear about the different quantitative and qualitative data collection techniques (e.g. questionnaires, interviews, focus groups and secondary data) and subsequent quantitative and qualitative data analysis procedures, which are dealt with in later chapters. We first outline the nature of quantitative and qualitative research and how these may be combined, to help you to choose and plan your research direction.

5.3 Choosing a quantitative, qualitative or multiple methods research design

One way of differentiating quantitative research from qualitative research is to distinguish between numeric data (numbers) and non-numeric data (words, images, video clips and other similar material). In this way, 'quantitative' is often used as a synonym for any data collection technique (such as a questionnaire) or data analysis procedure (such as graphs or statistics) that generates or uses numerical data. In contrast, 'qualitative' is often used as a synonym for any data collection technique (such as an interview) or data analysis procedure (such as categorising data) that generates or uses non-numerical data. This is an important way to differentiate this methodological choice; however, this distinction is both problematic and narrow.

It is problematic because, in reality, many business and management research designs are likely to combine quantitative and qualitative elements. This may be for a number of reasons. For example, a research design may use a questionnaire but it may be necessary to ask respondents to answer some 'open' questions in their words rather than ticking the appropriate box, or it may be necessary to conduct follow-up interviews to seek to explain findings from the questionnaire. Equally, some qualitative research data may be analysed quantitatively, or be used to inform the design of a subsequent questionnaire. In this way, quantitative and qualitative research may be viewed as two ends of a continuum, which in practice are often mixed. A research design may therefore combine methods in a number of ways, which we discuss later.

The distinction drawn earlier between quantitative research and qualitative research is also narrow. The purpose of Chapter 4 was to ask you to consider your research question through a philosophical lens. Given the way in which your philosophical assumptions inform your methodological choice, the initial distinction drawn earlier between numeric and non-numeric data appears insufficient for the purpose of designing research. From this broader perspective, we can reinterpret quantitative and qualitative methodologies through their associations to philosophical assumptions and also to research approaches and strategies. This will help you to decide how you might use these in a coherent way to address your research question. We now briefly outline some of these key associations.

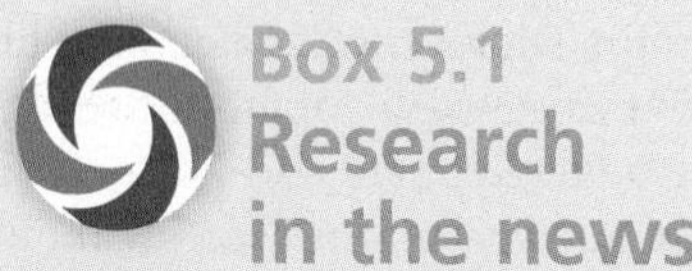

Comparing types of quantitative data

The 'Our Rivers campaign' is a coalition of a number of non-governmental organisations including the World Wildlife Fund, Royal Society for the Protection of Birds and the Angling Trust, concerned with the health of rivers. Part of its campaign involved a public opinion poll on the best or worst rivers in England and Wales in 2010. Respondents in this online survey voted the River Wye as the 'Best River', with the River Thames in second place, followed by the River Dart in third. The river voted the 'Worst River' was the River Thames, with the River Kennet and River Mersey in second and third places. Respondents were asked to give reasons for voting for the best and worst rivers. Pollution and sewage were the highest reasons for voting for a river as the 'worst'. A place to relax and wildlife were the highest reasons for voting for a river as the 'best'.

We may ask ourselves, 'how could the River Thames be voted the worst and the second best?' When the 'Our Rivers campaign' released the results of this public opinion poll, they also included data from the Government's Environment Agency, which show that '13 of the 14 sections of the main Thames river are below the required European standard, with high levels of phosphate and low numbers of fish being the two main reasons for failure.' Moreover, they also reported that 'only 3 of the 10 sections of the River Wye are achieving the European target status of "Good"', with data from the Environment Agency showing 'that agricultural diffuse pollution is the main problem on The Wye' (Our Rivers Campaign 2010).

These different sources of data on the same issue show important distinctions between types of quantitative data – one measured from subjective opinions, the other by objective criteria. Both types of data are valuable but neither should be used indiscriminately. We need to recognise the nature of a particular source of data to be able to use it appropriately.

Quantitative research design

Research philosophy

Quantitative research is generally associated with positivism, especially when used with predetermined and highly structured data collection techniques. However, a distinction needs to be drawn between data about the attributes of people, organisations or other things and data based on opinions, sometimes referred to as 'qualitative' numbers (Box 5.1). In this way, some survey research, whilst conducted quantitatively, may be seen to fit partly within an interpretivist philosophy. Quantitative research may also be used within the realist and pragmatist philosophies (see 'Multiple methods research design' later).

Research approach

Quantitative research is usually associated with a deductive approach, where the focus is on using data to test theory. However, it may also incorporate an inductive approach, where data are used to develop theory.

Characteristics

Quantitative research examines relationships between variables, which are measured numerically and analysed using a range of statistical techniques. It often incorporates controls to ensure the validity of data, as in an experimental design. Because data are collected in a standard manner, it is important to ensure that questions are expressed clearly so they are understood in the same way. This methodology often uses probability sampling techniques to ensure generalisability. The researcher is seen as independent from those being researched, who are usually called respondents.

Research strategies

Quantitative research is principally associated with experimental and survey research strategies, which we discuss in Section 5.5. In quantitative research, a survey research strategy is normally conducted through the use of questionnaires or structured interviews or, possibly, structured observation. Techniques associated with the use of these particular methods are considered in Chapters 9, 11 and 12.

Qualitative research design

Research philosophy

Qualitative research is associated with an interpretive philosophy (Denzin and Lincoln 2005). It is interpretive because researchers need to make sense of the subjective and socially constructed meanings expressed about the phenomenon being studied. Such research is sometimes referred to as naturalistic since researchers need to operate within a natural setting, or research context, in order to establish trust, participation, access to meanings and in-depth understanding. Like quantitative research, qualitative research may also be used within realist and pragmatist philosophies (see 'Multiple methods research design' later).

Research approach

Many varieties of qualitative research commence with an inductive approach, where a naturalistic and emergent research design is used to develop a richer theoretical perspective than already exists in the literature. However, some qualitative research strategies start with a deductive approach, to test an existing theoretical perspective using qualitative procedures (Yin 2009). In practice, much qualitative research uses an abductive approach, where inductive inferences are developed and deductive ones are tested iteratively throughout the research (Section 4.3).

Characteristics

Qualitative research studies participants' meanings and the relationships between them, using a variety of data collection techniques and analytical procedures, to develop a conceptual framework. Data collection is non-standardised so that questions and procedures may alter and emerge during a research process that is both naturalistic and interactive. It is likely to use non-probability sampling techniques. The success of the researcher's role is dependent not only on gaining physical access to participants but also building rapport and demonstrating sensitivity to gain cognitive access to their data.

Research strategies

Qualitative research is associated with a variety of strategies. Whilst these share ontological and epistemological roots and common characteristics, each strategy has a specific emphasis and scope as well as a particular set of procedures. Some of the principal strategies used with qualitative research are: action research, case study research, ethnography,

Grounded Theory and narrative research. These are discussed in Section 5.5. Some of these strategies can also be used in a quantitative research design such as a case study strategy, or used in a multiple methods research design as we now discuss. Techniques associated with the use of particular methods are considered in Chapters 9, 10 and 13.

Multiple methods research design

Research philosophy

We consider two philosophical positions that often lead to multiple methods research designs. In Section 4.2 we discussed the philosophical position of realism and in particular that of the critical realists. They believe that whilst there is an external, objective reality to the world in which we live, the way in which each of us interprets and understands it will be affected by our particular social conditioning. To accommodate this realist ontology and interpretivist epistemology (Tashakkori and Teddlie 2010), researchers may, for example, use quantitative analysis of officially published data followed by qualitative research methods to explore perceptions.

Pragmatism may also be likely to lead to a multiple methods research design. Pragmatists are not wedded to either positivism or interpretivism, which they see as a 'dualism', or theory of opposing concepts. They view this dichotomy as unhelpful and choose instead to see these philosophical positions as either end of a continuum, allowing a choice of whichever position or mixture of positions will help them to undertake their research (Tashakkori and Teddlie, 2010). For pragmatists, the nature of the research question, the research context and likely research consequences are driving forces determining the most appropriate methodological choice (Nastasi et al. 2010). Both quantitative and qualitative research are valued by pragmatists and the exact choice will be contingent on the particular nature of the research.

Research approach

A multiple methods research design may use either a deductive or inductive approach and is likely to combine both. For example, quantitative or qualitative research may be used to test a theoretical proposition or propositions, followed by further quantitative or qualitative research to develop a richer theoretical perspective. A theoretical perspective may also be used to provide some direction for the research. In this way a particular theory may be used to provide a focus for the research and to limit its scope (Tashakkori and Teddlie 2010).

Characteristics

An increasing number of variants of a multiple methods research design have recently been developed (e.g. Tashakkori and Teddlie 2010), and it is helpful to outline these in order to be able to consider their characteristics. Figure 5.2 shows the basic choice between using the single data collection technique and corresponding analytical procedure already discussed (either a quantitative or qualitative research design) known as a **mono method** and using more than one data collection technique and analytical procedure to answer your research question, known as **multiple methods**. This latter option is increasingly advocated within business and management research (Bryman 2006) because it is likely to overcome weaknesses associated with using only one method as well as providing scope for a richer approach to data collection, analysis and interpretation.

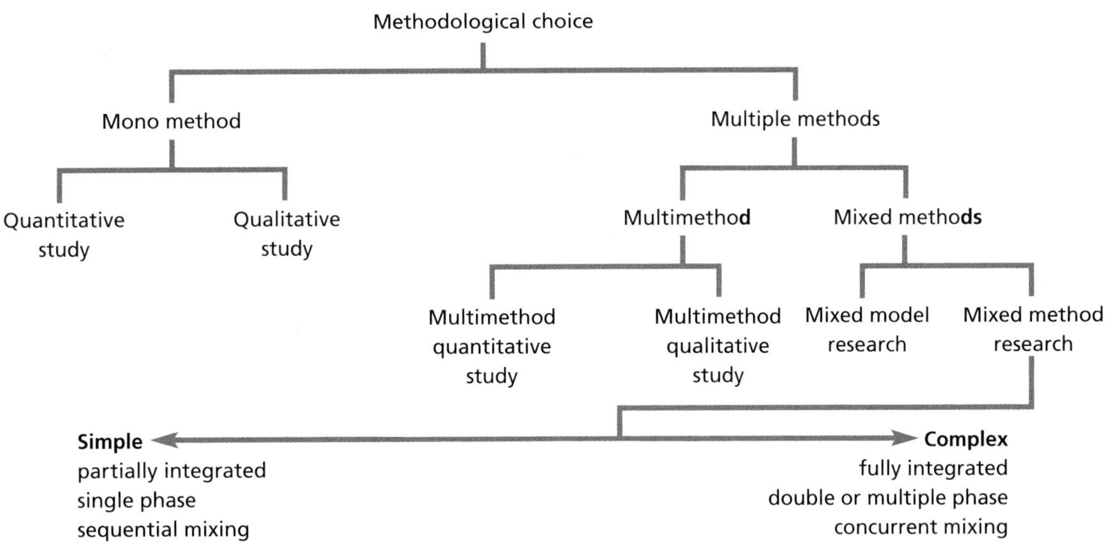

Figure 5.2 Methodological choice

Source: © Mark Saunders, Philip Lewis and Adrian Thornhill 2011

Multiple methods are in turn divided between multimethod research and mixed methods research (Figure 5.2). In **multimethod research** more than one data collection technique is used with associated analysis procedures, but this is restricted within either a quantitative or qualitative design (Tashakkori and Teddlie 2010). So you might choose to collect quantitative data using, for example, both questionnaires and structured observation, analysing these data using statistical (quantitative) procedures, known as a **multimethod quantitative study**. Alternatively, you might choose to collect qualitative data using, for example, in-depth interviews and diary accounts and analyse these data using qualitative procedures, known as a **multimethod qualitative study** (Box 5.2). Therefore, if you adopted multimethod research you would not mix quantitative and qualitative research.

Box 5.2 Focus on student research

Multimethod qualitative study

Harry wanted to establish how new supervisors learned to do their job. In order to do this he thought it essential that he should have the clearest possible grasp of what the supervisor's job entailed.

This involved him in:

- shadowing a new supervisor for a week (qualitative data);
- interviewing a day and a night shift supervisor to establish any differences in approach (qualitative data);
- interviewing the managers to whom these two supervisors reported (qualitative data).

This gave Harry a much better grasp of the content of the supervisor's job. It also did much to enhance his credibility in the eyes of the supervisors. He was then able to draw on the valuable data he had collected to complete his main research task: interviewing new supervisors to discover how they learned to do the job. This provided further qualitative data.

In **mixed methods research** both quantitative and qualitative research are combined in a research design. These may be combined in a variety of ways that range from simple, convergent forms to complex, fully integrated forms (Figure 5.2). The ways in which quantitative and qualitative research may be combined, as well as the extent to which this may occur, has led to the identification of a number of dimensions or characteristics of mixed methods research (Creswell and Plano Clark 2007; Nastasi et al. 2010) (Figure 5.2). We now consider each of these.

Stage of the research process at which mixing occurs and level of integration

In Chapter 1 we highlighted how the research process is composed of a number of stages, summarised as conceptualisation (including conceiving the research question, recognising the philosophical position, determining the approach and formulating the design), implementation (sampling, data collection and data analysis), interpretation and outcomes. During the implementation stages, mixing of quantitative and qualitative methodologies may occur at each stage, or at only one stage or at particular stages, such as during data collection but not in terms of choice of data analysis techniques. Use of both methodologies at every stage, including during the interpretation and presentation of the research, indicates **fully integrated mixed methods research**, whilst use of both at only one stage or at particular stages indicates **partially integrated mixed methods research** (Leech and Onwuegbuzie 2009; Nastasi et al. 2010; Ridenour and Newman 2008; Teddlie and Tashakkori 2009).

Questions about *when* qualitative and quantitative methods may be used in mixed methods research lead to a further question about *how* they are mixed, or integrated. The level of integration of these two methodologies may vary considerably. For example, both qualitative and quantitative methods may be used during a research project, but only in a complementary manner, so that each set of data are collected, analysed and presented separately in order to support the interpretation and conclusions reached. In this way, the quantitative data collected in this event are analysed quantitatively whilst the qualitative data are analysed qualitatively. Conversely, quantitative and qualitative methods may be used in a more integrated way so that data are merged and transformed, with qualitative data being '**quantitised**' (e.g. specific events in the data are counted as frequencies and numerically coded for statistical analysis) and quantitative data '**qualitised**' (e.g. frequencies are turned into text, although this is extremely rare in practice). Both types of data may also be presented together on a matrix, as well as qualitative data being presented using charts and graphs and quantitative data being presented using categorisation and narration. This approach to integration may be risky, since there is a danger that the respective value of each form of data may be diluted; for example, excessively 'quantising' qualitative data may lead to loss of its exploratory or explanatory richness.

An alternative way of looking at the integration of qualitative and quantitative methods in mixed methods research, which may be seen to combine the *when* and *how* of such mixing, involves the nature of the research process. Unless the use of quantitative and qualitative methods in mixed methods research occurs concurrently in a single phase, it must involve the use of two phases of data collection and analysis (a double-phase research design), or perhaps more than two phases (a multiphase research design). In such designs, the initial use of one methodology (qualitative or quantitative) will be followed by the other methodology, and perhaps so on. This dynamic approach to the research process recognises that mixed methods research is both interactive and iterative, where the use in a given phase of one methodology (qualitative or quantitative) subsequently informs and directs the next phase of data collection and analysis. The exact nature of this interaction and iteration in a particular research project therefore shapes the way in which qualitative and quantitative methods are chosen and integrated at each phase of the research (Greene 2007; Nastasi et al. 2010; Ridenour and Newman 2008; Teddlie and Tashakkori 2009). This leads us to consider the timing within the research process when mixing occurs.

Timing within the research process when mixing occurs

Mixed methods research may be conducted sequentially or concurrently (Creswell and Plano Clark 2007). **Sequential mixed methods research** involves more than one phase of data collection and analysis. In this design, the researcher will follow the use of one method with another in order to expand or elaborate on the initial set of findings. In a **double-phase research design** this leads to two alternative mixed methods research strategies, either a **sequential exploratory research design** (qualitative followed by quantitative) or a **sequential explanatory research design** (quantitative followed by qualitative). In a more complex, sequential**, multiphase design**, mixed methods research will involve multiple phases of data collection and analysis (e.g. qualitative followed by quantitative, then by a further phase of qualitative) (see Box 5.3 for an example).

Concurrent mixed methods research involves the use of both quantitative and qualitative methods within a single phase of data collection and analysis (a **single-phase research design**). This allows both sets of results to be interpreted together to provide a richer and more comprehensive response to the research question in comparison to the use of a mono-method design. This is referred to as a **concurrent triangulation design**.

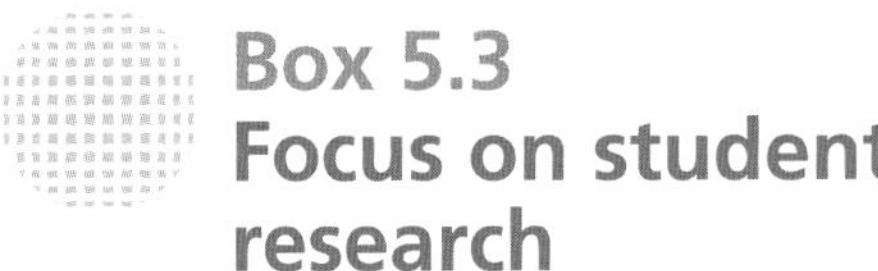

Box 5.3 Focus on student research

Mixed methods research

Adrian and Mark conducted research into organisational change in a county council, using a mixed methods research strategy. This was designed as a sequential mixed methods research project and consisted of four stages:

1 *Initial exploratory discussions* were held with key senior managers, which combined the purpose of helping to negotiate access, agree the scope of the project and gain essential contextual data. These data were analysed qualitatively in order to get a picture of important internal and external organisational issues.
2 *Individual in-depth interviews* were held with 30 directly employed staff (excluding for example school teachers), who formed a sample representing the organisation across its departments or 'Directorates' and throughout its grade structure. These data were also analysed qualitatively. This was to establish the issues that were important to staff, to help to inform the content of the questionnaire.
3 *A questionnaire* was designed, pilot-tested, amended and then administered to a representative sample of directly employed staff, producing a 36 per cent response rate. The quantitative data produced were analysed statistically to allow the views of employee groups to be compared for differences by age, gender, length of service, occupation and grade. The subsequent production of summary data based on these findings was particularly important to the county council.
4 A fourth stage consisted of *presentations to groups of employees*. This allowed employees' questions to be answered with care, whilst continuing to ensure anonymity. It also allowed discussion to occur to clarify the content of some of the questionnaire results. Notes from these presentations were analysed qualitatively.

Whilst potentially richer in outcome than a mono-method design, it is still likely to be shorter in timescale as well as more practical to undertake than a sequential mixed methods design.

Relative status of the quantitative and qualitative components in the research mix

Mixed methods research may use quantitative research and qualitative research equally or unequally (Creswell and Plano Clark 2007). In this way, the priority or weight given to either quantitative or qualitative research may vary, so that one methodology has a dominant role, while the other plays a supporting role, depending on the purpose of the research project. This prioritisation may also reflect the preferences of the researcher or the expectations of those who commission the research (such as your project tutor or the managers in an organisation). As we have also recognised, the direction of the research in an emergent design may determine the particular use and relative priority of each methodology as the research process 'unfolds'.

The purpose of the research may emphasise the initial use and prioritisation of qualitative research (as in an exploratory study, where qualitative precedes quantitative) or the initial use and prioritisation of quantitative research (as in a descriptive study, before the possible use of supporting qualitative research to explain particular findings further). The overall purpose of the research may also emphasise the dominance of either quantitative or qualitative research (e.g. as in a sequential project which commences with a qualitative, exploratory phase, followed by a quantitative, descriptive phase and which is completed by a further qualitative, explanatory phase). The purpose of other research projects may lead to the more equal use of quantitative and qualitative research methods. The research approach may also lead to the relative prioritisation of either quantitative or qualitative methods. In this way, an inductive approach designed to generate theoretical concepts and to build theory may lead to a greater emphasis on the use of qualitative methods.

Embedded mixed methods research is the term given to the situation where one methodology supports the other (Creswell and Plano Clark 2007). During data collection, this may occur in a number of ways. One methodology may be embedded within the other during a single means to collect data (e.g. some quantitative questions are included in an interview schedule, or some questions within a questionnaire require a qualitative response). This is known as a **concurrent embedded design**. Alternatively, a single-phase research design may use both quantitative and qualitative methods concurrently but collect these separately, one of which will be analysed to support the other. Within a double-phase, sequential research design, both quantitative and qualitative methods will be collected and analysed, one after the other, with one being used in a supporting role.

The characteristics that help to define mixed methods research (stage, level of integration, timing and relative status) highlight how quantitative and qualitative methods may be combined in a number of ways to provide you with better opportunities to answer your research question (Tashakkori and Teddlie 2010). Table 5.1 outlines a number of reasons for and advantages of using a mixed methods design. The specific nature of your mixed methods design will be related to particular reasons and advantages.

Research strategies

Different combinations of mixed methods research characteristics lead to various research strategies. The principal mixed methods research strategies summarised earlier in this section are: concurrent triangulation design, concurrent embedded design,

Table 5.1 Reasons for using a mixed methods design

Reason	Explanation
Initiation	Initial use of a qualitative or quantitative methodology may be used to define the nature and scope of sequential quantitative or qualitative research. May also be used to provide contextual background and to better understand the research problem (e.g. see Box 5.3). May also help in the formulation or redrafting of research questions, interview questions and questionnaire items and the selection of samples, cases and participants
Facilitation	During the course of the research, one method may lead to the discovery of new insights which inform and are followed up through the use of the other method
Complementarity	Use of mixed methods may allow meanings and findings to be elaborated, enhanced, clarified, confirmed, illustrated or linked
Interpretation	One method (e.g. qualitative) may be used to help to explain relationships between variables emerging from the other (e.g. quantitative)
Generalisability	Use of mixed methods may help to establish the generalisability of a study or its relative importance. In a similar way the use of mixed methods may help to establish the credibility of a study or to produce more complete knowledge
Diversity	Use of mixed methods may allow for a greater diversity of views to inform and be reflected in the study
Problem solving	Use of an alternative method may help when the initial method reveals unexplainable results or insufficient data
Focus	One method may be used to focus on one attribute (e.g. quantitative on macro aspects), while the other method may be used to focus on another attribute (e.g. qualitative on micro aspects)
Triangulation	Mixed methods may be used in order to combine data to ascertain if the findings from one method mutually corroborate the findings from the other method
Confidence	Findings may be affected by the method used. Use of a single method will make it impossible to ascertain the nature of that effect. To seek to cancel out this 'method effect', it is advisable to use mixed methods. This should lead to greater confidence in your conclusions

Source: Developed from Bryman (2006), Greene et al. (1989), Molina-Azorin (2010), and authors' experience

sequential explanatory design, sequential exploratory design (Creswell and Plano Clark 2007; Creswell 2009) and sequential, multi-phase design. Quantitative data collection techniques and analysis procedures that may be used as part of mixed methods research are considered in Chapters 9, 11 and 12 and qualitative techniques and procedures that may be used as part of mixed methods research are considered in Chapters 9, 10 and 13. Box 5.4 summarises how mixed methods have been used in management research.

Box 5.4 Focus on management research

Use of mixed methods in management research

Bryman (2006) examined 232 social science articles in which quantitative and qualitative research was combined. Approximately 23 per cent of these were concerned with management and organisational behaviour. He found that there often appeared to be a mismatch between the reasons given by authors for using a mixed methods approach and the ways in which they used these methods in practice. Bryman suggests that rationales for using mixed methods research may not be considered adequately. In only 10 articles in his sample was there clear evidence of research questions specifically designed to answer both the quantitative and qualitative aspects of the research. Bryman also suggests that because mixed methods research is likely to produce a rich data set, researchers will subsequently find more ways to use these than they may have expected. This leads him to conclude that researchers should seek to be explicit about the ways in which they intend to use mixed methods research whilst also recognising that the nature of the outcomes from this approach are unlikely to be entirely predictable.

Molina-Azorin (2010) has more recently examined the use and value of mixed methods in management research. Focusing on strategic management and entrepreneurship journals, he found that 11.4 per cent (152) of 1330 articles in his sample used mixed methods research. Mixed methods research was more prevalent in strategic management (14.6 per cent; n = 99) than entrepreneurship research (8.1 per cent; n = 53). In 80.9 per cent of these 152 articles quantitative or qualitative methods had been used as a dominant methodology in the mix, while 86.8 per cent of these mixed methods research projects had been conducted sequentially as opposed to concurrently.

Molina-Azorin also found that mixed methods articles in strategic management and entrepreneurship attracted more citations in subsequent publications than a comparison group of mono-method-based articles. He believes that this is because mixed methods research adds greater value to management research since the combination of quantitative and qualitative methods allows theory to be developed and extended, case-specific variables to be identified and explored or measured and the research process to produce analytical outcomes to a greater extent than might be the case with a mono-method design. However, he also found that management researchers may lack an adequate knowledge of the possibilities of and approaches to mixed methods research, limiting the potential of this methodological approach, reflecting a similar concern to that raised by Bryman.

5.4 Recognising the nature of your research design

In Section 5.3 we referred to your research following an exploratory, descriptive or explanatory purpose, or some combination of these. In Chapter 2 we encouraged you to think about your research project in terms of the question you wish to answer and your research objectives. The way in which you ask your research question will inevitably involve you in exploratory, descriptive or explanatory research leading to an answer that is either descriptive, descriptive and explanatory, or explanatory. The purpose of your research may also change over time. In this section we discuss each of these three in more detail to help you to choose which purpose or combination of these is appropriate to the nature of your research project.

Exploratory studies

An **exploratory study** is a valuable means to ask open questions to discover what is happening and gain insights about a topic of interest. It is particularly useful if you wish to clarify your understanding of a problem, such as if you are unsure of the precise nature of the problem. It may be that time is well spent on exploratory research, as it might show that the research is not worth pursuing!

There are a number of ways to conduct exploratory research. These include a search of the literature; interviewing 'experts' in the subject; conducting in-depth individual interviews or conducting focus group interviews. Because of their exploratory nature, these interviews are likely to be relatively unstructured and to rely on the quality of the contributions from those who participate to help guide the subsequent stage of your research (Section 10.2).

Exploratory research has the advantage that it is flexible and adaptable to change. If you are conducting exploratory research you must be willing to change your direction as a result of new data that appear and new insights that occur to you. A quotation from the travel writer V.S. Naipaul (1989: 222) illustrates this point beautifully:

> I had been concerned, at the start of my own journey, to establish some lines of enquiry, to define a theme. The approach had its difficulties. At the back of my mind was always a worry that I would come to a place and all contacts would break down . . . If you travel on a theme the theme has to develop with the travel. At the beginning your interests can be broad and scattered. But then they must be more focused; the different stages of a journey cannot simply be versions of one another. And . . . this kind of travel depended on luck. It depended on the people you met, the little illuminations you had. As with the next day's issue of fast-moving daily newspapers, the shape of the character in hand was continually being changed by accidents along the way.

Exploratory research may commence with a broad focus but this will become narrower as the research progresses.

Descriptive studies

The object of **descriptive research** is to gain an accurate profile of events, persons or situations. This may be an extension of, or a forerunner to, a piece of exploratory research or, more often, a piece of explanatory research. It is necessary to have a clear picture of the phenomenon on which you wish to collect data prior to the collection of the data. One of the earliest well-known examples of a descriptive survey is the Domesday Book, which described the population of England in 1085.

Often project tutors are rather wary of work that is too descriptive. There is a danger of their saying 'That's very interesting . . . but so what?' They will want you to go further and draw conclusions from the data you are describing. They will encourage you to develop the skills of evaluating data and synthesising ideas. These are higher-order skills than those of accurate description. Description in management and business research has a very clear place. However, it should be thought of as a means to an end rather than an end in itself. This means that if your research project utilises description it is likely to be a precursor to explanation. Such studies are known as **descripto-explanatory** studies.

Explanatory studies

Studies that establish causal relationships between variables may be termed **explanatory research**. The emphasis here is on studying a situation or a problem in order to explain the relationships between variables. You may find, for example, that a cursory analysis of quantitative data on manufacturing scrap rates shows a relationship between scrap rates and the age of the machine being operated. You could go ahead and subject the data to statistical tests such as correlation (discussed in Section 12.5) in order to get a clearer view of the relationship. As an alternative example, you might collect qualitative data to explain the reasons why customers of your company rarely pay their bills according to the prescribed payment terms.

Box 5.5 Focus on management research

Undertaking exploratory, descriptive and explanatory research to measure employees' perceptions about the actions necessary to implement organisational change successfully

Cinite and colleagues (2009) published a study in the *British Journal of Management* designed to develop and validate a series of questions to measure 'perceived organisational readiness for change'. This is concerned with employees' perceptions about the need for organisational change and whether the organisation is capable of implementing change successfully. Their study involved exploratory, descriptive and explanatory research. They commenced their research with two clearly articulated research questions: (1) 'What organizational actions are associated with employees' perceptions of organizational readiness for change?' (2) 'What organizational actions are associated with employees' perceptions of organizational unreadiness for change?'

A pre-stage of their research involved exploratory interviews with personnel responsible for implementing change in five organisations to gather background information. The first substantive stage of their research involved exploratory interviews with 88 employees in three organisations, who were asked to describe behaviours they had witnessed that indicated their organisation's readiness or unreadiness to implement change. This produced two lists, one of which described behaviours indicating readiness to implement change and the other unreadiness. These were edited to create 168 statements for a web-based survey, which was administered in the next stage of the research to a sample of 178 employees in four organisations, who were asked to rate their agreement or disagreement with each statement. Statements which were most highly rated as well as representative of both female and male employees and managers and non-managers were used to create a second web-based survey. This consisted of 21 items describing behaviours indicating organisational readiness to implement change and 19 items describing unreadiness. This was delivered to a large sample of employees from four organisations. The resulting data were analysed statistically to allow Cinite and colleagues to explain the relationship, based on employees' perceptions, between organisational actions and readiness or unreadiness to implement change posed in each of their research questions. They concluded that three actions indicated readiness to implement change: the commitment of senior managers, competence of change implementers and support of immediate line managers. Two actions indicated unreadiness to implement change: poor communication about change and adverse impact on work from the change.

From this summary, you can see that their research commenced with an exploratory phase allowing them to identify behaviours based on their participants' experiences of organisational change. This led to a descriptive phase, which was used as a forerunner to an explanatory stage, allowing them to explain the relationship between organisational actions and readiness or unreadiness to implement change, based on employees' perceptions.

5.5 Choosing a research strategy or strategies

The different research strategies

In this section we turn our attention to your choice of **research strategy**. In general terms, a strategy is a plan of action to achieve a goal. A research strategy may therefore be defined as a plan of how a researcher will go about answering her or his research question. It is the methodological link between your philosophy and subsequent choice of methods to collect and analyse data (Denzin and Lincoln 2005).

Different research traditions have led to a number of possible research strategies, as we have outlined earlier. In Section 5.3 we outlined the research strategies that are principally linked with quantitative, qualitative and multiple methods research designs respectively. Particular research strategies may be associated with one of the philosophies discussed in Chapter 4 and also to a deductive approach or to an inductive approach; however we also recognised in Section 5.3 that there are often open boundaries between research philosophies, research approaches and research strategies. In a similar way, a particular research strategy should not be seen as inherently superior or inferior to any other. Consequently, we believe that what is most important is not attaching labels for their own sake, or linking research elements to try to be methodologically aloof. For us, the key to your choice of research strategy or strategies is that you achieve a reasonable level of coherence throughout your research design which will enable you to answer your particular research question(s) and meet your objectives. Your choice of research strategy will therefore be guided by your research question(s) and objectives, the coherence with which these link to your philosophy, research approach and purpose, and also to more pragmatic concerns including the extent of existing knowledge, the amount of time and other resources you have available, and access to potential participants and to other sources of data. Finally, it must be remembered that these strategies should not be thought of as being mutually exclusive. For example, it is quite possible to use the survey strategy within a case study, or combine a number of different strategies within mixed methods.

The first two research strategies in the list below that we go on to consider in this section are principally or exclusively linked to a quantitative research design. The next two may involve quantitative or qualitative research, or a mixed design combining both – for example, Yin (2009) is emphatic on this point when discussing a case study research strategy. The final four strategies are principally or exclusively linked to a qualitative research design.

In our experience it is the choice between qualitative research strategies that is likely to cause the greatest confusion. Such confusion is often justified given the diversity of qualitative strategies (many more than those we consider), with their conflicting tensions and 'blurred genres' (Denzin and Lincoln 2005: 17). In our discussion we try to draw out the distinctions between these strategies to allow you to make an informed choice between qualitative strategies (as between or across quantitative and qualitative strategies). This is intended to help you avoid the vague assertion that you are 'doing qualitative research', without any further qualification! The strategies we now discuss are:

- Experiment;
- Survey;
- Archival Research;
- Case Study;
- Ethnography;
- Action Research;
- Grounded Theory;
- Narrative Inquiry.

Experiment

We start with discussion of the experiment strategy because its roots in natural science, laboratory-based research and the precision required to conduct them mean that the 'experiment' is often seen as the 'gold standard' against which the rigour of other strategies is assessed. **Experiment** is a form of research that owes much to the natural sciences, although it features strongly in psychological and social science research. The purpose of an experiment is to study the probability of a change in an **independent variable** causing a change in another, **dependent variable** (Hakim 2000) (see Table 5.2 for a description of types of variables). An experiment uses predictions, known as hypotheses, rather than research questions. This is because the researcher anticipates whether or not a relationship will exist between the variables. Two types of (opposing) **hypothesis** are formulated in a standard experiment: the **null hypothesis** and the **alternative hypothesis** (often referred to as the **hypothesis**). The null hypothesis predicts that there will not be a significant difference or relationship between the variables. An example of a null hypothesis might be that:

> customer services training of IT telephone support staff will not lead to a significant improvement in users' satisfaction feedback.

The alternative hypothesis predicts that there may be a significant difference or relationship between the variables. An example of a (directional) alternative hypothesis might be that:

> customer services training of IT telephone support staff will lead to a significant improvement in users' satisfaction feedback.

In an experiment, it is the null hypothesis which is tested statistically. Where the probability of there being no statistical difference is greater than a prescribed value (usually 0.05) the null hypothesis is accepted and the alternative hypothesis is rejected. Where the probability is less than or equal to the prescribed value (usually 0.05) this indicates that the alternative hypothesis is likely to be true. The simplest experiments are concerned with whether there is a link between two variables. More complex experiments also

Table 5.2 Types of variables

Variable	Meaning
Independent (IV)	Variable that is being manipulated or changed to measure its impact on a dependent variable
Dependent (DV)	Variable that may change in response to changes in other variables; observed outcome or result from manipulation of another variable
Mediating (MV)	A variable located between the independent and dependent variables, which explains the relationship between them (IV → MV → DV)
Moderator	A new variable that is introduced which will affect the nature of the relationship between the IV and DV
Control	Additional observable and measurable variables that need to be kept constant to avoid them influencing the effect of the IV on the DV
Confounding	Extraneous but difficult to observe or measure variables that can potentially undermine the inferences drawn between the IV and DV. Need to be considered when discussing results, to avoid spurious conclusions

consider the size of the change and the relative importance of two or more independent variables. Experiments therefore tend to be used in exploratory and explanatory research to answer 'what', 'how' and 'why' questions.

Different experimental designs may be used, each with different advantages and disadvantages, particularly in relation to **control variables** and **confounding variables** (Table 5.2). Experimental designs include classical experiments, quasi-experiments and within-subject designs. In a **classical experiment**, a sample of participants is selected and then randomly assigned to either an experimental group or to the control group. In the **experimental group**, some form of planned intervention or manipulation will be tested. In the **control group**, no such intervention is made. Random assignment means each group should be similar in all aspects relevant to the research other than whether or not they are exposed to the planned intervention or manipulation. In assigning the members to the control and experimental groups at random and using a control group, you try to control (that is, remove) the possible effects of an alternative explanation to the planned intervention (manipulation) and eliminate threats to internal validity. This is because the control group is subject to exactly the same external influences as the experimental group other than the planned intervention and, consequently, this intervention is the only explanation for any changes to the dependent variable.

A **quasi-experiment** will still use an experimental group(s) and a control group, but the researcher will not randomly assign participants to each group, perhaps because participants are only available in pre-formed groups (e.g. existing work groups). Differences in participants between groups may be minimised by the use of matched pairs. **Matched pair analysis** leads to a participant in an experimental group being paired with a participant in the control group based on matching factors such as age, gender, occupation, length of service, grade etc., to try to minimise the effect of extraneous variables on the experiment's outcomes. Those factors relevant to the nature of the experiment will need to be matched.

The basic experimental procedure in classical and quasi-experiments is the same (Figure 5.3), with the exception of random assignment, and we illustrate this procedure with an example related to the introduction of a sales promotion. The dependent variable in this example, purchasing behaviour, is measured for members of both the experimental group and control group before any intervention occurs. This provides a **pre-test** measure of purchasing behaviour. A planned intervention is then made to members of the experimental group in the form of a 'buy two, get one free' promotion. In the control group, no such intervention is made. The dependent variable, purchasing behaviour, is measured after the manipulation of the independent variable (the use of the 'buy two, get one free' promotion) for both the experimental group and the control group, so that a pre-test and **post-test** comparison can be made. On the basis of this comparison,

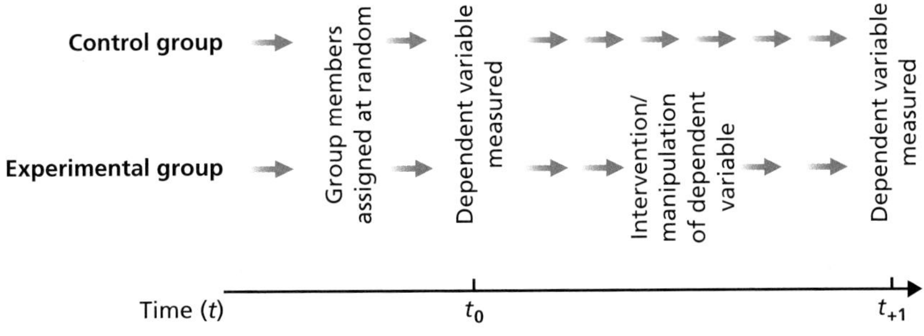

Figure 5.3 A classical experiment strategy

any difference between the experimental and control groups for the dependent variable (purchasing behaviour) is attributed to the intervention of the 'buy two, get one free' promotion. This experimental approach is known as a **between-subjects design**, where participants belong to either the experimental group or control group but not both. In a between-subjects design, if more than one intervention or manipulation is to be tested, a separate experimental group will be required for each test (known as **independent measures**). For example, if the experiment was designed to compare two separate interventions, such as a 'buy one, get one free' as well as the 'buy two, get one free' manipulation, two experimental groups would be required alongside the control group.

In a **within-subjects design**, or within-group design, there will only be a single group, rather than a separation into an experimental group and a control group. In this approach every participant is exposed to the planned intervention or series of interventions. For this reason, this approach is known as **repeated measures**. The procedure involves a pre-intervention observation or measurement, to establish a baseline (or control for the dependent variable). This is followed by a planned intervention (independent variable) and subsequent observation and measurement (related to the dependent variable). Following the withdrawal of the intervention and a period of 'reversal', to allow a return to the baseline, a further planned intervention may be attempted followed by subsequent observation and measurement. A within-subject design may be more practical than a between-subjects design because it requires fewer participants, but it may lead to carryover effects where familiarity or fatigue with the process distorts the validity of the findings. This may lead to a counterbalanced design, where some of the participants undertake tasks in a different order to see if familiarity or fatigue affects the outcomes.

Often experiments, including those in disciplines closely associated with business and management such as organisational psychology, are conducted in laboratories rather than in the field. This means that you have greater control over aspects of the research process such as sample selection and the context within which the experiment occurs. However, whilst this improves the **internal validity** of the experiment, that is, the extent to which the findings can be attributed to the interventions rather than any flaws in your research design, **external validity** is likely to be more difficult to establish (we discuss issues of validity in Section 5.8). Laboratory settings, by their very nature, are unlikely to be related to the real world of organisations. As a consequence, the extent to which the findings from a laboratory experiment are able to be generalised to all organisations is likely to be lower than for a field-(organisation-) based experiment.

The feasibility of using an experimental strategy will depend on the nature of your research question. As we noted, an experiment uses predictive hypotheses rather than open research questions. It may be appropriate to turn your question into hypotheses where you wish to test for expected relationships between variables. However, most business and management research questions will be designed to inquire into the relationships between variables, rather than to test a predicted relationship. This indicates the difference between experiments and other research strategies. Within quantitative research designs, it highlights a key difference between an experimental strategy and a survey strategy.

Survey

The **survey** strategy is usually associated with a deductive research approach. It is a popular and common strategy in business and management research and is most frequently used to answer 'what', 'who', 'where', 'how much' and 'how many' questions. It therefore tends to be used for exploratory and descriptive research. Surveys using questionnaires are popular as they allow the collection of standardised data from a sizeable population in a highly economical way, allowing easy comparison. In addition, the survey strategy is perceived as authoritative by people in general and is both comparatively easy to explain and to understand. Every day a news bulletin, news website or newspaper reports the results of a new survey that is designed to find out how a population thinks or behaves in relation to a particular issue. Box 5.6 illustrates how policymakers attempt to survey everything to collect both attitudinal and objective data.

The survey strategy allows you to collect quantitative data which you can analyse quantitatively using descriptive and inferential statistics (Sections 12.4 and 12.5). In addition, data collected using a survey strategy can be used to suggest possible reasons for particular relationships between variables and to produce models of these relationships. Using a survey strategy should give you more control over the research process

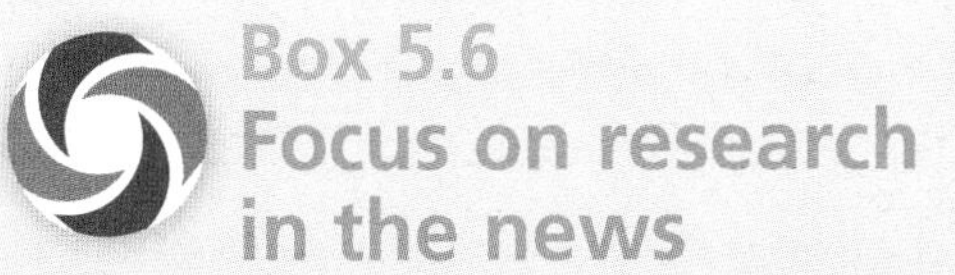

FT

Happiness: A measure of cheer

'The welfare of a nation can . . . scarcely be inferred from a measure of national income.'

So the US Congress was warned in 1934 by Simon Kuznets, who thus continued a long tradition of pointing out that there is more to life than money. But the economist's comments broke particular ground: they were attached to the first serious attempts to produce national income accounts – the tally of all that a country produces and earns – for the US. Kuznets and his small research team had built them, and he knew their limits. Where Kuznets led, others have followed. From the upper echelons of the administration of President Barack Obama to the offices of Nicolas Sarkozy, his French counterpart, to David Cameron, UK prime minister, the goal of gauging a nation's wellbeing has captured the imagination of policymakers. They join less likely countries such as Bhutan, whose mission to measure 'gross national happiness' has made the Himalayan mountain kingdom a trendsetter.

Mr Cameron was the most recent to take up the cause, saying Britain needed to look for alternative measures that would show national progress 'not just by how our economy is growing, but by how our lives are improving; not just by our standard of living, but by our quality of life'. While some analysts suspect each politician has his own motives – appearing nice to electors, flattering the economy and so on – the result has been to create a sense of momentum behind happiness economics.

Embracing happiness is one thing; measuring it another. There are, broadly speaking, three approaches to measuring a country's wellbeing. One is to use the long-established framework of national income accounts and adjust it to better reflect national welfare. The second is to collect data on objective measures that are plausibly related to wellbeing: anything from life expectancy to crime, suicide rates to income inequality. The third – and the three are not mutually exclusive – is to try to measure national welfare directly by asking people how they feel: the equivalent of measuring wealth by asking: 'On a scale of 1 to 10, how rich are you?'

Intellectually, the project of measuring national welfare seems to belong on the centre-left. National income accounts themselves – like unemployment statistics – rose to prominence in the 1930s as Franklin Roosevelt tried to lead the US out of the Great Depression and the government recognised it understood very little about how the economy was really doing – beyond very badly. The Second World War and the central planning mentality that came with it merely intensified the focus on the government being able to understand how the economy was functioning.

The countervailing view was most pithily expressed by John Cowperthwaite, the laissez-faire financial secretary of Hong Kong in the 1960s, who claimed he

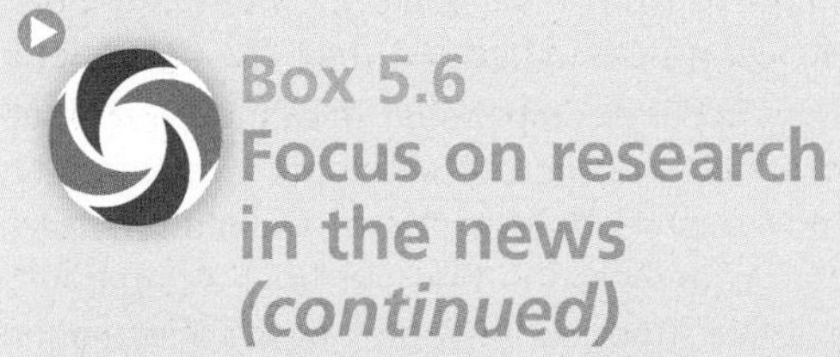

Box 5.6
Focus on research in the news (continued)

FT

refused to collect economic statistics because it would only provide ammunition to the planners. His views have not prevailed. Kuznets won the Nobel Prize in economics in 1971 – only the third year in which it was awarded – and it is hard to find serious economists who think that collecting national income accounts is pointless. The question is whether there is a benefit in trying to supplement those with accounts of national welfare – or, to put it cutely, an index of national happiness.

Mr Cameron says that there is. 'You cannot capture happiness on a spreadsheet any more than you can bottle it,' he declared last month. The happiness index project, he added, had a practical purpose: to help the government understand, 'with evidence', the best way of improving people's wellbeing. In short, Mr Cameron believes happiness indices can help his Conservative–Liberal Democrat coalition government plan its way to a happier nation in the same way Kuznets' national accounts helped policymakers respond to the Depression and the outbreak of war.

Source: Adapted from 'Happiness: a measure of cheer', Tim Harford (2010) *Financial Times*, 27 December. Copyright The Financial Times Ltd

and, when sampling is used, it is possible to generate findings that are representative of the whole population at a lower cost than collecting the data for the whole population (Section 7.2). You will need to spend time ensuring that your sample is representative, designing and piloting your data collection instrument and trying to ensure a good response rate. Analysing the data, even with readily available analysis software, will also be time-consuming. However, it will be your time and, once you have collected your data, you will be independent. Many researchers complain that their progress is delayed by their dependence on others for information.

The data collected by the survey strategy is unlikely to be as wide-ranging as those collected by other research strategies. For example, there is a limit to the number of questions that any questionnaire can contain if the goodwill of the respondent is not to be presumed on too much. Despite this, perhaps the biggest drawback with using a questionnaire as part of a survey strategy is, as emphasised in Section 11.2, the capacity to do it badly!

The questionnaire, however, is not the only data collection technique that belongs to the survey strategy. Structured observation, of the type most frequently associated with organisation and methods (O&M) research, and structured interviews, where standardised questions are asked of all interviewees, also often fall into this strategy. Structured observation techniques are discussed in Section 9.3 and structured interviews in Section 11.5.

Archival research

An **archival research** strategy makes use of administrative records and documents as the principal source of data. Although the term 'archival' has historical connotations, it can refer to recent as well as historical documents (Bryman 1989). Whilst the availability of these data is outlined in Section 8.2, it is important that an archival research strategy is not conflated with secondary data analysis discussed in Chapter 8. As we will discuss in Chapter 8, all research that makes use of data contained in administrative records is inevitably secondary data analysis. This is because these data were originally collected for a different purpose, the administration of the organisation. However, when these data are used in an archival research strategy they are analysed because they are a product of day-to-day activities (Hakim 2000). They are, therefore, part of the reality being studied rather than having been collected originally as data for research purposes.

An archival research strategy allows research questions which focus upon the past and changes over time to be answered, be they exploratory, descriptive or explanatory. However, your ability to answer such questions will inevitably be constrained by the nature of the administrative records and documents. Even where these records exist, they may not contain the precise information needed to answer your research question(s) or meet your objectives. Alternatively, data may be missing or you may be refused access or your data censored for confidentiality reasons. Using an archival research strategy therefore necessitates you establishing what data are available and designing your research to make the most of it.

Case study

A **case study** explores a research topic or phenomenon within its context, or within a number of real-life contexts. Yin (2009) also highlights the importance of context, adding that, within a case study, the boundaries between the phenomenon being studied and the context within which it is being studied are not always apparent. This is potentially an advantage of the case study strategy, which we discuss later. It is also the complete opposite of the experimental strategy we outlined earlier, where contextual variables are highly controlled as they are seen as a potential threat to the validity of the results. It also differs from the survey strategy where, although the research is undertaken in context, the ability to explore and understand this context is limited by the number of variables for which data can be collected.

The case study strategy will be relevant if you wish to gain a rich understanding of the context of the research and the processes being enacted (Eisenhardt and Graebner 2007). The case study strategy also has considerable ability to generate answers to the question 'why?' as well as 'what?' and 'how?' questions. For this reason the case study strategy is most often used in explanatory and exploratory research. It may use quantitative or qualitative methods and many case study designs use a mix of these methods to collect and analyse data (Yin 2009). These may include, for example, interviews, observation, documentary analysis and questionnaires. Consequently, if you are using a case study strategy you are likely to need to use and triangulate multiple sources of data. **Triangulation** refers to the use of different data collection techniques within one study in order to ensure that the data are telling you what you think they are telling you. For example, qualitative data collected using semi-structured group interviews may be a valuable way of triangulating quantitative data collected by other means such as a questionnaire.

Yin (2009) distinguishes between four case study strategies based upon two discrete dimensions:

- single case versus multiple cases;
- holistic case versus embedded case.

A single case is often used where it represents a critical case or, alternatively, an extreme or unique case. Conversely, a single case may be selected because it is typical or because it provides you with an opportunity to observe and analyse a phenomenon that few have considered before (Section 7.3). Inevitably, an important aspect of using a single case is defining the actual case. For many part-time students this is the organisation for which they work (see Box 5.7). The key here will be to ensure that this approach is suitable for the nature of your research question and objectives.

Box 5.7 Focus on student research

Using a single organisation as a case study

Simon was interested in discovering how colleagues within his organisation were using a recently introduced financial costing model in their day-to-day work. In discussion with his project tutor, he highlighted that he was interested in finding out how it was actually being used in his organisation as a whole, as well as seeing if the use of the financial costing model differed between senior managers, departmental managers and front-line operatives. Simon's project tutor suggested that he adopt a case study strategy, using his organisation as a single case within which the senior managers', departmental managers' and front-line operatives' groups were embedded cases. He also highlighted that, given the different numbers of people in each of the embedded cases, Simon would be likely to need to use different data collection techniques with each.

A case study strategy can also incorporate multiple cases, that is, more than one case. The rationale for using multiple cases focuses on whether findings can be replicated across cases. Cases will be carefully chosen on the basis that similar results are predicted to be produced from each one. Where this is realised, Yin (2009) terms this **literal replication**. Another set of cases may be chosen where a contextual factor is deliberately different. The impact of this difference on the anticipated findings is predicted by the researcher. Where this predicted variation is realised, Yin terms this a **theoretical replication**. Yin (2009) proposes that a multiple case study strategy may combine a small number of cases chosen to predict literal replication and a second small number chosen to predict theoretical replication. Where all of the findings from these cases are as predicted, this would clearly produce very strong support for the theoretical propositions on which these predictions were based. This particular approach to case study strategy therefore commences deductively, based on theoretical propositions and theory testing, before possibly incorporating an inductive or abductive approach (Section 4.3). Where the findings are in some way contrary to the predictions in the theoretical propositions being tested, it would be necessary to reframe these propositions and choose another set of cases to test them.

Yin's second dimension, holistic versus embedded, refers to the unit of analysis. For example, you may have chosen to use an organisation in which you have been employed or are currently employed as your case. If your research is concerned only with the organisation as a whole then you are treating the organisation as a holistic case study. Conversely, even if you are only researching within a single organisation, if you wish to examine a number of logical sub-units within the organisation, perhaps departments or work groups, then your case will inevitably involve more than one unit of analysis. Whichever way you select these units, this would be called an embedded case study (Box 5.7).

The procedural approach reported here is designed to demonstrate methodological rigour when using a case study strategy. We would argue that a case study strategy can be a very worthwhile way of exploring existing theory. In addition, a well-constructed case study strategy can enable you to challenge an existing theory and also provide a source of new research questions. Case study research is likely to prove to be intensive and demanding. We would advise you to read about the analytical procedures associated with case study research, which are outlined in Chapter 13 and discussed in more detail in Yin (2009), in order to understand this strategy better before committing to it.

As a student you are likely to find a single case study strategy to be more manageable. Alternatively, you may be able to develop a research design based on two to three cases, where you seek to achieve a literal replication, following Yin. However, as we have indicated earlier, choosing between a single or multiple case study is not simply related to producing more evidence. While a multiple case study is likely to produce more evidence, the purpose of each approach is different. A single case study approach is chosen because of the nature of the case (i.e. because it is a critical, unique or typical case etc.). A multiple case study approach is chosen because of its capacity to demonstrate one or both forms of replication. Where you are interested to use this strategy, you will therefore need to ensure that the approach chosen is suitable for the nature of your research question and objectives.

Ethnography

Ethnography is used to study groups. It is the earliest qualitative research strategy, with its origins in colonial anthropology. From the 1700s to early 1900s, ethnography was developed to study cultures in so-called 'primitive' societies that had been brought under the rule of a colonial power, to facilitate imperialist control and administration. Early anthropologists treated those amongst whom they lived and conducted their fieldwork as subjects and approached their ethnography in a detached way, believing that they were using a scientific approach, reminiscent of a positivist paradigm, to produce monographs that were meant to be accurate and timeless accounts of different cultures (Denzin and Lincoln 2005; Tedlock 2005). From the 1920s the use of ethnography changed through the work of the Chicago School (University of Chicago), which used ethnographic methods to study social and urban problems within cultural groups in the USA. A seminal example of this work is Whyte's 'Street Corner Society' published in 1943, which examined the lives of street gangs in Boston. This approach to ethnography involved researchers living amongst those whom they studied, to observe and talk to them in order to produce detailed cultural accounts of their shared beliefs, behaviours, interactions, language, rituals and the events that shaped their lives (Cunliffe 2010). This use of ethnography adopted a more interpretive and naturalistic focus by using the language of those being studied in writing up cultural accounts. However, the researcher remained the arbiter of how to tell the story and what to include, leading many to question how the socialisation and values of this person might affect the account being written (Geertz 1988).

This problem of 'representation' (Denzin and Lincoln 2005) meant that ethnography, as well as qualitative research more generally, was still in a fluid developmental state. Researchers developed a 'bewildering array' (Cunliffe 2010: 230) of qualitative research strategies in the second half of the twentieth century, associated with a great deal of 'blurring' across these strategies (Denzin and Lincoln 2005). We go on to discuss some of these new strategies (action research, grounded theory and narrative inquiry) in this section. As we shall see, these other strategies were designed for a different research focus to that of ethnography. Ethnographers are interested to study people in groups, who interact with one another and share the same space, whether this is at street level, within a work group, in an organisation or within a society. Conflict about how best to achieve this focus led ethnography to continue to develop and to fragment in this period, linked to the problem of representation and a second problem about how to judge the quality of qualitative research (which we return to in Section 5.8) (Denzin and Lincoln 2005). Out of the range of ethnographic strategies that resulted, Cunliffe (2010) describes three: Realist Ethnography, Impressionist or Interpretive Ethnography and Critical Ethnography.

Realist Ethnography is the closest to the ethnographic strategy described earlier. The realist ethnographer believes in objectivity, factual reporting and identifying 'true' meanings. She or he will report the situation observed through facts or data about structures and processes, practices and customs, routines and norms, artefacts and symbols. Such reporting is likely to use standardised categories that produce quantitative data from observations. The realist ethnographer will write up her or his account in the third person, portraying their role as the impersonal reporter of facts. This account will present a detailed contextual background, the nature of the cultural interactions observed, and identify patterns of behaviour and social processes. It will use edited quotations in a dispassionate way without personal bias or seeking to act as an agent for change. The realist ethnographer's final written account is his or her representation of what he or she has observed and heard.

In contrast, **Interpretive Ethnography** places much greater stress on subjective impressions than on objectivity. The interpretive ethnographer believes in the likelihood of multiple meanings rather than being able to identify a single, true meaning. Multiple meanings will be located in the socially constructed interpretations of the different participants. This suggests a more pluralistic approach, in which the interpretive ethnographer focuses on understanding meanings, with those being observed treated as participants rather than subjects. This is what Tedlock (2005: 467) calls the 'observation of participation'. The research report will reflect the participation of both the ethnographer (writing in the first person, editing herself into the text, rather than out of it) and those being observed, through devices such as personalisation, use of dialogue and quotations, dramatisation and presentation of different perspectives as well as contextualisation, orderly and progressive description, factual reporting, analysis and evaluation.

Critical Ethnography has a radical purpose, designed to explore and explain the impact of power, privilege and authority on those who are subject to these influences or marginalised by them. You may therefore ask if it can have any appeal to business and management research that is dependent on achieving organisational access. Critical ethnographers often adopt an advocacy role in their work to try to bring about change. A researcher may adopt a constrained or bounded version of Critical Ethnography to explore the impact of a problematic issue within an organisation or work group with a view to advocating internal or external change. Such an issue might be concerned with strategy, decision-making procedures, regulation, governance, organisational treatment, reward and promotion, communication and involvement and so forth.

We have partly presented our discussion of ethnography as a developmental account because it would be misleading to suggest that ideas about this strategy are unified. Whilst ethnography is a demanding strategy to use because you would need to develop some grounding in this approach and because of the time scale and intensity involved, it may possibly be relevant to you. For those of you who are currently working in an organisation, there may be scope to undertake participant observation of your work-group or another group in the organisation (Chapter 9). Alternatively, where you have recently undertaken a work placement, you will be familiar with the context and complexity of this workplace and you may be able to negotiate access based on your credibility to undertake an ethnographic study related to a work group that would enable you to answer your research question. Where an ethnographic strategy is appropriate and proves to be feasible (Sections 6.2–6.4), you will need to consider which ethnographic approach relates to the nature of your research question. You should then be in position to identify which issues to explore to commence fieldwork and the building of trust to be able to undertake this approach successfully.

Action Research

Lewin first used the term **Action Research** in 1946. It has been interpreted subsequently by management researchers in a variety of ways, but a number of common and related themes have been identified within the literature. In essence, Action Research is an emergent and iterative process of inquiry that is designed to develop solutions to real organisational problems through a participative and collaborative approach, which uses different forms of knowledge, and which will have implications for participants and the organisation beyond the research project (Coghlan and Brannick 2010; Reason 2006; Reason and Bradbury 2008; Shani and Pasmore 1985). Our definition identifies five themes, which we briefly consider in the following order: purpose, process, participation, knowledge and implications.

The purpose of an Action Research strategy is to promote organisational learning to produce practical outcomes through identifying issues, planning action, taking action and evaluating action. Coghlan and Brannick (2010: 4) state that Action Research is about, 'research in action rather than research about action'. This is because Action Research focuses on 'addressing worthwhile practical purposes' (Reason 2006: 188) and resolving real organisational issues (Shani and Pasmore 1985).

The process of Action Research is both emergent and iterative. An Action Research strategy commences within a specific context and with a research question but because it works through several stages or iterations the focus may change as the research develops. Each stage of the research involves a process of diagnosing or constructing issues, planning action, taking action and evaluating action (Figure 5.4). Diagnosing or constructing issues, sometimes referred to as fact finding and analysis, is undertaken to enable action planning and a decision about the actions to be taken. These are then taken and the actions evaluated (cycle 1). This evaluation provides a direction and focus for the next stage of diagnosing or constructing issues, planning action, taking action and evaluating action (cycle 2), demonstrating the iterative nature of the process. Subsequent cycles (cycle 3 and possibly beyond) involve further diagnosing or constructing of issues,

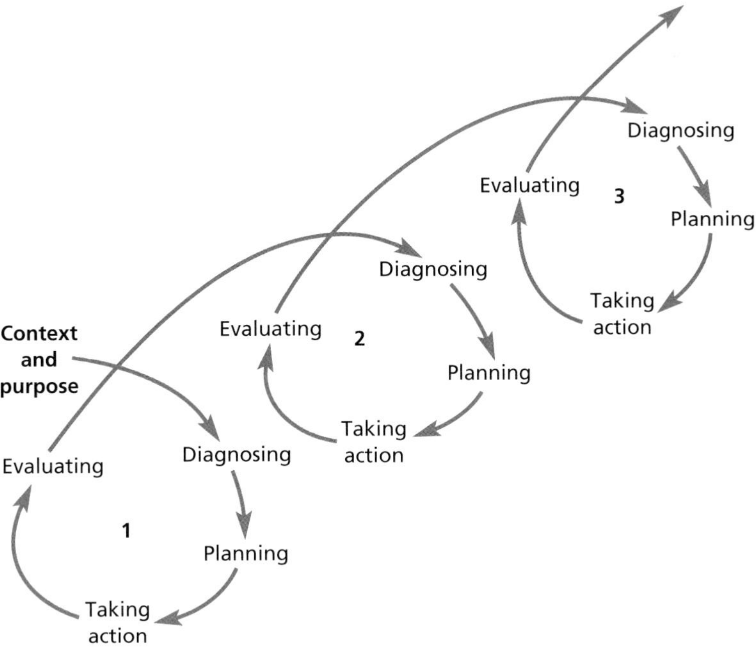

Figure 5.4 The action research spiral

taking into account previous evaluations, planning further actions, taking these actions and evaluating them. In this way, Action Research differs from other research strategies because of its explicit focus on action related to multiple stages, to explore and evaluate solutions to organisational issues and to promote change within the organisation.

Participation is a critical component of Action Research. Greenwood and Levin (2007) emphasise that Action Research is a social process in which an action researcher works with members in an organisation, as a facilitator and teacher, to improve the situation for these participants and their organisation. For Greenwood and Levin, a process can only be called Action Research if research, action and participation are all present. Participation by organisational members may take a number of forms. Firstly, organisational members need to cooperate with the researcher to allow their existing work practices to be studied. The process of Action Research then requires participation in the form of collaboration through its iterative cycles (as we described earlier) to facilitate the improvement of organisational practices. Collaboration means building a democratic approach to communication and decision making when constructing, planning, taking and evaluating each action research stage or cycle. The researcher passes on her or his skills and capabilities to participants so that they effectively become co-researchers in the action research process. Without such participation, this approach simply would not be viable, although creating such participation is likely to be difficult in practice and to meet with resistance at various levels (Reason 2006).

How then may this form of participation be developed? Eden and Huxham (1996: 75) argue that the participation of organisational members results from their involvement in 'a matter which is of genuine concern to them'. Schein (1999) emphasises that members of an organisation are more likely to implement change they have helped to create. Once the members of an organisation have identified a need for change and have widely shared this need, it becomes difficult to ignore, and the pressure for change comes from within the organisation. In this way, an Action Research strategy combines both data gathering and the facilitation of change. This outcome points to a further form of participation that may develop from an Action Research project and continue beyond its end, related to its potential to raise employees' expectations about their future treatment and involvement in decision making (Greenwood and Levin 2007; Reason 2006). It may also have the power to allow participants to redescribe and reanalyse (previous) organisational events and experiences, leading to their re-evaluation with implications for cultural change. In this way, Action Research may promote the re-evaluation of experience to encourage different expectations about future treatment to bring about bottom-up culture change (Reason 2006).

The nature of Action Research means that it will also be able to take advantage of different forms of knowledge. Action Research will not only be informed by abstract theoretical knowledge, known as propositional knowledge, but also by participants' everyday lived experiences (their experiential knowledge) and knowing-in-action (knowledge that comes from practical application) (Reason 2006). These forms of knowledge will inform and be incorporated into each stage or cycle of the Action Research process, encouraged by the collaborative approach that underpins this strategy.

Action Research also has implications beyond the research project. Implications for participants and the organisation have already been discussed, notably individuals' raised expectations about their future treatment, as well as the consequences for organisational development and culture change. There are also likely to be implications from the process that will inform other contexts. Academics will use the results from undertaking action research to develop theory to inform other contexts. Consultants will transfer knowledge gained in one context to inform their work in another. Such use of knowledge to inform other contexts, we believe, also applies to others undertaking action research, such as students undertaking research in their own organisations.

Where you think about using Action Research there will be a number of practical concerns to consider. Identifying an accommodating context, the emergent nature of this strategy, the need to engender participation and collaboration, the researcher's role as facilitator, and the stages or iterations involved are some of the reasons that make action research a demanding strategy in terms of the intensity involved and the resources and time required. As we have indicated, Action Research can be suited to part-time students who undertake research in their own organisation. The longitudinal nature of this strategy means that it is more appropriate for medium- or long-term research projects rather than short-term ones. There is the related issue of deciding how many Action Research cycles are sufficient. Where these practical as well as political concerns have been properly anticipated and evaluated in terms of a feasible design, Action Research has the potential to offer a worthwhile and rich experience for those involved.

Grounded Theory

'Grounded theory' can be used to refer to a methodological approach, a method of inquiry and the result of a research process (Bryant and Charmaz 2007; Charmaz 2005; Corbin and Strauss 2008). 'Grounded theory methodology' refers to the researcher's choice of this strategy as a way to conduct research. 'Grounded theory method' refers to the data collection techniques and analytic procedures that it uses (discussed in Chapter 13). 'Grounded theory' may be used loosely to incorporate methodology and method but more specifically it refers to a theory that is grounded in or developed inductively from a set of data. In this section we refer to '**Grounded Theory**' (i.e. as a proper noun), to indicate its use as a research strategy and to distinguish this from 'a grounded theory' (no capital letters).

Grounded Theory was developed by Glaser and Strauss (1967) as a response to the 'extreme positivism' of much social research at that time (Suddaby 2006: 633). They disputed the view that social research should use a paradigm based on a premise that theory will reveal a pre-existing reality. In positivism, reality is seen as existing independently and externally (to human cognition). Whilst positivism is suited to research in the natural sciences, they believed that social research should use a different philosophy. By adopting interpretivism in social research, 'reality' is seen as being socially constructed through the meanings that social actors ascribe to their experiences. Grounded Theory was therefore developed as a process to analyse, interpret and explain the meanings that social actors construct to make sense of their everyday experiences in specific situations (Charmaz 2006; Glaser and Strauss 1967; Suddaby 2006).

Grounded Theory is used to develop theoretical explanations of social interactions and processes in a wide range of contexts including business and management. As much of business and management is about people's behaviours, for example consumers' or employees', a Grounded Theory strategy can be used to explore a wide range of business and management issues. As the title of Glaser and Strauss's (1967) book indicates, the aim is to 'discover' or generate theory grounded in the data produced from the accounts of social actors. Grounded Theory methods are discussed further in Section 13.7; here we briefly outline the key elements of this strategy to enable you to assess whether it may be appropriate for the nature of your proposed research project to address your research question.

Grounded Theory is usually referred to as taking an inductive approach although, as we discuss later, it may be more appropriate to think of it as moving between induction and deduction (Strauss and Corbin 1998; Suddaby 2006). The researcher collects and analyses data simultaneously, developing analytical codes as these emerge from the data in order to reorganise these data into categories. In the Grounded Theory strategy of Strauss and Corbin (1998) there are three coding stages: the reorganisation of data into categories is called **open coding**, the process of recognising relationships between categories is referred to as **axial coding**, and the integration of categories to produce a theory is labelled **selective coding**. Charmaz (2006) simplifies this to two principal stages: **initial coding** and **focused coding**, supported by sufficient stages of sampling (Section 13.7). More recently, Corbin has altered the approach in Corbin and Strauss (2008), with axial coding being combined within open coding and selective coding simply becoming 'integration'. We expand on analytical coding in some detail in Section 13.7; needless to say here that coding is a key element of Grounded Theory.

Underpinning coding is the process of **constant comparison**. Each item of data collected is compared with others, as well as against the codes being used to categorise data. This is to check for similarities and differences, to promote consistency when coding data and to aid the process of analysis. Where appropriate, new codes are created and existing codes reanalysed as new data is collected. Constant comparison promotes the higher levels of analytical coding we referred to earlier because it involves moving between inductive and deductive thinking. As a researcher codes data into categories, a relationship may begin to suggest itself between specific codes (here, the researcher is using inductive thinking because she or he will be linking specific codes to form a general proposition). This emerging interpretation will need to be 'tested' through collecting data from new cases (here, the researcher will use deductive thinking to 'test' this abstract generalisation back to a new set of specific cases, to see if it stands up as an explanatory relationship to form a higher-level code) (Strauss and Corbin 1998). The process of gaining insights to create new conceptual possibilities which are then examined is termed **abduction** (Reichertz 2007; Suddaby 2006) (Section 4.3).

When using Grounded Theory you need to decide how to select cases for your research. As you analyse data, the categories being developed will indicate the type of new cases (e.g. new participants) to select for further data collection. The purpose of sampling is therefore to pursue theoretical lines of enquiry rather than to achieve representativeness. As you identify a core theme, relationship, or process around which to focus the research, a particular focus will be provided from which to select new cases to collect and analyse further data. This approach is a special form of purposive sampling, known as **theoretical sampling** (Section 7.3), which continues until **theoretical saturation** is reached. This occurs when data collection ceases to reveal any new properties that are relevant to a category, where categories have become well developed and understood and relationships between categories have been verified (Strauss and Corbin 2008). This is also referred to as achieving conceptual density (Glaser 1992) or conceptual saturation (Strauss and Corbin 2008). Using these elements of Grounded Theory means that the process of data collection and analysis becomes increasingly focused, leading to the generation of a contextually based theoretical explanation (Bryant and Charmaz 2007).

A number of implications have emerged from our discussion of this strategy as well as from Box 5.8. These may be summed up by saying that the use of Grounded Theory will involve you in processes that will be time-consuming, intensive and reflective. Before you commit yourself to this strategy, you will need to consider the time that you have to conduct your research, the level of competence you will need, your access to data, and the logistical implications of immersing yourself in such an intensive approach to research. There may also be a concern that either little of significance will emerge at the end of the research process or that what emerges is simply descriptive. It is therefore important for you to consider these possibilities when determining, and reflecting on, your research question. In particular you need to ask yourself whether you are using the analytical procedures of Grounded Theory in the way they were designed to be used: to generate theory grounded in your data. And of course to make use of existing theory to draw out the theoretical implications of what your data reveal (see Box 5.8).

Box 5.8 Focus on management research

Using Grounded Theory, or not!

Bryant and Charmaz (2007) in *The Sage Handbook of Grounded Theory* report that this strategy has, for the last couple of decades, been the qualitative research method used most widely across a range of subjects. They cite Titscher et al. (2000), who reported that out of 4134 citations for all types of research methods in the Social Science Citation Index between 1991 and 1998, Grounded Theory accounted for 2622 of these. However, Titscher et al. (2000, cited in Bryant and Charmaz 2007) question whether the ascendancy of Grounded Theory is as dominant as these data appear to suggest. Bryant and Charmaz (2007: 2) reflect back to Lee and Fielding (1996) in concluding that, 'the discrepancy between claiming use of [Grounded Theory] and actual evidence of this continues today'. Lee and Fielding (1996: 3.1) had stated in their *Sociological Research Online* comment that, 'When qualitative researchers are challenged to describe their approach, reference to "grounded theory" has the highest recognition value. But the very looseness and variety of researchers' schooling in the approach means that the tag may well mean something different to each researcher. A detailed examination of work claiming the label may deviate sharply from what Glaser and Strauss had in mind.'

Suddaby (2006) produced an excellent article in the *Academy of Management Journal* based on reviewing pre-publication management research manuscripts claiming to use Grounded Theory. He identifies six common misconceptions about Grounded Theory. We briefly summarise these, but where you are thinking about using Grounded Theory we would advise you to read Suddaby's article as we believe that it should help you to understand this approach and avoid these common misunderstandings:

1 Ignoring literature until late in the research project. It is a mistake to ignore existing literature before and during undertaking Grounded Theory.
2 Presenting raw data. Grounded Theory should never present unanalysed data. This is to ignore the essence of Grounded Theory, which is a conceptual process to develop a theory from the data.
3 Using inappropriate philosophical assumptions and testing theory rather than developing theory. Avoid methodological confusions or 'slurring' such as starting with positivist assumptions or commencing with interpretive assumptions but then proceeding to use objectivist rather than Grounded Theory methods.
4 Mechanically following Grounded Theory procedures without sufficient creative insight. The use of Grounded Theory procedures and techniques needs to be accompanied by creative insights and theoretical sensitivity to infer meanings in the data, to progress the research and in writing it up.
5 Following Grounded Theory procedures rigidly. In practice Grounded Theory procedures are 'messy' and require researchers to develop a tacit feel for their research to make judgements about issues such as deciding when theoretical saturation is achieved.
6 Grounded Theory is methodologically simple. Instead, it requires practice, dedication, creativity and sometimes good luck. Using it is also not an excuse to avoid developing a clear methodology based on the core principles and procedures of coding, constant comparison and theoretical sampling.

Narrative Inquiry

A narrative is a story; a personal account which interprets an event or sequence of events. Using the term 'narrative' requires a distinction to be drawn between its general meaning and the specific meaning used here. A qualitative research interview inevitably involves a participant in storytelling. In this way, the term 'narrative' can be applied generally to describe the nature or outcome of a qualitative interview. As a research strategy, however, **Narrative Inquiry** has a more specific meaning and purpose. There will be research contexts where the researcher believes that the experiences of her or his participants can best be accessed by collecting and analysing these as complete stories, rather than collecting them as bits of data that flow from specific interview questions and which are then fragmented during data analysis. A contrast may therefore be drawn between the approach to Grounded Theory which we discussed earlier and Narrative Inquiry which we consider here.

Several factors may encourage the use of Narrative Inquiry in order to preserve the continuity of the narrator's account and optimise the analytical potential of this strategy. The ways in which events in a story are linked, the actions that follow and their implications are more likely to be revealed by encouraging a participant to narrate his or her experiences than by responding to a series of pre-formed questions. Narrative Inquiry therefore seeks to preserve chronological connections and the sequencing of events as told by the narrator (participant), to enrich understanding and aid analysis. Chase (2005: 656) refers to this strategy as providing the opportunity to connect events and actions over time into a 'meaningful whole'. Through storytelling the narrator will also provide his or her interpretation of these events, allowing the narrative researcher to analyse the meanings which the narrator places on events. Where there is more than one participant providing a personal account of a given context, the narrative researcher will also be able to compare and to triangulate or contrast the narratives of these narrators.

The depth of this process is also likely to produce 'thick descriptions' of contextual detail and social relations which illustrate factors, such as financial, cultural, managerial or capability ones, that facilitate or constrain the context being researched (e.g. Chase 2005; Musson 2004). Gabriel and Griffiths (2004: 114) believe that using this strategy may allow researchers to 'gain access to deeper organizational realities, closely linked to their members' experiences'. A **narrative** may therefore be defined as an account of an experience that is told in a sequenced way, indicating a flow of related events that, taken together, are significant for the narrator and which convey meaning to the researcher (Coffey and Atkinson 1996).

In Narrative Inquiry, the participant is the narrator, with the researcher adopting the role of a listener facilitating the process of narration (see Box 5.9). The narrative provided may be a short story about a specific event; a more extended story (for example, about a work project, managing or setting up a business, or an organisational change programme); or a complete life history (Chase 2005). However, while in-depth interviews are the primary method to collect stories, other methods may be used by the narrative researcher to record stories as they occur naturally, such as participant observation in the research setting (Coffey and Atkinson 1996; Gabriel and Griffiths 2004). This raises the issue of the Narrative Researcher adopting the role of narrator in particular circumstances, which we will consider further later. It is also important to note that Narrative Inquiry may be used as the sole research strategy, or it may be used in conjunction with another strategy as a complementary approach (Musson 2004).

Narrative Inquiry may be used in different ways. It may be used with a very small number of participants (one, two or three), where these are selected because they are judged as being typical of a much larger culture-sharing population (Chase 2005). As an example, you may decide to interview a small number of accountants or marketing managers who are typical of their occupational population (Box 5.9). It may also be used with a very small sample because those selected are judged as being critical cases or extreme cases, from whom much may be learnt. In this context, in-depth narrative interviews with a small sample of company founders or entrepreneurs may prove to be valuable (Musson 2004). Narrative Inquiry may also be used with slightly larger samples, where, for example, narrative interviews are conducted with, or observations made of, participants from across an organisation, to be able to analyse how narratives are constructed around an event or series of events and to be able to compare how accounts differ, such as between departments, occupational groups, genders and/or grades.

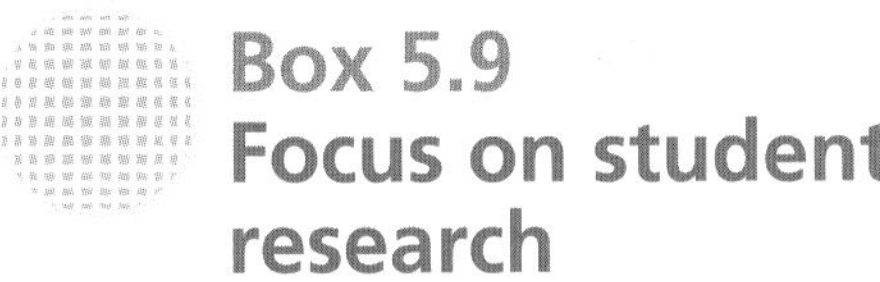

Box 5.9 Focus on student research

Using narrative inquiry to explore a marketing strategy

Kasia was undertaking a marketing degree and because of her longstanding interest in fashion and textiles, she hoped to find a job in that sector. Kasia's interests led her to focus her research project on factors that affected the success of marketing strategies in a small sample of fashion companies. After considering choice of research strategy and discussing this with her project tutor, she decided to use a narrative inquiry strategy, to conduct in-depth interviews with senior managers in a sample of carefully selected companies. She negotiated access to conduct interviews with the marketing directors or managers of three medium-sized fashion companies. Kasia realised that the outcome of her research would very much depend on the quality of these three in-depth interviews and the ways in which her interviewees responded to her request to participate in this narrative approach. She decided to send each of these three managers a letter very briefly outlining this approach and a list of the structural elements she had read about.

She was nervous going to the first interview and realised that her participant, Hetal, sensed this. Hetal had read Kasia's letter and knew a little about narrative inquiry from her own degree studies. Hetal provided Kasia with a full and useful narrative of the factors affecting the outcomes of her employer's marketing strategy over the past year. However, after the interview Kasia realised that she had interrupted Hetal unnecessarily with interview questions on several occasions, interrupting the flow of Hetal's narrative account. Kasia wrote and thanked Hetal for her very useful narrative account and resolved to read more about conducting this type of in-depth interview before conducting the second one. She read Czarniawska's (1997) account, *Narrating the Organization*, and learnt that she would need to move from the interviewer's standard role of asking questions and instead allow her interviewees to act as narrators, using their own voices to tell their stories. Kasia again wrote to her next participant and went to the interview with a list of elements and themes in which she was interested but resolved that her second participant, Jorg, should be allowed to use his own voice. Jorg provided Kasia with another full and useful narrative, with Kasia acting as listener rather than traditional interviewer, only seeking clarification occasionally, after explaining the nature and purpose of the process as they started. Kasia left this second interview feeling very pleased, and looked forward to the next one.

This strategy is generally associated with small, purposive samples (Section 7.3) because of its intensive and time-consuming nature. It is likely to generate large amounts of data in the form of interview transcripts or observational notes. The narratives that emerge may not do so in an easy-to-use structural and coherent form (Gabriel and Griffiths 2004). Coffey and Atkinson (1996) recognise this when they draw on previous research to outline the structural elements that are useful to facilitate analysis of narratives. These broadly take the following form:

- What is the story about?
- What happened, to whom, whereabouts and why?
- What consequences arose from this?
- What is the significance of these events?
- What was the final outcome?

To achieve such analytical coherence in a narrative account may therefore involve the narrative researcher in (re)constructing the story from the strands that emerge from conducting a number of in-depth interviews with one participant or with different participants. As we recognised earlier, this action will place the narrative researcher in a central role in telling the story. For example, decisions will need to be taken about to what to leave out, what to include and how to connect parts of the account. We consider this issue further in Section 13.7.

Where your research question and objectives suggest the use of an interpretive and qualitative strategy, Narrative Inquiry may be suitable for you to use. Narrative Inquiry will allow you to analyse the linkages, relationships and socially constructed explanations that occur naturally within narrative accounts in order 'to understand the complex processes which people use in making sense of their organisational realities' (Musson 2004: 42). The purpose of Narrative Inquiry is to derive theoretical explanations from narrative accounts whilst maintaining their integrity. Whilst analysis in Narrative Inquiry does not use the analytical fragmentation of Grounded Theory, neither does it offer a well-developed set of analytical procedures comparable to those used by grounded theorists. Despite this, analytical rigour is still important in order to derive constructs and concepts to develop theoretical explanations. Whilst narrative researchers may believe that predefined analytical procedures are neither advisable nor desirable, this may make the task of analysis more demanding for you. We return in Section 13.7 to consider some of the approaches that narrative researchers have used to analyse their data.

5.6 Choosing a time horizon

An important question to be asked in designing your research is, 'Do I want my research to be a "snapshot" taken at a particular time or do I want it to be more akin to a diary or a series of snapshots and be a representation of events over a given period?' This will, of course, depend on your research question. The 'snapshot' time horizon is what we call **cross-sectional** while the 'diary' perspective we call **longitudinal**.

Cross-sectional studies

It is probable that your research will be cross-sectional, the study of a particular phenomenon (or phenomena) at a particular time. We say this because we recognise that most research projects undertaken for academic courses are necessarily time constrained. However, the time horizons on many courses do allow sufficient time for a longitudinal study, provided, of course, that you start your research early!

Cross-sectional studies often employ the survey strategy. They may be seeking to describe the incidence of a phenomenon (for example, the IT skills possessed by managers in one organisation at a given point in time) or to explain how factors are related in different organisations (e.g. the relationship between expenditure on customer care training for sales assistants and sales revenue). However, they may also use qualitative or multiple research strategies. For example, many case studies are based on interviews conducted over a short period of time.

Longitudinal studies

The main strength of longitudinal research is its capacity to study change and development. This type of study may also provide you with a measure of control over some of the variables being studied. One of the best-known examples of this type of research comes from outside the world of business. It is the long-running UK television series, 'Seven Up'. This has charted the progress of a cohort of people every seven years of their life. Not only is this fascinating television, it has also provided the social scientist with a rich source of data on which to test and develop theories of human development.

Even with time constraints it is possible to introduce a longitudinal element to your research. As Section 8.2 indicates, there is a massive amount of published data collected over time just waiting to be reanalysed! An example is the Workplace Employee Relations Survey, conducted in 1980, 1984, 1990, 1998, 2004 and 2011/12 (Department for Business Innovation and Skills 2011). From these surveys you would be able to gain valuable secondary data, which would give you a powerful insight into developments in human resource management and employee relations over a period of wide-ranging change.

5.7 Establishing the ethics of the research design

Research ethics are a critical part of formulating your research design. This is discussed in detail in Chapter 6, which focuses on issues associated with negotiating access and research ethics. In particular, Sections 6.2–6.4 examine issues associated with gaining access (to people and to organisations), Section 6.5 defines research ethics and discusses why it is crucial to act ethically, and Section 6.6 highlights ethical issues at specific stages including when designing research and gaining access. Here we introduce two ethical issues that you need to consider when starting to design your research.

Your choice of topic will be governed by ethical considerations. You may be particularly interested to study the consumer decision to buy flower bouquets. Although this may provide some interesting data collection challenges (who buys, for whom and why?), there are not the same ethical difficulties as will be involved in studying, say, the funeral purchasing decision. Your research design in this case may have to concentrate on data collection from the undertaker and, possibly, the purchaser at a time as close to the death as delicacy permits. The ideal population, of course, may be the purchaser at a time as near as possible to the death. It is a matter of judgement as to whether the strategy and data collection method(s) suggested by ethical considerations will yield data that are valid. The general ethical issue here is that the research design should not subject those you are researching to the risk of embarrassment, pain, harm or any other material disadvantage.

Your research design may need to consider whether you should collect data if those you are researching are unaware they are the subject of research and so have not consented. There was a dispute between solicitors and the Consumers' Association (CA). Telephone enquiries were conducted by the CA with a sample of solicitors for the purpose of assessing the accuracy of legal advice given and the cost of specified work. The calls were, allegedly, made without the CA's identity or the purpose of the research being disclosed (Gibb 1995). Although it is for you to decide whether a similar covert research design for your project would be ethical, it is worth emphasising that many university research ethics procedures preclude the use of covert research. Circumstances related to the use of covert observation and issues related to privacy are considered further in Chapters 6 and 9.

5.8 Establishing the quality of the research design

Underpinning our discussion of research design is the issue of the quality of research findings. This is neatly expressed by Raimond (1993: 55) when he subjects findings to the 'how do I know?' test, 'Will the evidence and my conclusions stand up to the closest scrutiny?' For example, how do you know that the advertising campaign for a new product has resulted in enhanced sales? How do you know that manual employees in an electronics factory have more negative feelings towards their employer than their clerical counterparts? The answer, of course, is that, in the literal sense of the question, you cannot know. All you can do is reduce the possibility of getting the answer wrong. This is why good research design is important. This is aptly summarised by Rogers (1961; cited by Raimond 1993: 55): 'scientific methodology needs to be seen for what it truly is, a way of preventing me from deceiving myself in regard to my creatively formed subjective hunches which have developed out of the relationship between me and my material'.

A split often occurs at this point between positivist and interpretivist researchers. The former will use the 'canons of scientific inquiry' of reliability, construct validity, internal validity and external validity to assess the quality of their research or, perhaps more pertinently, that of others. The latter either seek to adapt these terms to assess their research, or reject them as inappropriate to interpretivist studies and use alternative constructs such as credibility, transferability, dependability and confirmability (Lincoln and Guba 1985). We briefly discuss each of these approaches to establish and assess research quality.

Scientific canons of inquiry: reliability, construct validity, internal validity and external validity

Reliability refers to whether your data collection techniques and analytic procedures would produce consistent findings if they were repeated on another occasion or if they were replicated by a different researcher. Ensuring reliability is not necessarily easy and a number of threats to reliability are described in Table 5.3. These threats imply that you will need to be methodologically rigorous in the way you devise and carry out your research to seek to avoid threatening the reliability of your findings and conclusions. More specific advice appears in other chapters but one key aspect is to ensure that your research process is clearly thought through and evaluated and does not contain 'logic leaps and false assumptions' (discussed later). You will need to report each part of your

Table 5.3 Threats to reliability

Threat	Definition and explanation
Participant error	Any factor which adversely alters the way in which a participant performs. For example, asking a participant to complete a questionnaire just before a lunch break may affect the way they respond compared to choosing a less sensitive time
Participant bias	Any factor which induces a false response. For example, conducting an interview in an open space may lead participants to provide falsely positive answers where they fear they are being overheard, rather than retaining their anonymity
Researcher error	Any factor which alters the researcher's interpretation. For example, a researcher may be tired or not sufficiently prepared and misunderstand some of the more subtle meanings of his or her interviewees
Researcher bias	Any factor which induces bias in the researchers' recording of responses. For example, a researcher may allow her or his own subjective view or disposition get in the way of fairly recording and interpreting participants' responses

work in a fully transparent way to allow others to judge for themselves and to replicate your study if they wished to do so.

Reliability is a key characteristic of research quality; however, whilst it is necessary, it is not sufficient by itself to ensure good quality research. Various forms of validity have also been identified to ensure the quality of research. **Construct validity** is concerned with the extent to which your research measures actually measure what you intend them to assess. Construct validity is associated with both positivist and quantitative research and we consider this in more detail in Section 11.4, along with other forms of validity to help to achieve it such as face validity, content validity and criterion-related validity.

Internal validity is established when your research demonstrates a **causal relationship** between two variables. For example, in an experiment internal validity would be established where an intervention can be shown statistically to lead to an outcome. In a questionnaire-based survey, internal validity would be established where a set of questions can be shown statistically to be associated with an analytical factor or outcome (see Chapter 11). Again this concept is associated with both positivist and quantitative research: it can be applied to causal or explanatory studies, but not to exploratory or purely descriptive studies.

Your research findings would be seen as spurious when an apparent relationship is really due to some other reason, such as a flaw in you research design. There are a number of reasons that might threaten the internal validity of your research (Cook and Campbell 1979). We offer definitions and examples of the most frequent in Table 5.4.

Table 5.4 Threats to internal validity

Threat	Definition and explanation
Past or recent events	An event which changes participants' perceptions. For example, a vehicle maker recalling its cars for safety modifications may affect its customers views about product quality and have an unforeseen effect on a planned study (unless the objective of the research is to find out about post-product recall opinions)
Testing	The impact of testing on participants' views or actions. For example, informing participants about a research project may alter their work behaviour or responses during the research if they believe it might lead to future consequences for them
Instrumentation	The impact of a change in a research instrument between different stages of a research project affecting the comparability of results. For example, in structured observational research on call centre operations, the definitions of behaviours being observed may be changed between stages of the research, making comparison difficult
Mortality	The impact of participants withdrawing from studies. Often participants leave their job or gain a promotion during a study
Maturation	The impact of a change in participants outside of the influence of the study that affects their attitudes or behaviours etc. For example, management training may make participants revise their responses during a subsequent research stage
Ambiguity about causal direction	Lack of clarity about cause and effect. For example, during a study, it was difficult to say if poor performance ratings were caused by negative attitudes to appraisal or if negative attitudes to appraisal were caused by poor performance ratings

External validity is concerned with the question: can a study's research findings be generalised to other relevant settings or groups? For example, a corporate manager may ask, 'Can the findings from the research study in one organisation in our corporation also be used to inform policy and practice in other organisations in the group?' The chief executive of a county council may ask, 'Are the findings from the survey in the Finance and Resources Department applicable to other departments in the Council?' Just as researchers take great care when selecting a sample from within a population to make sure that it represents that population, researchers and their clients are often concerned to establish the generalisability of their findings to other contexts. Even in such cases, however, it will be necessary to replicate the study in that other context, or contexts, to be able to establish such statistical generalisability.

Alternative criteria to assess the quality of research inquiry

All researchers take issues of research quality seriously if they wish others to accept their research as credible. However, the scientific canons of inquiry may be seen as placing interpretive, pragmatist, realist and qualitative researchers in something of a dilemma! If good quality research is to be judged against the criteria of reliability and validity, but these are seen as only applicable to positivist, quantitative research, how can a qualitative researcher demonstrate that their research is of high quality and credible? Three types of response are evident. Firstly, there are those who continue to use the concepts of reliability and validity, amending them to fit qualitative or multiple methods research designs (Yin 2009). Secondly, there are those who have formulated new names for versions of these criteria that recognise the nature of qualitative research. In this regard, Lincoln and Guba (1985) formulated 'dependability' for 'reliability', 'credibility' for 'internal validity' and 'transferability' for 'external validity'. Thirdly, there are those who have moved further away from the original concepts and have sought to develop new concepts through which to ensure and judge the quality of qualitative research. In this regard, Guba and Lincoln (1989, 2005) have developed a range of 'authenticity criteria' in place of validity.

A key concern in designing your research will be to familiarise yourself with the criteria to be used to assess your research project. Some of these will refer explicitly to the quality criteria which will be used to assess your research design and outcomes. Others will refer only to more generic criteria related to analytical and evaluative abilities, only implicitly recognising the need for valid/credible/authentic and reliable/dependable research in assessing your research design and outcomes. Familiarising yourself with the assessment criteria to be used will help you to decide how you should approach the way you describe and discuss the quality of your research.

Logic leaps and false assumptions

So far in this chapter we have shown that there are a host of research design decisions to be made in order that your research project can yield sufficient good quality data. These decisions will necessitate careful thought from you. Your research design will need to be logical and, along with any assumptions you make, to stand up to careful scrutiny. Raimond (1993: 128) advises you to 'stand back from your research [design] and take a critical, objective view of it, as though you were a detached observer'. This 'helicopter' view will allow you to see your design as others might, so that you can examine the logic of the research steps you propose to take to see if they will stand up to rigorous scrutiny (Box 5.10).

Box 5.10 Focus on management research

Examining the logic of research

Examining the logic of research has been illustrated skilfully by Raimond (1993). Raimond takes the research of Peters and Waterman on 'excellent' US companies and subjects it to such scrutiny. The ideas of Peters and Waterman (1982, 2004) have been enormously influential since *In Search of Excellence: Lessons from America's Best-Run Companies* was published in 1982. Their book gives managers a list of eight principles of organisations that were successful. As such, it is fairly typical of a prescriptive type of writing in management books that suggests 'the way it should be done'. Raimond's (1993) analysis of Peters and Waterman focuses on four 'logic step' queries.

1 About the implications of the way the research population was chosen:

   Raimond (1993: 129) says that as their sample of 63 successful companies was chosen 'because they are not representative', it is difficult to generalise findings from these, 'to the mass'.

2 About data collection:

   Raimond asks about the way data were collected. The key here is 'who was asked' (only senior managers or others as well?) and 'what were they asked' (what types of questions and how evaluative were these?).

3 About data analysis:

   Raimond asks about the way in which collected data was distilled into the principles for success. He (1993: 130) asks, 'How have they made the jump from thousands of interview reports to the eight attributes?'

4 About the conclusions:

   Raimond recognises the value of Peters and Waterman's research but questions its generalisability. He reports, 'A follow-up study ten years later found that, of the sixty-three companies . . . less than a quarter were successful ten years later, measured on the same criteria' (Raimond 1993: 131).

5.9 Taking into account your role as researcher

This chapter has discussed the decisions you will need to take to formulate your research design. You need to choose between a quantitative, qualitative or multiple methods research design; between research strategies; and between time frames. Each decision will have implications for the nature of your design (between an exploratory, descriptive or explanatory purpose, or some combination of these). Each decision also has implications for the ways in which you seek to establish the ethics and quality of your research design. As you have read through this chapter, you have probably been evaluating each of these decisions in relation to practical constraints as well as personal preferences. We have alluded to practical constraints in a number of places in the chapter in terms of the way they may affect each choice. An important practical consideration in deciding how to formulate a research design is related to your role as researcher.

The role of the external researcher

If you are a full-time student you are likely to adopt the role of an **external researcher**, where you need to identify an organisation within which to conduct your research. You will need to negotiate access to the organisation and to those from whom you would like to collect data. Having achieved this you will need to gain their trust so that they will participate meaningfully to allow you to collect these data. You will need to take these practical factors into account when formulating your research question and your research design. Sections 6.2 to 6.4 provide more detail about issues of access that you need to take into account as an external researcher before finalising your research design.

The role of the internal researcher or practitioner researcher

If you are currently working in an organisation, you may choose to undertake your research project within that organisation, adopting the role of an **internal researcher** or **practitioner researcher**. As a part-time student, you will be surrounded by numerous opportunities to pursue business and management research. You are unlikely to encounter one of the most difficult hurdles that an external researcher has to overcome: that of negotiating research access. Indeed, like many people in such a position, you may be asked to research a particular problem by your employer.

As an internal researcher, another advantage for you will be your knowledge of the organisation and all this implies about understanding the complexity of what goes on in that organisation. It will not be necessary to spend a great deal of time 'learning the context' in the same way as an external researcher will need to do. However, this advantage carries with it a significant disadvantage. You must be very conscious of the assumptions and preconceptions that you carry around with you. This is an inevitable consequence of knowing the organisation well and can prevent you from exploring issues that would enrich the research.

Familiarity may create other problems for the internal researcher. When we were doing case study work in a manufacturing company, we found it very useful to ask 'basic' questions revealing our ignorance about the industry and the organisation. These 'basic' questions are ones that as a practitioner researcher you would be less likely to ask because you, and your respondents, would feel that you should know the answers already. There is also the problem of status. If you are a junior employee you may feel that working with more senior colleagues inhibits your interactions as researcher practitioner. The same may be true if you are more senior than your colleagues.

A more practical problem is that of time. Combining two roles at work is obviously very demanding, particularly as it may involve you in much data recording 'after hours'. This activity is hidden from those who determine your workload. They may not appreciate the demands that your researcher role is making on you. For this reason, practitioner researchers may need to negotiate a proportion of their 'work time' to devote to their research. There are no easy answers to these problems. All you can do is be aware of the possible impact on your research of being too close to your research setting.

5.10 Summary

- Research design is the way a research question and objectives are operationalised into a research project. The research design process involves a series of decisions that need to combine into a coherent research project.
- Research design will be informed by your research philosophy.
- A choice has to be made between using a mono method or multiple methods.

- The nature of your research design will be exploratory, descriptive or explanatory, or a combination of these.
- A decision will be made to use one or more research strategies, related to the nature of the research question and objectives and to ensure coherence with the other elements of your research design.
- The research strategies discussed were: Experiment; Survey; Archival Research; Case Study; Ethnography; Action Research; Grounded Theory; and Narrative Inquiry.
- Choice of quantitative, qualitative or multiple methods and related research strategy or strategies will also be related to the choice of an appropriate time horizon.
- Research ethics play a critical part in formulating a research design. While the exact approach to research design will be governed by ethical considerations, different research designs will also reveal different ethical concerns.
- Establishing the quality of research is also a critical part of formulating a research design. Researchers from different research traditions have developed different criteria to judge and ensure the quality of research.
- Practical considerations will also affect research design, including the role of the researcher.

Self-check questions

Answers to these questions are available at the end of the chapter.

5.1 You wish to study the reasons why car owners join manufacturer-sponsored owners' clubs. You choose to use a qualitative methodology and narrative inquiry research strategy involving unstructured 'discussions' with some members of these owners' clubs. You are asked by a small group of marketing managers to explain why your chosen research design is as valid as a quantitative methodology, survey strategy that uses a questionnaire. What would be your answer?

5.2 You are working in an organisation that has branches throughout the country. The managing director is mindful of the fact that managers of the branches need to talk over common problems on a regular basis. That is why there have always been monthly meetings. However, she is becoming increasingly concerned that these meetings are not cost-effective. Too many managers see them as an unwelcome intrusion. They feel that their time would be better spent pursuing their principal job objectives. Other managers see it as a 'day off': an opportunity to recharge the batteries.

She has asked you to carry out some research on the cost-effectiveness of the monthly meetings. You have defined the research question you are seeking to answer as 'What are the managers' opinions of the value of their monthly meetings?'

Your principal research strategy will be a survey using a questionnaire to all managers who attend the monthly meetings. However, you are keen to triangulate your findings. How might you do this?

5.3 You have started conducting interviews in a university with the hourly paid staff (such as porters, gardeners and caterers). The research objective is to establish the extent to which those employees feel a sense of 'belonging' to the university. You have negotiated access to your interviewees through the head of each of the appropriate departments. In each case you have been presented with a list of interviewees.

It soon becomes apparent to you that you are getting a rather rosier picture than you expected. The interviewees are all very positive about their jobs, their managers and the university. This makes you suspicious. Are all the hourly paid staff as positive as this? Are you being given only the employees who can be relied on to tell the 'good news'? Have they been 'got at' by their manager?

There is a great risk that your results will not be valid. What can you do?

5.4 You are about to embark on a year-long study of customer service training for sales assistants in two supermarket companies. The purpose of the research is to compare the way in which the training develops and its effectiveness. What measures would you need to take in the research design stage to ensure that your results were valid?

Review and discussion questions

5.5 Agree with a friend to watch the same television documentary.

- **a** Does the documentary use a quantitative, qualitative or multiple methods research methodology?
- **b** To what extent is the nature of the documentary exploratory, descriptive or explanatory, or a combination of these?
- **c** What other observations can you make about the research strategy or strategies the documentary makers have used in their programme?

Do not forget to make notes regarding your reasons for your answers to each of these questions and to discuss these answers with your friend.

5.6 Use the search facilities of an online database to search for scholarly (peer-reviewed) articles which have used firstly a case study, secondly action research and thirdly experiment research strategy in an area of interest to you. Download a copy of each article. What reasons do the articles' authors give for the choice of strategy?

Progressing your research project

Deciding on your research design

- Review your research question and objectives. Make notes on your philosophy and how it will impact on your research (which philosophy and the likely impact?).
- Do your research question and objectives and philosophy support using a mono method qualitative, mono method quantitative or multiple methods research? Make notes for and against using each methodological choice. Decide which one is most appropriate.
- Based on the decisions you have made so far, create a shortlist of research strategies which may be appropriate to conduct your research, together with the advantages and disadvantages of each. Set this shortlist aside. Search for studies in the literature that are similar to your own. Use these to note which strategies have been used. What explanations do the researchers give for their choice of strategy? Evaluate your shortlist against the notes from your search of studies in the literature. Use this evaluation to decide which strategy or combination of strategies would be most appropriate for your own research.
- Decide on the time frame to conduct your proposed design.
- Ask yourself, 'What are the practical constraints on my proposed design?' Use this question to review your decisions above and if necessary make changes. Repeat this step until you are satisfied your proposals are practical.
- Use your draft research design, to list (1) potential threats to research quality and (2) ethical issues in your design and make notes about how you propose to deal with each. Where necessary, make further changes to the decisions in the steps above until you are satisfied with your research design.
- You should now be ready to discuss your proposed research design with your tutor.
- Use the questions in Box 1.4 to guide your reflective diary entry.

5.7 Visit the online gateway to the European Union website (http://europa.eu/) and click on the link in your own language. Discuss with a friend how you might you use the data available via links from this web page in archival research. In particular, you should concentrate on the research questions you might be able to answer using these data to represent part of the reality you would be researching.

References

Bryant, A. and Charmaz, K. (2007) *The Sage Handbook of Grounded Theory*. London: Sage.

Bryman, A. (1989) *Research Methods and Organisation Studies*. London: Unwin Hyman.

Bryman, A. (2006) 'Integrating quantitative and qualitative research: How is it done?', *Qualitative Research*, Vol. 6, No. 1, pp. 97–113.

Charmaz, K. (2005) 'Grounded theory in the 21st century', in N.K. Denzin and Y.S. Lincoln (eds) *The Sage Handbook of Qualitative Research* (3rd edn). London: Sage, pp. 507–36.

Charmaz, K. (2006) *Constructing Grounded Theory*. London: Sage.

Chase, S.E. (2005) 'Narrative inquiry', in N.K. Denzin and Y.S. Lincoln (eds) *The Sage Handbook of Qualitative Research* (3rd edn). London: Sage, pp. 651–80.

Cinite, I., Duxbury, L.E. and Higgins, C. (2009) 'Measurement of perceived organisational readiness for change in the public sector', *British Journal of Management*, Vol. 20, pp. 265–77.

Coffey, A. and Atkinson, P. (1996) *Making Sense of Qualitative Data*. London: Sage.

Coghlan, D. and Brannick, T. (2010) *Doing Action Research in Your Own Organisation* (3rd edn). London: Sage.

Cook, T.D. and Campbell, D.T. (1979) *Quasi-experimentation: Design and Analysis Issues for Field Settings*. Chicago: Rand McNally.

Corbin, J. and Strauss, A. (2008) *Basics of Qualitative Research* (3rd edn). London: Sage.

Cresswell, J.W. (2009) 'Mapping the field of mixed methods research', *Journal of Mixed Methods Research*, Vol. 3, No. 2, pp. 95–108.

Cresswell, J.W. and Plano Clark, V.L. (2007) *Designing and Conducting Mixed Methods Research*. Thousand Oaks, CA: Sage.

Cunliffe, A.L. (2010) 'Retelling tales of the field: In search of organisational ethnography 20 years on', *Organizational Research Methods*, Vol. 13, No. 2, pp. 224–39.

Czarniawska, B. (1997) *Narrating the Organization: Dramas of Institutional Identity*. Chicago: University of Chicago Press.

Denzin, N.K. and Lincoln, Y.S. (2005) *The Sage Handbook of Qualitative Research* (3rd edn). London: Sage.

Department for Business Innovation and Skills (2011) *Workplace employment relations study*. Available at www.bis.gov.uk/policies/employment-matters/research/wers [Accessed 14 August 2011].

Eden, C. and Huxham, C. (1996) 'Action research for management research', *British Journal of Management*, Vol. 7, No. 1, pp. 75–86.

Eisenhardt, K.M. and Graebner, M.E. (2007) 'Theory building from cases: Opportunities and challenges', *Academy of Management Journal*, Vol. 50, No. 1, pp. 25–32.

Gabriel, Y. and Griffiths, D.S. (2004) 'Stories in organizational research', in C. Cassell and G. Symon (eds) *Essential Guide to Qualitative Methods in Organizational Research*. London: Sage, pp. 114–26.

Geertz, C. (1988) *Works and Lives: The Anthropologist as Author*. Stanford, CA: Stanford University Press.

Gibb, F. (1995) 'Consumer group accuses lawyers of shoddy service', *The Times*, 5 October.

Glaser, B. and Strauss, A. (1967) *The Discovery of Grounded Theory*. Chicago, IL: Aldine.

Glaser, B.G. (1992) *Basics of Grounded Theory*. Mill Valley, CA: Sociology Press.

Greene, J.C. (2007) *Mixed Methods in Social Inquiry*. San Francisco: Jossey-Bass.

Greene, J.C., Caracelli, V.J. and Graham, W.F. (1989) 'Towards a conceptual framework for mixed-method evaluation designs', *Educational Evaluation and Policy Analysis*, Vol. 11, No. 3, pp. 255–74.

Greenwood, D.J. and Levin. M. (2007) *Introduction to Action Research* (2nd edn). London: Sage.

Guba, E.G. and Lincoln, Y.S. (1989) *Fourth Generation Evaluation*. Newbury Park, CA: Sage.

Guba, E.G. and Lincoln, Y.S. (2005) 'Paradigmatic controversies, contradictions, and emerging confluences' in N.K. Denzin and Y.S. Lincoln, *The Sage Handbook of Qualitative Research* (3rd edn). London: Sage, pp. 196–216.

Hakim, C. (2000) *Research Design: Successful Designs for Social and Economic Research* (2nd edn). London: Routledge.

Lee, R.M. and Fielding, N. (1996) 'Qualitative data analaysis: Representations of a technology', *Sociological Research Online*, Vol. 1, No. 4. Available at socresonline.org.uk/1/4/16.html [Accessed 11 October 2011].

Leech, N.L. and Onwuegbuzie, A.J. (2009) 'A typology of mixed methods research designs', *Quality and Quantity*, Vol. 43, pp. 265–75.

Lincoln , Y.S. and Guba, E.G. (1985) *Naturalistic Inquiry*. Beverly Hills, CA: Sage.

Molina-Azorin, J.F. (2011) 'The use and added value of mixed methods in management research', *Journal of Mixed Methods Research*, Vol. 5, No. 1, pp. 7–24.

Musson, G. (2004) 'Life histories', in C. Cassell and G. Symon (eds) *Essential Guide to Qualitative Methods in Organizational Research*. London: Sage, pp. 34–46.

Naipaul, V.S. (1989) *A Turn in the South*. London: Penguin.

Nastasi, B.K., Hitchcock, J.H. and Brown, L.M. (2010) 'An inclusive framework for conceptualising mixed methods typologies', in A. Tashakkori and C. Teddlie (eds) *The Sage Handbook of Mixed Methods in Social and Behavioural Research* (2nd edn). Thousand Oaks, CA: Sage.

Our Rivers Campaign (2010) Available at www.ourrivers.org.uk/results/ [Accessed 18 November 2010].

Peters, T. and Waterman, R. (1982) *In Search of Excellence*. New York: Harper & Row.

Peters, T. and Waterman, R. (2004) *In Search of Excellence* (2nd edn). New York: Profile Books.

Raimond, P. (1993) *Management Projects*. London: Chapman & Hall.

Reason, P. (2006) 'Choice and quality in action research practice', *Journal of Management Inquiry*, Vol. 15, No. 2, pp. 187–202.

Reason, P. and Bradbury, H. (2008) *Handbook of Action Research* (2nd edn). London: Sage.

Reichertz, J. (2007) Abduction: The logic of discovery of grounded theory', in A. Bryant and K. Charmaz (eds) *The Sage Handbook of Grounded Theory*. London: Sage.

Ridenour, C.S. and Newman, I. (2008) *Mixed Methods Research: Exploring the Interactive Continuum*. Carbondale, IL: South Illinois University Press.

Rogers, C.R. (1961) *On Becoming a Person*. London: Constable.

Schein, E. (1999) *Process Consultation Revisited: Building the Helping Relationship*. Reading, MA: Addison-Wesley.

Shani, A.B. and Pasmore, W.A. (1985) 'Organization inquiry: Towards a new model of the action research process', in D.D. Warrick (ed.) *Contemporary Organization Development*. Glenview, IL: Scott Foresman, pp. 438–48

Strauss, A. and Corbin, J. (1998) *Basics of Qualitative Research* (2nd edn) . London: Sage.

Suddaby, R. (2006) 'From the editors: What grounded theory is not', *Academy of Management Journal*, Vol. 49, No. 4, pp. 633–42.

Tashakkori, A. and Teddlie, C. (eds) (2010) *The Sage Handbook of Mixed Methods in Social and Behavioural Research* (2nd edn). Thousand Oaks, CA: Sage.

Teddlie, C. and Tashakkori, A. (2009) *Foundations of Mixed Methods Research: Integrating Quantitative and Qualitative Approaches in the Social and Behavioural Sciences*. Thousand Oaks, CA: Sage.

Tedlock, B. (2005) 'The observation of participation and the emergence of public ethnography', in N.K. Denzin and Y.S. Lincoln (eds) *The Sage Handbook of Qualitative Research* (3rd edn). London: Sage.

Titscher, S., Meyer, M., Wodak, R. and Vetter, E. (2000) *Methods of Text and Discourse Analysis*. London: Sage, pp. 467–82.

Whyte, W.F. (1993) *Street Corner Society: The Social Structure of an Italian Slum* (4th edn). Chicago, IL: University of Chicago Press.

Yin, R.K. (2009) *Case Study Research: Design and Method* (4th edn). London: Sage.

Further reading

Charmaz, K. (2006) *Constructing Grounded Theory*. London: Sage. Very useful and readable source for Grounded Theory strategy.

Coghlan, D. and Brannick, T. (2010). *Doing Action Research in Your Own Organisation* (3rd edn). London: Sage. Very useful and readable source for Action Research strategy

Cunliffe, A.L. (2010) 'Retelling tales of the field: In search of organisational ethnography 20 years on', *Organizational Research Methods*, Vol. 13, No. 2, pp. 224–39. Very useful and readable introduction to Organisational Ethnography.

Denzin, N.K. and Lincoln, Y.S. (2005) *The Sage Handbook of Qualitative Research* (3rd edn). London: Sage. This work contains many useful discussions about qualitative research and related strategies', including Chase's chapter on 'Narrative Inquiry'.

deVaus, D.A. (2002) *Surveys in Social Research* (5th edn). London: Routledge. Very useful source for survey strategy.

Hakim, C. (2000) *Research Design: Successful Designs for Social and Economic Research* (2nd edn). London: Routledge. This book provides a clear discussion of issues associated with a range of research designs. Chapter 9 is very useful for experiment strategy.

Tashakkori, A. and Teddlie, C. (eds) (2010) *The Sage Handbook of Mixed Methods in Social and Behavioural Research* (2nd edn). Thousand Oaks, CA: Sage. Useful introduction to mixed methods research.

Yin, R.K. (2009) *Case Study Research: Design and Method* (4th edn). London: Sage. Very useful source for case study strategy.

Case 5
Sangita's career

Sangita was interested in the topic of careers. She had taken a Human Resource Management module that involved studying issues related to career management, the psychological contract and developments in contemporary careers. She was interested in the distinction her tutor had drawn between traditional careers, where people spend their working lives in one organisation gradually gaining promotions, and so-called boundaryless careers, where people move between organisations to develop their careers. She decided that this was the research idea she wanted to work up into a research question. She discussed this idea with her friends, who joked with her that what she was really interested in was 'Sangita's career!'

Source: Pearson Education Photodisk/Kevin Peterson

She laughed at this idea but told her friends that she really did find the idea of careers fascinating! Her brother, who was four years older than Sangita, had just got his first career job. He had spent two years on an IT graduate training programme in a large market research company. At the end of this, the organisation had offered him the post of Information Services Analyst, Level 1, which he was delighted to accept. In this organisation there were five levels of services analyst. Sangita was really pleased for her brother and recognised that here was an organisation which was carefully managing the careers of its employees, offering them development and progression opportunities in return for their commitment, hard work and loyalty.

Her thoughts about the continued existence and importance of traditional careers were reinforced when she read some of the careers studies literature. She read a report from the Chartered Institute of Personnel and Development containing a number of case studies from a diverse range of organisations indicating that these approached 'talent management' and career development with great care and attention, even when confronted by the impact of economic downturn and uncertain times (McCartney 2010). She also read an insightful article by Rodrigues and Guest (2010). They used previously published literature and official data from a number of European countries, Japan and the USA to conclude that in overall terms there was little evidence to support the idea that job tenure had decreased significantly or that careers had become more boundaryless. This included evidence that core workers in these countries continued to experience similar levels of job tenure, measured in years with one employer. However, there was some evidence from these data that certain groups of employees, notably younger workers and those from lower socioeconomic groups, experienced less job stability.

Sangita concluded from this that traditional careers remained just as important for those who had benefited from them in the past. The idea of the boundaryless career was interesting but perhaps it was only of marginal importance. The boundaryless career suggested that employees would have to become much more individualistic about developing their careers as a consequence of job instability. However, the evidence that Sangita read pointed the other way. For most career-oriented employees, organisations continued to hold the key to career development (Rodrigues and Guest 2010). This set Sangita thinking about the distinction between individuals' self-managed career development and organisationally driven career management.

Sangita read a number of articles that used a theory-testing, deductive approach to explore the distinction between self-managed career development and organisational career management. These tended to test theoretical hypotheses using a questionnaire-based survey strategy (for example, Sturges et al. 2008). Sangita discovered that not only were organisationally driven career management interventions still important, but these were statistically linked to job performance, commitment to the organisation and also in some cultures to the promotion of individual career management behaviours. Organisational career management interventions that encourage employees to engage in their own career self-help could lead to promotion within an organisation or to a career move to another organisation. She also read an article by Zeitz et al. (2009) that highlighted the excessively individualistic nature of the boundaryless career idea and discussed several ways in which employees would need to be supported in order to develop their abilities to move between organisations, including organisationally based career management support.

Sangita thought that these articles were very useful as they helped her to understand that the reality of career development was much more complicated than was suggested by those who advocated the growth of the boundaryless career. However, she noted that employees did move between organisations to develop their careers, some groups such as younger graduate workers being more likely to do this (De Vos et al. 2009). If the concept of the boundaryless career was in doubt, Sangita felt that there was a need to understand more about the idea of career boundary crossing (Inkson et al. 2010; Zeitz et al. 2009) and the respective roles of self-managed career development and organisational career management in helping this.

Sangita felt that this would be a good topic for her research project. The question in her mind was how to focus and design her research. There were potentially many different ways in which she could explore this topic further. Her research might be employee focused. If this were to be the case, she thought that she could collect data from employees in different age groups, or occupational groups, or sectors of employment. Alternatively, she thought that she could collect data from employees in stable employment relationships who enjoyed a traditional career structure and contrast these with a second set from employees who moved between organisations to develop their careers across organisational boundaries. Conversely, her research might be management focused. If this were to be the case, she thought that she might collect data within a case study organisation, or sample of case study organisations, to examine the nature of their organisational career management policies and how these related to internal promotion decisions and boundary-crossing career turnover.

The research design possibilities for Sangita's research were not only numerous but also a little confusing. She thought about them carefully, especially in terms of what would be both interesting and practical to undertake. She decided to focus on analysing organisational career management policies using a case study organisation to evaluate how these related to career promotions and boundary-crossing career turnover in her research proposal. Her initial research question was: 'What organisational career management policies exist in [case study organisation name] to retain key employees and how have these policies been evaluated in relation to career-related employee turnover?'

On the morning of her meeting with her project tutor to discuss her draft research proposal, she reread her proposal and notes once more. She reflected on her research question and the notes she had made from various journal articles and books that she was going to develop into the first draft of her literature review. Finally she read through her proposed research design. She checked that she was satisfied with her methodological choice and research strategy and went to the meeting with her tutor.

References

De Vos, A., De Stobbeleir, K. and Meganck, A. (2009) 'The relationship between career-related antecedents and graduates' anticipatory psychological contracts', *Journal of Business Psychology,* Vol. 24, pp. 289–98.

Inkson, K., Ganesh, S., Roper, J. and Gunz, H. (2010). 'The boundaryless career: A productive concept that may have outlived its usefulness', *Academy of Management Annual Meeting Proceedings*, pp. 1-6.

McCartney, C. (2010) *Fightback through Talent Innovation: Talent Management under Threat in Uncertain Times.* London; Chartered Institute of Personnel and Development.

Rodrigues, R.A. and Guest, D. (2010) 'Have careers become boundaryless?', *Human Relations*, Vol. 63, No. 8, 1157–75.

Sturges, J., Conway, N. and Liefooghe, A. (2008) 'What's the deal? An exploration of career management behaviour in Iceland', *The International Journal of Human Resource Management*, Vol. 19, No. 4, pp. 752–68.

Zeitz, G., Blau, G. and Fertig, J. (2009) 'Boundaryless careers and institutional resources', *The International Journal of Human Resource Management*, Vol. 20, No. 2, pp. 372–98.

Questions

1 What are the possible research strategies from which Sangita might chose to address her research question?
2 What are the likely advantages and drawbacks of using each possible strategy?
3 Which research strategy would you use to conduct this research project and why?

Ongoing case: Researching emotional labour

Part 1: Some reading and a possible research design?

The magic and excitement of theme parks have enthralled Jessica since her first visit to a Disney theme park 14 years ago. The characters, the enchanted atmosphere, the immaculate park grounds and the stories told by the Disney employees – all of this made such a memorable impression that Jessica would now like to use a theme park as the focus for her Master's research project.

Source: Shutterstock/Tom Hirtreiter

Her interest in the sociology of work leads Jessica to read about theme park employees' accounts of their experience. These shed light on the burdens and troubles of being a theme park employee. She is particularly struck by the ethnography of the sociologist John van Maanen, who worked for three summers as a rides operator in a Disney theme park and wrote up his experiences as a participant observation ethnography of these workers (van Maanen and Kunda 1989).

Disney proclaims itself on its website as the 'happiest place on earth' (http://disneyland.disney.go.com). However, for employees, the picture may be less positive. John van Maanen describes Disney as 'the smile factory'. He observes that employees vie for status and respect in a highly regimented employment structure where standardised rules and procedures ensure that grimy operations such as cleaning are almost invisible, so that customers only experience joy and pleasure (and perhaps buy more from the concession outlets and merchandising stores). He writes about how employees find tricks to subvert the rules, for example, having more than the permitted number of 'time-outs'. But more often than not, employees come to accept and buy into the Disney culture. They 'glide into their kindly and smiling roles' with ease (van Maanen and Kunda 1989: 73). The success of this feat of social engineering is largely due, according to van Maanen and Kunda (1989) and Bryman (2003), to the socialisation process which employees go through.

A big part of the socialisation process is achieved through influencing employees' emotions, or at least the emotional aspect of their interactions with theme park visitors. Hochschild (2003: 186) argued that for many service industries such as air travel and hospitality, what used to be considered a private act of emotional display – idiosyncratic, spontaneous and personal to a customer and service worker – may now be controlled, managed and standardised through organisations' training and socialisation practices. This is perhaps the darker side of theme parks that Jessica never saw as an excited child. But with her interest in the sociology of work, she now feels that it reaches insidiously into all aspects of service work. Recently, scholars have talked of the 'emotional labour' which employees have to provide as part of their jobs. Their appearance, demeanour and emotional responses to customers are all aspects of work over which they usually have some control; but increasingly in organisations, employees' conduct is tightly scripted and regulated. It's not just a question of pretending to smile and be happy. The socialisation process into the organisation's culture and values aims to make employees want to smile all day.

Jessica wonders whether the stresses and strains of emotional labour have been ignored by many business researchers. She's particularly interested in getting the 'insider' view, and settles on a provisional title for her master's research project: 'Inside a theme park: what are employees' experiences of emotional labour?'

But what sort of research design would be best for doing this? Jessica has some university friends already working at a local theme park, and wants to ask them if they'll be interviewed for her project. However, having read Van Maanen's (1991) ethnographic study she has a nagging doubt: would semi-structured interviews be enough to expose the emotional labour which these employees have to perform?

References

Bryman, A. (2003) 'McDonald's as a Disneyized institution: Global implications', *American Behavioral Scientist*, Vol. 47, pp. 154–67.

Hochschild, A. (2003) *The Managed Heart* (2nd edn). Berkeley, CA: University of California Press.

Van Maanen, J. (1991) 'The smile factor: Work at Disneyland' in P.J. Frost, L.F. Moore, M.L. Louis, C.C. Lundberg and J. Martin (eds) *Reframing Organizational Culture*. Newbury Park, CA: Sage.

Van Maanen, J. and Kunda, G. (1989) '"Real feelings": Emotional expression and organizational culture', *Research in Organizational Behavior*, Vol. 11, pp. 43–103.

Questions for discussion for Part 1

1 Look at Jessica's research question; is the research 'purpose' exploratory, descriptive or explanatory?

2 Is Jessica's research design (based only on semi-structured interviews in one case study organisation) likely to be sufficient to answer the research question?

3 What are the possible issues associated with Jessica interviewing her university friends?

Additional case studies relating to material covered in this chapter are available via the book's companion website: **www.pearsoned.co.uk/saunders**. They are:

- The effectiveness of computer-based training at Falcon Insurance Company.
- Embedded quality at Zarlink Semi-conductor.
- The international marketing management decisions of UK ski tour operators.
- Managing the acquistion from the middle.

Self-check answers

5.1 You would need to stress here that your principal interest would be in getting a deep understanding of why car owners join manufacturer-sponsored owners' clubs. You would discover why the owners joined these clubs and what they thought of them. In other words, you would establish what you set out to establish and, no doubt, a good deal besides. There is no reason why your discussions with owners should not be as valid as a survey questionnaire. Your initial briefing should be skilful enough to elicit rich responses from your interviewees (see Chapter 10) and you may also use prompts to focus on themes that emerge in the narratives of your participants.

Of course, you may alleviate any fears about 'validity' by using a multiple methods research methodology and delivering a questionnaire as well, so that your findings may be triangulated!

5.2 The questionnaire will undoubtedly perform a valuable function in obtaining a comprehensive amount of data that can be compared easily, say, by district or age and gender. However, you would add to the understanding of the problem if you observed managers' meetings. Who does most of the talking? What are the non-verbal behaviour patterns displayed by managers? Who turns up late, or does not turn up at all? You could also consider talking to managers in groups or individually. Your decision here would be whether to talk to them before or after the questionnaire, or both. In addition, you could study the minutes of the meetings to discover who contributed the most. Who initiated the most discussions? What were the attendance patterns?

5.3 There is no easy answer to this question! You have to remember that access to organisations to research is an act of goodwill on the part of managers, and they do like to retain a certain amount of control. Selecting whom researchers may interview is a classic way of managers doing this. If this is the motive of the managers concerned then they are unlikely to let you have free access to their employees.

What you could do is ask to see all the employees in a particular department rather than a sample of employees. Alternatively, you could explain that your research was still uncovering new patterns of information and more interviews were necessary. This way you would penetrate deeper into the core of the employee group and might start seeing those who were rather less positive. All this assumes that you have the time to do this!

You could also be perfectly honest with the managers and confess your concern. If you did a sound job at the start of the research in convincing them that you are purely interested in academic research, and that all data will be anonymous, then you may have less of a problem.

Of course, there is always the possibility that the employees generally are positive and feel as if they really do 'belong'!

5.4 This would be a longitudinal study. Therefore, the potential of some of the threats to internal validity explained in Section 5.8 is greater simply because they have longer to develop. You would need to make sure that most of these threats were controlled as much as possible. For example, you would need to:

- account for the possibility of a major event during the period of the research (wide-scale redundancies, which might affect employee attitudes) in one of the companies but not the other;
- ensure that you used the same data collection devices in both companies;
- be aware of the 'mortality' problem. Some of the sales assistants will leave. You would be advised to replace them with assistants with similar characteristics, as far as possible.

Get ahead using resources on the companion website at: **www.pearsoned.co.uk/saunders**

- Improve your IBM SPSS for Windows and NVivo research analysis with practice tutorials.
- Save time researching on the Internet with the Smarter Online Searching Guide.
- Test your progress using self-assessment questions.
- Follow live links to useful websites.

Chapter 6

Negotiating access and research ethics

Learning outcomes

By the end of this chapter you should be:

- aware of issues associated with gaining traditional and Internet-mediated access;
- able to evaluate a range of strategies to help you to gain access to organisations and to individual participants;
- aware of the importance of research ethics and the need to act ethically;
- able to anticipate ethical issues at each stage of your research and in relation to particular techniques, and be aware of approaches to help you deal with these;
- aware of the principles of data protection and data management.

6.1 Introduction

Many students want to start their research as soon as they have identified a topic area, forgetting that access and ethics are critical aspects for the success of any research project. Such considerations are equally important whether you are using secondary data (Chapter 8), or collecting primary data through person-to-person, Internet-mediated or questionnaire-based methods. Over the past decade, concerns about the ethics of research practice have grown substantially. Consequently, you need to think carefully about how you will gain access to undertake your research and about possible ethical concerns that could arise throughout the conduct of your research project. Without paying careful attention to how you are going to gain access to the data you require and acting ethically, what seem like good ideas for research may flounder and prove impractical or problematic once you attempt to undertake them.

Business and management research almost inevitably involves human participants. Ethical concerns are greatest where research involves human participants, irrespective of whether the research is conducted person-to-person. In thinking about undertaking business and management research you need to be aware that most universities, as well as an increasing number of organisations, require researchers to obtain formal Research Ethics Committee approval (or a favourable ethical opinion) for their proposed research prior to granting permission to commence a project. Universities and other organisations help to facilitate the process of ethical scrutiny and approval by developing ethical guidelines for researchers to use in developing their research projects. We

Possibly the first statement of ethical principles was written by Hippocrates, a Greek physician considered by many to be the 'Father of Medicine', or by one of his followers. The Hippocratic Oath was written as an ethical guideline for the conduct of medical doctors. It required physicians to swear an oath upon the healing gods in whom the ancient Greeks believed, to uphold what we would now consider to be a number of professional standards. Translated from the original Greek (Edelstein, cited in Temkin and Temkin 1987: 6), these are extracts from the Hippocratic Oath,

> I will apply dietetic measures for the benefit of the sick according to my ability and judgment; I will keep them from harm and injustice.
>
> I will neither give a deadly drug to anybody if asked for it, nor will I make a suggestion to this effect. . . .
>
> Whatever houses I may visit, I will come for the benefit of the sick, remaining free of all intentional injustice, . . . be they free or slave.
>
> What I may see or hear in the course of the treatment or even outside of the treatment . . . I will keep to myself holding such things shameful to be spoken about.

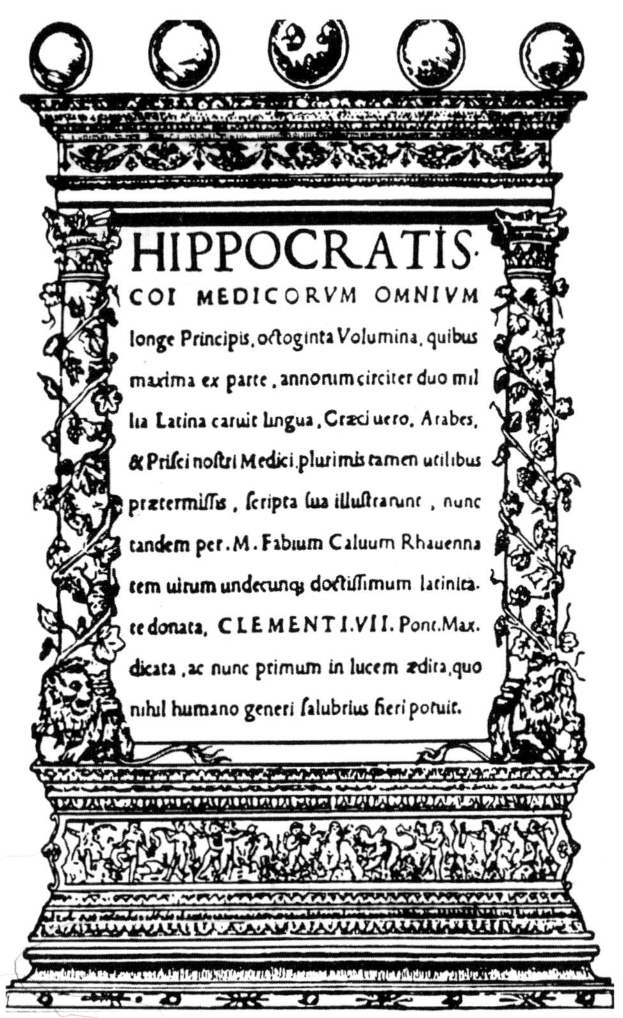

HIPPOCRATIS·
COI MEDICORVM OMNIVM
longe Principis, octoginta Volumina, quibus
maxima ex parte, annorum circiter duo mil
lia Latina caruit lingua, Græci uero, Arabes,
& Priſci noſtri Medici, plurimis tamen utilibus
prætermiſſis, ſcripta ſua illuſtrarunt, nunc
tandem per. M. Fabium Caluum Rhauenna
tem uirum undecunq; doctiſſimum latinita-
te donata, CLEMENTI.VII. Pont.Max.
dicata, ac nunc primum in lucem ædita, quo
nihil humano generi ſalubrius fieri potuit.

Source: Mary Evans Picture Hibrary

Some other parts of the original oath are seen as contentious or inappropriate. Where it has been used as an oath to swear in newly qualified doctors it has been reformulated through time to reflect different and changing cultural values. Clearly the original Hippocratic Oath reflected the beliefs and values of those who wrote and used it. Allowing for these caveats and recognising that it was devised approximately 2500 years ago, it established a number of ethical principles that are held by many as being universal and timeless. For doctors treating the sick, it established the division between healing and euthanasia. The ideal of treating the sick equally, irrespective of their class or rank, was also established. The ethical principle of avoiding harm and injustice has remained as a vital ethical principle for many professions, including researchers. Respecting privacy, another key ethical principle, was also established in the Hippocratic Oath.

consider ethical guidelines later but it is worth noting that the idea for these may be traced back some 2500 years to physicians in ancient Greece, as our opening vignette illustrates.

In this chapter we start by considering types and levels of traditional access and the issues associated with these (Section 6.2). In this section we also explore issues of feasibility and sufficiency in relation to gaining access and the impact of these on the nature and content of your research question and objectives. Section 6.3 examines Internet-mediated access and the issues associated with this. Section 6.4 discusses a number of established strategies to help you gain access to organisations and to your intended participants within these organisations. Section 6.5 provides an overview of research ethics and outlines why it is essential to act ethically. Section 6.6 anticipates the scope for ethical issues to occur during the various stages of your research project and in relation to the use of particular techniques. Section 6.7 introduces principles of data protection and data management, which you will need to consider in order to manage your data ethically.

6.2 Issues associated with gaining traditional access

Your ability to obtain either primary or secondary data will depend on gaining access to an appropriate source, or sources where there is a choice. The appropriateness of a source will, of course, depend on your research question, related objectives and research design (Chapter 5). In this discussion we refer to levels and **types of access**. It is useful to offer a definition of each at this point. The first type is **traditional access**, which involves face-to-face interactions (to conduct experiments, interviews, focus groups, observations or to administer questionnaires), 'phone conversations (for telephone interviews), correspondence (for postal questionnaires) or visiting data archives (such as record offices or organisational archives, where data are not available online). The second type is **Internet-mediated access**, which involves the use of different computing technologies (e.g. the Web, email, instant messaging, webcams), to gain virtual access to administer questionnaires, conduct archival research, discussions, experiments or interviews, or to gather secondary data. A variant of this is **intranet-mediated access**, where you seek to gain virtual access as an employee or worker in an organisation using its intranet. Even where you attempt to gain Internet- or intranet-mediated access it is likely that you will still need to use an element or some elements of traditional access. We therefore define a further type, **hybrid access**, which combines traditional and Internet-mediated approaches. We focus on traditional access in this section and on Internet, intranet and hybrid types of access in Section 6.3.

Levels of access vary depending on the nature and depth of the access that you achieve. We discuss three levels of access: physical, continuing and cognitive. Even where you seek to use the Internet or an intranet to gain virtual access you may first need to achieve physical access and, subsequently, to negotiate your access on a continuing basis. You will certainly need to achieve cognitive access where your research involves human participants. As a result, the discussion in this section is likely to be relevant to you irrespective of the type of access that you intend to use.

The first level of access is **physical access** or entry (Gummesson 2000). The Internet has undoubtedly made accessing some secondary data easier. However, for much secondary as well as primary data gaining physical access can be difficult. First, organisations, groups or individuals may not be prepared to engage in additional, voluntary activities because of the time and resources required. Many organisations receive frequent student requests for access and cooperation and would find it impossible to agree to all or even some of these. Second, the request for access and cooperation may fail to interest the **gatekeeper** or **broker** who receives it, and who makes the final decision whether or not to allow the researcher to undertake the research. This may be for a number of reasons, related to:

- a lack of perceived value in relation to the work of the organisation, group or the individual;
- the nature of the topic because of its potential sensitivity, or because of concerns about the confidentiality of the information that would be required;
- perceptions about your credibility and doubts about your competence.

Third, the organisation or group may find itself in a difficult situation owing to external events totally unrelated to any perceptions about the nature of the request or the person making it, so that they have no choice but to refuse access. There may be other reasons for refusing access, known to the organisation, group or individuals concerned. Even when someone is prepared to offer access this may be overruled at a higher level in the organisation. This may result in a 'false start' and an associated feeling of disappointment (Johnson 1975). Where you are unable to gain this type of access, you will need to find another organisation or group, or to modify your research question and objectives.

However, even when you are able to negotiate entry there are other levels of access that you will need to consider and plan for if your research strategy is to be realised. Many writers see access as a **continuing** process and not just an initial or single event (Gummesson 2000; Marshall and Rossman 2006; Okumus et al. 2007). This may take two forms. First, access may be an iterative and incremental process, so that you gain entry to carry out the initial part of your research and then seek further access in order to conduct another part (see Box 6.1).

Second, those from whom you wish to collect data may be a different set of people to those who agreed to your request for access. Physical access to an organisation will be granted formally through its management. Because of this it will also be necessary for you to gain the acceptance and trust of, as well as consent from, intended participants within the organisation or group in order to gain actual access to the data that they are able to provide. This type of access is referred to as **cognitive access**. Where you achieve this, you will have gained access to the data that you need your intended participants to share with you in order to be able to address your research question and objectives. Simply obtaining physical access to an organisation is likely to be inadequate unless you are also able to negotiate yourself into a position where you can collect data that reveal the reality of what is occurring in relation to your research question and objectives.

The nature of the access you manage to negotiate may impact upon your ability to select a suitable sample of participants, or of secondary data, affecting your attempt to produce reliable and valid data to fulfil your objectives and answer your research question in an unbiased way (Box 6.2). In order to select a suitable sample of, for example, customers, clients or employees you will require access to organisational data, either directly or indirectly,

Box 6.1 Focus on student research

Negotiating incremental access

Luc wished to undertake a series of interviews in the departments and sections of a data management company. He initially managed to negotiate access to commence his research in the management systems support department, where he was granted access to interview a sample of information systems support workers. As a result of conducting these interviews, he was then granted access within the same department to interview a sample of staff in the information technology section. Following the conduct of these interviews, the department's management team agreed to support his attempt to negotiate further access to interview staff in the company's accounting, human resources, marketing and sales departments.

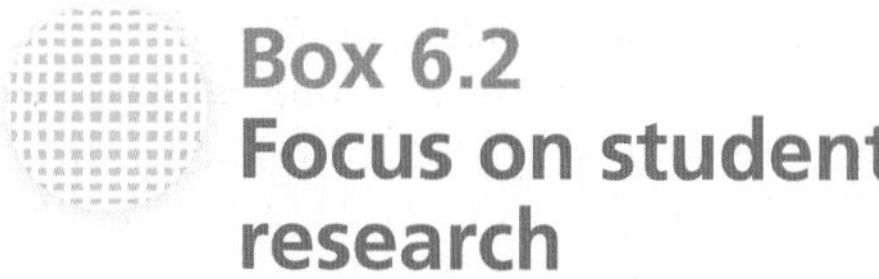

Box 6.2 Focus on student research

Gaining access to a suitable sample

Maria wished to discover how component suppliers viewed the just-in-time delivery requirements of large manufacturing organisations which they supplied. Two large manufacturing organisations agreed to introduce her to a sample of their component suppliers, whom Maria could then interview. Whilst undertaking the interviews Maria noted that all of the interviewees' responses were extremely positive about the just-in-time delivery requirements of both large manufacturing organisations. As both manufacturing organisations had selected who would be interviewed, Maria wondered whether these extremely positive responses were typical of all the component suppliers used by these organisations, or whether they were providing an unreliable and untypical picture.

through a request that outlines precisely how you require the sample to be selected (see Chapter 7 for a full discussion of sampling techniques). Where you wish to undertake a longitudinal study using primary data, you will require access to the organisation and your research participants on more than one occasion. The difficulty of obtaining access in relation to these more **intrusive methods** and approaches has been recognised many times in the literature (e.g. Buchanan et al. 1988; Easterby-Smith et al. 2008; Johnson 1975).

Negotiating access is therefore likely to be important to gain **personal entry** to an organisation (or, in the case of Internet-mediated research, virtual access) and develop cognitive access to allow you to collect the necessary data. In this context, there are two general concepts that you may consider, which will help you to evaluate the nature of the access that you will require. These concepts are feasibility and sufficiency. **Feasibility** is concerned with whether it is practicable to negotiate access for your proposed research project. A research proposal may be grand and elegant, but if it is not possible to gain access to data then it will be necessary to revise what is being proposed. Once you have a proposal that you believe will be feasible in general terms, the next point to consider is whether you will be able to gain sufficient access to fulfil all of your research objectives. **Sufficiency** is therefore concerned with the extent to which the access you negotiate will enable your proposed research project to be achieved. You do not want to have to say, 'I could achieve objectives a, b and c but not x, y and z!' Or, perhaps more likely, 'I can achieve objectives a, b, y and z, but now I think about this carefully, I'm going to find it difficult to collect much data for c and x!' You therefore need to consider fully the nature of the access that you will require and whether you will able to gain sufficient access in practice to fulfil all of your objectives, to answer your research question. These issues of feasibility and sufficiency will be related in practice but it is useful to consider them separately as you formulate your research proposal. Your clarity of thought, which should result from having considered the nature and extent of the access that you require, may also be helpful in persuading organisations or groups to grant entry since they are more likely to be convinced about your credibility and competence.

The issues of feasibility and sufficiency will determine the construction or refinement of your research question and objectives, and may sometimes lead to a clash with the hallmarks of good research (Cooper and Schindler 2008; Marshall and Rossman 2006; Sekaran and Bougie 2009). The ways in which these issues may clash with the hallmarks of good research and also affect the practice of research has been recognised by Buchanan et al. (1988: 53–4):

> Fieldwork is permeated with the conflict between what is theoretically desirable on the one hand and what is practically possible on the other. It is desirable to ensure

> representativeness in the sample, uniformity of interview procedures, adequate data collection across the range of topics to be explored, and so on. But the members of organisations block access to information, constrain the time allowed for interviews, lose your questionnaires, go on holiday, and join other organisations in the middle of your unfinished study. In the conflict between the desirable and the possible, the possible always wins.

This quotation highlights how, even when you consider feasibility and sufficiency carefully, you may still meet problems in practice. However, it should not be read as a justification for not considering these issues carefully. By considering these issues you will be more able to anticipate and overcome problems that occur in practice. The extent to which a careful consideration of feasibility will affect the approach that you adopt is made clear by Johnson (1975). He recognises that the reality of undertaking a research project may be to consider where you are likely to be able to gain access and to develop a topic to fit the nature of that access.

Problems of access may also vary in relation to your status as either a full-time or part-time student. We therefore consider further your role as either an external researcher or as an internal researcher. This latter role may involve you adopting the role of participant researcher.

Access issues as an external researcher

As a full-time student, approaching an organisation or group where you have little or no prior contact, you will be seeking to act as an **external researcher**. You will need to negotiate access at each level discussed earlier (physical, continuing and cognitive). Operating as an external researcher is likely to pose problems, although it may have some benefits. Your lack of status in relation to an organisation or group in which you wish to conduct research will mean not only that gaining physical access is a major issue to overcome but also that this concern will remain in relation to negotiating continued and cognitive access (Box 6.3). Goodwill on the part of the organisation or group and its members is something that external researchers have to rely on at each level of

Box 6.3 Focus on student research

The impact of a researcher's organisational status

David recalls a case of mistaken identity. His research involved gaining access to several employers' and trade union organisations. Having gained access to the regional office of one such organisation, David used various types of organisational documentation kept there over a period of a few days. During the first day David was located in a large, comfortable room and frequently brought refreshments by the caretaker of the building. This appeared to David to be very kind treatment. However, David did not know that a rumour had spread among some staff that he was from 'head office' and was there to 'monitor' in some way the work of the office. On attending the second day, David was met by the caretaker and taken to a small, plain room and no more refreshments appeared for the duration of the research visit. The rumour had been corrected!

Of course this example of the effect of the researcher's (lack of) organisational status is most unfair on the large number of people who treat those who undertake research within their organisation very well in full knowledge of their status. However, it illustrates the way in which some people may react to perceptions about status.

access. In this role, you need to remain sensitive to the issue of goodwill and seek to foster it at each level. Your ability to demonstrate clearly your research competence and integrity, and in particular your ability to explain your research project clearly and concisely, will also be critical at each level of access. These are key issues of access faced by all external researchers.

Where you are able to demonstrate competence (see Chapters 9 to 11) and integrity, your role as an external researcher may prove to be beneficial. This is because participants are usually willing to accept you as being objective and without a covert, often organisationally focused, agenda. In doing this your gatekeeper can play an important role, adding credibility and introducing you and your research project to the relevant people and creating an awareness of your research.

Access issues as an internal researcher or participant researcher

As an organisational employee or group member operating in the role of an **internal researcher** or a **participant researcher**, you are still likely to face problems of access to data, although these may differ compared to those faced by external researchers. As an internal researcher you may still face the problems associated with negotiating physical or continuing access, and may still need to obtain formal approval to undertake research in your organisation or group. In addition, your status in the organisation or group may pose particular problems in relation to cognitive access. This may be related to suspicions about why you are undertaking your research project and the use that will be made of the data, perceptions about the part of the organisation for which you work and your status in relation to those whom you wish to be your research participants. Any such problems may be exacerbated if you are given a project to research, perhaps by your line manager or mentor, where others are aware that this is an issue about which management would like to implement change. This is particularly likely to be the case where resulting change is perceived as being harmful to those whom you would wish to be your research participants. This will not only provide a problem for you in terms of gaining cognitive access but may also suggest ethical concerns as well (which we discuss in Section 6.5). As an internal researcher, you will need to consider these issues and, where appropriate, discuss them with those who provide you with the research project.

6.3 Issues associated with Internet-mediated access

The Internet enables access to research data and to research participants in a variety of ways, although its use also raises a number of data quality and ethical issues. We outline these ways before considering associated issues later. Quantitative and qualitative data collection techniques (Section 5.3 and Chapters 10 and 11) are increasing used via the Internet. Questionnaires may be delivered as a hyperlink within an email, completed and returned online. Certain types of experiment may be conducted via the Internet (Birnbaum 2004). Interviews or discussion groups may take place online. For example, Stieger and Goritz (2006) have explored the use of instant messaging, such as MSN Messenger and Facebook, to conduct Internet-based interviews. Interviews may also be conducted by email. They may also be conducted using a webcam, helping to overcome the impersonal nature of a text-based Internet interview.

Various types of online community have generated extremely large amounts of qualitative material, some of which has been accessed by researchers. Writing in 2006, Kozinets identified bulletin boards, email lists and linked web pages, amongst other types of online community. As online communities organised around an interest or a particular product, service, place or lifestyle, bulletin boards can be used to post messages and create a discussion over time amongst its members. Email lists also allow groups to converse around a subject or subjects of mutual interest. Linked web pages provide online community resources organised by interest, such as for consumer-to-consumer discussion. **Blogs** (web logs) and limited character blogs or tweets are also popular. As a form of online journal or diary, where an individual provides for public consumption a narrative about his or her everyday life, or some aspect of it, blogs provide a commentary on events at a group, organisational or societal level. For example, numerous bloggers comment on political events, often from the perspective of their political beliefs. Others comment on their shopping experiences and offer consumer advice, or on their employment (Schoneboom 2011). Many blogs are organised through content management systems, and can also be accessed through specialised blog search engines as well as Internet search engines (Hookway 2008; Kozinets 2006).

These Internet-mediated equivalents are subject to the same issues that affect traditional methods to gain research access. In some circumstances, issues associated with access may even be exacerbated using Internet-based methods. While the Internet, and more specifically the use of email, instant messaging or a webcam, may facilitate communication between you and your participants, it will first be necessary to determine the most suitable way to negotiate access and conduct your research. This will, of course, depend on the nature of your research question and research objectives. Where your research is designed to be conducted through an organisation, it may be more appropriate to negotiate traditional access to collect data. This is because you will need to obtain the permission of a broker or gatekeeper to gain access to organisational members. Where you wish to negotiate access on a continuing basis (Box 6.1) your chance of success is likely to be enhanced where you meet with participants and organisational managers to develop rapport, demonstrate your competence and establish trust. Finally, where you are using more intrusive forms of data collection, such as an in-depth interview, a personal approach may provide you with richer research data. This indicates circumstances where traditional access will continue to be the most effective way to conduct research (Box 6.4).

Even where you subsequently consider using Internet-mediated techniques, there may be circumstances where it would still be advantageous to negotiate initial access on a personal basis. This will remain the case where you require access to an organisation and need to obtain the permission of a broker or gatekeeper to gain access to a sample of organisational members. Where you are able to negotiate this, you may then be able to get the organisation to allow you to advertise your research by email, and provide a hyperlink to your questionnaire (Section 11.5). This highlights how access to organisations, intended participants and data may involve a **hybrid access strategy**, where access combines traditional and Internet-mediated approaches to achieve this.

Where your research will be conducted with a number of individuals there will be greater scope for you to identify an appropriate sample directly and then to negotiate **virtual access**, that is the equivalent of physical access, as well as cognitive access to your intended participants. The ability to identify your sample will be a key determinant of the feasibility of this approach. The choice of this access strategy will also depend on the nature of your research question and research objectives (Box 6.5).

Box 6.4 Focus on student research

Where sensitivity and context determined type of access

Sab had a keen interest in IT and thought that he would conduct his research using Internet-mediated access and data collection methods. His research focused on the ways in which senior managers influence board-level strategic decision making. His interest in this topic had developed after a fortuitous conversation with a senior personnel policy manager who worked for a large organisation, who had explained how in some cases strategy formation was influenced by promoting incremental changes rather than trying to bring about a radical change in one movement. This idea interested Sab and he formulated a research project to explore it in a range of organisational contexts. However, the more he thought about it and discussed it with his project tutor the more he realised that he would have to research it using traditional methods.

After negotiating physical access to interview six senior managers who worked in different functional areas in different organisations, he conducted an in-depth, exploratory interview with each one. Whilst conducting these interviews he realised that the value and depth of the data he collected would have been much less if he had tried to conduct these using the Internet. His questioning was shaped by the data each participant shared with him during the interview. Because of the sensitive nature of the topic most of the interviews took the form of discussions, allowing Sab to clarify points and ask for illustrative examples. As each interview progressed, he found that some of his participants were willing to show him quite sensitive documents in the privacy of the interview room (which was the manager's own office). He found that rapport and trust were vital to the conduct of each interview. He also found that conducting an interview at the organisation helped to focus his mind and enhance his understanding of the organisational context. This in turn helped him to make sense of the data his participants shared with him.

Sab concluded that first negotiating physical access and then cognitive access on a person-to-person basis had been the most appropriate strategy to adopt and also the most effective. However, as he had met with each participant and established some rapport and trust, he asked each one if he would be able to email any further questions for clarification. Some agreed but others said that they would prefer to undertake this either by telephone or a further face-to-face discussion.

6.4 Strategies to gain access

This section considers strategies that may help you to obtain physical, virtual, continuing and cognitive access to appropriate data. The applicability of the strategies discussed here to gain access will depend on the nature of your research design and research strategy (Chapter 5). It will also depend on your data collection methods (Chapters 8–11) and your use of traditional or Internet-mediated means to gain access. However, where you wish to gain access to an organisation, irrespective of whether you intend to use traditional or Internet-mediated means, or where your research involves human participants, irrespective of whether you wish to observe them or ask them to complete a postal or Internet-mediated questionnaire, the strategies discussed here should be applicable. In addition, some of the points that follow will apply to the way in which you construct the pre-survey contact and the written request to complete the questionnaire (see Sections 11.4 and 11.5). The applicability of these strategies will also vary in relation to your status as either an internal researcher or an external researcher. Table 6.1 presents the list of strategies that may help you to gain access.

Box 6.5 Focus on student research

Where topic and strategy determined type of access

Elina's research focused on consumers' purchasing decisions. She was interested in assessing the relative importance of information obtained from online shopping sites and from high street shops in informing purchasing decisions for a range of different product categories. These categories were all products that would be purchased by her age group, such as people on her marketing course.

Elina had formulated a mixed methods research design. She had designed an online questionnaire that asked respondents to identify actual recent purchasing decisions related to the categories in which she was interested. For each of these, where applicable, she asked questions about the product, the sources of information used to inform the purchase decision and the way in which these sources determined the purchasing decision. Following ethical approval from her university, an email was sent to each person on her course asking for their help and containing a hyperlink to the questionnaire. The questionnaire included a question asking each respondent if they were willing to help further by completing an electronic diary. Those who answered yes were asked to provide their email address so Elina could send them the diary.

Elina emailed the template of the electronic diary to all those willing to help further. She had designed this to allow respondents to record purchasing decisions related to her list of product categories, the sources of information used to inform these purchases and the way in which these sources determined the decision. Respondents returned the diary as an email attachment.

Elina was aware that her request to maintain an electronic diary of influences on purchasing decisions would sensitise respondents to their use of different information sources, so had distributed the questionnaire first. This she felt would help her judge the extent the participant had been sensitised as well as about the relative impact of these different sources.

Her use of an Internet-mediated access strategy proved successful in gaining access to both questionnaire respondents and a group of people who would keep a diary.

Ensuring familiarity with the organisation or group

Before attempting to gain physical access it is essential that you familiarise yourself fully with the characteristics of the organisation or group. The knowledge that you gain will enable you to signal to the gatekeeper that you have thought carefully about your research, as you will be able to provide a credible case to justify your request to grant access to the organisation or group.

Table 6.1 Strategies that may help you to gain access

- Ensuring you are familiar with the organisation or group before making contact
- Allowing yourself sufficient time
- Using existing contacts and developing new ones
- Providing a clear account of the purpose of your research and the type of access required
- Overcoming organisational concerns about granting access
- Identifying possible benefits to the organisation of granting you access
- Using suitable language
- Facilitating replies when requesting access
- Developing access incrementally
- Establishing your credibility

Allowing yourself sufficient time

Physical access may take weeks or even months to arrange, and in many cases the time invested will not result in access being granted (Buchanan et al. 1988). An approach to an organisation or group will result in either a reply or no response at all. A politely worded but clearly reasoned refusal at least informs you that access will not be granted. The non-reply situation means that if you wish to pursue the possibility of gaining access you will need to allow sufficient time before sending further correspondence, emailing or making a follow-up telephone call. Great care must be taken in relation to this type of activity so that no grounds for offence are given. Seeking access to a large, complex organisation, where you do not have existing contacts, may also necessitate several telephone calls to contact the most appropriate person to consider your request for access, or to establish who this will be. As highlighted in Box 6.6, even after the person to contact has been established, access can still take months to achieve. You may also consider using email as a way of making contact, although great care needs to be taken given the ease with which emails may sent 'in all directions'. Care also needs to taken in the composition of any email, as with any 'phone call or letter.

If you can contact a participant directly, such as a manager, an exchange of correspondence may be sufficient to gain access. Here you should clearly set out what you require from this person and persuade them of the value of your work and your credibility. Even so, you will still need to allow time for your request to be received and considered and an interview meeting to be arranged at a convenient time for your research participant. This may take a number of weeks, and you may have to wait for longer to schedule the actual interview.

Box 6.6 Focus on management research

Spending time gaining access

In a paper in the *Annals of Tourism Research* Okumus et al. (2007) reflect on their experiences of gaining access for three distinct research projects. For one of these studies, eight companies were initially approached by letter in which the background, aims and potential benefits to the companies were explained alongside issues of confidentiality and resource and time requirements. Subsequent to this letter, follow-up telephone calls were made and further explanations provided. Five of the eight companies responded that they were unable to participate in the research.

After months of negotiation, three companies had shown interest. Access to the first was gained through a university professor acting as an intermediary between the researchers and the company. In the negotiations it was made clear that the research would need to be of value to the company. The process of gaining access to the first company had taken more than four months from initial contact to starting to collect data.

During data collection, gatekeepers in each of the three companies identified potential informants to approach for interview. These informants then identified others to be interviewed. Okumus and colleagues comment that, although this might be considered a 'snowball sample', they prefer not to use this term. Initially the three companies selected themselves by agreeing to take part in the research. Subsequently, although the researchers had sought to reach and interview all key informants at different management levels and locations this was in some cases not possible. Potential informants had been identified by the gatekeepers and only those willing to take part could be interviewed.

Where you are seeking access to conduct a number of interviews, to undertake a questionnaire, to engage in observation or to use secondary data, your request may be passed 'up' the organisation or group for approval and is likely be considered by a number of people. Where you are able to use a known contact in the organisation or group this may help, especially where they are willing to act as a sponsor for your research. Even so, you will still need to allow for this process to take weeks rather than days. Where the organisation or group is prepared to consider granting access, it is likely that you will be asked to attend a meeting to discuss your research. There may also be a period of delay after this stage while the case that you have made for access is evaluated in terms of its implications for the organisation or group, and it may be necessary to make a number of telephone calls or emails to pursue your request politely.

In the situation where your intended participants or respondents are not the same people who grant you physical access, you will need to allow further time to gain their acceptance. This may involve you making **pre-survey contact** by telephoning these people (Section 11.5), engaging in correspondence or holding an explanatory meeting with them (discussed later). You may well need to allow a couple of weeks or more to establish contact and to secure cooperation, especially given any operational constraints that restrict individuals' availability.

Once you have gained physical access to the organisation or group and to your participants or respondents, you will be concerned with gaining cognitive access. Whichever method you are using to gather data will involve you in a time-consuming process, although some methods will require that more of your time be spent within the organisation or group to understand what is happening. The use of a questionnaire will mean less time spent in the organisation compared with the use of non-standardised interviews, whereas the use of some observation techniques can result in even more time being spent gathering data (Chapter 9). Where you are involved in a situation of continuing access, as outlined in this section, there will also be an issue related to the time that is required to negotiate, or renegotiate, access at each stage. You will need to consider how careful planning may help to minimise the possibility of any 'stop–go' approach to your research activity.

Using existing contacts and developing new ones

Most management and organisational researchers suggest that you are more likely to gain access where you are able to use **existing contacts** (Buchanan et al. 1988; Easterby-Smith et al. 2008; Johnson 1975). Buchanan et al. (1988: 56) say that, 'we have been most successful where we have a friend, relative or student working in the organisation'. We have also found this to be the case. In order to request access we have approached those whom we would consider to be professional colleagues, who may also be present or past students, course advisers, external examiners or otherwise known to us through our networks. Their knowledge of us means that they can trust our stated intentions and the assurances we give about the use of any data provided. It can also be useful to start a research project by utilising these existing contacts in order to establish a track record that you can refer to in approaches you make to other organisations or groups where you do not have such contacts. This should help your credibility with these new contacts.

Use of known contacts will depend largely on your choice of research strategy, approach to selecting a sample, research question and objectives. It is likely to be easier to use this approach where you are using a case study, action research or ethnographic research strategy (Section 5.3). This will certainly be likely where you undertake an in-depth study that focuses on a small, purposively selected sample (Section 7.3). There will clearly be a high level of convenience in terms of gaining access through contacts who are familiar; however, these contacts may also be cases in other non-probability samples (Section 7.3).

In many instances it may be possible for you to use your work placement organisation as the context for your research project. Where you have enjoyed a successful work placement, you will undoubtedly have made a number of contacts who may be able to be very helpful in terms of cooperating with you and granting access. You may have become interested in a particular topic because of the time that you spent in your placement organisation. Where this is so, you can spend time reading theoretical work that may be relevant to this topic, then identify a research question and objectives, and plan a research project to pursue your interest within the context of your placement organisation. The combination of genuine interest in the topic and relatively easy access to organisational participants should help towards the production of a good-quality and useful piece of work.

Where you need to develop **new contacts**, there may be several ways of finding these, depending on your research topic. You may consider asking the local branch of an appropriate professional association for the names and business addresses of key employees to contact in organisations where it would be suitable for you to conduct research. You could also contact this professional association at national level, where this is more appropriate to your research question and objectives. It might also be appropriate to contact either an employers' association for a particular industry, or a trade union, at local or national level. Alternatively, it might be appropriate for you to contact one or more chambers of commerce, learning skills councils or other employers' network. However, you need to be mindful that such associations and organisations are likely to receive literally hundreds of requests from students every year and so may have insufficient time or resources to respond.

You may also consider making a direct approach to an organisation or group in an attempt to identify the appropriate person to contact in relation to a particular research project. This has the advantage of potentially providing access to organisations or groups that you would like to include in your research project; however, great care needs to be exercised at each stage of the process (Box 6.7).

Using the approach outlined in Box 6.7 may result in you obtaining the business email addresses of possible organisational 'leads'. In this case you will need to send an email request to each person (Box 6.8). Where you consider this to be appropriate you will, of course, still need to follow the standards of care that you should use in drafting and sending a letter. The ease of using email may tempt some to use a lower level of care about the way their written communication is constructed. It may also lead to a temptation to send repeated messages. Use of email is considered later in our discussion about 'netiquette'; however, from a practical point of view using this means to make contact may result in a greater danger that the recipient of your email request simply deletes the message! People who receive large numbers of email may cope by deleting any that are not essential. Conversely, sending a letter to a potential gatekeeper may result in that person considering your request more carefully!

Using the type of contact outlined in Box 6.7 may result in identifying the person whom you wish to participate in your research. Alternatively, your reason for making contact with this person may be to ask them to grant you access to others in the organisation or group whom you wish to be your participants, or to secondary data. This type of contact may be the functional manager or director of those staff to whom you would like access. Having identified a gatekeeper you will have to persuade that person about your credibility, overcome any issues that exist about the sensitivity of your research project and demonstrate the potential value of this for the organisation.

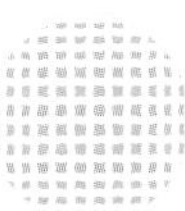

Box 6.7 Focus on student research

Identifying possible contacts through whom to request access

Andrew identified a number of specific organisations that matched the criteria established for the types of business he wished to include in his research project. Many of these were organisations where he did not have an appropriate contact, or indeed any contact at all. The different types of organisational structure in these organisations added to his difficulties in tracking down the most appropriate employee to contact in order to request access.

Organisations' websites were used to identify the corporate headquarters of each organisation, which was then contacted by telephone. When talking to each organisation, Andrew explained that he was a student and gave the title of his course and the name of his university. He also gave a very brief explanation of his research to the person who answered the telephone. This resulted in him being provided with a telephone number or email address for that part of the organisation the person who answered the telephone thought was appropriate, or being connected directly. Andrew always ended this initial telephone conversation by thanking the person for the help that they had provided.

At the next stage, Andrew again explained that he was a student and gave the title of his course and the name of his university. The purpose of the research was also explained briefly to the personal assistant who inevitably answered the telephone. Andrew asked for the name and business address of the person whom the personal assistant thought would be the most appropriate person to write to, or to email. In most cases the people to whom he spoke at this stage were helpful and provided some excellent leads.

Sometimes, particularly in relation to complex organisations, Andrew found that he was not talking to someone in the appropriate part of the organisation. He therefore asked the person to help by transferring the telephone call. Sometimes this led to a series of calls to identify the right person. Andrew always remained polite, thanking the person to whom he spoke for her or his help. He always gave his name and that of his university to reduce the risk of appearing to be threatening in any way. It was most important to create a positive attitude in what could be perceived as a tiresome enquiry.

Andrew chose to ask for the name and business address of a hoped-for organisational 'lead'. Using this he could send a written request to this person, which could be considered when it was convenient, rather than attempt to talk to them then, when it might well have not been a good time to make such a request. This process resulted in many successes, and Andrew added a number of good contacts to his previous list. However, the key point to note is the great care that was exercised when using this approach.

Box 6.8 Focus on student research

Email requesting access

Annette was undertaking her research project on the use of lean production systems. Having made telephone contact with the Production Controller's personal assistant, she was asked to send an email requesting access (see below).

Unfortunately, Annette relied on her email software's spellcheck to proofread her email. This resulted in the Production Controller receiving an email containing four mistakes:

- the addition of the word 'I' at the end of the first paragraph;
- the phrase 'between 30 minutes and half an hour' instead of 'between 30 minutes and an hour' at the end of the second paragraph;
- two digits being transposed in the mobile telephone number at the end of the last paragraph, resulting in it being incorrect;
- the second sentence of the final paragraph being poorly worded.

Not surprisingly, Annette was denied access.

Box 6.8 Focus on student research *(continued)*

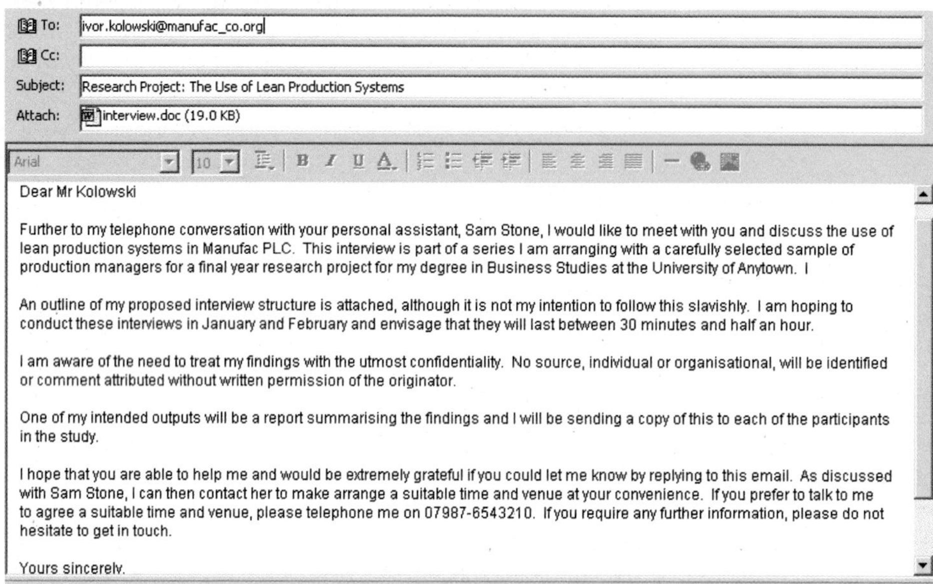

To: ivor.kolowski@manufac_co.org
Cc:
Subject: Research Project: The Use of Lean Production Systems
Attach: interview.doc (19.0 KB)

Dear Mr Kolowski

Further to my telephone conversation with your personal assistant, Sam Stone, I would like to meet with you and discuss the use of lean production systems in Manufac PLC. This interview is part of a series I am arranging with a carefully selected sample of production managers for a final year research project for my degree in Business Studies at the University of Anytown. I

An outline of my proposed interview structure is attached, although it is not my intention to follow this slavishly. I am hoping to conduct these interviews in January and February and envisage that they will last between 30 minutes and half an hour.

I am aware of the need to treat my findings with the utmost confidentiality. No source, individual or organisational, will be identified or comment attributed without written permission of the originator.

One of my intended outputs will be a report summarising the findings and I will be sending a copy of this to each of the participants in the study.

I hope that you are able to help me and would be extremely grateful if you could let me know by replying to this email. As discussed with Sam Stone, I can then contact her to make arrange a suitable time and venue at your convenience. If you prefer to talk to me to agree a suitable time and venue, please telephone me on 07987-6543210. If you require any further information, please do not hesitate to get in touch.

Yours sincerely,

Providing a clear account of the purpose and type of access required

Providing a clear account of your requirements will allow your intended participants to be aware of what will be required from them (Robson 2011). Asking for access and cooperation without being specific about your requirements will probably lead to a cautious attitude on their part since the amount of time that could be required might prove to be disruptive. It is also likely to be considered unethical (Section 6.5). Even where the initial contact or request for access involves a telephone call, it is still probably advisable to send a letter or email that outlines your proposed research and requirements (Box 6.8). Your **introductory letter** requesting access should outline in brief the purpose of your research, how the person being contacted might be able to help, and what is likely to be involved in participating. The success of this letter will be helped by the use of short and clear sentences. Its tone should be polite, and it should seek to generate interest on the part of intended respondents.

Establishing your credibility will be vital in order to gain access. The use of known contacts will mean that you can seek to trade on your existing level of credibility. However, when you are making contact with a potential participant for the first time, the nature of your approach will be highly significant in terms of beginning to establish credibility – or not doing so! Any telephone call, introductory letter or email will need to be well presented, and demonstrate your clarity of thought and purpose. Any lack of preparation at this stage will be apparent and is likely to reduce the possibility of gaining access. These issues are discussed in more detail in Section 10.4.

Overcoming organisational concerns about granting access

Organisational concerns may be placed into one of three categories. First, concerns about the amount of time or resources that will be involved in the request for access. Easterby-Smith et al. (2008) suggest that your request for access is more likely to be accepted if the amount of time and resources you ask for are kept to a minimum. As a complementary point, Healey (1991) reports earlier work which found that introductory letters containing multiple requests are also less likely to be successful. However, while the achievement of access may be more likely to be realised where your demands are kept to a minimum, there is still a need to maintain honesty. For example, where you wish to conduct an interview you may be more likely to gain access if the time requested is kept within reason. Remember, stating falsely that it will last for only a short time and then deliberately exceeding this is very likely to upset your participant and may prevent you gaining further access.

The second area of concern is related to **sensitivity** about the topic. We have found that organisations are less likely to cooperate where the topic of the research has negative implications. Organisations do not normally wish to present themselves as not performing well in any aspect of their business. If this is likely to be the case you will need to consider carefully the way in which your proposed research topic may be perceived by those whom you ask to grant access. In such cases you may be able to highlight a positive approach to the issue by, for example, emphasising that your work will be designed to identify individual and organisational learning in relation to the topic (a positive inference). You should avoid sending any request that appears to concentrate on aspects associated with non-achievement or failure if you are to gain access. Your request for access is therefore more likely to be favourably considered where you are able to outline a research topic that does not appear to be sensitive to the organisation (Easterby-Smith et al. 2008).

The third area of concern is related to the **confidentiality** of the data that would have to be provided and the **anonymity** of the organisation or individual participants. To overcome this concern, you will need to provide clear assurances about these aspects (Box 6.8). When offering these you must be sure that you will be able to keep to your agreement. Strictly, if you have promised confidentiality you should not share your raw data with anyone, not even your project tutor, or present this as it may be recognised or identified. Data remain confidential; it will be the analysed results that you present at a sufficient level of generalisation that identification is not possible. Anonymity ensures that no one will know who participated in your research and that no one is able to identify the source of any response. One advantage of using an introductory letter is to give this guarantee in writing at the time of making the request for access, when this issue may be uppermost in the minds of those who will consider your approach. Once initial access has been granted you will need to repeat any assurances about anonymity and confidentiality to your participants as you seek their consent (Section 6.6). You will also need to consider how to maintain these assurances when you write up your work in situations where particular participants could be indirectly identified (Section 14.5). Illustrations of how not to do this are provided in Box 6.17!

Possible benefits to the organisation of granting access

Apart from any general interest that is generated by the subject of your proposed research, you may find that it will be useful to the jobs undertaken by those whom you approach for access. Practitioners often wrestle with the same subjects as researchers and may therefore welcome the opportunity to discuss their own analysis and course of action related to an issue, in a non-threatening, non-judgemental environment. A discussion may allow them to think through an issue and to reflect on the action that they have adopted to manage it. For this reason, in our own interviews with practitioners we are pleased when told that the discussion has been of value to them.

For those who work in organisations where they are perhaps the only subject practitioner, this may be the first time they have had this type of opportunity. You therefore need to consider whether your proposed research topic may provide some advantage to those from whom you wish to gain access, although this does not mean that you should attempt to 'buy' your way in based on some promise about the potential value of your work. Where it is unlikely that your proposed research may assist those whose cooperation you seek, you will need to consider what alternative course of action to take.

It may help to offer a summary report of your findings to those who grant access. The intention would be to provide something of value and to fulfil any expectations about exchange between the provider and receiver of the research data, thereby prompting some of those whom you approach to grant access (Johnson 1975). We believe it is essential that this summary report is designed specifically to be of use to those who granted access rather than, say, a copy of the research report you need to submit to your university. It is also possible that feedback from the organisation about this summary report may help you further with your research.

Where access is granted in return for supplying a report of your findings it may be important to devise a simple 'contract' to make clear what has been agreed. This should state the broad form of the report and the nature and depth of the analysis that you agree to include in it, and how you intend to deal with issues of confidentiality and anonymity. This may vary from a summary report of key findings to a much more in-depth analysis. For this reason it will be important to determine what will be realistic to supply to those who grant you access.

Using suitable language

Some researchers advise against referring to certain terms used in relation to research activity when making an approach to an organisation for access, because these may be perceived as threatening or not interesting to the potential participant (e.g. Buchanan et al. 1988; Easterby-Smith et al. 2008). Buchanan et al. (1988: 57) suggest using 'learn from your experience' in place of research, 'conversation' instead of interview and 'write an account' rather than publish.

Use of language will depend largely on the nature of the people you are contacting. Your language should be appropriate to the type of person being contacted, without any hint of being patronising, threatening or just boring. Given the vital role of initial telephone conversations, introductory letters or emails, we would suggest allowing adequate time to consider and draft these and using someone to check through your message. You may find Section 11.4, and in particular Box 11.16, helpful in this process. Do not forget that you are intending to engender interest in your research project, and the initial point of contact needs to convey this.

Facilitating replies when requesting access

We have found that the inclusion of a number of different contact methods (telephone, mobile phone, fax, email) in our written requests for access helps to ensure a reply. These may not be suitable in all cases, and should be selected to fit the data collection technique you intend to use. Inclusion of a stamped or postage prepaid (freepost) addressed envelope may also facilitate a reply.

Developing access incrementally

We have already referred to the strategy of achieving access by stages, as a means of overcoming organisational concerns about time-consuming, multiple requests. Johnson (1975) provides an example of developing access on an incremental basis. He used a three-stage strategy to achieve his desired depth of access. The first stage involved a request to conduct interviews. This was the minimum requirement in order to commence his research. The next stage involved negotiating access to undertake observation. The final stage was in effect an extension to the second stage and involved gaining permission to audio-record the interactions being observed.

There are potentially a number of advantages related to the use of this strategy. As suggested earlier, a request to an organisation for multiple access may be sufficient to cause them to decline entry. Using an incremental strategy at least gains you access to a certain level of data. This strategy will also allow you the opportunity to develop a positive relationship with those who are prepared to grant initial access of a restricted nature. As you establish your credibility, you can develop the possibility of achieving a fuller level of access. A further advantage may follow from the opportunity that you have to design your request for further access specifically to the situation and in relation to opportunities that may become apparent from your initial level of access. On the other hand, this incremental process will be time-consuming, and you need to consider the amount of time that you will have for your research project before embarking on such a strategy. In addition, it can be argued that it is unethical not to explain your access requirements fully.

Establishing your credibility

In Section 6.2 we differentiated between physical and cognitive access. Just because you have been granted entry into an organisation you will not be able to assume that those whom you wish to interview, survey or observe will be prepared to provide their cooperation. Indeed, assuming that this is going to happen raises an ethical issue that is considered in the next section. Robson (2011) says that gaining cooperation from these intended participants is a matter of developing relationships. This will mean repeating much of the process that you will have used to gain entry into the organisation. You will need to share with them the purpose of your research project, state how you believe that they will be able to help your study and provide assurances about confidentiality and anonymity. This may involve writing to your intended participants or talking to them individually or in a group. Which of these means you use will depend on the intended data collection technique, your opportunity to make contact with them, the number of participants involved and the nature of the setting. However, your credibility and the probability of individuals' participation are likely to be enhanced if the request for participation is made jointly with a senior person from the organisation (Box 6.9). Where your intended data collection technique may be considered intrusive, you may need to exercise even greater care and take longer to gain acceptance. This might be the case, for example, where you wish to undertake observation (Chapter 9). The extent to which you succeed in gaining cognitive access will depend on this effort.

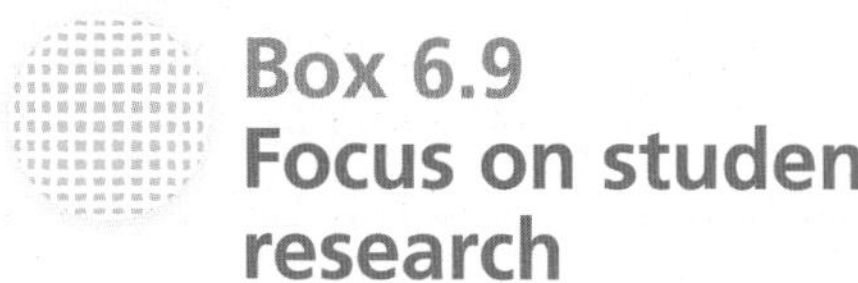

Box 6.9 Focus on student research

Email request to participate in a focus group

Sara's research project involved her in undertaking a communication audit for an organisation near her university. As part of her research design she had chosen to use mixed method research using focus groups followed by a questionnaire. Those selected to attend the focus groups were invited by individual emails sent jointly from herself and a senior manager within the organisation:

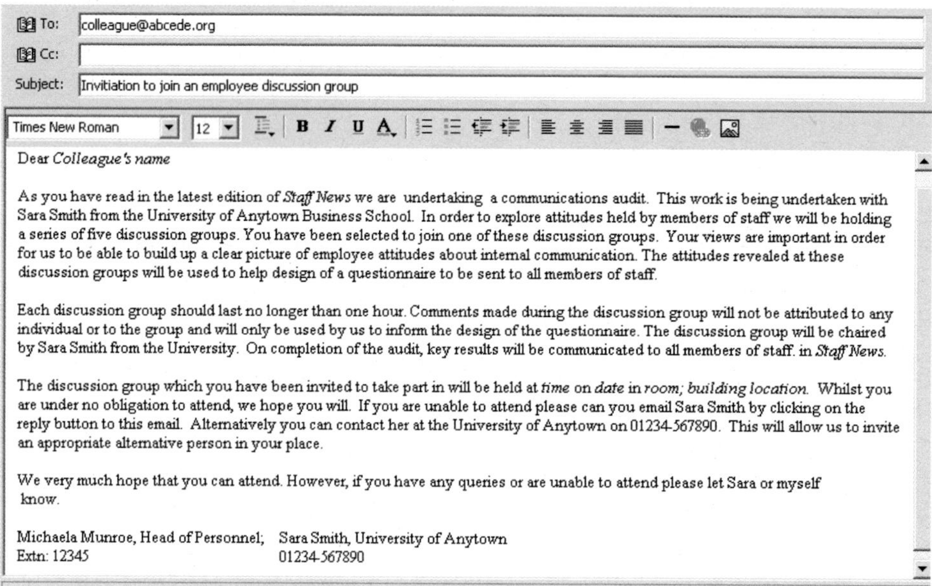

To: colleague@abcede.org

Cc:

Subject: Invitiation to join an employee discussion group

Dear *Colleague's name*

As you have read in the latest edition of *Staff News* we are undertaking a communications audit. This work is being undertaken with Sara Smith from the University of Anytown Business School. In order to explore attitudes held by members of staff we will be holding a series of five discussion groups. You have been selected to join one of these discussion groups. Your views are important in order for us to be able to build up a clear picture of employee attitudes about internal communication. The attitudes revealed at these discussion groups will be used to help design of a questionnaire to be sent to all members of staff.

Each discussion group should last no longer than one hour. Comments made during the discussion group will not be attributed to any individual or to the group and will only be used by us to inform the design of the questionnaire. The discussion group will be chaired by Sara Smith from the University. On completion of the audit, key results will be communicated to all members of staff. in *Staff News*.

The discussion group which you have been invited to take part in will be held at *time* on *date* in *room; building location*. Whilst you are under no obligation to attend, we hope you will. If you are unable to attend please can you email Sara Smith by clicking on the reply button to this email. Alternatively you can contact her at the University of Anytown on 01234-567890. This will allow us to invite an appropriate alternative person in your place.

We very much hope that you can attend. However, if you have any queries or are unable to attend please let Sara or myself know.

Michaela Munroe, Head of Personnel; Extn: 12345

Sara Smith, University of Anytown 01234-567890

The strategies that we have outlined to help you to gain access to organisations and to those whom you wish to participate in your research project are summarised as a checklist in Box 6.10.

6.5 Research ethics and why you should act ethically

Defining research ethics

Ethical concerns will emerge as you design and plan your research, seek access to organisations and to individuals, collect, analyse, manage and report your data. In the context of research, **ethics** refer to the standards of behaviour that guide your conduct in relation to the rights of those who become the subject of your work, or are affected by it. Standards of behaviour will be guided by a number of influences. The appropriateness or acceptability of a researcher's conduct will be influenced by broader social norms of

Box 6.10 Checklist

To help to gain access

- ✔ Have you allowed yourself plenty of time for the entire process?
- ✔ Are you clear about the purpose of your research project?
- ✔ Are you clear about your requirements when requesting access (at least your initial requirements)?
- ✔ Can you use existing contacts, at least at the start of your research project, in order to gain access and gather data?
- ✔ (If you have been on a work placement) Is your work placement organisation an appropriate setting for your research project?
- ✔ Have you approached appropriate local and/or national employer, or employee, professional or trade bodies to see if they can suggest contacts through whom you might gain access?
- ✔ Have you considered making a direct approach to an organisation to identify the most appropriate person to contact for access?
- ✔ Have you identified the most appropriate person and been willing to keep on trying to make contact?
- ✔ Have you drafted a list of the points you wish to make, including your thanks to those to whom you speak?
- ✔ Have you considered and thought about how you will address likely organisational concerns such as:
  - the amount of time or resources that would be involved on the part of the organisation;
  - the sensitivity of your research topic;
  - the need for confidentiality and anonymity?
- ✔ Have you considered the possible benefits for the organisation should access be granted to you, and the offer of a report summarising your findings to enhance your chance of achieving access?
- ✔ Are you willing to attend a meeting to present and discuss your request for access?
- ✔ Where your initial request for access involves a telephone conversation, have you followed this with an introductory letter to confirm your requirements?
- ✔ Is the construction, tone and presentation of an introductory letter likely to support you gaining access?
- ✔ Have you ensured that your use of language is appropriate to the person who receives it without any hint of being patronising, threatening or boring?
- ✔ Have you considered including a range of contact methods for recipients to use to reply?
- ✔ Are you prepared to work through organisational gatekeepers in order to gain access to intended participants?
- ✔ Have you allowed sufficient time to contact intended participants and gain their acceptance once physical access has been granted?
- ✔ Have you allowed sufficient time within your data collection to gain 'cognitive access' to data?

behaviour. A **social norm** indicates the type of behaviour that a person ought to adopt in a particular situation; however, the norms of behaviour that prevail will in reality allow for a range of ethical positions.

The philosophical foundations of research ethics also illustrate that a researcher's conduct may be open to competing and conflicting ethical positions (Berry 2004; Thomas 1996). Two dominant and conflicting philosophical positions have been identified: deontological and teleological. A **deontological view** is based on following rules to guide researchers' conduct. According to this view, acting outside the rules can never be justified. Where the rules are inadequate or contested, it would be necessary to reappraise and if required amend them. In contrast, the **teleological view** argues that deciding whether an act of conduct is justified or not should be determined by its consequences, not by a set of predetermined rules. This would involve deciding whether the benefits of undertaking an act outweigh the negative consequences from this action. However, it is unlikely that a simple comparison between the benefits to one group and costs to another would provide you with a clear answer to such an ethical dilemma.

Attempts to overcome ethical dilemmas arising from different social norms and conflicting philosophical approaches have resulted in the widespread development of **codes of ethics**, which generally contain a list of principles outlining the nature of ethical research and a statement of ethical standards to accompany these principles that are intended to guide your research conduct. As a member of a university (and where appropriate a professional association) you are likely to be required to abide by such an ethical code or adhere to its ethical guidelines for research. Codes of ethics explicitly or implicitly recognise that ethical dilemmas exist and that it will often be necessary to exercise some choice about conduct. For example, the Statement of Ethical Practice produced by British Sociological Association (see Table 6.2) expressly recognises that it is not possible to produce 'a set of recipes' to deal with all ethical dilemmas but that researchers need to exercise choice based on ethical principles and standards (British Sociological Association 2002: 1). The key point is that by producing such ethical principles and standards, researchers and ethical reviewers (discussed shortly) have an ethical basis against which to anticipate issues and risk, and exercise choice to avoid conflict and harm.

The conduct of your research is therefore likely to be guided by your university's code of ethics or ethical guidelines, highlighting what is and what is not considered ethical. This will be helpful and, where followed, should ensure that you do not transgress the behavioural norms established by your university or professional association. However, as Bell and Bryman (2007) point out, such codes tend to be written in abstract terms and

Table 6.2 Internet addresses for ethical codes, guidelines and statements of practice

Name	Internet address
Academy of Management's Code of Ethics	www.aomonline.org/aom.asp?id=268
American Psychological Association's Ethical Principles of Psychologists and Code of Conduct	www.apa.org/ethics/code/index.aspx
Association of Business Schools' Ethics Guide	www.the-abs.org.uk/?id=717
British Psychological Society's Code of Ethics and Conduct	www.bps.org.uk/the-society/code-of-conduct/code-of-conduct_home.cfm
British Sociological Association's Statement of Ethical Practice	www.britsoc.co.uk/equality/Statement+Ethical+Practice.htm
Economic and Social Research Council's (ESRC) Framework for Research Ethics (FRE)	www.esrcsocietytoday.ac.uk/about-esrc/information/research-ethics.aspx
European Union's Respect Code of Practice for Socio-Economic Research (The Respect Project)	www.respectproject.org/code
Market Research Society's Code of Conduct	www.mrs.org.uk/standards/codeconduct.htm
Researcher Development Initiative Research Ethics Guidebook	www.ethicsguidebook.ac.uk
Social Research Association's Ethical Guidelines	www.the-sra.org.uk/guidelines.htm

are designed to prevent misconduct. This means you will need to interpret the principles and standards contained in the code of ethics with care and apply them to the context of your own proposed research project. The Internet can also provide direct links to a number of codes of ethics and ethical guidelines, which may be potentially useful for your research. A selection of these is contained in Table 6.2.

You should expect to submit your research proposal for ethical review. Students' research will be expected to comply with a university's code of ethics or ethical guidelines and the principles and standards that it contains. The nature of ethical review will depend on the nature of the research being proposed. Ethical review may be conducted by your project tutor or by two or more academic staff using an ethics protocol. This 'light touch' or 'fast track' review, overseen by the school or faculty ethics committee, is likely to allow non-controversial research proposals that pose minimal risk to participants and others to be considered without too much delay. A fuller ethical review conducted by the school or faculty ethics committee may be required where proposals raise ethical concerns or are considered to have higher levels of risk. You will need to be aware of potential ethical concerns and risks to those involved as you design your research proposal so that you can seek to avoid them. You should not assume that using particular techniques will reduce the possibility of ethical concerns or risk. While the use of observation or interviews may appear to be more intrusive than designing a questionnaire, it is possible that the latter may raise ethical concerns and risk to participants. It is the nature of the questions that you wish to ask and the nature of your intended participants that may raise ethical concerns rather than the research method that you intend to use.

Research ethics committees fulfil a number of objectives. These may include a proactive role, such as developing an ethical code, and an educational one, such as disseminating advice about conducting research ethically. The primary role of a research ethics committee will be to review all research conducted by those in the institution that involves human participants and personal data. The research ethics committee will be responsible for examining aspects of research quality that relate to ethics; protecting the rights, dignity and welfare of those who participate in this research as well as others who may be affected by it; and considering the safety of researchers. A research ethics committee is therefore responsible for all aspects of ethical review and approval. A research ethics committee is likely to be composed of experienced researchers from a variety of backgrounds, including both men and women, who are able to draw on their range of experience and knowledge of different ethical perspectives to provide advice. It will be expected to act in an impartial and independent way and its independence is supported by the inclusion of at least one external member, who otherwise has no connection to the institution.

In some cases you may also have to satisfy the requirements of an ethics committee established in your host organisation as well as your university. This may apply where your research is based in the health service. For example, many of our students undertaking research within the UK's National Health Service (NHS) have had to meet the requirements established by their local NHS Trust's ethics committee (Box 6.11). Such a requirement is often time-consuming to meet.

Approval of your research proposal should not be interpreted as the end of your consideration of ethical issues. Consideration of ethical issues should remain at the forefront of your thinking throughout the course of your research project and even beyond it. In Section 6.6 we consider ethical issues that arise at specific stages in the research process. In preparation for this consideration we firstly consider a range of general ethical issues that permeate research and which therefore form the focus of codes of ethical conduct. We also consider a range of general issues that are associated with Internet-mediated research.

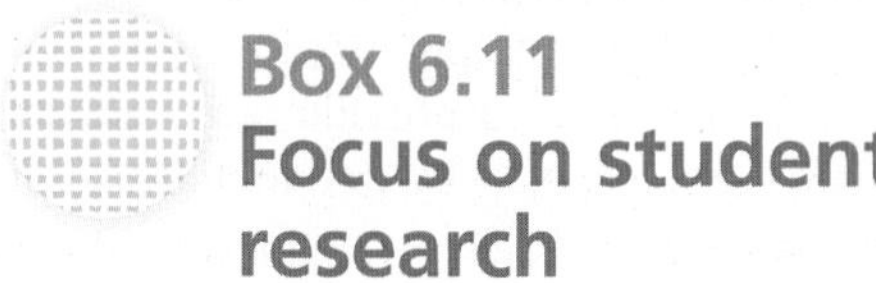

Box 6.11 Focus on student research

Establishing whether research warrants mandated ethical review

Rachel worked for a local hospital. At her first meeting with her project tutor, he had reminded her to check with the hospital and establish if she would need to submit her research project to the hospital's research ethics committee for review. Subsequently, she discussed this with her line manager who suggested she check with the National Health Service's National Research Ethics Service. Using the Google search engine, Rachel found the Service's website and downloaded their two-page leaflet, *Defining Research* (National Patient Safety Agency 2007).

The *Defining Research* leaflet highlighted that, although research always required a Research Ethics Committee review, it was not mandatory for either audit or service evaluation. This did not mean there were no ethical issues associated with audit or service evaluation, only that there was not a mandatory requirement for a Research Ethics Committee review. The leaflet also provided clear definitions of what was meant by the terms 'research', 'audit' and 'service evaluation':

> Research is 'the attempt to derive generalisable new knowledge including studies that aim to generate hypotheses, as well as studies that aim to test them'.
>
> Audit is 'designed and conducted to produce information to inform delivery of best care'.
>
> Service evaluation is 'designed and conducted solely to define or judge current care'.

Based on these definitions and the other information in the leaflet, Rachel felt that her research project was 'service evaluation' rather than research. She discussed this with her line manager who agreed, but suggested that she also confirm with the Chair of the Research Ethics Committee that her project was a 'service evaluation'. The Committee Chair agreed with Rachel and her line manager.

General categories of ethical issues and the formulation of principles to recognise and overcome or minimise these

General categories of ethical issues are recognised in codes of ethics. These are ethical issues that occur across many approaches to research. Rather than write highly detailed and prescriptive regulations to anticipate and deal with these for each research approach, codes of ethics instead contain a set of principles that allow researchers to apply these principles to the context of their own research and to that of others. We now consider a number of principles that have been developed to recognise ethical issues that occur across many different approaches to research. These are outlined in Table 6.3.

Codes of ethics are intended to avoid poor practice, malpractice and harm (**non-maleficence**) as well as to promote ethical practice and private or public good (**beneficence**). To avoid harm, or at the very least to minimise it, it is necessary to evaluate risk. Evaluating risk involves thinking about the likelihood of harm occurring and the extent or severity of the harm that would be caused. As we indicated in Table 6.3, harm may take a number of forms and lead to a range of consequences. Estimating risk is not straightforward and it may be affected by a number of contextual or cultural factors. However, it is important to anticipate risk in each research situation to attempt to avoid the likelihood of causing harm. Box 6.12 suggests a number of questions that you may ask to seek to assess risk, although others may suggest themselves related to the research context within you are operating (Section 6.6).

Table 6.3 Ethical principles and the ethical rationale for and development of each principle

Ethical principle	Ethical rationale for and development of this principle
Integrity and objectivity of the researcher	The quality of research depends in part on the integrity and objectivity of the researcher. This means acting openly, being truthful and promoting accuracy. Conversely it also means avoiding deception, dishonesty, misrepresentation (of data and findings etc), partiality, reckless commitments or disingenuous promises. Where appropriate, any conflict of interest or commercial association should be declared
Respect for others	A researcher's position is based on the development of trust and respect. The conduct of research entails social responsibility and obligations to those who participate in or at affected by it. The rights of all persons should be recognised and their dignity respected
Avoidance of harm (non-maleficence)	Any harm to participants must be avoided. Harm may occur through risks to emotional wellbeing, mental or physical health, or social or group cohesion. It may take a number of forms including embarrassment, stress, discomfort, pain or conflict. It may be caused by using a research method in an intrusive or zealous way that involves mental or social pressure causing anxiety or stress. It may also be caused by violating assurances about confidentiality and anonymity, or through harassment or discrimination
Privacy of those taking part	Privacy is a key principle that links to or underpins several other principles considered here. Respect for others, the avoidance of harm, the voluntary nature of participation, informed consent, ensuring confidentiality and maintaining anonymity, responsibility in the analysis of data and reporting of findings, and compliance in the management of data are all linked to or motivated by the principle of ensuring the privacy of those taking part
Voluntary nature of participation and right to withdraw	The right not to participate in a research project is unchallengeable. This is accompanied by the right not to be harassed to participate. It is also unacceptable to attempt to extend the scope of participation beyond that freely given. Those taking part continue to exercise the right to determine how they will participate in the data collection process, including rights: not to answer any question, or set of questions; not to provide any data requested; to modify the nature of their consent; to withdraw from participation; and possibly to withdraw data they have provided
Informed consent of those taking part	The principle of informed consent involves researchers providing sufficient information and assurances about taking part to allow individuals to understand the implications of participation and to reach a fully informed, considered and freely given decision about whether or not to do so, without the exercise of any pressure or coercion. This leads to the right of those taking part to expect the researcher to abide by the extent of the consent given and not to find that the researcher wishes to prolong the duration of an interview or observation, or to widen the scope of the research without first seeking and obtaining permission, or to commit any subsequent breach of the consent given
Ensuring confidentiality of data and maintenance of anonymity of those taking part	Research is designed to answer 'who', 'what', 'when', 'where', 'how' and 'why' questions, not to focus on those who provide the data to answer these. Individuals and organisations should therefore remain anonymous and the data they provide should be processed to make it non-attributable, unless there is an explicit agreement to attribute comments. Harm may result from unauthorised attribution or identification. Reliability of data is also likely to be enhanced where confidentiality and anonymity are assured. This principle leads to the right to expect assurances about anonymity and confidentiality to be observed strictly

(continued)

Table 6.3 (*Continued*)

Ethical principle	Ethical rationale for and development of this principle
Responsibility in the analysis of data and reporting of findings	Assurances about privacy, anonymity and confidentiality must be upheld when analysing and reporting data. Primary data should not be made up or altered and results should not be falsified. Findings should be reported fully and accurately, irrespective of whether they contradict expected outcomes. The same conditions apply to secondary data, the source or sources of which should also be clearly acknowledged. Analyses and the interpretations that follow from these should be checked carefully and corrections made to ensure the accuracy of the research report and any other outcome
Compliance in the management of data	Research is likely to involve the collection of personal data. Many governments have passed legislation to regulate the processing of personal data. There is therefore a statutory requirement to comply with such legislation. In the European Union, European Directive 95/46/CE has led member states to pass data protection legislation. Other laws may exist in particular countries relating to the processing, security and possible sharing of data. It will therefore be essential for researchers to understand and comply with the legal restrictions and regulations that relate to the management of research data within the country or countries within which they conduct research
Ensuring the safety of the researcher	The safety of researchers is a very important consideration when planning and conducting a research project. The Social Research Association's Code of Practice for the Safety of Social Researchers identifies possible risks from social interactions including 'risk of physical threat or abuse; risk of psychological trauma ...; risk of being in a compromising situation . . .; increased exposure to risks of everyday life' (Social Research Association 2001: 1). Research design therefore needs to consider risks to researchers as well as to participants

Notes and Sources: The ethical codes and guidelines listed in Table 6.2 were helpful in informing the contents of this table. Table 6.3 seeks to synthesise key points from many different approaches to writing ethical principles. It should not therefore be interpreted as providing completely comprehensive guidance. You are advised to consult the Code of Ethics defined as being appropriate for your research project. References to legislation in Table 6.3 and elsewhere only provide general indications and should not be interpreted as providing legal advice, or the existence of such types of law in all countries.

Research may result in benefits for the researcher, research participants, the group or organisation being researched, or for the community or society within which it occurs. As we discussed in Section 6.4, it is important and ethical to be realistic about the benefits you claim for your research project and to honour any promises made about sharing findings, such as promising to send a summary report to an organisation that provides access to host your research. Adopting ethical behaviour means more than just using a code of ethics as a way to get your research proposal approved. Acting ethically means thinking about each aspect and each stage of your research from an ethical perspective. Where you do this, you will have internalised the values of acting ethically and this should help you to anticipate concerns at each stage of your research.

General ethical issues associated with Internet-mediated research

While the Internet may help to facilitate access to some categories of participants and certain types of data, its use raises a number of issues and even dilemmas about the applicability of the ethical principles referred to in Table 6.3 to Internet-mediated research. The

Box 6.12 Checklist

Assessing risk in research

- ✔ Is your proposed research likely to harm the wellbeing of those participating?
- ✔ Will others be harmed by the process or outcomes of your proposed research?
- ✔ How may this harm occur and what characteristics may make this more likely?
- ✔ How likely is it that harm might result?
- ✔ How severe would be any resulting harm?
- ✔ Which features or what aspects of your research may cause harm?
- ✔ How intrusive is your proposed research method or methods?
- ✔ How sensitive are your proposed questions, observations, searches or requests for data?
- ✔ Can you justify your choice of research method or methods and tactics; in particular, can you explain why alternatives that involve fewer potential risks cannot be used?
- ✔ Where anticipated risk cannot be reduced any further during the design of the research and ethical review is favourable, how will the implementation of your research seek to avoid the occurrence of risk in practice, or at the very least to seek to minimise it?
- ✔ Does the information you provided to intended participants to facilitate informed consent also allow them to contact you to discuss potential concerns? How have you facilitated this whilst maintaining your own privacy (e.g. using a university email address not your personal email or home address)?
- ✔ How will you commence a data collection activity to allow potential concerns to be raised first? How will you make yourself aware of themes that may be sensitive for particular participants?
- ✔ How will you reinforce the voluntary nature of participation to allow participants not to answer a particular question, set of questions, or to decline any request for data?
- ✔ Other potential risks are likely to be evident within the context of your particular research project. What might these be?

ethical issues and dilemmas raised by the use of blogs, bulletin boards, chat rooms, email lists, instant messaging and web pages include the following points:

- ***Scope for deception***. Where researchers join online communities with the intention of collecting data rather than participating and seeking consent (known as 'passive analysis' or 'lurking') this may be seen as a form of deception (e.g. British Psychological Society 2007). Declaring your real intention after a period of 'lurking' may increase the chance of you as a researcher being asked to leave (Madge 2006).
- ***Lacking respect and causing harm***. 'Harvesting' data from online communities without the knowledge and permission of those who create it may also be seen as disrespectful and opposed to the principle of gaining trust (e.g. Barkardjieva and Feenberg 2000; Berry 2004). Deception and the development of mistrust may cause damage to online communities and to their members (Eysenbach and Till 2001).
- ***Respecting privacy***. While it may be technically possible to access online communities because they operate in a publicly accessible virtual space, it may be argued that content on these websites should be treated as private conversations, albeit 'publicly private' ones (e.g. Barkardjieva and Feenberg 2000; Waskul and Douglass 1996)?
- ***Nature of participation and scope to withdraw***. 'Harvesting' data may be seen as violating the principle of the voluntary nature of participation. Lack of consent whilst using accessible material also negates the right to limit the nature of data used or to withdraw.

- ***Informed consent***. Is it ethical to waive the need to obtain consent because material is seen as being in the public domain and because it may be difficult to achieve this (e.g. Eysenbach and Till 2001; Hookway 2008)? Informed consent in a virtual setting may be obtained by contacting an online community's moderator; or by specifically asking participants in the case of a web questionnaire or online interview, for example. Informed consent for online research may include agreed limits about the scope of participation. It may also include procedures to allow concerns to be raised or for withdrawal to take place. Such procedures will be important in Internet-mediated research because the issue of distance and lack of face-to-face contact makes it difficult to anticipate participants' concerns and attitudes (British Psychological Society 2007). Signed consent may be facilitated by issuing a consent form by email or online using electronic checkboxes.
- ***Confidentiality of data and anonymity of participants' identities***. Even though members of an online community may produce discussions that are publicly accessible and which create a permanent record, they may do this in the belief that no one will be 'harvesting' or analysing this material, or using it subsequently. Barkardjieva and Feenberg (2000) found that members of an online community expected to be asked for consent before access was achieved in practice; and that access was then only granted for subsequently generated online discussions, not to archived discussions that took place before community members knew they were to be the subject of research. This approach enables members of online communities to control data that is available to researchers. Barkardjieva and Feenberg (2000) provide an example of how members of an online community went further to exercise control and to protect the confidentiality of their discussions and their anonymity. The researchers were not permitted to save these online discussions or to use quotations from them. Instead they were allowed to read these discussions and then ask members questions about what they had read. The researchers were allowed to use these answers and to take suitably anonymised quotations from them for their research. This effectively separated the private nature of members' online discussions from public access to research data, enabling members of the online community to control their participation and to ensure the confidentiality of their discussions as well as maintaining their anonymity.
- ***Analysis of data and reporting of findings***. Issues of confidentiality, anonymity, privacy and copyright are raised when Internet data are analysed and reported. Where data are 'harvested' the researcher is confronted with the dilemma of whether to use these data openly or anonymously. Since 'harvesting' occurs without obtaining consent, at least initially, should the researcher use pseudonyms and other changes to disguise the identities of those who created the material? Where the researcher wishes to quote from this material, there is the possibility that others could use Internet search engines to identify the author of a quotation (Eysenbach and Till 2001; Madge 2006). This raises issues about the confidentiality of the data and researchers are advised to avoid using quotations that would be traceable without first obtaining consent (British Psychological Society 2007). These issues are compounded by copyright. Blogs are protected by copyright laws and those who create them have exclusive rights in relation to their reproduction (Hookway 2008). Web pages are also protected by copyright laws (British Psychological Society 2007). Those who author or create web materials may wish their work to be properly attributed; conversely they may wish to protect its use, or for any permitted use to be anonymised (Eysenbach and Till 2001). Seeking informed consent should help to overcome the dilemmas associated with using materials from the Internet as data.

- ***Management of data***. Data protection legislation has (or is likely to have, depending on country) implications for Internet-mediated research, including in the UK the need for notification and consent if personal data are to be processed (British Psychological Society 2007). Researchers using the Internet need to comply with current data protection legislation as well as with any other legal requirements. A further set of issues concerns the potential insecurity of data transmission and storage. This may be because of errors. For example, emails containing personal data may be sent to the wrong address. Questionnaire software may contain errors. Insecurity may also occur because others have access to a website and are able to alter data or to copy and direct it elsewhere. As researchers do not control websites or networks, risks associated with data transmission and storage need to be recognised and participants told about these in relation to confidentiality, anonymity and possible 'data hacking' or misuse as part of seeking informed consent (e.g. British Psychological Society 2007; Madge 2006).
- ***Safety of the researcher***. The researcher may help to ensure her or his safety when conducting Internet-mediated research by using a university email address, not a personal one. Researchers also need to be diligent when setting up access rights to their own personal information on social network sites to protect their privacy.

This review has highlighted some of the issues and dilemmas associated with the use of Internet-mediated research, although several more exist in practice. In addition, many more details associated with these issues need to be considered before using this approach to research. Table 6.4 refers to sets of guidelines for Internet-mediated research. Internet-mediated research is still in a formative stage and it is noticeable how opinions and guidance about its use varies across sources. There is scope for a greater consensus about its ethical use but achieving this may not be an easy matter. You will therefore need to refer very carefully to your university's guidelines about Internet-mediated research (or those that they recommend you to use), where you consider the possibility of using this approach.

A further aspect of Internet use concerns **netiquette**, which refers to user standards to encourage courtesy. The principal focus of netiquette concerns the use of email and messaging. The ease of creating these may lead to issues that impair your attempt to use Internet-mediated research. Emails and messages may be poorly worded (Box 6.8), and they may appear unfriendly or unclear so that they fail to interest those whom you approach. Emails and messages need to be worded appropriately for their intended audience and to be clearly structured, relevant and succinct. The ease of sending emails and messages may lead to 'spamming' potential and actual participants. 'Spamming' involves sending large numbers of unwanted mail and should be avoided. Another netiquette custom involves respecting the intentions of other users, so that private messages should not subsequently be made public. We consider netiquette further in Sections 6.6, 10.9 (Internet-mediated interviews) and 11.5 (Internet-mediated questionnaires).

Table 6.4 Internet addresses for ethical guidelines for the conduct of online research

Name	Internet address
Association of Internet Researchers' Ethics Guide	http://aoir.org/documents/ethics-guide/
British Psychological Society's Report of the Working Party on Conducting Research on the Internet	www.bps.org.uk/publications/policy-guidelines/research-guidelines-policy-documents/

6.6 Ethical issues at specific stages of the research process

As can be seen in Figure 6.1, ethical issues are likely to be of importance throughout your research. This will require ethical integrity from you in your role as the researcher, any organisational gatekeeper(s) involved and, where appropriate, your research sponsor. Where you are undertaking research for an organisation you will need to find the middle ground between the organisation's expectation of useful research and your right not to be

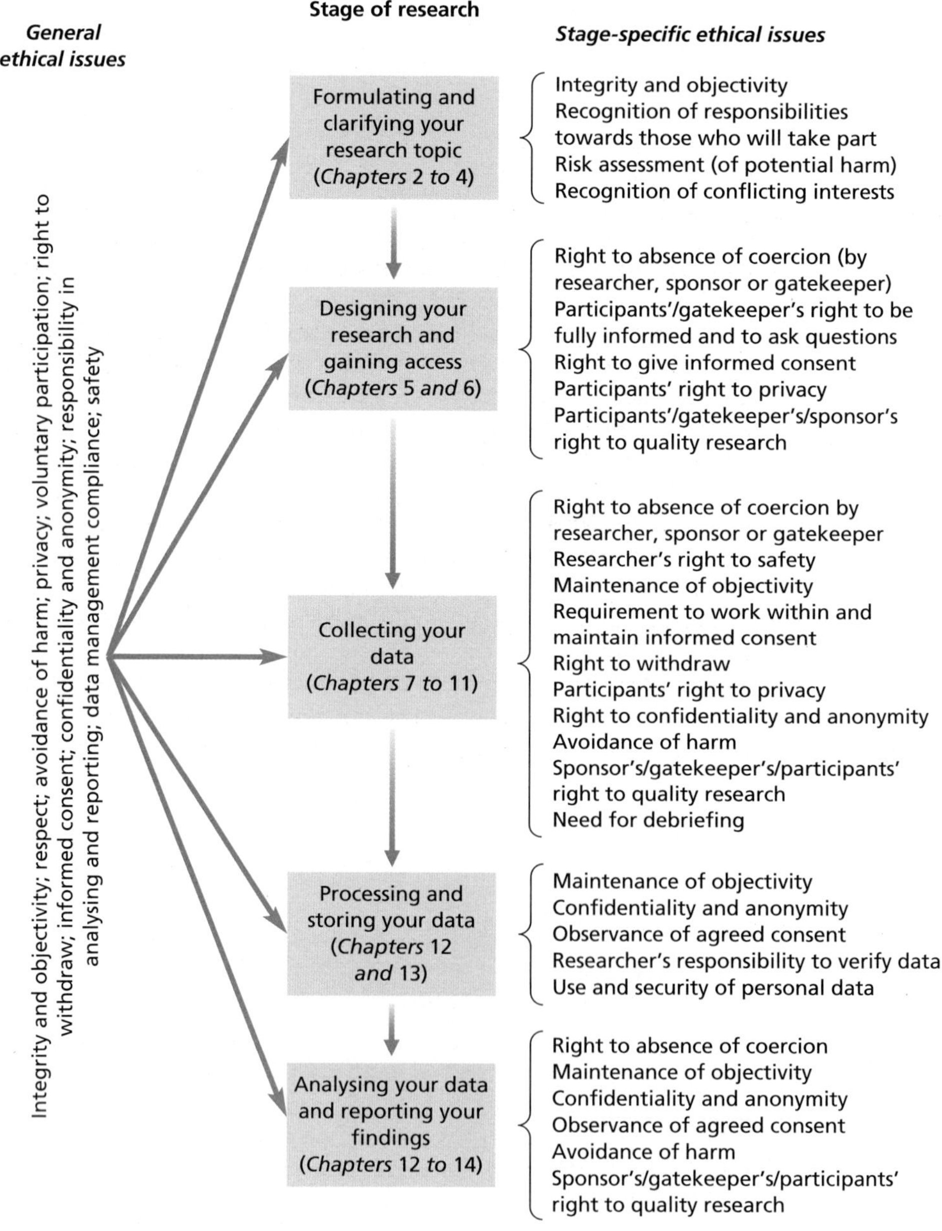

Figure 6.1 Ethical issues at different stages of research

coerced into researching a topic in which you are not interested or that does not satisfy the assessment requirements of your university.

Ethical issues during design and gaining access

Most ethical issues can be anticipated and dealt with during the design stage of any research project. This should be attempted by planning to conduct the research project in line with the ethical principle of not causing harm (discussed earlier) and by adapting your research strategy or choice of methods where appropriate. Evidence that ethical issues have been considered and evaluated at this stage is likely to be one of the criteria against which your research proposal is judged (Cooper and Schindler 2008; Marshall and Rossman 2006).

One of the key stages at which you need to consider the potential for ethical issues to arise is when you seek access. As noted earlier, you should not attempt to apply any pressure on intended participants to grant access. This is unlikely to be the case where you are approaching a member of an organisation's management to request access. However, where you are undertaking a research project as an internal researcher within your employing organisation (Section 6.2), in relation to a part-time qualification, there may be a temptation to apply pressure on others (colleagues or subordinates) to cooperate. Individuals have a right to privacy and should not feel pressurised or coerced into participating. By not respecting this, you may well be causing harm.

Consequently, you will have to accept any refusal to take part (Cooper and Schindler 2008; Robson 2011). Box 6.13 contains a short checklist to help you ensure that you are not putting pressure on individuals to participate. You may also cause harm by the nature and timing of any approach that you make to intended participants – perhaps by telephoning at 'unsociable' times, or, if possible, by 'confronting' those from whom you would like to collect data. Access to secondary data may also raise ethical issues in relation to harm. Where you happen to obtain access to personal data about individuals who have not consented to let you have this (through personnel or client records), you will be obliged to anonymise these or to seek informed consent from those involved.

Consent to participate in a research project is not a straightforward matter. In general terms, an approach to a potential participant is an attempt to gain consent. However, this raises a question about the scope of any consent given. Where someone agrees to participate in a particular data collection method, this does not necessarily imply consent about the way in which the data provided may be used. Clearly, any assurances that you

Assessing your research in relation to not pressurising individuals to participate

- ✔ Have you ensured that participants have not been coerced into participating?
- ✔ Have you made sure that no inducements (e.g. financial payments), other than reimbursement for travel expenses or in some cases time, are offered?
- ✔ Have you checked that the risks involved in participation are likely to be acceptable to those participating?
- ✔ Are participants free to withdraw from your study at any time and have you informed them of this?

provide about anonymity or confidentiality will help to develop an understanding of the nature of the consent being entered into, but even these may be inadequate in terms of clarifying the nature of that consent.

This suggests a continuum that ranges from a lack of consent, involving some form of deception, through **inferred consent**, where agreement to take part leads the researcher to assume that data may be analysed, used, stored and reported as he or she wishes without clarifying this with the participant, to informed consent. **Informed consent** involves participants being given sufficient information (discussed next), the opportunity to ask questions, time to consider without any pressure or coercion, to be able to reach a fully informed, considered and freely given decision about whether or not to take part (see Table 6.3). This continuum is shown in Figure 6.2.

Three points are described in Figure 6.2, although in reality this is likely to operate as a continuum because a multitude of positions are possible around the points described. For example, research that is conducted with those who have agreed to participate can still involve an attempt to deceive them in some way. This **deception** may be related to deceit over the real purpose of the research (Sekaran and Bougie 2009), or in relation to some undeclared sponsorship (Zikmund 2000), or related to an association with another organisation that will use any data gained for commercial advantage. Where this is the case, it could cause embarrassment or harm to those who promote your request for access within their employing organisation, as well as to yourself.

The information that is required for prospective participants to reach a fully informed decision about whether or not to participate should be produced formally as a **participant information sheet**. This may be given or sent to intended participants, or emailed or made available online in the case of Internet-mediated research. It should include information about the nature of the research, the requirements and implications of taking part, participants' rights, how their data will be analysed, reported and stored and who to contact in the case of concerns. These points are developed in Box 6.14, where they are presented as a checklist.

The nature of information required for informed consent may vary according to your research strategy, as will the way in which you seek to establish consent. If you are intending to use a questionnaire where personal data are not collected or where data are completely anonymised, the return of a completed questionnaire by a respondent is taken to grant consent. However, this will require you to include an information sheet detailing how these data will be analysed and reported, for what purpose, and what will then happen to them, as well as your identity (UK Data Archive 2011a). If you are intending to interview a senior manager, correspondence may be exchanged, such as that discussed in Section 6.4, to establish informed consent. When interviewing individuals, informed consent should be supplemented by a more detailed written agreement, such

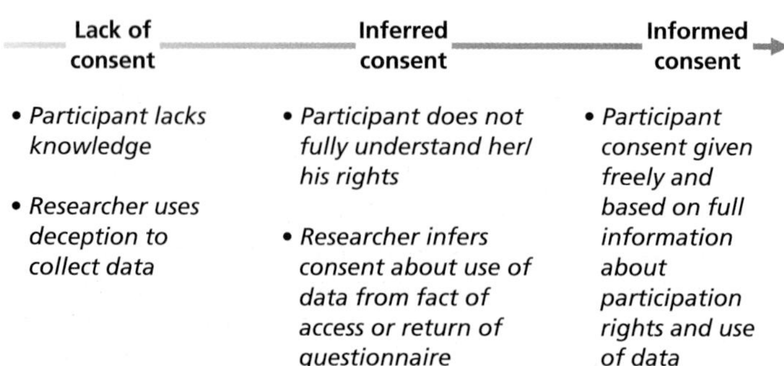
Lack of consent
Inferred consent
Informed consent
• Participant lacks knowledge
• Researcher uses deception to collect data
• Participant does not fully understand her/his rights
• Researcher infers consent about use of data from fact of access or return of questionnaire
• Participant consent given freely and based on full information about participation rights and use of data

Figure 6.2 The nature of participant consent

Box 6.14 Checklist

Requirements for a participant information sheet

Organisational 'gatekeepers' (discussed earlier in Section 6.4) and intended participants need to be informed about the following aspects of the research. This information can be drawn together in a participant information sheet.

About the nature of the research

- ✔ What is its purpose?
- ✔ Who is or will be undertaking it?
- ✔ Is it being funded or sponsored – if so, by whom and why?
- ✔ Who is being asked to participate – i.e. broad details about the sampling frame, sample determination and size?
- ✔ How far has the research project progressed?

About the requirements of taking part

- ✔ What type of data will be required from those who agree to take part?
- ✔ How will these data be collected (e.g. interview, observation or questionnaire)?
- ✔ How much time will be required, and on how many occasions?
- ✔ What are the target dates to undertake the research and for participation?

About the implications of taking part and participant's rights

- ✔ Recognition that participation is voluntary.
- ✔ Recognition that participants have the right to decline to answer a question or set of questions; or to be observed in particular circumstances.
- ✔ Recognition that participants have control over the right to record any of their responses where a voice recorder is used.
- ✔ Recognition that participants may withdraw at any time.
- ✔ What will be the consequences of participating – possible risks, depending on the nature of the approach and purpose, and expected benefits?
- ✔ What assurances will be provided about participant anonymity and data confidentiality?

About the use of the data collected and the way in which it will be reported

- ✔ Who will have access to the data collected?
- ✔ How will the results of the research project be disseminated?
- ✔ How will assurances about anonymity and confidentiality be observed at this stage?
- ✔ What will happen to the data collected after the project is completed?
- ✔ Where data are to be destroyed, what is the date by which this will happen?
- ✔ Where data are to be preserved, where and how will these be stored securely, who might be given access to them, and what safeguards will be established to ensure the continuing future confidentiality of these data and anonymity of the participants?

Who to contact to raise any concerns and questions about the research

- ✔ Have you established how you will provide the participant with a person to contact about the research, including name, work address, email and contact phone number?

as a **consent form** (Box 6.15), which is signed by both parties. Use of a written consent form helps to clarify the boundaries of consent and should help you to comply with data protection legislation where your research involves the collection of confidential, personal or sensitive personal data (see Section 6.7) (UK Data Archive 2011a). Depending on the nature of your research project you may also seek consent to photograph or video-ecord data. Where the nature of the data make this a possibility, it would be necessary to gain a participant's consent to do this before the event, given potential reluctance or sensitivity about using these types of recording media. Your consent form should be amended to record such consent formally.

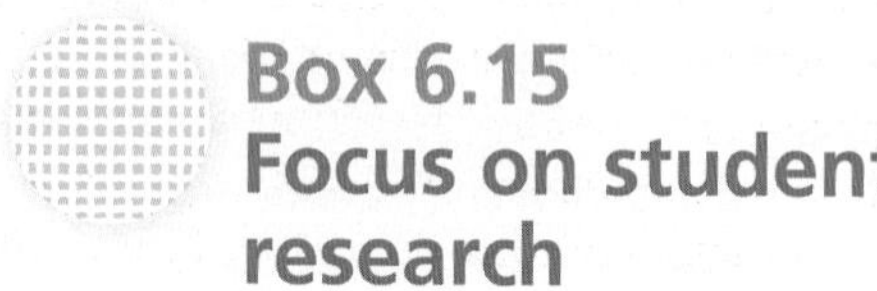

Box 6.15 Focus on student research

Consent form

Anna's research involved interviewing a number of franchisees who had expanded their franchises to run multiple outlets, to understand the competence required to achieve this expansion successfully and how they had developed this. Prior to commencing each interview, Anna gave each participant an information sheet that summarised her research project, including the possible benefits and disadvantages of taking part. After carefully explaining her research, the reasons why (with the participant's permission) she wished to audio-record the interview and emphasising that individuals were not obliged to participate unless they wished, Anna asked them if they wished to participate. Those who did were asked to complete and sign the following consent form:

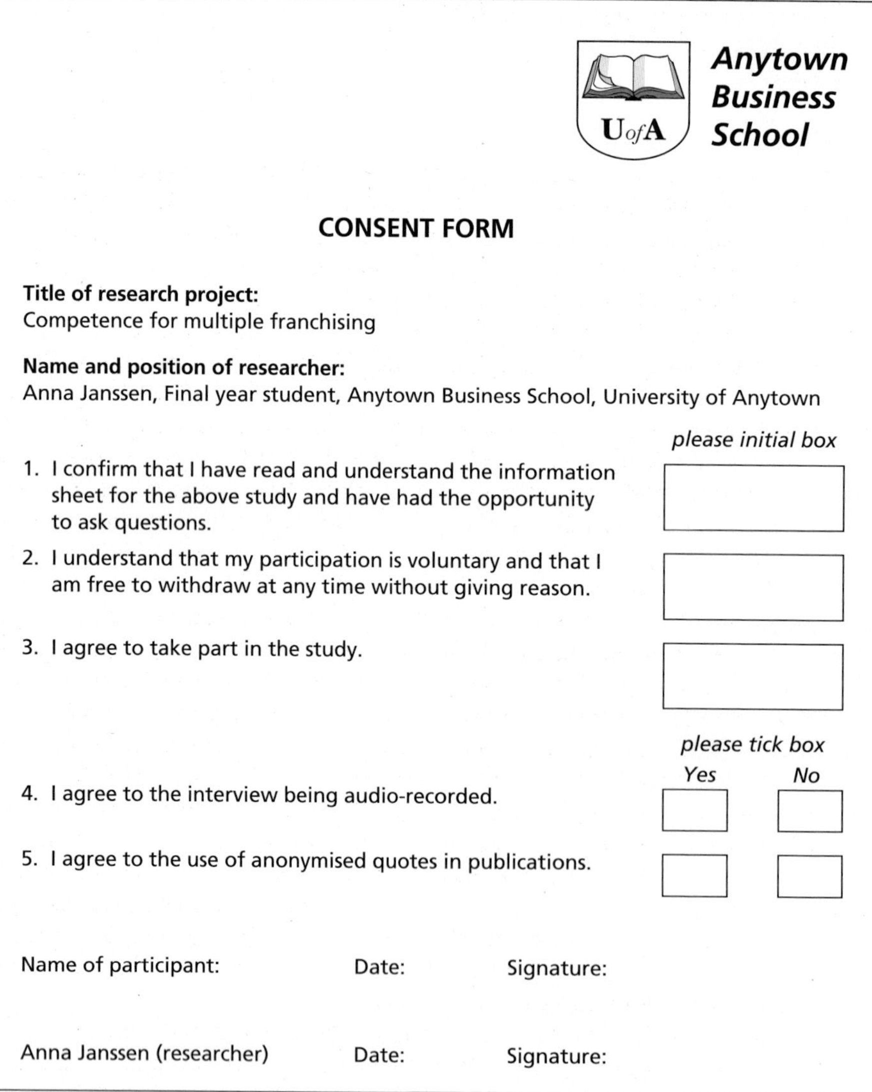

Anytown Business School

UofA

CONSENT FORM

Title of research project:
Competence for multiple franchising

Name and position of researcher:
Anna Janssen, Final year student, Anytown Business School, University of Anytown

please initial box

1. I confirm that I have read and understand the information sheet for the above study and have had the opportunity to ask questions. ☐
2. I understand that my participation is voluntary and that I am free to withdraw at any time without giving reason. ☐
3. I agree to take part in the study. ☐

please tick box

	Yes	*No*
4. I agree to the interview being audio-recorded.	☐	☐
5. I agree to the use of anonymised quotes in publications.	☐	☐

Name of participant: Date: Signature:

Anna Janssen (researcher) Date: Signature:

You will also need to operate on the basis that informed consent is a continuing requirement for your research. This, of course, will be particularly significant where you seek to gain access on an incremental basis (Section 6.4). Although you may have established informed consent through prior written correspondence, it is still worthwhile to reinforce this at the point of collecting data. An example of this is provided in Box 10.9, which contains a worked example about opening a semi-structured interview. You will also need to gain informed consent from those whom you wish to be your intended participants as well as those who act as organisational gatekeepers, granting you access.

Earlier (Section 6.4) we discussed possible strategies to help you to gain access. One of these was related to possible benefits to an organisation of granting you access. You should be realistic about this. Where you are anxious to gain access, you may be tempted to offer more than is feasible. Alternatively, you may offer to supply information arising from your work without intending to do this. Such behaviour would be unethical and, to make this worse, the effect of such action (or inaction) may result in a refusal to grant access to others who come after you.

Ethical issues during data collection

As highlighted in Figure 6.1, the data collection stage is associated with a range of ethical issues. Some of these are general issues that will apply to whichever technique is being used to collect data. Other issues are more specifically related to a particular data collection technique. Finally, and of equal importance, there are issues associated with ensuring your own safety whilst collecting your data.

Irrespective of data collection technique, there are a number of ethical principles to which you need to adhere. In the previous subsection we referred to the importance of not causing harm or intruding on privacy. This was in relation to the right not to take part. Once individuals or organisations have consented to take part in your research, they still maintain their rights. This means that they have the right to withdraw, and that they may decline to take part in a particular aspect of your research. You should not ask them to participate in anything that will cause harm or intrude on their privacy, where this goes beyond the scope of the access agreed. We have also referred to rights in relation to deceit. Once access has been granted, you should keep to the aims of your research project that you agreed (Zikmund 2000). To do otherwise, without raising this with those taking part and renegotiating access, would be, in effect, another type of deceit. This would be likely to cause upset, and could result in the premature termination of your data collection. There are perhaps some situations where deception may be accepted in relation to 'covert' research, and we shall discuss this later in this subsection.

Another general ethical principle is related to the maintenance of your objectivity. During the data collection stage this means making sure that you collect your data accurately and fully – that you avoid exercising subjective selectivity in what you record. The importance of this action also relates to the validity and reliability of your work, which is discussed in Chapters 5 and 7–11. Without objectively collected data, your ability to analyse and report your work accurately will also be impaired. We return to this as an ethical issue in the next subsection. Obviously, fabrication of any data is also a totally unacceptable and unethical course of action.

Confidentiality and anonymity may be important in gaining access to organisations and individuals (Section 6.4). Once such promises have been given, it is of great importance to make sure that these are maintained. Where confidentiality has been promised, then you must ensure the data collected remain confidential. This is particularly important in relation to personal and sensitive personal data (see Section 6.7). Ways of ensuring anonymity are inevitably research method specific. Whilst the main concern is likely to be individuals or organisations being able to be identified, it is worth recognising that permission may be given for data to be attributed directly to them. Anonymising quantitative data by aggregating or removing key variables is relatively straightforward. However, where qualitative data are being reported it may be less straightforward. New points of significance will emerge as the research progresses which you will wish to explore with others. Your key concern is to ensure that you do not cause harm (Easterby-Smith et al. 2008). For example, within interviews, participants can often infer what earlier interviewees might have said from the questions being asked. This may lead to participants indirectly identifying which person was responsible for making the earlier point that you now wish to explore with them, with repercussions for the person whose openness allowed you to identify this point for exploration. Where you wish to get others to discuss a potentially sensitive point you may attempt to steer the discussion to see if they will raise it without in any way making clear that one of the other participants has already referred to it.

Use of the Internet and email during data collection will lead to the possibility of serious ethical and netiquette issues, related to confidentiality and anonymity. For example, it would be technically possible to forward the email (or interview notes) of one research participant to another participant in order to ask this second person to comment on the issues being raised. Such an action would infringe the right to confidentiality and anonymity, perhaps causing harm. It should definitely be avoided. It may also lead to data protection issues related to the use of personal data (discussed in Section 6.7).

The ability to explore data or to seek explanations through interview-based techniques means that there will be greater scope for ethical and other issues to arise in relation to this approach to research (Easterby-Smith et al. 2008). The resulting personal contact, scope to use non-standardised questions or to observe on a 'face-to-face' basis, and capacity to develop your knowledge on an incremental basis, mean that you will be able to exercise a greater level of control (Chapter 10). This contrasts with the use of a quantitative approach based on structured interviews or self-administered questionnaires (Chapter 11).

The relatively greater level of research control associated with interview-based techniques should be exercised with care so that your behaviour remains within appropriate and acceptable parameters. In face-to-face interviews, you should avoid over-zealous questioning and pressing your participant for a response. Doing so may make the situation stressful for your participant (Sekaran and Bougie 2009). You should also make clear to your interview participants that they have the right to decline to respond to any question (Cooper and Schindler 2008). The nature of questions to be asked also requires consideration. Sekaran and Bougie (2009) state that you should avoid asking questions that are in any way demeaning to your participant (Sections 10.5, 10.6, 10.8 and 10.9 provide a fuller consideration of related issues). In face-to-face interviews it will clearly be necessary to arrange a time that is convenient for your participant; however, where you wish to conduct an interview by telephone (Sections 10.9, 11.2 and 11.5) you should not attempt to do this at an unreasonable time of the day. In interviews, whether face to face or using a telephone, it would also be unethical to attempt to prolong the discussion when it is apparent that your participant has other commitments (Zikmund 2000).

The use of observation techniques raises its own ethical concerns (Chapter 9). The boundaries of what is permissible to observe need to be drawn clearly. Without this type of agreement those being observed may feel that their actions are constrained (Bryman 1988). You should also avoid attempting to observe behaviour related to private life, such as personal telephone calls and so forth. Without this, the relationship between observer and observed will break down, with the latter finding the process to be an intrusion on their right to privacy. There is, however, a second problem related to the use of this method. This is the issue of '"**reactivity**" – the reaction on the part of those being investigated to the researcher and their research instruments' (Bryman 1988: 112). This issue applies to a number of strategies and methods (Bryman 1988) but is clearly a particular problem in observation.

One solution to this problem could be to undertake a **covert** study so that those being observed are not aware of this fact. In a situation of likely 'reactivity' to the presence of an observer you might use this approach in a deceitful yet benign way, since to declare your purpose at the outset of your work might lead to non-participation or to problems related to validity and reliability if those being observed altered their behaviour (Bryman, 1988; Gummesson 2000; Wells 1994). The rationale for this choice of approach would thus be related to a question of whether 'the ends justify the means', provided that other ethical aspects are considered (Wells 1994: 284). However, the ethical concern with deceiving those being observed may prevail over any pragmatic view (Bryman 1988; Cooper and Schindler 2008). Indeed, the problem of reactivity may be a diminishing one where those being observed adapt to your presence as declared observer (Bryman 1988). Their adaptation is known as **habituation** (Section 9.2).

Where access is denied after being requested you may decide you have no other choice but to carry out covert observation – where this would be practical (Gummesson 2000). We strongly advise against this. Covert observation after access has been denied will prove to be a considerable source of irritation. Indeed, many universities' ethical codes prohibit any form of research being carried out if access has been denied. Irrespective of the reason why a deception occurred, it is widely accepted that after the observation has taken place you should inform those affected about what has occurred and why. This process is known as **debriefing**.

One group of students who sometimes consider using a covert approach are internal researchers or practitioner-researchers. There are recognised advantages and disadvantages associated with being an internal researcher (see Sections 6.2 and 9.3). One of the possible disadvantages is related to your relationship with those from whom you will need to gain cooperation in order to acquire cognitive access to their data. This may be related to the fact that your status is relatively junior to these colleagues, or that you are more senior to them. Any status difference can impact negatively on your intended data collection. One solution would therefore be to adopt a covert approach in order to seek to gain data. You may therefore decide to interview subordinate colleagues, organise focus groups through your managerial status or observe interactions during meetings without declaring your research interest. The key question to consider is: will this approach be more likely to yield trustworthy data than declaring your real purpose and acting overtly? The answer will depend on a number of factors:

- the existing nature of your relationships with those whom you wish to be your participants;
- the prevailing managerial style within the organisation or that part of it where these people work;
- the time and opportunity that you have to attempt to develop the trust and confidence of these intended participants in order to gain their cooperation.

Absolute assurances about the use of the data collected may also be critical to gain trust, and the time you invest in achieving this may be very worthwhile. You will also need to consider the impact on yourself of adopting a covert approach when others learn of it.

In comparison with the issues discussed in the preceding paragraphs, Dale et al. (1988) believe that the ethical problems associated with questionnaires and other research using the survey strategy are fewer. This is due to the nature of structured questions that are rarely designed to explore responses, and the avoidance of the in-depth interview situation, where the ability to use probing questions can lead to more revealing information (Dale et al. 1988). Zikmund (2000) believes that the ethical issues linked with a survey strategy are those associated with more general issues discussed earlier: privacy, deception, openness, confidentiality and objectivity.

When thinking about avoiding harm, many researchers forget about themselves! The possibility of harm to you as the researcher is an important ethical issue that you should not ignore. You should not reveal personal information about yourself such as your home address or telephone number. Careful consideration needs to given to a range of risk factors including the nature of the research, the location and timing of data collection activities, and health and safety considerations. Researchers need to consider risks to their safety and to seek to avoid these through strategies such as meeting participants in safe spaces, conducting data collection during the daytime and letting other people know your arrangements, including where you will be.

In discussing the safety of researchers with our students, we have found the guidance sheets provided by the Suzy Lamplugh Trust (2011) to be extremely helpful (Box 6.16). As the Trust's guidance sheets emphasise, you should never allow your working practices (research design) to put your own safety in danger. The Social Research Association (2001) has also published, 'A Code of Practice for the Safety of Social Researchers' (Table 6.2) that contains very helpful advice for research managers and researchers, including a range of strategies to promote safety.

Box 6.16 Checklist

Personal safety when collecting primary data

In its guidance sheet, 'Personal Safety Alone in the Workplace', the Suzy Lamplugh Trust (2011) highlights how many people find themselves working alone in the workplace, emphasising the corresponding need to make adequate arrangements to ensure they are safe at all times, especially when clients visit. The advice offered by the Trust also applies to you as a researcher if you are intending to collect primary data. In particular, the Trust advises that you should:

- ✔ let other people know whom you are meeting, when and where so that someone is looking after your welfare;
- ✔ set up a system where you contact someone every day with a full list of whom you are meeting, where and at what times;
- ✔ make a telephone call just after a visitor has arrived, telling someone at the other end of the line that you will contact them again at a certain time after the visitor has left;
- ✔ be careful not to tell anyone that you are alone in a workplace.

As part of this leaflet, the Trust also offers the following general advice for anyone working alone:

- ✔ **P**lan your first meeting with a person in a busy public place if at all possible.
- ✔ **L**og your visits/meetings with someone and telephone them afterwards to let them know you are safe.
- ✔ **A**void situations that might be difficult or dangerous.
- ✔ **N**ever assume it will not happen to you.

However, as emphasised by the Trust, these are suggestions only and should not be regarded as comprehensive sources of advice.

Ethical issues related to analysis and reporting

The maintenance of your objectivity will be vital during the analysis stage to make sure that you do not misrepresent the data collected. This will include not being selective about which data to report or, where appropriate, misrepresenting its statistical accuracy (Zikmund 2000). A great deal of trust is placed in each researcher's integrity, and it would clearly be a major ethical issue were this to be open to question. This duty to represent your data honestly extends to the analysis and reporting stage of your research. Lack of objectivity at this stage will clearly distort your conclusions and any associated recommendations.

The ethical issues of confidentiality and anonymity also come to the fore during the reporting stage of your research. Wells (1994) recognises that it may be difficult to maintain the assurances that have been given. However, allowing a participating organisation to be identified by those who can 'piece together' the characteristics that you reveal may result in embarrassment and also in access being refused to those who seek this after you. Great care therefore needs to be exercised to avoid this situation. You also have the option of requesting permission from the organisation to use their name. To gain this permission you will almost certainly need to let them read your work to understand the context within which they would be named.

This level of care also needs to be exercised in making sure that the anonymity of individuals is maintained (Box 6.17). Embarrassment and even harm could result from reporting data that are clearly attributable to a particular individual (Cooper and Schindler 2008; Robson 2011). Care therefore needs to be taken to protect those who participate in your research. Do not collect data that identify individuals where it is not necessary to do so, e.g. full names where you do not need this type of data. Always seek to anonymise participants' identities by using a level of generalisation which ensures that others are not able to identify the organisation, group, community or individuals who participated in your data collection. For example, do not refer to specific ages, dates, locations, names of countries, real names, actual organisational names or job positions and so forth that will

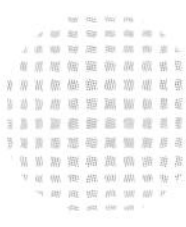

Box 6.17 Focus on students' research

Inadvertently revealing participants' identities

Over the years we have been fortunate to read a large number of student research projects. The following examples, drawn from some of these, highlight how easy it is to inadvertently reveal the identities of research participants when presenting your findings:

- reporting a comment made by a female accounts manager when in fact there is only one such person;
- referring to a comment made by a member of the sales team, when only one salesperson would have had access to the information referred to in the comment;
- reporting data and comments related to a small section of staff, where you state the name or job title of the one person interviewed from that section elsewhere in your research report;
- referring to an 'anonymous' organisation by name on the copy of the questionnaire placed in an appendix;
- attributing comments to named employees;
- thanking those who participated in the research by name;
- using pseudonyms where the initials of the pseudonym are the same as those of the actual person interviewed, or where the name is similar, e.g. using Tim Jennings for Tom Jenkins;
- including a photograph of the interview site or interviewee in your project report.

make it easy to identify participants or participating organisations, groups or communities (UK Data Archive 2011b), unless there is express permission to identify any of these.

A further ethical concern stems from the use made by others of the conclusions that you reach and any course of action that is explicitly referred to or implicitly suggested, based on your research data. How ethical would it be to use the data collected from a group of participants effectively to disadvantage them because of the decisions that are then made in the light of your research? On the other hand, there is a view which says that while the identity of your participants should not be revealed, they cannot be exempt from the way in which research conclusions are then used to make decisions (Dale et al. 1988). This is clearly an ethical issue, requiring very careful evaluation.

Where you are aware that your findings may be used to make a decision that could adversely affect the collective interests of those who were your participants, it may be ethical to refer to this possibility even though it reduces the level of access that you achieve. An alternative position is to construct your research question and objectives to avoid this possibility, or so that decisions taken as a result of your research should have only positive consequences for the collective interests of those who participate. You may find that this alternative is not open to you, perhaps because you are a part-time student in employment and your employing organisation directs your choice of research topic. If so, it will be more honest to concede to your participants that you are in effect acting as an internal consultant rather than in a (dispassionate) researcher's role.

This discussion about the impact of research on the collective interests of those who participate brings us back to the reference made earlier to the particular ethical issues that arise in relation to the analysis of secondary data derived from questionnaires. Dale et al. (1988) point out that where questionnaire data are subsequently used as secondary data the original assurances provided to those who participated in the research may be set aside, with the result that the collective interests of participants may be disadvantaged through this use of data. The use of data for secondary purposes therefore also leads to ethical concerns of potentially significant proportions, and you will need to consider these in the way in which you make use of this type of data.

A final checklist to help you anticipate and deal with ethical issues is given in Box 6.18.

Box 6.18 Checklist

To help anticipate and deal with ethical issues

- ✔ Attempt to recognise potential ethical issues that will affect your proposed research.
- ✔ Utilise your university's code on research ethics to guide the design and conduct of your research.
- ✔ Anticipate ethical issues at the design stage of your research and discuss how you will seek to control these in your research proposal.
- ✔ Seek informed consent through the use of openness and honesty, rather than using deception.
- ✔ Do not exaggerate the likely benefits of your research for participating organisations or individuals.
- ✔ Respect others' rights to privacy at all stages of your research project.
- ✔ Maintain objectivity and quality in relation to the processes you use to collect data.
- ✔ Recognise that more intrusive approaches to research will be associated with greater scope for ethical issues to arise, and seek to avoid the particular problems related to interviews and observation.
- ✔ Avoid referring to data gained from a particular participant when talking to others, where this would allow the individual to be identified with potentially harmful consequences to that person.

- ✔ Only consider covert research where reactivity is likely to be a significant issue and a covert presence is practical. However, other ethical aspects of your research should still be respected when using this approach and where possible debriefing should occur after the collection of data.
- ✔ Maintain your objectivity during the stages of analysing and reporting your research.
- ✔ Maintain the assurances that you gave to participating organisations with regard to confidentiality of the data obtained and their organisational anonymity.
- ✔ Recognise that use of the Internet may raise particular ethical issues and dilemmas. Anticipate these in relation to your project to determine how you will conduct your Internet-mediated research ethically. You should be able to justify your approach to those who review and assess it.
- ✔ Where you use Internet-mediated research, seek informed consent and agreement from your virtual participants; maintain confidentiality of data and anonymity of participants, unless they expressly wish to be acknowledged; consider issues related to copyright of Internet sources.
- ✔ Avoid using the Internet or email to share data with other participants.
- ✔ Protect those involved by taking great care to ensure their anonymity in relation to anything that you refer to in your project report unless you have their explicit permission to do otherwise.
- ✔ Consider how the collective interests of those involved may be adversely affected by the nature of the data that you are proposing to collect, and alter the nature of your research question and objectives where this possibility is likely. Alternatively, declare this possibility to those whom you wish to participate in your proposed research.
- ✔ Consider how you will use secondary data in order to protect the identities of those who contributed to its collection or who are named within it.
- ✔ Unless necessary, base your research on genuinely anonymised data. Where it is necessary to process personal data, ensure that you comply carefully with all current data protection legal requirements.

6.7 An introduction to the principles of data protection and data management

This section outlines the principles of data protection and data management, which you will need to consider in order to manage your data ethically and even lawfully. Within the European Union, issues of data protection have assumed an even greater importance since the implementation of Directive 95/46/EC. This provides protection for individuals in relation to the processing, storing and movement of personal data. Data protection legislation is likely to exist in countries outside the European Union, and you will need to be familiar with legislative requirements where you undertake your research project.

Article 1 of Directive 95/46/EC requires member states to protect individuals' rights and freedoms, including their right to privacy, with regard to the processing of personal data. Article 2 provides a number of definitions related to the purpose of the Directive. **Personal data** are defined as data that relate to a living person which allow that individual to be identified, perhaps in combination with other information known to the controller of the data. Where you control and process this type of data your research will become subject to the provisions of the data protection legislation of the country in which you live. In the context of UK legislation, this refers to the provisions of the Data Protection Act 1998 (Stationery Office 1998). This Act, in following the Articles of the Directive, outlines the principles with which anyone processing personal data must comply. Although the following list provides a summary of these principles, you are strongly advised to familiarise yourself with the definitive legal version and to determine its implications for your research project and approach to collecting, processing, storing and use of data.

Personal data must be:

1 processed fairly and lawfully;
2 obtained for specified, explicit and lawful purposes and not processed further in a manner incompatible with those purposes;
3 adequate, relevant and not excessive in relation to the purpose for which they are processed;
4 accurate and, where necessary, kept up to date;
5 kept (in a form that allows identification of data subjects) for no longer than is necessary;
6 processed in accordance with the rights granted to data subjects by the Act;
7 kept securely;
8 not transferred to a country outside the European Economic Area unless it ensures an adequate level of protection in relation to the rights of data subjects.

These principles have implications for all research projects that involve the processing of personal data. There are certain, limited exemptions to the second, fifth and seventh data principles (and to Section 7 of the 1998 Act) related to the processing and use of personal data for research purposes. These are contained in Section 33 of the Data Protection Act 1998. Where data are not processed to support measures or decisions with respect to particular individuals and are not processed in a way that will cause substantial damage or distress to a data subject:

- personal data may be processed further for a research purpose, although it may be necessary to inform data subjects about this new purpose and who controls these data;
- personal data, where processed only for research purposes, may be kept indefinitely;
- personal data that are processed only for research will be exempt from Section 7, which provides data subjects with rights to request information, where the results of the research, including any statistics, are not made available in a form that identifies any data subject.

In addition, there is a further category of personal data, known as **sensitive personal data**, which covers information held about a data subject's racial or ethnic origin, political opinions, religious or other similar beliefs, trade union membership, physical or mental health or condition, sexual life, commission or alleged commission of any offence, or any proceedings or sentence related to an (alleged) offence. This type of data may be processed only if at least one of the conditions in Schedule 3 of the 1998 Act is met. The first of these conditions refers to the data subject providing their explicit consent to the processing of such data. Effective explicit consent is likely to mean clear and unambiguous written consent in this context.

Our brief summary of this legislation should be treated as only providing a general outline and not as providing advice. You should instead seek advice that is appropriate to the particular circumstances of your research project where this involves the collection, processing, storage or use of personal data.

These legally based data protection concerns have hopefully focused your mind on the question of keeping personal data and also on whether the use of these data allows any participant to be identified. Unless there is a clear reason for processing these types of data, the best course of action is likely to be to ensure that your data are completely and genuinely anonymised and that any 'key' to identify data subjects is not retained by those who control these data.

Files containing confidential or personal data will also need to be properly labelled and securely kept. This refers not only to your original notes or recordings, but also to any subsequent drafts, transcriptions, rerecordings, backup and anonymised versions. Original notes or recordings will be likely to include personal identifiers such as names, job titles, workplace locations and so forth that clearly identify the person being interviewed or observed. Personal identifiers may also exist on completed questionnaire forms. Anonymised versions of data will have used tactics such as aggregating data, pseudonyms and higher levels of generalisation to remove personal identifiers. Nevertheless, where these personal identifiers still exist in another document, there remains the possibility that they may be used to reveal the identities of participants or respondents. Original and anonymised data therefore need to be stored securely to protect these from unauthorised access. Particular care needs to be exercised when storing original versions of data that include personal identifiers, or when storing personal identifiers that relate to anonymised versions of data where these identifiers hold the key to revealing the identities of individuals in these anonymised versions. Data that contain personal identifiers therefore need to be held securely but separately to anonymised versions of data to which they relate (UK Data Archive 2011a).

Security will take a number of forms. Paper copies of interview or observation notes, signed consent forms, structured observation forms, questionnaires, transcriptions and other documents that contain confidential or personal data need to be held in a restricted, secure and safe place. Data held on external hard disc drives, compact discs and other audio recordings will also need to be held under the same conditions. Data held on a computer hard drive will need to be protected through the use of a password as well as by firewall and network protection software. When data are to be destroyed this needs to be carried out with due care so that paper documents are shredded, not just placed in a bin, and computer files and other digital material are permanently deleted (UK Data Archive 2011a). The management of your data in these ways illustrates how ethical concerns are likely to remain beyond the end of your research project in order to continue to maintain the confidentiality of the data that was collected, the anonymity of participants, their privacy and to ensure that harm is not caused to those who helped you.

6.8 Summary

- Access and ethics are critical aspects for the conduct of research.
- Different types of access exist: traditional access, Internet-mediated access, intranet-mediated access and hybrid access. Each of these types of access is associated with issues that may affect your ability to collect suitable, high-quality data.
- Different levels of access have been identified: physical access, continuing access and cognitive access.
- Feasibility and sufficiency are important determinants of what you choose to research and how you will conduct it.
- Issues related to gaining access will depend to some extent on your role as either an external researcher or a participant researcher.
- Your approach to research may combine traditional access with Internet- or intranet-mediated access leading to the use of a hybrid access strategy.
- There are a range of strategies to help you to gain access to organisations and to intended participants within them.
- Research ethics refers to the standards of behaviour that guide your conduct in relation to the rights of those who become the subject of your work, or are affected by it.

- Potential ethical issues should be recognised and considered from the outset of your research and are one of the criteria against which your research is judged. Issues may be anticipated by using codes of ethics, ethical guidelines and ethical principles.
- The Internet has facilitated access for particular types of research strategy; however its use is associated with a range of ethical concerns and even dilemmas in certain types of research, notably related to respecting rights of privacy and copyright.
- Ethical concerns can occur at all stages of your research project: when seeking access, during data collection, as you analyse data and when you report your findings.
- Qualitative research is likely to lead to a greater range of ethical concerns in comparison with quantitative research, although all research methods have specific ethical issues associated with them.
- Ethical concerns are also associated with the 'power relationship' between the researcher and those who grant access, and the researcher's role (as external researcher, internal researcher or internal consultant).
- Researchers also need to consider their own safety very carefully when planning and conducting research.
- Further ethical and legal concerns are associated with data protection and data management, affecting the collection, processing, storage and use of personal and confidential data. Researchers need to comply carefully with data protection legislation when using personal data, to protect the privacy of their data subjects and to avoid the risk of any harm occurring.

Self-check questions

Help with these questions is available at the end of the chapter.

6.1 How can you differentiate between types of access, and why is it important to do this?

6.2 What do you understand by the use of the terms 'feasibility' and 'sufficiency' when applied to the question of access?

6.3 Which strategies to help to gain access are likely to apply to the following scenarios:

a an 'external' researcher seeking direct access to managers who will be the research participants;

b an 'external' researcher seeking access through an organisational gatekeeper/broker to their intended participants;

c an internal researcher planning to undertake a research project within their employing organisation?

6.4 What are the principal ethical issues you will need to consider irrespective of the particular research methods that you use?

6.5 What problems might you encounter in attempting to protect the interests of participating organisations and individuals despite the assurances that you provide?

Review and discussion questions

6.6 In relation to your proposed research project, evaluate your scope to use: (a) a traditional approach to gain access; (b) an Internet- or intranet-mediated approach to gain access; (c) a hybrid access strategy to gain access to participants and potential data. Make notes about the advantages and disadvantages of each access strategy.

6.7 With a friend, discuss the outcomes of the evaluation you carried out for Question 6.6. From this, discuss how you intend to gain access to the data you need for your research project. In your discussion make a list of possible barriers to your gaining access and how

Progressing your research project

Negotiating access and addressing ethical issues

Consider the following aspects:

- Which types of data will you require in order to be able to answer sufficiently your proposed research question and objectives?
- Which research methods will you attempt to use to yield these data (including secondary data as appropriate)?
- What type(s) of access will you require in order to be able to collect data?
- What problems are you likely to encounter in gaining access?
- Which strategies to gain access will be useful to help you to overcome these problems?
- Depending on the type of access envisaged and your research status (i.e. as external researcher or practitioner-researcher), produce appropriate requests for organisational access and/or requests to individuals for their cooperation.
- Describe the ethical issues that are likely to affect your proposed research project, including your own personal safety. Discuss how you might seek to overcome or control these. This should be undertaken in relation to the various stages of your research project.
- Note down your answers. Use the questions in Box 1.4 to guide your reflective diary entry.

these might be overcome. Make sure that the ways you consider for overcoming these barriers are ethical!

6.8 Agree with a friend to each obtain a copy of your university's or your own professional association's ethical code. Make notes regarding those aspects of the ethical code you have obtained that you feel are relevant to each other's proposed research. Discuss your findings.

6.9 Visit the Suzy Lamplugh Trust website at www.suzylamplugh.org and browse their guidance leaflets/web pages. Make a list of the actions you should take to help ensure your own personal safety when undertaking your research project. Make sure you actually put these into practice.

6.10 Visit the Research Ethics Guidebook at www.ethicsguidebook.ac.uk and browse through the sections of this guide. In relation to the context of your proposed research project, make a note of points that provide additional guidance to help you to anticipate and deal with potential ethical concerns.

References

Bakardjieva, M. and Feenberg, A. (2000) 'Involving the virtual subject', *Ethics and Information Technology*, Vol. 2, pp. 233–40.

Bell, E. and Bryman, A. (2007) 'The ethics of management research: An exploratory content analysis', *British Journal of Management*, Vol. 18, No. 1, pp. 63–77.

Berry, D. (2004) 'Internet research: privacy, ethics and alienation: An open source approach', *Internet Research*, Vol. 14, No. 4, pp. 323–32.

Birnbaum, M.H. (2004) 'Human research and data collection via the internet', *Annual Review of Psychology*, Vol. 55, pp. 803–32.

British Psychological Society (2007) *Report of the Working Party on Conducting Research on the Internet, Guidelines for ethical practice in psychological research online*. Available at www.bps.org.uk/publications/policy-guidelines/research-guidelines-policy-documents/ [Accessed 1 June 2011].

British Sociological Association (2002) *Statement of Ethical Practice*. Available at www.britsoc.co.uk/equality/Statement+Ethical+Practice.htm [Accessed 1 June 2011].

Bryman, A. (1988) *Quantity and Quality in Social Research*. London: Unwin Hyman.

Buchanan, D., Boddy, D. and McCalman, J. (1988) 'Getting in, getting on, getting out and getting back', in A. Bryman (ed.) *Doing Research in Organisations*. London: Routledge, pp. 53–67.

Cooper, D.R. and Schindler, P.S. (2008) *Business Research Methods* (10th edn). Boston, MA and Burr Ridge, IL: McGraw-Hill.

Dale, A., Arber, S. and Procter, M. (1988) *Doing Secondary Research*. London: Unwin Hyman.

Easterby-Smith, M., Thorpe, R. and Jackson, P.R. (2008) *Management Research* (3rd edn). London: Sage.

Eysenbach, G. and Till, J.E. (2001) 'Ethical issues in qualitative research on internet communities', *British Medical Journal*, Vol. 323, pp. 1103–5.

Gummesson, E. (2000) *Qualitative Methods in Management Research* (2nd edn). Thousand Oaks, CA: Sage.

Healey, M.J. (1991) 'Obtaining information from businesses', in M.J. Healey, (ed.) *Economic Activity and Land Use*. Harlow: Longman, pp. 193–251.

Hookway, N. (2008) 'Entering the blogosphere: Some strategies for using blogs in social research', *Qualitative research*, Vol. 8, No. 1, pp. 91–113.

Johnson, J.M. (1975) *Doing Field Research*. New York: Free Press.

Kozinets, R.V. (2006) 'Netography 2.0', in R.W. Belk (ed.) *Handbook of Qualitative Research Methods in Marketing*. Cheltenham: Edward Elgar Publishing, pp. 129–42.

Madge, C. (2006) *Online research ethics*. Available at www.geog.le.ac.uk/orm/ethics/ethprint.htm [Accessed 1 June 2011].

Marshall, C. and Rossman, G.B. (2006) *Designing Qualitative Research* (4th edn). Thousand Oaks, CA: Sage.

National Patient Safety Agency (2007) *Defining Research*, Issue 3. London: National Patient Safety Agency.

Okumus, F., Altinay, L. and Roper, A. (2007) 'Gaining access for research: Reflections from experience', *Annals of Tourism Research*, Vol. 34, No. 1, pp. 7–26.

Robson, C. (2011) *Real World Research: A Resource for Users of Social Research Methods in Applied Settings* (3rd edn). Chichester: John Wiley.

Schoneboom, A. (2011) 'Workblogging in a Facebook age', *Work, Employment and Society*, Vol. 25, No. 1, pp. 132–40.

Sekaran, U. and Bougie, R. (2009) *Research Methods for Business: A Skill-Building Approach* (5th edn). Chichester: John Wiley.

Social Research Association (2001) *A Code of Practice for the Safety of Social Researchers*. Available at www.the-sra.org.uk/guidelines.htm [Accessed 1 June 2011].

Stationery Office, The (1998) *Data Protection Act 1998*. London: The Stationery Office.

Stieger, S. and Goritz, A.S. (2006) 'Using instant messaging for internet-based interviews', *CyberPsychology and Behavior*, Vol. 9, No. 5, pp. 552–9.

Suzy Lamplugh Trust, The (2011) *Personal safety alone in the workplace*. Available at www.suzylamplugh.org/personal-safety/personal-safety-tips/workplace-safety/alone-in-the-workplace/ [Accessed 1 June 2011].

Temkin, O. and Temkin, C.L. (1987) *Ancient Medicine: Selected Papers of Ludwig Edelstein*. Baltimore, MD: John Hopkins University Press.

Thomas, J. (1996) 'Introduction: A debate about the ethics of fair practices for collecting social science data in cyberspace', *The Information Society*, Vol. 12, No. 2, pp. 107–17.

UK Data Archive (2011a) *Managing and Sharing Data: Best Practice for Researchers* (3rd edn). Available at www.esds.ac.uk/support/datamanguides.asp [Accessed 1 June 2011].

UK Data Archive (2011b) *Create and Manage Data – Anonymisation*. Available at www.data-archive.ac.uk/create-manage/consent-ethics/anonymisation [Accessed 17 May 2011] .

Waskul, D. and Douglass, M. (1996) 'Considering the electronic participant: some polemical observations on the ethics of on-line research', *The Information Society*, Vol. 12, No. 2, pp. 129–39.

Wells, P. (1994) 'Ethics in business and management research', in V.J. Wass and P.E. Wells (eds) *Principles and Practice in Business and Management Research*. Aldershot: Dartmouth, pp. 277–97.

Zikmund, W.G. (2000) *Business Research Methods* (6th edn). Fort Worth, TX: Dryden Press.

Further reading

Bakardjieva, M. and Feenberg, A. (2000) 'Involving the virtual subject', *Ethics and Information Technology*, Vol. 2, pp. 233–40. This provides a thoughtful and thought-provoking account of the ethical issues associated with Internet-mediated research. Bakardjieva and Feenberg advance an important ethical principle of 'non-alienation', so that members of online communities may genuinely become virtual participants in research that relates to their online output.

Buchanan, D., Boddy, D. and McCalman, J. (1988) 'Getting in, getting on, getting out and getting back', in A. Bryman (ed.) *Doing Research in Organisations*. London: Routledge, pp. 53–67. This continues to provide a highly readable, relevant and very useful account of the negotiation of access.

Hookway, N. (2008) 'Entering the blogosphere: Some strategies for using blogs in social research', *Qualitative Research*, Vol. 8, No. 1, pp. 91–113. This provides an interesting and useful account of the author's experience of using blogs in social research. Hookway provides a practical account of the steps that he took along with discussion of the data quality and ethical issues associated in attempting to use this approach.

Suzy Lamplugh Trust, The (2011) *Personal safety tips*. Available at www.suzylamplugh.org/personal-safety/personal-safety-tips/ [Accessed 1 June 2011]. This web page provides links to the Trust's guidance sheets. These are designed to give you useful tips and information to help improve your personal safety.

Case 6
The impact of colour on children's brand choices

Helen had decided that her master's research project would lie within the area of branding, specifically focusing on the role that colour plays in brand choice. From her review of the literature she knew that colour could prompt a swifter response to a brand than either the written word or imagery and was the quickest path to emotion creation (Hayes et al. 2006). She was very interested in children as a consumer group, especially as they are becoming increasingly targeted as influential consumers. She had read that the average child in the UK sees 20–40,000 television adverts every year (Lindstrom 2003) and in research conducted by Roper and Shah (2007) 90 per cent of children had agreed if they saw a brand in a television or magazine advert it would have a positive affect on their purchase intentions. Helen wanted to explore this attachment with brands, further focusing on the question of whether colour played a role in brand choice and, if so, what strategies could be recommended for use by brand managers?

Source: Shutterstock/Dimitry Shironosov

Helen decided an experiment would be the best strategy for researching this question. Initially she designed the experiment procedure which included producing mock-up packaging of fictitious brands within the confectionery market. The only difference being the dominant colour in the brand logo. In her experiment she planned to ask children which one they preferred and why. She decided on colour as a variable as she learnt that on average people make judgements with respect to products within 90 seconds of their initial interactions, and up to 90 per cent of that assessment is based on colour alone (Singh 2006).

The first step was to gain ethical approval. She designed the experiment in line with her university's Code of Ethics and applied to the ethics committee. Her research proposal was however initially rejected on the grounds that it involved confectionery products and therefore could potentially encourage unhealthy eating in children. The committee also questioned whether schools would agree to participate in research on confectionery products for the same reason, commenting that obesity in children under 11 years old had risen by over 40 per cent in 10 years and the UK now had the highest obesity rate in Europe (Mayo and Nairn 2009). Bearing this in mind, Helen changed her proposal to focus instead on healthy snack food products and resubmitted her application, which was approved. Now with ethical approval, she needed to obtain official clearance that she was safe to work with children from the UK's Criminal Records Bureau (CRB). She completed the relevant forms and received a letter stating that she was 'cleared' to work with children.

Now she was ready to contact schools. She was interested in younger children, aged 4 to 11, so needed to conduct her research in primary schools. She was convinced that, now her research had a healthy eating focus, schools would be responsive to her requests; but also appreciated that schools were very busy and that she had to minimise their time and resources disruption. She understood that the head teacher was the key decision maker (and gatekeeper) so therefore telephoned her sample of schools to ascertain the head teacher details and whether an email or letter introduction would be best. Once this information was ascertained Helen emailed or sent a letter to the head teacher explaining her research and the possible benefits to the school for participating in her research. She was met with a very positive response, with many of the schools saying that they would use her research to work towards their Healthy Eating Charter status.

Once the schools had agreed to participate, the next challenge was to obtain permission from parents for their children to participate in her research. Helen produced packs for the schools to post to their children's parents. Each pack contained:

- a covering letter to the parent detailing the experiment and the healthy eating aspect,
- an appropriately worded participant information sheet for both the parent and the child explaining exactly what would happen in the experiment and emphasising that the child could withdraw at any time from the experiment,
- a consent form for the parent to complete and give to their child to return to their class teacher.

Helen found this a very lengthy process which took between two and three months from the initial contact with a school to the time when Helen had sufficient children with consent to proceed with the experiment. Additionally, on the day of the experiment some of the children who had returned the form were absent from school whilst others (especially the older children) were not allowed out of their lessons due to important topics being covered that day. Out of the 765 packs she distributed, Helen eventually undertook 301 experiments.

When the experiments were completed Helen entered the results into the IBM SPSS Statistics analysis software. She coded each child with a unique number in order to maintain the confidentiality of their responses. She then analysed her results.

References

Hayes, J.B., Alford, B.L., Silver, L. and York, R.P. (2006) 'Looks matter in developing consumer–brand relationships', *Journal of Product and Brand Management,* Vol. 15, No. 5, pp. 306–15.

Lindstrom, M. (2003) *Marketing Targets Tweens' Dreams*. London: Kogan Page.

Mayo, E. and Nairn, A. (2009) *Consumer Kids: How Big Business is Grooming Our Children for Profit.* London: Constable and Robinson Ltd.

Roper, S. and Shah, B. (2007) 'Vulnerable consumers: The social impact of branding on children', *Equal Opportunities International*, Vol. 26, No. 7, pp. 712–28.

Singh, S. (2006) 'Impact of color on marketing', *Management Decision*, Vol. 44, No. 6, pp.783–89.

Questions

1 List the problems researchers can encounter when conducting research on children.
2 What did Helen do to help her gain access to the head teachers?
3 What impact did the decision to change to healthy snack foods have on the research's success?
4 Outline the ethical issues Helen had to consider and how she addressed them.

Additional case studies relating to material covered in this chapter are available via the book's companion website: **www.pearsoned.co.uk/saunders**.

They are:

- The effects of a merger in a major UK building society.
- The quality of service provided by the accounts department.
- Misreading issues related to access and ethics in a small-scale enterprise.
- Mystery customer research in restaurant chains.
- Gaining access to business angels networks.

Self-check answers

6.1 The types of access that we have referred to in this chapter are: physical entry or initial access to an organisational setting; continuing access, which recognises that researchers often need to develop their access on an incremental basis; and cognitive access, where you will be concerned to gain the cooperation of individual participants once you have achieved access to the organisation in which they work. We also referred to personal access, which allows you to consider whether you actually need to meet with participants in order to carry out an aspect of your research as opposed to corresponding with them or sending them a self-administered, postal questionnaire. Access is strategically related to the success of your research project and needs to be carefully planned. In relation to many research designs, it will need to be thought of as a multifaceted aspect and not a single event.

Table 6.5 Considering access

	Scenario A	Scenario B	Scenario C
Allowing yourself sufficient time to gain access	Universally true in all cases. The practitioner-researcher will be going through a very similar process to those who wish to gain access from the outside in terms of contacting individuals and organisations, meeting with them to explain the research, providing assurances, etc. The only exception will be related to a covert approach, although sufficient time for planning, etc. will of course still be required		
Using any existing contacts	Where possible		Yes
Developing new contacts	Probably necessary		This may still apply within large, complex organisations, depending on the nature of the research
Providing a clear account of the purpose of your research and what type of access you require, with the intention of establishing your credibility	Definitely necessary		Still necessary although easier to achieve (verbally or internal memo) with familiar colleagues. Less easy with unfamiliar colleagues, which suggests just as much care as for external researchers
Overcoming organisational concerns in relation to the granting of access	Definitely necessary	Absolutely necessary. This may be the major problem to overcome since you are asking for access to a range of employees	Should not be a problem unless you propose to undertake a topic that is highly sensitive to the organisation! We know of students whose proposal has been refused within their organisation
Outlining possible benefits of granting access to you and any tangible outcome from doing so	Probably useful		Work-based research projects contain material of value to the organisation although they may largely be theoretically based
Using suitable language	Definitely necessary		Still necessary at the level of individuals in the organisation
Facilitating ease of reply when requesting access	Definitely useful		Might be useful to consider in relation to certain internal individuals
Developing your access on an incremental basis	Should not be necessary, although you may wish to undertake subsequent work	Definitely worth considering	Might be a useful strategy depending on the nature of the research and the work setting
Establishing your credibility	Access is not being sought at 'lower' levels within the organisation: however, there is still a need to achieve credibility in relation to those to whom you are applying directly	Definitely necessary	May still be necessary with unfamiliar individuals in the organisation

6.2 Gaining access can be problematic for researchers for a number of reasons. The concept of feasibility recognises this and suggests that in order to be able to conduct your research it will be necessary to design it with access clearly in mind. Sufficiency refers to another issue related to access. There are two aspects to the issue of sufficiency. The first of these relates to whether you have sufficiently considered and therefore fully realised the extent and nature of the access that you will require in order to be able to answer your research question and objectives. The second aspect relates to whether you are able to gain sufficient access in practice in order to be able to answer your research question and objectives.

6.3 We may consider the three particular scenarios outlined in the question in Table 6.5.

6.4 The principal ethical issues you will need to consider irrespective of which research method you use are:

- maintaining your integrity and objectivity during the data collection, analysis and reporting stages;
- avoiding deception about why you are undertaking the research, its purpose and how the data collected will be used;
- respecting rights to privacy and not to be exposed to the risk of harm;
- emphasising that participation is voluntary and that participants retain the right not to answer any questions that they do not wish to, or to provide any data requested. Those involved also retain the right to withdraw;
- achieving consent that is fully informed, considered and freely given. Research without prior fully informed consent should only be acceptable in very specific and previously approved circumstances;
- respecting assurances provided to organisations about the confidentiality of (certain types of) data and their anonymity;
- respecting assurances given to individuals about the confidentiality of the data they provide and their anonymity;
- considering the collective interests of individuals and organisations in the way you analyse, use and report the data which they provide;
- complying with legislation and other legal requirements relating to the processing and management of personal and confidential data;
- considering your own personal safety and that of other researchers.

6.5 A number of ethical problems might emerge. These are considered in turn. You may wish to explore a point made by one of your participants but to do so might lead to harmful consequences for this person where the point was attributed to him or her. It may be possible for some people who read your work to identify a participating organisation, although you do not actually name it. This may cause embarrassment to the organisation. Individual participants may also be identified by the nature of the comments that you report, again leading to harmful consequences for them. Your report may also lead to action being taken within an organisation that adversely affects those who were kind enough to take part in your research. Finally, others may seek to reuse any survey data that you collect, and this might be used to disadvantage those who provided the data by responding to your questionnaire. You may have thought of other problems that might also emerge.

Get ahead using resources on the companion website at:
www.pearsoned.co.uk/saunders

- Improve your IBM SPSS Statistics and NVivo research analysis with practice tutorials.
- Save time researching on the Internet with the Smarter Online Searching Guide.
- Test your progress using self-assessment questions.

Chapter 7

Selecting samples

Learning outcomes

By the end of this chapter you should:

- understand the need for sampling in business and management research;
- be aware of a range of probability and non-probability sampling techniques and the possible need to combine techniques within a research project;
- be able to select appropriate sampling techniques for a variety of research scenarios and be able to justify their selection;
- be able to use a range of sampling techniques;
- be able to assess the representativeness of the sample selected;
- be able to assess the extent to which it is reasonable to generalise from a sample;
- be able to apply the knowledge, skills and understanding gained to your own research project.

7.1 Introduction

Whatever your research question(s) and objectives you will need to consider whether you need to use sampling. Occasionally, it may be possible to collect and analyse data from every possible case or group member; this is termed a **census**. However, for many research questions and objectives it will be impossible for you either to collect or to analyse all the potential data available to you owing to restrictions of time, money and often access. In the vignette it was not possible to use a list of all outdoor advertising posters from all times, or to obtain opinions of the entire 'general public'. Sampling techniques enable you to reduce the amount of data you need to collect by considering only data from a subgroup rather than all possible cases or **elements** (Figure 7.1). Some research questions will require sample data to generalise statistically about all the cases from which your **sample** has been selected. For example, if you asked a sample of consumers what they thought of a new chocolate bar and 75 per cent said that they thought it was too expensive, you might infer that 75 per cent of all consumers felt that way. Other research questions may not involve such generalisations. To gain an understanding

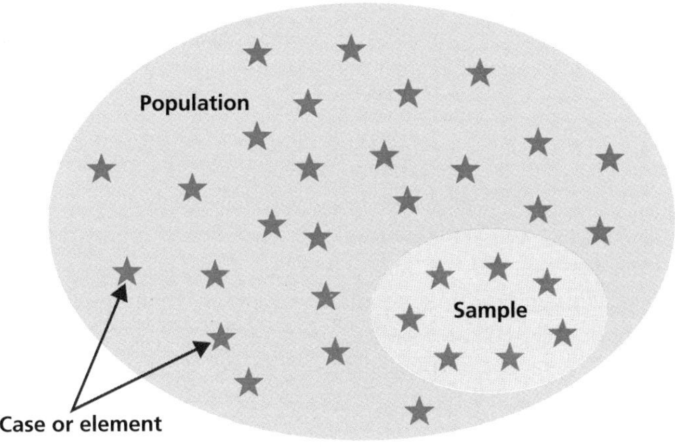

Figure 7.1 Population, sample and individual cases

In February 2011 the UK's Outdoor Media Centre launched its 'Hall of Fame' competition to identify the 100 best advertising posters of all time. Working with the History of Advertising Trust, they generated a list of 500 advertising campaigns. This was reduced to a shortlist of 228 campaigns by a committee of media and creative experts together with the editor of the weekly magazine for the advertising media and communications industry – *Campaign*. These were displayed on a dedicated website www.outdoorhalloffame.co.uk

Creative agencies, media planners, advertisers, media owners and the general public were invited in an article in *Campaign* to go to the website, view the advertising campaigns and cast their votes for what they considered to be the best outdoor posters (Bidlake 2011). Each person was able to cast a total of 10 votes, the best advertisements being chosen after more than 10,000 reader votes had been cast (Farey-Jones 2011).

On 31 March 2011 the results were announced, being reported widely in the UK media. TBWA's 1995 'Hello Boys' billboard poster advertising Wonderbra was voted the best poster ever created. In second place was Saatchi & Saatchi's 'Labour Isn't Working' poster created for the Conservative Party in the late 1970s. The 1914 UK First World War army recruiting poster 'Lord Kitchener Wants You' by Caxton Advertising took third place. The highest ranking outdoor poster from the last decade was TBWA's 2002/3 iTunes silhouette poster for Apple.

iTunes silhouette poster for Apple

Source: © Apple Inc. Used with permission. All rights reserved. Apple® and the Apple logo are registered trademarks of Apple Inc.

of how people manage their careers, you may select a sample of company chief executives. For such research your sample selection would be based on the premise that, as these people have reached executive level and have been successful in managing their own careers, they are most likely to be able to offer insights from which you can build understanding. Even if you are adopting a case study strategy using one large organisation and collecting your data using unstructured interviews, you will still need to select your case study (sample) organisation and a group (sample) of employees and managers to interview. For example, in the vignette, a report of findings in some UK media inferred they were based on a statistically representative public vote. Consequently, whatever your research question an understanding of techniques for selecting samples is likely to be very important.

In selecting a sample to study, it should represent the full set of cases in a way that is meaningful and which we can justify (Becker 1998). In the opening vignette, the Outdoor Media Centre provides information regarding how its sample of 228 advertising posters were selected. This allows us to assess whether this was meaningful with regard to establishing the 100 best advertising posters of all time. It also outlines briefly how the people who voted (creative agencies, media planners, advertisers, media owners and the general public) were selected, providing an indication of whom the sample were: predominantly people employed in media industries. This allows us to assess whether the claim that those receiving the most votes were the 100 best advertising posters of all time is justifiable.

The full set of cases from which a sample is taken is called the **population**. In sampling, the term 'population' is not used in its normal sense, as the full set of cases need not necessarily be people. For research to discover the level of service at Chinese restaurants throughout a country, the population from which you would select your sample would be all Chinese restaurants in that country. Alternatively, you might need to establish the normal 'range' in miles that can be travelled by electric cars in everyday use produced by a particular manufacturer. Here the population would be all the electric cars in everyday use produced by that manufacturer.

The need to sample

For some research questions it is possible to collect data from an entire population as it is of a manageable size. However, you should not assume that a census would necessarily provide more useful results than collecting data from a sample which represents the entire population. Sampling provides a valid alternative to a census when:

- it would be impracticable for you to survey the entire population;
- your budget constraints prevent you from surveying the entire population;
- your time constraints prevent you from surveying the entire population.

For all research questions where it would be impracticable for you to collect data from the entire population, you need to select a sample. This is equally important whether you are planning to use interviews, questionnaires, observation or some other data collection technique. You might be able to obtain permission to collect data from only two or three organisations. Alternatively, testing an entire population of products to destruction, such as to establish the actual duration of long-life batteries, would be impractical for any manufacturer.

With other research questions it might be theoretically possible for you to collect data from the entire population but the overall cost would prevent it. It is obviously cheaper for you to collect, prepare for analysis and check data from 250 customers than from

2500, even though the cost per case for your study (in this example, customer) is likely to be higher than with a census. Your costs will be made up of new costs such as sample selection, and the fact that overhead costs such as the questionnaire, interview or observation schedule design and general preparation for data for analysis are spread over a smaller number of cases. Sampling also saves time, an important consideration when you have tight deadlines. The organisation of data collection is more manageable as fewer people are involved. As you have fewer data to prepare for analysis and then to analyse, the results will be available more quickly.

Many researchers, for example Barnett (2002), argue that using sampling makes possible a higher overall accuracy than a census. The smaller number of cases for which you need to collect data means that more time can be spent designing and piloting the means of collecting these data. Collecting data from fewer cases also means that you can collect information that is more detailed. If you are employing people to collect the data (perhaps as interviewers) you can afford higher-quality staff. You can also devote more time to trying to obtain data from more difficult to reach cases. Once your data have been collected, proportionally more time can be devoted to checking and testing the data for accuracy prior to analysis. However, one point remains crucial when selecting a sample: it must enable you to answer your research question!

An overview of sampling techniques

Sampling techniques available to you can be divided into two types:

- probability or representative sampling;
- non-probability sampling.

Those discussed in this chapter are highlighted in Figure 7.2. With **probability samples** the chance, or probability, of each case being selected from the population is known and is usually equal for all cases. This means it is possible to answer research questions and to achieve objectives that require you to estimate statistically the characteristics of

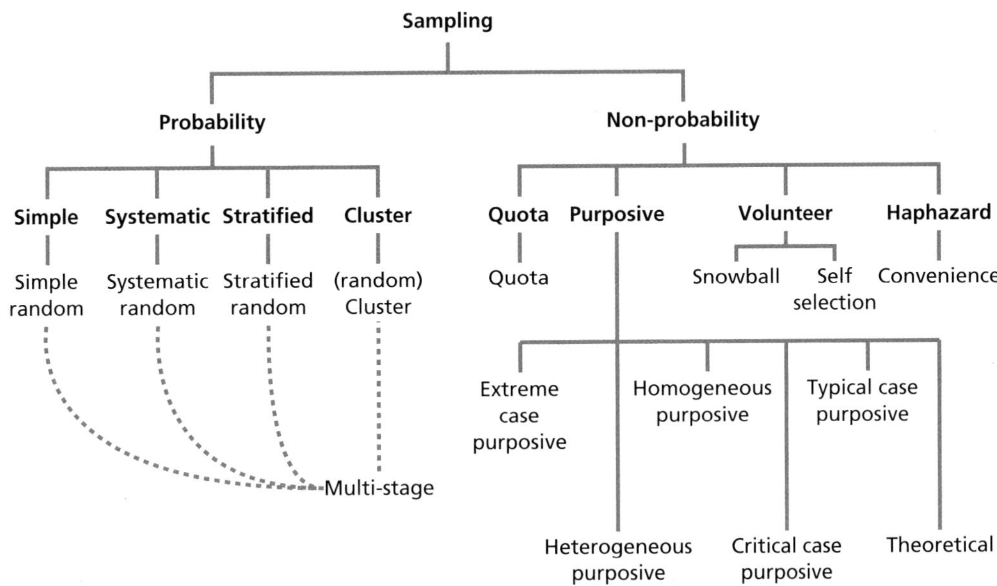

Figure 7.2 Sampling techniques

the population from the sample. Consequently, probability sampling is often associated with survey and experiment research strategies (Section 5.5). For **non-probability samples**, the probability of each case being selected from the total population is not known and it is impossible to answer research questions or to address objectives that require you to make statistical inferences about the characteristics of the population. You may still be able to generalise from non-probability samples about the population, but not on statistical grounds. However, with both types of sample you can answer other forms of research questions, such as 'What job attributes attract people to jobs?' or 'How are financial services institutions adapting their services in response to the post-2009 crash liquidity rules?'

Subsequent sections of this chapter outline the most frequently used probability (Section 7.2) and non-probability (Section 7.3) sampling techniques, discuss their advantages and disadvantages, and give examples of how and when you might use them. Although each technique is discussed separately, for many research projects you will need to use a combination of sampling techniques, some projects involving both probability and non-probability sampling techniques.

7.2 Probability sampling

Probability sampling (or **representative sampling**) is associated most commonly with survey research strategies where you need to make inferences from your sample about a population to answer your research question(s) and to meet your objectives. The process of probability sampling can be divided into four stages:

1 Identify a suitable sampling frame based on your research question(s) and objectives.
2 Decide on a suitable sample size.
3 Select the most appropriate sampling technique and select the sample.
4 Check that the sample is representative of the population.

Each of these stages will be considered in turn. However, for populations of fewer than 50 cases Henry (1990) advises against probability sampling. He argues that you should collect data on the entire population as the influence of a single extreme case on subsequent statistical analyses is more pronounced than for larger samples.

Identifying a suitable sampling frame and the implications for generalisability

The **sampling frame** for any probability sample is a complete list of all the cases in the population from which your sample will be drawn. Without a sampling frame, you will not be able to select a probability sample and so will have to consider using non-probability sampling. If your research question or objective is concerned with members of a student society, your sampling frame will be the complete membership list for that society. If your research question or objective is concerned with registered childminders in a local area, your sampling frame will be the directory of all registered childminders in this area. Alternatively, if your research question is concerned with organisations in a particular sector, you may be thinking of creating a sampling frame from an existing database of companies available at your university, such as Fame or Amadeus. You then select your sample from your list.

Obtaining a sampling frame is therefore essential if you are going to use probability sampling. However, as highlighted in research by Edwards et al. (2007), you need to be aware of the possible problems of using existing databases for your sampling frame. In their work on multinationals in Britain, they found that:

- individual databases are often incomplete;
- the information held about organisations in databases is sometimes inaccurate;
- the information held in databases soon becomes out of date.

This emphasises the importance of ensuring your sampling frame is as complete, accurate and up to date as possible. An incomplete or inaccurate list means that some cases will have been excluded and so it will be impossible for every case in the population to have a chance of selection. If this is the case you need to state it clearly (Box 7.1).

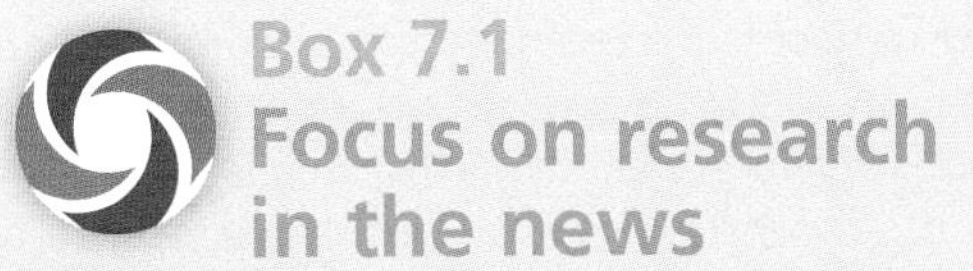

Box 7.1
Focus on research in the news
FT

More top graduates chase fewer jobs

Investment banks are offering one-quarter fewer entry-level roles than before the recession, and graduate intakes at engineering companies are down a third, according to a study. Despite two years of growth, there are still 6 per cent fewer graduate vacancies being offered by large recruiters than in 2007, according to High Fliers Research, a market research company, which surveyed 100 big graduate recruiters.

From this sample, which is skewed towards higher-paying service industry companies, the report shows a 9.4 per cent rise in recruitment for 2011, and a 12.6 per cent increase in 2010. There were steep declines in the previous two years.

The largest recruiters are the accountancy companies: PwC, Deloitte and KPMG each recruit between 900 and 1200 graduates a year. Teach First, a programme to encourage high-flying graduates to become teachers, is fourth, recruiting 780 graduates. The national graduate labour market remains tight and cohorts leaving university are growing. Unemployment among people aged 18 to 24 is 18 per cent, compared with 8 per cent for the population at large.

Martin Birchall, managing director of High Fliers, said: 'The "class of 2011" will be disappointed to hear that graduate recruitment has yet to return to the pre-recession levels seen in 2007, especially as there are an estimated 50,000 extra graduates leaving university in 2011 compared with four years ago.' After rising throughout the recession, the average graduate starting salary offered by the companies surveyed by High Fliers for 2011 is unchanged at £29,000. This is markedly higher than the national average for graduate starting salaries.

Average national pay for all full-time employees, according to official statistics, was about £26,000 in 2010. About half of new graduate jobs offered by companies in the High Fliers sample group start at a salary above this level. Within the survey group, average starting salaries vary, the survey shows, from £42,000 in banking down to £22,200 in the public sector. Outside the City, the highest paying graduate recruiter, Aldi, the supermarket, pays £40,000 a year.

The survey also revealed that half of all entrants at investment banks and law firms had already completed some time working for their employer before joining. The survey revealed that 60 per cent of employers said graduates with no work experience would be unlikely to be offered a job.

Lee Elliot Major, research director at the Sutton Trust, a social mobility charity, expressed concern that this could limit the ability of poorer students to get good jobs. 'Our fear is that work experience opportunities are too often the exclusive preserve of those from more privileged backgrounds – with the contacts and the support to survive on little or no pay', he said.

Source: Adapted from 'More top graduates chase fewer jobs', Chris, Cook (2011) *Financial Times*, 18 January.

Where no suitable list exists, and you wish to use probability sampling, you will have to compile your own sampling frame (perhaps drawing upon existing lists). It is important to ensure that your sampling frame is valid. You might decide to use a telephone directory as the sampling frame from which to select a sample of typical householders. However, the telephone directory covers only subscribers in one geographical area who rent a telephone landline from that company. Your survey will therefore be biased towards householders who have a landline telephone. Because the telephone directory is only published biennially, the sampling frame will be out of date ('non-current'). As some householders choose to be ex-directory, or only have mobile telephones, it will not be a valid representation as it does not include all those who own telephones. This means that you will be selecting a sample of landline telephone subscribers at the date the directory was compiled by a particular company who chose not to be ex-directory!

The way you define your sampling frame also has implications regarding the extent to which you can generalise from your sample. As we have already discussed, sampling is used when it is impracticable or unnecessary to collect data from the entire population. Within probability sampling, by defining the sampling frame you are defining the population about which you want to generalise. This means that if your sampling frame is a list of all customers of an organisation, strictly speaking you can only generalise, that is apply the findings based upon your sample, to that population. Similarly, if your sampling frame is all employees of an organisation (the list being the organisation's payroll) you can only generalise to employees of that organisation. This can create problems, as often we hope that our findings have wider applicability than the population from which our sample was selected. However, even if your probability sample has been selected from one large multinational organisation, you should not claim that what you have found will also occur in similar organisations. In other words, you should not generalise beyond your sampling frame. Despite this, researchers often do make such claims, rather than placing clear limits on the generalisability of the findings.

An increasing number of organisations specialise in selling machine readable lists of names, addresses and email addresses. These lists include a wide range of people such as company directors, chief executives, marketing managers, production managers and human resource managers, for public, private and non-profit-making organisations, and can be merged into standard letters such as those included with questionnaires (Section 11.4). Some organisations also specialise in delivering your questionnaire to an online 'survey panel' of potential respondents, guaranteeing you obtain a specified number of completed questionnaires for a sample tailored to your specific requirements. Because you pay for the list or completed questionnaire by the case (named individual), the organisations that provide them usually select your sample. It is therefore important to establish precisely how they will select your sample as well as obtaining an indication of the organisation database's completeness, accuracy and currency. For example, when obtaining a list of email addresses don't forget that some people change their Internet service provider and their email address regularly. This means the sampling frame is likely to under-represent this group. Usage patterns of the Internet both in organisations and at home are changing rapidly; you therefore need to ensure your intended sampling frame is relevant to your research population. If you are intending to use an online survey panel you need to establish whether or not the organisation offers panel members an incentive to encourage response and the likely implications of this for the characteristics of respondents and consequently their responses (Section 11.2). Box 7.2 provides a checklist against which to check your sampling frame.

Box 7.2
Checklist

Selecting your sampling frame

- ✔ Are cases listed in the sampling frame relevant to your research topic, in other words will they enable you to answer your research question and meet your objectives?
- ✔ How recently was the sampling frame compiled, in particular is it up to date?
- ✔ Does the sampling frame include all cases, in other words is it complete?
- ✔ Does the sampling frame contain the correct information, in other words is it accurate?
- ✔ Does the sampling frame exclude irrelevant cases, in other words is it precise?
- ✔ (For purchased lists and online panels) Can you establish and control precisely how the sample will be selected?
- ✔ (For an online panel) Can you establish whether incentives will be used to enhance the likely response and provide an assessment of the impact of this on respondent characteristics and consequently responses.

Deciding on a suitable sample size

Generalisations about populations from data collected using any probability samples are based on statistical probability. The larger your sample's size the lower the likely error in generalising to the population. Probability sampling is therefore a compromise between the accuracy of your findings and the amount of time and money you invest in collecting, checking and analysing the data. Your choice of sample size within this compromise is governed by:

- the confidence you need to have in your data – that is, the level of certainty that the characteristics of the data collected will represent the characteristics of the total population;
- the margin of error that you can tolerate – that is, the accuracy you require for any estimates made from your sample;
- the types of analyses you are going to undertake – in particular, the number of categories into which you wish to subdivide your data, as many statistical techniques have a minimum threshold of data cases for each cell (e.g. chi square, Section 12.5); and, to a lesser extent,
- the size of the total population from which your sample is being drawn.

Given these competing influences, it is not surprising that the final sample size is almost always a matter of judgement as well as of calculation. However, as we discuss in Section 12.5, if your sample is extremely large you may find that whilst relationships are statistically significant, the practical implications (effect size) of this difference are small (Lenth 2001). For many research questions and objectives, your need to undertake particular statistical analyses (Section 12.5) will determine the threshold sample size for individual categories. In particular, an examination of virtually any statistics textbook (or Sections 12.3 and 12.5 of this book) will highlight that, in order to ensure spurious results do not occur, the data analysed must be normally distributed. Whilst the normal distribution is discussed in Chapter 12, its implications for sample size need to be considered here. Statisticians have proved that the larger the absolute size of a sample, the closer its distribution will be to the normal distribution and thus the more robust it will be. This relationship, known as the **central limit theorem**, occurs even if the population from which the sample is drawn is not normally distributed. Statisticians have also shown that a sample size of 30 or more will usually result in a sampling distribution for the mean that is very close to a normal distribution. For this reason, Stutely's (2003) advice of a minimum number of 30 for statistical analyses provides a useful rule of thumb for the smallest number in each category within your overall sample. Where the population in the category is less than 30, and you wish to undertake your analysis at this level of detail, you should normally collect data from all cases in that category. Alternatively, you may have access to an expert system such as Ex-Sample™. This software calculates the minimum sample size required for different statistical analyses as well as the maximum possible sample size given resources such as time, money and response rates. In addition, it provides a report justifying the sample size calculated (Idea Works 2011).

It is likely that, if you are undertaking statistical analyses on your sample, you will be drawing conclusions from these analyses about the population from which your sample was selected. This process of coming up with conclusions about a population on the basis of data describing the sample is called **statistical inference** and allows you to calculate how probable it is that your result, given your sample size, could have been obtained by chance. Such probabilities are usually calculated automatically by statistical analysis software. However, it is worth remembering that, providing they are not biased, samples of larger absolute size are more likely to be representative of the population from which they are drawn than smaller samples and, in particular, the mean (average) calculated for the sample is more likely to equal the mean for the population. This is known as the **law of large numbers**.

Researchers normally work to a 95 per cent level of certainty. This means that if your sample was selected 100 times, at least 95 of these samples would be certain to represent the characteristics of the population. The confidence level states the precision of your estimates of the population as the percentage that is within a certain range or margin of error. Table 7.1 provides a rough guide to the different minimum sample sizes required

Table 7.1 Sample sizes for different sizes of population at a 95 per cent confidence level (assuming data are collected from all cases in the sample)

	Margin of error			
Population	**5%**	**3%**	**2%**	**1%**
50	44	48	49	50
100	79	91	96	99
150	108	132	141	148
200	132	168	185	196
250	151	203	226	244
300	168	234	267	291
400	196	291	343	384
500	217	340	414	475
750	254	440	571	696
1 000	278	516	706	906
2 000	322	696	1091	1655
5 000	357	879	1622	3288
10 000	370	964	1936	4899
100 000	383	1056	2345	8762
1 000 000	384	1066	2395	9513
10 000 000	384	1067	2400	9595

from different sizes of population given a 95 per cent confidence level for different margins of error. It assumes that data are collected from all cases in the sample (full details of the calculation for minimum sample size and adjusted minimum sample size are given in Appendix 2). For most business and management research, researchers are content to estimate the population's characteristics at 95 per cent certainty to within plus or minus 3 to 5 per cent of its true values. This means that if 45 per cent of your sample are in a particular category then you will be 95 per cent certain that your estimate for the total population within the same category will be 45 per cent plus or minus the margin of error – somewhere between 42 and 48 per cent for a 3 per cent margin of error.

As you can see from Table 7.1, the smaller the absolute size of the sample and, to a far lesser extent, the smaller the relative proportion of the total population sampled, the greater the margin of error. Within this, the impact of absolute sample size on the margin of error decreases for larger sample sizes. deVaus (2002) argues that it is for this reason that many market research companies limit their samples' sizes to approximately 2000. Unfortunately, from many samples, a 100 per cent response rate is unlikely and so your sample will need to be larger to ensure sufficient responses for the margin of error you require.

The importance of a high response rate

The most important aspect of a probability sample is that it represents the population. A perfect **representative sample** is one that exactly represents the population from which it is taken. If 60 per cent of your sample were small service sector companies then, provided the sample was representative, you would expect 60 per cent of the population to be small service sector companies. You therefore need to obtain as high a response rate as possible to reduce the risk of non-response bias and ensure your sample is representative (Groves and Peytcheva 2008). This is not to say that a low response rate will necessarily result in your sample being biased, just that it is more likely!

In reality, you are likely to have non-responses. Non-respondents are different from the rest of the population because they have refused to be involved in your research for whatever reason. Consequently, your respondents will not be representative of the total population, and the data you collect may be biased. In addition, each non-response will necessitate an extra respondent being found to reach the required sample size, increasing the cost of your data collection.

You should therefore collect data on refusals to respond to both individual questions and entire questionnaires or interview schedules to check for bias (Section 12.2) and report this briefly in your project report. For returned questionnaires or structured interviews, the American Association for Public Opinion Research (2008) defines four levels of non-response that can be reported for questionnaires and structured interviews:

- **complete refusal**: none of the questions answered;
- **break-off**: less than 50 per cent of all questions answered other than by a refusal or no answer (this therefore includes complete refusal);
- **partial response**: 50 per cent to 80 per cent of all questions answered other than by a refusal or no answer;
- **complete response**: over 80 per cent of all questions answered other than by a refusal or no answer.

Non-response is due to four interrelated problems:

- refusal to respond;
- ineligibility to respond;

- inability to locate respondent;
- respondent located but unable to make contact.

The most common reason for non-response is that your respondent refuses to answer all the questions or be involved in your research, but does not give a reason. Such non-response can be minimised by paying careful attention to the methods used to collect your data (Chapters 9, 10 and 11). Alternatively, some of your selected respondents may not meet your research requirements and so will be **ineligible** to respond. Non-location and non-contact create further problems; the fact that these respondents are **unreachable** means they will not be represented in the data you collect.

As part of your research report, you will need to include your **response rate**. Neumann (2005) suggests that when you calculate this you should include all eligible respondents:

$$\text{total response rate} = \frac{\text{total number of responses}}{\text{total number in sample} - \text{ineligible}}$$

This he calls the **total response rate**. A more common way of doing this excludes ineligible respondents and those who, despite repeated attempts (Sections 10.3 and 11.5), were unreachable. This is known as the **active response rate**:

$$\text{active response rate} = \frac{\text{total number of responses}}{\text{total number in sample} - (\text{ineligible} + \text{unreachable})}$$

An example of the calculation of both the total response rate and the active response rate is given in Box 7.3.

Even after ineligible and unreachable respondents have been excluded, it is probable that you will still have some non-responses. You therefore need to be able to assess how representative your data are and to allow for the impact of non-response in your calculations of sample size. These issues are explored in subsequent sections.

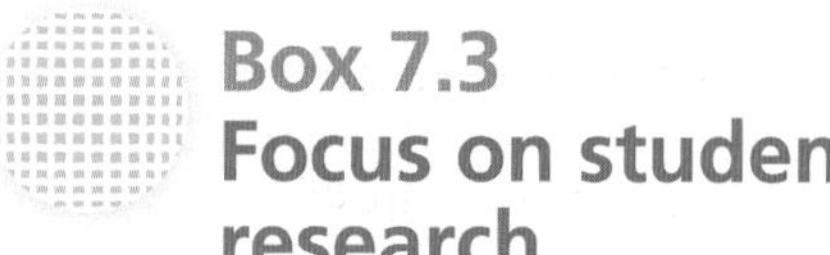

Box 7.3 Focus on student research

Calculation of total and active response rates

Ming had decided to administer a telephone questionnaire to people who had left his company's employment over the past five years. He obtained a list of the 1034 people who had left over this period (the total population) and selected a 50 per cent sample. Unfortunately, he could obtain current telephone numbers for only 311 of the 517 ex-employees who made up his total sample. Of these 311 people who were potentially reachable, he obtained a response from 147. In addition, his list of people who had left his company was inaccurate, and nine of those he contacted were ineligible to respond, having left the company over five years earlier.

$$\text{His total response rate} = \frac{147}{517 - 9} = \frac{147}{508} = 28.9\%$$

His active response rate

$$= \frac{147}{311 - 9} = \frac{147}{302} = 48.7\%$$

Estimating response rates and actual sample size required

With all probability samples, it is important that your sample size is large enough to provide you with the necessary confidence in your data. The margin of error must be within acceptable limits, and you must ensure that you will be able to undertake your analysis at the level of detail required. You therefore need to estimate the likely response rate – that is, the proportion of cases from your sample who will respond or from which data will be collected – and increase the sample size accordingly. Once you have an estimate of the likely response rate and the minimum or the adjusted minimum sample size, the actual sample size you require can be calculated using the following formula:

$$n^a = \frac{n \times 100}{re\%}$$

where n^a is the actual sample size required,
n is the minimum (or adjusted minimum) sample size (see Table 7.1 or Appendix 2),
$re\%$ is the estimated response rate expressed as a percentage.

This calculation is shown in Box 7.4.

If you are collecting your sample data from a secondary source (Section 8.2) within an organisation that has already granted you access, for example a database recording customer complaints, your response rate should be virtually 100 per cent. Your actual sample size will therefore be the same as your minimum sample size.

In contrast, estimating the likely response rate from a sample to which you will be sending a questionnaire or interviewing is more difficult. One way of obtaining this estimate is to consider the response rates achieved for similar surveys that have already been undertaken and base your estimate on these. Alternatively, you can err on the side of caution. For most academic studies involving individuals or organisations' representatives, response rates of approximately 50 per cent and 35 to 40 per cent respectively are reasonable (Baruch and Holtom 2008).

However, beware: response rates can vary considerably when collecting primary data. Willimack et al. (2002) report response rates for North American university-based

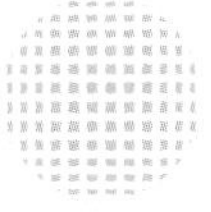

Box 7.4 Focus on student research

Calculation of actual sample size

Jan was a part-time student employed by a large manufacturing company. He had decided to send a questionnaire to the company's customers and calculated that an adjusted minimum sample size of 439 was required. From previous questionnaires that his company had used to collect data from customers, Jan knew the likely response rate would be approximately 30 per cent. Using these data he could calculate his actual sample size:

$$n^a = \frac{439 \times 100}{30} = \frac{43\,900}{30} = 1463$$

Jan's actual sample, therefore, needed to be 1463 customers. The likelihood of 70 per cent non-response meant that Jan needed to include a means of checking that his sample was representative when he designed his questionnaire.

Box 7.5 Focus on management research

Reporting response rates

In their 2008 *Human Relations* paper 'Survey responses rates: Levels and trends in organizational research', Baruch and Holtom offer useful advice regarding reporting responses rates from questionnaires. Within this they stress that authors should make it clear whether their questionnaire was administered (in other words respondents filled it in as part of their job, role or studies) or truly voluntary. They also offer a checklist for authors (and editors), which covers information that should be included about the sample and the questionnaires returned. In particular:

- ✔ Number of respondents to whom the questionnaire was sent.
- ✔ How the questionnaire was distributed.
- ✔ Whether prior consent was obtained from respondents.
- ✔ The number of questionnaires returned.
- ✔ Of those returned, the numbers that were useable.
- ✔ Reasons (if known) for questionnaires not being useable.
- ✔ Where different populations received a questionnaire, differences (if any) in response rates.
- ✔ Techniques (if any) used to increase response rates.
- ✔ Where response rates differ from likely norms, possible reasons for this.

questionnaire surveys of business ranging from 50 to 65 per cent, with even higher non-response for individual questions. Neuman (2005) suggests response rates of between 10 and 50 per cent for postal questionnaire surveys and up to 90 per cent for face-to-face interviews. The former rate concurs with a questionnaire survey we undertook for a multinational organisation that had an overall response rate of 52 per cent. In our survey, response rates for individual sites varied from 41 to 100 per cent, again emphasising variability. Our examination of response rates to recent business surveys reveals rates as low as 10–20 per cent for postal questionnaires, an implication being that respondents' questionnaire fatigue was a contributory factor! With regard to telephone questionnaires, response rates have fallen from 70 to 80 per cent to less than 40 per cent, due principally to people using answering services to screen calls (Dillman 2009). Fortunately a number of different techniques, depending on your data collection method, can be used to enhance your response rate. These are discussed with the data collection method in the appropriate sections (Sections 10.3 and 11.5).

Selecting the most appropriate sampling technique and the sample

Having chosen a suitable sampling frame and established the actual sample size required, you need to select the most appropriate sampling technique to obtain a representative sample. Five main techniques can be used to select a probability sample (Figure 7.3):

- simple random;
- systematic random;
- stratified random;
- cluster;
- multi-stage.

Your choice of probability sampling technique depends on your research question(s) and your objectives. Subsequently, your need for face-to-face contact with respondents, and the geographical area over which the population is spread further influence your choice of probability sampling technique (Figure 7.3). The structure of the sampling

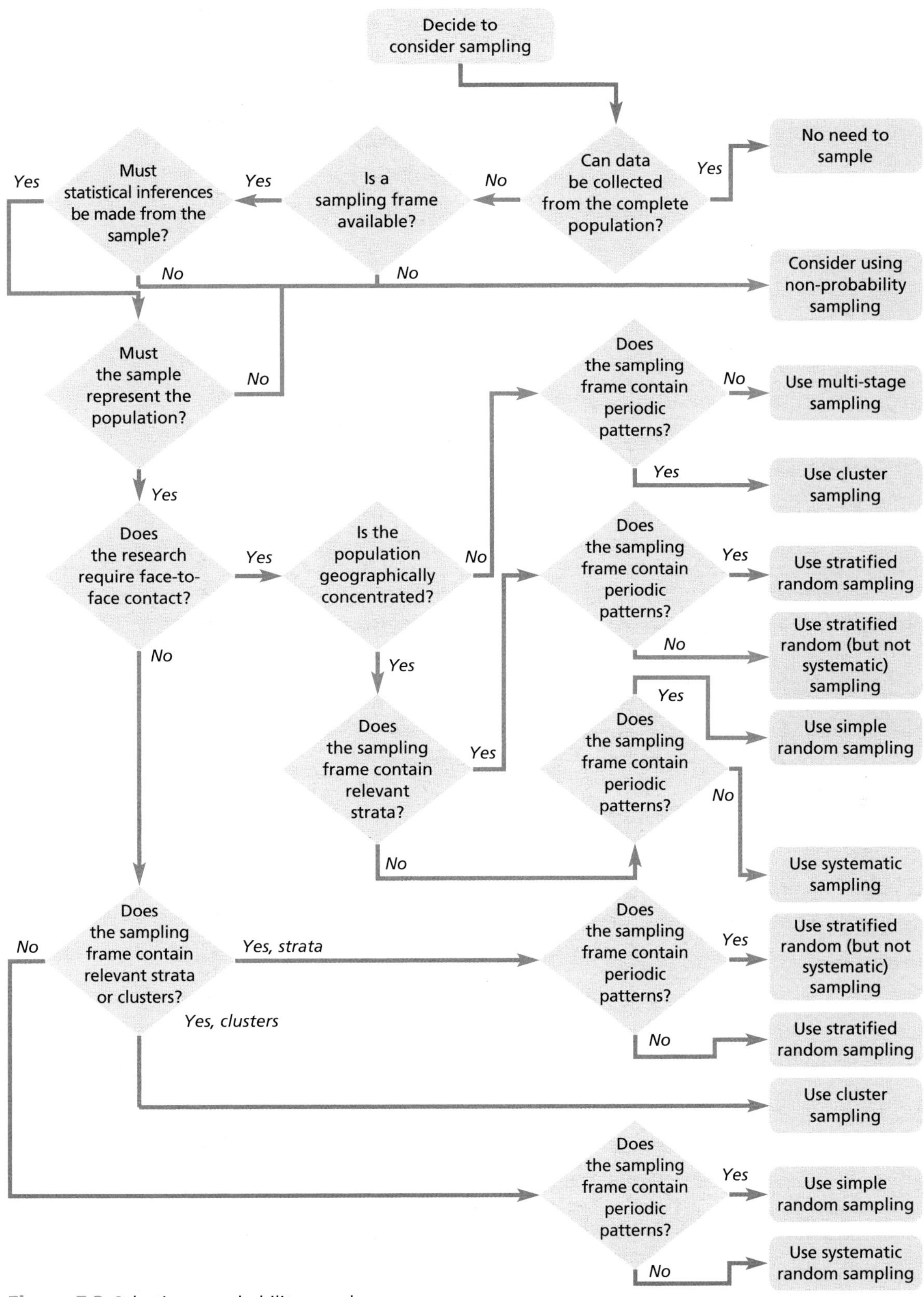

Figure 7.3 Selecting a probability sample

Note: Simple random sampling ideally requires a sample size of over a few hundred.

Table 7.2 Impact of various factors on choice of probability sampling techniques

Sample technique	Sampling frame required	Size of sample needed	Geographical area to which suited	Relative cost	Easy to explain to support workers?	Advantages compared with simple random
Simple random	Accurate and easily accessible	Better with over a few hundred	Concentrated if face-to-face contact required, otherwise does not matter	High if large sample size or sampling frame not computerised	Relatively difficult to explain	
Systematic random	Accurate, easily accessible and not containing periodic patterns. Actual list not always needed	Suitable for all sizes	Concentrated if face-to-face contact required, otherwise does not matter	Low	Relatively easy to explain	Normally no difference
Stratified random	Accurate, easily accessible, divisible into relevant strata (see comments for simple random and systematic random as appropriate)	See comments for simple random and systematic random as appropriate	Concentrated if face-to-face contact required, otherwise does not matter	Low, provided that lists of relevant strata available	Relatively difficult to explain (once strata decided, see comments for simple random and systematic random as appropriate)	Better comparison and hence representation across strata. Differential response rates may necessitate reweighting
Cluster	Accurate, easily accessible, relates to relevant clusters, not individual population members	As large as practicable	Dispersed if face-to-face contact required and geographically based clusters used	Low, provided that lists of relevant clusters available	Relatively difficult to explain until clusters selected	Quick but reduced precision
Multi-stage	Initial stages: geographical. Final stage: needed only for geographical areas selected see comments for simple random and systematic random as appropriate	Initial stages: as large as practicable. Final stage: see comments for simple random and systematic random as appropriate	Dispersed if face-to-face contact required, otherwise no need to use this technique!	Low, as sampling frame for actual survey population required only for final stage	Initial stages: relatively difficult to explain. Final stage: see comments for simple random and systematic random as appropriate	Difficult to adjust for differential response rates. Substantial errors possible! However, often only practical approach when sampling a large complicated population

Source: © Mark Saunders, Philip Lewis and Adrian Thornhill 2011

frame, the size of sample you need and, if you are using support workers, the ease with which the technique may be explained will also influence your decision. The impact of each of these is summarised in Table 7.2

Simple random sampling

Simple random sampling (sometimes called just **random sampling**) involves you selecting the sample at random from the sampling frame using either a computer or random number tables (Appendix 3). To do this you:

1. Number each of the cases in your sampling frame with a unique number. The first case is numbered 0, the second 1 and so on.
2. Select cases using random numbers (e.g. Table 7.3, Appendix 3) until your actual sample size is reached.

If using random number tables you must select your first random number at random (closing your eyes and pointing with your finger is one way!) as this ensures that the set of random numbers obtained for different samples is unlikely to be the same. If you do not, you will obtain sets of numbers that are random but identical.

Starting with this number, you read off the random numbers (and select the cases or elements) in a regular and systematic manner until your sample size is reached. If the same number is read off a second time it must be disregarded as you need different cases. This means that you are not putting each case's number back into the sampling frame after it has been selected and is termed 'sampling without replacement'. If a number is selected that is outside the range of those in your sampling frame, you simply ignore it and continue reading off numbers until your sample size is reached (Box 7.6).

If you are using an online random number generator or program such as a spreadsheet to generate random numbers, you must ensure that the numbers generated are within your range and that if a number is repeated it is ignored and replaced. If details of your population are stored on the computer it is possible to generate a sample of randomly selected cases. For telephone interviews, many market research companies now use computer-aided telephone interviewing (CATI) software to select and dial telephone numbers at random from an existing database or random digit dialling and to contact each respondent in turn.

Random numbers allow you to select your sample without bias. The sample selected, therefore, can be said to be representative of the whole population. However, the selection that simple random sampling provides is more evenly dispersed throughout the population

Table 7.3 Extract from random number tables

78	41	11	62	72	18	66	69	58	71	31	90	51	36	78	09	41	00
70	50	58	19	68	26	75	69	04	00	25	29	16	72	35	73	55	85
32	78	14	47	**01**	55	10	91	83	21	13	32	59	53	03	38	79	32
71	60	20	53	86	78	50	57	42	30	73	48	68	09	16	35	21	87
35	30	15	57	99	96	33	25	56	43	65	67	51	45	37	99	54	89
09	08	05	41	66	54	01	49	97	34	38	85	85	23	34	62	60	58
02	59	34	51	98	71	31	54	28	85	23	84	49	07	33	71	17	88
20	13	44	15	22	95												

Source: Appendix 3

Box 7.6 Focus on student research

Simple random sampling

Jemma was undertaking her work placement at a large supermarket, where 5011 of the supermarket's customers used the supermarket's Internet purchase and delivery scheme. She was asked to interview customers and find out why they used this scheme. As there was insufficient time to interview all of them she decided to interview a sample using the telephone. Her calculations revealed that to obtain acceptable levels of confidence and accuracy she needed an actual sample size of approximately 360 customers. She decided to select them using simple random sampling.

Having obtained a list of Internet customers and their telephone numbers, Jemma gave each of the cases (customers) in this sampling frame a unique number. In order that each number was made up in exactly the same way she used 5011 four-digit numbers starting with 0000 through to 5010. So customer 677 was given the number 0676.

The first random number she selected was 01 (shown in bold in Table 7.3). Starting with this number she read off the two-digit random numbers in a regular and systematic manner (in this example continuing along the line):

01 55 10 91 83 21 13 32 59 53 03 38 79 32 71 60 20. . . .

Jemma combined the first two-digit random number (01) with second (55) to get her first four-digit random number 0155. She continued combining random numbers in this manner until 360 different cases had been selected. These formed her random sample. Numbers selected that were outside the range of those in her sampling frame (such as 8321, 5953 and 7932) were simply ignored.

for samples of more than a few hundred cases. The first few hundred cases selected using simple random sampling normally consist of groups of cases whose numbers are close together followed by a gap and then a further grouping. For more than a few hundred cases, this pattern occurs far less frequently. Because of the technique's random nature it is possible that a chance occurrence of such patterns will result in certain parts of a population being over- or under-represented.

Simple random sampling is best used when you have an accurate and easily accessible sampling frame that lists the entire population, preferably in electronic format. While you can often obtain these for employees within organisations or members of clubs or societies, adequate lists are less likely to be available for organisations. If your population covers a large geographical area, random selection means that selected cases are likely to be dispersed throughout the area. Consequently, this form of sampling is not suitable if collecting data over a large geographical area using a method that requires face-to-face contact, owing to the associated high travel costs. Simple random sampling would still be suitable for a geographically dispersed area if you used an alternative technique of collecting data such as Internet-based or postal questionnaires or telephone interviewing (Chapter 11).

Sampling frames used for telephone interviewing have been replaced increasingly by random digital dialling. By selecting particular within-country area dialling codes this provides a chance to reach any household within that area represented by that code which has a telephone, regardless of whether or not the number is ex-directory. However, care must be taken as, increasingly, households have more than one telephone number. Consequently there is a higher probability of people in such households being selected as part of the sample. In addition, such a sample would exclude people who use only mobile telephones as their dialling codes are telephone network operator rather than geographical area specific (Tucker and Lepkowski 2008).

Systematic random sampling

Systematic random sampling (often called just **systematic sampling**) involves you selecting the sample at regular intervals from the sampling frame. To do this you:

1. Number each of the cases in your sampling frame with a unique number. The first case is numbered 0, the second 1 and so on.
2. Select the first case using a random number.
3. Calculate the sampling fraction.
4. Select subsequent cases systematically using the sampling fraction to determine the frequency of selection.

To calculate the **sampling fraction** – that is, the proportion of the total population that you need to select – you use the formula:

$$\text{sampling fraction} = \frac{\text{actual sample size}}{\text{total population}}$$

If your sampling fraction is 1/3 you need to select one in every three cases – that is, every third case from the sampling frame. Unfortunately, your calculation will usually result in a more complicated fraction. In these instances it is normally acceptable to round your population down to the nearest 10 (or 100) and to increase your minimum sample size until a simpler sampling fraction can be calculated.

On its own, selecting one in every three would not be random as every third case would be bound to be selected, whereas those between would have no chance of selection. To overcome this, a random number is used to decide where to start on the sampling frame. If your sampling fraction is 1/3 the starting point must be one of the first three cases. You therefore select a random number (in this example a one-digit random number between 0 and 2) as described earlier and use this as the starting point. Once you have selected your first case at random you then select, in this example, every third case until you have gone right through your sampling frame (Box 7.7).

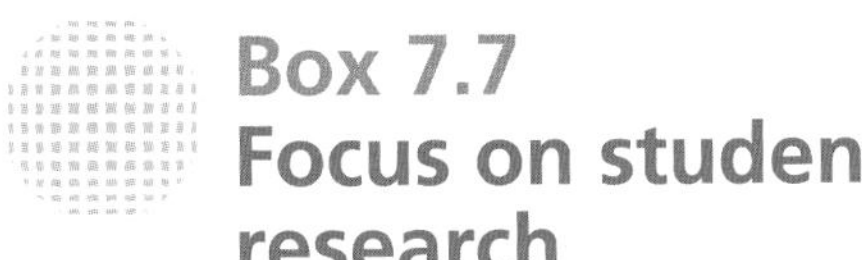

Systematic random sampling

Stefan worked as a receptionist in a dental surgery with approximately 1500 patients. He wished to find out their attitudes to the new automated appointments scheme. As there was insufficient time and money to collect data from all patients using a questionnaire he decided to send the questionnaire to a sample. The calculation of sample size revealed that to obtain acceptable levels of confidence and accuracy he needed an actual sample size of approximately 300 patients. Using the patient files kept in the filing cabinet as a sampling frame, he decided to select his sample systematically.

First he calculated the sampling fraction:

$$\frac{300}{1500} = \frac{1}{5}$$

This meant that he needed to select every fifth patient from the sampling frame. Next he used a random number to decide where to start on his sampling frame. As the sampling fraction was 1/5, the starting point had to be one of the first five patients. He therefore selected a one-digit random number between 0 and 4.

Once he had selected his first patient at random he continued to select every fifth patient until he had gone right through his sampling frame (the filing cabinet). If the random number Stefan had selected was 2, then he would have selected the following patient numbers:

2 7 12 17 22 27 32 37

and so on until 300 patients had been selected.

Table 7.4 The impact of periodic patterns on systematic random sampling

Number	Customer	Sample	Number	Customer	Sample
000	Mr L. Baker	✓	006	Mr A. Saunders	✓
001	Mrs B. Baker	*	007	Mrs C. Saunders	*
002	Mr P. Knight	✓	008	Mr J. Smith	✓
003	Ms J. Farnsworth	*	009	Mrs K. Smith	*
004	Mr J. Lewis	✓	010	Ms L. Williams	✓
005	Mrs P. Lewis	*	011	Ms G. Catling	*

✓ Sample selected if you start with 000. * Sample selected if you start with 003.

In some instances it is not necessary to actually construct a list for your sampling frame. For online questionnaires, such as pop-up questionnaires that appear in a window on the computer screen, there is no need to create an actual list if an invitation to participate is triggered at random. For systematic random sampling, a random selection could be triggered by a mechanism such as every tenth visitor to the site over a specified time period (Bradley 1999).

Despite the advantages, you must be careful when using existing lists as sampling frames. You need to ensure that the lists do not contain periodic patterns. A high street bank needs you to administer a questionnaire to a sample of individual customers with joint bank accounts. A sampling fraction of 1/2 means that you will need to select every second customer on the list. The names on the customer lists, which you intend to use as the sampling frame, are arranged alphabetically by joint account, with predominantly males followed by females (Table 7.4). If you start with a male customer, the majority of those in your sample will be male. Conversely, if you start with a female customer, the majority of those in your sample will be female. Consequently your sample will be biased (Table 7.4). Systematic random sampling is therefore not suitable without reordering or stratifying the sampling frame (discussed later).

Unlike simple random sampling, systematic random sampling works equally well with a small or large number of cases. However, if your population covers a large geographical area, the random selection means that the sample cases are likely to be dispersed throughout the area. Consequently, systematic random sampling is suitable for geographically dispersed cases only if you do not require face-to-face contact when collecting your data.

Stratified random sampling

Stratified random sampling is a modification of random sampling in which you divide the population into two or more relevant and significant strata based on one or a number of attributes. In effect, your sampling frame is divided into a number of subsets. A random sample (simple or systematic) is then drawn from each of the strata. Consequently, stratified random sampling shares many of the advantages and disadvantages of simple random or systematic random sampling.

Dividing the population into a series of relevant strata means that the sample is more likely to be representative, as you can ensure that each of the strata is represented proportionally within your sample. However, it is only possible to do this if you are aware of, and can easily distinguish, significant strata in your sampling frame. In addition, the extra stage in the sampling procedure means that it is likely to take longer, to be more expensive, and to be more difficult to explain than simple random or systematic random sampling.

In some instances, as pointed out by deVaus (2002), your sampling frame will already be divided into strata. A sampling frame of employee names that is in alphabetical order will automatically ensure that, if systematic random sampling is used (discussed earlier), employees will be sampled in the correct proportion to the letter with which their name begins. Similarly, membership lists that are ordered by date of joining will automatically result in stratification by length of membership if systematic random sampling is used. However, if you are using simple random sampling or your sampling frame contains periodic patterns, you will need to stratify it. To do this you:

1 Choose the stratification variable or variables.
2 Divide the sampling frame into the discrete strata.
3 Number each of the cases within each stratum with a unique number, as discussed earlier.
4 Select your sample using either simple random or systematic random sampling, as discussed earlier.

The stratification variable (or variables) chosen should represent the discrete characteristic (or characteristics) for which you want to ensure correct representation within the sample (Box 7.8).

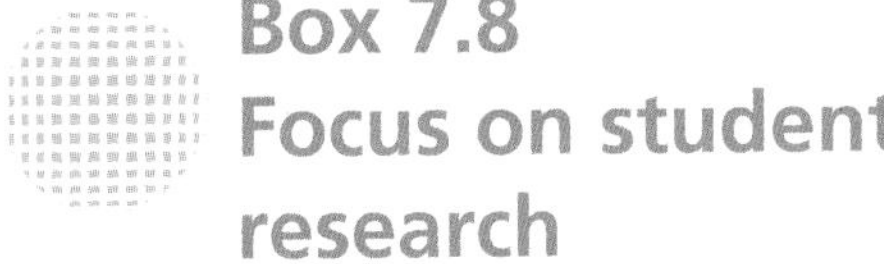

Box 7.8 Focus on student research

Stratified random sampling

Dilek worked for a major supplier of office supplies to public and private organisations. As part of her research into her organisation's customers, she needed to ensure that both public and private-sector organisations were represented correctly. An important stratum was, therefore, the sector of the organisation. Her sampling frame was thus divided into two discrete strata: public sector and private sector. Within each stratum, the individual cases were then numbered (see at below).

She decided to select a systematic random sample. A sampling fraction of 1/4 meant that she needed to select every fourth customer on the list. As indicated by the ticks (✓), random numbers were used to select the first case in the public sector (001) and private sector (003) strata. Subsequently, every fourth customer in each stratum was selected.

Public sector stratum			Private sector stratum		
Number	Customer	Selected	Number	Customer	Selected
000	Anyshire County Council		000	ABC Automotive manufacturer	
001	Anyshire Hospital Trust	✓	001	Anytown printers and bookbinders	
002	Newshire Army Training Barracks		002	Benjamin Toy Company	
003	Newshire Police Force		003	Jane's Internet Flower shop	✓
004	Newshire Housing		004	Multimedia productions	
005	St Peter's Secondary School	✓	005	Roger's Consulting	
006	University of Anytown		006	The Paperless Office	✓
007	West Anyshire Council		007	U-need-us Ltd	

Samples can be stratified using more than one characteristic. You may wish to stratify a sample of an organisation's employees by both department and salary grade. To do this you would:

1 divide the sampling frame into the discrete departments.
2 Within each department divide the sampling frame into discrete salary grades.
3 Number each of the cases within each salary grade within each department with a unique number, as discussed earlier.
4 Select your sample using either simple random or systematic random sampling, as discussed earlier.

In some instances the relative sizes of different strata mean that, in order to have sufficient data for analysis, you need to select larger samples from the strata with smaller populations. Here the different sample sizes must be taken into account when aggregating data from each of the strata to obtain an overall picture. More sophisticated statistical analysis software packages enable you to do this by differentially weighting the responses for each stratum (Section 12.2).

Cluster sampling

Cluster sampling (sometimes known as **one-stage cluster sampling**) is, on the surface, similar to stratified random sampling as you need to divide the population into discrete groups prior to sampling (Barnett 2002). The groups are termed *clusters* in this form of sampling and can be based on any naturally occurring grouping. For example, you could group your data by type of manufacturing firm or geographical area (Box 7.9).

For cluster sampling, your sampling frame is the complete list of clusters rather than a complete list of individual cases within the population. You then select a few clusters, normally using simple random sampling. Data are then collected from every case within the selected clusters. The technique has three main stages:

1 Choose the cluster grouping for your sampling frame.
2 Number each of the clusters with a unique number. The first cluster is numbered 0, the second 1 and so on.
3 Select your sample of clusters using some form of random sampling, as discussed earlier.

Selecting clusters randomly makes cluster sampling a probability sampling technique. Despite this, the technique normally results in a sample that represents the total population

Box 7.9 Focus on student research

Cluster sampling

Ceri needed to select a sample of firms to undertake an interview-based survey about the use of large multi-purpose digital printer copiers. As she had limited resources with which to pay for travel and other associated data collection costs, she decided to interview firms in four geographical areas selected from a cluster grouping of local administrative areas. A list of all local administrative areas formed her sampling frame. Each of the local administrative areas (clusters) was given a unique number, the first being 0, the second 1 and so on. The four sample clusters were selected from this sampling frame of local administrative areas using simple random sampling.

Ceri's sample was all firms within the selected clusters. She decided that the appropriate telephone directories would probably provide a suitable list of all firms in each cluster.

less accurately than stratified random sampling. Restricting the sample to a few relatively compact geographical sub-areas (clusters) maximises the amount of data you can collect using face-to-face methods within the resources available. However, it may also reduce the representativeness of your sample. For this reason you need to maximise the number of sub-areas to allow for variations in the population within the available resources. Your choice is between a large sample from a few discrete subgroups and a smaller sample distributed over the whole group. It is a trade-off between the amount of precision lost by using a few subgroups and the amount gained from a larger sample size.

Multi-stage sampling

Multi-stage sampling, sometimes called *multi-stage cluster sampling,* is a development of cluster sampling. It is normally used to overcome problems associated with a geographically dispersed population when face-to-face contact is needed or where it is expensive and time-consuming to construct a sampling frame for a large geographical area. However, like cluster sampling, you can use it for any discrete groups, including those that are not geographically based. The technique involves modifying a cluster sample by adding at least one more stage of sampling that also involves some form of random sampling. This aspect is represented by the dotted lines in Figure 7.2, the drawing these samples being termed sub-sampling. Multi-stage sampling can be divided into four phases. These are outlined in Figure 7.4

Phase 1

- Choose sampling frame of relevant discrete groups
- Number each group with a unique number. The first is numbered 0, the second two and so on
- Select a small sample of relevant discrete groups using some form of random sampling

Phase 2

- From these relevant discrete groups select a sampling frame of relevant discrete subgroups
- Number each subgroup with a unique number as described in Phase 1
- Select a small sample of relevant discrete subgroups using some form of random sampling

Phase 3

- *Repeat Phase 2 if necessary*

Phase 4

- From these relevant discrete subgroups choose a sampling frame of relevant discrete sub-subgroups
- Number each sub-subgroup with a unique number as described in Phase 1
- Select your sample using some form of random sampling

Figure 7.4 Phases of multi-stage sampling

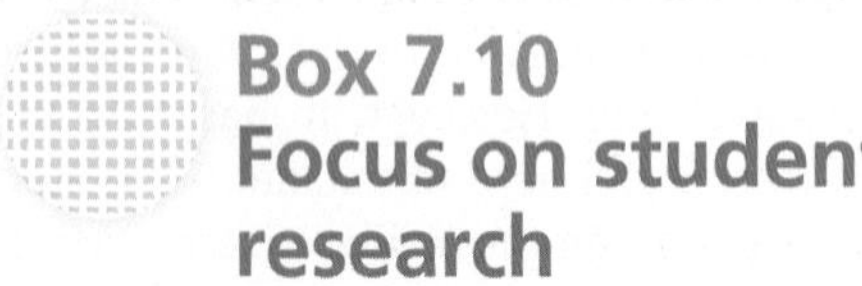

Box 7.10 Focus on student research

Multi-stage sampling

Laura worked for a market research organisation that needed her to interview a sample of 400 households in England and Wales. She decided to use the electoral register as a sampling frame. Laura knew that selecting 400 households using either systematic or simple random sampling was likely to result in these 400 households being dispersed throughout England and Wales, resulting in considerable amounts of time spent travelling between interviewees as well as high travel costs. By using multi-stage sampling Laura felt these problems could be overcome.

In her first stage the geographical area (England and Wales) was split into discrete sub-areas (counties). These formed her sampling frame. After numbering all the counties, Laura selected a small number of counties using simple random sampling. Since each case (household) was located in a county, each had an equal chance of being selected for the final sample.

As the counties selected were still too large, each was subdivided into smaller geographically discrete areas (electoral wards). These formed the next sampling frame (stage 2). Laura selected another simple random sample. This time she selected a larger number of wards to allow for likely important variations in the nature of households between wards.

A sampling frame of the households in each of these wards was then generated using a combination of the electoral register and the UK Royal Mail's postcode address file. Laura finally selected the actual cases (households) that she would interview using systematic random sampling.

Because multi-stage sampling relies on a series of different sampling frames, you need to ensure that they are all appropriate and available. In order to minimise the impact of selecting smaller and smaller subgroups on the representativeness of your sample, you can apply stratified random sampling techniques (discussed earlier). This technique can be further refined to take account of the relative size of the subgroups by adjusting the sample size for each subgroup. As you have selected your sub-areas using different sampling frames, you only need a sampling frame that lists all the members of the population for those subgroups you finally select (Box 7.10). This provides considerable savings in time and money.

Checking that the sample is representative

Often it is possible to compare data you collect from your sample with data from another source for the population, such as data contained in an 'archival' database. For example, you can compare data on the age and socioeconomic characteristics of respondents in a marketing survey with these characteristics for the population in that country as recorded by the latest national census of population. If there is no statistically significant difference, then the sample is representative with respect to these characteristics.

When working within an organisation, comparisons can also be made. In a questionnaire Mark administered recently to a sample of employees in a large UK organisation, he asked closed questions about salary grade, gender, length of service and place of work. Possible responses to each question were designed to provide sufficient detail to compare the characteristics of the sample with the characteristics of the entire population of employees as recorded by the organisation's personnel database. At the same time he kept the categories sufficiently broad to preserve, and to be seen to preserve, the confidentiality of individual respondents. The two questions on length of service and salary grade from a questionnaire he developed illustrate this:

97 How long have you worked for ***organisation's name?***

less than 1 year ❑ 1 year to less than 3 years ❑ 3 or more years ❑

98 Which one of the following best describes your job?

Clerical (grades 1–3)	❑	Management (grades 9–11)	❑
Supervisory (grades 4–5)	❑	Senior management (grades 12–14)	❑
Professional (grades 6–8)	❑	Other (please say)	❑

Using the Kolmogorov test (Section 12.5), Mark found there was no statistically significant difference between the proportions of respondents in each of the length of service groups and the data obtained from the organisation's personnel database for all employees. This meant that the sample of respondents was representative of all employees with respect to length of service. However, those responding were (statistically) significantly more likely to be in professional and managerial grades than in technical, administrative or supervisory grades. He therefore added a note of caution about the representativeness of his findings.

You can also assess the representativeness of samples a variety of other ways (Rogelberg and Stanton 2007). Those our students have used most often, in order of quality of assessment of possible bias, include:

- replicating your findings using a new sample selected using different sampling techniques, referred to as 'demonstrate generalisability';
- resurveying non-respondents, the 'follow-up approach';
- analysing whether non-response was due to refusal, ineligibility or some other reason through interviews with non-respondents, known as 'active non-response analysis';
- comparing late respondents' responses with those from early respondents, known as 'wave analysis'.

In relation to this list, the quality of the assessment of bias provided by archival analysis, as outlined earlier, is similar to that provided by the follow-up approach and active non-response analysis.

7.3 Non-probability sampling

The techniques for selecting samples discussed earlier have all been based on the assumption that your sample will be chosen at random from a sampling frame. Consequently, it is possible to specify the probability that any case will be included in the sample. However, within business research, such as market surveys and case study research, this may either not be possible (as you do not have a sampling frame) or not be appropriate to answering your research question. This means your sample must be selected some other way. Non-probability sampling (or **non-random sampling**) provides a range of alternative techniques to select samples, the majority of which include an element of subjective judgement. In the exploratory stages of some research projects, such as a pilot survey, a non-probability sample may be the most practical, although it will not allow the extent of the problem to be determined. Subsequent to this, probability sampling techniques may be used. For other business and management research projects your research question(s), objectives and choice of research strategy (Sections 2.4, 5.5) may dictate non-probability sampling. To answer your research question(s) and to meet your objectives you may need to undertake an in-depth study that focuses on a small number of cases, perhaps one,

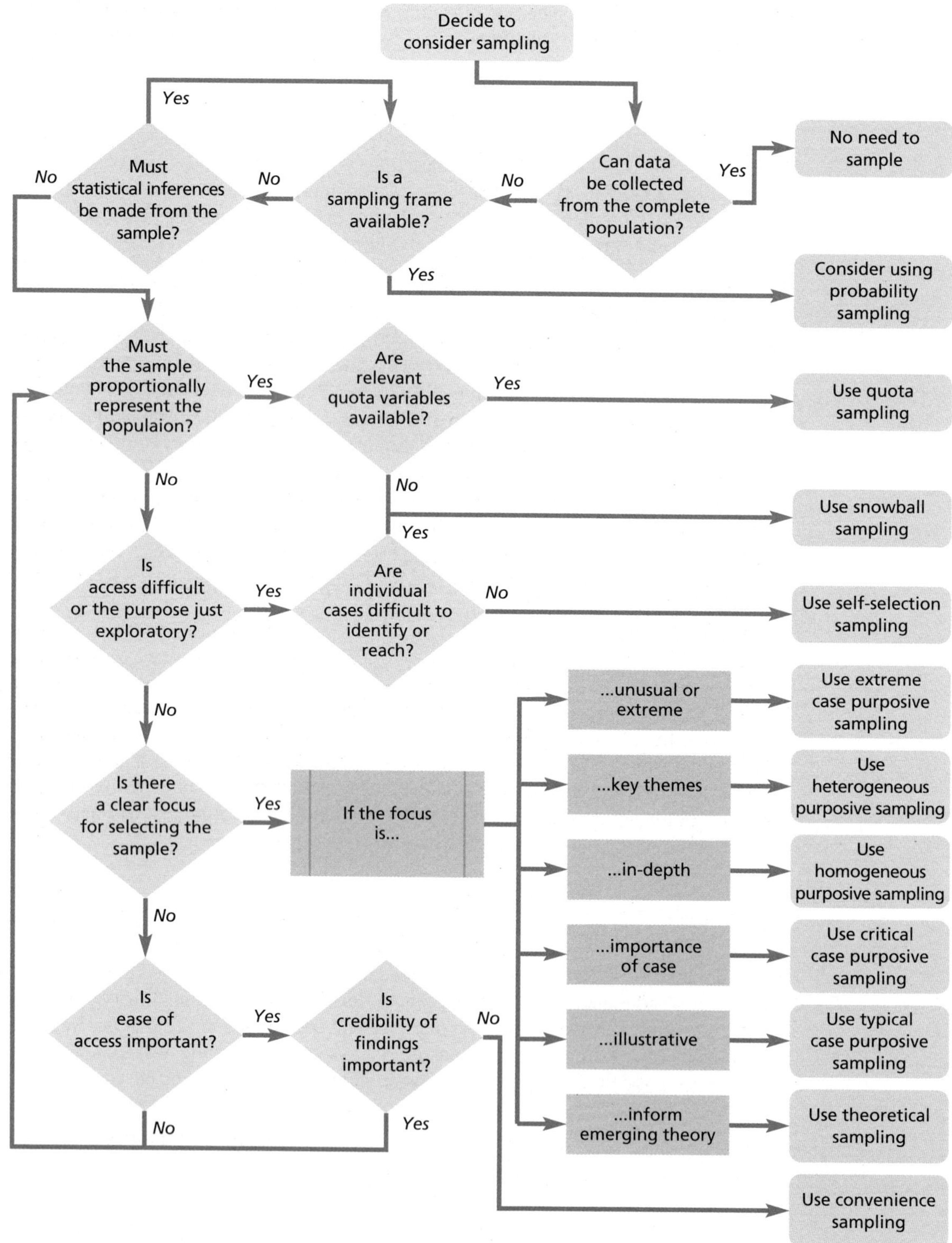

Figure 7.5 Selecting a non-probability sampling technique

selected for a particular purpose. This sample would provide you with an information-rich case study in which you explore your research question and gain theoretical insights.

Deciding on a suitable sample size

For all non-probability sampling techniques, other than for quota samples (which we discuss later), the issue of sample size is ambiguous and, unlike probability sampling, there are no rules. Rather the logical relationship between your sample selection technique and the purpose and focus of your research is important (Figure 7.5), generalisations being made to theory rather than about a population. Consequently, your sample size is dependent on your research question(s) and objectives – in particular, what you need to find out, what will be useful, what will have credibility and what can be done within your available resources (Patton 2002). This is particularly so where you are intending to collect qualitative data using semi or unstructured interviews (Chapter 10). Although the validity, understanding and insights that you will gain from your data will be more to do with your data collection and analysis skills than with the size of your sample (Patton 2002), it is possible to offer guidance as to the sample size to ensure you have conducted sufficient interviews or undertaken sufficient observations.

In addressing this issue, many research textbooks simply recommend continuing to collect qualitative data, such as by conducting additional interviews, until **data saturation** is reached: in other words until the additional data collected provides few, if any, new information or suggests new themes. While this is essential, it does not answer the question of how many participants you are likely to need in your sample. Fortunately, Saunders (2012) summarises the limited guidance available for different types of study (Table 7.5). For research where your aim is to understand commonalities within a fairly homogenous group, 12 in-depth interviews should suffice (Guest et al. 2006). However, Guest et al. also note that 12 interviews are unlikely to be sufficient where the sample is drawn from a heterogeneous population or the focus of the research question is wide-ranging. Given this, we would suggest that, for a general study, you should expect to undertake between 25 and 30 interviews (Creswell 2007). Additionally, where your research requires comparison between distinct groups, the sample size will need to be larger, treating each group as a separate homogeneous population.

Selecting the most appropriate sampling technique and the sample

Having decided the likely suitable sample size, you need to select the most appropriate sampling technique to enable you to answer your research question from the range of

Table 7.5 Minimum non-probability sample size

Nature of study	Minimum sample size
Semi structure/in-depth Interviews	5–25
Ethnographic	35–36
Grounded theory	20–35
Considering a homogeneous population	4–12
Considering a heterogeneous population	12–30

Source: Developed from Saunders (2012)

Table 7.6 Impact of various factors on choice of non-probability sampling techniques

Group	Technique	Likelihood of sample being representative	Types of research in which useful	Relative costs	Control over sample contents
Quota	Quota	Reasonable to high, although dependent on selection of quota variables	Where costs constrained or data needed very quickly so an alternative to probability sampling needed	Moderately high to reasonable	Specifies quota selection criteria
Purposive	Extreme case	Low	Unusual or special	Reasonable	Specifies selection criteria
	Heterogeneous	Low, although dependent on researcher's choices	Reveal/illuminate key themes	Reasonable	Specifies selection criteria
	Homogeneous	Low	In-depth focus	Reasonable	Specifies selection criteria
	Critical case	Low	Importance	Reasonable	Specifies selection criteria
	Typical case	Low, although dependent on researcher's choices	Illustrative	Reasonable	Specifies selection criteria
	Theoretical	Low	Inform emerging theory	Reasonable	Specifies selection criteria
Volunteer	Snowball	Low, but cases likely to have characteristics desired	Where cases difficult to identify	Reasonable	Selects initial participant
	Self-selection	Low, as cases self-selected	Where access difficult, research exploratory	Reasonable	Offers only general invitation
Haphazard	Convenience	Very low (often lacks credibility)	Ease of access	Low	Haphazard

Sources: Developed from Kervin (1999); Patton (2002); Saunders (2012)

non-probability sampling techniques available (Figure 7.2). At one end of this range is quota sampling, which, like probability samples, tries to represent the total population. At the other end of this range is haphazard sampling, based on the need to obtain a sample as quickly as possible. With this technique you have virtually no control over the cases that will be included in your sample. Purposive sampling and volunteer sampling techniques lie between these extremes (Table 7.6).

Quota sampling

Quota sampling is entirely non-random and is often used for structured interviews as part of a survey strategy. It is based on the premise that your sample will represent the population as the variability in your sample for various quota variables is the same as that in the population. Quota sampling is therefore a type of stratified sample in which selection of cases within strata is entirely non-random (Barnett 2002). Quota sampling has similar requirements for sample size as probabilistic sampling techniques (Section 7.2). To select a quota sample you:

1 Divide the population into specific groups.
2 Calculate a quota for each group based on relevant and available data.
3 Give each interviewer an 'assignment', which states the number of cases in each quota from which they must collect data.
4 Combine the data collected by interviewers to provide the full sample.

Quota sampling has a number of advantages over the probability sampling techniques. In particular, it is less costly and can be set up very quickly. If, as with television audience research surveys, your data collection needs to be undertaken very quickly then quota sampling may be the only possibility. In addition, it does not require a sampling frame and therefore may be the only technique you can use if one is not available. Quota sampling is normally used for large populations. Decisions on sample size are governed by the need to have sufficient responses in each quota to enable subsequent statistical analyses to be undertaken. This often necessitates a sample size of between 2000 and 5000.

Calculations of quotas are based on relevant and available data and are usually relative to the proportions in which they occur in the population (Box 7.11). Without sensible and relevant quotas, data collected may be biased. For many market research

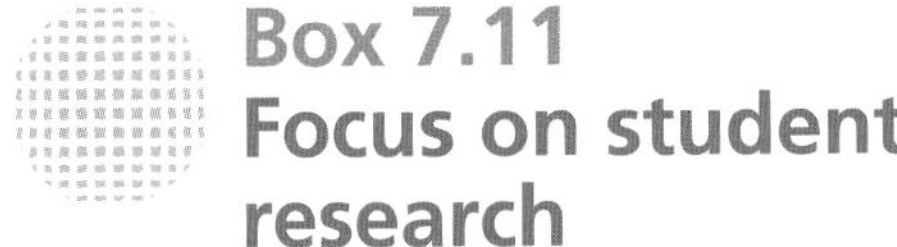

Box 7.11 Focus on student research

Devising a quota sample

Mica was undertaking the data collection for his dissertation as part of his full-time employment. For his research he needed to interview a sample of people representing those aged 20–64 who were in work in his country. No sampling frame was available. Once the data had been collected, he was going to disaggregate his findings into subgroups dependent on respondents' age and type of employment. Previous research had suggested that gender would also have an impact on responses and so he needed to make sure that those interviewed in each group also reflected the proportions of males and females in the population. Fortunately, his country's national census of population contained a breakdown of the number of people in employment by gender, age and socioeconomic status. These formed the basis of the categories for his quotas:

gender ×	age group ×	socioeconomic status
male	20–29	professional managers/ employers
female	30–34	intermediate and junior non-manual
	45–64	skilled manual
		semi-skilled manual
		unskilled manual

As he was going to analyse the data for individual age and socioeconomic status groups, it was important that each of these categories had sufficient respondents (at least 30) to enable meaningful statistical analyses. Mica calculated that a 0.5 per cent quota for each of the groups would provide sufficient numbers for all groups, provided his analyses were not also disaggregated by gender. This gave him the following quotas:

Box 7.11 Focus on student research *(continued)*

Gender	Age group	Socioeconomic status	Population (10 per cent sample)	Quota
Male	20–29	Professional	11 210	56
		managers/employers	7 983	40
		Intermediate and junior non-manual	9 107	43
		Skilled manual	16 116	79
		Semi-skilled manual	12 605	63
		Unskilled manual	5 039	25
	30–44	Professional	21 431	107
		managers/employers	23 274	116
		Intermediate and junior non-manual	7 997	40
		Skilled manual	21 410	107
		Semi-skilled manual	19 244	96
		Unskilled manual	4 988	25
	45–64	Professional	16 612	83
		managers/employers	23 970	120
		Intermediate and junior non-manual	9 995	49
		Skilled manual	20 019	100
		Semi-skilled manual	17 616	88
		Unskilled manual	5 763	29
Female	20–29	Professional	8 811	44
		managers/employers	6 789	34
		Intermediate and junior non-manual	21 585	108
		Skilled manual	1 754	9
		Semi-skilled manual	9 632	48
		Unskilled manual	3 570	18
	30–44	Professional	16 380	82
		managers/employers	9 765	49
		Intermediate and junior non-manual	28 424	142
		Skilled manual	2 216	11
		Semi-skilled manual	11 801	59
		Unskilled manual	8 797	41
	45–64	Professional	8 823	44
		managers/employers	7 846	39
		Intermediate and junior non-manual	21 974	110
		Skilled manual	1 578	8
		Semi-skilled manual	9 421	47
		Unskilled manual	8 163	41
Total sample			441 604	2 200

These were then divided into assignments of 50 people for each interviewer.

projects, quotas are derived from census data. Your choice of quota is dependent on two main factors:

- usefulness as a means of stratifying the data;
- ability to overcome likely variations between groups in their availability for interview.

Where people who are retired are likely to have different opinions from those in work, a quota that does not ensure that these differences are captured may result in the data being biased as it would probably be easier to collect the data from those people who are retired. Quotas used in market research surveys and political opinion polls usually include measures of age, gender and socioeconomic status or social class. These may be supplemented by additional quotas dictated by the research question(s) and objectives (Box 7.11).

Once you have given each interviewer their particular assignment, they decide whom to interview until they have completed their quota. You then combine the data from this assignment with those collected by other interviewers to provide the full sample. Because the interviewer can choose within quota boundaries whom they interview, your quota sample may be subject to bias. Interviewers tend to choose respondents who are easily accessible and who appear willing to answer the questions. Clear controls may therefore be needed. In addition, it has been known for interviewers to fill in quotas incorrectly. This is not to say that your quota sample will not produce good results; they can and often do! However, you cannot measure the level of certainty or margins of error as the sample is not probability based.

Purposive sampling

With **purposive sampling** you need to use your judgement to select cases that will best enable you to answer your research question(s) and to meet your objectives. For this reason it is sometimes known as **judgemental sampling**. It is often used when working with very small samples such as in case study research and when you wish to select cases that are particularly informative (Neuman 2005). A particular form of purposive sampling, theoretical sampling, is used by researchers adopting the Grounded Theory strategy (Section 13.8).

Purposive samples cannot be considered to be statistically representative of the total population. The logic on which you base your strategy for selecting cases for a purposive sample should be dependent on your research question(s) and objectives (Box 7.12). Patton (2002) emphasises this point by contrasting the need to select information-rich cases in purposive sampling with the need to be statistically representative in probability sampling. The more common purposive sampling strategies were outlined in Figure 7.2 and are discussed on the next page.

Extreme case or **deviant sampling** focuses on unusual or special cases on the basis that the data collected about these unusual or extreme outcomes will enable you to learn the most and to answer your research question(s) and to meet your objectives most effectively. This is often based on the premise that findings from extreme cases will be relevant in understanding or explaining more typical cases (Patton 2002).

Heterogeneous or **maximum variation sampling** uses your judgement to choose participants with sufficiently diverse characteristics to provide the maximum variation possible in the data collected. It enables you to collect data to describe and explain the key themes that can be observed. Although this might appear a contradiction, as a small sample may contain cases that are completely different, Patton (2002) argues that this is in fact a strength. Any patterns that do emerge are likely to be of particular interest and value and represent the key themes. In addition, the data collected should enable you to

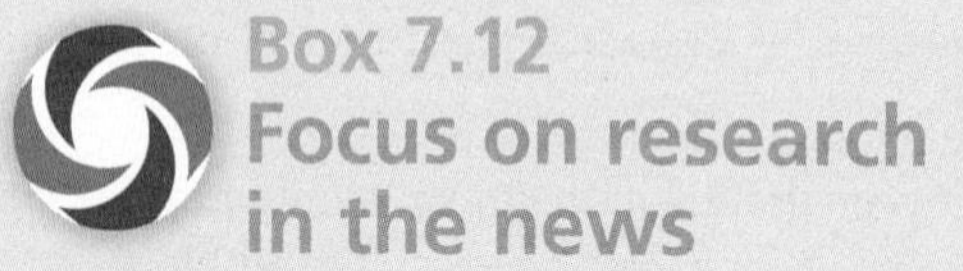

FT

Primed and en primeur

Bordeaux has been showing off its 2010s, its second very promising vintage in a row. The Americans are back in the market, Asian demand is showing no sign of abating and myriad retailers and commentators are blogging daily from Bordeaux about last week's tastings of hundreds of barrel samples. But it is worth stopping for a moment to consider just how approximate these samples are.

Over the past few decades the Bordelais have become increasingly dependent on selling their young wine en primeur: showing barrel samples to the hordes of black-tongued visitors in late March and early April; waiting for scores and comments on them to be published; and then, in May, June and sometimes July, announcing their prices and eking out various tranches to their favoured middlemen.

The presentation and judgement of samples of these six-month-old babies from the barrels in which they will be aged for nearly two years is crucial. The notes, and especially scores, handed out to these infants can make all the difference to the opening price of a specific wine, so producers make every effort to ensure the wine is drawn out of cask as recently as possible and does not oxidise en route to the tasting table.

But the samples we pore over so assiduously may bear remarkably little relation to the final wines once all the ingredients have been blended and the wine has been bottled. There can be enormous variation between different barrels, as a discreet tasting I was treated to last week showed. The eventual wine will be made up of a blend of hundreds of barrels that may have come from a range of different forests, coopers and barrel treatments. Some barrels produce wines that look particularly good one day but not the next week. It must be tempting, to say the least, to choose a sample from the most flattering barrel type for the primeurs tastings, but that wine will not be truly representative of the final blend.

Wine is a living, petulant thing that goes through all sorts of phases during its two years in barrel. Some producers make their final assemblage of the various lots they decide will go into their top wine – the *grand vin* – and into the second and sometimes third wines, quite early on. They do the requisite blend and age the final blends as long as possible in oak. But the fleshy Merlot grape is likely to be much more seductive at six months old than the tougher Cabernet Sauvignon. In years in which the tannins and acids are particularly pronounced, a Merlot-heavy sample may win more approbation than a more representative Cabernet-heavy one at six months, while in a vintage that tended towards over-ripeness, the reverse could be the case.

Even in the grander parts of Bordeaux, producers may make up for nature's deficiencies by either deacidifying their wines, generally adding potassium bicarbonate, as some did in 2010, or by adding extra tartaric acid in riper vintages. However, there is an argument that a wine from a vat that was acidified, for example, might not look at its best after only six months of integration between acid and fruit, so you might not want to include that vat in the blend from which primeurs samples were taken . . .

Source: Adapted from 'Primed and *en primeur*', Jancis Robinson (2011) *Financial Times* 8 April. Copyright © 2011 The Financial Times Ltd

document uniqueness. To ensure maximum variation within a sample, Patton (2002) suggests you identify your diverse characteristics (sample selection criteria) prior to selecting your sample.

In direct contrast to heterogeneous sampling, **homogeneous sampling** focuses on one particular subgroup in which all the sample members are similar, such as a particular occupation or level in an organisation's hierarchy. Characteristics of the selected participants are similar, allowing them to be explored in greater depth and minor differences to be more apparent.

Critical case sampling selects critical cases on the basis that they can make a point dramatically or because they are important. The focus of data collection is to understand what is happening in each critical case so that logical generalisations can be made (Box 7.12). Patton (2002) outlines a number of clues that suggest critical cases. These can be summarised by the questions such as:

- If it happens there, will it happen everywhere?
- If they are having problems, can you be sure that everyone will have problems?
- If they cannot understand the process, is it likely that no one will be able to understand the process?

In contrast, **typical case sampling** is usually used as part of a research project to provide an illustrative profile using a representative case. Such a sample enables you to provide an illustration of what is 'typical' to those who will be reading your research report and may be unfamiliar with the subject matter. It is not intended to be definitive.

Theoretical sampling is a special case of purposive sampling, being particularly associated with Grounded Theory and analytic induction (Section 13.8). Initially you need to have some idea of where to sample, although not necessarily what to sample for, participants being chosen as they are needed. Subsequent sample selection is dictated by the needs of the emerging theory and the evolving storyline, your participants being chosen purposively to inform this. A theoretical sample is therefore cumulatively chosen according to developing categories and emerging theory based upon your simultaneous collecting, coding and analysis of the data.

Volunteer sampling

Snowball sampling is the first of two techniques we look at where participants are volunteered to be part of the research rather than being chosen. It is used commonly when it is difficult to identify members of the desired population, for example people who are working while claiming unemployment benefit. You, therefore, need to:

1. Make contact with one or two cases in the population.
2. Ask these cases to identify further cases.
3. Ask these new cases to identify further new cases (and so on).
4. Stop when either no new cases are given or the sample is as large as is manageable.

The main problem is making initial contact. Once you have done this, these cases identify further members of the population, who then identify further members, and so the sample snowballs (Box 7.13). For such samples the problems of bias are huge, as respondents are most likely to identify other potential respondents who are similar to themselves, resulting in a homogeneous sample (Lee 1993). The next problem is to find these new cases. However, for populations that are difficult to identify, snowball sampling may provide the only possibility.

Self-selection sampling is the second of the volunteer sampling techniques we look at. It occurs when you allow each case, usually individuals, to identify their desire to take part in the research. You therefore:

1. Publicise your need for cases, either by advertising through appropriate media or by asking them to take part.
2. Collect data from those who respond.

Publicity for convenience samples can take many forms. These include articles and advertisements in magazines that the population are likely to read, postings on appropriate Internet newsgroups and discussion groups, hyperlinks from other websites as well as letters or emails of invitation to colleagues and friends (Box 7.14). Cases that self-select

Box 7.13 Focus on management research

Critical case and snowball sampling

In their 2008 *International Journal of Tourism Research* article 'Tourist satisfaction and beyond: Tourism migrants in Mallorca', Bowen and Schouten discuss an exploratory case study of the role of tourists' experiences in subsequent migration from the UK to Mallorca, Spain. Primary data for their research were collected through a series of elite interviews with key political appointees in the region connected with foreign residents, in-depth interviews with eight individual migrants to provide micro-case studies and a questionnaire completed by 42 migrants.

Through personal contacts, the authors were able to interview a number of key political appointees who were connected with foreign residents in the region. These had a special interest in migrants and so can be considered a 'critical' case sample.

The sample for the micro-case studies was developed initially through personal contacts followed by snowballing. Bowen and Schouten argue that this approach was necessary to both identify migrants and ensure trust between themselves and their interviewees.

Three participants in the in-depth interviews subsequently agreed to act as gatekeepers to other migrants, distributing and collecting a set of questionnaires. These gatekeepers were chosen on the basis of their range of contacts with the British migrant network and their interest in the research. Bowen and Schouten explain in their article how these gatekeepers were instructed regarding the need to maintain confidentiality, be organised in their approach and distribute the questionnaire to a wide range of contacts rather than just close friends in order to avoid bias. They argue that although the questionnaire responses could not provide sufficient data for statistical generalisation, the depth of response provided was more important for their exploratory study.

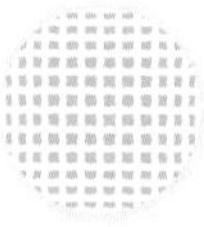

Box 7.14 Focus on student research

Self-selection sampling

Siân's research was concerned with the impact of student loans on studying habits. She had decided to administer her questionnaire using the Internet. She publicised her research on Facebook in a number of groups' pages, using the associated description to invite people to self-select and clicking on the link to the questionnaire. Those who self-selected by clicking on the hyperlink were automatically taken to the online questionnaire she had developed using the SurveyMethods.com online survey software.

often do so because of their feelings or opinions about the research question(s) or stated objectives. In some instances, as in research undertaken by Adrian, Mark and colleagues on the management of the survivors of downsizing (Thornhill et al. 1997), this is exactly what the researcher wants. In this research a letter in the personnel trade press generated a list of self-selected organisations that were interested in the research topic, considered it important and were willing to devote time to being interviewed.

Haphazard sampling

Haphazard sampling occurs when sample cases are selected without any obvious principles of organisation in relation to your research question, the most common form being

convenience sampling (also known as **availability sampling**). This involves selecting cases haphazardly only because they are easily available (or most convenient) to obtain for your sample, such as the person interviewed at random in a shopping centre for a television programme 'vox pop'. Although convenience sampling is used widely (for example, Facebook polls or questions), it is prone to bias and influences that are beyond your control. Cases appear in the sample only because of the ease of obtaining them; consequently all you can do is make some statement about the people who were using Facebook during the period your poll was available who felt strongly enough about the subject of your question to answer it! Not surprisingly, as emphasised in Figure 7.5, findings from convenience samples are often given very little credibility. Despite this, Saunders (2012) points out that samples ostensibly chosen for convenience often meet purposive sample selection criteria that are relevant to the research aim. It may be that an organisation you intend to use as a case study is 'convenient' because you have been able to negotiate access through existing contacts. Where this organisation also represents a 'typical' case, it can also offer an appropriate illustrative scenario, providing justification regarding its purpose when addressing the research aim. Alternatively, whilst a sample of operatives in another division of an organisation for which you work might be easy to obtain and consequently 'convenient', the fact that such participants allow you to address a research aim necessitating an in-depth focus on a particular homogenous group is more crucial.

Where the reasons for using a convenience sample have little, if any relevance to the research aim, participants appear in the sample only because of the ease of obtaining them. Whilst this may not be problematic if there is little variation in the population, where the population is more varied it can result in participants that are of limited use in relation to the research question. Often a sample is intended to represent the total population, for example managers taking a part-time MBA course as a surrogate for all managers. In such instances the selection of individual cases is likely to have introduced bias to the sample, meaning that subsequent interpretations must be treated with caution.

7.4 Summary

- Your choice of sampling techniques is dependent on the feasibility and sensibility of collecting data to answer your research question(s) and to address your objectives from the entire population. For populations of fewer than 50 it is usually more sensible to collect data from the entire population where you are considering using probability sampling.
- Choice of sampling technique or techniques is dependent on your research question(s) and objectives:
  - Research question(s) and objectives that need you to estimate statistically the characteristics of the population from a sample require probability samples.
  - Research question(s) and objectives that do not require such generalisations can, alternatively, make use of non-probability sampling techniques.
- Probability sampling techniques all necessitate some form of sampling frame, so they are often more time-consuming than non-probability techniques.
- Where it is not possible to construct a sampling frame you will need to use non-probability sampling techniques.
- Factors such as the confidence that is needed in the findings, accuracy required and likely categories for analyses will affect the size of the sample that needs to be collected:
  - Statistical analyses usually require a minimum sample size of 30.
  - Research question(s) and objectives that do not require statistical estimation may need far smaller samples.

- Sample size and the technique used are also influenced by the availability of resources, in particular financial support and time available to select the sample and to collect, enter into a computer and analyse the data.
- Non-probability sampling techniques also provide you with the opportunity to select your sample purposively and to reach difficult-to-identify members of the population.
- For many research projects you will need to use a combination of different sampling techniques.
- All your choices will be dependent on your ability to gain access to organisations. The considerations summarised earlier must therefore be tempered with an understanding of what is practically possible.

Self-check questions

Help with these questions is available at the end of the chapter.

7.1 Identify a suitable sampling frame for each of the following research questions.

a How do company directors of manufacturing firms of over 500 employees think a specified piece of legislation will affect their companies?

b Which factors are important in accountants' decisions regarding working in mainland Europe?

c How do employees at Cheltenham Gardens Ltd think the proposed introduction of compulsory Saturday working will affect their working lives?

7.2 Lisa has emailed her tutor with the following query regarding sampling and dealing with non-response. Imagine you are Lisa's tutor. Draft a reply to answer her query.

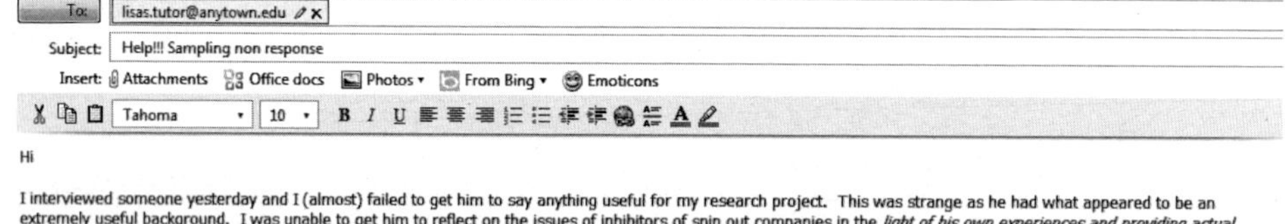

To: lisas.tutor@anytown.edu

Subject: Help!!! Sampling non response

Insert: Attachments Office docs Photos From Bing Emoticons

Tahoma 10

Hi

I interviewed someone yesterday and I (almost) failed to get him to say anything useful for my research project. This was strange as he had what appeared to be an extremely useful background. I was unable to get him to reflect on the issues of inhibitors of spin out companies in the *light of his own experiences and providing actual examples*. He clearly wanted to follow a format he had decided on prior to my arrival. This was that there was a right or wrong answer and he was guessing at what inhibited people rather than giving me actual examples, which was what I asked for. This did not allow for feedback loops or linkages of ideas which, as you know, is what my research is about. It was a very linear model of innovation. My attempts to get the conversation onto my research were gently, but firmly, put aside. ***He had his format on paper when I arrived!***

My question is... can I just exclude this interview from my sample/ He was a super guy and I enjoyed meeting him. But, because I could not get him to answer my questions the interview did not yield any insights. What should I do?

Lisa

7.3 You have been asked to select a sample of manufacturing firms using the sampling frame below. This also lists the value of their annual output in tens of thousands of pounds over the past year. To help you in selecting your sample the firms have been numbered from 0 to 99.

a Select two simple random samples, each of 20 firms, and mark those firms selected for each sample on the sampling frame.

b Describe and compare the pattern on the sampling frame of each of the samples selected.

c Calculate the average (mean) annual output in tens of thousands of pounds over the past year for each of the samples selected.

d Given that the true average annual output is £6,608,900, is there any bias in either of the samples selected?

	Output		Output		Output		Output		Output
0	1163	20	1072	40	1257	60	1300	80	1034
1	10	21	7	41	29	61	39	81	55
2	57	22	92	42	84	62	73	82	66
3	149	23	105	43	97	63	161	83	165
4	205	24	157	44	265	64	275	84	301
5	163	25	214	45	187	65	170	85	161
6	1359	26	1440	46	1872	66	1598	86	1341
7	330	27	390	47	454	67	378	87	431
8	2097	28	1935	48	1822	68	1634	88	1756
9	1059	29	998	49	1091	69	1101	89	907
10	1037	30	1298	50	1251	70	1070	90	1158
11	59	31	10	51	9	71	37	91	27
12	68	32	70	52	93	72	88	92	66
13	166	33	159	53	103	73	102	93	147
14	302	34	276	54	264	74	157	94	203
15	161	35	215	55	189	75	168	95	163
16	1298	36	1450	56	1862	76	1602	96	1339
17	329	37	387	57	449	77	381	97	429
18	2103	38	1934	58	1799	78	1598	98	1760
19	1061	39	1000	59	1089	79	1099	99	898

7.4 You have been asked to select a 10 per cent sample of firms from the sampling frame used for self-check question 7.3.

- **a** Select a 10 per cent systematic random sample and mark those firms selected for the sample on the sampling frame.
- **b** Calculate the average (mean) annual output in tens of thousands of pounds over the past year for your sample.
- **c** Given that the true average annual output is £6,608,900, why does systematic random sampling provide such a poor estimate of the annual output in this case?

7.5 You need to undertake a face-to-face interview survey of managing directors of small to medium-sized organisations. From the data you collect you need to be able to generalise about the attitude of such managing directors to recent changes in government policy towards these firms. Your generalisations need to be accurate to within plus or minus 5 per cent. Unfortunately, you have limited resources to pay for interviewers, travelling and other associated costs.

- **a** How many managing directors will you need to interview?
- **b** You have been given the choice between cluster and multi-stage sampling. Which technique would you choose for this research? You should give reasons for your choice.

7.6 You have been asked to undertake a survey of residents' opinions regarding the siting of a new supermarket in an inner city suburb (estimated catchment population 111,376 at

Gender	Age group 0–4	5–15	16–19	20–29	30–44	45–59/64*	60/65#–74	75+
Males	3498	7106	4884	7656	9812	12892	4972	2684
Females	3461	6923	6952	9460	8152	9152	9284	4488

*59 females, 64 males; #60 females, 65 males.

the last census). The age and gender distribution of the catchment population at the last census is listed above.

a Devise a quota for a quota sample using these data.

b What other data would you like to include to overcome likely variations between groups in their availability for interview and replicate the total population more precisely? Give reasons for your answer.

c What problems might you encounter in using interviewers?

7.7 For each of the following research questions it has not been possible for you to obtain a sampling frame. Suggest the most suitable non-probability sampling technique to obtain the necessary data, giving reasons for your choice.

a What support do people sleeping rough believe they require from social services?

b Which television advertisements do people remember watching last weekend?

c How do employers' opinions vary regarding the impact of European Union legislation on age discrimination?

d How are manufacturing companies planning to respond to the introduction of road tolls?

e Would users of the squash club be prepared to pay a 10 per cent increase in subscriptions to help fund two extra courts (answer needed by tomorrow morning!)?

Review and discussion questions

7.8 With a friend or colleague choose one of the following research questions (or one of your own) in which you are interested.

- What attributes attract people to jobs?
- How are financial institutions adapting the services they provide to meet recent legislation?

Use the flow charts for both probability sampling (Figure 7.3) and non-probability sampling (Figure 7.5) to decide how you could use each type of sampling independently to answer the research question.

7.9 Agree with a colleague to watch a particular documentary or consumer rights programme on the television. If possible, choose a documentary with a business or management focus. During the documentary, pay special attention to the samples from which the data for the documentary are drawn. Where possible, note down details of the sample such as who were interviewed, or who responded to questionnaires and the reasons why these people were chosen. Where this is not possible, make a note of the information you would have liked to have been given. Discuss your findings with your colleague and come to a conclusion regarding the nature of the sample used, its representativeness and the extent to which it was possible for the programme maker to generalise from that sample.

7.10 Obtain a copy of a quality daily newspaper and, within the newspaper, find an article which discusses a 'survey' or 'poll'. Share the article with a friend. Make notes of the process used to select the sample for the 'survey' or 'poll'. As you make your notes, note down any areas where you feel there is insufficient information to fully understand the sampling process. Aspects for which information may be lacking include the total population, size of sample, how the sample were selected, representativeness and so on. Discuss your findings with your friend.

Progressing your research project

Using sampling as part of your research

- Consider your research question(s) and objectives. You need to decide whether you will be able to collect data on the entire population or will need to collect data from a sample.
- If you decide that you need to sample, you must establish whether your research question(s) and objectives require probability sampling. If they do, make sure that a suitable sampling frame is available or can be devised, and calculate the actual sample size required, taking into account likely response rates. If your research question(s) and objectives do not require probability sampling, or you are unable to obtain a suitable sampling frame, you will need to use non-probability sampling.
- Select the most appropriate sampling technique or techniques after considering the advantages and disadvantages of all suitable techniques and undertaking further reading as necessary.
- Select your sample or samples following the technique or techniques as outlined in this chapter.
- Remember to note down the reasons for your choices when you make them, as you will need to justify your choices when you write about your research method.
- Use the questions in Box 1.4 to guide your reflective diary entry.

References

American Association for Public Opinion Research (2008) *Standard Definitions: Final Dispositions of Case Codes and Outcome Rates for Surveys* (5th edn). Lenexa, KA: AAPOR.

Barnett, V. (2002) *Sample Survey Principles and Methods* (3rd edn). Chichester: Wiley.

Baruch, Y. and Holtom, B.C. (2008) 'Survey response rate levels and trends in organizational research', *Human Relations*, Vol. 61, pp. 1139–60.

Becker, H.S. (1998) *Tricks of the Trade: How to Think About Your Research While You're Doing It.* Chicago: Chicago University Press.

Bidlake, S. (2011) 'Outdoor hall of fame contest opens', *Campaign,* 10 February. Available at www.campaignlive.co.uk/News/MostRead/1054277/Outdoor-Hall-Fame-contest-opens/ [Accessed 6 April 2011].

Bowen, D. and Schouten, A.F. (2008) 'Tourist satisfaction and beyond: Tourism migrants in Mallorca', *International Journal of Tourism Research*, Vol. 10, No. 2, pp. 141–53.

Bradley, N. (1999) 'Sampling for Internet surveys: An examination of respondent selection for Internet research', *Journal of the Market Research Society*, Vol. 41, No. 4, pp. 387–95.

Creswell, J. (2007) *Qualitative Inquiry and Research Design: Choosing among Five Approaches* (2nd edn). Thousand Oaks, CA: Sage.

deVaus, D.A. (2002) *Surveys in Social Research* (5th edn). London: Routledge.

Dillman, D.A. (2009) *Internet, Mail and Mixed Mode Surveys: The Tailored Design Method* (3rd edn). New York: Wiley.

Edwards, T., Tregaskis, O., Edwards, P., Ferner, A., Marginson, A. with Arrowsmith, J., Adam, D., Meyer, M. and Budjanovcanin, A. (2007) 'Charting the contours of multinationals in Britain: Methodological challenges arising in survey-based research', *Warwick Papers in Industrial Relations*, No. 86. Available at www2.warwick.ac.uk/fac/soc/wbs/research/irru/wpir/ [Accessed 2 February 2008].

Farey-Jones, D. (2011) '"Hello Boys" voted greatest poster ever', *Campaign,* 31 March. Available at www.campaignlive.co.uk/news/1063405/Hello-Boys-voted-greatest-poster-ever-created/ [Accessed 6 April 2011].

Groves, R.M. and Peytcheva, E. (2008) 'The impact of nonresponse rates on nonresponse bias', *Public Opinion Quarterly,* Vol. 72, No. 2, pp. 167–89.

Guest, G., Bunce, A. and Johnson, L. (2006) 'How many interviews are enough? An experiment with data saturation and validity', *Field Methods*, Vol. 18, No. 1, pp. 59–82.

Henry, G.T. (1990) *Practical Sampling.* Newbury Park, CA: Sage.

Idea Works (2011) *Methodologist's toolchest ex-sample*. Available at www.ideaworks.com/mt/exsample.html [Accessed 27 March 2011].

Kervin, J.B. (1999). *Methods for Business Research* (2nd edn). New York: HarperCollins.

Lee, R.M. (1993) *Doing Research on Sensitive Topics*. London: Sage.

Lenth, R.V. (2001) 'Some practical guidelines for effective sample size determination', *The American Statistician,* Vol. 55, No. 3, pp. 187–93.

Neuman, W.L. (2005) *Social Research Methods* (6th edn). London: Pearson.

Patton, M.Q. (2002) *Qualitative Research and Evaluation Methods* (3rd edn). Thousand Oaks, CA: Sage.

Rogelberg, S.G. and Stanton, J.M. (2007) 'Introduction: Understanding and dealing with organizational survey non-response', *Organizational Research Methods*, Vol. 10, No. 2, pp. 195–209.

Saunders, M.N.K. (2012) 'Choosing research participants', in G. Symons and C. Cassell (eds) *The Practice of Qualitative Organizational Research: Core Methods and Current Challenges.* London: Sage, pp. 37–55.

Stutely, M. (2003) *Numbers Guide: The Essentials of Business Numeracy*. London: Bloomberg Press.

Thornhill, A., Saunders, M.N.K. and Stead, J. (1997) 'Downsizing, delayering but where's the commitment? The development of a diagnostic tool to help manage survivors', *Personnel Review*, Vol. 26, No. 1/2, pp. 81–98.

Tucker, C. and Lepkowski, J.M. (2008) 'Telephone survey methods: Adapting to change', in J.M. Lepkowski, C. Tucker, J.M. Brick, E.D. De Leeuw, L. Japec, P.J. Lavrakas, M.W. Link and R.L. Sangster, *Advances in Telephone Survey Methodology*. Hoboken, NJ: Wiley, pp. 3–28.

Willimack, D.K., Nichols, E. and Sudman, S. (2002) 'Understanding unit and item nonresponse in business surveys', in D.A. Dillman, J.L. Eltringe, J.L. Groves and R.J.A. Little (eds) *Survey Nonresponse.* New York: Wiley Interscience, pp. 213–27.

Further reading

Barnett, V. (2002) *Sample Survey Principles and Method* (3rd edn) Chichester: Wiley. Chapters 2, 4 and 5 provide an explanation of statistics behind probability sampling and quota sampling as well as the techniques.

Baruch, Y. and Holtom, B.C. (2008) *'Survey response rate levels and trends in organizational research', Human Relations*, Vol. 61, pp. 1139–60. This examines 490 academic studies using surveys published in 2000 and 2005 covering 100,000 organisations and over 400,000 individual respondents. The paper suggests likely response rates for different types of study and offers useful advice for reporting response rates.

deVaus, D.A. (2002) *Surveys in Social Research* (5th edn). London: Routledge. Chapter 6 provides a useful overview of both probability and non-probability sampling techniques.

Dillman, D.A., Eltringe, J.L., Groves, J.L. and Little, R.J.A. (eds) (2002) *Survey Nonresponse*. New York: Wiley Interscience. This book contains a wealth of information on survey non-response. Chapter 1 provides a useful overview in relation to the impact of survey design on non-response. This is discussed in more detail in Chapters 7 to 17, Chapter 14 referring specifically to business surveys and Chapter 15 to Internet-based surveys.

Patton, M.Q. (2002) *Qualitative Research and Evaluation Methods* (3rd edn). Thousand Oaks, CA: Sage. Chapter 5, 'Designing qualitative studies', contains a useful discussion of non-probability sampling techniques, with examples.

Case 7
Comparing UK and French perceptions and expectations of online supermarket shopping

How did I end up here? Daniel mused as he sat staring at his computer screen. Six months earlier, as he left family and friends in France to complete his master's degree on an exchange to the UK, the future seemed bright. Hundreds of kilometres away from home, with a deadline looming that could make or break his future career, he did not know where to start. He had left university with a bachelor's degree in Marketing and Management three years before and since that time had been on a graduate recruitment scheme with one of the largest supermarket chains in France. His performance in the early stages of a part-time master's programme in Retail Management sponsored by his employer had been good. This, combined with his high standard of English, meant he had been offered the opportunity to travel to the UK to study for one year on a full-time basis and obtain a double qualification from both his French and a British institution. The taught classes in the first semester had complemented his previous studies and he had soon identified the area he wanted to investigate for his research project – online supermarket shopping. He decided the aim of his project would be to compare and contrast UK and French consumers' perceptions and expectations of supermarkets' online shopping offerings.

Source: Getty Images/Bloomberg

In class Daniel's lecturers had identified the key problems faced by online retailers, in particular customer concerns around security and trust (Beldad et al. 2010; Koufari and Hampton-Sosa 2004). They had also discussed in tutorials the impact of social network sites and the 'online word of mouth' interactions (Gruen et al. 2006), which were changing the way marketing was undertaken. Organisations were initiating interactions by using blogs and noticeboards where customers could post their views of company products and service levels (Godes et al. 2005). Almost every student he knew had bought something on eBay or Amazon, and many chose to do their supermarket shopping online to avoid wasting time standing in checkout queues. In addition, many supermarkets had diversified their offer away from daily consumables into white goods such as washing machines and even financial services (Colgate and Alexander 2001), meaning consumers were now looking to these organisations for more than just the weekly household shopping. Against the advice of his project tutor, Daniel had decided the results of his Marketing assignment on online buyer behaviour, where his classmates had been his population, would be his pilot study.

It had been a revelation to him to see how well developed the retail websites were in the UK, compared with those in France, and how different the webscape was in the two countries. Statistics he had found showed that in June 2010 there were 51.4 million Internet users in the UK, 82.5 per cent of the population, an increase of 234 per cent between 2000 and 2010. In France the figures were 44.6 million users, 68.9 per cent of the population, a 425 per cent increase over the decade (Miniwatts Marketing Group 2011).

Through browsing the Internet he observed that French retailers seemed to have developed their Internet sites as an advertising tool. Potential customers could browse the site to look at the products but often had to send an email to obtain information. His mother had been very frustrated when renovating the bathroom; she waited several weeks for a response to her online request and then received brochures in the post. Although some companies, like his employer, had moved towards offering a complete online shopping experience from first view to receipt of the product, their sites were far less developed than those of the UK online stores he accessed. A paper he read about French supermarkets had also identified problems managing home delivery of purchases bought online (Durand 2008).

Daniel decided he needed to identify his population, and from that draw a representative sample. He thought his organisation's database of existing online customers would be a useful place to start, but he was unsure whether he would be allowed access. In addition, he did not simply want to undertake a large-scale quantitative survey of existing customers as did not think it would produce a picture of the wider situation. One of his objectives was, after all, to identify the French consumers' expectations of these online offerings. How could he ensure he limited bias in the respondents' answers, which would be a threat to the reliability of his findings?

His initial idea to use Facebook to gain access to a bigger population had not been received enthusiastically by his project tutor but he had anticipated the need to justify this suggestion. He argued that by using this informal network, and building simple instructions and collecting demographic data in an Internet questionnaire, he would be able to categorise respondents and identify which supermarket website they were evaluating.

So here he was, with an interesting project that fitted perfectly with the needs of his employer, which wanted to develop its presence on the Web. His intention was to get an overview of online consumer perceptions and expectations of the online supermarket sites available in the UK and France. He then planned to compare the data collected from the participants to identify the differences between the online activities of the British and French supermarkets and produce some guidelines to help his employer develop this side of its activities. However, the problem he came back to again was how to select his sample.

Daniel thought a non-probability approach would fit this exploratory research but, if he was honest, the research methods lectures had totally confused him. A great deal of time had been spent on the explanation of the formula to work out the optimum sample size for a survey, and the need to collect data from a representative sample to make statistical inferences about the population. His concern was how to build the argument for using non-probability sampling and be able to justify it to his project tutor, whose own research activity involved large-scale marketing research projects run in conjunction with companies in the USA.

So here he was preparing his argument to produce a questionnaire using SurveyMonkey and post the link on Facebook. In addition, he would send the link via emails to other friends who did not use Facebook. He would make the request that they all pass the link on to their friends and family who fell within the parameters that would be defined in the message accompanying the link.

One point he felt that was in his favour was he had been able to develop a network of contacts during his time in the UK. As one of the few French students on campus he had taken advantage of his gregarious nature and tried to meet as many people as possible. His Facebook wall had thousands of postings from his 'friends'. He was convinced this was the place to start but really needed to get his head around non-probability sampling if he was going to do it well.

References

Beldad, A., De Jong, M. Steehouder, M. (2010) 'How shall I trust the faceless and intangible? A literature on the antecedents of online trust', *Computers in Human Behaviour*, Vol. 26, No. 5, pp. 857–69.

Colgate, M. and Alexander, N. (2001) 'Retailers and diversification: The financial service dimension', *Journal of Retailing and Consumer Services*, Vol. 9, No. 1, pp. 1–11.

Durand, B. (2008) 'Les magasins de proximité: Un atout logistique pour l'épicerie en ligne', *La Revue des Sciences de Gestion, Direction et Gestion, Spécial Marketing*, Vol. 229, pp. 75–83.

Godes, D., Mayzlin, D., Chen, Y., Das, S., Dellarocas, C., Pfeiffer, B., Libai, B., Sen, S., Shi, M. and Verlegh, P. (2005) 'The firm's management of social interactions', *Marketing Letters*, Vol. 16, No. 3, pp. 415–28.

Gruen, T.W., Osmonbekov, T. and Czaplewski, A.J. (2006) 'eWOM: The impact of customer-to-customer online know-how exchange on customer value and loyalty', *Journal of Business Research*, Vol. 59, pp. 449–56.

Koufari, M. and Hampton-Sosa, W. (2004) 'The development of initial trust in an online company by new users', *Journal of Information and Management*, Vol. 41, No. 3, pp. 377–97.

Miniwatts Marketing Group (2011) *Internet World Stats.* Available at www.internetworldstats.com/stats/4.htm [Accessed 1 April 2011].

Questions

1 Outline the problems Daniel is likely to face by using his Marketing assignment as his pilot study.
2 Discuss how the distribution of a link to the Internet questionnaire using Facebook via email might jeopardise the statistical representativeness of Daniel's findings.
3 Identify a sampling technique that could enable Daniel to collect reliable data from which he could make statistical inferences. Give reasons for your choice and explain the steps you would take to select your sample.

Additional case studies relating to material covered in this chapter are available via the book's companion website: **www.pearsoned.co.uk/saunders**.

They are:

- Change management at Hattersley Electronics.
- Employment networking in the Hollywood film industry.
- Auditor independence and integrity in accounting firms.
- Implementing strategic change initiatives.

Self-check answers

7.1 **a** A complete list of all directors of large manufacturing firms could be purchased from an organisation that specialised in selling such lists to use as the sampling frame. Alternatively, a list that contained only those selected for the sample could be purchased to reduce costs. These data are usually in a format suitable for being read by word-processing and database computer software, and so they could easily be merged into standard letters such as those included with questionnaires.

b A complete list of accountants, or one that contained only those selected for the sample, could be purchased from an organisation that specialised in selling such lists. Care would need to be taken regarding the precise composition of the list to ensure that it included those in private practice as well as those working for organisations. Alternatively, if the research was interested only in qualified accountants then the professional accountancy bodies' yearbooks, which list all their members and their addresses, could be used as the sampling frame.

c The personnel records or payroll of Cheltenham Gardens Ltd could be used. Either would provide an up-to-date list of all employees with their addresses.

7.2 Your draft of Lisa's tutor's reply is unlikely to be worded the same way as the one below. However, it should contain the same key points:

From: "tutor's name" <lisas.tutor@anytown.ac.uk>
To: <lisa@anytown.ac.uk>
Sent: today's date 7:06
Subject: Re: Help!!! Sampling non-response?

Hi Lisa
Many thanks for the email. This is not in the least unusual. I reckon to get about 1 in 20 interviews which go this way and you just have to say 'c'est la vie'. This is not a problem from a methods perspective as, in sampling terms, it can be treated as a non-response due to the person refusing to respond to your questions. This would mean you could not use the material. However, if he answered some other questions then you should treat this respondent as a partial non-response and just not use those answers.
Hope this helps.
'Tutor's name'

7.3 **a** Your answer will depend on the random numbers you selected. However, the process you follow to select the samples is likely to be similar to that outlined. Starting at randomly selected points, two sets of 20 two-digit random numbers are read from the random number tables (Appendix 3). If a number is selected twice it is disregarded. Two possible sets are:

Sample 1: 38 41 14 59 53 03 52 86 21 88 55 87 85 90 74 18 89 40 84 71
Sample 2: 28 00 06 70 81 76 36 65 30 27 92 73 20 87 58 15 69 22 77 31

These are then marked on the sampling frame (sample 1 is shaded in blue, sample 2 is shaded in brown) as shown below:

0	1163	*20*	1072	*40*	1257	*60*	1300	*80*	1034
1	10	*21*	7	*41*	29	*61*	39	*81*	55
2	57	*22*	92	*42*	84	*62*	73	*82*	66
3	149	*23*	105	*43*	97	*63*	161	*83*	165
4	205	*24*	157	*44*	265	*64*	275	*84*	301
5	163	*25*	214	*45*	187	*65*	170	*85*	161
6	1359	*26*	1440	*46*	1872	*66*	1598	*86*	1341
7	330	*27*	390	*47*	454	*67*	378	*87*	431
8	2097	*28*	1935	*48*	1822	*68*	1634	*88*	1756
9	1059	*29*	998	*49*	1091	*69*	1101	*89*	907
10	1037	*30*	1298	*50*	1251	*70*	1070	*90*	1158
11	59	*31*	10	*51*	9	*71*	37	*91*	27
12	68	*32*	70	*52*	93	*72*	88	*92*	66
13	166	*33*	159	*53*	103	*73*	102	*93*	147
14	302	*34*	276	*54*	264	*74*	157	*94*	203
15	161	*35*	215	*55*	189	*75*	168	*95*	163
16	1298	*36*	1450	*56*	1862	*76*	1602	*96*	1339
17	329	*37*	387	*57*	449	*77*	381	*97*	429
18	2103	*38*	1934	*58*	1799	*78*	1598	*98*	1760
19	1061	*39*	1000	*59*	1089	*79*	1099	*99*	898

b Your samples will probably produce patterns that cluster around certain numbers in the sampling frame, although the amount of clustering may differ, as illustrated by samples 1 and 2 above.

c The average (mean) annual output in tens of thousands of pounds will depend entirely upon your sample. For the two samples selected the averages are:

Sample 1 (shaded in blue): £6,752,000
Sample 2 (shaded in brown): £7,853,500

d There is no bias in either of the samples, as both have been selected at random. However, the average annual output calculated from sample 1 represents the total population more closely than that calculated from sample 2, although this has occurred entirely at random.

7.4 **a** Your answer will depend on the random number you select as the starting point for your systematic sample. However, the process you followed to select your sample is likely to be similar to that outlined. As a 10 per cent sample has been requested, the sampling fraction is 1/10. Your starting point is selected using a random number between 0 and 9, in this case 2. Once the firm numbered 2 has been selected, every tenth firm is selected:

2 12 22 32 42 52 62 72 82 92

These are shaded in brown on the sampling frame and will result in a regular pattern whatever the starting point:

0	1163	*20*	1072	*40*	1257	*60*	1300	*80*	1034
1	10	*21*	7	*41*	29	*61*	39	*81*	55
2	57	*22*	92	*42*	84	*62*	73	*82*	66
3	149	*23*	105	*43*	97	*63*	161	*83*	165
4	205	*24*	157	*44*	265	*64*	275	*84*	301
5	163	*25*	214	*45*	187	*65*	170	*85*	161
6	1359	*26*	1440	*46*	1872	*66*	1598	*86*	1341
7	330	*27*	390	*47*	454	*67*	378	*87*	431
8	2097	*28*	1935	*48*	1822	*68*	1634	*88*	1756
9	1059	*29*	998	*49*	1091	*69*	1101	*89*	907
10	1037	*30*	1298	*50*	1251	*70*	1070	*90*	1158
11	59	*31*	10	*51*	9	*71*	37	*91*	27
12	68	*32*	70	*52*	93	*72*	88	*92*	66
13	166	*33*	159	*53*	103	*73*	102	*93*	147
14	302	*34*	276	*54*	264	*74*	157	*94*	203
15	161	*35*	215	*55*	189	*75*	168	*95*	163
16	1298	*36*	1450	*56*	1862	*76*	1602	*96*	1339
17	329	*37*	387	*57*	449	*77*	381	*97*	429
18	2103	*38*	1934	*58*	1799	*78*	1598	*98*	1760
19	1061	*39*	1000	*59*	1089	*79*	1099	*99*	898

b The average (mean) annual output of firms for your sample will depend upon where you started your systematic sample. For the sample selected above it is £757,000.

c Systematic sampling has provided a poor estimate of the annual output because there is an underlying pattern in the data, which has resulted in firms with similar levels of output being selected.

7.5 **a** If you assume that there are at least 100,000 managing directors of small to medium-sized organisations from which to select your sample, you will need to interview approximately 380 to make generalisations that are accurate to within plus or minus 5 per cent (Table 7.1).

b Either cluster or multi-stage sampling could be suitable; what is important is the reasoning behind your choice. This choice between cluster and multi-stage sampling is dependent on the amount of limited resources and time you have available. Using multi-stage sampling will take longer than cluster sampling as more sampling stages will need to be undertaken. However, the results are more likely to be representative of the total population owing to the possibility of stratifying the samples from the sub-areas.

7.6 **a** Prior to deciding on your quota you will need to consider the possible inclusion of residents who are aged under 16 in your quota. Often in such research projects residents aged under 5 (and those aged 5–15) are excluded. You would need a quota of between 2000 and 5000 residents to obtain a reasonable accuracy. These should be divided proportionally between the groupings as illustrated in the possible quota below:

	Age group					
Gender	**16–19**	**20–29**	**30–44**	**45–59/64**	**60/65–74**	**751**
Males	108	169	217	285	110	59
Females	154	209	180	203	205	99

b Data on social class, employment status, socioeconomic status or car ownership could also be used as further quotas. These data are available from the Census and are likely to affect shopping habits.

c Interviewers might choose respondents who were easily accessible or appeared willing to answer the questions. In addition, they might fill in their quota incorrectly or make up the data.

7.7 **a** Either snowball sampling as it would be difficult to identify members of the desired population or, possibly, convenience sampling because of initial difficulties in finding members of the desired population.

b Quota sampling to ensure that the variability in the population as a whole is represented.

c Purposive sampling to ensure that the full variety of responses are obtained from a range of respondents from the population.

d Self-selection sampling as it requires people who are interested in the topic.

e Convenience sampling owing to the very short timescales available and the need to have at least some idea of members' opinions.

Get ahead using resources on the companion website at:
www.pearsoned.co.uk/saunders

- Improve your IBM SPSS Statistics and NVivo research analysis with practice tutorials.
- Save time researching on the Internet with the Smarter Online Searching Guide.
- Test your progress using self-assessment questions.
- Follow live links to useful websites.

Chapter 8

Using secondary data

Learning outcomes

By the end of this chapter you should be able to:

- identify the full variety of secondary data that are available;
- appreciate ways in which secondary data can be utilised to help to answer your research question(s) and to meet your objectives;
- understand the advantages and disadvantages of using secondary data in research projects;
- use a range of techniques to locate secondary data;
- evaluate the suitability of secondary data for answering your research question(s) and meeting your objectives in terms of coverage, validity, reliability and measurement bias;
- apply the knowledge, skills and understanding gained to your own research project.

8.1 Introduction

When thinking about how to obtain data to answer their research question(s) or meet their objectives, students are increasingly expected to consider undertaking further analyses of data that have already been collected for some other purpose. Such data are known as **secondary data** and include both raw data and published summaries. Once obtained, these data can be further analysed to provide additional or different knowledge, interpretations or conclusions (Bulmer et al. 2009). Despite this, many students automatically think in terms of collecting new (**primary**) **data** specifically for that purpose. Yet, unlike national governments, non-governmental agencies and other organisations, they do not have the time, money or access to collect detailed large data sets themselves. Fortunately, over the past decade the number of sources of potential secondary data and the ease of gaining access have expanded rapidly alongside the growth of the Internet. These may provide useful data from which to answer, or partially to answer, your research question(s).

Most organisations collect and store a variety of data to support their operations: for example, payroll details, copies of letters, minutes of meetings and accounts of sales of goods or services.

Quality daily newspapers contain a wealth of data, including reports about takeover bids and companies' share prices. Government departments undertake surveys and publish official statistics covering social, demographic and economic topics. Consumer research organisations collect data that are used subsequently by different clients. Trade organisations collect data from their members on topics such as sales that are subsequently aggregated and published. Social networking sites (such as Facebook) host web pages for particular interest groups, including those set up by organisations, storing alongside other data group members' posts and photographs.

These days, data about people's whereabouts, purchases, behaviour and personal lives are gathered, stored and shared on a scale that no repressive political dictator would ever have thought possible. Much of the time there is nothing obviously sinister about this. Governments say they need to gather data to assist in the fight against terrorism or protect public safety; commercial organisations argue that they do it to deliver goods and services more effectively. But the widespread use of electronic data gathering and processing is remarkable compared with the situation even as recently as 10 years ago.

Source: © Philip Lewis 2008

We can all think of examples of how the technology reveals information about what we have been doing. The Oyster payment card used for travel on public transport in London such as the Underground and buses tells those who want to know where we have travelled and at what time. The mobile phone allows identification of where we are at a particular time and the credit card will show where and when we make purchases. Many of our telephone calls to call centres are recorded and the search engine Google stores data on our web searches.

Such data are obtained every time we interact directly or indirectly with these organisations' electronic systems. These data are often reused for purposes other than that for which they were originally collected. They are aggregated to provide information about, for example, different geographical regions or social groups. They are merged with other data to form new data sets, the creation of these secondary data sets allowing new relationships to be explored. They are also made available or sold to other people and organisations for further analysis as secondary data.

Some of these data, in particular documents such as company minutes, are available only from the organisations that produce them, and so access will need to be negotiated (Sections 6.2 to 6.4). Others, such as web pages on social networking sites, can range from being 'open' for everyone using the site to view to being completely 'secret' other than to group members. Governments' survey data, such as a censuses of population, are widely available to download in aggregated form via the Internet as governments allow open access to data they have collected. Such survey data are also often deposited in, and available from, data archives. Online computer databases containing company information such as Amadeus and Datamonitor can often be accessed via your university library web pages (Table 8.1). In addition, companies and professional organisations usually have their own websites which may contain data that are useful to your research project.

For certain types of research project, such as those requiring national or international comparisons, secondary data will probably provide the main source to answer your research question(s) and to address your objectives. However, if you are undertaking your research project as part of a course of study, we recommend that you check the assessment regulations before deciding whether you are going to use primary or secondary or a combination of both types of data. Some universities explicitly require students to collect primary data for their research projects. Most research questions are answered using some combination of secondary and primary data. Invariably where limited appropriate secondary data are available, you will have to rely mainly on data you collect yourself.

In this chapter we examine the different types of secondary data that are likely to be available to help you to answer your research question(s) and meet your objectives,

Table 8.1 Selected online databases with potential secondary data

Name	Secondary data
Amadeus	Financial, descriptive and ownership information for 250,000 companies in Europe
British Newspapers 1600–1900	Full text of British newspapers
Datamonitor	Company profiles for world's 10,000 largest companies, Industry profiles for various industries
Datastream	Company, financial and economic information
Euromonitor International	Global market information database searchable by industry, product, country etc.
Key Note Reports	1600 market reports covering a range of sectors
Mintel Reports	Market research reports on wide range of sectors
Nexis	Full text of UK national and regional newspapers. Some international coverage and company data
QIN	Company accounts, ratios and activities for over 300,000 companies in mainland China
Regional Business News	Full text of United States business journals, newspapers and newswires. Updated daily
Times Digital Archive 1785–1985	Digital editions (including photographs, illustrations and advertisements) from *The Times* national newspaper (UK)

how you might use them (Section 8.2), and a range of methods for locating these data (Section 8.3). We then consider the advantages and disadvantages of using secondary data (Section 8.4) and discuss ways of evaluating their validity and reliability (Section 8.5). We do not attempt to provide a comprehensive list of secondary data sources because, as these are expanding rapidly, it would be an impossible task.

8.2 Types of secondary data and uses in research

Secondary data include both quantitative (numeric) and qualitative (non-numeric) data (Section 5.3), and are used principally in both descriptive and explanatory research. The secondary data you analyse further may be **raw data**, where there has been little if any processing, or **compiled data** that have received some form of selection or summarising. Within business and management research such data are used most frequently as part of a case study or survey research strategy. However, there is no reason not to include secondary data in other research strategies, including archival research, action research and experimental research.

Different researchers (e.g. Bryman 1989; Dale et al. 1988; Hakim 1982, 2000) have generated a variety of classifications for secondary data. These classifications do not, however, capture the full variety of data. We have therefore built on their ideas to create three main subgroups of secondary data: documentary, survey-based and those compiled from multiple sources (Figure 8.1).

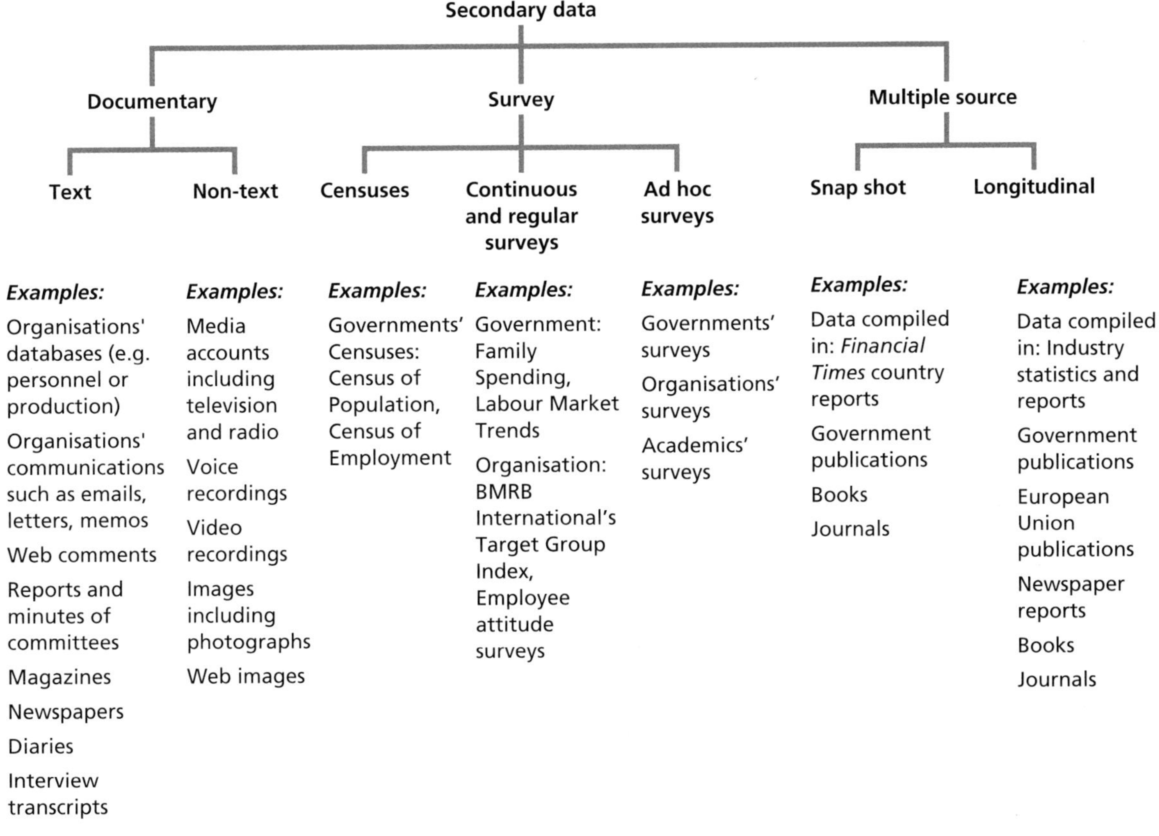

Figure 8.1 Types of secondary data
Source: © Mark Saunders, Philip Lewis and Adrian Thornhill 2011

Documentary secondary data

Documentary secondary data are often used in research projects that also collect primary data. However, you can also use them on their own or with other sources of secondary data, for example for business history research within an archival research strategy. Documentary secondary data include text materials such as notices, correspondence (including emails), minutes of meetings, reports to shareholders, diaries, transcripts of speeches and conversations, administrative and public records and text of web pages (Box 8.1). Text data can also include books, journal and magazine articles and newspapers. Although these are usually just a storage medium for compiled data, they can be important raw data sources in their own right. You could use such documents to provide qualitative data such as managers' espoused reasons for decisions. They could also be used to generate statistical measures such as data on absenteeism and profitability derived from company records (Bryman 1989).

Documentary secondary data also include non-text materials (Figure 8.1), such as voice and video recordings, pictures, drawings, films and television programmes (Robson 2011), DVDs and CD-ROMs as well as web pages. These data can be analysed both quantitatively and qualitatively, including transcribing spoken words and analysing them as text (Section 13.4). In addition, these secondary data can be used to help to triangulate findings based on other data, such as text material and primary data collected through observation, interviews or questionnaires (Chapters 9, 10 and 11).

Increasingly researchers are making use of web-based materials generated by online communities as documentary secondary data. Whilst data stored in the majority of web pages such as blogs and those set up by social networking sites' user groups were never intended to be used in this way, they can still provide secondary data for research projects. There are, however, a number of issues related to using such data, including locating it, evaluating its usefulness in relation to your research question and objectives and associated ethical issues (Sections 6.5 and 6.6).

For your research project, the documentary sources you have available can depend on whether you have been granted access to an organisation's records as well as on your

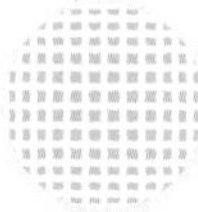

Box 8.1 Focus on student research

Using organisation-based documentary secondary data

Sasha was interested in how her work placement organisation dealt with complaints by customers. Her mentor within the organisation arranged for her to have access to the electronic files containing copies of customers' letters and emails of complaint and the replies sent by the organisation's customer relations team (text documentary secondary data). Reading through these customers' letters, Sasha soon realised that many of these customers complained in writing because they had not received a satisfactory response when they had complained earlier by telephone. She therefore asked her mentor if records were kept of complaints made by customers by telephone. Her mentor said that summary details of all telephone conversations by the customer relations team, including complaints (text documentary secondary data), were stored in their database and offered to find out precisely what data were held. Her mentor was, however, doubtful as to whether these data would be as detailed as the customers' written complaints.

On receiving details of the data stored in the customer relations database, Sasha realised that the next stage would be to match the written complaints data with telephone complaints data. The latter, she hoped, would enable her to obtain a complete list of all complaints and set the written complaints in the context of all complaints received by the organisation.

success in locating data archives, and other Internet, commercial and library sources (Section 8.3). Access to an organisation's data will be dependent on gatekeepers within that organisation (Sections 6.2–6.4). In our experience, those research projects that make use of documentary secondary data often do so as part of a within-company action research project or a case study of a particular organisation (Box 8.1).

When you analyse text and non-text materials such as the text of a web page, a television news report or a newspaper article directly as part of your research, you are using those materials as secondary data. However, often such materials are just the source of your secondary data, rather than the actual secondary data you are analysing (Box 8.2).

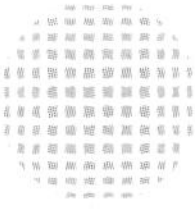

Box 8.2 Focus on student research

When are the reports in newspapers and on YouTube secondary data?

Jana's research question was 'to what extent is the media's reporting of government policies on pension reform biased?' She had downloaded and read journal articles about the case for pension reform as well as a number of government documents on the subject. The latter included an information pack about the Pensions Bill 2011 from the UK government's Department of Work and Pensions' website which she used to establish the government's stated reasons for pension reform. She had also obtained copies of newspaper reports about pension reform for the past two years and found YouTube clips of television news reports uploaded by television companies such as the BBC, Sky News and Independent Television News.

As she began to write the method chapter of her research project Jana became confused. She knew that the journal articles about the case for pension reform were literature rather than secondary data. However, she was unclear whether the government's information pack, the newspaper reports and the YouTube clips were secondary data. She emailed her tutor who responded:

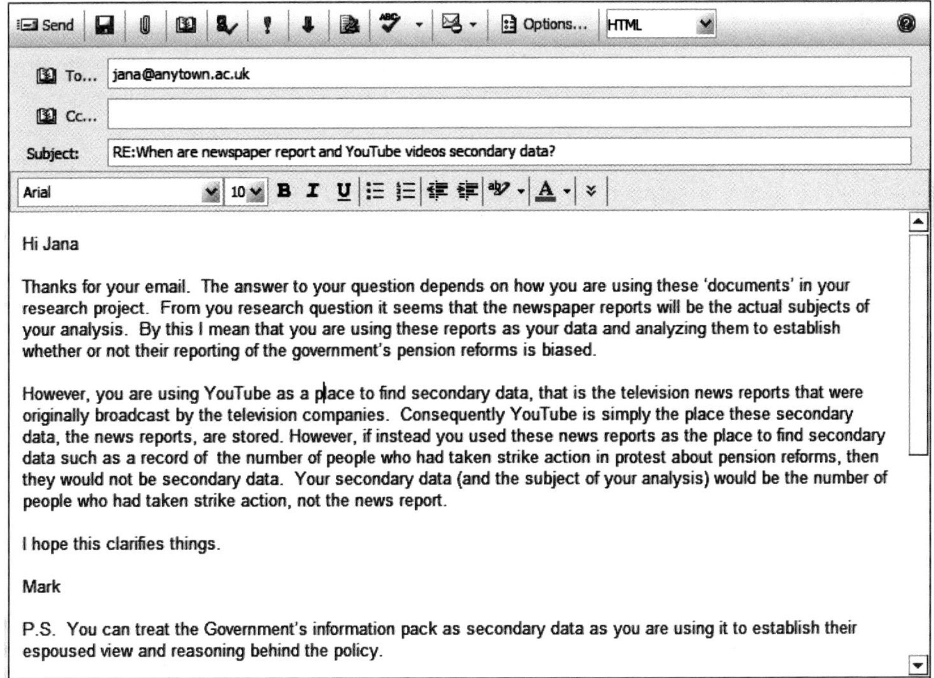

To... jana@anytown.ac.uk

Cc...

Subject: RE:When are newspaper report and YouTube videos secondary data?

Hi Jana

Thanks for your email. The answer to your question depends on how you are using these 'documents' in your research project. From you research question it seems that the newspaper reports will be the actual subjects of your analysis. By this I mean that you are using these reports as your data and analyzing them to establish whether or not their reporting of the government's pension reforms is biased.

However, you are using YouTube as a place to find secondary data, that is the television news reports that were originally broadcast by the television companies. Consequently YouTube is simply the place these secondary data, the news reports, are stored. However, if instead you used these news reports as the place to find secondary data such as a record of the number of people who had taken strike action in protest about pension reforms, then they would not be secondary data. Your secondary data (and the subject of your analysis) would be the number of people who had taken strike action, not the news report.

I hope this clarifies things.

Mark

P.S. You can treat the Government's information pack as secondary data as you are using it to establish their espoused view and reasoning behind the policy.

Survey-based secondary data

Survey-based secondary data refers to existing data collected for some other purpose using a survey strategy, usually questionnaires (Chapter 11). Such data normally refer to organisations, people or households. They are made available as compiled data tables or, increasingly frequently, as a downloadable matrix of raw data (Section 12.2) for secondary analysis.

Survey-based secondary data will have been collected through one of three distinct subtypes of survey strategy: censuses, continuous/regular surveys or ad hoc surveys (Figure 8.1). Censuses are usually carried out by governments and are unique because, unlike surveys, participation is obligatory. Consequently, they provide very good coverage of the population surveyed. They include censuses of population, which have been carried out in many countries since the eighteenth century and in the UK since 1801 (Office for National Statistics 2011a). Published tabulations are available via the Internet for more recent UK censuses, and the raw data 100 years after the census was conducted can be accessed via the Internet. The data from censuses conducted by many governments are intended to meet the needs of government departments as well as of local government. As a consequence they are usually clearly defined, well documented and of a high quality. Such data are easily accessible in compiled form, and are widely used by other organisations and individual researchers.

Continuous and regular surveys are those, excluding censuses, that are repeated over time (Hakim 1982). They include surveys where data are collected throughout the year, such as the UK's General LiFestyle Survey (GLF) (Office for National Statistics 2011b), and those repeated at regular intervals. The latter include the EU Labour Force Survey, which since 1998 has been undertaken quarterly using a core set of questions by member states throughout the European Union. This means that some comparative data are available for member states, although access to these data is limited by European and individual countries' legislation (European Commission 2010). Non-governmental bodies also carry out regular surveys. These include general-purpose market research surveys such as BMRB International's Target Group Index. Because of the commercial nature of such market research surveys, the data are likely to be costly to obtain. Many large organisations also undertake regular surveys, a common example being the employee attitude survey. However, because of the sensitive nature of such information, it is often difficult to gain access to such survey data, especially in its raw form.

Census and continuous and regular survey data provide a useful resource with which to compare or set in context your own research findings from primary data. Aggregate data are usually available via the Internet (Section 8.3), in particular for government surveys. When using these data you need to check when they were collected, as there can be over a year between collection and publication! If you are undertaking research in one UK organisation, you could use these data to place your case study organisation within the context of its industry group or division using the Annual Employment Survey. Aggregated results of the Annual Employment Survey can be found via the UK government's statistics information gateway, the *Office for National Statistics* (Table 8.2). Alternatively, you might explore issues already highlighted by undertaking further analysis of data provided by an earlier organisation survey through in-depth interviews.

Survey secondary data may be available in sufficient detail to provide the main data set from which to answer your research question(s) and to meet your objectives. They may be the only way in which you can obtain the required data. If your research question is concerned with national variations in consumer spending it is unlikely that you will be able to collect sufficient data. You will therefore need to rely on secondary data such as those contained in the report *Family Spending: A Report of the Living Costs and Food*

Table 8.2 Selected Internet secondary data gateways and archives

Name	Internet address	Comment
General focus		
RBA Business Information on the Internet	www.rba.co.uk/sources/	Gateway with links to business, statistical, government and country sites
UK Data Archive	www.data-archive.ac.uk/	Archive of UK digital data in the social science and humanities fields. Links to data archives worldwide
University of Michigan Documents Center	www.lib.umich.edu/government-documents-center/	Although predominantly American focus gateway, has excellent annotated links to international agencies, non-American governmental websites and their statistical agencies
Economic and Social DataService (ESDS)	www.esds.ac.uk/	Gateway to and support for economic and social data, both quantitative and qualitative for both the UK and other countries
Euromonitor International	www.euromonitor.com/	Business intelligence on countries, companies, markets, and consumers
Hemscott	www.hemscott.com/	Hemscott's guide to companies and investment trusts, report service and market activity analysis
MIMAS	www.mimas.ac.uk/	National data centre for UK higher education institutions providing gateway to key data such as UK census. NB: for some data sets you will need to register through your university
Country focus		
Australia: Australian Social Science Data Archive	www.assda.edu.au/	Archive of Australian social science data sets including Census. Includes data from other Asia Pacific countries. Links to other secondary data sites
Canada: Statistics Canada	www.statcan.gc.ca/start-debut-eng.html	Gateway to statistics on economy, culture, society and culture (including Census) of Canada
China: Universities Service Centre Databank for Chinese Studies	www.usc.cuhk.edu.hk/Eng/AboutDCS.aspx	Archive of social science data about People's Republic of China (see also University of Michigan site)
European Union: Europa	http://europa.eu/	Gateway to information (including press releases, legislation, fact sheets) published by European Union. Links include Eurostat statistics information gateway

(*continued*)

Table 8.2 (*Continued*)

Name	Internet address	Comment
France: National Institute for Statistics	www.insee.fr/en/default.asp	France's National Institute for Statistics gateway for both statistics and government publications. Much of this website is available in English
Germany: Federal Statistics Office	www.destatis.de/jetspeed/portal/cms/Sites/destatis/Internet/EN/Navigation/Homepage__NT.psml;jsessionid=0F34E9926750985B7ABAA700B0403184.internet2	Germany's Federal Statistical Office providing a gateway to data. Much of this website is available in English
Ireland (Eire)	www.cso.ie/	Irish Central Statistical Office (CSO), the government body providing a gateway to Irish official statistics
Japan: Social Science Japan Data Archive	ssjda.iss.u-tokyo.ac.jp/en/	Archive of social science datasets available providing details in both Japanese and English. Datasets in Japanese only
Korea: Korean Social Science Data Centre	www.ksdc.re.kr/unisql/engjap/eindex.html	Archive of social science statistical data including Census available in Korean, English and Japanese
The Netherlands: Central Bureau of Statistics	www.cbs.nl/en-GB/menu/home/default.htm?Languageswitch=on	Site of the Netherland's Central Bureau of Statistics (CBS). Much of this website is available in English. Provides gateway to StatLine, which contains statistical data that can be downloaded free of charge
Norway: Norwegian Social Science Data Services	www.nsd.uib.no/nsd/english/index.html	Archive of social science data on Norway
South Africa: South African Data Archive	sada.nrf.ac.za/	Archive of social science data such as the Census on South Africa
United Kingdom: Direct.gov	www.direct.gov.uk/	UK government information service providing a gateway to government departments, official statistics, etc.
United Kingdom: Office for National Statistics	www.statistics.gov.uk/default.asp	The official UK statistics gateway containing official UK statistics and information about statistics, which can be accessed and downloaded free of charge

Survey (Office for National Statistics 2010). For some research questions and objectives suitable data will be available in published form. For others, you may need more disaggregated data. This is most likely to be available via the Internet, often from data archives (Section 8.3). We have found that for most business and management research requiring secondary data you are unlikely to find all the data you require from one source. Rather, your research project is likely to involve detective work in which you build your own multiple-source data set using different data items from a variety of secondary data sources (Box 8.3). Like all detective work, finding data that help to answer a research question or meet an objective is immensely satisfying.

Box 8.3 Focus on management research

Undertaking further analysis of consumer trial data

One way in which firms market their products is through campaigns that encourage consumers to talk about the product, thereby helping win new customers by what is termed 'Word of Mouth' advertising. Research by Alain Samson published in the *International Journal of Market Research* (2010) discusses findings drawn from combining and reanalysing data originally generated during a variety of product sampling consumer trials by Yooster Ltd for five fast-moving consumer goods comprising:

- breakfast food (muesli) – sample size 1541;
- skincare product one – sample size 1765;
- skincare product two – sample size 941;
- dietary supplement one – sample size 1837;
- dietary supplement two – sample size 1252.

These data had been originally collected from consumer panels for each of the products using pre- and post-campaign questionnaire surveys. Within each of these, each panel member had been asked questions about specific brands used in the previous 12 months, the most frequently used brand as well as their intention to recommend, word-of-mouth conversations and their sharing of product samples they had been given with others and the like.

Based on his reanalysis of these data Samson was able to state that within the health and beauty product category usage of a product had a pervasive effect on consumers' pre-trial intentions to recommend a product as well the number of word-of-mouth conversations generated by the trial and their effectiveness. In contrast, frequency of product use only affected significantly the number of word-of-mouth conversations. He also found that, compared to non-users, being a loyal user of a product in the trial had a negative effect on the effectiveness of the word-of-mouth conversations generated by the trial. Based on this, he concluded that loyal users were not necessarily the best targets of word-of-mouth marketing campaigns.

Ad hoc surveys are usually one-off surveys and are far more specific in their subject matter. They include data from questionnaires that have been undertaken by independent researchers as well as interviews undertaken by organisations and governments. Because of their ad hoc nature, you will probably find it more difficult to discover relevant surveys. However, it may be that an organisation in which you are undertaking research has conducted its own questionnaire or interview-based survey on an issue related to your research. Some organisations will provide you with a report containing aggregated data; others may be willing to let you undertake further analyses using the raw data from this ad hoc survey. Alternatively, you may be able to gain access to and use raw data from an ad hoc survey that has been deposited in a data archive (Section 8.3).

Multiple-source secondary data

Multiple-source secondary data can be compiled entirely from documentary or survey secondary data, or can be an amalgam of the two. The key factor is that different data sets have been combined to form another data set prior to your accessing the data. One of the more common types of multiple-source data that you are likely to come across are online compilations of company information stored in databases such as *Amadeus* (Table 8.1). This contains comparable financial data about over 18 million public and private European companies. Other multiple-source secondary data include the various share price listings for different stock markets reported in the financial pages of quality newspapers. Whilst newspapers are usually available online, there may be a charge to view their web pages. Fortunately university libraries usually have recent paper copies, whilst national and regional newspapers can also be accessed using online databases such as *Nexis* and, for older newspapers, *British Newspapers 1600–1900* (Table 8.1).

The way in which a multiple-source data set has been compiled will dictate the sorts of research question(s) or objectives with which you can use it. One method of compilation is to extract and combine selected comparable variables from a number of surveys or from the same survey that has been repeated a number of times to provide **longitudinal** data. For many undergraduate and taught master's courses' research projects, this is one of the few ways in which you will be able to obtain data over a long period. Other ways of obtaining time-series data are to use a series of company documents, such as appointment letters or public and administrative records, as sources from which to create your own longitudinal secondary data set. Examples of such data sets include the UK Employment Department's stoppages at work data held by the UK Data Archive (Table 8.2) and those derived by researchers from nineteenth and early twentieth century population census returns, the raw data for which can often be accessed through national governments' information gateways such as the UK's Office for National Statistics (Table 8.2).

Data can also be compiled for the same population over time using a series of 'snapshots' to form **cohort studies**. Such studies are relatively rare, owing to the difficulty of maintaining contact with members of the cohort from year to year. An example is the UK television series 'Seven Up', which has followed a cohort since they were schoolchildren at seven-year intervals since 1964.

Secondary data from different sources can also be combined, if they have the same geographical basis, to form area-based data sets (Hakim 2000). Such data sets usually draw together quantifiable information and statistics. They are commonly compiled by national governments for their country and their component standard economic planning regions and by regional and local administrations for their own region. Such area-based multiple-source data sets are increasingly only available online either through national governments' information gateways, regional administration's information gateways or data archives (Table 8.2). Widely used European examples include the European Union's annually published *Europe in Figures: Eurostat Yearbook* (Eurostat 2010) and collections such as Eurostat's (2011) statistical data for member countries.

8.3 Locating secondary data

Unless you are approaching your research project with the intention of analysing one specific secondary data set that you already know well, your first step will be to ascertain whether the data you need are available. Your research question(s), objectives and the literature you have already reviewed will guide this. For many research projects you are likely to be unsure as to whether the data you require are available as secondary data. Fortunately, there are a number of pointers to the sorts of data that are likely to be available.

The breadth of data discussed in the previous sections serves only to emphasise that, despite the increasing importance of the Internet, potential secondary data may be stored in a variety of locations. Finding relevant secondary data requires detective work, which has two interlinked stages:

1 establishing whether the sort of data you require are likely to be available as secondary data;
2 locating the precise data you require.

Establishing the likely availability of secondary data

There are a number of clues to whether the secondary data you require are likely to be available. As part of your literature review you will have already read journal articles and books on your chosen topic. Where these have made use of secondary data (as in Box 8.3), they will provide you with an idea of the sort of data that are available. In addition, these articles and books should contain full references to the sources of the data. Where these refer to published secondary data such as those stored in online databases or multiple-source or survey reports it is usually relatively easy to find the original source. Your university library will have subscriptions to a number of these online databases (Table 8.1) and is well worth browsing to establish the secondary data that are available. Quality national newspapers are also often a good source as they often report summary findings of recent reports (Box 8.4). Your tutors have probably already suggested that you read a quality national newspaper on a regular basis, advice we would fully endorse as it is an excellent way of keeping up to date with recent events in the business world. In addition, there are now many online news services, although some charge a subscription.

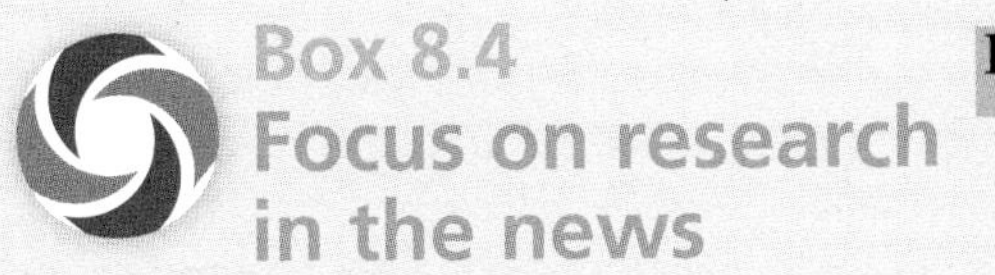

Box 8.4
Focus on research in the news
FT

University fees system mystery to many

One-third of children wrongly believe they will need to pay tuition fees upfront if they wish to go to an English university, underlining the challenge faced by the government as it sets out its higher education strategy this week. The finding is from a poll by the Sutton Trust, the social mobility charity, which found that only one-third of 11 to 16 year olds understands that the government will lend them money to pay fees and that student loans are not conventional debt.

Sir Peter Lampl, chairman of the Sutton Trust and England's leading educational philanthropist, said: 'Our survey reveals widespread misunderstanding of the new fees system among school pupils.' Martin Lewis, founder of MoneySavingExpert.com, is heading a taskforce to combat the misinformation problem. He said: 'The political spittle . . . has clouded many people's view of the practical impact on students' pockets.' Gareth Thomas, shadow universities minister, said that he shared 'the concern that too many young people will be put off from going to university in the future'.

The survey results find that older children are better informed, with half of 15–16 year olds understanding that they do not need to save up to go to an English university or start repaying their loans immediately upon graduation. Sir Peter also noted that there was still a strong appetite for a university education. The survey, he said, 'once again demonstrates high levels of aspirations to go to university among 11–16 year olds of all backgrounds who realise education is increasingly the key to future employment'. Some 78 per cent of the 2739 pupils surveyed said they were fairly likely or very likely to go to university, with a further 10 per cent saying they were uncertain. These figures are similar to those found last year, before it was known that the cap on tuition fees, now £3290, would rise to £9000.

The survey results have been released as the government is finalising its long-delayed white paper on higher education, due for release this week. The principal aim of the document will be to allow popular universities to expand, so sharpening the competitive pressure to which universities are subjected. A spokesman for the business department, which has responsibility for universities, said: 'The government is committed to making sure no one is put off going to university because they do not understand how the new system works. It is encouraging that close to a third of the 11–16 year olds questioned in the survey already understand that going to university will continue to depend on ability – not the ability to pay.'

Source: From 'University fees system mystery to many', Chris Cook, *Financial Times*, 27 June 2011.

References for unpublished and documentary secondary data are often less specific, referring to 'unpublished survey results' or an 'in-house company survey'. Although these may be insufficient to locate or access the actual secondary data, they still provide useful clues about the sort of data that might be found within organisations and which might prove useful. Subject-specific textbooks such as Bradley's (2010) *Marketing Research: Tools and Techniques* can provide a clear indication of secondary data sources available in your research area, in this instance marketing. Other textbooks, such as Kavanagh and Thite's (2009) *Human Resource Information Systems: Basics, Applications and Future Directions*, can provide you with valuable clues about the sort of documentary secondary data that are likely to exist within organisations' management information systems.

Establishing the availability of relevant web-based materials generated by online communities which can be used as secondary data such as blogs and pages set up by social networking sites' user groups can be even more difficult. With the number of blogs growing rapidly and more than 160 million blogs now in existence (Nielson Company 2011), there are almost certainly going to be blogs about your research topic. However, as we discuss later in this section, actually finding them is more difficult! In contrast, although estimates suggest similar rapid growth for organisation web pages, with more than 105 million .com and .net domain names in existence (VeriSign Inc. 2011), finding these organisations on their Facebook pages is far easier.

Tertiary literature such as indexes and catalogues can also help you to locate secondary data (Sections 3.3–3.5). Online searchable data archive catalogues, such as for the UK Data Archive, may prove a useful source of the sorts of secondary data available (Table 8.2). This archive holds the UK's largest collection of qualitative and quantitative digital social science and humanities data sets for use by the research community (UK Data Archive 2011). These data have been acquired from academic, commercial and government sources, and relate mainly to post-war Britain. However, it should be remembered that the supply of data and documentation for all of the UK Data Archive's data sets is charged at cost, and there may be additional administrative and royalty charges.

Increasingly, online indexes and catalogues are being provided with direct linkages to downloadable files, often in spreadsheet format. Government websites (Table 8.2) such as the UK government's *Direct.gov* and the European Union's *Europa* provide useful gateways to a wide range of reports, legislative documents and statistical data as well as links to other sites. However, although data from such government sources are usually of good quality, those from other sources may be neither valid nor reliable. It is important, therefore, that you evaluate the suitability of such secondary data for your research (Section 8.5).

Finally, informal discussions are also often a useful source. Acknowledged experts, colleagues, librarians or your project tutor may well have knowledge of the sorts of data that might be available.

Locating secondary data

Once you have ascertained that secondary data are likely to exist, you need to find their precise location. For secondary data held in online databases to which your university subscribes, published by governments or held by data archives this will be relatively easy, especially where other researchers have made use of them and a full reference exists! All you will need to do is search the appropriate online database (Table 8.1) data archive or gateway (Table 8.2), find and download your data. Locating published secondary data held by specialist libraries is also relatively straightforward. Within the UK, specialist libraries with specific subject collections can usually be located using the most recent Chartered Institute of Library and Information Professional's (2010) publication *Libraries and Information Services in the UK and ROI*. If you are unsure where to start, confess your ignorance and ask a librarian. This will usually result in a great deal of helpful advice, as well as saving you time. Once the appropriate abstracting tool or catalogue has been located and its use demonstrated, it can be searched using similar techniques to those employed in your literature search (Section 3.5).

Data that are held by organisations are more difficult to locate. For within-organisation data we have found that the information or data manager within the appropriate department is most likely to know the precise secondary data that are held. This is the person who will also help or hinder your eventual access to the data and can be thought of as the gatekeeper to the information (Section 6.2).

One way to locate relevant web-based materials generated by online communities is to use Blog Content Management Systems such as Blogster and Blogit, which contain their own search engines, to identify potentially relevant blogs (Hookway 2008). Another is to use a general search engine such as Google or Bing. However, as highlighted by Hookway (2008), who spent four months working through some 200 blogs composed of an indeterminate number of postings only to locate 11 that were useful, this can be extremely time-consuming! You may find it easier to set up your own blog and collect primary data (Section 10.9). In contrast, home and Facebook pages of organisations can be located easily using a general search engine or, in the case of UK-based companies, the links provided by the Yellow Pages UK subject directory (Table 3.5). However, you will still need to assess their relevance.

Data sets on the Internet can also be located using information gateways such as the University of Michigan's Documents Center and archives such as the UK Data Archive (Table 8.2), or search engines where you search for all possible locations that match search terms associated with your research question(s) or objectives (Section 3.5). In some cases data will be stored at sites hosted by companies and professional organisations or trade associations and other than for aggregated data there is likely to be a charge. Additional guidance regarding how to use general search engines such as Google is given in Marketing Insights' *Smarter Internet Searching Guide*, which is available via this book's web page. However, searching for relevant data is often very time-consuming. In addition, although the amount of data on the Internet is increasing rapidly, much of it is, in our experience, of dubious quality. Consequently the evaluation of secondary data sources is crucial (Section 8.5).

Once you have located a possible secondary data set, you need to be certain that it will meet your needs. For most forms of secondary data the easiest way is to obtain and evaluate a sample copy of the data and a detailed description of how it was collected. For survey-derived data this is may involve some cost. One alternative is to download and evaluate detailed definitions for the data set variables (which include how they are coded; Section 12.2) and the documentation that describes how the data were collected. This evaluation process is discussed in Section 8.5

8.4 Advantages and disadvantages of secondary data

Advantages

May have fewer resource requirements

For many research questions and objectives the main advantage of using secondary data is the enormous saving in resources, in particular your time and money (Ghauri and Grønhaug 2010). In general, it is much less expensive to use secondary data than to collect the data yourself. Consequently, you may be able to analyse far larger data sets such as those collected by governments. You will also have more time to think about theoretical aims and substantive issues, as your data will already be collected, and subsequently you will be able to spend more time and effort analysing and interpreting the data. If you need your data quickly, secondary data may be the only viable alternative. In addition, they are often higher-quality data than could be obtained by collecting your own (Smith 2006).

Unobtrusive

Using secondary data within organisations may also have the advantage that, because they have already been collected, they provide an unobtrusive measure. Cowton (1998) refers to this advantage as eavesdropping, emphasising its benefits for sensitive situations.

Longitudinal studies may be feasible

For many research projects time constraints mean that secondary data provide the only possibility of undertaking longitudinal studies. This is possible either by creating your own or by using an existing multiple-source data set (Section 8.2). Comparative research may also be possible if comparable data are available. You may find this to be of particular use for research questions and objectives that require regional or international comparisons. However, you need to ensure that the data you are comparing were collected and recorded using methods that are comparable. Comparisons relying on unpublished data or data that are currently unavailable in that format, such as the creation of new tables from existing census data, are likely to be expensive, as such tabulations will have to be specially prepared. In addition, your research is dependent on access being granted by the owners of the data, principally governments (Dale et al. 1988), although this is becoming easier as more data are made available via the Internet. In addition, many countries are enshrining increased rights of access to information held by public authorities through freedom of information legislation such as the UK's Freedom of Information Act 2005. This gives a general right to access to recorded information held by public authorities, although a charge may be payable (Information Commissioner's Office 2011). However, this is dependent upon your request not being contrary to relevant data protection legislation or agreements (Section 6.7).

Can provide comparative and contextual data

Often it can be useful to compare data that you have collected with secondary data. This means that you can place your own findings within a more general context or, alternatively, triangulate your findings (Section 5.3). If you have used a questionnaire, perhaps to collect data from a sample of potential customers, secondary data such as a national Census can be used to assess the generalisability of findings, in other words how representative these data are of the total population (Section 7.2).

Can result in unforeseen discoveries

Reanalysing secondary data can also lead to unforeseen or unexpected new discoveries. Dale et al. (1988) cite establishing the link between smoking and lung cancer as an example of such a serendipitous discovery. In this example the link was established through secondary analysis of medical records that had not been collected with the intention of exploring any such relationship.

Permanence of data

Unlike data that you collect yourself, secondary data generally provide a source of data that is often permanent and available in a form that may be checked relatively easily by others (Denscombe 2007). This means that the data and your research findings are more open to public scrutiny.

Disadvantages

May be collected for a purpose that does not match your need

Data that you collect yourself will be collected with a specific purpose in mind: to answer your research question(s) and to meet your objectives. Unfortunately, secondary data will have been collected for a specific purpose that differs from your research question(s) or objectives (Denscombe 2007). Consequently, the data you are considering may be inappropriate to your research question. If this is the case then you need to find an alternative source, or collect the data yourself! More probably, you will be able to answer your research question or address your objective only partially. Common reasons for this include the data being collected a few years earlier and so not being current, or the methods of collection differing between the original data sources which have been amalgamated subsequently to form the secondary data set you intend to use (Box 8.5). For example, the 2011 UK National Census question on marital status

Box 8.5 Focus on student research

The pitfalls of secondary data

Alison Wolf is the Sir Roy Griffiths Professor of Public Sector Management at King's College, London. In a 2007 article in *The Times Higher Education Supplement* (Wolf 2007), she issues some warnings to students using secondary data in their research, particularly in an era when such data are readily available on the Internet. Her main concern is the lack of questioning that many of us adopt when approaching secondary data. In her view, many of us 'have a tendency to assume that quantitative data must be out there waiting to be found: on the Web, organised and collated. How the figures get there and who collected the data and analysed them are not questions they seem to ask. Nor do they probe definitions (let alone response rates) – or not unless and until they start trying to locate, manipulate and integrate a variety of data on a specific subject' (Wolf 2007).

According to Wolf, some of the major pitfalls are assuming that samples are representative; and that the people who filled in questionnaires all did so in such a way that we can put faith in the results. They may not have been truthful in their responses, have taken the questions seriously or, indeed, have understood the questions fully. Moreover, Wolf notes that it should not be assumed that whoever coded and entered the data knew what they were doing; and that it was clear what all the observations meant.

Wolf gives the example of one of her recent students who wanted to track how many history graduates from a given university enter teaching over a 20-year period. She points out that 'teaching' as a recorded student destination sometimes includes further education as well as schools, sometimes includes higher education as well, sometimes neither. Also, what counts as a 'history' graduate may not be clear.

Wolf sounds other warnings, using the example of official UK government statistics. First, statistics that were routinely calculated can suddenly disappear. She gives the example of the decision, by the Office for National Statistics, suddenly to stop calculating average non-manual earnings. This caused major problems for one of her students. In addition, and more frequently, definitions change constantly in ways that seem to be dictated by changing government priorities which makes it difficult to track changes over time. Wolf cites the example of education, where statistics are reported in terms of performance targets that keep changing. She concludes that this is a serious matter as good statistics are at the heart of governmental accountability, as well as good policymaking.

asked 'What is your legal marital or same-sex civil partnership status?' whilst the 2001 question on marital status asked 'What is your marital status?' (Office for National Statistics 2011a), reflecting changes in social norms and legislation. Where the data are non-current and you have access to primary data, such as in a research project that is examining an issue within an organisation, you are likely to have to combine secondary and primary data. Alternatively the secondary data you rely on may 'leave things out because the people whose information we are using don't think it's important, even if we do' (Becker 1998: 101).

Access may be difficult or costly

Where data have been collected for commercial reasons, gaining access may be difficult or costly. Market research reports, such as those produced by Mintel or KeyNote (Table 8.2), may cost a great deal if the report(s) that you require are not available online via your library.

Aggregations and definitions may be unsuitable

The fact that secondary data were collected for a different purpose may result in other, including ethical (Section 6.6), problems. Much of the secondary data you use is likely to be in published reports. As part of the compilation process, data will have been aggregated in some way. These aggregations, while meeting the requirements of the original research, may not be quite so suitable for your research. The definitions of data variables may not be the most appropriate for your research question(s) or objectives. In addition, where you are intending to combine data sets, definitions may differ markedly or have been revised over time (Box 8.6). Alternatively, the documents you are using may represent the interpretations of those who produced them, rather than offer an objective picture of reality.

No real control over data quality

Although many of the secondary data sets available from governments and data archives are of higher quality than you could ever collect yourself, this is not always the case. For this reason care must be taken and data sources must be evaluated carefully, as outlined in Section 8.5.

Initial purpose may affect how data are presented

When using data that are presented as part of a report you also need to be aware of the purpose of that report and the impact that this will have on the way the data are presented. This is especially so for internal organisational documents and external documents such as published company reports and newspaper reports. Reichman (1962; cited by Stewart and Kamins 1993) emphasises this point referring to newspapers, although the sentiments apply to many documents. He argues that newspapers select what they consider to be the most significant points and emphasise these at the expense of supporting data. This, Reichman states, is not a criticism as the purpose of the reporting is to bring these points to the attention of readers rather than to provide a full and detailed account. However, if we generalise from these ideas, we can see that the culture, predispositions and ideals of those who originally collected and collated the secondary data will have influenced the nature of these data at least to some extent. For these reasons you must evaluate carefully any secondary data you intend to use. Possible ways of doing this are discussed in the next section.

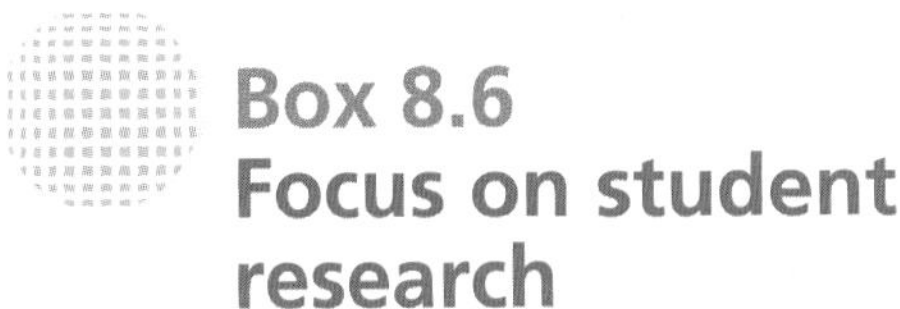

Box 8.6 Focus on student research

Changing definitions

As part of his research, Jeremy wished to use longitudinal data on the numbers of males and females disaggregated by some form of social grouping. Using the UK government's national statistics website (Table 8.2), he quickly found and downloaded data which classified males and females using the National Statistics Socio-economic Classification (NS-SEC). However, this classification appeared to have been used only from 2001. Prior to this date, two separate classifications had been used: social class (SC) and socio-economic group (SEG), for which much longer time series of data were available. Before arranging an appointment with his project tutor to discuss this potential problem, Jeremy made a note of the two classifications:

NS-SEC		SC	
1	Higher managerial and professional occupations	I	Professional
2	Lower managerial and professional occupations	II	Managerial and technical
3	Intermediate occupations	IIIa	Skilled non-manual
4	Small employers and own account workers	IIIb	Skilled manual
5	Lower supervisory and technical occupations	IV	Semi-skilled
6	Semi-routine occupations	V	Unskilled
7	Routine occupations		

During their meeting later that week, Jeremy's tutor referred him to research on the NS-SEC which compared this with the old measures of SC and SEG and made suggestions regarding the continuity of the measures. Jeremy noted down the reference:

Heath, A., Martin, J. and Beerten, R. (2003) 'Old and new social class measures – a comparison', in D. Rose and D.J. Pevalin (eds) *A Researcher's Guide to the National Statistics Socio-economic Classification.* London: Sage, pp. 226–42.

8.5 Evaluating secondary data sources

Secondary data must be viewed with the same caution as any primary data that you collect. You need to be sure that:

- they will enable you to answer your research question(s) and to meet your objectives;
- the benefits associated with their use will be greater than the costs;
- you will be allowed access to the data (Sections 6.2 to 6.4).

Secondary sources that appear relevant at first may not on closer examination be appropriate to your research question(s) or objectives. It is therefore important to evaluate the suitability of secondary data sources for your research.

Stewart and Kamins (1993) argue that, if you are using secondary data, you are at an advantage compared with researchers using primary data. Because the data already

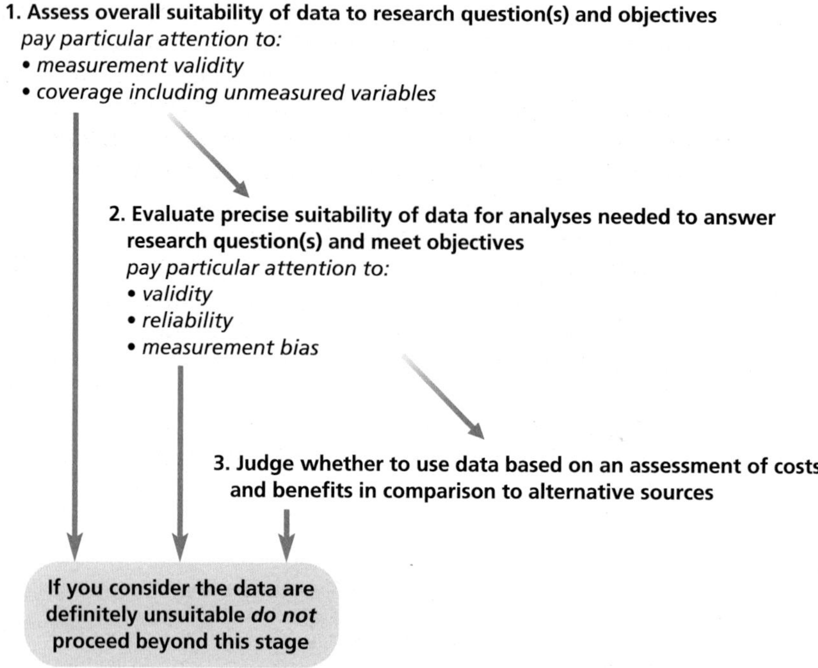

Figure 8.2 Evaluating potential secondary data sources

exist you can evaluate them prior to use. The time you spend evaluating any potential secondary data source is time well spent, as rejecting unsuitable data earlier can save much wasted time later! Such investigations are even more important when you have a number of possible secondary data sources you could use. Most authors suggest a range of validity and reliability (Section 5.8) criteria against which you can evaluate potential secondary data. These, we believe, can be incorporated into a three-stage process (Figure 8.2).

Alongside this process you need also to consider the accessibility of the secondary data. For some secondary data sources, in particular those available via the Internet or in your library, this will not be a problem. It may, however, still necessitate long hours working in the library if the sources are 'for reference only'. For other data sources, such as those within organisations, you need to obtain permission prior to gaining access. This will be necessary even if you are working for the organisation. These issues are discussed in Sections 6.2 to 6.4, so we can now consider the evaluation process in more detail.

Overall suitability

Measurement validity

One of the most important criteria for the suitability of any data set is **measurement validity.** Secondary data that fail to provide you with the information that you need to answer your research question(s) or meet your objectives will result in invalid answers (Smith 2006). Often when you are using secondary survey data you will find that the measures used do not quite match those that you need. For example, a manufacturing organisation may record monthly sales whereas you are interested in monthly orders.

This may cause you a problem when you undertake your analyses believing that you have found a relationship with sales whereas in fact your relationship is with the number of orders. Alternatively, you may be using minutes of company meetings as a proxy for what actually happened in those meetings. These are likely to reflect a particular interpretation of what happened, the events being recorded from a particular viewpoint, often the chairperson's. You therefore need to be cautious before accepting such records at face value (Denscombe 2007).

Unfortunately, there are no clear solutions to problems of measurement invalidity. All you can do is try to evaluate the extent of the data's validity and make your own decision (Box 8.7). A common way of doing this is to examine how other researchers have coped with this problem for a similar secondary data set in a similar context. If they found that the measures, while not exact, were suitable, then you can be more certain that they will be suitable for your research question(s) and objectives. If they had problems, then you may be able to incorporate their suggestions as to how to overcome them. Your literature search (Sections 3.4 and 3.5) will probably have identified other such studies already.

Coverage and unmeasured variables

The other important suitability criterion is **coverage**. You need to be sure that the secondary data cover the population about which you need data, for the time period you need, and contain data variables that will enable you to answer your research question(s) and to meet your objectives. For all secondary data sets coverage will be concerned with two issues:

- ensuring that unwanted data are or can be excluded;
- ensuring that sufficient data remain for analyses to be undertaken once unwanted data have been excluded (Hakim 2000).

When analysing secondary survey data, you will need to exclude those data that are not relevant to your research question(s) or objectives. Service companies, for example, need to be excluded if you are concerned only with manufacturing companies. However, in doing this it may be that insufficient data remain for you to undertake the quantitative analyses you require (Sections 12.4 and 12.5). For documentary sources, you will need to ensure that the data contained relate to the population identified in your research. For example, check that the social media content on an organisation's social media pages actually relate to the organisation. Where you are intending to undertake a longitudinal study, you also need to ensure that the data are available for the entire period in which you are interested.

Some secondary data sets, in particular those collected using a survey strategy, may not include variables you have identified as necessary for your analysis. These are termed unmeasured variables. Their absence may not be particularly important if you are undertaking descriptive research. However, it could drastically affect the outcome of explanatory research as a potentially important variable has been excluded.

Precise suitability

Reliability and validity

The reliability and validity (Section 5.8) you ascribe to secondary data are functions of the method by which the data were collected and the source. You can make a quick assessment of these by looking at the source of the data. Dochartaigh (2007) and others

Box 8.7 Focus on Student Research

Using a Social Networking site as a source of secondary data

Mike's research project was concerned with the impact of social media on brand awareness and brand loyalty. He was particularly interested in how small automobile manufacturers used social networking sites in their marketing, His research question was: 'How effectively do small automotive manufacturers use social networking sites in their marketing?'

Mike was aware from the academic (Neelotpaul 2010) and trade (Mangold and Faulds 2009) literature that social media was of major importance in marketing and could influence various aspects of consumer behaviour such as product awareness, information acquisition and purchase behaviour. Based on the academic literature on branding and social media, Mike argued that, to use social media most effectively, organisations needed to follow a three-stage process of providing material of interest, engaging people and using them as advocates for their products.

Mike was also aware from Internet searches and his own interest in cars that automotive manufacturers had each created their own Facebook presence, providing content, and using their pages to interact with their fans (customers). Mike was already a fan of the Morgan Motor Company's Facebook page which was 'liked' by over 800 Facebook members. Morgan's wall contained company posts about their products and comments and other posts from fans. Although the data in these posts were not originally intended to answer Mike's research question, after careful evaluation he considered further analysis of the posts and comments would enable him to do this.

Because Morgan's Facebook page was open to everyone, Mike considered that the information was in the public domain and so he could use it for his research project without seeking consent. He now needed to analyse the posts (data) available on Morgan's Facebook wall to establish the extent to which this form of social media was being used by the organisation to provide consumers with material of interest, engage them and allow them to become advocates for the product.

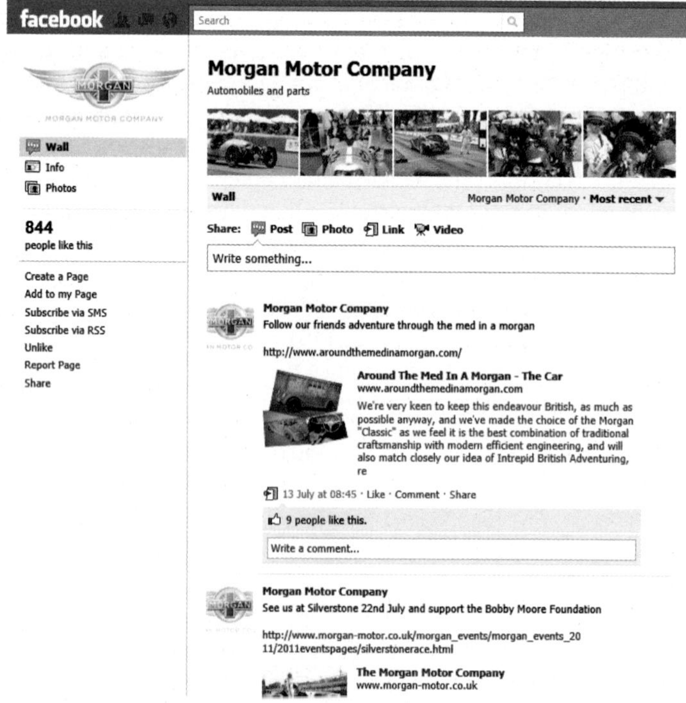

Source: © Morgan Motor Company, 2011. Reproduced with permission

refer to this as assessing the authority or reputation of the source. Survey data from large, well-known organisations such as those found in Mintel and Key Note market research reports (Table 8.1) are likely to be reliable and trustworthy. The continued existence of such organisations is dependent on the credibility of their data. Consequently, their procedures for collecting and compiling the data are likely to be well thought through and accurate. Survey data from government organisations are also likely to be reliable, although they may not always be perceived as such (Box 8.8). However, you will probably find the validity of documentary data such as organisations' records more difficult to assess. While organisations may argue that their records are reliable, there are often inconsistencies and inaccuracies. You therefore need also to examine the method by which the data were collected and try to ascertain the precision needed by the original (primary) user.

Dochartaigh (2007) suggests a number of areas for initial assessment of the authority of documents available via the Internet. These, we believe, can be adapted to assess the authority of all types of secondary data. First, as suggested in the previous paragraph, it is important to discover the person or organisation responsible for the data and to be able to obtain additional information through which you can assess the reliability of the source. For data in printed publications this is usually reasonably straightforward (Section 3.6).

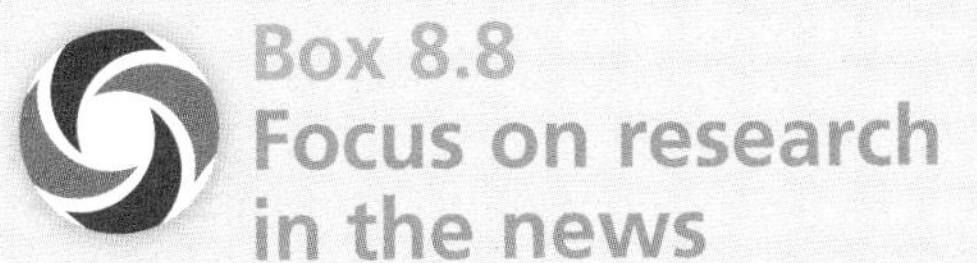

Box 8.8
Focus on research in the news
FT

Builders reject ONS sector data

The Office for National Statistics is looking into whether a change in the way it collects data about the construction industry has distorted reported levels of activity, with gross domestic product growth likely to have been stronger in the first quarter of 2011 than had been reported, but weaker at the end of 2010.

Construction executives said a change to the methods used for the agency's monthly survey led companies to submit data about business completed up to six weeks earlier. Until 2010, the survey measured the value of new orders won during the month. The new survey asks for the volume of output in the period. 'It's not just a problem with this first quarter, but for a while now we've been concerned about the reliability of the [ONS] numbers', said Geoff Cooper, chief executive of Travis Perkins, the UK's largest builders' merchant. This view was echoed by executives from contractors and building materials companies including Kier, Tarmac and McLaren Construction.

If the complaints are correct, UK GDP is likely to have grown about 0.8 per cent in the first quarter of 2011 rather than the 0.5 per cent reported. The higher level of output is in line with forecasts in March from the Office for Budget Responsibility and in February from the Bank of England. However, any upgrade also suggests the economy contracted by more than the 0.5 per cent decline in GDP in the fourth quarter of 2010. The ONS said activity was 'flattish' after accounting for the effects of snow. Now, it emerges, output may have contracted. Construction accounts for about 6 per cent of national output but has been volatile since Britain emerged from recession and has affected calculations of GDP disproportionately.

Economists expressed concern about the strength of first-quarter GDP in early April when construction orders for February were made public. These showed that the expected rebound from snow-related delays not only failed to materialise but that orders fell. Economists scaled back forecasts for GDP growth for the quarter and futures markets, where predictions of a rate rise in May prevailed, began to roll back the timing of a near-term rise in spite of high inflation. Joe Grice, ONS chief economist, said the agency routinely evaluated the performance of all its output and had 'no reason at present to believe the construction series is giving a distorted picture of what is going on in the sector'.

Source: From 'Builders reject ONS sector data', Ed Hammond and Norma Cohen (2011) *Financial Times*, 8 May.

However, for secondary data obtained via the Internet it may be more difficult. Although organisation names, such as the 'Center for Research into . . .' or 'Institute for the Study of . . . ', may appear initially to be credible, publication via the Internet is not controlled, and such names are sometimes used to suggest pseudo-academic credibility. Dochartaigh (2007) therefore suggests that you look also for a copyright statement and the existence of published documents relating to the data to help validation. The former of these, when it exists, can provide an indication of who is responsible for the data. The latter, he argues, reinforces the data's authority, as printed publications are regarded as more reliable. In addition, Internet sources often contain an email address or other means of contacting the author for comments and questions about the Internet site and its contents. However, beware of applying these criteria too rigidly as sometimes the most authoritative web pages do not include the information outlined above. Dochartaigh (2007) suggests that this is because those with most authority often feel the least need to proclaim it!

For all secondary data, a detailed assessment of the validity and reliability will involve you in an assessment of the method or methods used to collect the data (Dale et al. 1988). These may be provided as hyperlinks for Internet-based data sets. Alternatively, they may be discussed in the methodology section of an associated report. Your assessment will involve looking at who were responsible for collecting or recording the information and examining the context in which the data were collected. From this you should gain some feeling regarding the likelihood of potential errors or biases. In addition, you need to look at the process by which the data were selected and collected or recorded. Where sampling has been used to select cases (usually as part of a survey strategy), the sampling procedure adopted and the associated sampling error and response rates (Section 7.2) will give clues to validity. Secondary data collected using a questionnaire with a high response rate are also likely to be more reliable than those from one with a low response rate. However, commercial providers of high-quality, reliable data sets may be unwilling to disclose details about how data were collected. This is particularly the case where these organisations see the methodology as important to their competitive advantage.

For some documentary sources, such as blogs, social media pages and transcripts of interviews or meetings, it is unlikely that there will be a formal methodology describing how the data were collected. The reliability of these data will therefore be difficult to assess, although you may be able to discover the context in which the data were collected. For example, blogs, emails and memos contain no formal obligation for the writer to give a full and accurate portrayal of events. Rather they are written from a personal point of view and expect the recipient to be aware of the context (Hookway 2008). This means that these data are more likely to be useful as a source of the writer's perceptions and views than as an objective account of reality. The fact that you did not collect and were not present when these data were collected will also affect your analyses. Dale et al. (1988) argue that full analyses of in-depth interview data require an understanding derived from participating in social interactions that cannot be fully recorded on tape or by transcript.

The validity and reliability of collection methods for survey data will be easier to assess where you have a clear explanation of the techniques used to collect the data (Box 8.9). This needs to include a clear explanation of any sampling techniques used and response rates (discussed earlier) as well as a copy of the data collection instrument, which is usually a questionnaire. By examining the questions by which data were collected, you will gain a further indication of the validity.

Where data have been compiled, as in a report, you need to pay careful attention to how these data were analysed and how the results are reported. Where percentages (or proportions) are used without actually giving the totals on which these figures are based, you need to examine the data very carefully. For example, a 50 per cent increase in the

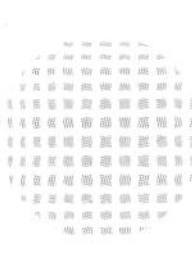

Box 8.9 Focus on student research

Assessing the suitability of online multiple-source longitudinal data

As part of her research project on changing consumer spending patterns in Europe, Jocelyn wished to establish how the cost of living had altered in the European Union since the accession of the 10 new member states in 2004. Other research that she had read as part of her literature review had utilised the European Union's Harmonized Index of Consumer Prices (HICPs). She therefore decided to see whether this information was available via the Internet from the European Union's *Europa* information gateway. She clicked on the link to the *Eurostat Official EU Statistics* home page and she searched for 'Harmonized Indices of Consumer Prices'. This revealed that there were publications, monthly data and indices data of consumer prices.

Jocelyn then clicked on the link to the Harmonized Indices of Consumer Prices (HCIP) Metadata and read the data description. As the data were relevant to her research she clicked on and viewed the content revealed by a number of different links, eventually finding the one that enabled her to specify the data she wanted 'HICP (2005=100) – Annual data'.

She clicked on this link and looked briefly at the data table. It appeared to be suitable in terms of coverage for her research so she downloaded and saved it as an Excel spreadsheet on her MP3 player.

Jocelyn was happy with the data's overall suitability and the credibility of the source, the data having been compiled for the European Union using data collected each year by each of the member states. She also discovered that the actual data collected were governed by a series of European Union regulations.

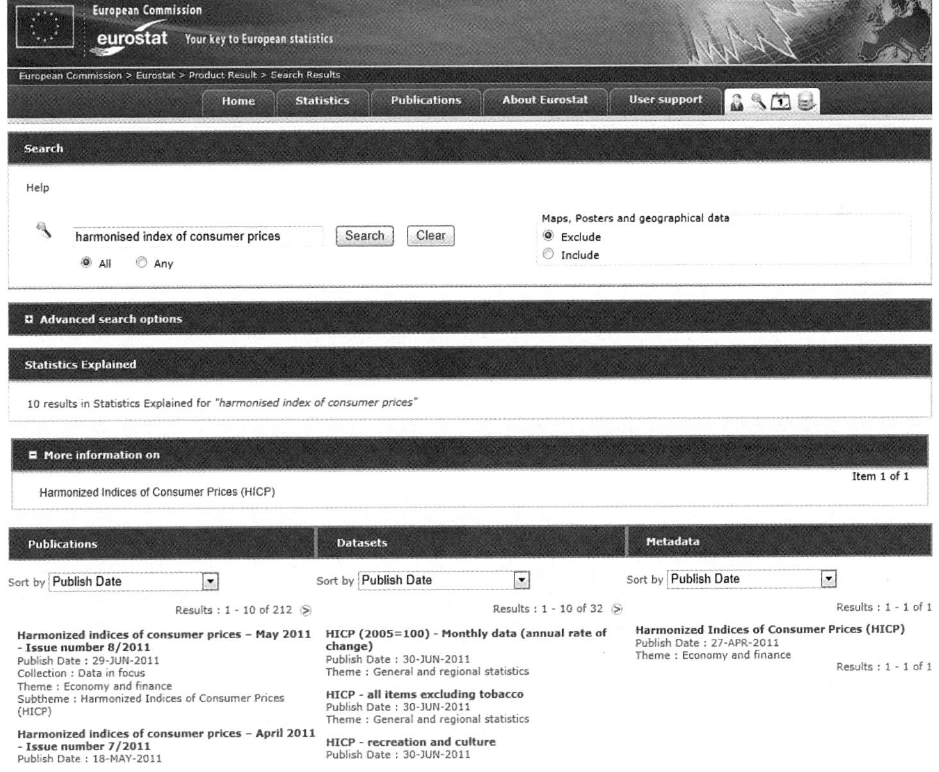

Source: Eurostat (2011). Copyright European Communities, 2011. Reproduced with permission

Box 8.9 Focus on student research *(continued)*

In order to be certain about the precise suitability of the HICPs, Jocelyn needed to find out exactly how the index had been calculated and how the data on which it was based had been collected. Hyperlinks from the data description web page provided an overview of how the index was calculated, summarising the nature of goods and services that were included. The data for the HICPs were collected in each member state using a combination of visits to local retailers and service providers and central collection (via mail, telephone, email and the Internet), over 1 million price observations being used each month! One potential problem was also highlighted: there was no uniform basket of goods and services applying to all member states. Rather, the precise nature of some goods and services included in the HICPs varied from country to country, reflecting the reality of expenditure in each of the countries. Jocelyn decided that this would not present too great a problem as she was going to use these data only to contextualise her research.

The Eurostat web pages emphasised that the HICP was a price rather than a cost of living index. However, it also emphasised that, despite conceptual differences between price and the cost of living, there were unlikely to be substantial differences in practice. Jocelyn therefore decided to use the HICPs as a surrogate for the cost of living.

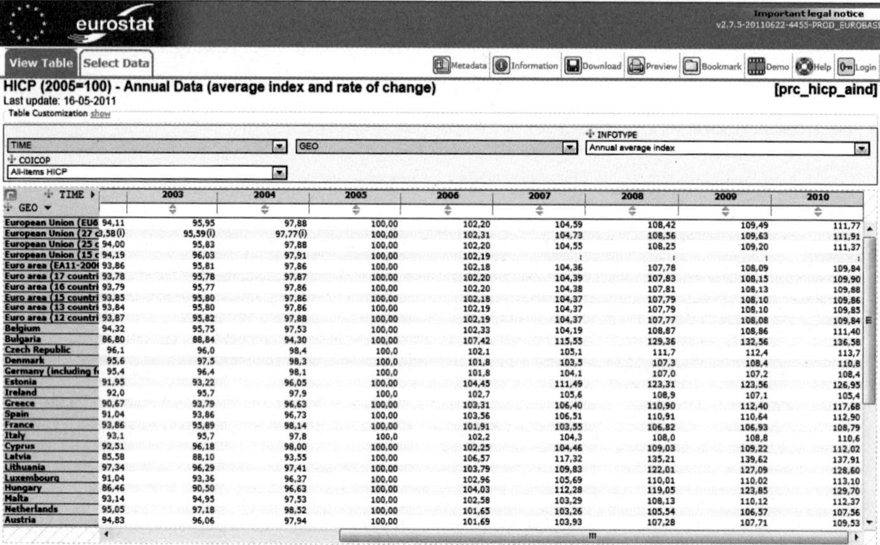

GEO / TIME		2003	2004	2005	2006	2007	2008	2009	2010
European Union (EU6	94,11	95,95	97,88	100,00	102,20	104,59	108,42	109,49	111,77
European Union (27 c	93,58 (i)	95,59 (i)	97,77 (i)	100,00	102,31	104,73	108,56	109,63	111,91
European Union (25 c	94,00	95,83	97,88	100,00	102,20	104,55	108,25	109,20	111,37
European Union (15 c	94,19	96,03	97,91	100,00	102,19	:	:	:	:
Euro area (EA11-200(	93,86	95,81	97,86	100,00	102,18	104,36	107,78	108,09	109,84
Euro area (17 countri	93,78	95,78	97,87	100,00	102,20	104,39	107,83	108,15	109,90
Euro area (16 countri	93,79	95,77	97,86	100,00	102,20	104,38	107,81	108,13	109,88
Euro area (15 countri	93,85	95,80	97,86	100,00	102,18	104,37	107,79	108,10	109,86
Euro area (13 countri	93,84	95,80	97,86	100,00	102,19	104,37	107,79	108,10	109,85
Euro area (12 countri	93,87	95,82	97,88	100,00	102,19	104,37	107,77	108,08	109,84
Belgium	94,32	95,75	97,53	100,00	102,33	104,19	108,87	108,86	111,40
Bulgaria	86,80	88,84	94,30	100,00	107,42	115,55	129,36	132,56	136,58
Czech Republic	96,1	96,0	98,4	100,0	102,1	105,1	111,7	112,4	113,7
Denmark	95,6	97,5	98,3	100,0	101,8	103,5	107,3	108,4	110,8
Germany (including f	95,4	96,4	98,1	100,0	101,8	104,1	107,0	107,2	108,4
Estonia	91,95	93,22	96,05	100,00	104,45	111,49	123,31	123,56	126,95
Ireland	92,0	95,7	97,9	100,0	102,7	105,6	108,9	107,1	105,4
Greece	90,67	93,79	96,63	100,00	103,31	106,40	110,90	112,40	117,68
Spain	91,04	93,86	96,73	100,00	103,56	106,51	110,91	110,64	112,90
France	93,86	95,89	98,14	100,00	101,91	103,55	106,82	106,93	108,79
Italy	93,1	95,7	97,8	100,0	102,2	104,3	108,0	108,8	110,6
Cyprus	92,51	96,18	98,00	100,00	102,25	104,46	109,03	109,22	112,02
Latvia	85,58	88,10	93,55	100,00	106,57	117,32	135,21	139,62	137,91
Lithuania	97,34	96,29	97,41	100,00	103,79	109,83	122,01	127,09	128,60
Luxembourg	91,04	93,36	96,37	100,00	102,96	105,69	110,01	110,02	113,10
Hungary	86,46	90,50	96,63	100,00	104,03	112,28	119,05	123,85	129,70
Malta	93,14	94,95	97,53	100,00	102,58	103,29	108,13	110,12	112,37
Netherlands	95,05	97,18	98,52	100,00	101,65	103,26	105,54	106,57	107,56
Austria	94,83	96,06	97,94	100,00	101,69	103,93	107,28	107,71	109,53

Source: Eurostat (2011). Copyright European Communities, 2011. Reproduced with permission

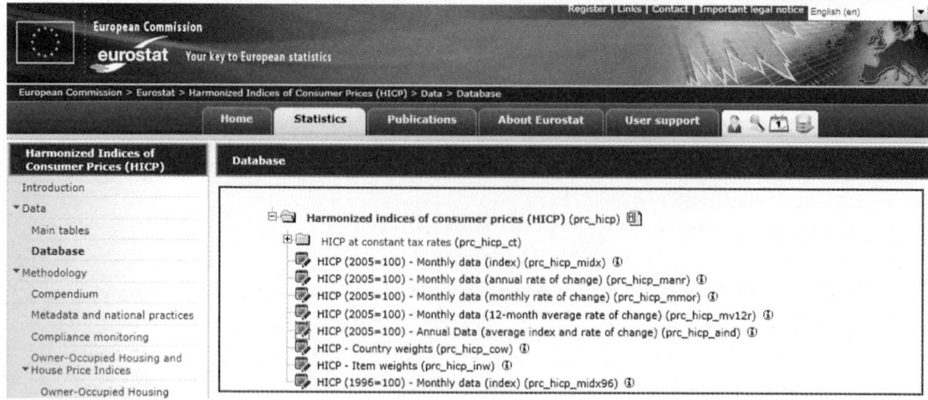

Source: Eurostat (2011). Copyright European Communities, 2011. Reproduced with permission

number of clients from two to three for a small company may be of less relevance than the 20 per cent increase in the number of clients from 1000 to 1200 for a larger company in the same market! Similarly, where quotations appear to be used selectively without other supporting evidence you should beware, as the data may be unreliable.

Measurement bias

Measurement bias can occur for two reasons (Kervin 1999):

- deliberate or intentional distortion of data;
- changes in the way data are collected.

Deliberate distortion occurs when data are recorded inaccurately on purpose, and is most common for secondary data sources such as organisational records. Managers may deliberately fail to record minor accidents to improve safety reports for their departments. Data that have been collected to further a particular cause or the interests of a particular group are more likely to be suspect as the purpose of the study may be to reach a predetermined conclusion (Smith 2006). Reports of consumer satisfaction surveys may deliberately play down negative comments to make the service appear better to their target audience of senior managers and shareholders, and graphs may deliberately be distorted to show an organisation in a more favourable light.

Other distortions may be deliberate but not intended for any advantage. Employees keeping time diaries might record only the approximate time spent on their main duties rather than accounting precisely for every minute. People responding to a structured interview (questionnaire) might adjust their responses to please the interviewer (Section 11.2).

Unfortunately, measurement bias resulting from deliberate distortion is difficult to detect. While we believe that you should adopt a neutral stance about the possibility of bias, you still need to look for pressures on the original source that might have biased the data. For written documents such as minutes, reports and memos the intended target audience may suggest possible bias, as indicated earlier in this section. Therefore, where possible you will need to triangulate the findings with other independent data sources. Where data from two or more independent sources suggest similar conclusions, you can have more confidence that the data on which they are based are not distorted. Conversely, where data suggest different conclusions you need to be more wary of the results.

Changes in the way in which data were collected can also introduce changes in measurement bias. Provided that the method of collecting data remains constant in terms of the people collecting it and the procedures used, the measurement biases should remain constant. Once the method is altered, perhaps through a new procedure for taking minutes or a new data collection form, then the bias also changes. This is very important for longitudinal data sets such as the UK's Retail Price Index where you are interested in trends rather than actual numbers. Your detection of biases is dependent on discovering that the way data are recorded has changed. Within-company sources are less likely to have documented these changes than government-sponsored sources.

Costs and benefits

Kervin (1999) argues that the final criterion for assessing secondary data is a comparison of the costs of acquiring them with the benefits they will bring. Costs include both time and financial resources that you will need to devote to locating and obtaining the data. Some data will be available in your local library and so will be free, although you will have to pay for any photocopying you need. Other data will require lengthy negotiations to gain access, the outcome of which may be a polite 'no' (Sections 6.2 to 6.4). Data from market research companies or special tabulations from government surveys will have to be ordered specially and will normally be charged for: consequently, these will be relatively costly.

Benefits from data can be assessed in terms of the extent to which they will enable you to answer your research question(s) and meet your objectives. You will be able to form a judgement on the benefits from your assessment of the data set's overall and precise suitability (discussed earlier in this section). This assessment is summarised as a checklist of questions in Box 8.10. An important additional benefit is the form in which you receive the data. If the data are already in spreadsheet format this will save you considerable time as you will not need to re-enter the data prior to analysis (Sections 12.2 and 13.3).

Box 8.10 Checklist

Evaluating your secondary data sources

Overall suitability

- ✔ Does the data set contain the information you require to answer your research question(s) and meet your objectives?
- ✔ Do the measures used match those you require?
- ✔ Is the data set a proxy for the data you really need?
- ✔ Does the data set cover the population that is the subject of your research?
- ✔ Does the data set cover the geographical area that is the subject of your research?
- ✔ Can data about the population that is the subject of your research be separated from unwanted data?
- ✔ Are the data for the right time period or sufficiently up to date?
- ✔ Are data available for all the variables you require to answer your research question(s) and meet your objectives?
- ✔ Are the variables defined clearly?

Precise suitability

- ✔ How reliable is the data set you are thinking of using?
- ✔ How credible is the data source?
- ✔ Is it clear what the source of the data is?
- ✔ Do the credentials of the source of the data (author, institution or organisation sponsoring the data) suggest it is likely to be reliable?
- ✔ Do the data have an associated copyright statement?
- ✔ Do associated published documents exist?
- ✔ Does the source contain contact details for obtaining further information about the data?
- ✔ Is the method described clearly?
- ✔ If sampling was used, what was the procedure and what were the associated sampling errors and response rates?
- ✔ Who was responsible for collecting or recording the data?
- ✔ (For surveys) Is a copy of the questionnaire or interview checklist included?
- ✔ (For compiled data) Are you clear how the data were analysed and compiled?
- ✔ Are the data likely to contain measurement bias?
- ✔ What was the original purpose for which the data were collected?
- ✔ Who was the target audience and what was its relationship to the data collector or compiler (were there any vested interests)?
- ✔ Have there been any documented changes in the way the data are measured or recorded including definition changes?
- ✔ How consistent are the data obtained from this source when compared with data from other sources?
- ✔ Have the data have been recorded accurately?

Costs and benefits

- ✔ What are the financial and time costs of obtaining these data?
- ✔ Can the data be downloaded into a spreadsheet, statistical analysis software or word processor?
- ✔ Do the overall benefits of using these secondary data sources outweigh the associated costs?

Source: Authors' experience; Blumberg et al. (2008); Dale et al. (1988); Dochartaigh (2007); Kervin (1999); Smith (2006); Stewart and Kamins (1993)

However, when assessing the costs and benefits you must remember that data that are not completely reliable and contain some bias are better than no data at all, if they enable you to start to answer your research question(s) and achieve your objectives.

8.6 Summary

- Secondary data are data that you analyse further which have already been collected for some other purpose, perhaps processed and subsequently stored. There are three main types of secondary data: documentary, survey and multiple source.
- Most research projects require some combination of secondary and primary data to answer your research question(s) and to meet your objectives. You can use secondary data in a variety of ways. These include:
  - to provide your main data set;
  - to provide longitudinal (time-series) data;
  - to provide area-based data;
  - to compare with, or set in context, your own research findings.
- Any secondary data you use will have been collected for a specific purpose. This purpose may not match that of your research. Secondary data are often less current than any data you collect yourself.
- Finding the secondary data you require is a matter of detective work. This will involve you in:
  - establishing whether the sort of data that you require are likely to be available;
  - locating the precise data.
- Once located, you must assess secondary data sources to ensure their overall suitability for your research question(s) and objectives. In particular, you need to pay attention to the measurement validity and coverage of the data.
- You must also evaluate the precise suitability of the secondary data. Your evaluation should include both reliability and any likely measurement bias. You can then make a judgement on the basis of the costs and benefits of using the data in comparison with alternative sources.
- When assessing costs and benefits, you need to be mindful that secondary data that are not completely reliable and contain some bias are better than no data at all if they enable you partially to answer your research question(s) and to meet your objectives.

Self-check questions

Help with these questions is available at the end of the chapter.

8.1 Give three examples of different situations where you might use secondary data as part of your research.

8.2 You are undertaking a research project as part of your course. Your initial research question is 'How has the UK's import and export trade with other countries altered since its entry into the European Union?' List the arguments that you would use to convince someone of the suitability of using secondary data to answer this research question.

8.3 Suggest possible secondary data that would help you answer the following research questions. How would you locate these secondary data?

a To what extent do organisations' employee relocation policies meet the needs of employees?

b How have consumer spending patterns in your home country changed in the last 10 years?

c How have governments' attitudes to the public sector altered in the twenty-first century?

8.4 As part of case study research based in a manufacturing company with over 500 customers, you have been given access to an internal market research report. This was undertaken by the company's marketing department. The report presents the results of a recent customer survey as percentages. The section in the report that describes how the data were collected and analysed is reproduced below:

> Data were collected from a sample of current customers selected from our customer database. The data were collected using an Internet-mediated questionnaire designed and administered via the online software tool SurveyMonkey™. Twenty-five customers responded, resulting in a 12.5 per cent response rate. These data were analysed using IBM SPSS Statistics. Additional qualitative data based on in-depth interviews with customers were also included.

a Do you consider these data are likely to be reliable?
b Give reasons for your answer.

Review and discussion questions

8.5 With a friend revisit Figure 8.1, types of secondary data, and reread the accompanying text in Section 8.2 Agree to find and, where possible, make copies (either electronic or photocopy) of at least two examples of secondary data for each of the seven subheadings:
a text materials;
b non-text materials;
c snapshot;
d longitudinal;
e censuses;
f continuous and regular surveys;
g ad hoc surveys.
Compare and contrast the different examples of secondary data you have found.

Progressing your research project

Assessing the suitability of secondary data for your research

- Consider your research question(s) and objectives. Decide whether you need to use secondary data or a combination of primary and secondary data to answer your research question. (If you decide that you need only use secondary data and you are undertaking this research as part of a course of study, check your course's assessment regulations to ensure that this is permissible.)
- If you decide that you need to use secondary data, make sure that you are clear why and how you intend to use these data.
- Locate the secondary data that you require and make sure that, where necessary, permission for them to be used for your research is likely to be granted. Evaluate the suitability of the data for answering your research question and make your judgement based on assessment of its suitability, other benefits and the associated costs.
- Note down the reasons for your choice(s), including the possibilities and limitations of the data. You will need to justify your choice(s) when you write about your research methods.
- Use the questions in Box 1.4 to guide your reflective diary entry.

8.6 Choose an appropriate information gateway from Table 8.2 to search the Internet for secondary data on a topic which you are currently studying as part of your course.

a 'Add to favourites' (bookmark) those sites which you think appear most relevant.

b Make notes regarding any secondary data that are likely to prove useful to either seminars for which you have to prepare or coursework you have still to undertake.

8.7 Agree with a friend to each evaluate the same secondary data set obtained via the Internet. This could be one of the data sets you found when undertaking question 8.6. Evaluate independently your secondary data set with regard to its overall and precise suitability using the checklist in Box 8.10. Do not forget to make notes regarding your answers to each of the points raised in the checklist. Discuss your answers with your friend.

References

Becker, H.S. (1998) *Tricks of the Trade*. Chicago, IL: Chicago University Press.

Blumberg, B., Cooper, D.R. and Schindler, P.S. (2008) *Business Research Methods*. (International student edn). Maidenhead: McGraw-Hill Education.

Bradley, N. (2010) *Marketing Research: Tools and Techniques* (2nd edn). Oxford: Oxford University Press.

Bryman, A. (1989) *Research Methods and Organisation Studies*. London: Unwin Hyman.

Bulmer, M., Sturgis, P.J. and Allum, N. (2009) 'Editors' introduction, in M. Bulmer, P.J. Sturgis and N. Allum (eds) *Secondary Analysis of Survey Data*. Los Angeles: Sage, pp. xviii–xxvi.

Chartered Institute of Library and Information Professionals (2010) *Libraries and Information Services in the UK and ROI 2010–11* (37th edn). London: Facet Publishing.

Cowton, C.J. (1998) 'The use of secondary data in business ethics research', *Journal of Business Ethics*, Vol. 17, No. 4, pp. 423–34.

Dale, A., Arber, S. and Proctor, M. (1988) *Doing Secondary Analysis*. London: Unwin Hyman.

Denscombe, M. (2007) *The Good Research Guide* (3rd edn). Buckingham: Open University Press.

Dochartaigh, N.O. (2007) *Internet Research Skills: How to do your Literature Search and Find Research Information Online*. London: Sage.

European Commission (2010) *Employment and Unemployment (LFS)*. Available at http://epp.eurostat.ec.europa.eu/portal/page/portal/employment_unemployment_lfs/introduction [Accessed 1 July 2011].

Eurostat (2010) *Europe in Figures: Eurostat Yearbook 2010*. Available at http://epp.eurostat.ec.europa.eu/portal/page/portal/product_details/publication?p_product_code=KS-CD-10-220 [Accessed 1 July 2011].

Eurostat (2011) *Eurostat home page*. Available at http://epp.eurostat.ec.europa.eu/portal/page/portal/eurostat/home/ [Accessed 2 July 2011].

Ghauri, P. and Grønhaug, K. (2010) *Research Methods in Business Studies: A Practical Guide* (4th edn). Harlow: Financial Times Prentice Hall.

Hakim, C. (1982) *Secondary Analysis in Social Research*. London: Allen & Unwin.

Hakim, C. (2000) *Research Design: Successful Designs for Social and Economic Research* (2nd edn). London: Routledge.

Hookway, N. (2008). 'Entering the blogosphere: Some strategies for using blogs in social research', *Qualitative Research*, Vol. 8, No. 1, pp. 91–113.

Information Commissioners Office (2011) *Freedom of Information Act*. Available at www.ico.gov.uk/for_the_public.aspx [Accessed 3 July 2011].

Kavanagh, M.J. and Thite, M. (2009) *Human Resource Information Systems: Basics, Applications, and Future Directions*. Los Angeles, CA: Sage.

Kervin, J.B. (1999) *Methods for Business Research* (2nd edn). New York: HarperCollins.

Mangold, W. and Faulds, D. (2009) 'Social media: The new hybrid element of the promotion mix', *Business Horizons*, Vol. 52, pp. 357–65.

Neelotpaul, B. (2010) 'A study on interactivity and online branding', *Advances in Management*, Vol. 3, No. 3, pp. 13–15.

Nielson Company (2011) *BlogPulse*. Available at www.blogpulse.com/ [Accessed 3 July 2011].

Office for National Statistics (2010) *Family Spending: A Report on the 2009 Living Costs and Food Survey*. Cardiff: Office for National Statistics. Available at www.statistics.gov.uk/StatBase/Product.asp?vlnk=361&Pos=1&ColRank=1&Rank=272 [Accessed 1 July 2011].

Office for National Statistics (2011a) *Census history*. Available at http://2011.census.gov.uk/Censushistory [Accessed 1 July 2011].

Office for National Statistics (2011b) *Results from the General LiFestyle Survey*. Available at www.statistics.gov.uk/StatBase/Product.asp?vlnk=5756&Pos=&ColRank=1&Rank=272; www.statistics.gov.uk/StatBase/Product.asp?vlnk=361 [Accessed 1 July 2011].

Reichman, C.S. (1962) *Use and Abuse of Statistics.* New York: Oxford University Press.

Robson, C. (2011) *Real World Research: A Resource for Users of Social Research Methods in Applied Settings* (3rd edn). Chichester: John Wiley.

Samson, A. (2010) 'Product useage and firm-generated word of mouth: Some results from fmcg product trials', *International Journal of Market Research*, Vol. 52, No. 4, pp. 459–82.

Smith, E. (2006) *Using Secondary Data in Educational and Social Research.* Maidenhead: Open University Press.

Stewart, D.W. and Kamins, M.A. (1993) *Secondary Research: Information Sources and Methods* (2nd edn). Newbury Park, CA: Sage.

UK Data Archive (2011) *UK Data Archive*. Available at www.data-archive.ac.uk/ [Accessed 2 July 2011].

Verisign Inc. (2011) *The Domain Name Industry Brief*, Vol. 8, No. 1. Available at www.verisigninc.com/assets/domain-name-report-feb-2011.pdf [Accessed 3 July 2011].

Wolf, A. (2007) 'People have a tendency to assume that quantitative data must be out there on the web waiting to be found', *The Times Higher Education Supplement*, 12 October. Available at www.timeshighereducation.co.uk/story.asp?sectioncode=26&storycode=310797 [Accessed 4 July 2011].

Further reading

Hakim, C. (2000) *Research Design: Successful Designs for Social and Economic Research* (2nd edn). London: Routledge. Chapter 4 contains a good discussion with a series of examples from the social sciences regarding using administrative records and documents as secondary data.

Levitas, R. and Guy, W. (eds) (1996) *Interpreting Official Statistics.* London: Routledge. Although published more than a decade ago, this book provides a fascinating insight into UK published statistics. Of particular interest are Chapter 1, which outlines the changes in UK statistics since the 1980 Raynor review, Chapter 3, which looks at the measurement of unemployment, the discussion in Chapter 6 of the measurement of industrial injuries and their limitations, and Chapter 7, which examines gender segregation in the labour force, utilising data from the Labour Force Survey.

Smith, E. (2006) *Using Secondary Data in Educational and Social Research*. Maidenhead: Open University Press. This provides a good discussion on the pitfalls (Chapter 2) and promises (Chapter 3) of secondary data analysis. Chapter 4 discusses some of the things you need to think about when using secondary data and includes, amongst others, a detailed example using the UK's General Household Survey.

Case 8
Trust repair in a major finance company

Liam was interested in understanding how senior managers try to recover a damaged corporate reputation, whether from a scandal or an act of incompetence. He had ambitions to be a management consultant, and could see that immersing himself in one such case for his research project would be invaluable in terms of knowledge building and problem analysis. One of his lecturers had discussed in class the theoretical framework for organisation-level trust repair put forward by Gillespie and Dietz (2009), and shown a DVD of how a large organisation had responded to negative publicity caused by their product failing. The DVD had illustrated vividly some of the key points of Gillespie and Dietz's argument. Liam was keen to explore another high-profile case.

Source: Alamy Images/Gavin Hellier

That month he read in the financial press that an investment bank was being prosecuted by the regulator. The bank was accused of creating an investment portfolio designed to fail, thereby allowing those with inside knowledge to profit. Liam wanted his career to involve work in the lucrative banking industry. This was his ideal case. His research project would be a single case study of trust repair in 'The bank versus the regulator'.

Although Liam could have analysed the case using theories of crisis management, or brand/reputation management, he was most interested in the trust angle. Gillespie and Dietz had proposed a four-stage systemic trust repair process: an immediate response in the first 24–72 hours, a system-wide diagnostic investigation of the failure, comprehensive reforming interventions throughout the organisational system, and finally an evaluation of progress. Actions and communications at each stage should tap into two underlying mechanisms of trust repair: 'distrust regulation' (preventing a reoccurrence), and 'trustworthiness demonstration' (renewed displays of the organisation's ability, benevolence and integrity). Gillespie and Dietz had a series of propositions for each stage. So, applying their theory would mean finding out how the bank had reacted at each stage of the developing crisis, mapping its responses against Gillespie and Dietz's framework, and reflecting on similarities and differences.

Data collection

His first challenge, therefore, was to understand what had happened, when, and the impact the developing crisis and senior management's response was having inside the firm. Primary sources would be best, and testimonies from current bank staff would have been ideal. After discussion with his project supervisor Liam suspected that access would be highly unlikely, and so decided to use only secondary sources.

He began by consulting the bank's corporate website. In the media section, he found press releases and statements from the firm responding to the regulator's charges. These were official statements, direct from the bank itself, and so were essential material for analysing how they had responded. He printed them all off, also saving them as web archive (mht) files, amassing a complete collection of the bank's official press statements in chronological order. As there was no RSS feed, Liam realised he would have to check in with the bank's media section every day, so as not to miss anything.

But Liam knew that relying on the interpretation of the case produced by the accused bank was prone to bias. Plus, in order to truly understand the systemic aspects of the failure, he needed background information and expert analysis. That left him needing additional documentary forms of secondary data to work with. This material would have to come from reliable sources.

He first logged onto the BBC website and found some useful material. But when he tried *The Times*, he was put off by its paywall, which prevented him from reading any of its articles for free. The same thing happened with the *Financial Times* after 10 free articles. Fortunately, at the start of the year he had subscribed to *The Economist* for a discounted rate, and so he was able to go onto their site and download all of its coverage, including several useful comment pieces. Friends suggested that he use a range of other media, which he found to be useful. He also decided to look on a range of websites for news coverage.

Every day Liam followed the case on the bank's own website and in a range of reliable media sources. Some articles pointed him toward others he would probably not have found. He opted not to follow any blogs as he could not be sure of their veracity and reliability.

Liam collected as many articles as he could for as long as he could before having to stop in order to begin writing up the case. The regulator case was settled with a fine for the bank (which denied any wrongdoing). The repercussions would continue to reverberate around the bank, and the industry as a whole, for months, however. Liam had three months' worth of articles, a good body of secondary data that would be considered reliable (although some details in some reports were not corroborated by other media outlets, he was satisfied that his source newspapers were credible and trustworthy, and had checked the facts on his behalf). Liam also felt he had reached something akin to a 'saturation point' as the different sources had begun to provide similar content.

Data analysis

Liam's first task was to construct a basic timeline of events, to create a detailed narrative of what happened. He went through all the materials, putting them in chronological order, then going through them source by source to identify the essential details of the case. He wrote this factual account up first, without any detail.

After producing the timeline, he went through them all again, source by source, embellishing the narrative with details and pertinent quotes, prioritising official bank statements (e.g. from official press releases, or reporters quoting verbatim comments from senior bank executives) over journalist sources, and corroborating where possible using different sources. He was careful to cite where he had found each (author, source, date), and to maintain an exhaustive list of references.

With the detailed narrative written up, Liam returned to the Gillespie and Dietz article that would provide the theoretical framework for his analysis. Gillespie and Dietz had proposed a four-stage sequential model, so Liam began to structure his case study accordingly, identifying how the bank had responded in each phase and coding each action or statement according to Gillespie and Dietz's framework and propositions. For example, was the firm's immediate statement an acknowledgement of the incident, with a tone of regret and a commitment to investigate thoroughly what had happened, as recommended? Liam quoted it verbatim in his case study then coded the content manually, noting that it was in fact an emphatic denial, backed up with a robust point-by-point refutation of the allegations. (Interestingly, though Gillespie and Dietz warn against such a statement, it did fit the theory on interpersonal trust repair, a point Liam discussed in his Analysis chapter.) Liam critiqued the bank's internal enquiry, and examined each of their trust repair responses, to see which elements of the bank's system had been targeted for reform, and whether the interventions were designed to prevent a future reoccurrence or to demonstrate renewed positive indicators of the bank's trustworthiness.

By the time he had completed his analysis, Liam had produced a rich and dense case study, vivid in its detail, with complex analytical commentary on each phase and each action and each statement. His analysis suggested some counterintuitive implications for organisation-level trust repair. The experience had been fascinating, immersing himself in a single crisis, considering different options for response and speculating on the implications for the emerging theory on organisation-level trust repair.

Reference

Gillespie, N. and Dietz, G. (2009) 'Trust repair after an organization-level failure', *Academy of Management Review*, Vol. 34, No. 1, pp. 127–45.

Questions

1 How might Liam have got around the various subscription paywalls on certain media websites that prevented him from accessing their material?
2 In terms of his coding procedure, Liam opted to annotate the documents by hand. How else might he have done the coding in a more systematic and transparent manner?
3 How might Liam write up his case study, in terms of a structure?
4 What limitations would Liam need to concede in his write-up?

Ongoing Case: Researching emotional labour

Part 2: Permission to collect data is unlikely so what about secondary data?

Jessica talks to her friends about asking the local theme park if she can conduct in-depth interviews with 10 employees about their experience of working there. They say she's unlikely to get permission: the time she wants to collect data is their peak season, so employees are unlikely to be released from their duties to be interviewed.

Emotional labour in the airline industry

Source: Alamy Images/David R. Frazier Photolibrary Inc.

Jessica is disappointed; but more than that, she's now worried about whether she can save her project. How can she abandon it after spending so much time reading extensively on the context of theme parks, and the conceptual topics of emotional labour, workplace socialisation and how organisations 'manage' the emotions of their employees? Jessica arranges a meeting with her project tutor so that she can ask about next steps. She wants to be proactive and show that she's already thought about alternative research designs, but realises that she might also need to rethink her topic. She notes down a number of questions to ask her project tutor:

1 What's the difference between primary and secondary data, and what sort of secondary data could be relevant for the research project?
2 Can I (Jessica) just interview employees about their emotional labour at the local theme park without asking the theme park's permission?
3 Can I use data from personal blogs and unofficial websites which expose grievances felt by employees?
4 Is there scope for me to undertake an empirically based master's project on theme parks and emotional labour using only secondary data? If so, what kind of secondary data might be available that relates to emotional labour within the theme park context?

Question

1 Imagine you are Jessica's project tutor. How would you respond to Jessica's four questions?

Additional case studies relating to material covered in this chapter are available via the book's companion website: **www.pearsoned.co.uk/saunders**. They are:

- The involvement of auditors in preliminary profit announcements.
- Research and development in the UK pharmaceutical industry.
- Small firms' internationalisation.
- Patent grants and the implications for business.

Self-check answers

8.1 Although it would be impossible to list all possible situations, the key features that should appear in your examples are listed below:
- to compare findings from your primary data;
- to place findings from your primary data in a wider context;
- to triangulate findings from other data sources;
- to provide the main data set where you wish to undertake research over a long period, to undertake historical research or to undertake comparative research on a national or international scale with limited resources.

8.2 The arguments you have listed should focus on the following issues:
- The study suggested by the research question requires historical data so that changes that have already happened can be explored. These data will, by definition, have already been collected.
- The timescale of the research (if part of a course) will be relatively short. One solution for longitudinal studies in a short time frame is to use secondary data.
- The research question suggests an international comparative study. Given your likely limited resources, secondary data will provide the only feasible data sources.

8.3 **a** The secondary data required for this research question relate to organisations' employee relocation policies. The research question assumes that these sorts of data are likely to be available from organisations. Textbooks, research papers and informal discussions would enable you to confirm that these data were likely to be available. Informal discussions with individuals responsible for the personnel function in organisations would also confirm the existence and availability for research of such data.

b The secondary data required for this research question relate to consumer spending patterns in your home country. As these appear to be the sort of data in which the government would be interested, they may well be available via the Internet or in published form. For the UK, examination of the Office for National Statistics and direct.gov information gateways (Table 8.2) would reveal that these data were collected by the annual Expenditure and Food Survey providing hyperlinks to a series of reports including *Family Spending: A Report of the 2009 Living Costs and Food Survey* (Office for National Statistics 2010), summary results of which are published (Office for National Statistics 2010). Summary data could also be downloaded. In addition, reports could be borrowed either from your university library or by using inter-library loan.

c The secondary data required for this research question are less clear. What you require is some source from which you can infer past and present government attitudes. Relative changes in spending data, such as appears in quality newspapers, might be useful; although this would need to be examined within each department budget. Transcripts of ministers' speeches and newspaper reports might prove useful. However, to establish suitable secondary sources for this research question you would need to pay careful attention to those used by other researchers. These would be outlined in research papers and textbooks. Informal discussions could also prove useful.

8.4 **a** The data are unlikely to be reliable.

b Your judgement should be based on a combination of the following reasons:

- Initial examination of the report reveals that it is an internally conducted survey. As this has been undertaken by the marketing department of a large manufacturing company, you might assume that those undertaking the research had considerable expertise. Consequently, you might conclude the report contains credible data. However:
- The methodology is not clearly described. In particular:
  - The sampling procedure and associated sampling errors are not given.
  - It does not appear to contain a copy of the questionnaire. This means that it is impossible to check for bias in the way that questions were worded.
  - The methodology for the qualitative in-depth interviews is not described.
- In addition, the information provided in the methodology suggests that the data may be unreliable:
- The reported response rate of 12.5 per cent is very low for a telephone survey (Section 7.2).
- Responses from 25 people means that all tables and statistical analyses in the report are based on a maximum of 25 people. This may be too few for reliable results (Sections 7.2 and 12.5).

Get ahead using resources on the companion website at:
www.pearsoned.co.uk/saunders

- Improve your IBM SPSS Statistics and NVivo research analysis with practice tutorials.
- Save time researching on the Internet with the Smarter Online Searching Guide.
- Test your progress using self-assessment questions.
- Follow live links to useful websites.

Chapter 9

Collecting primary data through observation

Learning outcomes

By the end of this chapter you should:

- appreciate the role of observation as a data collection method;
- be able to differentiate between participant observation and structured observation, and understand their differing applications;
- be aware of approaches to data collection and analysis for each type of observation;
- be able to identify threats related to validity and reliability for each type of observation and appreciate how to reduce these.

9.1 Introduction

Observation has been a somewhat neglected aspect of business and management research. Yet it can be rewarding and enlightening to pursue and, what is more, add considerably to the richness of your research data. Technological changes even mean that observation may become a more popular research method, as the opening vignette suggests. If your research question(s) and objectives are concerned with what people do, an obvious way in which to discover this is to watch them do it. This is essentially what **observation** involves: the systematic observation, recording, description, analysis and interpretation of people's behaviour.

Two types of observation are examined in this chapter. **Participant observation** (Section 9.2) is qualitative and derives from the work of social anthropology early in the twentieth century. Its emphasis is on discovering the meanings that people attach to their actions. In contrast, **structured observation** (Section 9.3) is quantitative and is more concerned with the frequency of actions.

In other approaches to research, those who take part are called either respondents or participants. Those who complete a questionnaire are usually called respondents. Those who agree to take part in most forms of qualitative research are usually called participants. These labels don't work for observation since it is the researcher who is participating in the environment of other people, responding to the ways in which they carry out their usual activities. In observational research, those who agree to be observed are usually called **informants** (Monahan and Fisher 2010). This is the term that we will use throughout this chapter.

A common theme in this book is our effort to discourage you from thinking of the various research methods as the sole means you should employ in your study. This is equally true of observation methods. It may meet the demands of your research question(s) and objectives to use participant observation or structured observation in your study as either the main method of data collection or to supplement other methods.

Barack Obama is the first President of the United States of America to have an online video diary produced of his presidential activities, known as the White House Blog or 'West Wing Week' (Vaidyanathan 2011). Edited and approved footage is posted weekly on the White House website and also on YouTube. This provides coverage of the previous week's events at the White House, or from the places where the President has visited (West Wing Week 2011). The producer of this online video diary, Arun Chaudhary, has been given extensive access to the President. This means being able to film inside the Oval Office at the White House and travelling with the President to record events.

Prior to this online video diary or blog, the official record of each President's work was produced by the official White House photographer, who recorded important events using still photographs. In addition, some key events were filmed by military camera personnel, to provide a motion picture record. The advent of this online video diary has resulted in an (almost) all-seeing and all-hearing approach, capable of producing a far more intrusive and revealing record of the President's activities. Arun Chaudhary is quoted by Vaidyanathan (2011: 2), 'My favourite thing to film is what I call "awkward world leader moments", which are basically world leaders having chit-chat like you and I would.' He is also quoted as commenting on the scope of this observational approach, 'I think people enjoy seeing how their institutions work from the inside, and they're going to demand more of it' (Vaidyanathan, 2011: 4). Vaidyanathan (2011) also reports that other world leaders including the President of Russia and the Prime Minister of Canada have employed people to produce video records of their work activities.

Source: Press Association Images (PA Photos)/Jacquelyn Martin

Observation has traditionally been associated with ethnography (see Section 5.5). The use of the Internet to conduct types of observation led to the invention of the term, 'netnography' (Kozinets 2006). Now, this use of online video diaries or blogs has lead to another new term to describe this data collection method: 'videography.'

9.2 Participant observation

What is participant observation?

If you have studied sociology or anthropology in the past you are certain to be familiar with participant observation. This is where 'the researcher attempts to participate fully in the lives and activities of members and thus becomes a member of their group, organisation or community. This enables the researcher to share their experiences by not merely observing what is happening but also feeling it' (Gill and Johnson 2010: 161). It has been used extensively in these disciplines to attempt to get to the root of 'what is going on' in a wide range of social settings.

Participant observation has its roots in social anthropology, but it was the Chicago School (at the University of Chicago) that changed its focus by using ethnographic methods to study social and urban problems within cultural groups in the USA. A seminal example of this work is Whyte's (1943) *Street Corner Society*, which examined the lives of street gangs in Boston. This approach to ethnography involved researchers living amongst those whom they studied, to observe and talk to them to produce detailed cultural accounts of their shared beliefs, behaviours, interactions, language, rituals and the events that shaped their lives (Cunliffe 2010). Participant observation has not been used that much in management and business research. However, this does not mean to say that it has limited value for management and business researchers. Indeed, it can be a very valuable tool, usually as the principal research method, but possibly in combination with other methods.

Delbridge and Kirkpatrick (1994: 37) note that participant observation implies, 'immersion [by the researcher] in the research setting, with the objective of sharing in peoples' lives while attempting to learn their symbolic world'. It is worth dwelling on this explanation. Whichever role you adopt as the participant observer (the choice open to you will be discussed later), there will be a high level of immersion. This is quite different from data collection by means of questionnaire, where you will probably know little of the context in which the respondents' comments are set or the delicate nuances of meaning with which the respondents garnish their responses. In participant observation the purpose is to discover those delicate nuances of meaning. As Delbridge and Kirkpatrick (1994: 39) state, 'in the social sciences we cannot hope to adequately explain the behaviour of social actors unless we at least try to understand their meanings'.

This last comment gives a clue to the point that Delbridge and Kirkpatrick make about 'attempting to learn the [informants'] symbolic world'. Some understanding of this point is vital if you are to convince yourself and others of the value of using participant observation.

The symbolic frame of reference is located within the school of sociology known as **symbolic interactionism**. In symbolic interactionism the individual derives a sense of identity from interaction and communication with others. Through this process of interaction and communication the individual responds to others and adjusts his or her understandings and behaviour as a shared sense of order and reality is 'negotiated' with others. Central to this process is the notion that people continually change in the light of the social circumstances in which they find themselves. The transition from full-time student to career employee is one example of this. (How often have you heard people say, 'she's so different since she's worked at that new place'?) The individual's sense of identity is constantly being constructed and reconstructed as he or she moves through differing social contexts and encounters different situations and different people.

This is a necessarily brief explanation of symbolic interactionism. However, we hope that you can see why Delbridge and Kirkpatrick (1994: 37) think that participant

Box 9.1 Focus on student research

Managers and their use of power: a cross-cultural approach

Mong was a young Chinese business graduate who had recently been working in a Chinese/German joint venture in the automobile industry. She was located in the supply chain department. Mong was completing the latter stages of her MBA. As part of the course, she had to submit a research project on a management topic of her choice.

Mong was fascinated by the international management component of her course that dealt with cross-cultural matters. This was particularly significant in her case as she worked at a company site that comprised both Chinese and German managers.

Mong felt that a body of theory which she could profitably link to the issue of cross-cultural integration was that of power. With help from her project tutor she developed a research question that allowed her to explore the way in which Chinese and German managers used power to 'negotiate' their relationships in a situation which was unfamiliar to both sets of managers. Mong's question was: 'What strategies are used by different groups of national managers collaborating in an international joint venture to negotiate their transnational relationships and how effective are these?'

Mong was fortunate that one of her duties was to take minutes at the twice-weekly management meetings in the department. She obtained permission to use these meetings to collect her data. She developed an observation schedule which related to her research objectives and used this to collect data during each meeting.

Data collection was not easy for Mong as she had to take minutes in addition to noting the type and frequency of responses of managers. However, as time progressed she became very skilled at fulfilling both her minute-taking and data-collection roles. She also gained permission to audio-record the meetings. At the end of four months, when she had attended over 30 meetings, she had collected a wealth of data and was in a good position to analyse them and draw some fascinating conclusions.

Mong's observation role raised ethical questions as she did not reveal her researcher role to the meeting delegates. She discussed these questions with her senior manager in the company and project tutor and completed the necessary university ethics committee documentation. It was agreed by all concerned that Mong's research objectives justified the data collection approach chosen and that the university's ethical code had not been breached.

observation is about 'attempting to learn the [informants'] symbolic world'. It is a quest to understand the identity of the individual, but, more importantly, it is about trying to get to the bottom of the processes by which the individual constantly constructs and reconstructs his or her identity (Box 9.1).

Different types of participant observation

There are four types of participant observation. These four types are distinguished by two separate dimensions (see Figure 9.1). One dimension relates to whether the researcher's identity is revealed (overt observation) or concealed (covert observation). In overt observation, the researcher is open about the fact that she or he is conducting research; in covert observation, the researcher conceals what he or she is doing. The other dimension relates to the extent to which the researcher participates in the activities of the organisation, group or community that she or he is observing.

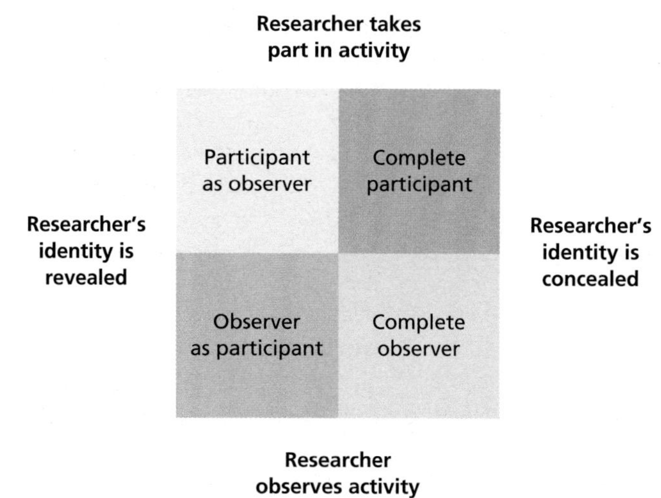

Figure 9.1 Typology of participant observation researcher roles

Based on earlier work, Gill and Johnson (2010) labelled the roles indicated by these four types (Figure 9.1):

- complete participant;
- complete observer;
- observer-as-participant;
- participant-as-observer.

Complete participant

The **complete participant** role sees you as the researcher attempting to become a member of the group in which you are performing research. You do not reveal your true purpose to the group members. You may be able to justify this role on pure research grounds in the light of your research questions and objectives. For example, you may be interested to know the extent of lunchtime drinking in a particular work setting. You would probably be keen to discover which groups of employees drink at lunchtimes, what they drink, how much they drink and how they explain their drinking. Were you to explain your research objectives to the group you wished to study, it is rather unlikely that they would cooperate since employers would usually discourage lunchtime drinking. In addition, they might see your research activity as prying.

This example raises questions of ethics. You would be in a position where you were 'spying' on people who have probably become your friends as well as colleagues. They may have learned to trust you with information that they would not share were they to know your true purpose. This example suggests the researcher should not adopt this role where the focus of the research may cause harm to individuals (see Section 6.5). However, there may be other foci where you might consider adopting the role of complete participant, where there would not be any risks of breaching trust or creating harm. An example might be where you were researching working practices in an organisation, to evaluate the relationship between theory and practice, where it would be possible to maintain the anonymity of both the organisation and informants as you participated as a co-worker.

Complete observer

Here too you would not reveal the purpose of your activity to those you were observing. However, unlike the complete participant role, you would not take part in the activities of the group. For example, the **complete observer** role may be used in studying consumer behaviour in supermarkets. Your research question may concern your wish to observe consumers at the checkout. Which checkouts do they choose? How much interaction is there with fellow shoppers and the cashier? How do they appear to be influenced by the attitude of the cashier? What level of impatience is displayed when delays are experienced? This behaviour may be observed by the researcher being located near the checkout in an unobtrusive way. The patterns of behaviour displayed may be the precursor to research by structured observation (Section 9.3), in which case this would be the exploratory stage of such a research project.

Observer-as-participant

Acting in the role of **observer-as-participant** will primarily involve you in observing, although your purpose will be known to those whom you are studying. In some cases this role may verge on that of participant-as-observer, where it becomes necessary to have some interaction with informants. For example, adopting the role of observer-as-participant in an outward-bound course to assist team building would mean that you were there as a spectator but it may be necessary to interact with participants and take part in some activities to be able to conduct your observation.

As an observer-as-participant, your identity as a researcher would be clear to all concerned and they would know your purpose. This would present the advantage of you being able to focus on your researcher role. For example, you would be able to jot down insights as they occurred to you. You would be able to concentrate on your discussions with the informants. What you would lose, of course, would be the emotional involvement: really knowing what it feels like to be on the receiving end of the experience.

Participant-as-observer

In the role of **participant-as-observer** you would both take part and reveal your purpose as a researcher. This role is potentially a broad one. On the one hand, you may become a fully accredited participant by becoming, for example, an employee in order to undertake your observation study in a particular context. As a part-time business or management student you may be able to use your existing employment status to adopt the role of participant-as-observer.

Alternatively, you may participate in a group without taking on all of the attributes of its members. For example, Waddington (2004) describes his experiences of being a participant-as-observer, in which he participated in a strike, spending long hours on the picket line and socialising with those on strike, without being an employee of the company involved. To achieve this, it was necessary to gain the support and trust of those involved. Waddington describes how he immersed himself in this context, how he experienced the emotional involvement of participating in this event and how he experienced the same feelings as the defeated strikers at the end of the strike.

Factors that will determine the choice of participant observer role

The purpose of your research

You should always be guided by the appropriateness of the method for your research question(s) and objectives. A research question that seeks to develop an understanding of a phenomenon about which the research informants would be naturally defensive is one that lends itself to the complete participant role. Discovering what it is like to be a participant on a particular training course is more appropriate to the participant-as-observer role.

Your status

If you are a part-time student who otherwise works full-time in an organisation, there may be a range of opportunities for you to use one of the participant observation roles as the means to collect data to answer your research question and address your research objectives. Depending on the nature and focus of your research question and objectives you may be able to adopt the role of either complete participant, or participant-as-observer, or observer-as-participant. As a part-time student you will be likely to encounter advantages as well some issues where you conduct research as an insider within your employing organisation (Box 9.2).

If you are a full-time student you will need to secure access before adopting this approach but may still be able to adopt any of the four roles depending on the nature of your research question and objectives, the time you have to devote to your research and your circumstances.

Box 9.2 Focus on management research

The case for doing research in your own organisation

In an *Organisational Research Methods* article, Brannick and Coghlan (2007) question the established tradition that academic theory-driven research in organisations is conducted best by outsiders, arguing that this can be done acceptably by insider researchers. They define insider researchers as those undertaking research in their own organisations while a complete member, which in this context means both having insider pre-understanding and access and wanting to remain a member on a desired career path when the research is completed. Insider research may be frowned upon because it is perceived as not conforming to standards of intellectual rigour, because internal researchers have a personal stake and substantive emotional investment in the setting. It is argued that insider researchers are native to the setting and, therefore, they are perceived to be prone to charges of being too close and thereby not attaining the distance and objectivity necessary for valid research. Brannick and Coghlan challenge this view and show how insider research, in whatever research tradition it is undertaken, is not only valid and useful but also provides important knowledge about what organisations are really like, which traditional approaches may not be able to uncover.

Brannick and Coghlan assemble a number of points to substantiate their argument. They argue that researchers, through a process of reflexive awareness, are able to articulate tacit knowledge that has become deeply segmented because of socialisation in an organisational system and reframe it as theoretical knowledge. Reflexivity is the concept used in the social sciences to explore and deal with the relationship between the researcher and the object of research. Insider researchers are already members of the organisation and so have primary access.

Clearly, any researcher's status in the organisation has an impact on access. Access at one level automatically may lead to limits or access at other levels. The higher the status of the researcher, the more access they have or the more networks they can access, particularly downward through the hierarchy. However, being in a high hierarchical position may exclude access to many informal and grapevine networks.

Insider researchers derive benefits from their experience and pre-understanding. Managers have knowledge of their organisation's everyday life. They know

the everyday jargon. They know the legitimate and taboo phenomena of what can be talked about and what cannot. They know what occupies colleagues' minds. They know how the informal organisation works and to whom they should turn for information and gossip. They know the critical events and what they mean within the organisation. They are able to see beyond objectives that are merely window dressing. When they are inquiring, they can use the internal jargon, draw on their own experience in asking questions and interviewing, be able to follow up on replies, and so obtain richer data. They are able to participate in discussions or merely observe what is going on without others necessarily being aware of their presence. They can participate freely without drawing attention to themselves and creating suspicion.

There are also some disadvantages to being close to the data. Insider researchers may assume too much and so not probe as much as if they were outsiders or ignorant of the situation. They may think they know the answer and not expose their current thinking to alternative reframing. They may find it difficult to obtain relevant data because, as a member, they have to cross departmental, functional or hierarchical boundaries, or because, as an insider, they may be denied deeper access that might not be denied an outsider.

Insider researchers may have a strong desire to influence and change the organisation. They may feel empathy for their colleagues and so be motivated to keep up the endeavour. These are beneficial in that they may sustain researchers' energy and a drawback in that they may lead to erroneous conclusions. Insider researchers have to deal with the dilemma of writing a report on what they have found. When they are observing colleagues at work and recording their observations, they may be perceived as spying or breaking peer norms. Probably the most important issue for insider researchers, particularly when they want to remain and progress in the organisation, is managing organisational politics.

The time you have to devote to your research

Some of the roles outlined earlier may be very time-consuming. If you are to develop a rich and deep understanding of an organisational phenomenon, it will need much careful study. A period of attachment to the organisation will often be necessary. However, many full-time courses have placement opportunities that may be used for this purpose. In addition, most full-time students have part-time jobs, which provide wonderful opportunities to understand the 'meanings' that their fellow employees, for whom the work is their main occupation, attach to a variety of organisational processes. What is needed is a creative perspective on what constitutes research and research opportunities. The possibilities are potentially numerous.

The degree to which you feel suited to participant observation

Delbridge and Kirkpatrick (1994) note that not everybody is suited to observational research. Much of it relies on the building of relationships with others. A certain amount of personal flexibility is also needed. As the participant observer you have to be 'all things to all people'. Your own personality must be suppressed to a greater extent. This is not something with which you may feel comfortable.

Organisational access

This may present a problem for some researchers as it is obviously a key issue. More is said about gaining access to organisations for research in Sections 6.2 to 6.4.

Ethical considerations

The degree to which you reveal your identity as the researcher or adopt a covert stance will be dictated by ethical considerations. The topic of ethics in research is dealt with in detail in Sections 6.5 and 6.6.

Data collection and analysis

Note making and recording data

Note making is very important in observation-based studies. Your notes are likely to be composed of different types of data. Delbridge and Kirkpatrick (1994) categorise the types of data generated by participant observation as 'primary', 'secondary' and 'experiential' (Table 9.1). In addition, you will find it helpful to record contextual data.

Data collection

It is likely that the nature of the primary data you collect will go through various phases, as you first seek to become familiar with the setting in which you are conducting observation before focusing on those aspects that will allow you to answer your research question and meet your objectives. Robson (2011) outlines a process that involves descriptive observation, then creating a narrative account before possibly undertaking a phase of focused observation. In **descriptive observation** you will concentrate on observing and describing the physical setting, the key informants and their activities, particular events and their sequence and the attendant processes and emotions involved. This description may be the basis for you to write a **narrative account**, in much the same way as an investigative journalist would write one. However, Robson (2011) makes the point forcefully that the researcher must go much further than the journalist. Your job as researcher is to go on and develop a framework of theory that will help you to understand, and to explain to others, what is going on in the research setting you are studying. To achieve this it may become evident to you that your observation needs to focus

Table 9.1 Types of data generated by participant observation

Data type	Explanation
Primary observations	Those data where you would note what happened or what was said at the time. Keeping a diary is a good way of doing this
Secondary observations	Statements by observers of what happened or was said. This necessarily involves observers' interpretations
Experiential data	Those data on your perceptions and feelings as you experience the process you are researching. Keeping a diary of these perceptions proves a valuable source of data when the time comes to write up your research. This may also include notes on how you feel that your values have intervened, or changed, over the research process
Contextual data	Those data related to the research setting; for example, roles played by key informants and how these may have changed; organisational structures and communication patterns that will help you to interpret other data

Source: Developed from Delbridge and Kirkpatrick (1994)

on particular events or on the interactions between key informants, which will lead you to undertake a phase of **focused observation**.

What will be clear from the types of data you will collect as participant observer is that formal set-piece interviewing is unlikely to take place. Such 'interviewing' as does take place is likely to be informal discussion. It will be part of the overall approach of asking questions that should be adopted in this research method. These questions are of two types (Robson 2011): first, to informants to clarify the situations you have observed and, second, to yourself to clarify the situation and the accounts given of the situation.

How you record your data will depend to a great extent on the role you play as observer. The more 'open' you are the more possible it will be for you to make notes at the time the event is being observed or reported. In any event, there is one golden rule: recording must take place on the same day as the fieldwork in order that you do not forget valuable data. The importance placed on this by one complete participant observer, working in a bakery, is evident from the following quotation:

> Right from the start I found it impossible to keep everything I wanted in my head until the end of the day . . . and had to take rough notes as I was going along. But I was 'stuck on the line', and had nowhere to retire to privately to note things down. Eventually, the wheeze of using innocently provided lavatory cubicles occurred to me. Looking back, all my notes for that third summer were on Bronco toilet paper! Apart from the awkward tendency for pencilled notes to be self-erasing from hard toilet paper . . . my frequent requests for 'time out' after interesting happenings or conversations in the bakehouse and the amount of time that I was spending in the lavatory began to get noticed . . .
>
> Ditton (1977), cited in Bryman (1989: 145)

Other ways of conducting observation and collecting data

Participant observation means that the researcher needs to be present in some way. The traditional way to conduct observation involves the researcher being present in the physical setting of those being observed. Internet and video technologies mean that an event may be streamed to a different location, or recorded in its entirety, so that the researcher may still be able to operate as a participant observer in the role of either complete observer or observer-as-participant (Figure 9.1). Clearly, what they would not be able to do is operate as either complete participant or participant-as-observer if observing a previously recorded event in which they had not taken part.

The advent of these technologies also means that other forms of observation are now possible. These may be linked to participant observation but they cannot be categorised as such. The opening vignette indicates that edited video recording can also facilitate observational analysis. There are a number of ways in which this approach may be used, with different advantages and disadvantages. Recorded material that is suitable may be available to be downloaded from the Internet, perhaps through social networking sites. The key here is suitability. Such material may provide you with a source of data but this is very likely to have been collected and edited for a different purpose to that of your research question and objectives and so may be of limited use.

In some cases it may be possible to ask your informant or informants to create a video diary that you subsequently analyse. This would have the advantage of being designed to address your research question and objectives but would be a logistically demanding task to plan for and undertake, making this an unlikely event in practice. However, this approach may be useful where considerable distances exist between informants, making face-to-face observation difficult or impossible to undertake. In such a case, this type of video diary or blog could be uploaded to the Internet by willing informants and downloaded for analysis by the researcher. The key would be to ensure that recorded material matched the focus of your research question and objectives. This method of assembling information may open up the possibility of a new area of observational research. Starr and Fernandez (2007) outline an innovative approach in which advanced miniaturised video-recording equipment provides observational data from the perspective of the research informant, not the researcher (i.e. a first-person perspective). These data may then be used as stimuli in an in-depth interview process (see Box 9.3).

Box 9.3 Focus on management research

Using 'mindcam' in observational marketing research

In their article in *Qualitative Market Research*, Starr and Fernandez (2007) argue that a film-making approach to consumer marketing research, which they call 'mindcam', is better for understanding the narrative, conveying a rich understanding of a subject. They assert that it is better for understanding precise details, exact cognitions, differences between perceptions/recollections and reality, and informant thoughts and feelings about the processes portrayed.

The mindcam apparatus consists of concealed video equipment, using a small, battery-operated pinhole video camera and microphone mounted in an unobtrusive, nearly invisible way. The camera moves with the person and requires no attention or effort to operate. The camera is mounted either on the consumer's head by concealing it in a hat or eyeglass frames; or the consumer's body by concealing it in a handbag, or other object such as a button, piece of jewellery or mobile phone case. The camera and microphone are connected to other required hardware such as a battery, video recorder or video transmitter. The mindcam technique can be used in wired or wireless form. It can be viewed by the researcher in real time via a wireless transmission, recorded for later analysis, or both. The camera can be placed anywhere on the informant's person, as long as it captures some aspect of their point of view.

Starr and Fernandez explain three distinct stages in a mindcam research project. After the research domain and issues are established, the first stage is recording video data from the informant's point of view. When this is complete, the second stage uses this first-person video as a memory prompt in a detailed and video-recorded interview with the informant. The third stage is final analysis, editing and presentation of the findings.

The authors point out that there are serious ethical issues to consider when using this technology. They express concern about the ethics of employing hidden cameras and emphasise the need for good research ethics protocols. They note that the observational research guidelines set out by market research societies are quite suitable to protect the interests of research respondents, non-participants who are inadvertently filmed and researchers, albeit that it should be recognised that filming for mindcam purposes has not yet been specifically considered by market research societies, and there are areas which remain unclear.

Starr and Fernandez note that there are several advantages and disadvantages regarding using mindcams. Among the former, they list: an unobtrusive first-person perspective; an unedited, unfiltered record; a versatile research methodology; a rich record of behaviour; and a verifiable record of behaviour and perceptions. The major disadvantage is a loss of external physical clues (researchers see what the informant sees and hear everything they may say and can watch much of what they do, but do not see what the informant looks like while doing it). The mindcam does not capture informants' facial expressions or body language while they are engaging in the focal activity.

Although they accept that substantial development is necessary, Starr and Fernandez believe the mindcam technique is now ready for use in research, and they encourage other researchers to employ the technology where appropriate.

Data analysis

Data from participant observation are analysed like other qualitative data and we consider this more fully in Chapter 13. Like other qualitative data, those from participant observation will start to be analysed at the time you collect them. That is, you will be carrying out data collection and analysis simultaneously. Let us say you were acting as the complete participant observer in attempting to establish 'what is going on' in terms of sex discrimination at the workplace in which you were researching. You would observe informal banter, hear conversations of a discriminatory nature and talk to those who 'approved' and 'disapproved' of the activity. All this would be part of your everyday work. You might mix socially with colleagues in situations where discriminatory attitudes and behaviour might be evident. All these events would yield data that you would record, as far as possible, on the spot, or at least note soon afterwards. You would turn these rough notes into something rather more systematic along the lines of the types of data outlined in Table 9.1 and discussed more fully in Chapter 13. What would be emerging is what an investigative journalist might call 'promising lines of enquiry' that you wish to follow up in your continued observation. However, remember that the journalist is interested in the story, while you are interested in generating a theory to help you understand 'what is going on'. This will lead you to adopt the researcher's equivalent of 'promising lines of enquiry'. A common approach to this is what is called analytic induction (Box 9.4).

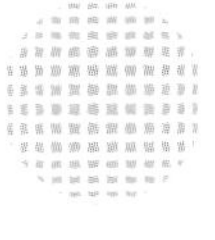

Box 9.4 Focus on student research

Using analytic induction

Parvati had already gained a strong impression from the news media to form an initial hypothesis that the giant supermarkets impose restrictive trading conditions upon their small suppliers. These conditions are such that the suppliers lose effective control of many of their daily operations. Her impression was reinforced by data collected from the literature, both academic and practitioner.

She spent a period of time working with a small organisation which supplies specialist dairy products to one of the supermarkets. Her research objectives were specifically written in order that her period of time with the supplier would result in data collection which responded to her research objectives.

Parvati's initial findings confirmed the overall hypothesis that the giant supermarkets impose restrictive trading conditions upon their small suppliers. However, the situation was rather more complex than she imagined. She found that while the supermarket buyers conduct stringent checks on product quality matters, they are less demanding when it comes to such issues as dictating the number of hours worked by employees.

This led her to redefine the initial hypothesis to one stating that that the giant supermarkets impose stringent product quality conditions upon their small suppliers but less restrictive conditions in relation to non-product quality issues.

In the next data collection phase she needed to extend the category of both product quality and non-product quality issues to see if the revised hypothesis required further revision and sophistication.

Note: This Focus on student research is a simplified version of analytic induction. It involves only *one* redefinition of the hypothesis whereas several may be involved. Moreover, an alternative to the redefining of the hypothesis is redefining the phenomenon to be explained so that the particular instance that casts doubt on the hypothesis is excluded (Denzin 1989).

Issues related to reliability and validity

Participant observation has high **ecological validity** because it involves studying social actors and social phenomena (i.e. informants and their activities) in their natural settings. However, using participant observation may lead to a number of threats to reliability and validity. This is because the setting is unknown to the observer and he or she needs to understand the cultural and interpersonal nuances that characterise it in order to interpret it; or because, as an insider, the observer is so familiar with it that she or he may take some things for granted instead of 'standing back' and analysing these through a more objective, theoretical lens. In relation to participant observation, we discuss three such issues related to observer error, observer bias and observer effect.

Observer error

Your lack of understanding of, or overfamiliarity with, the setting in which you are trying to operate as a participant observer may lead you unintentionally to misinterpret what is happening. This would be **observer error**. This error would not be because of any deliberate bias but because you need to understand the setting better before you seek to interpret it. Interpretation arises from understanding and the insights that follow from understanding. This point helps to illustrate that observation is a process that involves immersion in a context in order to produce valid and reliable results.

Observer bias

Conversely, an observer may not allow herself or himself the time necessary to develop the depth of understanding required in order to interpret the setting objectively. This would lead to **observer bias** where the observer uses his or her own subjective view or disposition to interpret events in the setting being observed. The observer may be unaware that she or he is doing this. As Delbridge and Kirkpatrick (1994: 43) note, 'because we are part of the social world we are studying we cannot detach ourselves from it, or for that matter avoid relying on our common sense knowledge and life experiences when we try to interpret it'.

When you are using observation, you will need to be aware that every observation you record may be open to more than one interpretation. This may appear to be a daunting thought! However, it shouldn't be read as such. Instead it should encourage you to give yourself enough time in the setting to begin to understand it and then to develop a rigorous analytical approach to the way you make interpretations.

Your attempts to make objective interpretations will depend on whether you are using covert or overt observation. As a covert researcher, you will not be able to check your interpretations with informants. You will therefore need to think about the possible ways that a particular type of observation may be interpreted and then, as you continue to observe and collect more primary observations (see Table 9.1), you will need to test out which interpretation appears to fit best. This process illustrates the interactive nature of data collection and data analysis.

Where you are using overt observation, you have the possibility of asking your informants to read some of the secondary observations that relate to them. This would provide you with the opportunity to check some of your interpretations with your informants and perhaps to benefit from the insights that they are able to add to your own views (see Box 9.5). This process is known as **informant verification**.

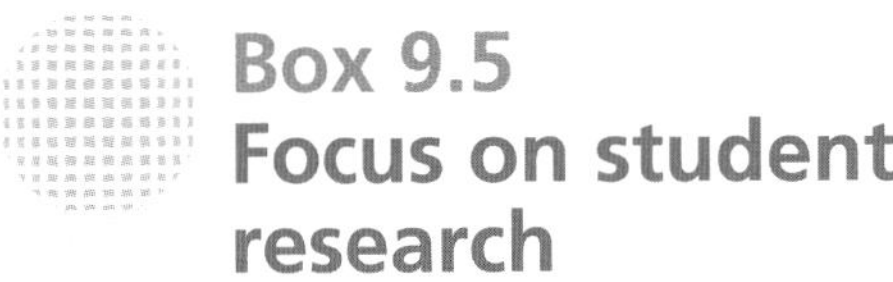

Box 9.5 Focus on student research

Informant verification

Susanna undertook participant observation in the customer services call centre of a retail company. Her research focused on the training and quality assurance of call centre staff. One of the aspects of her research project focused on the training needed to be able to deal with complex customer issues. For this aspect of her research project, Susanna negotiated access to spend a period in the call centre, in the role of observer-as-participant. This gave her access to observe call centre staff dealing with complex customer issues, to understand how they used their discretion to deal with customers sensitively while seeking to adhere to their training and to any scripted parts of their telephone conservations with callers. To achieve cognitive access (Chapter 6), she gained the consent of individual informants to observe each for a day or part of a day. This provided her with the opportunity to observe a number of informants during the period of her agreed access.

Susanna negotiated to meet each informant during part of his or her main rest break on the following day. This provided Susanna with the opportunity to describe and discuss her secondary observations about a particular call that the informant had taken. Most of these informants were interested to help and provided Susanna with their own interpretations and insights, often recalling what they had been thinking as they had dealt with the call being discussed. These additional interpretations, directly from the informants, were very helpful to Susanna as she continued to observe and interpret and later when she wrote up her research project.

Observer effect

A more tricky threat to the reliability and validity of data collected through observation relates to the presence of the observer. By simply being present, the researcher may affect the behaviour of those being observed, potentially resulting in unreliable and invalid data (LeCompte and Goetz 1982; Spano 2005). This is referred to as the **observer effect**. The implication of this effect is that informants will work harder or act more ethically when they know they are being observed (Monahan and Fisher 2010). Conversely, those being observed may decide to slow their work if they feel that any measurements of this will lead to them being given more demanding targets. Either way, observations will not be reliable.

One solution to this is for the observer to act covertly. This solution assumes that it would be appropriate for the researcher to adopt the role of complete participant or of complete observer (Figure 9.1). However, this may not be appropriate, even if it were ethically acceptable. Another solution to this is for the observer to achieve **minimal interaction**, where the observer tries as much as possible to 'melt into the background' – having as little interaction as possible with informants (Robson 2011). This may involve sitting in an unobtrusive position in the room and avoiding eye contact with those being observed. In relation to Figure 9.1, this would mean adopting a purely observing role, rather than a participatory one – acting in the role of observer-as-participant. However, as we discussed earlier, adopting this role may not be appropriate to the nature of the research.

A further solution where the observation is overtly conducted is related to familiarisation. As you operate in the role of participant-as-observer or observer-as-participant your informants will become familiar with you and take less notice of your presence, where they feel they can trust you. This is known as **habituation**, where the informants being observed become familiar with the process of observation so that they take it for

Box 9.6 Focus on management research

Observer effects

Monahan and Fisher (2010) in an article in *Qualitative Research* challenge some of the assumptions about observer effects. They argue that all research methods can have researcher effects that may lead to bias. In this way qualitative research including participant observation may be no more prone to bias than quantitative approaches to research, which are often held up as being more objective.

They also cast doubt on the idea that observer effects will always be negative and negate the value of the observer's results. Instead they believe that while the presence of an observer may have an effect on those whom they observe, the result of this effect may actually lead to the collection of valuable data. For them, observer effects may prove to be positive rather than being negative. They refer to the possibilities that informants may either 'stage' a performance for an observer or 'self-censor' their activities.

Monahan and Fisher suggest that staged performances may be welcomed because informants demonstrate an idealised set of behaviours to observers. They show what the informants think the observer ought to know and see. This idealised performance may then be compared to other observations where the performance cannot be staged or managed so easily. This may occur when the observer is watching a more pressured or stressful situation, or perhaps where other organisational participants are involved and the ability to manage a staged performance is not possible. Observations made of other informants in the same or a similar setting may also be compared to those that are being staged. Such situations offer the possibility of gaining rich and multilayered data that would be very valuable to the observer in understanding the setting and when undertaking data analysis and interpretation.

Another way in which informants may try to manage their performance is through self-censorship. This may be designed to hide any behaviour that informants feel would be undesirable for the observer to see. Monahan and Fisher suggest that informants may behave worse when not being observed but are unlikely to behave better. Habituation may result in such cloaking behaviour being dropped. Apart from habituation, observers may try to check the validity of their observations by looking for inconsistencies in the data they observe and also by identifying differences between informants, to identify any facade of self-censorship.

Monahan and Fisher conclude that irrespective of whether a performance is being staged, or whether self-censorship is occurring, or whether neither of these is affecting what is being observed, the process of observation allows researchers to get close to and interact with informants. This may be seen as providing observation with an advantage over other research methods where distance and separation mean that data cannot be as intricate and rich. Rather than only focusing on observer effects, there is scope to focus on these other attributes of observation in assessing its value as a research method.

granted and behave normally. To achieve habituation it will probably be necessary for you to undertake several observation sessions in the same research setting with the same informants before you begin to achieve reliable and valid data. In fact, it will probably be necessary for you to undertake several sessions in order to begin to understand the dynamics of this setting, so this would be time well spent.

Not all researchers agree that observer effects inevitably lead to unreliable results. In addition, other strategies have been proposed to recognise and manage observer effects (Box 9.6).

The advantages and disadvantages of participant observation are summarised in Table 9.2.

Table 9.2 Advantages and disadvantages of participant observation

Advantages	Disadvantages
• It is good at explaining 'what is going on' in particular social situations • It heightens the researcher's awareness of significant social processes • It is particularly useful for researchers working within their own organisations • Some participant observation affords the opportunity for the researcher to the experience 'for real' the emotions of those who are being researched • Virtually all data collected are useful	• It can be very time-consuming • It can pose difficult ethical dilemmas for the researcher • There can be high levels of role conflict for the researcher (e.g. 'colleague' versus researcher) • The closeness of the researcher to the situation being observed can lead to significant observer bias • The participant observer role is a very demanding one, to which not all researchers will be suited • Access to organisations may be difficult • Data recording is often very difficult for the researcher

9.3 Structured observation

What is structured observation?

In contrast to participant observation, structured observation has a high level of predetermined structure. If you use this data collection method as part of your research strategy you will be adopting a more detached stance. Your concern will be to quantify behaviour. As such, structured observation may form only a part of your data collection approach because its function is to tell you how often things happen rather than why they happen. Once again, we see that all research methods may have a place in an overall research strategy. What is important is choosing the method that meets your research questions and objectives.

Structured observation has a long history that extends into the present, linked to computer technologies. It has been used for many years to analyse how factory workers carry out their tasks and the times that it takes to complete these. This is known as a 'time-and-motion' study and was used by employers to increase their control over the way in work was conducted. It has been used to 'speed up' work by reducing the time required to undertake different tasks. This approach has more recently been facilitated by computer technologies. Computers may be used to record the work activities of those who work in call centres and on checkouts in shops, for example. Video recording adds another layer of observation to monitor those in particular types of workplace as well as within areas covered by CCTV, such as in city and town centres, shopping centres and within retail outlets. We live in a world where in many situations our movements are routinely observed while we go about our daily lives, often without being aware that this is happening. Adrian uses an independent retail outlet which makes light of this situation: at various places in the store there are signs which state, 'Smile, you're on camera!'

Structured observation by itself may be little more than surveillance or fact-finding. It is the ways in which such data are analysed that can transform this activity into valuable research findings. One of the best-known examples of managerial research that used structured observation as part of its data collection approach was the study of the work of senior managers by Mintzberg (1973). This led Mintzberg to cast doubt on the long-held theory that managerial work was a rational process of planning, controlling and directing. Mintzberg studied what five chief executives actually did during one of each of the executives' working weeks. He did this by direct observation and the recording of events on three predetermined coding schedules. This followed a period of 'unstructured' observation in which the categories of activity that formed the basis of the coding schedules he used were developed. In this way Mintzberg 'grounded' (Grounded Theory is explained in Section 5.5 and in Chapter 13) his structured observation on data collected in an initial period of participant observation.

Modern uses of structured observation do not have to rely on computer technologies. Structured observation is still used as a tool to assess the way in which workers in modern workplaces carry out their tasks, as Box 9.7 indicates.

The Internet has widened the scope to conduct forms of structured observation. The Internet may be used in 'real time' to make virtual structured observations. These range from simple to more complex structured observations. Every time you 'visit' a website this will be recorded electronically. This allows organisations to count the number of visits to their websites in a given period. Internet behaviour may also be tracked and analysed. Search engines such as Google regularly do research on the search behaviour of their users. This has been termed 'indirect observation', where traces of users' behaviour are recorded and analysed (Hewson et al. 2003: 46). Box 9.8 illustrates how marketing and advertising companies are investing in ways to obtain more detailed online data that will allow them to observe and analyse the links between online behaviour. Hewson et al. (2003) point out that using the Internet for structured observation offers researchers the advantage of non-intrusiveness and the removal of possible observer bias.

Box 9.7 Focus on student research

Observing staff behaviours at Fastfoodchain

Sangeeta worked at Fastfoodchain for her vacation job. She became interested in measuring service quality in her course and decided to do a preliminary study of customer interaction at Fastfoodchain.

Fastfoodchain has restaurants all over the world. Central to its marketing strategy is that the customer experience should be the same in every restaurant in every country of the world. An important part of this strategy is ensuring that customer-facing staff observe the same behavioural standards in every restaurant. This is achieved by defining precise standards of behaviour that customers should experience in every transaction undertaken. These standards are used in the training of staff and assessment of their performance. Reproduced below is part of the section of the standards schedule concerned with dealing with the customer. (There are also sections which deal with the behaviours needed to prepare for work, e.g. till readiness, and general issues, e.g. hygiene.)

The standards schedule is as an observation document used by trainers in order to evaluate the degree to which their training is effective with individual employees. It is also used by managers in their assessment of the performance of employees. Sangeeta was very impressed with the level of precision contained in this schedule and wondered whether it could form the basis of her research project.

Section 2: Delighting the customer

Staff member:...		
Behaviour	**Was the behaviour observed?**	**Comments**
Smiles and makes eye contact with the customer		
Greets the customer in a friendly manner		
Gives the customer undivided attention throughout the transaction		
Suggests extra items that have not been ordered by the customer		
Places items on clean tray with tray liner facing customer		
Ensures that customer is told where all relevant extras (e.g. cream, sugar) are located		
Explains to customer reasons for any delays and indicates likely duration of delay		
Neatly double-folds bags containing items with the Fastfoodchain logo facing the customer		
Price of order is stated and customer thanked for payment		
Lays all money notes across till drawer until change is given and clearly states the appropriate amount of change		
Customer is finally thanked for transaction, hope expressed that the meal will be enjoyed, and an invitation to return to the restaurant issued		

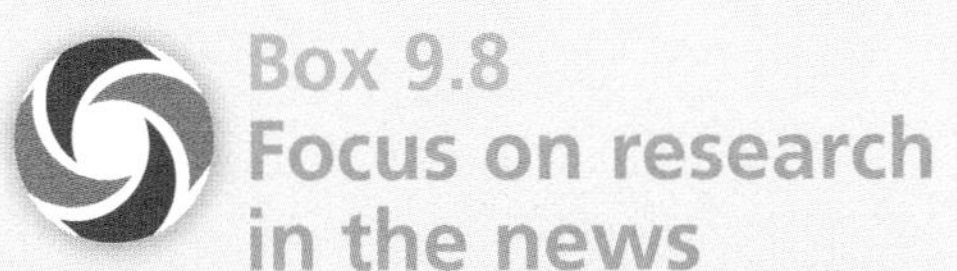

FT

Online advertising: it is hard to tell if the ads work

As advertising dollars speed to the web, marketers are scrambling to find ways to measure the effectiveness of their search, display and social media efforts. While companies such as Nielsen and Omniture provide some ways of doing this, they give an incomplete picture of online behaviour. In addition to the 'last click' (which records how a user came to a site, and if it was from an ad), the bigger question of how online advertising influences brand awareness is exceedingly hard to address.

Measuring the effectiveness of online advertising is 'very difficult', says Tony Palmer, chief marketing officer of Kimberly-Clark, a consumer products group. Mr Palmer's team has developed a strategy that is tailored to each product launch or new campaign. And yet even years of internal development have not delivered an adequate solution. 'We're probably at 50 per cent of where we want to be in being able to measure our media mix', he says. 'It's a competitive advantage to have better analytics.' In an effort to close this gap, new companies are emerging with the aim of providing more 'holistic' measurement systems. MarketShare, which tries to measure how online spending works in concert with offline campaigns, has lured half the Fortune 50 as clients. Wes Nichols, its chief executive, says: 'Rather than look at just who's seeing something from outdoor, or online or in-store, we're looking at how does it drive sales? How do they combine to create a reaction?' Mr Nichols cautions that it 'is not as simple as looking at media mix'. Instead, he likens it to the human genome project. 'It's not like one gene causes cancer', he says. 'It's a combination of factors.' For example, a consumer might see a Toyota ad on

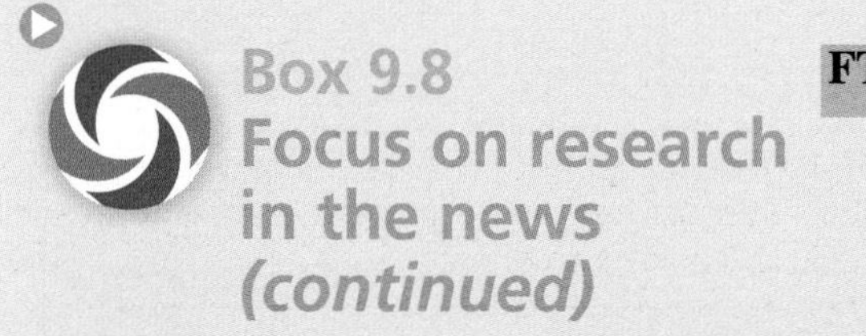

Box 9.8 Focus on research in the news (continued)

FT

Yahoo, do a Google search for Toyota later and then go to Edmunds.com, the car guide, to look at ratings. 'There are a lot of things that impacted what got that person to the dealership, but it's usually the last click that gets all the credit', says Mr Nichols.

Another way that brands are working to get more out of online adverts is by rigorous experimentation and testing. 'Kayak is a brand that lives online', says Robert Birge, chief marketing officer of travel website Kayak.com. 'Like many internet start-ups, we took an approach that was very online-focused.' Mr Birge says Kayak initially invested in paid search advertising, and relied on reputation and word-of-mouth. Recently, the company has invested in display adverts. But Mr Birge concedes that 'online display is very complicated', even for professionals. Kayak works with MediaMath, a company that provides advertising management services and technology, to buy search advertising. Equally important is brand awareness. To hone this, Kayak runs experiments to test which adverts are most effective and how many clicks and sales different versions of adverts can generate. Some marketers think social media are an online arena that provides more clarity on what works. Nielsen has partnered with Facebook to track the effectiveness of adverts on the social network, and companies avidly count their Twitter followers, re-tweets, mentions, and 'shares' on Facebook. Salesforce, the web-based customer management software provider, has embraced social media. 'YouTube is transformational for us', says Kendall Collins, chief marketing officer of Salesforce. 'An event with our chief executive on stage is great, but a video is super-high fidelity, and the cost per video engagement can be very [low].' Mr Collins has sought to tie engagement in social media and the Web to conversions into customers. 'If you're statistically minded and have the tools, you can correlate behaviour on your website with other behaviour', he says.

In 2007, Salesforce integrated its CRM system with the Google AdWords service. That allowed it to see quickly which keywords attract customers. But not all brands are rushing to social media. '[It] is a very hard nut to crack', says Mr Birge. 'The challenge is turning it into something that has a material impact on business. It's hard to be a CMO and say social media aren't your top priority'. In the absence of established metrics for online advertising, some marketers have created their own. Jim Farley, CMO of Ford, says his European team has developed a metric for the company: 'cost per minute of engagement'. Encompassing the benefits of social engagement, the cost of producing content and the need to drive sales, Mr Farley says more companies may use this type of metric in years to come. 'This is a highly relevant new metric in the world of social media', he says. 'If 6m people watch a minute-long video on YouTube, how does that compare with an advert on TV? The number of engagements, and the amount of time people spend with your content [can be much greater] online.'

Source: From 'Online advertising: it is hard to tell if the ads work', David Gelles (2011) *Financial Times*, 15 March.

The advantages and disadvantages of structured observation are summarised in Table 9.3.

Data collection and analysis

Using coding schedules to collect data

One of the key decisions you will need to make before undertaking structured observation is whether to use an 'off-the-shelf' coding schedule or to design your own. You will hardly be surprised to hear us say that this should depend on your research questions and objectives. What follows are two sets of guidelines for assessing the suitability of existing tailor-made coding schedules.

Table 9.3 Advantages and disadvantages of structured observation

Advantages
• It can be used by anyone after suitable training in the use of the measuring instrument. Therefore, you could delegate this extremely time-consuming task. In addition, structured observation may be carried out simultaneously in different locations. This would present the opportunity of comparison between locations • It should yield highly reliable results by virtue of its replicability. The easier the observation instrument is to use and understand, the more reliable the results will be • Structured observation is capable of more than simply observing the frequency of events. It is also possible to record the relationship between events. For example, does a visit to a website lead to the exploration of related pages and video recordings; does this lead to a decision to purchase? • The method allows the collection of data at the time they occur in their natural setting. Therefore, there is no need to depend on 'second-hand' accounts of phenomena from participants who put their own interpretation on events • Structured observation secures data that most informants would ignore because to them these are too mundane or irrelevant
Disadvantages
• Unless virtual observation is used, the observer must be in the research setting when the phenomena under study are taking place • Research results are limited to overt action or surface indicators from which the observer must make inferences • Data are slow (and may be expensive) to collect

Choosing an 'off-the-shelf' coding schedule

There are a number of questions that you need to ask yourself when choosing an 'off-the-shelf' coding schedule. These are listed in Box 9.9.

One of the most frequent uses of established coding schedules in management and business is for recording interpersonal interactions in social situations such as meetings or negotiations. This lends itself to structured observation particularly well. Figure 9.2 is an example of just such an 'off-the-shelf' coding schedule that may be used for this purpose.

Box 9.9 Checklist

Questions to ask when choosing an 'off-the-shelf' coding schedule

✔ For what purpose was the coding schedule developed? Is it consistent with your research question(s) and objectives? (It should be.)
✔ Is there overlap between the behaviours to be observed? (There should not be.)
✔ Are all behaviours in which you are interested covered by the schedule? (They should be.)
✔ Are the behaviours sufficiently clearly specified so that all observers will place behaviours in the same category? (They should be.)
✔ Is any observer interpretation necessary? (It should not be.)
✔ Are codes to be used indicated on the recording form to avoid the necessity for memorisation by the observer? (They should be.)
✔ Will the behaviours to be observed be relevant to the inferences you make? (They should be.)
✔ Have all sources of observer bias been eliminated? (They should have been.)

Source: Developed from Walker (1985) *Doing Research: A Handbook for Teachers*, London: Routledge. Reproduced with permission

Nature of group:

Nature of activity:

Date: Name of observer:

Initial arrangement of group:

C D
B E
A F

	Name of group members (or reference letters)					
	A	B	C	D	E	F
Taking initiative – e.g. attempted leadership, seeking suggestions, offering directions						
Brainstorming – e.g. offering ideas or suggestions, however valid						
Offering positive ideas – e.g. making helpful suggestions, attempting to problem-solve						
Drawing in others – e.g. encouraging contributions, seeking ideas and opinions						
Being responsive to others – e.g. giving encouragement and support, building on ideas						
Harmonising – e.g. acting as peacemaker, calming things down, compromising						
Challenging – e.g. seeking justification, showing disagreement in a constructive way						
Being obstructive – e.g. criticising, putting others down, blocking contributions						
Clarifying/Summarising – e.g. linking ideas, checking progress, clarifying objectives/proposals						
Performing group roles – e.g. spokesperson, recorder, time-keeper, humorist						
Other comments						

Figure 9.2 Recording sheet for observing behaviour in groups

Source: Reproduced from Figure 9.4 in L.J. Mullins (2010). *Management and Organisational Behaviour* (9th edn). Harlow: Financial Times Prentice Hall. Copyright © L.J. Mullins 2010. Reprinted with permission of Pearson Education Ltd

We would encourage you to use an 'off-the-shelf' coding schedule if you can find one that is suitable. Not only will it save you a lot of time, but it will be tried and tested. Therefore, it is likely to make your results and conclusions more reliable and valid.

However, you may decide that no 'off-the-shelf' coding schedule is suitable for your purposes. In this case you will need to develop your own schedule. Box 9.10 contains a checklist to guide this activity, to help to ensure the reliability and ease of use of the

Box 9.10 Checklist

Developing your own coding scheme

- ✔ Are the meanings of codes to used transparent and have you written these down?
- ✔ Have you ensured that the meanings of different codes do not overlap?
- ✔ Are the codes you have developed flexible enough in practice to be applied across different settings?
- ✔ Are the codes you have developed strictly relevant for the behaviours that you wish to observe and record?
- ✔ Do the range of codes you have developed cover all of the behaviours you wish to observe and record?
- ✔ Are the codes you have developed simple to understand and undemanding to apply so that you will not need to memorise or check their meanings?

codes you devise. The observation categories in this schedule should also be devised to be consistent with your research question(s) and objectives.

An alternative to the use of an 'off-the-shelf' coding schedule or the development of your own may be a combination of the two. If this is the option that seems most appropriate in the light of your research question(s) and objectives, we recommend that you still use the checklists in Boxes 9.9 and 9.10 to ensure that your schedule is as valid and reliable as possible.

Data analysis

The complexity of your analysis will depend on your research question(s) and objectives. It may be that you are using Figure 9.2 to establish the number of interactions by category in order to relate the result to the output of the meeting. This may enable you to conclude that 'positive' behaviours (e.g. brainstorming) may be more strongly associated with meetings that make clear decisions than with 'negative' behaviours (e.g. being obstructive). Simple manual analysis may be sufficient for this purpose.

Alternatively, you may be using Figure 9.2 to see what patterns emerge. It may be that the amount of interaction varies by the nature of the group or its activity, or that seating position is associated with the number of contributions. Patterns reflecting relationships between numbers of interaction categories may become evident (e.g. when 'drawing in others' was high 'clarifying/summarising' was also high). This level of analysis is obviously more complex and will usually need statistical software to calculate the cross-tabulations. Section 12.2 contains guidance on preparing data for quantitative analysis by computer.

Issues related to validity and reliability

The main issues for structured observation relate to aspects of reliability: observer error, informant error, time error and observer effects. We discussed observer error and observer effects earlier, in Section 9.2. Here we consider informant error and time error.

Informant error

Informant error may cause your data to be unreliable. You may be concerned with observing the normal output of sales administrators as measured by the amount of orders they process in a day. Informant error may be evident if you chose administrators in a section that was short-staffed owing to illness. This may mean that they were spending more time answering telephones and less time processing orders, as there were fewer people available to handle telephone calls. The message here is clear: select your sample of informants using the sampling technique that best enables you to answer your research question and meet your aims (Chapter 7).

Time error

Closely related to the issue of informant error is that of **time error**. It is essential that the time at which you conduct an observation does not provide data that are untypical of the total time period in which you are interested. For example, the number of calls taken in a call centre is often higher in the hours surrounding lunchtime in comparison to any other two-hour period. Conversely, they may be lower in the hours just before the lines close than in any other two-hour period. It would therefore be necessary to conduct periods of observation at intervals throughout the day in order to gain a reliable set of data. Of course, computer technology would allow a researcher with access to computer-collected data to know not only which periods were busiest but also other data such as average call times, the number of calls taken by particular members of staff and how many callers were waiting to be answered at particular times of the day!

9.4 Summary

- Participant observation is an approach that allows the researcher to participate in or closely observe the lives and activities of those whom they are studying. It is used to attempt to get to the root of 'what is going on' in a wide range of social settings.
- Four types of participant observation are distinguished by two separate dimensions: whether the researcher's identity is revealed or concealed and the extent to which the researcher participates in the activities being observed.
- As a full-time student your choice of one of these types will be influenced by a number of factors including the nature of your research question and objectives, your ability to negotiate access, the time you have to devote to your research and your circumstances.
- As a part-time student in employment your choice of one of these types will be influenced by factors including the nature of your research question and objectives, your ability to simultaneously undertake your job and manage the demands of participant observation, being able to maintain objectivity and ensuring that your closeness to informants does not lead to conflict.
- Participant observation is principally conducted through the researcher being physically present although variations may involve the use of streamed, recorded or downloaded material. It leads to the production of different types of data that facilitate data analysis. Data are normally analysed like other qualitative data, with the intention of developing theory.
- A prevalent form of data analysis used in participant observation is analytic induction. This may lead to an initial hypothesis being redeveloped more than once.
- Participant observation has high ecological validity but may be affected by observer error, observer bias and observer effects. These issues may be minimised or overcome by observer familiarisation, interpretive rigour, informant verification, habituation and the observer using

strategies to explore and validate interpretations. Using these strategies can allow the benefits of gaining intricate and rich data to prevail over concerns about unreliable data.
- Structured observation is concerned with the frequency of events. It is characterised by a high level of predetermined structure and quantitative analysis.
- When collecting observational data, a choice will need to be made between using an 'off-the-shelf' coding schedule and one that you design for your own purpose. Alternatively, you may decide to develop a hybrid schedule that fulfils your research objectives more effectively.
- Structured observation may be affected by observer error, informant error, time error and observer effects. These issues may also be minimised or overcome by those strategies discussed in relation to participant observation and by designing a coding schedule that is free from interpretive ambiguity.

Self-check questions

Help with these questions is available at the end of the chapter.

9.1 You are a project manager responsible for the overall management of a large project to introduce your company's technology into the development of a new hospital. Most of the members of your team are from the UK, France and Germany. However, several of the engineers are from newer EU member states, principally Poland. You notice at project meetings that the Polish engineers tend to be far more reticent than the other team members in volunteering ideas for solving problems.

This issue has coincided with the arrival on the scene of a management student from the local university who is keen to study a real-life management problem for her final-year undergraduate dissertation. You have asked her to study the assimilation experience of 'new EU member state' engineers into your company with a view to recommending any changes that may be necessary to change the programme designed to effect the assimilation process.

You ask her to start the research by sitting in on the project team meetings and, in particular, observing the behaviour of the 'new EU member state' engineers. What suggestions would you make to your student to help her structure her observation of the meetings?

9.2 You have been asked to give a presentation to a group of managers at the accountancy firm in which you are hoping to negotiate access for research. You wish to pursue the research question: 'What are the informal rules that govern the way in which trainee accountants work, and how do they learn these rules?'

You realise that talk of 'attempting to learn the trainee accountants' symbolic world' would do little to help your cause with this group of non-research-minded businesspeople. However, you wish to point out some of the benefits to the organisation that your research may yield. Outline what you believe these would be.

9.3 You are a building society branch manager. You feel your staff are too reluctant to generate sales 'leads' from ordinary investors and borrowers, which may be passed on to the society's consultants in order that they can attempt to sell life insurance policies, pensions and unit trusts. You would like to understand the reasons for their reluctance. As the participant observer, how would you go about this?

How would you record your observations?

9.4 Look again at Box 9.9. Ask the questions contained in Box 9.9 in relation to the coding schedule in Figure 9.2. How well does it match?

Progressing your research project

Deciding on the appropriateness of observation

- Return to your research question(s) and objectives. Decide how appropriate it would be to use observation as part of your research strategy.
- If you decide that this is appropriate, explain the relationship between your research question(s) and objectives and observation. If you decide that using observation is not appropriate, justify your decision.
- Look again at the previous paragraph and ensure that you have responded for both participant observation and structured observation separately.
- If you decide that participant observation is appropriate, what practical problems do you foresee? Are you likely to be faced with any ethical dilemmas (see Chapter 6)? How might you overcome both sets of problems?
- If you decide that participant observation is appropriate, what threats to validity and reliability are you likely to encounter? How might you overcome these?
- If you decide that structured observation is appropriate, what practical problems do you foresee? How might you overcome these?
- If you decide that structured observation is appropriate, what threats to validity and reliability are you likely to encounter? How might you overcome these?
- If you decide that structured observation is appropriate, use an existing design or design your own research instrument.
- Use the questions in Box 1.4 to guide your reflective diary entry.

Review and discussion questions

9.5 Compile a behaviour observation sheet similar to that in Box 9.7 in respect of either your job or that of a friend. Use this to compile a record of the behaviours observed.

9.6 Choose an everyday example of social behaviour, such as the way that motorists park their cars in 'open' (not multi-storey) car parks. Observe this behaviour (for example, the distance from the entrance/exit that they park) and draw general conclusions about observed behaviour patterns.

9.7 Video record a current affairs (or similar) discussion on TV. Use the recording sheet in Figure 9.2 to record the interactions and then assess interaction patterns.

References

Brannick, T. and Coghlan, D. (2007) 'In defense of being native: The case for insider academic research', *Organizational Research Methods*, Vol. 10, No. 1, pp. 59–74.

Bryman, A. (1989) *Research Methods and Organisation Studies*. London: Unwin Hyman.

Cunliffe, A.L. (2010) 'Retelling tales of the field: In search of organisational ethnography 20 years on', *Organizational Research Methods*, Vol. 13, No. 2, pp. 224–39.

Delbridge, R. and Kirkpatrick, I. (1994) 'Theory and practice of participant observation', in V. Wass and P. Wells (eds) *Principles and Practice in Business and Management Research*. Aldershot, Dartmouth, pp. 35–62.

Denzin, N. (1989) *The Research Act: A Theoretical Introduction to Sociological Methods* (3rd edn). Englewood Cliffs, NJ: Prentice-Hall.

Ditton, J. (1977) *Part-Time Crime: An Ethnography of Fiddling and Pilferage*. London: Macmillan.

Gill, J. and Johnson, P. (2010) *Research Methods for Managers* (4th edn). London: Sage.

Hewson, C., Yule, P., Laurent, D. and Vogel, C. (2003) *Internet Research Methods*. London: Sage.

Kozinets, R.V. (2006) 'Netnography 2.0', in R.W. Belk (ed.) *Handbook of Qualitative Research Methods in Marketing*. Cheltenham: Edward Elgar Publishing, pp. 129–42.

Le Compte, M.D. and Goetz, J.P. (1982) 'Problems of reliability and validity in ethnographic research', *Review of Educational Research*, Vol. 52, No. 1, pp. 31–60.

Mintzberg, H. (1973) *The Nature of Managerial Work*. New York: Harper & Row.

Monahan, T. and Fisher, J.A. (2010) 'Benefits of "observer effects": Lessons from the field', *Qualitative Research*, Vol. 10, No. 3, pp. 357–76.

Mullins, L.J. (2010) *Management and Organisational Behaviour* (9th edn). Harlow: Financial Times Prentice Hall.

Robson, C. (2011) *Real World Research: A Resource for Users of Social Research Methods in Applied Settings* (3rd edn). Chichester: John Wiley.

Spano, R. (2005) 'Potential sources of observer bias in police observational data', *Social Science Research*, Vol. 34, pp. 591–617.

Starr, R. and Fernandez, K. (2007) 'The mindcam methodology: Perceiving through the natives eye', *Qualitative Market Research*, Vol. 10, No. 2, pp. 168–82.

Vaidyanathan, R. (2011) 'Barack Obama's shadow – the man who films the president', BBC News US and Canada. Available at: www.bbc.co.uk/news/world-us-canada-13148700?print=true [Accessed 6 June 2011].

Waddington, D. (2004) 'Participant observation', in C. Cassell and G. Symon (eds) *Essential Guide to Qualitative Methods in Organizational Research*. London: Sage, pp. 154–64.

Walker, R. (1985) *Doing Research: A Handbook for Teachers*. London: Methuen.

West Wing Week (2010) *The White House Blog*. Available at www.whitehouse.gov/blog/2010/04/02/west-wing-week [Accessed 6 June 2011].

Whyte, W.F. (1943) *Street Corner Society: The Social Structure of an Italian Slum*. Chicago: University of Chicago Press.

Further reading

Mintzberg, H. (1973) *The Nature of Managerial Work*. New York: Harper & Row. Appendix C has a full account of the methodology that Mintzberg employed. You will be struck by how such a seemingly simple methodology can lead to such important conclusions.

Monahan, T. and Fisher, J.A. (2010) 'Benefits of "observer effects": Lessons from the field', *Qualitative Research*, Vol. 10, No. 3, pp. 357–76. A very useful article that draws on observational research to evaluate observer effects and the benefits to be gained from using observation as a research method.

Robson, C. (2011) *Real World Research: A Resource for Users of Social Research Methods in Applied Settings* (3rd edn). Chichester: John Wiley. Chapter 13 provides a comprehensive discussion of observational methods related to both participant observation and structured observation.

Waddington, D. (2004) 'Participant observation', in C. Cassell and G. Symon (eds) *Essential Guide to Qualitative Methods in Organizational Research*. London: Sage, pp. 154–64. This provides a very readable account of participant observation in practice and useful evaluation of this method.

Case 9
Strategy options in a mature market

Siphiwe worked as a planner in the strategy department of a leading South African poultry producer which has invested heavily in recent years to increase production capacity as it targeted the lower income market. She was currently studying part-time for an MBA at her local university and had decided to use her organisation as a case study for her research project. Over the previous year her organisation's sales of the existing range of poultry products had remained stable and forecasts indicated that, unless something was done, they were likely to decline. From her work in the strategy department Siphiwe was already aware that the South African poultry market was regarded as being mature. Oversupply of poultry was placing downward pressure on prices (Beeld 2010; Smith 2010) whilst, at the same time, producer inflation was rising faster than consumer inflation, resulting in profit margins being reduced still further.

Flatties cooking on the braai
Source: © Mark Saunders 2011

Not surprisingly, Siphiwe felt her research should look at strategies her organisation could use to increase profit margins. Talking to her line manager, she discovered that her organisation had very little information about consumers' poultry-buying behaviours other than for their own range of products. In addition, no secondary data were available as Statistics South Africa, the body responsible for official statistics, no longer published wholesale and retail sales figures. Siphiwe therefore decided that she needed to collect her own comparative data on consumers' poultry-buying behaviours for both her own organisation's products and those of the competition. Her line manager asked her to ensure her organisation remained anonymous and suggested she called their company 'Cheeky Chicken'. He also agreed that a sensible research question would be: 'To what extent do customers' poultry-buying behaviours differ between "Cheeky Chicken's" and other poultry producers' products, and why?'

Siphiwe remembered that in her module on strategic management her lecturer had talked about how, when an organisation is at the mature stage of its lifecycle, it is often characterised by stabilising and even declining sales, which adversely affect profits. Rereading her module textbook (Aaker and McLoughlin 2010) and two other books she had found in the library (Barney and Hesterley 2010; Carpenter and Sanders 2009), she noted that organisations in such situations had a range of strategic options to try and ensure profitable survival:

- *Maintenance strategies* to protect market share, pursuing either:
  - forward integration by expanding activities toward end users of products such as obtaining a share in a retailing outlet;
  - backward integration by expanding activities to include the supply of inputs;
  - horizontal integration by merging with or taking over the competition.

- *Diversification strategies* to expand the market by adding products and/or new markets to reach more consumers and hence increase sales.
- *Cooperation strategies* through joint ventures and/or strategic alliances.
- *Harvest strategies* by limiting investment in mature products and 'harvesting' the income to invest in products that are likely to be more profitable.

From her knowledge of the South African poultry industry Siphiwe was aware that the Competition Commission were already suspicious regarding collusion in the industry (Marud 2010). This meant cooperation strategies might be difficult as they would attract attention from the competition authorities. Maintenance strategies were likely to involve increased investment and so put the organisation's declining profits further under pressure. In contrast, harvesting strategies, if introduced at the right time, could generate cash to invest elsewhere, perhaps used to diversify. Despite feeling that harvesting and diversification was probably the way forward, Siphiwe knew any such decision needed to be based both on reasoned argument and data. Without talking to her project supervisor, she therefore decided to observe consumers' poultry buying behaviour to get an insight into poultry sales across the product range. This she believed would provide the data she needed to inform the investment decision.

Siphiwe decided to visit two retailers in her immediate vicinity to observe the poultry-buying behaviour of shoppers. Given that she would be observing buyers in a public space, where anyone has a right to be, she considered there was no need to request permission from either retailer to observe their shoppers. On a late December Monday morning at 11.15 Siphiwe walked into the first retailer, a shop located in and serving an upper-middle-class neighbourhood. With her shopping trolley, notepad (that looked like a shopping list) and pen, she blended with the shoppers. Walking into the cold storage area, she observed that nobody was paying attention to the frozen poultry. Everyone who seemed interested in poultry was at the fresh poultry fridge. She slowly approached this fridge and inspected its contents. On one side were 'flatties' (splayed chicken in marinade) ready for the 'braai' (barbeque), in the middle skinless and regular cuts and on the other side whole birds. According to the price tags on the fridge, flatties, regular cuts and whole birds were all on 'special offer' with reduced prices. Siphiwe noted all the prices. Virtually all the regular poultry cuts had been sold and all the remaining poultry was the shop's own brand. She noted it was unclear which producer had supplied this poultry. Siphiwe moved to the next aisle where she had a clear view of the activities in front of the poultry fridge. Fortunately the shop was not too busy, which made observation easier.

Siphiwe observed and noted on her 'shopping list' what was happening at the poultry fridge. The majority of buyers (16), regardless of age, race and gender, whether alone or with someone, purchased one pack of regular poultry cuts, consisting of eight pieces (four thighs and four drumsticks) offered at the 'special price'. In one instance, a young male accompanied by a female smelled the cuts before he put the package in his basket. Skinless cuts were bought by only three customers – two older women accompanied by teenage girls and a middle-aged female, accompanied by a male, who also bought a 'special offer' whole bird. This was the second most popular product, particularly with the elderly of all races. One elderly woman stocked her basket with two such birds after consulting her male companion. Only one young male bought a flattie. After 20 minutes she had observed and noted the behaviour of 34 individuals. At this point she felt that someone might realise she was conducting research and decided to leave.

At the same time on the following day, Siphiwe entered her second retailer, this time in a large shopping centre close to a major road. This meant this retailer served a wide range of customers living in different neighbourhoods and even different towns. From their advertisements Siphiwe knew this retailer competed on price, targeting lower-income earners. Siphiwe walked towards the fridges and observed again that shoppers were ignoring frozen poultry in favour of fresh poultry. She examined this fridge and saw that the shelves were well stocked with a variety of brands (including five brands produced by her own organisation and four from competitors). When writing down the prices she observed that whilst prices for whole chickens were higher than the 'special offer' in the first shop, prices for the various cuts were lower, 'Cheeky Chicken's' most well-known brand being the least expensive. Siphiwe observed the packaging of this brand was more appealing than those of the others. As before, Siphiwe observed shoppers' behaviours, but this time she decided not to note down their race or age but concentrate more on their behaviours. In three instances, the shoppers walked straight to the fridge, took a product and moved on. In five cases, the shoppers first inspected the fridges and only then actually took a product. Two of these people appeared to be undecided because they put the selected item down before picking up another. A further three people walked away with nothing only to return after a while and take a product. Eight shoppers left the fridges without taking any product. The well-known competitor brand poultry cuts were most popular, being selected by eight buyers. One male, on picking up some cuts from another brand immediately put them down, remarking to his female companion: 'I don't buy junk'. 20 minutes later she left the shop having observed only 19 shoppers as no more people seemed to be visiting this part of the shop.

Based on her observation of poultry-buying behaviours, Siphiwe concluded that 'Cheeky Chicken' should consider reducing the number of brands offered to the market. She wished she could have asked shoppers why they had made the decisions they did. When she mentioned to a friend at work that she was puzzled when someone had sniffed the package, she discovered that a competitor poultry producer has recently publicly admitted that it reworked expired frozen poultry to be sold as fresh poultry to some shops (Van Wyk 2010). The management of the first shop had informed the press that they had inspected the facilities and the products of this particular supplier and were certain that none of their supplies had been reworked. The management of the second shop had not been available for comment.

References

Aaker, D. and McLoughlin, D. (2010) *Strategic Market Management: Global perspectives.* Chichester: John Wiley & Sons Ltd.

Barney, J.B. and Hesterley, W.S. (2010) *Strategic Management and Competitive Advantage: Concepts* (3rd edn). Upper Saddle River, NJ: Pearson.

Beeld (2010) 'Hier kiep-kiep, daar kiep-kiep (Cluck, cluck)', *Beeld*, 30 April.

Carpenter, M.A. and Sanders, W.G. (2009) *Strategic Management: A Dynamic Perspective, Concepts* (2nd edn). Upper Saddle River, NJ: Pearson.

Marud, M. (2010). 'Importers hope poultry probe will curb process', *Cape Argus*, 2 March.

Smith, C. (2010) 'Pluimveebedryf grootste in land (Poultry industry biggest in country)', *Volksblad*, 30 July.

Van Wyk, A. (2010) 'Supreme Poultry admits to selling expired chicken', *Eye Witness News*, 22 December. Available at http://eyewitnessnews.co.za/wintess.aspx [accessed 22 December 2010.]

Questions

1 Given Siphiwe's research question, do you think the observation method she used was the best option? Give reasons for your answer.
2 Do you think it was ethical for Siphiwe to use covert observation?
3 Do you consider Siphiwe's observations were of any value? Give reasons for your answer.
4 To what extent do you feel Siphiwe's presence in the shop could have affected the behaviour of the shoppers?
5 Comment on the validity and reliability of the data Siphiwe has collected.

Additional case studies relating to material covered in this chapter are available via the book's companion website: **www.pearsoned.co.uk/saunders**. They are:

- Manufacturing in a textile company.
- Customer satisfaction on a long-haul tour holiday.
- Exploring service quality in bank customers' face-to-face experience.
- Online images of tourist detinations.

Self-check answers

9.1 It may be as well to suggest to her that she start her attendance at meetings with an unstructured approach in order to simply get the 'feel' of what is happening. She should make notes of her general impressions of the 'new EU member states' team members' general participation in meetings. She could then analyse these data and develop an observational instrument which could be used in further meetings she attends. This instrument would be based on a coding schedule that allowed her to record, among other things, the amount of contribution by each person at the meeting and the content of that contribution.

Data collection at the meetings does, of course, raise questions of research ethics. In our view, you, as the project manager, should explain to the team the role that the researcher is playing at the meetings. It would be quite truthful to say that the meeting participation of all team members is being observed with the overall purpose of making the meetings more effective, although it need not be emphasised what gave rise to the project manager's initial concern.

9.2 The research question is very broad. It allows you plenty of scope to discover a host of interesting things about the world of the trainee accountant. Without doubt, one of the things you will emerge with a clear understanding of is what they like about their work and what they do not like. This has practical implications for the sort of people that the firm ought to recruit, and how they should be trained and rewarded. You may learn about some of the short cuts practised by all occupations that may not be in the interest of the client. By the same token you will probably discover aspects of good practice that managers can disseminate to other accountants. The list of practical implications is numerous.

All this assumes, of course, that you will supply the managers with some post-research feedback. This does raise issues of confidentiality, which you must have thought through beforehand.

9.3 This is a difficult one. The question of status may be a factor. However, this would depend on your relationship with the staff. If you are, say, of similar age and have an open, friendly, 'one of the team' relationship with them, then it may not be too difficult. The element of threat that would attend a less open relationship would not be present.

You could set aside a time each day to work on the counter in order really to get to know what life is like for them. Even if you have done their job, you may have forgotten what it is like! It may have changed since your day. Direct conversations about lead generation would probably not feature in your research times. However, you would need to have a period of reflection after each 'research session' to think about the implications for your research question of what you have just experienced.

9.4 Clearly, there are some question marks about the coding schedule in Figure 9.2. There does appear to be some overlap in the behavioural categories covered in the schedule. For example, it could be difficult to distinguish between what is 'offering directions' (taking initiative) and 'offering ideas' (brainstorming). It might be even more difficult to draw a distinction between 'offering suggestions' (brainstorming) and 'making helpful suggestions' (offering positive ideas). Similarly, there does not appear to be much difference between the behaviours in 'drawing in others' and 'being responsive to others'. You may argue that the first is defined by invitation, the second by response. But making the distinction when the interactions are coming thick and fast in the research setting will be much less easy.

The point about all these potential confusions is that different observers may make different estimations. This obviously has potentially harmful implications for the reliability of the coding schedule.

A much smaller point is: How does the observer indicate on the schedule the occurrence of a particular interaction?

Get ahead using resources on the companion website at:
www.pearsoned.co.uk/saunders

- Improve your IBM SPSS Statistics and NVivo research analysis with practice tutorials.
- Save time researching on the Internet with the Smarter Online Searching Guide.
- Test your progress using self-assessment questions.
- Follow live links to useful websites.

Chapter 10

Collecting primary data using semi-structured, in-depth and group interviews

Learning outcomes

By the end of this chapter you should be:

- able to classify research interviews in order to help you to understand the purpose of each type;
- aware of research situations favouring the use of semi-structured and in-depth interviews, and their limitations;
- able to analyse potential data quality issues and evaluate how to overcome these;
- able to consider the development of your competence to undertake semi-structured and in-depth interviews, and the logistical and resource issues that affect their use;
- aware of the advantages and disadvantages of using one-to-one and group interviews, including focus groups, in particular contexts;
- aware of the issues and advantages of conducting interviews by telephone and via the Internet or intranet.

10.1 Introduction

The **research interview** is a purposeful conversation between two or more people, requiring the interviewer to establish rapport, to ask concise and unambiguous questions, to which the interviewee is willing to respond, and to listen attentively. Essentially it is about asking purposeful questions and carefully listening to the answers to be able to explore these further. The use of interviews can help you to gather valid and reliable data that are relevant to your research question(s) and objectives. Interviews can also be used to help you refine your ideas where you have not yet formulated a research question and objectives.

In reality, the research interview is a general term for several types of interview. This fact is important since the nature of any interview should be consistent with your research question(s) and objectives, the purpose of your research and the research strategy that you have adopted. We provide an overview of types of interview in the next section of this chapter

(Section 10.2) and show how each type is related to a research purpose. Our main focus in this chapter is on semi-structured, in-depth and group interviews, with structured interviews (interviewer-administered questionnaires) being discussed in Chapter 11.

Section 10.3 considers situations favouring the use of semi-structured and in-depth interviews. Section 10.4 identifies data quality issues associated with their use and discusses how to overcome these. Section 10.5 discusses preparing for semi-structured and in-depth

Interviews are occurring constantly. There is probably not a day that goes by without you reading about, listening to and watching interviews. We read interviews such as those given by business leaders in quality newspapers, listen to interviews such as those with celebrities on radio programmes and watch interviews about news events on television programmes. Every time an event happens, those who witness it, those who are involved in it and those who have some expertise associated with it will be interviewed. However, despite the seeming ease with which interviews may be conducted, using the interview to collect research data requires considerable skill.

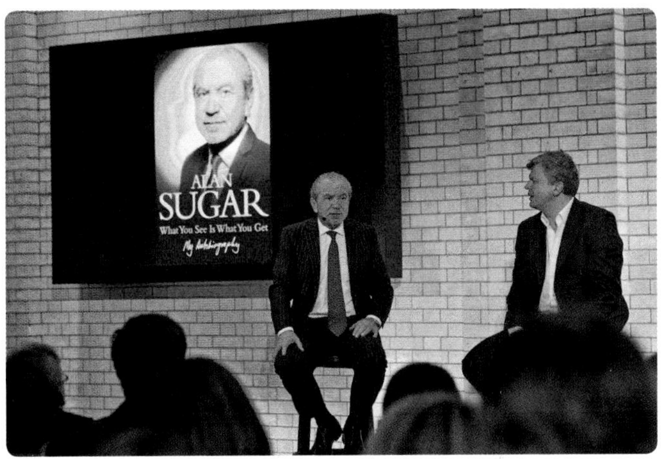

A television interview with Lord Sugar
Source: Getty Images

One profession that relies on good-quality interview skills is journalism. The BBC College of Journalism outlines a number of key interviewing skills on its website. It advises interviewers to think clearly about the purpose of each interview. Interviewers need to be aware that their first question will set the direction of an interview and establish its style. Think of the interview style of a 'hard' interviewer you have seen or heard and contrast that with the style of a 'friendly, inviting' interviewer! Interviewers are also advised to be clear in the way they ask questions and not to be obscure or to use jargon. One key way to achieve clarity is to achieve simplicity. This means finding ways to ask questions about complex issues that are simple and direct. Interviewers should also ask questions that are appropriate. Open questions invite interviewees to describe or explain, or to develop a previous answer. Closed questions seek straightforward answers, like 'yes' or 'no'. In journalism, this type of question can be used to get to the heart of a particular matter and for this reason it is often called the 'killer' question. Where an interviewee wants to avoid directly answering such a question, its use will expose this reluctance to give a straightforward answer. The use of a 'killer' question isn't likely to be appropriate in business and management interviewing, but the other skills outlined on the BBC College of Journalism website (2011) are likely to be helpful to business and management researchers and the website contains video guides that you can access to watch highly skilled journalists demonstrating each of these interview skills.

interviews and Section 10.6 conducting these. Section 10.7 considers logistical and resource issues and how to manage these. Section 10.8 considers the particular advantages and issues associated with the use of group interviews and focus groups. Finally, Section 10.9 explores the advantages and issues associated with telephone, Internet- and intranet-mediated (electronic) interviews.

10.2 Types of interview and their link to the purpose of research and research strategy

Types of interview

Interviews may be highly formalised and structured, using standardised questions for each research participant (called a **respondent** in this type of interview) (Section 11.2), or they may be informal and unstructured conversations. In between there are intermediate positions depending on the level of formality and structure used. For example, an interview may contain some highly structured sections and some unstructured parts, depending on its purpose. One typology that is commonly used relates to these levels of formality and structure, where interviews are categorised as either:

- structured interviews;
- semi-structured interviews;
- unstructured or in-depth interviews.

Another commonly used typology differentiates between:

- standardised interviews;
- non-standardised interviews.

Robson (2011), based on the work of Powney and Watts (1987), refers to a different typology:

- focused interviews;
- non-directive interviews.

There is overlap between these different typologies, although consideration of each typology adds to our overall understanding of the nature of research interviews.

Structured interviews use questionnaires based on a predetermined and 'standardised' or identical set of questions and we refer to them as interviewer-administered questionnaires (Section 11.2). You read out each question and then record the response on a standardised schedule, usually with pre-coded answers (Sections 11.4 and 12.2). While there is social interaction between you and the respondent, such as the preliminary explanations that you will need to provide, you should read out the questions exactly as written and in the same tone of voice so that you do not indicate any bias. As structured interviews are used to collect quantifiable data they are also referred to as 'quantitative research interviews'.

By comparison, semi-structured and in-depth (unstructured) interviews are 'non-standardised'. These are often referred to as qualitative research interviews (King, 2004). In **semi-structured interviews** the researcher will have a list of themes and possibly some key questions to be covered, although their use may vary from interview to interview. This means that you may omit some questions in particular interviews, given a specific organisational context that is encountered in relation to the research topic. The order of questions may also be varied depending on the flow of the conversation. On the other hand, additional questions may be required to explore your research question and objectives given the nature of events within particular organisations. The nature of the questions and the ensuing discussion mean that data will be captured by audio-recording the conversation or perhaps note taking (Section 10.5). Apart from containing the list of themes and questions to be covered, the **interview schedule** for this type of interview will also be likely to contain some comments to open the discussion, a possible list of prompts to promote and further discussion, and some comments to close it. These are discussed in more detail later.

Unstructured interviews are informal. You would use these to explore in depth a general area in which you are interested. We therefore refer to these as 'in-depth interviews' in this chapter and elsewhere in this book. There is no predetermined list of questions to work through in this situation, although you need to have a clear idea about the aspect or aspects that you want to explore. The interviewee is given the opportunity to talk freely about events, behaviour and beliefs in relation to the topic area, so that this type of interaction is sometimes called non-directive. It has been labelled as an **informant interview** since it is the interviewee's perceptions that guide the conduct of the interview. In comparison, a **focused interview** is one where the interviewer exercises greater direction over the interview while allowing the interviewee's opinions to emerge as he or she responds to the questions of the researcher (Easterby-Smith et al. 2008; Ghauri and Grønhaug 2010; Robson 2011).

We can also differentiate between types of interview according to the nature of interaction between the researcher and those who participate in this process. Interviews may be conducted on a one-to-one basis, between you and a single participant. Such interviews are most commonly conducted by meeting your participant 'face to face', but there may be some situations where you conduct an interview by telephone or using the Internet or an organisation's intranet. There may be other situations where you conduct a semi-structured or in-depth interview on a group basis, where you meet with a small number of participants to explore an aspect of your research through a group discussion that you facilitate. These forms of interview are summarised in Figure 10.1. The discussion throughout most of this chapter applies to each of these forms. However, the final two sections (10.8 and 10.9) include specific consideration of the issues and advantages related to the use of one to many group interviews and focus groups and to the use of a telephone and Internet-mediated interviews as an alternative to a 'face-to-face' meeting, respectively.

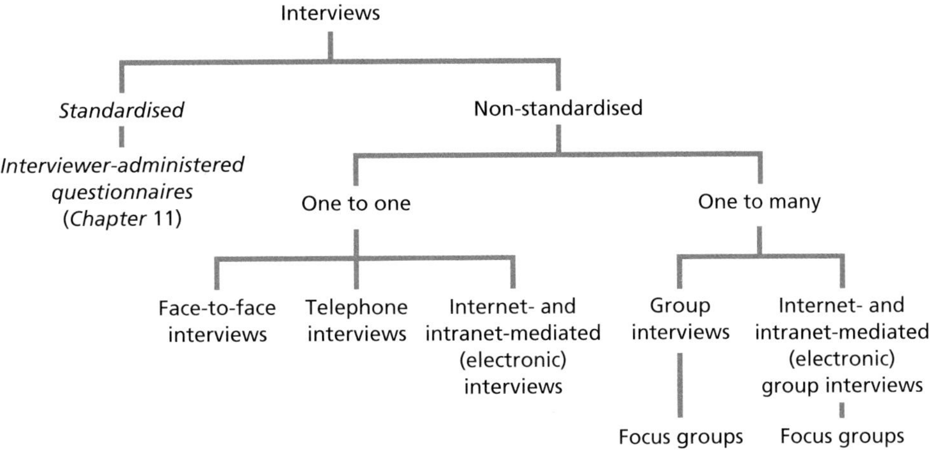

Figure 10.1 Forms of interview

Links to the purpose of research and research strategy

Each form of interview outlined above has a distinct purpose. Structured, standardised interviews are normally used to gather data which will then be the subject of quantitative analysis (Sections 12.3–12.5), for example as part of a survey strategy. Semi-structured and in-depth interviews are used to gather data which are normally analysed qualitatively (Chapter 13), for example as part of a case study or Grounded Theory strategy. These data are likely to be used not only to understand the 'what' and the 'how' but also to place more emphasis on 'why' (Box 10.1).

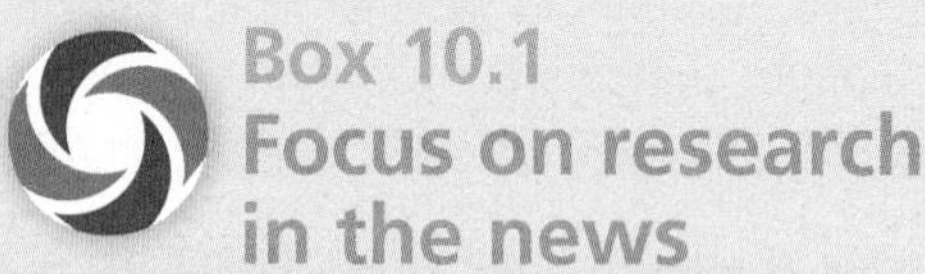

FT

Users' trust of online news rises

British web surfers say they now trust online news sources more than television bulletins and newspapers, ignoring the adage never to believe what you read on the Internet. A survey of media literacy by Ofcom, the media regulator, also found that almost half of the UK population had created a profile on a social networking site, but added that adults were becoming more savvy about who they befriended online.

According to 1824 in-depth interviews with people over the age of 16 conducted last year, Britain has become an even more tech-happy nation since Ofcom's last audit in 2007, with usage of digital television, Internet and mobile phones all increasing.

With seven in 10 people now using the Internet, booking holidays online has become just as popular as visiting a travel agent in person, while about half of all Internet users have used price comparison websites to save money or research an illness using the Web.

Even so, many people remain sceptical of the reliability of the information they find online. More than half of those surveyed rated television and radio content as 'reliable and accurate', compared with less than a third lending the same credence to the Internet for general use. But for the first time the Web overtook television as the more trusted source of news, Ofcom found. Although both were outstripped by radio at 66 per cent, 58 per cent of people said they trusted online news and 54 per cent believed television. People aged 25 to 34 were by far the most confident that television news was accurate, with women more convinced than men.

The press was deemed the least trustworthy medium, with more adults saying they thought newspapers were unreliable than said they believed in them.

That increase in trust for online sources may stem from an increase in the use of social networks, where people frequently share news and links, lending a personal endorsement to the story or website, Ofcom found. It also said the proportion of Internet users with a social networking profile had doubled since 2007, with the biggest increases among women, 25 to 34-year-olds, and the lowest socioeconomic grouping, DE. Facebook is by far the most popular, with MySpace and Bebo both seeing falls in usage, and Twitter used by just one in 10.

Two in five people visit a social network every day, with half of all Internet users saying the Web has increased the frequency of their contact with friends and family.

More than three-quarters of those who have an online identity allow only friends or family to see it, Ofcom found, marking a large increase in the number of people restricting who can see their personal information since 2007. Only 17 per cent said they had profiles that can now be seen by 'anyone', compared with 44 per cent in 2007.

Source: From 'Users' trust of online news rises', Tim Bradshaw, *Financial Times*, 18 May 2010.

In Chapter 5 we outlined how the purpose of your research could be classified as either exploratory, descriptive or explanatory (Section 5.4). By examining these categories we can see how the various types of interview may be used to gather information for, and assist the progress of, each kind of study:

- In an exploratory study, in-depth interviews can be very helpful to find out what is happening and to understand the context. Semi-structured interviews may also be used in an exploratory study. Both of these types of interview may provide important background or contextual material for your study. You will find it helpful to conduct exploratory, qualitative interviews where your research design adopts an inductive approach, as in the development of grounded theory (Section 4.3 and 5.5)
- In a descriptive study, structured interviews (Section 11.2) can be used as a means to identify general patterns. You may find it helpful to conduct structured interviews where your research design uses a deductive approach to test a theory, as the standardised nature of the data will make it easier to test statistical propositions or hypotheses (Chapter 12).
- In an explanatory study, semi-structured interviews may be used in order to understand the relationships between variables, such as those revealed from a descriptive study (Section 5.4). Structured interviews may also be used in relation to an explanatory study, in a statistical sense (Section 12.5). Research interviews used for an explanatory purpose may be useful in both inductive and deductive approaches because of the intention to explain why relationships exist (Section 2.4).

This is summarised in Table 10.1.

Your research may incorporate more than one type of interview (multiple methods). As part of a survey strategy, for example, you may decide to use in-depth or semi-structured interviews initially to help identify the questions that should be asked in a questionnaire administered as a structured interview. The data that you gather from such exploratory interviews will be used in the design of your structured interview. Alternatively, semi-structured interviews may be used to explore and explain themes that have emerged from the use of a questionnaire. In addition to the use of multiple methods, different types of interview questions may be used within one interview. For example, one section of an interview may be composed of a set of questions with pre-coded responses, while another section may use semi-structured questions to explore responses. Increasingly authors also emphasise how semi-structured or in-depth interviews may also be used as part of mixed methods research, such as a means to validate findings from questionnaires (Teddlie and Tashakkori 2009). We can therefore see that the various types of interview have a number of potentially valuable uses in terms of undertaking your research project. The key point for you to consider is the consistency between your research question and objectives, the strategy you will employ and the methods of data collection you will use.

Table 10.1 Uses of different types of interview in each of the main research categories

	Exploratory	Descriptive	Explanatory
Structured		✓✓	✓
Semi-structured	✓		✓✓
Unstructured	✓✓		

✓✓ = more frequent, ✓ = less frequent.

10.3 When to use semi-structured and in-depth interviews

There are many situations in which the use of semi-structured or in-depth research interviews as a method of data collection may be advantageous. These situations can be grouped into four categories:

- the purpose of the research;
- the significance of establishing personal contact;
- the nature of the data collection questions;
- length of time required and completeness of the process.

We examine each of these in turn.

The purpose of the research

Where you are undertaking an exploratory study, or a study that includes an exploratory element, it is likely that you will include in-depth or semi-structured research interviews in your design (Cooper and Schindler 2008). Similarly, an explanatory study is also likely to include interviews in order for the researcher to be able to infer causal relationships between variables (Sections 2.4 and 11.4). Where it is necessary for you to understand the reasons for the decisions that your research participants have taken, or to understand the reasons for their attitudes and opinions, you are likely to need to conduct an in-depth or semi-structured interview.

Semi-structured and in-depth interviews also provide you with the opportunity to 'probe' answers, where you want your interviewees to explain, or build on, their responses. This is important if you are adopting an interpretivist epistemology, where you will be concerned to understand the meanings that participants ascribe to various phenomena (Section 4.2). Interviewees may use words or ideas in a particular way, and the opportunity to probe these meanings will add significance and depth to the data you obtain. They may also lead the discussion into areas that you had not previously considered but which are significant for your understanding, and which help you to address your research question and objectives, or indeed help you formulate such a question. Interviews also afford each interviewee an opportunity to hear themself 'thinking aloud' about things they may not have previously thought about. The result should be that you are able to collect a rich and detailed set of data. However, you need to be aware that the manner in which you interact with your interviewees and ask questions will impact on the data you collect.

The significance of establishing personal contact

We have found that managers are more likely to agree to be interviewed, rather than complete a questionnaire, especially where the interview topic is seen to be interesting and relevant to their current work. An interview provides them with an opportunity to reflect on events without needing to write anything down. This situation also provides the opportunity for interviewees to receive feedback and personal assurance about the way in which information will be used (Sections 6.2 and 6.5).

Potential research participants who receive a questionnaire via the Internet, the intranet or through the post may be reluctant to complete it for a number of reasons. They may feel that it is not appropriate to provide sensitive and confidential information to someone they have never met. They may also not completely trust the way in which the information is to be used. They may be reluctant to spend time providing written explanatory answers, where these are requested, especially if the meaning of any question is not entirely clear. The use of personal interviews, where appropriate, may therefore achieve a higher response rate than using questionnaires (Sections 7.2 and 7.3). Where a questionnaire is received by a manager who is not inclined to complete it, it may also be passed to another person to complete which will adversely affect your control over those whom you wish to answer your questions and also possibly the reliability of the data that you receive.

The nature of the questions

An in-depth or semi-structured interview will undoubtedly be the most advantageous approach to attempt to obtain data in the following circumstances (Easterby-Smith et al. 2008; Jankowicz 2005):

- where there are a large number of questions to be answered;
- where the questions are either complex or open-ended;
- where the order and logic of questioning may need to be varied (Box 10.2).

Length of time required and completeness of the process

Often the complexity of issues to be covered or their number and variety mean that an interview is the best or only means of collecting data. In our experience, where expectations have been established clearly about the length of time required and participants understand and agree with the objectives of the research interview, they have generally been willing to agree to be interviewed. Some negotiation is, in any case, possible and the interview can be arranged at a time when the interviewee will be under least pressure.

Box 10.2 Focus on student research

The need to vary the order and logic of questioning

Val undertook a series of semi-structured interviews into the approach used to manage public relations (PR) activities in 30 organisations. It soon became evident that it would not be meaningful to ask exactly the same questions in each organisation. For example, some organisations had centralised PR as part of the marketing function, whereas in other organisations it was devolved to individual business units. Another significant variable was associated with the public relations styles adopted. Some organisations adopted a 'press agency' approach where the main focus was to get the organisation or product mentioned in the media as often as possible, the nature of the mention being of secondary importance. Others adopted a 'public information' approach where the main aim was to get media exposure for the organisation or product.

The impact of these and other variables meant that it was not sensible to ask exactly the same questions at each interview, even though many questions remained applicable in all cases and the underlying intention was to ensure consistency between interviews. It was not until each interview had started that Val was able to learn which of these different variables operated within the particular organisation. Fortunately, the flexibility offered by the use of semi-structured interviews enabled her to do this.

Box 10.3 Checklist

To help you decide whether to use in-depth or semi-structured interviews

- ✔ Does the purpose of your research suggest using semi-structured and/or in-depth interviews?
- ✔ Will it help to seek personal contact in terms of gaining access to participants and their data?
- ✔ Are your data collection questions large in number, complex or open-ended?
- ✔ Will there be a need to vary the order and logic of questioning?
- ✔ Will it help to be able to probe interviewees' responses to build on or seek explanation of their answers?
- ✔ Will the data collection process with each individual involve a relatively lengthy period?

We have found that our participants tend to be generous with their time, and sometimes when interviews have been organised to start at mid-morning they will arrange for lunch, which can allow the discussion and exploration of issues to continue. However, for those of you who fancy a free lunch, we do not want to raise your expectations falsely, and the start time for an interview should not be set with this in mind!

Your aim will be to obtain data to enable you to answer all your research questions, allowing for the right of participants to decline to respond to any question you ask. Where you conduct the interaction skilfully an interview is more likely to achieve this than the use of a self-administered or interviewer-administered questionnaire. Where your participant does not provide an answer to a particular question or questions in an in-depth or semi-structured interview, you should be able to form some indication of why a response could not be provided. This may even lead you to modify the question or to compose another where this would be appropriate. Section 6.6 provides a consideration of the ethical issues associated with seeking to obtain answers.

While there are a number of situations favouring the use of in-depth or semi-structured interviews, you still need to decide whether or not to use these types of interview to collect your data and, of equal importance, to justify your choice. Silverman (2007) emphasises that your choice should depend on what is the best way to answer your research question. He refers to a discussion by Speer (2002, cited in Silverman, 2007: 57) as an illustration: 'if you are studying gender . . . you should be wary of basing your research on interviews where participants are asked to comment on gender issues . . . You are much more likely to gather reliable data by studying how people actually *do* gender in everyday environments, e.g. in meetings, email messages, etc'. Box 10.3 provides a checklist to help you in your deliberations as to whether or not to use in-depth or semi-structured interviews.

10.4 Data quality issues associated with semi-structured and in-depth interviews

Data quality issues

Before discussing how to prepare for and conduct semi-structured or in-depth interviews we consider data quality issues associated with these types of research interview. This is because your preparation for and conduct of these interviews will be influenced by the need to avoid these issues. We use the language of the positivist tradition to describe these data quality issues, in order to show how well-designed qualitative research interviews respond to the standards used to assess quantitative research (Section 5.8). These data quality issues are related to:

- reliability;
- forms of bias;
- generalisability;
- validity.

We discuss these in turn.

The lack of standardisation in these types of interview may lead to concerns about **reliability**. In relation to qualitative research, reliability is concerned with whether alternative researchers would reveal similar information (Easterby-Smith et al. 2008; Silverman 2007). The concern about reliability in these types of interview is also related to issues of bias. There are three types of potential bias to consider. The first of these is related to **interviewer bias**. This is where the comments, tone or non-verbal behaviour of the interviewer creates bias in the way that interviewees respond to the questions being asked. This may be because you attempt to impose your own beliefs and frame of reference through the questions that you ask. It is also possible that you will demonstrate bias in the way you interpret responses. Where you are unable to develop the trust of the interviewee, or perhaps where your credibility is seen to be lacking, the value of the information given may also be limited, raising doubts about its validity and reliability.

Related to this is **interviewee** or **response bias**. This type of bias may be caused by perceptions about the interviewer, as we have referred to, or in relation to perceived interviewer bias. However, the cause of this type of bias may not be linked to any perception related to the interviewer. Taking part in an interview is an intrusive process. This is especially true in the case of in-depth or semi-structured interviews, where your aim will be to explore events or to seek explanations. An interviewee may, in principle, be willing to participate but may nevertheless be sensitive to the unstructured exploration of certain themes. Interviewees may therefore choose not to reveal and discuss an aspect of the topic that you wish to explore, because this would lead to probing questions that would intrude on sensitive information that they do not wish, or are not empowered, to discuss with you. The outcome of this may be that the interviewee provides a partial 'picture' of the situation that casts himself or herself in a 'socially desirable' role, or the organisation for which they work in a positive or even negative fashion.

Bias may also result from the nature of the individuals or organisational participants who agree to be interviewed (Box 10.4). This may be labelled as **participation bias**.

Box 10.4 Focus on student research

Willingness (or otherwise) to be interviewed

Saffron's research project involved her interviewing people about their perceptions of the real benefits of different hair products. She decided that the best way to conduct these interviews was, with the permission of the owner, to interview customers at her local hairdresser. Saffron discovered that although some of the customers were willing to be interviewed, others were not. A minority of customers, often smartly dressed in business suits, refused outright, saying that they had insufficient time. In contrast, others, particularly pensioners, were happy to answer her questions in considerable detail and appeared to wish to prolong the interview.

The time-consuming requirements of the interview process may result in a reduction in willingness to take part of some of those to whom you would like to talk. This may bias your sample from whom data are collected. This is an issue that you will need to consider carefully and attempt to overcome through the approach taken to sampling (Sections 7.2 and 7.3).

An issue is often raised about the generalisability of findings from qualitative research interviews, although the validity of the data they produce is generally seen as less of an issue. **Generalisability** refers to the extent to which the findings of a research study are applicable to other settings. This is frequently questioned in relation to the statistical generalisability of qualitative research studies where these are based on a small sample. However, this should not be interpreted as meaning that a qualitative study is intrinsically less generalisable than a quantitative study. The generalisability of each will depend equally on the nature of the sample on which it is based. **Validity** refers to the extent to which the researcher has gained access to a participant's knowledge and experience, and is able to infer meanings that the participant intends from the language used by that person.

Overcoming data quality issues

Reliability

One response to the issue of reliability is that the findings derived from using in-depth or semi-structured interviews are not necessarily intended to be repeatable since they reflect reality at the time they were collected, in a situation which may be subject to change (Marshall and Rossman 2006). The assumption behind this type of research is that the circumstances to be explored are complex and dynamic. The value of using in-depth or semi-structured interviews is derived from the flexibility that you may use to explore the complexity of the topic. Therefore, an attempt to ensure that qualitative, non-standardised research could be replicated by other researchers would not be realistic or feasible without undermining the strength of this type of research. Marshall and Rossman (2006) suggest that researchers using a qualitative, non-standardised approach need to make this clear – perhaps to transform an aspect perceived to be a weakness by some into a strength based on realistic assumptions about the ability to replicate research findings.

However, they suggest that where you use this approach you should make and retain notes relating to your research design, the reasons underpinning the choice of strategy and methods, and the data obtained. These records can be referred to by other researchers in order to understand the processes you used and to enable them to reanalyse the data that you collected. The use of in-depth or semi-structured interviews should not lead to a lack of rigour in relation to the research process – if anything, greater rigour is required to overcome the views of those who may be wedded to the value of quantitative research to the exclusion of any other approach.

Interviewer and interviewee bias

Overcoming these forms of bias is related to the ways in which these types of interview are prepared for and conducted. Bias may be avoided by acting on the points indicated in Box 10.5, which lists the key measures that you will need to consider as you prepare for and conduct semi-structured or in-depth interviews. These measures are discussed in Sections 10.5 and 10.6.

Box 10.5 Checklist

Measures to overcome interviewer and interviewee bias as you prepare for and conduct semi-structured or in-depth interviews

- ✔ Your level of knowledge about the context of the organisation or culture of the group within which research interviews will be conducted
- ✔ The level of information supplied by you to each interviewee
- ✔ The appropriateness of the interview location
- ✔ The appropriateness of your appearance at the interview
- ✔ The nature of your opening comments at the interview
- ✔ Your approach to questioning
- ✔ Appropriate use of open, probing, specific and closed questions and avoidance of leading questions
- ✔ The impact of your behaviour during the interview
- ✔ Your ability to demonstrate attentive listening skills
- ✔ Your scope to summarise and test your understanding
- ✔ Your ability to recognise and deal with difficult participants, where this becomes appropriate
- ✔ Your ability to record data accurately and fully

Generalisability

Earlier we stated that there is likely to be a concern surrounding the generalisability of findings from qualitative research, based on the use of a small and unrepresentative number of cases. However, two arguments have been advanced that seek to clarify and modify the approach often adopted to the generalisability of qualitative research. The first of these relates to the situation where a single case study is used because of the unstructured nature of the research. Bryman (1988: 90) states that 'within a case study a wide range of different people and activities are invariably examined so that the contrast with survey samples is not as acute as it appears at first glance'. The single case may in fact encompass a number of settings, where for example it involves a study in a large organisation with sites across the country, or even around the world. By contrast, Bryman (1988) points out that many research projects adopting a survey strategy use samples restricted to one particular locality. A well-completed and rigorous case study is thus more likely to be useful in other contexts than one that lacks such rigour.

The second argument with the approach that questions the generalisability of qualitative research or a case study is related to the significance of this type of research to theoretical propositions (Bryman 1988; Yin 2009). Where you are able to relate your research project to existing theory you will be in a position to demonstrate that your findings have a broader theoretical significance than the case or cases that form the basis of your work (Marshall and Rossman 2006). It will clearly be up to you to establish this relationship to existing theory in order to be able to demonstrate the broader significance of your particular case study findings.

This relationship will allow your study to test the applicability of existing theory to the setting(s) that you are examining and where this is found wanting to suggest why. It will also allow theoretical propositions to be advanced that can then be tested in another context. As Bryman (1988) points out, this also has implications for the relationship between theory and research, since the identification of existing theory and its application will be necessary before the researcher embarks on the collection of data.

However, in seeking to counter arguments about the generalisability of qualitative research studies using semi-structured or in-depth interviews, it is important to recognise that such studies cannot be used to make statistical generalisations about an entire population (whatever this may be in the context of the research topic) where your data are from a small non-probability sample.

Validity

In semi-structured and in-depth interviews a high level of validity may be achieved where these are conducted carefully due to the scope to clarify questions, to probe meanings and to be able to explore responses and themes from a variety of angles. This use of questioning in such interviews is discussed in detail in Section 10.6.

10.5 Preparing for semi-structured or in-depth interviews

Like all research methods, the key to a successful interview is careful preparation. When using in-depth or semi-structured interviews, the 'five Ps' will be useful to remember: prior planning prevents poor performance. In particular, we believe it is crucial that you plan precisely how you are going to demonstrate your competence and credibility to obtain the confidence of your interviewees.

In order to avoid data quality issues when you conduct in-depth or semi-structured interviews, we consider some key measures that your preparations will need to include. These are:

- Your level of knowledge.
- Developing interview themes and supplying information to the interviewee before the interview.
- The appropriateness of the intended interview location.

We discuss these in turn.

Level of knowledge

You need to be knowledgeable about the research topic and organisational or situational context in which the interview is to take place. In addition to your literature review, a prior search in your university library (Sections 3.4 and 3.5) may reveal journal articles written by senior employees of the organisation that is participating in your research. There may also be other material about the organisation, and this is particularly likely to be found on the Internet, in the 'trade' press and the quality newspapers. This is likely to include company annual reports and other publications, as well as financial data relating to the organisation. The ability to draw on this type of information in the interview should help to demonstrate your credibility, assess the accuracy of responses and encourage the interviewee to offer a more detailed account of the topic under discussion. As you undertake your interviews, you will also be able to draw on the initial analysis that you make of data previously collected.

Interviewing participants from different cultures will also require you to develop some knowledge about those cultures to be able to undertake interviews successfully and to obtain reliable data. Without adequate preparation, there may be misinterpretation because of the cultural differences between the interviewee and the interviewer

(Marshall and Rossman 2006). An in-depth interview at least offers the opportunity to explore meanings, including those that may be culturally specific, but you will need to be aware of cultural differences and their implications (see, for example, Hofstede 2001). Kvale and Brinkmann (2009) highlight some of the verbal and non-verbal cues that may have contrary or different meanings between cultures. For example, answering 'yes' to a question may be taken to indicate agreement but in some cultures it may be a way of telling the interviewer that the question has been understood, or in others to recognise its importance. A nod of the head may be taken as agreement in some cultures but in others it may mean something else. Kvale and Brinkmann (2009) note the importance of being aware of social conventions in a culture in order to understand the way answers are constructed and also not to cause offence, both of which may affect the conduct of the interview. Cultural differences not only exist between countries but between groups, social classes and organisations and some prior knowledge about those you wish to interview will probably be helpful to the conduct of each interview.

Developing interview themes and supplying information to the interviewee before the interview

Credibility may also be promoted through the supply of relevant information to participants before the interview. Providing participants with a list of the interview themes before the event, where this is appropriate, should help this. This list of themes (Box 10.6) may help to promote validity and reliability because it informs the interviewee about the information you are interested in and provides them with the opportunity to prepare for the interview by assembling supporting organisational documentation from their files. We can testify to this approach and the value of allowing participants to prepare themselves for the discussion in which they are to engage. Access to organisational documentation also allows for triangulation of the data provided (Sections 8.2 and 8.3). Our experience is that participants are generally willing to supply a pdf file or photocopy of such material, although of course it will be necessary to conceal any confidential or personal details that this contains.

Box 10.6 Focus on student research

Developing interview themes

Karl was interested in understanding why some employees in his organisation used the IT Help Desk whilst others did not. This subject was felt to be significant in relation to the perceptions of service-level agreements, service relationships and service quality. He decided to provide his interviewees with a list of themes that he wished to explore during the interviews. After some deliberation and reading of the academic literature he came up with the following list of themes to explore (the question):

what do employees understand by the term 'IT Help Desk'?:

- the extent to which the IT Help Desk is meeting employees' needs;
- the nature of support employees feel they are receiving;
- the extent to which employees feel they know how to use the IT Help Desk;
- the services employees feel the IT Help Desk should be providing;
- knowledge of service-level agreements.

He subsequently used this list of themes to develop his interview guide (Box 10.7).

Box 10.7 Focus on student research

Extract from an interview guide

Karl was interested in understanding why some employees in his organisation used the IT Help Desk whilst others did not. Using his interview themes (Box 10.6), he began to develop his guide:

Help Desk Support

1 To what extent does the IT Help Desk meet your needs?

Probe: In what ways? [ask for real-life examples]
Probe: Can you give me an example (if possible) of when you received good support from the IT Help Desk?
Probe: Can you give me an example (if possible) of when you received insufficient support from the IT Help Desk?

2 Do you consider you have enough support from the IT Help Desk?

Probe: How is this support provided (e.g. telephone, face to face)?
Probe: What else (if anything) could usefully be done?

Interview themes may be derived from the literature that you read, the theories that you consider, your experience of a particular topic, common sense, discussions with co-workers, fellow students, tutors and research participants, or a combination of these approaches. You will need to have some idea of the theme or themes that you wish to discuss with your participants even if you intend to commence with exploratory, in-depth interviews as part of a Grounded Theory strategy to your research project (Section 5.5). Without at least some focus, your work will clearly lack a sense of direction and purpose. It will be necessary for you to formulate a focus if your work is to make progress. You should therefore start with a set of themes that reflect the variables being studied, or at least one or more general questions related to your research topic that you could use to start your interview. These can be incorporated into your interview guide (Box 10.7). This lists topics that you intend to cover in the interview along with initial questions and probes that may be used to follow up initial responses and obtain greater detail from the participants (King 2004). When creating your guide, you need to try to ensure that the order of questions is likely to be logical to your participants and that the language you use will be comprehensible. Using your guide, you will be able to develop and/or explore research themes through the in-depth or semi-structured interviews that you conduct to see whether you can identify and test relationships between them (Chapter 13).

Appropriateness of location

It is possible that the place where you conduct your interviews will influence the data you collect. As we discussed in Section 6.6, you should choose the location for your interviews with regard to your own personal safety. However, it is also important that you think about the impact that the location will have upon your participants and the responses they are likely to give. In particular, you should choose a location which is convenient for your participants, where they will feel comfortable and where the interview is unlikely to be disturbed (Box 10.8).

Finally, you need to choose a place that is quiet so that outside noise will not reduce the quality of your audio-recording of the interview. Each of us has experienced situations when conducting interviews where noise from outside the building

Box 10.8 Focus on student research

Choosing an appropriate location

Anne was pleased that the manufacturing company in which she was undertaking her research had arranged for her to use a room in the Human Resources Department. The room contained a low table and chairs, and she had been provided with bottled water and glasses as well. However, after her third interview she was beginning to doubt her own interviewing skills. Her participants, the company's production line workers, seemed unwilling to be open in their responses. She began to wonder if something was wrong with the interview location and decided to ask the next participant about this. At the end of that interview she had her answer. Her participants were unhappy with the interview location. Prior to being interviewed by Anne, the only time they or their colleagues had visited the Human Resources Department was to receive a reprimand. The location was, therefore, inappropriate!

or even from within it has been disruptive. In particular, Mark recalls an interview in a room where noise from building work outside meant that although he was able to hear the participant's responses clearly whilst the interview was taking place, much of the audio-recording of this interview was unintelligible due to the sound of a very loud pneumatic drill!

In many cases, the interview location will be arranged by those whom you interview. When you interview organisational participants such as managers in their offices, this has the advantage that they are able to find documents which support points they are making and in some cases they may be prepared to supply you with a copy of an extract from such a source.

Box 10.9 provides a checklist of the key points considered in this section to help you to prepare for semi-structured or in-depth interviews.

Box 10.9 Checklist

To help you prepare for your semi-structured or in-depth interview

- ✔ What level of knowledge about your research topic will be required in order to demonstrate your competence and credibility to gain the confidence of your interviewees?
- ✔ What level of knowledge about the research context will be required in order to demonstrate your competence and credibility to gain the confidence of your interviewees?
- ✔ What level of knowledge about the culture of your interviewees will be required in order to gain their confidence before they are willing to share data?
- ✔ What will be the broad focus of your in-depth interview, or what are the themes that you wish to explore or seek explanations for during a semi-structured interview?
- ✔ What type of information, if any, will it be useful to send to your interviewee prior to the interview?
- ✔ What did you agree to supply to your interviewee when you arranged the interview? Has this been supplied?
- ✔ Have you considered the impact that your interview location may have on participants' responses and on your own personal safety?

10.6 Conducting semi-structured or in-depth interviews

This section is about actually conducting semi-structured or in-depth interviews. The aspects we discuss here are intended to avoid forms of bias that would affect the reliability and validity of the data produced. These aspects relate to the:

- appropriateness of the researcher's appearance at the interview;
- nature of the opening comments when the interview commences;
- approach to questioning;
- appropriate use of different types of questions;
- nature and impact of the researcher's behaviour during the interview;
- demonstration of attentive listening skills;
- scope to summarise and test understanding;
- ability to recognise and deal with difficult participants;
- ability to record data accurately and fully.

We discuss these in turn. Key points are summarised as a checklist at the end of this section (Box 10.14).

Appropriateness of the researcher's appearance at the interview

Your appearance may affect the perception of the interviewee. Where this has an adverse affect on your credibility in the view of interviewees, or results in a failure to gain their confidence, the resulting bias may affect the reliability of the information provided. Where appropriate you should consider wearing a similar style of dress to those to be interviewed, although this may not always be appropriate. For example, your interviewees would not expect you to wear the same work wear that they need to put on to work on the production line. Essentially, this means that you will need to wear clothing that will be generally acceptable for the setting within which the interview is to occur (Box 10.10).

Box 10.10 Focus on student research

Checking out the dress code

Mal arranged to visit the administration centre of a large insurance company on a Friday to conduct a group interview with staff drawn from one of its telephone sales divisions and two one-to-one interviews with senior managers. He felt that it was appropriate to wear fairly 'formal' clothes to match what he thought would be the dress code of the organisation. Indeed, for four days of the working week this assumption would have been appropriate. However, the organisation had recently introduced the practice of not wearing such formal work clothes on Fridays. Thus he found himself the only one dressed formally in the organisation on the day of his visit. Taking lunch proved to be a memorable experience, as he intermingled with everyone else dressed in jeans and tee shirts, etc. His 'mistake' proved to be an amusing opening at the start of each interview rather than a barrier to gaining access to participants' data. Indeed, it might not have been appropriate for him to match too closely the 'dress-down' style of participants. Nevertheless, it does provide a useful example of the way in which expectations about appearance are likely to be noticed.

Nature of the opening comments when the interview commences

Where the interviewee has not met you before, the first few minutes of conversation will have a significant impact on the outcome of the interview – again related to the issue of your credibility and the level of the interviewee's confidence. Often such interviews occur in a setting that is unfamiliar to you. Despite this, it is your responsibility to shape the start of the conversation. You will need to explain your research to the participant and, hopefully, gain consent (Section 6.6). As part of this you will need to establish your credibility and gain the interviewee's confidence. During these initial discussions we have found that the interviewee often has some uncertainties about sharing information, and about the manner in which these data may be used. Alternatively, she or he may still need clarification about the exact nature of the data that you wish to obtain. We have found that a pre-prepared participant information sheet (Section 6.6, Box 6.14) and consent form (Box 6.15) are both extremely helpful in reducing such anxieties. There may also be a degree of curiosity on the part of the interviewee and probably a genuine level of interest in the research, related to the reason why the request to participate was accepted. This curiosity and interest will offer an opening for both parties to start a conversation, probably before the 'intended discussion' commences. You may find it appropriate to follow the initial discussion by demonstrating interest in the interviewee by asking about her or his role within the host organisation (Ghauri and Grønhaug 2010). However, you need to make sure that these opening moves to demonstrate credibility and friendliness, and to relax and develop a positive relationship, are not overstated, so that too much time is used and the interviewee starts to become bored or restive.

The start of the intended conversation therefore needs to be shaped by you. It is your opportunity to allay, wherever possible, the interviewee's uncertainties about providing information, establish the participant's rights and, based upon this, hopefully, obtain informed consent. Box 10.11 provides a structure that you can adapt for starting your interviews.

An assurance from you that confidential information is not being sought should make interviewees more relaxed and open about the information that they are willing to discuss. Combined with assurances about anonymity, this should increase the level of confidence in your trustworthiness and reduce the possibility of interviewee or response bias. You can also demonstrate your commitment to confidentiality by not naming other individuals or organisations that have participated in your research, or by talking about the data you obtained from them.

Approach to questioning

When conducted appropriately, your approach to questioning should reduce the scope for bias during the interview and increase the reliability of the information obtained. Your questions need to be phrased clearly, so that the interviewee can understand them, and you should ask them in a neutral tone of voice. Easterby-Smith et al. (2008) point out that the use of open questions should help to avoid bias. These can then be followed up by the use of appropriately worded probing questions. The use of these types of question will help you to explore the topic and to produce a fuller account. These types of questions are discussed more fully in the following subsection. Conversely, questions that seek to lead the interviewee or which indicate bias on your part should be avoided. Perceived interviewer bias may well lead to interviewee or response bias. Long questions or those that are really made up of two or more questions (known as double-barrel

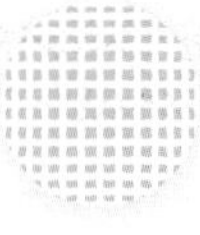

Box 10.11 Focus on student research

Opening a semi-structured interview

As part of her research project, Beth undertook a series of semi-structured interviews with freelance consultants working for a range of organisations. She covered the following points at the start of each interview:

- The participant was thanked for considering the request for access and for agreeing to the meeting.
- The purpose of the research and its progress to date were outlined briefly. As part of this, the participant was given an information sheet to keep.
- The previously agreed right to confidentiality and anonymity was reiterated by stating that nothing said by the participant would be attributed to them without first seeking and obtaining permission.
- The participant's right not to answer any question was emphasised and that the interview would be stopped if the participant wished.
- The participant was told about the nature of the outputs to which the research was intended to lead and what would happen to the data collected during and after the project.
- The offer to provide a summary of the research findings to the interviewee was also restated and the participant was told when this would happen.
- The request to record the interview electronically was restated and, where agreed, this was used subsequently.
- Before the substantive discussion started, Beth again requested permission to undertake the interview, summarised the themes to be covered, confirmed the amount of time available and requested that the participant read and signed the informed consent form.

All of these points were dealt with within five minutes.

questions) should also be avoided if you are to obtain a response to each aspect that you are interested to explore.

Questions should also avoid too many theoretical concepts or jargon since your understanding of such terms may vary from that of your interviewees. Where theoretical concepts or specific terminology need to be used, you will have to ensure that both you and the interviewee have the same understanding (Box 10.12; Easterby-Smith et al. 2008; Ghauri and Grønhaug 2010).

When asking questions it is important that wherever possible these are grounded in the real-life experiences of your participants rather than being discussed as abstract concepts. One approach to questioning which makes use of key participant experiences is the **critical incident technique**, in which participants are asked to describe in detail a

Box 10.12 Focus on student research

(Mis)understanding terminology

Sven was conducting an interview with the European sales manager of a large multinational corporation. Throughout the interview the sales manager referred to the European Division. Sven assumed that the sales manager meant continental Europe. However, by chance, later questions revealed that, for this organisation, Europe extended into parts of Asia, including Turkey, the United Arab Emirates, Saudi Arabia, Kuwait and Israel. Until this point in the interview, Sven had assumed that these countries were the responsibility of another sales manager!

Box 10.13 Focus on student research

Establishing trust and asking sensitive questions

Sam recalls an occasion when her treatment by her participants altered as her group interview progressed. For the first hour of a two-hour interview it appeared to her that the participants were convinced that she was really there to sell them a consultancy service. When they accepted that she was not going to try to sell them something, the mood of the interview changed and they became much more relaxed and responsive to the questions that Sam wished to ask. It was at this point that she was able to ask and pursue more sensitive questions that could have led to the interview being terminated during the period when the participants mistrusted her motives.

critical incident or number of incidents that are relevant to the research question. A **critical incident** is defined as an activity or event where the consequences were so clear that the participant has a definite idea regarding the effects (Keaveney 1995).

It will also be important to consider when to ask sensitive questions. Leaving these until near the end of an interview will provide your participant with some time to build up trust and confidence in you and to allay any doubts about your intentions, as Box 10.13 illustrates. This will also affect the nature of the questions that you may ask during the early part of an interview, as you attempt to build trust and gain your participant's confidence.

Once this position of trust has been reached and you wish to seek responses to potentially sensitive questions, Ghauri and Grønhaug (2010) point out that the wording of these deserves very particular attention in order to avoid any negative inferences related to, for example, responsibility for failure or error. Care taken over the exploration of sensitive questions should help towards the compilation of a fuller and more reliable account.

Appropriate use of different types of questions

Formulating appropriate questions to explore areas in which you are interested will be critical to achieving success in semi-structured or in-depth interviews. It will also be important to word your questions in a factual way, avoiding emotional language. We now discuss the types of question that you can use during semi-structured and in-depth interviews to seek to achieve this.

Open questions

The use of **open questions** will allow participants to define and describe a situation or event. An open question is designed to encourage the interviewee to provide an extensive and developmental answer, and may be used to reveal attitudes or obtain facts. It encourages the interviewee to reply as they wish. An open question is likely to start with, or include, one of the following words: 'what', 'how' or 'why'. Examples of open questions include:

'Why did the organisation introduce its marketing strategy?'
'What methods have been used to make employees redundant?'
'How has corporate strategy changed over the past five years?'

Probing questions

Probing questions can be used to explore responses that are of significance to the research topic. They may be worded like open questions but request a particular focus or direction. Examples of this type of question include:

'How would you evaluate the success of this new marketing strategy?'
'Why did you choose a compulsory method to make redundancies?'
'What external factors caused the corporate strategy to change?'

These questions may be prefaced with, for example, 'That's interesting . . .' or 'Tell me more about . . .'.

Probing questions may also be used to seek an explanation where you do not understand the interviewee's meaning or where the response does not reveal the reasoning involved. Examples of this type of question include:

'What do you mean by "bumping" as a means to help to secure volunteers for redundancy?'
'What is the relationship between the new statutory requirements that you referred to and the organisation's decision to set up its corporate affairs department?'

The use of reflection may also help you to probe a theme. This is where you will 'reflect' a statement made by the interviewee by paraphrasing their words. An example of this might be:

'Why don't you think that the employees understand the need for advertising?'

The intention will be to encourage exploration of the point made without offering a view or judgement on your part.

Where an open question does not reveal a relevant response, you may also probe the area of interest by using a supplementary question that finds a way of rephrasing the original question.

Specific and closed questions

These types of question may be loosely used as introductory questions when you commence questioning about a particular interview theme. Examples of this might be,

'Could you tell me about the change to the pricing policy' or
'Can you describe the production process?'

They can be used to obtain specific information or to confirm a fact or opinion (Section 11.4):

'How many people responded to the customer survey?'
'Has the old Central Region been merged with the Southern Region?'
'Do you prefer the new training programme?'

Other means to further your questioning

There are a number of devices that you may use to prompt further answers to a question you have asked. These include:

- follow-up expressions, such as: 'Ah', 'Oh' or 'Um';
- short follow-up statements, such as: 'That's interesting' or 'Really!';
- short follow-up questions, such as: 'Please tell me more', 'When did that happen' or 'What happened then';

- short reflective questions where you rephrase what you have just been told to reflect it back, such as: 'So that was when . . .' or 'They felt the investment had been worthwhile';
- interpretation and extension questions, where you seek to explore the implications of an answer, such as: 'Because they have diversified into Internet sales, does that mean that they are also going to build new distribution centres'?
- silence, where the participant is effectively invited to fill this by offering more information;
- using these devices in combination to explore a theme, but you will need to be very careful if you use this approach as it may be interpreted as being overbearing, stressful and confrontational. It will be more productive and ethical to maintain an even pace and respectful stance when asking questions.

Types of question to avoid

In phrasing questions, remember that you should avoid using leading or proposing types of question in order to control any bias that may result from their use (Section 11.4).

Nature and impact of the interviewer's behaviour during the interview

Appropriate behaviour by the researcher should also reduce the scope for bias during the interview. Comments or non-verbal behaviour, such as gestures, which indicate any bias in your thinking, should be avoided. A neutral (but not an uninterested) response should be projected in relation to the interviewee's answers in order not to provide any lead that may result in bias. Robson (2011) says that you should enjoy the interview opportunity, or at least appear to do so. An appearance of boredom on your part is hardly likely to encourage your interviewee!

Your posture and tone of voice may also encourage or inhibit the flow of the discussion. You should sit slightly inclined towards the interviewee and adopt an open posture, avoiding folded arms. This should provide a signal of attentiveness to your interviewee. Tone of voice can also provide a signal to the interviewee. You need to project interest and enthusiasm through your voice, avoiding any impression of anxiety, disbelief, astonishment or any other negative signal.

Demonstration of attentive listening skills

The purpose of a semi-structured or in-depth interview will be to understand your participant's explanations and meanings. This type of interaction will not be typical of many of the conversations that you normally engage in, where those involved often compete to speak rather than concentrate on listening. You therefore need to recognise that different skills will be emphasised in this kind of interaction. Attentive listening will involve you attending to and being sensitive to your participants by spending the time needed to listen to them to build your understanding. You will need to hold back your own thoughts where these would compete with those of your participant(s), or stray from the theme being explored.

It will be necessary for you to explore and probe explanations and meanings, but you must also provide the interviewee with reasonable time to develop their responses, and you must avoid projecting your own views (Easterby-Smith et al. 2008; Ghauri and Grønhaug 2010; Robson 2011).

Scope to summarise and test understanding

You may test your understanding by summarising an explanation provided by the interviewee. This will allow your participant to tell you whether your summary is adequate and to add points to this to further or correct your understanding where appropriate. This can be a powerful tool for avoiding a biased or incomplete interpretation. It may also act as a means to explore and probe the interviewee's responses further.

In addition to this opportunity to test understanding at the interview, you may also ask the interviewee to read through the factual account that you produce of the interview. Where the interviewee is prepared to undertake this, it will provide a further opportunity for you to test your understanding and for the interviewee to add any further points of relevance that may not previously have been apparent.

Dealing with difficult participants

Inevitably, during the course of your interviews you will meet some participants who are difficult to interview. In such circumstances it is imperative that you remain polite and do not show any irritation. Although it is impossible for us to highlight all the possible variations, the most common difficulties are summarised in Table 10.2, along with suggestions about how you might attempt to deal with them. However, whilst reading Table 10.2 will give you some ideas of what to do, the best advice we can give is to undertake practice interviews in which a colleague introduces one or more of these 'difficulties' and you have to deal with them!

Approach to recording data

Where possible we believe it is beneficial to audio-record an interview and make notes as it progresses. Using both methods to record interview data has a number of advantages. Notes provide a back-up if the audio-recording does not work. Making notes may help you to maintain your concentration, formulate points to summarise back to the interviewee to test your understanding and devise follow-up probing questions. Note taking demonstrates to your interviewee that her or his responses are important to you. Making notes also allows you to record your own thoughts and any events that would not be evident from the audio-recording. For example, if you think there may be a relationship between two variables that you wish to explore later, if your interviewer uses a facial expression or provides another non-verbal cue, or if someone enters the room, you can make a note about each of these. Most people have their own means of making notes, which may range from an attempt to create a verbatim account to a diagrammatic style that records key words and phrases, perhaps using mind mapping (Section 2.3).

The task of note making in this situation will be a demanding one. As you seek to test your understanding of what your interviewee has told you, this will allow some time to complete your notes concurrently in relation to the particular aspect being discussed. Most interviewees recognise the demands of the task and act accordingly. For example, Adrian recalls one particular interviewee who paused at the end of the main part of each of his answers to allow notes of this to be completed before adding some supplementary data which could also be noted down. Such pacing is the ideal way to make sure that all data can be noted down. However, the interview will not be the occasion to perfect your style, and we advise you to practise in a simulated situation: for example, by watching an interview on television and attempting to produce a set of notes.

Table 10.2 Difficult interview participants and suggestions on how to address them

Recognised difficulty	Suggestion
Participant appears willing only to give monosyllabic answers, these being little more than 'yes' or 'no'	Reasons for this are varied If it is due to limited time, or worries about anonymity, then this can be minimised by careful opening of the interview (Box 10.11). If the participant gives these answers despite such precautions, try phrasing your questions in as open a way as possible; also use long pauses to signify that you want to hear more
Participant repeatedly provides long answers which digress from the focus of your interview	Although some digression should be tolerated, as it can lead to aspects about which you are interested, you will need to impose more direction This must be done subtly so as not to cause offence, such as by referring back to an earlier relevant point and asking them to tell you more, or requesting that they pause so you can note down what they have just said
Participant starts interviewing you	This can suggest that you have created rapport. However, you need to stress that you are interested in their opinions and that, if they wish, they can ask you questions at the end
Participant is proud of their status relative to you and wants to show off their knowledge, criticising what you do	This is extremely difficult and at times like this you will have to listen attentively and be respectful Remember that you are also likely to be knowledgeable about the research topic, so be confident and prepared to justify your research and the research design you have chosen
Participant becomes noticeably upset during the interview and, perhaps, starts to cry	Another difficult one for you You need to give your participant time to answer your question and, in particular, do not do anything to suggest that you are feeling impatient If your participant starts crying or is obviously very distressed, it is probably a good idea to explain that the question does not have to be answered Do not end the interview straight away as this is likely to make the participant even more upset

Sources: King (2004); authors' experiences

To optimise the value from the interview you should compile a full record of the interview, including contextual data. If you cannot do this immediately after the interview, this should be done as soon as possible. Where you do not do this, the exact nature of explanations provided may be lost as well as general points of value. There is also the possibility that you may mix up data from different interviews, where you carry out several of these within a short period of time and you do not complete a record of each one at the time it takes place. Either situation will clearly lead to an issue about the trustworthiness of any data. You therefore need to allocate time to write up a full set of notes soon after the event. In addition to your notes from the actual interview, you should also record the following **contextual data**:

- the location of the interview (e.g. the organisation, the place);
- the date and time;
- the setting of the interview (e.g. was the room quiet or noisy, could you be overheard, were you interrupted?);
- background information about the participant (e.g. role, post title, gender);
- your immediate impression of how well (or badly) the interview went (e.g. was the participant reticent, were there aspects about which you felt you did not obtain answers in sufficient depth?).

You may be wondering how, if you are recording both of these types of data, you can still ensure the confidentiality and anonymity of your participants where this has been promised. As we outlined in Section 6.6, the best course of action is to ensure that your data are completely and genuinely anonymised. To help to achieve this you should store the contextual data separately from your interview transcripts. We suggest that you should only be able to link these two sets of data by using a 'key', such as an impersonal code number. Where it is absolutely necessary to retain a 'key' that allows participants to be linked to their data using their real name, this 'key' should be kept securely and separately, not by those who control the data.

Audio-recording your data where permission is given, making notes, compiling a full record of the interview immediately or soon after it has occurred and producing a set of contextual data and related memos (Chapter 13) are all means to control bias and produce reliable data. Most interviewers audio-record their interviews, where permission is given. Audio-recording interviews has both advantages and disadvantages and these are summarised in Table 10.3.

Permission should always be sought to audio-record an interview. You should also seek to justify why you believe it would be beneficial to use an audio-recorder and to offer guarantees about your participant's rights over its use. Where it is likely to have a detrimental effect, it is better not to use a recorder. However, most interviewees adapt

Table 10.3 Advantages and disadvantages of audio-recording the interview

Advantages	Disadvantages
Allows the interviewer to concentrate on questioning and listening Allows questions formulated at an interview to be accurately recorded for use in later interviews where appropriate Can re-listen to the interview Accurate and unbiased record provided Allows direct quotes to be used Permanent record for others to use	May adversely affect the relationship between interviewee and interviewer (possibility of 'focusing' on the audio-recorder) May inhibit some interviewee responses and reduce reliability Possibility of a technical problem Time required to transcribe the audio-recording (Section 13.4)

Sources: authors' experience; Easterby-Smith et al. (2008); Ghauri and Grønhaug (2010)

Box 10.14 Checklist

To help you conduct your semi-structured or in-depth interview

Appearance at the interview

- ✔ How will your appearance at the interview affect the willingness of the interviewee to share data?

Opening the interview

- ✔ How will you commence the interview to gain the confidence of your interviewee?
- ✔ What will you tell your interviewee about yourself, the purpose of your research, its funding and your progress?
- ✔ What concerns, or need for clarification, may your interviewee have?
- ✔ How will you seek to overcome these concerns or provide this clarification?
- ✔ In particular, how do you intend to use the data to which you are given access, ensuring, where appropriate, its confidentiality and your interviewee's anonymity?
- ✔ What will you tell your interviewee about their right not to answer particular questions and to end the interview should they wish?
- ✔ How do you wish to conduct (or structure) the interview?

Asking questions and behaviour during the interview

- ✔ How will you use appropriate language and tone of voice, and avoid jargon when asking questions or discussing themes?
- ✔ How will you word open questions appropriately to obtain relevant data?
- ✔ How will you word probing questions to build on, clarify or explain your interviewee's responses?
- ✔ How will you avoid asking leading questions that may introduce forms of bias?
- ✔ Have you devised an appropriate order for your questions to avoid asking sensitive questions too early where this may introduce interviewee bias?
- ✔ How will you maintain a check on the interview themes that you intend to cover and to steer the discussion where appropriate to raise and explore these aspects?
- ✔ How will you avoid overzealously asking questions and pressing your interviewee for a response where it should be clear that they do not wish to provide one?
- ✔ How will you avoid projecting your own views or feelings through your actions or comments?
- ✔ How might you identify actions and comments made by your interviewee that indicate an aspect of the discussion that should be explored in order to reveal the reason for the response?
- ✔ How will you listen attentively and demonstrate this to your interviewee?
- ✔ How will you summarise and test your understanding of the data that are shared with you in order to ensure accuracy in your interpretation?
- ✔ Where appropriate, how will you deal with difficult participants whilst remaining polite?

Recording data during the interview

- ✔ How would you like to record the data that are revealed to you during the interview? Where this involves using an audio recorder, have you raised this as a request and provided a reason why it would help you to use this technique?
- ✔ How will you allow your interviewee to maintain control over the use of an audio recorder, where used, where they may wish to exercise this?
- ✔ Have you practised to ensure you can carry out a number of tasks at the same time, including listening, note taking and identifying where you need to probe further?

Closing the interview

- ✔ How do you plan to draw the interview to a close within the agreed time limit and to thank the interviewee for their time and the data they have shared with you?

quickly to the use of the recorder. It is more ethical to allow your interviewee to maintain control over the recorder so that if you ask a question that they are prepared to respond to, but only if their words are not audio-recorded, they have the option to switch it off (Section 6.6). It will inevitably be necessary to make notes in this situation.

10.7 Managing logistical and resource issues

Logistical and resource issues

Time issues

Interviewing is a time-consuming process. Where the purpose of the interview is to explore themes or to explain findings, the process may call for a fairly lengthy discussion. In such cases the time required to obtain data is unlikely to be less than one hour and could easily exceed this, perhaps taking two hours or longer. This may have an adverse impact on the number and representativeness of those who are willing to be interview participants, as we discussed earlier. Where managers or other potential participants receive frequent requests to participate in research projects, they will clearly need to consider how much of their time they may be willing to devote to such activities. It will therefore be important for you to establish credibility with, and to engender the interest of, potential interviewees.

Cost and other resource issues

Your decision to collect data through interviewing will have particular resource issues. Conducting interviews may become a costly process where it is necessary to travel to the location of participants, although this can be kept to a minimum by cluster sampling (Section 7.2) or using the Internet (Section 10.9). Interviews are almost certainly likely to be more expensive than using self-completed or telephone questionnaires to collect data. Choice of method should be determined primarily by the nature of the research question and objectives rather than by cost considerations. This highlights the need to examine the feasibility of the proposed question and research strategy in relation to resource constraints, including time available and expense, before proceeding to the collection of data.

Logistical issues

Where your research question and objectives require you to undertake semi-structured or in-depth interviews, you need to consider the logistics of scheduling interviews. Thought needs to be given to the number of interviews to be arranged within a given period, and to the time required to compose notes and/or transcribe audio-recordings of each one, and undertake an initial analysis of the data collected (Section 13.4).

Managing logistical and resource issues

Time management

In the preceding subsection, the issue of time required to collect data through interviewing was raised. You need to consider very carefully the amount of time that will be required to conduct an interview. In our experience, the time required to undertake qualitative research interviews is usually underestimated. The likely time required should be clearly referred to in any initial contact, and it may be better to suggest that interviews are envisaged to last up to, say, one, one and a half, or two hours, so that a willing participant sets aside sufficient time. Some negotiation is in any case possible with an interested participant who feels unable to agree to a request for, say, two hours but who is prepared to agree to a briefer meeting. The interview can also be arranged at a time when the interviewee will be under least pressure.

Interview scheduling

Another possible strategy is to arrange two or more shorter interviews in order to explore a topic thoroughly. This might have the added advantage of allowing participants to reflect on the themes raised and questions being asked, and therefore to provide a fuller account and more accurate set of data. In order to establish this option, it may be beneficial to arrange an initial meeting with a potential participant to discuss this request, where you will be able to establish your credibility. A series of exploratory interviews may then be agreed. Consideration also needs to be given to the number of interviews that may be undertaken in a given period. It is easy to overestimate what is practically possible (Box 10.15).

These are all factors that need to be considered in the scheduling of semi-structured and in-depth interviews. Where you are involved in a study at one establishment, it may be more practical to undertake a number of interviews in one day, although there is still a need to maintain concentration, to make notes and write up information and to conduct your initial analysis. Even in this situation, undertaking up to three interviews per day is likely to be enough.

Interview management

The nature of semi-structured or in-depth interviews also has implications for the management of the time available during the meeting. The use of open-ended questions and reliance on participant responses means that, while you must remain responsive to the objectives of the interview and the time constraint, interviewees need the opportunity to provide full answers. You should avoid making frequent interruptions but will need to cover the themes and questions indicated and probe responses in the time available (Ghauri and Grønhaug 2010). The intensive nature of the discussion and the need to optimise your understanding of what has been revealed means that time must be found to write up notes as soon as possible after an interview.

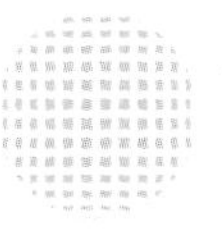

Box 10.15 Focus on student research

Calculating the number of in-depth interviews to be undertaken in one day

Feroz arranged two interviews in a capital city during the course of a day, which involved travelling some miles across the city during the lunch hour. Two interviews appeared to be a reasonable target. However, a number of logistical issues were experienced even in relation to the plan to undertake two such interviews in one day. These issues included the following: the total travelling time to and from the city; the time to find the appropriate buildings; the transfer time during a busy period; the time to conduct the interviews; the need to maintain concentration, to probe responses, to make initial notes and then to write these up without too much time elapsing. Because of his experience, Feroz took a decision not to conduct more than one interview per day where significant travel was involved, even though this necessitated more journeys and greater expense.

Recording and transcription

Where an audio-recorder has been used (Section 10.6), you will need to decide whether to work directly from the recording or to produce a transcription of all or parts of the recording. This decision will depend on your research strategy and the way in which you intend to analyse your qualitative data (Chapter 13). For example, using a Grounded Theory strategy (Sections 5.5 and 13.7) is likely to mean that you will need to transcribe the whole of each interview. Each hour of recording is likely to take several hours to transcribe or to process ready for entry into computer-assisted qualitative data analysis software, unless you are a very competent audio-typist, or you know one who will undertake this task for you! Use of software to assist the transcription of audio-recordings may also be helpful.

10.8 Group interviews and focus groups

Semi-structured and in-depth interviews may also be conducted on a group basis, where the interviewer asks questions to a group of participants. Figure 10.1 summarised these variations earlier in this chapter. Currently there are a variety of terms that are used interchangeably to describe group interviews and which are often assumed to have equivalent meanings (Boddy 2005). These include focus group, group interview, group discussion and various combinations of these words! In this section we use **group interview** as a general term to describe all semi-structured and in-depth interviews conducted with two or more people. In contrast, and as suggested by Figure 10.1, the term **focus group** is used to refer to those group interviews where the topic is defined clearly and precisely and there is a focus on enabling and recording interactive discussion between participants (Carson et al. 2001; Krueger and Casey 2009; Box 10.16).

Typically group interviews (and focus groups) involve between 4 and 12 participants, the precise number depending upon the nature of the participants, the topic matter and the skill of the interviewer. Inevitably, the more complex the subject matter the smaller

Box 10.16 Focus on management research

Using focus group interviews

Dick (2009) published a study in the *British Journal of Management* exploring the management of flexible working in the UK Police Service that used qualitative interviews conducted with police officers to collect data. Semi-structured interviews were conducted on a one-to-one basis and on a group basis. The one-to-one interviews were held with those responsible for developing flexible working practices and also with those who had responsibility for managing it in practice.

Data were also gathered from conducting three focus group interviews, one with each of the three police forces which participated in this study. Dick reports that each of these focus groups was made up of between 8 and 12 participants. These focus groups were comprised of officers working reduced hours, their managers and colleagues, members of the Force's human resource management department and also representatives of the Police Federation. These focus groups were composed of a mix of those involved in order to gain a 'pluralistic account' of the experiences and management of this working practice (Dick 2009: 185).

Participants agreed for the data produced to be audio-recorded and these were then transcribed in their entirety before being checked and analysed.

the number of interviewees. Participants are normally chosen using non-probability sampling, often with a specific purpose in mind (Section 7.3). For many group interviews this purpose is that you feel that you can learn a great deal from these specific individuals. Krueger and Casey (2009: 21) refer to such participants as being 'information rich'.

If you are thinking about using group interviews, or specifically focus groups, consideration of the following issues may help.

- Where your research project (or part of it) occurs within an organisation the request to participate in a group interview may be received by individuals as an instruction rather than allowing them a choice about whether to take part. This may be the case where an organisation is acting as a host for your research and the request is sent in the name of a manager, or because of your own position in the organisation. Where this is the case it is likely to lead to some level of non-attendance, or to unreliable data. In our experience, participants often welcome the chance to 'have their say'. However, where any request may be perceived as indicating lack of choice, to gain their confidence and participation you will need to exercise care over the wording to be used in the request that is sent to them to take part. You will also need to exercise similar care in your introduction to the group when the interview occurs in order to provide a clear assurance about confidentiality.
- Once your sample has been selected, participants should be grouped so as not to inhibit individuals' possible contributions. Inhibitions may be related to lack of trust, to perceptions about status differences, or because of the dominance of certain individuals. The nature and selection of each group will affect the first two elements. We would advise using a series of horizontal slices through an organisation so that, within each group, participants have a similar status and similar work experiences. (Using a vertical slice would introduce perceptions about status differences and variations in work experience.) In this way, group interviews can be conducted at a number of levels within an organisation. A reference may be made about the nature of the group to provide reassurance, and you may consider asking people to introduce themselves by their first name only without referring to their exact job.
- Where one or two people dominate the discussion, you should seek to reduce their contributions by encouraging others. This may be attempted in a general way:

  'What do you think, Yuksel?'
  'What do other people think about this?'

  Alternatively, more specifically:

  'How does Emma's point relate to the one that you raised, Kristie?'

  A question posed to other group members should also have the effect of inhibiting the contribution of a dominant member:

  'What do you think about Johan's suggestion?'

- You will need to ensure that participants understand each other's contributions and that you develop an accurate understanding of the points being made. Asking a participant to clarify the meaning of a particular contribution, where it has not been understood, and testing understanding through summarising should help to ensure this.
- You will need to consider the location and setting for a group interview. It is advisable to conduct the interview in a neutral setting rather than, say, in a manager's office, where participants may not feel relaxed. There should be no likelihood of interruption or being overheard. You should consider the layout of the seating in the room where the interview is to be held. Where possible, arrange the seating in a circular fashion so that everyone will be facing inward and so that they will be an equal distance from the central point of this circle.

- Finally, students often ask, 'When will I know that I have undertaken sufficient group interviews or focus groups?' Writing about focus groups, Krueger and Casey (2009) suggest that you should plan to undertake three or four group interviews with any one type of participant. If after the third or fourth group interview you are no longer receiving new information you will have reached **saturation**, in which case you will have heard the full range of ideas.

The demands of conducting all types of group interview, including focus groups, and the potential wealth of ideas that may flow from them mean that it is likely to be difficult to manage the process and note key points at the same time. We have managed to overcome this in two ways: by audio-recording group interviews or using two interviewers. Where two interviewers are used, one person facilitates the discussion and the other person makes notes. We would recommend that you use two interviewers, even if you are audio-recording the group interview, as it will allow one interviewer to concentrate fully on managing the process whilst the other ensures the data are recorded. Where you cannot audio-record the group interview, you will need to write up any notes immediately afterwards so as not to lose data. As with one-to-one interviews, your research will benefit from the making of notes about the nature of the interactions that occur in the group interviews that you conduct. We would not advise you to undertake more than one group interview in a day on your own because of the danger of losing or confusing data.

Group interviews

In a group interview your role will be to ensure that all participants have the opportunity to state their points of view in answer to your questions, and to record the resulting data. This type of interview can range from being highly structured to unstructured, although it tends to be relatively unstructured and fairly free-flowing (Zikmund 2000) in terms of both breadth and depth of topics. The onus will be placed firmly on you to explain the interview's purpose, to encourage participants to relax, and to initiate, encourage and direct the discussion. The use of this method is likely to necessitate a balance between encouraging participants to provide answers to a particular question or questions that you introduce and allowing them to range more freely in discussion where this may reveal data that provide you with important insights. Thus once you have opened the interview (Box 10.10) and the discussion is established, it will need to be managed carefully.

Group interactions may lead to a highly productive discussion as interviewees respond to your questions and evaluate points made by the group. However, as your opportunity to develop an individual level of rapport with each participant will not be present (compared with a one-to-one interview), there may also emerge a group effect where certain participants effectively try to dominate the interview whilst others may feel inhibited. This may result in some participants publicly agreeing with the views of others, whilst privately disagreeing. As a consequence a reported consensus may, in reality, be a view that nobody wholly endorses and nobody disagrees with (Stokes and Bergin 2006). You will therefore need to test the validity of emergent views by trying to encourage involvement of all group members and pursuing the interview's exploratory purpose through the use of open and probing questions. A high level of skill will be required in order for you to be able to conduct this type of discussion successfully, as well as to try to record its outcomes.

Despite this reference to the potential difficulties of using group interviews, there are distinct advantages arising from their use. Because of the presence of several participants, this type of situation allows a breadth of points of view to emerge and for the group to respond to these views. A dynamic group can generate or respond to a number of ideas and evaluate them, thus helping you to explain or explore concepts. You are also likely to benefit from the opportunity that this method provides in terms of allowing your participants to consider points raised by other group members and to challenge one another's views. In one-to-one interviews, discussion is of course limited to the interviewer and interviewee. Stokes and Bergin (2006) highlight that whilst group interviews, and in particular focus groups, are able to identify principal issues accurately, they are not able to provide the depth and detail in relation to specific issues that can be obtained from individual interviews.

The use of group interviews may also provide an efficient way for you to interview a larger number of individuals than would be possible through the use of one-to-one interview. Linked to this point, their use may allow you to adopt an interview-based strategy that can more easily be related to a representative sample, particularly where the research project is being conducted within a specific organisation or in relation to a clearly defined population. This may help to establish the credibility of this research where an attempt is made to overcome issues of bias associated with interviews in general and this type in particular.

Group interviews can also help to identify key themes that will be used to develop items that are included in a survey questionnaire. This particular use of group interviews may inform subsequent parts of your data collection, providing a clearer focus. For example, in an attitude questionnaire the initial use of group interviews can lead to a 'bottom-up' generation of concerns and issues, which subsequently inform its content.

Focus groups

Focus groups are well known because of the way they have been used by political parties to test voter reactions to particular policies and election strategies, and through their use in market research to test reactions to products. A **focus group**, sometimes called a 'focus group interview', is a group interview that focuses upon a particular issue, product, service or topic by encouraging discussion amongst participants and the sharing of perceptions in an open and tolerant environment (Krueger and Casey 2009). This means that, in comparison with other forms of group interview, individual group members' interactions and responses are both encouraged and more closely controlled to maintain the focus. Participants are selected because they have certain characteristics in common that relate to the topic being discussed and they are encouraged to discuss and share their points of view without any pressure to reach a consensus (Krueger and Casey 2009). These discussions are conducted several times, with similar participants, to enable trends and patterns to be identified when the data collected are analysed.

If you are running a focus group, you will probably be referred to as the **moderator** or 'facilitator'. These labels emphasise the dual role of the person running the focus group, namely to:

- keep the group within the boundaries of the topic being discussed;
- generate interest in the topic and encourage discussion, whilst at the same time not leading the group towards certain opinions.

Where focus groups are being used this is likely to be associated with a higher level of interviewer-led structure and intervention to facilitate discussion than where group interviews are being used. The size of groups may also be related to topic. Thus a focus group designed to obtain views about a product range is likely to be larger than a group interview that explores a topic related to a more emotionally involved construct, such as attitudes to performance-related pay or the way in which employees rate their treatment by management. You may also choose to design smaller groups as you seek to develop your competence in relation to the use of this interviewing technique to collect qualitative data.

10.9 Telephone, Internet- and intranet-mediated interviews

Most semi-structured or in-depth interviews occur on a face-to-face basis. However, such qualitative interviews may also be conducted by telephone or electronically via the Internet or intranet. These pose particular problems as well as providing advantages in certain circumstances that we discuss in this section.

Telephone interviews

Attempting to conduct semi-structured or in-depth interviews by telephone may offer potential advantages associated with access, speed and lower cost. This method may allow you to make contact with participants with whom it would be impractical to conduct an interview on a face-to-face basis because of the distance and prohibitive costs involved and time required. Even where 'long-distance' access is not an issue, conducting interviews by telephone may still offer advantages associated with speed of data collection and lower cost. In other words, this approach may be seen as more convenient (Box 10.17).

However, there are a number of significant issues that militate against attempting to collect qualitative data by telephone contact. We have already discussed the importance of establishing personal contact in this type of interviewing. The intention of semi-structured or in-depth interviewing is to be able to explore the participant's responses. This is likely to become more feasible once a position of trust has been established, as discussed earlier. This situation, of establishing trust, will become particularly important where you wish to ask sensitive questions. For these reasons, seeking to conduct qualitative interviews by telephone may lead to issues of (reduced) reliability, where your participants are less willing to engage in an exploratory discussion, or even a refusal to take part.

Box 10.17 Focus on management research

Using telephone interviews in a longitudinal study to understand the development of dynamic capabilities

Narayanan et al. (2009) report how they used telephone interviews in a longitudinal study that focused on the development of dynamic capabilities in a major pharmaceutical company. Their study published in the *British Journal of Management* involved conducting semi-structured interviews with managers in two different parts of this company. Interviews were conducted on a person-to-person basis where this was possible. However, some of these managers were required to travel and work abroad and interviews with these had to be conducted by telephone.

Narayanan et al. report that the person-to-person interviews were all recorded and then transcribed. For the interviews conducted by telephone, elaborate notes were taken by the interviewer. These were then summarised and sent to the appropriate managers to check and to make corrections to the 'scientific terms and ideas' (Narayanan et al. 2009: 29). They report that this study was focused on a process perspective, where the research question is designed to understand how decisions are made rather than what decisions were taken. It would therefore appear that their ability to conduct research interviews by telephone was vital to the outcome of this longitudinal study because of the critical periods when some participants were placed out of reach of person-to-person interviews.

There are also some other practical issues that would need to be managed. These relate to your ability to control the pace of a telephone interview and to record any data that were forthcoming. Conducting an interview by telephone and taking notes is an extremely difficult process and so we would recommend using audio-recording. In addition, the normal visual cues that allow your participant to control the flow of the data that they share with you would be absent. With telephone interviews you lose the opportunity to witness the non-verbal behaviour of your participant, which may adversely affect your interpretation of how far to pursue a particular line of questioning. Your participant may be less willing to provide you with as much time to talk to them in comparison with a face-to-face interview. You may also encounter difficulties in developing more complex questions in comparison with a face-to-face interview situation. Finally, attempting to gain access through a telephone call may lead to ethical issues, as we discussed in Section 6.6.

For these reasons, we believe that semi-structured or in-depth interviewing by telephone is likely to be appropriate only in particular circumstances. It may be appropriate to conduct a short, follow-up telephone interview to clarify the meaning of some data, where you have already undertaken a face-to-face interview with a participant with whom you have been able to establish your integrity and to demonstrate your competence. It may also be appropriate where access would otherwise be prohibited because of long distance, where you have already been able to establish your credibility through prior contact, perhaps through correspondence, and have made clear that your requirements are reasonable and guided by ethical principles. Where this situation involves a request to undertake a telephone interview with a participant from another country, you will need to be aware of any cultural norms related to the conduct and duration of telephone conversations.

Internet-and intranet-mediated interviewing

Morgan and Symon (2004) use the term **electronic interviews** to refer to interviews held both in real time using the Internet and organisations' intranets as well as those that are, in effect, undertaken offline. This subdivision into asynchronous and synchronous (Figure 10.2) offers a useful way of categorising electronic interviews as there are significant differences in electronic interviews dependent upon whether the interview is undertaken in real time (**synchronous**) or offline (**asynchronous**).

Using the Internet or an organisation's intranet has significant advantages where the population you wish to interview are geographically dispersed. In addition, with all forms of electronic interview the software automatically records data as they are typed in, thereby removing problems associated with audio-recording and transcription such as cost, accuracy and participants' apprehension. However, as you will remember from Sections 6.5 and 6.6, electronic interviews have their own set of ethical issues that you will need to consider.

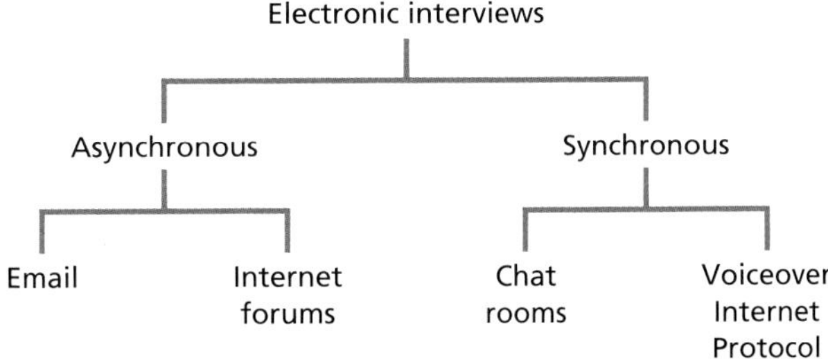

Figure 10.2 Forms of electronic interviews

Synchronous modes to conduct electronic interviews include chat rooms and Voiceover Internet Protocol services. A **chat room** is an online forum operating in synchronous mode. By far the most common form of chat room is instant messaging such as MSN Messenger™. Although some would argue that this is not a true chat room as conversations are restricted to those named in a user's list, such instant messaging can be used to undertake real-time one-to-one and group interviews, providing netiquette is observed. Social networking websites, such as facebook.com, also provide a means to conduct both synchronous and asynchronous electronic interviews through their messaging services.

Voiceover Internet Protocol services such as Skype™ allow users to conduct electronic interviews in real time. In addition to voice chat facilities, this technology facilitates video-conferencing between users. Video-conferencing facilities are being enhanced by improvements to this technology and the use of high-definition quality webcams. Skype™ also provides other facilities through which to conduct electronic interviews such as instant messaging. This type of software also facilitates file transfers.

Web conferencing software can be used for both synchronous (real-time) and asynchronous one-to-one and group interviews. Where this requires participants to have the software loaded onto their computers this can cause problems, especially where they are unfamiliar with the software or there is incompatibility with hardware or operating systems.

The considerable debate regarding the suitability of Internet- and intranet-mediated communication for synchronous interviewing has been reviewed by Mann and Stewart (2000). Some researchers argue that interviewing participants online such as through web conferencing or chat rooms is unlikely to achieve the same high levels of interactivity and rich and spontaneous communication that can be obtained with face-to-face interviewing. This is often explained by the relatively narrow bandwidth of these electronic media when compared with face-to-face communication, it being argued that electronic media transmit fewer social cues. Others argue that this is not the case and that, after the initial invitation to participate, it is possible to build up considerable rapport between the interviewer and the interviewee during an online interview. It has also been suggested that the relative anonymity of online interviews facilitates more open and honest responses, in particular with regard to sensitive issues where participants have adopted pseudonyms (Sweet 2001). Where group interviews or focus groups are being conducted, participants are less likely to be influenced by characteristics such as age, ethnicity or appearance. Overbearing participants are less likely to predominate, although variations in keyboard skills are likely to impact on participation levels.

For asynchronous interviewing, email and Internet forums or discussion groups mean that interviews are normally conducted over an extended time period of weeks. An **Internet forum** usually deals with one topic only and personal exchanges are discouraged. Forums are commonly referred to as web forums, message boards, discussion boards, discussion forums, discussion groups and bulletin boards. Although forums do not allow people to edit each other's messages, there is usually a moderator or forum administrator who typically is responsible for netiquette being observed (Sections 6.5 and 11.5) and has the ability to edit, delete or modify any content. Hookway (2008) describes the strategy he used to advertise within online communities to gain access to data, with scope to conduct Internet-mediated interviews. Hookway sets out the following steps to achieve access:

- An invitation is devised that will invite bloggers to participate in the research;
- This invitation is emailed to the moderators of previously identified online communities relevant to the research topic, who are each asked for permission to post this on the site they moderate;

- Where permission is granted, the researcher will be allowed to join the online community and granted access to post the invitation;
- Bloggers interested in the researcher's post can then make contact by posting a comment or sending an email;
- The researcher will need to reply to those expressing an interest to thank them, either by email where the address has been provided or by posting a return comment;
- Interested bloggers should then email the list of URLs to posts that are relevant to the research which will grant the researcher access to use these.

Hookway (2008) reports that his experience of using this procedure to gain access to data was very productive. There may then be further scope to conduct electronic interviews with consenting participants to explore the meanings of these data further. A similar approach to invite data contributions may be made by using a 'Wiki', which is a website that allows other users to edit pages and to create new ones (Box 10.18).

An **email interview** consists of a series of emails each containing a small number of questions rather than one email containing a series of questions (Morgan and Symon 2004). Although you can send one email containing a series of questions, this is really an Internet- or intranet-mediated questionnaire (Sections 11.2 and 11.5). After making contact and obtaining agreement to participate, you initially email a small number of questions or introduce a topic to which the participant will (hopefully) reply. You then need

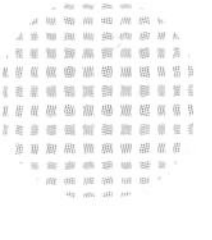

Box 10.18 Focus on student research

Using a Wiki to collect data

Lindsay's project title was 'Targeted Advertising to Attract the Gay Consumer: Consumer Interpretations and Preferences'. Within her research she was interested in finding out how gay consumers perceived images used in different types of advertisements and how these images might influence (positively or negatively) their purchasing decisions. In order to collect her data she set up a Wiki and invited gay people to comment on a series of advertisements that she had selected on the basis of whether or not they contained implicit or explicit gay images, and whether the advertisement was placed in gay or mainstream or both gay and mainstream magazines. For each type of advertisement Lindsay asked a range of questions to stimulate discussion amongst the Wiki users, such as:

Do you remember this advertisement?
Who do you think it is aimed at?
Why?

Over a period of six weeks Lindsay had over 200 comments added to her Wiki. In response to one clothing advertisement comprised of two men, which appeared in a mainstream magazine, that she had categorised as an 'implicit gay image' comments included:

'Yes, I remember this ad. One of my straight friends said it didn't even occur to him that this was also aimed at gay men! Once I pointed out that there wasn't a woman in the ad and that the guys might be a couple on holiday together the penny dropped!'

'It's so clearly aimed at gay men too!! Look at how close their hands are together and they've only got one bag between them – you could definitely think they were a couple!!'

'It's very clever marketing really. It would be nice though if they were more obviously a gay couple. I think if more companies put gay people in their ads it would definitely make me buy their products more.'

'I don't know if that would work for me. I buy products based on whether I need them, not who's in the advert. But I guess I'm quite a practical person like that.'

From this she was able to theorise that, in addition to gay people perceiving when a range of advertisement types were being targeted towards them, their purchasing decisions were positively influenced by a number of other factors in addition to the way they were portrayed in advertisements.

to respond to these ideas, specifically asking further questions, raising points of clarification and pursuing ideas that are of further interest. Morgan and Symon (2004) emphasise that, because of the nature of email communications, such interviews may last for some weeks, there being a time delay between a question being asked and it being answered. This, they argue, can be advantageous as it allows both the interviewer and the interviewee to reflect on the questions and responses prior to providing a considered response.

10.10 Summary

- The use of semi-structured and in-depth interviews should allow you to collect a rich and detailed set of data, although you will need to develop a sufficient level of competence to conduct these and to be able to gain access to the type of data associated with their use.
- Interviews can be differentiated according to the level of structure and standardisation adopted.
- Semi-structured and in-depth research interviews can be used to explore topics and explain findings.
- There are situations favouring semi-structured and in-depth interviews that will lead you to use either or both of these to collect data. Apart from the purpose of your research, these are related to the significance of establishing personal contact, the nature of your data collection questions, and the length of time required from those who provide data.
- Your research design may incorporate more than one type of interview.
- Semi-structured and in-depth interviews can be used in a variety of research strategies.
- Data quality issues related to reliability, forms of bias and generalisability may be overcome by considering why you have chosen to use interviews, recognising that all research methods have limitations and through careful preparation to conduct interviews to avoid bias that would threaten the reliability and validity of your data.
- The conduct of semi-structured and in-depth interviews will be affected by the appropriateness of the researcher's appearance, opening comments when the interview commences, approach to questioning, appropriate use of different types of question, nature of the interviewer's behaviour during the interview, demonstration of attentive listening skills, scope to summarise and test understanding, ability to deal with difficult participants and ability to record data accurately and fully.
- Logistical and resource matters will need to be considered and managed when you use in-depth and semi-structured interviews.
- Apart from one-to-one interviews conducted on a face-to-face basis, you may consider conducting such interviews by telephone or electronically.
- You may consider using group interviews or focus group interviews. There may be particular advantages associated with group interviews, but these are considerably more difficult to manage than one-to-one interviews.

Self-check questions

Help with these questions is available at the end of the chapter.

10.1 What type of interview would you use in each of the following situations:

a a market research project?

b a research project seeking to understand whether trade union attitudes have changed?

c following the analysis of a questionnaire?

10.2 What are the advantages of using semi-structured and in-depth interviews?

10.3 During a presentation of your proposal to undertake a research project, which will be based on semi-structured or in-depth interviews, you feel that you have dealt well with the relationship between the purpose of the research and the proposed methodology when one of the panel leans forward and asks you to discuss the trustworthiness and usefulness of your work for other researchers. This is clearly a challenge to see whether you can defend such an approach. How do you respond?

10.4 Having quizzed you about the trustworthiness and usefulness of your work for other researchers, the panel member decides that one more testing question is in order. He explains that interviews are not an easy option. 'It is not an easier alternative for those who want to avoid statistics', he says. 'How can we be sure that you're competent to get involved in interview work, especially where the external credibility of this organisation may be affected by the impression that you create in the field?' How will you respond to this concern?

10.5 What are the key issues to consider when planning to use semi-structured or in-depth interviews?

10.6 What are the key areas of competence that you need to develop in order to conduct an interview successfully?

Review and discussion questions

10.7 Watch and, if possible, video-record a television interview such as one that is part of a chat show or a documentary. It does not matter if you only record an interview of 10 to 15 minutes' duration.

- **a** As you watch the interview, make notes about what the participant is telling the interviewer. After the interview review your notes. How much of what was being said did you manage to record?
- **b** If you were able to video-record the television interview, watch the interview again and compare your notes with what was actually said. What other information would you like to add to your notes?
- **c** Either watch the interview again or another television interview that is part of a chat show or a documentary. This time pay careful attention to the questioning techniques used by the interviewer. How many of the different types of question discussed in Section 10.5 can you identify?
- **d** How important do you think the non-verbal cues given by the interviewer and the interviewee are in understanding the meaning of what is being said?

10.8 With a friend, each decide on a topic about which you think it would be interesting to interview the other person. Separately develop your interview themes and prepare an interview guide for a semi-structured interview. At the same time, decide which one of the 'difficult' participants in Table 10.2 you would like to role-play when being interviewed.

- **a** Conduct both interviews and, if possible, make a video-recording. If this is not possible either audio-record or ensure the interviewer takes notes.
- **b** Watch each of the video-recordings – what aspects of your interviewing technique do you each need to improve?
- **c** If you were not able to video-record the interview, how good a record of each interview do you consider the notes to be? How could you improve your interviewing technique further?

10.9 Obtain a transcript of an interview that has already been undertaken. If your university subscribes to online newspapers such as ft.com, these are a good source of

Progressing your research project

Using semi-structured or in-depth interviews in your research

- Review your research question(s) and objectives. How appropriate would it be to use non-standardised (qualitative) interviews to collect data? Where it is appropriate, explain the relationship between your research question(s) and objectives, and the use of such interviews. Where this type of interviewing is not appropriate, justify your decision.
- If you decide that semi-structured or in-depth interviews are appropriate, what practical problems do you foresee? How might you attempt to overcome these practical problems?
- Think about how your interviews are likely to be analysed before you conduct them. This will guide your preparation of the list of interview themes as well as the conduct of your subsequent interviews and data transcription (Chapter 13).
- What threats to the trustworthiness of the data collected are you likely to encounter? How might you overcome these?
- Draft a list of interview themes to be explored and compare these thoroughly with your research question(s) and objectives.
- Ask your project tutor to comment on your judgement about the use of non-standardised (qualitative) interviews, the issues and threats that you have identified, your suggestions to overcome these, and the fit between your interview themes and your research question(s) and objectives.
- Use the questions in Box 1.4 to guide your reflective diary entry.

business-related transcripts. Alternatively, typing 'interview transcript' into a search engine such as Google or Bing will generate numerous possibilities on a vast range of topics!

a Examine the transcript, paying careful attention to the questioning techniques used by the interviewer. To what extent do you think that certain questions have led the interviewee to certain answers?

b Now look at the responses given by the interviewer. To what extent do you think these are the actual verbatim responses given by the interviewee? Why do you think this?

References

BBC College of Journalism (2011) *Interviews*. Available at www.bbc.co.uk/journalism/skills/interviewing [Accessed 29 June 2011].

Boddy, C. (2005) 'A rose by any other name may smell as sweet but "group discussion" is not another name for "focus group" nor should it be', *Qualitative Market Research*, Vol. 8, No. 3, pp. 248–55.

Bryman, A. (1988) *Quantity and Quality in Social Research*. London: Unwin Hyman.

Carson, D., Gilmore, A., Perry, C. and Grønhaug, K. (2001) *Qualitative Marketing Research*. London: Sage.

Cooper, D.R. and Schindler, P.S. (2008) *Business Research Methods* (10th edn). London: McGraw-Hill.

Dick, P. (2009) 'Bending over backwards? Using a pluralistic framework to explore the management of flexible working in the UK police service', *British Journal of Management*, Vol. 20, pp. 182–93.

Easterby-Smith, M., Thorpe, R. and Jackson, P. (2008) *Management Research: An Introduction* (3rd edn) London: Sage.

Ghauri, P. and Grønhaug, K. (2010) *Research Methods in Business Studies: A Practical Guide* (4th edn). Harlow: FT Prentice Hall.

Hofstede, G. (2001) *Culture's Consequences: Comparing Values, Behaviors, Institutions and Organizations Across Nations*. Thousand Oaks, CA: Sage.

Hookway, N. (2008) 'Entering the blogosphere: Some strategies for using blogs in social research', *Qualitative Research*, Vol. 8, No. 1, pp. 91–113.

Jankowicz, A.D. (2005) *Business Research Projects* (4th edn). London: Business Press Thomson Learning.

Keaveney, S.M. (1995) 'Customer switching behaviour in service industries: an exploratory study', *Journal of Marketing*, Vol. 59, No. 2, pp. 71–82.

King, N. (2004) 'Using interviews in qualitative research', in C. Cassell and G. Symon (eds) *Essential Guide to Qualitative Methods in Organizational Research*. London: Sage, pp. 11–22.

Krueger, R.A. and Casey, M.A. (2009) *Focus Groups: A Practical Guide for Applied Research* (4th edn). Thousand Oaks, CA: Sage.

Kvale, S. and Brinkmann, S. (2009) *InterViews* (2nd edn). Thousand Oaks, CA: Sage.

Mann, C. and Stewart, F. (2000) *Internet Communication and Qualitative Research: A Handbook for Researching Online*. London: Sage.

Marshall, C. and Rossman, G.B. (2006) *Designing Qualitative Research* (4th edn). Thousand Oaks, CA: Sage.

Morgan, S.J. and Symon, G. (2004) 'Electronic interviews in organizational research', in C. Cassell and G. Symon (eds) *Essential Guide to Qualitative Methods in Organizational Research*. London: Sage, pp. 3–33.

Narayanan, V.K., Colwell, K. and Douglass, F.L. (2009) 'Building organizational and scientific platforms in the pharmaceutical industry: A process perspective on the development of dynamic capabilities', *British Journal of Management*, Vol. 20, pp. 25–40.

Powney, J. and Watts, M. (1987) *Interviewing in Educational Research*. London: Routledge and Kegan Paul.

Robson, C. (2011) *Real World Research: A Resource for Users of Social Research Methods in Applied Settings* (3rd edn). Chichester: John Wiley.

Silverman, D. (2007) *A Very Short, Fairly Interesting and Reasonably Cheap Book about Qualitative Research*. London: Sage.

Speer, S. (2002) '"Natural" and "contrived" data: A sustainable distinction?', *Discourse Studies*, Vol. 4, No. 4, pp. 511–25.

Stokes, D. and Bergin, R. (2006) 'Methodology or "methodolatry"? An evaluation of focus groups and depth interviews', *Qualitative Market Research*, Vol. 9, No. 1, pp. 26–37.

Sweet, C. (2001) 'Designing and conducting virtual focus groups', *Qualitative Market Research*, Vol. 4, No. 3, pp. 130–35.

Teddlie, C. and Tashakkori, A. (2009) *Foundations of Mixed Methods Research: Integrating Quantitative and Qualitative Approaches in the Social and Behavioural Sciences*. Thousand Oaks, CA: Sage.

Yin, R.K. (2009) *Case Study Research: Design and Methods* (4th edn). Thousand Oaks, CA: Sage.

Zikmund, W.G. (2000) *Business Research Methods* (6th edn). Fort Worth, TX: Dryden Press.

Further reading

Krueger, R.A. and Casey, M.A. (2009) *Focus Groups: A Practical Guide for Applied Research* (3rd edn). Thousand Oaks, CA: Sage. This provides a very useful source for those considering the use of this method of group interviewing.

Kvale, S. and Brinkmann, S. (2009) *InterViews* (2nd edn). Thousand Oaks, CA: Sage. A useful general guide to interviewing skills.

Mann, C. and Stewart, F. (2000) *Internet Communication and Qualitative Research: A Handbook for Researching Online*. London: Sage. Although written in 2000, Chapter 6 still provides a useful guide to using online interviews and Chapter 5 to online focus groups.

Symon, G. and Cassell, C. (eds) (2012) *The Practice of Qualitative Research: Core Methods and Current Challenges*. London: Sage. This edited work contains an excellent range of chapters related to qualitative data collection with useful examples.

Case 10
Organisations in a flash?

Anthony is interested in the way Internet and mobile communications technologies are changing the way it is possible for people to organise themselves. He has a personal interest in technology so decided to undertake a research project in this area. To gain ideas as to suitable research questions, he took a trip to the university library to browse through the 'tables of contents' of recently published journals. One particular article in the journal *Culture and Organization* about 'flash-mobs' caught his eye (Kaulingfreks and Warren 2010). The authors had written that the recent craze for 'flash-mobbing' in public places could be seen as a new organisational form based on Hardt and Negri's (2004) idea of the 'swarm' – where people who do not know each other come together to do a particular task and dissipate again straight away. Importantly, these 'swarms' used mobile phone and Internet technologies to send messages to one another through viral communication, and had no clear leadership or management. The authors of the flash-mobs article suggested that these forms could be seen in 'collaborative innovation networks' (Gloor 2006) and were also politically powerful, given they were so difficult to 'find' – and to stop by police or other authorities. Anthony was intrigued.

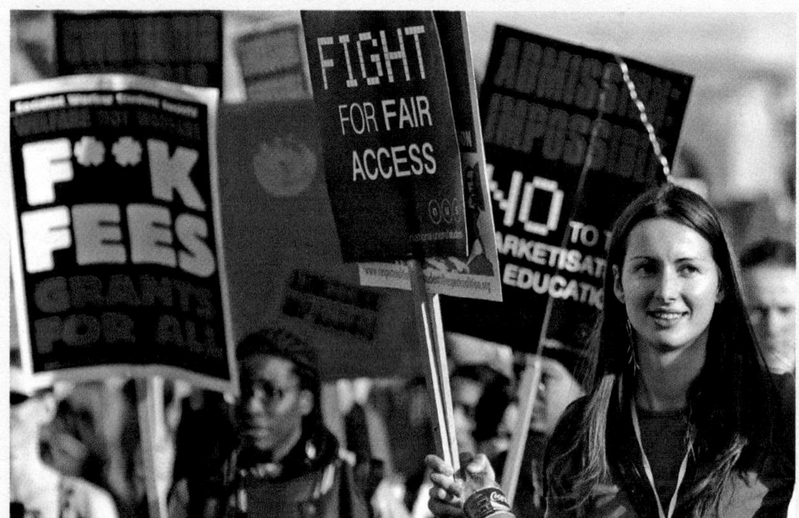

Students protesting against tuition fees
Source: Getty Images

Anthony had read this particular journal article because he had recently taken part in a couple of flash-mobs. The first one had been a bit of harmless fun – around 50 or 60 people had gathered in the town centre and had a water pistol fight for exactly 1 minute 27 seconds before running away. The second one had been more of an 'event' – hundreds of people of all ages and walks of life had brought the mainline railway station to a standstill by crowding into the ticket hall and dancing to music on their MP3 players. This had been a protest against government spending cuts and rising tuition fees. Once again, the event lasted for only a few minutes and the participants disappeared as fast as they came. The first time, Anthony had received a text message from a friend about the event – which he then forwarded on to all his contacts on his phone. He had found out about the second event via Twitter and he had been amazed at the number of people who had turned out for it!

He continued his literature search and as far as he could see there was virtually no empirical research into the flash-mob phenomenon, and certainly nothing that tried to investigate this as a new form of organisation. Anthony decided that he wanted to explore his topic for his research project. He tried to phrase this as a research aim: 'to get a feel for the purpose and motivation of flash-mob events and also the role of technology in their organisation'. He felt that while the last part of his research aim might have been suitable for a short research-administered survey or structured interview, in order to gain the data he needed to answer the first part of his aim, he would need to do more in-depth research. His supervisor suggested that he conduct semi-structured interviews. This would enable him to keep some degree of control over the discussion whilst also being flexible enough to allow participants to digress into areas of importance for them. Given that there are no 'leaders' of flash-mobs in a traditional sense – only the person that instigated the idea and sent the first text message, tweet or Facebook event – Anthony and his supervisor agreed that his sample should be drawn from the participants. A couple of Anthony's friends had attended the flash mobs with him and his supervisor suggested Anthony interview them first and select his sample on a 'snowball' basis – with each interviewee recommending one or two more people to interview. This seemed like a practically 'do-able' method for his research and he set off from his supervisor's office eager to start interviewing. He arranged to meet Josh later that week and, armed with a digital voice recorder, a notepad and a list of general topics he wanted to cover, he began his first interview.

Anthony was concerned to feel the interview did not go very well. He was surprised because Josh was a good friend of his. He hadn't had to spend any time building the rapport that his research methods textbooks had said was so important in getting quality data from interviews, because he'd known Josh for years! They had covered all his questions and Josh had offered some interesting insights into the feeling of being in a community of flash-mobbers he didn't even know, which confirmed some of the ideas in the Kaulingfreks and Warren (2010) journal article. But the problem was that the interview was much more like a conversation and Anthony felt he was talking too much. Several times he had to remind himself that he was supposed to be trying to stay objective. He felt he had said things that had led Josh to discuss areas that he might not have thought of on his own, like the community issue – did Anthony bias the interview by raising this idea? Was the whole interview wasted because he couldn't keep quiet?!

The whole process didn't feel very scientific and a dejected Anthony came away with over an hour of recorded conversation, a list of three more possible interviewees to contact, and a nagging feeling that he was not a particularly good research interviewer.

He made an appointment with his project tutor and was very surprised that she was not at all bothered by his concerns. Rather, as they listened to the recording of the interview together, she seemed to think it had gone extremely well. Anthony was confused. How could the interviews provide him with truthful, valid data when he was so involved in the interview? He felt it was all just subjective.

References

Gloor, P. (2006) *Swarm Creativity: Competitive Advantage through Collaborative Innovation Networks*. Oxford: Oxford University Press.

Hardt, M., and A. Negri (2004) *Multitude, War and Democracy in the Age of Empire*. NewYork: Penguin.

Kaulingfreks, R. and Warren, S. (2010) 'SWARM: Flash mobs, mobile clubbing and the city', *Culture and Organization*, Vol. 16, No. 3, pp. 211–27.

Questions

1 Why do you think Anthony's supervisor thought the interview went very well?
2 What is the difference between bias and subjectivity?
3 What does the interpretive research paradigm have to say about truth and subjectivity in research?
4 Do you think Anthony is right to be concerned about 'talking too much' in his interview? Give reasons for your answer.

Additional case studies relating to material covered in this chapter are available via the book's companion website: **www.pearsoned.co.uk/saunders**. They are:

- Equal opportunities in the publishing industry.
- The practices and styles of public relations practitioners.
- Students' use of work-based learning in their studies.
- Students' and former students' debt problems.

Self-check answers

10.1 The type of interview that is likely to be used in each of these situations is as follows: A standardised and structured interview where the aim is to develop response patterns from the views of people. The interview schedule might be designed to combine styles so that comments made by interviewees in relation to specific questions could also be recorded. The situation outlined suggests an exploratory approach to research, and therefore an in-depth interview would be most appropriate. The situation outlined here suggests that an explanatory approach is required in relation to the data collected, and in this case a semi-structured interview is likely to be appropriate.

10.2 Reasons that suggest the use of interviews include:

- the exploratory or explanatory nature of your research;
- situations where it will be significant to establish personal contact, in relation to interviewee sensitivity about the nature of the information to be provided and the use to be made of this;
- situations where the researcher needs to exercise control over the nature of those who will supply data;
- situations where there are a large number of questions to be answered;
- situations where questions are complex or open-ended;
- situations where the order and logic of questioning may need to be varied.

10.3 Certainly politely! Your response needs to show that you are aware of the issues relating to reliability, bias and generalisability that might arise. It would be useful to discuss how these might be overcome through the following: the design of the research; the keeping of records or a diary in relation to the processes and key incidents of the research project as well as the recording of data collected; attempts to control bias through the process of collecting data; the relationship of the research to theory.

10.4 Perhaps it will be wise to say that you understand his position. You realise that any approach to research calls for particular types of competence. Your previous answer touching on interviewee bias has highlighted the need to establish credibility and to gain the interviewee's confidence. While competence will need to be developed over a period of time, allowing for any classroom simulations and dry runs with colleagues, probably the best approach will be your level of preparation before embarking on interview work. This relates first to the nature of the approach made to those whom you would like to participate in the research project and the information supplied to them, second to your intellectual preparation related to the topic to be explored and the particular context of the organisations participating in the research, and third to your ability to conduct an interview. You also recognise that piloting the interview themes will be a crucial element in building your competence.

10.5 Key issues to consider include the following:

- planning to minimise the occurrence of forms of bias where these are within your control, related to interviewer bias, interviewee bias and sampling bias;
- considering your aim in requesting the research interview and how you can seek to prepare yourself in order to gain access to the data that you hope your participants will be able to share with you;
- devising interview themes that you wish to explore or seek explanations for during the interview;
- sending a list of your interview themes to your interviewee prior to the interview, where this is considered appropriate;
- requesting permission and providing a reason where you would like to use an audio recorder during the interview;
- making sure that your level of preparation and knowledge (in relation to the research context and your research question and objectives) is satisfactory in order to establish your credibility when you meet your interviewee;
- considering how your intended appearance during the interview will affect the willingness of the interviewee to share data.

10.6 There are several areas where you need to develop and demonstrate competence in relation to the conduct of semi-structured and in-depth research interviews. These areas are:

- opening the interview;
- using appropriate language;
- questioning;
- listening;
- testing and summarising understanding;
- behavioural cues;
- recording data.

Get ahead using resources on the companion website at:
www.pearsoned.co.uk/saunders

- Improve your IBM SPSS Statistics and NVivo research analysis with practice tutorials.
- Save time researching on the Internet with the Smarter Online Searching Guide.
- Test your progress using self-assessment questions.
- Follow live links to useful websites.

Chapter 11

Collecting primary data using questionnaires

Learning outcomes

By the end of this chapter you should:

- understand the advantages and disadvantages of questionnaires as a data collection method;
- be aware of a range of self-completed and interviewer-completed questionnaires;
- be aware of the possible need to combine data collection methods within a research project;
- be able to select and justify the use of appropriate questionnaire methods for a variety of research scenarios;
- be able to design, pilot and deliver a questionnaire to answer research questions and to meet objectives;
- be able to take appropriate action to enhance response rates and to ensure the validity and reliability of the data collected;
- be able to apply the knowledge, skills and understanding gained to your own research project.

11.1 Introduction

Within business and management research, the greatest use of questionnaires is made within the survey strategy (Section 5.5). However, both experiment and case study research strategies can make use of these methods. Although you probably have your own understanding of the term 'questionnaire', it is worth noting that there are a variety of definitions in common usage (Oppenheim 2000). Some people reserve it exclusively for questionnaires where the person answering the question actually records their own answers. Others use it as a more general term to also include interviews in which the questions are asked either face to face or by telephone.

In this book we use **questionnaire** as a general term to include all methods of data collection in which each person is asked to respond to the same set of questions in a predetermined order (deVaus 2002). It therefore includes both structured interviews and telephone questionnaires as well as those in which the questions are answered without an interviewer being present, such as the Auchentoshan distillery's online questionnaire. The range of data

collection methods that fall under this broad heading are outlined in the next section (11.2), along with their relative advantages and disadvantages.

The use of questionnaires is discussed in many research methods texts. These range from those that devote a few pages to it to those that specify precisely how you should construct and use them, such as Dillman's (2009) **tailored design method**. Perhaps not surprisingly, the questionnaire is one of the most widely used data collection methods within the survey strategy. Because each person (respondent) is asked to respond to the same set of questions, it provides an efficient way of collecting responses from a large sample prior to quantitative analysis (Chapter 12). However, before you decide to use a questionnaire we should like to include a note of caution. Many authors (for example, Bell 2010; Oppenheim 2000) argue that it is far harder to produce a good questionnaire than you might think. You need to ensure that it will collect the precise data that you require to answer your research question(s) and achieve your objectives. This is of paramount importance because, like the Auchentoshan Distillery, you are unlikely to

Questionnaires are a part of our everyday lives. For modules in your course, your lecturers have probably asked you and your fellow students to complete module evaluation questionnaires, thereby collecting data on students' views. Similarly, when we visit a tourist attraction or have a meal in a restaurant there is often the opportunity to complete a comment card or visitor feedback form. Auchentoshan Whisky Distillery, part of the Morrison Bowmore Distilleries Ltd, is no exception. Visitors to the distillery can take a guided tour during which they see the complete single malt whisky production process, including the triple distillation process, usually only associated with Irish whiskey. They can also taste one of the range of Auchentoshan single malt whiskies. At the end of the tour visitors are asked by their tour guide if they would be willing to complete a one-page feedback form. It starts with a brief introduction emphasising the importance of visitors opinions in helping the Distillery to improve:

Auchentoshan Distillery
Source: © Morrison Bowmore Distillers Ltd

Here at Auchentoshan Distillery we are dedicated to the continual improvement of our products, services and to the company itself. To assist us in achieving this and to be in with a chance of winning a free bottle of our Single Malt Whisky, we would be grateful if you could tell us what you thought of your experience today – thank you.

This is followed by eight questions including:

Please score the following topics according to the ratings shown:

1. Distillery Tour & Shop	**Score**	**Ratings**
Welcome and friendliness of our staff.	☐	5 = Excellent
How informative was the tour?	☐	4 = Very Good
How interesting was the tour?	☐	3 = Good
The knowledge of the tour guide.	☐	2 = Fair
Our tour in comparison with any other distilleries you may have visitied	☐	1 = Poor
Value for money.	☐	
Product range within the shop	☐	
What did you think of the DVD presentation?	☐	
Name of your tour guide:	☐	

4. Have you visited Auchentoshan Distillery before? **Yes** ☐ **No** ☐

5. Would you recommend us to others or return in the future? **Yes** ☐ **No** ☐

7. Comments/Improvements (please tell us what you thought or where we could improve).

Extract from Auchentoshan questionnaire reproduced with permission of Morrison Bowmore Distillers Ltd.

Details about the respondent including their name, country and email address are also collected, visitors being asked to tick a box ☑ if they are over 18 years of age, the legal drinking age in the United Kingdom. Anne Kinnes, the Visitor Centre Operations and Development Manager for Morrison Bowmore, says 'We are committed to offering world class service at all our visitors' centres and the most effective way for us to improve our service is to listen to our customers. One of the methods we use is the feedback form, by using the information we collect this enables us to make improvements to our visitor experience.' These data help the Auchentoshan Distillery maintain high levels of visitor satisfaction.

have more than one opportunity to collect the data. In particular, you will be unable to go back to those individuals who choose to remain anonymous and collect additional data using another questionnaire. These issues are discussed in Section 11.3.

The design of your questionnaire will affect the response rate and the reliability and validity of the data you collect. These, along with response rates, can be maximised by:

- careful design of individual questions;
- clear and pleasing layout of the questionnaire;
- lucid explanation of the purpose of the questionnaire;
- pilot testing;
- carefully planned and executed delivery and return of completed questionnaires.

Together these form Sections 11.4 and 11.5. In Section 11.4 we discuss designing your questionnaire. Delivery and return of the questionnaire is considered in Section 11.5 along with actions to help ensure high response rates.

11.2 An overview of questionnaires

When to use questionnaires

We have found that many people use a questionnaire to collect data without considering other methods such as examination of secondary sources (Chapter 8), observation (Chapter 9), and semi-structured or unstructured interviews (Chapter 10). Our advice is to evaluate all possible data collection methods and to choose those most appropriate to your research question(s) and objectives. Questionnaires are usually not particularly good for exploratory or other research that requires large numbers of open-ended questions (Sections 10.2 and 10.3). They work best with standardised questions that you can be confident will be interpreted the same way by all respondents (Robson 2011).

Questionnaires therefore tend to be used for descriptive or explanatory research. Descriptive research, such as that undertaken using attitude and opinion questionnaires and questionnaires of organisational practices, will enable you to identify and describe the variability in different phenomena. In contrast, explanatory or analytical research will enable you to examine and explain relationships between variables, in particular cause-and-effect relationships. These two purposes have different research design requirements (Gill and Johnson 2010), which we shall discuss later (Section 11.3).

Although questionnaires may be used as the only data collection method, it may be better to link them with other methods in a multimethod research design (Sections 5.3 and 5.5). For example, a questionnaire to discover customers' attitudes can be complemented by in-depth interviews to explore and understand these attitudes (Section 10.3). In addition, questionnaires, if worded correctly, normally require less skill and sensitivity to undertake than semi-structured or in-depth interviews (Jankowicz 2005).

Types of questionnaire

The design of a questionnaire differs according to how it is delivered, returned or collected, and the amount of contact you have with the respondents (Figure 11.1). **Self-completed questionnaires** are usually completed by the respondents. Such questionnaires are sent electronically using the Internet (**Internet-mediated** or **Web-based questionnaires**) or intranet (**intranet-mediated questionnaires**), posted to respondents who return them by post after completion (**postal** or **mail questionnaires**), or delivered by hand to each respondent and collected later (**delivery and collection questionnaires**). Responses to

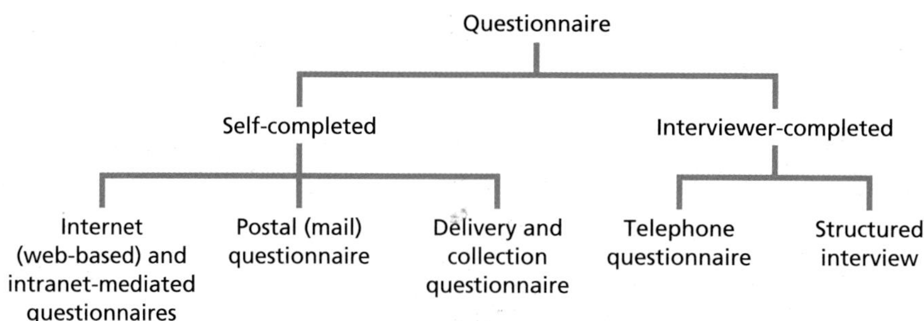

Figure 11.1 Types of questionnaire

interviewer-completed questionnaires are recorded by the interviewer on the basis of each respondent's answers. Questionnaires undertaken using the telephone are known as **telephone questionnaires**. The final category, **structured interviews**, refers to those questionnaires where interviewers physically meet respondents and ask the questions face to face. These differ from semi-structured and unstructured (in-depth) interviews (Section 10.2), as there is a defined schedule of questions, from which interviewers should not deviate.

The choice of questionnaire

Your choice of questionnaire will be influenced by a variety of factors related to your research question(s) and objectives (Table 11.1), and in particular the:

- characteristics of the respondents from whom you wish to collect data;
- importance of reaching a particular person as respondent;
- importance of respondents' answers not being contaminated or distorted;
- size of sample you require for your analysis, taking into account the likely response rate;
- types of question you need to ask to collect your data;
- number of questions you need to ask to collect your data.

These factors will not apply equally to your choice of questionnaire, and for some research questions or objectives may not apply at all. The type of questionnaire you choose will dictate how sure you can be that the respondent is the person whom you wish to answer the questions and thus the reliability of responses (Table 11.1). Even if you address a postal questionnaire to a company manager by name, you have no way of ensuring that the manager will be the respondent. The manager's assistant or someone else could complete it! Internet- and intranet-mediated questionnaires, and in particular those delivered in conjunction with email, offer greater control because most people read and respond to their own email. With delivery and collection questionnaires, you can sometimes check who has answered the questions at collection. By contrast, interviewer-completed questionnaires enable you to ensure that the respondent is whom you want. This improves the reliability of your data. In addition, you can record some details about non-respondents, allowing you to give some assessment of the impact of bias caused by refusals.

Any contamination of respondents' answers will reduce your data's reliability (Table 11.1). Sometimes, if they have insufficient knowledge or experience, they may deliberately guess at the answer, a tendency known as **uninformed response**. This is particularly likely when the questionnaire has been incentivised (Section 11.5). Respondents to self-completed questionnaires are relatively unlikely to answer to please you or because they believe certain responses are more **socially desirable** (Dillman

Table 11.1 Main attributes of questionnaires

Attribute	Internet- and intranet-mediated	Postal	Delivery and collection	Telephone	Structured interview
Population's characteristics for which suitable	Computer-literate individuals who can be contacted by email, or accessed using the Internet or intranet	Literate individuals who can be contacted by post; selected by name, household, rganisation, etc.		Individuals who can be telephoned; selected by name, household, organisation, etc.	Any; selected by name, household, organisation, in the street etc.
Confidence that right person has responded	High if using email	Low	Low but can be checked at collection	High	
Likelihood of contamination or distortion of respondent's answer	Low	May be contaminated by consultation with others		Occasionally distorted or invented by interviewer	Occasionally contaminated by consultation or distorted/invented by interviewer
Size of sample	Large, can be geographically dispersed		Dependent on number of field workers	Dependent on number of interviewers	
Likely response rate[a]	Variable, 30–50% reasonable within organisations/via intranet, 11% or lower using Internet	Variable, 30–50% reasonable		High, 50–70% reasonable	
Feasible length of questionnaire	Equivalent of 6–8 A4 pages, minimise scrolling down	6–8 A4 pages		Up to half an hour	Variable depending on location
Suitable types of question	Closed questions but not too complex; complicated sequencing fine if uses software; must be of interest to respondent	Closed questions but not too complex; simple sequencing only; must be of interest to respondent		Open and closed questions, including complicated questions; complicated sequencing fine	
Time taken to complete collection	2–6 weeks from distribution (dependent on number of follow-ups)	4–8 weeks from posting (dependent on number of follow-ups)	Dependent on sample size, number of field workers, etc.	Dependent on sample size, number of interviewers, etc., but slower than self-completed for same sample size	
Main financial resource implications	If via a web page, web page design. Subscription to online software	Outward and return postage, photocopying, clerical support, data entry	Field workers, travel, photocopying, clerical support, data entry	Interviewers, telephone calls, clerical support; photocopying and data entry if not using CATI;[c] programming, software and computers if using CATI	Interviewers, travel, clerical support; photocopying and data entry if not using CAPI;[d] programming, software and computers if using CAPI
Role of the interviewer/field worker	None		Delivery and collection of questionnaires; enhancing respondent participation	Enhancing respondent participation; guiding the respondent through the questionnaire; answering respondents' questions	
Data input[b]	Automated	Closed questions can be designed so that responses may be entered using optical mark readers after questionnaire has been returned		Response to all questions entered at time of collection using CATI[c]	Response to all questions can be entered at time of collection using CAPI[d]

[a]Discussed in Chapter 7. [b]Discussed in Section 12.2. [c]Computer-aided telephone interviewing. [d]Computer-aided personal interviewing.

Sources: Authors' experience; Baruch and Holtom (2008); deVaus (2002); Dillman (2009); Oppenheim (2000)

2009). They may, however, discuss their answers with others, thereby contaminating their response. Respondents to telephone questionnaires and structured interviews are more likely to answer to please due to their contact with you, although the impact of this can be minimised by good interviewing technique (Sections 10.5 and 10.6). Responses can also be contaminated or distorted when recorded. In extreme instances, interviewers may invent responses. For this reason, random checks of interviewers are often made by survey organisations. When writing your project report you will be expected to state your response rate. When doing this you need to be careful not to make unsubstantiated claims if comparing with other surveys' response rates. Whilst such comparisons place your survey's response rate in context, a higher than normal response rate does not prove that your findings are unbiased (Rogelberg and Stanton 2007). Similarly, a lower than normal response rate does not necessarily mean that responses are biased.

The type of questionnaire you choose will affect the number of people who respond (Section 7.2). Interviewer-completed questionnaires will usually have a higher response rate than self-completed questionnaires (Table 11.1). The size of your sample and the way in which it is selected will have implications for the confidence you can have in your data and the extent to which you can generalise (Section 7.2).

Longer questionnaires are best presented as a structured interview. In addition, they can include more complicated questions than telephone questionnaires or self-completed questionnaires (Oppenheim 2000). The presence of an interviewer (or the use of online software) means that it is also easier to route different subgroups of respondents to answer different questions using a filter question (Section 11.4). The suitability of different types of question also differs between methods.

Your choice of questionnaire will also be affected by the resources you have available (Table 11.1), and in particular the:

- time available to complete the data collection;
- financial implications of data collection and entry;
- availability of interviewers and field workers to assist;
- use of automated data entry.

The time needed for data collection increases markedly for delivery and collection questionnaires and structured interviews where the samples are geographically dispersed (Table 11.1). One way you can overcome this constraint is to select your sample using cluster sampling (Section 7.2). Unless your questionnaire is Internet- or intranet-mediated, or **computer-aided personal interviewing (CAPI)** or **computer-aided telephone interviewing (CATI)** is used, you will need to consider the costs of reproducing the questionnaire, clerical support and entering the data for computer analysis. For postal and telephone questionnaires, cost estimates for postage and telephone calls will need to be included. If you are working for an organisation, postage costs may be reduced by using *Freepost* for questionnaire return. This means that you pay only postage and a small handling charge for those questionnaires that are returned by post. However, the use of Freepost rather than a stamp may adversely affect your response rates (see Table 11.4 below).

Virtually all data collected by questionnaires will be analysed by computer. Some online survey tools (e.g. Snap Surveys™, Sphinx Survey™ and SurveyMonkey™) allow you to design your questionnaire, and collect, enter and analyse the data within the same software. Once your data have been coded and entered into the computer you will be able to explore and analyse them far more quickly and thoroughly than by hand (Section 12.2). As a rough rule, you should analyse questionnaire data by computer if they have been collected from 30 or more respondents. For larger surveys, you may wish to automate the capture and input of data. For Internet- and intranet-mediated questionnaires, this is normally undertaken at the questionnaire design stage and, where the software is automated, costs

Box 11.1 Focus on student research

Closed question designed for an optical mark reader

Ben's research project involved sending out a questionnaire to a large number of people. Because of this he obtained permission to use his university's optical mark reader to input the data from his questionnaire. In his questionnaire, respondents are given clear instructions on how to mark their responses:

> Please use a pencil to mark your answer as a solid box like this: [—]
>
> If you make a mistake use an eraser to rub out your answer.

1 Please mark all the types of music that you regularly listen to:	Rock and Pop	[ ]
	Dance and Urban	[ ]
	Soundtracks	[ ]
	Jazz and Blues	[ ]
	Country	[ ]
	Easy listening	[ ]
	Folk	[ ]
	World	[ ]
	Classical	[ ]
	Other	[ ]
	(please describe):	
	....	

are minimal. For example, SurveyMonkey™, an online survey tool for creating, delivering and collecting responses using web-based questionnaires, at the time of writing charged £23.99 for up to 1000 responses a month, whilst a survey of 10 or fewer questionnaires and with 100 or fewer responses was free (SurveyMonkey 2011). For self-completed questionnaires, data capture and input is most straightforward for closed questions where respondents select and mark their answer from a prescribed list (Box 11.1).

The mark is read using an **optical mark reader**, which recognises and converts marks into data at rates often exceeding 200 pages a minute. Data for interviewer-completed questionnaires can be entered directly into the computer at the time of interview using CATI or CAPI software. With both types of software you read the questions to the respondent from the screen and enter their answers directly into the computer. Because of the costs of high-speed and high-capacity scanning equipment, software and pre-survey programming, CATI and CAPI are financially viable only for very large surveys or where repeated use of the hardware and software will be made.

In reality, you are almost certain to have to make compromises in your choice of questionnaire. These will be unique to your research as the decision about which questionnaire is most suitable cannot be answered in isolation from your research question(s) and objectives and the population or sample from which you are collecting data.

11.3 Deciding what data need to be collected

Research design requirements

Unlike in-depth and semi-structured interviews (Chapter 10), the questions you ask in questionnaires need to be defined precisely prior to data collection. Whereas you can prompt and explore issues further with in-depth and semi-structured interviews, this will not be possible for questionnaires. In addition, the questionnaire offers only one chance to collect the data as it is often difficult to identify respondents or to return to collect additional information. This means that the time you spend planning precisely what data you need to collect, how you intend to analyse them (Chapter 12) and designing your questionnaire to meet these requirements is crucial if you are to answer your research question(s) and meet your objectives.

For most business and management research the data you collect using questionnaires will be used for either descriptive or explanatory purposes. For questions where the main purpose is to describe the population's characteristics either at a fixed time or at a series of points over time to enable comparisons, you will normally need to deliver your questionnaire to a sample. The sample needs to be as representative and accurate as possible where it will be used to generalise about the total population (Sections 7.1–7.3). You will also probably need to relate your findings to earlier research. It is therefore important that you select the appropriate characteristics to answer your research question(s) and to address your objectives. You will need to have:

- reviewed the literature carefully;
- discussed your ideas with colleagues, your project tutor and other interested parties.

For research involving organisations, we have found it essential to understand the organisational context in which we are undertaking the research. Similarly, for international or cross-cultural research it is important to have an understanding of the countries and cultures in which you are undertaking the research. Without this it is easy to make mistakes, such as using the wrong terminology or language, and to collect useless data. For many research projects an understanding of relevant organisations can be achieved through browsing company publications or their websites (Section 8.3), observation (Chapter 9) and in-depth and semi-structured interviews (Chapter 10).

Explanatory research requires data to test a theory or theories. This means that, in addition to those issues raised for descriptive research, you need to define the theories you wish to test as relationships between variables prior to designing your questionnaire. You will need to have reviewed the literature carefully, discussed your ideas widely and conceptualised your own research clearly prior to designing your questionnaire (Ghauri and Grønhaug 2010). In particular, you need to be clear about which relationships you think are likely to exist between variables:

- a **dependent variable** changes in response to changes in other variables;
- an **independent variable** causes changes in a dependent variable;
- a **mediating variable** that transmits the effect of an independent variable to a dependent variable;
- a **moderating variable** that affects the relationship between an independent variable and a dependent variable (Box 11.2 and Table 5.2).

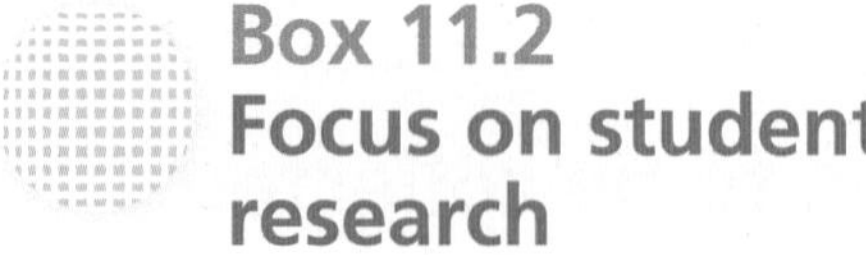

Box 11.2 Focus on student research

Defining theories in terms of relationships between variables

As part of her research, Marie-Claude wished to test the theory that the use of professional fundraisers in charitable fundraising altered the donations made by members of the public.

The relationship that she thought existed between these two variables was that the donations made were higher when professional fundraisers were used. The dependent variable was the value of donations received, and the independent variable was the use of professional fundraisers.

Marie-Claude thought that mediating factors such as the tactics devised by the professional fundraisers (such as media events and advertising) would transmit the effect of the use of professional fundraisers, acting as mediating variables. In contrast, factors such as public opinion about the cause the charity represented and potential donors' disposable income would act as moderating variables. Data were collected on each of these variables.

As these relationships are likely to be tested through statistical analysis (Section 12.5) of the data collected by your questionnaire, you need to be clear about the detail in which they will be measured at the design stage. Where possible, you should ensure that measures are compatible with those used in other relevant research so that comparisons can be made (Section 12.2).

Types of data variable

Dillman (2009) distinguishes between three types of data variable that can be collected through questionnaires:

- opinion;
- behaviour;
- attribute.

These distinctions are important, as they will influence the way your questions are worded (Box 11.3). **Opinion variables** record how respondents feel about something or what they think or believe is true or false. In contrast, data on behaviours and attributes record what respondents do and are. When recording what respondents do, you are recording their behaviour. This differs from respondents' opinions because you are recording a concrete experience. **Behavioural variables** contain data on what people (or their organisations) did in the past, do now or will do in the future. By contrast, **attribute variables** contain data about the respondents' characteristics. Attributes are best thought of as things a respondent possesses, rather than things a respondent does (Dillman 2009). They are used to explore how opinions and behaviour differ between respondents as well as to check that the data collected are representative of the total population (Section 7.2). Attributes include characteristics such as age, gender, marital status, education, occupation and income.

Ensuring that essential data are collected

A problem experienced by many students and organisations we work with is how to ensure that the data collected will enable the research question(s) to be answered and the objectives achieved. Although no method is infallible, one way is to create a **data requirements table** (Table 11.2). This summarises the outcome of a six-step process:

1. Decide whether the main outcome of your research is descriptive or explanatory.
2. Subdivide each research question or objective into more specific investigative questions about which you need to gather data.
3. Repeat the second stage if you feel that the investigative questions are not sufficiently precise.
4. Identify the variables about which you will need to collect data to answer each investigative question.
5. Establish the level of detail required from the data for each variable.
6. Develop measurement questions to capture the data at the level of data required for each variable.

Table 11.2 Data requirements table

Research question/objective:			
Type of research:			
Investigative questions	Variable(s) required	Detail in which data measured	Check measurement question included in questionnaire ✓

Box 11.3 Focus on student research

Opinion, behaviour and attribute questions

Sally was asked by her employer to undertake an anonymous survey of financial advisers' ethical values. In particular, her employer was interested in the advice given to clients. After some deliberation she came up with three questions that addressed the issue of putting clients' interests before their own:

2 How do you feel about the following statement? 'Financial advisors should place their clients' interest before their own.'

	strongly agree	❑
	mildly agree	❑
(please tick the appropriate box)	neither agree or disagree	❑
	mildly disagree	❑
	strongly disagree	❑

3 In general, do financial advisors place their clients' interests before their own?

	always yes	❑
	usually yes	❑
(please tick the appropriate box)	sometimes yes	❑
	seldom yes	❑
	never yes	❑

4 How often do you place your clients' interests before your own?

	81–100% of my time	❑
	61–80% of my time	❑
(please tick the appropriate box)	41–60% of my time	❑
	21–40% of my time	❑
	0–20% of my time	❑

Sally's choice of question or questions to include in her questionnaire was dependent on whether she needed to collect data on financial advisors' opinions or behaviours. She designed question 2 to collect data on respondents' opinions about financial advisors placing their clients' interest before their own. This question asks respondents how they feel. In contrast, question 3 asks respondents whether financial advisors in general place their clients' interests before their own. It is therefore concerned with their individual beliefs regarding how financial advisors act. Question 4 focuses on how often the respondents actually place their clients' interests before their own. Unlike the previous questions, it is concerned with their actual behaviour rather than their opinion.

To answer her research questions and to meet her objectives Sally also needed to collect data to explore how ethical values differed between subgroupings of financial advisors. One theory she had was that ethical values were related to age. To test this she needed to collect data on the attribute age. After some deliberation she came up with question 5:

5 How old are you?

	Less than 30 years	❑
	30 to less than 40 years	❑
(please tick the appropriate box)	40 to less than 50 years	❑
	50 to less than 60 years	❑
	60 years or over	❑

Investigative questions are the questions that you need to answer in order to address satisfactorily each research question and to meet each objective (Bloomberg et al. 2008). They need to be generated with regard to your research question(s) and objectives. For some investigative questions you will need to subdivide your first attempt into more detailed investigative questions. For each you need to be clear whether you are interested in respondents' opinions, behaviours or attributes (discussed earlier), as what appears to be a need to collect one sort of variable frequently turns out to be a need for another. We have found the literature review, discussions with interested parties and pilot studies to be of help here.

You should then identify the variables about which you need to collect data to answer each investigative question and to decide the level of detail at which these are measured. Again, the review of the literature and associated research can suggest possibilities. However, if you are unsure about the detail needed you should measure at a more precise level. Although this is more time-consuming, it will give you flexibility in your analyses. In these you will be able to use computer software to group or combine data (Section 12.2).

Once your table is complete (Box 11.4), it must be checked to make sure that all data necessary to answer your investigative questions are included. When checking, you need to be disciplined and ensure that only data which are essential to answering your research question(s) and meeting your objectives are included. The final column is to remind you to check that your questionnaire actually includes a measurement question that collects the precise data required!

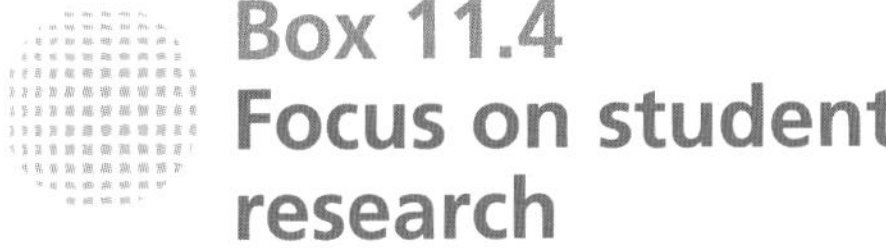

Box 11.4 Focus on student research

Data requirements table

As part of his work placement Greg was asked to discover customer attitudes to the outside smoking area at restaurants and bars. Discussion with senior management and colleagues and reading relevant literature helped him to firm up his objective and investigative questions. A selection of these is included in the extract from his table of data requirements:

• **Research question/objective:** To establish customers' attitudes to the outside smoking area at restaurants and bars			
• **Type of research:** Predominantly descriptive, although wish to examine differences between restaurants and bars, and between different groups of customers			
• ***Investigative questions***	• ***Variable(s) required***	• ***Detail in which data measured***	• ***Check included in questionnaire ✓***
• *Do customers feel that they should have an outside smoking area at restaurants and bars as a right? (opinion)*	• *Opinion of customer on restaurants and bars providing an outside smoking area as a right*	• *Feel . . . should be a right, should not be a right, no strong feelings [N.B. will need separate questions for restaurants and for bars]*	

Box 11.4 Focus on student research *(continued)*

• ***Investigative questions***	• ***Variable(s) required***	• ***Detail in which data measured***	• ***Check included in questionnaire ✓***
• *Do customers feel that restaurants and bars should provide an out-side smoking area for smokers? (opinion)*	• *Opinion of customer to the provision of an outside smoking area for smokers*	• *Feel . . . very strongly that it should, quite strongly that it should, no strong opinions, quite strongly that it should not, very strongly that it should not [N.B. will need separate questions for restaurants and for bars]*	
• *Do customers' opinions differ depending on*	• *(Opinion of employee – outlined above)*	• *(Included above)*	
• *age? (attribute)*	• *Age of employee*	• *To nearest 5-year band (youngest 16, oldest 65+)*	
• *whether or not a smoker? (behaviour)*	• *Smoker*	• *Non-smoker, smokes but not in own home, smokes in own home*	
• *How representative are the responses of customers? (attributes)*	• *Age of customer; Gender of customer; Job [Note: must be able to compare with Office for National Statistics (2005) Socio-Economic Classification]*	• *(Included above) Male, female; Higher managerial and professional occupa-tions, Lower managerial and professional occupations, Intermediate occupations, Small employers and own account workers, Lower supervisory and technical occupations, Semi-routine occupations, Routine occu-pations, Never worked and long-term unemployed*	

11.4 Designing the questionnaire

The internal validity and reliability of the data you collect and the response rate you achieve depend, to a large extent, on the design of your questions, the structure of your questionnaire, and the rigour of your pilot testing (all discussed in this section). A valid questionnaire will enable accurate data that actually measure the concepts you are interested in to be collected, whilst one that is reliable will mean that these data are collected

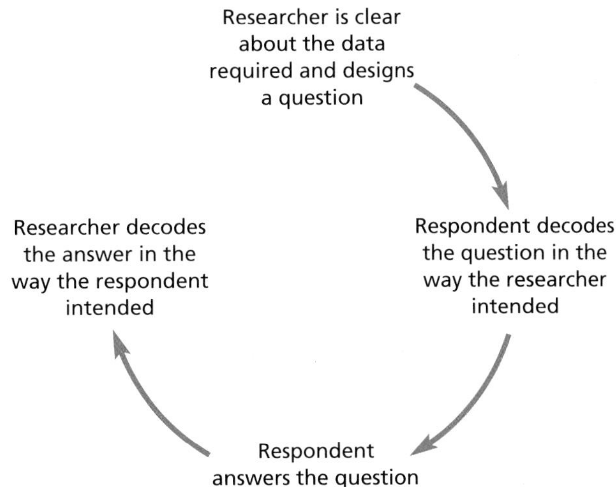
Researcher is clear about the data required and designs a question
Respondent decodes the question in the way the researcher intended
Respondent answers the question
Researcher decodes the answer in the way the respondent intended

Figure 11.2 Stages that must occur if a question is to be valid and reliable
Source: Developed from Foddy (1994) *Constructing Questions from Interviews and Questionnaires.* Reproduced with permission from Cambridge University Press

consistently. Foddy (1994: 17) discusses validity and reliability in terms of the questions and answers making sense. In particular, he emphasises that 'the question must be understood by the respondent in the way intended by the researcher and the answer given by the respondent must be understood by the researcher in the way intended by the respondent'. This means that there are at least four stages that must occur if the question is to be valid and reliable (Figure 11.2). It also means that the design stage is likely to involve you in substantial rewriting in order to ensure that the respondent decodes the question in the way you intended. We therefore recommend that you use a word processor or online survey tool such as SurveyMonkey™, Snap Surveys™ or Sphinx Survey™.

Assessing validity

Internal validity in relation to questionnaires refers to the ability of your questionnaire to measure what you intend it to measure. It is sometimes termed **measurement validity** as it refers to concerns that what you find with your questionnaire actually represents the reality of what you are measuring. This presents you with a problem as, if you actually knew the reality of what you were measuring, there would be no point in designing your questionnaire and using it to collect data! Researchers get round this problem by looking for other relevant evidence that supports the answers found using the questionnaire, relevance being determined by the nature of their research question and their own judgement.

Often, when discussing the validity of a questionnaire, researchers refer to content validity, criterion-related validity and construct validity (Bloomberg et al. 2008). **Content validity** refers to the extent to which the measurement device, in our case the measurement questions in the questionnaire, provides adequate coverage of the investigative questions. Judgement of what is 'adequate coverage' can be made in a number of ways. One is through careful definition of the research through the literature reviewed and, where appropriate, prior discussion with others. Another is to use a panel of individuals to assess whether each measurement question in the questionnaire is 'essential' 'useful but not essential' or 'not necessary'.

Criterion-related validity, sometimes known as **predictive validity**, is concerned with the ability of the measures (questions) to make accurate predictions. This means that if you are using the measurement questions within your questionnaire to predict customers' future buying behaviours then a test of these measurement questions' criterion-related validity will be the extent to which they actually predict these customers' buying behaviours. In assessing criterion-related validity, you will be comparing the data from your questionnaire with that specified in the criterion in some way. Often this is undertaken using statistical analysis such as correlation (Section 12.5).

Construct validity refers to the extent to which your measurement questions actually measure the presence of those constructs you intended them to measure. This term is normally used when referring to constructs such as attitude scales, aptitude and personality tests and the like (Section 11.4) and can be thought of as answering the question: 'How well can you generalise from your measurement questions to your construct?' Because validation of such constructs against existing data is difficult, other methods are used. These are discussed in more detail in a range of texts, including Bloomberg et al. (2008).

Testing for reliability

As we outlined earlier, reliability refers to consistency. Although for a questionnaire to be valid it must be reliable, this is not sufficient on its own. Respondents may consistently interpret a question in your questionnaire in one way, when you mean something else! As a consequence, although the question is reliable, it does not really matter as it has no internal validity and so will not enable your research question to be answered. Reliability is therefore concerned with the robustness of your questionnaire and, in particular, whether or not it will produce consistent findings at different times and under different conditions, such as with different samples or, in the case of an interviewer-completed questionnaire, with different interviewers (Box 11.5).

Mitchell (1996) outlines three common approaches to assessing reliability, in addition to comparing the data collected with other data from a variety of sources. Although the analysis for each of these is undertaken after data collection, they need to be considered at the questionnaire design stage. They are:

- test re-test;
- internal consistency;
- alternative form.

Test re-test estimates of reliability are obtained by correlating data collected with those from the same questionnaire collected under as near equivalent conditions as possible. The questionnaire therefore needs to be delivered and completed twice by respondents. This may create problems, as it is often difficult to persuade respondents to answer the same questionnaire twice. In addition, the longer the time interval between the two questionnaires, the lower the likelihood that respondents will answer the same way. We therefore recommend that you use this method only as a supplement to other methods.

Internal consistency involves correlating the responses to questions in the questionnaire with each other. It thus measures the consistency of responses across either a subgroup of the questions or all the questions from your questionnaire. There are a variety of methods for calculating internal consistency, of which one of the most frequently used is **Cronbach's alpha**. This statistic is usually used to measure the consistency of responses to a set of questions (scale items) that are combined as a scale (discussed later in this section) to measure a particular concept. It consists of an alpha coefficient with a value between 0 and 1. Values of 0.7 or above indicate that the questions combined in the scale are measuring the same thing. Further details of this and other approaches can be found in Mitchell (1996) and in books discussing more advanced statistics and analysis software such as Field (2009).

The final approach to testing for reliability outlined by Mitchell (1996) is 'alternative form'. This offers some sense of the reliability within your questionnaire through comparing responses to alternative forms of the same question or groups of questions. Where

FT

Builders reject ONS sector data

The Office for National Statistics is looking into whether a change in the way it collects data about the construction industry has distorted reported levels of activity, with gross domestic product growth likely to have been stronger in the first quarter of 2011 than had been reported, but weaker at the end of 2010.

Construction executives said a change to the methods used for the agency's monthly survey led companies to submit data about business completed up to six weeks earlier. Until 2010, the survey measured the value of new orders won during the month. The new survey asks for the volume of output in the period. 'It's not just a problem with this first quarter, but for a while now we've been concerned about the reliability of the [ONS] numbers', said Geoff Cooper, chief executive of Travis Perkins, the UK's largest builders' merchant. This view was echoed by executives from contractors and building materials companies including Kier, Tarmac and McLaren Construction.

If the complaints are correct, UK GDP is likely to have grown about 0.8 per cent in the first quarter of 2011 rather than the 0.5 per cent reported. The higher level of output is in line with forecasts in March from the Office for Budget Responsibility and in February from the Bank of England. However, any upgrade also suggests the economy contracted by more than the 0.5 per cent decline in GDP in the fourth quarter of 2010. The ONS said activity was 'flattish' after accounting for the effects of snow. Now, it emerges, output may have contracted. Construction accounts for about 6 per cent of national output but has been volatile since Britain emerged from recession and has affected calculations of GDP disproportionately.

Economists expressed concern about the strength of first-quarter GDP in early April when construction orders for February were made public. These showed that the expected rebound from snow-related delays not only failed to materialise but that orders fell. Economists scaled back forecasts for GDP growth for the quarter and futures markets, where predictions of a rate rise in May prevailed, began to roll back the timing of a near-term rise in spite of high inflation. Joe Grice, ONS chief economist, said the agency routinely evaluated the performance of all its output and had 'no reason at present to believe the construction series is giving a distorted picture of what is going on in the sector'.

Source: From 'Builders reject ONS sector data', Ed Hammond and Norma Cohen, *Financial Times,* 8 May 2011.

questions are included for this purpose, usually in longer questionnaires, they are often called 'check questions'. However, it is often difficult to ensure that these questions are substantially equivalent. Respondents may suffer from fatigue owing to the need to increase the length of the questionnaire, and they may spot the similar question and just refer back to their previous answer! It is therefore advisable to use check questions sparingly.

Designing individual questions

The design of each question should be determined by the data you need to collect (Section 11.3). When designing individual questions researchers do one of three things (Bourque and Clark 1994):

- adopt questions used in other questionnaires;
- adapt questions used in other questionnaires;
- develop their own questions.

Adopting or adapting questions may be necessary if you wish to replicate, or to compare your findings with, another study. This can allow reliability to be assessed. It is also more efficient than developing your own questions, provided that you can still collect the data you need to answer your research question(s) and to meet your objectives. Some survey design software includes questions that you may use. Alternatively, you may find questions and coding schemes that you feel will meet your needs in existing questionnaires, journal articles or in Internet-based question banks, such as the Survey Question Bank hosted by the Survey Resource Network (2011). This provides access to fully searchable questionnaires in pdf format from a range of UK and cross-national surveys since the mid-1990s. It also has a question search facility allowing access to over 200,000 questions from more than 50 surveys and is available from **http://surveynet.ac.uk/sqb/about/introduction.asp**.

However, before you adopt questions, beware! There are a vast number of poor questions in circulation, so always assess each question carefully. In addition, you need to check whether they are under copyright. If they are, you need to obtain the author's permission to use them. Even where there is no formal copyright you should, where possible, contact the author and obtain permission. In your project report you should state where you obtained the questions and give credit to their author.

Initially, you need only consider the type and wording of individual questions rather than the order in which they will appear on the form. Clear wording of questions using terms that are likely to be familiar to, and understood by, respondents can improve the validity of the questionnaire. Most types of questionnaire include a combination of open and closed questions. **Open questions**, sometimes referred to as open-ended questions, allow respondents to give answers in their own way (Fink 2009). **Closed questions**, sometimes referred to as closed-ended questions (Fink 2009) or **forced-choice questions** (deVaus 2002), provide a number of alternative answers from which the respondent is instructed to choose. The latter type of question is usually quicker and easier to answer, as they require minimal writing. Responses are also easier to compare as they have been predetermined. However, if these responses cannot be easily interpreted then these benefits are, to say the least, marginal (Foddy 1994). Within this chapter we highlight six types of closed question that we discuss later:

- list, where the respondent is offered a list of items, any of which may be selected;
- category, where only one response can be selected from a given set of categories;
- ranking, where the respondent is asked to place something in order;
- rating, in which a rating device is used to record responses;
- quantity, to which the response is a number giving the amount;
- matrix, where responses to two or more questions can be recorded using the same grid.

Prior to data analysis, you will need to group and code responses to each question. Detailed coding guidance is given in Section 12.2. You are strongly advised also to read this chapter prior to designing your questions.

Open questions

Open questions are used widely in in-depth and semi-structured interviews (Section 10.5). In questionnaires they are useful if you are unsure of the response, such as in exploratory research, when you require a detailed answer or when you want to find out what is uppermost in the respondent's mind. An example of an open question (from a self-completed questionnaire) is:

6 Please list up to three things you like about your job:

1 ....

2 ....

3 ....

With open questions, the precise wording of the question and the amount of space partially determine the length and fullness of response. However, if you leave too much space the question becomes off-putting. Question 6 collects data about what each respondent believes they like about their job. Thus if salary had been the reason uppermost in their mind this would probably have been recorded first. Unfortunately, when questionnaires are returned by large numbers of respondents, responses to open questions are extremely time-consuming to code (Section 12.2). For this reason, it is usually advisable keep their use to a minimum.

List questions

List questions offer the respondent a list of responses, any of which they can choose. Such questions are useful when you need to be sure that the respondent has considered all possible responses. However, the list of responses must be defined clearly and meaningfully to the respondent. For structured interviews, it is often helpful to present the respondent with a prompt card listing all responses. The response categories you can use vary widely and include 'yes/no', 'agree/disagree' and 'applies/does not apply' along with 'don't know' or 'not sure'. If you intend to use what you hope is a complete list, you may wish to add a catch-all category of 'other'. This has been included in question 7, which collects data on respondents' religion. However, as you can read in Box 11.6, the use of 'other' can result in unforeseen responses, especially where the question is considered intrusive!

7 What is your religion?

Please tick ✓ the appropriate box.

Buddhist	❑	None	❑
Christian	❑	Other	❑
Hindu	❑		
Jewish	❑	(Please say:)	
Muslim	❑		
Sikh	❑		

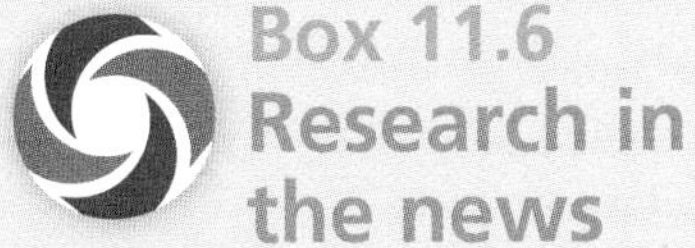

Box 11.6 Research in the news

FT

Concensus on the census is lacking

Censuses have been controversial ever since Mary and Joseph checked into a Bethlehem stable, but Notebook will miss them if, as seems likely, this year's is the UK's last. Not only is the 10-yearly census still valued by genealogists and demographers, it has also become a useful focus for debate about how much an intrusive state should know about its citizens.

That, of course, is one reason for its likely downfall. People who object to the questions either sabotage the answers – such as 390,000 who claimed to be Jedi in answer to a voluntary question on religion in 2001 – or avoid filling in the form, as 3m did last time. That tends to make it inaccurate, which, coupled with the fact that data go rapidly out of date and that it costs £480m, probably means it is doomed.

The UK began its census in 1801. Early concerns included fears that the government would use the information to direct labour to where it was required and that the census would allow an enemy to know where populations were concentrated. Some said it would incur the wrath of God, as when King David ordered a census of the Israelites and 70,000 died in a plague.

Yet, in a society with 4m CCTV cameras, where millions of people's DNA is stored by law enforcement agencies and where hundreds of agencies can carry out surveillance, not to mention the myriad commercial databases that trade data, the degree of intrusion involved in the census appears mild.

The government believes, based on Scandinavian experience, that a cheaper and more accurate count can be obtained by using data held by the NHS, the electoral roll, tax records and even credit card and telecom companies.

Yet I wonder how well these sources can be married. The census has continuity and consistency and remains the biggest source of demographic and social statistics. Will future generations, seeking to learn about us, get what they need from a rolling wave of data?

Source: Adapted from 'Concensus on the census is lacking', Brian Groom, *Financial Times*, 14 March 2011.

Question 7 collects data on the religion of the respondent. In this list question, the common practice of omitting negative response boxes has been adopted. Consequently, negative responses in this question not being, for example, a Christian, are inferred from each unmarked response. If you choose to do this, beware: non-response could also indicate uncertainty, or for some questions that an item does not apply!

Category questions

In contrast, **category questions** are designed so that each respondent's answer can fit only one category. Such questions are particularly useful if you need to collect data about behaviour or attributes. The number of categories that you can include without affecting the accuracy of responses is dependent on the type of questionnaire. Self-completed questionnaires and telephone questionnaires should usually have no more than five response categories (Fink 2009). Structured interviews can have more categories provided that a *prompt card* is used (Box 11.7) or, as in question 8, the interviewer categorises the responses.

8 How often do you visit this shopping centre?

Interviewer: listen to the respondent's answer and tick ✓ as appropriate.

❑ First visit	2 or more times a week ❑
❑ Once a week	Less than once a week to fortnightly ❑
❑ Less than fortnightly to once a month	Less often ❑

You should arrange responses in a logical order so that it is easy to locate the response category that corresponds to each respondent's answer. Your categories should be mutually exclusive (not overlapping), and should cover all possible responses. The layout of your questionnaire should make it clear which boxes refer to which response category by placing them close to the appropriate text.

Ranking questions

A **ranking question** asks the respondent to place things in rank order. This means that you can discover their relative importance to the respondent. In question 9, taken from a postal questionnaire, the respondents are asked their beliefs about the relative importance of a series of features when choosing a new car. The catch-all feature of 'other' is included to allow respondents to add one other feature.

9 Please number each of the factors listed below in order of importance to you in your choice of a new car. Number the most important 1, the next 2 and so on. If a factor has no importance at all, please leave blank.

Factor	**Importance**
Carbon dioxide emissions	[ ]
Boot size	[ ]
Depreciation	[ ]
Safety features	[ ]
Fuel economy	[ ]
Price	[ ]
Driving enjoyment	[ ]
Other	[ ]
....	(⇐ Please describe)

Box 11.7 Focus on student research

Use of a prompt card as part of a structured interview

As part of his interview schedule, Peter asked the following question:

> Which of the following newspapers have you read during the past month?

[Show respondent card 3 with the names of the newspapers. Read out names of the newspapers one at a time. Record their response with a ✓ in the appropriate box].

	Read	Not read	Don't know
The Daily Express	❑	❑	❑
Daily Mail	❑	❑	❑
The Daily Mirror	❑	❑	❑
Daily Star	❑	❑	❑
Financial Times	❑	❑	❑
The Guardian	❑	❑	❑
The Daily Telegraph	❑	❑	❑
The Independent	❑	❑	❑
The Sun	❑	❑	❑
The Times	❑	❑	❑

Peter gave card 3 to each respondent prior to reading out newspaper names and collected the card after the question had been completed.

FINANCIAL TIMES

theguardian

The Daily Telegraph

3

Source: *Financial Times* masthead © *Financial Times*.

With such questions, you need to ensure that the instructions are clear and will be understood by the respondent. In general, respondents find that ranking more than seven items takes too much effort, reducing their motivation to complete the questionnaire, so you should keep your list to this length or shorter (Bloomberg et al. 2008). Respondents can rank accurately only when they can see or remember all items. This can be overcome with face-to-face questionnaires by using prompt cards on which you list all of the features to be ranked. However, telephone questionnaires should ask respondents to rank fewer items, as the respondent will need to rely on their memory.

Rating questions

Rating questions are often used to collect opinion data. They should not be confused with **scales** (discussed later in this section), which are a coherent set of questions or scale items that are regarded as indicators of a construct or concept (Corbetta 2003). Rating questions most frequently use the **Likert-style rating** in which the respondent is asked how strongly she or he agrees or disagrees with a statement or series of statements, usually on a four-, five-, six- or seven-point rating scale. Possible responses to rating questions should be presented in a straight line (such as in question 10) rather than in multiple lines or columns as this is how respondents are most likely to process the data (Dillman 2009). If you intend to use a series of statements, you should keep the same order of response categories to avoid confusing respondents (Dillman 2009). You should include both positive and negative statements so as to ensure that the respondent reads each one carefully and thinks about which box to tick.

10 For the following statement please tick ✓ the box that matches your view most closely.

	Agree	**Tend to agree**	**Tend to disagree**	**Disagree**
I feel employees' views have influenced the decisions taken by management.	❑	❑	❑	❑

Question 10 has been taken from a delivery and collection questionnaire to employees in an organisation and is designed to collect opinion data. In this rating question, an even number of points (four) has been used to force the respondent to express their feelings towards the statement. By contrast, question 11, also from a delivery and collection questionnaire, contains an odd number (five) of points. This rating allows the respondent to 'sit on the fence' by ticking the middle 'not sure' category when considering an implicitly negative statement. The phrase 'not sure' is used here as it is less threatening to the respondent than admitting they do not know. This rating question is designed to collect data on employees' opinions of the situation now.

11 For the following statement please tick ✓ the box that matches your view most closely.

	Agree	**Tend to agree**	**Not sure**	**Tend to disagree**	**Disagree**
I believe there are 'them and us' barriers to communication in the company now.	❑	❑	❑	❑	❑

Table 11.3 Response categories for different types of rating questions

Type of rating	Five categories	Seven categories
Agreement	Strongly agree Agree Neither agree nor disagree/not sure/uncertain* Disagree Strongly disagree	Strongly agree Agree/moderately agree/ mostly agree* Slightly agree Neither agree nor disagree/not sure/uncertain* Slightly disagree Disagree/moderately disagree/ mostly disagree* Strongly disagree
Amount	Far too much/nearly all/very large* Too much/more than half/large* About right/about half/some* Too little/less than half/small* Far too little/almost none/not at all*	Far too much/nearly all/very large* Too much/more than half/large* Slightly too much/quite large* About right/about half/some* Slightly too little/quite small* Too little/less than half/small* Far too little/almost none/not at all*
Frequency	All the time/always* Frequently/very often/most of the time* Sometimes/about as often as not/about half the time* Rarely/seldom/less than half the time* Never/practically never*	All the time/always* Almost all the time/almost always* Frequently/very often/most of the time* Sometimes/about as often as not/ about half the time* Seldom Almost never/practically never* Never/not at all*
Likelihood	Very Good Reasonable Slight/bit* None/not at all*	Extremely Very Moderately Quite/reasonable* Somewhat Slight/bit* None/not at all*

*Response dependent on investigative question.

Source: Developed from Tharenou et al. (2007) and authors' experience

You can expand this form of rating question further to record finer shades of opinion, a variety of which are outlined in Table 11.3. However, respondents to telephone questionnaires find it difficult to distinguish between values when rating more than five points plus 'don't know'. In addition, there is little point in collecting data for seven or nine response categories, if these are subsequently combined in your analysis (Chapter 12). Colleagues and students often ask us how many points they should have on their rating scale. This is related to the likely measurement error. If you know that your respondents can only respond accurately to a three-point rating, then it is pointless to have a finer rating scale with more points!

12 For the following statement please circle O the number that matches your view most closely.

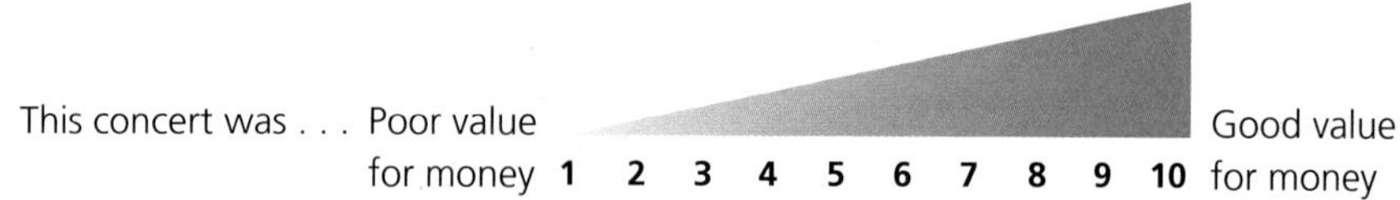

In question 12 the respondent's attitude is captured on a 10-point numeric rating scale. In such rating questions it is important that the numbers reflect the feeling of the respondent. Thus, 1 reflects poor value for money and 10 good value for money. Only these end categories (and sometimes the middle) are labelled and are known as self-anchoring rating scales. As in this question, graphics may also be used to reflect the rating scale visually, thereby aiding the respondent's interpretation. An additional category of 'not sure' or 'don't know' may be added and should be separated slightly from the rating scale.

Another variation is the **semantic differential rating question**. These are often used in consumer research to determine underlying attitudes. The respondent is asked to rate a single object or idea on a series of bipolar rating scales (Box 11.8). Each bipolar scale is described by a pair of opposite adjectives (question 13) designed to anchor respondents' attitudes towards service. For these rating scales, you should vary the position of positive and negative adjectives from left to right to reduce the tendency to read only the adjective on the left (Bloomberg et al. 2008).

Box 11.8 Focus on management research

Students' use of information sources

Kyung Sum Kim and Sei-Ching Joanna Sin (2011) published findings from a study of the information sources undergraduates use frequently and what criteria they consider important when selecting these sources in the *Journal of Information Science*.

Following an email request to participate, students at one university were invited to complete an Internet-mediated questionnaire. This questionnaire asked for demographic information such as age, gender as well as a series of seven-point semantic differential rating questions to discover how each respondent perceived nine different information sources. Each of the 576 participating students rated each of nine information sources using 13 pairs of characteristics framed as bipolar adjectives. Although their paper does not detail the 13 pairs of adjectives used to rate each of the characteristics, the authors state these were derived initially from earlier studies.

As part of the research students were also asked to rank in order of importance both the nine information sources and the 13 characteristics of information sources. The five characteristics of information sources that were ranked as most important were 'accurate/trustworthy', 'accessible', 'easy to use', 'free' and 'active/updated'. The top five sources used by these students were 'web search engines', 'websites/portals', 'online journal databases', 'books' and 'OPACs' (Online Public Access Catalogues).

Despite students recognising that the most important information source characteristic was 'accurate/trustworthy', they did not rate their most frequently used sources, web search engines and websites/portals, highly in this regard. Rather, students' responses to the semantic differential rating questions imply they use such web sources most frequently because they are perceived as 'accessible', 'free' and 'easy to use'. Based on this, Kim and Sin concluded that although students know which sources would be the best to use, they prefer the immediate benefits associated with ease of access and use to the long-term investment required for a larger gain.

13 On each of the lines below, place a x to show how you feel about the service you received at our restaurant.

Fast	__|__|__|__|__|__|__|__|__|__	Slow
Unfriendly	__|__|__|__|__|__|__|__|__|__	Friendly
Value for money	__|__|__|__|__|__|__|__|__|__	Overpriced

Rating questions have been combined to measure a wide variety of concepts such as customer loyalty, service quality and job satisfaction. For each concept the resultant measure or **scale** is represented by a scale score created by combining the scores for each of the rating questions. Each question is often referred to as a **scale item**. In the case of a simple Likert-type scale, for example, the scale score for each case would be calculated by adding together the scores of each of the rating questions (items) selected (deVaus 2002). A detailed discussion of creating scales, including those by Likert and Guttman, can be found in Corbetta (2003). However, rather than developing your own scales, it often makes sense to use or adapt existing scales (Schrauf and Navarro 2005). Since scaling techniques were first used in the 1930s, literally thousands of scales have been developed to measure attitudes and personality dimensions and to assess skills and abilities. Details of an individual scale can often be found by following up references in an article reporting research that uses that scale. In addition, there are a wide variety of handbooks that list these scales (e.g. Miller and Salkind 2002). These scales can, as highlighted in Box 11.9, be used in your own research providing they:

- measure what you are interested in;
- have been empirically tested and validated;
- were designed for a reasonably similar group of respondents.

It is worth remembering that you should only make amendments to the scale where absolutely necessary as significant changes could impact upon both the validity of the scale and, subsequently, your results! You also need to be aware that existing scales may be subject to copyright constraints. Even where there is no formal copyright, you should, where possible, contact the author and ask for permission. In your project report you should note where you obtained the scale and give credit to the author.

Box 11.9 Focus on student research

Using existing scales from the literature

When planning his questionnaire David, like most students, presumed he would need to design and develop his own measurement scale. However, after reading Schrauf and Navarro's (2005) paper on using existing scales, he realised that it would probably be possible to adopt an existing scale which had been reported in the academic literature. As he pointed out to his project tutor, this was particularly fortunate because the process of scale development was hugely time-consuming and could distract his attention from answering the actual research question.

In looking for a suitable published scale David asked himself a number of questions:

- Does the scale measure what I am interested in?
- Has the scale been empirically tested and validated?
- Was the scale designed for a similar group of respondents as my target population?

Fortunately, the answer to all these questions was 'yes'. David, therefore, emailed the scale's author to ask for formal permission.

Quantity questions

The response to a **quantity question** is a number, which gives the amount of a characteristic. For this reason, such questions tend to be used to collect behaviour or attribute data. A common quantity question, which collects attribute data, is:

14 What is your year of birth? | 1 | 9 | | |

(for example, for 1988 write:) | 1 | 9 | 8 | 8 |

Because the data collected by this question could be entered into the computer without coding, the question can also be termed a **self-coded** question, that is one which each respondent codes her or himself.

Matrix questions

A **matrix** or grid of questions enables you to record the responses to two or more similar questions at the same time. As can be seen from question 15, created in SurveyMonkey™, questions are listed down the left-hand side of the page, and responses listed across the top. The appropriate response to each question is then recorded in the cell where the row and column met. Although using a matrix saves space, Dillman (2009) suggests that respondents may have difficulties comprehending these designs and that they are a barrier to response.

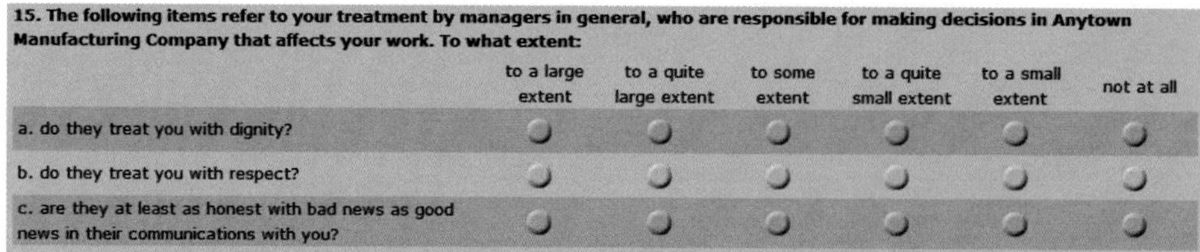
15. The following items refer to your treatment by managers in general, who are responsible for making decisions in Anytown Manufacturing Company that affects your work. To what extent:

	to a large extent	to a quite large extent	to some extent	to a quite small extent	to a small extent	not at all
a. do they treat you with dignity?	○	○	○	○	○	○
b. do they treat you with respect?	○	○	○	○	○	○
c. are they at least as honest with bad news as good news in their communications with you?	○	○	○	○	○	○

Source: Question layout created by SurveyMonkey.com, LLC (2011) Palo Alto, California. Reproduced with permission

Question wording

The wording of each question will need careful consideration to ensure that the responses are valid – that is, measure what you think they do. Your questions will need to be checked within the context for which they were written rather than in abstract to ensure they are not misread (Box 11.10). Given this, the checklist in Box 11.11 should help you to avoid the most obvious problems associated with wording that threaten the validity of responses.

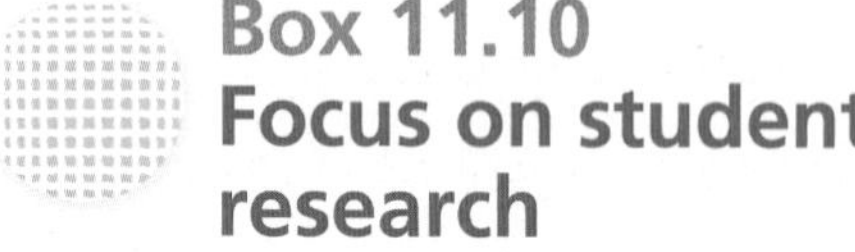

Box 11.10 Focus on student research

Misreading questions

Before becoming a student, Tracey worked for a UK-based market research agency and was responsible for much of their questionnaire design and analysis work. During her time at the agency she noted that certain words in questions were likely to be misread by respondents. The question 'In which county do you live?' was often answered as if the question had been 'In which country do you live?' This meant that rather than answering 'Worcestershire', the respondent would answer either 'England' or 'UK'. Later questionnaires for which Tracey was responsible used the question 'In which town do you live?', the response being used to establish and code the county in which the respondent lived.

Box 11.11 Checklist

Your question wording

- ✔ Does your question collect data at the right level of detail to answer your investigative question as specified in your data requirements table?
- ✔ Will respondents have the necessary knowledge to answer your question? A question on the implications of a piece of European Union legislation would yield meaningless answers from those who were unaware of that legislation.
- ✔ Does your question appear to talk down to respondents? It should not!
- ✔ Are the words used in your question familiar to, and will all respondents understand them in the same way? In particular, you should use simple words and avoid jargon, abbreviations and colloquialisms.
- ✔ Are there any words that sound similar and might be confused with those used in your question? This is a particular problem with interviewer-completed questionnaires.
- ✔ Are there any words that look similar and might be confused if your question is read quickly? This is particularly important for self-completed questionnaires.
- ✔ Are there any words in your question that might cause offence? These might result in biased responses or a lower response rate.
- ✔ Can your question be shortened? Long questions are often difficult to understand, especially in interviewer-completed questionnaires, as the respondent needs to remember the whole question. Consequently, they often result in no response at all.
- ✔ Are you asking more than one question at the same time? The question 'How often do you visit your mother and father?' contains two separate questions, one about each parent, so responses would probably be impossible to interpret.
- ✔ Does your question include a negative or double negative? Questions that include the word 'not' are sometimes difficult to understand. The question 'Would you rather not use a non-medicated shampoo?' is far easier to understand when rephrased as: 'Would you rather use a medicated shampoo?'
- ✔ Is your question unambiguous? This can arise from poor sentence structure, using words with several different meanings or having an unclear investigative question. If you ask 'When did you leave school?' some respondents might state the year, others might give their age, while those still in education might give the time of day! Ambiguity can also occur in category questions. If you ask employers how many employees they have on their payroll and categorise their answers into three groups (up to 100, 100–250, 250 plus), they will not be clear which group to choose if they have 100 or 250 employees.
- ✔ Does your question imply that a certain answer is correct? If it does, the question is biased and will need to be reworded, such as with the question 'Many people believe that too little money is spent on our public Health Service. Do you believe this to be the case?' For this question, respondents are more likely to answer 'yes' to agree with and please the interviewer.
- ✔ Does your question prevent certain answers from being given? If it does, the question is biased and will need to be reworded. The question 'Is this the first time you have pretended to be sick?' implies that the respondent has pretended to be sick whether they answer yes or no!
- ✔ Is your question likely to embarrass the respondent? If it is, then you need either to reword it or to place it towards the end of the survey when you will, it is to be hoped, have gained the respondent's confidence. Questions on income can be asked as either precise amounts (more embarrassing), using a quantity question, or income bands (less embarrassing), using a category question.
- ✔ Have you incorporated advice appropriate for your type of questionnaire (such as the maximum number of categories) outlined in the earlier discussion of question types?
- ✔ Are answers to closed questions written so that at least one will apply to every respondent and so each of the list of responses is mutually exclusive ?
- ✔ Are the instructions on how to record each answer clear?

Translating questions into other languages

Translating questions and associated instructions into another language requires care if your translated or target questionnaire is to be decoded and answered by respondents in the way you intended. For international research this is extremely important if the questions are to have the same meaning to all respondents. For this reason Usunier (1998) suggests that when translating the source questionnaire attention should be paid to:

- **lexical meaning** – the precise meaning of individual words (e.g. the French word *chaud* can be translated into two concepts in English and German, 'warm' and 'hot');
- **idiomatic meaning** – the meanings of a group of words that are natural to a native speaker and not deducible from those of the individual words (e.g. the English expression for informal communication, 'grapevine', has a similar idiomatic meaning as the French expression *téléphone arabe,* meaning literally 'Arab telephone' and the German expression *Mundpropaganda,* meaning literally 'mouth propaganda');
- **experiential meaning** – the equivalence of meanings of words and sentences for people in their everyday experiences (e.g. terms that are familiar in the source questionnaire's context such as 'dual career household' may be unfamiliar in the target questionnaire's context);
- **grammar and syntax** – the correct use of language, including the ordering of words and phrases to create well-formed sentences (e.g. in Japanese the ordering is quite different from English or Dutch, as verbs are at the end of sentences).

Usunier (1998) outlines a number of techniques for translating your source questionnaire. These, along with their advantages and disadvantages, are summarised in Table 11.4. In

Table 11.4 Translation techniques for questionnaires

	Direct translation	Back-translation	Parallel translation	Mixed techniques
Approach	Source questionnaire to target questionnaire	Source questionnaire to target questionnaire to source questionnaire; comparison of two new source questionnaires; creation of final version	Source questionnaire to target questionnaire by two or more independent translators; comparison of two target questionnaires; creation of final version	Back-translation undertaken by two or more independent translators; comparison of two new source questionnaires; creation of final version
Advantages	Easy to implement, relatively inexpensive	Likely to discover most problems	Leads to good wording of target questionnaire	Ensures best match between source and target questionnaires
Disadvantages	Can lead to many discrepancies (including those relating to meaning) between source and target questionnaire	Requires two translators, one a native speaker of the source language, the other a native speaker of the target language	Cannot ensure that lexical, idiomatic and experiential meanings are kept in target questionnaire	Costly, requires two or more independent translators. Implies that the source questionnaire can also be changed

Source: Developed from Usunier (1998) 'Translation techniques for questionnaires' in *International and Cross-Cultural Management Research.* Copyright © 1998 Sage Publications, reprinted with permission

this table, the **source questionnaire** is the questionnaire that is to be translated, and the **target questionnaire** is the translated questionnaire. When writing your final project report, remember to include a copy of both the source and the target questionnaire as appendices. This will allow readers familiar with both languages to check that equivalent questions in both questionnaires have the same meaning.

Question coding

As you will be analysing your data by computer, question responses will need to be coded prior to entry. For numerical responses, actual numbers can be used as codes. For other responses, you will need to design a coding scheme. Whenever possible, you should establish the coding scheme prior to collecting data and incorporate it into your questionnaire. This should take account of relevant existing coding schemes to enable comparisons with other data sets (Section 12.2).

For most closed questions you should be able to add codes to response categories. These can be printed on the questionnaire, thereby **pre-coding** the question and removing the need to code after data collection. Two ways of doing this are illustrated by questions 16 and 17, which collect data on the respondents' opinions.

16	Is the service you receive? (Please circle O the number)	Excellent 5	Good 4	Reasonable 3	Poor 2	Awful 1
17	Is the service you receive? (Please tick ✓ the box)	Excellent ❑5	Good ❑4	Reasonable ❑3	Poor ❑2	Awful ❑1

The codes allocated to response categories will affect your analyses. In both questions 16 and 17 an ordered scale of numbers has been allocated to adjacent responses. This will make it far easier to aggregate responses using a computer (Section 12.2) to 'satisfactory' (5, 4 or 3) and 'unsatisfactory' (2 or 1).

If you are considering using an Internet- (or intranet-) mediated questionnaire you can create an **online form (questionnaire)** using online software tools such as containing text boxes where the respondent enters information, check boxes that list the choices available to the respondent allowing them to 'check' or 'tick' one or more of them, and drop-down list boxes that restrict the respondent to selecting only one of the answers you specify. Alternatively, as for question 18, you can use online survey tools such as SurveyMonkey™ to create your online form. Both allow you to create a professional questionnaire and the respondent to complete the questionnaire online and return the data electronically in a variety of formats such as Excel™, IBM SPSS Statistics compatible or a comma-delimited file.

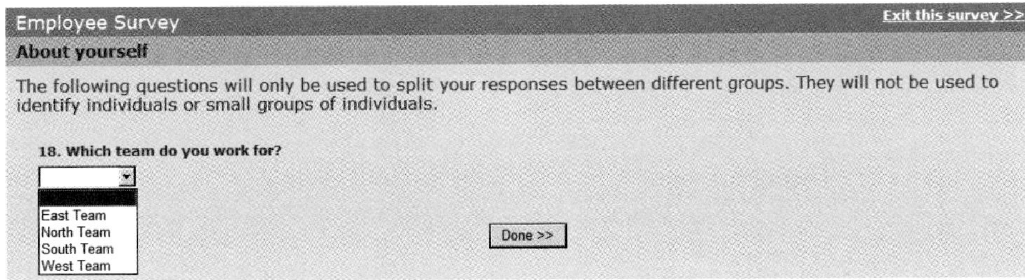

Source: Question layout created by SurveyMonkey.com, LLC (2011) Palo Alto, California. Reproduced with permission

For open questions you will need to reserve space on your data collection form to code responses after data collection. Question 19 has been designed to collect attribute data in a sample survey of 5000 people. Theoretically there could be hundreds of possible responses, and so sufficient spaces are left in the 'For office use only' box.

19 What is your full job title?

....

For Office use only
❑ ❑ ❑

Open questions, which generate lists of responses, are likely to require more complex coding using either the multiple-response or the multiple-dichotomy method. These are discussed in Section 12.2, and we recommend that you read this prior to designing your questions.

Constructing the questionnaire

The order and flow of questions

When constructing your questionnaire it is a good idea to spend time considering the order and flow of your questions. These should be logical to the respondent (and interviewer) rather than follow the order in your data requirements table (Table 11.2). To assist the flow of the questions it may be necessary to include **filter questions**. These identify those respondents for whom the following question or questions are not applicable, so they can skip those questions. You should beware of using more than two or three filter questions in self-completed questionnaires, as respondents tend to find having to skip questions annoying. More complex filter questions can be programmed using online survey tools and CAPI and CATI software so that skipped questions are never displayed on the screen and as a consequence never asked (Dillman 2009). In such situations the respondent is unlikely to be aware of the questions that have been skipped. The following example uses the answer to question 20 to determine whether questions 21 to 24 will be answered. (Questions 20 and 21 both collect data on attributes.)

20 Are you currently registered as unemployed? Yes ❑ 1

If 'no' go to question 25 No ❑ 2

21 How long have you been registered as unemployed? ☐☐ years ☐☐ months

(for example, for no years and six months write: ☐**0** years ☐**6** months)

Where you need to introduce new topics, phrases such as 'the following questions refer to . . .' or 'I am now going to ask you about . . .' are useful. And when wording your questions, you should remember the particular population for whom your questionnaire is designed. For interviewer-completed questionnaires, you will have to include instructions for the interviewer (Box 11.12). The checklist in Box 11.13 should help you to avoid the most obvious problems associated with question order and flow. For some questionnaires the advice contained may be contradictory. Where this is the case, you need to decide what is most important for your particular population.

The layout of the questionnaire

Layout is important for both self-completed and interviewer-completed questionnaires. Interviewer-completed questionnaires should be designed to make reading questions and filling in responses easy. The layout of self-completed questionnaires should, in addition,

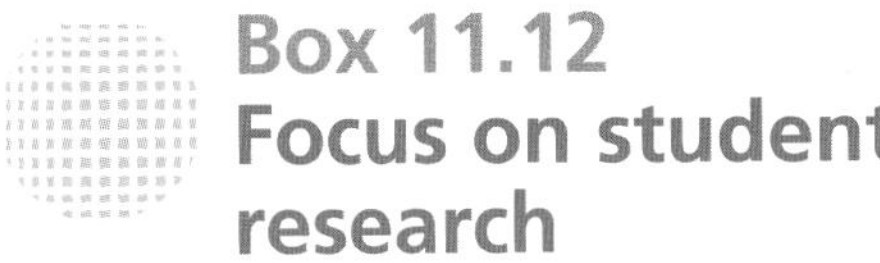

Box 11.12 Focus on student research

Introducing a series of rating questions in a telephone questionnaire

As part of a telephone questionnaire, Stefan needed to collect data on respondents' attitudes to motorway service stations. To do this he asked respondents to rate a series of statements using a Likert-type rating scale. These were recorded as a matrix. Because his survey was conducted by telephone the rating scale was restricted to four categories: strongly agree, agree, disagree, strongly disagree.

In order to make the questionnaire easy for the interviewer to follow, Stefan used italic script to highlight the interviewer's instructions and the words that the interviewer needed to read in bold. An extract is given below:

Now I'm going to read you several statements. Please tell me whether you strongly agree, agree, disagree or strongly disagree with each.

Interviewer: read out statements 22 to 30 one at a time and after each ask ...

Do you strongly agree, agree, disagree or strongly disagree?

Record respondent's response with a tick ✓

	strongly agree	agree	disagree	strongly disagree
22 I wish there were a greater number of service stations on motorways	□4	□3	□2	□1

Box 11.13 Checklist

Your question order

- ✔ Are questions at the beginning of your questionnaire more straightforward and ones the respondent will enjoy answering? Questions about attributes and behaviours are usually more straightforward to answer than those collecting data on opinions.
- ✔ Are questions at the beginning of your questionnaire obviously relevant to the stated purpose of your questionnaire? For example, questions requesting contextual information may appear irrelevant.
- ✔ Are questions and topics that are more complex placed towards the middle of your questionnaire? By this stage most respondents should be undertaking the survey with confidence but should not yet be bored or tired.
- ✔ Are personal and sensitive questions towards the end of your questionnaire, and is their purpose clearly explained? On being asked these a respondent may refuse to answer; however, if they are at the end of an interviewer-completed questionnaire you will still have the rest of the data!
- ✔ Are filter questions and routing instructions easy to follow so that there is a clear route through the questionnaire?
- ✔ (For interviewer-completed questionnaires) Are instructions to the interviewer easy to follow?
- ✔ Are questions grouped into obvious sections that will make sense to the respondent?
- ✔ Have you re-examined the wording of each question and ensured it is consistent with its position in the questionnaire as well as with the data you require?

be attractive to encourage the respondent to fill it in and to return it, while not appearing too long. However, where the choice is between an extra page and a cramped questionnaire the former is likely to be more acceptable to respondents (Dillman 2009). Online survey tools such as Snap™, Sphinx Survey™ and SurveyMonkey™ contain a series of style templates for typefaces, colours and page layout, which are helpful in producing a professional-looking questionnaire more quickly (Le Sphinx 2011; Snap Surveys 2011; SurveyMonkey 2011). For paper-based surveys, the use of colour will increase the printing costs. However, it is worth noting that the best way of obtaining valid responses to questions is to keep both the visual appearance of the questionnaire and the wording of each question simple (Dillman 2009).

Research findings on the extent to which the length of your questionnaire will affect your response rate are mixed (deVaus 2002). There is a widespread view that longer questionnaires will reduce response rates relative to shorter questionnaires (Edwards et al. 2002). However, a very short questionnaire may suggest that your research is insignificant and hence not worth bothering with. Conversely, a questionnaire that takes over two hours to complete might just be thrown away by the intended respondent. In general, we have found that a length of between four and eight A4 pages has been acceptable for within-organisation self-completed questionnaires. Telephone questionnaires of up to half an hour have caused few problems, whereas the acceptable length for structured interviews can vary from only a few minutes in the street to over two hours in a more comfortable environment (Section 10.6). Based on these experiences, we recommend you follow deVaus' (2002) advice:

- Do not make the questionnaire longer than is really necessary to meet your research questions and objectives.
- Do not be too obsessed with the length of your questionnaire.

Remember you can reduce apparent length without reducing legibility by using matrix questions (discussed earlier). Box 11.14 discusses the impact on responses of delivering a questionnaire using the Internet (Web) rather than by mail and Box 11.15 summarises the most important layout issues as a checklist.

Explaining the purpose of the questionnaire

The covering letter

Most self-completed questionnaires are accompanied by a **covering letter** or email, which explains the purpose of the survey. This is the first part of the questionnaire that a respondent should look at. Unfortunately, some of your sample will ignore it, while others use it to decide whether to answer the accompanying questionnaire.

Research by Dillman (2009) and others has shown that the messages contained in a self-completed questionnaire's covering letter will affect the response rate. The results of this research, along with requirement of most ethics committees to stress that participation is voluntary, are summarised in the annotated letter (Figure 11.3).

For some research projects you may also send a letter prior to delivering your questionnaire. This will be used by the respondent to decide whether to grant you access. Consequently, it is often the only opportunity you have to convince the respondent to participate in your research. Ways of ensuring this are discussed in Section 6.3.

Introducing the questionnaire

At the start of your questionnaire you need to explain clearly and concisely why you want the respondent to complete the survey. Dillman (2009) argues that, to achieve as

Box 11.14 Focus on management research

Comparing responses to Internet (Web) and postal (mail) questionnaires

Saunders' (2012) paper, 'Web versus mail: The influence of survey distribution mode on employees' response' in the journal *Field Methods*, uses an experimental design to examine implicitly the impact of distribution mode where employees are IT literate and already have access to the Internet as part of their everyday work. Within this paper the 'Web' was used to refer to Internet-delivered questionnaires, whilst 'mail' referred to postal questionnaires.

Using an employee attitude survey distributed to a 50 per cent systematic sample of 3338 employees by mail, remaining employees receiving the survey via a web link (hyperlink), Saunders found, in contrast to many earlier studies, the return rate for the Web (49.1 per cent) was higher than that for mail (33.5 per cent). Although utility of web returns was reduced by a higher number of partial responses and abandonments (particularly for demographic questions), the rate for complete responses was still higher for the Web than for mail. Significant differences between web and mail responses were small other than those for open question: 'If there are any other areas or issues that concern you, please feel free to comment below . . .' Nearly 20 per cent of respondents provided written response to this question, there being no significant association between the distribution modes regarding whether or not a comment was provided, its tone or the topics covered. However, length of responses to this open question differed significantly, the mean length for web responses being twice that for mail distribution.

Drawing on his findings and the literature reviewed, Saunders offered a series of recommendations concerning the use of web surveys:

1 For research in organisations, the use of web-based questionnaires should be considered only where respondents are IT literate and have ready access to the Internet at work.

Partial response and, in particular abandonment and complete non-response of demographic questions, prompted his second recommendation:

2 Web-based questionnaires should be designed to allow the impact of people not responding to be assessed.

As the literature reviewed had highlighted that the use of web questionnaires might influence responses where this is related to the survey topic, his third recommendation was:

3 Caution should be exercised regarding the inclusion of questions on topics related to the use of the Web or associated technologies.

Finally, based on the difference in length between responses to the Internet and mail delivered questionnaires he recommended:

4 Care should be taken when comparing or aggregating responses to open (write in) questions from web-based questionnaires with those from questionnaires delivered using other methods due to the impact of the technology on response length.

Box 11.15 Checklist

Your questionnaire layout

- ✔ (For self-completed questionnaires) Do questions appear squashed on the page or screen? This will put the respondent off reading it and reduce the response rate. Unfortunately, a thick questionnaire is equally off-putting!
- ✔ (For paper-based self-completed questionnaires) Is the questionnaire going to be printed on good-quality paper? This will imply that the survey is important.

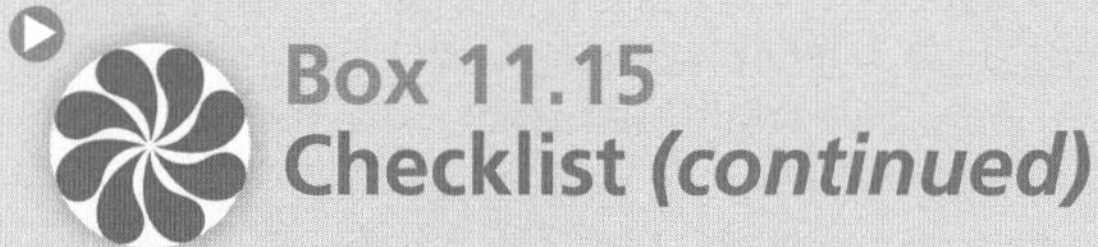

Box 11.15 Checklist *(continued)*

- ✔ (For self-completed questionnaires) Is the questionnaire going to be printed or displayed on a warm-pastel colour? Warm pastel shades, such as yellow and pink, generate slightly more responses than white (Edwards et al. 2002) or cool colours, such as green or blue. White is a good neutral colour but bright or fluorescent colours should be avoided.
- ✔ (For structured interviews) Will the questions and instructions be printed on one side of the paper only? You will find it difficult to read the questions on the back of pages if you are using a questionnaire attached to a clipboard!
- ✔ Is your questionnaire easy to read? Questionnaires should be typed in 12 point or 10 point using a plain font. Excessively long and excessively short lines reduce legibility. Similarly, respondents find CAPITALS, *italics* and shaded backgrounds more difficult to read. However, if used consistently, they can make completing the questionnaire easier.
- ✔ Have you ensured that the use of shading, colour, font sizes, spacing and the formatting of questions is consistent throughout the questionnaire?
- ✔ Is your questionnaire laid out in a format that respondents are accustomed to reading? Research has shown that many people skim-read questionnaires (Dillman 2009). Instructions that can be read one line at a time from left to right moving down the page are, therefore, more likely to be followed correctly.

high a response rate as possible, this should be done on the first page of the questionnaire in addition to the covering letter. He suggests that in addition to a summary of the main messages in the covering letter (Figure 11.3) you include:

- a clear unbiased banner or title, which conveys the topic of the questionnaire and makes it sound interesting;
- a subtitle, which conveys the research nature of the topic (optional);
- a neutral graphic illustration or logo to add interest and to set the questionnaire apart (self-completed questionnaires).

This advice also applies to Internet- and intranet-mediated questionnaires and is discussed later in this section.

Interviewer-completed questionnaires will require this information to be phrased as a short introduction; given in the interviewer's own words to each respondent. A template for this (developed from deVaus 2002), which the interviewer would paraphrase, is given in the next paragraph, while Box 11.16 provides an example from a self-completed questionnaire.

> Good morning/afternoon/evening. My name is [your name] from [your organisation]. I am doing a research project to find out [brief description of purpose of the research]. Your telephone number was drawn from a random sample of [brief description of the total population]. The questions I should like to ask will take about [number] minutes. If you have any queries, I shall be happy to answer them. [Pause] Before I continue please can you confirm that this is [read out the telephone number] and that I am talking to [read out name/occupation/position in organisation to check that you have the right person]. Please can I confirm that you consent to answering the questions and ask you them now?

You will also need to have prepared answers to the more obvious questions that the respondent might ask you. These include the purpose of the survey, how you obtained the respondent's telephone number, who is conducting or sponsoring the survey, and why someone else should not answer the questions instead (Lavrakas 1993).

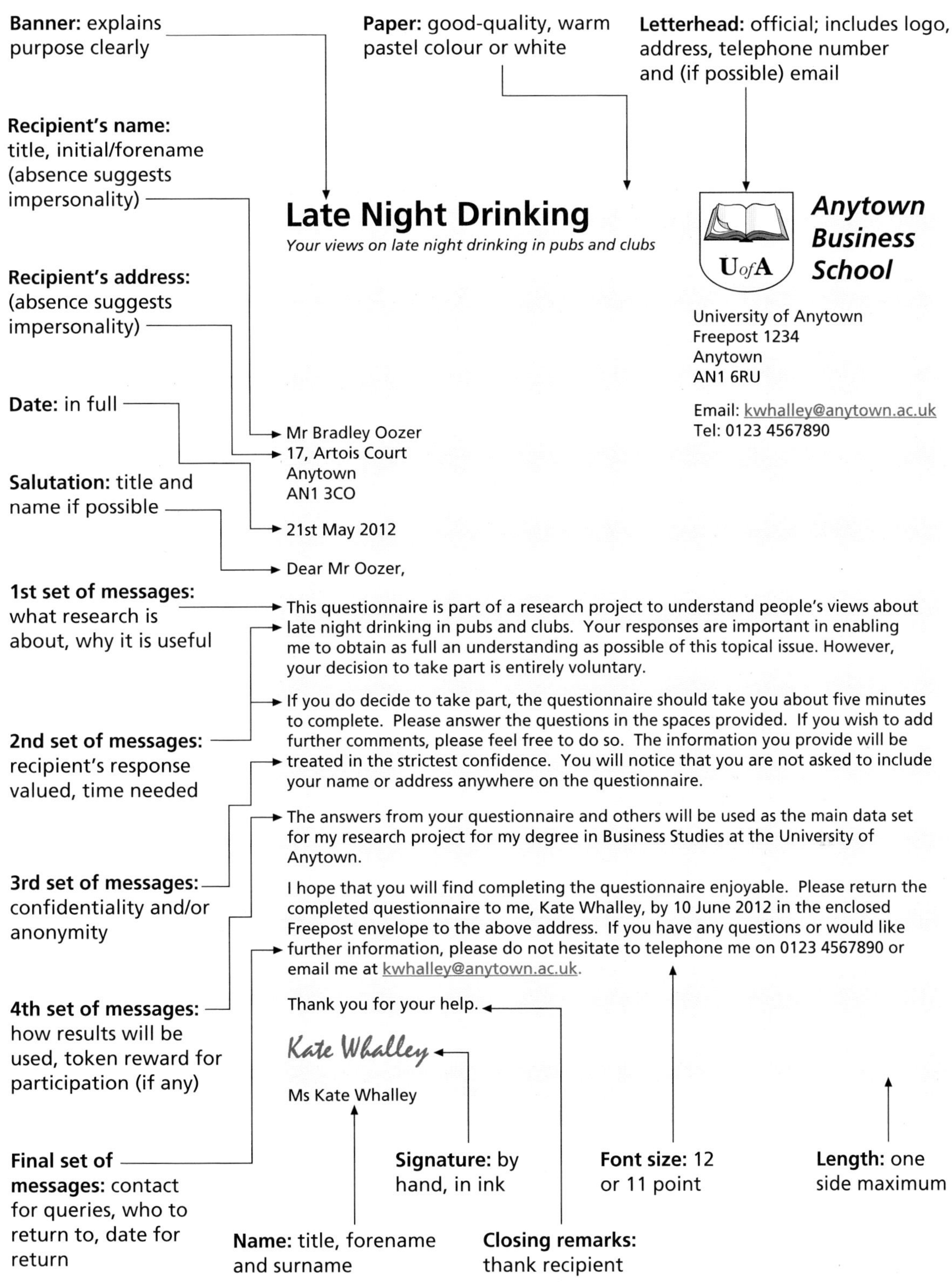

Late Night Drinking

Your views on late night drinking in pubs and clubs

UofA **Anytown Business School**

University of Anytown
Freepost 1234
Anytown
AN1 6RU

Email: kwhalley@anytown.ac.uk
Tel: 0123 4567890

Mr Bradley Oozer
17, Artois Court
Anytown
AN1 3CO

21st May 2012

Dear Mr Oozer,

This questionnaire is part of a research project to understand people's views about late night drinking in pubs and clubs. Your responses are important in enabling me to obtain as full an understanding as possible of this topical issue. However, your decision to take part is entirely voluntary.

If you do decide to take part, the questionnaire should take you about five minutes to complete. Please answer the questions in the spaces provided. If you wish to add further comments, please feel free to do so. The information you provide will be treated in the strictest confidence. You will notice that you are not asked to include your name or address anywhere on the questionnaire.

The answers from your questionnaire and others will be used as the main data set for my research project for my degree in Business Studies at the University of Anytown.

I hope that you will find completing the questionnaire enjoyable. Please return the completed questionnaire to me, Kate Whalley, by 10 June 2012 in the enclosed Freepost envelope to the above address. If you have any questions or would like further information, please do not hesitate to telephone me on 0123 4567890 or email me at kwhalley@anytown.ac.uk.

Thank you for your help.

Kate Whalley

Ms Kate Whalley

Figure 11.3 Structure of a covering letter

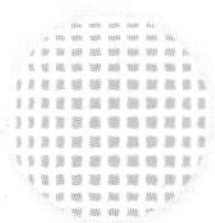

Box 11.16
Focus on student research

Introducing a self-completed questionnaire

Lil asked her project tutor to comment on what she hoped was the final draft of her questionnaire. This included the following introduction:

> ANYTOWN PRIVATE HOSPITAL STAFF SURVEY
>
> All your responses will be treated in the strictest of confidence and only aggregated data will be available to the Hospital. All questionnaires will be shredded once the data have been extracted. The Hospital will publish a summary of the results.

Not surprisingly, her project tutor suggested that she redraft her introduction. Her revised introduction follows:

Anytown Private Hospital

Staff Survey 2012

Caring for All

This survey is being carried out to find out how you feel about the Hospital's policies to support colleagues like you in your work. Please answer the questions freely. You cannot be identified from the information you provide, and no information about individuals will be given to the Hospital.

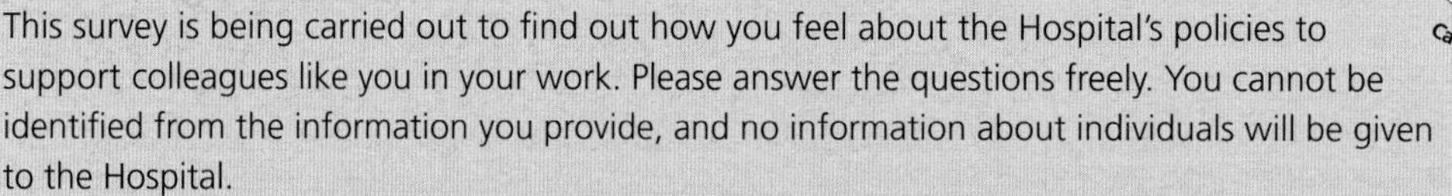

ALL THE INFORMATION YOU PROVIDE WILL BE TREATED IN THE STRICTEST CONFIDENCE. YOUR DECISION TO PARTICIPATE IN THIS RESEARCH IS ENTIRELY VOLUNTARY.

If you do not wish to take part, just do not return the questionnaire to me. If you do decide to take part, the questionnaire should take you about five minutes to complete. Please answer the questions in the space provided. Try to complete the questions at a time when you are unlikely to be disturbed. Also, do not spend too long on any one question. Your first thoughts are usually your best! Even if you feel the items covered may not apply directly to your working life please do not ignore them. Your answers are essential in building an accurate picture of the issues that are important to improving our support for people working for this Hospital.

There are no costs associated with completing the questionnaire other than your time.

WHEN YOU HAVE COMPLETED THE QUESTIONNAIRE PLEASE RETURN IT TO US IN THE ENCLOSED FREEPOST ENVELOPE NO LATER THAN 6 APRIL.

I hope you will be willing to complete and return the questionnaire and thank you for your time. A summary of the findings will be published on the Hospital intranet. If you have any queries or would like further information about this project, please telephone me on 01234-5678910 or email me on l.woollons@anytownhealthcare.com.
Thank you for your help.

Lily Woollons

Lily Woollons
Human Resources Department
Anytown Private Hospital
Anytown AN99 9HS

Closing the questionnaire

At the end of your questionnaire you need to explain clearly what you want the respondent to do with their completed questionnaire. It is usual to start this section by thanking the respondent for completing the questionnaire, and restating the contact name and telephone number for any queries they may have from the covering letter (Figure 11.3). You should restate details of the date by which you would like the questionnaire returned and how and where to return it. A template for this is given in the next paragraph:

> **Thank you for taking the time to complete this questionnaire. If you have any queries please do not hesitate to contact [your name] by telephoning [contact telephone number with answer machine/voice mail] or emailing [email address].**
>
> **Please return the completed questionnaire by [date] in the envelope provided to:**
>
> **[your name]**
>
> **[your address]**

Sometimes, as in Box 11.16, you may wish to offer your respondents a summary of your research findings. If you do make this offer, don't forget to actually provide the summary!

Pilot testing and assessing validity

Prior to using your questionnaire to collect data it should be pilot tested. The purpose of the **pilot test** is to refine the questionnaire so that respondents will have no problems in answering the questions and there will be no problems in recording the data. In addition, it will enable you to obtain some assessment of the questions' validity and the likely reliability of the data that will be collected. Preliminary analysis using the pilot test data can be undertaken to ensure that the data collected will enable your investigative questions to be answered.

Initially you should ask an expert or group of experts to comment on the representativeness and suitability of your questions. As well as allowing suggestions to be made on the structure of your questionnaire, this will help establish content validity and enable you to make necessary amendments prior to pilot testing with a group as similar as possible to the final population in your sample. For any research project there is a temptation to skip the pilot testing. We would endorse Bell's (2010: 151) advice, 'however pressed for time you are, do your best to give the questionnaire a trial run', as, without a trial run, you have no way of knowing whether your questionnaire will succeed.

The number of people with whom you pilot your questionnaire and the number of pilot tests you conduct are dependent on your research question(s), your objectives, the size of your research project, the time and money resources you have available, and how well you have initially designed your questionnaire. Very large questionnaire surveys such as national censuses will have numerous field trials, starting with individual questions and working up to larger and more rigorous pilots of later drafts.

For smaller-scale questionnaires you are unlikely to have sufficient financial or time resources for large-scale field trials. However, it is still important that you pilot test your questionnaire. The number of people you choose should be sufficient to include any major variations in your population that you feel are likely to affect responses. For most student questionnaires this means that the minimum number for a pilot is 10 (Fink 2009), although for large surveys between 100 and 200 responses is usual (Dillman 2009). Occasionally you may be extremely pushed for time. In such instances it is better to pilot test the questionnaire using friends or family than not at all! This will provide you with at least some idea of your questionnaire's **face validity**: that is, whether the questionnaire appears to make sense.

As part of your pilot you should check each completed pilot questionnaire to ensure that respondents have had no problems understanding or answering questions and have followed all instructions correctly (Fink 2009). Their responses will provide you with an idea of the reliability and suitability of the questions. For self-completed questionnaires additional information about problems can be obtained by giving respondents a further short questionnaire. Bell (2010) suggests you should use this to find out:

- how long the questionnaire took to complete;
- the clarity of instructions;
- which, if any, questions were unclear or ambiguous;
- which, if any, questions the respondent felt uneasy about answering;
- whether in their opinion there were any major topic omissions;
- whether the layout was clear and attractive;
- any other comments.

Interviewer-completed questionnaires need to be tested with the respondents for all these points other than layout. One way of doing this is to form an assessment as each questionnaire progresses. Another is to interview any interviewers you are employing. However, you can also check by asking the respondent additional questions at the end of their interview. In addition, you will need to pilot test the questionnaire with interviewers to discover whether:

- there are any questions for which visual aids should have been provided;
- they have difficulty in finding their way through the questionnaire;
- they are recording answers correctly.

Once you have completed pilot testing you should write to your respondents thanking them for their help.

11.5 Delivering and collecting the questionnaire

Once your questionnaire is designed, pilot tested and amended and your sample selected, the questionnaire can be used to collect data. Within business and management research reports, it is often not clear whether respondents felt compelled to respond to the questionnaire (Baruch and Holtom 2008). Respondents' feelings of compulsion are usually signified by stating the questionnaire was 'administered', whereas non-compulsion is signified by phrases such as 'invited to fill out a questionnaire voluntarily' or 'voluntary response'. In collecting data using your questionnaire it is important that you abide by your university's or professional body's code of ethics (Sections 6.5 and 6.6). Although, when a respondent answers questions and returns their questionnaire they are giving their implied consent, they have rights just like all research participants.

Inevitably you will need to gain access to your sample (Sections 6.2 to 6.4) and attempt to maximise the response rate. A large number of studies have been conducted to assess the impact of different strategies for increasing the response to postal questionnaires. Fortunately, the findings of these studies have been analysed and synthesised by Edwards et al. (2002) and, more recently by Anseel et al. (2010). As you can see from Table 11.5, response rates can be improved by careful attention to a range of factors including questionnaire appearance, length, content, delivery methods and associated communication as well as being clearly worded and well laid out. In addition, it must be remembered that organisations and individuals are increasingly being bombarded with requests to respond to questionnaires and so may be unwilling to answer your questionnaire. Which of these techniques you use to help to maximise responses will inevitably be dependent, at least

Table 11.5 Relative impact of strategies for raising postal questionnaire response rates

Strategy	Relative impact
Incentives	
Monetary incentive v. no incentive	Very high
Incentive sent with questionnaire v. incentive on questionnaire return	High
Non-monetary incentive v. no incentive	Low
Length	
Shorter questionnaire v. longer questionnaire	Very high
Appearance	
Brown envelope v. white envelope	High but variable
Coloured ink v. standard	Medium
Folder or booklet. v. stapled pages	Low
More personalised (name, hand signature etc.) v. less personalised	Low
Coloured questionnaire v. white questionnaire	Very low
Identifying feature on the return v. none	Very low but variable
Delivery	
Recorded delivery v. standard delivery	Very high
Stamped return envelope v. business reply or franked	Medium
First class post outwards v. other class	Low
Sent to work address v. sent to home address	Low but variable
Pre-paid return v. not pre-paid	Low but variable
Commemorative stamp v. *ordinary stamp*	Low but variable
Stamped outward envelope v. franked	Negligible
Contact	
Pre-contact (advanced notice) v. no pre-contact	Medium
Follow-up v. no follow-up	Medium
Postal follow-up including questionnaire v. postal follow-up excluding questionnaire	Medium
Pre-contact by telephone v. *pre-contact by post*	Low
Mention of follow-up contact v. none	Negligible
Content	
More interesting/relevant v. less interesting/relevant topic	Very high
User friendly language v. standard	Medium
Attribute and behaviour questions only v. attribute, behaviour and attitude questions	Medium
More relevant questions first v. other questions first	Low
Most general question first v. *last*	Low
Sensitive questions included v. *sensitive questions not included*	Very low
Demographic questions first v. other questions first	Negligible
'Don't know' boxes included v. not included	Negligible
Origin	
University sponsorship as a source v. other organisation	Medium
Sent by more senior or well-known person v. *less senior or less well-known*	Low but variable
Ethnically unidentifiable/white name v. other name	Low but variable
Communication	
Explanation for not participating requested v. not requested	Medium
Anonymity stressed v. not mentioned	Medium
Choice to opt out from study offered v. *not given*	Low
Instructions given v. *not given*	Low but variable
Benefits to respondent stressed v. other benefits	Very low
Benefits to sponsor stressed v. other benefits	Negligible
Benefits to society stressed v. other benefits	Negligible
Response deadline given v. no deadline	Negligible

Note: strategies in italics increase response rates relative to those in normal font.

Source: developed from Anseel et al. (2010); Edwards et al. (2002)

in part, on the way in which your questionnaire is delivered. It is the processes associated with delivering each of the five types of questionnaire that we now consider.

Internet- and intranet-mediated questionnaires

For Internet- and intranet-mediated questionnaires, it is important to have a clear timetable which identifies the tasks that need to be done and the resources that will be needed. A good response is dependent on the recipient being motivated to answer the questionnaire and to send it back. Although the covering email (Section 11.4) and good design will help to ensure a high level of response, it must be remembered that, unlike paper questionnaires, the designer and respondent may see different images displayed on their monitors. Alternative computer operating systems, Internet browsers and display screens can all result in the image being displayed differently, emphasising the need to ensure the questionnaire design is clear (Dillman 2009).

Internet- and intranet-mediated questionnaires are usually delivered via email or via a website. The first of these uses email to 'post' and receive the hyperlink (web link) to the questionnaire and is dependent on having a list of addresses. Although it is possible to obtain such lists from an Internet-based employment directory or via a search engine (Section 3.5), we would not recommend you obtain them this way. If you are using the Internet for research, you should abide by the general operating guidelines or **netiquette**. This includes (Hewson et al. 2003):

- ensuring emails and postings to user groups are relevant and that you do not send junk emails (spam);
- remembering that invitations to participate sent to over 20 user groups at once are deemed as unacceptable by many net vigilantes and so you should not exceed this threshold;
- avoiding sending your email to multiple mailing lists as this is likely to result in individuals receiving multiple copies of your email (this is known as **cross-posting**);
- avoiding the use of email attachments as these can contain viruses.

Failure to do this is likely to result in 'few responses and a barrage of emails informing the researcher of their non-compliance' (Coomber 1997: 10). Despite this, questionnaires can be easily delivered by email as a direct hyperlink within organisations provided all of the sample have access to it and use it. If you choose to use email with a direct hyperlink to the questionnaire, we suggest that you:

1 contact recipients by email and advise them to expect a questionnaire – a **pre-survey contact** (Section 6.3);
2 email the hyperlink to the questionnaire with a covering email. Where possible, the letter and questionnaire or hyperlink should be part of the email message rather than an attached file to avoid viruses. You should make sure that this will arrive when recipients are likely to be receptive. For most organisations Fridays and days surrounding major public holidays have been shown to be a poor time;
3 include an explicit request for the respondent's consent at the start of the questionnaire (Box 11.17);
4 email the first **follow-up** one week after emailing out the questionnaire to all recipients. This should thank early respondents and remind non-respondents to answer (a copy of the hyperlink should be included);
5 email the second follow-up to people who have not responded after three weeks. This should include another covering letter and a copy of the hyperlink. The covering letter should be reworded to further emphasise the importance of completing the questionnaire;
6 also use a third follow-up if time allows or your response rate is low.

Box 11.17 Focus on student research

Request for respondent's consent in an Internet-mediated questionnaire

Meg had decided to collect her data using an Internet-mediated questionnaire. She emailed potential respondents explaining the purpose of her research and requesting their help. At the end of her email she included a hyperlink to the online questionnaire created in SurveyMonkey™.

The first page of Meg's online questionnaire included a summary of the main messages in her email. This was followed by a formal request to the respondent for their consent which stressed that the decision to participate was entirely voluntary and that they could withdraw at any time:

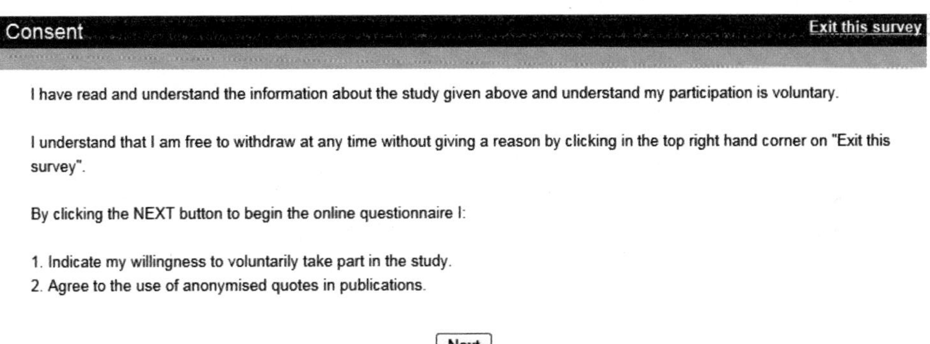

Source: Question layout created by SurveyMonkey.com, LLC (2011) Palo Alto, California. Reproduced with permission

Alternatively, the questionnaire can be advertised on the Internet or on the intranet and respondents invited to access the questionnaire via a hyperlink and fill it in. Adopting this web-based approach observes netiquette and means that respondents can remain anonymous and, of equal importance, are unable to modify the questionnaire (Witmer et al. 1999). The stages involved are:

1. Ensure that a website has been set up that explains the purpose of the research and how to complete the questionnaire (this takes the place of the covering letter).
2. Ensure that the questionnaire has been set up on the Web and has a hyperlink from the website.
3. Advertise the website widely using a range of media (for example, an email pre-survey contact or a banner advertisement on a page that is likely to be looked at by the target population), using a hyperlink to the questionnaire and highlighting the closing date.
4. When the respondent completes the questionnaire, ensure that the data file is generated and saved automatically and that the web-based software prevents multiple responses from one respondent.

Response rates from web advertisements are likely to be very low, and there are considerable problems of non-response bias as the respondent has to take extra steps to locate and complete the questionnaire (Coomber 1997). Consequently, it is likely to be very difficult to obtain a representative sample from which you might generalise. This is not to say that this approach should not be used as it can, for example, enable you to contact difficult-to-access groups. It all depends, as you would expect us to say, on your research question and objectives!

Postal questionnaires

For postal questionnaires, it is also important to have a well-written covering letter and good design to help to ensure a high level of response. As with online questionnaires, a clear timetable and well-executed administration process are important (Box 11.18).

Box 11.18 Focus on management research

Questionnaire administration

Mark undertook an attitude survey of employees in a large organisation using a questionnaire. Within the organisation, 50 per cent of employees received the questionnaire by a hyperlink in an email, the remaining 50 per cent receiving a paper questionnaire by post.

General information regarding the forthcoming survey was provided to employees using the staff intranet, the normal method for such communications. Subsequently each employee received five personal contacts including the questionnaire:

- One week before the questionnaire was delivered a pre-survey notification letter, jointly from the organisation's chief executive and Mark, was delivered in the same manner as the potential respondent would receive their questionnaire.
- Covering letter/email and questionnaire/hyperlink to online questionnaire.
- Personal follow-up/reminder designed as an information sheet re-emphasising the deadline for returns at the end of that week.
- First general reminder (after the deadline for returns) posted on the staff intranet.
- Second general reminder (after the deadline for returns) posted on the staff intranet.

The following graph records the cumulative responses for both the Internet-mediated and postal questionnaire, emphasising both the impact of deadlines, follow-up/reminders and the length of time required (over seven weeks) to collect all the completed questionnaires.

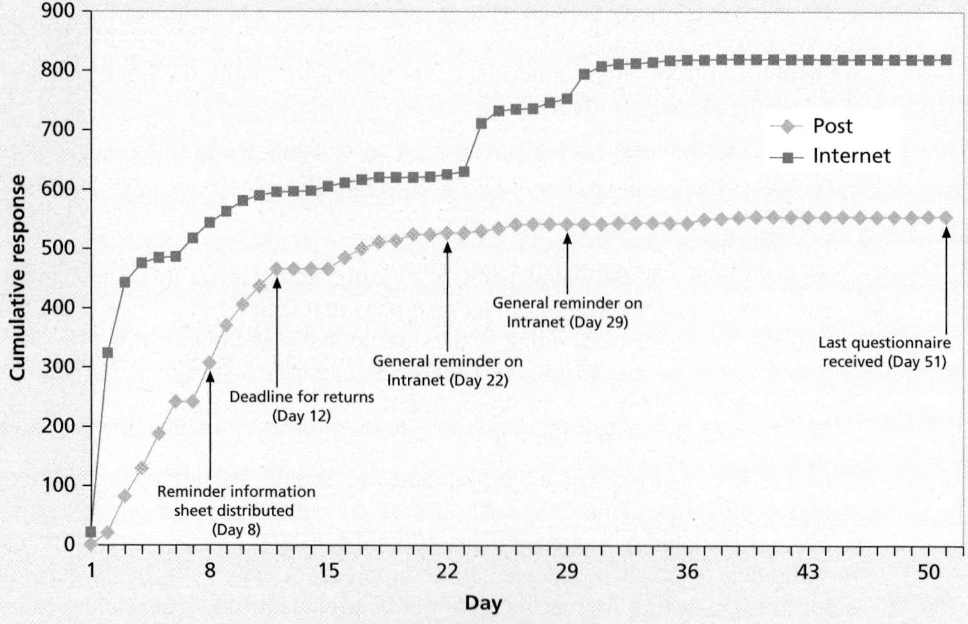

Cumulative questionnaires returned by Internet and post

Source: Unpublished data; details of research from Saunders (2012)

Our advice for postal questionnaires (developed from deVaus 2002) can be split into six stages:

1 Ensure that questionnaires and letters are printed, and envelopes addressed.
2 Contact recipients by post, telephone or email and advise them to expect a questionnaire – a pre-survey contact (Section 6.3). This stage is often omitted for cost reasons.
3 Post the survey with a covering letter and a return envelope (and fax cover sheet). You should make sure that this will arrive when recipients are likely to be receptive. For most organisations Fridays and days surrounding major public holidays have been shown to be a poor time.
4 Post (or email) the first follow-up one week after posting out the survey to all recipients. For posted questionnaires this should take the form of a postcard designed to thank early respondents and to remind rather than to persuade non-respondents.
5 Post the second follow-up to people who have not responded after three weeks. This should contain another copy of the questionnaire, a new return envelope and a new covering letter. The covering letter should be reworded to emphasise further the importance of completing the questionnaire. For anonymous questionnaires a second follow-up will not be possible, as you should not be able to tell who has responded!
6 Also use a third follow-up if time allows or your response rate is low. For this it may be possible to use recorded delivery (post), telephone calls or even call in person to emphasise the importance of responding.

Additionally, deVaus (2002) advises placing a unique identification number on each questionnaire, which is recorded on your list of recipients. This makes it easy to check and follow up non-respondents and, according to Dillman (2009) and Edwards et al. (2002), has little, if any, effect on response rates. However, identification numbers should not be used if you have assured respondents that their replies will be anonymous!

Delivery and collection questionnaires

For delivery and collection questionnaires either you or field staff will deliver and call to collect the questionnaire. It is therefore important that your covering letter states when the questionnaire is likely to be collected. As with postal questionnaires, follow-ups can be used, calling at a variety of times of day and on different days to try to catch the respondent.

A variation on this process that we have used widely in organisations allows for delivery and collection of questionnaires the same day and eliminates the need for a follow-up. The stages are:

1 Ensure that all questionnaires and covering letters are printed and a collection box is ready.
2 Contact respondents by email, internal post or telephone advising them to attend a meeting or one of a series of meetings to be held (preferably) in the organisation's time (Section 6.3).
3 At the meeting or meetings, hand out the questionnaire with a covering letter to each respondent.
4 Introduce the questionnaire, stress its anonymous or confidential nature and that participation is voluntary.
5 Ensure that respondents place their questionnaires in a collection box before they leave the meeting.

Although this adds to costs, as employees are completing the questionnaire in work time, response rates as high as 98 per cent are achievable!

Telephone questionnaires

The quality of data collected using telephone questionnaires will be affected by the researcher's competence to conduct interviews. This is discussed in Sections 10.5 and 10.6. Once your sample has been selected, you need to:

1 ensure that all questionnaires are printed or, for CATI, that the software has been programmed and tested;
2 where it is possible and resources allow, contact respondents by email, post or telephone advising them to expect a telephone call (Section 6.3);
3 telephone each respondent, recording the date and time of call and whether or not the questionnaire was completed. You should note any specific times that have been arranged for call-backs. For calls that were not successful you should note the reason, such as no reply or telephone disconnected;
4 for unsuccessful calls where there was no reply, try three more times, each at a different time and on a different day, and note the same information;
5 make call-back calls at the time arranged.

Structured interviews

Conducting structured interviews uses many of the skills required for in-depth and semi-structured interviews (Sections 10.5 and 10.6). Issues such as interviewer appearance and preparedness are important and will affect the response rate. However, once your sample has been selected you need to:

1 ensure that all questionnaires are printed or, for CAPI, that the software has been programmed and tested;
2 contact respondents by email, post or telephone advising them to expect an interviewer to call within the next week. This stage is often omitted for cost reasons;
3 (for large-scale surveys) divide the sample into assignments that are of a manageable size (50–100) for one interviewer;
4 contact each respondent or potential respondent in person, recording the date and time of contact and whether or not the interview was completed. You should note down any specific times that have been arranged for return visits. For contacts that were not successful, you should note down the reason;
5 try unsuccessful contacts at least twice more, each at a different time and on a different day, and note down the same information;
6 visit respondents at the times arranged for return visits.

11.6 Summary

- Questionnaires collect data by asking people to respond to exactly the same set of questions. They are often used as part of a survey strategy to collect descriptive and explanatory data about opinions, behaviours and attributes. Data collected are normally analysed by computer.
- Your choice of questionnaire will be influenced by your research question(s) and objectives and the resources that you have available. The five main types are Internet- or intranet-mediated, postal, delivery and collection, telephone and interview schedule.
- Prior to designing a questionnaire, you must know precisely what data you need to collect to answer your research question(s) and to meet your objectives. One way of helping to ensure that you collect these data is to use a data requirements table.

- The validity and reliability of the data you collect and the response rate you achieve depend largely on the design of your questions, the structure of your questionnaire, and the rigour of your pilot testing.
- When designing your questionnaire you should consider the wording of individual questions prior to the order in which they appear. Questions can be divided into open and closed. Six types of closed questions are list, category, ranking, rating, quantity and matrix.
- Wherever possible, closed questions should be pre-coded on your questionnaire to facilitate data input and subsequent analyses.
- The order and flow of questions in the questionnaire should be logical to the respondent. This can be assisted by filter questions and linking phrases.
- The questionnaire should be laid out so that it is easy to read and the responses are easy to fill in.
- Questionnaires must be introduced carefully to the respondent to ensure a high response rate. For self-completed questionnaires this should take the form of a covering letter; for interviewer-completed questions it will be done by the interviewer.
- All questionnaires should be pilot tested prior to their delivery to assess the validity and likely reliability of the questions.
- Delivery of questionnaires needs to be appropriate to the type of questionnaire.

Self-check questions

Help with these questions is available at the end of the chapter.

11.1 In what circumstances would you choose to use a delivery and collection questionnaire rather than a postal questionnaire? Give reasons for your answer.

11.2 The following questions have been taken from a questionnaire about flexibility of labour.

i Do you agree or disagree with the use of nil hours contracts by employers?

(Please tick appropriate box)

Strongly agree ❑ $_4$
Agree ❑ $_3$
Disagree ❑ $_2$
Strongly disagree ❑ $_1$

ii Have you ever been employed on a nil hours contract?

(Please tick appropriate box)

Yes ❑ $_1$
No ❑ $_2$
Not sure ❑ $_3$

iii What is your marital status?

(Please tick appropriate box)

Single ❑ $_1$
Married or living in long-term relationship ❑ $_2$
Widowed ❑ $_3$
Divorced ❑ $_4$
Other ❑ $_5$
.... (⇐ Please describe)

iv Please describe what you think would be the main impact on employees of a nil hours contract.

For each question identify:

a the type of data variable for which data are being collected;

b the type of question.

You should give reasons for your answers.

11.3 You are undertaking research on the use of children's book clubs by householders within mainland Europe. As part of this, you have already undertaken in-depth interviews with households who belong and do not belong to children's book clubs. This, along with a literature review, has suggested a number of investigative questions from which you start to construct a table of data requirements.

a For each investigative question listed, decide whether you will need to collect data on opinions, behaviours or attributes.

Research question/objective: To establish mainland Europe's householders' opinions about children's book clubs			
Type of research: Predominantly descriptive, although wish to explain differences between householders			
Investigative questions	**Variable(s) required**	**Detail in which data measured**	**Check measurement question included in questionnaire ✓**
A Do householders think that children's book clubs are a good or a bad idea?			
B What things do householders like most about children's book clubs?			
C Would householders be interested in an all-ages book club?			
D How much per year do households spend on children's books?			
E Do households' responses differ depending on (i) number of children? (ii) whether already members of a children's book club?			

b Complete the table of data requirements for each of the investigative questions already listed. (You may embellish the scenario to help in your choice of variables required and how the data will be measured as you feel necessary.)

11.4 Design pre-coded or self-coded questions to collect data for each of the investigative questions in self-check question 11.3. Note that you will need to answer self-check question 11.3 first (or use the answer at the end of this chapter).

11.5 What issues will you need to consider when translating your questionnaire?

11.6 You work for a major consumer research bureau that has been commissioned by 11 major UK companies to design, deliver and analyse the data collected from a telephone questionnaire. The purpose of this questionnaire is to describe and explain relationships between adult consumers' lifestyles, opinions and purchasing intentions. Write the introduction to this telephone questionnaire, to be read by an interviewer to each respondent. You may embellish the scenario and include any other relevant information you wish.

11.7 You have been asked by a well-known national charity 'Work for All' to carry out research into the effects of long-term unemployment throughout the UK. The charity intends to use the findings of this research as part of a major campaign to highlight public awareness about the effects of long-term unemployment. The charity has drawn up a list of names and addresses of people who are or were long-term unemployed with whom they have had contact over the past six months. Write a covering letter to accompany the postal questionnaire. You may embellish the scenario and include any other relevant information you wish.

11.8 You have been asked to give a presentation to a group of managers at an oil exploration company to gain access to undertake your research. As part of the presentation you outline your methodology, which includes piloting the questionnaire. In the ensuing question and answer session one of the managers asks you to justify the need for a pilot study, arguing that 'given the time constraints the pilot can be left out'. List the arguments that you would use to convince him that pilot testing is essential to your methodology'.

Review and discussion questions

11.9 If you wish for more help with designing questionnaires, visit the website www.statpac.com/surveys/ and download and work through the tutorial 'Designing Surveys and Questionnaires'.

11.10 Obtain a copy of a 'customer questionnaire' from a department store or restaurant. For each question on the questionnaire establish whether it is collecting data about opinions, behaviours or attributes. Do you consider any of the questions are potentially misleading? If yes, how do you think the question could be improved? Discuss the answer to these questions in relation to your questionnaire with a friend.

11.11 Visit the website of an online questionnaire provider. A selection of possible providers can be found by typing 'online questionnaire provider' or 'online survey provider' into the Google search engine. Use the online software to design a simple questionnaire. To what extent does the questionnaire you have designed meet the requirements of the checklists in Boxes 11.11, 11.13 and 11.15?

Using questionnaires in your research

- Return to your research question(s) and objectives. Decide on how appropriate it would be to use questionnaires as part of your research strategy. If you do decide that this is appropriate, note down the reasons why you think it will be sensible to collect at least some of your data in this way. If you decide that using a questionnaire is not appropriate, justify your decision.
- If you decide that using a questionnaire is appropriate, reread Chapter 7 on sampling and, in conjunction with this chapter, decide which of the five types of questionnaire will be most appropriate. Note down your choice of questionnaire and the reasons for this choice.
- Construct a data requirements table and work out precisely what data you need to answer your investigative questions. Remember that you will need to relate your investigative questions and data requirements back to the literature you have reviewed and any preliminary research you have already undertaken.
- Design the separate questions to collect the data specified in your data requirements table. Wherever possible, try to use closed questions and to adhere to the suggestions in the question wording checklist. If you are intending to analyse your questionnaire by computer, read Section 12.2 and pre-code questions on the questionnaire whenever possible.
- Order your questions to make reading the questions and filling in the responses as logical as possible to the respondent. Wherever possible, try to adhere to the checklist for layout. Remember that interviewer-completed questionnaires will need instructions for the interviewer.
- Write the introduction to your questionnaire and, where appropriate, a covering letter.
- Pilot test your questionnaire with as similar a group as possible to the final group in your sample. Pay special attention to issues of validity and reliability.
- Deliver your questionnaire and remember to send out a follow-up survey to non-respondents whenever possible.
- Use the questions in Box 1.4 to guide your reflective diary entry.

11.12 Visit your university library or use the Internet to view a copy of a report for a recent national government survey in which you are interested. If you are using the Internet, the national government websites listed in Table 8.2 are a good place to start. Check the appendices in the report to see if a copy of the questionnaire used to collect the data is included. Of the types of question – open, list, category, ranking, rating, quantity and grid – which is most used and which is least frequently used? Note down any that may be of use to you in your research project.

References

Anseel, F., Lievens, F., Schollaert, E. and Choragwicka, B. (2010) 'Response rates in organizational science, 1995–2008: A meta-analytic review and guidelines for survey researchers', *Journal of Business Psychology*, Vol. 25, pp. 335–49.

Baruch, Y. and Haltom, B.C. (2008) 'Survey response rate levels and trends in organizational research', *Human Relations*, Vol. 61, pp. 1139–60.

Bell, J. (2010) *Doing Your Research Project* (5th edn). Maidenhead: Open University Press.

Bloomberg, B., Cooper, D.R. and Schindler, P.S. (2008) *Business Research Methods* (2nd European edn). Boston, MA and Burr Ridge, IL: McGraw-Hill.

Bourque, L.B. and Clark, V.A. (1994) 'Processing data: The survey example', in M.S. Lewis-Beck (ed.) *Research Practice*. London: Sage, pp. 1–88.

Coomber, R. (1997) 'Using the Internet for survey research', *Sociological Research Online*, Vol. 2, No. 2. Available at www.socresonline.org.uk/socresonline/2/2/2.html [Accessed 20 April 2008].

Corbetta, P. (2003) *Social Research: Theory, Methods and Techniques*. London: Sage.

deVaus, D.A. (2002) *Surveys in Social Research* (5th edn). London: Routledge.

Dillman, D.A. (2009) *Internet, Mail and Mixed Mode Surveys: The Tailored Design Method* (3rd edn). New York: Wiley.

Edwards, P., Roberts, I., Clarke, M., Di Giuseppe, C., Pratap, S., Wentz, R. and Kwan, I. (2002) 'Increasing response rates to postal questionnaires: Systematic review', *British Medical Journal*, No. 324, May, pp. 1183–91.

Field, A. (2009) *Discovering Statistics Using SPSS* (3rd edn). London: Sage.

Fink, A. (2009) *How to Conduct Surveys* (4th edn). Thousand Oaks, CA: Sage.

Foddy, W. (1994) *Constructing Questions for Interviews and Questionnaires*. Cambridge: Cambridge University Press.

Ghauri, P. and Grønhaug, K. (2010) *Research Methods in Business Studies: A Practical Guide* (4th edn). Harlow: Financial Times Prentice Hall.

Gill, J. and Johnson, P. (2010) *Research Methods for Managers* (4th edn). London: Sage.

Hewson, C., Yule, P., Laurent, D. and Vogel, C. (2003) *Internet Research Methods: A Practical Guide for the Social and Behavioural Sciences*. London: Sage.

Jankowicz, A.D. (2005) *Business Research Projects* (4th edn). London: Thomson Learning.

Kim, K.S. and Sin, S.-C.J. (2011) 'Selecting sources: Bridging the gap between perception and use of information sources', *Journal of Information Science*, Vol. 37, No. 2, pp. 178–88.

Lavrakas, P.J. (1993) *Telephone Survey Methods: Sampling, Selection and Supervision*. Newbury Park, CA: Sage.

Le Sphinx (2011) *Sphinx survey and statistical software*. Available at www.sphinxsurvey.com/ [Accessed 7 May 2011].

Miller, D.C. and Salkind, N.J. (eds) (2002) *Handbook of Research Design and Social Measurement* (6th edn). Thousand Oaks, CA: Sage.

Mitchell, V. (1996) 'Assessing the reliability and validity of questionnaires: An empirical example', *Journal of Applied Management Studies*, Vol. 5, No. 2, pp. 199–207.

Office for National Statistics (2005) *The National Statistics Socio-economic Classification User Manual.* Basingstoke: Palgrave Macmillan.

Oppenheim, A.N. (2000) *Questionnaire Design, Interviewing and Attitude Measurement* (new edn). London: Continuum International.

Robson, C. (2011) *Real World Research: A Resource for Users of Social Research Methods in Applied Settings* (3rd edn). Chichester: John Wiley.

Rogelberg, S.G. and Stanton, J.M. (2007) 'Introduction: Understanding and dealing with organizational survey non-response', *Organizational Research Methods*, Vol. 10, No. 2, pp. 195–209.

Saunders, M.N.K. (2012) 'Web versus mail: The influence of survey distribution mode on employees' response', *Field Methods*, Vol. 24, No. 1.

Schrauf, R.W. and Navarro, E. (2005) 'Using existing tests and scales in the field', *Field Methods*, Vol. 17, No. 4, pp. 373–93.

Snap Surveys (2011) *Snap Survey Software Research Services*. Available at www.snapsurveys.com [Accessed 9 May 2011].

SurveyMonkey (2011) *SurveyMonkey.com*. Available at www.surveymonkey.com [Accessed 17 May 2011].

Survey Resource Network (2011) *Survey Resource Network.* Available at http://surveynet.ac.uk/ [Accessed 11 June 2011].

Tharenou, P., Donohue, R. and Cooper, B. (2007) *Management Research Methods.* Melbourne: Cambridge University Press.

Usunier, J.-C. (1998) *International and Cross-Cultural Management Research*. London: Sage.

Witmer, D.F., Colman, R.W. and Katzman, S.L. (1999) 'From paper and pen to screen and keyboard: Towards a methodology for survey research on the Internet', in S. Jones (ed.) *Doing Internet Research.* Thousand Oaks, CA: Sage, pp. 145–62.

Further reading

deVaus, D.A. (2002) *Surveys in Social Research* (5th edn). London: Routledge. Chapters 7 and 8 provide a detailed guide to constructing and delivering questionnaires, respectively.

Dillman, D.A. (2009) *Internet, Mail and Mixed Mode Surveys: The Tailored Design Method* (3rd edn.). New York: Wiley. The third edition of this classic text contains an extremely detailed and well-researched discussion of how to design postal and Internet-based questionnaires to maximise response rates.

Foddy, W. (1994) *Constructing Questions for Interviews and Questionnaires.* Cambridge: Cambridge University Press. This contains a wealth of information on framing questions, including the use of scaling techniques.

Case 11
A quantitative evaluation of students' desire for self-employment

Thomas is a part-time master's student who has been successfully self-employed for the last six years in the web technologies industry. As a consequence of his current employment status and area of expertise, he has chosen to research the impact of enterprise modules on undergraduate students at his university. He is interested in seeing whether there has been an increase over the past 10 years in students considering self-employment after their studies, particularly in the high-technology industries. Furthermore, as he is an expert in technology he wishes to put his skills to use in obtaining his data.

Source: Shutterstock.com/Eimantas Buzas

Thomas began his research project with a comprehensive search and review of the literature. He broke down his search into three main areas: research methods, enterprise education and technologically oriented students. Following his review of the literature on research methods, Thomas felt his world view was most closely related to an objectivist paradigm within a positivist philosophy. Thomas used his review of enterprise education literature to develop his research aims and form four hypotheses to test. These were:

H1: Students' desires to enter self-employment following graduation are greater compared with 10 years ago

H2: More female students are considering self-employment following graduation compared with 10 years ago

H3: More students wish become self-employed in the technology industry following graduation compared with 10 years ago

H4: Students who take at least one enterprise module are more likely to wish to enter self-employment following graduation than those who do not

Thomas decided that the way forward for his research was to use an online questionnaire delivered via an email with a weblink, as opposed to paper completion. His reasons for this were twofold:

- literature had highlighted that students were now more technologically orientated than in the past (Greenlaw and Welty-Brown 2009; Oblinger 2003) and so, he assumed, would be willing to complete his online questionnaire;

- he did not want to input the data from numerous questionnaires completed on paper by hand.

Thomas decided his population would be all third-year students studying for undergraduate degrees within the faculty in which his degree programme was based. He decided to initially select a purposive sample from this population because he wanted to include only those degree programmes that offered the enterprise modules. The purposive sample selected consisted of two degree programmes.

In addition to his rationale for purposive sampling, Thomas remembered that a sample should also be representative of its population. He knew that the purposive sample of degree programmes could not be statistically representative, but wanted the sample of students from each of the two programmes to be representative of all students on both of these programmes.

Each of the two programmes identified had 200 students in the third year of study. He decided that 50 per cent (100) from each would form part of a representative sample. Following a discussion about research ethics, declaration of use of human participants and the Data Protection Act, Thomas was given an alphabetical list of students' names for these two programmes from which he selected the sample systematically. As he had not been provided with the students' email addresses, Thomas had to search for each student's individual email address using the student email search facility on the student portal.

After searching for and identifying almost all student email addresses Thomas had an electronic list of 196 students to whom to send the weblink to his Internet-mediated questionnaire. Once Thomas had finalised his questionnaire and had piloted it with five of his friends and fellow students he felt confident that he could now use it. He imported all the email addresses into the online software tool and distributed the link electronically to his intended participants.

An element of the questionnaire that Thomas felt was important for the intended participants was the 'cover email' accompanying his questionnaire and providing details about his research, completion deadlines and issues associated with research ethics such as confidentiality and anonymity of both the data and participants' details. In this he wrote:

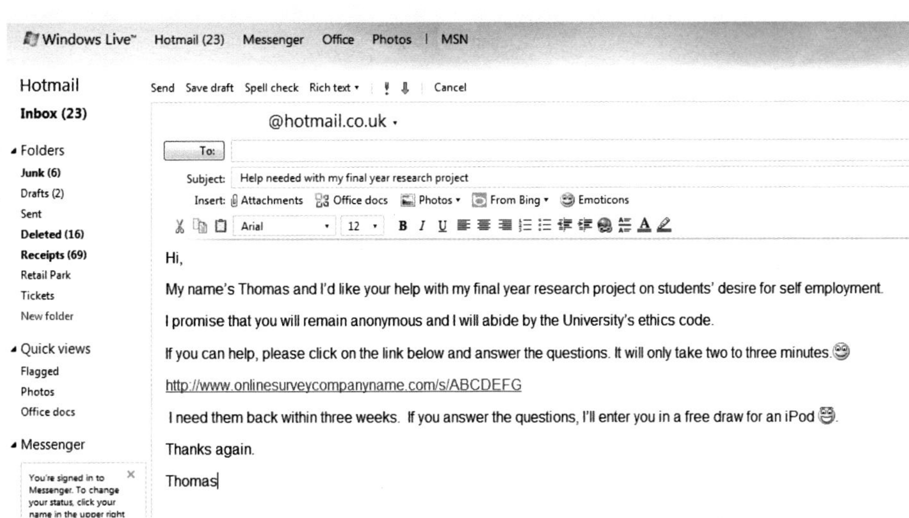

Clicking on the link took the respondent to the questionnaire, which consisted of 48 questions about self-employment followed by four demographic questions, asking for information about age, gender, degree programme and whether or not they had taken at least one enterprise module. A final open question stated:

Anything else?

***53. If there is anything else you would like to add on this topic, please do**

Done

Source: Question layout created by SurveyMonkey.com, LLC (2011) Palo Alto, California. Reproduced with permission

As indicated in his introductory email, Thomas had decided initially to give potential respondents three weeks to complete the online questionnaire, sending a follow-up email two weeks after the weblink had been delivered. However, after one week he had only received 11 responses and so decided to send the follow-up email earlier than planned: at the beginning of the second week. In conversations with his project tutor Thomas remembered she had said that as a general rule response rates should be around 30 per cent of the chosen sample size. This meant he should expect at least 60 questionnaires to be returned.

Unfortunately, Thomas was struggling to get the response rate he needed and despite three follow-up emails to his intended participants by the end of the third week he only had 27 responses. Even worse, two of these were partial completions, reducing his response rate to 25!

Worse still, the three responses to his open question did not appear relevant to his questionnaire or his research project. One male respondent had commented: 'a few minute mate!!!!!!, more like half a ****ing hour!!!!!' Another who had declined to answer the question on gender, had commented 'I bet this questionnaire is not really anonymous, you can tell who sent it from the IP address. You must, otherwise how could you enter me in a free draw for an iPod'. The third, female, had queried how some of the questions he had asked were relevant to his stated topic: 'I've left out all your questions on the industry I intend to work in as I can't see why these are relevant to the research'.

Finally, after a last attempt at generating more responses that resulted in four more returns, Thomas gave up on his online questionnaire. He had 31 responses, a rate of 16.5 per cent. Thomas was extremely disappointed with this and asked himself many times about what could have had gone wrong.

References

Greenlaw, C. and Welty-Brown, S. (2009) 'A comparison of web-based and paper-based survey methods: Testing assumptions of survey mode and response cost', *Evaluation Review*, Vol. 33, No. 5, pp. 464–80.

Oblinger, D. (2003) 'Boomers, Gen-Xers, and millennials: Understanding the "new students"', *EDUCAUSE Review*, Vol. 38, No. 4 pp. 36–40, 42, 44–5.

Questions

1 Would the data Thomas collected from the third-year students have enabled him to test his four hypotheses?
2 What mistake might Thomas have made in his assumption that because students were more technologically orientated now than in the past they would be willing to complete his questionnaire online?
3 What are the possible disadvantages of using an online questionnaire sent to students' university email address?
4 What possible factors should Thomas consider as reasons for non-completion of his online questionnaire?
5 How could Thomas have redesigned his research to increase his questionnaire response rate?

Additional case studies relating to material covered in this chapter are available via the book's companion website: **www.pearsoned.co.uk/saunders**. They are:

- The provision of leisure activities for younger people in rural areas.
- Job satisfaction in an Australian organisation.
- Service quality in health-care supply chains.
- Downsizing in the Middle East.

Self-check answers

11.1 When you:

- wanted to check that the person whom you wished to answer the questions had actually answered the questions;
- have sufficient resources to devote to delivery and collection and the geographical area over which the questionnaire is delivered is small;
- can use field workers to enhance response rates. Delivery and collection questionnaires have a moderately high response rate of between 30 and 50 per cent compared with 30 per cent offered on average by a postal questionnaire;
- are delivering a questionnaire to an organisation's employees and require a very high response rate. By delivering the questionnaire to groups of employees in work time and collecting it on completion, response rates of up to 98 per cent can be achieved.

11.2 **a** **i** Opinion data: the question is asking how the respondent *feels* about the use of nil hours contracts by employees.

ii Behaviour data: the question is asking about the *concrete experience* of being employed on a nil hours contract.

iii Attribute data: the question is asking about the respondent's *characteristics*.

iv Opinion data: the question is asking the respondent what they *think* or *believe* would be the impact on employees.

b **i** Rating question using a Likert-type scale in which the respondent is asked how strongly they agree or disagree with the statement.

ii Category question in which the respondent's answer can fit only one answer.

iii Category question as before.

iv Open question in which the respondent can answer in their own way.

11.3 Although your answer is unlikely to be precisely the same, the completed table of data requirements below should enable you to check you are on the right lines.

Research question/objective: To establish householders' opinions about children's book clubs			
Type of research: Predominantly descriptive, although wish to explain differences between householders			
Investigative questions	**Variable(s) required**	**Detail in which data measured**	**Check measurement question included in questionnaire ✓**
Do householders think that children's book clubs are a good or a bad idea? (opinion – this is because you are really asking how householders feel)	Opinion about children's book clubs	Very good idea, good idea, neither a good nor a bad idea, bad idea, very bad idea	
What things do householders like most about children's book clubs? (opinion)	What householders like about children's book clubs	Get them to rank the following things (generated from earlier in-depth interviews): monthly magazine, lower prices, credit, choice, special offers, shopping at home	
Would householders be interested in an all-ages book club?(behaviour)	Interest in a book club which was for both adults and children	Interested, not interested, may be interested	
How much per year do households spend on children's books? (behaviour)	Amount spent on children's books by adults and children per year by household	(Answers to the nearest €) €0 to €10, €11 to €20, €21 to €30, €31 to €50, €51 to €100, over €100	
Do households' responses differ depending on: Number of children? (attribute) Whether already members of a children's book club? (behaviour)	Number of children aged under 16 Children's book club member	Actual number yes, no	

11.4 **a** Please complete the following statement by ticking the phrase that matches your feelings most closely . . .

I feel children's book clubs are . . . . . . a very good idea ☐5
. . . a good idea ☐4
. . . neither a good nor a bad idea ☐3
. . . a bad idea ☐2
. . . a very bad idea ☐1

b Please number each of the features of children's book clubs listed below in order of how much you like them. Number the most important 1, the next 2 and so on. The feature you like the least should be given the highest number.

Feature	**How much liked**
Monthly magazine	☐
Lower prices	....
Credit	....
Choice	....
Special offers	....
Shopping at home	....

c Would you be interested in a book club that was for both adults and children?

(Please tick the appropriate box)	Yes	❑1
	No	❑2
	Not sure	❑3

d How much money is spent in total each year on children's books by all the adults and children living in your household?

(Please tick the appropriate box)	€0 to €10	❑1
	€11 to €20	❑2
	€21 to €30	❑3
	€31 to €50	❑4
	€51 to €100	❑5
	Over €100	❑6

e i How many children aged under 16 are living in your household?

	☐	children
(for example, for 3 write:)	3	children

ii Is any person living in your household a member of a children's book club?

(Please tick the appropriate box)	Yes	❑1
	No	❑2

11.5 When translating your questionnaire you will need to ensure that:

- the precise meaning of individual words is kept (lexical equivalence);
- the meanings of groups of words and phrases that are natural to a native speaker but cannot be translated literally are kept (idiomatic equivalence);
- the correct grammar and syntax are used.

In addition, you should, if possible, use back translation, parallel translation or mixed translation techniques to ensure that there are no differences between the source and the target questionnaire.

11.6 Although the precise wording of your answer is likely to differ, it would probably be something like this:

Good morning/afternoon/evening. My name is ____ from JJ Consumer Research. We are doing an important national survey covering lifestyles, opinions and likely future purchases of adult consumers. Your telephone number has been selected at random. The questions I need to ask you will take about 15 minutes. If you have any queries I shall be happy to answer them [*pause*]. Before I continue please can you confirm that this is [*read out telephone number including dialling code*] and that I am talking to a person aged 18 or over. Please can I confirm that you are willing to take part and ask you the first question now?

11.7 Although the precise wording of your answer is likely to differ, it would probably be something like the letter below.

Work for All

Registered charity No: 123456789

B&J Market Research Ltd
St Richard's House
Malvern
Worcestershire WR14 12Z
Phone 01684–56789101
Fax 01684–56789102

Respondent's name

Respondent's address

Email andy@b&jmarketresearch.co.uk

Today's date

Dear *title name*

Work for All is conducting research into the effects of long-term unemployment. This is an issue of great importance within the UK and yet little is currently known about the consequences.

You are one of a small number of people who are being asked to give your opinion on this issue. You were selected at random from Work for All's list of contacts. In order that the results will truly represent people who have experienced long-term unemployment, it is important that your questionnaire is completed and returned.

All the information you give us will be totally confidential. You will notice that your name and address do not appear on the questionnaire and that there is no identification number. The results of this research will be passed to Work for All, who will be mounting a major campaign in the New Year to highlight public awareness about the effects of long-term unemployment.

If you have any questions you wish to ask or there is anything you wish to discuss please do not hesitate to telephone me, or my assistant Benjamin Marks, on 01684–56789101 during the day. You can call me at home on 01234–123456789 evenings and weekends. Thank you for your help.

Yours sincerely

Andy Nother

Mr Andy Nother

Project Manager

11.8 Despite the time constraints, pilot testing is essential to your methodology for the following reasons:

- to find out how long the questionnaire takes to complete;
- to check that respondents understand and can follow the instructions on the questionnaire (including filter questions);
- to ensure that all respondents understand the wording of individual questions in the same way and that there are no unclear or ambiguous questions;

- to ensure that you have the same understanding of the wording of individual questions as the respondents;
- to check that respondents have no problems in answering questions; for example:
  - all possible answers are covered in list questions;
  - whether there are any questions that respondents feel uneasy about answering;
- to discover whether there are any major topic omissions;
- to provide an idea of the validity of the questions that are being asked;
- to provide an idea of the reliability of the questions by checking responses from individual respondents to similar questions;
- to check that the layout appears clear and attractive;
- to provide limited test data so you can check that the proposed analyses will work.

Get ahead using resources on the companion website at: **www.pearsoned.co.uk/saunders**

- Improve your IBM SPSS Statistics and NVivo research analysis with practice tutorials.
- Save time researching on the Internet with the Smarter Online Searching Guide.
- Test your progress using self-assessment questions.
- Follow live links to useful websites.

Chapter 12

Analysing quantitative data

Learning outcomes

By the end of this chapter, you should be able to:

- identify the main issues that you need to consider when preparing quantitative data for analysis and when analysing these data by computer;
- recognise different types of data and understand the implications of data type for subsequent analyses;
- create a data matrix and code data for analysis by computer;
- select the most appropriate tables and diagrams to explore and illustrate different aspects of your data;
- select the most appropriate statistics to describe individual variables and to examine relationships between variables and trends in your data;
- interpret the tables, diagrams and statistics that you use correctly.

12.1 Introduction

Quantitative data in a raw form, that is, before these data have been processed and analysed, convey very little meaning to most people. These data, therefore, need to be processed to make them useful, that is, to turn them into information. Quantitative analysis techniques such as graphs, charts and statistics allow us to do this, helping us to explore, present, describe and examine relationships and trends within our data.

Virtually any business and management research you undertake is likely to involve some numerical data or contain data that could usefully be quantified to help you answer your research question(s) and to meet your objectives. **Quantitative data** refer to all such primary and secondary data and can be a product of all research strategies (Section 5.5) as well as secondary data. They can range from simple counts such as the frequency of occurrences to more complex data such as test scores, prices or rental costs. To be useful these data need to be analysed and interpreted. Quantitative analysis techniques assist you in this process. They range from creating simple tables or diagrams that show the frequency of occurrence and using

statistics such as indices to enable comparisons, through establishing statistical relationships between variables to complex statistical modelling.

Within quantitative analysis, calculations and chart drawing are undertaken using analysis software ranging from spreadsheets such as Excel™ to more advanced data management and statistical analysis software packages such as Minitab™, SAS™, IBM SPSS Statistics™ and Statview™. You might also use more specialised survey design and analysis packages such as

Source: Shutterstock.com/Paul Prescott

The Big Mac Index is published annually by the *Economist* to provide a simple way of measuring differences in purchasing power between currencies. The index provides an idea of the extent to which currency exchange rates actually result in goods costing the same in different countries. Obviously the index does not take into account that Big Mac hamburgers are not precisely the same in every country; nutritional values, weights and sizes often differ. Similarly it does not allow for prices within a country differing between McDonald's restaurants, McDonald's providing the *Economist* with a single price for each country. However, it does provide an indication of whether purchasing power parity exists between different currencies.

The Big Mac Index is calculated by first converting the country price of a Big Mac (in the local currency) to US dollars using the current exchange rate. Using Big Mac Index figures available on the Internet (Bigmacindex.com 2011), the British price of a Big Mac was £2.29 in 2010. Using the exchange rate at that time of £1 equals $1.52, this converts to $3.48. At this time, the price of a Big Mac in the USA was $3.73, 25 cents more than was charged in Britain. This means theoretically you could buy a Big Mac in Britain for $3.48 and sell it in the USA for $3.73, a profit of 25 cents. Unlike most index numbers which use the value 100 to express parity, the difference between the country price and the USA price is expressed as a percentage in the Big Mac Index. Consequently, as the British price for a Big Mac was 25 cents less than the USA price, the value of the index was – 7 per cent. This suggests that purchasing power of the British pound was greater than the US dollar by 7 per cent, suggesting the currency was overvalued. According to the 2010 index, one of the currencies with the greatest difference in purchasing power to the US dollar was the Ukranian Hryvnia; a Big Mac cost the equivalent of $1.84, less than half the price in the USA (with a Big Mac index value of – 51 per cent). This suggests the currency was overvalued. In contrast, the Norwegian Kroner could be considered undervalued; a Big Mac costing the equivalent of $7.20, nearly twice the price in the USA (with a Big Mac Index value of 93 per cent). Where there is a parity of purchasing power, the index value is zero. This allows for easy comparisons between countries.

SNAP™ and Sphinx Survey™ or statistical shareware such as the R Project for Statistical Computing. However, whilst this means you do not have to be able to draw charts by hand or undertake calculations manually, if your analyses are to be straightforward and of any value you need to:

- have prepared your data with quantitative analyses in mind;
- be aware of and know when to use different charting and statistical techniques.

Robson (2011: 414) summarises this, arguing that quantitative data analysis is:

> **a field where it is not at all difficult to carry out an analysis which is simply wrong, or inappropriate for your data or purposes. And the negative side of readily available specialist statistical software is that it becomes that much easier to generate elegantly presented rubbish.**

He also emphasises the need to seek advice regarding statistical analyses, a sentiment that we support strongly.

This chapter builds on the ideas outlined in earlier chapters about secondary data and primary data collection including issues of sample size. It assumes that you will use a computer (with at least a spreadsheet) to undertake all but the most simple quantitative analyses. Although it does not focus on one particular piece of analysis software, you will notice in the Focus on Student Research boxes that many of the analyses were undertaken using widely available software such as Excel and IBM SPSS Statistics. If you wish to develop your skills in either of these software packages, self-teach packages are available via our companion website. In addition, there are numerous statistics books already published that concentrate on specific software packages. These include Dancey and Reidy (2008), Field (2009) or Kinnear and Gray (2010) on IBM SPSS Statistics, and Curwin and Slater (2007) or Morris (2012) on Excel. Likewise, this chapter does not attempt to provide an in-depth discussion of the wide range of graphical and statistical techniques available or to cover more complex statistical modelling, as these are already covered elsewhere (e.g. Dancey and Reidy 2008; Everitt and Dunn 2001; Hair et al. 2006; Hays 1994; Henry 1995). Rather it discusses issues that need to be considered at the planning and analysis stages of your research project, and outlines analytical techniques that our students have found to be of most use. In particular, the chapter is concerned with:

- preparing, inputting into a computer and checking your data (Section 12.2);
- choosing the most appropriate tables and diagrams to explore and present your data (Section 12.3);
- choosing the most appropriate statistics to describe your data (Section 12.4);
- choosing the most appropriate statistics to examine relationships and trends in your data (Section 12.5).

12.2 Preparing, inputting and checking data

If you intend to undertake quantitative analysis we recommend that you consider the:

- number of cases of data, that is the sample size (already discussed in Section 7.2);
- type or types of data (scale of measurement);
- data layout and format required by the analysis software;
- impact of data coding on subsequent analyses (for different types of data);
- process of entering data;
- need to weight cases;
- process of checking the data for errors.

Ideally, all of these should be considered before obtaining your data. This is equally important for both primary and secondary data analysis, although you obviously have far greater control over the type, format and coding of primary data. We shall now consider each of these.

Types of Data

Many business statistics textbooks classify quantitative data into *data types* using a hierarchy of measurement, often in ascending order of numerical precision (Berman Brown and Saunders 2008; Dancey and Reidy 2008). These different levels of numerical measurement dictate the range of techniques available to you for the presentation, summary and analysis of your data. They are discussed in more detail in subsequent sections of this chapter.

Quantitative data can be divided into two distinct groups: categorical and numerical (Figure 12.1). **Categorical data** refer to data whose values cannot be measured numerically but can be either classified into sets (categories) according to the characteristics that identify or describe the variable or placed in rank order (Berman Brown and Saunders 2008). They can be further subdivided into descriptive and ranked. A car manufacturer might categorise the types of cars it produces as hatchback, saloon and estate. These are known as **descriptive data** or **nominal data** as it is impossible to define the category numerically or to rank it. Rather, these data simply count the number of occurrences in each category of a variable. For virtually all analyses the categories should be unambiguous and discrete; in other words, having one particular feature, such as a car being a hatchback, excludes all other features for that variable. This prevents questions arising regarding which category an individual case belongs to. Although these data are purely descriptive, you can count them to establish which category has the most and whether cases are spread evenly between categories (Morris 2012). Some statisticians (and statistics) also separate descriptive data where there are only two categories. These are known as **dichotomous data**, as the variable is divided into two categories, such as the variable gender being divided into female and male. **Ranked** (or **ordinal**) **data** are a more precise form of categorical data. In such instances you know the relative position of each case within your data set, although the actual numerical measures (such as scores) on which the position is based are not recorded (Box 12.1). Rating or scale questions, such as where a respondent is asked to rate how strongly she or he agrees with a statement, collect ranked (ordinal) data. Despite this, some researchers argue that, where such data are likely to have similar size gaps between data values, they can be analysed as if they were numerical interval data (Blumberg et al. 2008).

Numerical data are those whose values are measured or counted numerically as quantities (Berman Brown and Saunders 2008). This means that numerical data are more precise than categorical as you can assign each data value a position on a numerical scale. It also means that you can analyse these data using a far wider range of statistics. There are two possible ways of subdividing numerical data: into interval or ratio data and, alternatively, into continuous or discrete data (Figure 12.1). If you have **interval data** you can state the difference or 'interval' between any two data values for a particular variable, but you cannot state the relative difference. This means that values on an interval scale can meaningfully be added and subtracted, but not multiplied and divided. The Celsius temperature scale is a good example of an interval scale. Although the difference between, say, 20°C and 30°C is 10°C it does not mean that 30°C is one and a half times as warm. This is because 0°C does not represent a true zero. When it is 0°C outside, there is still some warmth, rather than none at all! In contrast, for **ratio data**, you can also calculate the relative difference or ratio between

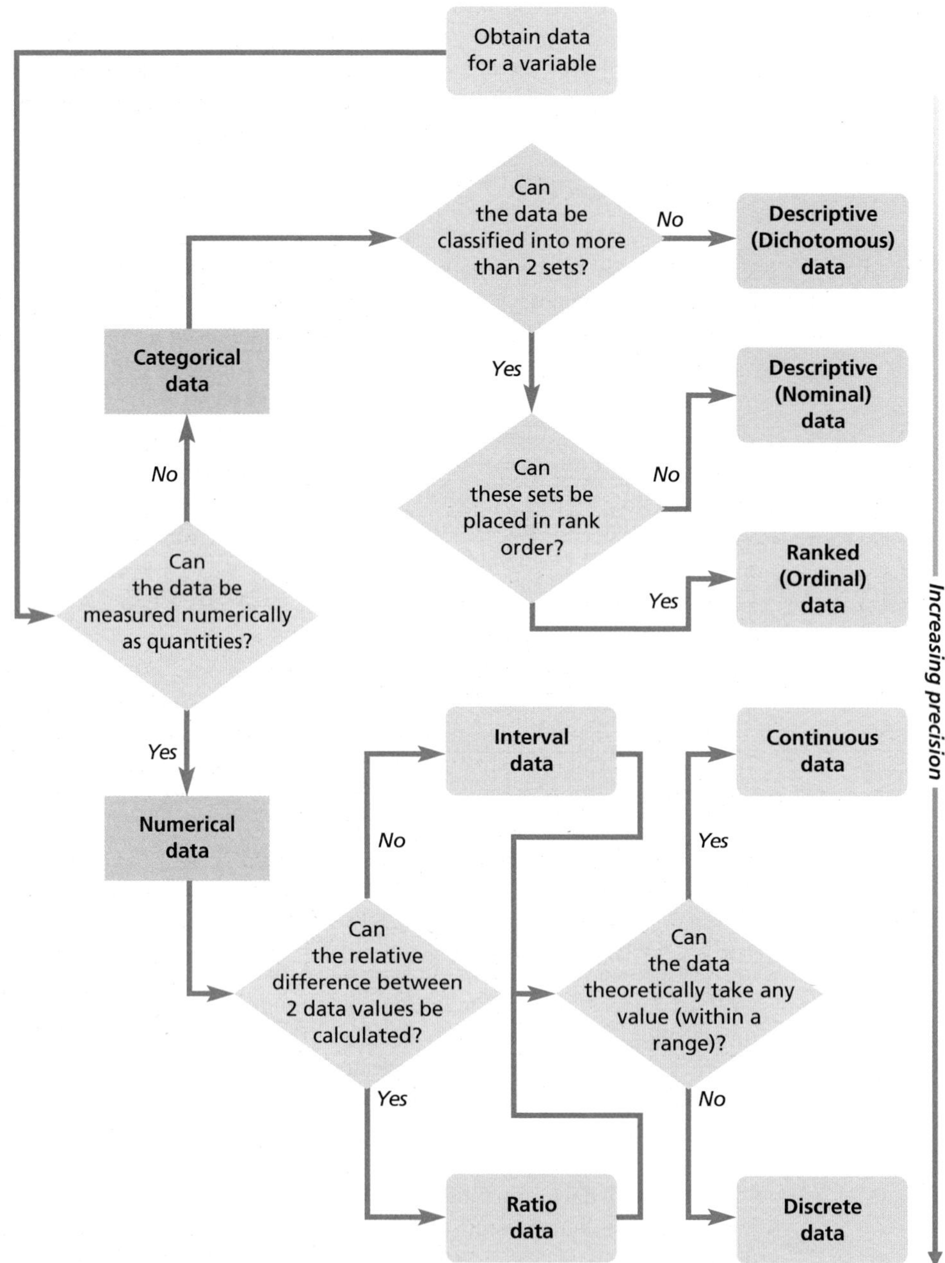

Figure 12.1 Defining the data type

any two data values for a variable. Consequently, if a multinational company makes a profit of $300,000,000 in one year and $600,000,000 the following year, we can say that profits have doubled.

Continuous data are those whose values can theoretically take any value (sometimes within a restricted range) provided that you can measure them accurately enough (Dancey and Reidy 2008). Data such as furnace temperature, delivery distance and length of service are therefore continuous data. **Discrete data** can, by contrast, be measured precisely. Each case takes one of a finite number of values from a scale that measures

Box 12.1 Focus on student research

Scales of measurement

As part of a marketing questionnaire, Rashid asked individual customers to rank up to five features of a new product in order of importance to them. Data collected were, therefore, categorical and ranked (ordinal). Initial analyses made use of these ranked data. Unfortunately, a substantial minority of customers had ticked, rather than ranked, those features of importance to them.

All responses that had been ranked originally were therefore recoded to 'of some importance'. This reduced the precision of measurement from ranked (ordinal) to descriptive (nominal) but enabled Rashid to use all responses in the subsequent analyses.

changes in discrete units. These data are often whole numbers (**integers**) such as the number of mobile telephones manufactured or customers served. However, in some instances (e.g. UK shoe size) discrete data will include non-integer values. Definitions of discrete and continuous data are, in reality, dependent on how your data values are measured. The number of customers served by a large organisation is strictly a discrete datum as you are unlikely to get a part customer! However, for a large organisation with many customers you might treat this as a continuous datum, as the discrete measuring units are exceedingly small compared with the total number being measured.

Understanding differences between types of data is extremely important when analysing your data quantitatively, for two reasons. Firstly, it is extremely easy with analysis software to generate statistics from your data that are inappropriate for the data type and are consequently of little value (Box 12.2). Secondly, the more precise the scale of measurement, the greater the range of analytical techniques available to you (Box 12.3). Data that have been collected and coded using a precise numerical scale of measurement can also be regrouped to a less precise level where they can also be analysed (Box 12.1). For example, a student's score in a test could be recorded as the actual mark (discrete data) or as the position in their class (ranked data). By contrast, less precise data cannot be made more precise. Therefore, if you are not sure about the scale of measurement you require, it is usually better to collect data at the highest level of precision possible and to regroup them if necessary.

Data layout

Some primary data collection methods, such as computer-aided personal interviewing (CAPI), computer-aided telephone interviewing (CATI) and online questionnaires automatically enter and save data to a computer file at the time of collection, normally using predefined codes. These data can subsequently be exported in a range of formats to ensure they are compatible with different analysis software. Survey design and analysis software such SNAP™ Surveys and SurveyMonkey™ go one stage further and integrates the analysis software in the same package as the questionnaire design/data input software (Snap Surveys 2011; SurveyMonkey 2011). Alternatively, secondary data (Section 8.3) downloaded from the Internet can be saved to a file, removing the need for re-entering. For such data, it is often possible to specify a data layout compatible with your analysis software. For other data collection methods, you will have to prepare and enter your data for computer analysis. You therefore need to be clear about the precise data layout requirements of your analysis software.

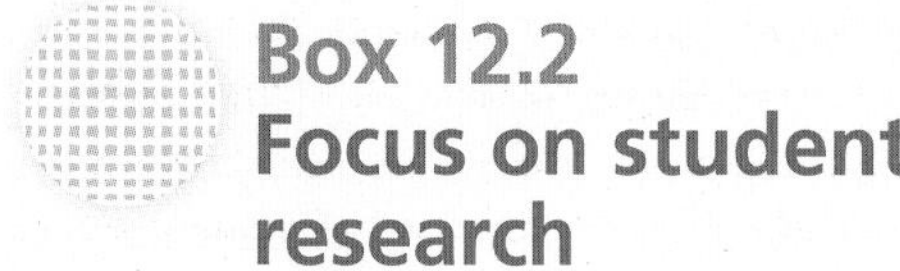

Box 12.2 Focus on student research

The implications of data types for analysis

Pierre's research was concerned with customers' satisfaction for a small hotel group of six hotels. In collecting the data he had asked 760 customers to indicate the hotel at which they were staying when they completed their questionnaires. Each hotel was subsequently allocated a numerical code and this data entered into the computer in the variable 'Hotel'.

Hotel	Code
Amsterdam	1
Antwerp	2
Eindhoven	3
Nijmegen	4
Rotterdam	5
Tilburg	6

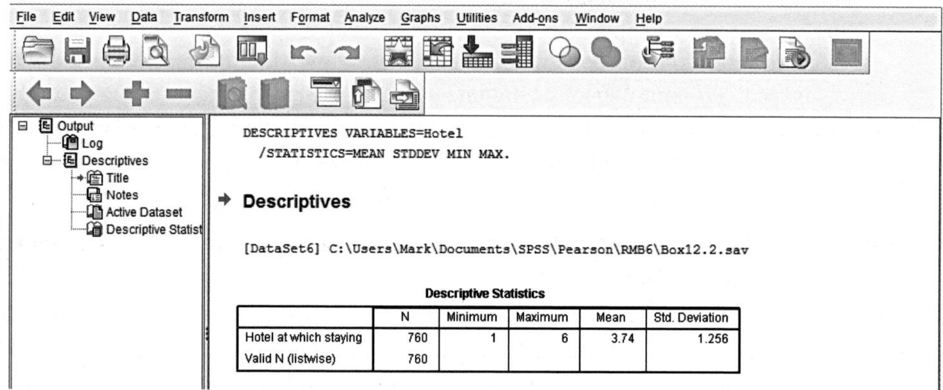

	N	Minimum	Maximum	Mean	Std. Deviation
Hotel at which staying	760	1	6	3.74	1.256
Valid N (listwise)	760				

In his initial analysis, Pierre used the computer to calculate descriptive statistics for every data variable including the variable 'Hotel'. These included the minimum value (the code for Amsterdam), the maximum value (the code for Tilburg), the mean and the standard deviation. Looking at his computer screen, Pierre noted that the mean (average) was 3.74 and the standard deviation was 1.256. He had forgotten that the data for this variable were categorical and, consequently, the descriptive statistics he had chosen were inappropriate.

Virtually all analysis software will accept your data if they are entered in table format. This table is called a **data matrix** (Table 12.1). Once data have been entered into your analysis software, it is usually possible to save them in a format that can be read by other software. Within a data matrix, each column usually represents a separate **variable** for which you have obtained data. Each matrix row contains the variables for an individual **case**, that is, an individual unit for which data have been obtained. If your data have been collected using a questionnaire, each row will contain the data from one completed questionnaire. Secondary data that have already been stored in computer-readable form are almost always held as a large data matrix. For such data sets you usually select the subset of variables and cases you require and save these as a separate matrix. If you are entering your own data, they are typed directly into your chosen analysis software one

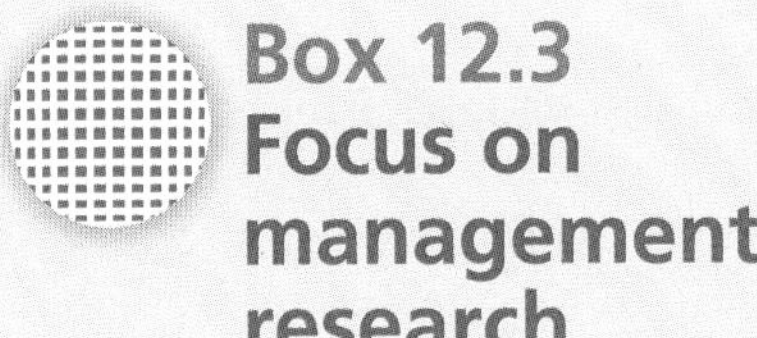

Box 12.3 Focus on management research

The effect of dominant chief executive officers (CEOs) on firm strategy and performance

At the start of the introduction to their article 'Dominant CEO, deviant strategy, and extreme performance: The moderating role of a powerful board' published online in the *Journal of Management Studies* (2011) Tang, Crossan and Rowe use the well-known quotation 'Power tends to corrupt and absolute power corrupts absolutely', attributing this to Lord Acton (1887). In their article they question this pessimistic view that a leader with dominant power tends to do harm. Based on data collected from a sample of 51 publicly traded firms in the US computer industry, they suggest that firms with dominant CEOs tend to have a strategy deviant from the industry central tendency and thus extremely good or extremely poor performance.

In the article Tang and colleagues outline clearly the variables used in their analysis to test statistically six hypotheses. The variables associated with executive power are listed below along with how they were measured and the data type in brackets:

Variable	How measured
Percentage with higher titles	Percentage of individuals in a firm's top management team with higher official titles than the executive in question (continuous data)
Compensation	Executive in question's total cash compensation (continuous data)
Number of titles	Number of official titles executive in question had, as stated in annual reports (discrete data)
Executive shares	Percentage of a firm's shares owned by the executive in question and their spouse and dependent children (continuous data)
Founder or relative	Whether or not the executive was a founder of the firm, or was related to the founder;
	whether or not the executive had a family relationship with another executive of the firm
	Coded: 0 if neither; 1 if either but not both, 2 if both (nominal data)

Table 12.1 A simple data matrix

	Id	Variable 1	Variable 2	Variable 3	Variable 4
Case 1	1	27	1	2	1
Case 2	2	19	2	1	2
Case 3	3	24	2	3	1

case (row) at a time using codes to record the data (Box 12.4). Larger data sets with more data variables and cases are recorded using larger data matrices. Although data matrices store data using one column for each variable, this may not be the same as one column for each question for data collected using surveys.

We strongly recommend that you save your data regularly as you are entering it, to minimise the chances of deleting it all by accident! In addition, you should save a backup or security copy on your MP3 player or other mass storage device, or email it to yourself.

If you intend to enter data into a spreadsheet, the first variable is in column A, the second in column B and so on. Each cell in the first row (1) should contain a short variable name to enable you to identify each variable. Subsequent rows (2 onwards) will each contain the data for one case (Box 12.4). Statistical analysis software follows the same logic, although the variable names are usually displayed 'above' the first row (Box 12.5).

The **multiple-response method** of coding uses the same number of variables as the maximum number of different responses from any one case. For question 2 these were named 'like1', 'like2', 'like3', 'like4' and 'like5' (Box 12.5). Each of these

Box 12.4 Focus on student research

An Excel data matrix

Lucy's data related to employees who were working or had worked for a large public sector organisation. In her Excel spreadsheet, the first variable (id) was the *survey form identifier*. This meant that she could link data for each case (row) in her matrix to the survey form when checking for errors (discussed later). The second variable (age) contained numerical data, the age of each respondent (case) at the time her questionnaire was administered. Subsequent variables contained the remaining data: the third (gender) recorded this dichotomous data using code 1 for male and 2 for female; the fourth (service) recorded numerical data about each case's length of service to the nearest year in the organisation. The final dichotomous variable (employed) recorded whether each respondent was (code 1) or was not (code 2) employed by the organisation at the time the data were collected. The codes used by Lucy, therefore, had different meanings for different variables.

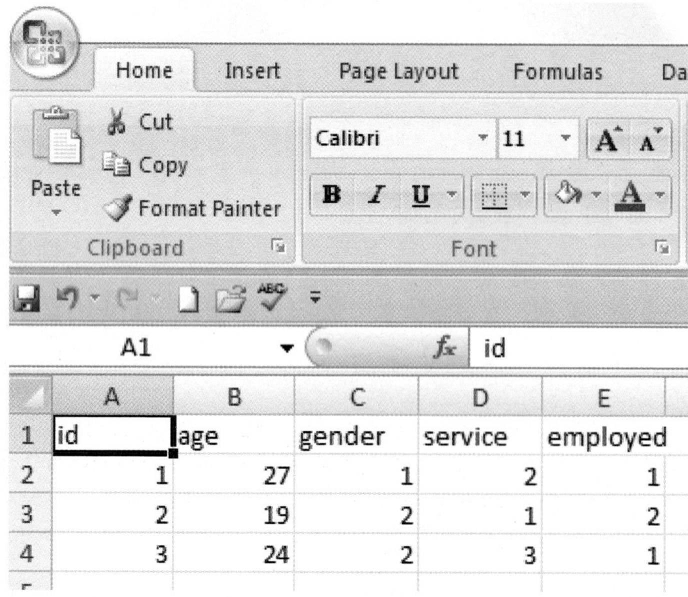

	A	B	C	D	E
1	id	age	gender	service	employed
2	1	27	1	2	1
3	2	19	2	1	2
4	3	24	2	3	1

Box 12.5 Focus on student research

Data coding

As part of a market research interview survey, Zack needed to discover which of four products (tomato ketchup, brown sauce, soy sauce, vinegar) had been purchased within the last month by consumers. He therefore needed to collect four data items from each respondent:

- Tomato ketchup purchased within the last month? Yes/No
- Brown sauce purchased within the last month? Yes/No
- Soy sauce purchased within the last month? Yes/No
- Salad dressing purchased within the last month? Yes/No

Each of these data items is a separate variable. However, the data were collected using one question:

1 Which of the following items have you purchased within the last month?

Item	**Purchased**	**Not purchased**	**Not sure**
Tomato ketchup	❑ 1	❑ 2	❑ 3
Brown sauce	❑ 1	❑ 2	❑ 3
Soy sauce	❑ 1	❑ 2	❑ 3
Salad dressing	❑ 1	❑ 2	❑ 3

The data Zack collected from each respondent formed four separate variables in the data matrix using numerical codes (1 = purchased, 2 = not purchased, 3 = not sure). This is known as multiple-dichotomy coding.

File Edit View Data Transform Analyze Graphs Utilities Add-ons Window Help

	tomato	brown	soy	saladdre	like1	like2
1	1	1	1	2	23	31
2	2	2	2	3	12	15
3	1	2	3	1	23	12

Zack also included a question (question 2 below) that could theoretically have millions of possible responses for each of the 'things'. For such questions, the number that each respondent mentions may also vary. Our experience suggests that virtually all respondents will select five or fewer. Zack therefore left space to code up to five responses after data had been collected.

Box 12.5 Focus on student research *(continued)*

For office use only

2 List up to five things you like about tomato ketchup

....	❑	❑	❑	❑
....	❑	❑	❑	❑
....	❑	❑	❑	❑
....	❑	❑	❑	❑
....	❑	❑	❑	❑

variables would use the same codes and could include any of the responses as a category. Statistical analysis software often contains special multiple-response procedures to analyse such data. The alternative, the **multiple-dichotomy method** of coding, uses a separate variable for each different answer (Box 12.5). For question 2 (Box 12.5) a separate variable could have been used for each 'thing' listed: for example, flavour, consistency, bottle shape, smell, price and so on. You subsequently would code each variable as 'listed' or 'not listed' for each case. This makes it easy to calculate the number of responses for each 'thing' (deVaus 2002).

Coding

All data types should, with few exceptions, be recorded using numerical codes. This enables you to enter the data quickly using the numeric keypad on your keyboard and with fewer errors. It also makes subsequent analyses, in particular those that require re-coding of data to create new variables, more straightforward. Unfortunately, meaningless analyses are also easier, such as calculating a mean (average) gender from codes 1 and 2, or the mean hotel location (Box 12.2)! A common exception to using a numerical code for categorical data is where a postcode is used as the code for a geographical reference. If you are using a spreadsheet, you will need to keep a list of codes for each variable. Statistical analysis software can store these so that each code is automatically labelled.

Coding numerical data

Actual numbers are often used as codes for numerical data, even though this level of precision may not be required. Once you have entered your data as a matrix, you can use analysis software to group or combine data to form additional variables with less detailed categories. This process is referred to as **re-coding**. For example, a Republic of Ireland employee's salary could be coded to the nearest euro and entered into the matrix as 43543 (numerical discrete data). Later, re-coding could be used to place it in a group of similar salaries, from €40,000 to €49,999 (categorical ranked data).

Coding categorical data

Codes are often applied to categorical data with little thought, although you can design a coding scheme that will make subsequent analyses far simpler. For many secondary data sources (such as government surveys), a suitable coding scheme will have already been devised when the data were first collected. However, for some secondary and all primary data you will need to decide on a coding scheme. Prior to this, you need to establish the highest level of precision required by your analyses (Figure 12.1).

Existing coding schemes can be used for many variables. These include industrial classification (Prosser 2009), occupation (Office for National Statistics 2010a, 2010b), social class and socioeconomic classification (Office for National Statistics 2005), and ethnic group (Smith 2002) as well as social attitude variables (Park et al. 2007). Wherever possible, we recommend you use these as they:

- save time;
- are normally well tested;
- allow comparisons of your results with other (often larger) surveys.

These codes should be included on your data collection form as **pre-set codes** provided that there are a limited number of categories (Section 11.4), and they will be understood by the person filling in the form. Even if you decide not to use an existing coding scheme, perhaps because of a lack of detail, you should ensure that your codes are still compatible. This means that you will be able to compare your data with those already collected.

Coding at data collection occurs when there is a limited range of well-established categories into which the data can be placed. These are included on your data collection form, and the person filling in the form selects the correct category.

Coding after data collection is necessary when you are unclear of the likely responses or there are a large number of possible responses in the coding scheme. To ensure that the coding scheme captures the variety in responses (and that it will work!) it is better to wait until data from the first 50 to 100 cases are available and then develop the coding scheme. This is called the **codebook** (Box 12.6). As when designing your data collection

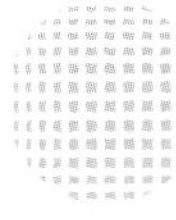

Box 12.6 Focus on student research

Creating a codebook, coding multiple responses and entering data

As part of his research project, Amil used a questionnaire to collect data from the customers of a local themed restaurant. The questionnaire included an open question which asked 'List up to three things you like about this restaurant'. The answers included over 50 different 'things' that the 186 customers responding liked about the restaurant, although the maximum number mentioned by any one customer was three.

Once data had been collected, Amil devised a hierarchical coding scheme based on what the customers liked about the restaurant. Codes were allocated to each 'thing' a customer liked, as shown in the extract below.

Codes were entered into three (the maximum number customers were asked to list) variables, like1, like2 and like3 in the data matrix using the multiple-response method for coding. This meant that any response could appear in any of the three variables. When there were fewer than three responses given, the code '.' was entered automatically by the software into empty cells in the remaining outlet variables, signifying missing data. The first customer in the extract below listed 'things' coded 11, 21 and 42, the next 3 and 21 and so on. No significance was attached to the order of variables to which responses were coded.

Box 12.6 Focus on student research *(continued)*

File Edit View Data Transform Analyze Graphs Utilities Add-ons Window Help

	numvisit	reason	like1	like2	like3	offer
1	3	14	11	21	42	.
2	5	12	3	21	.	2
3	6	22	32	11	38	1

Extract from coding scheme used to classify responses

Grouping	**Subgrouping**	**Response**	**Code**
Physical surroundings			1–9
		Decoration	1
		Use of colour	2
		Comfort of seating	3
Dining experience	*Menu*		10–19
		Choice	11
		Regularly changed	12
	Food		20–29
		Freshly prepared	21
		Organic	22
		Served at correct temperature	23
	Staff attitude		30–39
		Knowledgeable	31
		Greet by name	32
		Know what diners prefer	33
		Discreet	34
		Do not hassle	35
		Good service	36
		Friendly	37
		Have a sense of humour	38
	Drinks		40–49
		Value for money	41
		Good selection of wines	42
		Good selection of beers	43
		Served at correct temperature	44

The hierarchical coding scheme meant that individual responses could subsequently be re-coded into subgroupings and groupings such as those indicated earlier to facilitate a range of different analyses. These were undertaken using statistical analysis software.

method(s) (Chapters 8, 9, 10 and 11), it is essential to be clear about the intended analyses, in particular:

- the level of precision required;
- the coding schemes used by surveys with which comparisons are to be made.

To create your codebook for each variable you:

1. examine the data and establish broad groupings;
2. subdivide the broad groupings into increasingly specific subgroups dependent on your intended analyses;
3. allocate codes to all categories at the most precise level of detail required;
4. note the actual responses that are allocated to each category and produce a codebook;
5. ensure that those categories that may need to be aggregated are given adjacent codes to facilitate re-coding.

Coding missing data

Each variable for each case in your data set should have a code, even if no data have been collected. The choice of code is up to you, although some statistical analysis software have a code that is used by default. A missing data code is used to indicate why data are missing. Four main reasons for missing data are identified by deVaus (2002):

- The data were not required from the respondent, perhaps because of a skip generated by a filter question in a survey.
- The respondent refused to answer the question (a **non-response**).
- The respondent did not know the answer or did not have an opinion. Sometimes this is treated as implying an answer; on other occasions it is treated as missing data.
- The respondent may have missed a question by mistake, or the respondent's answer may be unclear.

In addition, it may be that:

- leaving part of a question in a survey blank implies an answer; in such cases the data are not classified as missing (Section 11.4).

Statistical analysis software often reserves a special code for missing data. Cases with missing data can then be excluded from subsequent analyses when necessary (Box 12.6). For some analyses it may be necessary to distinguish between reasons for missing data using different codes.

Entering data

Once your data have been coded, you can enter them into the computer. Although some data analysis software contain algorithms that check the data for obvious errors as it is entered, it is essential that you take considerable care to ensure that your data are entered correctly. When entering data the well-known maxim 'rubbish in, rubbish out' certainly applies! More sophisticated analysis software allows you to attach individual labels to each variable and the codes associated with each of them. If this is feasible, we strongly recommend that you do this. By ensuring the labels replicate the exact words used in the data collection, you will reduce the number of opportunities for misinterpretation when analysing your data. Taking this advice for the variable 'like1' in Box 12.6 would result in the variable label 'List up to three things you like about this restaurant', each value being labelled with the actual response in the coding scheme.

Checking for errors

No matter how carefully you code and subsequently enter data there will always be some errors. The main methods to check data for errors are as follows:

- Look for illegitimate codes. In any coding scheme, only certain numbers are allocated. Other numbers are, therefore, errors. Common errors are the inclusion of letters O and o instead of zero, letters l or I instead of 1, and number 7 instead of 1.
- Look for illogical relationships. For example, if a person is coded to the 'higher managerial occupations' socioeconomic classification category and she describes her work as 'manual' it is likely an error has occurred.
- Check that rules in filter questions are followed. Certain responses to filter questions (Section 11.4) mean that other variables should be coded as missing values. If this has not happened there has been an error.

For each possible error, you need to discover whether it occurred at coding or data entry and then correct it. By giving each case a unique identifier (normally a number), it is possible to link the matrix to the original data. You must, however, remember to ensure the identifier is on the data collection form and entered along with the other data into the matrix.

Data checking is very time-consuming and so is often not undertaken. Beware: not doing it is very dangerous and can result in incorrect results from which false conclusions are drawn!

Weighting cases

Most data you use will be a sample. For some forms of probability sampling, such as stratified random sampling (Section 7.2), you may have used a different sampling fraction for each stratum. Alternatively, you may have obtained a different response rate for each of the strata. To obtain an accurate overall picture you will need to take account of these differences in response rates between strata. A common method of achieving this is to use cases from those strata that have lower proportions of responses to represent more than one case in your analysis (Box 12.7). Most statistical analysis software allows you to do this by **weighting** cases. To weight the cases you:

1. Calculate the percentage of the population responding for each stratum.
2. Establish which stratum had the highest percentage of the population responding.
3. Calculate the weight for each stratum using the following formula:

$$\text{weight} = \frac{\text{highest proportion of population responding for any stratum}}{\text{proportion of population responding in stratum for which calculating weight}}$$

(Note: if your calculations are correct this will always result in the weight for the stratum with the highest proportion of the population responding being 1.)

4. Apply the appropriate weight to each case.

Beware: many authors (for example, Hays 1994) question the validity of using statistics to make inferences from your sample if you have weighted cases.

Box 12.7 Focus on student research

Weighting cases

Doris had used stratified random sampling to select her sample. The percentage of each stratum's population that responded is given below:

- Upper stratum: 90%
- Lower stratum: 65%

To account for the differences in the response rates between strata she decided to weight the cases prior to analysis.

The weight for the upper stratum was: $\frac{90}{90} = 1$

This meant that each case in the upper stratum counted as 1 case in her analysis.

The weight for the lower stratum was: $\frac{90}{65} = 1.38$

This meant that each case in the lower stratum counted for 1.38 cases in her analysis.

Doris entered these as a separate variable in her data set and used the statistical analysis software to apply the weights.

12.3 Exploring and presenting data

Once your data have been entered and checked for errors, you are ready to start your analysis. We have found Tukey's (1977) **exploratory data analysis (EDA)** approach useful in these initial stages. This approach emphasises the use of diagrams to explore and understand your data, emphasising the importance of using your data to guide your choice of analysis techniques. As you would expect, we believe that it is important to keep your research question(s) and objectives in mind when exploring your data. However, the exploratory data analysis approach allows you flexibility to introduce previously unplanned analyses to respond to new findings. It therefore formalises the common practice of looking for other relationships in data, which your research was not initially designed to test. This should not be discounted, as it may suggest other fruitful avenues for analysis. In addition, computers make this relatively easy and quick.

Even at this stage it is important that you structure and label clearly each diagram and table to avoid possible misinterpretation. Box 12.8 provides a summary checklist of the points to remember when designing a diagram or table.

We have found it best to begin exploratory analysis by looking at individual variables and their components. The key aspects you may need to consider will be guided by your research question(s) and objectives, and are likely to include (Sparrow 1989):

- specific values;
- highest and lowest values;
- trends over time;
- proportions;
- distributions.

Once you have explored these, you can then begin to compare and look for relationships between variables, considering in addition (Sparrow 1989):

- conjunctions (the point where values for two or more variables intersect);
- totals;
- interdependence and relationships.

Box 12.8 Checklist

Designing your diagrams and tables

For both diagrams and tables

- ✔ Does it have a brief but clear and descriptive title?
- ✔ Are the units of measurement used stated clearly?
- ✔ Are the sources of data used stated clearly?
- ✔ Are there notes to explain abbreviations and unusual terminology?
- ✔ Does it state the size of the sample on which the values in the table are based?

For diagrams

- ✔ Does it have clear axis labels?
- ✔ Are bars and their components in the same logical sequence?
- ✔ Is more dense shading used for smaller areas?
- ✔ Have you avoided misrepresenting or distorting the data
- ✔ Is a key or legend included (where necessary)?

For tables

- ✔ Does it have clear column and row headings?
- ✔ Are columns and rows in a logical sequence?

These are summarised in Table 12.2. Most analysis software contains procedures to create tables and diagrams. Your choice will depend on those aspects of the data that you wish to emphasise and the scale of measurement at which the data were recorded. This section is concerned only with tables and two-dimensional diagrams, including pictograms, available on most spreadsheets (Table 12.2). Three-dimensional diagrams are not discussed, as these can often hinder interpretation. Those tables and diagrams most pertinent to your research question(s) and objectives will eventually appear in your research report to support your arguments. You should therefore save an electronic copy of all tables and diagrams which you create.

Exploring and presenting individual variables

To show specific values

The simplest way of summarising data for individual variables so that specific values can be read is to use a **table** (**frequency distribution**). For categorical data, the table summarises the number of cases (frequency) in each category. For variables where there are likely to be a large number of categories (or values for numerical data), you will need to group the data into categories that reflect your research question(s) and objectives.

To show highest and lowest values

Tables attach no visual significance to highest or lowest values unless emphasised by alternative fonts. Diagrams can provide visual clues, although both categorical and numerical data may need grouping. For categorical and discrete data, bar charts and pictograms are both suitable. Generally, bar charts provide a more accurate representation and should be used for research reports, whereas pictograms convey a general impression and can be used to gain an audience's attention. In a **bar chart**, the height or length of each bar represents the frequency of occurrence. Bars are separated by gaps, usually half the width of the bars. Bar charts where the bars are vertical (as in Figure 12.2) are sometimes called column charts. This bar chart emphasises that the European Union member state with the highest total greenhouse gas emissions in 2008 was Germany, whilst either Iceland, Liechtenstein or Malta had the lowest total greenhouse gas emissions.

Table 12.2 Data presentation by data type: a summary

	Categorical		**Numerical**	
	Descriptive	**Ranked**	**Continuous**	**Discrete**
To show one variable so that any specific value can be read easily	Table/frequency distribution (data often grouped)			
To show the frequency of occurrences of categories or values for one variable so that highest and lowest are clear	Bar chart or pictogram (data may need grouping)		Histogram or frequency polygon (data must be grouped)	Bar chart or pictogram (data may need grouping)
To show the trend for a variable		Line graph or bar chart	Line graph or histogram	Line graph or bar chart
To show the proportion of occurrences of categories or values for one variable	Pie chart or bar chart (data may need grouping)		Histogram or pie chart (data must be grouped)	Pie chart or bar chart (data may need grouping)
To show the distribution of values for one variable			Frequency polygon, histogram (data must be grouped) or box plot	Frequency polygon, bar chart (data may need grouping) or box plot
To show the *interdependence* between two or more variables so that any *specific* value can be read easily	Contingency table/cross-tabulation (data often grouped)			
To compare the frequency of occurrences of categories or values for two or more variables so that *highest* and *lowest* are clear	Multiple bar chart (continuous data must be grouped, other data may need grouping)			
To compare the *trends* for two or more variables so that *conjunctions* are clear		Multiple line graph or multiple bar chart		
To compare the *proportions* of occurrences of categories or values for two or more variables	Comparative pie charts or percentage component bar chart (continuous data must be grouped, other data may need grouping)			
To compare the *distribution* of values for two or more variables			Multiple box plot	
To compare the frequency of occurrences of categories or values for two or more variables so that *totals* are clear	Stacked bar chart (continuous data must be grouped, other data may need grouping)			
To compare the *proportions* and *totals* of occurrences of categories or values for two or more variables	Comparative proportional pie charts (continuous data must be grouped, other data may need grouping)			
To show the *relationship* between cases for two variables		Scatter graph/scatter plot		

Source: © Mark Saunders, Philip Lewis and Adrian Thornhill 2011

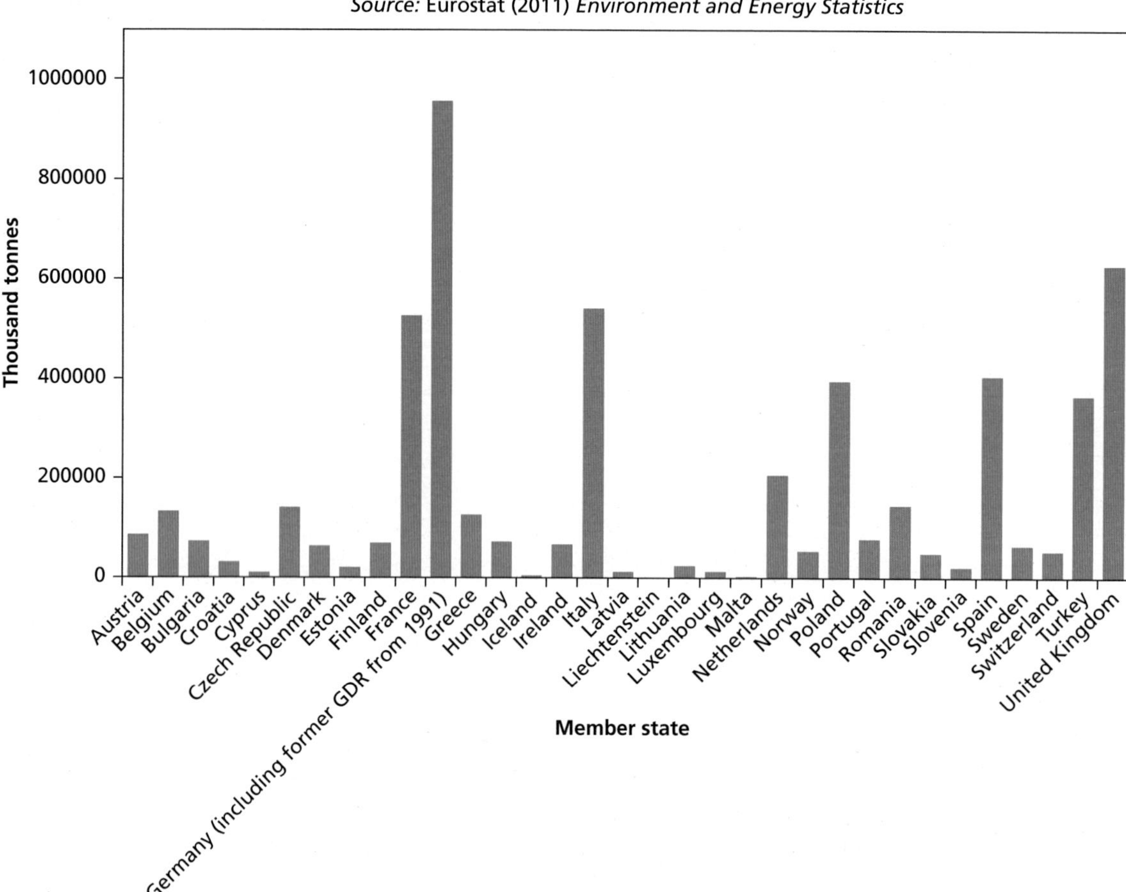

Figure 12.2 Bar chart

Source: Adapted from Eurostat (2011) © European Communities, 2011. Reproduced with permission

To emphasise the relative values represented by each of the bars in a bar chart, the bars may be reordered in either descending or ascending order of the frequency of occurrence represented by each bar (Figure 12.3). It is now from the order of the bars that Liechtenstein has the lowest greenhouse gas emissions.

Most researchers use a histogram to show highest and lowest values for continuous data. Prior to being drawn, data will often need to be grouped into class intervals. In a **histogram**, the area of each bar represents the frequency of occurrence and the continuous nature of the data is emphasised by the absence of gaps between the bars. For equal width class intervals, the height of your bar still represents the frequency of occurrences (Figures 12.4 and 12.5) and so the highest and lowest values are easy to distinguish. For histograms with unequal class interval widths, this is not the case. In Figure 12.4 the histogram emphasises that the most frequent amount spent is £40 to £60, whilst the least frequent amount spent is £160 to £180. In Figure 12.5 the histogram emphasises that the highest number of Harley-Davidson motorcycles shipped worldwide was in 2006, and the lowest number in 2000.

Analysis software treats histograms for data of equal width class intervals as a variation of a bar chart. Unfortunately, few spreadsheets will cope automatically with the calculations required to draw histograms for unequal class intervals. Consequently, you may have to use a bar chart owing to the limitations of your analysis software.

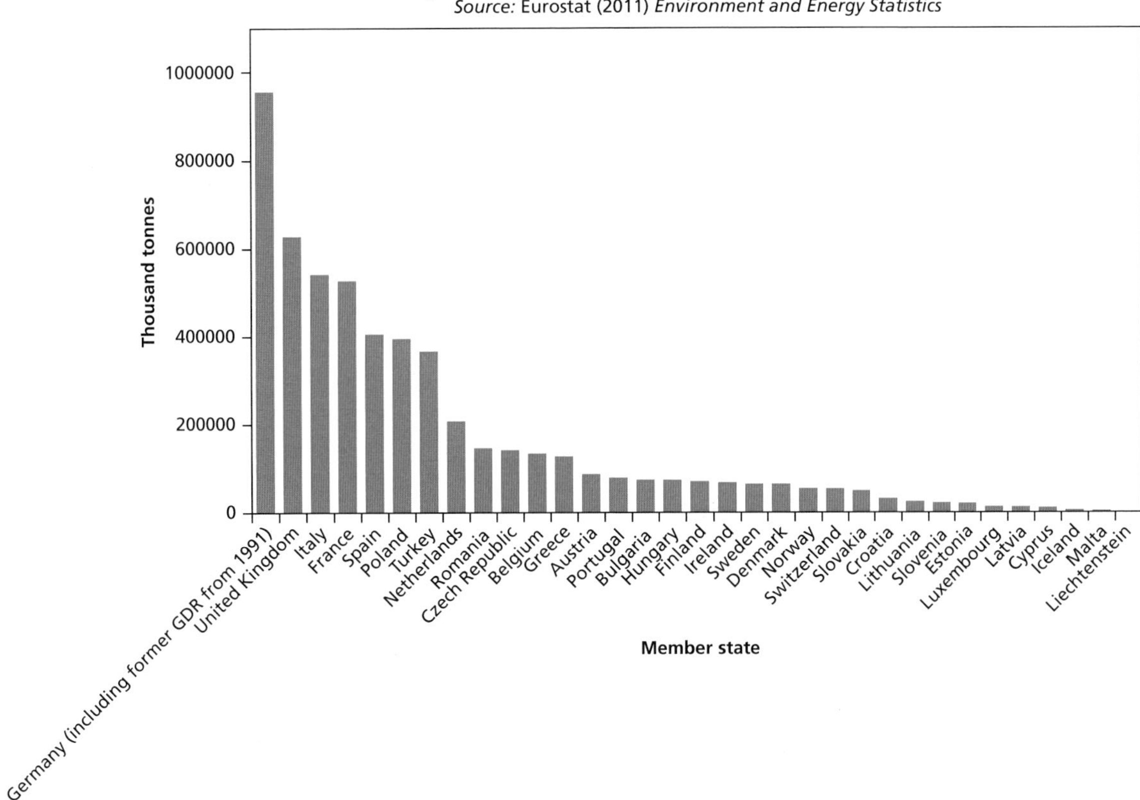

Figure 12.3 Bar chart (data reordered)

Source: Adapted from Eurostat (2011) © European Communities, 2011. Reproduced with permission

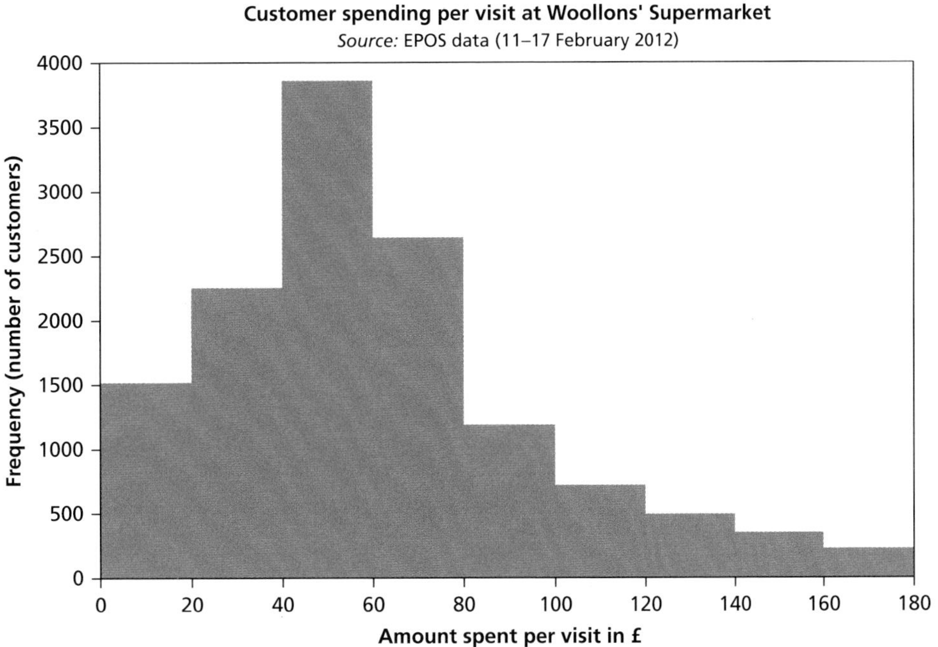

Figure 12.4 Histogram

Source: EPOS data (11–17 February 2012)

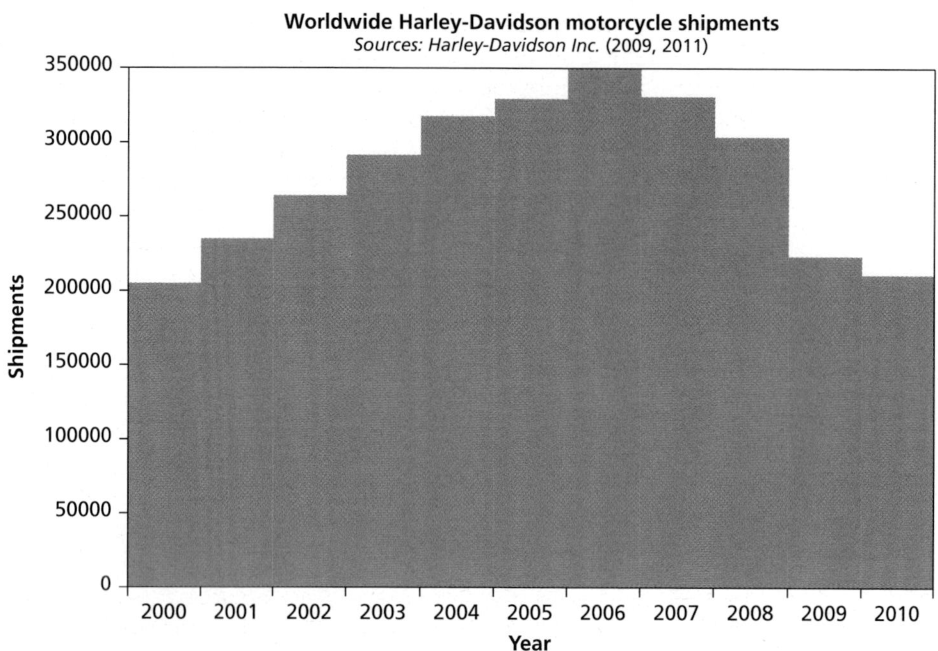

Figure 12.5 Histogram

Sources: Adapted from Harley-Davidson Inc. (2009) *Annual Report 2008* and (2011) *Form 10K (Annual Report) 2010*

In a **pictogram**, each bar is replaced by a picture or series of pictures chosen to represent the data. To illustrate the impact of doing this, we have used data of worldwide Harley-Davidson motorcycle shipments to generate both a histogram (Figure 12.5) and a pictogram (Figure 12.6). In the pictogram each picture represents 20,000 motorcycles. Pictures in pictograms can, like bars in bar charts and histograms, be shown in

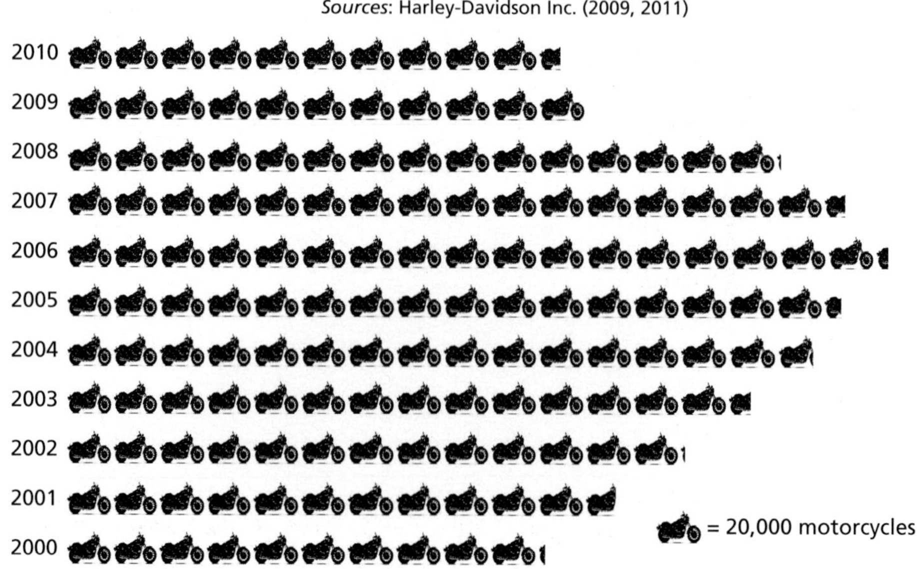

Figure 12.6 Pictogram

Sources: Adapted from Harley-Davidson Inc. (2009) *Annual Report 2008* and (2011) *Form 10K (Annual Report) 2010*

columns or horizontally. The height of the column or length of the bar made up by the pictures represents the frequency of occurrence. In this case we felt it was more logical to group the pictures as a horizontal bar rather than vertically on top of each other. You will have probably also noticed that, in the pictogram, there are gaps between the bars. Whilst this normally signifies discrete categories of data, it is also acceptable to do this for continuous data (such as years) when drawing a pictogram, to aid clarity. Although analysis software allows you to convert a bar chart or histogram to a pictogram easily and accurately, it is more difficult to establish the actual data values from a pictogram. This is because the number of units part of a picture represents is not immediately clear. For example, in Figure 12.6, how many motorcycles shipped would a rear wheel represent?

Pictograms have a further drawback, namely that it is very easy to misrepresent the data. Both Figure 12.5 and Figure 12.6 show that shipments of Harley-Davidson motorcycles declined between 2006 and 2010. Using our analysis software, this could have been represented using a picture of a motorcycle in 2006 that was nearly one and a half times as long as the picture in 2010. However, in order to keep the proportions of the motorcycle accurate, the picture would have needed to be nearly one and a half times as tall. Consequently, the actual area of the picture for 2006 would have been over twice as great and would have been interpreted as motorcycle shipments being twice as large in 2006 and 2010! Because of this we would recommend that, if you are using a pictogram, you decide on a standard value for each picture and do not alter its size. In addition, you should include a key or note to indicate the value each picture represents.

Frequency polygons are used less often to illustrate limits. Most analysis software treats them as a version of a line graph (Figure 12.7) in which the lines are extended to meet the horizontal axis, provided that class widths are equal.

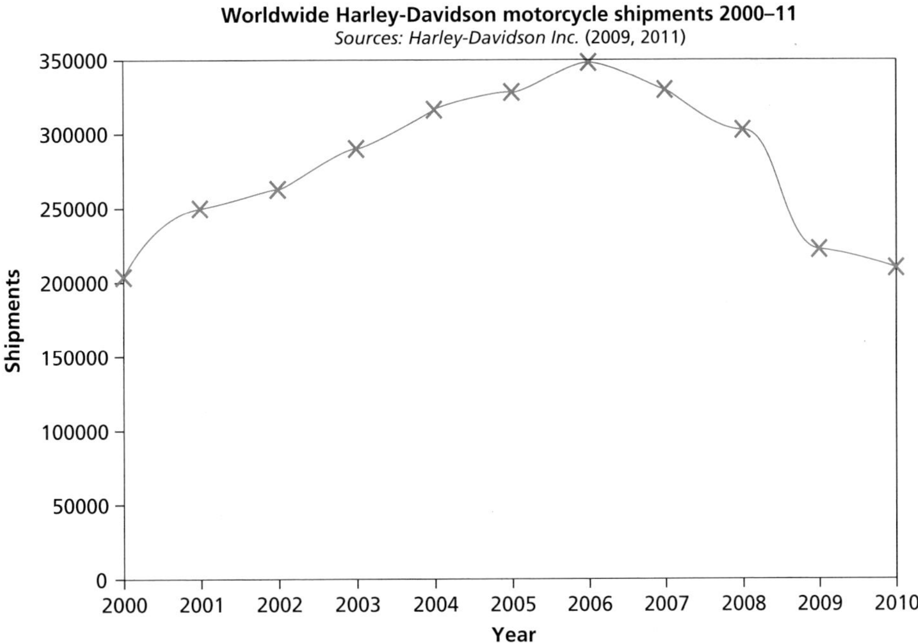

Figure 12.7 Line graph

Sources: Adapted from Harley-Davidson Inc. (2009) *Annual Report 2008* and (2011) *Form 10K (Annual Report) 2010*

To show a trend

Trends can only be presented for variables containing numerical (and occasionally ranked) longitudinal data. The most suitable diagram for exploring the trend is a **line graph** (Anderson et al. 2010) in which your data values for each time period are joined with a line to represent the trend (Figure 12.7, Box 12.9). In Figure 12.7 the line graph reveals the rise and decline in the number of Harley-Davidson motorcycles shipped worldwide between 2000 and 2010. You can also use histograms (Figure 12.5) to show trends over continuous time periods and bar charts (Figure 12.2) to show trends between discrete time periods. The trend can also be calculated using time-series analysis (Section 12.5).

Box 12.9 Focus on research in the news

FT

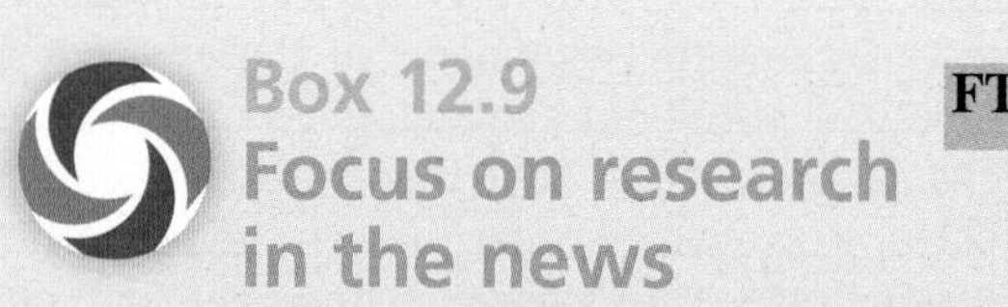

Producers acquiring the taste
World coffee consumption
%
World total 2000
105.5m
60kg bags
Emerging markets 15
Producing countries 25
Traditional markets 60
World total 2010*
134m
60kg bags
Emerging markets 17
Producing countries 30
Traditional markets 53
* Estimate
Consumption in Brazil climbs inexorably...
60kg bags (m)
20
15
10
5
0
1990
95
2000
05
10
... Arabica coffee price hits 34-year high
New York (cents per lb)
350
300
250
200
150
100
50
0
1976
80
85
90
95
2000
05
11
Sources: International Coffee Organisation, Associação Brasileira da Indústria de CO; Bloomberg

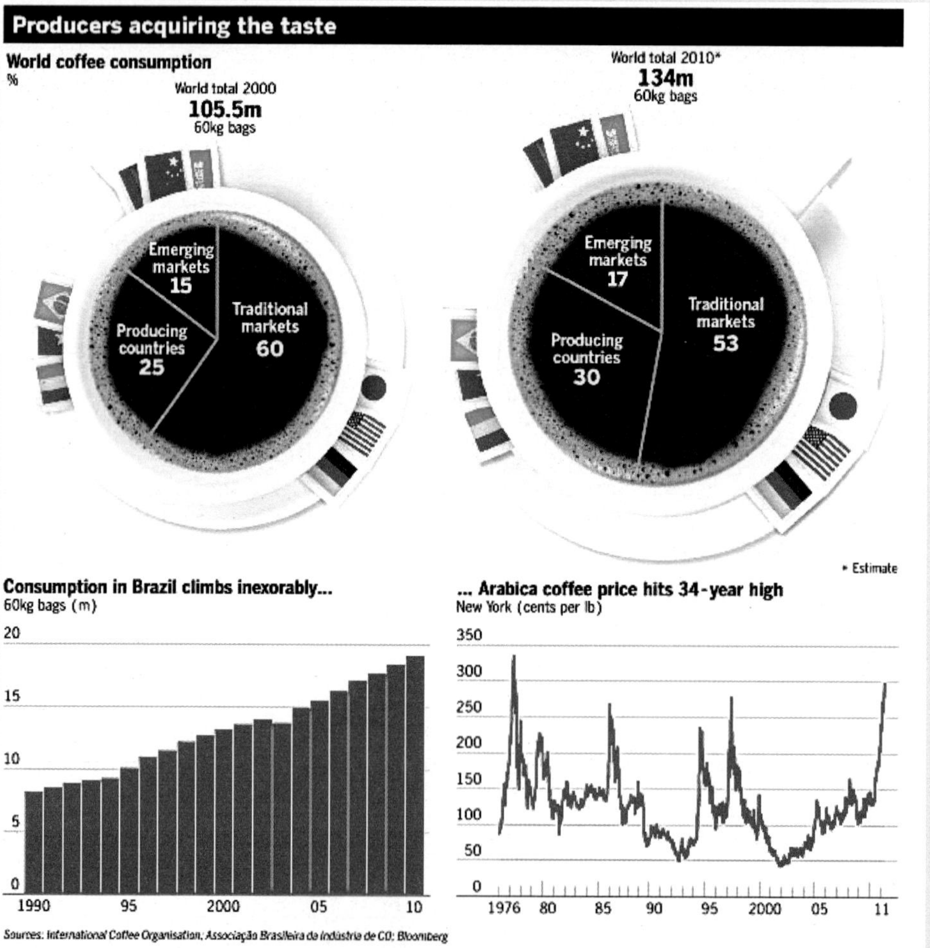

Source: From International Coffee Organisation: Associacao Brasileira de CO; Bloomberg

To show proportions

Research has shown that the most frequently used diagram to emphasise the proportion or share of occurrences is the pie chart, although bar charts have been shown to give equally good results (Anderson *et al.* 2010). A **pie chart** is divided into proportional segments according to the share each has of the total value (Box 12.9). For numerical and some categorical data you will need to group data prior to drawing the pie chart, as it is difficult to interpret pie charts with more than six segments (Morris 2012).

To show the distribution of values

Prior to using many statistical tests it is necessary to establish the distribution of values for variables containing numerical data (Sections 12.4, 12.5). This can be seen by plotting either a frequency polygon or a histogram (Figure 12.4) for continuous data or a frequency polygon or bar chart for discrete data. If your diagram shows a bunching to the left and a long tail to the right as in Figure 12.4 the data are **positively skewed**. If the converse is true, the data are **negatively skewed**. If your data are equally distributed either side of the highest frequency then they are **symmetrically distributed**. A special form of the symmetric distribution, in which the data can be plotted as a bell-shaped curve, is known as **normal distribution**.

The other indicator of the distribution's shape is **kurtosis** – the pointedness or flatness of the distribution compared with normal distribution. If a distribution is more pointed or peaked, it is said to be leptokurtic and the kurtosis value is positive. If a distribution is flatter, it is said to be platykurtic and the kurtosis value is negative. A distribution that is between the extremes of peakedness and flatness is said to be mesokurtic and has a kurtosis value of zero (Dancey and Reidy 2008).

An alternative often included in more advanced statistical analysis software is the **box plot** (Figure 12.8). This diagram provides you with a pictorial representation of the distribution of the data for a variable. The plot shows where the middle value or median is,

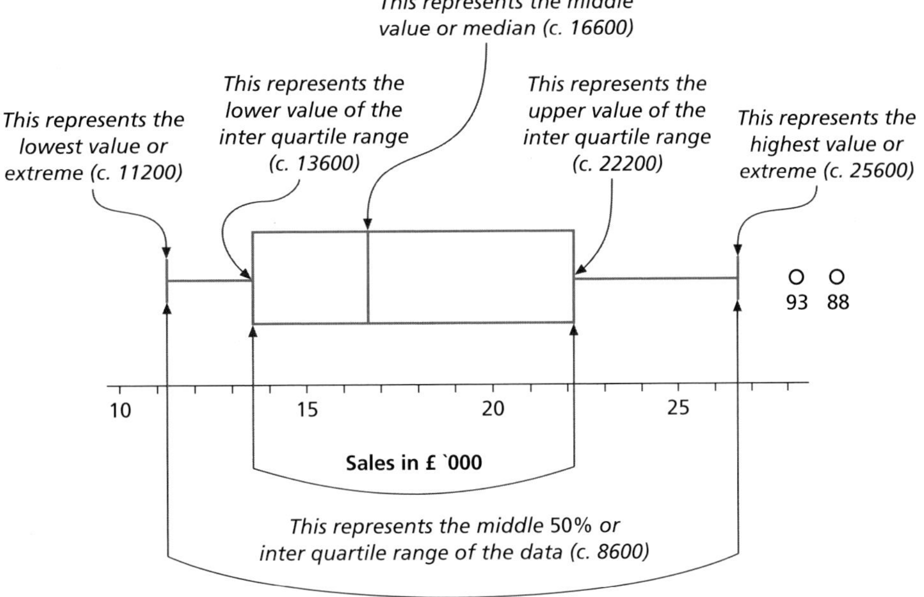

Figure 12.8 Annotated box plot

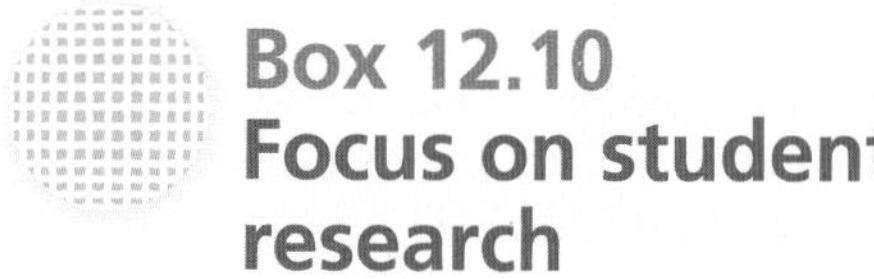

Box 12.10 Focus on student research

Exploring and presenting data for individual variables

As part of audience research for his dissertation, Valentin asked people attending a play at a provincial theatre to complete a short questionnaire. This collected responses to 25 questions including:

3 How many plays (including this one) have you seen at this theatre in the past year?

11 This play is good value for money

strongly disagree ❑$_1$ disagree ❑$_2$
agree ❑$_3$ strongly agree ❑$_4$

24 How old are you?

Under 18 ❑$_1$ 18 to 34 ❑$_2$
35 to 64 ❑$_3$ 65 and over ❑$_4$

Exploratory analyses were undertaken using analysis software and diagrams and tables generated. For question 3, which collected discrete data, the aspects that were most important were the distribution of values and the highest and lowest numbers of plays seen. A bar chart, therefore, was drawn:

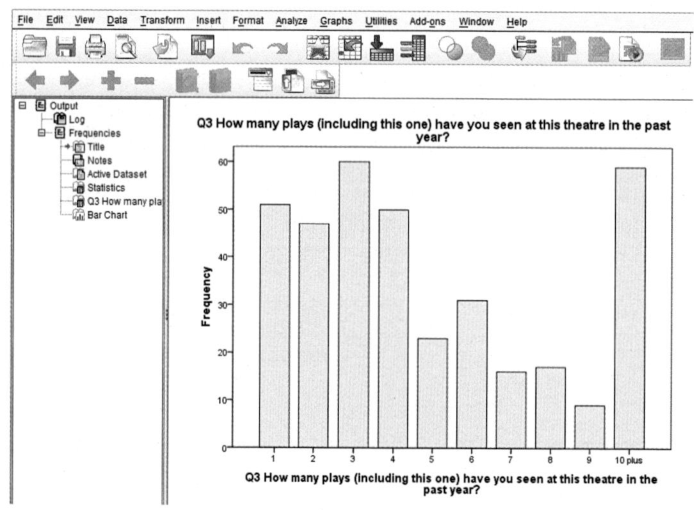

This emphasised that the most frequent number of plays seen by respondents was three and the least frequent number of plays seen by the respondents was either nine or probably some larger number. It also suggested that the distribution was positively skewed towards lower numbers of plays seen.

For question 11 (categorical data), the most important aspect was the proportions of people agreeing and disagreeing with the statement. A pie chart was therefore drawn although unfortunately the shadings were not similar for the two agree categories and for the two disagree categories.

This emphasised that the vast majority of respondents (95 per cent) agreed that the play was good value for money.

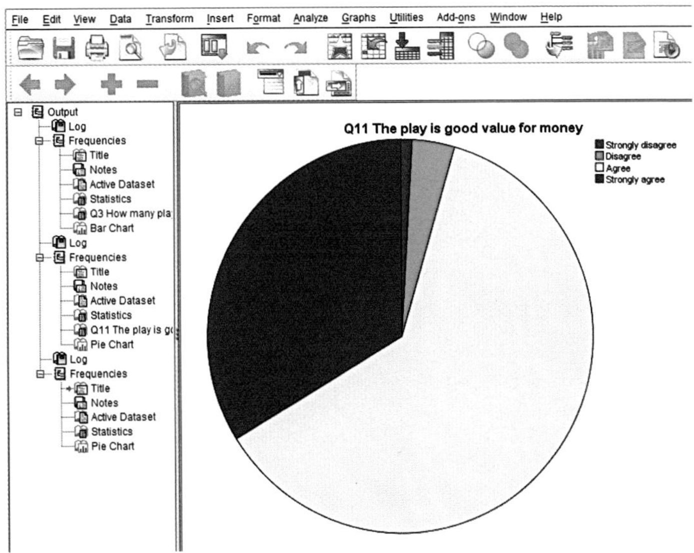

Question 24 collected data on each respondent's age. This question had grouped continuous data into four unequal-width age groups. For this analysis, the most important aspects were the specific number and percentage of respondents in each age category and so a table was constructed.

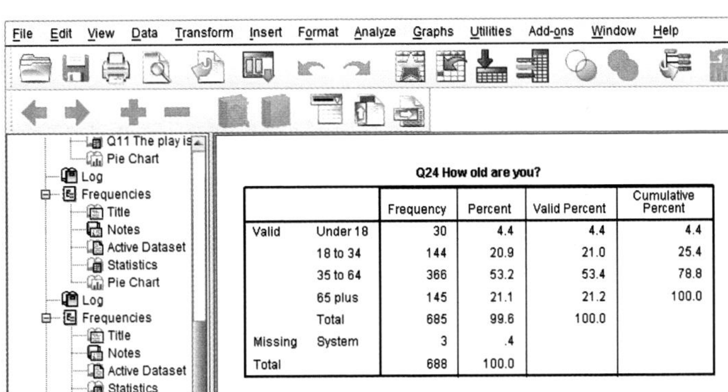

Q24 How old are you?

		Frequency	Percent	Valid Percent	Cumulative Percent
Valid	Under 18	30	4.4	4.4	4.4
	18 to 34	144	20.9	21.0	25.4
	35 to 64	366	53.2	53.4	78.8
	65 plus	145	21.1	21.2	100.0
	Total	685	99.6	100.0	
Missing	System	3	.4		
Total		688	100.0		

how this relates to the middle 50 per cent of the data or inter-quartile range, and highest and lowest values or *extremes* (Section 12.4). It also highlights outliers, those values that are very different from the data. In Figure 12.9 the two outliers might be due to mistakes in data entry. Alternatively, they may be correct and emphasise that sales for these two cases (93 and 88) are far higher. In this example we can see that the data values for the variable are positively skewed as there is a long tail to the right.

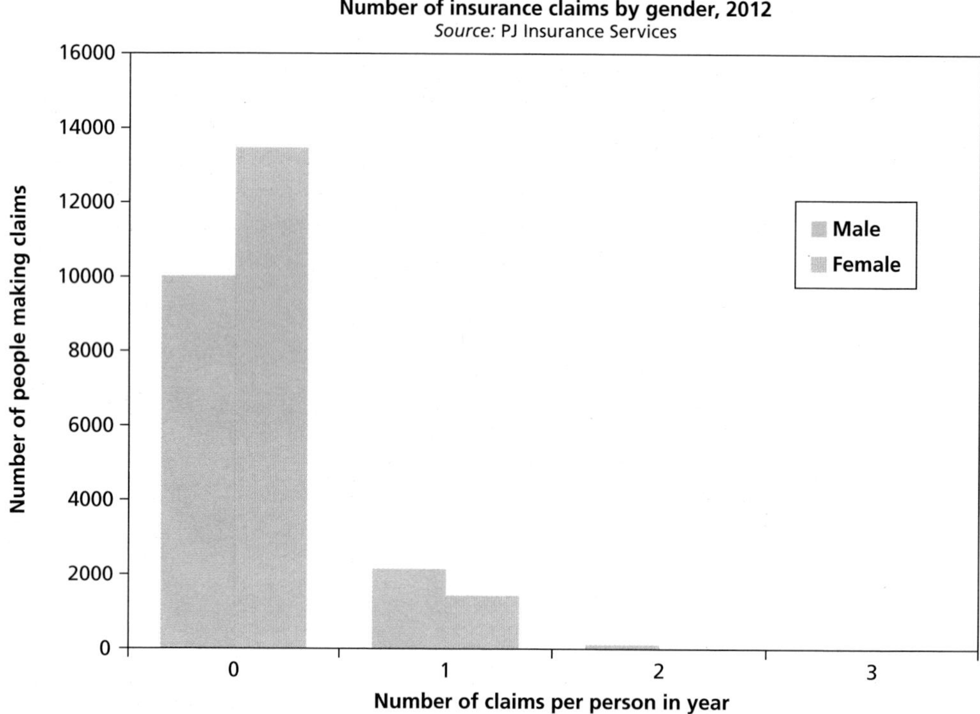

Figure 12.9 Multiple bar chart

Comparing variables

To show specific values and interdependence

As with individual variables, the best method of finding specific data values is a table. This is known as a **contingency table** or **cross-tabulation** (Table 12.3), and it also enables you to examine interdependence between the variables. For variables where there are likely to be a large number of categories (or values for numerical data), you may need to group the data to prevent the table from becoming too large.

Most statistical analysis software allows you to add totals, and row and column percentages when designing your table. Statistical analyses such as chi square can also be undertaken at the same time (Section 12.5).

Table 12.3 Contingency table: number of insurance claims by gender, 2012

Number of claims*	Male	Female	Total
0	10032	13478	23510
1	2156	1430	3586
2	120	25	145
3	13	4	17
Total	12321	14937	27258

*No clients had more than three claims.
Source: PJ Insurance Services

To compare highest and lowest values

Comparisons of variables that emphasise the highest and lowest rather than precise values are best explored using a **multiple bar chart** (Anderson et al. 2010), also known as a *compound bar chart*. As for a bar chart, continuous data – or data where there are many values or categories – need to be grouped. Within any multiple bar chart you are likely to find it easiest to *compare* between adjacent bars. The multiple bar chart (Figure 12.9) has therefore been drawn to emphasise comparisons between males and females rather than between numbers of claims.

To compare proportions

Comparison of proportions between variables uses either a **percentage component bar chart** or two or more pie charts. Either type of diagram can be used for all data types, provided that continuous data, and data where there are more than six values or categories, are grouped. Percentage component bar charts are more straightforward to draw than comparative pie charts when using most spreadsheets. Within your percentage component bar chart, comparisons will be easiest between adjacent bars. The chart in Figure 12.10 has been drawn to emphasise the proportions of males and females for each number of insurance claims in the year. Males and females, therefore, form a single bar.

To compare trends and conjunctions

The most suitable diagram to compare trends for two or more numerical (or occasionally ranked) variables is a **multiple line graph** where one line represents each variable (Henry 1995). You can also use multiple bar charts (Box 12.11) in which bars for the same time period are placed adjacent to each other.

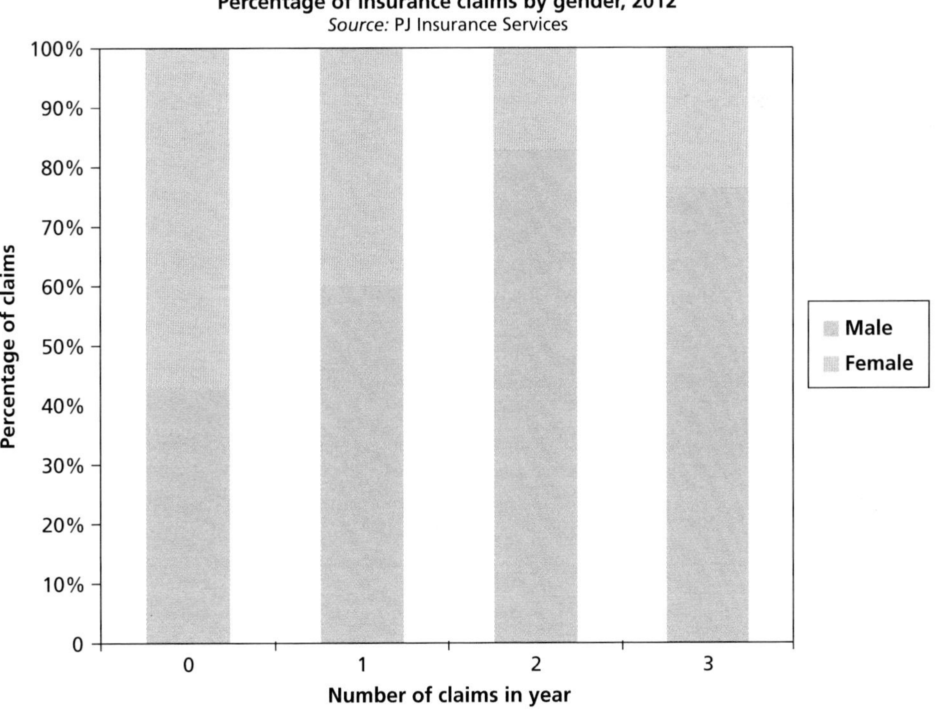

Figure 12.10 Percentage component bar chart

Box 12.11 Focus on student research

Comparing variables

Francis was asked by his uncle, an independent ice cream manufacturer, to examine the records of monthly sales of ice cream for 2011 and 2012. In addition, his uncle had obtained longitudinal data on average (mean) daily hours of sunshine for each month for the same time period from their local weather station. Francis decided to explore data on sales of the three best-selling flavours (vanilla, strawberry and chocolate), paying particular attention to:

- comparative trends in sales;
- the relationship between sales and amount of sunshine.

To compare trends in sales between the three flavours he plotted a multiple line graph using a spreadsheet.

This indicated that sales for all flavours of ice cream were following a seasonal pattern but with an overall upward trend. It also showed that sales of vanilla ice cream were highest, and that those of chocolate had overtaken strawberry. The multiple line graph highlighted the conjunction when sales of chocolate first exceeded strawberry, September 2012.

To show relationships between sales and amount of sunshine Francis plotted scatter graphs for sales of each ice cream flavour against average (mean) daily hours of sunshine for each month. He plotted sales on the vertical axis, as he presumed that these were dependent on the amount of sunshine, (see below).

The scatter graph showed that there was a positive relationship between the amount of sunshine and sales of vanilla flavour ice cream. Subsequent scatter plots revealed similar relationships for strawberry and chocolate flavours.

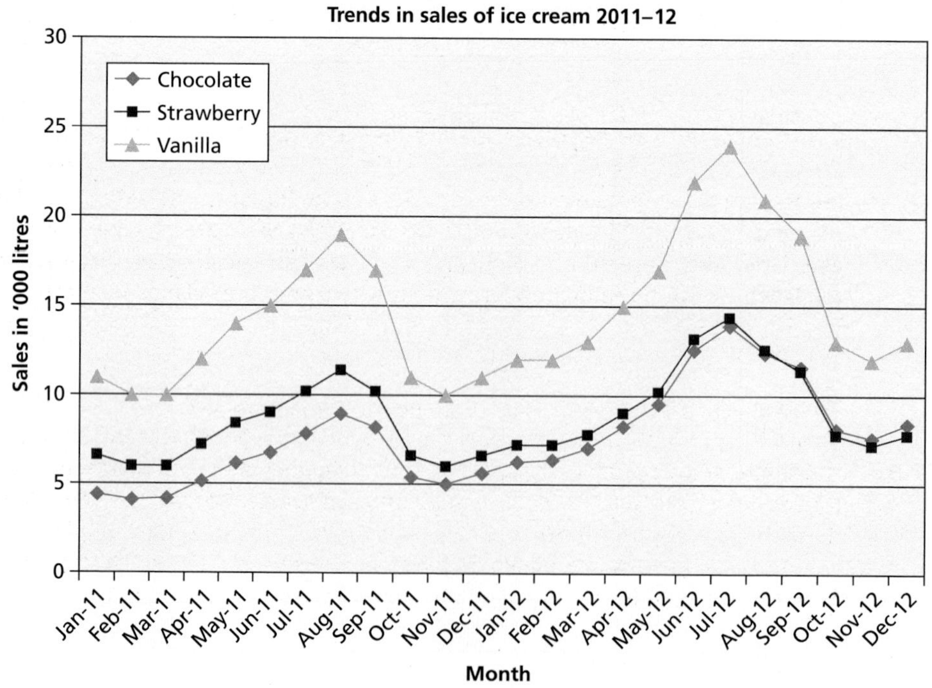

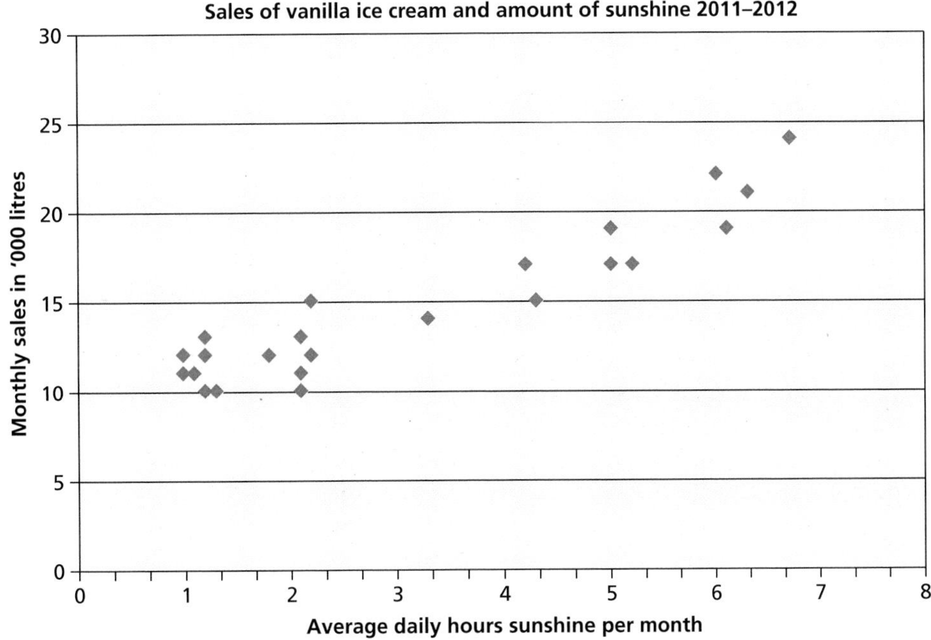

If you need to look for conjunctions in the trends – that is, where values for two or more variables intersect – this is where the lines on a multiple line graph cross.

To compare totals

Comparison of totals between variables uses a variation of the bar chart. A **stacked bar chart** can be used for all data types provided that continuous data and data where there are more than six possible values or categories are grouped. As with percentage component bar charts, the design of the stacked bar chart is dictated by the totals you want to compare. For this reason, in Figure 12.11 males and females have been stacked to give totals which can be compared for zero, one, two and three claims in a year.

To compare proportions and totals

To compare both proportions of each category or value and the totals for two or more variables it is best to use **comparative proportional pie charts** for all data types. For each comparative proportional pie chart the total area of the pie chart represents the total for that variable. By contrast, the angle of each segment represents the relative proportion of a category within the variable (Box 12.9). Because of the complexity of drawing comparative proportional pie charts, they are rarely used for exploratory data analysis, although they can be used to good effect in research reports.

To compare the distribution of values

Often it is useful to compare the distribution of values for two or more variables. Plotting multiple frequency polygons or bar charts (Box 12.11) will enable you to compare

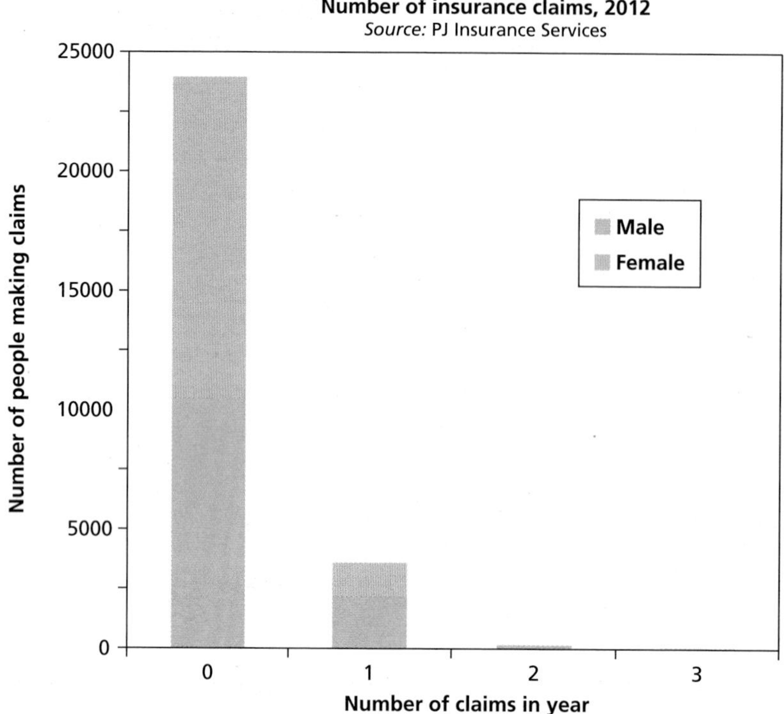

Figure 12.11 Stacked bar chart

distributions for up to three or four variables. After this your diagram is likely just to look a mess! An alternative is to use a diagram of multiple box plots, similar to the one in Figure 12.8. This provides a pictorial representation of the distribution of the data for the variables in which you are interested. These plots can be compared and are interpreted in the same way as the single box plot.

To show the relationship between cases for variables

You can explore possible relationships between ranked and numerical data variables by plotting one variable against another. This is called a **scatter graph** or **scatter plot**, and each cross (point) represents the values for one case (Figure 12.12). Convention dictates that you plot the **dependent variable** – that is, the variable that changes in response to changes in the other **(independent) variable** – against the vertical axis. The strength of the relationship is indicated by the closeness of the points to an imaginary straight line. If as the values for one variable increase so do those for the other then you have a positive relationship. If as the values for one variable decrease those for the other variable increase then you have a negative relationship. Thus, in Figure 12.12 there is a negative relationship between the two variables. The strength of this relationship can be assessed statistically using techniques such as correlation or regression (Section 12.5).

12.4 Describing data using statistics

The exploratory data analysis approach (Section 12.3) emphasised the use of diagrams to understand your data. **Descriptive statistics** enable you to describe (and compare) variables numerically. Your research question(s) and objectives, although limited by the

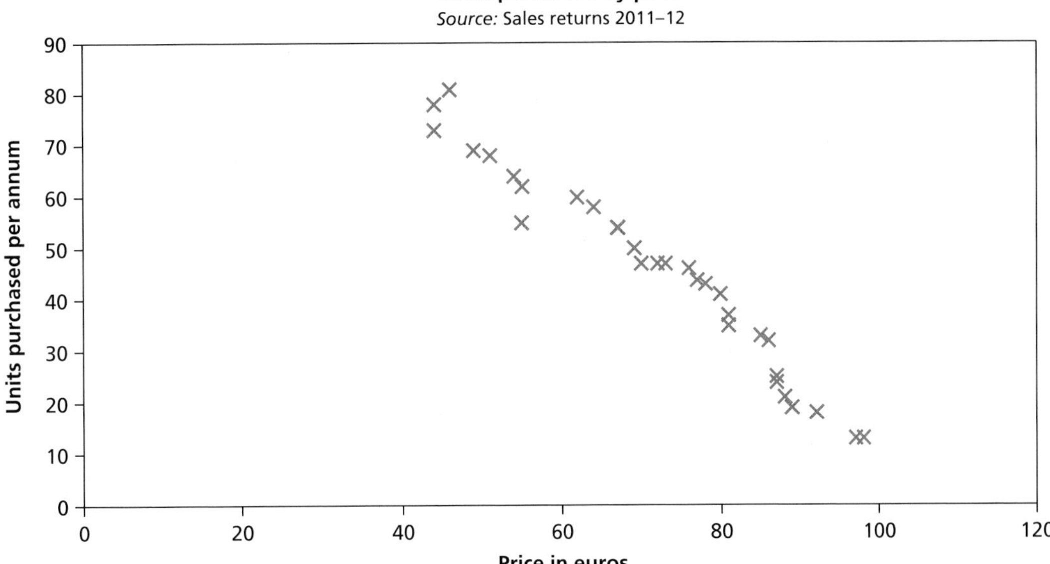

Figure 12.12 Scatter graph

type of data (Table 12.4), should guide your choice of statistics. Statistics to describe a variable focus on two aspects:

- the central tendency;
- the dispersion.

These are summarised in Table 12.4. Those most pertinent to your research question(s) and objectives will eventually be quoted in your project report as support for your arguments.

Describing the central tendency

When describing data for both samples and populations quantitatively it is usual to provide some general impression of values that could be seen as common, middling or average. These are termed measures of **central tendency** and are discussed in virtually all statistics textbooks. The three ways of measuring the central tendency most used in business research are the:

- value that occurs most frequently (mode);
- middle value or mid-point after the data have been ranked (median);
- value, often known as the average, that includes all data values in its calculation (mean).

However, as we saw in Box 12.2, beware: if you have used numerical codes, most analysis software can calculate all three measures whether or not they are appropriate!

To represent the value that occurs most frequently

The **mode** is the value that occurs most frequently. For descriptive data, the mode is the only measure of central tendency that can be interpreted sensibly. You might read in a report that the most common (modal) colour of motor cars sold last year was silver, or that the two equally most popular makes of motorcycle in response to a questionnaire were Honda and Yamaha. In such cases where two categories occur equally most

Table 12.4 Descriptive statistics by data type: a summary

To calculate a measure of:		Categorical		Numerical	
		Descriptive	Ranked	Continuous	Discrete
Central tendency that . . .	. . . represents the value that occurs most frequently	Mode			
	. . . represents the middle value			Median	
	. . . includes all data values (average)			Mean	
Dispersion that . . .	. . . states the difference between the highest and lowest values			Range (data need not be normally distributed but must be placed in rank order)	
	. . . states the difference within the middle 50% of values			Inter-quartile range (data need not be normally distributed but must be placed in rank order)	
	. . . states the difference within another fraction of the values			Deciles or percentiles (data need not be normally distributed but must be placed in rank order)	
	. . . describes the extent to which data values differ from the mean			Variance, or more usually, the standard deviation (data should be normally distributed)	
	. . . compares the extent to which data values differ from the mean between variables			Coefficient of variation (data should be normally distributed)	
	. . . allows the relative extent that different data values differ to be compared			Index numbers	

Source: © Mark Saunders, Philip Lewis and Adrian Thornhill 2011

frequently, this is termed bi-modal. The mode can be calculated for variables where there are likely to be a large number of categories (or values for numerical data), although it may be less useful. One solution is to group the data into suitable categories and to quote the most frequently occurring or **modal group**.

To represent the middle value

If you have quantitative data it is also possible to calculate the middle or **median** value by ranking all the values in ascending order and finding the mid-point (or **50th percentile**) in the distribution. For variables that have an even number of data values the median will occur halfway between the two middle data values. The median has the advantage that it is not affected by extreme values in the distribution.

To include all data values

The most frequently used measure of central tendency is the **mean** (average in everyday language), which includes all data values in its calculation. However, it is usually only possible to calculate a meaningful mean using numerical data.

Box 12.12 Focus on student research

Measuring the central tendency

As part of her research project, Kylie had obtained secondary data from the service department of her organisation on the length of time for which their customers had held service contracts:

Length of time held contract	Number of customers
< 3 months	50
3 to < 6 months	44
6 months to < 1 year	71
1 to < 2 years	105
2 to < 3 years	74
3 to < 4 years	35
4 to < 5 years	27
5+ years	11

Her exploratory analysis revealed a positively skewed distribution (long tail to the right).

From the table, the largest single group of customers were those who had contracts for 1 to 2 years. This was the modal time period (most commonly occurring). However, the usefulness of this statistic is limited owing to the variety of class widths. By definition, half of the organisation's customers will have held contracts below the median time period (approximately 1 year 5 months) and half above it. As there are 11 customers who have held service contracts for over 5 years, the mean time period (approximately 1 year 9 months) is pulled towards longer times. This is represented by the skewed shape of the distribution.

Kylie needed to decide which of these measures of central tendency to include in her research report. As the mode made little sense she quoted the median and mean when interpreting her data:

> The length of time for which customers have held service contracts is positively skewed. Although mean length of time is approximately 1 year 9 months, half of customers have held service contracts for less than 1 year 5 months (median). Grouping of these data means that it is not possible to calculate a meaningful mode.

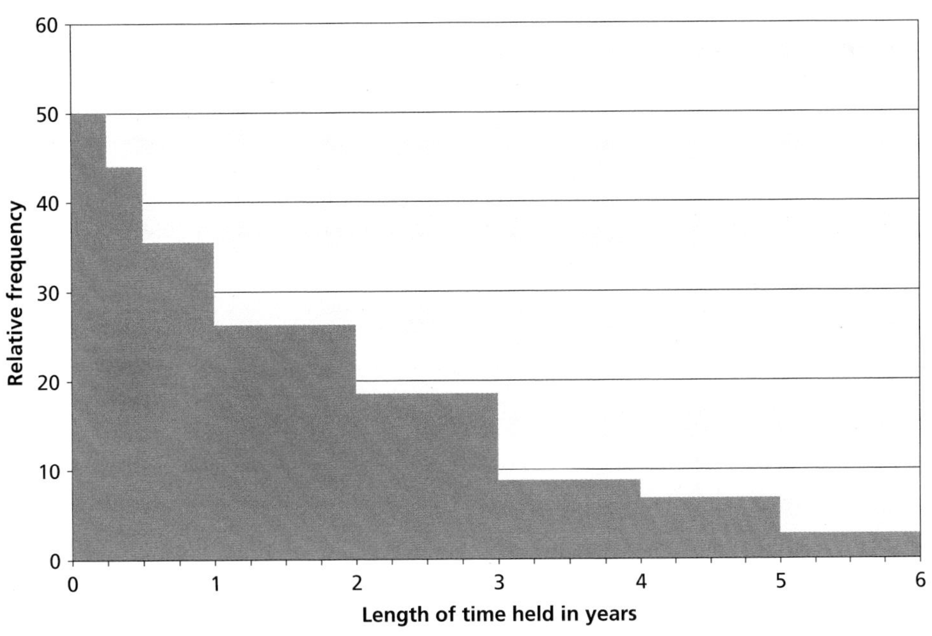

The value of your mean is unduly influenced by extreme data values in skewed distributions (Section 12.3). In such distributions the mean tends to get drawn towards the long tail of extreme data values and may be less representative of the central tendency. For this and other reasons Anderson et al. (2010) suggest that the median may be a more useful descriptive statistic. However, because the mean is the building block for many of the statistical tests used to explore relationships (Section 12.5), it is usual to include it as at least one of the measures of central tendency for numerical data in your report. This is, of course, provided that it makes sense!

Describing the dispersion

As well as describing the central tendency for a variable, it is important to describe how the data values are dispersed around the central tendency. As you can see from Table 12.4, this is only possible for numerical data. Two of the most frequently used ways of describing the dispersion are the:

- difference within the middle 50 per cent of values (inter-quartile range);
- extent to which values differ from the mean (standard deviation).

Although these **dispersion measures** are suitable only for numerical data, most statistical analysis software will also calculate them for categorical data if you have used numerical codes!

To state the difference between values

In order to get a quick impression of the distribution of data values for a variable you could simply calculate the difference between the lowest and the highest values – that is, the **range**. However, this statistic is rarely used in research reports as it represents only the extreme values.

A more frequently used statistic is the **inter-quartile range**. As we discussed earlier, the median divides the range into two. The range can be further divided into four equal sections called **quartiles**. The **lower quartile** is the value below which a quarter of your data values will fall; the **upper quartile** is the value above which a quarter of your data values will fall. As you would expect, the remaining half of your data values will fall between the lower and upper quartiles. The difference between the upper and lower quartiles is the inter-quartile range (Morris 2012). As a consequence, it is concerned only with the middle 50 per cent of data values and ignores extreme values.

You can also calculate the range for other fractions of a variable's distribution. One alternative is to divide your distribution using **percentiles**. These split your distribution into 100 equal parts. Obviously the lower quartile is the 25th percentile and the upper quartile the 75th percentile. However, you could calculate a range between the 10th and 90th percentiles so as to include 80 per cent of your data values. Another alternative is to divide the range into 10 equal parts called **deciles**.

To describe and compare the extent by which values differ from the mean

Conceptually and statistically in research it is important to look at the extent to which the data values for a variable are spread around their mean, as this is what you need to know to assess its usefulness as a typical value for the distribution. If your data values are all close to the mean, then the mean is more typical than if they vary widely. To describe the extent of spread of numerical data you use the **standard deviation**. If your data are

Box 12.13 Focus on student research

Describing variables and comparing their dispersion

Cathy was interested in the total value of transactions at the main and sub-branches of a major bank. The mean value of total transactions at the main branches was approximately five times as high as that for the sub-branches. This made it difficult to compare the relative spread in total value of transactions between the two types of branches. By calculating the coefficients of variation Cathy found that there was relatively more variation in the total value of transactions at the main branches than at the sub-branches. This is because the coefficient of variation for the main branches was larger (23.62) than the coefficient for the sub-branches (18.08).

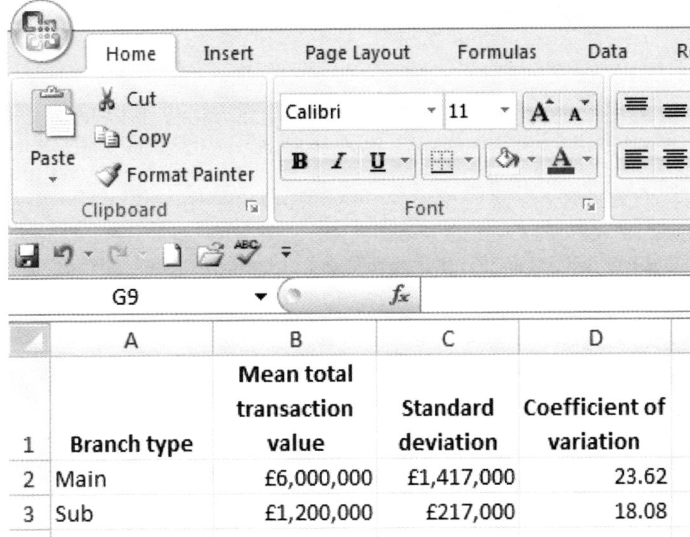

	A	B	C	D
1	Branch type	Mean total transaction value	Standard deviation	Coefficient of variation
2	Main	£6,000,000	£1,417,000	23.62
3	Sub	£1,200,000	£217,000	18.08

a sample (Section 7.1), this is calculated using a slightly different formula than if your data are a population, although if your sample is larger than about 30 cases there is little difference in the two statistics (Morris 2012).

You may need to compare the relative spread of data between distributions of different magnitudes (e.g. one may be measured in hundreds of tonnes, the other in billions of tonnes). To make a meaningful comparison you will need to take account of these different magnitudes. A common way of doing this is:

1 to divide the standard deviation by the mean;
2 then to multiply your answer by 100.

This results in a statistic called the **coefficient of variation** (Black 2009). The values of this statistic can then be compared. The distribution with the largest coefficient of variation has the largest relative spread of data (Box 12.13).

Alternatively, as discussed in the introduction in relation to the cost of Big Mac hamburgers in different countries, you may wish to compare the relative extent to which data values differ. One way of doing this is to use **index numbers** and consider the relative differences rather than actual data values. Such indices compare each data value against a base value that is normally given the value of 100, differences being calculated relative to this value. An index number greater than 100 would represent a larger or higher data value relative to the base value and an index less than 100, a smaller or lower data value.

To calculate an index number for each case for a data variable you use the following formula:

$$\text{index number for case} = \frac{\text{data value for case}}{\text{base data value}} \times 100$$

12.5 Examining relationships, differences and trends using statistics

One of the questions you are most likely to ask in your analysis is: 'How does a variable relate to another variable?' In statistical analysis you answer this question by testing the likelihood of a relationship (or one more extreme) occurring by chance alone, if there really was no difference in the population from which the sample was drawn (Robson 2011). This process is known as significance or hypothesis testing as, in effect, you are comparing the data you have collected with what you would theoretically expect to happen. Significance testing can therefore be thought of as helping to rule out the possibility that your result could be due to random variation in your sample.

There are two main groups of statistical significance tests: non-parametric and parametric. **Non-parametric statistics** are designed to be used when your data are not normally distributed. Not surprisingly, this most often means they are used with categorical data. In contrast, **parametric statistics** are used with numerical data. Although parametric statistics are considered more powerful because they use numerical data, a number of assumptions about the actual data being used need to be satisfied if they are not to produce spurious results (Blumberg et al. 2008). These include:

- the data cases selected for the sample should be independent, in other words the selection of any one case for your sample should not affect the probability of any other case being included in the same sample;
- the data cases should be drawn from normally distributed populations (Section 12.3 and later in Section 12.5);
- the populations from which the data cases are drawn should have equal variances (don't worry, the term variance is explained later in Section 12.5);
- the data used should be numerical.

In addition, as we will discuss later, you need to ensure that your sample size is sufficiently large to meet the requirements of the statistic you are using (see also Section 7.2). If the assumptions are not satisfied, it is often still possible to use non-parametric statistics.

The way in which this significance is tested using both non-parametric and parametric statistics can be thought of as answering one from a series of questions, dependent on the data type:

- Is the association statistically significant?
- Are the differences statistically significant?
- What is the strength of the relationship, and is it statistically significant?
- Are the predicted values statistically significant?

These are summarised in Table 12.5 along with statistics used to help examine trends.

Table 12.5 Statistics to examine relationships, differences and trends by data type: a summary

	Categorical		Numerical	
	Descriptive	**Ranked**	**Continuous**	**Discrete**
To test normality of a distribution			Kolmogorov–Smirnov test, Shapiro–Wilk test	
To test whether two variables are associated	Chi square (data may need grouping)		Chi square if variable grouped into discrete classes	
	Cramer's V and Phi (both variables must be dichotomous)			
To test whether two groups (categories) are different		Kolmogorov–Smirnov (data may need grouping) or Mann– Whitney *U* test	Independent ***t***-test or paired ***t***-test (often used to test for changes over time) or Mann–Whitney *U* test (where data skewed or a small sample)	
To test whether three or more groups (categories) are different			Analysis of variance (ANOVA)	
To assess the strength of relationship between two variables		Spearman's rank correlation coefficient (Spearman's rho) or Kendall's rank order correlation coefficient (Kendall's tau)	Pearson's product moment correlation coefficient (PMCC)	
To assess the strength of a relationship between one dependent and one independent variable			Coefficient of determination (regression coefficient)	
To assess the strength of a relationship between one dependent and two or more independent variables			Coefficient of multiple determination (multiple regression coefficient)	
To predict the value of a dependent variable from one or more independent variables			Regression equation (regression analysis)	
To explore relative change (trend) over time			Index numbers	
To compare relative changes (trends) over time			Index numbers	
To determine the trend over time of a series of data			Time series: moving averages or Regression equation (regression analysis)	

Source: © Mark Saunders, Philip Lewis and Adrian Thornhill 2011

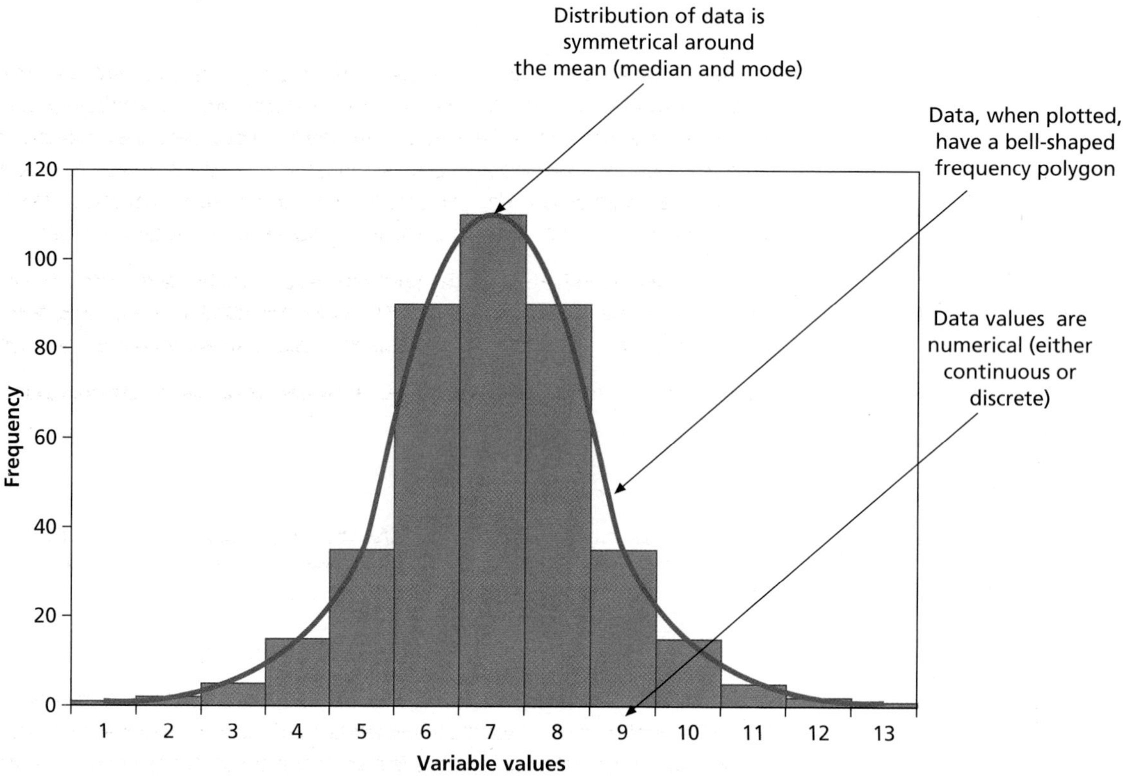

Figure 12.13 Annotated frequency polygon showing a normal distribution

Testing for normality

As we have already noted, parametric tests assume that the numerical data cases in your sample are drawn from normally distributed populations. This means that the data values for each quantitative variable should also be normally distributed, being clustered around the variable's mean in a symmetrical pattern forming a bell-shaped frequency distribution. Fortunately, it is relatively easy to check if data values for a particular variable are distributed normally, both using graphs and statistically.

In Section 12.3 we looked at a number of different types of graphs including histograms (Figures 12.4 and 12.5), box plots (Figure 12.8) and frequency polygons (Figure 12.13). All of these can be used to assess visually whether the data values for a particular numerical variable are clustered around the mean in a symmetrical pattern, and so normally distributed. For normally distributed data, the value of the mean, median and mode are also likely to be the same.

Another way of testing for normality is to use statistics to establish whether the distribution as a whole for a variable differs significantly from a comparable normal distribution. Fortunately, this is relatively easy to do in statistical software such as IBM SPSS statistics using the **Kolmogorov–Smirnov test** and the **Shapiro–Wilk test** (Box 12.14), as the software also calculates a comparable normal distribution automatically. For both these tests the calculation consists of the test statistic (labelled *D* and *W* respectively), the degrees of freedom[1] (*df*) and, based on this, the probability *(p-value)* that the data for

[1]Degrees of freedom are the number of values free to vary when computing a statistic. The number of degrees of freedom for a contingency table of at least 2 rows and 2 columns of data is calculated from: (number of rows in the table – 1) × (number of columns in the table – 1).

Box 12.14 Focus on student research

Testing for normality

As part of his research project, Osama had collected quantitative data about music piracy and illegal downloading of music from a number of student respondents. Before undertaking his statistical analysis Osama decided to test his quantitative variables for normality using the Kolmogorov–Smirnov test and the Shapiro–Wilk test. The output from IBM SPSS Statistics for one of his data variables, 'number of legal music downloads made in the past month', follows:

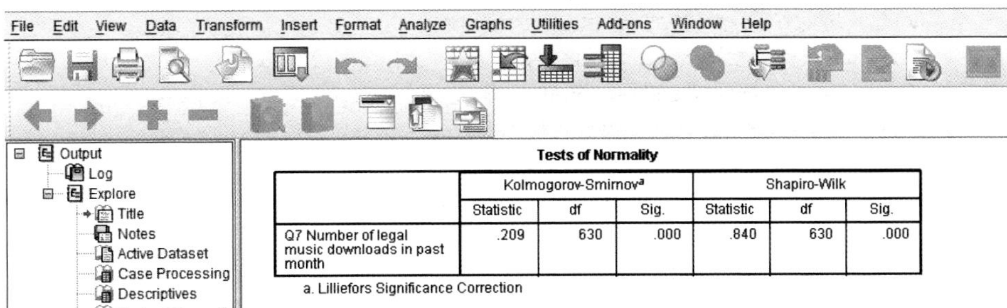

Tests of Normality

	Kolmogorov-Smirnov[a]			Shapiro-Wilk		
	Statistic	df	Sig.	Statistic	df	Sig.
Q7 Number of legal music downloads in past month	.209	630	.000	.840	630	.000

a. Lilliefors Significance Correction

This calculated the significance (Sig.) for both the Kolmogorov–Smirnov test and the Shapiro–Wilk test as '000', meaning that for this variable the likelihood of the actual distribution differing from a normal distribution occurring by chance alone was less than 0.001. Consequently the data values for variable 'Number of legal music downloads in past month' were not normally distributed, reducing his choice of statistics for subsequent analyses. This was confirmed by a bar chart showing the distribution of the data for the variable:

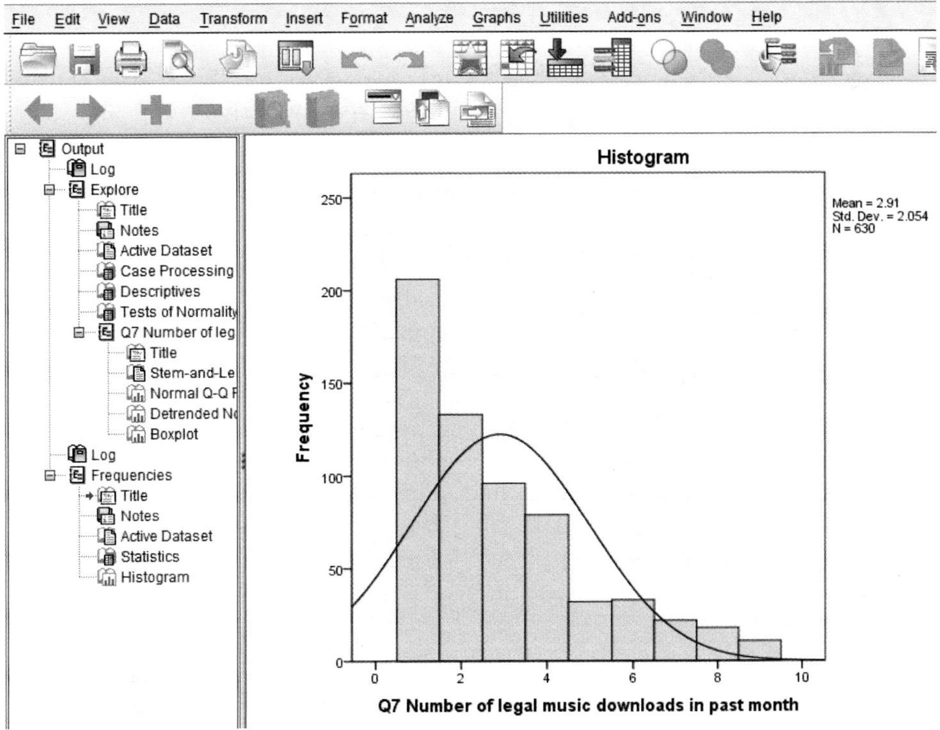

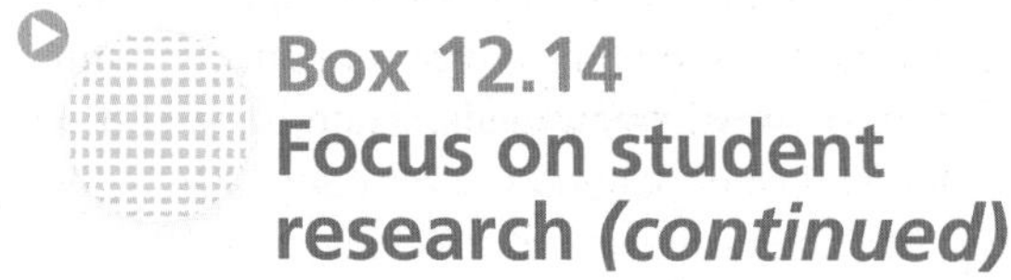

Box 12.14 Focus on student research (continued)

Osama reported the outcome of this analysis in his project report quoting the test statistics '*D*' and '*W*' and their associated degrees of freedom 'df' and probabilities 'p' in brackets:

> Tests for normality revealed that data for the variable 'number of legal music downloads in the past month' were not normally distributed [$D = 0.201$, $df = 674$, $p < 0.001$; $W = 0.815$, $df = 674$, $p < 0.001$].

your variable differ by chance from a comparable normal distribution for that variable. For either statistic, a probability of 0.05 means there is only a 5 per cent likelihood of the actual data distribution differing from a comparable normal distribution by chance alone. Therefore a probability of 0.05 or lower[2] for either statistic means that these data are not normally distributed. When interpreting probabilities from software packages, beware: owing to statistical rounding of numbers a probability of 0.000 does not mean zero, but that it is less than 0.001 (Box 12.14). If the probability is greater than 0.05, then the data are considered to be normally distributed. However, you need to be careful. With very large samples it is easy to get significant differences between a sample variable and a comparable normal distribution when actual differences are quite small. For this reason it is often helpful to also use a graph to make an informed decision.

Testing for significant relationships and differences

Testing the probability of a pattern such as a relationship between variables occurring by chance alone is known as **significance testing** (Berman Brown and Saunders 2008). As part of your research project, you might have collected sample data to examine the relationship between two variables. Once you have entered data into the analysis software, chosen the statistic and clicked on the appropriate icon, an answer will appear as if by magic! With most statistical analysis software this consists of a test statistic, the degrees of freedom (*df*) and, based on these, the probability (*p-value*) of your test result or one more extreme occurring by chance alone. If the probability of your test statistic or one more extreme having occurred by chance alone is very low (usually $p < 0.05$ or lower[3]), then you have a statistically significant relationship. Statisticians refer to this as rejecting the null hypothesis and accepting the hypothesis, often abbreviating the terms null hypothesis to H_0 and hypothesis to H_1. Consequently, rejecting a null hypothesis will mean rejecting a testable statement something like 'there is no significant difference between . . .' and accepting a testable statement something like 'there is a significant difference between . . .'. If

[2]A probability of 0.05 means that the probability of your test result or one more extreme occurring by chance alone, if there really was no difference, is 5 in 100, that is 1 in 20.

[3]A probability of 0.05 means that the probability of your test result or one more extreme occurring by chance alone, if there really was no difference in the population from which the sample was drawn, is 5 in 100, that is 1 in 20.

the probability of obtaining the test statistic or one more extreme by chance alone is higher than 0.05, then you conclude that the relationship is not statistically significant. Statisticians refer to this as accepting the **null hypothesis**. There may still be a relationship between the variables under such circumstances, but you cannot make the conclusion with any certainty.

Despite our discussion of hypothesis testing, albeit briefly, it is worth mentioning that a great deal of quantitative analysis, when written up, does not specify actual hypotheses. Rather, the theoretical underpinnings of the research and the research questions provide the context within which the probability of relationships between variables occurring by chance alone is tested. Thus, although hypothesis testing has taken place, it is often only discussed in terms of statistical significance.

The statistical significance of the relationship indicated by a test statistic is determined in part by your sample size (Section 7.2). One consequence of this is that it is very difficult to obtain a significant test statistic with a small sample. Conversely, by increasing your sample size, less obvious relationships and differences will be found to be statistically significant until, with extremely large samples, almost any relationship or difference will be significant (Anderson 2003). This is inevitable as your sample is becoming closer in size to the population from which it was selected. You therefore need to remember that small populations can make statistical tests insensitive, while very large samples can make statistical tests overly sensitive. There are two consequences to this:

- If you expect a difference, relationship or association will be small, you need to have a larger sample size.
- If you have a large sample and the difference, relationship or association is significant, you need to assess the practical significance of this relationship by calculating an effect size index such as Cohen's *d*. An excellent discussion of these can be found in Ellis (2010).

Type I and Type II errors

Inevitably, errors can occur when making inferences from samples. Statisticians refer to these as Type I and Type II errors. Blumberg et al. (2008) use the analogy of legal decisions to explain Type I and Type II errors. In their analogy they equate a Type I error to a person who is innocent being unjustly convicted and a Type II error to a person who is guilty of a crime being unjustly acquitted. In business and management research we would say that an error made by wrongly rejecting a null hypothesis and therefore accepting the hypothesis is a **Type I error**. Type I errors might involve you concluding that two variables are related when they are not, or incorrectly concluding that a sample statistic exceeds the value that would be expected by chance alone. This means you are rejecting your null hypothesis when you should not. The term '**statistical significance**' discussed earlier therefore refers to the probability of making a Type I error. A **Type II error** involves the opposite occurring. In other words, you accept your null hypothesis when it should be rejected. This means that Type II errors might involve you in concluding that two variables are not related when they are, or that a sample statistic does not exceed the value that would be expected by chance alone.

Given that a Type II error is the inverse of a Type I error, it follows that if we reduce our likelihood of making a Type I error by setting the significance level to 0.01 rather than 0.05, we increase our likelihood of making a Type II error by a corresponding amount. This is not an insurmountable problem, as researchers usually consider Type I errors more serious and prefer to take a small likelihood of saying something is true when it is not (Figure 12.14). It is therefore generally more important to minimise Type I than Type II errors.

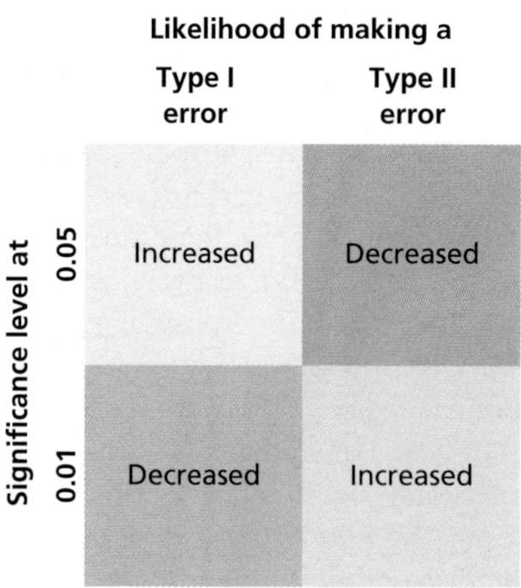

Figure 12.14 Type I and Type II errors

To test whether two variables are associated

Often descriptive or numerical data will be summarised as a two-way contingency table (such as Table 12.3). The **chi square test** enables you to find out how likely it is that the two variables are associated. It is based on a comparison of the observed values in the table with what might be expected if the two distributions were entirely independent. Therefore you are assessing the likelihood of the data in your table, or data more extreme, occurring by chance alone by comparing it with what you would expect if the two variables were independent of each other. This could be phrased as the null hypothesis: 'there is no significant association . . .'.

The test relies on:

- the categories used in the contingency table being mutually exclusive, so that each observation falls into only one category or class interval;
- no more than 25 per cent of the cells in the table having expected values of less than 5. For contingency tables of two rows and two columns, no expected values of less than 10 are preferable (Dancey and Reidy 2008).

If the latter assumption is not met, the accepted solution is to combine rows and columns where this produces meaningful data.

The chi square (χ^2) test calculates the probability that the data in your table, or data more extreme, could occur by chance alone. Most statistical analysis software does this automatically. However, if you are using a spreadsheet you will usually need to look up the probability in a 'critical values of chi square' table using your calculated chi square value and the degrees of freedom.[4] This table is included in most statistics textbooks. A probability of 0.05 means that there is only a 5 per cent likelihood of the data in your table occurring by chance alone, and is termed statistically significant. Therefore, a probability of 0.05 or smaller means you can be at least 95 per cent certain that the association between your two variables could not have occurred by chance factors alone. Remember, when interpreting probabilities from software packages, beware: owing to statistical rounding of numbers a probability of 0.000 does not mean zero, but that it is less than 0.001 (Box 12.15).

[4]Degrees of freedom are the number of values free to vary when computing a statistic. The number of degrees of freedom for a contingency table of at least 2 rows and 2 columns of data is calculated from (number of rows in the table 31) 3 (number of columns in the table 31).

Box 12.15 Focus on student research

Testing whether two variables are associated

As part of his research project, John wanted to find out whether there was a significant association between grade of respondent and gender. Earlier analysis using IBM SPSS Statistics had indicated that there were 385 respondents in his sample with no missing data for either variable. However, it had also highlighted the small numbers of respondents in the highest grade (GC01 to GC05) categories:

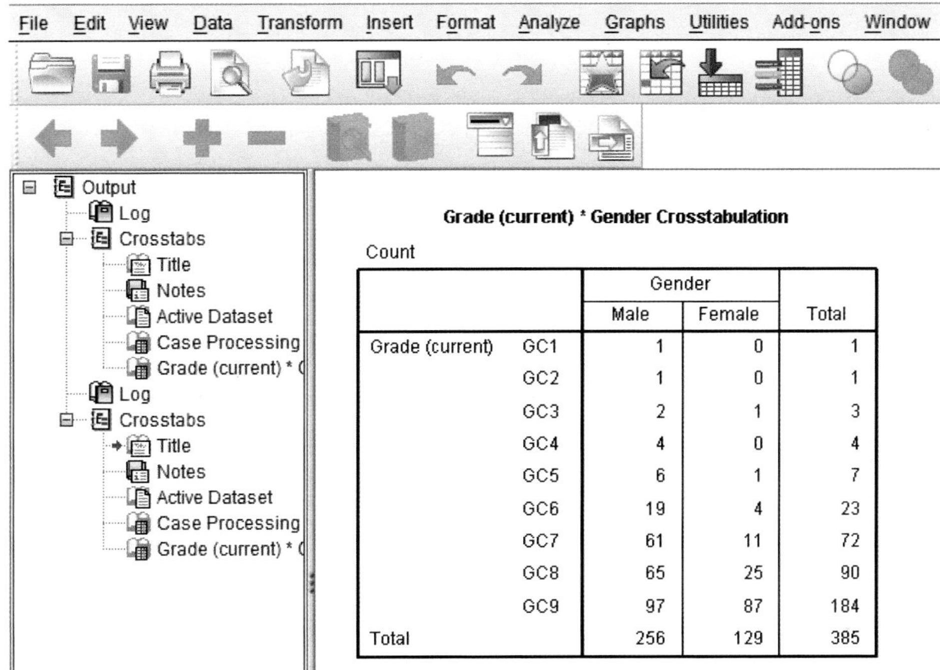

Grade (current) * Gender Crosstabulation

Count

		Gender		Total
		Male	Female	
Grade (current)	GC1	1	0	1
	GC2	1	0	1
	GC3	2	1	3
	GC4	4	0	4
	GC5	6	1	7
	GC6	19	4	23
	GC7	61	11	72
	GC8	65	25	90
	GC9	97	87	184
Total		256	129	385

Bearing in mind the assumptions of the chi square test, John decided to combine categories GC01 through GC05 to create a new grade GC01-5 using IBM SPSS Statistics (see top of next page).

He then used his analysis software to undertake a chi square test and calculate Cramer's V (see bottom of next page).

As can be seen, this resulted in an overall chi square value of 33.59 with 4 degrees of freedom (df).

The significance of .000 (Asymp. Sig.) meant that the probability of the values in his table occurring by chance alone was less than 0.001. He therefore concluded that the relationship between gender and grade was extremely unlikely to be explained by chance factors alone and quoted the statistic in his project report:

$$[x^2\ 33.59,\ df = 4,\ p < 0.001]^*$$

The Cramer's V value of .295, significant at the .000 level (Approx. Sig.), showed that the association between gender and grade, although weak, was positive. This meant that men (coded 1 whereas females were coded 2) were more likely to be employed at higher grades GC01–5 (coded using lower numbers). John also quoted this statistic in his project report:

$$[V_c = 0.295, p < 0.001]3 \quad v_c = 0.295, p = 0.0014$$

*You will have noticed that the computer printout in this box does not have a zero before the decimal point. This is because most software packages follow the North American convention, in contrast to the UK convention of placing a zero before the decimal point.

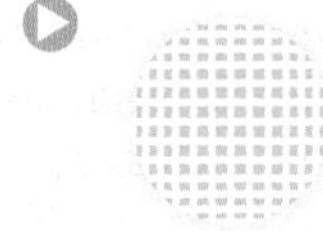

Box 12.15 Focus on student research *(continued)*

To explore this association further, John examined the cell values in relation to the row and column totals. Of males, 5 per cent were in higher grades (GC01–5) compared to less than 2 per cent of females. In contrast, only 38 per cent of males were in the lowest grade (GC09) compared with 67 per cent of females.

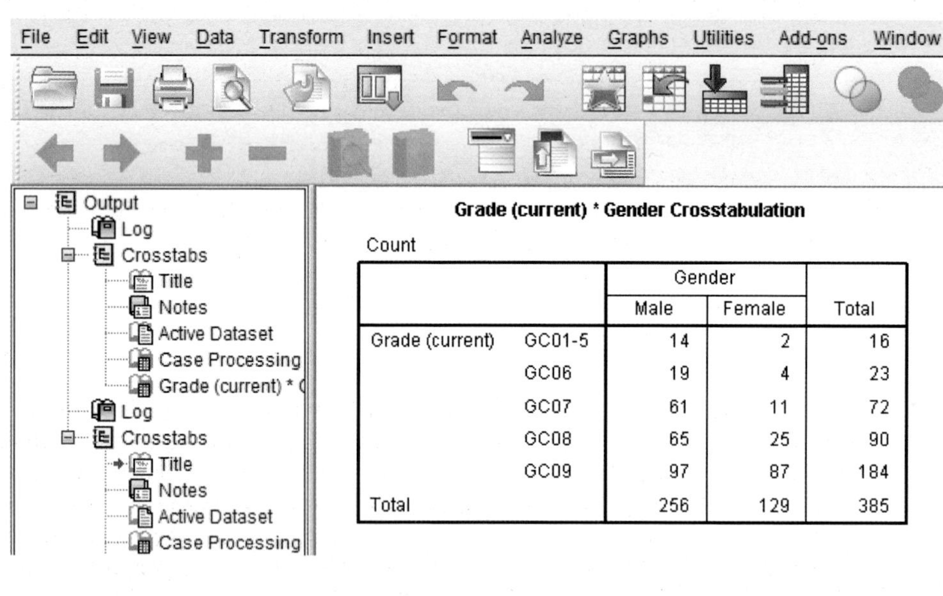

Grade (current) * Gender Crosstabulation

Count

		Gender		Total
		Male	Female	
Grade (current)	GC01-5	14	2	16
	GC06	19	4	23
	GC07	61	11	72
	GC08	65	25	90
	GC09	97	87	184
Total		256	129	385

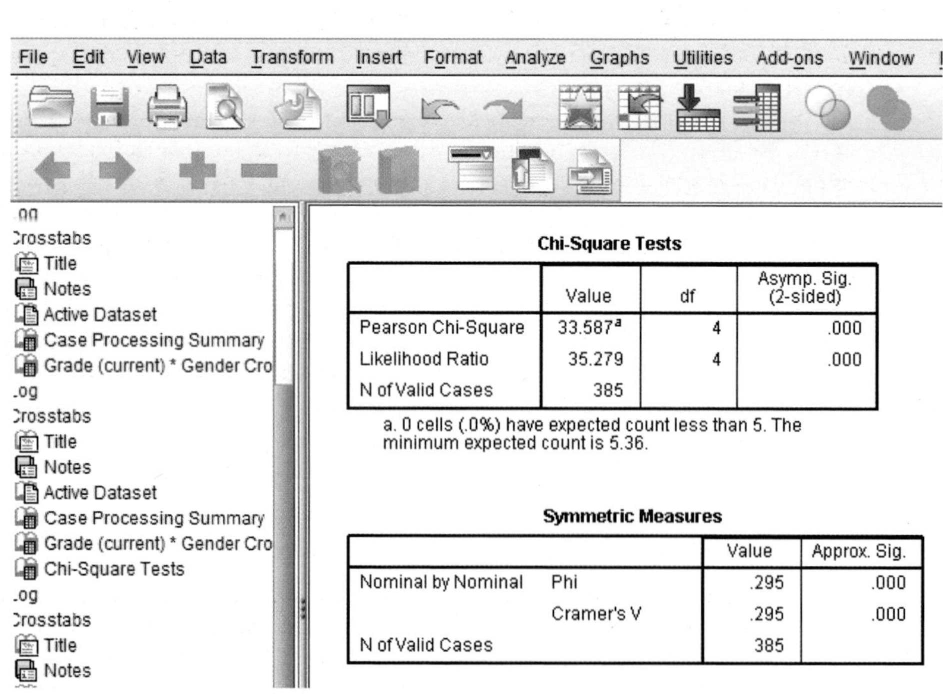

Chi-Square Tests

	Value	df	Asymp. Sig. (2-sided)
Pearson Chi-Square	33.587[a]	4	.000
Likelihood Ratio	35.279	4	.000
N of Valid Cases	385		

a. 0 cells (.0%) have expected count less than 5. The minimum expected count is 5.36.

Symmetric Measures

		Value	Approx. Sig.
Nominal by Nominal	Phi	.295	.000
	Cramer's V	.295	.000
N of Valid Cases		385	

Some software packages, such as IBM SPSS Statistics calculate the statistic **Cramer's V** alongside the chi square statistic (Box 12.15). If you include the value of Cramer's V in your research report, it is usual to do so in addition to the chi square statistic. Whereas the chi square statistic gives the probability that data in a table, or data more extreme, could occur by chance alone; Cramer's V measures the association between the two variables within the table on a scale where 0 represents no association and 1 represents perfect association. Because the value of Cramer's V is always between 0 and 1, the relative strengths of significant associations between different pairs of variables can be compared.

An alternative statistic used to measure the association between two variables is **Phi**. This statistic measures the association on a scale between – 1 (perfect negative association), through 0 (no association) to 1 (perfect association). However, unlike Cramer's V, using Phi to compare the relative strengths of significant associations between pairs of variables can be problematic. This is because, although values of Phi will only range between – 1 and 1 when measuring the association between two dichotomous variables, they may exceed these extremes when measuring the association for categorical variables where at least one of these variables has more than two categories. For this reason, we recommend that you use Phi only when comparing pairs of dichotomous variables.

To test whether two groups are different

Ranked data

Sometimes it is necessary to see whether the distribution of an observed set of values for each category of a variable differs from a specified distribution other than the normal distribution, for example whether your sample differs from the population from which it was selected. The **Kolmogorov–Smirnov test** enables you to establish this for ranked data (Kanji 2006). It is based on a comparison of the cumulative proportions of the observed values in each category with the cumulative proportions in the same categories for the specified population. Therefore you are testing the likelihood of the distribution of your observed data differing from that of the specified population by chance alone.

The Kolmogorov–Smirnov test calculates a *D* statistic to work out the probability of the two distributions differing by chance alone. Although the test statistic is not often found in analysis software other than for comparisons with a normal distribution (discussed earlier), it is relatively straightforward to calculate using a spreadsheet (Box 12.16). A reasonably clear description of this can be found in Cohen and Holliday (1996). Once calculated, you will need to look up the significance of your *D* value in a 'critical values of *D* for the Kolmogorov–Smirnov test' table. A probability of 0.05 means that there is only a 5 per cent likelihood that the two distributions differ by chance alone, and is termed statistically significant. Therefore a probability of 0.05 or smaller means you can be at least 95 per cent certain that the difference between your two distributions cannot be explained by chance factors alone.

Numerical data

If a numerical variable can be divided into two distinct groups using a descriptive variable, you can assess the likelihood of these groups being different using an **independent groups *t*-test**. This compares the difference in the means of the two groups using a measure of the spread of the scores. If the likelihood of any difference between these two groups occurring by chance alone is low, this will be represented by a large *t* statistic with a probability less than 0.05. This is termed statistically significant.

Box 12.16 Focus on student research

Testing the representativeness of a sample

Benson's research question was, 'To what extent do the espoused values of an organisation match the underlying cultural assumptions?' As part of his research, he sent a questionnaire to the 150 employees in the organisation where he worked and 97 of these responded. The responses from each category of employee in terms of their seniority within the organisation's hierarchy were as shown in the spreadsheet below.

The maximum difference between his observed cumulative proportion (that for respondents) and his specified cumulative proportion (that for total employees) was 0.034. This was the value of his *D* statistic. Consulting a 'critical values of *D* for the Kolmogorov–Smirnov test' table for a sample size of 97 revealed the probability that the two distributions did not differ by chance alone was less than 0.01, in other words, less than 1 per cent. He concluded that those employees who responded did not differ significantly from the total population in terms of their seniority within the organisation's hierarchy. This was stated in his research report:

> Statistical analysis showed the sample selected did not differ significantly from all employees in terms of their seniority within the organisation's hierarchy [$D = .034$, $p = .014$].

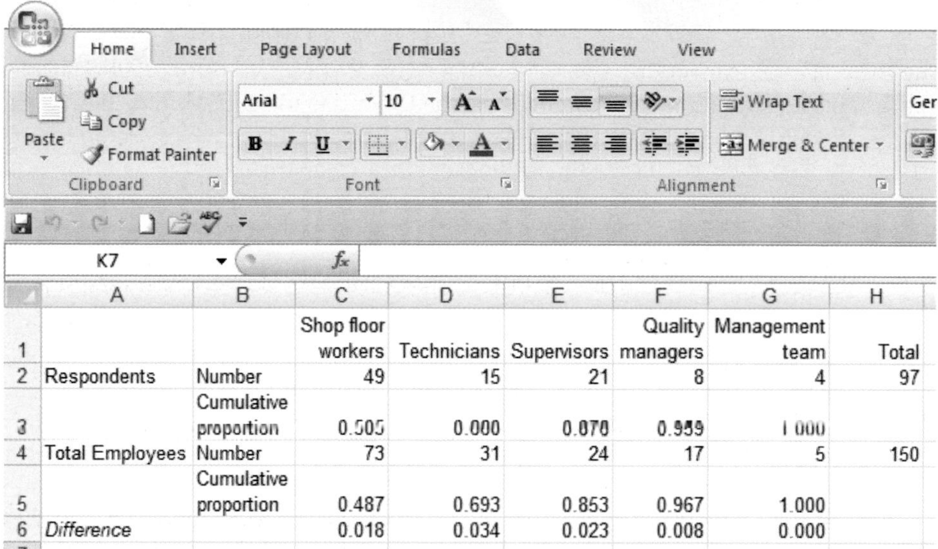

	A	B	C	D	E	F	G	H
1			Shop floor workers	Technicians	Supervisors	Quality managers	Management team	Total
2	Respondents	Number	49	15	21	8	4	97
3		Cumulative proportion	0.505	0.660	0.876	0.959	1.000	
4	Total Employees	Number	73	31	24	17	5	150
5		Cumulative proportion	0.487	0.693	0.853	0.967	1.000	
6	*Difference*		0.018	0.034	0.023	0.008	0.000	

Alternatively, you might have numerical data for two variables that measure the same feature but under different conditions. Your research could focus on the effects of an intervention such as employee counselling. As a consequence, you would have pairs of data that measure work performance before and after counselling for each case. To assess the likelihood of any difference between your two variables (each half of the pair) occurring by chance alone, you would use a **paired *t*-test** (Box 12.17). Although the calculation of this is slightly different, your interpretation would be the same as for the independent groups *t*-test.

Although the ***t*-test** assumes that the data are normally distributed (discussed earlier and Section 12.3), this can be ignored without too many problems even with sample

Box 12.17 Focus on management research

Testing whether groups are different

Millward and Postmes's (2010) paper in the *British Journal of Management* considers the relationship between the extent employees identify with their organisation and their productivity, demonstrating that organisational identification does result in a benefit to sales.

Using an online questionnaire delivered to 51 customer business managers, data collected included responses to a one-item statement to measure their strength of identification (measured on a seven-point scale of agreement/disagreement) with each of four foci:

- The specific customer team in the retail outlet in which the employee worked (customer team).
- The operating company to whom the manager reported (operating company).
- The fellow customer managers within the operating company irrespective of retail outlet (sales managers).
- The total business unit (organisation).

These were integrated with secondary data recording sales turnover prior to analysis..

Initial analysis focused upon significant differences in strength of identification across the four foci (customer team, operating company, sales managers, organisation), these differences being tested using ANOVA and paired *t*-tests. ANOVA was used to see if there was a significant difference in strength of identification across the four foci. The *F* ratio value of 2730.56 with 1 and 54 degrees of freedom meaning the probability of the differences in strength across the four foci occurring by chance alone was less than 0.01. This allowed Millward and Postmes (2010: 332) to state that there was 'a significant difference across foci in strength of identification.'

Millward and Postmes presented the results of a series of paired t-tests between the four foci as part of a single table:

t-tests[b]

Foci	operating company identity	organisational identity	sales manager identity
customer team identity	0.285	6.25*	4.10*
operating company identity		5.17*	4.16*
organisational identity			2.25**

[b]$df = 54$; *$p < 0.01$; **$p < 0.05$

These *t*-tests allowed Millward and Postmes to state that social identification with the customer team was significantly greater than with the organisation [$t = 6.25$, $df = 54$, $p < 0.01$] or with the sales managers [$t = 4.10$, $df = 54$, $p < 0.01$]. They were also able to report that there was no significant difference between customer team identification and operating company identification [$t = 0.285$, $df = 54$, $p > 0.05$]. Finally they could state that identification with the operating company was significantly greater than with the organisation [$t = 5.17$, $df = 54$, $p < 0.01$], or with the sales managers [$t = 4.16$, $df = 54$, $p < 0.01$].

These results were also considered in relation to three of their hypotheses: (Millward and Postmes 2010: 330), namely:

> *H1a: Customer team identification will be stronger than operating company, sales manager and business unit (organisational) identification.*
>
> *H1b: Operating company identification will be significantly stronger than customer team, sales manager and business unit (organisational) identification.*

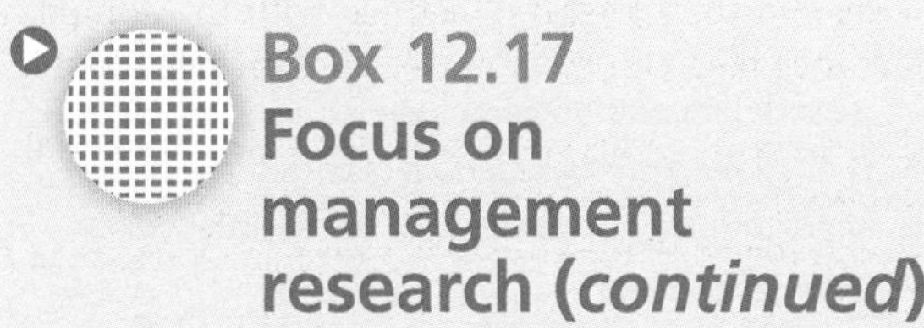

Box 12.17 Focus on management research (*continued*)

H2: Business unit (organisational) identification is less likely to be as strong as for either customer team or operating company memberships.

They argued that the findings provided partial support for hypotheses 1a and 1b, in so far as both customer team and operating company identification affording the highest levels of identification together. For hypothesis 2, both customer team and operating company foci were significantly higher than organisational identification.

sizes of less than 30 (Hays 1994). The assumption that the data for the two groups have the same variance (standard deviation squared) can also be ignored provided that the two samples are of similar size (Hays 1994). If the data are skewed or the sample size is small, the most appropriate statistical test is the Mann-Whitney *U* Test. This test is the non-parametric equivalent of the independent groups *t*-test (Dancey and Reidy 2008). Consequently, if the likelihood of any difference between these two groups occurring by chance alone is low, this will be represented by a large *U* statistic with a probability less than 0.05. This is termed statistically significant.

To test whether three or more groups are different

If a numerical variable is divided into three or more distinct groups using a descriptive variable, you can assess the likelihood of these groups being different occurring by chance alone by using **one-way analysis of variance** or one-way **ANOVA** (Table 12.5). As you can gather from its name, ANOVA analyses the **variance**, that is, the spread of data values, within and between groups of data by comparing means. The *F* ratio or *F* statistic represents these differences. If the likelihood of any difference between groups occurring by chance alone is low, this will be represented by a large *F* ratio with a probability of less than 0.05. This is termed statistically significant (Box 12.17).

The following assumptions need to be met before using one-way ANOVA. More detailed discussion is available in Hays (1994) and Dancey and Reidy (2008).

- Each data value is independent and does not relate to any of the other data values. This means that you should not use one-way ANOVA where data values are related in some way, such as the same case being tested repeatedly.
- The data for each group are normally distributed (discussed earlier and Section 12.3). This assumption is not particularly important provided that the number of cases in each group is large (30 or more).
- The data for each group have the same variance (standard deviation squared). However, provided that the number of cases in the largest group is not more than 1.5 times that of the smallest group, this appears to have very little effect on the test results.

Assessing the strength of relationship

If your data set contains ranked or numerical data, it is likely that, as part of your exploratory data analysis, you will already have plotted the relationship between cases for these ranked or numerical variables using a scatter graph (Figure 12.12). Such relationships might include those between weekly sales of a new product and those of a similar established product, or age of employees and their length of service with the company. These examples emphasise the fact that your data can contain two sorts of relationship:

- those where a change in one variable is accompanied by a change in another variable but it is not clear which variable caused the other to change, a **correlation**;
- those where a change in one or more (independent) variables causes a change in another (dependent) variable, a cause-and-effect relationship.

To assess the strength of relationship between pairs of variables

A **correlation coefficient** enables you to quantify the strength of the linear relationship between two ranked or numerical variables. This coefficient (usually represented by the letter *r*) can take on any value between +1 and − 1 (Figure 12.15). A value of +1 represents a perfect **positive correlation**. This means that the two variables are precisely related and that as values of one variable increase, values of the other variable will increase. By contrast, a value of − 1 represents a perfect **negative correlation**. Again, this means that the two variables are precisely related; however, as the values of one variable increase those of the other decrease. Correlation coefficients between +1 and − 1 represent weaker positive and negative correlations, a value of 0 meaning the variables are perfectly independent. Within business research it is extremely unusual to obtain perfect correlations.

For data collected from a sample you will need to know the probability of your correlation coefficient having occurred by chance alone. Most analysis software calculates this probability automatically (Box 12.18). As outlined earlier, if this probability is very low (usually less than 0.05) then it is considered statistically significant. If the probability is greater than 0.05 then your relationship is not statistically significant.

If both your variables contain numerical data you should use **Pearson's product moment correlation coefficient** (PMCC) to assess the strength of relationship (Table 12.5). Where these data are from a sample then the sample should have been selected at random. However, if one or both of your variables contain rank data you cannot use PMCC, but will need to use a correlation coefficient that is calculated using ranked data. Such rank correlation coefficients represent the degree of agreement between the two sets of rankings. Before calculating the rank correlation coefficient, you will need to ensure that the data for both variables are ranked. Where one of the variables is numerical this will necessitate converting these data to ranked data. Subsequently, you have a choice of rank correlation coefficients. The two used most widely in business and management research are **Spearman's rank correlation coefficient** (Spearman's rho) and **Kendall's rank correlation coefficient** (Kendall's tau). Where data is being used from a sample, both these rank correlation coefficients assume that the sample is selected at random and the data are ranked (ordinal). Given this, it is not surprising that whenever you can use

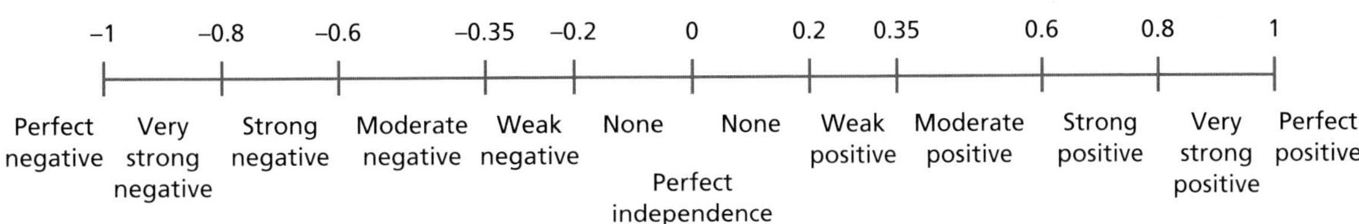

Figure 12.15 Values of the correlation coefficient
Sources: Developed from earlier editions; Hair et al. (2006)

Box 12.18 Focus on student research

Assessing the strength of relationship between pairs of variables

As part of his research project, Hassan obtained data from a company on the number of television advertisements, number of enquiries and number of sales of their product. These data were entered into the statistical analysis software. He wished to discover whether there were any relationships between the following pairs of these variables:

- number of television advertisements and number of enquiries;
- number of television advertisements and number of sales;
- number of enquiries and number of sales.

As the data were numerical, he used the statistical analysis software to calculate Pearson's product moment correlation coefficients for all pairs of variables. The output was a correlation matrix below.

Hassan's matrix is symmetrical because correlation implies only a relationship rather than a cause-and-effect relationship. The value in each cell of the matrix is the correlation coefficient. Thus, the correlation between the number of advertisements and the number of enquiries is 0.362. This coefficient shows that there is a weak to moderate positive relationship between the number of television advertisements and the number of enquiries. The (**) highlights that the probability of this correlation coefficient occurring by chance alone is less than or equal to 0.01 (1 per cent). This correlation coefficient is therefore statistically significant.

Using the data in this matrix Hassan concluded that:

> There is a statistically significant strong positive relationship between the number of enquiries and the number of sales ($r = .726, p < .01$) and a statistically significant but weak to moderate relationship between the number of television advertisements and the number of enquiries ($r = .362$, $p < .01$). However, there is no statistically significant relationship between the number of television advertisements and the number of sales ($r = .204$, $p > .05$).

File Edit View Data Transform Insert Format Analyze Graphs Utilities Add-ons Window Help

Output
Log
Correlations
Title
Notes
Active Dataset
Correlations
Log
Frequencies
Title
Notes
Active Dataset
Statistics
Number of adverti

Correlations

		Number of advertisements	Number of enquiries	Number of sales
Number of advertisements	Pearson Correlation	1	.362**	.204
	Sig. (2-tailed)		.006	.131
	N	61	57	56
Number of enquiries	Pearson Correlation	.362**	1	.726**
	Sig. (2-tailed)	.006		.000
	N	57	62	59
Number of sales	Pearson Correlation	.204	.726**	1
	Sig. (2-tailed)	.131	.000	
	N	56	59	61

**. Correlation is significant at the 0.01 level (2-tailed).

Spearman's rank correlation coefficient you can also use Kendall's rank correlation coefficient. However, if your data for a variable contain tied ranks, Kendall's rank correlation coefficient is generally considered to be the more appropriate of these coefficients to use. Although each of the correlation coefficients discussed uses a different formula in its calculation, the resulting coefficient is interpreted in the same way as PMCC.

To assess the strength of a cause-and-effect relationship between dependent and independent variables

In contrast to the correlation coefficient, the **coefficient of determination** (sometimes known as the **regression coefficient**) enables you to assess the strength of relationship between a numerical dependent variable and one or more numerical independent variables. Once again, where these data have been selected from a sample, the sample must have been selected at random. For a dependent variable and one (or perhaps two) independent variables you will have probably already plotted this relationship on a scatter graph. If you have more than two independent variables this is unlikely as it is very difficult to represent four or more scatter graph axes visually!

The coefficient of determination (represented by r^2) can take on any value between 0 and +1. It measures the proportion of the variation in a dependent variable (amount of sales) that can be explained statistically by the independent variable (marketing expenditure) or variables (marketing expenditure, number of sales staff, etc.). This means that if all the variation in amount of sales can be explained by the marketing expenditure and the number of sales staff, the coefficient of determination will be 1. If 50 per cent of the variation can be explained, the coefficient of determination will be 0.5, and if none of the variation can be explained, the coefficient will be 0 (Box 12.19). Within our research we have rarely obtained a coefficient above 0.8.

The process of calculating coefficient of determination and regression equation using one independent variable is normally termed **regression analysis**. Calculating a **coefficient of multiple determination** (or **multiple regression coefficient**) and regression equation using two or more independent variables is termed **multiple regression analysis**. The calculations and interpretation required by multiple regression are relatively complicated, and we advise you to use statistical analysis software and consult a detailed statistics textbook that also explains how to use the software, such as Field (2009). Most statistical analysis software will automatically calculate the significance of the coefficient of multiple determination for sample data. A very low significance value (usually less than 0.05) means that your coefficient is unlikely to have occurred by chance alone. A value greater than 0.05 means you can conclude that your coefficient of multiple determination could have occurred by chance alone.

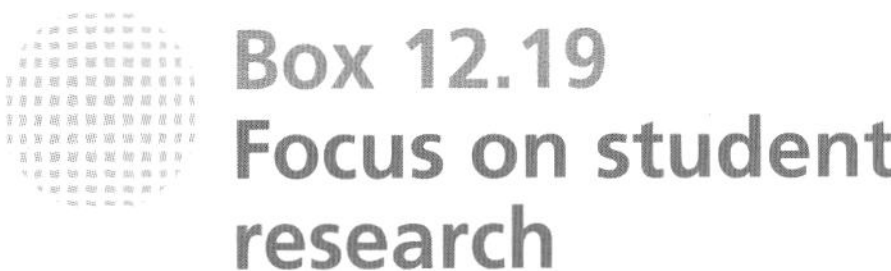

Box 12.19 Focus on student research

Assessing a cause-and-effect relationship

As part of her research project, Arethea wanted to assess the relationship between all the employees' annual salaries and the number of years each had been employed by an organisation. She believed that an employee's annual salary would be dependent on the number of years for which she or he had been employed (the independent variable). Arethea entered these data into her analysis software and calculated a coefficient of determination (r^2) of 0.37.

As she was using data for all employees of the firm (the total population) rather than a sample, the probability of her coefficient occurring by chance alone was 0. She therefore concluded that 37 per cent of the variation in current employees' salary could be explained by the number of years they had been employed by the organisation.

To predict the value of a variable from one or more other variables

Regression analysis can also be used to predict the values of a dependent variable given the values of one or more independent variables by calculating a **regression equation**. You may wish to predict the amount of sales for a specified marketing expenditure and number of sales staff. You would represent this as a regression equation:

$$AoS_i = \alpha + \beta_1 ME_i + \beta_2 NSS_i$$

where:
AoS is the amount of sales
ME is the marketing expenditure
NSS is the number of sales staff
α is the regression constant
β_1 and β_2 are the beta coefficients

This equation can be translated as stating:

$$\textit{Amount of sales}_i = \textit{value} + (\beta_1 * \textit{Marketing expenditure}_i) + (\beta_2 * \textit{Number of sales staff}_i)$$

Using regression analysis you would calculate the values of the constant coefficient α and the slope coefficients β_1 and β_2 from data you had already collected on amount of sales, marketing expenditure and number of sales staff. A specified marketing expenditure and number of sales staff could then be substituted into the regression equation to predict the amount of sales that would be generated. When calculating a regression equation you need to ensure the following assumptions are met:

- The relationship between dependent and independent variables is linear. **Linearity** refers to the degree to which the change in the dependent variable is related to the change in the independent variables. Linearity can easily be examined through residual plots (these are usually drawn by the analysis software). Two things may influence the linearity. First, individual cases with extreme values on one or more variables (outliers) may violate the assumption of linearity. It is, therefore, important to identify these outliers and, if appropriate, exclude them from the regression analysis. Second, the values for one or more variables may violate the assumption of linearity. For these variables the data values may need to be transformed. Techniques for this can be found in other, more specialised books on multivariate data analysis, for example Anderson (2003).
- The extent to which the data values for the dependent and independent variables have equal variances (this term was explained earlier in Section 12.4), also known as **homoscedasticity**. Again, analysis software usually contains statistical tests for equal variance. For example, the Levene test for homogeneity of variance measures the equality of variances for a single pair of variables. If **heteroscedasticity** (that is, unequal variances) exists, it may still be possible to carry out your analysis. Further details of this can again be found in more specialised books on multivariate analysis, such as Anderson (2003).
- Absence of correlation between two or more independent variables (**collinearity** or **multicollinearity**), as this makes it difficult to determine the separate effects of individual variables. The simplest diagnostic is to use the correlation coefficients, extreme collinearity being represented by a correlation coefficient of 1. The rule of thumb is that the presence of high correlations (generally 0.90 and above) indicates substantial collinearity (Hair et al. 2006). Other common measures include the tolerance value and its inverse – the **variance inflation factor** (VIF). Hair *et al.* (2006) recommend

that a very small tolerance value (0.10 or below) or a large VIF value (10 or above) indicates high collinearity.
- The data for the independent variables and dependent variable are normally distributed (discussed earlier in this section and Section 12.3).

The coefficient of determination, r^2 (discussed earlier), can be used as a measure of how good a predictor your regression equation is likely to be. If your equation is a perfect predictor then the coefficient of determination will be 1. If the equation can predict only 50 per cent of the variation, then the coefficient of determination will be 0.5, and if the equation predicts none of the variation, the coefficient will be 0. The coefficient of multiple determination (R^2) indicates the degree of the goodness of fit for your estimated multiple regression equation. It can be interpreted as how good a predictor your multiple regression equation is likely to be. It represents the proportion of the variability in the dependent variable that can be explained by your multiple regression equation. This means that when multiplied by 100, the coefficient of multiple determination can be interpreted as the percentage of variation in the dependent variable that can be explained by the estimated regression equation. The adjusted R^2 statistic (which takes into account the number of independent variables in your regression equation) is preferred by some researchers as it helps avoid overestimating the impact of adding an independent variable on the amount of variability explained by the estimated regression equation.

The *t*-test and *F*-test are used to work out the probability of the relationship represented by your regression analysis having occurred by chance. In simple linear regression (with one independent and one dependent variable), the *t*-test and *F*-test will give you the same answer. However, in multiple regression, the *t*-test is used to find out the probability of the relationship between each of the individual independent variables and the dependent variable occurring by chance. In contrast, the *F*-test is used to find out the overall probability of the relationship between the dependent variable and all the independent variables occurring by chance. The *t* distribution table and the *F* distribution table are used to determine whether a *t*-test or an *F*-test is significant by comparing the results with the *t* distribution and *F* distribution respectively, given the degrees of freedom and the predefined significance level.

Examining trends

When examining longitudinal data the first thing we recommend you do is to draw a line graph to obtain a visual representation of the trend (Figure 12.7). Subsequent to this, statistical analyses can be undertaken. Three of the more common uses of such analyses are:

- to explore the trend or relative change for a single variable over time;
- to compare trends or the relative change for variables measured in different units or of different magnitudes;
- to determine the long-term trend and forecast future values for a variable.

These were summarised earlier in Table 12.5.

To explore the trend

To answer some research question(s) and meet some objectives you may need to explore the trend for one variable. One way of doing this is to use **index numbers** to compare the relative magnitude for each data value (case) over time rather than using the actual data value. Index numbers are also widely used in business publications and by organisations.

Box 12.20 Focus on student research

Forecasting number of road injury accidents

As part of her research project, Nimmi had obtained data on the number of road injury accidents and the number of drivers breath tested for alcohol in 39 police force areas. In addition, she obtained data on the total population (in thousands) for each of these areas from the most recent census. Nimmi wished to find out if it was possible to predict the number of road injury accidents (*RIA*) in each police area (her dependent variable) using the number of drivers breath tested (*BT*) and the total population in thousands (*POP*) for each of the police force areas (independent variables). This she represented as an equation:

$$RIA_i = \alpha + \beta_1 BT_i + \beta_2 POP_i$$

Nimmi entered her data into the analysis software and undertook a multiple regression. She scrolled

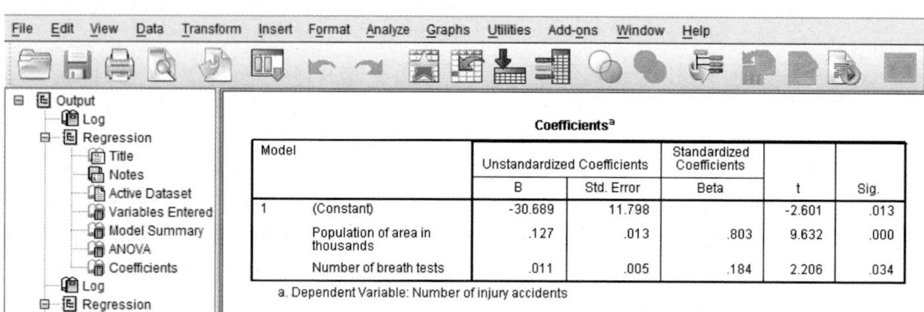

Coefficients[a]

Model		Unstandardized Coefficients B	Unstandardized Coefficients Std. Error	Standardized Coefficients Beta	t	Sig.
1	(Constant)	-30.689	11.798		-2.601	.013
	Population of area in thousands	.127	.013	.803	9.632	.000
	Number of breath tests	.011	.005	.184	2.206	.034

a. Dependent Variable: Number of injury accidents

down the output file and found the table headed 'Coefficients' (see above). Nimmi substituted the 'unstandardized coefficients' into her regression equation (after rounding the values):

$$RIA_i = -30.689 + 0.011\ BT_i + 0.127\ POP_i$$

This meant she could now predict the number of road injury accidents for a police area of different populations for different numbers of drivers breath tested for alcohol. For example, the number of road injury accidents for an area of 500,000 population in which 10,000 drivers were breath tested for alcohol can now be estimated:

$$-30.689 + (0.011 \times 10000) + (0.127 \times 500)$$
$$= -30.689 + 110 + 49 + 63.5$$
$$= 81.8$$

In order to check the usefulness of these estimates, Nimmi scrolled back up her output and looked at the results of R^2, *t* test and *F*-test.

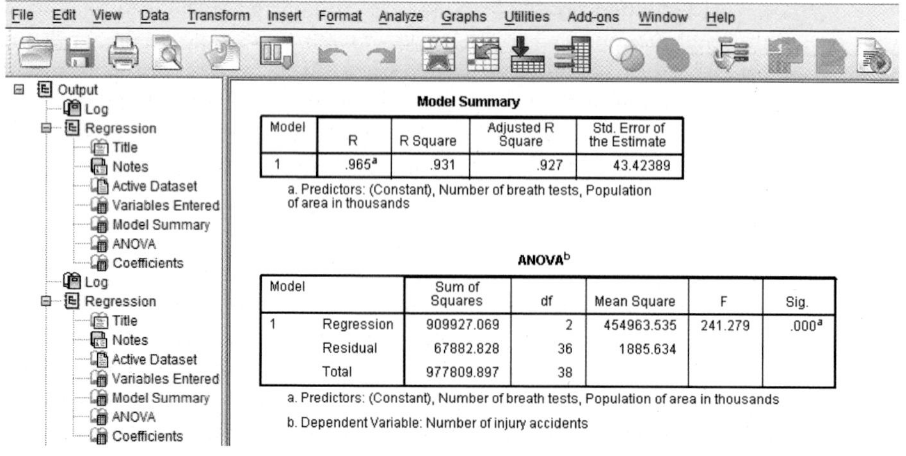

Model Summary

Model	R	R Square	Adjusted R Square	Std. Error of the Estimate
1	.965[a]	.931	.927	43.42389

a. Predictors: (Constant), Number of breath tests, Population of area in thousands

ANOVA[b]

Model		Sum of Squares	df	Mean Square	F	Sig.
1	Regression	909927.069	2	454963.535	241.279	.000[a]
	Residual	67882.828	36	1885.634		
	Total	977809.897	38			

a. Predictors: (Constant), Number of breath tests, Population of area in thousands

b. Dependent Variable: Number of injury accidents

The R^2 and adjusted R^2 values of 0.965 and 0.931 respectively both indicated that there was a high degree of goodness of fit of her regression model. It also meant that over 90 per cent of variance in the dependent variable (the number of road injury accidents) could be explained by the regression model. The F-test result was 241.279 with a significance ('Sig.') of .000. This meant that the probability of these results occurring by chance was less than 0.001. Therefore, a significant relationship was present between the number of road injury accidents in an area and the population of the area, and the number of drivers breath tested for alcohol.

The t-test results for the individual regression coefficients (shown in the first extract) for the two independent variables were 9.632 and 2.206. Once again, the probability of both these results occurring by chance was less than 0.05, being less than 0.001 for the independent variable population of area in thousands and 0.034 for the independent variable number of breath tests. This means that the regression coefficients for these variables were both statistically significant at the $p < 0.05$ level.

The *Financial Times* share indices such as the FTSE 100 (Box 12.21) and the Retail Price Index are well-known examples.

Although such indices can involve quite complex calculations, they all compare change over time against a base period. The **base period** is normally given the value of 100 (or 1000 in the case of many share indices, including the FTSE 100), and change is calculated relative to this. Thus a value greater than 100 would represent an increase relative to the base period, and a value less than 100 a decrease.

To calculate simple index numbers for each case of a longitudinal variable you use the following formula:

$$\text{data value for case index number of case} = \frac{\text{data value for case}}{\text{data value for base period}} \times 100$$

Thus, if a company's sales were 125, 000 units in 2007 (base period) and 150 000 units in 2008, the index number for 2007 would be 100 and for 2008 it would be 120.

To compare trends

To answer some other research question(s) and to meet the associated objectives you may need to compare trends between two or more variables measured in different units or at different magnitudes. For example, to compare changes in prices of fuel oil and coal over time is difficult as the prices are recorded for different units (litres and tonnes). One way of overcoming this is to use index numbers (Section 12.4) and compare the relative changes in the value of the index rather than actual figures. The index numbers for each variable are calculated in the same way as outlined earlier.

To determine the trend and forecasting

The trend can be estimated by drawing a freehand line through the data on a line graph. However, these data are often subject to variations such as seasonal fluctuations, and so this method is not very accurate. A straightforward way of overcoming this is to calculate a moving average for the time series of data values. Calculating a **moving average** involves replacing each value in the time series with the mean of that value and those values directly preceding and following it (Morris 2012). This smoothes out the variation

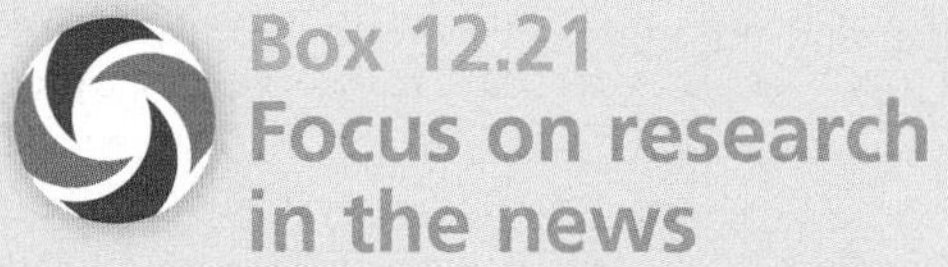

Box 12.21
Focus on research in the news

FT

Resource stocks set to skew FTSE 100

The Dow Jones Industrial Average has long had its critics. As the index is weighted by share prices and not market value, it can be skewed by the performance of companies with the highest nominal stock price. It is for that reason many investment banks and brokerages ignore the Dow and use the S&P 500 instead, which adjusts for the size of its constituents.

Might the same be about to happen to the FTSE 100? Not because of the way it is calculated (like the S&P, it is weighted by market capitalisation) but because of the growing influence of oil and commodity stocks. Could investors turn to other indices much better balanced than the UK's benchmark?

Mining, and oil and gas companies – led by BP, Royal Dutch Shell, BG, BHP Billiton, Rio Tinto and Anglo American – now account for just over one-third of the blue-chip FTSE 100 capitalisation, according to index compiler FTSE. And that figure is likely to rise over the next six months. The anticipated inclusion of Glencore, the Swiss-based commodities group, in the FTSE 100 at the end of the month will tilt the index further towards resources and overseas trade. At the midpoint of the IPO range, Glencore will be valued at £37bn (including money raised). To put that figure in perspective, it is about 2.4 per cent of the FTSE 100.

Glencore, which is being fast-tracked into the benchmark index, could be joined later this year by Vallar, the natural resources investment company founded by Nathaniel Rothschild, and New World Resources, a Czech coal producer in the process of reincorporating in Britain. That would bring the proportion of resources stocks in the FTSE 100 to almost one-fifth and increase the index's exposure to emerging markets and countries such as the Democratic Republic of Congo, Indonesia and Colombia. That could make the FTSE 100 and, by extension, the FTSE All-Share index – which also has a large amount of cash benchmarked against it – more prone to sharper one-day rises and falls. This is because resource stocks are tied to commodities prices which, as we have seen this week, can be very volatile.

The mining sector has a beta – a measure of how it performs relative to the overall market – of 1.9, according to Bloomberg. That means it goes up or down 1.9 times as fast as the market. However, the sensitivity of resource stocks can be exaggerated. BP and Shell have not been pure plays on the oil price for the past decade, while Randgold Resources and Fresnillo have respectively lagged behind the gold and silver price this year. Arguably, resource stocks are more influenced by the performance of the global economy (in particular the US and China) than by any underlying commodity. Glencore's impact on the London stock market has been overstated. As it has a limited free float (for the first year anyway), it will have a weighting of just 0.44 per cent. And, in any case, what is so wrong with tracking an index that reflects the performance of the global economy?

Surely, if you work in the UK and own UK assets, it is a good idea to have some investments that aren't geared to the performance of the UK economy, even if that brings some currency risk. An increasing number of companies report and declare dividends in dollars and these have to be translated into sterling. That said, the weighting of resource stocks in the FTSE 100 is a concern, but so too is the fact that 15 companies now account for half its market capitalisation. For a variety of reasons, including the fact that they are bid-proof, these mega-cap companies have performed poorly over the past decade and acted as a drag on the entire London market. Since 2000, they have delivered negative returns and have hugely underperformed the faster growing mid-caps. So it's not just domicile or sector exposure that investors need to think about, size also matters. Big has not been beautiful in recent years, which is something to ponder ahead of the Glencore flotation.

Source: From 'Resource stocks set to skew FTSE 100', Neil Hume (2011) *Financial Times*, 6 May.

in the data so that you can see the trend more clearly. The calculation of a moving average is relatively straightforward using either a spreadsheet or statistical analysis software.

Once the trend has been established, it is possible to forecast future values by continuing the trend forward for time periods for which data have not been collected. This involves calculating the **long-term trend** – that is, the amount by which values are changing in each time period after variations have been smoothed out. Once again, this is relatively straightforward to calculate using analysis software. Forecasting can also be undertaken using other statistical methods, including regression analysis.

If you are using regression for your time series analysis, the **Durbin–Watson statistic** can be used to discover whether the value of your dependent variable at time t is related to its value at the previous time period, commonly referred to as $t - 1$ This situation, known as **autocorrelation** or **serial correlation**, is important as it means that the results of your regression analysis are less likely to be reliable. The Durbin–Watson statistic ranges in value from zero to four. A value of two indicates no autocorrelation. A value towards zero indicates positive autocorrelation. Conversely, a value towards four indicates negative autocorrelation. More detailed discussion of the Durbin–Watson test can be found in other, more specialised books on multivariate data analysis, for example Anderson (2003).

12.6 Summary

- Data for quantitative analysis can be collected and subsequently coded at different scales of measurement. The data type (precision of measurement) will constrain the data presentation, summary and analysis techniques you can use.
- Data are entered for computer analysis as a data matrix in which each column usually represents a variable and each row a case. Your first variable should be a unique identifier to facilitate error checking.
- All data should, with few exceptions, be recorded using numerical codes to facilitate analyses.
- Where possible, you should use existing coding schemes to enable comparisons.
- For primary data you should include pre-set codes on the data collection form to minimise coding after collection. For variables where responses are not known, you will need to develop a codebook after data have been collected for the first 50 to 100 cases.
- You should enter codes for all data values, including missing data.
- Your data matrix must be checked for errors.
- Your initial analysis should explore data using both tables and diagrams. Your choice of table or diagram will be influenced by your research question(s) and objectives, the aspects of the data you wish to emphasise, and the measurement precision with which the data were recorded.

  This may involve using:
  - tables to show specific values;
  - bar charts, multiple bar charts, histograms and, occasionally, pictograms to show highest and lowest values;
  - line graphs to show trends;
  - pie charts and percentage component bar charts to show proportions;
  - box plots to show distributions;
  - scatter graphs to show relationships between variables.
- Subsequent analyses will involve describing your data and exploring relationships using statistics. Your choice of statistics will be influenced by your research question(s) and objectives, your sample size the measurement precision at which the data were recorded

and whether the data are normally distributed. Your analysis may involve using statistics such as:

- the mean, median and mode to describe the central tendency;
- the inter-quartile range and the standard deviation to describe the dispersion;
- chi square, Cramer's V and phi to test whether two variables are significantly associated;
- Kolmogorov–Smirnov to test whether the values differ significantly from a specified population;
- *t*-tests and ANOVA to test whether groups are significantly different;
- correlation and regression to assess the strength of relationships between variables;
- regression analysis to predict values.

- Longitudinal data may necessitate selecting different statistical techniques such as:
  - index numbers to establish a trend or to compare trends between two or more variables measured in different units or at different magnitudes;
  - moving averages and regression analysis to determine the trend and forecast.

Self-check questions

Help with these questions is available at the end of the chapter.

12.1 The following secondary data have been obtained from the Park Trading Company's audited annual accounts:

Year end	Income	Expenditure
2004	11000000	9500000
2005	15200000	12900000
2006	17050000	14000000
2007	17900000	14900000
2008	19000000	16100000
2009	18700000	17200000
2010	17100000	18100000
2011	17700000	19500000
2012	19900000	20000000

a Which are the variables and which are the cases?

b Sketch a possible data matrix for these data for entering into a spreadsheet.

12.2 a How many variables will be generated from the following request?

Please tell me up to five things you like about this film. For office use

.... ❑ ❑ ❑

.... ❑ ❑ ❑

.... ❑ ❑ ❑

.... ❑ ❑ ❑

.... ❑ ❑ ❑

b How would you go about devising a coding scheme for these variables from a survey of 500 cinema patrons?

12.3 a Illustrate the data from the Park Trading Company's audited annual accounts (self-check question 12.1) to show trends in income and expenditure.

b What does your diagram emphasise?

c What diagram would you use to emphasise the years with the lowest and highest income?

12.4 As part of research into the impact of television advertising on donations by credit card to a major disaster appeal, data have been collected on the number of viewers reached and the number of donations each day for the past two weeks.

a Which diagram or diagrams would you use to explore these data?

b Give reasons for your choice.

12.5 a Which measures of central tendency and dispersion would you choose to describe the Park Trading Company's income (self-check question 12.1) over the period 2004–12?

b Give reasons for your choice.

12.6 A colleague has collected data from a sample of 74 students. He presents you with the following output from the statistical analysis software:

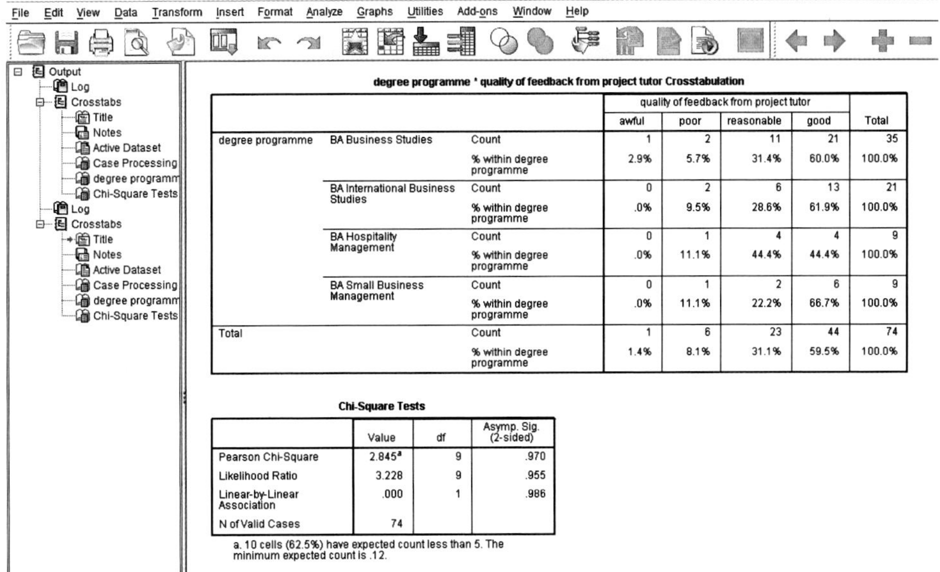

degree programme * quality of feedback from project tutor Crosstabulation

			quality of feedback from project tutor				Total
			awful	poor	reasonable	good	
degree programme	BA Business Studies	Count	1	2	11	21	35
		% within degree programme	2.9%	5.7%	31.4%	60.0%	100.0%
	BA International Business Studies	Count	0	2	6	13	21
		% within degree programme	.0%	9.5%	28.6%	61.9%	100.0%
	BA Hospitality Management	Count	0	1	4	4	9
		% within degree programme	.0%	11.1%	44.4%	44.4%	100.0%
	BA Small Business Management	Count	0	1	2	6	9
		% within degree programme	.0%	11.1%	22.2%	66.7%	100.0%
Total		Count	1	6	23	44	74
		% within degree programme	1.4%	8.1%	31.1%	59.5%	100.0%

Chi-Square Tests

	Value	df	Asymp. Sig. (2-sided)
Pearson Chi-Square	2.845[a]	9	.970
Likelihood Ratio	3.228	9	.955
Linear-by-Linear Association	.000	1	.986
N of Valid Cases	74		

a. 10 cells (62.5%) have expected count less than 5. The minimum expected count is .12.

Explain what this tells you about students' opinions about feedback from their project tutor.

12.7 Briefly describe when you would use regression analysis and correlation analysis, using examples to illustrate your answer.

12.8 a Use an appropriate technique to compare the following data on share prices for two financial service companies over the past six months, using the period six months ago as the base period:

	EJ Investment Holdings	AE Financial Services
Price 6 months ago	€10	€587
Price 4 months ago	€12	€613
Price 2 months ago	€13	€658
Current price	€14	€690

b Which company's share prices have increased most in the last six months? (Note: you should quote relevant statistics to justify your answer.)

Review and discussion questions

12.9 Use a search engine to discover coding schemes that already exist for ethnic group, family expenditure, industry group, socioeconomic class and the like. To do this you will probably find it best to type the phrase 'coding ethnic group' into the search box.

- **a** Discuss how credible you think each coding scheme is with a friend. To come to an agreed answer pay particular attention to:
  - the organisation (or person) that is responsible for the coding scheme;
  - any explanations regarding the coding scheme's design;
  - use of the coding scheme to date.
- **b** Widen your search to include coding schemes that may be of use for your research project. Make a note of the web address of any that are of interest.

12.10 With a friend, choose a large company in which you are interested. Obtain a copy of the annual report for this company. If it is not readily available via the Internet, hard copy can often be obtained from your university library. Examine the use of tables, graphs and charts in your chosen company's report.

- **a** To what extent does the use of graphs and charts in your chosen report follow the guidance summarised in Box 12.8 and Table 12.2?
- **b** Why do you think this is?

12.11 With a group of friends, each choose a different share price index. Well-known indices you could choose include the Nasdaq Composite Index, France's CAC 40, Germany's Xetra Dax, Hong Kong's HIS-Hang Seng, Japan's Nikkei Average Index, the UK's FTSE 100 and the USA's Dow Jones Industrial Average Index.

- **a** For each of the indices, find out how it is calculated and note down its daily values for a one-week period.
- **b** Compare your findings regarding the calculation of your chosen index with those for the indices chosen by your friends, noting down similarities and differences.

Progressing your research project

Analysing your data quantitatively

- Examine the technique(s) you are proposing to use to collect data to answer your research question. You need to decide whether you are collecting any data that could usefully be analysed quantitatively.
- If you decide that your data should be analysed quantitatively, you must ensure that the data collection methods you intend to use have been designed to make analysis by computer as straightforward as possible. In particular, you need to pay attention to the coding scheme for each variable and the layout of your data matrix.
- Once your data have been entered into a computer and the dataset opened in your analysis software, you will need to explore and present them. Bearing your research question in mind, you should select the most appropriate diagrams and tables after considering the suitability of all possible techniques. Remember to label your diagrams clearly and to keep an electronic copy, as they may form part of your research report.
- Once you are familiar with your data, describe and explore relationships using those statistical techniques that best help you to answer your research questions and are suitable for the data type. Remember to keep an annotated copy of your analyses, as you will need to quote statistics to justify statements you make in the findings section of your research report.
- Use the questions in Box 1.4 to guide you in your reflective diary entry

c To what extent do the indices differ in the changes in share prices they show? Why do you think this is?

12.12 Find out whether your university provides you with access to IBM SPSS Statistics. If it does, visit this book's companion website and download the self-teach package and associated data sets. Work through this to explore the features of IBM SPSS Statistics.

References

Anderson, T.W. (2003) *An Introduction to Multivariate Statistical Analysis*. New York: John Wiley.

Anderson, D.R., Sweeney, D.J. and Williams, T.A. (2010) *Statistics for Business and Economics* (11th edn). London: Thomson Learning.

Berman Brown, R. and Saunders, M. (2008) *Dealing with Statistics: What You Need to Know.* Maidenhead: McGraw-Hill Open University Press.

Bigmacindex.com (2011) *Big Mac Index Data.* Available at www.bigmacindex.org/index.html [Accessed 3 May 2011].

Black, K. (2009) *Business Statistics* (6th edn). Hoboken, NJ: Wiley.

Blumberg, B., Cooper, D.R. and Schindler, D.S. (2008) *Business Research Methods.* Maidenhead: McGraw-Hill.

Cohen, L. and Holliday, M. (1996) *Practical Statistics for Students.* London: Paul Chapman.

Curwin, J. and Slater, R. (2007) *Quantitative Methods: A Short Course*. London: Thomson Learning EMEA.

Dancey, C.P. and Reidy, J. (2008) *Statistics Without Maths for Psychology: Using SPSS for Windows* (4th edn). Harlow: Prentice Hall.

deVaus, D.A. (2002) *Surveys in Social Research* (5th edn). London: Routledge.

Ellis, P. (2010) *The Essential Guide to Effect Sizes.* Cambridge: Cambridge University Press.

Eurostat (2011) *Environment and energy statistics – total greenhouse gas emissions.* Available at http://epp.eurostat.ec.europa.eu/portal/page/portal/environment/data/main_tables [Accessed 5 May 2011].

Everitt, B.S. and Dunn, G. (2001) *Applied Multivariate Data Analysis* (2nd edn). London: Arnold.

Field, A. (2009) *Discovering Statistics Using SPSS* (3rd edn). London: Sage.

Hair, J.F., Black, B., Babin, B., Anderson, R.E. and Tatham, R.L. (2006) *Multivariate Data Analysis* (6th edn). Harlow: Pearson Education.

Harley Davidson Inc. (2009) *Harley-Davidson Inc. 2008 Annual Report* Available at www.harley-davidson.com/en_US/Media/downloads/Annual_Reports/2008/HD_Annual2008.pdf?locale=en_US&bmLocale=en_US [Accessd 2 May 2011].

Harley Davidson Inc. (2011) H*arley Davidson Inc. Form 10K (Annual Report).* Available at www.harley-davidson.com/en_US/Media/downloads/Annual_Reports/2010/10k_2010.pdf [Accessed 2 May 2011].

Hays, W.L. (1994) *Statistics* (4th edn). London: Holt-Saunders.

Henry, G.T. (1995) *Graphing Data: Techniques for Display and Analysis.* Thousand Oaks, CA: Sage.

Kanji, G.K. (2006) *100 Statistical Tests* (3rd edn). London: Sage.

Kinnear, P.R. and Gray, C.D. (2010) *SPSS 18 Made Simple: For IBM SPSS Statistics Software*. Hove: Psychology Press.

Millward, L.J. and Postmes, T. (2010) 'Who we are affects how we do. The financial benefits of organisational identification', *British Journal of Management,* Vol. 21, pp. 327–39.

Morris, C. (2012) *Quantitative Approaches in Business Studies* (8th edn). Harlow: FT Prentice-Hall.

Office for National Statistics (2005) *The National Statistics Socio-economic Classification User Manual.* Basingstoke: Palgrave Macmillan.

Office for National Statistics (2010a) *Standard Occupation Classification Volume 1: Structure and Description of Unit Groups.* Basingstoke: Palgrave Macmillan.

Office for National Statistics (2010b) *Standard Occupation Classification Volume 2: The Structure and Index.* Basingstoke: Palgrave Macmillan.

Park, A., Curtice, J., Thomson, K., Phillips, M., Johnson M. and Clery, E. (2007) *British Social Attitudes: 24th Report.* London: Sage.

Prosser, L. (2009) *Office for National Statistics UK Standard Industrial Classification of Activities 2007 (SIC 2007).* Basingstoke: Palgrave Macmillan.

Robson, C. (2011) *Real World Research: A Resource for Users of Social Research Methods in Applied Settings* (3rd edn). Chichester: John Wiley.

Smith, A. (2002) 'The new ethnicity classification in the Labour Force Survey', *Labour Market Trends*, December, pp. 657–66.

Snap Surveys (2011) *Snap Survey Software Research Services.* Available at www.snapsurveys.com [Accessed 9 May 2011].

Sparrow, J. (1989) 'Graphic displays in information systems: Some data properties influencing the effectiveness of alternate forms', *Behaviour and Information Technology*, Vol. 8, No. 1, pp. 43–56.

SurveyMonkey (2011) *SurveyMonkey home page.* Available at www.surveymonkey.com/ [Accessed 9 May 2011].

Tang, J., Crossan, M. and Rowe, W.G. (2011) 'Dominant CEO, deviant strategy, and extreme performance: The moderating role of a powerful board', *Journal of Management Studies.* Available at https://remote.surrey.ac.uk/doi/10.1111/j.1467-6486.2010.00985.x/,DanaInfo=.aoonlrjrpj0k2-M-x1vESw98+pdf [Accessed 9 May 2011].

Tukey, J.W. (1977) *Exploratory Data Analysis.* Reading, MA: Addison-Wesley.

Further reading

Berman Brown, R. and Saunders, M. (2008) *Dealing with Statistics: What You Need to Know.* Maidenhead: McGraw Hill Open University Press. This is a statistics book that assumes virtually no statistical knowledge, focusing upon which test or graph, when to use it and why. It is written for people who are fearful and anxious about statistics and do not think they can understand numbers!

Blastland, M. and Dilnot, A. (2008) *The Tiger than Isn't.* London: Profile Books. This is a very different type of book on statistics. Rather than explaining how to calculate different statistics it explains how to make sense of the numbers and statistics which we are confronted with in the news media and other publications. It is well worth reading and will almost certainly help you to better understand and interpret numbers and statistics.

Dancey, C.P. and Reidy, J. (2008) *Statistics Without Maths for Psychology: Using SPSS for Windows* (4th edn). Harlow: Prentice Hall. This book introduces key statistical concepts and techniques, avoiding as much maths as possible. It also provides clear descriptions of how to perform statistical tests using IBM SPSS Statistics and how to report your results both graphically and in texts.

deVaus, D.A. (2002) *Surveys in Social Research* (5th edn). London: Routledge. Chapters 9 and 10 contain an excellent discussion about coding data and preparing data for analysis. Part IV (Chapters 12–18) provides a detailed discussion of how to analyse survey data.

Field, A. (2009) *Discovering Statistics Using SPSS* (3rd edn). London: Sage. This book offers a clearly explained guide to statistics and using SPSS. It is divided into four levels, the lowest of which assumes no familiarity with the data analysis software and very little with statistics. It covers inputting data and how to generate and interpret a wide range of tables, diagrams and statistics using SPSS versions 16 and 17. If you are using an earlier version of SPSS, particularly pre-version 9, be sure to use a book written specifically for that version as there are a number of changes between versions.

Hair, J.F., Black, B., Babin, B., Anderson, R.E. and Tatham, R.L. (2006) *Multivariate Data Analysis* (6th edn). Harlow: Pearson Education. This book provides detailed information on statistical concepts and techniques. Issues pertinent to design, assumptions, estimation and interpretation are systematically explained for users of more advanced statistical techniques.

Morris, C. (2012) *Quantitative Approaches in Business Studies* (8th edn). Harlow: Pearson. This gives a clear introduction to the use of mathematical and statistical techniques and diagrams in business. Guidance is given on using the Excel spreadsheet.

Case 12
Food miles, carbon footprints and supply chains

During her business degree, Rebecca had become interested in the environmental impacts of business activity and, in particular, the concept that lean supply chains use less resources per unit of output and that the leaner systems tended to be larger scale. The modules she had taken, particularly in sustainable business management, introduced several case studies and literature which appeared to have conflicting messages, in particular surrounding the 'food miles' debate. Some literature suggested smaller-scale, localised systems may be better for the environment and others advocated larger-scale systems. She decided to try to find some answers to this by collecting data for her research project, which she titled: 'How do small- and large-scale distribution systems differ in terms of distance travelled and their carbon footprint?'

Rebecca's project tutor felt this was a good question to ask but suggested she might want to take it further by examining, within whichever system seemed to have the lowest carbon footprint, how different aspects of that supply chain affect total carbon emissions for different products (raw materials, production, processing, manufacture, retail and consumption). Her tutor also recommended some useful secondary data and literature to help work out the carbon footprint of different distribution options.

During her literature search Rebecca found three papers that were particularly useful as they outlined the type of data she needed to collect (Bimpeh et al. 2006; Coley et al. 2009; Oglethorpe 2010). To discover whether small- and large-scale distribution systems differed in terms of distance travelled and their carbon footprint, she needed data about the distance travelled using different distribution systems and how much carbon was emitted for each kilometre travelled, by different vehicles. Rebecca then needed to compare small-scale distribution systems using small-scale vehicles with large-scale distribution systems using large-scale vehicles. To try and make any differences between these systems obvious, she decided to contrast farm shops with supermarkets.

Collecting data for farm shops

Rebecca contacted regional food groups and obtained names and addresses of 100 farm shops. She emailed each of them asking if she could provide a very brief questionnaire for their shoppers to complete. This questionnaire asked shoppers two simple questions and was to be distributed on paper at the checkout, customers placing their completed questionnaire in a box. The questionnaire was as follows:

Farm Shop Questionnaire

Dear Customer

My name is Rebecca Smith and I am a student at the University of Anytown. For my research project I am studying the distance people travel to do shopping at different types of shops. The farm shop has kindly let me ask you two very simple questions about your visit today and I would be very grateful if you would be able to fill your answers in below and post your completed questionnaire in the box provided. Your help is very much appreciated.

1 How far have you travelled to come to the farm shop today?

________ miles, or ________ kilometres

2 What type of transport did you use to get to the farm shop today?

Please tick:

On foot	
Bicycle	
Car	
Public transport	

Thank you very much again for your help.

Rebecca Smith

Student, University of Anytown

Eventually, Rebecca was able to obtain responses to her questionnaire from shoppers at 35 farm shops. From these she calculated the mean (average) distance that shoppers travelled, all shoppers having travelled by car, which Rebecca had to assume was an 'average car' as defined by Defra (2010). Rebecca remembered to convert all 'miles' to kilometres'.

Once she had gathered these data, Rebecca contacted each of these 35 farm shops and, having thanked them for their generous help so far, asked how far their produce travelled from the distribution centre they used and what sort of vehicle was used. 28 farm shops were able to provide this information, all using a light freight vehicle, rigid body, weighing between 3.5 to 7.5 tonnes (Figure C12.1).

Rebecca now had complete data for 28 farm shops detailing the mean distance that shoppers travelled, the type of transport shoppers used and the distance produce travelled from the distribution centre to the shop.

Figure C12.1 A typical light freight vehicle, rigid body, weighing between 3.5 to 7.5 tonnes

Source: Shutterstock.com/max blain

Collecting data for supermarkets

Rebecca now needed to collect equivalent data for supermarkets. One particular supermarket group had a loyalty card scheme. Through this the supermarket collected data on the produce bought, as well storing where the shopper lived and how they travelled to the supermarket.

Rebecca contacted this supermarket group and asked if they could provide the average distance customers travelled to a sample of 28 different stores and, for each store, how far produce travelled from their distribution centre to that store. The supermarket chain provided Rebecca with the data she needed but she had to assume all journeys to the supermarkets were made using an 'average car'. They also told her that all produce was transported using by 33-tonne articulated heavy goods vehicles (Figure C12.2)

Figure C12.2 A typical 33 tonne articulated heavy goods vehicle

Source: Shutterstock/Adrian Reynolds

Data analysis

Rebecca typed the data for the 28 Farm Shops and 28 Supermarkets into her spreadsheet software in preparation for her analysis (Figure C12.3)

Rebecca decided to use an independent sample *t*-test (assuming unequal variances) to see if there was a significant difference between the total mean distances (kilometres) travelled by food purchased from the farm shops and supermarkets. This was referred to as a 'two sample *t*-test', its alternative name, in her spreadsheet software. Using the spreadsheet, Rebecca obtained the output in Figure C12.4.

To work out the carbon footprint of each farm shop's or supermarket's mean distance (km) travelled by food purchased, Rebecca needed to know how much carbon dioxide was emitted per tonne of produce for each type of vehicle for every kilometre travelled. Fortunately this data is published by the UK's Department of Environment, Food and Rural Affairs (Defra) assuming average loads are carried (Table C12.1).

	A	B	C	D	E	F
1	**Farm shops**			**Supermarkets**		
2	**Average customer car journey (km)**	**Distance from distribution centre (km) by 3.5–7.5t truck**	**Total mean distance (km) travelled by food purchased**	**Average customer car journey (km)**	**Distance from distribution centre (km) by 33t HGV**	**Total mean distance (km) travelled by food purchased**
3	10	35	45	2	95	97
4	15	37	52	4	101	105
5	14	45	59	2	96	98
6	13	42	55	3	102	105
7	11	39	50	3	102	105
8	14	40	54	4	102	106
9	13	45	58	3	97	100
10	13	43	56	3	114	117
11	13	43	56	3	107	110
12	10	44	54	2	100	102
13	13	36	49	2	97	99
14	12	39	51	3	112	115
15	14	37	51	3	114	117
16	12	40	52	4	96	100
17	14	42	56	2	103	105
18	14	37	51	4	97	101
19	14	39	53	4	96	100
20	15	38	53	3	108	111
21	12	41	53	3	96	99
22	13	44	57	4	107	111
23	15	42	57	4	105	109
24	13	43	56	3	96	99
25	12	44	56	3	104	107
26	11	42	53	3	99	102
27	11	41	52	4	108	112
28	13	44	57	3	101	104
29	14	42	56	2	98	100
30	10	38	48	2	109	111

Figure C12.3 Data for the mean customer and distribution journey distances at 28 farm shops and 28 supermarkets

	A	B	C
1	t-Test: Two-Sample Assuming Unequal Variances		
2			
3		*Variable 1*	*Variable 2*
4	Mean	53.5	105.1786
5	Variance	11.07407	34.37434
6	Observations	28	28
7	Hypothesized Mean Difference	0	
8	df	43	
9	t Stat	-40.563	
10	P(T<=t) one-tail	3.28E-36	
11	t Critical one-tail	1.681071	
12	P(T<=t) two-tail	6.56E-36	
13	t Critical two-tail	2.016692	
14			

Figure C12.4 Spreadsheet output for an independent sample *t*-test for the difference between the mean total journeys

Table C12.1 Carbon dioxide-equivalent (CO_2-e) emissions from different vehicles used in the journeys

Vehicle type	Carbon dioxide-equivalent emissions
Average car (unknown fuel)[1]	0.24579 kg CO_2-e per km traveled
Rigid truck, 3.5t–7.5t (diesel)[2]	0.79456 kg CO_2-e per tonne-km travelled
Articulated HGV, 33t (diesel)[2]	0.10462 kg CO_2-e per tonne-km travelled

Source: Developed from Defra (2010) [1]Table 6e; [2]Table 7e

By multiplying each total mean distance in Figure C12.3 by the corresponding carbon dioxide-equivalent emissions in Table C12.1, Rebecca transformed all the mean distance (km) travelled by food purchased data into a corresponding carbon footprint for each of the 28 farm shops and supermarkets. Again, Rebecca decided to use an independent sample *t*-test (assuming unequal variances) to test if there was a significant difference between the total carbon emissions for each of the two systems.

Using her spreadsheet as before, Rebecca obtained the output in Figure C12.5.

	A	B	C
1	t-Test: Two-Sample Assuming Unequal Variances		
2			
3		*Variable 1*	*Variable 2*
4	Mean	35.4985	11.42185
5	Variance	5.505866	0.3952
6	Observations	28	28
7	Hypothesized Mean Difference	0	
8	df	31	
9	t Stat	52.44569	
10	P(T<=t) one-tail	3.83E-32	
11	t Critical one-tail	1.695519	
12	P(T<=t) two-tail	7.67E-32	
13	t Critical two-tail	2.039513	
14			

Figure C12.5 Spreadsheet output for independent sample *t*-test for the difference between the mean carbon emissions

Questions

1 Explain what the *t*-test results in Figures. C12.4 and C12.5 mean, stating an appropriate hypothesis and null hypothesis for each.

2 With regard to Rebecca's research question, what would you conclude from these results about the importance of distance travelled as opposed to type of vehicle used?

3 Comment on Rebecca's analysis and the assumptions she has made. What are the implications of this for the validity and reliability of her findings?

4 What data would Rebecca need and what sort of analysis could Rebecca do in order to take her research further as her project tutor suggests such as seeing how different aspects of the supply chain affect total carbon emissions for different products within that supply chain?

References

Bimpeh, M., Djokoto, E., Doe, H. and Jequier, R. (2006) *Life Cycle Assessment (LCA) of the Production of Home Made and Industrial Bread in Sweden*. KTH, Life Cycle Assessment Course (1N1800), May 2006.

Coley D., Howard M. and Winter M. (2009) 'Local food, food miles and carbon emissions: A comparison of farm shop and mass distribution approaches', *Food Policy,* Vol. 34, No. 2, pp. 150–155.

Defra (2010) *Guidelines to Defra/DECC's GHG Conversion Factors for Company Reporting*. Produced by AEA for the Department of Energy and Climate Change (DECC) and the Department for Environment, Food and Rural Affairs (Defra). Version 1.2.1 FINAL. Updated 6 October 2010.

Oglethorpe, D.R. (2010) 'Optimising economic, environmental and social objectives: A goal programming approach in the food sector', *Environment and Planning A*, Vol. 42, No. 5, pp. 1239–1254.

Additional case studies relating to material covered in this chapter are available via the book's companion website: **www.pearsoned.co.uk/saunders**. They are:

- The marketing of arts festivals.
- Marketing a golf course.
- The impact of family ownership on financial performance.
- Small business owner managers' skill sets.

Self-check answers

12.1 **a** The variables are 'income', 'expenditure' and 'year'. There is no real need for a separate case identifier as the variable 'year' can also fulfil this function. Each case (year) is represented by one row of data.

b When the data are entered into a spreadsheet the first column will be the case identifier, for these data the year. Income and expenditure should not be entered with the £ sign as this can be formatted subsequently using the spreadsheet:

	A	B	C
1	*Year*	*Income (£)*	*Expenditure (£)*
2	2004	11000000	9500000
3	2005	15200000	12900000
4	2006	17050000	14000000
5	2007	17900000	14900000
6	2008	19000000	16100000
7	2009	18700000	17200000
8	2010	17100000	18100000
9	2011	17700000	19500000
10	2012	19900000	20000000
11			

12.2 **a** There is no one correct answer to this question as the number of variables will depend on the method used to code these descriptive data. If you choose the multiple-response method, five variables will be generated. If the multiple-dichotomy method is used, the number of variables will depend on the number of different responses.

b Your first priority is to decide on the level of detail of your intended analyses. Your coding scheme should, if possible, be based on an existing coding scheme. If this is of insufficient detail then it should be designed to be compatible to allow comparisons. To design the coding scheme you need to take the responses from the first 50–100 cases and establish broad groupings. These can be subdivided into increasingly specific subgroups until the detail is sufficient for the intended analysis. Codes can then be allocated to these subgroups. If you ensure that similar responses receive adjacent codes, this will make any subsequent grouping easier. The actual responses that correspond to each code should be noted in a codebook. Codes should be allocated to data on the data collection form in the 'For office use' box. These codes need to include missing data, such as when four or fewer 'things' have been mentioned.

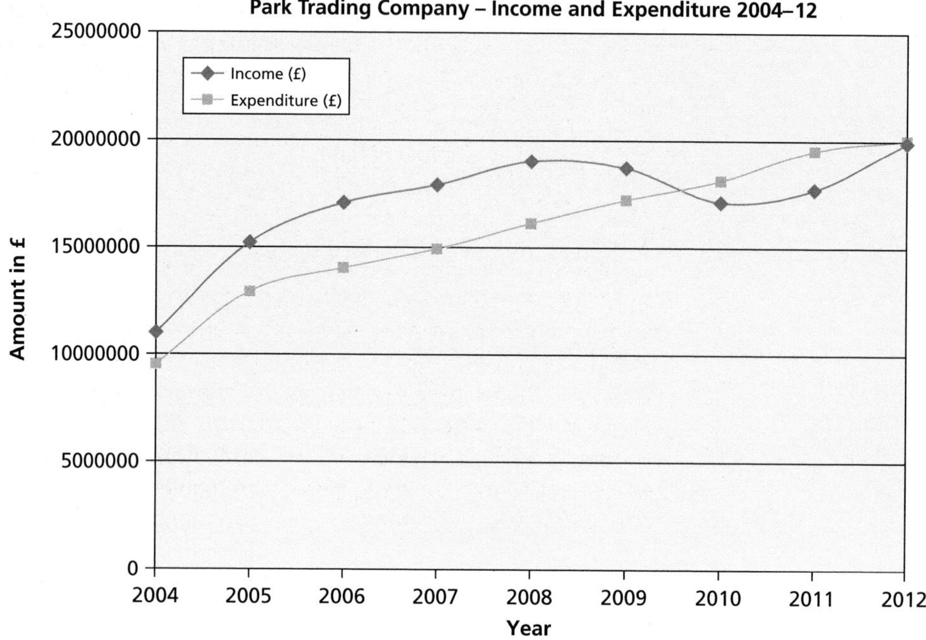

12.3 **a** Park Trading Company – Income and Expenditure 2004–12.

b Your diagram (it is hoped) emphasises the upward trends of expenditure and (to a lesser extent) income. It also highlights the conjunction where income falls below expenditure in 2010.

c To emphasise the years with the lowest and highest income, you would probably use a histogram because the data are continuous. A frequency polygon would also be suitable.

12.4 **a** You would probably use a scatter graph in which number of donations would be the dependent variable and number of viewers reached by the advertisement the independent variable.

b This would enable you to see whether there was any relationship between number of viewers reached and number of donations.

12.5 **a** The first thing you need to do is to establish the data type. As it is numerical, you could theoretically use all three measures of central tendency and both the standard deviation and inter-quartile range. However, you would probably calculate the mean and perhaps the median as measures of central tendency and the standard deviation and perhaps the interquartile range as measures of dispersion.

b The mean would be chosen because it includes all data values. The median might be chosen to represent the middle income over the 2004–12 period. The mode would be of little use for these data as each year has different income values.

If you had chosen the mean you would probably choose the standard deviation, as this describes the dispersion of data values around the mean. The inter-quartile range is normally chosen where there are extreme data values that need to be ignored. This is not the case for these data.

12.6 The probability of a chi square value of 2.845 with 9 degrees of freedom occurring by chance alone for these data is 0.970. This means that statistically the association between students' degree programmes and their opinion of the quality of feedback from project tutors is extremely likely to be explained by chance alone. In addition, the assumption of the chi square test that no more than 20 per cent of expected values should be less than 5 has not been satisfied.

To explore this lack of association further, you examine the cell values in relation to the row and column totals. For all programmes, over 80 per cent of respondents thought the quality of feedback from their project tutor was reasonable or good.

12.7 Your answer needs to emphasise that correlation analysis is used to establish whether a change in one variable is accompanied by a change in another. In contrast, regression analysis is used to establish whether a change in a dependent variable is caused by changes in one or more independent variables – in other words, a cause-and-effect relationship. Although it is impossible to list all the examples you might use to illustrate your answer, you should make sure that your examples for regression illustrate a dependent and one or more independent variables.

12.8 **a** These quantitative data are of different magnitudes. Therefore, the most appropriate technique to compare these data is index numbers. The index numbers for the two companies are:

	EJ Investment Holdings	AE Financial Services
Price 6 months ago	100	100.0
Price 4 months ago	120	104.4
Price 2 months ago	130	112.1
Current price	140	117.5

b The price of AE Financial Services' shares has increased by €103 compared with an increase of €4 for EJ Investment Holdings' share price. However, the proportional increase in prices has been greatest for EJ Investment Holdings. Using six months ago as the base period (with a base index number of 100), the index for EJ Investment Holdings' share price is now 140 while the index for AE Financial Services' share price is 117.5.

Get ahead using resources on the companion website at:
www.pearsoned.co.uk/saunders

- Improve your IBM SPSS Statistics and NVivo research analysis with practice tutorials.
- Save time researching on the Internet with the Smarter Online Searching Guide.
- Test your progress using self-assessment questions.
- Follow live links to useful websites.

Chapter 13

Analysing qualitative data

Learning outcomes

By the end of this chapter you should be:

- able to understand the nature of qualitative data and appreciate the implications of this for their analysis;
- able to evaluate different approaches to analyse your qualitative data (inductive or deductive);
- able to identify the main issues that you need to consider when preparing your qualitative data for analysis including preparation to use computer aided qualitative data analysis software (CAQDAS);
- able to transcribe a recorded interview or notes of an interview or observation and create a data file for analysis by computer;
- aware of different analytical aids to help you to analyse your qualitative data, including keeping a reflective or reflexive journal;
- able to select an appropriate set of procedures to undertake qualitative data analysis;
- able to describe and evaluate reasons for quantifying qualitative data as a means of analysis;
- able to identify the common functions of CAQDAS and describe the issues associated with its use.

13.1 Introduction

This chapter is designed to help you analyse qualitative data. The nature of qualitative data is discussed in Section 13.2. It is possible to approach qualitative data analysis from either a deductive or inductive perspective and we outline this choice in Section 13.3. As you read through the sections of this chapter you will recognise the interrelated and interactive nature of qualitative data collection and analysis. Because of this it will be necessary to plan your qualitative research as an interconnected process where you collect, analyse and interpret data as you undertake each interview or observation. To help you to with this process, we discuss the preparation of your data for analysis in Section 13.4 and outline a number of aids that will help you analyse these data and record your ideas about how to progress your research in Section 13.5.

Sections 13.6–13.8 discuss different types of procedure to analyse your qualitative data. Section 13.6 outlines a generic approach to analyse qualitative data. Section 13.7 outlines different sets of procedures to analyse qualitative data that commence from an inductive perspective. Section 13.8 outlines two sets of procedures to analyse qualitative data that commence from a deductive perspective. Section 13.6 also briefly discusses reasons for quantifying qualitative data and recognises the limits to the use of such an approach. Qualitative analysis is based on an interpretivist paradigm (Chapter 4) irrespective of which of these analytical approaches you adopt, as the opening vignette illustrates.

Nearly all of us have, at some time in our lives, completed a jigsaw puzzle. As children we may have played with jigsaw puzzles and, as we grew older, those we were able to complete became more complex. In some ways, qualitative data analysis can be likened to the process of completing a jigsaw puzzle in which the pieces represent data. These pieces of data and the relationships between them help us as researchers to create a picture of what we think the data are telling us!

When trying to complete a jigsaw puzzle, most of us begin by looking at the picture on the lid of our puzzle's box. This is where the analogy between qualitative analysis and completing a jigsaw can break down. Puzzles for which there is no picture are usually more challenging as we have no idea of the picture we are trying to create! In qualitative analysis there may be no well-defined external reality, so there is no pre-existing picture that we strive to recreate.

Perhaps you haven't tried to complete a jigsaw puzzle for many years but you might find the following useful as well as entertaining! Get a friend to give you the contents of a jigsaw in a bag without the box (since this normally shows the picture of what it is!). Turn all of the pieces picture side up. Think about how you will categorise these data that lie in front of you. What do they mean? You will be likely to group pieces with similar features such as those of a particular colour together. Normally you might then try to fit these similar pieces together to begin to reveal the picture that the fitted pieces are designed to show. Perhaps completing jigsaws reinforces a sense of positivism in us – there's an external reality 'out there', so all we need to do is reveal it! Where qualitative analysis is based on an interpretivist paradigm, we may reveal many pieces of data but the picture we eventually make of these will be socially constructed depending on the nature of our research question and our own ways of making sense of what we see!

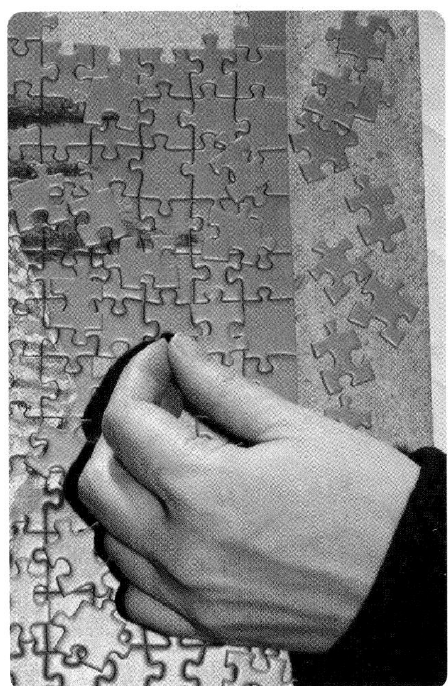

The key is for the pieces to be sorted
Source: Marshall Ikonography/Alamy.

Section 13.9 discusses the use of computer aided qualitative data analysis software (**CAQDAS**). Until the advent of powerful personal computers and readily available CAQDAS, qualitative data analysis was undertaken manually. Indeed, it is only comparatively recently that CAQDAS such as NVivo™, ATLAS.ti™, and HyperRESEARCH™ have begun to be made accessible to students taking undergraduate and master's programmes in universities. Consequently, at an increasing number of universities, it may no longer necessary for you to undertake routine qualitative data management tasks manually, such as sorting your data into categories and locating subsets of these data according to specified criteria. However, we would like to sound a note of caution. Whilst the use of analysis software for quantitative data is almost universal, the use of CAQDAS for qualitative data is not so widely practised and the associated software is not always available. As a result, this chapter does not assume that you will necessarily have access to and use a computer to organise and analyse your data.

Consequently, although we make reference to, and include screenshots of, different software packages in some worked examples, these are used to illustrate generic issues associated with analysis rather than imply that you must use such software. If you wish to develop your skills in one of the more widely used CAQDAS packages called NVivo™, a self-teach package is available via our companion website.

13.2 Qualitative data

It is helpful to commence our discussion by understanding what we mean by qualitative data. Understanding **qualitative data** will help you to analyse these meaningfully. In Sections 4.2 and 5.3 we recognised that qualitative research is often associated with an interpretive philosophy because researchers need to make sense of the subjective and socially constructed meanings expressed by those who take part in research about the phenomenon being studied. **Social constructionism** indicates that meanings are dependent on human cognition – people's interpretation of the events that occur around them. Since meanings in qualitative research depend on social interpretation, qualitative data are likely to be more ambiguous, elastic and complex than quantitative data. Analysis and understanding of these data therefore needs to be sensitive to these characteristics to be meaningful.

Qualitative data are likely to be characterised by their richness and fullness, based on your opportunity to explore a subject in as real a manner as is possible (Box 13.1). A contrast can thus be drawn between the 'thin' abstraction or description that principally results from quantitative data collection and the 'thick' or 'thorough' abstraction or description associated with qualitative data (Brekhus et al. 2005; Dey 1993).

A further way to understand qualitative data is to distinguish them from quantitative data. Table 13.1 highlights three distinct differences between quantitative and qualitative data.

In qualitative research, meanings are principally derived from words not numbers. Since words may have multiple meanings as well as unclear meanings, it is necessary to explore and clarify these with great care. This indicates that the quality of qualitative research depends on the interaction between data collection and data analysis to allow meanings to be explored and clarified. We discuss this aspect of quality later.

The nature of qualitative data has further implications for their analysis. These non-standardised data will be likely to be large in volume and complex in nature. You will therefore be confronted by a mass of paper or electronic files that you will need to explore, analyse, synthesise and transform in order to address your research objectives and answer your research question. This will be likely to involve you in processes where you summarise some parts of your data to condense them, categorise data in order to group them according to themes that begin to make sense of these data, and then to link

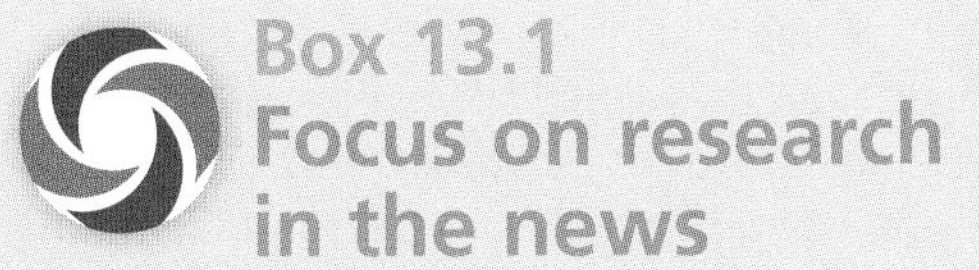

FT

Rank sets out to discover home truths

Rank Group, the company behind Grosvenor casinos and Mecca bingo, has become the latest UK group to employ immersive market research to better understand its customers. Rank is sending senior staff into the homes of customers to probe daily habits that would sometimes seem to have little to do with its products and services. In addition to long interviews, researchers photograph the subjects at home, travel with them on their journeys to bingo clubs or casinos and observe them throughout their visits. The process can take six hours or more.

And yet while qualitative market research – of which immersive observational studies are one part – is usually more time-consuming and expensive to conduct than quantitative surveys, it now takes a chunk of many R&D budgets. 'Qualitative research has grown as fast if not faster as a proportion of the total', said Ben Page, chief executive of Ipsos Mori, the UK arm of global research group Ipsos. He estimates that 15 to 20 per cent of his company's work is qualitative.

Unlike other companies, however, Rank wants its top executives to take part. Ian Burke, chief executive, has already spent a day following a couple from their home to one of the company's casinos and observing them there. 'At Mecca, there are already back-to-floor initiatives [in which head office staff work at the clubs]', said Jon McPherson, Rank's group head of insight and analytics. 'But immersion with a customer is very different from seeing things through the eyes of the employee.'

The push follows a year in which Rank stemmed a decline in Mecca revenues by getting customers to spend more per visit – in part through new offerings, such as food and drink table service and 'After Dark' bingo, a looser form of the game. Luring more people in is the next task – and one Mr Burke has said cannot be accomplished without a better understanding of why people go to bingo halls. Mecca has paid out . . . £500,000 a year for the past two years on 'customer insight'. Rank spent £1.5m ($2.4m) a year in 2009 and 2010 – about 2 per cent of operating profits – divided equally between qualitative and quantitative approaches.

'It's been Ian's passion', said Mark Jones, managing director of Mecca. 'It's not just research, it's "insight", which is more intrusive, but in a positive way.' Mr McPherson hopes even to involve Rank Interactive, the group's online division. 'We have good technology for measuring how people move around a [web] page, but we don't know if people come home, put the children in bed, make a cup of tea and then sit down at the computer.' He admits these immersions could be difficult to arrange. The Mecca research might involve two hours in a customer's home before going to the club, but with Rank Interactive it may mean 'staying in the customer's spare bedroom'.

Source: From 'Rank sets out to discover home truths', Rose Jacobs (2011) *Financial Times*, 7 February.

Table 13.1 Distinctions between quantitative and qualitative data

Quantitative data	Qualitative data
Based on meanings derived from numbers	Based on meanings expressed through words
Collection results in numerical and standardised data	Collection results in non-standardised data requiring classification into categories
Analysis conducted through the use of diagrams and statistics	Analysis conducted through the use of conceptualisation

Sources: Developed from Dey (1993); Healey and Rawlinson (1994); authors' experience

these categories in ways that provide you with a structure or structures to answer your research question. Without undertaking one or more of these processes, the most that may result may be an impressionistic view of what these qualitative data mean.

While it might be possible to make some use of diagrams and statistics at this stage, such as the frequency of occurrence of certain categories of data (Sections 12.3, 12.4 and 13.6), the way in which you are likely to analyse the qualitative data that you collect is through the development of research-specific concepts that you may then link into a conceptual framework. This framework may be developed before, during or after your data collection and then refined as your research progresses. These analytical processes are discussed in much greater detail in Sections 13.6–13.8.

13.3 Deciding on your approach to analysis

Research commences from either a deductive or an inductive approach (Section 4.3). Where you commence your research project using a deductive approach you will seek to use existing theory to shape the approach that you adopt to the qualitative research process and to aspects of data analysis. Where you commence your research project using an inductive approach you will seek to build up a theory that is adequately grounded in your data. In this section we discuss the difference between using theory at the start of your research to analyse qualitative data and commencing your research by collecting and exploring your data without a predetermined theoretical or descriptive framework (Yin 2009).

Using a deductive approach

Yin (2009) suggests that, where you have made use of existing theory to formulate your research question and objectives, you may also use the theoretical propositions that helped you do this as a means to devise a framework to help you to organise and direct your data analysis. There is debate about this approach as applied to qualitative analysis. Bryman (1988: 81) sums up the argument against it as follows:

> The prior specification of a theory tends to be disfavoured because of the possibility of introducing a premature closure on the issues to be investigated, as well as the possibility of the theoretical constructs departing excessively from the views of participants in a social setting.

If this occurs when you use a theoretical framework to design and analyse your research, you will clearly need to adapt your approach (Box 13.2).

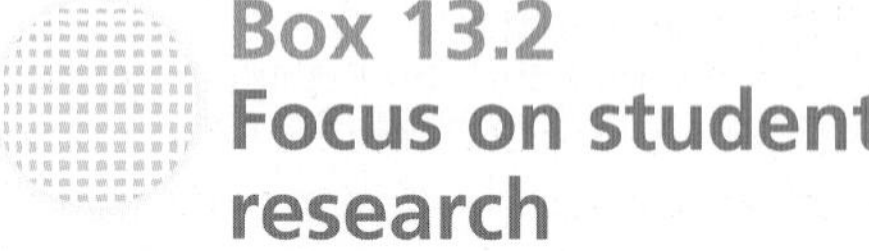

Box 13.2 Focus on student research

Incorporating an inductive approach

Phil commenced a research project by adopting a deductive approach, but found that the theoretical framework he adopted did not yield a sufficiently convincing answer to his research questions and objectives. He therefore decided to reanalyse his data inductively. This revealed themes that had not figured prominently in the deductive analysis. A combination of the two approaches generated a more convincing answer to Phil's research questions and objectives.

Even though you may incorporate an inductive approach in your research, commencing your work from a theoretical perspective may have certain advantages. It will link your research into the existing body of knowledge in your subject area, help you to get started and provide you with an initial analytical framework.

To devise a theoretical or descriptive framework you need to identify the main variables, components, themes and issues in your research project and the predicted or presumed relationships between them (Yin 2009). A descriptive framework will rely more on your prior experience and what you expect to occur, although it is of course possible to develop an explanatory framework based on a mixture of theory derived from the literature you used and your own expectations. You will use this framework as the means to start and direct the analysis of your data.

Using an inductive approach

The alternative to the deductive approach is to start to collect data and then explore them to see which themes or issues to follow up and concentrate on (e.g. Glaser and Strauss 1967; Schatzman and Strauss 1973; Corbin and Strauss 2008; Yin 2009). Yin (2009) believes that this inductive approach may be a difficult strategy to follow and may not lead to success for someone who is an inexperienced researcher. This is likely to happen where you simply go ahead and collect data without examining them to assess which themes are emerging from the data as you progress. Where you commence your data collection with this type of approach – related initially to an exploratory purpose – you should analyse the data as you collect them and develop a conceptual framework to guide your subsequent work. This is also referred to as a grounded approach because of the nature of the theory or explanation that emerges as a result of the research process. In this approach:

- you do not commence such a study with a clearly defined theoretical framework;
- instead you identify relationships between your data and develop questions and hypotheses or propositions to test these;
- theory emerges from the process of data collection and analysis.

You will, however, still need to commence this type of approach with a clear research purpose. To use an inductive approach successfully may involve a lengthy period of time and prove to be resource intensive. It is also likely that this approach will combine some elements of a deductive approach as you seek to develop a theoretical position and then test its applicability through subsequent data collection and analysis (see the discussion of abduction in Section 4.3). Consequently, while you may commence with either an inductive or a deductive approach, in practice your research is likely to combine elements of both.

We develop the discussion about these approaches to qualitative analysis in Sections 13.6 to 13.8. In practice you will need to have thought about your approach to analysis before embarking on the collection of qualitative data because of the interactive nature of data collection and analysis, which we also discuss further in Section 13.6. Once you have started to collect data you will need to prepare these data for analysis and we consider this in the next section. As you collect and analyse qualitative data there are a number of aids, including the creation of summaries and self-memos and the keeping of a research notebook and/or reflective diary, that will help you progress your research and we discuss these in Section 13.5 before returning to consider approaches to qualitative analysis in greater detail.

13.4 Preparing your data for analysis

As we have seen in Chapters 8, 9, 10 and 11, qualitative data can be found in many forms. In Chapter 8, when we considered different secondary data, we highlighted how documentary data were available in both written form, including organisational documents, reports, emails and newspapers, and non-written form such as audio- and video-recordings. Subsequently, in Chapter 9, we noted how, in addition to recording your observation on a schedule, it could also be video-recorded. Chapter 10 highlighted the role of audio-recording as well as note taking, emphasising the importance of transcribing both recordings and notes to ensure data were not lost. Finally, Chapter 11, although focusing on collecting data that could be quantified, noted that open questions could be used to collect qualitative data from respondents, these being recorded in writing by either the respondent or an interviewer. In this section we focus upon the conversion of qualitative data from oral or handwritten form to word-processed text, as this is the way that you are most likely to use these in your analysis. As part of this, we discuss the general requirements of CAQDAS packages.

Transcribing qualitative data

In Chapter 10 we emphasised that, in qualitative research interviews, the interview is normally audio-recorded and subsequently **transcribed**, that is, reproduced as a written (word-processed) account using the actual words. We also emphasised that, as an interviewer, you would be interested not only in what participants said, but in the way they said it as well. This means that the task of transcribing audio-recorded interviews is likely to be time-consuming as you will need not only to record exactly what was said and by whom, but also try to give an indication of the tone in which it was said and the participants' non-verbal communications. Without this additional contextual information, your data will be impoverished to some extent (Kvale and Brinkmann 2009). You also need to ensure it can be linked to the contextual information that locates the interview (Section 10.4).

Even if you are a touch-typist, you will find the task of transcribing an audio-recording extremely time-consuming. Most research methods texts suggest that it takes a touch-typist between 6 and 10 hours to transcribe every hour of audio-recording. Consequently, it is helpful if your interviews are transcribed as soon as possible after they are undertaken in order to avoid a build-up of audio-recordings and associated transcription work. Fortunately, there are a number of possible ways of reducing the vast amount of personal time needed to transcribe interviews verbatim. These are summarised in Table 13.2 along with some of the associated potential problems. As you will see in Table 13.2, one problem, however you choose to transcribe the data, is making sure that the transcription is accurate by correcting any transcription errors. This process is known as data cleaning. Once this has been done, some researchers send a copy of the transcript to the participant for final checking. Whilst this can be helpful for ensuring factual accuracy, we have found that interviewees often want to correct their own grammar and use of language as well! This is because spoken and written language are very different. For this reason, you need to think carefully before offering to provide each interviewee with a full copy of their transcript.

Each interview you transcribe should be saved as a separate word-processed file. As part of this we recommend that you use a filename that maintains confidentiality and preserves anonymity but that you can easily recognise and which codifies important information. When doing this Mark always starts his transcription filenames with the interview number and saves the word-processed transcripts for each research project in a separate subdirectory. Subsequent parts of the filename provide more detail. Thus the file '26MPOrg1.doc' is the transcript of the **26**th interview, **M**ale, **P**rofessional, undertaken at

Table 13.2 Alternative ways of reducing the time needed to transcribe audio-recordings

Alternative	Potential problems
Pay a touch-typist to transcribe your audio-recordings	• Expense of paying someone else • Important data such as pauses, coughs, sighs and the like may not be included • You will not be familiarising yourself with the data as you are not transcribing it yourself • The transcription will still require careful checking as errors can creep in
Borrow a transcription machine with a foot-operated start–play–stop play mechanism	• Although this will allow you to control the audio-recorder more easily, the speed of transcription will still be dependent upon your typing ability • The transcription will still require careful checking
'Dictate' your audio-recordings to your computer using voice-recognition software	• You will need to discover which voice-recognition software works best with your voice • You will also need to discover which voice-recognition software is suited to the needs of your research project • You will need to 'teach' the voice-recognition software to understand your voice • You will need to listen to and dictate the entire audio-recording • The transcription will still require careful checking as the software is not entirely accurate
Only transcribe those sections of each audio-recording that are pertinent to your research (**data sampling**)	• You will need to listen to the entire recording carefully first, at least twice • You may miss certain things, meaning you will have to go back to the audio-recording later • Those sections you transcribe will still require careful checking

Organisation1. As some CAQDAS programs require filenames of eight or fewer characters, you may need to limit your filenames to this length.

When transcribing interviews and group interviews, you need to be able to distinguish between the interviewer and the participant or participants. This means you need to have clear speaker identifiers such as '17FA' for the seventeenth interviewee who is a female administrator. This tends to be more visible in the transcript if they are in capitals (Box 13.3). Similarly, you need to be able to distinguish between any topic headings you use, questions and responses. One way of doing this, dependent upon the precise requirements of your CAQDAS, is to put topic headings in CAPITALS, questions in *italics* and responses in normal font. The most important thing is to be consistent within and across all your transcriptions. Some authors also recommend the use of specific transcription symbols to record intakes of breath, overlapping talk and changes in intonation. A useful list of transcription symbols is provided as an appendix by Silverman (2007).

In a transcription of a more structured interview, you also need to include the question number and the question in your transcription. For example, by including the question number 'Q27' at the start of the question you will be able to search for and find question 27 quickly. In addition, by having the full question in your transcript you will be far less likely to misinterpret the question your respondent is answering.

When transcribing audio-recordings or your own notes you need to plan in advance how you intend to analyse your transcriptions. If you only have access to a black and white printer, there is little point in using different coloured fonts to distinguish between participants in a group interview or to distinguish non-verbal responses such as nervous

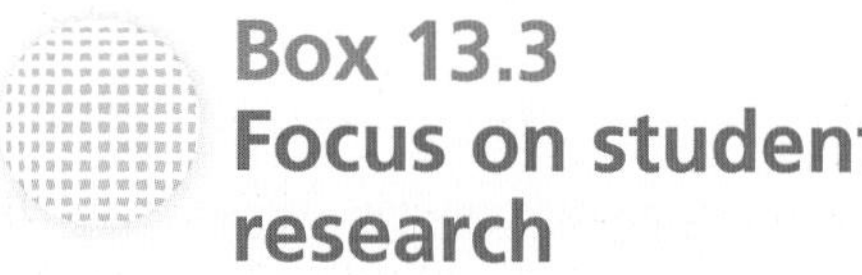

Box 13.3 Focus on student research

Extract from an interview transcript

Martin had decided to use the code IV to represent himself in the transcripts of his in-depth interviews and 01FS to represent his first interviewee, a female student. By using capital letters to identify both himself and the interviewee Martin could identify clearly where questions and responses started. In addition, it reduced the chance of a mistype in the transcription as identifiers were always a combination of capital letters and numbers. Martin used transcription symbols such as '(.)' to represent a brief pause and '.hhh' to represent an in-breath. He also included brief comments relating to a respondent's actions in the interview transcript. These he enclosed with double parentheses (( )). A brief extract from a transcript follows:

> IV: So tell me, why do you use the Student Union Bar?
>
> 01FS: Well, erm (.), a lot of my friends go there for the final drink of the evening (.) there is an atmosphere and the drinks are cheap. I don't feel embarrassed to walk in on my own and there's always someone to talk to and scrounge a fag off ((laughs)) . . .

laughter in your transcripts as these will be difficult to discern when working from the paper copies. You also need to be careful about using these and other word-processing software features if you are going to analyse the data using CAQDAS. These programs often have precise file formats which can mean that word-processing software features such as **bold** and *italics* generated by your word-processing software will disappear when your data file is imported (Lewins and Silver 2009). For example, although you may transcribe your interviews using a word processor such as Microsoft Word, your chosen CAQDAS package may require this textual data to be saved as a text-only file (.txt) or using rich text format (.rtf), resulting in the loss of some of these features. These are summarised as a checklist in Box 13.4.

Box 13.4 Checklist

Transcribing your interviews

- ✔ Have you thought about how you intend to analyse your data and made sure that your transcription will facilitate this?
- ✔ Have you chosen clear interviewer and respondent identifiers and used them consistently?
- ✔ Have you included the interviewer's questions in full in your transcription?
- ✔ Have you saved your transcribed data using a separate file for each interview?
- ✔ Does your filename maintain confidentiality and preserve anonymity whilst still allowing you to recognise important information easily?
- ✔ Have you checked your transcript for accuracy and, where necessary, 'cleaned up' the data?
- ✔ (If you intend to use CAQDAS) Will the package you are going to use help you to manage and analyse your data effectively? In other words, will it do what you need it to do?
- ✔ (If you intend to use CAQDAS) Are your saved transcriptions compatible with the CAQDAS package you intend to use, so you will not lose any features from your word-processed document when you import the data?
- ✔ (If you intend to use CAQDAS) Have you checked your transcript for accuracy and 'cleaned up' the data *prior* to importing into your chosen CAQDAS package?
- ✔ Have you stored a separate backup or security copy of each data file on your USB mass storage device or burnt one onto a CD?

Using electronic textual data including scanned documents

For some forms of textual data such as, for example, email interviews (Section 10.9) or electronic versions of documents (Section 8.2), including organisational emails, blogs and web-based reports, your data may already be in electronic format. Although these data have already been captured electronically, you are still likely to need to spend some time preparing them for analysis. This is likely to involve you in ensuring that, where necessary, the data are:

- suitably anonymised, such as by using separate codes for yourself and different participants;
- appropriately stored for analysis, for example one file for each interview, each meeting's minutes or each organisational policy;
- free of typographical errors that you may have introduced, and, where these occurred, they have been 'cleaned up'.

Consequently, you are likely to find much of the checklist in Box 13.4 helpful. If you intend to use CAQDAS to help you to manage and analyse documents which are not available electronically, you will need to scan these into your word-processing software and ensure they are in a format compatible with your chosen CAQDAS.

13.5 Aids to help your analysis

In addition to transcribing your audio-recording or notes, it will also help your analysis if you have made a record of contextual information (Section 10.4). This will help you to recall the context and content of the interview or observation as well as informing your interpretation as you will be more likely to remember the precise circumstances to which your data relate. Various researchers have suggested ways of recording information and developing reflective ideas to supplement your written-up notes or transcripts and your categorised data (e.g. Gerstl-Pepin and Patrizio 2009; Glaser 1978; Kvale and Brinkmann 2009; Miles and Huberman 1994; Riley 1996; Strauss and Corbin 2008). These include:

- interim or progress summaries;
- transcript summaries;
- document summaries;
- self-memos;
- a research notebook;
- a reflective diary or journal.

Interim or progress summaries

As your analysis progresses you may wish to write an **interim summary** of your progress to date. This outlines:

- what you have found so far;
- what level of confidence you have in your findings and conclusions to date;
- what you need to do in order to improve the quality of your data and/or to seek to substantiate your apparent conclusions, or to seek alternative explanations;
- how you will seek to achieve the needs identified by the above interim analysis.

This can become a working document that you modify and continue to refer to, as your research project progresses.

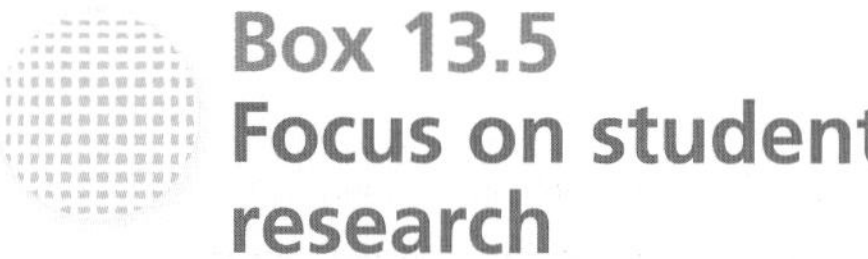

Box 13.5 Focus on student research

Noting an event that affected the nature of data collection

Birjit was facilitating a focus group whose participants were the customers of a large department store. Approximately halfway through the allotted time, an additional participant joined the group. This person almost immediately took control of the discussion, two other participants appearing to become reticent and withdrawing from the group's discussion. Despite this, all Birjit's questions were answered fully and she felt the data she had obtained was valuable. However, she recorded the point at which the new participant joined the group in a post-transcript summary in case any divergence was apparent between the nature of the data in the two parts of the focus group.

Transcript summaries

After you have written up your notes, or produced a transcript, of an interview or observation session, you can also produce a summary of the key points that have emerged from undertaking this activity. A **transcript summary** compresses long statements into briefer ones in which the main sense of what has been said or observed is rephrased in a few words (Kvale and Brinkmann 2009). Through summarising you will become conversant with the principal themes that have emerged from each interview or observation. You may be able to identify apparent relationships between themes that you wish to note down so that you can return to these to seek to establish their validity. It will also be useful to make some comments about the person(s) you interviewed or observed, the setting in which this occurred and whether anything occurred during the interview or observation which might have affected the nature of the data that you collected (Box 13.5).

Once you have produced a summary of the key points that emerge from the interview or observation and its context, you should attach a copy to the set of your written-up notes or transcript for further reference.

Document summaries

Documents may also be summarised. These data may be an important source in their own right (e.g. using minutes of meetings, internal reports, briefings, planning documents and schedules), or you may use such documentation as a means of triangulating other data that you collect (Section 8.2). Where you use any sort of documentation it is helpful to produce a **document summary** that, in addition to providing a list of the key points it contains, also describes the purpose of the document, how it relates to your work and why it is significant. This type of summary is useful when you undertake further analysis if you want to refer to sources of data (that is, the document) as well as the way in which your categorical data have been categorised into their component parts.

Self-memos

Self-memos allow you to record ideas that occur to you about any aspect of your research, as you think of them. Where you omit to record any idea as it occurs to you it may well be forgotten. The occasions when you are likely to want to write a memo include:

- when you are writing up interview or observation notes, or producing a transcript of this event;

- when you are constructing a narrative;
- when you are categorising these data;
- as you continue to categorise and analyse these data;
- when you engage in writing your research project.

Most CAQDAS programs include some form of writing tool that allows you make notes, add comments or write self-memos as you are analysing your data (Lewins and Silver 2009). This is extremely helpful and, as your self-memos are automatically dated, you can also trace the development of your ideas. Ideas may also occur as you engage in an interview or observation session. In this case you may record the idea very briefly as a margin note and write it as a memo to yourself after the event. Similarly, ideas may occur as you work through a documentary source. It may be useful to carry a reporter's notebook or an e-notebook in order to be able to record your ideas, whenever and wherever they occur. When you are undertaking the production of notes, or a transcript, or any aspect of qualitative analysis, the notebook will be available for you to record your ideas.

Self-memos may vary in length from a few words to one or more pages. They can be written as simple notes – they do not need to be set out formally. Miles and Huberman (1994) suggest it will be useful to date them and to provide cross-references to appropriate places in your written-up notes or transcripts, where appropriate. Alternatively, an idea that is not grounded in any data (which may nevertheless prove to be useful) should be recorded as such. Memos should be filed together, not with notes or transcripts, and may themselves be categorised where this will help you to undertake later stages of your qualitative analysis. Memos may also be updated as your research progresses, so that your bank of ideas continues to have currency and relevance (Glaser 1978).

Research notebook

An alternative approach to recording your ideas about your research is to keep a **research notebook**. You may of course keep such a notebook alongside the creation of self-memos. Its purpose will be similar to the creation of self-memos: to record your ideas and your reflections, and to act as an aide-memoire about your intentions for the direction of your research. Using a chronological format may help you to identify the development of certain ideas (such as data categories, propositions or hypotheses) and the way in which your research has progressed, as well as providing an approach that suits the way in which you like to think (Riley 1996).

Reflective diary

In Chapter 1 we recommended you also keep a **reflective diary** or journal. This is devoted to reflections about your experiences of undertaking research, what you have learnt from these experiences, how you will seek to apply this learning as your research progresses and what you will need to do to develop your competence to further your research. Increasingly universities require students to reflect on their research as part of their project reports to be able to evaluate their learning from the research process. In Section 1.5 we talked about keeping a reflective diary and provided you with a checklist (Box 1.4).

Reflection may occur in a number of ways. It may occur during an event, so that you one reflect on your approach while you conducting an activity. This type of reflection may occur, for example, while you are interviewing or observing. Reflection may also occur after an activity has taken place so that you reflect on what occurred and how you might be able to do better next time. A more fundamental type of reflection, known as **reflexivity**, involves you examining your reactions to what is being researched, the nature of your relationship with those who take part in the research and evaluating the way in which you interpret data to construct knowledge (Finlay 2002; Gerstl-Pepin and Patrizio 2009). Given its interpretivist nature, Finlay (2002: 211) says that reflexivity is, 'now the defining feature of qualitative research'. Your reactions, your interactions with those taking part and your attitudes and beliefs may each impact on your interpretation of the data that are shared with you. Engaging in forms of reflexivity may enable you to develop greater insights as you explore and analyse these data. Developing a reflexive focus in your reflective diary may therefore prove to be a valuable aid to further your research.

13.6 Generic approaches to analysis

We recognised in Section 13.3 that there is not a standardised approach to analyse your qualitative data. A key determinant of the approach you use will depend on whether you commence your research inductively or deductively. Each may lead to different options about how to analyse the qualitative data that you collect. There are few prescriptions about the approach that you ought to use: you will need to make a choice, perhaps after discussing this with your tutor, and be able to justify this. You will need to be able to show that your choice of procedure(s) to analyse your qualitative data is consistent with your research philosophy (Chapter 4), research strategy (Chapter 5) and nature of your data collection method(s) in order to be able to justify your approach.

Some procedures for analysing qualitative data are highly structured, whereas others adopt a much lower level of structure. Related to this, some approaches to analysing qualitative data are associated with specific rules, whereas others rely much more on the researcher's interpretation. These means of differentiating qualitative analysis procedures, together with the distinction between using a deductive or inductive approach, while not comprehensive, are shown as three independent dimensions in Figure 13.1. For example, Grounded Theory (Sections 13.7 and 5.5) is more structured, relies on rules and is principally inductive.

These means to differentiate qualitative analysis can be problematic when used to map some analytic strategies or procedures. For example, Grounded Theory Method analysis procedures (Section 13.7) may be more or less structured dependent upon the precise Grounded Theory strategy adopted and still require interpretation even when following one of its more rule-bound models. However, in general terms the use of these dimensions will help you to compare different qualitative analysis procedures more easily. Care also needs to be taken in relation to any decisions that result from a consideration of these dimensions. For example, the use of a procedure that relies on your interpretation should not be seen as implying less analytical rigour (Coffey and Atkinson 1996; Tesch 1990). These three dimensions should not therefore be used to indicate higher quality at one end of a particular continuum.

Figure 13.1 Dimensions of qualitative analysis

Various researchers have developed and used specific analytical procedures for qualitative data (e.g. Corbin and Strauss 2008; Johnson 2004; King 2012; Yin 2009). As we have discussed, these may be divided into inductively based procedures (Section 13.7) or deductively based procedures (Section 13.8). There is also a third category of generic approaches to analyse qualitative data that are not necessarily linked to a specific theoretical approach but which follow the general principles of analysing this type of data to enable you to:

1 comprehend often large and disparate amounts of qualitative data;
2 integrate related data drawn from different transcripts and notes;
3 identify key themes or patterns from them for further exploration;
4 develop and/or test theories based on these apparent patterns or relationships;
5 draw and verify conclusions.

We outline a generic approach to analyse your qualitative data that follows these five points by: identifying categories or codes that allow you to comprehend your data; attaching data from disparate sources to appropriate categories or codes to integrate these data; developing analytical categories further to identify relationships and patterns; developing testable propositions; drawing and verifying conclusions. This generic analytical approach, outlined by many qualitative researchers (e.g. Dey 1993; Robson 2011), is not restricted to one theoretical approach and is often used in a more particularised or distinct form in a range of other specific approaches (e.g. as in forms of Grounded Theory Method). Outlining this generic approach here may provide you with an adequate means to analyse your qualitative data or, alternatively, provide an introduction to some of the analytical processes contained in the specific approaches discussed in Sections 13.7 and 13.8.

In this section we also outline two further generic approaches to analyse your qualitative data. The first of these briefly outlines some of the ideas of Miles and Huberman (1994) related to data reduction, data display and the drawing and verification of conclusions. The second relates to the use of a quasi-statistical approach, where qualitative data are quantitised.

Categorising data

The first activity involves identifying categories, to which you will subsequently attach meaningful 'bits' or 'chunks' of your original data (see the next subsection). This allows you to rearrange your original data into analytical categories. Each category is given a suitable name, usually referred to as a code or label. This simple process provides you with an emergent structure that is relevant to your research project to organise and analyse your data further.

Your identification of categories will be guided by the purpose of your research as expressed through your research question and objectives. Another researcher with different objectives to you may derive different categories from the same data (Dey 1993). Categories can either be developed in advance by consulting the literature (concept-driven category) or from the data collected (data-driven category), or both. Strauss and Corbin (1998) suggest that there are three main sources to derive codes or labels for these categories:

- you utilise terms that emerge as you analyse your data;
- they are based on the actual terms used by your participants ('in vivo' codes); or
- they are derived from terms used in existing theory and the literature.

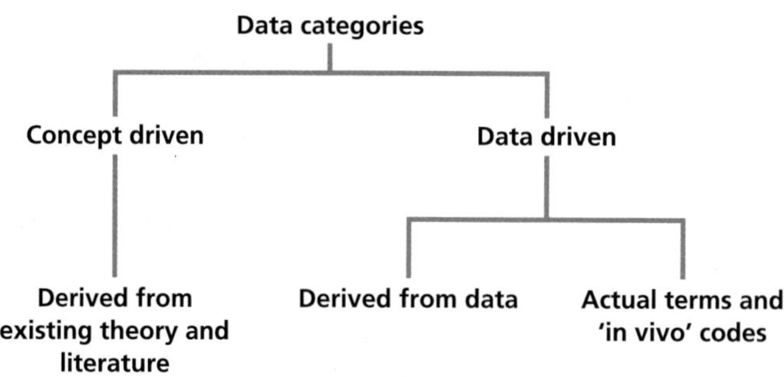

Figure 13.2 Types of category and codes

These types of category and codes or labels are shown in Figure 13.2 to illustrate their relationship.

The categories that you devise need to be part of a coherent set so that they provide you with a well-structured analytical framework to pursue your analysis. Dey (1993: 96–7) states that 'categories must have two aspects, an internal aspect – they must be meaningful in relation to the data – and an external aspect – they must be meaningful in relation to the other categories'. Categories you develop initially, especially where you use an inductive, grounded approach, are likely to be essentially descriptive. As your analysis progresses you may develop a more hierarchical approach to the categorisation of your data, whereby some category codes or labels will be developed and used to indicate emerging analytical linkages between your data (Corbin and Strauss 2008; King 2012; Box 13.6). Categories may also show the occurrence or non-occurrence of a phenomenon, or the strength of opinion in some instances. For example, Adrian undertook a research project where some categories had large amounts of data attached to them, while other categories attracted relatively small amounts of data. As we discuss later, this was helpful in pursuing the analysis and led to the large categories being subdivided into further categories (Box 13.7).

'Unitising' data

The next activity of the analytical process will be to attach relevant 'bits' or 'chunks' of your data, which we refer to as 'units' of data, to the appropriate category or categories that you have devised. A **unit of data** may be a number of words, a line of a transcript, a sentence, a number of sentences, a complete paragraph, or some other chunk of textual data that fits the category (Boxes 13.6 and 13.7).

You may use CAQDAS to help you to process your data (Section 13.9) or you may use a manual approach. Where you use the second approach, you can label a unit of data with the appropriate category (or categories) in the margin of your transcript or set of notes (Box 13.6). This may then be copied, cut up and stuck onto a data card, or otherwise transferred, and filed so that you end up with piles of related units of data. When doing this, it is essential to label each unit of data carefully so that you know its precise source (Section 13.4). An alternative is to index categories by recording precisely where they occur in your transcripts or notes (e.g. interview 7, page 2, line 16) on cards headed with particular category labels (Easterby-Smith et al. 2008). Undertaking this stage of the analytic process means that you are engaging in a selective process, guided by the aim of your research and your research objectives, which has the effect of reducing and rearranging your data into a more manageable and comprehensible form.

Box 13.6 Focus on student research

Interview extract with categories attached

Adrian's research project was concerned with how human resource management professionals from a range of organisations had managed the downsizing process in their own organisation. He derived his initial categories from existing theory in the academic literature and attached them subsequently to units of each transcript. His initial categories were hierarchical, the codes he used being shown in brackets:

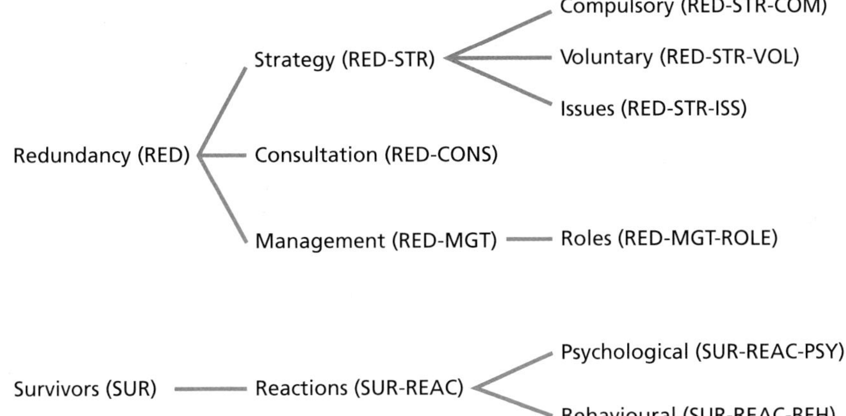

These were then attached to the interview transcript, using sentences as units of data. Like our jigsaw example at the start of this chapter, those units of data that were coded with more than one category suggested interrelationships:

RED–CONS	27MM The first stage is to find out what particular employees
	want for themselves and how they want this to happen. Staff are
RED–CONS	seen by their line manager and/or a member of personnel.
RED–MGT–ROLE	Employees might want to talk to someone from personnel rather
	than talk with their line manager – well, you know, for obvious
	reasons, at least as they see it – and this would be acceptable to the
RED–STR–VOL	organisation. This meeting provides them with the opportunity to
	opt for voluntary redundancy. We do not categorise employees
RED–STR–ISS	into anything like core or non-core, although we will tell a group
RED–CONS	of employees something like 'there are four of you in this
	particular function and we only need two of you, so you think
RED–CONS	about what should happen'. Sometimes when we attempt to give
	employees a choice about who might leave, they actually ask us to
	make the choice. This is one such situation where a compulsory
RED–STR–COM	selection will occur. We prefer to avoid this compulsory selection
SUR–REAC–PSY	because of the impact on those who survive – negative feelings,
	guilt and so on.

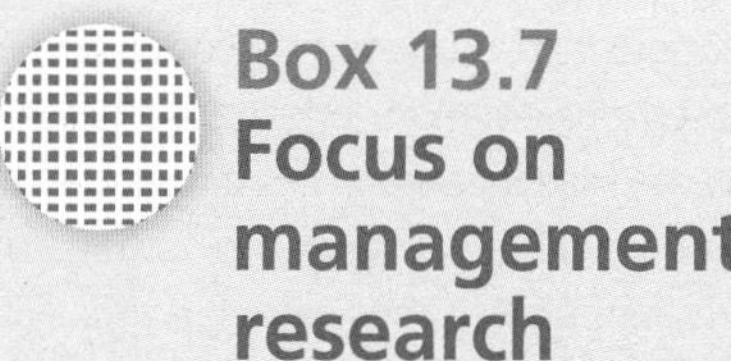

Box 13.7 Focus on management research

Assigning data to and developing categories

'After each interview, I transcribed the interview verbatim and filed its material according to the categorisation then in use. The material was typically in the form of paragraphs [that] were cross-classified to several categories. As I filed each statement, I compared it with previous statements in that category and kept running notes on the content of the category. The categories changed over time; some disappeared and were merged under more general titles. Some emerged out of previous categories that became too heterogeneous. Some categories became parts of matched pairs or triads in which any given comment would typically be filed in each constituent category. For example, comments [that] described instances of lax work or bad workmanship also typically mentioned abusive management. Similarly, statements that described devising one's own procedures also typically included statements of satisfaction with the autonomy that provided. This helped to reveal connections between categories.'

Source: Hodson (1991), cited in Erlandson *et al.* (1993: 119) *Journal of Contemporary Ethnography*. Copyright © 1991 by Sage Publications, Inc. Reprinted by permission

One way of achieving this reduction and rearrangement of your data, depending on the suitability of the data, is to use one or more of the analytical techniques described by Miles and Huberman (1994). These are considered later in this section.

Recognising relationships and developing categories

Generating categories and reorganising your data according to them means that you are engaging in the process of analysing your data (Dey 1993; Yin 2009). This analysis will continue as you search for key themes and patterns or relationships in your rearranged data. This may lead you to revise your categories and continue to rearrange your data as you search for meaning in your data set. You may decide to 'subdivide or integrate categories as ways of refining or focusing [your] analysis' (Dey 1993: 95).

There may be practical reasons for seeking to divide or join your initial categories. Some categories, for example, may attract large numbers of units of data and prove to be too broad for further analysis without being subdivided. You may also gain new insights within existing categories that suggest new ones. Because of this we would strongly recommend you keep an up-to-date definition of each of the categories you are using, so that you can maintain consistency when assigning further units of data to these as you continue to undertake interviews or observations (Miles and Huberman 1994). Subsequently you will continue to generate a more hierarchical approach to the categorisation and coding of your data as you move towards the generation of an explanation for the research question and objectives that form the focus of your research (Box 13.7).

Developing testable propositions

As you seek to reveal patterns within your data and to recognise relationships between categories, you will be able to develop testable propositions (Box 13.8). The appearance of an apparent relationship or connection between categories will need to be tested if you are to be able to conclude that there is an actual relationship. However, while this is sometimes referred to as 'testing a hypothesis', it is not the same as the statistical hypothesis or significance testing we discussed in relation to quantitative analysis in Section 12.5.

Box 13.8 Focus on student research

Research propositions

During the process of qualitative data analysis a student evaluating the growth of online retailing formulated the following proposition:

Customers' willingness to trust online retailers depends on the ease of use of their website.

A student exploring mortgage borrowers' decision making drew up this proposition:

Potential mortgage borrowers' choice of lending institution is strongly affected by the level of customer service that they receive during the initial inquiry stage.

Another student investigating cause-related marketing formulated the following proposition:

Companies engaging in cause-related marketing are motivated principally by altruism.

A relationship is evident in each of these propositions. Each was tested using the data that had been collected or that were to be collected.

It is important to test the propositions that emerge inductively from the data by seeking alternative explanations and negative examples that do not conform to the pattern or relationship being tested. Alternative explanations frequently exist, and only by testing the propositions that you identify will you be able to move towards formulating valid conclusions and an explanatory theory, even a simple one (Miles and Huberman 1994). Dey (1993: 48) points out that 'the association of one variable with another is not sufficient ground for inferring a causal or any other connection between them'. The existence of an intervening variable may offer a more valid explanation of an association that is apparent in your data (Box 13.9).

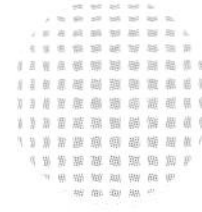

Box 13.9 Focus on student research

The impact of an intervening variable

Kevin's research project involved looking at the use of subcontractors by an organisation. A relationship appeared to emerge between the total value of contracts a particular subcontractor had been awarded and the size of that contractor in terms of number of employees; in particular, those contractors with larger numbers of employees had a larger total value of contracts. This could have led Kevin to conclude that the value of work undertaken by a particular subcontractor was related to that organisation's size and that, in particular, the organisation tended to use subcontractors with large numbers of employees.

The organisational reality was not so simple. The organisation had originally used over 2500 subcontractors but had found this exceedingly difficult to manage. To address this issue the organisation had introduced a system of preferred contractors. All 2500 subcontractors had been graded according to the quality of their work, and those whose work had been consistently of high quality being awarded preferred contractor status. This meant that they were invited by the organisation Kevin was researching to tender for all relevant contracts. The intervening variable was therefore the introduction of preferred contractor status dependent upon the quality of work previously undertaken. The fact that the majority of these subcontractors also had relatively large numbers of employees was not the reason why the organisation had awarded them contracts.

By rigorously testing your propositions against your data, looking for alternative explanations and seeking to explain why negative cases occur, you will be able to move towards the development of valid and well-grounded conclusions. The validity of your conclusions needs to be verified by their ability to withstand alternative explanations and the nature of **negative cases**. Negative cases are those that do not support your explanations and the emergence of your grounded theory. Finding cases that do not fit with your analysis should be seen positively as these will help to refine your explanations and direct the selection of further cases to collect and analyse data.

This will help you to avoid interpretations that prove to be unreliable because you only notice evidence that supports your own opinions. This relates to our discussion of reflexivity in Section 13.5. As a researcher you need to recognise your own attitudes and beliefs about the topic being researched, perhaps by writing about these to make them explicit, in order to understand how this affects your judgement about what the research data might mean and to gain greater insights while analysing these data. Kvale and Brinkmann (2009: 242) refer to this process as seeking to achieve 'reflexive objectivity'. This important aspect of your analysis is considered further in Sections 13.7 and 13.8.

The interactive nature of the process

Data collection, data analysis and the development and verification of propositions are very much an interrelated and interactive set of processes. Analysis occurs during the collection of data as well as after it. This analysis helps to shape the direction of data collection, especially where you are following a more inductive, grounded approach (Section 13.7). The propositions that emerge from your data or those you commenced with at the start of your data collection (Section 13.8) will be tested as you compare them against the cases in your study (Erlandson et al. 1993; Glaser and Strauss 1967). The key point here is the relative flexibility that this type of process permits you.

The interactive nature of data collection and analysis allows you to recognise important themes, patterns and relationships as you collect data: in other words, to allow these to emerge from the process of data collection and analysis. As a result you will be able to re-categorise your existing data to see whether these themes, patterns and relationships are present in the cases where you have already collected data. You will also be able to adjust your future data collection to see whether data exist in cases where you intend to conduct your research (Corbin and Strauss 2008).

The concurrent process of data collection and analysis also has implications for the way in which you manage your time and organise your data and related documentation. As we discussed in Section 10.6, it will be necessary to arrange interviews or observations with enough space between them to allow yourself sufficient time to word process a transcript or set of notes, and to analyse this before proceeding to your next data-collection session. Where you conduct a small number of interviews in one day, you will need time during the evening to undertake some initial analysis on these before carrying out further interviews. You may also be able to find a little time between interviews to carry out a cursory level of analysis. As part of this we have found it extremely helpful to listen to audio-recordings of interviews we have undertaken while travelling to and from the university.

There is a clear limit to the value of continuing to undertake interviews or observations without properly analysing these in the manner described earlier. There is a danger of data overload where you continue to collect data without sufficiently analysing these. This will be associated with a lost opportunity to understand what your data reveal in relation to your research question and the directions that might be worth pursuing for your research.

Reporting qualitative data results

The process of analysing your data will reveal themes, patterns and relationships which, having been verified, will be important to report. A quantitative study may use an assortment of diagrams, tables and statistics to present the results from the use of questionnaires (Sections 12.3 and 12.4). Qualitative studies do not use such standard devices to report results. Instead it will be necessary to devise other means to present your qualitative findings. These will need to achieve a balance between providing necessary contextual description and presenting analytical findings. One means might be to use your research objectives as the way to structure and present your analytical findings. The role of your research objectives is to operationalise your aim or research question (Section 2.4). As your objectives are designed to help you to arrive at an answer to your research question, they can be used an organising device to present your results in a logical way. Within such a structure you will need to report the themes, patterns and verified relationships that your data collection and analysis have revealed.

You may seek to report these by using your own text and a selection of quotations from those who took part in your research. Care needs to be exercised when using quotations from interviews, observations or verbatim documentary sources. Kvale and Brinkmann (2009) offer some useful advice about the use of quotations when reporting qualitative data results. Quotations need to support your own text not be a replacement for it. You should be very selective about which quotations to use to support a particular finding. Not all qualitative results will need to be supported by the use of a quotation. Those that you use should be short and clearly related to the finding being reported. You will also need to interpret the quotations that you use so that these are clearly contextualised. You will need to avoid stringing together a number of quotations that in effect leave the reader of your project report to make sense of what these all mean and what it is that you found. You should avoid using quotations in a formulaic way, such as starting or ending a section of findings with a quotation. You will also need to ensure that the use of a quotation does not undo the anonymity of the person who voiced it, or attribute the quotation to a named person unless he or she has expressly agreed to such an attribution.

Quantifying your qualitative data

There may be reasons why you decide to quantify some of your qualitative data (Box 13.10). This is likely to be the case when you wish to count the frequency of certain events, or of particular reasons that have been given, or in relation to specific references to a phenomenon. These frequencies can then be displayed using a table or diagram (Section 12.3) and can usually be produced using CAQDAS programs and exported to statistical analysis software such as IBM SPSS Statistics. They can also often be exported directly to your word processor.

This approach to describing and presenting your data will provide you with a very useful supplement to the principal means of analysing your qualitative data discussed above. It may also enable you to undertake other quantitative analyses, such as those discussed in Sections 12.4 and 12.5. However, it is should only be used as an additional means to achieve this (Box 13.11), as there is clearly only limited purpose in collecting qualitative data if you intend to ignore the nature and value of these data by reducing most of them to a simplified form (Box 13.10).

Box 13.10 Focus on management research

Whether to count your qualitative data

Hannah and Lautsch (2011) in an article published in the *Journal of Management Inquiry* discuss whether or not to quantify some of your qualitative data. They recognise that there are different opinions about quantifying qualitative data based on the opposing views of different researchers and research traditions. They discuss four reasons why you might decide to count your data in a qualitative study:

1 so that this becomes the principal means to present your findings;
2 to support or supplement your qualitatively analysed findings;
3 to confirm or corroborate your qualitatively analysed results;
4 to demonstrate the rigour of your data collection.

For example, Hannah and Lautsch suggest you might provide quantified data about the number of interviews or observations you undertook, the characteristics of your participants (e.g. numbers of female and male participants) and the quantity of data you collected. They also suggest you might present quantified data to establish the credibility of your findings by, for example, showing that the categories you used in your analysis were representative of the data you collected. This might involve stating the number and percentage of units of data attached to a particular analytical category.

Hannah and Lautsch also discuss two reasons when you would avoid quantifying your qualitative data. You wouldn't quantify your qualitative data:

1 where this would mean losing the perspectives of participants or informants;
2 where this would inhibit your scope to understand meanings and generate insights from using an inductive approach to explore your qualitative data.

Hannah and Lautsch go on to discuss circumstances when you might decide to conceal your efforts to quantify data, in this interesting and helpful article.

Data display and analysis

The data display and analysis approach is based on the work of Miles and Huberman (1994), whose book focuses on the process of 'doing analysis'. For them, the process of analysis consists of three concurrent sub-processes:

- data reduction;
- data display;
- drawing and verifying conclusions.

As part of the process, **data reduction** includes summarising and simplifying the data collected and/or selectively focusing on some parts of this data. The aim of this process is to transform the data and to condense it. Miles and Huberman outline a number of methods for summarising data, some of which we have already referred to in Section 13.5. These include the production of interview or observation summaries, document summaries, coding and categorising data and perhaps constructing a narrative.

Data display involves organising and assembling your data into summary diagrammatic or visual displays. Miles and Huberman describe a number of ways of displaying data, and refer to two main families of data display: matrices and networks. Matrices are generally tabular in form, with defined columns and rows, where data are entered selectively into the appropriate cells of such a matrix, to facilitate further data analysis

Box 13.11 Focus on student research

Using a data cloud to display the frequency of key terms

Luca undertook a research project evaluating types of pay structure. This involved him conducting interviews in organisations that each used a different pay structure. Luca wanted to explore why each had decided to adopt a particular structure and to evaluate perceptions about that structure's use in practice. He was interested to use multiple forms of data analysis and this led him to consider quantifying or counting some of his data. To demonstrate the frequency of terms used by his interview participants he thought it might be useful to produce a data cloud for each set of interviews exploring a particular pay structure. Since these data clouds would represent the actual terms used by his interview participants, they helped Luca to demonstrate how he had derived the 'in vivo' codes he used in his Grounded Theory analytical approach. This data cloud represents the terms used by interview participants in an organisation that had implemented a Job Families pay structure:

(Box 13.12). A network is a collection of nodes or boxes that are joined or linked by lines, perhaps with arrows to indicate relationships. The boxes or nodes contain brief descriptions or labels to indicate variables or key points from the data.

Miles and Huberman (1994) believe that there are a number of advantages associated with using these forms of data display. Qualitative data collection tends to produce hours of audio-recorded interviews or extensive piles of notes. Once these have been transcribed or word processed, they are generally referred to as 'extended text'. Extended text is considered an unreduced form of display that is difficult to analyse because it is both extensive and poorly ordered. Based on the logic that 'you know what you display', the analysis of data and the drawing of conclusions from these will be helped by using matrices, networks or other visual forms to display reduced or selected data drawn from your extended text. Miles and Huberman argue that these forms of display are relatively easy to generate, can be developed to fit your data specifically, and will help you develop your analytical thinking as you work through several iterations to develop a visual form that represents your data well.

Recognising relationships and patterns in the data, as well as drawing conclusions and verifying these, are helped by the use of data displays. A display allows you to make comparisons between the elements of the data and to identify any relationships, key themes, patterns and trends that may be evident. These will be worthy of further exploration and analysis. In this way, the use of data displays can help you to interpret your data and to draw meaning from it.

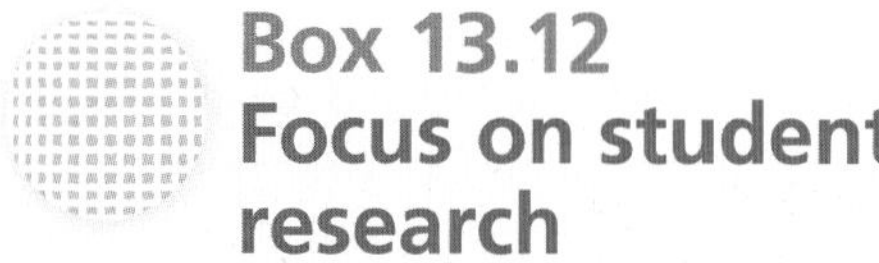

Box 13.12 Focus on student research

Using CAQDAS to explore how key words are used in context

Marcus' research was concerned with how staff were responding to the managed changes in the organisation where he worked. He had collected his data using an online questionnaire, which contained the open question: 'If there is any further you would like to add in relation to the changes at OrgCo, please type your comment in the box'. Marcus downloaded the responses verbatim from the online survey tool as a data file and spellchecked them, correcting words that had been misspelled or used American spellings to the English spelling. This ensured he would pick up all occurrences of particular words such as 'staff' or 'OrgCo', the pseudonym he used to anonymise the organisation. He then loaded the spellchecked data into Provalis Research's text analysis software WordStat. These were displayed in a tabular form. During the next stage of his analysis Marcus wanted to see which respondents had mentioned staff or staffing in their responses to the question and the context in which the words had been used. He therefore searched for the keyword 'staff' within his data.

Scanning the responses suggested that those respondents who had answered this question appeared to often talk about how staff had been treated by Orgco. Marcus decided to investigate further.

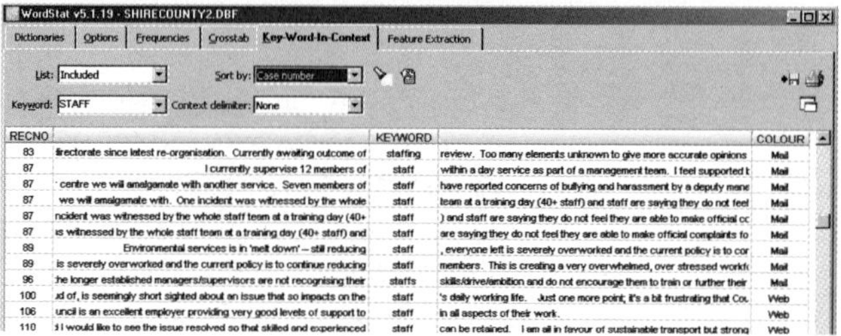

RECNO		KEYWORD		COLOUR
83	irectorate since latest re-organisation. Currently awaiting outcome of	staffing	review. Too many elements unknown to give more accurate opinions	Mail
87	I currently supervise 12 members of	staff	within a day service as part of a management team. I feel supported t	Mail
87	centre we will amalgamate with another service. Seven members of	staff	have reported concerns of bullying and harassment by a deputy mane	Mail
87	we will amalgamate with. One incident was witnessed by the whole	staff	team at a training day (40+ staff) and staff are saying they do not feel	Mail
87	ncident was witnessed by the whole staff team at a training day (40+	staff	) and staff are saying they do not feel they are able to make official cc	Mail
87	is witnessed by the whole staff team at a training day (40+ staff) and	staff	are saying they do not feel they are able to make official complaints fo	Mail
89	Environmental services is in 'melt down' – still reducing	staff	, everyone left is severely overworked and the current policy is to cor	Mail
89	is severely overworked and the current policy is to continue reducing	staff	members. This is creating a very overwhelmed, over stressed workfc	Mail
96	he longer established managers/supervisors are not recognising their	staffs	skills/drive/ambition and do not encourage them to train or further their	Mail
100	ad of, is seemingly short sighted about an issue that so impacts on the	staff	's daily working life. Just one more point; it's a bit frustrating that Cou	Web
106	uncil is an excellent employer providing very good levels of support to	staff	in all aspects of their work.	Web
110	d I would like to see the issue resolved so that skilled and experienced	staff	can be retained. I am all in favour of sustainable transport but strong	Web

Use of data display and analysis can provide you with an appropriate set of procedures to analyse your qualitative data, or alternatively one or more of the techniques that Miles and Huberman (1994) outline can be useful as part of your approach to analysing this type of data. They describe the analysis of qualitative data as an interactive process, and in this sense their approach includes many aspects of analysis that complement the generic processes discussed earlier in this section. Their approach is a systematic and structured one, and they recognise that the procedures they outline are often associated with a fairly high level of formalisation. However, unlike grounded theory, the exact procedures to be followed within their framework of data reduction, display and conclusion drawing and verification are not specified. Miles and Huberman (1994) refer to their book as a 'sourcebook', and as such they offer a number of possible techniques that may be appropriate within their overall approach. If you intend to use their book we suggest you take care in identifying what is useful for you in the context of your own research question and objectives.

Data display and analysis is suited to an inductive strategy to analyse qualitative data, although it is also compatible with a more deductive strategy. Miles and Huberman's (1994) book is useful both for its overall discussion of the analysis of qualitative data and in relation to the many suggestions relating to particular aspects of, and techniques for, the successful conduct of this process.

13.7 Specific approaches to analysis: inductive procedures

This section outlines and briefly discusses a number of inductively based analytical procedures to analyse qualitative data. These are:

- Grounded Theory Method;
- Template Analysis;

- Analytic Induction;
- Narrative Analysis;
- Discourse Analysis.

While most of these analytical procedures commence from an inductive perspective, in practice they may incorporate a deductive approach to analyse qualitative data, as we discuss. Template Analysis is the exception as it commences from a deductive perspective and then uses an inductive approach.

There may be a number of good reasons for adopting an inductive approach to your research project and the analysis of the data that you collect. First, as we discussed in Section 13.3, you may commence an exploratory project seeking to generate a direction for further work. Second, the scope of your research may be constrained by adopting theoretical propositions that do not reflect your participants' views and experience. In this case, the use of a theoretically based approach to qualitative analysis would prove inadequate. The use of an inductive approach in such a case should allow a good 'fit' to develop between the social reality of the research participants and the theory that emerges – it will be 'grounded' in that reality. This relationship should also mean that those who participated in the research process would understand any theory that emerges. Third, the theory may be used to suggest subsequent, appropriate action to be taken because it is specifically derived from the events and circumstances of the setting in which the research was conducted. Finally, the theory's generalisability may also be tested in other contexts (e.g. Corbin and Strauss 2008; Glaser and Strauss 1967).

You should not, however, use an inductive approach as a means of avoiding a proper level of preparation before commencing your research project. Researchers who use such an approach do not start to research a subject area without a competent level of knowledge about that area. Their research commences with a clearly defined research question and objectives, even though this may be altered by the nature of the data that they collect. For example, Hodson (1991, cited in Erlandson et al. 1993) reported that his initial purpose was focused on organisational sabotage, although the research process led him to develop and seek to verify a hypothesis related to more subtle forms of non-cooperation with an employer. The avoidance of a predetermined theoretical basis in this type of approach is related to the desire to search for and recognise meanings in the data and to understand the social context and perceptions of your research participants. It is not to avoid the burden of producing this before the process of data collection! You will need to compare your explanations with existing theory once these have emerged. The use of an inductive approach may also involve you in a lengthy period of data collection and concurrent analysis in order to analyse a theme adequately or to derive a well-grounded theory. Corbin and Strauss (2008) suggest that this type of approach may take months to complete. This is an important consideration if, like many of our students, your research project is time-constrained by a submission date.

Grounded Theory Method

We discussed Grounded Theory as a research strategy in Section 5.5. The aim of this strategy is to use an inductive approach to develop a grounded theory around the core category that emerges from your data. Analytical procedures have been designed to achieve this aim. Grounded Theory Method is associated with a number of defined procedures to collect and analyse data and some prominent advocates of this method state fairly precise procedures to be followed in relation to each of its analytic processes. The exact nature of these procedures varies between sources that outline this method and even between editions of the same book (e.g. Bryant and Charmaz 2007; Charmaz 2006; Corbin and Strauss 2008; Glaser and Strauss 1967; Strauss and Corbin 1998).

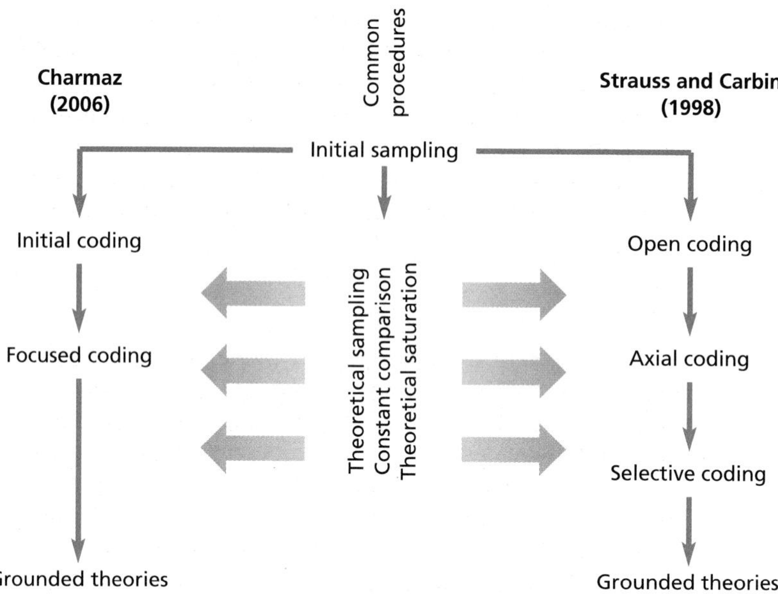

Figure 13.3 Comparing approaches to grounded theory method
Source: © Mark Saunders, Philip Lewis and Adrian Thornhill 2011

For example, the Grounded Theory Method of Strauss and Corbin (1998) and Corbin and Strauss (2008) is highly structured and systematic, with set procedures to follow at each stage of analysis. However, between the two editions of this book, advice about some of these analytical procedures changed. In the Grounded Theory Method of Strauss and Corbin (1998) the disaggregation of data into units is called open coding, the process of recognising relationships between categories is referred to as axial coding, and the integration of categories around a core category to develop a theory is labelled selective coding. In the 2008 edition, open coding and axial coding have been merged and selective coding has been relabelled as integration. Alternatively, the more flexible approach to Grounded Theory Method of Charmaz (2006) consists of two major phases of coding: initial coding and focused coding, while she also discusses and evaluates axial coding (Strauss and Corbin 1998) and the theoretical coding approach developed by Glaser (1978, 1998).

As an introduction to the analytical procedures associated with using Grounded Theory Method, we focus on those of Strauss and Corbin (1998) and Charmaz (2006) (Figure 13.3). Where you decide to use a Grounded Theory strategy (Section 5.5) you will not only find it useful to consult these two books but also the others to which we have referred briefly. However, we believe the key to Grounded Theory Method is the rigour with which you undertake this, rather than a need to follow the procedures of one particular approach unquestioningly. This is an aspect that we would advise you to discuss with your project tutor. In Section 5.5 we introduced three other Grounded Theory Method procedures that are important for the analysis of data. These are constant comparison, theoretical sampling and theoretical saturation (Charmaz 2006; Corbin and Strauss 2008; Glaser and Strauss 1967; Strauss and Corbin 1998).

Within Grounded Theory Method, choice of cases is purposive (Section 7.3). Your **initial sample** will be deliberately chosen to provide you with an appropriate case through which to gather data related to your research question and objectives, or at least to the topic you wish to explore. Following analysis of these initial data, further cases will be chosen from which to collect data, to further the development of your analytical categories and concepts to be able to explore relationships between these to develop a grounded theory. This approach to choosing cases is termed **theoretical sampling** (Section 7.3). Underpinning this is the process of **constantly comparing** the data being collected with the categories and concepts being used, so as to aid the process of developing an emerging theory that will be thoroughly grounded in that data. Theoretical sampling continues until **theoretical saturation** is reached. This occurs when data collection ceases to reveal new data that are relevant to a category, where categories have become well developed and understood and relationships between categories have been verified (Figure 13.3).

Initial coding or open coding

Initial coding or **open coding** is similar to the unitisation and categorisation procedures outlined in Section 13.6. The data that you collect will be disaggregated into conceptual units and provided with a label. The same label or name will be given to similar units of data. However, because this research process commences without an explicit basis in existing theory, the result may be the creation of a multitude of conceptual labels related to the lower level of focus and structure with which you commence your research (Box 13.13). The emphasis in Grounded Theory Method is to derive meaning from the subjects and settings being studied. In Section 13.6 we stated that a unit of data might relate to a few words, a line, a sentence or number of sentences, or a paragraph. The need to understand meanings and to generate categories to encompass these in Grounded Theory Method is likely to lead you to conduct your early analysis by looking at smaller rather than larger units of data. The resulting multitude of code labels will therefore need to be compared and placed into broader, related groupings or categories. This will allow you to produce a more manageable and focused research project and to develop the analytical process. This is discussed in focused coding and axial coding.

There are three main sources to derive names for codes: you utilise terms that emerge from your data; they are based on actual terms used by your participants (**'in vivo' codes**); or they come from terms used in existing theory and the literature (Charmaz 2006; Corbin and Strauss 2008; Strauss and Corbin 1998). However, Strauss and Corbin counsel against names being derived from existing theory and literature in Grounded Theory Method. This is because their use in the written account of your research may lead readers to interpret these according to their prior understanding of such theoretical concepts rather than the particular meaning now being placed on such terms.

The categorisation of your data should lead you to identify significant concepts and themes and help you to consider where data collection should be focused in the future (theoretical sampling). It may also help you to develop the focus of your research question. Using a Grounded Theory strategy may mean that your initial research question is broadly focused, although still within manageable exploratory confines. As you develop a narrower focus through this process, you will be able to refine and limit the scope of your research question.

Focused coding

In the approach of Charmaz (2006), **focused coding** involves reanalysing your data to test which of your initial codes may be used to categorise larger units of these data. By definition, codes with the capability to categorise larger units of your data are likely to be those that proved to be the most important or frequently used during initial coding. Charmaz (2006) believes that progressing from initial coding to focused coding is unlikely to be a simple, linear process. As you gain insights about what your data mean, you should use these insights to evaluate which codes will have the analytical capability to become focused codes to progress your analysis. These conceptually more useful focused codes also allow you to code and compare data across different

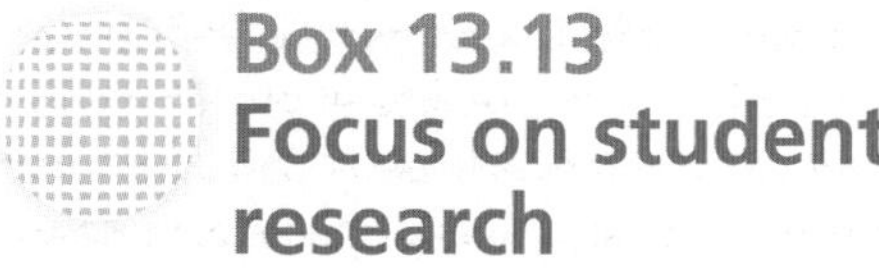

Box 13.13 Focus on student research

Using open coding

James's research was concerned with the micro-strategising activities of individuals in small enterprises. He was particularly interested in how 'firm-level' strategy might evolve from 'day-to-day' mundane and routine activities. He undertook a series of semi-structured interviews with owner-managers of small enterprises. The audio recordings of each interview were subsequently transcribed into a text file and imported into the CAQDAS package NVivo™. Open codes such as 'sharing knowledge' and 'formal strategy' and 'strategy as lived' were then applied to each transcript as illustrated in the extract.

Based upon analysis using his codes James noticed that these small organisations all seemed to have at least one individual (Karen in the extract) who was performing at least some micro-strategising activities (indicated by her strategic vision 'concerning what we might do in the future'). He theorised that most small organisations performed at least some micro-strategising activities, although the accumulation of such actions into an explicit and disseminated strategy was not so prevalent. Taking the theoretical perspective of 'Strategy-as-Practice', James developed his analysis to argue that even those firms which did not believe they were indulging in strategic thinking were actually creating some of its precursors.

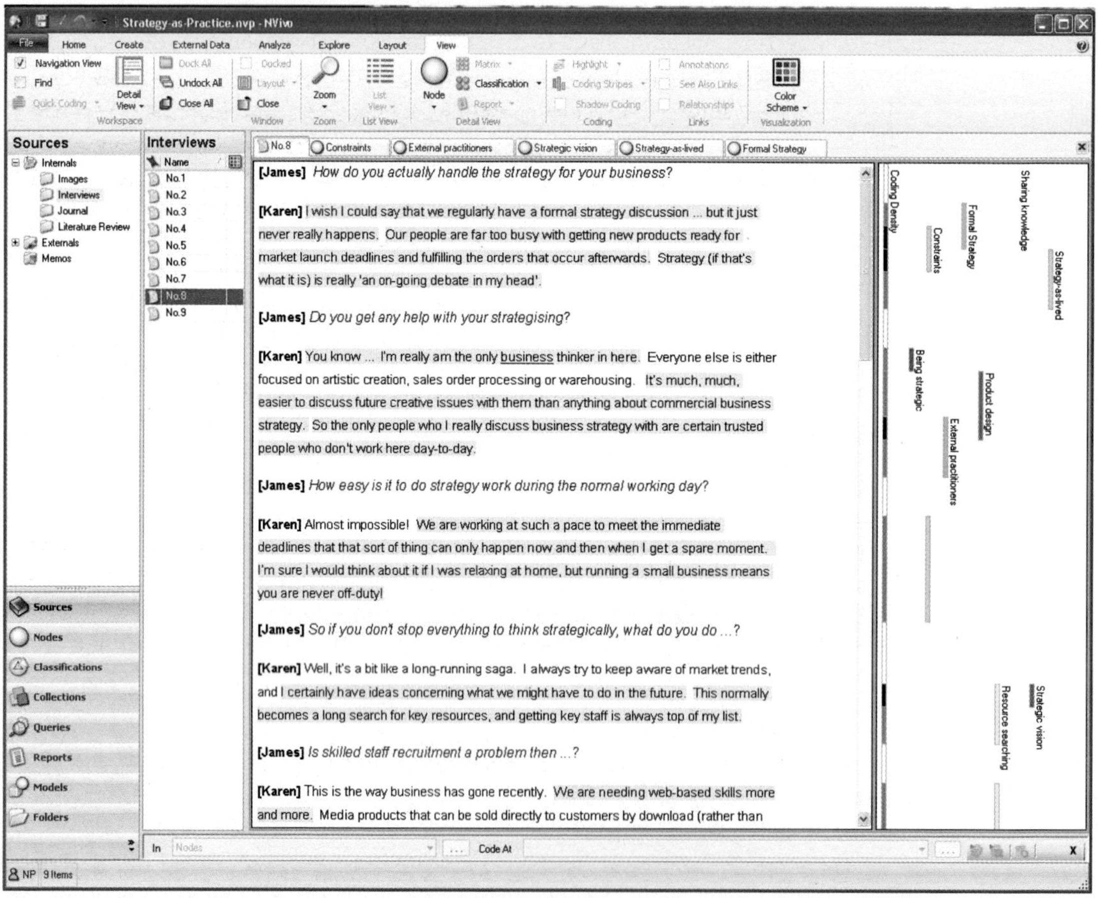

Strategy-as-Practice.nvp - NVivo

[James] *How do you actually handle the strategy for your business?*

[Karen] I wish I could say that we regularly have a formal strategy discussion ... but it just never really happens. Our people are far too busy with getting new products ready for market launch deadlines and fulfilling the orders that occur afterwards. Strategy (if that's what it is) is really 'an on-going debate in my head'.

[James] *Do you get any help with your strategising?*

[Karen] You know ... I'm really am the only business thinker in here. Everyone else is either focused on artistic creation, sales order processing or warehousing. It's much, much, easier to discuss future creative issues with them than anything about commercial business strategy. So the only people who I really discuss business strategy with are certain trusted people who don't work here day-to-day.

[James] *How easy is it to do strategy work during the normal working day?*

[Karen] Almost impossible! We are working at such a pace to meet the immediate deadlines that that sort of thing can only happen now and then when I get a spare moment. I'm sure I would think about it if I was relaxing at home, but running a small business means you are never off-duty!

[James] *So if you don't stop everything to think strategically, what do you do ...?*

[Karen] Well, it's a bit like a long-running saga. I always try to keep aware of market trends, and I certainly have ideas concerning what we might have to do in the future. This normally becomes a long search for key resources, and getting key staff is always top of my list.

[James] *Is skilled staff recruitment a problem then ...?*

[Karen] This is the way business has gone recently. We are needing web-based skills more and more. Media products that can be sold directly to customers by download (rather than

interviews and observations. You will be able to develop your analysis by constantly comparing the codes you are using to categorise your data with the data you have collected, to gain further insights and work towards an emergent explanation of what your data mean to you.

In this way, Charmaz's approach to Grounded Theory Method may be seen as being less prescriptive than other approaches. She adopts a constructivist approach, which assumes that people construct their social realities, with both the participants' and the researcher's interpretations being socially constructed. Charmaz emphasises a Grounded Theory Method that is interactive, flexible and less defined. Analysis develops from constantly comparing data to codes and codes to data, to develop higher levels of abstraction rather than necessarily using axial coding or selective coding (discussed later). Analysis is shaped by the researcher's interaction with and interpretation of these constant comparisons. As a result, this approach to Grounded Theory Method does not follow the more tightly defined prescriptive procedures of other approaches.

For these reasons, Charmaz (2006) believes that axial coding (Strauss and Corbin 1998) may be too rigid for some grounded theory researchers. As we go on to describe, axial coding is a way of rearranging the data that were fragmented during open or initial coding into a new whole, based on a hierarchical structure. In some Grounded Theory Method prescriptions, this may involve identifying structural elements such as the situation involved, the issue at the centre of this situation, the interactions that took place and the outcomes or consequences of these actions to develop a hierarchical structure. Charmaz believes that this approach may be appropriate where you wish to use a prescribed analytical framework to develop your analysis. But she believes that some will find it to be too prescriptive and will prefer to use a simpler, more flexible approach. For these, axial coding as specified by Strauss and Corbin will not be useful. The use of initial coding and focused coding, combined with the use of theoretical sampling, constant comparison and theoretical saturation, will provide a more suitable and flexible approach (Figure 13.3). Where axial coding is still used in this more flexible Grounded Theory Method it may be used in a less prescriptive and more flexible way. Charmaz also believes that Glaser's (1978, 1998) theoretical coding procedure is too prescriptive for the same types of reason, so that this particular procedure may be useful for some but not for all approaches using Grounded Theory Method.

We now go on to describe Strauss and Corbin's (1998) approach to axial coding and the approach to selective coding of Strauss and Corbin (1998) and Corbin and Strauss (2008) (see also Figure 13.3).

Axial coding

Axial coding refers to the process of looking for relationships between the categories of data that have emerged from open coding. It indicates a process of theoretical development. As relationships between categories are recognised, they are rearranged into a hierarchical form, with the emergence of subcategories. The essence of this approach is to explore and explain a phenomenon (a subject of your research project) by identifying what is happening and why, the environmental factors that affect this (such as economic, technological, political, legal, social and cultural ones), how it is being managed within the context being examined, and the outcomes of action that has been taken. Clearly, there will be a relationship between these aspects, or categories, and the purpose of your analysis will be to explain this.

Once these relationships have been recognised, you will then seek to verify them against actual data that you have collected. Strauss and Corbin (1998) recommend that you undertake this by formulating questions or statements, which can then be phrased as hypotheses, to test these apparent relationships. As you undertake this process you will be looking for evidence that supports these 'hypotheses' and for negative cases that will demonstrate variations from these relationships.

Selective coding

Strauss and Corbin (1998) suggest that after a lengthy period of data collection, which may take several months, you will have developed a number of principal categories and related subcategories. The stage that follows is called **selective coding**. This is intended to identify one of these principal categories, which becomes known as the central or core category, in order to relate the other categories to this with the intention of integrating the research and developing a grounded theory (Corbin and Strauss 2008; Strauss and Corbin 1998). In the previous stage the emphasis was placed on recognising the relationships between categories and their subcategories. In this stage the emphasis is placed on recognising and developing the relationships between the principal categories that have emerged from this grounded approach in order to develop an explanatory theory.

Implications of using Grounded Theory Method

A number of implications have emerged from this brief outline of the main procedures involved in the use of grounded theory. These may be summed up by saying that the use of Grounded Theory Method will involve you in processes that will be time-consuming, intensive and reflective. Before you commit yourself to this method, you will need to consider the time that you have to conduct your research, the level of competence you will need, your access to data, and the logistical implications of immersing yourself in such an intensive approach to research. There may also be a concern that little of significance will emerge at the end of the research process, and this will be an important aspect for you to consider when determining the focus of your research if you use Grounded Theory Method.

Template Analysis

This subsection is based on the work of King (2012). He describes and discusses a procedure to analyse qualitative data known as **Template Analysis**. A template is essentially a list of the codes or categories that represent the themes revealed from the data that have been collected. Like the data display approach discussed in Section 13.6, Template Analysis combines a deductive and an inductive approach to qualitative analysis in the sense that codes can be predetermined and then amended or added to as data are collected and analysed.

King (2012) provides a number of ways of differentiating Template Analysis from the procedures used in Grounded Theory Method, which he says it resembles. Grounded Theory Method, as we discussed earlier in this section, does not permit the prior specification of any codes to analyse data, holding as it does to a more purely inductive analytical approach as far as is practically possible. Grounded Theory Method is also more structured than Template Analysis, specifying a set of procedures to be used (Strauss and Corbin 2008). In this sense King (2012) comments that Grounded Theory Method is much more prescriptive whilst Template Analysis is similar to the data display and analysis approach in that it offers a more flexible route to analysis, which would allow you to amend its use to the needs of your own research project.

Like the generic approach to categorising data outlined earlier in Section 13.6, Template Analysis involves developing categories and attaching these to units of data. Data are coded and analysed to identify and explore themes, patterns and relationships. The template approach allows codes and categories to be shown hierarchically to help this analytical process. In Box 13.14 a hierarchical relationship is shown between the codes listed, there being (in the example) three levels of codes and greater depth of

Box 13.14 Focus on student research

Part of an initial template to analyse an advertising campaign's impact

Joss had been asked to analyse the impact of a recent advertising campaign. Using her interview topic guide, she used the main questions to set higher-order codes (shown in CAPITALS). Subsidiary questions and probes were used to generate lower-order codes, shown in lower case and italic script. An extract of her initial template follows:

1 CONTEXTUAL FACTORS
- 1 Reasons for campaign
- 2 Environment
  - 1 *Political*
  - 2 *Economic*
  - 3 *Socio-cultural*
  - 4 *Technological*
  - 5 *Legal*
- 3 Nature of the product
  - 1 *Cost*
  - 2 *Features*
  - 3 *Target groups*

2 NATURE OF THE CAMPAIGN
- 1 Media
- 2 Coverage

3 AWARENESS BY TARGET GROUPS AND OTHERS
- 1 Those in target groups
- 2 Others

analysis being indicated by the lower-level codes shown towards the right-hand side of the template. Codes are also grouped together in levels 2 and 3 to show how higher-order codes are constituted.

As data collection proceeds, your template will be subject to revision as part of the process of qualitative analysis. The process of analysing interview transcripts or observation notes will lead to some of the codes being revised and even changes to their place or level in the template hierarchy. This process will also involve unitising data according to the list of codes currently in use. Where you consider introducing a new code or altering the level of an existing code in the template, you will need to verify this action and explore its implications in relation to your previous coding activity. This is usually more straightforward using CAQDAS (Lewins and Silver 2009). As part of this, it is helpful to use self-memos to remind you later of the reasons for these changes.

King (2012) outlines five ways in which a template may be reorganised and revised:

- insertion of a new code into the hierarchy as the result of a relevant issue being identified through data collection for which there is no existing code;
- deletion of a code from the hierarchy if it is not needed;
- merging codes that were originally considered distinctive;
- changing the scope of a code, that is altering its level within the hierarchy;
- changing a higher-order classification.

The issue or theme indicated by a lower-order code may assume a greater importance than expected once data collection and analysis occurs. For example, in Box 13.14, the third-level code 'Features' may prove to be of greater importance in relation to the research project and therefore require to be reclassified as a level 1 code or category. Equally, the analytical relevance of some higher-order codes may be restricted in practice so that they are reclassified at a lower level as a subset of another higher-order code. A template may also be modified when a code originally included as a subcategory of one higher-order code is reclassified as a subcategory of another as you begin to immerse yourself in your transcripts more fully.

The template may continue to be revised until all of the data collected have been coded and analysed carefully. It will therefore serve as an analytical device through which to devise an initial conceptual framework that subsequently will be revised and then finalised as a means to represent and explore key themes and relationships in your data. Using a template will also help you to select key themes to explore and to identify emergent issues that arise through the process of data collection and analysis that you may not have intended to focus on as you commenced your research project (King 2012).

Analytic Induction

Analytic Induction is an inductive version of the explanation-building procedure outlined in Section 13.8 (Yin 2009). This means that the process of collecting and analysing data to understand the research topic or phenomenon is composed of a number of repeated steps to find a valid explanation. Johnson (2004: 165) defines **Analytic Induction** as 'the intensive examination of a strategically selected number of cases so as to empirically establish the causes of a specific phenomenon'. It seeks to develop an explanation by intensively examining the phenomenon being explored, rather than commencing the search for this by using existing theory or predetermined categories. Its approach may therefore be contrasted with that of Template Analysis. It resembles Grounded Theory Method with two main exceptions. As we have noted, Analytic Induction emphasises cycles of developing and testing propositions, albeit that both it and Grounded Theory Method are inductively grounded in participants' data rather than existing knowledge and theory. Second, unlike Grounded Theory Method (but perhaps because there are few published examples in business and management research) its analytical procedures are not as highly developed or formalised. As a result, where you use Analytic Induction, you may also find the generic procedures outlined in Section 13.6 helpful to guide your analysis within each step of this approach.

Data will need to be collected from an initial case study, by conducting exploratory interviews or observations. These data will then be analysed to identify categories and to recognise relationships between them to develop an initial definition of a proposition that seeks to explain the phenomenon. This initial proposition is then tested through the purposive selection of a further case study (Section 7.3), involving further exploratory interviews or observations. Given the loosely defined nature of this initial proposition, it is likely that it will either need to be redefined or that the scope of the phenomenon to be explained will need to be narrowed. Redefining the proposition leads to a third iteration or step in the analytic induction process, involving the purposive selection of a third case study to explore the phenomenon and test this redefined proposition. If at this stage your redefined proposition appears to explain the phenomenon, you may either cease data collection on the basis that you believe you have found a valid explanation or seek to test the explanation in other purposively selected cases to see whether it is still valid. Where the explanation is not adequate, it will again be necessary to redefine your proposition and to test this in the context of another purposively selected case. This process may continue until a redefined proposition is generated that reasonably explains the phenomenon in relevant cases where you collected and analysed data. In practice several redefinitions of the proposition may be necessary to develop a valid explanation of the phenomenon being studied.

As an inductive and incremental way of collecting and analysing data qualitatively this process has the capability to lead to the development of well-grounded explanations. Analytic Induction encourages the collection of data that are thorough and rich by exploring the actions and meanings of those who participate in this process, through in-depth interviews or observation, or some combination of these methods. However, it has been evaluated in different ways in relation to the nature of the explanations that are likely to be produced. On the one hand, it has been claimed that thorough and rigorous use of analytic induction may lead to unassailable explanations where all negative cases are either accounted for by the final revised explanation or excluded by redefining the phenomenon being studied.

On the other hand, Analytic Induction has been criticised because of issues about its limited representativeness and generalisability. Because the final explanation of the research phenomenon will be completely grounded in the cases that give rise to it, this explanation may be without the ability to predict what may be found in other cases, even those containing the same characteristics or conditions. This is the type of criticism which is often made about all inductive research. Two points may be made to rebuff such criticism. First, this type of criticism misses the point of inductive research, which is to find explanations that are well grounded in the context being researched. These explanations will exhibit high levels of reliability and internal validity (or dependability and credibility; see Section 5.8). Others may subsequently seek to test these explanations in other settings. Secondly, such criticism may also be made in relation to much survey research. While survey research will be representative of a wider population, the nature of that population may be restricted to a particular case or number of cases.

Narrative Analysis

We discussed Narrative Inquiry as a research strategy in Section 5.5. Our discussion here focuses on the analysis of narrative data. We noted in Section 5.5 that collecting data through narratives may be advantageous in certain circumstances. These include research contexts where the experiences of your participants can best be understood by collecting and analysing these as complete stories or narratives, rather than as fragmented data (Mello 2002). The ways in which events in a story are linked, the actions that follow and their implications are more likely to be revealed by encouraging a participant to narrate his or her experiences than by responding to a series of pre-formed questions. Narrative Inquiry allows chronological connections and the sequencing of events as told by the narrator to be preserved, with the potential to enrich understanding and aid analysis (Box 13.15).

If this approach is useful to your research project, the question arises about how to analyse the narrative data that you collect in order to preserve these beneficial characteristics and to ensure dependability and credibility (Section 5.8). De Fina and Georgakopoulou (2008) outline what they refer to as the conventional approach to narrative analysis. This centres on analysing narratives according to their structural elements. Two types of structural elements are used in this approach. One of these is to order the analysis of the narrative using a temporal sequence – that is the order in which events occurred. The other is to analyse the narrative using a logical sequence. This involves describing the situation around which the narrative is organised, the issue or complicating variable at the centre of this situation, the events or actions that occurred in relation to this situation and the way in which the situation was resolved, or the outcomes and consequences associated with this situation. Using this approach allows the transcripts of narratives to be left complete, without being fragmented into units of data, as is the case in grounded theory method or in the generic form of categorisation and unitisation outlined in Section 13.6.

Instead of fragmenting these data, your narratives may either be left intact in their original form, or they can be 're-storied' so that they are reconstructed into a new narrative that remains a holistic account albeit in a new, more coherent form. We discuss

Box 13.15 Focus on management research

Using narratives in an organisational context

An article published in *Qualitative Research* by Syrjala, Takala and Sintonen (2009) discusses the use of narratives to explore the wellbeing of an organisation's personnel during corporate mergers. Syrjala et al. studied the impact on employees of a series of corporate mergers that affected a company operating in Finland's electricity distribution industry. Workplace-based interviews were conducted three times over a four-year period with the same sample of employees – each time a corporate merger affected the case study company. Syrjala et al. report that this resulted in a large body of interview data that was fairly chaotic to start with, characterised by a multitude of details and diverse meanings. At this stage these data were not in a narrative form so that it was the role of the researchers to analyse and transform these data into a more comprehensible form.

They choose to use narrative analysis because they felt that this would allow their data to tell stories and reveal insights that would be difficult to make known by any other analytical approach. Whilst they had collected their data by using interviews, these had revealed a series of personal stories reflecting the meanings participants had developed to understand events and make sense of these changes. Narratives were particularly relevant given events within the case study company, where a number of changes affected the same group of employees. Using narratives allowed Syrjala et al. to represent the changing nature of their participants' experiences as they worked through these changes. Narratives allowed them to reflect the different layers of their participants' experiences related to each of these changes. By 'storying' and 're-storying' the data they collected, they were able to present a rich and insightful set of narratives that reflected the experiences of their participants across different levels in the case study company.

're-storying' later in this subsection. In order to analyse these narratives as complete accounts you may colour-code different structural elements such as the defining situation, key issue, action and outcomes. This will allow you identify different analytical themes without fragmenting the narratives you have collected. This simple procedure will also allow you to compare different narrative accounts relating to the same situation more easily as you read and reread each one. Reading and rereading transcripts of narrative accounts several times is recognised as being an important aid to their analysis.

De Fina and Georgakopoulou (2008) believe that this conventional approach may be appropriate for narratives that consist of 'an active teller, highly tellable account, relatively detached from surrounding talk and activity, linear temporal and causal organisation, and certain, constant moral stance' (Ochs and Capps 2001: 20 cited in DeFina and Georgakopoulou 2008), but may not be suitable for other narratives that do not conform to these characteristics. Types of narrative that exhibit less transparent, or more complex, structures, or which do not follow a linear timeline, or do not exhibit identifiable cause-and-effect relationships may therefore need to adopt a different analytical approach.

Mello (2002) discusses a range of approaches to analyse narratives that focus not only on their structural elements but also on other features of their content. These include analysing the text of narratives to identify patterns and themes that occur across the narratives of different participants. This may be achieved by coding within a set of narratives. (For example, you may decide to print several sets of narratives and code a particular theme or pattern within one such set.) They also include analysing differences between individuals' responses to a particular aspect or issue. Mello (2002) says that it can be valuable to compare related parts of different narratives to understand contrasting perspectives between informants. The views from several narratives may be more insightful than using the view from only one. This approach may be repeated in relation to many different aspects that occur in a set of narratives. These aspects may include cultural differences and similarities, beliefs and identity.

Mello (2002) believes that findings will be more dependable and credible where multiple approaches are used to analyse narratives. Using the content of narratives as well as their structural elements to conduct your analysis may therefore provide you with complementary approaches, as well as greater flexibility. In order to demonstrate analytical rigour you will need to explain the approach you use with great care and justify this in relation to your research question and objectives, and your research strategy.

One way to analyse your narrative data involves the process of 're-storying' or 'retelling' (Box 13.15). This can be similar to the structural analytical approach we outlined earlier, using the situation, issue, actions and outcomes in a narrative as the way to re-story and analysis it. You can also analyse a number of related narratives, collected from different participants, to create a new narrative that incorporates all of their stories into one account. This may have analytical value but you will need to remain sensitive to the fact that these re-storied narratives will reflect your construction of events. In achieving this re-storying you will also need to remain sensitive to the reasons why you exclude any material from the original narrative or narratives and whether such material contains relevant meaning that you have not yet grasped!

Discourse analysis

Discourse analysis is a general term that covers an extremely wide variety of approaches to the analysis of language in its own right and is concerned with how and why individuals' language is used by individuals in specific social contexts. In particular, it explores how language (discourse) in the form of talk and text both constructs and simultaneously reproduces and/or changes the social world rather than using it as a means to reveal the social world as a phenomenon (Phillips and Hardy 2002). The focus is therefore on identifying how this reproduction or change occurs. Given these concerns, you will not be surprised that researchers using discourse analysis usually adopt a subjectivist ontology (Section 4.2). In choosing a discourse analysis approach you would explore the use of language in specific contexts such as holiday brochures to construct a social reality of a package holiday or the minutes of meetings to reflect the meaning of the meeting from the perspective of the chairperson. Although there are many forms of discourse analysis (Dick 2004), within this subsection we concern ourselves with one, critical discourse analysis.

Critical discourse analysis assumes that the constructions that individuals make operate not only in a sense-making way but also reproduce or challenge the underlying ideological belief systems of society at large (Dick 2004). Consequently, different discourses will produce different explanations of the same practice such as a meeting, a holiday or a day at work. They will also produce different versions of the same concept. For example, the discourse related to the norms of behaviour that are expected in a classroom are likely to differ between students attending primary school, secondary school and university. In addition, the concept of being a student in a classroom can only be constructed in those societies where some form of organised education exists.

The data that are analysed in critical discourse analysis are texts which can be, as discussed in Section 13.4, collected from a wide variety of sources. Dick (2004) argues that for some research it is useful to identify specific contexts such as the career identities of graduates or the resistance to diversity initiatives in a particular type of organisation. Interview data are transcribed in full prior to analysis and, as the focus is content, Dick (2004) advises that there is no need to indicate pauses or overlaps between speakers

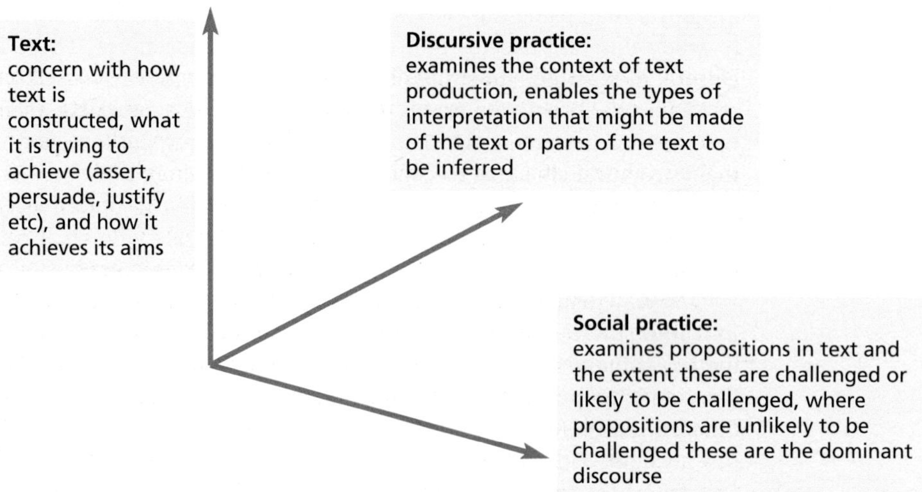
Text:
concern with how text is constructed, what it is trying to achieve (assert, persuade, justify etc), and how it achieves its aims
Discursive practice:
examines the context of text production, enables the types of interpretation that might be made of the text or parts of the text to be inferred
Social practice:
examines propositions in text and the extent these are challenged or likely to be challenged, where propositions are unlikely to be challenged these are the dominant discourse

Figure 13.4 A three-dimensional analytical framework for critical discourse analysis

(Box 13.3 above). She also suggests that it may be possible to use data sampling rather than transcribe and analyse entire interviews (Table 13.2). Once data have been collected, they can be analysed qualitatively, using the procedures outlined in Section 13.6, through a three-dimensional analytical framework. This analyses each discourse from the perspectives of its being (Figure 13.4):

- text;
- discursive practice;
- social practice.

It is this final dimension, social practice, that is likely to reveal where discourses are multiple and contradictory. The extent to which the text defends a particular position provides a clear indication as to the degree to which that position is contested. Where positions are challenged or defended vigorously with the text, these are examples of hegemonic struggle where two or more ideologies compete for dominance.

Discourse analysis therefore focuses on understanding how language is used to construct and change aspects of the world. This means it encourages you not to accept your research data at face value. Its main disadvantages are that it is time-consuming and requires considerable experience before you feel comfortable with the process. In addition, it is a contentious method which is subject to much debate (Dick 2004).

13.8 Specific approaches to analysis: deductive procedures

Yin's (2009) preference for devising theoretical propositions prior to data collection as a means to analyse data is associated with a number of specific analytical procedures. This section outlines two analytical procedures described by Yin (2009) that are particularly applicable to qualitative analysis and examines how the deductive perspective that underpins these impacts upon processes for analysing qualitative data (Section 13.6).

Pattern matching

Pattern matching involves predicting a pattern of outcomes based on theoretical propositions to explain what you expect to find from analysing your data. Using this approach, you will need to develop a conceptual or analytical framework, utilising existing theory, and then test the adequacy of the framework as a means to explain your findings. If the pattern of your data matches that which has been predicted through the conceptual framework you will have found an explanation, where possible threats to the validity of your conclusions can be discounted. We discuss examples related to two variations of this procedure. These variations depend on the nature of the variables being used for pattern matching.

The first variation is associated with a set of dependent variables where you suggest the likely outcomes arising from another, independent variable. For example, based on theoretical propositions drawn from appropriate literature you specify a number of related outcomes (dependent variables) that you expect to find as a result of the implementation of a particular change management programme (independent variable) in an organisation where you intend to undertake research. Having specified these expected outcomes, you then engage in the process of data collection and analysis. Where your predicted outcomes are found, it is likely that your theoretically based explanation is appropriate to explain your findings. If, however, you reveal one or more outcomes that have not been predicted by your explanation, you will need to seek an alternative one (Yin 2009).

The second variation is associated with variables that are independent of each other. In this case you would identify two or more alternative explanations to explain the pattern of outcomes that you expect to find (Box 13.16). As a consequence, only one of these predicted explanations may be valid. In other words, if one explanation is found to explain your findings then the others may be discarded. Where you find a match between one of these predicted explanations and the pattern of your outcomes you will have evidence to suggest that this is indeed an explanation for your findings. Further evidence that this is a correct explanation will flow from finding the same pattern of outcomes in other similar cases (Yin 2009).

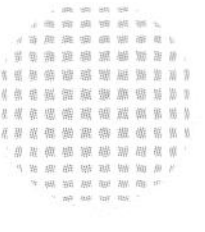

Box 13.16 Focus on student research

Alternative predicted explanations

The objective of Linzi's research project was to explain why productivity had increased in a case study organisation even though a number of factors had been held constant (technology, numbers of staff employed, pay rates and bonuses, and the order book) during the period of the increase in productivity. She developed two alternative explanations based on different theoretical propositions to explain why this increase in productivity had occurred in the organisation. Her explanations were related to the following propositions:

1 the productivity increase is due to better management, which has been able to generate greater employee commitment, where this proposition is based on theory related to strategic human resource management;

2 the productivity increase is due to fears about change and uncertainty in the future, where this proposition is, in addition, based on theory related to organisational behaviour and the management of change.

These propositions offered her two possible and exclusive reasons why the described phenomenon had occurred, so that where evidence could be found to support one of these, the other, which did not match her outcomes, could be discounted.

Explanation building

Another pattern-matching procedure involves an attempt to build an explanation while collecting data and analysing them, rather than testing a predicted explanation as set out above. Yin (2009) recognises that this procedure, which he labels **explanation building**, appears to be similar to Grounded Theory Method (and analytic induction) (Section 13.7). However, unlike these, explanation building is designed to test a theoretical proposition, albeit in an iterative manner, rather than to generate theory inductively (Section 13.7). Yin states that his proposition-testing approach is related to explanatory case studies, while the hypothesis-generating approach developed by Glaser and Strauss (1967) is relevant for exploratory studies. The explanation-building procedure uses the following stages (Yin 2009):

1. Devise a theoretically based proposition, which you will then seek to test.
2. Undertake data collection through an initial case study in order to be able to compare the findings from this in relation to this theoretically based proposition.
3. Where necessary, amend the theoretically based proposition in the light of the findings from the initial case study.
4. Undertake a further round of data collection in order to compare the findings from this in relation to the revised proposition.
5. Where necessary, further amend the revised proposition in the light of the findings from the second case study.
6. Undertake further iterations of this process until a satisfactory explanation is derived.

Impact of a deductive approach on the analysis process

In relation to pattern matching and explanation building, you will still be able to follow the generic processes outlined earlier for analysing qualitative data (Section 13.6), with some modification. First, you will be in a position to commence your data collection with a well-defined research question and set of objectives, and a clear framework and propositions, derived from the theory that you have used. Second, with regard to sampling (Section 7.3), you will be in a position to identify the number and type of organisations to which you wish to gain access in order to undertake data collection. Using non-probability sampling to achieve this should not be offered as an excuse for adopting a less than rigorous approach to selecting sufficient cases to test the propositions that have been advanced and to answer your research question and meet your objectives. Third, the literature that you used and the theory within it will shape the data collection questions that you ask those who participate in your research project (Section 3.2). It is also to be expected that categories for analysis will emerge from the nature of your interview questions. Therefore you will be able to commence data collection with an initial set of categories derived from your theoretical propositions and conceptual framework, linked to your research question and objectives (Miles and Huberman 1994).

Of course, these categories may be subject to change, depending on their appropriateness for the data that your participants provide (Dey 1993). However, where your predicted theoretical explanations appear to fit the data being revealed, your predetermined categories may prove to be useful, subject to some revision and development (Miles and Huberman 1994).

Your use of this deductive approach will also provide you with key themes and patterns to search for in your data. For example, as you carry out your research and conduct analysis through attaching units of data to categories, and examine these for emergent patterns, your analysis will be guided by the theoretical propositions and explanations with which you commenced. Your propositions will still need to be tested with rigour – associated with the thoroughness with which you carry out this analytical process and by seeking negative examples and alternative explanations that do not conform to the pattern or association being tested for.

The use of predicted explanations should mean that the pathway to an answer to your research question and objectives is reasonably defined. The extent to which this is the case will depend on two factors:

- your level of thoroughness in using existing theory to define clearly the theoretical propositions and conceptual framework that will guide your research project;
- the appropriateness of these theoretical propositions and the conceptual framework for the data that you reveal.

The use of a deductive approach is underpinned by the need to specify theoretical propositions before the commencement of data collection and its analysis. Even in explanation building, a theoretically based proposition is suggested initially, although this may be revised through the iterative stages of the process involved. The general processes outlined earlier for analysing qualitative data will be useful to you in carrying out these deductive analytical procedures. In particular, the stages of the process related to devising categories and indentifying patterns are likely to be more apparent, at least initially, because this approach is based on existing theory.

13.9 Using CAQDAS

The use of CAQDAS offers a number of advantages in relation to the analytical procedures we have been discussing. In particular, when used systematically, it can aid continuity and increase both transparency and methodological rigour. These latter points were summarised by one of our students as 'it forces you to do your analysis properly!' However, the use of this type of software may be problematic, not least due to its not being available at some universities!

The literature that evaluates CAQDAS raises a number of issues associated with its use. While there are a number of different CAQDAS programs available, these vary in relation to the type of facilities that they offer and, therefore, potentially in their usefulness for different analytic situations. Consequently, you need to develop some familiarity with a range of programs to be able to evaluate their applicability for the particular analyses you wish to undertake. At the same time, it is likely that only one or perhaps two of these programs will be available for you to explore and evaluate in your university. Lewins and Silver (2009: 1) summarise this situation, stating:

> It is not always easy to visualise exactly what a CAQDAS package offers when exploring it for the first time yourself. Equally when asking someone else for their opinion, it is not always easy to know which questions you should be asking. Most of the software packages we are aware of and discuss regularly are excellent products in several ways. Sometimes you choose a package that is already *in situ* and make good use of it – but if you have a choice about which software to purchase for your research project, you may be in some uncertainty about how to proceed.

Functions

Despite differences between CAQDAS programs, the basic ways in which they can facilitate your qualitative data analysis are similar. Lewins and Silver (2009) summarise these as:

- *Structure of work:* ability to store or provide connections between all data files within the research project.
- *Closeness to data and interactivity:* almost instantaneous access to all your data once it has been introduced.
- *Explore the data:* text search tools enable a word, a phrase or a collection of words to be searched and retrieved within context.
- *Code and retrieve:* complete freedom over the use of inductive, deductive or a combination of coding schema to code, retrieve, recode and output data.
- *Project management and data organisation:* powerful means to manage the research project as a whole and organise your data. Data organisation allows you to focus on subsets of data.
- *Searching and interrogating:* on basis of language used, including automatically coding data, on basis of relationships between codes, for different units of data to build hypotheses and theorise.
- *Writing memos, comments, notes, etc.* to record thoughts systematically in relation to the data.
- *Output:* reports allowing you to view material in hard copy or export it to other applications such as word processors and spreadsheets as well as produce tabular reports.

What is not apparent from this list is that the functions contained in some CAQDAS packages are better at supporting certain types of qualitative data analysis procedures than others. This means that you may need to experiment with more than one package before you find the CAQDAS that meets your needs. Your final choice of CAQDAS package will be dependent on a range of factors, including, not least, the relative benefits you will gain relative to the time you need to invest to learn a CAQDAS program. These factors are summarised in Box 13.17 as a checklist.

Box 13.17 Checklist

Choosing a CAQDAS package

- ✔ How much data do you have that needs to be analysed qualitatively?
- ✔ How important are these data, relative to other data you have collected for your research project?
- ✔ How much time do you have to learn how to use the package?
- ✔ How much support is available in your university to help you learn to use the package?
- ✔ What is the operating system of your computer?
- ✔ How much memory does your computer have?
- ✔ How much time do you have to undertake your analysis?
- ✔ Do you want software that will allow you to take an inductive (or a deductive) approach to your analysis?
- ✔ Do you want a package that will help you manage your thinking and allow you to develop your own codes?
- ✔ Do you want a package that will allow you to explore the way language is used in your data?
- ✔ Do you want a package that allows you display relationships within your data diagrammatically?
- ✔ Do you want a package that will allow you to quantify your data?

Table 13.3 Internet addresses for a range of selected CAQDAS developers

Name	Internet address	Brief comments
ATLAS.ti	www.atlasti.de	Windows version only, offers great flexibility
HyperRESEARCH	www.researchware.com	Windows and MAC versions, simple to use
MAXqda2	www.maxqda.de	Windows version only, intuitive, easy to get to grips with
NVivo	www.qsrinternational.com	Windows version only, very powerful software, large range of searching possibilities
QDA Miner	www.provalisresearch.com	Windows and MAC versions, offering mixed methods analytical capabilities. WordStat is an 'add on' to QDA Miner
QSR N6	www.qsrinternational.com	Windows version only, excellent range of search tools

Sources: Developed from Lewins and Silver (2006); authors' experiences

Exploring the latest versions of CAQDAS

Published information about CAQDAS programs is likely to become out of date fairly quickly. Fortunately, there is a wealth of up-to-date information available from the CAQDAS Networking project's website hosted by the University of Surrey.[1] If you are considering using CAQDAS, we would strongly recommend a visit to this website which, in addition to a wealth of useful articles, also contains weblinks to commercial software producers' sites including downloadable demonstration versions of the software. We would also advise you to explore the Internet sites of CAQDAS producers to obtain details and demonstrations of the latest versions of these packages and the features that they offer. Some of those most widely used are listed in Table 13.3.

13.10 Summary

- Qualitative data are rich and full textual and/or visual data. They may also be characterised as non-standardised and non-numerical data.
- A qualitative approach involves commencing your research from an inductive or deductive perspective.
- Qualitative data need to be carefully prepared for manual or computer-assisted analysis, usually involving transcription.
- There are a number of aids that you might use to help you through the process of qualitative analysis, including: interim summaries, event summaries, document summaries, self-memos, maintaining a research notebook and keeping a reflective diary or reflexive journal.
- There are different approaches to analyse your data, including generic, inductive and deductive approaches.

[1]The Internet address for the CAQDAS Networking Project is www.surrey.ac.uk/sociology/research/researchcentres/caqdas/

- Procedures to analyse your data generally share a number of characteristics, including: the interrelated nature of data collection and analysis; the categorisation and unitisation of data; recognising relationships and developing analytical categories and concepts; and developing testable propositions to build or test theory.
- There are some reasons why you might consider counting or quantifying your qualitative data and other reasons when you would avoid this.
- Displaying data is also a useful way to summarise, analyse and understand it.
- A number of specific analytic procedures have been discussed that commence from an inductive perspective: Grounded Theory Method; Template Analysis; Analytic Induction; Narrative Analysis; Discourse Analysis.
- Specific analytic procedures have been discussed that commence from a deductive perspective: pattern matching and explanation building.
- The use of computer-assisted qualitative data analysis software (CAQDAS) can help you during qualitative analysis with regard to project management and data organisation, keeping close to your data, exploration, coding and retrieval of your data, searching and interrogating to build propositions and theorise, and recording your thoughts systematically.

Self-check questions

Help with these questions is available at the end of the chapter.

13.1 Why do we describe qualitative analysis as an 'interactive process'?

13.2 What types of data will you need to retain and file while you are undertaking qualitative research?

13.3 How would you differentiate between a deductive and an inductive analytical approach?

13.4 What are the main implications of using a deductive analytical approach for the way in which you conduct the process of qualitative analysis?

13.5 What are the main implications of using an inductive analytical approach for the way in which you conduct the process of qualitative analysis?

Review and discussion questions

13.6 With a friend, obtain a transcript of an interview that has already been undertaken. If your university subscribes to online newspapers such as ft.com, these are a good source of business-related transcripts. Alternatively, typing 'interview transcript' into a search engine such as Google will generate numerous possibilities on a vast range of topics!

- **a** With your friend, decide on the unit of analysis you wish to use. We suggest you use either lines or paragraphs and subsequently agree on a coding template.
- **b** Independently, apply your template to your transcript, using it to code your data units.
- **c** How well did your coding template work?
- **d** To what extent does your coding differ from that of your friend?
- **e** Why do you think this is?

13.7 Visit one of the CAQDAS websites listed in Table 13.3. Find and download a demonstration version of the CAQDAS package and explore its features. How useful do you think this will be for analysing your research data?

13.8 Find out whether your university provides you with access to the NVivo™ CAQDAS. If it does, visit this book's companion website and download the self-teach package and associated data sets. Work through this to explore the features of NVivo™.

Progressing your research project

Analysing your data qualitatively

- Undertake and audio-record an initial semi-structured or in-depth interview related to your research project, transcribe this interview, and make a few copies of your transcript. Alternatively obtain a copy of a relevant document.
- Decide whether it is most appropriate to summarise, categorise or develop a narrative using your data in order to answer your research question.
- Where a summary is most appropriate develop this, ensuring you also include contextual data.
- Where a narrative is most appropriate, develop this paying particular attention to the temporal order and the organisational and social contexts.
- Where categorising is most appropriate and your research project is based on a deductive approach, develop a provisional set of categories from your research question and objectives, conceptual framework, research themes and initial propositions. Produce a description of each of these categories. Evaluate these categories to see whether they appear to form a coherent set in relation to the aim of your research.
- Using one of your transcripts, attempt to allocate units of data to appropriate categories by using CAQDAS or writing their code labels alongside the text in the left-hand margin. Again, evaluate this provisional set of categories and modify any that appear to be inappropriate.
- Where categorising is most appropriate and your research project is based on an inductive approach, work through one of the transcript copies and seek to identify categories related to your research purpose. Allocate units of data to appropriate categories by using CAQDAS or writing appropriate code labels for these categories alongside the text in the left-hand margin. List these categories and their labels and produce a description for each of the categories that you have devised.
- Once you have allocated units of data to the set of categories, use the CAQDAS program to organise your data by different categories. Alternatively, cut out the units of data related to different categories and transfer them to an appropriately labelled index card (reference to the interview, location of the text in the transcript and the date and so forth). Read through the units of data within each category.
- Analyse these data by asking questions such as: What are the points of interest that emerge within each category? How will you seek to follow these up during your next data collection session? How does the material that has been revealed through this interview relate to any theoretical explanation or initial propositions with which you commenced your data collection? Are any connections evident between the categories?
- Produce a summary of the interview and attach it to a copy of the transcript. Memo any ideas that you have and file these.
- Repeat the procedures for the remaining qualitative data as appropriate and revise your ideas as necessary.
- Use the questions in Box 1.4 to guide your reflective diary entry.

References

Brekhus, W.H., Galliher, J.F. and Gubrium, J.F. (2005) 'The need for thin description', *Qualitative Inquiry*, Vol. 11, No. 6, pp. 861–79.

Bryant, A. and Charmaz, K. (2007) *The Sage Handbook of Grounded Theory*. London: Sage.

Bryman, A. (1988) *Quantity and Quality in Social Research.* London: Unwin Hyman.

Charmaz, K. (2006) *Constructing Grounded Theory*. London, Sage.

Coffey, A. and Atkinson, P. (1996) *Making Sense of Qualitative Data*. Thousand Oaks, CA: Sage.

Corbin, J. and Strauss, A. (2008) *Basics of Qualitative Research* (3rd edn). Thousand Oaks, CA: Sage.

DeFina, A. and Georgakopoulou, A. (2008) 'Analysing narratives as practices', *Qualitative Research*, Vol. 8, No. 3, pp. 379–87.

Dey, I. (1993) *Qualitative Data Analysis*. London: Routledge.

Dick, P. (2004) 'Discourse analysis', in C. Cassell and G. Symon (eds) *Essential Guide to Qualitative Methods and Analysis in Organizational Research*. London: Sage, pp. 203–13.

Easterby-Smith, M., Thorpe, R. and Jackson, P. (2008) *Management Research: An Introduction* (3rd edn). London: Sage.

Erlandson, D.A., Harris, E.L., Skipper, B.L. and Allen, S.D. (1993) *Doing Naturalistic Inquiry*. Newbury Park, CA: Sage.

Finlay, L. (2002). 'Negotiating the swamp: The opportunity and challenge of reflexivity in research practice', *Qualitative Research*, Vol. 2, No. 2, pp. 209–30.

Gerstl-Pepin, C. and Patrizio, K. (2009) 'Learning from Dumbledore's Pensieve: Metaphor as an aid in teaching reflexivity in qualitative research', *Qualitative Research*, Vol. 9, No. 3, pp. 299–308.

Glaser, B. (1978) *Theoretical Sensitivity: Advances in the Methodology of Grounded Theory*. Mill Valley, CA: Sociology Press.

Glaser, B. (1998) *Doing Grounded Theory: Issues and Discussions*. Mill Valley, CA: Sociology Press.

Glaser, B. and Strauss, A. (1967) *The Discovery of Grounded Theory*. Chicago, IL: Aldine.

Hannah, D.R. and Lautsch, B.A. (2011) 'Counting in qualitative research: Why to conduct it, when to avoid it, and when to closet it', *Journal of Management Inquiry*, Vol. 20, No. 1, pp. 14–22.

Healey, M.J. and Rawlinson, M.B. (1994) 'Interviewing techniques in business and management research', in V.J. Wass and P.E. Wells (eds) *Principles and Practice in Business and Management Research*. Aldershot: Dartmouth, pp. 123–45.

Hodson, R. (1991) 'The active worker: Compliance and autonomy at the workplace', *Journal of Contemporary Ethnography*, Vol. 20, No. 1, pp. 47–8.

Johnson, P. (2004) 'Analytic induction', in G. Symon and C. Cassell (eds) *Essential Guide to Qualitative Methods and Analysis in Organizational Research*. London: Sage, pp. 165–79.

King, N. (2012) 'Doing template analysis', in G. Symon and C. Cassell (eds) *The Practice of Qualitative Organizational Research: Core Methods and Current Challenges*. London: Sage.

Kvale, S. and Brinkmann, S. (2009). *InterViews* (2nd edn). Thousand Oaks, CA: Sage.

Lewins, A. and Silver, C. (2009) 'Choosing a CAQDAS package – 6th edition', CAQDAS Networking Project Working Paper. Available at http://caqdas.soc.surrey.ac.uk/sociology/researchcentres/caqdas/files/2009ChoosingaCAQDASPack [Accessed 14 July 2011].

Mello, R.A. (2002). 'Collocation analysis: A method for conceptualizing and understanding narrative data', *Qualitative Research*, Vol. 2, No. 2, pp. 231–43.

Miles, M.B. and Huberman, A.M. (1994) *Qualitative Data Analysis* (2nd edn). Thousand Oaks, CA: Sage.

Ochs, E. and Capps, L. (2001) *Living Narrative*. Cambridge, MA, Harvard University Press.

Phillips, N. and Hardy, C. (2002) *Discourse Analysis: Investigating Processes of Social Construction*. London: Sage.

Riley, J. (1996) *Getting the Most from your Data: A Handbook of Practical Ideas on How to Analyse Qualitative Data* (2nd edn). Bristol: Technical and Educational Services Ltd.

Robson, C. (2011) *Real World Research: A Resource for Users of Social Research Methods in Applied Settings* (3rd edn). Chichester, John Wiley.

Schatzman, L. and Strauss, A. (1973) *Field Research: Strategies for a Natural Sociology*. Englewood Cliffs, NJ: Prentice-Hall.

Silverman, D. (2007) *A Very Short, Fairly Interesting and Reasonably Cheap Book about Qualitative Research*. London: Sage.

Strauss, A. and Corbin, J. (1998) *Basics of Qualitative Research* (2nd edn). Thousand Oaks, CA: Sage.

Syrjala, J, Takala, T. and Sintonen, T. (2009) 'Narratives as a tool to study personnel wellbeing in corporate mergers', *Qualitative Research*, Vol. 9, No. 3, pp. 263–84.

Tesch, R. (1990) *Qualitative Research: Analysis Types and Software Tools.* New York: Falmer.

Yin, R.K. (2009) *Case Study Research: Design and Methods* (4th edn). Thousand Oaks, CA: Sage.

Further reading

Charmaz, K. (2006) *Constructing Grounded Theory*. London: Sage. Provides an accessible and useful discussion and evaluation of Grounded Theory and grounded theory method.

Lewins, A. and Silver, C. (2009) 'Choosing a CAQDAS package – 6th edition', CAQDAS Networking Project Working Paper. Available at http://caqdas.soc.surrey.ac.uk/ChoosingLewins&SilverV5July06.pdf [Accessed 18 June 2008]. This working paper provides an excellent summary of types of software for managing qualitative data. It covers both code-based theory-building and text retrievers and text-based managers software.

Miles, M.B. and Huberman, A.M. (1994) *Qualitative Data Analysis* (2nd edn). Thousand Oaks, CA: Sage. Provides an excellent source of reference to the elements involved in qualitative research as well as offering a number of particular techniques that may help you to analyse your data.

Symon, G. and Cassell, C. (eds) (2012) *The Practice of Qualitative Research: Core Methods and Current Challenges*. London: Sage. This edited work contains an excellent range of chapters related to analytical strategies.

Yin, R.K. (2009) *Case Study Research: Design and Methods* (4th edn). Thousand Oaks, CA: Sage. Chapter 5 very usefully examines analytical strategies and procedures based on a deductive approach.

Case 13
Creating environmentally friendly office spaces

Stephanie is a part-time student conducting a masters in management at a UK university. Stephanie's research project is focused upon how organisations can make their office spaces more environmentally friendly, and what are the barriers to that process. As a committed green activist, Stephanie has relished the chance to investigate this issue in two separate international locations. One of these is her own organisation, which is a branch of a large multinational bank, and the other is in a New Zealand government office where she had the opportunity to interview staff when she was in Wellington on vacation. Stephanie decided she wanted to do two comparative case studies of how the different organisations approached environmental issues so her data comes from a range of different sources. She has interviewed and audio-recorded 10 employees at each of the different locations about their views and transcribed these interviews. She has also collected documents that relate to the different company policies

Source: Alamy Images/Jaak Nilson

and practices regarding environmental issues. Furthermore she has spent a week conducting participant observation in both offices on the everyday practices around recycling and other environmentally friendly practices. As part of this she has made extensive field notes in her research diary.

This is the first time that Stephanie has conducted any qualitative data analysis and she is concerned to find an appropriate method that will enable her to draw upon the three different sources of data she has across the two case studies. Initially it all seemed a bit bewildering and she was unsure where to start. In her research methods lectures her tutor had talked about three different types of qualitative data analysis as examples of the variety of data analytic processes available. These were content analysis, narrative analysis and thematic analysis using templates, but Stephanie was unsure about which of these would be appropriate in her case.

Initially Stephanie considered how she could use content analysis for this data. She thought about how she could draw up a codebook and the initial terms that she could use. Words and phrases such as *recycling* and *turning off lights* were typical of the phrases that could go in the codebook. She could then go through her interview transcripts, documents and research diary to see precisely how many times each of these words was used. Stephanie designed what she thought was an appropriate codebook, but after coding a couple of interviews, she began to worry about precisely what this kind of analysis would give her. Specifically she had two concerns. One was that it might simplify the complex data that she had, in that everything would be reduced to counting terms rather than addressing meanings about issues. Secondly, she felt that she would lose some of the sense of passion and commitment that came through in the interviews when people talked about environmental issues. This was particularly true in her experience of the New Zealand interviewees.

Given these concerns Stephanie then considered how an analysis of the narratives in the data may be helpful. In reading and rereading her data she had been interested to see that there were some underlying narratives that came through particularly in the interviews and the documents. One of these was the way in which interviewees would draw upon the consequences of climate change in how they talked about their own environmentally friendly practices. There was also an ongoing reference to being part of some collective or community that has some form of shared responsibility for the environment. Stephanie felt that the use of narrative analysis might particularly enable her to identify this shared sense of what environmentally friendly practices were about. However, despite being potentially useful she had two concerns about going down the narrative analysis route. One was that she wasn't sure how the data from her own research dairies could be used in this kind of approach. Where would it fit? Her observations had focused upon practices, rather than what people talked about. Secondly, Stephanie wasn't sure how this kind of narrative analysis would help to address her research question. A narrative analysis couldn't comprehensively address the question of the various barriers that might exist in both the organisations.

Eventually Stephanie settled upon a template analysis for the analytic process. Firstly, she designed a set of themes for the template. She then coded the interview data into those themes in line with the processes of template analysis (King 2004). As part of this process Stephanie soon realised that not every piece of data could clearly be fitted into one theme or another, and in some places she had to create a new theme or splice two sub-themes together to accommodate new data. Therefore at the end of the interview coding process she was surprised that the template structure was somewhat different than it was when she originally started. She then remembered her tutor's advice that she should keep a copy of the original template and the revised template so that she could account for changes she had made along the way. These were, after all, important analytic decisions. Stephanie was surprised how easy it was to then code the data from the participant observation and her research diary into the same template. She was pleased that this process meant that she could see all the data from the different research methods under the different themes in the template. So, for example, the data on what people said in interviews about paper recycling; what the company policy was about paper recycling; and observations on what people did about paper recycling were all in the same part of the template.

Although Stephanie felt a great sense of satisfaction once all the data had been coded, she realised that there was still quite a lot of work left to be done and that the processes of interpretation were only just beginning. She studied her template carefully to see what patterns there were within the various themes and what conclusions she could make. However, there was a nagging doubt in her mind that in coding all of the data into the same template she had somehow lost sense of how to identify differences between the two organisations in their practices. Thinking about this she decided that interpreting the data from the full template would help her answer her overall research questions, but in order to be able to evaluate potentially subtle differences between approaches in the two countries she might also have to separate the UK and New Zealand data and have two identical templates, one containing the UK data and one containing the New Zealand data. After constructing these templates Stephanie felt more confident about summarising the different approaches that the two separate organisations took towards the greening of office space, and the underlying differences between the two countries that might underpin this. Stephanie now felt more confident that as well as addressing her research questions she had something interesting to say from her international comparisons.

Reference

King, N. (2004) 'Templates in the thematic analysis of text', in C.M. Cassell and G. Symon (eds) *Essential Guide to Qualitative Methods in Organizational Research*. London: Sage, pp. 256–70.

Questions

1 Did Stephanie organise her template analysis to make best use of her data? Could she have organised the template analysis differently?
2 We know that Stephanie conducted research in her own organisation and that she is a committed green activist. Should she have taken these issues into account as part of the analytic process and if so, in what ways?
3 What other forms of qualitative data analysis could Stephanie have used and how would these have enabled her to address her research questions?

Ongoing case: Researching emotional labour

Part 3: A revised research question, a variety of secondary data, but what about the analysis?

Although disappointed that her original plan to interview employees has come to nothing, Jessica resolves to develop a slightly different project using secondary data which are publicly available.

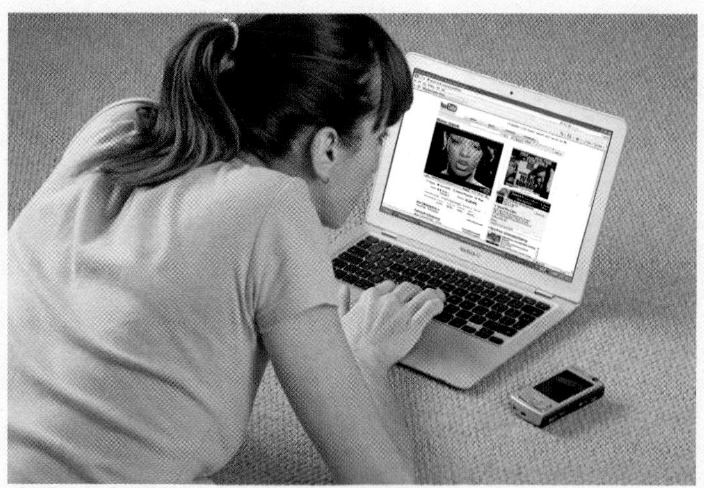

Source: Alamy Images/David J. Green – Lifestyle 2

First of all, she thought about researching how theme parks manage the emotions of their employees. But this still requires an 'insider' perspective, which she doesn't have. So she thought more about the 'public face' of theme parks. What information do these parks present to the outside world?

Jessica thinks again about the analytic concept that first grabbed her attention – 'emotional labour'. She reflects on whether theme parks might use their recruitment processes to attract certain types of people whom the theme park predict will suit jobs requiring emotional labour. The organisation might also have a public-facing 'employer branding' strategy (e.g. Backhaus and Tikoo 2004) to convey a particular image to potential employees (as well as those already working for the theme park) which conveys the sort of employee who might 'fit' in terms of organisational values and the behaviours and attitudes that entails.

Jessica focuses on the recruitment angle. Although she cannot find any data about precisely how many people are employed in theme parks there are numerous tables that she can download giving numbers of people employed in different parts of the service sector. She finds recruitment websites from theme parks as well as mediating recruitment agencies. There are job adverts, articles about employee development potential and the working culture, visual images showing employees at work and social media uploads showcasing how it feels to work for the recruiting theme parks and how important employees are in creating the 'magic' for visitors. These are all artefacts created by the theme parks or their agents which – as they weren't originally intended for research purposes – could be useful as secondary data.

Delving more deeply, Jessica also finds Youtube clips from theme parks' employees and from individuals who've been through the recruitment process. Some are disgruntled; others who've just been accepted for a job are overjoyed, and are even mirroring the 'style' of the theme park culture.

Having found this new source of data, Jessica amends her title, and goes to her project tutor with the new one: 'Recruiting for the smile factories: what is the public face of theme parks' recruitment process, and how do applicants respond to it?'

Reference

Backhaus, K. and Surinder Tikoo, S. (2004) 'Conceptualizing and researching employer branding', *Career Development International*, Vol. 9, No. 5, pp. 501–17.

Questions

1 Jessica has already obtained statistical, visual and textual material including visual images of employees, and recruitment adverts (combining text and imagery). What other secondary data could she use for her research?'

2 Undertake your own search using online databases discussed in Chapter 8 and search engines such as Google or Bing for possible data to answer Jessica's research question. Make notes about each secondary data source you find. Don't forget to include the full reference including the URL and data of retrieval.

3 What methods of data analysis could Jessica use for each of these types of data you have identified?

Additional case studies relating to material covered in this chapter are available via the book's companion website: **www.pearsoned.co.uk/saunders.** They are:

- Communicating bad news at Abco.
- Paying for competence at Investco.
- Internet abuse in universities.
- The influence of film on tourist decision making.

Self-check answers

13.1 There are a number of reasons why we may describe qualitative analysis as an 'interactive process'. Analysis needs to occur during the collection of data as well as after it. This helps to shape the direction of data collection, especially where you are following a grounded theory approach. The interactive nature of data collection and analysis allows you to recognise important themes, patterns and relationships as you collect data. As a result, you will be able to re-categorise your existing data to see whether these themes, patterns and relationships are present in the cases where you have already collected data. In addition, you will be able to adjust your future data collection approach to see whether they exist in cases where you intend to conduct your research.

13.2 You will generate three broad types of data that you will need to retain and file as the result of undertaking qualitative research.

The first of these may be referred to as raw data files. These are your original notes and audio-recordings made during the conduct of interviews or observations, or from consulting documentation. In addition, you will also retain transcripts and written-up notes of interviews and observations, although these may also be contained in a computer file.

The second of these is analytical files containing your categorised data. Alternatively, this may contain your summary or your narrative. These may of course also be contained in a computer file.

The third of these may be referred to as a supporting file, or indeed it may be different files, containing working papers, self-memos, interim reports and so forth. Again, these may also be contained in a computer file. You are well advised to keep all of this until the end of your research project.

Eventually you will create a fourth file – containing your finished work!

13.3 A *deductive* analytical approach is one where you will seek to use existing theory to shape the approach that you adopt to the qualitative research process and to aspects of data analysis. An *inductive* analytical approach is one where you will seek to build up a theory that is adequately grounded in a number of relevant cases. The design of qualitative research requires you to recognise this choice and to choose an appropriate approach to guide your research project.

13.4 There are a number of implications of using a deductive analytical approach for the way in which you conduct the process of qualitative analysis:

- You will be in a position to commence your data collection with a well-defined research question and objectives and a clear framework and propositions, derived from the theory that you will have used.
- With regard to sampling, you will be in a position to identify the number and type of organisations to which you wish to gain access in order to undertake data collection to answer your research question and meet your objectives.

- The use of literature and the theory within it will shape the data collection questions that you wish to ask those who participate in your research project.
- You will be able to commence data collection with an initial set of categories derived from your theoretical propositions/hypotheses and conceptual framework linked to your research question and objectives.
- This approach will provide you with key themes and patterns to search for in your data, and your analysis will be guided by the theoretical propositions and explanations with which you commenced.

13.5 The main implications of using an inductive analytical approach for the process of qualitative analysis are likely to be related to:

- managing and categorising a large number of code labels, which will probably emerge from the data that you collect;
- working with smaller rather than larger units of data;
- recognising significant themes and issues during early analysis to help you to consider where data collection should be focused in the future;
- recognising the relationships between categories and rearranging these into a hierarchical form, with the emergence of subcategories;
- seeking to verify apparent relationships against the actual data that you have collected;
- understanding how negative cases broaden (or threaten) your emerging explanation;
- recognising the relationships between the principal categories that have emerged from this grounded approach in order to develop an explanatory theory;
- being rigorous in your use of the procedures that are advocated in order to be able to produce a research report that contains findings that are sufficiently 'grounded' to substantiate the analysis or theory that you are seeking to advance.

Get ahead using resources on the companion website at: **www.pearsoned.co.uk/saunders**

- Improve your IBM SPSS Statistics and NVivo research analysis with practice tutorials.
- Save time researching on the Internet with the Smarter Online Searching Guide.
- Test your progress using self-assessment questions.
- Follow live links to useful websites.

Chapter 14

Writing and presenting your project report

Learning outcomes

By the end of this chapter you should be able to:

- view the writing of your project report as an exciting prospect;
- write in such a way that you can reflect on all you have learned while conducting the research;
- write a final project report that presents an authoritative account of your research;
- adopt an appropriate format, structure and style for the final project report;
- differentiate between a project report and a consultancy report;
- ensure that your report meets the necessary assessment criteria;
- plan and design an oral presentation of your report.

14.1 Introduction

Some of you may view the process of writing your **project report** and presenting it orally as an exciting prospect. However, it is more likely that you will approach this stage of your research with some trepidation. This would be a great pity. We believe that writing about your work is the most effective way of clarifying your thoughts. Writing may be the time when we think most deeply. This suggests that writing should not be seen as the last stage of your research but, as we illustrated at the start of this book in Figure 1.2, thought of as something that is continuous throughout the research process. In this way your project report may be seen as something you develop throughout your research rather than leaving it until every other part has been completed.

Writing is a powerful way of learning. Most teachers will tell you that the best way to learn is to teach. This is because of the necessity to understand something thoroughly yourself before you can begin to explain it to others. This is the position you are in as the writer of your project report. You have to explain a highly complex set of ideas and facts to an audience that you must assume has little or no knowledge of your subject. There is another problem here, which has a parallel with teaching. Often, the more familiar you are with a subject, the more difficult it is to explain it to others with no knowledge of that subject. You will be so familiar with your

research topic that, like the teacher, you will find it difficult to put yourself in the place of the reader. The result of this is that you may fail to explain something that you assume the reader will know. Even worse, you may leave out important material that should be included.

However, why do most of us view writing with such concern? Veroff (2007) argues that much of this is rooted in the experience we have of writing. Many of us are afraid of exposing our efforts to an audience that we feel will be more likely to criticise than encourage. In our education much of our writing has been little more than rehashing the ideas of others. This has taught us to think of writing as a boring, repetitive process. Some of us are impatient. We are unwilling to devote the time and energy (and inevitable frustration) that is needed for writing.

This fear of criticism is captured perfectly by Richards (2007), who recites the story of being asked by the distinguished sociologist Howard Becker to adopt his method of sitting down and

If you have ever thought about visiting London, you will have a list of places that you would like to visit. One that is on many people's list is the Tower of London. This is a complex of historical buildings dating from the twelfth century, which has served a number of purposes, including being a royal palace and fortress. Parts of the Tower of London have also been a prison and visitors to the Tower see 'attractions' including Traitors Gate, the Bloody Tower, Torture at the Tower and the Scaffold Site. During the reign of England's Tudor kings and queens, important prisoners were held in the Beauchamp Tower. In the Prisoners' Room on the first floor of this tower you will see an extraordinary collection of graffiti carved into its walls. Unlike much modern graffiti these are carefully preserved as an historical record of those who were imprisoned there. These political and religious prisoners carved not only their names but also statements about their situation and their innocence.

The White Tower, Tower of London
Source: © Mark Saunders 2011

If they had been alive today these prisoners would have wanted to send emails, instant messages and tweets and to use a range of social media to bring attention to their plight and to represent their points of view. Increasingly our world is being connected through the use of these media, so that individuals can talk, share information and coordinate their activities. Even in the isolation of a prison in a tower our ancestors sought to express themselves through carving words in a wall. Today we have many more means to express ourselves by writing to others. The speed with which we can write and communicate with others means that we are likely to take writing for granted, without seeing this as something to be fearful about.

writing what came into her head about the research she had done without even consulting her notes. Her fears of producing poor-quality material, which would be derided by colleagues who saw her work, are described vividly. It is a fear most of us experience. Set against this, most of us write a lot more than we imagine. We all have thoughts that we want to express and the desire to write about these has always been common, as the opening vignette illustrates. This vignette should be interpreted as giving you the confidence to write, even when you do this for formal reasons, rather than being fearful about writing.

In this chapter we begin by looking at issues concerned with getting started in the writing process including the importance of generating a plan (Section 14.2). Sections 14.3 and 14.4 are devoted to the core issues of writing your project report – structure and content – and explaining the differences between a project report and a consultancy report. We then consider the topic of writing style (Section 14.5) before examining how to meet the assessment criteria (Section 14.6). For many of us the fear of making an oral presentation is even more daunting than writing. As we note in Section 14.7, some of this apprehension can be overcome by thorough preparation and this section examines the preparation and delivery of the oral presentation.

14.2 Getting started with writing

If writing is synonymous with thinking, it follows that writing is something you should do throughout the whole research process. Chapter 2 emphasises the need for clear ideas in writing about research questions and objectives. If you have done this already you will know the difficulty of committing your vague ideas to paper and amending them continually until they express your ideas with brevity, clarity and accuracy. However, there is no reason why your research proposal and plan should be the last writing you do before you finally write up your research in the project report. We encourage you to write as a continual process throughout the research.

Many researchers find it helpful to write the literature review early on in their research. This has clear benefits. It gets you writing about a part of your research that necessarily comes early in that process. Also, it focuses your thinking on the way in which the literature will inform the research strategy you adopt. You will be pleased you wrote this part of the report when the time pressure is on as the submission deadline for your report approaches. Do not worry that early writing of the literature review means that subsequently published relevant literature is ignored in your review. It can always be incorporated at a later date. This is one of the advantages of using a word processor, a topic that we shall cover later in this section.

Having discouraged you from thinking of writing as a process you leave until the end of your research, this section goes on to consider a number of practical hints to assist you to get started.

Create time for your writing

Writing is not an activity that can be allocated an odd half-hour whenever it is convenient. It requires sustained concentration. The amount of time needed to make real progress in your writing is dependent on the way in which you prefer to work. Most people find that it takes at least a day to write about 2000 words, but we all work in different ways. Once some people have started, they prefer to continue until they drop from exhaustion! Others like to set a strict timetable where three or four hours a day are devoted to writing. Whichever category you are in, make sure that you have time for writing allocated in your diary. We have found that it is helpful to have blocks of time where writing can take place on successive days. This ensures a degree of continuity of ideas, which is not as easy if you keep having to 'think your way back' into your research.

Write when your mind is fresh

We have emphasised so far in this chapter that writing should be a highly creative process. It is important, therefore, that you write at the time of day when your mind is at its freshest. All of us have jobs to do during the day that require little or no creativity. Arrange your day so that the uncreative jobs are done in the time when you are at your least mentally alert.

Find a regular writing place

Most of us have a place where we do our writing. It is so important that we often cannot write in unfamiliar surroundings. If this is the case with you then it is essential that you combine this psychological comfort with a few practical features of your writing place that will enhance your productivity. One of the most important of these is to ensure that you are not interrupted. A simple 'do not disturb' sign on the door may work wonders. This may allow you to write in your own room although you will probably need to switch off all distractions such as your mobile phone, social media and television as well as remove computer games and magazines. Some of you may concentrate better by listening to the radio or some music tracks on your MP3 player. However, like some of our students, you may be able to concentrate better if you find a neutral space, such as an area in the library, where you can write without your possessions or your friends being able to distract you! What is important is to know what distracts you and to remove those distractions.

Set goals and achieve them

This is the height of self-discipline. Most writers set themselves targets for the period of writing. Usually this is a set number of words. It is better to be realistic about these goals. If you are too ambitious the quality of your work may suffer as you rush to meet the goal. You may be as self-disciplined as Mark, who sets himself sub-goals during the day and rewards the achievement of these goals with coffee breaks. What is important is that you see this as entering into a contract with yourself. If you break this contract by not meeting your goal, you are the one who should feel guilty. You may like to enter into a similar arrangement with a close friend on the understanding that each of you will insist on the other meeting your goals.

Use word processing

Word processing has revolutionised writing (Box 14.1). There are still a few students who prefer to write longhand before word processing the final report. However, for the vast majority who 'think onto the screen' the main advantage of word processing is that it enables us to keep amending copy without having to fill the waste paper basket with numerous unsatisfactory attempts. In addition, word processing enables you to keep updating your project report as you develop new ideas or become dissatisfied with old ones. There is, however, a potential problem here. The ease with which you can keep inserting and deleting text means that relevant 'flagging' material will need to

Box 14.1 Focus on student research

Using word processing to transcribe field notes to the final project report

Samuel made interview notes in longhand during the interviews that he conducted with managers about the stock control systems in their retail outlets. He was particularly careful to note verbatim especially relevant comments from the managers.

Samuel ensured that he word processed these notes, either on his notebook on the return train journey at the end of the day, or at home in the evening.

When writing his project report, Samuel found these word-processed notes to be invaluable. He wanted to use some of the verbatim quotes to illustrate key arguments that he was developing from the data. He was able to insert many of these into the report, thus saving time and ensuring accuracy of transcription.

be changed. At its simplest, this may be the contents page or the announcement at the beginning of a chapter that the chapter will cover certain ground. However, it is just as likely to be an obscure reference buried in the text to a table that you have deleted, thus making the reference redundant.

Other advantages of word processing may have occurred to you. First, most packages have a word count facility. You can use this to check your progress towards the word goal you have set yourself for the writing session. A second advantage is the readability statistics that are a feature of Microsoft Word. This allows you to check not only spelling, but also the average number of sentences per paragraph and words per sentence. To do this click on the 'Review' tab, then click 'Spelling & Grammar' and select 'Options'. In the 'Word Options' window, click the 'Show readability statistics' check box and then 'OK'. Next time you click on 'Spelling & Grammar', Word will display readability statistics.

Word processing also allows you to keep copies of your work. This has two benefits. You may keep copies of every version of your work so that you do not throw away anything that may be useful later on. Sometimes you may rewrite part of your work, only to realise later that the earlier version contains something that you would still like to include. It is therefore useful to keep every version of your work providing that you carefully label each, e.g. Project report Section 3 V1, V2, V3 etc. Work processing also allows you to make backup copies of every document. The necessity of keeping backup copies of your work should go without saying. However, the drawback to this is the possibility that you may lose all of your work where you do not do this (Box 14.2)!

Generate a plan

Few of us can sit down and write without a lot of thought and planning. We all have our own systems for doing this. However, most people find it essential to construct a plan before they start writing. Veroff (2007) describes the 'clustering' method. This may be familiar to you. The method's stages are:

1 Write the main topic in the middle of a sheet of paper.
2 Jot down the other ideas that occur to you at other points on the page.
3 As the page begins to fill, relationships between the ideas suggest themselves and lines between the ideas may be drawn.
4 This allows you to group the ideas into discrete but related 'chunks', which enables you to devise an outline structure for a section, or chapter.

Box 14.2 Focus on student research

"Help I've lost my research project"

Ross had heard of cases where others hadn't been able to submit their assignments because of computer problems. He had always found his course demanding and wondered how he would cope if the same happened to him.

This made him determined to keep at least one backup copy of every document that he created or altered. It would be disastrous that if he lost any of his files without these being backed up. He very carefully followed the same routine every time he worked on his project. At the end of every session working on his project, he backed up files he had worked on or new files he had created on to a USB mass storage device that he kept specifically for his research. On every Sunday afternoon he also emailed all of his project files to himself.

Some weeks into his project he encountered a problem with the Notebook that he carried and used for all of his work. He took it along to the Students' Union, where there was an IT shop. They examined the machine and told Ross that his hard disc drive had failed. Ross was annoyed and shocked by this. This was another expense for Ross to have the component replaced. This left him feeling pretty low. He was reassured however because his work had been carefully filed and fully backed up.

Box 14.3 Focus on student research

Devising an outline structure

Andrea found the task of writing each part of her project report to be demanding. She started her literature review in the early stages of her research project. She felt that this early attempt lacked coherence and development. She returned to the planning phase of her literature review and mapped her ideas onto an A3 sheet.

This process provided her with a number of discrete ideas from the literature related to her research question that she wanted to include in her review. She worked on the order of these ideas until they matched the flow of her research objectives. This provided her with an idea or ideas for each section of her review. She then devised headings for each section and for the various subsections. She typed these into a Word file, so that she now had the 'skeleton' or framework of her literature review. This provided Andrea with an outline structure to start to write her literature review and she now worked on each section in turn.

The wording of some these headings changed, as did the order of some of the subheadings. However, she found the creation of this type of structural outline or framework to be very helpful, both in terms of facilitating her writing and providing targets to complete, such as a section in a given period. She used the same approach to write each of the other parts of each project report.

This chapter started out as just such a pencilled plan written on four pieces of A4 held together with sticky tape. It is essential to get your ideas into some form of order at the outset. This will give you encouragement to start writing (Box 14.3).

Finish a writing session on a high point and provide a link to a new session

Some writers prefer to finish their writing session while they are in the middle of a section to which they will look forward to returning. Others prefer to get to the end of a section before they finish writing so that they do not lose any ideas they have developed

Box 14.4 Focus on student research

Getting restarted

Veronika always tried to complete a section or subsection within a writing session. This allowed her to concentrate on a set of ideas without interruption. When she did not have time to complete a section or subsection, she typed in notes about her ideas to act as an aide-memoire for her next writing session.

Veronika also found it useful to start a writing session by reading the section on which she had worked previously. Her mind was very 'clear' at the start of a new writing session and she was able to read and improve her previous work. This also had the benefit of refreshing her thoughts about what she had completed previously and directing her thoughts about what she wanted to achieve next.

during that session. This allows them to tidy up one set of materials and to lay out the set for the next session of writing. Whichever approach you prefer, your aim will be to ease your progress the next time you write (Box 14.4). The worst thing you can do is to leave a complex section half completed as it will be difficult to pick up your thoughts and ideas.

Get friends to read your work

Writing is creative and exciting, but checking our work is not. The importance of getting someone else to read through your material cannot be overemphasised. Your project tutor should not be the first person who reads your report, even in its draft form.

Ask a friend to be constructively critical. Your friend must be prepared to tell you about things in the text that are not easy to understand – to point out omissions, spelling, punctuation and grammatical errors. Overall, your friend must tell you whether the piece of writing makes sense and achieves its purpose.

This is not an easy process for you or your critical friend. Most of us are sensitive to criticism, particularly when the consequence of it is the necessity to do a lot more work. Many of us are also hesitant about giving criticism. However, if your project report does not communicate to the reader in the way it should, you will get it back for revision work in the long run. It is much better to try to ensure that this does not happen.

14.3 Structuring your project report

Suggested structure

The conventional way to structure your project report is to produce the following sections:

- Abstract;
- Introduction;
- Literature review;
- Method;
- Findings;
- Discussion;
- Conclusions;
- References;
- Appendices.

In addition many universities also require a reflective statement or essay as part of your project. This can be developed from the entries you have made in your reflective diary throughout the research process when answering the questions in Box 1.4 (Section 1.5).

However, this conventional structure should not inhibit you from adopting something different. The structure outlined above fits the deductive approach particularly closely. It assumes that the literature was reviewed to establish the current state of knowledge on the topic and this informed the method adopted. Reporting the findings in a factual manner gives rise to a detailed consideration of what these findings mean to the specific piece of research that has been conducted and to the current state of knowledge on the topic. However, if your research is essentially inductive, it may be that you prefer to structure the report in a different way. You may prefer to tell your story (that is, to explain your conclusions) in the early part of the report. This may include a clear explanation of how this story relates to the existing literature on the topic. This could be followed by a detailed explanation of how you arrived at these conclusions (a combination of an explanation of method adopted and findings established). The precise structure you adopt is less important than the necessity for your reader to be absolutely clear about what you are saying and for you to meet the assessment criteria.

Phillips and Pugh (2010) note that these general sections can be subdivided into one or more relevant chapters depending on the topic and the way in which you want to present your particular **storyline**. This is a vital point. Your structure should have a logical flow. Your readers should know the journey on which they are being taken, and should know at all times the point in the journey that has been reached. Above all, the structure you adopt should enable your reader, having read the report, to identify the storyline clearly.

We shall now explain how to distinguish between these broad sections by outlining their purpose and content.

The abstract

The **abstract** is probably the most important part of your report because it may be the only part that some will read. It is a short summary of the complete content of the project report. This enables those who are not sure whether they wish to read the complete report to make an informed decision. For those who intend to read the whole report the abstract prepares them for what is to come. It should contain four short paragraphs with the answers to the following questions:

1 What were my research questions, and why were these important?
2 How did I go about answering the research questions?
3 What did I find out in response to my research questions?
4 What conclusions do I draw regarding my research questions?

The academic publisher, Emerald, gives advice to potential academic authors on how to compile an abstract. This is shown in Box 14.5. Although referring to academic journal articles (papers), it is useful to consider in terms of preparation of your research report and any subsequent publication.

Smith (1991) lists five principles for the writing of a good abstract. He argues that:

1 It should be short. Try to keep it to a maximum of two sides of A4. (Some universities stipulate a maximum length, often between 300 and 500 words.)
2 It must be self-contained. Since it may be the only part of your project report that some people see, it follows that it must summarise the complete content of your report.

Box 14.5 Focus on management research

Advice on the preparation of an abstract for publication

Abstracts should contain no more than 250 words. Write concisely and clearly. The abstract should reflect only what appears in the original paper.

Purpose

What are the reason(s) for writing the paper or the aims of the research?

Design/methodology/approach

How are the objectives achieved? Include the main method(s) used for the research. What is the approach to the topic and what is the theoretical or subject scope of the paper?

Findings

What was found in the course of the work? This will refer to analysis, discussion or results.

Research limitations/implications (if applicable)

If research is reported on in the paper this section must be completed and should include suggestions for future research and any identified limitations in the research process.

Practical implications (if applicable)

What outcomes and implications for practice, applications and consequences are identified? How will the research impact on the business or enterprise? What changes to practice should be made as a result of this research? Not all papers will have practical implications.

Originality/value

What is new in the paper? State the value of the paper and to whom.

Source: From Emerald Group Publishing (2011) 'How to . . . write an abstract'. From The Emerald website, www.emeraldinsight.com/authors/guides/write/abstracts.htm. Reproduced with permission

3. It must satisfy your reader's needs. Your reader must be told about the problem, or central issue, that the research addressed and the method adopted to pursue the issue. It must also contain a brief statement of the main results and conclusions.
4. It must convey the same emphasis as the project report, with the consequence that the reader should get an accurate impression of the report's contents from the abstract.
5. It should be objective, precise and easy to read. The project report contents page should give you the outline structure for the abstract. Summarising each section should give you an accurate résumé of the content of the report. Do ensure that you stick to what you have written in the report. The abstract is not the place for elaborating any of your main themes. Be objective. You will need to write several drafts before you eliminate every word that is not absolutely necessary. The purpose is to convey the content of your report in as clear and brief a way as possible.

Writing a good abstract is difficult. The obvious thing to do is to write it after you have finished the report. We suggest that you draft it at the start of your writing so that you have got your storyline abundantly clear in your mind. You can then amend the draft when you have finished the report so that it conforms to the five principles above. Box 14.6 contains an example of a short abstract by Mark and colleagues that meets most of the criteria for an effective abstract that we list above.

Box 14.6 Focus on management research

Abstract from a refereed journal article

This paper explores employees' reactions to the management of post-merger cultural integration in the hotel industry. Using a mixed method design incorporating a structured card sort of possible emotions and subsequent in-depth interview, data were collected from 30 head office employees. Findings highlight the importance of the human dynamics of a merger, emphasising the importance of strong leadership, open and honest communication as precursors to integration and suggest the need for a pre-merger cultural audit. Merging two organisations involves the dedication of a remarkable level of resources and activities both before and after the merger and yet, a successful outcome is uncertain and is subject to effective management of cultural integration.

Source: Saunders, M.N.K., Altinay, L. and Riordan, K. (2009) 'The management of post merger cultural integration: Implications from the hotel industry', *Service Industries Journal,* Vol. 29, No. 10, pp. 359–75. Reproduced with permission

The introductory chapter

The **introduction** should give the reader a clear idea about the central issue of concern in your research and why you thought that this was worth studying. It should also include a full statement of your aim or research question(s) and research objectives. If your research is based in an organisation, we think that it is a good idea to include in this chapter some details of the organisation, such as its history, size, products and services. This may be a general background to the more specific detail on the research setting you include in the method chapter. It is also important to include in this chapter a 'route map' to guide the reader through the rest of the report. This will give brief details of the content of each chapter and present an overview of how your storyline unfolds.

This will usually be a fairly brief chapter, but it is vitally important.

The literature review

Chapter 3 deals in detail with the writing of a literature review. All that it is necessary to comment on here is the position of this chapter in the project report. We suggest that this is placed before the methodology chapter.

The main purposes of your literature review are to set your study within its wider context and to show the reader how your study supplements the work that has already been done on your topic. The literature review, therefore, may directly inform your research questions (see Box 14.7) and any specific hypotheses that your research is designed to test. These hypotheses will also suggest a particular research approach, strategy and data collection techniques. If, on the other hand, you are working inductively (that is, from data to theory) your literature review may serve the purpose of illuminating and enriching your conclusions.

The title of your literature review chapter should reflect the content of the chapter. It may draw on one of the main themes in the review. We recommend that you do not call it simply 'literature review'. It may be that your literature is reviewed in more than one chapter. This would be the case, for example, where you were using more than one body of literature in your research.

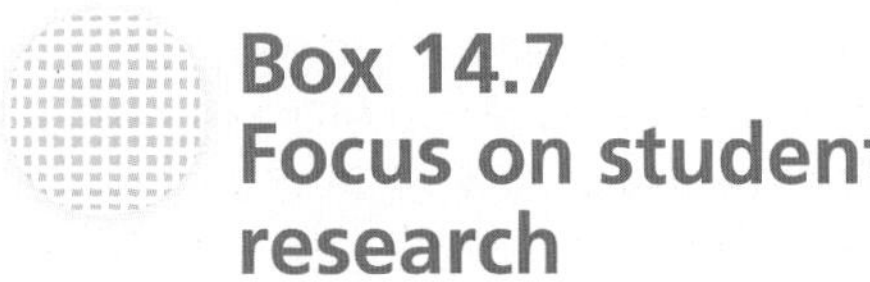

Box 14.7 Focus on student research

Using the literature review to inform the research questions

Guiyan was a Chinese student studying for a master's degree. In her research dissertation she was interested to know whether Chinese managers would be able to conduct performance appraisal schemes effectively in China with Chinese employees. She was aware that there were certain aspects of Chinese culture that would make this difficult. Guiyan studied two bodies of literature: one relating to the managerial skills of performance appraisal, and a second concerned with the effects of Chinese culture on the ways in which Chinese managers manage their employees. She presented both in a literature review chapter. She structured her chapter around three questions:

1 What are the key skills needed by managers to conduct performance appraisal effectively?
2 What are the most important aspects of Chinese culture which impact upon on the ways in which Chinese managers manage their employees?
3 To what extent will the aspects of Chinese culture, explained in the answer to question 2, affect the ability of Chinese managers to conduct performance appraisal effectively?

From this, Guiyan developed a theoretical proposition that supported her initial idea that certain aspects of Chinese culture would make the conduct of performance appraisal by Chinese managers with Chinese employees difficult. She was then ready to move on to her method chapter, which was an explanation of the way in which she would test her theoretical proposition.

The methodology chapter

This should be a detailed and transparent chapter giving the reader sufficient information to make an estimate of the reliability and validity of your methods, and trustworthiness of your findings. Box 14.8 provides a useful checklist of the points that you should include in the method chapter.

The findings chapter(s)

It may well be that your report will contain more than one findings (sometimes called 'results') chapter. The question you should ask yourself is: 'Is more than one findings chapter necessary to communicate my findings clearly?'

The findings chapter or chapters are probably the most straightforward to write. It is your opportunity to report the facts that your research discovered. This is where you will include such tables and graphs that will illustrate your findings (do not put these in the appendices). The chapter may also contain verbatim quotes from interviewees, or sections of narrative account that illustrate periods of unstructured observation. This is a particularly powerful way in which you can convey the richness of such data. It is the qualitative equivalent of tables and graphs. Often, a short verbatim quote can convey with penetrating simplicity a particularly difficult concept that you are trying to explain. Do not be afraid to capture precisely what the interviewee said. Slang and swear words are often the most revealing, and may provide amusement for the reader!

There are two important points to bear in mind when writing about your findings. The first is to stress that the purpose is to present facts. It is normally not appropriate in this chapter to begin to offer opinions on the facts. This is for the following chapter(s). Many

Box 14.8
Checklist

Points to include in your methodology chapter

Setting

- ✔ What was the research setting?
- ✔ Why did you choose that particular setting?
- ✔ What ethical issues were raised by the study, and how were these addressed?

Participants

- ✔ How many?
- ✔ How were they selected?
- ✔ What were their characteristics?
- ✔ How were refusals/non-returns handled?

Materials

- ✔ What tests/scales/interview or observation schedules/questionnaires were used?
- ✔ How were purpose-made instruments developed?
- ✔ How were the resulting data analysed?

Procedures

- ✔ What were the characteristics of the interviewers and observers, and how were they trained?
- ✔ How valid and reliable do you think the procedures were?
- ✔ In what context were the data collected?
- ✔ What instructions were given to participants?
- ✔ How many interviews/observations/questionnaires were there; how long did they last; where did they take place?
- ✔ When was the research carried out?

Source: Developed from authors' experience; Kvale and Brinkmann (2009); Robson (2011)

of us become confused about the difference between findings and the conclusions drawn from these which form the basis of the discussion and conclusions chapters. One way of overcoming the confusion is to draw up a table with two columns. The first should be headed 'What I found out' and the second 'What judgements I have formed on the basis of what I found out'. The first list is entirely factual (e.g. 66 per cent of responding customers indicated they preferred to receive email messages rather than mailshots) and therefore the content of your findings chapter. The second list will be your judgements based on what you found out (e.g. it appears that electronic forms of communication are preferred to traditional) and therefore the content of your conclusions section.

The second point links to the first. Drawing up a table will lead you to a consideration of the way in which you present your findings. The purpose of your project report is to communicate the answer to your research question to your audience in as clear a manner as possible. Therefore you should structure your findings in a clear, logical and easily understood manner. There are many ways of doing this. One of the simplest is to return to the research objectives and let these dictate the order in which you present your findings. Alternatively, you may prefer to report your findings thematically. You could present the themes in descending order of importance. Whichever method you choose should be obvious to the reader. As with the literature review, the chapter(s) devoted to research should be titled in an interesting way that reflects the content of findings.

The clarity of your findings should be such that they may find their way into a news report similar to that in Box 14.9.

The discussion chapter

Findings presented without reflective thought run the risk of your reader asking 'so what?': what meaning do these findings have for me?; for my organisation?; for professional practice?; for the development of theory? So the main focus of the discussion

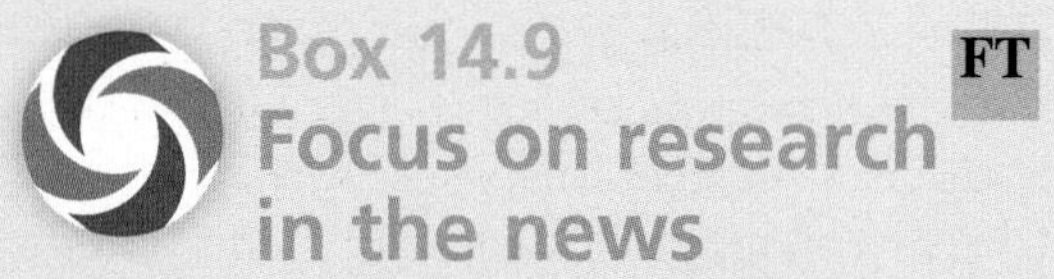

Box 14.9 Focus on research in the news

FT

Green jobs boost for the UK

More than three-quarters of small and medium-sized cleantech businesses in the UK plan to recruit in the next 12 months, according to a report. The findings, from a survey of 312 companies by the CleanTech Group on behalf of the Carbon Trust, will give a boost to government hopes for a recovery founded on green jobs.

Benj Sykes, director of innovations at the Carbon Trust, told Energy Source: 'This is evidence that green growth is going to be an engine for growth. There is a recognition that this is an agenda that is not going to fail because of financial constraints.'

The report found remarkable optimism in the UK cleantech industry: average confidence on a scale of 1 to 10 is up from 6 a year ago to 8 this year. Some 37 per cent of companies are thinking of expanding into foreign markets in the next year. This comes despite multiple reports pointing to a lack of finance for companies in the sector, as well as the government's move to reduce solar subsidies. Sykes said the reduction to solar subsidies was a worry, and may not yet have been factored into the mood of the sector as a whole. Besides, as he pointed out, entrepreneurs tend to be an optimistic bunch, so perhaps some overenthusiasm is to be expected.

Just under a third still regard a lack of finance as the main obstacle to growth, and the number of companies with revenues of under £2m that are concerned about finance rose to 40 per cent. Unsurprisingly, wind energy remains one of the biggest areas for optimism, and there is a sense within the industry that the UK's burgeoning expertise on offshore wind could be exported to other countries. China would be an obvious market for such knowledge, as it is now the fastest growing wind energy market in the world.

But a word of warning for anyone who thinks this signals the start of a new green recovery: these companies are small, and recruitment is likely to be on a similarly small scale. Many are just starting and are still looking to recruit people into research and development. Once the core expertise has been developed here, Sykes said, it is likely that China or other markets with cheaper labour would benefit from the mass creation of jobs in manufacturing. After all, nothing has changed since Ditlev Engel, boss of Vestas, the world's biggest turbine maker, told Energy Source that western Europe was simply too expensive to build its turbines in.

Source: From 'Green jobs boost for the UK', Kiran Stacey (2011) *Financial* Times, 14 April.

chapter is on the interpretation of the results that you presented in the previous chapter. You should state the relation of the findings to the goals, questions and hypotheses that you stated in the introductory chapter. In addition, the discussion chapter will benefit from a consideration of the implications of your research for the relevant theories which you detailed in your literature review. It is usual to discuss the strengths, weaknesses and limitations of your study. However, it is not a good idea to be too modest here and draw attention to aspects of your research which you may consider to be a limitation but that the reader has not noticed!

The discussion chapter is where you have the opportunity to shine. It will show the degree of insight that you exhibit in reaching your conclusions. However, it is the part of the report that most of us find difficult. It is the second major opportunity in the research process to demonstrate real originality of thought (the first time being at the stage where you choose the research topic). Because of that, we urge you to pay due attention to the discussion chapter. In our view it should normally be at least as long as your results chapter(s). Crucially, here you are making judgements rather than reporting facts, so this is where your maturity of understanding can shine through.

Box 14.10 Checklist

Do your conclusions answer these questions?

- ✔ Did the research project meet your research objectives?
- ✔ Did the research project meet your aim or answer your research question(s)?
- ✔ What are the main findings of the research?
- ✔ Are there any recommendations for future action based on the conclusions you have drawn?
- ✔ Do you have any overall conclusions on the research process itself?
- ✔ Where should further research be focused? (Typically this will consider two points: firstly, new areas of investigation implied by developments in your project, and secondly parts of your work which were not completed due to time constraints and/or problems encountered.)

The conclusion chapter

This chapter should not be used to present any new material and should be a conclusion to the whole project (not just the research findings). Check your chapter using the questions in Box 14.10.

You may find that the clearest way to present your conclusions is to follow a similar structure to the one used in your findings section. If that structure reflects the research objectives then it should make certain that your conclusions would address them. Drawing up a matrix similar to that in Figure 14.1 may help you in structuring your findings and conclusions. The result should be a clear statement of conclusions drawn similar to that shown in Box 14.11.

An alternative approach to the matrix is to draw a 'mind map' (see Section 2.3), which places the findings randomly on a blank page and links conclusions to these findings by way of lines and arrows. For some of you this may be a more creative approach, which enables you to associate groups of findings with conclusions and vice versa.

Answering the research question(s), meeting the objectives and, if appropriate, supporting or otherwise the research hypotheses is the main purpose of the conclusions chapter. This is where you will consider the findings presented in the previous chapter. You should also return to your literature review and ask yourself 'What do my conclusions add to the understanding of the topic displayed in the literature?'

It may be that there are practical implications of your findings. In a management report this would normally form the content of a chapter specifically devoted to recommendations.

Research questions	***Results*** *(what factual information did I discover in relation to the specific research questions?)*	***Conclusions*** *(what judgements can I make about the results in relation to the specific research questions?)*
What are the operational differences between different shifts in the production plant?	Cases of indiscipline in the last six months have been twice as frequent on the night shift as on the day shift	The night shift indiscipline problems may be due to the reluctance of operators to work on this shift

Figure 14.1 Using a matrix in the planning of the content for the results and conclusions chapters

Box 14.11 Focus on management research

Have careers become boundaryless?

In an article published in *Human Relations*, Rodrigues and Guest (2010) ask the research question, 'Have careers become boundaryless?' The term 'boundaryless' is defined primarily as a career that develops across different employers rather than within one organisation. Rodrigues and Guest analyse international secondary data sets to produce a clear set of conclusions to answer this research question.

They conclude that job tenure has not changed dramatically and that there is insufficient evidence to support the idea of a growing prevalence of boundaryless careers. Instead they conclude that job turnover and tenure continue to remain broadly stable in the USA, Japan and those European countries for which they analysed data. They also conclude that job mobility has not increased significantly amongst managerial and professional groups, whose careers have traditionally been anchored within a particular organisation.

In spite of the lack of empirical evidence to support the growth of boundaryless careers, Rodrigues and Guest conclude that the concept is still a useful one. They provide three reasons to justify this conclusion. First it provides a new perspective through which to evaluate the possibility of change in contemporary career patterns. Second it develops understanding of different career models. Third it raises our understanding of the issues associated with career boundaries.

Rodrigues and Guest discuss the direction for further research in the area of career boundaries. They argue that career boundaries remain crucial to understanding careers. They conclude that there is a need to improve our understanding of the factors that affect the nature of career boundaries such as occupation, employment contracts, the location of work and family influences, so that their effects are understood not just separately but also jointly and simultaneously.

Their conclusions provide a clear example of the way in which these flow from their findings and relate back to the research question they sought to answer. They also demonstrate how sound conclusions are related to the literature that has been reviewed to discuss the meaning and impact of the research and how further research may be developed to further our understanding.

We suggest that you check your assessment criteria carefully to establish whether this is expected. In the reports that students are required to prepare on some professional courses this is an important requirement. For some academic degree programmes it is not required.

Even if you do not specify any practical implications of your research you may comment in the conclusions chapter on what your research implies for any future research. This is a logical extension of a section in the conclusions chapter that should be devoted to the limitations of your research. These limitations may be about the size of sample, the snapshot nature of the research, or the restriction to one geographical area of an organisation. Virtually all research has its limitations. This section should not be seen as a confession of your weaknesses, but as a mature reflection on the degree to which your findings and conclusions can be said to be generalisable.

References

A range of conventions are used to reference other writers' material that you have cited in your text. Appendix 1 illustrates three of the most popular of these, the Harvard, footnotes and American Psychological Association (APA) systems. However, we suggest that you check your project assessment criteria to establish the system that is required for your project report, as many universities require their own variation of these systems.

It is a good idea to start your references section at the beginning of the writing process and add to it as you go along. It will be a tedious and time-consuming task if left until you have completed the main body of the text. If you do leave it until the end, the time spent on compiling the reference section is time that would have been better spent on checking and amending your report.

At the start of your report you must acknowledge all those who have contributed to your research (including your project tutor!). In addition, you should ensure that you have cited in your reference section all those sources to which you have referred in the text. In order to avoid charges of plagiarism you should also ensure that all data and material taken verbatim (that is copied exactly) from another person's published or unpublished written or electronic work is explicitly identified and referenced to its author (see Neville 2010; Section 3.9) giving the page numbers(s) of the copied material if possible. This also extends to work which is referred to in the written work of others. Even if this work is not quoted verbatim, the originator should be cited in your references. If you are in any doubt about this it is important that you consult your university's guidelines on how to ensure that you do not plagiarise. The proliferation of online material now is such that all academic institutions are very mindful of plagiarism and will almost certainly check your work carefully.

Appendices

In general, **appendices** should be kept to the minimum. If they are so important that your reader's understanding of the points you are making in the text makes their inclusion in the report necessary, then they should be in the main body of the text. If, on the other hand, the material is 'interesting to know' rather than 'essential to know' then it should be in the appendices. Often students feel tempted to include appendices to 'pad out' a project report. Resist this temptation. Your readers will not be reading your report for leisure reading. They will be pressed for time and will probably not look at your appendices. Your project report will stand or fall on the quality of the main text. However, your appendices should include a blank copy of your questionnaire, interview or observation schedule. Where these have been conducted in a language different from that in which you write your submitted project report you will need to submit both this version and the translation.

Recommendations

You may have wondered why we make little reference to recommendations in the report structure. In the typical management report or consultancy report (discussed later) this may be the most important section. The hard-pressed executive reading your report may turn to your recommendations first to see what action needs to be taken to tackle the issue.

Whether you include a recommendation section depends on the objectives of your research. If you are doing exploratory research you may well write recommendations, among which will be suggestions for the pursuit of further research. However, if your research is designed to explain or describe, recommendations are less likely. For example, the research question 'Why do small engineering companies in the UK reinvest less of their profits in their businesses than their German counterparts?' may imply clear points for action. However, strictly speaking, recommendations are outside the scope of the research question, which is to discover 'Why?' not 'What can be done about it?' The message is clear. If you want your research to change the situation that you are researching, then include the need to develop recommendations in your research objectives.

Length of the project report

You will probably have guidelines on the number of words your project report should contain. Do stick to these. However interesting your report, your tutors will have others to read, so they will not thank you for exceeding the limit. Reports that exceed the word limit are usually excessively verbose. It is more difficult to be succinct. Do not fall into the trap of writing a long report because you did not have the time to write a shorter one.

14.4 Organising the project report's content

Choosing a title

This is the part of the project report on which most of us spend the least time. Yet it is the only knowledge that many people have of the project. Day and Gastel (2011) comment that a good title is one that has the minimum possible number of words that describe accurately the content of the paper. Try choosing a title and then ask a colleague who knows your subject what they think the title describes. If their description matches your content then stick with your title.

Tell a clear story

Be prepared for your project tutor to ask you 'What's your main storyline?' Your storyline (your central argument or thesis) should be clear, simple and straightforward. It should be so clear that you can stop the next person you see walking towards you and tell that person what your project report's storyline is and he or she will say 'Yes, I understand that'. This is where writing the abstract helps. It forces you to think clearly about the storyline because you have to summarise it in so few words.

A simple format for developing the storyline is shown in Figure 14.2.

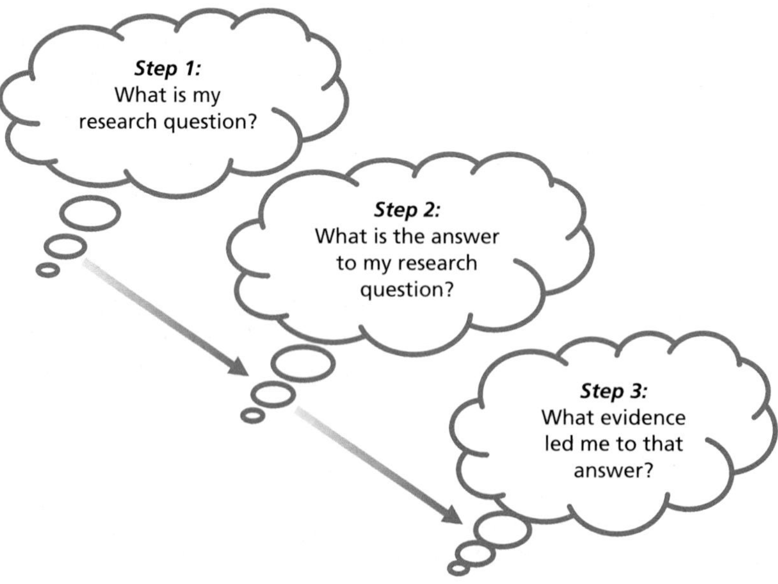

Figure 14.2 A format for developing the storyline

Source: Developed from Raimond (1993:175) *Management Project: Design, Research and Presentation*. Reproduced with permission of Thompson Publishing Services

Another way of checking to see whether your storyline is clear is to 'reason backwards'. An example of this may be a report that ends in clear recommendations for action. Start by explaining your recommendations to the manager who, for example, may have to spend money on their implementation. This invites the question from that manager: 'What makes you recommend this action?' Your answer should be: 'I came to the conclusion in my report that they are necessary.' The follow-up question from the manager here could be: 'On what basis do you draw these conclusions?' Here your answer is, of course, on the findings that you established. The next question asked by the manager is: 'How did you arrive at these findings?' in response to which you explain your method. The manager may counter by asking you why she should take any notice of your findings. The response to this is that you took care to design a research strategy that would lead to valid and reliable findings. Moreover, that research strategy is based on clear research objectives and a detailed review of the relevant literature. Such 'reasoning backwards' is a useful check to see not only whether your storyline is clear but also that it stands up to logical analysis.

Helping the reader to get all the information out

Dividing your work

One of us once received the first draft of a 20,000-word project report that had virtually no divisions except the chapters. It was like looking at a road map that did not include any road numbers or towns. It was just as difficult to find your way around that report as it would be to journey between two cities using a townless road map. The content of the project report seemed fine. However, it was hard to be sure about this because it was so difficult to spot any gaps in the ground it covered. What was needed were some signposts and some town names. Do not think about how you can put in all your information. Instead, concentrate on helping the reader to get all the information out (Box 14.12).

The message is simple. Divide your work in such a way that it is easy for readers to find their way round it and for them always to be clear where they are, where they have come from, and where they are going.

To do this you may find it helpful to return to the matrix idea in Figure 14.1. You will see that each column of the matrix represents the broad content of a chapter. The cells indicate the way in which the chapters may be divided. Each division may have a subdivision.

Developing a storyline

Step 1

I wanted to know whether, as the literature suggested, organisational structures are determined by the organisations' strategies.

Step 2

The answer is that organisation structures are in part determined by strategies and in part by ad hoc factors that owe little to strategy considerations.

Step 3

I based this answer on interviews with senior managers in three large UK organisations and examination of the minutes of meetings at which structural issues were discussed. The particular focus was on the removal of management positions.

We hope you have noticed that we have employed a similar system in this book. However, this book is printed in more than one colour. The equivalent would be that each chapter section is identified by bold upper-case letters. The subheadings are bold lower-case, and further divisions of the subsection content are denoted by bold, lower-case italics. Smith (1991) explains various ways of organising and signposting text. It is not important which way you do this as long as your approach is consistent and it helps the reader around the report and matches the ways specified by your examining institution.

Previewing and summarising chapters

A further way in which you can signpost your work is to 'top and tail' each chapter. This is to include a few words at the beginning of the chapter (Smith 1991) that provide a description of how the chapter is to contribute to answering the research question, the methods used in this part of the study, and the points that are covered. At the end of each chapter it is useful if the reader has a brief summary of the content of the chapter and a very brief indication of how this content links to the following chapter. This may seem like repetition. However, it helps the reader on her or his journey through your report and ensures that you, the writer, are on the correct road.

Tables and graphics

Your reader will find your project report more accessible and easier to read if you present some of your data and ideas in tables and graphics. It is not only numerical data that can be presented in tables. You can also present ideas that can be easily compared. Table 13.1 is an example of this.

Do not be tempted to put your numerical tables in the appendices. They will probably be some of your most important data. Include them and comment on them in the text. Your commentary should note the significance of the data in the tables. It should not simply describe the table's contents.

Section 12.3, and in particular Box 12.8, provide details on the design and presentation of tables and diagrams.

A final note of caution should be sounded. To avoid confusing your reader, do make sure that, wherever possible, you have introduced the table or diagram before it appears in the text.

One report?

Many researchers of management topics face the dilemma of having to write for more than one audience. In addition to the academic audience, who possibly will mark and grade the report for a degree or a diploma, it may be necessary to prepare a report for the management of the employing organisation, or, indeed, a non-employing organisation, both of whom who will be interested in the practical benefit that the report promises. This raises the thorny question, 'For whom should the report be written?'

Many people have resolved this dilemma by writing two reports: one for each audience. The academic report will usually be much longer and contain contextual description that the organisational audience does not require. Similarly, those managers reading the report will probably be less interested in the literature review and the development of theory than the academic audience. If the research question did not imply the necessity for recommendations for future action, these may need to be written for the organisational version. The content of this chapter concentrates on the academic report. However, in the subsection below we include a brief discussion on consultancy reports.

Fortunately, the advent of word processing makes the job of compiling more than one report quite easy. Some careful cutting and pasting along with subsequent careful proof-reading will be necessary. However, what should always be kept in mind is the audience that each specific report is addressing. Take care not to fall between two stools. Write each report for its audience in style and content.

The consultancy report

Here we assume that the report that you write for the management of the employing organisation, or a non-employing organisation, follow the same format. For this reason we refer to both as **consultancy reports**.

Advice from the Institute of Management Consultancy (now the Institute of Business Consulting) suggests that a number of key questions need to be asked before the consultancy report is planned. Among these are: what information does management expect?; with what level of detail?; how much knowledge does management already have?; for what purpose will the report be used?; who will read it? Another fundamental question is: what key messages and recommendations do you want to impart? To be consistent with the main thrust of this chapter a report structure such as:

- Executive summary;
- Introduction;
- Results;
- Conclusions;
- Recommendations.

is the most straightforward.

There is, however, an alternative structure which, arguably, is simpler and delivers the message more forcibly. In this you start with your main message and then provide the information that supports it. This second structure will, however, involve you in more alteration of the academic report you have written.

Decisions about what to include in (and, just as importantly, to exclude from) the report requires ruthlessness. Only information that is essential to management should go in the main body of the report; any information that is 'important' or 'of interest' should be relegated to appendices. Additional detail, for example figures, references or diagrams, are all examples of 'important' information. The Institute of Management Consultancy suggests that you should put yourself in the reader's shoes. The management reader will be short of time and want only essential detail. That said, the management reader will be interested in the background to the project and in how you carried out the research. But the main purpose of the report will be to tell management your recommendations. Recommendations equate with action, and managers are paid to act! As with the academic report, division of the report content into logical sections with clear subheadings will lead management through the report and show them where to find specific topics.

The executive summary is likely to be the part of the report on which managers will concentrate. It is important that it can stand alone and that it contains real information, including hard facts and figures. If your report includes recommendations, the executive summary should make it clear what these are and include their implications, values and costs. As with the abstract, the executive summary should be short (no more than two pages) and designed to get your main message across.

Two final points about the writing style of the consultancy report. The reader will not appreciate long words, complicated language, 'management speak' or a multitude of acronyms and abbreviations. If it is necessary to use complex technical terms, make sure you provide a glossary in the appendix.

Finally, it is more appropriate to use the first person in the consultancy report. Language like 'it was found', 'it is estimated', 'it is recommended' does not sound more professional; it simply depersonalises your report and makes it less accessible. Be bold and put yourself at the heart of your writing!

As well as presenting two written reports you may have to present your report orally. In the next two sections we address the writing of reports, and in the final section (14.7), we turn our attention to their oral presentation.

14.5 Developing an appropriate writing style

Much of your concern in writing your project report will be about what you write. In this section of the chapter we ask you to think about the way you write. Your writing style is just as important as the content, structure and layout of your report. That said, it is often observed that good writing cannot substitute for flawed thinking (Phillips and Pugh 2010). In fact, the clearer the writing the more flawed thinking is exposed. However, poor writing can spoil the effect of good-quality thought.

Clarity and simplicity

> The . . . lack of ready intelligibility [in scholarly writing], I believe, usually has little or nothing to do with the complexity of the subject matter, and nothing at all to do with profundity of thought. It has to do almost entirely with certain confusions of the academic writer about his own status . . . To overcome the academic prose you first of all have to overcome the academic pose.
>
> Wright Mills (1970: 239–40)

Each Christmas, Mark accompanies his Christmas cards with a family newsletter. It is written in a simple, direct and friendly manner that is easy and enjoyable to read. Few of the project reports we read are written in such a simple, direct manner. They are more elaborate in their explanation: they use difficult words where Mark's family newsletter would use simple ones. They adopt the academic pose.

Phil tells a story that reinforces the point made by Wright Mills in the above quotation. He was asked by a student to comment on her thesis in progress, which was about the impact of a particular job advertising strategy. He thought that it was written in an over-elaborate and 'academic' way. After many suggestions for amendments Phil came across a sentence that explained that the strategy his student was studying 'was characterised by factors congruent with the results of a lifestyle analysis of the target market'. Phil thought that this was too wordy. He suggested making it simpler. His student examined the sentence at length and declared she could see no way of improving it. Phil thought that it could say 'it was a strategy that matched the lifestyles of those at whom it was aimed'. His student protested. She agreed it was shorter and clearer but protested that it was less 'academic'. We think that clarity and simplicity are more important than wishing to appear academic. Your project report is a piece of communication in the same way as Mark's Christmas newsletter.

Phillips and Pugh (2010) advise that you should aim to provide readers with a report that they cannot put down until 2.00 a.m. or later for fear of spoiling the flow. (If you are reading this chapter at 2.30 a.m. we have succeeded!)

Box 14.13 Focus on student research

Writing clearer sentences

Consider the following sentence:

> While it is true to say that researchers have illusions of academic grandeur when they sit down to write their project report, and who can blame them because they have had to demonstrate skill and resilience to get to this point in their studies, they nonetheless must consider that writing a project report is an exercise in communication, and nobody likes reading a lot of ideas that are expressed in such a confusing and pretentious way that nobody can understand them, let alone the poor tutor who has to plough through it all to try and make some sense of it.

There appear to be at least six separate ideas in this sentence. It contains 101 words (when marking, we sometimes come across sentences with over 150!). In addition, it contains a common way of introducing multiple ideas into a sentence: the embedded clause. In the sentence above the embedded clause is '. . . , and who can blame them because they have had to demonstrate skill and resilience to get to this point in their studies, . . .' The give-away is the first word in the sentence: 'While'. This invites an embedded clause. The point here is that potentially rich ideas get buried in the literary undergrowth. Dig them up and replant them. Let them flourish in a sentence of their own.

The sentence needs to be clearer and simpler. However, it should not lose any of its meaning. Halving the number of words and dividing up the sentence into smaller, clearer sentences results in the following:

> Researchers have illusions of academic grandeur when they write their project report. This is understandable. They have demonstrated skill and resilience to reach this point in their studies. However, writing a project report is an exercise in communication. Nobody likes confusing and pretentious writing that is difficult to understand. Pity the tutor who has to make sense of it.

Write simple sentences

A common source of lack of clarity is the confusing sentence (see Box 14.13). This is often because it is too long. A simple rule to adopt is: one idea – one sentence. Try reading your work out loud. If your sentences are too long, you will run out of breath!

Avoid jargon

Jargon should not be confused with technical terminology. Some technical terms are unavoidable. To assist your reader, it is best to put a glossary of such terms in the appendices. However, do not assume that your reader will have such a full knowledge as you of the subject and, in particular, the context. Here, and in all cases, try to put yourself in the position of the reader. Phil makes this point to students who use organisations as vehicles to write assignments. He asks them to 'mark' past (anonymous) assignments. They are usually horrified at the assumptions that their fellow students make about the tutor's prior knowledge of the organisation.

What can be avoided is the sort of jargon that *The Free Online Dictionary* (2011) defines as 'gibberish' and 'debased language'. You will know the sort of phrases: 'ongoing situation'; 'going down the route of'; 'at the end of the day'; 'the bottom line'; 'at this moment in time'. It is not just that they are ugly but they are not clear and simple. For example, 'now' is much clearer and simpler than 'at this moment in time'.

Beware of using large numbers of quotations from the literature

We believe that quotations from the literature should be used infrequently in your project report. Occasionally we receive draft projects that consist of little more than a series of quotations from books and journal articles that a student has linked together with a few sentences of her or his own. This tells us very little about the student's understanding of the concepts within the quotations. All it shows is that he or she has looked at the book or journal article and, it is hoped, can acknowledge sources correctly! In addition, by using quotations in this way the student's line of argument tends to become disjointed and less easy to follow. It is therefore usually better to explain other people's ideas in your own words.

That is not to say that you should never use quotations. As you have seen, we have used direct quotations from other people's work in this book. Rather we would advise you to use them sparingly to create maximum impact in supporting your storyline.

Check your spelling and grammar

Spelling is still a problem for many of us, in spite of the word-processing software's spell-check facility. It will not correct your 'moral' when you wished to say 'morale' or sort out when you should write 'practise' rather than 'practice'. This is where the friend who is reading your draft can help, provided that friend is a competent speller. Tutors tend to be more patient with errors of this kind than those that reflect carelessness. However, the point remains that spelling errors detract from the quality of your presentation and the authority of your ideas.

Avoiding common grammatical errors

Grammatical errors threaten the credibility of our writing. In Table 14.1. we outline 10 of the most common errors, most of which, with some careful checking, can be avoided.

It is not our intention here to conduct an English grammar lesson. Some of the common errors in Table 14.1 are self-explanatory.

You may argue that the **split infinitive** is not often thought of as an error these days. However, 'to boldly go' ahead with your project report ignoring this rule risks irritating your reader – something you can ill afford to do. You want the reader to concentrate on your ideas.

Day's 'dangling participle' warning is amusingly illustrated by the draft questionnaire shown to us by a student. This asked for 'the amount of people you employ in your organisation, broken down by sex'. The tutor had written: 'We haven't got people in that category: they've not got the energy when they work here!' (Remember that when writing your questionnaire!)

Some of the more obvious grammatical errors you can spot by reading your text aloud to yourself. You need not know the grammatical rules; they often just sound wrong.

Person, tense and gender

Traditionally, academic writing has been dry and unexciting. This is partly because the convention has been to write impersonally, in the past **tense** and in the **passive voice** (e.g. 'interviews were conducted following the administration of questionnaires').

Table 14.1 Ten common grammatical errors

Often we write	The correct way is
Each pronoun should agree with their antecedent	Each pronoun should agree with its antecedent
Just between you and I, case is important	Just between you and me, case is important
A preposition is a poor word to end a sentence with	A preposition is a poor word with which to end a sentence
Verbs has to agree with their subject	Verbs have to agree with their subject
Do not use no double negatives	Do not use double negatives
Remember to never split an infinitive	Remember never to split an infinitive
When dangling, do not use participles	Do not use dangling participles
Avoid clichés like the plague	To avoid clichés like the plague!
Do not write a run-on sentence it is difficult when you have got to punctuate it so it makes sense when the reader reads what you wrote	Do not write a run-on sentence. It is difficult to punctuate it so that it makes sense to the reader
The data is included in this section	The data are included in this section

Source: Developed from Day (1998: 160)

The writer was expected to be distanced from the text. This convention is no longer as strong. It is now a matter of preferred style rather than rules. The research approach that dominates your methods may dictate your choice of **personal pronoun**. Section 4.2 notes that one feature of positivism is that 'the researcher is independent of, and neither affects nor is affected by, the subject of the research'. It follows from this that an impersonal style may be more appropriate. By contrast, Section 9.2 notes that the participant observer 'participates in the daily life of people under study'. The researcher is an intrinsic part of the research process. Use of the first person seems more logical here. However, style is important. Use of the term 'the author' sounds too impersonal and stilted. In contrast, excessive use of 'I' and 'we' may raise questions in your readers' minds about your ability to stand outside your data and to be objective.

Day (1998) identifies rules for the correct use of tense. He suggests that you should normally use the present tense when referring to previously published work (e.g. Day identifies . . .) and the past tense when referring to your present results (e.g. I found that . . .)'. Although he notes exceptions to this rule, it serves as a useful guide.

Day and Gastel (2011) and Becker (2007) both stridently attack the passive voice (it was found that) and champion the use of the **active voice** (I found that). Certainly, it is clearer, shorter and unambiguous. It is a good idea to check with your project tutor here which is most likely to be acceptable.

Finally, a note about the use of language that assumes the gender of a classification of people. The most obvious example of these is the constant reference to managers as 'he'. Not only is this inaccurate in many organisations, it also gives offence to many people of both sexes. Those offended will probably include your readers! It is simple enough to avoid (e.g. 'I propose to interview each executive unless he refuses' becomes 'I propose to interview each executive unless I receive a refusal') but often less easy to spot. The further reading section in the first draft of this chapter referred to Becker as a 'master craftsman'. These notes on language and gender prompted us to change it to 'an expert in the field'. Appendix 4 gives more detailed guidance on the use of non-discriminatory language.

It is a good idea to be aware of any specific discriminatory or potentially insulting concepts, terms and expressions which may be used in your research due to the particular context of the research (e.g. the industry or organisation in which you work). If your work has an international dimension, it is also a good idea to be aware of any country-specific or national guidelines on the non-discriminatory use of language.

Preserving anonymity

You may have given those people (and the organisations) from whom you collected data an undertaking that you would not disclose their identity in anything you write. In this case you will need to conceal their identity in your project report. The usual way of doing this is to invent pseudonyms for organisations and not to name individual participants. This should not detract from the impact of your report.

Similarly, your sponsoring organisation(s) may have requested sight of your report before it is submitted. Should there be misgivings about the content of the report you should be able to alleviate these by the use of pseudonyms. This is usually a better option than significant text changes.

The need for continual revision

Phil asked a group of undergraduate students how many of them did more than one draft of their assignment papers. He did not expect that many would reply that they did. What he did not predict was that many of them had not even thought this was necessary.

Submitting the first attempt is due partly to the heavy assessment loads on many courses, which means that students are constantly having to 'keep up with the clock'. On part-time courses, students these days have so many demands in their daily work that writing an assignment just once is all that is possible. This is the way most of us learned to write at school. The work is usually seen only by the teacher. The arrangement is a private one.

However, project reports are different. They will be seen by an audience much wider than one tutor. They will usually be lodged in the library to be read by succeeding students. You will be judged on the quality of your work. For that reason we urge you most strongly to polish your work with successive drafts until you are happy that you can do no better (Box 14.14).

Having been through this checklist you may decide to make minor alterations to your text. On the other hand you may rewrite sections or move sections within chapters to other chapters. Keep asking yourself 'How can I make the reader's task easier?'

After each successive draft do leave a space of time for your thoughts to mature. It is amazing how something you wrote a few days before will now make no sense to you. However, you will also be impressed with the clarity and insight of some passages.

Having completed a second draft you may now feel confident enough to give it to your colleague or friend to read. Ask your reader to use the checklist in Box 14.14 to which you can add specific points that you feel are important (e.g. are my arguments well reasoned?).

Box 14.14
Checklist

To evaluate each draft of your project report

- ✔ Is there a clear structure?
- ✔ Is there a clear storyline?
- ✔ Does your abstract reflect accurately the whole content of the report?
- ✔ Does your introduction state clearly the research question(s) and objectives?
- ✔ Does your literature review inform the later content of the report?
- ✔ Are your methods clearly explained?
- ✔ Have you made a clear distinction between findings and conclusions in the two relevant chapters?
- ✔ Have you checked all your references and presented these in the required manner?
- ✔ Is there any text material that should be in the appendices or vice versa?
- ✔ Does your title reflect accurately your content?
- ✔ Have you divided up your text throughout with suitable headings?
- ✔ Does each chapter have a preview and a summary?
- ✔ Are you happy that your writing is clear, simple and direct?
- ✔ Have you eliminated all jargon?
- ✔ Have you eliminated all unnecessary quotations?
- ✔ Have you checked spelling and grammar?
- ✔ Have you checked for assumptions about gender?
- ✔ Is your report in a format that will be acceptable to the assessing body?
- ✔ Would you be proud of your project if it was placed in the university's library as it is now?

14.6 Meeting the assessment criteria

Your readers will be assessing your work against the assessment criteria that apply to your research programme. Therefore, it is essential that you familiarise yourself with these criteria. Easterby-Smith *et al.* (2008) cite Bloom's (1971) well-known taxonomy of educational objectives to illustrate the level that project reports should meet. At the lower levels project reports should show knowledge and comprehension of the topic covered. At the intermediate levels they should contain evidence of application and analysis. Application is thought of as the ability to apply certain principles and rules in particular situations. Your method section should be the principal vehicle for demonstrating application. Analysis may be illustrated by your ability to break down your data and to clarify the nature of the component parts and the relationship between them. Whatever your assessment criteria, it is certain that you will be expected to demonstrate your ability at these lower and intermediate levels.

The higher levels are synthesis and evaluation. **Synthesis** is the process of putting together or assembling various elements so as to create a new statement or conclusion. The emphasis put on conclusions and, in particular, on the development of a storyline in your project report suggests that we feel that you should be showing evidence of synthesis. **Evaluation** is the process of judging materials or methods in terms of their accuracy and internal consistency or by comparing them against external criteria. You have the chance to show this ability in the literature review and in the awareness of the limitations of your own research (see Section 14.3). Each of these levels of educational objectives should be demonstrated in your project report.

In addition to meeting these, you will also need to make sure that you meet any other assessment criteria. You will need to make sure that your project is correctly formatted, does not exceed the maximum permitted length and contains all of the elements specified for inclusion. A final, more holistic consideration that many of our students find useful is to ask yourself whether you would be proud for your project to be placed in the university's library as it is now. If your honest answer is 'no, not yet' you will have more work to do! Conversely, you will need to submit by the due date and so you will need to make sure that you do not keep polishing one part to the exclusion of completing the whole project. You will therefore need to manage your time carefully in terms of drafting the whole and then refining each part.

14.7 Oral presentation of the report

Many students, particularly on professional courses, have to present their project report orally as part of the assessment process. The skills required here are quite different from those involved with writing. We discuss them here under three headings: planning and preparing; the use of visual aids; and presenting.

Planning and preparing

We make no apology for starting this section with the trainer's old adage 'Failing to prepare is preparing to fail'. Your assessors will forgive any inadequacies that stem from inexperience, but they will be much less forgiving of students who have paid little attention to preparation. You can be sure of one thing about insufficient preparation: it shows, particularly to the experienced tutor.

All presentations should have clear aims and objectives. This is not the place to analyse the difference between these. Suffice to say that your aim should be to give the audience members an overview of your report in such a way that it will capture their interest. Keep it clear and simple. By doing so you will meet the most basic assessment criterion: that some time later the tutor in the audience can remember clearly your main project storyline. Your objectives are more specific. They should start you thinking about the interests of your audience. These should be phrased in terms of what it is you want your audience members to be able to do after your presentation. Since your presentation will usually be confined to the imparting of knowledge, it is sufficient to phrase your objectives in terms of the audience members being able, for example, to define, describe, explain or clarify. It is a good idea to share the objectives with your audience members so they know about the journey on which they are being taken (Box 14.15).

Setting clear objectives for your presentation leads you neatly to deciding the content. This should be straightforward because your abstract should serve as your guide to the content. After all, the purpose of the abstract is to give the reader a brief overview of the report, which is precisely the same purpose as the presentation. How much detail you go into on each point will be determined largely by the time at your disposal. But the audience member who wants more detail can always ask you to elaborate, or read it in the report.

The final point to note here is to think about the general approach you will adopt in delivering your presentation. It is a good idea to involve the audience members rather than simply tell them what it is you want them to know. Thirty minutes of you talking at the audience members can seem like an age, for you and sometimes for them! Inviting them to ask questions throughout the presentation is a good way of ensuring that the talk is not all in one direction. Rarely will tutors miss the opportunity of asking you to 'dig

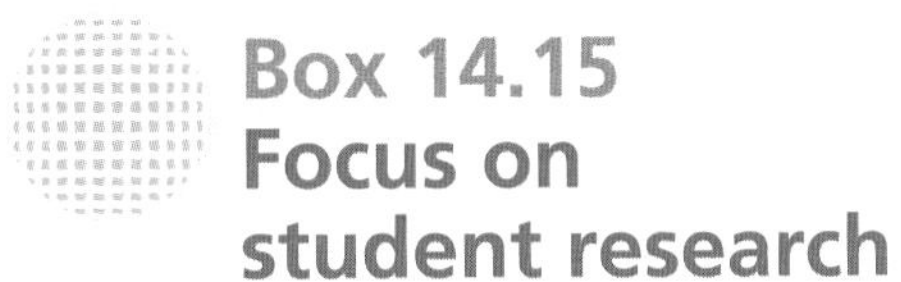

Box 14.15 Focus on student research

Presenting the objectives for a project

Phil created the following slides in Microsoft PowerPoint as part of a lecture on project presentation. This allowed him to produce various designs of slide to meet his purpose, examples of which are shown in the following versions:

Version 1: Standard PowerPoint slide

Objectives for a presentation

- To describe the purpose of the research project
- To explain the context in which the research project research was set
- To identify the research strategy adopted and the reasons for its choice
- To list the main findings, conclusions and recommendations flowing from the research
- *N.B. Detail related to the specific project may be added*

Version 2: PowerPoint slide using design template

Objectives for a presentation

- To describe the purpose of the research project
- To explain the context in which the research project research was set
- To identify the research strategy adopted and the reasons for its choice
- To list the main findings, conclusions and recommendations flowing from the research
- *N.B. Detail related to the specific project may be added*

Box 14.15 Focus on student research

Version 3: PowerPoint slide using more colour

Objectives for a presentation

- To describe the purpose of the research project
- To explain the context in which the research project research was set
- To identify the research strategy adopted and the reasons for its choice
- To list the main findings, conclusions and recommendations flowing from the research
- *N.B. Detail related to the specific project may be added*

Version 4: PowerPoint slide with photograph inserted

OBJECTIVES FOR A PRESENTATION

- To describe the purpose of the research project
- To explain the context in which the research project research was set
- To identify the research strategy adopted and the reasons for its choice
- To list the main findings, conclusions and recommendations flowing from the research

- *N.B. Detail related to the specific project may be added*

Version 5: PowerPoint slide with space for audience to add notes

OBJECTIVES FOR A PRESENTATION

- To describe the purpose of the research project
- To explain the context in which the research project research was set
- To identify the research strategy adopted and the reasons for its choice
- To list the main findings, conclusions and recommendations flowing from the research

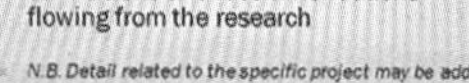

a little deeper' to test your understanding, so don't worry that no questions will arise. However, you must be careful to ensure that you do not let questions and answers run away with time. The more you open up your presentation to debate, the less control you have of time. In general we do not think it is a good idea to attempt to emulate tutors and turn your presentation into a teaching session. We have seen students set the audience mini-exercises to get them involved, but often these tend to fall flat. Play to your strengths and enjoy the opportunity to share your detailed knowledge with an interested audience.

Using visual aids

Now another old adage: 'I hear and I forget, I see and I remember' (Rawlins 1999: 37). The use of **visual aids** will do more than enhance the understanding of your audience. It will help you to look better prepared and therefore more professional. It is unlikely that you will have the time in your presentation to incorporate visual aids such as videoclips, and often your subject matter will not lend itself to their use. So we shall confine our discussion here to using slides with a digital video projector and using the whiteboard.

A simple set of slides will perform the same function as a set of notes, in that it will ensure that you do not forget key points, and will help you to keep your presentation on track. You will know the material so well that a key point noted on the overhead will be enough to trigger your thought process and focus the attention of the audience. Key points will also ensure that you are not tempted to read a script for your presentation, something that will not sustain the attention of your audience for very long.

The use of Microsoft PowerPoint™ has revolutionised the preparation of overhead presentation slides and handouts (Box 14.15). It is now easy to produce a highly professional presentation, using slides which can include simple illustrations to reinforce a point or add a little humour. Virtually all organisations have digital video projectors to project the slides directly from a computer, which adds to the degree of professionalism. This allows you electronically to reveal each point as you talk about it while concealing forthcoming points. PowerPoint also allows you to print miniature versions of your slides as a handout or note pages (Box 14.15, version 5), which is a very useful aide-memoire for the audience.

You may want to supplement your pre-prepared slides with the use of the whiteboard. This may be useful for explaining points in relation to questions you receive. A word of warning here: ensure that you use dry markers that can be wiped from the board. A vain attempt to erase the results of a permanent pen in front of your audience will do nothing to enhance your confidence. Ensuring that you have dry wipe markers (use only black and blue pens – red and green are too faint), and checking computers and overhead projectors before the presentation, serve to emphasise the need for careful preparation.

Making the presentation

The first thing to say here is: don't worry about nerves. You may expect to be a little nervous as you commence your presentation and your audience may also expect this. The best way to minimise nervousness is to have prepared your presentation carefully and to have practised it beforehand.

Be positive about your presentation and your report. Trial your presentation on a friend to ensure that it flows logically and smoothly and that you can deliver it in the allotted time. In our experience most students put too much material in their presentations, although they worry beforehand that they have not got enough.

It is important that your presentation has a clear structure. We can do no better than repeat the words of a famous evangelist: when asked how he held the attention of his audience, he replied 'First I tell them what I'm going to say, then I say it, then I tell them what I've said' (Parry 1991: 17). Parry (1991) notes that audiences like to know where they are going, they like to know how they are progressing on the journey and they like to know when they have arrived.

Finally some practical points that will help:

- Think about whether you would prefer to sit or stand at the presentation. The former may be better to foster debate, the latter is likely to give you a sense of 'control' (Rawlins 1999). Which one you choose may depend upon the circumstances of the presentation, including the approach you wish to adopt, the room layout, the equipment you are using and your preferred style.
- Consider how you will deal with difficult questions. Rehearse these and your answers in your mind so that you can deal with them confidently during the presentation.
- Avoid jargon.
- Check the room before the presentation to ensure you have everything you need, you are happy and familiar with the layout, and all your equipment is working.

14.8 Summary

- Writing is a powerful way of clarifying your thinking.
- Writing is a creative process, which needs the right conditions if it is to produce successful results.
- Your project report should have a clear structure that enables you to develop a clear storyline.
- Your report should be laid out in such a way that your reader finds all the information readily accessible.
- You should try to develop a clear, simple writing style that will make reading the report an easy and enjoyable experience.
- Spelling and grammatical errors should be avoided.
- Do not think of your first draft as your last. Be prepared to rewrite your report several times until you think it is the best you can do.
- Failing to prepare for your presentation is preparing to fail.
- Visual aids will enhance the understanding of your audience and lend your presentation professionalism.
- Remember: tell them what you're going to say, say it, then tell them what you've said.

Self-check questions

Help with these questions is available at the end of the chapter.

14.1 Your project tutor has returned your draft project report with the suggestion that you make a clearer distinction between your results and your conclusions. How will you go about this?

14.2 Why is it considered good practice to acknowledge the limitations of your research in the project report?

14.3 Look again at the quote from Wright Mills cited early in Section 14.5. Rewrite this so that his idea is communicated to the reader in the clearest way possible.

14.4 There are other problems that must be avoided when repositioning sections of your report in the redrafting processes. What are they?

14.5 Your friend or colleague is concerned about preparing her or his project presentation. What advice will you give to help him or her prepare this presentation?

Review and discussion questions

14.6 Draft a plan for your project report, show it to your friends and compare your plan with those they have drafted. Explain the reason for any differences between your plan and those of your friends.

14.7 Look through several of the refereed academic journals that relate to your subject area. Choose an article that is based upon some primary research and note the structure of the article. Decide whether you agree with the way in which the author has structured the article and think of ways in which you may have done this differently.

14.8 Share pieces of your writing with a group of your friends. Look at the example in Box 14.13 and subject all the pieces to the 'write clearer sentences' test.

Writing your project report

- Design a clear structure for your report that broadly fits the structure suggested in Section 14.3. Ensure that the structure you design accommodates a clear storyline and meets the expectations of your audience.
- Write the report's abstract. Remember that you will need to rewrite this when you have finished your first draft.
- Compile the main body of the report. How will you ensure that the literature review relates to the following chapters? What method will you adopt to make the distinction between result and conclusions?
- Give your report the 'reader-friendly' test to ensure that the style is easy to read and free from avoidable errors.
- Use the question in Box 1.4 to guide your reflective diary entry.

References

Becker, H. (2007) *Writing for Social Scientists* (2nd edn) Chicago, IL: University of Chicago Press.

Bloom, B. (ed.) (1971) *Taxonomy of Educational Objectives: Cognitive Domain*. New York: McKay.

Day, R. (1998) *How to Write and Publish a Scientific Paper* (5th edn). Phoenix, AZ: Oryx Press.

Day, R. and Gastel, B. (2011) *How to Write and Publish a Scientific Paper* (7th edn). Oxford, Greenwood.

Easterby-Smith, M., Thorpe, R. and Jackson, P. (2008) *Management Research* (3rd edn). London: Sage.

Emerald Group Publishing (2011) *How to . . . write an abstract*. Available at www.emeraldinsight.com/authors/guides/write/abstracts.htm [Accessed 9 August 2011].

Free Online Dictionary (2011) 'Gibberish'. Available at www.thefreedictionary.com/gibberish [Accessed 18 August 2011].

Kvale, S. and Brinkmann, S (2009) *InterViews* (2nd edn). London: Sage.

Neville, C. (2010) *The Complete Guide to Referencing and Plagiarism* (2nd edn). Maidenhead: Open University Press McGraw Hill.

Parry, H. (1991) *Successful Business Presentations*. Kingston-upon-Thames: Croner.

Phillips, E.M. and Pugh, D.S. (2010) *How to get a PhD* (5th edn). Maidenhead: Open University Press McGraw Hill.

Raimond, P. (1993) *Management Projects: Design, Research and Presentation*. London: Chapman & Hall.

Rawlins, K. (1999) *Presentation and Communication Skills: A Handbook for Practitioners*. London: Emap Healthcare Ltd.

Richards, P. (2007) 'Risk', in H. Becker (ed.) *Writing for Social Scientists* (2nd edn). Chicago, IL: University of Chicago Press, pp. 108–20.

Robson, C. (2011) *Real World Research: A Resource for Users of Social Research Methods in Applied Settings* (3rd edn). Chichester: John Wiley.

Rodrigues, R. A. and Guest, D. (2010) 'Have careers become boundaryless?', *Human Relations*, Vol. 63, No. 8, pp. 1157–75.

Smith, C.B. (1991) *A Guide to Business Research*. Chicago, IL: Nelson-Hall.

Veroff, J. (2007) 'Writing', in K. Rudestam and R. Newton (eds) *Surviving your Dissertation* (3rd edn). Newbury Park, CA: Sage pp. 227–8.

Wright Mills, C. (1970) 'On intellectual craftsmanship', in C. Wright Mills, *The Sociological Imagination*. London: Pelican.

Further reading

Becker, H. (2007) *Writing for Social Scientists* (2nd edn). Chicago, IL: University of Chicago Press. This is a highly readable book, full of anecdotes, from an expert in the field. It is rich in ideas about how writing may be improved. Most of these have been developed by Becker from his own writing and teaching. Such is the emphasis that Becker puts on rewriting that the title would more accurately be 'Rewriting for Social Scientists'.

Day, R. and Gastel, B. (2011) *How to Write and Publish a Scientific Paper* (7th edn). Oxford: Greenwood. This takes the reader through the whole process, with a host of useful advice. It is funny and irreverent but none the less valuable for that!

Fisher, C. (2010) *Researching and Writing a Dissertation* (3rd edn). Harlow: FT Prentice Hall. Chapter 6 has lots of useful tips for the writing-up process.

Neville, C. (2010) *The Complete Guide to Referencing and Plagiarism* (2nd edn). Maidenhead: Open University Press McGraw Hill. A very useful guide to both how to reference and how to help ensure you do not inadvertently plagiarise the work of others.

Rawlins, K. (1999). *Presentation and Communication Skills: A Handbook for Practitioners*. Basingstoke: Palgrave MacMillan. A very useful and practical guide for the inexperienced.

Case 14
Clare's research project presentation

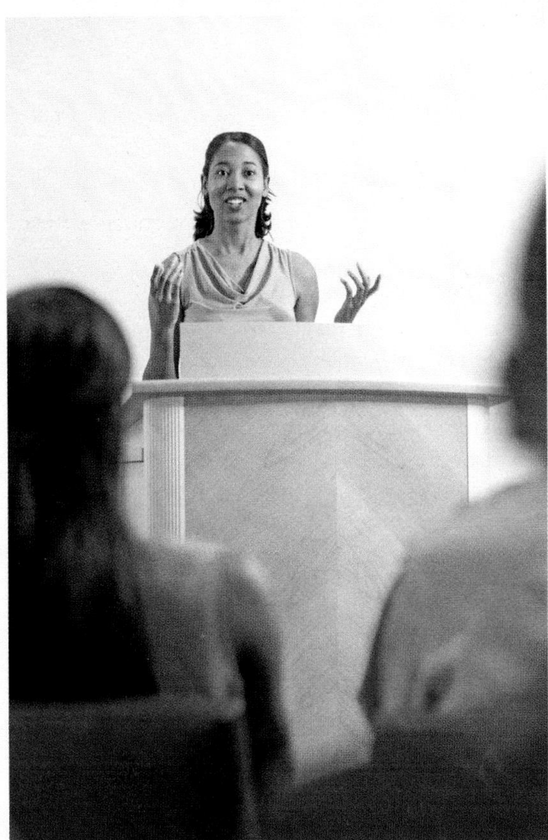
Source: Corbis ER productions/Blend Images

Clare was slightly nervous when she heard that she had to give a presentation about her undergraduate research project. She had done presentations previously, but they had always been in groups. This time it was a 10-minute individual presentation in front of five students and two tutors using PowerPoint. Ten minutes seemed a very long time; and there were also the two minutes devoted to audience questions to think about.

Remembering that last year she had taken part in a group presentation for another module where each member of the group had to speak for two minutes, she looked back at the helpful feedback the group had received from the tutor which had been divided into five sub-sections:

- Structure;
- Visual aids;
- Delivery;
- Audience interaction;
- Question handling.

She also found her copy of Cameron's (2009) *The Business Student's Handbook – Skills for Study and Employment*. The two things she remembered vividly from both her reading and her previous experience was that preparation was the key and, practice helped combat nerves. Clare's research project was entitled 'To what extent can the retail industry reduce the threat of terrorism?' She had enjoyed researching it as it had increased her understanding of the impact that current world issues had on a sector that she planned to work in; providing her with the opportunity to focus on strategic actions taken by both global and local hotel groups. Deciding to start with the structure of her presentation, Clare worked on the '1 slide per minute' rule-of-thumb that a friend had found on the Internet. She drew a set of eight boxes on a piece of paper as a previous tutor had shown her, and allocated the first to be a 'Title of presentation' and the final one to 'Any questions' – that left six to fill.

Clare knew that the students in the audience and one of the tutors would not have read her research report, and so she decided to outline her research in slides 2, 3 and 4. This would provide her with the opportunity to clarify the scope of her research question, use images to highlight the problem, and describe her research method. She could then use slides 5 and 6 to outline her findings, and slide 7 to summarise her conclusions.

Looking back at her project report, she was pleased to see that her chosen structure followed the sections on the contents page. However, opening up PowerPoint to create a new presentation, her confidence faded as blank pages with boxes that seemed to demand information in specific formats stared back at her. She returned to her 8-slide plan and started to scribble in each box.

Title of presentation Name Date Degree programme and student number	Research project question scope reason for choice of topic	Setting context Visuals (showing the effect of terrorism and speed of recovery)	Research methodology used (+ limitations)
Findings 1 Bullet points	Findings 2 (graph or chart)	Conclusions Bullet points	Any questions?

Feeling much more in control, she returned to PowerPoint and quickly created slide layouts that supported what she wanted to say or show at each stage. She created a master slide to ensure consistency in looking for each slide and, prompted by memories of unreadable lectures slides in some teaching rooms, checked in which room her presentation would take place. Based on this she chose a theme that had a dark background with light text. This would provide the best contrast in a room with some natural light or undimmable lighting. Adding suitable text and two images was then quite straightforward. However, viewing the slideshow on her laptop screen Clare noticed that there seemed to be a lot of text, each bullet point taking at least two lines of text. One of the feedback points from her previous experience was to ensure the slides 'supported' what the speaker had to say, not 'said it with them'. The lecturer had commented that the audience primarily needs to listen to the speaker, not read the slide; and they can't do both. Editing the bullet points was difficult because the shorter they got, the more information Clare felt she needed to commit to memory. Adding 'notes' to each slide helped, but she still felt uneasy.

Having finally reached the point when her slideshow was almost complete, she stopped work for the day and went for a drink with her friends. She knew from her experience of previous presentations that when she revisited the slideshow the next day she would look at it with new eyes and spot things that needed attention. As expected, when she returned to her presentation the following day she noticed some formatting errors and a couple of spelling mistakes. Using the spellchecker and showing the slides to a trusted friend helped ensure her edited presentation looked professional and was error-free. It was at this stage that Clare started to consider the actual delivery of the presentation and wondered whether some custom animation and slide transitions might enhance her presentation. Adding basic transitions didn't detract from her message, and setting up the pictures to appear 'on next click' showed the before and after shots in sequence effectively. Clare's decision not to add more 'effects' was led by memories of her previous group presentation when things whizzed in and out making noises like bullets and fireworks – not the sort of image she wanted to portray this time.

She knew it was not appropriate to read her notes out loud, having listened to several student groups doing that last year and noticing how stilted it sounded. She considered memorising it as a speech, but remembered someone saying 'Don't memorise – just rehearse out loud!'.

Asking another friend to act as an audience, she ran through the presentation. She finished in four minutes and only remembered to ask for questions when her final slide appeared. Her friend looked slightly stunned and kindly suggested that she went through it again, remembering to talk more slowly and pause after each slide so that the listener could take in what she'd said. Her second attempt at the presentation took six minutes and this time Clare was able to glance sideways at her 'audience' whilst she was talking, gauging her friend's understanding. At the appropriate moment in the presentation her friend asked a question relating to the chart in slide 6: 'I'm confused. Can you explain the chart in slide 6 to me?' Whilst initially slightly flustered, Clare was able to access that slide to answer the question. She recognised that the chart was not clearly labelled, not even stating the date of the terrorist attach in question. She also noted that she needed to explain why she was focusing on comparing quarterly data rather than looking at the overall trend after the terrorist attack.

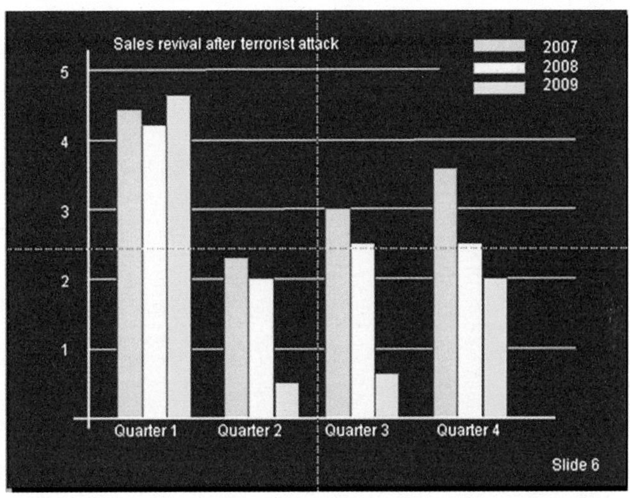

She'd emailed the slides to the tutor; she knew which room she would be presenting in; she knew her material; she'd practised out loud; and her presentation had a clear logical structure. However, she was still nervous. On the day of the presentation she sat through three other student's presentations which did nothing to help her nerves, but when she stood up to speak, she took a deep breath, as her friend had advised, and introduced herself clearly. Her hands shook as she clicked on to slide 2, checked her notes and then, looking directly over the heads of the audience, started to tell them about her research project in a clear voice. Clare worked through her notes and slides without noticing the intense reaction to the pictures on slide 3 and the slightly quizzical faces when she explained the chart in slide 6. Reaching the end of her slide show Clare glanced at the audience and asked in a quiet voice if there were any questions. Two people raised their hands. The first question related to the chart in slide 6 and, in answering it, she reiterated some of the things she had said earlier. The second question was a simple query about the images used in Slide 3 and, having answered it and the remaining questions Clare sat down to listen to the final student presentation in that group. It was over.

Looking back on the experience later, Clare decided that she would probably always be nervous in that sort of situation, but that provided she understood the subject she was talking about and had spent sufficient time developing a simple slideshow then the outcome would be relatively professional; and every time would be easier that the last. Feedback from the tutor later confirmed that the presentation was well structured, her voice pace, pitch and tone were appropriate and the visual aids, other than slide 6, enhanced the spoken words. The feedback suggested that she needed to work on her audience interaction and question handling.

Reference

Cameron, S. (2009) *The Business Student's Handbook – Skills for Study and Employment* (5th edn). Harlow: Prentice Hall.

Questions

1 In what way did starting with the eight boxes limit or help Clare's planning of her presentation?
2 What advice would you give Clare in relation to interacting with her audience more effectively?
3 In what ways might 'telling them what you're going to say, saying it, and then telling them what you've just said' have helped Clare's audience?
4 Even if you think you aren't nervous, why is practising a presentation in front of a critical friend a good idea?

Additional case studies relating to material covered in this chapter are available via the book's companion website: **www.pearsoned.co.uk/saunders**. They are:

- Writing Lata's project report.
- Amina's story.
- Akasma's draft disappointment.
- James' consultancy report on managers' financial information needs.

Self-check answers

14.1 This is easier said than done. Start by going through your results chapter, continually asking yourself 'Did I find this out?' You will probably weed out a lot of things that you have thought about that are related to points you found out. These belong in the conclusions (or discussion) chapter.

Now turn to the conclusions chapter, asking yourself the question: 'Is this a reflection of what I found out?' If the points are a repeat of what you covered in your findings section, then cut them out and make sure you write reflections on the findings.

14.2 It will demonstrate good practice in two respects. First it will demonstrate that you have evaluated your research design. Second it will help you to evaluate how you would alter this design if you were going to repeat your research, or if you were going to undertake further research. Remember that there is no perfect research design.

14.3 Academic writing is often difficult to understand. This is not usually because the subject matter is complex or the thoughts profound. It is because the writer thinks it necessary to write in an 'academic' way.

14.4 The 'road map' you announced in the introduction may not now be correct. The previews and summaries at the beginning and end of the relevant chapters may need changing. A more serious potential problem is that the storyline may be altered. This should not be the case. Nonetheless, it would important to reread the whole report to ensure that any repositioning does not alter its sense of coherence.

14.5 You may emphasise the general point that preparation is very important, not least because this will help to overcome any nervousness that your friend will feel when he or she makes the presentation. You may also emphasise that she or he should think about the audience and what is it that he or she will want to tell them. You may tell her or him to make sure that the presentation has clear objectives and that it should be kept simple so that there is no danger of overloading the audience with too much information in a short period. This will mean telling the audience what they need to know and eliminating other information. You may also tell him or her that using visual aids will be important but that these should support the key points you wish to make and not be used to show off your technical skills as this may only serve to annoy or confuse your audience. Clear visual aids will also be helpful to your friend in delivering her or his presentation. You may also advise your friend to practise his or her presentation, to invite members of the audience to ask some questions during the actual performance to help to engage them but to remain mindful of the time allowed to complete it.

Get ahead using resources on the companion website at: **www.pearsoned.co.uk/saunders**

- Improve your IBM SPSS Statistics and NVivo research analysis with practice tutorials.
- Save time researching on the Internet with the Smarter Online Searching Guide.
- Test your progress using self-assessment questions.
- Follow live links to useful websites.

Bibliography

A

American Association for Public Opinion Research (2008) *Standard Definitions: Final Dispositions of Case Codes and Outcome Rates for Surveys* (5th edn). Lenexa, KA: AAPOR.

American Psychological Association (2009) *Concise Rules of the APA Style*. Washington, DC: American Psychological Association.

Anderson, D.R., Sweeney, D.J. and Williams, T.A. (2010) *Statistics for Business and Economics* (11th edn). London: Thomson Learning.

Anderson, T.W. (2003) *An Introduction to Multivariate Statistical Analysis*. New York: John Wiley.

Anseel, F., Lievens, F., Schollaert, E. and Choragwicka, B. (2010) 'Response rates in organizational science, 1995–2008: A meta-analytic review and guidelines for survey researchers', *Journal of Business Psychology*, Vol. 25, pp. 335–49.

B

Backhaus, K. and Surinder Tikoo, S. (2004) 'Conceptualizing and researching employer branding', *Career Development International*, Vol. 9, No. 5, pp. 501–17.

Bakardjieva, M. and Feenberg, A. (2000) 'Involving the virtual subject', *Ethics and Information Technology*, Vol. 2, pp. 233–40.

Barnett, V. (2002) *Sample Survey Principles and Methods* (3rd edn). Chichester: Wiley.

Baruch, Y. and Holtom, B.C. (2008) 'Survey response rate levels and trends in organizational research', *Human Relations*, Vol. 61, pp. 1139–60.

BBC (2011) *Shopping may improve health*'. Available at www.bbc.co.uk/news/health-12990071 [Accessed 7 April 2011].

BBC College of Journalism (2011) *Interviews*. Available at www.bbc.co.uk/journalism/skills/interviewing [Accessed 29 June 2011].

Becker, H.S. (1998) *Tricks of the Trade: How to Think about Your Research While You're Doing It*. Chicago, IL. University of Chicago Press.

Becker, H. (2007) *Writing for Social Scientists* (2nd edn). Chicago, IL: University of Chicago Press.

Bell, E. and Bryman, A. (2007) 'The ethics of management research: an exploratory content analysis', *British Journal of Management*, Vol. 18, No. 1, pp. 63–77.

Bell, J. (2010) *Doing Your Research Project* (5th edn). Maidenhead: Open University Press.

Berman Brown, R. and Saunders, M. (2008) *Dealing with Statistics: What You Need to Know*. Maidenhead: McGraw-Hill Open University Press.

Berry, D. (2004) 'Internet research: Privacy, ethics and alienation: an open source approach', *Internet Research*, Vol. 14, No. 4, pp. 323–32.

Bhaskar, R. (1989) *Reclaiming Reality: A Critical Introduction to Contemporary Philosophy*. London: Verso.

Bidlake, S. (2011) 'Outdoor hall of fame contest opens', *Campaign*, 10 February. Available at www.campaignlive.co.uk/News/MostRead/1054277/Outdoor-Hall-Fame-contest-opens/ [Accessed 6 April 2011].

Bigmacindex.com (2011) *Big Mac Index Data*. Available at www.bigmacindex.org/index.html [Accessed 3 May 2011].

Birnbaum, M.H. (2004) 'Human research and data collection via the internet', *Annual Review of Psychology*, Vol. 55, pp. 803–32.

Black, K. (2009) *Business Statistics* (6th edn). Hoboken, NJ: Wiley.

Blaikie, N. (2010) *Designing Social Research* (2nd edn). Cambridge: Polity.

Blastland, M. and Dilnot, A. (2008) *The Tiger than Isn't*. London: Profile Books.

Bloom, B. (ed.) (1971) *Taxonomy of Educational Objectives: Cognitive Domain*. New York, McKay.

Blumberg, B., Cooper, D.R. and Schindler, D.S. (2008) *Business Research Methods*. Maidenhead: McGraw-Hill.

Boddy, C. (2005) 'A rose by any other name may smell as sweet but "group discussion" is not another name for "focus group" nor should it be', *Qualitative Market Research*, Vol. 8, No. 3, pp. 248–55.

Bourque, L.B. and Clark, V.A. (1994) 'Processing data: the survey example', in M.S. Lewis-Beck (ed.) *Research Practice*. London: Sage, pp. 1–88.

Bowen, D. and Schouten, A.F. (2008) 'Tourist satisfaction and beyond: Tourism migrants in Mallorca', *International Journal of Tourism Research*, Vol. 10, No. 2, pp. 141–53.

Bradley, N. (1999) 'Sampling for Internet surveys: An examination of respondent selection for Internet research', *Journal of the Market Research Society*, Vol. 41, No. 4, pp. 387–95.

Bradley, N. (2010) *Marketing Research: Tools and Techniques* (2nd edn). Oxford: Oxford University Press.

Bradshaw, D. (2011) 'Rotterdam dean eyes China', *Financial Times*, 11 March. Available at www.ft.com/ [Accessed 17 March 2011].

Brannick, T. and Coghlan, D. (2007) 'In defense of being native: The case for insider academic research', *Organizational Research Methods*, Vol. 10, No. 1, pp. 59–74.

Brekhus, W.H., Galliher, J.F. and Gubrium, J.F. (2005) 'The need for thin description', *Qualitative Inquiry*, Vol. 11, No. 6, pp. 861–79.

British Psychological Society (1988) 'Guidelines for the use of non-sexist language', *The Psychologist*, Vol. 1, No. 2, pp. 53–4.

British Psychological Society (2004) *Style guide*. Available at www.bps.org.uk/document-download-area/document-download$.cfm?file_uuid=1B29ADB1-7E96-C67F-D51D3ADFC581A906&ext=pdf [Accessed 10 May 2011].

British Psychological Society (2007) *Report of the Working Party on Conducting Research on the Internet, Guidelines for ethical practice in psychological research online.* Available at www.bps.org.uk/publications/policy-guidelines/research-guidelines-policy-documents/ [Accessed 1 June 2011].

British Sociological Association (2002) *Statement of ethical practice.* Available at www.britsoc.co.uk/equality/Statement+ Ethical+Practice.htm [Accessed 1 June 2011].

British Sociological Association (2004a) *Language and the BSA: Sex and gender*. Available at www.britsoc.co.uk/equality/ [Accessed 10 May 2011].

British Sociological Association (2004b) *Language and the BSA: Non-disablist*. Available at www.britsoc.co.uk/equality/ [Accessed 10 May 2011].

British Sociological Association (2011) *Equality and diversity. Language and the BSA: Ethnicity and race*. Available at www.britsoc.co.uk/equality/ [Accessed 21 June 2011].

Bryant, A. and Charmaz, K. (2007) *The Sage Handbook of Grounded Theory*. London: Sage.

Bryman, A. (1988) *Quantity and Quality in Social Research*. London: Unwin Hyman.

Bryman, A. (1989) *Research Methods and Organisation Studies*. London: Unwin Hyman.

Bryman, A. (2006) 'Integrating quantitative and qualitative research: How is it done?', *Qualitative Research*, Vol. 6, No. 1, pp. 97–113.

Bryson, B. (1995) *Made in America*. London: Minerva.

Buchanan, D., Boddy, D. and McAlman, J. (1988) 'Getting in, getting on, getting out and getting back', in A. Bryman (ed.) *Doing Research in Organisations*. London: Routledge, pp. 53–67.

Bulmer, M., Sturgis, P.J. and Allum, N. (2009) 'Editors' introduction', in M. Bulmer, P.J. Sturgis and N. Allum (eds) *Secondary Analysis of Survey Data*. Los Angeles: Sage, pp. xviii–xxvi.

Burrell, G. and Morgan, G. (1982) *Sociological Paradigms and Organisational Analysis*. London: Heinemann.

Buzan, T. (2011) *Buzan's Study Skills: Mind Maps, Memory Techniques, Speed Reading and More*. London: BBC.

C

Canals, J. (2010) 'Crisis offers a chance to reflect on strategy', *Financial Times*, 17 October. Available at www.ft.com/ [Accessed 17 March 2011].

Carroll, L. (1989). *Alice's Adventures in Wonderland*. London: Hutchinson.

Carson, D., Gilmore, A., Perry, C. and Grønhaug, K. (2001) *Qualitative Marketing Research*. London: Sage.

Cassell, C. and Lee, B. (eds) (2011a) *Challenges and Controversies in Management Research*. New York: Routledge.

Cassell, C. and Lee, B. (2011b) 'Introduction: Key debates, challenges and controversies in management research', C. Cassell and B. Lee (eds) *Challenges and Controversies in Management Research*. New York: Routledge, pp. 1–16.

Chang, Y.H, Chen, R.C.Y., Wahlqvist, M.L. and Lee, M.S. (2011) 'Frequent shopping by men and women increases survival in the older Taiwanese population', *Journal of Epidemiology and Community Health Online*, 6 April. Available at http://jech.bmj.com/ [Accessed 7 April 2011].

Charmaz, K. (2005) 'Grounded theory in the 21st century', in N.K. Denzin and Y.S. Lincoln (eds) *The Sage Handbook of Qualitative Research* (3rd edn). London: Sage, pp. 507–36.

Charmaz, K. (2006) *Constructing Grounded Theory*. London: Sage.

Chartered Institute of Library and Information Professionals (2010) *Libraries and Information Services in the UK and ROI 2010–11* (37th edn). London: Facet Publishing.

Chase, S.E. (2005) 'Narrative inquiry', in N.K. Denzin and Y.S. Lincoln (eds) *The Sage Handbook of Qualitative Research* (3rd edn). London, Sage, pp. 651–80.

Cinite, I., Duxbury, L.E. and Higgins, C. (2009) 'Measurement of perceived organisational readiness for change in the public sector', *British Journal of Management*, Vol. 20, pp. 265–77.

CIPD (2010) *Research Insight: Harnessing the Power of Employee Communication*. London: Chartered Institute of Personnel and Development.

Clausen, H. (1996) 'Web information quality as seen from libraries', *New Library World*, Vol. 97, No. 1130, pp. 4–8.

Clough, P. and Nutbrown, C. (2002) *A Student's Guide to Methodology*. London: Sage.

Coffey, A. and Atkinson, P. (1996) *Making Sense of Qualitative Data*. Thousand Oaks, CA: Sage.

Coghlan, D. and Brannick, T. (2010) *Doing Action Research in Your Own Organisation* (3rd edn). London: Sage.

Cohen, L. and Holliday, M. (1996) *Practical Statistics for Students*. London: Paul Chapman.

Cook, T.D. and Campbell, D.T. (1979) *Quasi-experimentation: Design and Analysis Issues for Field Settings*. Chicago: Rand McNally.

Coomber, R. (1997) 'Using the Internet for survey research', *Sociological Research Online*, Vol. 2, No. 2. Available at www.socresonline.org.uk/socresonline/2/2/2.html [Accessed 20 April 2008].

Cooper, D.R. and Schindler, P.S. (2008) *Business Research Methods* (10th edn). London: McGraw-Hill.

Corbetta, P. (2003) *Social Research: Theory, Methods and Techniques*. London: Sage.

Corbin, J. and Strauss, A. (2008) *Basics of Qualitative Research* (3rd edn). Thousand Oaks, CA: Sage.

Cowton, C.J. (1998) 'The use of secondary data in business ethics research', *Journal of Business Ethics*, Vol. 17, No. 4, pp. 423–34.

Cresswell, J.W. (2007) *Qualitative Inquiry and Research Design: Choosing Among Five Approaches*. Thousand Oaks, CA: Sage.

Cresswell, J.W. (2009) 'Mapping the field of mixed methods research', *Journal of Mixed Methods Research*, Vol. 3, No. 2, pp. 95–108.

Cresswell, J.W. and Plano Clark, V.L. (2007) *Designing and Conducting Mixed Methods Research*. Thousand Oaks, CA: Sage.

Crotty, M. (1998) *The Foundations of Social Research*. London: Sage.

Cunliffe, A.L. (2010) 'Retelling tales of the field: In search of organisational ethnography 20 years on', *Organizational Research Methods*, Vol. 13, No. 2, pp. 224–39.

Curwin, J. and Slater, R. (2007) *Quantitative Methods: A Short Course*. London: Thomson Learning EMEA.

D

Dale, A., Arber, S. and Procter, M. (1988) *Doing Secondary Research*. London: Unwin Hyman.

Dancey, C.P. and Reidy, J. (2008) *Statistics Without Maths for Psychology: Using SPSS for Windows* (4th edn). Harlow: Prentice Hall.

Davies, J. (2001) 'International comparisons of labour disputes in 1999', *Labour Market Trends*, Vol. 109, No. 4, pp. 195–201.

Day, R. (1998) *How to Write and Publish a Scientific Paper* (5th edn). Phoenix, AZ: Oryx Press.

Day, R. and Gastel, B. (2011) *How to Write and Publish a Scientific Paper* (7th edn). Oxford: Greenwood.

Dees, R. (2000) *Writing the Modern Research Paper*. Boston, MA: Allyn and Bacon.

Dees, R. (2003) *Writing the Modern Research Paper* (4th edn). Boston, MA: Allyn and Bacon.

DeFina, A. and Georgakopoulou, A. (2008) 'Analysing narratives as practices', *Qualitative Research*, Vol. 8, No. 3, pp. 379–87.

Delbridge, R. and Kirkpatrick, I. (1994) 'Theory and practice of participant observation', in V. Wass and P. Wells (eds) *Principles and Practice in Business and Management Research*. Aldershot: Dartmouth, pp. 35–62.

Denscombe, M. (2007) *The Good Research Guide* (3rd edn). Buckingham: Open University Press.

Denyer, D. and Neely, A. (2004) 'Introduction to special issue: Innovation and productivity performance in the UK', *International Journal of Management Reviews*, Vol. 5/6, Nos. 3 and 4, pp. 131–5.

Denyer, D. and Tranfield, D. (2009) 'Producing a systematic review', in D.A. Buchanan and A. Bryman (eds) *The Sage Handbook of Organizational Research Methods*. London: Sage, pp. 671–89.

Denzin, N. (1989) *The Research Act: A Theoretical Introduction to Sociological Methods* (3rd edn). Englewood Cliffs, NJ: Prentice-Hall.

Denzin, N.K. and Lincoln, Y.S. (2005) *The Sage Handbook of Qualitative Research* (3rd edn). London: Sage.

Department for Business Innovation and Skills (2011) *Workplace Employment Relations Study*. Available at www.bis.gov.uk/policies/employment-metters/research/wers [Accessed 14 August 2011].

deVaus, D.A. (2002) *Surveys in Social Research* (5th edn). London: Routledge.

Devinney, T. (2011) 'Research generates better business scholarship', *Financial Times*, 31 January. Available at www.ft.com/ [Accessed 17 March 2011].

Dey, I. (1993) *Qualitative Data Analysis*. London: Routledge.

Dick, P. (2004) 'Discourse analysis', in C. Cassell and G. Symon (eds) *Essential Guide to Qualitative Methods and Analysis in Organizational Research*. London: Sage, pp. 203–13.

Dick, P. (2009) 'Bending over backwards? Using a pluralistic framework to explore the management of flexible working in the UK police service', *British Journal of Management*, Vol. 20, pp. 182–93.

Dillman, D.A. (2009) *Internet, Mail and Mixed Mode Surveys: The Tailored Design Method* (3rd edn). New York: Wiley.

Dillman, D.A., Eltringe, J.L., Groves, J.L. and Little, R.J.A. (eds) (2002) *Survey Nonresponse*. New York: Wiley Interscience.

Ditton, J. (1977). *Part-Time Crime: An Ethnography of Fiddling and Pilferage*. London: Macmillan.

Dobson, P. (2002) 'Critical realism and information systems research: Why bother with philosophy?', *Information Research*, Vol. 7, No. 2. Available at http://informationr.net/ir/7-2/paper124.html [Accessed 11 July 2011].

Dochartaigh, N.O. (2007) *Internet Research Skills: How to do your Literature Search and Find Research Information Online*. London: Sage.

Dyer, O. (2003) 'Lancet accuses AstraZeneca of sponsoring biased research', *British Medical Journal*, Vol. 327, No. 1, p. 1005.

E

Easterby-Smith, M., Thorpe, R. and Jackson, P. (2008) *Management Research: An Introduction* (3rd edn). London: Sage.

Eddy, E.R., D'Abate, C.P. and Thurston Jr, P.W. (2010) 'Explaining engagement in personal activities on company time', *Personnel Review*, Vol. 39, No. 5, pp. 639–54.

Eden, C. and Huxham, C. (1996) 'Action research for management research', *British Journal of Management*, Vol. 7, No. 1, pp. 75–86.

Edwards, P., Roberts, I., Clarke, M., Di Giuseppe, C., Pratap, S., Wentz, R., and Kwan, I. (2002) 'Increasing response rates to postal questionnaires: Systematic review', *British Medical Journal*, No. 324, May, pp. 1183–91.

Edwards, T., Tregaskis, O., Edwards, P., Ferner, A., Marginson, A. with Arrowsmith, J., Adam, D., Meyer, M. and Budjanovcanin, A. (2007) 'Charting the contours of multinationals in Britain: Methodological challenges arising in survey-based research', *Warwick Papers in Industrial Relations* No. 86. Available at www2.warwick.ac.uk/fac/soc/wbs/research/irru/wpir/ [Accessed 2 February 2008].

Eisenhardt, K.M. and Graebner, M.E. (2007) 'Theory building from cases: Opportunities and challenges', *Academy of Management Journal*, Vol. 50, No. 1, pp. 25–32.

Ellis, P. (2010) *The Essential Guide to Effect Sizes*. Cambridge: Cambridge University Press.

Elsbach, K.D., Cable, D.M. and Sherman, J.W. (2010) 'How passive "face time" affects perceptions of employees: Evidence of spontaneous trait inference', *Human Relations*, Vol. 63, No. 6, pp. 735–60.

Emerald Group Publishing (2011) *How to . . . write an abstract*. Available at www.emeraldinsight.com/authors/guides/write/abstracts.htm [Accessed 9 August 2011].

Erlandson, D.A., Harris, E.L., Skipper, B.L. and Allen, S.D. (1993) *Doing Naturalistic Inquiry*. Newbury Park, CA: Sage.

European Commission (2010) *Employment and Unemployment (LFS)*. Available at http://epp.eurostat.ec.europa.eu/portal/page/portal/employment_unemployment_lfs/introduction [Accessed 1 July 2011].

Eurostat (2010) *Europe in Figures: Eurostat Yearbook 2010*. Available at http://epp.eurostat.ec.europa.eu/portal/page/portal/product_details/publication?p_product_code=KS-CD-10-220 [Accessed 1 July 2011].

Eurostat (2011) *Environment and energy statistics – total greenhouse gas emissions*. Available at http://epp.eurostat.ec.europa.eu/portal/page/portal/environment/data/main_tables [Accessed 5 May 2011].

Eurostat (2011) *Eurostat home page*. Available at http://epp.eurostat.ec.europa.eu/portal/page/portal/eurostat/home/ [Accessed 2 July 2011].

Everitt, B.S. and Dunn, G. (2001) *Applied Multivariate Data Analysis* (2nd edn). London: Arnold.

Eysenbach, G. and Till, J.E. (2001) 'Ethical issues in qualitative research on internet communities', *British Medical Journal*, Vol. 323, pp. 1103–5.

F

Farey-Jones, D. (2011) "Hello Boys" voted greatest poster ever', *Campaign*, 31 March. Available at www.campaignlive.co.uk/news/1063405/Hello-Boys-voted-greatest-poster-ever-created/ [Accessed 6 April 2011].

Festinger, L. (1957) *A Theory of Cognitive Dissonance*. Stanford, CA: Stanford University Press.

Field, A. (2009) *Discovering Statistics Using SPSS* (3rd edn). London: Sage.

Fink, A. (2009) *How to Conduct Surveys* (4th edn). Thousand Oaks, CA: Sage.

Finlay, L. (2002) 'Negotiating the swamp: The opportunity and challenge of reflexivity in research practice', *Qualitative Research*, Vol. 2, No. 2, pp. 209–30.

Fisher, C. (2010) *Researching and Writing a Dissertation for Business Students* (3rd edn). Harlow: Financial Times Prentice Hall.

Foddy, W. (1994) *Constructing Questions for Interviews and Questionnaires*. Cambridge: Cambridge University Press.

Free Online Dictionary (2011) 'Gibberish'. Available at www.thefreedictionary.com/gibberish [Accessed 18 August 2011].

Fukami, C. (2007) 'The third road', *Journal of Management Education*, Vol. 31, pp. 358–64.

G

Gabriel, Y. and Griffiths, D.S. (2004) 'Stories in organizational research', in C. Cassell and G. Symon (eds) *Essential Guide to Qualitative Methods in Organizational Research*. London: Sage, pp. 114–26.

Gall, M.D., Gall, J.P. and Borg, W. (2006) *Educational Research: An Introduction* (8th edn). New York: Longman.

Geertz, C. (1988) *Works and Lives: The Anthropologist as Author*. Stanford, CA: Stanford University Press.

Gerstl-Pepin, C. and Patrizio, K. (2009) 'Learning from Dumbledore's Pensieve: Metaphor as an aid in teaching reflexivity in qualitative research', *Qualitative Research*, Vol. 9, No. 3, pp. 299–308.

Ghauri, P. and Grønhaug, K. (2010) *Research Methods in Business Studies: A Practical Guide* (4th edn). Harlow: FT Prentice Hall.

Gibb, F. (1995) 'Consumer group accuses lawyers of shoddy service', *The Times*, 5 October.

Gibbons, M.L., Limoges, H., Nowotny, S., Schwartman, P., Scott, P. and Trow, M. (1994) *The New Production of Knowledge: The Dynamics of Science and Research in Contemporary Societies*. London: Sage.

Gill, J. and Johnson, P. (2010) *Research Methods for Managers* (4th edn). London: Sage.

Glaser, B. (1978) *Theoretical Sensitivity: Advances in the Methodology of Grounded Theory*. Mill Valley, CA: Sociology Press.

Glaser, B. (1998) *Doing Grounded Theory: Issues and Discussions*. Mill Valley, CA: Sociology Press.

Glaser, B. and Strauss, A. (1967) *The Discovery of Grounded Theory*. Chicago, IL: Aldine.

Glaser, B.G. (1992) *Basics of Grounded Theory*. Mill Valley, CA: Sociology Press.

Greene, J.C. (2007) *Mixed Methods in Social Inquiry*. San Francisco: Jossey-Bass.

Greene, J.C., Caracelli, V.J. and Graham, W.F. (1989) 'Towards a conceptual framework for mixed-method evaluation designs', *Educational Evaluation and Policy Analysis*, Vol. 11, No. 3, pp. 255–74.

Greenhalgh, T. (1997) 'Papers that summarize other papers (systematic reviews and meta-analyses)', *British Medical Journal*, Vol. 315, pp. 672–5.

Greenwood, D.J. and Levin. M. (2007) *Introduction to Action Research* (2nd edn). London: Sage.

Groves, R.M. and Peytcheva, E. (2008) 'The impact of nonresponse rates on nonresponse bias', *Public Opinion Quarterly*, Vol. 72, No. 2, pp. 167–89.

Guba, E.G. and Lincoln, Y.S. (1989) *Fourth Generation Evaluation*. Newbury Park, CA: Sage.

Guba, E.G. and Lincoln, Y.S. (2005) 'Paradigmatic controversies, contradictions, and emerging confluences', in N.K. Denzin and Y.S. Lincoln (eds) *The Sage Handbook of Qualitative Research* (3rd edn). London: Sage, pp. 191–216.

Guest, G., Bunce, A. and Johnson, L. (2006) 'How many interviews are enough? An experiment with data saturation and validity', *Field Methods*, Vol. 18, No. 1, pp. 59–82.

Gummesson, E. (2000) *Qualitative Methods in Management Research* (2nd edn). Thousand Oaks, CA: Sage.

H

Hair, J.F., Black, B., Babin, B., Anderson, R.E. and Tatham, R.L. (2006) *Multivariate Data Analysis* (6th edn). Harlow: Pearson Education.

Hakim, C. (1982) *Secondary Analysis in Social Research*. London: Allen & Unwin.

Hakim, C. (2000) *Research Design: Successful Designs for Social and Economic Research* (2nd edn). London: Routledge.

Hannah, D.R. and Lautsch, B.A. (2011) 'Counting in qualitative research: Why to conduct it, when to avoid it, and when to closet it', *Journal of Management Inquiry*, Vol. 20, No. 1, pp. 14–22.

Harley Davidson Inc. (2009) *Harley-Davidson Inc. 2008 Annual Report*. Available at www.harley-davidson.com/en_US/Media/downloads/Annual_Reports/2008/HD_Annual2008.pdf?locale=en_US&bmLocale=en_US [Accessd 2 May 2011].

Harley Davidson Inc. (2011) H*arley Davidson Inc. Form 10K (Annual Report)*. Available at available from www.harley-davidson.com/en_US/Media/downloads/Annual_Reports/2010/10k_2010.pdf [Accessed 2 May 2011].

Hart, C. (1998) *Doing a Literature Review*. London: Sage.

Harvard College Library (2006) *Interrogating texts: 6 reading habits to develop in your first year at Harvard*. Available at http://hcl.harvard.edu/research/guides/lamont_handouts/interrogatingtexts.html [Accessed 20 May 2008].

Hatch, M.J. and Yanow, D. (2008) 'Methodology by metaphor: Ways of seeing in painting and research', *Organization Studies*, Vol. 29, No. 1, pp. 23–44.

Hays, W.L. (1994) *Statistics* (4th edn). London: Holt-Saunders.

Healey, M.J. and Rawlinson, M.B. (1994) 'Interviewing techniques in business and management research', in V.J. Wass and P.E. Wells (eds) *Principles and Practice in Business and Management Research*. Aldershot: Dartmouth, pp. 123–45.

Healey, M.J. (1991) 'Obtaining information from businesses', in M.J. Healey (ed.) *Economic Activity and Land Use*. Harlow: Longman, pp. 193–251.

Hedrick, T.E., Bickmann, L. and Rog, D.J. (1993) *Applied Research Design*. Newbury Park, CA: Sage.

Henry, G.T. (1990) *Practical Sampling*. Newbury Park, CA: Sage.

Henry, G.T. (1995) *Graphing Data: Techniques for Display and Analysis*. Thousand Oaks, CA: Sage.

Heron, J. (1996) *Co-operative Inquiry: Research into the Human Condition*. London: Sage.

Hewson, C., Yule, P., Laurent, D. and Vogel, C. (2003) *Internet Research Methods*. London: Sage.

Hodgkinson, G.P. and Rousseau, D. (2009) 'Bridging the rigour–relevance gap in management research. It's already happening!', *Journal of Management Studies*, Vol. 46, No. 3, pp. 534–46.

Hodgkinson, G.P., Herriot, P. and Anderson, N. (2001) 'Re-aligning the stakeholders in management research: Lessons from industrial, work and organizational psychology', *British Journal of Management*, Vol. 12, Special Issue, pp. 41–8.

Hodson, R. (1991) 'The active worker: Compliance and autonomy at the workplace', *Journal of Contemporary Ethnography*, Vol. 20, No. 1, pp. 47–8.

Hofstede, G. (2001) *Culture's Consequences: Comparing Values, Behaviors, Institutions and Organizations Across Nations*. Thousand Oaks, CA: Sage.

Hookway, N. (2008) 'Entering the blogosphere: Some strategies for using blogs in social research', *Qualitative Research,* Vol. 8, No. 1, pp. 91–113.

Huff, A.S. and Huff, J.O. (2001) 'Re-focusing the business school agenda', *British Journal of Management*, Vol. 12, Special Issue, pp. 49–54.

I

Idea Works (2011) *Methodologist's toolchest ex-sample*. Available at www.ideaworks.com/mt/exsample.html [Accessed 27 March 2011].

Information Commissioners Office (2011) *Freedom of Information Act*. Available at www.ico.gov.uk/for_the_public.aspx [Accessed 3 July 2011].

Inspiration (2011) *Inspiration homepage*. Available at www.inspiration.com/Inspiration [Accessed 21 March 2011].

J

Jankowicz, A.D. (2005) *Business Research Projects* (4th edn). London: Thomson Learning.

Johnson, J.M. (1975) *Doing Field Research*. New York: Free Press.

Johnson, P. (2004) 'Analytic induction', in C. Cassell and G. Symon (eds) *Essential Guide to Qualitative Methods and Analysis in Organizational Research*. London: Sage, pp. 165–79.

Johnson, P. and Clark, M. (2006) 'Editors' introduction: Mapping the terrain: An overview of business and management research methodologies', in P. Johnson and M. Clark (eds) *Business and Management Research Methodologies*. London: Sage, pp. xxv–lv.

K

Kanji, G.K. (2006) *100 Statistical Tests* (3rd edn). London: Sage.

Kavanagh, M.J. and Thite, M. (2009) *Human Resource Information Systems: Basics, Applications, and Future Directions*. Los Angeles, CA: Sage.

Keaveney, S.M. (1995) 'Customer switching behaviour in service industries: An exploratory study', *Journal of Marketing*, Vol. 59, No. 2, pp. 71–82.

Kelemen, M. and Rumens, N. (2008) *An Introduction to Critical Management Research*. London: Sage.

Kelly, G.A. (1955) *The Psychology of Personal Constructs*. New York: Norton.

Kervin, J.B. (1999) *Methods for Business Research* (2nd edn). New York: HarperCollins.

Ketokivi, M. and Mantere, S. (2010) 'Two strategies for inductive reasoning in organizational research', *Academy of Management Review*, Vol. 35, No. 2, pp. 315–33.

Kilduff, M. (2006) 'Editors' comments: Publishing theory', *Academy of Management Review*, Vol. 31, No. 2, pp. 252–5.

Kim, K.S. and Sin, S.-C.J. (2011) 'Selecting sources: Bridging the gap between perception and use of information sources', *Journal of Information Science*, Vol. 37, No. 2, pp. 178–88.

King, N. (2004) 'Using interviews in qualitative research', in C. Cassell and G. Symon (eds) *Essential Guide to Qualitative Methods in Organizational Research*. London: Sage, pp. 11–22.

King, N. (2012) 'Doing template analysis', in C. Cassell and G. Symons (eds) *The Practice of Qualitative Organizational Research: Core Methods and Current Challenges*. London: Sage.

Kinnear, P.R. and Gray, C.D. (2010) *SPSS 18 Made Simple: For IBM SPSS Statistics Software*. Hove: Psychology Press.

Kozinets, R.V. (2006) 'Netography 2.0', in R.W. Belk (ed.) *Handbook of Qualitative Research Methods in Marketing*. Cheltenham, Edward Elgar Publishing, pp. 129–42.

Krueger, R.A. and Casey, M.A. (2009) *Focus Groups: A Practical Guide for Applied Research* (4th edn). Thousand Oaks, CA: Sage.

Kvale, S. and Brinkmann, S. (2009) *InterViews* (2nd edn). Thousand Oaks, CA: Sage.

L

Lavrakas, P.J. (1993) *Telephone Survey Methods: Sampling, Selection and Supervision*. Newbury Park, CA: Sage.

Le Compte, M.D. and Goetz, J.P. (1982) 'Problems of reliability and validity in ethnographic research', *Review of Educational Research*, Vol. 52, No. 1, pp. 31–60.

Le Sphinx (2011) *Sphinx Survey and Statistical Software*. Available at www.sphinxsurvey.com/ [Accessed 7 May 2011].

Lee, R.M. (1993) *Doing Research on Sensitive Topics*. London: Sage.

Lee, R.M. and Fielding, N. (1996) 'Qualitative data analaysis: Representations of a technology', *Sociological Research*

Online, Vol. 1, No. 4. Available at www.socresonline.org.uk/1/4/1f.html [Accessed 11 October 2011].

Leech, N.L. and Onwuegbuzie, A.J. (2009) 'A typology of mixed methods research designs', *Quality and Quantity*, Vol. 43, pp. 265–75.

Lenth, R.V. (2001) 'Some practical guidelines for effective sample size determination', *The American Statistician*, Vol. 55, No. 3, pp. 187–93.

Levitas, R. and Guy, W. (eds) (1996) *Interpreting Official Statistics*. London: Routledge.

Lewin, K. (1945), 'The Research Center for Group Dynamics at Massachusetts Institute of Technology', *Sociometry*, Vol. 8, No. 2, pp. 126–36.

Lewins, A. and Silver, C. (2009) 'Choosing a CAQDAS package – 6th edition', CAQDAS Networking Project Working Paper. Available at http://caqdas.soc.surrey.ac.uk/sociology/researchcentres/caqdas/files/2009ChoosingaCAQDASPack [Accessed 14 July 2011].

Lincoln, Y.S. and Guba, E.G. (1985) *Naturalistic Inquiry*. Beverly Hills, CA: Sage.

M

Mackenzie, K.D. (2000a) 'Knobby analyses of knobless survey items, part I: The approach', *International Journal of Organizational Analysis*, Vol. 8, No. 2, pp. 131–54.

Mackenzie, K.D. (2000b) 'Knobby analyses of knobless survey items, part II: An application', *International Journal of Organizational Analysis*, Vol. 8, No. 3, pp. 238–61.

Madge, C. (2006). *Online research ethics*. Available at www.geog.le.ac.uk/orm/ethics/ethprint.htm [Accessed 1 June 2011].

Mangold, W. and Faulds, D. (2009) 'Social media: The new hybrid element of the promotion mix', *Business Horizons*, Vol. 52, pp. 357–65.

Mann, C. and Stewart, F. (2000) *Internet Communication and Qualitative Research: A Handbook for Researching Online*. London: Sage.

Marchington, M. and Wilkinson, A. (2008) *Human Resource Management at Work* (4th edn). London: Chartered Institute of Personnel and Development.

Marshall, C. and Rossman, G.B. (2006) *Designing Qualitative Research* (4th edn). Thousand Oaks, CA: Sage.

McDonald, S. (2005) 'Studying actions in context: A qualitative shadowing method for organizational research', *Qualitative Research*, Vol. 5, No. 4, pp. 455–73.

McNeill, P. (2005) *Research Methods* (3rd edn). London: Routledge.

McNiff, J. with Whitehead, J. (2000) *Action Research in Organizations*. London: Routledge.

Meier, M. (2011) 'Knowledge management in strategic alliances: A review of empirical evidence', *International Journal of Management Reviews*, Vol. 13, pp. 1–23.

Mello, R.A. (2002) 'Collocation analysis: A method for conceptualizing and understanding narrative data', *Qualitative Research*, Vol. 2, No. 2, pp. 231–43.

Miles, M.B. and Huberman, A.M. (1994) *Qualitative Data Analysis* (2nd edn). Thousand Oaks, CA: Sage.

Miller, D.C. and Salkind, N.J. (eds) (2002) *Handbook of Research Design and Social Measurement* (6th edn). Thousand Oaks, CA: Sage.

Millmore, M., Lewis, P., Saunders, M., Thornhill, A. and Morrow, T. (2007) *Strategic Human Resource Management*. Harlow: FT Prentice Hall.

Millward, L.J. and Postmes, T. (2010) 'Who we are affects how we do. The financial benefits of organizational identification', *British Journal of Management*, Vol. 21, pp. 327–39.

MindGenius (2011) *MindGenius homepage*. Available at www.mindgenius.com/home.aspx [Accessed 21 March 2011].

Mingers, J. (2000) 'What is it to be critical? Teaching a critical approach to management undergraduates', *Management Learning*, Vol. 31, No. 2, pp. 219–37.

Mintzberg, H. (1973) *The Nature of Managerial Work*. New York: Harper & Row.

Mitchell, V. (1996) 'Assessing the reliability and validity of questionnaires: An empirical example', *Journal of Applied Management Studies*, Vol. 5, No. 2, pp. 199–207.

Moher, D., Liberati, A., Tetzlaff, J. and Altman, D.G. (2009) 'Preferred reporting for systematic reviews and meta-analyses: The PRISMA statement', *British Medical Journal (BMJ)*, No. 338, p. b2535. Available from www.bmj.com/content/339/bmj.b2535.full?view=long&pmid=19622551 [Accessed 27 March 2011].

Molina-Azorin, J.F. (2011) 'The use and added value of mixed methods in management research', *Journal of Mixed Methods Research*, Vol. 5, No. 1, pp. 7–24.

Monahan, T. and Fisher, J.A. (2010) 'Benefits of "observer effects": Lessons from the field', *Qualitative Research*, Vol. 10, No. 3, pp. 357–76.

Morgan, S.J. and Symon, G. (2004) 'Electronic interviews in organizational research', in C. Cassell and G. Symon (eds) *Essential Guide to Qualitative Methods in Organizational Research*. London: Sage, pp. 3–33.

Morris, C. (2012) *Quantitative Approaches in Business Studies* (8th edn). Harlow: Pearson.

Morrison, E. (2010) 'OB in *AMJ*: What is hot and what is not?', *Academy of Management Journal*, Vol. 53, No. 5, pp. 932–6.

Mullins, L.J. (2010) *Management and Organisational Behaviour* (9th edn). Harlow: Financial Times Prentice Hall.

Musson, G. (2004) 'Life histories', in C. Cassell and G. Symon (eds) *Essential Guide to Qualitative Methods in Organizational Research*. London: Sage, pp. 34–46.

N

Naipaul, V.S. (1989) *A Turn in the South*. London: Penguin.

Narayanan, V.K., Colwell, K. and Douglass, F.L. (2009) 'Building organizational and scientific platforms in the pharmaceutical industry: A process perspective on the development of dynamic capabilities', *British Journal of Management*, Vol. 20, pp. 25–40.

Nastasi, B.K., Hitchcock, J.H. and Brown, L.M. (2010) 'An inclusive framework for conceptualising mixed methods typologies', in A. Tashakkori and C. Teddlie (eds) *The Sage Handbook of Mixed Methods in Social and Behavioural Research* (2nd edn.). Thousand Oaks, CA: Sage, pp. 305–38.

National Patient Safety Agency (2007) *Defining Research*, Issue 3. London: National Patient Safety Agency.

Neelotpaul, B. (2010) 'A study on interactivity and online branding', *Advances in Management*, Vol. 3, No. 3, pp. 13–15.

Neuman, W.L. (2005) *Social Research Methods* (6th edn). London: Pearson.

Neville, C. (2010) *The Complete Guide to Referencing and Avoiding Plagiarism* (2nd edn). Maidenhead: Open University Press.

Nielson Company (2011) *BlogPulse*. Available at www.blogpulse.com/ [Accessed 3 July 2011].

Niglas, K. (2010) 'The multidimensional model of research methodology: An integrated set of continua', in A. Tashakkori, and C. Teddlie (eds) *The Sage Handbook of Mixed Methods in Social and Behavioural Research*. Thousand Oaks, CA: Sage, pp. 215–36.

O

Ochs, E. and Capps, L. (2001) *Living Narrative*. Cambridge, MA: Harvard University Press.

Office for National Statistics (2005) *The National Statistics Socio-economic Classification User Manual*. Basingstoke: Palgrave Macmillan.

Office for National Statistics (2010a) *Family Spending: A Report on the 2009 Living Costs and Food Survey*. Cardiff: Office for National Statistics. Available at www.statistics.gov.uk/StatBase/Product.asp?vlnk=361&Pos=1&ColRank=1&Rank=272 [Accessed 1 July 2011].

Office for National Statistics (2010b) *Standard Occupation Classification Volume 1: Structure and Description of Unit Groups*. Basingstoke: Palgrave Macmillan.

Office for National Statistics (2010c) *Standard Occupation Classification Volume 2: The Structure and Index*. Basingstoke: Palgrave Macmillan.

Office for National Statistics (2011a) *Census history*. Available at http://2011.census.gov.uk/Censushistory [Accessed 1 July 2011].

Office for National Statistics (2011b) *Results from the General LiFestyle Survey*. Available at www.statistics.gov.uk/StatBase/Product.asp?vlnk=5756&Pos=&ColRank=1&Rank=272; www.statistics.gov.uk/StatBase/Product.asp?vlnk=361 [Accessed 1 July 2011].

Office for National Statistics (2011c) *Annual Survey of Hours and Earnings (ASHE)*. Available at www.statistics.gov.uk/StatBase/Product.asp?vlnk=15236&More=Y [Accessed 1 July 2011].

Okumus, F., Altinay, L. and Roper, A. (2007) 'Gaining access for research: Reflections from experience', *Annals of Tourism Research*, Vol. 34, No. 1, pp. 7–26.

Oppenheim, A.N. (2000) *Questionnaire Design, Interviewing and Attitude Measurement* (new edn). London: Continuum International.

Our Rivers Campaign (2010) Available at www.ourrivers.org.uk/results/ [Accessed 18 November 2010].

P

Pandza, K. and Thorpe, R. (2010) 'Management as design, but what kind of design? An appraisal of the design science analogy for management', *British Journal of Management*, Vol. 21, No. 2, pp. 171–86.

Park, A., Curtice, J., Thomson, K., Phillips, M., Johnson M. and Clery, E. (2007) *British Social Attitudes: 24th Report*. London: Sage.

Park, C. (2003) 'In other (people's) words: Plagiarism by university students – literature and lessons', *Assessment and Evaluation in Higher Education*, Vol. 28, No. 5, pp. 471–88.

Parry, H. (1991) *Successful Business Presentations*. Kingston-upon-Thames: Croner.

Patton, M.Q. (2002) *Qualitative Research and Evaluation Methods* (3rd edn). Thousand Oaks, CA: Sage.

Pearsall, J. (ed.) (1998) *The New Oxford English Dictionary*. Oxford: Oxford University Press.

Peters, T. and Waterman, R. (1982) *In Search of Excellence*. New York: Harper & Row.

Petticrew, M. and Roberts, H. (2006) *Systematic Review in the Social Sciences: A Practical Guide*. Malden, MA: Blackwell.

Phillips, E.M. and Pugh, D.S. (2010) *How to get a PhD* (5th edn). Maidenhead: Open University Press McGraw Hill.

Phillips, N. and Hardy, C. (2002) *Discourse Analysis: Investigating Processes of Social Construction*. London: Sage.

Post-it (2011) *Post-it history and facts*. Available at http://solutions.3m.co.uk/wps/portal/3M/en_GB/Post-Its/Post-It/Solutions/History/ [Accessed 15 July 2011].

Powney, J. and Watts, M. (1987) *Interviewing in Educational Research*. London: Routledge and Kegan Paul.

Prosser, L. (2009) *Office for National Statistics UK Standard Industrial Classification of Activities 2007 (SIC 2007).* Basingstoke: Palgrave Macmillan.

R

Raimond, P. (1993) *Management Projects*. London: Chapman & Hall.

Rawlins, K. (1999) *Presentation and Communication Skills: A Handbook for Practitioners*. London: Emap Healthcare Ltd.

Reason, P. (2006) 'Choice and quality in action research practice', *Journal of Management Inquiry*, Vol. 15, No. 2, pp. 187–202.

Reason, P. and Bradbury, H. (2008) *Handbook of Action Research* (2nd edn). London: Sage.

Reichertz, J. (2007) 'Abduction: The logic of discovery of grounded theory', in A. Bryant and K. Charmaz (eds) *The Sage Handbook of Grounded Theory*. London: Sage.

Reichman, C.S. (1962) *Use and Abuse of Statistics*. New York: Oxford University Press.

Research Randomizer (2011) 'Research Randomizer'. Available at www.randomizer.org/ [Accessed 24 April 2011].

Richards, P. (2007) 'Risk', in H. Becker (ed.) *Writing for Social Scientists* (2nd edn). Chicago, IL: University of Chicago Press, pp. 108–20.

Ridenour, C.S. and Newman, I. (2008) *Mixed Methods Research: Exploring the Interactive Continuum*. Carbondale, IL: South Illinois University Press.

Riley, J. (1996) *Getting the Most from your Data: A Handbook of Practical Ideas on How to Analyse Qualitative Data* (2nd edn). Bristol: Technical and Educational Services Ltd.

Robson, C. (2011) *Real World Research: A Resource for Users of Social Research Methods in Applied Settings* (3rd edn). Chichester: John Wiley.

Rodrigues, R.A. and Gust, D. (2010) 'Have careers become boundaryless?', *Human Relations*, Vol. 63, No. 8, pp. 1157–75.

Rogelberg, S.G. and Stanton, J.M. (2007) 'Introduction: Understanding and dealing with organizational survey non-response', *Organizational Research Methods*, Vol. 10, No. 2, pp. 195–209.

Rogers, C.R. (1961) *On Becoming a Person*. London: Constable.

Rouseau, D. (2006) 'Is there such a thing as "Evidence-based management"?', *Academy of Management Review*, Vol. 31, No. 2, pp. 256–69.

S

Salmon, P. (2003) 'How do we recognise good research?', *The Psychologist*, Vol. 16, No. 1, pp. 24–7.

Samson, A. (2010) 'Product useage and firm-generated word of mouth: Some results from fmcg product trials', *International Journal of Market Research*, Vol. 52, No. 4, pp. 459–82.

Saunders, M.N.K. (2011) 'The management researcher as practitioner', in B. Lee and C. Cassell (eds) *Challenges and Controversies in Management Research*. New York: Routledge, pp. 243–57.

Saunders, M.N.K. (2012a) 'Choosing research participants', in G. Symons and C. Cassell (eds) *The Practice of Qualitative Organizational Research: Core Methods and Current Challenges*. London: Sage, pp. 37–55.

Saunders, M.N.K. (2012b) 'Web versus mail: The influence of survey distribution mode on employees' response', *Field Methods*, Vol. 24, No. 1.

Saunders, M.N.K. and Lewis, P. (1997) 'Great ideas and blind alleys? A review of the literature on starting research', *Management Learning*, Vol. 28, No. 3, pp. 283–99.

Saunders, M.N.K., Altinay, L. and Riordan, K. (2009) 'The management of post-merger cultural integration: Implications from the hotel industry', *Service Industries Journal*, Vol. 29, No. 10, pp. 1359–75.

Schatzman, L. and Strauss, A. (1973) *Field Research: Strategies for a Natural Sociology*. Englewood Cliffs, NJ: Prentice-Hall.

Schein, E. (1999) *Process Consultation Revisited: Building the Helping Relationship*. Reading, MA: Addison-Wesley.

Schoneboom, A. (2011) 'Workblogging in a Facebook age', *Work, Employment and Society*, Vol. 25, No. 1, pp. 132–40.

Schrauf, R.W. and Navarro, E. (2005) 'Using existing tests and scales in the field', *Field Methods*, Vol. 17, No. 4, pp. 373–93.

Searcy, D.L. and Mentzer, J.T. (2003) 'A framework for conducting and evaluating research', *Journal of Accounting Literature*, Vol. 22, pp. 130–67.

Sekaran, U. and Bougie, R. (2009) *Research Methods for Business: A Skill-Building Approach* (5th edn). Chichester: John Wiley.

Shani, A.B. and Pasmore, W.A. (1985) 'Organization inquiry: Towards a new model of the action research process', in D.D. Warrick (ed.) *Contemporary Organization Development*. Glenview. IL: Scott Foresman.

Sharp, J.A., Peters, J. and Howard, K. (2002) *The Management of a Student Research Project* (3rd edn). Aldershot: Gower.

Silverman, D. (2007) *A Very Short, Fairly Interesting and Reasonably Cheap Book about Qualitative Research*. London: Sage.

Skapinker, M. (2008) 'Why business ignores business schools', *Financial Times*, 7 January. Available at www.ft.com/ [Accessed 17 March 2011].

Skapinker, M. (2011) 'Why business still ignores business schools', *Financial Times*, 24 January. Available at www.ft.com/ [Accessed 17 March 2011].

Smith, A. (2002) 'The new ethnicity classification in the Labour Force Survey', *Labour Market Trends*, December, pp. 657–66.

Smith, C.B. (1991) *A Guide to Business Research*. Chicago, IL: Nelson-Hall.

Smith, E. (2006) *Using Secondary Data in Educational and Social Research*. Maidenhead: Open University Press.

Smith, N.C. and Dainty, P. (1991) *The Management Research Handbook*. London: Routledge.

Snap Surveys (2011) *Snap Survey Software Research Services*. Available at www.snapsurveys.com [Accessed 9 May 2011].

Snap Surveys (2011) *Snap Survey Software Research Services*. Available at www.snapsurveys.com [Accessed 9 May 2011].

Snow, B (2007) *The ten worst-selling games consoles of all time*. Available at www.gamepro.com/article/features/111822/the-10-worst-selling-consoles-of-all-time/ [Accessed 15 July 2011].

Social Research Association (2001) 'A code of practice for the safety of social researchers'. Available at www.the-sra.org.uk/guidelines.htm [Accessed 1 June 2011].

Spano, R. (2005) 'Potential sources of observer bias in police observational data', *Social Science Research*, Vol. 34, pp. 591–617.

Sparrow, J. (1989) 'Graphic displays in information systems: Some data properties influencing the effectiveness of alternate forms', *Behaviour and Information Technology*, Vol. 8, No. 1, pp. 43–56.

Speer, S. (2002) '"Natural" and "contrived" data: A sustainable distinction?', *Discourse Studies*, Vol. 4, No. 4, pp. 511–25.

Spence, M., Gherib, J.B.B. and Biwolé, V.O. (2011) 'Sustainable development: Is entrepreneurial will enough?', *Journal of Business Ethics*, Vol. 99, No. 3, pp. 335–67.

Starkey, K. and Madan, P. (2001) 'Bridging the relevance gap: Aligning stakeholders in the future of management research', *British Journal of Management*, Vol. 12, Special Issue, pp. 3–26.

Starr, R. and Fernandez, K. (2007) 'The mindcam methodology: Perceiving through the natives eye', *Qualitative Market Research*, Vol. 10, No. 2, pp. 168–82.

Stationery Office, The (1998) *Data Protection Act 1998*. London: The Stationery Office.

Stewart, D.W. and Kamins, M.A. (1993) *Secondary Research: Information Sources and Methods* (2nd edn). Newbury Park, CA: Sage.

Stieger, S. and Goritz, A.S. (2006) 'Using instant messaging for internet-based interviews', *CyberPsychology and Behavior*, Vol. 9, No. 5, pp. 552–9.

Stokes, D. and Bergin, R. (2006) 'Methodology or "methodolatry"? An evaluation of focus groups and depth interviews', *Qualitative Market Research*, Vol. 9, No. 1, pp. 26–37.

Strauss, A. and Corbin, J. (1998) *Basics of Qualitative Research* (2nd edn). Thousand Oaks, CA: Sage.

Stutely, M. (2003) *Numbers Guide: The Essentials of Business Numeracy*. London: Bloomberg Press.

Suddaby, R. (2006) 'From the editors: What grounded theory is not', *Academy of Management Journal*, Vol. 49, No. 4, pp. 633–42.

Survey Resource Network (2011) *Survey Resource Network*. Available at http://surveynet.ac.uk/ [Accessed 11 June 2011].

SurveyMonkey (2011) *SurveyMonkey home page*. Available at www.surveymonkey.com/ [Accessed 9 May 2011].

SurveyMonkey (2011) *SurveyMonkey.com*. Available at www.surveymonkey.com [Accessed 17 May 2011].

Sutton, R. and Staw, B. (1995) 'What theory is not', *Administrative Science Quarterly*, Vol. 40, No. 3, pp. 371–84.

Suzy Lamplugh Trust, The (2011) *Personal safety alone in the workplace*. Available at www.suzylamplugh.org/personal-safety/personal-safety-tips/workplace-safety/alone-in-the-workplace/ [Accessed 1 June 2011].

Sweet, C. (2001) 'Designing and conducting virtual focus groups', *Qualitative Market Research*, Vol. 4, No. 3, pp. 130–35.

Syed, J., Mingers, J., and Murray, P.A. (2010) 'Beyond rigour and relevance: A critical realist approach to business education', *Management Learning*, Vol. 41, No. 1, pp. 71–85.

Symon, G. and Cassell, C. (eds) (2012) *The Practice of Qualitative Research: Core Methods and Current Challenges*. London: Sage.

Syrjala, J., Takala, T. and Sintonen, T. (2009) 'Narratives as a tool to study personnel wellbeing in corporate mergers', *Qualitative Research*, Vol. 9, No. 3, pp. 263–84.

T

Tang, J., Crossan, M. and Rowe, W.G. (2011) 'Dominant CEO, deviant strategy, and extreme performance: The moderating role of a powerful board, *Journal of Management Studies*. Available at https://remote.surrey.ac.uk/doi/10.1111/j.1467-6486.2010.00985.x/,DanaInfo=.aoonlrjrpj0k2-M-x1vESw98+pdf [Accessed 9 May 2011].

Tashakkori, A. and Teddlie, C. (eds) (2010) *The Sage Handbook of Mixed Methods in Social and Behavioural Research* (2nd edn). Thousand Oaks, CA: Sage.

Teddlie, C. and Tashakkori, A. (2009) *Foundations of Mixed Methods Research: Integrating Quantitative and Qualitative Approaches in the Social and Behavioural Sciences*. Thousand Oaks, CA: Sage.

Tedlock, B. (2005) 'The observation of participation and the emergence of public ethnography', in N.K. Denzin and Y.S. Lincoln (eds) *The Sage Handbook of Qualitative Research* (3rd edn). London: Sage, pp. 467–82.

Temkin, O. and Temkin, C.L. (1987) *Ancient Medicine: Selected Papers of Ludwig Edelstein*. Baltimore, MD: John Hopkins University Press.

Tesch, R. (1990) *Qualitative Research: Analysis Types and Software Tools.* New York: Falmer.

Tharenou, P., Donohue, R. and Cooper, B. (2007) *Management Research Methods*. Melbourne: Cambridge University Press.

Thomas, J. (1996) 'Introduction: A debate about the ethics of fair practices for collecting social science data in cyberspace', *The Information Society*, Vol. 12, No. 2, pp. 107–17.

Thompson, L. F. and Surface, E. A. (2007) 'Employee surveys administered online – attitudes to the medium, non-response, and data representativeness', *Organizational Research Methods*, Vol. 10, No. 2, pp. 241–61.

Thornhill, A., Saunders, M.N.K. and Stead, J. (1997) 'Downsizing, delayering but where's the commitment? The development of a diagnostic tool to help manage survivors', *Personnel Review*, Vol. 26, No. 1/2, pp. 81–98.

Titscher, S., Meyer, M., Wodak, R. and Vetter, E. (2000) *Methods of Text and Discourse Analysis*. London: Sage.

Tranfield, D. and Denyer, D. (2004) 'Linking theory to practice: A grand challenge for management research in the 21st century?', *Organization Management Journal*, Vol. 1, No. 1, pp. 10–14.

Tranfield, D. and Starkey, K. (1998) 'The nature, social organization and promotion of management research: Towards policy', *British Journal of Management*, Vol. 9, pp. 341–53.

Tranfield, D., Denyer, D. and Smart, P. (2003) 'Towards a methodology for developing evidence-informed management knowledge by means of systematic review', *British Journal of Management*, Vol. 14, No. 3, pp. 207–22.

Tucker, C. and Lepkowski, J.M. (2008) 'Telephone survey methods: Adapting to change', in J.M. Lepkowski, C. Tucker, J.M. Brick, E.D. De Leeuw, L. Japec, P.J. Lavrakas, M.W. Link and R.L. Sangster (eds) *Advances in Telephone Survey Methodology*. Hoboken, NJ: Wiley, pp. 3–28.

Tukey, J.W. (1977) *Exploratory Data Analysis*. Reading, MA: Addison-Wesley.

U

UK Data Archive (2011) *UK Data Archive*. Available at www.data-archive.ac.uk/ [Accessed 2 July 2011].

UK Data Archive (2011) *Managing and Sharing Data: Best Practice for Researchers* (3rd edn). Available at www.esds.ac.uk/support/datamanguides.asp [Accessed 1 June 2011].

UK Data Archive (2011) *Create and manage data – Anonymisation*. Available at www.data-archive.ac.uk/create-manage/consent-ethics/anonymisation [Accessed 17 May 2011].

Usunier, J.-C. (1998) *International and Cross-Cultural Management Research*. London: Sage.

V

Vaidyanathan, R. (2011) 'Barack Obama's shadow – the man who films the president', BBC News US & Canada. Available at: www.bbc.co.uk/news/world-us-canada-13148700?print=true [Accessed 6 June 2011].

Van Aken, J.E. (2005) 'Management research as a design science: Articulating the research products of Mode 2 knowledge production in management', *British Journal of Management*, Vol. 16, No. 1, pp. 19–36.

Van de Ven, A.H. (1989) 'Nothing is quite so practical as a good theory', *Academy of Management Review*, Vol. 14, No. 4, pp. 486–9.

Van Maanen, J., Sørensen, J.B. and Mitchell, T.R. (2007) 'The interplay between theory and method', *Academy of Management Review*, Vol. 32, No. 4, pp. 1145–54.

Verisign Inc. (2011) *The Domain Name Industry Brief*, Vol. 8, No. 1. Available at www.verisigninc.com/assets/domain-name-report-feb-2011.pdf [Accessed 3 July 2011].

Vermeulen, F. (2011) 'Popular fads replace relevant teaching', *Financial Times*, 24 January. Available at www.ft.com/ [Accessed 17 March 2011].

Veroff, J. (2007) 'Writing', in K. Rudestam and R. Newton. (eds) *Surviving your Dissertation* (3rd edn). Newbury Park, CA: Sage.

W

Waddington, D. (2004) 'Participant observation', in C. Cassell and G. Symon (eds) *Essential Guide to Qualitative Methods in Organizational Research*. London: Sage, pp. 154–64.

Walker, R. (1985) *Doing Research: A Handbook for Teachers*. London: Methuen.

Wallace, M. and Wray, A. (2011) *Critical Reading and Writing for Postgraduates* (2nd edn). London: Sage.

Walliman, N. (2011) *Your Research Project: A Step by Step Guide for the First-Time Researcher* (3rd edn). London: Sage.

Waskul, D. and Douglass, M. (1996) 'Considering the electronic participant: Some polemical observations on the ethics of on-line research', *The Information Society*, Vol. 12, No. 2, pp. 129–39.

Watson, T. (2011) 'Ethnography, reality and truth: The vital need for studies of "how things work" in organizations and management', *Journal of Management Studies*, Vol. 48, No. 1, pp. 202–17.

Wells, P. (1994) 'Ethics in business and management research', in V.J. Wass and P.E. Wells (eds) *Principles and Practice in Business and Management Research*. Aldershot: Dartmouth, pp. 277–97.

Wensley, R. (2011) 'Seeking relevance in management research', in C. Cassell and B. Lee (eds) *Challenges and Controversies in Management Research*. New York: Routledge, pp. 258–74.

West Wing Week (2010) The White House Blog. Available at www.whitehouse.gov/blog/2010/04/02/west-wing-week [Accessed 6 June 2011].

Whetten, D. (1989) 'What constitutes a theoretical contribution?', *Academy of Management Review*, Vol. 14, No. 4, pp. 490–95.

Whyte, W.F. (1943) *Street Corner Society: The Social Structure of an Italian Slum*. Chicago: University of Chicago Press.

Whyte, W.F. (1993) *Street Corner Society: The Social Structure of an Italian Slum* (4th edn). Chicago: University of Chicago Press.

Wikipedia (2011) *Wikipedia:About*. Available at http://en.wikipedia.org/wiki/Wikipedia:About [Accessed 20 March 2011].

Willimack, D.K., Nichols, E. and Sudman, S. (2002) 'Understanding unit and item nonresponse in business surveys', in D.A. Dillman, J.L. Eltringe, J.L. Groves and R.J.A. Little (eds) *Survey Nonresponse*. New York: Wiley Interscience, pp. 213–27.

Witmer, D.F., Colman, R.W. and Katzman, S.L. (1999) 'From paper and pen to screen and keyboard: Towards a methodology for survey research on the Internet', in S. Jones (ed.) *Doing Internet Research*. Thousand Oaks, CA: Sage, pp. 145–62.

Wolf, A. (2007) 'People have a tendency to assume that quantitative data must be out there on the web waiting to be found', *The Times Higher Education Supplement*, 12 October. Available at www.timeshighereducation.co.uk/story.asp?sectioncode=26&storycode=310797 [Accessed 4 July 2011].

Wright Mills, C. (1970) 'On intellectual craftsmanship', in C. Wright Mills, *The Sociological Imagination*. London: Pelican.

Y

Yin, R.K. (2009) *Case Study Research: Design and Methods* (4th edn). Thousand Oaks, CA: Sage.

Yip, G. (2011) 'Business research needs to be more relevant for managers', *Financial Times*, 14 February. Available at www.ft.com/ [Accessed 17 March 2011].

Z

Zikmund, W.G. (2000) *Business Research Methods* (6th edn). Fort Worth, TX: Dryden Press.

Appendix 1 Systems of referencing

Preferred styles of referencing differ both between universities and between departments within universities. Even styles that are in wide use such as 'Harvard' vary in how they are used in practice by different institutions. When this is combined with the reality that some lecturers apply an adopted style strictly, whilst others are more lenient, it emphasises the need for you to use the precise style prescribed in your assessment criteria. Within business and management, two author–date referencing systems predominate, the Harvard style and the American Psychological Association (APA) style, both of which are author–date systems. The alternative, numeric systems, are used far less widely.

Five points are important when referencing:

- Full credit must be given to the author or originator (the person or organisation taking main responsibility for the source) when quoting or citing other's work.
- Adequate information must be provided in the reference to enable that work to be located.
- References must be consistent and complete.
- References must be recorded using precisely the style required by your university and are often part of the marking criteria.
- If you fail to reference fully you are likely to be accused of plagiarism (Section 3.9).

As you will see later in this appendix, when referring to electronic documents accessed via the Internet, it is preferable to give the documents DOI (digital object identifier) rather than their URL (Uniform resource locator – usually its web address). This is because the DOI for an electronic document is permanent whereas its URL may change.

Author–date systems

The Harvard style

Referencing in the text

The Harvard style is an *author–date system*, a variation of which we use in this book. It appears to have its origins in a referencing practice developed by a professor of anatomy at Harvard University (Neville 2010) and usually uses the author's or originator's name and year of publication to identify cited documents within the text. All references are listed alphabetically at the end of the text. Common institutional variations within the Harvard style which are applied consistently include (Neville 2010):

- Where there are more than two authors, the names of the second and subsequent authors may or may not be replaced in the text by et al.
- Name(s) of authors or originators may or may not be in UPPER CASE in the list of references.

- The year of publication may or may not be enclosed in (brackets) in the list of references.
- Capitalisation of words in the title is usually kept to a minimum rather than being used for Many of the Words in the Title
- The title of the publication may be in *italics* or may be underlined in the list of references.

The style for referencing work in the text and in the list of references or bibliography is outlined in Table A1.1, additional conventions for referencing in the text being given in Table A1.2.

Table A1.1 Conventions when using the Harvard style to reference

To cite	In the text		In the list of references/bibliography	
	General format	**Example**	**General format**	**Example**
Books				
Book (first edition)	*1 author:* (Family name year)	*1 author:* (Silverman 2007)	Family name, Initials. (year). *Title.* Place of publication: Publisher.	Silverman, D. (2007). *A very short, fairly interesting and reasonably cheap book about qualitative research.* London: Sage.
	2 or 3 authors: (Family name, Family name and Family name year)	*2 or 3 authors:* (Berman Brown and Saunders 2008)	Family name, Initials. and Family name, Initials. (year). *Title.* Place of publication: Publisher.	Berman Brown, R. and Saunders, M. (2008). *Dealing with statistics: What you need to know.* Maidenhead: Open University Press.
	4+ authors: (Family name et al. year)	*4+ authors:* (Millmore *et al.* 2010)	Family name, Initials., Family name, Initials. and Family name, Initials [can be discretionary to include more than first author] (year). *Title.* Place of publication: Publisher.	Millmore, M., Lewis, P., Saunders, M., Thornhill, A. and Morrow, T. (2007). *Strategic human resource management: Contemporary Issues.* Harlow: FT Prentice Hall.
Book (other than first edition)	*As for* 'Book (first edition)'	(Morris 2008)	Family name, Initials. and Family name, Initials. (year). *Title.* (# edn). Place of publication: Publisher.	Morris, C. (2008). *Quantitative approaches to business studies.* (7th edn). London: Financial Times Pitman Publishing.
Book (edited)	*As for* 'Book (first edition)'	(Saunders et al. 2010)	Family name, Initials. and Family name, Initials. (eds.) (year). *Title.* Place of publication: Publisher.	Saunders, M.N.K, Skinner, D., Gillespie, N., Dietz, G. and Lewicki, R. (eds.) (2010). *Organizational trust: a cultural perspective.* Cambridge: Cambridge University Press.

Table A1.1 *(Continued)*

To cite	In the text		In the list of references/bibliography	
	General format	**Example**	**General format**	**Example**
Book (not in English language)	*As for* 'Book (first edition)'	(Fontaine, Salti and Thivard 2010)	Family name, Initials. and Family name, Initials. (year). *Title* [English translation of title]. Place of publication: Publisher.	Fontaine, C., Salti, S. and Thivard, T. (2010). *100 CV et lettres de motivation* [100 CV and cover letters]. Paris: Studyrama.
Book (translated into English)	*As for* 'Book (first edition)'	(Hugo 2003)	Family name, Initials. and Family name, Initials. (year). *Title.* (Initials of translator. Family name of translator. Trans). Place of publication: Publisher. (Original work published year).	Hugo, V. (2003). *Les Miserables*. (N. Denny. Trans.). London: Penguin. (Original work published 1862).
Republished book	*As for* 'Book (first edition)'	*As for* 'Book (first edition)'	Family name, Initials. and Family name, Initials. (year). *Title*. Place of publication: Publisher (originally published by Publisher year).	Marshall, J.D. (1981). *Furness and the industrial revolution.* Beckermont: Michael Moon (originally published by Barrow Town Council 1958).
Online book	*As for* 'Book (first edition)'	(Saunders et al. 2007)	Family name, Initials. and Family name, Initials. (year). *Title.* (# edn) Place of publication: Publisher. [Accessed day month year from Database name].	Saunders M., Lewis, P. and Thornhill A. (2007). *Research Methods for Business Students.* (4th edn) Harlow: FT Prentice Hall. [Accessed 6 Apr. 2010 from MyLibrary.com]
Book (no known author)	(Originator name *or* *Publication title* year)	(Mintel Marketing Intelligence 2008)	Originator name *or* Publication title. (year). *Title*. Place of publication: Publisher.	Mintel Marketing Intelligence. (1998). *Designerwear: Mintel marketing intelligence report.* London: Mintel International Group Ltd.
Chapters in books				
Chapter in a book	*As for* 'Book (first edition)'	(Robson 2002)	Family name, Initials. and Family name, Initials. (year). *Title*. Place of publication: Publisher. Chapter #.	Robson, C. (2002). *Real World Research*. (2nd edn). Oxford: Blackwell. Chapter 3.
Chapter in an edited book containing a collection of articles (sometimes called a reader)	(Chapter author family name year)	(King 2004)	Family name, Initials. (year). Chapter title. In Initials. Family name and Initials. Family name (eds) *Title*. Place of publication: Publisher. pp. ###–###.	King, N. (2004). Using templates in the thematic analysis of text. In C. Cassell and G. Symon (eds) *Essential guide to qualitative methods in organizational research*. London: Sage. pp. 256–270.

Table A1.1 *(Continued)*

To cite	In the text		In the list of references/bibliography	
	General format	**Example**	**General format**	**Example**
Chapter in an online book	(Chapter author family name year)	(Roper 2007)	Chapter author family name, Initials. (year). Chapter title. In Initials. Family name and Initials. Family name (eds) *Title.* Place of publication: Publisher. pp. ###–###. [Accessed day month year from Database name].	Roper, A. (2007). The international marketing management decisions of UK ski tour operators. In M. Saunders, P. Lewis and A. Thornhill. *Research Methods for Business Students.* (4th edn) Harlow: FT Prentice Hall. pp. 158–9. [Accessed 6 Apr. 2010 from MyLibrary.com]
Dictionaries and other reference books				
. . . where author known	*As for* 'Book (first edition)'	*As for* 'Book (first edition)'	Family name, Initials. (year). *Title.* (# edn). Place of Publication: Publisher. pp. ###–###.	Vogt, W.P. (2005). *Dictionary of statistics and methodology: a nontechnical guide for the social sciences.* (3rd edn). Thousand Oaks, CA: Sage. pp. 124–5.
. . . where no author or editor	(*Publication title* year)	(*The right word at the right time* 1985)	*Publication tiitle.* (year). (# edn). Place of Publication: Publisher. pp. ###–###.	*The right word at the right time.* (1985). Pleasantville, NY: Readers Digest Association. pp. 563–4.
. . . where editor known and author for particular entry	(Entry author family name data)	(Watson 2008)	Entry author family name, Initials. (year). Entry title. In Initials. Family name and Initials. Family name (eds) *Title.* Place of publication: Publisher. pp. ###–###.	Watson, T. (2008). Field research. In R. Thorpe and R. Holt (eds) *The SAGE dictionary of qualitative management research.* London: Sage. pp. 99–100.
. . . where accessed online and is no author or editor	(*Publication title* year)	(*Encyclopaedia Britannica Online* 2010)	*Publication title.* (year). Available at http:/ /www .remainderoffullInternet-address/ [Accessed day month year].	*Encyclopaedia Britannica Online* (2010). Available at http://www.britannica.com/ [Accessed 1 May 2010].
. . . where accessed online and no author or editor for a particular entry	(*Publication title* year)	(*Encyclopaedia Britannica Online* 2010)	*Publication title.* (year). Title of entry. Available at http:// www.remainderoffullInternet-address/ [Accessed day month year].	*Encyclopaedia Britannica Online* (2010). Definition of 'Marketing'. Available at http://www.britannica.com/ EBchecked/topic/365730/ marketing [Accessed 1 May 2010].
Reports				
Report	*As for* 'Book (first edition)'	(Howard 2010)	Family name, Initials. and Family name, Initials. (year). *Title.* Place of publication: Publisher.	Howard, G. (2010). *Employee sickness and fitness for work (Thorogood Reports).* London: Thorogood.

Table A1.1 *(Continued)*

To cite	In the text		In the list of references/bibliography	
	General format	**Example**	**General format**	**Example**
Report (no named author)	(Originator name *or* *Publication title* year)	(Mintel Marketing Intelligence 2008)	Originator name *or* Publication title. (year). *Title*. Place of publication: Publisher.	Mintel Marketing Intelligence. (1998). *Designerwear: Mintel marketing intelligence report.* London: Mintel International Group Ltd.
Organisation's annual report	*As for* 'Book (first edition)'	(Cable and Wireless Plc 2010)	Organisation name. (year). *Title*. Place of publication: as author.	Cable and Wireless Plc. (2010). *Annual report 2009.* Bracknell: as author.
Online report	*As for* 'Book (first edition)'	(Birkinshaw and Pass 2008)	Family name, Initials. and Family name, Initials. (year). *Title of report*. Available at http:/ /www .remainderoffullInternet-address/ [Accessed day month year].	Birkinshaw, J. and Pass, S. (eds.) (2006). *Innovation in the workplace: How are organisations responding to generation Y employees and Web 2.0 technologies?* Available at http://www .cipd.co.uk/NR/rdonlyres/ C2682F1A-0442-492C-831C-E7E3D828050D/0/ innovation_workplace.pdf [Accessed 30 Apr. 2010].
Online report (no named author)	(Originator name *or* *Publication title* year)	(African Development Bank Group 2008)	Originator name. (year). *Title of report*. Available at http://www .remainderoffullInternet-address/ [Accessed day month year].	African Development Bank Group. (2008). *Madagascar young rural entrepreneurs project completion report.* Available at http://www .afdb.org/fileadmin/ uploads/afdb/Documents/ Project-and-Operations/ Madargascar.%20Young%20 Rural%20Entrepreneurs%20 %28PROJER%29%20_%20 EN.pdf [Accessed 9 May 2010].
Government publications				
Parliamentary papers including acts and bills	(Country of origin year)	(United Kingdom 2005)	Country of origin. (year). *Title*. Place of publication: Publisher.	United Kingdom. (2005). *The Prevention of Terrorism Act*. London: The Stationery Office.
Parliamentary debates (Hansard)	(Country Parliament year)	(United Kingdom Parliament 2001)	Country Parliament. House of Commons (HC) or House of Lords (HL) Deb. day month year command paper #.	United Kingdom Parliament HC Deb 13 November 2001 c 345.

Table A1.1 *(Continued)*

To cite	In the text		In the list of references/bibliography	
	General format	**Example**	**General format**	**Example**
Other	*As for* 'Books'	(Skentelbery 2009)	*As for* 'Books'	Skentelbery, R. (Ed.) (2009). *Family spending: A report on the 2008 living costs and food survey*. Basingstoke: Palgrave Macmillan.
Other (no named author or editor)	(Department name *or* Committee name year)	(Department of Trade and Industry 1992)	Department name or Committee name. (year). *Title*. Place of publication: Publisher.	Department of Trade and Industry. (1992). *The Single Market: Europe Open for Professions, UK Implementation*. London: HMSO.
Other (online)	(Family name year)	(Browne and Alstrup 2006)	Family name, Initials. and Family name, Initials. (year). *Title of report*. Available at http://www.remainderoffullInternet-address/ [Accessed day month year].	Browne, L. and Alstrup, P. (Eds.) (2006). *What exactly is the Labour Force Survey?* Available at http://www.statistics.gov.uk/downloads/_theme_labour/_What_exactly_is_LFS1.pdf [Accessed 25 Dec. 2007].
Journal articles				
Journal article (print form or facsimile of print form accessed via full text database)	*As for* 'Book (first edition)'	(Storey et al. 1997)	Family name, Initials. and Family name, Initials. (year). Title of article. *Journal name*. Vol. ##, No. ##, pp. ###–####.	Storey, J., Cressey, P., Morris, T. and Wilkinson, A. (1997). Changing employment practices in UK banking: case studies. *Personnel Review*. Vol. 26, No. 1, pp. 24–42.
Journal article (facsimile of print form, where full text database details required by University)	*As for* 'Book (first edition)'	(Storey et al., 1997)	Family name, Initials. and Family name, Initials. (year). Title of article. *Journal name*. Vol. ##, No. ##, pp. ###–####. [Accessed day month year from Database name].	Storey, J., Cressey, P., Morris, T. and Wilkinson, A. (1997). Changing employment practices in UK banking: case studies. *Personnel Review*. Vol. 26, No. 1, pp. 24–42. [Accessed 6 Apr. 2010 from Emerald Fulltext].
Journal article only published online	*As for* 'Book (first edition)'	(Illingworth 2001)	Family name, Initials. and Family name, Initials. (year). Title of article, *Journal name*. Available at full doi or Internet address [Accessed day month year].	Illingworth, N. (2001). The Internet matters: exploring the use of the Internet as a research tool. *Sociological Research Online*, Vol. 6, No. 2. Available at http://www.socresonline.org.uk/6/2/illingworth.html [Accessed 20 Mar. 2002].

Table A1.1 *(Continued)*

To cite	In the text		In the list of references/bibliography	
	General format	**Example**	**General format**	**Example**
Journal article for which corrected proofs are available online but which is still to be published	*As for* 'Book (first edition)'	(Yang 2008)	Family name, Initials. and Family name, Initials. (year). Title of article, *Journal name*. Available at full doi or Internet address/ [Accessed day month year].	Yang, D. (2008). Pendency and grant ratios on invention patents: A comparative study of the US and China, *Research Policy*. Available at http://dx.doi.org/10.1016/ j.respol.2008. 03.008 [Accessed 14 May 2008].
Magazine articles				
Magazine article	*As for* 'Book (first edition)'	(Saunders 2004)	Family name, Initials. and Family name, Initials. (year). Title of article. *Magazine name*. Vol. ##, No. ## (*or* Issue *or* day *and/or* month), pp. ###–###.	Saunders, M. (2004). Land of the long white cloud. *HOG News UK*. Issue 23, Oct. pp. 24–6.
Magazine article (no named author)	(Originator name *or Publication name* year)	(*Quality World* 2007)	Originator name *or* Publication *name*. (year). Title of article. *Magazine name*. Vol. ##, No. ## (*or* Issue *or* day *and/or* month), pp. ###–###.	Quality World. (2007). Immigration abuse. *Quality World*. Vol. 33, No. 12, p. 6.
Newspapers				
Newspaper article	*As for* 'Book (first edition)'	(Hawkes 2007)	Family name, Initials. and Family name, Initials. Title of article. *Newspaper name*, day month year, p. ###.	Hawkes, S. Umbro slashes England shirt production. *The Times*. 24 Nov. 2007, p. 63.
Newspaper article (no named author)	(*Newspaper name* year)	(*The Times* 2007)	*Newspaper name*. Title of article, day month year, p. ##.	*The Times*. Business big shot Steve Mankin, 24 Nov. 2007, p. 63.
Newspaper article (published online)	*As for* other Newspaper articles	(Barboza 2010)	Family name, Initials. and Family name, Initials. Title of article. *Newspaper name*, day month year. Available at http://www.full-Internet address/ [Accessed day month year].	Barboza, D. Market defies fear of real estate bubble in China. *The New York Times*. 5 Mar. 2010. Available at http://www .nytimes.com/2010/03/05/ business/global/05yuan. html?src=linkedin [Accessed 5 Mar. 2010].
Newspaper article (from electronic database)	*As for* other Newspaper articles	(Anderson 2009)	Family name, Initials. and Family name, Initials. Title of article. *Newspaper name*, day month year, p. ### (if known). [Accessed day month year from Database name]	Anderson, L. How to choose a Business School. *Financial Times*, 23 Jan. 2009. [Accessed 20 Mar. 2010 from ft.com]

Table A1.1 *(Continued)*

To cite	In the text		In the list of references/bibliography	
	General format	**Example**	**General format**	**Example**
CD-ROMS				
CD-ROM	*As for* 'Book (first edition)'	(Friedman et al. 2007)	Family name, Initials. and family name, initials. (year). *Title of CD-ROM.* [CD-ROM]. Place of publication: Publisher.	Friedman, M., Friedman, R. and Adams, J. (2007). *Free to chase.* [CD-ROM]. Ashland, OR: Blackstone Audiobooks.
CD-ROM (no named author)	(*CD-ROM title* year)	(*Encarta 2006 Encyclopaedia* 2005)	*Title of CD-ROM*. (year). [CD-ROM]. Place of publication: Publisher.	*Encarta 2006 Encyclopaedia*. (2005). [CD-ROM]. Redmond, WA: Microsoft.
Brochures and Media/Press releases				
Brochure	(Originator name *or* Brochure title year)	(Harley-Davidson Europe 2007)	Originator name *or* Brochure title. (year). *Title*. Place of publication: as author.	Harley-Davidson Europe. (2007). *2008 make every day count.* Oxford: as author.
Media/press releases	(Originator name *or Release title* year).	(BBC 2010)	Originator name *or Release title*. (year). *Title*. Place of publication: as author.	BBC. (2010). *Trust publishes proposed strategy for reshaping BBC.* London: as author.
Internet/websites				
Internet site or specific site pages	(Source organisation year)	(European Commission 2007)	Source organisation. (year). *Title of site or page within site.* Available at http://www .remainderoffullInternet address/ [Accessed day month year].	European Commission. (2007). *Eurostat – structural indicators.* Available at http:// epp .eurostat.ec.europa .eu/ portal/page?_pageid=1133, 47800773,1133_ 47802558&_dad= portal&_ schema= PORTAL [Accessed 27 Nov. 2007].
Blogs (weblogs), Wikis, web forums				
Blogs (weblogs)	(Owners family name year of posting)	(Bonham-Carter 2007)	Owner's family name, Owner's Initials. (year of posting). Specific subject. *Title of blog*. Day Month Year (of posting). [Blog] Available at http://www.remainder offullInternetaddress/ [Accessed day month year].	Bonham-Carter, D. (2007) Career change questionnaire. *David's life coaching blog.* 10 Dec 2007. [Blog] Available at http://www.davidbonham-carter.com/2007/12/career-change-questionnaire.html [Accessed 11 Dec. 2007].
Wiki	(Originator name or *Wiki title* year of posting)	(Microformats Wiki 2009)	Originator name or *Wiki title*. *Title of Wiki.* Day Month Year (of posting). [Wiki article]. Available at http:// www.remainderoffullInternet address/ [Accessed day month year].	Microfromats Wiki. *Tag cloud examples.* 8 Jan. 2009. [Wiki article] Available at http://microformats.org/wiki/ tagcloud-examples [Accessed 5 Mar. 2010].

Table A1.1 *(Continued)*

To cite	In the text		In the list of references/bibliography	
	General format	**Example**	**General format**	**Example**
Web forums (Usenet groups, bulletin boards etc.)	(Author's family name year of posting)	(Seth 2009)	Authors family name, Authors initials. (year of posting). Title of posting. *Name of forum*. Posted day month year (of posting). [Web forum]. Available at http://www.remainderoffull Internetaddress/ [Accessed day month year].	Seth, S. (2009). Using twitter to get leads. *Small Business Forum*. Posted 27 Nov. 2008. [Web forum] Available at http://www.small-business-forum.com/showthread.php?t=57833 [Accessed 9 May 2010].
Discussion list email (where email sender known)	(Author's family name year of posting)	(Manno 2007)	Sender's Family name, Sender's Initials. (year of posting). Re. Subject of discussion. Posted day month year. Sender's email address (see note below). [Accessed day month year].	Manno, D.F. (2007). Re. I got an email solicitation. Posted 6 Dec. 2007. dfma...@mail.com [Accessed 10 Dec. 2007].
Letters and personal emails				
Letter	(Sender's family name year)	(Saunders 2008)	Sender's family name, Sender's Initials. (year). Unpublished letter to Recipient's Initials. Recipient's Family name re. Subject matter, day, month, year.	Saunders, J. (2008). Unpublished letter to M.N.K. Saunders re. French Revolution, 10 Sept. 2008.
Personal email	(Sender's family name year)	(McPartlin 2008)	Sender's family name, Sender's initials. (year). Email to recipient's initials. recipient's family name re. Subject matter, day month year.	McPartlin, A. (2008). Email to M.N.K. Saunders re. Reviewers' feedback, 23 Nov. 2008.
Online images and diagrams				
Online image or diagram	*As for* 'Book (first edition)'	(Gilroy 1936)	Author's name, Author's initials. (year of production if available). *Title of image or diagram*. Format, name and place of source if available. Available at http://www.remainderoffullInternet address/ [Accessed day month year].	Gilroy, J. (1936). *Lovely day for a Guinness*. Advertising poster, Guinness Webstore. Available at http://www.guinnesswebstore.com/imagesEdp/p82866b.jpg [Accessed 20 Mar. 2010].

Table A1.1 *(Continued)*

To cite	In the text		In the list of references/bibliography	
	General format	Example	General format	Example
Online image or diagram (no named author)	(*Diagram or image title* year)	*Iron Maiden, A matter of life and death* 2006)	*Title of image or diagram.* (year of production if available). Format, name and place of source if available. Available at http://www .remainderoffullInternet address/ [Accessed day month year].	*Iron Maiden, A matter of life and death.* (2006). Tour poster, Starstore.com. Available at http://www .starstore.com/acatalog/ Starstore_Catalogue_IRON_ MAIDEN_POSTERS__IRON_ MAIDEN_POSTER_1815.html [Accessed 20 Mar. 2010].
Conference papers				
Conference paper published as part of proceedings	*As for* 'Book (first edition)'	(Saunders 2009)	Family name, Initials. and Family name, Initials. (year). Title of paper. In Initials. Family name and Initials. Family name (eds) *Title.* Place of publication: Publisher. pp. ###–###.	Saunders, M.N.K. (2009). A real world comparison of responses to distributing questionnaire surveys by mail and web. In J. Azzopardi (Ed.) *Proceedings of the 8th European Conference on Research Mehods in Business and Management.* Reading: ACI, pp. 323–30
Unpublished conference paper	*As for* 'Book (first edition)'	(Saunders et al. 2010)	Family name, Initials. and Family name, Initials. (year). *Title of paper.* Unpublished paper presented at 'Conference name'. Location of conference, day month year.	Saunders, M.N.K., Slack, R. and Bowen, D. (2010). *Location, the development of swift trust and learning: insights from two doctoral summer schools.* Unpublished paper presented at the 'EIASM 5th Workshop on Trust Within and Between Organizations'. Madrid, 28–29 January 2010.
Film, Video, TV, Radio, Downloads				
Television or radio programme	(*Television or radio programme title* year)	(*Today Programme* 2008)	*Programme title.* (year of production). Transmitting organisation and nature of transmission, day month year of transmission.	*The Today Programme.* (2008). British Broadcasting Corporation Radio broadcast, 6 Apr. 2008.
Television or radio programme that is part of a series	(*Television or radio programme series title* year)	(*Money Programme* 2007)	*Series title.* (year of production). Episode. episode title. Transmitting organisation and nature of transmission, day month year of transmission.	*The Money Programme.* (2007). Episode. Last orders for Guinness. British Broadcasting Corporation Television broadcast, 11 Dec. 2007.

Table A1.1 *(Continued)*

To cite	In the text		In the list of references/bibliography	
	General format	**Example**	**General format**	**Example**
Commercial DVD	(DVD title year)	(*Bruce Springsteen live in New York City* 2003)	*DVD title.* (Year of production). [DVD]. Place of publication: Publisher.	*Bruce Springsteen live in New York City* (2003). [DVD]. New York: Sony.
Commercial DVD that is part of a series	(DVD series title year)	(*The Office complete series 1 and 2 and the Christmas specials* 2005)	*DVD series title* (Year of production) Episode. Episode title. [DVD]. Place of publication: Publisher.	*The Office complete series 1 and 2 and the Christmas specials.* (2005). Episode. Series 1 Christmas Special. [DVD]. London: British Broadcasting Corporation.
Video download (e.g. YouTube)	(Company name *or* Family name year)	(Miller 2010)	Company name *or* Family name, Initials. (year). Title of audio download. *YouTube.* Available at http://www.remainderoffullInternet address/ [Accessed day month year].	Miller, L. (2010). Harvard style referencing made easy. *YouTube.* Available at http://www.youtube.com/watch?v=RH1lzyn7Exc [Accessed 20 Mar. 2010].
Audio CD	(Family name *or* Artist *or* Group year)	(Goldratt 2005)	Family name, Initials. *or* Artist. *or* Group. (year). *Title of CD.* [Audio CD]. Place of Publication: Publisher.	Goldratt, E.M. (2005). *Beyond the goal.* [Audio CD]. Buffalo NY: Goldratt's Marketing Group.
Audio download (e.g. Podcast)	(Company name *or* Family name year)	(Harvard Business IdeaCast 2010)	Company name *or* Family name, Initials. (year). Title of audio download.*Title of series* ### [Audio podcast] Available at http://www.remainder offullInternetaddress/ [Accessed day month year].	Harvard Business IdeaCast (2010). Better decisions through analytics. *Harvard Business IdeaCast 180.* [Audio podcast] Available at http://hbsp.libsyn.com/rss [Accessed 10. Sept. 2010].
Course materials and online teaching materials from virtual learning environments (VLEs)				
Lecture*	(Lecturer family name year)	(Saunders 2010)	Lecturer family name, Initials. (year). *Lecture on title of lecture.* Module title. Year (if appropriate) and course title. Place of lecture: Institution. Day month year.	Saunders, M.N.K. (2010). *Lecture on analyzing secondary data using statistics.* Project module. Final year undergraduate business and management degree. Guildford: University of Surrey. 17 Feb. 2010.
Module and course notes*	*As for* 'Book (first edition)'	(Nuri 2010)	Lecturer family name, Initials. (year). *Title of material.* Module title (if appropriate). Level (if appropriate) and course title. Institution, Department or School.	Nuri, J. (2010). *Postgraduate dissertation handbook 2009–10.* MSc Management. University of Surrey, School of Management.

Table A1.1 *(Continued)*

To cite	In the text		In the list of references/bibliography	
	General format	**Example**	**General format**	**Example**
Materials available on a VLE*	(Author family name year)	(Warren 2009)	Author family name, Initials. (year of production). *Title of material* [nature of material]. Module title (if appropriate). Level (if appropriate) and course title. Institution *name of VLE* [online]. Available at http://www .remainderoffullInternet address/ [Accessed day month year].	Warren, S. (2009). *Qualitative data analysis* [PowerPoint slides]. Research methods. MSc Management. University of Surrey ULearn [Online]. Available at http://vle.surrey. ac.uk/webct/urw/lc20935. tp0/cobaltMainFrame. dowebct [Accessed 1 May 2010).

Notes: Where date is not known or unclear, follow conventions outlined towards the end of Table A1.2.
Email addresses should not be included except when they are in the public domain. Even where this is the case, permission should be obtained or the email address replaced by '. . .' after the fourth character, for example: 'abcd . . . @isp.ac.uk'.
*Be warned, most lecturers consider citing of lectures as 'lazy' scholarship.

Table A1.2 Additional conventions when using the Harvard style to reference in the text

To refer to	Use the general format	For example
Work by different authors generally	(Family name year, Family name year) in alphabetical order	(Cassell 2004, Dillman 2000, Robson 2002)
Different authors with the same family name	(Family name Initial year)	(Smith J. 2008)
Different works by the same author	(Family name year, year) in ascending year order	(Saunders 2004, 2005)
Different works by the same author from the same year	(Family name year letter), make sure the letter is consistent throughout	(de Vita 2006a)
An author referred to by another author where the original has not been read (*secondary reference*)*	(Family name year, cited by Family name year)	(Granovetter 1974, cited by Saunders 1993)
A work for which the year of publication cannot be identified	(Family name or Originator name nd), where 'nd' means no year	(Woollons nd)
	(Family name or Originator name c. year) where 'c.' means circa	(Hattersley c. 2004)
A direct quotation	(Family name or Originator name year, p. ###) where 'p.' means 'page' and ### is the page in the original publication on which the quotation appears	'Whenever an employee's job ceases to exist it is potentially fair to dismiss that person.' (Lewis et al. 2003, p. 350)

*For secondary references, whilst many universities only require you to give details of the source you looked at in your list of references, you may also be required the reference for the original source in your list of references.

Referencing in the references or bibliography

In the references or bibliography all the sources are listed alphabetically in one list by the originator or author's family name, and all authors' family names and initials are normally listed in full. If there is more than one work by the same author or originator, these are listed chronologically. A style for referencing work in the references or bibliography is outlined in Table A1.1. While it would be impossible for us to include an example of every type of reference you might need to include, the information contained in this table should enable you to work out the required format for all your references. If there are any about which you are unsure, Colin Neville's (2010) book *The Complete Guide to Referencing and Avoiding Plagiarism* is one of the most comprehensive sources we have found.

For copies of journal articles from printed journals that you have obtained electronically via the Internet it is usually acceptable to reference these using exactly the same format as printed journal articles (Table A1.1), provided that you have obtained and read a facsimile (exact) copy of the article. Exact copies of journal articles have precisely the same format as the printed version, including page numbering, tables and diagrams. They are usually obtained by downloading the article via the Internet as a pdf file that can be read on the screen and printed using Adobe Acrobat Reader. The Adobe Acrobat Reader can be downloaded free of charge from: www.adobe.com/

Finally, remember to include a, b, c etc. immediately after the year when you are referencing different publications by the same author from the same year. Do not forget to ensure that these are consistent with the letters used for the references in the main text.

The American Psychological Association (APA) style

The *American Psychological Association style* or *APA style* is a variation on the author–date system. Like the Harvard style it dates from the 1930s and 1940s, and has been updated subsequently. The latest updates are outlined in the latest edition of the American Psychological Association's (2009) *Concise rules of the APA style,* which is likely to be available for reference in your university's library.

Relatively small but significant differences exist between the Harvard and APA styles, and many authors adopt a combination of the two styles. The key differences are outlined in Table A1.3.

Numeric systems

Referencing in the text

When using *a* Numeric system such as the Vancouver style, references within the project report are shown by a number that is either bracketed or in superscript. This number refers directly to the list of references at the end of the text, and it means it is not necessary for you to include the authors' names or year of publication:

'Research[1] indicates that . . .'

[1]Ritzer, G *The McDonaldization of Society.* (6th edn). Thousand Oaks, CA: Sage, Pine Forge Press, 2011.

Table A1.3 Key differences between Harvard and APA styles of referencing

Harvard style	APA style	Comment
Referencing in the text		
(Lewis 2001)	(Lewis, 2001)	Note punctuation
(Williams and Saunders 2006)	(Williams & Saunders, 2006)	'&' not 'and'
(Saunders et al. 2005)	(Saunders, Skinner, Wang & Beresford, 2005)	For first occurrence if three to five authors
(Saunders et al. 2005)	(Saunders et al., 2005)	For first occurrence if six or more authors; not punctuation and use of italics
(Saunders et al. 2005)	(Saunders et al., 2005)	For subsequent occurrences of two or more authors; note punctuation and use of italics
Referencing in the references or bibliography		
Berman Brown, R. and Saunders, M. (2008). *Dealing with statistics: What you need to know.* Maidenhead: Open University Press.	Berman Brown, R. & Saunders, M. (2008). *Dealing with statistics: What you need to know.* Maidenhead: Open University Press.	Note: use of 'and' and '&'
Varadarajan, P.R. (2003). Musings on relevance and rigour of scholarly research in marketing. *Journal of the Academy of Marketing Science*. Vol. 31, No. 4, pp. 368–376. [Accessed 6 Apr. 2010 from Business Source Complete].	Varadarajan, P.R. (2003). Musings on relevance and rigour of scholarly research in marketing. *Journal of the Academy of Marketing Science*. 31 (4): 368–376. doi: 10.1177/0092070303258240	Note: Volume, part number and page numbers; DOI (digital object identifier) number given in APA. Name of database not given in APA if DOI number given; Date accessed site not included in APA.

Referencing in the references

The references list sequentially the referenced items in the order they are referred to in your project report. This means that they are unlikely to be in alphabetical order. When using the Numeric system you need to ensure that:

- The layout of individual references is that prescribed by the style you have adopted. This is likely to differ from both the Harvard and APA styles (Table A1.3) and will be dependent upon precisely which style has been adopted. The reference to Ritzer's book in the previous subsection (indicated by the number and the associated endnote at the end of this appendix) follows the Vancouver style. Further details of this and other numeric styles can be found in Neville's (2010) book.
- The items referred to include only those you have cited in your report. They should therefore be headed 'References' rather than 'Bibliography'.
- Only one number is used for each item, except where you refer to the same item more than once but need to refer to different pages. In such instances you use standard bibliographic abbreviations to save repeating the reference in full (Table A1.4).

Table A1.4 Bibliographic abbreviations

Abbreviation	Explanation	For example
Op. cit. (opere citato)	Meaning 'in the work cited'. This refers to a work previously referenced, and so you must give the author and year and, if necessary, the page number	Robson (2002) *op. cit.* pp. 23–4.
Loc. cit. (loco citato)	Meaning 'in the place cited'. This refers to the same page of a work previously referenced, and so you must give the author and year	Robson (2002) *loc. cit.*
Ibid. (ibidem)	Meaning 'the same work given immediately before'. This refers to the work referenced immediately before, and replaces all details of the previous reference other than a page number if necessary	*Ibid.* p. 59.

References

American Psychological Association (2009) *Concise Rules of the APA Style*. Washington, DC: American Psychological Association.

Neville, C. (2010) *The Complete Guide to Referencing and Avoiding Plagiarism* (2nd edn). Maidenhead: Open University Press.

Further reading

American Psychological Association (2009) *Concise Rules of the APA Style*. Washington, DC: American Psychological Association. The most recent version of this manual contains full details of how to use this form of the author–date system of referencing as well as how to lay out tables, figures, equations and other statistical data. It also provides guidance on grammar and writing.

Neville, C. (2010) *The Complete Guide to Referencing and Avoiding Plagiarism* (2nd edn). Maidenhead: Open University Press. This fully revised edition provides a comprehensive, up-to-date discussion of the layout required for a multitude of information sources including those from the Internet. It includes guidance on the Harvard, American Psychological Association, numerical and other referencing styles as well as chapters on plagiarism and answering frequently asked questions.

Taylor & Francis (n.d.) *Taylor & Francis Reference Style APA Quick Guide.* Available at www.tandf.co.uk/journals/authors/style/quickref/tf_A.pdf [Accessed 27 November 2010]. This site provides an excellent one-page guide to using the American Psychological Association author–date system as well as a direct link to a document providing full details of this style including how to cite references in the text.

University of New South Wales (2009) *Harvard Referencing Electronic Sources*. Available at www.lc.unsw.edu.au/onlib/pdf/elect_ref.pdf [Accessed 27 November 2010]. This site provides an excellent guide to referencing electronic sources and has useful 'troubleshooting' and 'frequently asked questions' sections.

Appendix 2 Calculating the minimum sample size

In some situations, such as experimental research, it is necessary for you to calculate the precise minimum sample size you require. This calculation assumes that data will be collected from all cases in the sample and is based on:

- how confident you need to be that the estimate is accurate (the level of confidence in the estimate);
- how accurate the estimate needs to be (the margin of error that can be tolerated);
- the proportion of responses you expect to have some particular attribute.

Provided that you know the level of confidence and the margin of error, it is relatively easy to estimate the proportion of responses you expect to have a particular attribute. To do this, ideally you need to collect a pilot sample of about 30 observations and from this to infer the likely proportion for your main survey. It is therefore important that the pilot sample uses the same methods as your main survey. Alternatively, you might have undertaken a very similar survey and so already have a reasonable idea of the likely proportion. If you do not, then you need either to make an informed guess or to assume that 50 per cent of the sample will have the specified attribute – the worst scenario. Most surveys will involve collecting data on more than one attribute. It is argued by deVaus (2002) that for such multi-purpose surveys you should determine the sample size on the basis of those variables in the sample that are likely to have the greatest variability.

Once you have all the information you substitute it into the formula,

$$n = p\% \times q\% \times \left[\frac{z}{e\%}\right]^2$$

where
n is the minimum sample size required
$p\%$ is the percentage belonging to the specified category
$q\%$ is the percentage not belonging to the specified category
z is the z value corresponding to the level of confidence required (see Table A2.1)
$e\%$ is the margin of error required.

Table A2.1 Levels of confidence and associated z values

Level of confidence	*z* value
90% certain	1.65
95% certain	1.96
99% certain	2.57

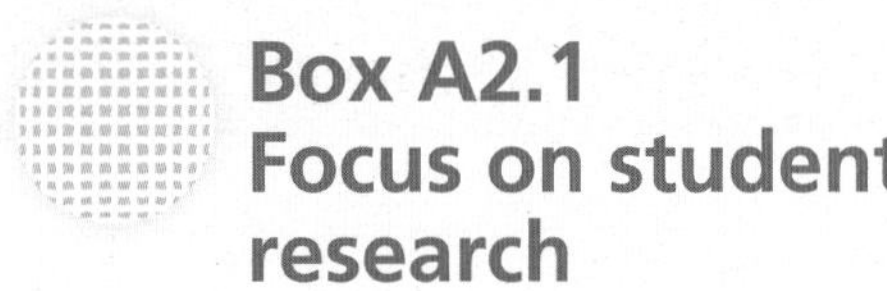

Box A2.1 Focus on student research

Calculating the minimum sample size

To answer a research question Jon needed to estimate the proportion of a total population of 4000 home care clients who receive a visit from their home care assistant at least once a week. Based on his reading of the research methods literature he decided that he needed to be 95 per cent certain that his 'estimate' was accurate (the level of confidence in the estimate); this corresponded to a z score of 1.96 (Table A2.1). Based on his reading he also decided that his 'estimate' needed to be accurate to within plus or minus 5 per cent of the true percentage (the margin of error that can be tolerated).

In order to calculate the minimum sample size, Jon still needed to estimate the proportion of respondents who received a visit from their home care assistant at least once a week. From his pilot survey he discovered that 12 out of the 30 clients receive a visit at least once a week – in other words, that 40 per cent belonged to this specified category. This meant that 60 per cent did not.

Jon substituted these figures into the formula:

$$n = 40 \times 60 \times \left(\frac{1.96}{5}\right)^2$$

$$= 2400 \times (0.392)^2$$

$$= 2400 \times 0.154$$

$$= 369.6$$

His minimum sample size, therefore, was 370 returns.

As the total population of home care clients was 4000, Jon could now calculate the adjusted minimum sample size:

$$n' = \frac{369.6}{1 + \left(\frac{369.6}{4000}\right)}$$

$$= \frac{369.6}{1 + 0.092}$$

$$= \frac{369.6}{1.092}$$

$$= 338.46$$

Because of the small total population, Jon needed a minimum sample size of only 339. However, this assumed he had a response rate of 100 per cent

Where your population is less than 10000, a smaller sample size can be used without affecting the accuracy. This is called the *adjusted minimum sample size* (Box A2.1). It is calculated using the following formula:

$$n' = \frac{n}{1 + \left(\frac{n}{N}\right)}$$

where
n' is the adjusted minimum sample size
n is the minimum sample size (as calculated above)
N is the total population.

Reference

deVaus, D.A. (2002) *Surveys In Social Research* (5th edn). London: Routledge.

Appendix 3 Random sampling numbers

78 41	11 62	72 18	66 69	58 71	31 90	51 36	78 09	41 00
70 50	58 19	68 26	75 69	04 00	25 29	16 72	35 73	55 85
32 78	14 47	01 55	10 91	83 21	13 32	59 53	03 38	79 32
71 60	20 53	86 78	50 57	42 30	73 48	68 09	16 35	21 87
35 30	15 57	99 96	33 25	56 43	65 67	51 45	37 99	54 89
09 08	05 41	66 54	01 49	97 34	38 85	85 23	34 62	60 58
02 59	34 51	98 71	31 54	28 85	23 84	49 07	33 71	17 88
20 13	44 15	22 95	98 97	60 02	85 07	17 57	20 51	01 67
36 26	70 11	63 81	27 31	79 71	08 11	87 74	85 53	86 78
00 30	62 19	81 68	86 10	65 61	62 22	17 22	96 83	56 37
38 41	14 59	53 03	52 86	21 88	55 87	85 59	14 90	74 87
18 89	40 84	71 04	09 82	54 44	94 23	83 89	04 59	38 29
34 38	85 56	80 74	22 31	26 39	65 63	12 38	45 75	30 35
55 90	21 71	17 88	20 08	57 64	17 93	22 34	00 55	09 78
81 43	53 96	96 88	36 86	04 33	31 40	18 71	06 00	51 45
59 69	13 03	38 31	77 08	71 20	23 28	92 43	92 63	21 74
60 24	47 44	73 93	64 37	64 97	19 82	27 59	24 20	00 04
17 04	93 46	05 70	20 95	42 25	33 95	78 80	07 57	86 58
09 55	42 30	27 05	27 93	78 10	69 11	29 56	29 79	28 66
46 69	28 64	81 02	41 89	12 03	31 20	25 16	79 93	28 22
28 94	00 91	16 15	35 12	68 93	23 71	11 55	64 56	76 95
59 10	06 29	83 84	03 68	97 65	59 21	58 54	61 59	30 54
41 04	70 71	05 56	76 66	57 86	29 30	11 31	56 76	24 13
09 81	81 80	73 10	10 23	26 29	61 15	50 00	76 37	60 16
91 55	76 68	06 82	05 33	06 75	92 35	82 21	78 15	19 43
82 69	36 73	58 69	10 92	31 14	21 08	13 78	56 53	97 77
03 59	65 34	32 06	63 43	38 04	65 30	32 82	57 05	33 95
03 96	30 87	81 54	69 39	95 69	95 69	89 33	78 90	30 07
39 91	27 38	20 90	41 10	10 80	59 68	93 10	85 25	59 25
89 93	92 10	59 40	26 14	27 47	39 51	46 70	86 85	76 02
99 16	73 21	39 05	03 36	87 58	18 52	61 61	02 92	07 24
93 13	20 70	42 59	77 69	35 59	71 80	61 95	82 96	48 84
47 32	87 68	97 86	28 51	61 21	33 02	79 65	59 49	89 93
09 75	58 00	72 49	36 58	19 45	30 61	87 74	43 01	93 91
63 24	15 65	02 05	32 92	45 61	35 43	67 64	94 45	95 66
33 58	69 42	25 71	74 31	88 80	04 50	22 60	72 01	27 88
23 25	22 78	24 88	68 48	83 60	53 59	73 73	82 43	82 66
07 17	77 20	79 37	50 08	29 79	55 13	51 90	36 77	68 69
16 07	31 84	57 22	29 54	35 14	22 22	22 60	72 15	40 90
67 90	79 28	62 83	44 96	87 70	40 64	27 22	60 19	52 54
79 52	74 68	69 74	31 75	80 59	29 28	21 69	15 97	35 88
69 44	31 09	16 38	92 82	12 25	10 57	81 32	76 71	31 61
09 47	57 04	54 00	78 75	91 99	26 20	36 19	53 29	11 55
74 78	09 25	95 80	25 72	88 85	76 02	29 89	70 78	93 84

Source: from Morris, C. (2012) *Quantitative Approaches in Business Studies* (8th edn). Reproduced by permission of Pearson Education Ltd

Reference

Morris, C. (2012). *Quantitative Approaches in Business Studies* (8th edn). Harlow: Pearson.

Appendix 4 Guidelines for non-discriminatory language

Writing in a non-discriminatory manner is important in all areas of business and management. For example, in Section 14.5 we noted how the use of language that assumes the gender of a group of people, such as referring to a clerical assistant as 'she', not only is inaccurate but also gives offence to people of both sexes. Similar care needs to be exercised when using other gender-based terms, referring to people from different ethnic groups, and people with disabilities. Without this, the language used may reinforce beliefs and prejudices, as well as being oppressive, offensive, unfair or even incorrect. The impact of this is summarised clearly by Bill Bryson (1995: 425) in his book, *Made in America*, when he observes: 'at the root of the bias-free language movement lies a commendable sentiment: to make language less wounding or demeaning to those whose sex, race, physical condition or circumstances leave them vulnerable to the raw power of words'.

Therefore, although the task of ensuring that the language you use is non-discriminatory may at first seem difficult, it is important that you do so. Some universities have developed their own guidelines, which are available via their intranet or the Internet. However, if your university has not developed its own guidelines, we hope those in this appendix will help you to ensure that your language is not discriminatory.

Guidelines for gender

When referring to both sexes, it is inappropriate to use the terms 'men' or 'women' and their gender-based equivalents; in other words, do not use gender-specific terms generically. Some of the more common gender-neutral alternatives are listed in Table A4.1.

Guidelines for ethnicity

Attention needs to be paid when referring to different ethnic groups. This is especially important where the term used refers to a number of ethnic groups. For example, the term 'Asian' includes a number of diverse ethnic groups that can be recognised with the terms 'Asian peoples' or 'Asian communities'. Similarly, the diversity of people represented by the term 'Black' can be recognised by referring to 'Black peoples' or 'Black communities'. Where possible, the individual groups within these communities should be identified separately.

'Black' is used as a term to include people who are discriminated against due to the colour of their skin. It is often used to refer to people of Caribbean, South Asian and African descent. 'African-Caribbean' has replaced the term Afro-Caribbean and is used to describe Caribbean people who are of African descent. Increasingly, there is a view that hyphenated terms such as 'Afro-Caribbean', 'Black-British' or 'African-American' should not be used. Rather terms such as African Caribbean, Black British

Table A4.1 Gender-specific terms and gender-neutral alternatives

Gender-specific term	Gender-neutral alternative
chairman	chair, chairperson
Dear Sir	Dear Sir/Madam
disseminate	broadcast, inform, publicise
forefathers	ancestors
foreman	supervisor
layman	lay person
man	person
man hours	work hours
mankind	humanity, humankind, people
man-made	manufactured, synthetic
manning	resourcing, staffing
manpower	human resources, labour, staff, workforce
master copy	original, top copy
masterful	domineering, very skilful
policewoman/policeman	police officer
rights of man	people's/citizens' rights, rights of the individual
seminal	classical, formative
women	people
working man/working woman	worker, working people

Source: Adapted from 'Language and the BSA: sex and gender', pp. 35–6, http://www.britsoc.co.uk/equality. You can find the latest BPS advice on gender-specific terms and gender-neutral alternatives in its *Style Guide* (2004), available at: www.bps.org.uk/publications/submission-guidelines/submission-guidelines_home.cfm. Advice on sex-specific language can be found on pp. 35–6 in the guide.

or African American should be used to refer to second or subsequent generations whom, although born in the country, often wish to retain their origins.

If you are unsure of the term to use, then ask someone from the appropriate community for the most acceptable current term. Alternatively, consult a more comprehensive text such as the British Sociological Association's (2011) guidelines which are available via the Internet.

Guidelines for disability

Disability is also an area where terminology is constantly changing as people voice their own preferences. Despite this, general guidelines can be offered:

- Do not use medical terms as these emphasise the condition rather than the person.
- Where it is necessary to refer to a person's medical condition, make the person explicit (see Table A4.2).
- Where referring to historical and some contemporary common terms, place speech marks around the term.

Table A4.2 Disablist terms and non-disablist alternatives

Disablist term	Non-disablist alternative
the blind	blind and partially sighted people, visually impaired people
cripple	mobility impaired person
the deaf	deaf or hard of hearing people
the disabled, the handicapped, invalid	disabled people, people with disabilities, employees with disabilities
dumb, mute	person with a speech impairment
epileptic, epileptics	person who has epilepsy
handicap	disability
mentally handicapped	person with a learning difficulty or learning disability
mentally ill, mental patient	mental health service user
patient	person
spastic	person who has cerebral palsy
wheelchair-bound	wheelchair user
victim of, afflicted by, suffering from, crippled by	person who has, person with

Source: Adapted from 'Language and the BSA: non-disablist', pp. 35–6, http://www.britsoc.co.uk/equality

There are non-disablist alternatives for the more common disablist terms. These are summarised in Table A4.2. However, if you are unsure of the term to use, ask someone from the appropriate group for the most acceptable current term.

References

British Psychological Society (1988) 'Guidelines for the use of non-sexist language', *The Psychologist*, Vol. 1, No. 2, pp. 53–4.

British Psychological Society (2004) *Style guide*. Available at www.bps.org.uk/document-download-area/document-download$.cfm?file_uuid=1B29ADB1-7E96-C67F-D51D3ADFC581A906&ext=pdf [Accessed 10 May 2011].

British Sociological Association (2004a) *Language and the BSA: Sex and gender*. Available at www.britsoc.co.uk/equality/ [Accessed 10 May 2011].

British Sociological Association (2004b) *Language and the BSA: Non-disablist*. Available at www.britsoc.co.uk/equality/ [Accessed 10 May 2011].

British Sociological Association (2011) *Equality and diversity. Language and the BSA: Ethnicity and race*. Available at www.britsoc.co.uk/equality/ [Accessed 21 June 2011].

Bryson, B. (1995) *Made in America*. London: Minerva.

Glossary

50th percentile The middle value when all the values of a variable are arranged in rank order; usually known as the median.

A

abductive approach Research approach involving the collection of data to explore a phenomenon, identify themes and explain patterns, to generate a new – or modify an existing – theory which is subsequently tested.

abstract (1) Summary, usually of an article or book, which also contains sufficient information for the original to be located. (2) Summary of the complete content of the project report.

access (1) The process involved in gaining entry into an organisation to undertake research. (2) The situation where a research participant is willing to share data with a researcher. *See also* cognitive access, continuing access, physical access.

action research Research strategy concerned with the management of a change and involving close collaboration between practitioners and researchers. The results flowing from action research should also inform other contexts.

active response rate The total number of responses divided by the total number in the sample after ineligible and unreachable respondents have been excluded. *See* ineligible respondent, unreachable respondent. *See also* break off, complete response, complete refusal, partial response total response rate.

active voice The voice in which the action of the verb is attributed to the person. For example, '*I* conducted interviews'.

ad hoc survey A general term normally used to describe the collection of data that only occurs once due to the specificity of focus. Although the term is normally interpreted as referring to questionnaires, it also includes other techniques such as structured observation and structured interviews. *See also* survey.

alpha coefficient *see* Cronbach's alpha.

alternative hypothesis Testable proposition stating that there is a significant difference or relationship between two or more variables. Often referred to as H_a. *See also* hypothesis, null hypothesis.

analysis The ability to break down data and to clarify the nature of the component parts and the relationship between them.

analysis of variance Statistical test to determine the probability (likelihood) that the values of a numerical data variable for three or more independent samples or groups are different. The test assesses the likelihood of any difference between these groups occurring by chance alone.

analytic induction Analysis of qualitative data that involves the iterative examination of a number of strategically selected cases to identify the cause of a particular phenomenon.

anonymity (1) The process of concealing the identity of participants in all documents resulting from the research. (2) The promise that even the researcher will not be able to identify by whom responses are made.

ANOVA *see* analysis of variance.

appendix A supplement to the project report. It should not normally include material that is essential for the understanding of the report itself, but additional relevant material in which the reader may be interested.

application The ability to apply certain principles and rules in particular situations.

applied research Research of direct and immediate relevance to practitioners that addresses issues they see as important and is presented in ways they can understand and act upon.

archival research Research strategy that analyses administrative records and documents as principal sources of data because they are products of day-to-day activities.

asynchronous Not undertaken in real time, working offline.

attribute variable Variable that records data about respondents' characteristics, in other words things they possess.

autocorrelation The extent to which the value of a variable at a particular time (t) is related to its value at the previous time period ($t - 1$).

availability sampling *see* convenience sampling.

axial coding The process of recognising relationships between categories in grounded theory.

axiology A branch of philosophy that studies judgements about the role of values.

B

bar chart Diagram for showing frequency distributions for a categorical or grouped discrete data variable, which highlights the highest and lowest values.

base period The period against which index numbers are calculated to facilitate comparisons of trends or changes over time. *See also* index number.

basic research Research undertaken purely to understand processes and their outcomes, predominantly in universities as a result of an academic agenda, for which the key consumer is the academic community.

behaviour variable Variable that records what respondents actually do.

beneficence Actions designed to promote beneficial effects. *See also* code of ethics.

between-subjects design Experimental design allowing a comparison of results to be made between an experimental group and a control group. *See also* experiment, within-subjects design.

bibliographic details The information needed to enable readers to find original items consulted or used for a research project. These normally include the author, date of publication, title of article, title of book or journal.

bibliography Alphabetical list of the bibliographic details for all relevant items consulted and used, including those items not referred to directly in the text. The university will specify the format of these.

blog A personal online journal on which an individual or group of individuals record opinions, information and the like on a regular basis for public consumption. Most blogs are interactive allowing visitors to leave comments. 'Blog' is an abbreviation of 'weblog'.

Boolean logic System by which the variety of items found in a search based on logical propositions that can be either true or false can be combined, limited or widened.

box plot Diagram that provides a pictorial representation of the distribution of the data for a variable and statistics such as median, inter-quartile range, and the highest and lowest values.

brainstorming Technique that can be used to generate and refine research ideas. It is best undertaken with a group of people.

break off The level of response to questionnaires or structured interviews in which less than 50% of all questions answered other than by a refusal or no answer. Break off therefore includes complete refusal.

broker *see* gatekeeper.

C

CAQDAS Computer Aided Qualitative Data Analysis Software.

case (1) Individual element or group member within a sample or population such as an employee. (2) Individual unit for which data have been collected.

case study Research strategy that involves the empirical investigation of a particular contemporary phenomenon within its real-life context, using multiple sources of evidence.

categorical data Data whose values cannot be measured numerically but can either be classified into sets (categories) or placed in rank order.

categorising The process of developing categories and subsequently attaching these categories to meaningful units of data. *See also* unitising, units of data

category question Closed question in which the respondent is offered a set of mutually exclusive categories and instructed to select one.

causality Relationship between cause and effect. Everything that happens will have a cause, while each action will cause an effect.

causal relationship Relationship between two or more variables in which the change (effect) in one variable is caused by the other variable(s).

census The collection and analysis of data from every possible case or group member in a population.

central limit theorem The larger the absolute size of a sample, the more closely its distribution will be to the normal distribution. *See* normal distribution.

central tendency measure The generic term for statistics that can be used to provide an impression of those values for a variable that are common, middling or average.

chat room An online forum operating in synchronous mode. *See also* synchronous.

chi square test Statistical test to determine the probability (likelihood) that two categorical data variables are associated. A common use is to discover whether there are statistically significant associations between the observed frequencies and the expected frequencies of two variables presented in a cross-tabulation.

classic experiment Experiment in which two groups are established and members assigned at random to each. *See also* experiment, experimental group.

closed question Question that provides a number of alternative answers from which the respondent is instructed to choose.

cluster sampling Probability sampling procedure in which the population is divided into discrete groups or clusters prior to sampling. A random sample (systematic or simple) of these clusters is then drawn.

codebook Complete list of all the codes used to code data variables.

code of ethics Statement of principles and procedures for the design and conduct of research. *See also* privacy, research ethics, research ethics committee.

coding *see* axial coding, categorising, focused coding, initial coding, open coding, selective coding, unitising data

coefficient of determination *see* regression coefficient.

coefficient of multiple determination *see* multiple regression coefficient.

coefficient of variation Statistic that compares the extent of spread of data values around the mean between two or more variables containing numerical data.

cognitive access The process of gaining access to data from intended participants. This involves participants agreeing to be interviewed or observed, within agreed limits. *See also* informed consent.

cohort study Study that collects data from the same cases over time using a series of 'snapshots'.

collinearity The extent to which two or more independent variables are correlated with each other. Also termed multicollinearity.

comparative proportional pie chart Diagram for comparing both proportions and totals for all types of data variables.

compiled data Data that have been processed, such as through some form of selection or summarising.

complete observer Observational role in which the researcher does not reveal the purpose of the research activity to those being observed. However, unlike the complete participant role, the researcher does not take part in the activities of the group being studied.

complete participant Observational role in which the researcher attempts to become a member of the group in which research is being conducted. The true purpose of the research is not revealed to the group members.

complete refusal The level of response to questionnaires or structured interviews in which none of the questions are answered.

complete response The level of response to questionnaires or structured interviews in which over 80% of all questions answered other than by a refusal or no answer.

computer-aided personal interviewing (CAPI) Type of interviewing in which the interviewer reads questions from a computer screen and enters the respondent's answers directly into the computer.

computer-aided telephone interviewing (CATI) Type of telephone interviewing in which the interviewer reads questions from a computer screen and enters the respondent's answers directly into the computer.

conclusion The section of the project report in which judgements are made rather than just facts reported. New material is not normally introduced in the conclusion.

concurrent embedded design Mixed methods research design where the collection of either quantitative or qualitative data is embedded within the collection of the other. *See also* concurrent mixed methods research, embedded mixed methods research.

concurrent mixed methods research Research using both quantitative and qualitative methods that are conducted concurrently during a single phase of data collection and analysis. *See also* concurrent embedded design, concurrent triangulation design, mixed methods research, single-phase research design.

concurrent triangulation design Mixed methods research design where quantitative and qualitative data are collected in the same phase so that these data can be compared to see where they converge or diverge in relation to addressing your research question. *See also* concurrent mixed methods research.

confidentiality (1) Concern relating to the right of access to the data provided by the participants and, in particular the need to keep these data secret or private. (2) Promise made by the researcher not to reveal the identity of participants or present findings in a way that enables participants to be identified.

confounding variables Extraneous but difficult to observe or measure variables than can potentially undermine the inferences drawn about the relationship between the independent variable and the dependent variable. *See also* control variables, experiment.

consent *see* implied consent, informed consent.

consent form Written agreement, signed by both parties in which the participant agrees to take part in the research and gives her or his permission for data to be used in specified ways.

constant comparison Process of constantly comparing data to analytical categories and vice versa, as well comparing data with other data and each category with other categories, to develop higher level categories and further your analysis towards the emergence of a grounded theory. *See also* inductive approach; Grounded Theory Method.

construct validity Extent to which your measurement questions actually measure the presence of those constructs you intended them to measure.

consultancy report *see* management report.

content validity *see* face validity.

contextual data Additional data recorded when collecting primary or secondary data that reveals background information about the setting and the data collection process.

contingency table Technique for summarising data from two or more variables so that specific values can be read.

continuing access Gaining agreed research access to an organisation on an incremental basis.

continuous data Data whose values can theoretically take any value (sometimes within a restricted range) provided they can be measured with sufficient accuracy.

control group Group in an experiment that, for the sake of comparison, does not receive the intervention in which you are interested. *See also* experiment, experimental group.

control variables Unwanted but measurable variables that need to be kept constant to avoid them influencing the effect of the independent variable on the dependent variable. *See also* confounding variables, experiment.

controlled index language The terms and phrases used by databases to index items within the database. If search terms do not match the controlled index language, the search is likely to be unsuccessful.

convenience sampling Non-probability haphazard sampling procedure in which cases are selected only on the basis that they are easiest to obtain. *See also* haphazard sampling, non-probability sampling.

correlation The extent to which two variables are related to each other. *See also* correlation coefficient, negative correlation, positive correlation.

correlation coefficient Number between −1 and +1 representing the strength of the relationship between two ranked or numerical variables. A value of +1 represents a perfect positive correlation. A value of −1 represents a perfect negative correlation. Correlation coefficients between +1 and −1 represent weaker positive and negative correlations, a value of 0 meaning the variables are perfectly independent. *See also* negative correlation, Pearson's product moment correlation coefficient, positive correlation, Spearman's rank correlation coefficient.

coverage The extent to which a data set covers the population it is intended to cover.

covering letter Letter accompanying a questionnaire, which explains the purpose of the survey. *See also* introductory letter.

covert research Research undertaken where those being researched are not aware of this fact.

Cramer's V Statistical test to measure the association between two variables within a table on a scale where 0 represents no association and 1 represents perfect association. Because the value of Cramer's V is always between 0 and 1, the relative strengths of significant associations between different pairs of variables can be compared.

creative thinking technique One of a number of techniques for generating and refining research ideas based on non-rational criteria. These may be, for example, biased heavily in favour of the individual's preferences or the spontaneous ideas of the individual or others. *See also* brainstorming, Delphi technique, relevance tree.

criterion-related validity Ability of a statistical test to make accurate predictions.

critical case sampling A purposive sampling method which focuses on selecting those cases on the basis of making a point dramatically or because they are important. *See also* purposive sampling.

critical ethnography Ethnographic strategy that questions the status quo and often adopts an advocacy role to bring about change. *See also* ethnography, interpretive ethnography, realist ethnography.

critical incidence technique A technique in which respondents are asked to describe in detail a critical incident or number of incidents that is key to the research question. *See also* critical incident.

critical incident An activity or event where the consequences were so clear that the respondent has a definite idea regarding its effects.

critical (literature) review Detailed and justified analysis and commentary of the merits and faults of the literature within a chosen area, which demonstrates familiarity with what is already known about your research topic.

critical realism The epistemological position that what we experience are sensations, the images of the things in the real world, not the things directly. *See also* direct realism, realism.

Cronbach's alpha Statistic used to measure the consistency of responses across a set of questions (scale items) designed to measure a particular concept together (scale). It consists of an alpha coefficient with a value between 0 and 1. Values of 0.7 or above suggest that the questions in the scale are measuring the same thing. *See also* scale item, scale.

cross-posting Receipt by individuals of multiple copies of an email, often due to the use of multiple mailing lists on which that individual appears.

cross-sectional research The study of a particular phenomenon (or phenomena) at a particular time, i.e. a 'snapshot'.

cross-tabulation *see* contingency table.

D

data Facts, opinions and statistics that have been collected together and recorded for reference or for analysis.

data display and analysis A process for the collection and analysis of qualitative data that involves three concurrent subprocesses of data reduction, data display, and drawing and verifying conclusions.

data matrix The table format in which data are usually entered into analysis software consisting of rows (cases) and columns (variables).

data reduction Condensing data by summarising or simplifying these as a means to analyse them. *See also* data display and analysis.

data requirements table A table designed to ensure that, when completed, the data collected will enable the research question(s) to be answered and the objectives achieved.

data sampling The process of only transcribing those sections of an audio-recording that are pertinent to your research, having listened to it repeatedly beforehand.

data saturation The stage when any additional data collected provides few, if any, new insights.

debriefing Providing research participants with a retrospective explanation about a research project and its purpose where covert observation has occurred.

deception Deceiving participants about the nature, purpose or use of research by the researcher(s). *See also* informed consent, research ethics.

decile One of 10 sections when data are ranked and divided into 10 groups of equal size.

deductive approach Research approach involving the testing of a theoretical proposition by the employment of a research strategy specifically designed for the purpose of its testing.

deliberate distortion Form of bias that occurs when data are recorded inaccurately on purpose. It is most common for secondary data sources such as organisational records.

delivery and collection questionnaire Data collection technique in which the questionnaire is delivered to each respondent. She or he then reads and answers the same set of questions in a predetermined order without an interviewer being present before the completed questionnaire is collected.

Delphi technique Technique using a group of people who are either involved or interested in the research topic to generate and select a more specific research idea.

deontological view View that the ends served by research can never justify research which is unethical.

dependent variable Variable that changes in response to changes in other variables.

descriptive data Data whose values cannot be measured numerically but can be distinguished by classifying into sets (categories).

descriptive observation Observation where the researcher concentrates on observing the physical setting, the key participants and their activities, particular events and their sequence and the attendant processes and emotions involved.

descriptive research Research for which the purpose is to produce an accurate representation of persons, events or situations.

descriptive statistics Generic term for statistics that can be used to describe variables.

descripto-explanatory study A study whose purpose is both descriptive and explanatory where, usually, description is the precursor to explanation.

deviant sampling *see* extreme case sampling.

dichotomous data Descriptive data that are grouped into two categories. *See also* descriptive data.

direct realism The epistemological position that what you see is what you get: what we experience through our senses portrays the world accurately. *See also* critical realism, realism.

discourse analysis General term covering a variety of approaches to the analysis of language in its own right. It explores how language constructs and simultaneously reproduces and/or changes the social world rather than using it as a means to reveal the social world as a phenomenon.

discrete data Data whose values are measured in discrete units and therefore can take only one of a finite number of values from a scale that measures changes in this way.

discussion The section of the project report in which the wider implications of the findings (and conclusions) are considered.

dispersion measures Generic term for statistics that can be used to provide an impression of how the values for a variable are dispersed around the central tendency.

dissertation The usual name for research projects undertaken as part of undergraduate and taught masters degrees. Dissertations are usually written for an academic audience.

documentary secondary data Written documents such as notices, minutes of meetings, diaries, administrative and public records and reports to shareholders as well as non-written documents such as tape and video recordings, pictures, films and television programmes.

document summary Type of summary used an analytical aid. *See also* interim summary; transcript summary.

DOI Digital object identifier name used to uniquely identify an electronic document such as a specific journal article stored in an online database.

double-phase research design Research involving two phases of data collection and analysis. *See also* sequential mixed methods research.

Durbin–Watson statistic Statistical test to measure the extent to which the value of a dependent variable at time t is related to its value at the previous time period, $t - 1$ (autocorrelation). The statistic ranges in value from zero to four. A value of two indicates no autocorrelation. A value of towards zero indicates positive autocorrelation. A value towards four indicates negative autocorrelation. *See also* autocorrelation.

E

ecological validity A type of external validity referring to the extent to which findings can be generalised from one group to another. *See also* external validity.

effect size index A measure of the practical significance of a statistically significant difference, association or relationship. The statistic is normally used when the data sample is large.

electronic interview An Internet- or intranet-mediated interview conducted through either a chat room, Internet forum, web conferencing or email. *See also* email interview, chat room, Internet forum.

electronic questionnaire An Internet- or intranet-mediated questionnaire. *See also* Internet-mediated questionnaire, intranet-mediated questionnaire.

element Individual case or group member within a sample or population such as an employee.

email interview A series of emails each containing a small number of questions rather than one email containing a series of questions.

embedded mixed methods research Use of quantitative and qualitative methods in research design where use of one is embedded within the other. *See also* concurrent embedded design, concurrent mixed methods research.

epistemology A branch of philosophy that studies the nature of knowledge and what constitutes acceptable knowledge in a field of study.

ethics *See* research ethics, research ethics committees, code of ethics.

ethnography Research strategy that focuses upon describing and interpreting the social world through first-hand field study.

evaluation The process of judging materials or methods in terms of internal accuracy and consistency or by comparison with external criteria.

existing contacts Colleagues, friends, relatives or fellow students who may agree to become research informants, participants or respondents.

experiential data Data about the researcher's perceptions and feelings as the research develops.

experiential meaning The equivalence of meaning of a word or sentence for different people in their everyday experiences.

experiment Research strategy whose purpose is to study the probability of a change in an independent variable causing a change in another, dependent variable. Involves the definition of null and alternative hypotheses; random allocation of participants to either an experimental group(s) or a control group; manipulation of the independent variable; measurement of changes in the dependent variable and; control of other variables. *See also* between-subjects design, control group, experimental group, quasi-experiment.

experimental group Group in an experiment that receives the intervention in which you are interested. *See also* control group, experiment.

explanation building Deductive process for analysing qualitative data that involves the iterative examination of a number of strategically selected cases to test a theoretical proposition.

explanatory research Research that focuses on studying a situation or a problem in order to explain the relationships between variables.

exploratory data analysis (EDA) Approach to data analysis that emphasises the use of diagrams to explore and understand the data.

exploratory study Research that aims to seek new insights into phenomena, to ask questions, and to assess the phenomena in a new light.

external researcher Researcher who wishes to gain access to an organisation for which she or he does not work. *See also* access, internal researcher.

external validity The extent to which the research results from a particular study are generalisable to all relevant contexts.

extreme case sampling A purposive sampling method which focuses on unusual or special cases. *See also* purposive sampling.

F

face validity Agreement that a question, scale, or measure appears logically to reflect accurately what it was intended to measure.

feasibility [of access] Being able to negotiate access to conduct research.

filter question Closed question that identifies those respondents for whom the following question or questions are not applicable, enabling them to skip these questions.

focused coding Analysis or re-analysis of data to identify which of the initial codes may be used as higher level codes to categorise larger units of data to further the analysis towards the emergence of a grounded theory.

focused interview Interviewer exercises direction over the interview while allowing the interviewee's opinions to emerge as he or she responds to the questions of the researcher.

focused observation Phase in an observation study when the researcher focuses her or his observations on particular events or interactions between key informants.

focus group Group interview, composed of a small number of participants, facilitated by a 'moderator', in which the topic is defined clearly and precisely and there is a focus on enabling and recording interactive discussion between participants. *See also* group interview.

follow-up Contact made with respondents to thank them for completing and returning a survey and to remind non-respondents to complete and return their surveys.

forced-choice question *see* closed question.

forum *see* Internet forum.

frequency distribution Table for summarising data from one variable so that specific values can be read.

full text online database Online database that indexes and provides a summary and full text of articles from a range of journals. Sometimes includes books, chapters from books, reports, theses and conference papers.

fully integrated mixed methods research Use of both quantitative and qualitative methods throughout the research. *See also* partially integrated mixed methods research.

functionalist paradigm A philosophical position which is concerned with a rational explanation of behaviours and institutions such as why a particular organisational problem is occurring in terms of the functions they perform.

fundamental research *see* basic research.

G

Gantt chart Chart that provides a simple visual representation of the tasks or activities that make up a project, each being plotted against a time line.

gatekeeper The person, often in an organisation, who controls research access.

general focus research question Question that flows from the research idea and may lead to several more detailed questions or the definition of research objectives.

generalisability The extent to which the findings of a research study are applicable to other settings.

generalisation The making of more widely applicable propositions based upon the process of deduction from specific cases.

Goldilocks test A test to decide whether research questions are either too big, too small, too hot or just right. Those that are too big probably demand too many resources. Questions that are too small are likely to be of insufficient substance, while those that are too hot may be so because of sensitivities that may be aroused as a result of doing the research.

grammatical error Error of grammar that detracts from the authority of the project report.

grey literature *see* primary literature.

grounded theory (1) Including both Grounded Theory Methodology and Grounded Theory Method. (2) Theory that is grounded or developed using an inductive approach. *See also* Grounded Theory Methodology, Grounded Theory Method, inductive approach.

Grounded Theory (Methodology) Research strategy in which theory is developed from data collected by a series of observations or interviews principally involving an inductive approach. *See also* deductive approach, Grounded Theory Method, inductive approach.

Grounded Theory Method Data collection techniques and analytic procedures used in a Grounded Theory research strategy to derive meaning from the subjects and settings being studied. *See also* Grounded Theory (Methodology)

group interview General term to describe all non-standardised interviews conducted with two or more people.

H

habituation Situation where, in observation studies, the subjects being observed become familiar with the process of observation so that they take it for granted. This is an attempt to overcome 'observer effect' or reactivity.

haphazard sampling Non-probability sampling procedure in which cases are selected without any obvious principles of organization. *See also* convenience sampling, non-probability sampling.

heterogeneous sampling A purposive sampling method which focuses on obtaining the maximum variation in the cases selected. *See also* purposive sampling.

heteroscedasticity Extent to which the data values for the dependent and independent variables have unequal variances. *See also* variance.

histogram Diagram for showing frequency distributions for a grouped continuous data variable in which the area of each bar represents the frequency of occurrence.

homogeneous sampling A purposive sampling method which focuses on selecting cases from one particular subgroup in which all the members are similar. *See also* purposive sampling.

homoscedasticity Extent to which the data values for the dependent and independent variables have equal variances. *See also* variance.

hybrid access Use of both traditional access and Internet-mediated access to conduct research.

Hypothesis (1) Testable proposition stating that there is a significant difference or relationship between two or more variables. Often referred to as H_1. *See also* alternative hypothesis, null hypothesis. (2) Testable proposition about the relationship between two or more events or concepts.

I

idiomatic meaning The meaning ascribed to a group of words that are natural to a native speaker, but which is not deducible from the individual words.

independent groups *t*-test Statistical test to determine the probability (likelihood) that the values of a numerical data variable for two independent samples or groups are different. The test assesses the likelihood of any difference between these two groups occurring by chance alone.

independent measures Use of more than one experimental group in an experiment where more than one intervention or manipulation is to be tested and measured. *See also* experiment.

independent variable Variable that causes changes to a dependent variable or variables.

in-depth interview *See* unstructured interview.

index number Summary data value calculated from a base period for numerical variables, to facilitate comparisons of trends or changes over time. *See also* base period.

inductive approach Research approach involving the development of a theory as a result of the observation of empirical data.

ineligible respondent Respondent selected for a sample who does not meet the requirements of the research.

inference, statistical *see* statistical inference.

inferred consent Informants, participants or respondents may or may not fully understand the implications of taking part but their consent to participate, is inferred from their participating in the research. The researcher assumes that data may be recorded, analysed, used, stored or reported as she or he wishes without clarifying such issues with those who take part. *See also* informed consent.

informant error Errors that occur when informants are observed in situations that are inconsistent with their normal behaviour patterns, leading to atypical responses. *See also* informants.

informant interview Interview guided by the perceptions of the interviewee.

informants Those who agree to be observed in participant observation or structured observation studies.

informant verification Form of triangulation in which the researcher presents written accounts of, for example, interview notes to informants for them to verify the content. *See also* triangulation.

informed consent Position achieved when intended participants are fully informed about the nature, purpose and use of research to be undertaken and their role within it, and where their consent to participate, if provided, is freely given. *See also* deception, implied consent.

initial coding *see* open coding.

initial sample Purposively selected initial case from which to collect and analyse data used in Grounded Theory. *See also* Grounded Theory Method.

integer A whole number.

inter-library loan System for borrowing a book or obtaining a copy of a journal article from another library.

interim summary Type of summary used to outline progress and to aid analysis. *See also* document summary; transcript summary.

internal researcher Person who conducts research within an organisation for which they work. *See also* cognitive access, external researcher.

internal validity Extent to which findings can be attributed to interventions rather than any flaws in your research design. *See also* measurement validity.

Internet forum Commonly referred to as web forums, message boards, discussion boards, discussion forums, discussion groups and bulletin boards. Usually only deal with one topic and discourage personal exchanges.

Internet-mediated access Use of Internet technologies to gain virtual access to conduct research.

Internet-mediated questionnaire Questionnaire administered electronically using the Internet.

interpretive ethnography Ethnographic strategy stressing subjectivity, reflection and identifying multiple meanings. *See also* ethnography, critical ethnography, realist ethnography.

interpretive paradigm A philosophical position which is concerned with understanding the way we as humans make sense of the world around us.

interpretivism The epistemological position that advocates the necessity to understand differences between humans in their role as social actors.

inter-quartile range The difference between the upper and lower quartiles, representing the middle 50% of the data when the data values for a variable have been ranked.

interval data Numerical data for which the difference or 'interval' between any two data values for a particular variable can be stated, but for which the relative difference can not be stated. *See also* numerical data.

interview schedule *see* structured interview.

interviewee bias Attempt by an interviewee to construct an account that hides some data or when she or he presents herself or himself in a socially desirable role or situation.

interviewer bias Attempt by an interviewer to introduce bias during the conduct of an interview, or where the appearance or behaviour of the interviewer has the effect of introducing bias in the interviewee's responses.

interviewer-completed questionnaire Data collection technique in which an interviewer reads the same set of questions to the respondent in a predetermined order and records his or her responses. *See also* structured interview, telephone questionnaire.

intranet-mediated access Use of an intranet within an organisation to gain access to conduct research.

intranet-mediated questionnaire Questionnaire administered electronically using an organisation's intranet.

introduction The opening to the project report, which gives the reader a clear idea of the central issue of concern of the research, states the research question(s) and research objectives, and explains the research context and the structure of the project report.

introductory letter Request for research access, addressed to an intended participant or organisational broker/gatekeeper, stating the purpose of the research, the nature of the help being sought, and the requirements of agreeing to participate. *See also* covering letter, gatekeeper.

intrusive research methods Methods that involve direct access to participants, including qualitative interviewing, observation, longitudinal research based on these methods and phenomenologically based approaches to research. *See also* access, cognitive access.

investigative question One of a number of questions that need to be answered in order to address satisfactorily each research question and meet each objective.

'in vivo' codes Names or labels for codes based on actual terms used by those who take part in research.

J

journal *see* professional journal, refereed academic journal.

judgemental sampling *see* purposive sampling.

K

Kendall's rank correlation coefficient Statistical test that assesses the strength of the relationship between two ranked data variables, especially where the data for a variable contain tied ranks. For data collected from a sample, there is also a need to calculate the probability of the correlation coefficient having occurred by chance alone.

key word Basic term selected from the controlled index language specified by the online database to describe the research question(s) and objectives to search the tertiary literature.

Kolmogorov–Smirnov test Statistical test to determine the probability (likelihood) that an observed set of values for each category of a variable differs from a specified distribution. Common uses are to discover whether a data variable's distribution differs significantly from a normal distribution, or an alternative distribution such as that of the population from which it was selected.

kurtosis The pointedness or flatness of a distribution's shape compared with the normal distribution. If a distribution is pointier or peaked, it is leptokurtic and the kurtosis value is positive. If a distribution is flatter, it is platykurtic and the kurtosis value is negative. *See also* normal distribution.

L

law of large numbers Samples of larger absolute size are more likely to be representative of the population from which they are drawn than smaller samples and, in particular, the mean (average) calculated for the sample is more likely to equal the mean for the population, providing the samples are not biased.

level of access The nature and depth of access to participants required and achieved. *See also* cognitive access, continuing access, physical access.

lexical meaning The precise meaning of an individual word.

Likert-style rating question Rating question that allows the respondent to indicate how strongly she or he agrees or disagrees with a statement.

linearity Degree to which change in a dependent variable is related to change in one or more independent variables. *See also* dependent variable, independent variable

line graph Diagram for showing trends in longitudinal data for a variable.

list question Closed question, in which the respondent is offered a list of items and instructed to select those that are appropriate.

literal replication Replication of findings across selected multiple case studies in a case study strategy. *See also* case study, theoretical replication.

literature review *see* critical (literature) review.

logical reasoning Process used in theory development to explain why relationships may exist based on what is already known.

longitudinal study The study of a particular phenomenon (or phenomena) over an extended period of time.

long-term trend The overall direction of movement of numerical data values for a single variable after variations have been smoothed out. *See also* moving average.

lower quartile The value below which a quarter of the data values lie when the data values for a variable have been ranked.

M

mail questionnaire *see* postal questionnaire.

management report Abbreviated version of the project report, usually written for a practitioner audience. Normally includes a brief account of objectives, method, findings, conclusions and recommendations.

Mann-Whitney *U* Test Statistical test to determine the probability (likelihood) that the values of a ordinal data variable for two independent samples or groups are different. The test assesses the likelihood of any difference between these two groups occurring by chance alone and is often used when the assumptions of the independent samples *t*-test are not met.

matched pair analysis Used in an experimental design to match participants in an experimental group with those in a control group before conducting the experiment where random assignment is not possible. *See also* quasi-experiment.

matrix question Series of two or more closed questions in which each respondent's answers are recorded using the same grid.

maximum variation sampling *see* heterogeneous sampling.

mean The average value calculated by adding up the values of each case for a variable and dividing by the total number of cases.

measurement validity The extent to which a scale or measuring instrument measures what it is intended to measure. *See also* internal validity.

median The middle value when all the values of a variable are arranged in rank order; sometimes known as the 50th percentile.

mediating variable A variable that transmits the effect of an independent variable to a dependent variable. *See also* dependent variable, independent variable.

method The techniques and procedures used to obtain and analyse research data, including for example questionnaires, observation, interviews, and statistical and non-statistical techniques.

methodology The theory of how research should be undertaken, including the theoretical and philosophical assumptions upon which research is based and the implications of these for the method or methods adopted.

minimal interaction Process in which the observer tries as much as possible to 'melt into the background', having as little interaction as possible with the subjects of the observation. This is an attempt to overcome observer effect. *See also* observer effect.

mixed-methods research Use of both quantitative and qualitative data collection techniques and analysis procedures either at the same time (concurrent) or one after the other (sequential).

mixed-model research Combination of quantitative and qualitative data collection techniques and analysis procedures as well as combining quantitative and qualitative approaches in other phases of the research such as research question generation.

mode The value of a variable that occurs most frequently.

modal group The most frequently occurring category for data that have been grouped.

Mode 1 knowledge creation Research of a fundamental rather than applied nature, in which the questions are set and solved by academic interests with little, if any, focus on exploitation of research by practitioners.

Mode 2 knowledge creation Research of an applied nature, governed by the world of practice and highlighting the importance of collaboration both with and between practitioners.

Mode 3 knowledge creation Research growing out of Mode 1 and Mode 2 whose purpose is 'to assure survival and promote the common good at various levels of social aggregation' (Huff and Huff 2001:S53).

moderating variable A variable that affects the relationship between an independent variable and a dependent variable. *See also* dependent variable, independent variable.

moderator Facilitator of focus group interviews. *See also* focus group, group interview.

mono method Use of a single data collection technique and corresponding analysis procedure or procedures.

moving average Statistical method of smoothing out variations in numerical data recorded for a single variable over time to enable the long-term trend to be seen more clearly. *See also* long-term trend.

multicollinearity *see* collinearity.

multi-method Use of more than one data collection technique and corresponding analysis procedure or procedures.

multi-method qualitative study Use of more than one qualitative data collection technique and corresponding qualitative analysis procedure or procedures.

multi-method quantitative study Use of more than one quantitative data collection technique and corresponding quantitative analysis procedure or procedures.

multi-phase research design Research involving more than two phases of data collection and analysis. *See also* sequential mixed methods research.

multiple bar chart Diagram for comparing frequency distributions for categorical or grouped discrete or continuous data variables, which highlights the highest and lowest values.

multiple-dichotomy method Method of data coding using a separate variable for each possible response to an open question or an item in a list question. *See also* list question, open question.

multiple line graph Diagram for comparing trends over time between numerical data variables.

multiple methods Use of more than one data collection technique and analysis procedure or procedures. *See also* mixed methods.

multiple regression analysis The process of calculating a coefficient of multiple determination and regression equation using two or more independent variables and one dependent variable. For data collected from a sample, there is also a need to calculate the probability of the regression coefficient having occurred by chance alone. *See also* multiple regression coefficient, regression analysis, regression equation.

multiple regression coefficient Number between 0 and +1 that enables the strength of the relationship between a numerical dependent variable and two or more numerical independent variables to be assessed. The coefficient represents the proportion of the variation in the dependent variable that can be explained statistically by the independent variables. A value of 1 means that all the variation in the dependent variable can be explained statistically by the independent variables. A value of 0 means that none of the variation in the dependent variable can be explained by the independent variables. *See also* multiple regression analysis.

multiple-response method Method of data coding using the same number of variables as the maximum number of different responses to an open question or a list question by any one case. *See also* list question, open question.

multiple-source secondary data Secondary data created by combining two or more different data sets prior to the data being accessed for the research. These data sets can be based entirely on documentary or on survey data, or can be an amalgam of the two.

multi-stage sampling Probability sampling procedure that is a development of cluster sampling. It involves taking a series of cluster samples, each of which uses random sampling (systematic, stratified or simple).

N

narrative A personal account that interprets an event or series of events, which is significant for the narrator and which convey meaning to the researcher, and which are narrated in a sequenced way. *See also* narrative inquiry.

narrative analysis The collection and analysis of qualitative data that preserves the integrity and narrative value of data collected, thereby avoiding their fragmentation.

narrative inquiry Qualitative research strategy to collect the experiences of participants as whole accounts or narratives, or which attempts to reconstruct such experiences into narratives. *See also* narrative.

naturalistic Adopting an ethnographic strategy in which the researcher researches the phenomenon within the context in which it occurs.

negative cases Cases that do not support emergent explanations, but which help the refining of these explanations and direct the selection of further cases to collect data.

negative correlation Relationship between two variables for which, as the values of one variable increase, the values of the other variable decrease. *See also* correlation coefficient.

negative skew Distribution of numerical data for a variable in which the majority of the data are found bunched to the right, with a long tail to the left.

netiquette General operating guidelines for using the Internet, including not sending junk emails.

new contacts People approached to become research informants, participants or respondents previously unknown to the researcher.

nominal data *see* descriptive data.

non-maleficence Avoidance of harm.

non-parametric statistic Statistic designed to be used when data are not normally distributed. Often used with categorical data. *See also* categorical data.

non-probability sampling Selection of sampling techniques in which the chance or probability of each case being selected is not known.

non-random sampling *See* non-probability sampling.

non-response When the respondent refuses to take part in the research or answer a question.

non-response bias Bias in findings caused by respondent refusing to take part in the research or answer a question.

non-standardised interview *See* semi-structured interview, unstructured interview.

normal distribution Special form of the symmetric distribution in which the numerical data for a variable can be plotted as a bell-shaped curve.

notebook of ideas Technique for noting down any interesting research ideas as you think of them.

null hypothesis Testable proposition stating that there is no significant difference or relationship between two or more variables. Often referred to as H_0. *See also* alternative hypothesis, hypothesis.

numerical data Data whose values can be measured numerically as quantities.

numeric rating question Rating question that uses numbers as response options to identify and record the respondent's response. The end response options, and sometimes the middle, are labelled.

O

objectivism An ontological position that asserts that social entities exist in a reality external to, and independent of, social actors concerned with their existence. *See also* ontology, subjectivism.

objectivity Avoidance of (conscious) bias and subjective selection during the conduct and reporting of research. In some research philosophies the researcher will consider that interpretation is likely to be related to a set of values and therefore will attempt to recognise and explore this.

observation The systematic observation, recording, description, analysis and interpretation of people's behaviour. *See also* participant observation, structured observation.

observer as participant Observational role in which the researcher observes activities without taking part in those activities in the same way as the 'real' research subjects. The researcher's identity as a researcher and research purpose is clear to all concerned. *See also* participant as observer.

observer bias This may occur when observers give inaccurate responses in order to distort the results of the research.

observer effect The impact of being observed on how people act. *See also* habituation, reactivity.

observer error Systematic errors made by observers, as a result of tiredness, for example.

one stage cluster sampling *see* cluster sampling.

one-way analysis of variance *see* analysis of variance.

online form (questionnaire) *See* online questionnaire.

online questionnaire Data collection technique in which the questionnaire is delivered via the Internet or an intranet to each respondent. She or he then reads and answers the same set of questions in a predetermined order without an interviewer being present before returning it electronically.

ontology Branch of philosophy that studies the nature of reality or being. *See also* axiology, epistemology.

open coding The process of disaggregating data into units in grounded theory.

open question Question allowing respondents to give answers in their own way.

operationalisation The translation of concepts into tangible indicators of their existence.

opinion variable Variable that records what respondents feel about something or what they think or believe is true or false.

optical mark reader Data input device that recognises and converts marks on a data collection form such as a questionnaire into data that can be stored on a computer.

ordinal data *see* ranked data.

P

paired *t*-test Statistical test to determine the probability (likelihood) that the values of two (a pair of) numerical data variables collected for the same cases are different. The test assesses the likelihood of any difference between two variables (each half of the pair) occurring by chance alone.

paradigm A way of examining social phenomena from which particular understandings of these phenomena can be gained and explanations attempted.

parametric statistic Statistic designed to be used when data are normally distributed. Used with numerical data. *See also* numerical data.

partially integrated mixed methods research Use of both quantitative and qualitative methods at only one stage or at particular stages of the research. *See also* fully integrated mixed methods research.

partial response The level of response to questionnaires or structured interviews in which 50% to 80% of all questions answered other than by a refusal or no answer.

participant The person who answers the questions, usually in an interview or group interview.

participant as observer Observational role in which the researcher takes part in and observes activities in the same way as the 'real' research subjects. The researcher's identity as a researcher and research purpose is clear to all concerned. *See also* observer as participant.

participation bias Type of bias resulting from the nature of the individuals or organisational participants who agree to take part in a research study.

participant information sheet Document providing information required by gatekeepers and intended participants in order for informed consent to be given.

participant observation Observation in which the researcher attempts to participate fully in the lives and activities of the research subjects and thus becomes a member of the subjects' group(s), organisation(s) or community. *See also* complete observer, complete participant, observer as participant, participant as observer.

participant researcher *see* internal researcher.

passive voice The voice in which the subject of the sentence undergoes the action of the verb: for example, 'interviews were conducted'.

pattern matching Analysis of qualitative data involving the prediction of a pattern of outcomes based on theoretical propositions to seek to explain a set of findings.

Pearson's product moment correlation coefficient Statistical test that assesses the strength of the relationship between two numerical data variables. For data collected from a sample there is also a need to calculate the probability of the correlation coefficient having occurred by chance alone.

percentage component bar chart Diagram for comparing proportions for all types of data variables.

percentile One of 100 sections when data are ranked and divided into 100 groups of equal size.

personal data Category of data, defined in law, relating to identified or identifiable persons. *See also* sensitive personal data.

personal entry Situation where the researcher needs to conduct research within an organisation, rather than rely on the use and completion of self-administered, postal questionnaires or the use of publicly available secondary data. *See* access.

personal pronoun One of the pronouns used to refer to people: I, me, you, he, she, we, us, they, him, her, them.

phenomenology Research philosophy that sees social phenomena as socially constructed, and is particularly concerned with generating meanings and gaining insights into those phenomena.

phi Statistic to measure association between two variables using a scale between −1 (perfect negative association), through 0 (no association) to +1 (perfect association).

physical access The initial level of gaining access to an organisation to conduct research. *See also* cognitive access, continuing access, gatekeeper.

pictogram Diagram in which a picture or series of pictures are used to represent the data proportionally.

pie chart Diagram frequently used for showing proportions for a categorical data or a grouped continuous or discrete data variable.

pilot test Small-scale study to test a questionnaire, interview checklist or observation schedule, to minimise the likelihood of respondents having problems in answering the questions and of data recording problems as well as to allow some assessment of the questions' validity and the reliability of the data that will be collected.

plagiarism Presenting work or ideas as if they are your own when in reality they are the work or ideas of someone else, and failing to acknowledge the original source.

population The complete set of cases or group members.

positive correlation Relationship between two variables for which, as the value of one variable increases, the values of the other variable also increase. *See also* correlation coefficient.

positive skew Distribution of numerical data for a variable in which the majority of the data are found bunched to the left, with a long tail to the right.

positivism The epistemological position that advocates working with an observable social reality. The emphasis is on highly structured methodology to facilitate replication, and the end product can be law-like generalisations similar to those produced by the physical and natural scientists.

postal questionnaire Data collection technique in which the questionnaire is delivered by post to each respondent. She or he then reads and answers the same set of questions in a predetermined order without an interviewer being present before returning it by post.

post-test Outcome measurement for the dependent variable in an experiment. *See also* pre-test.

PowerPoint™ Microsoft computer package that allows the presenter to design overhead slides using text, pictures, photographs etc., which lend a professional appearance.

practitioner-researcher Role occupied by a researcher when she or he is conducting research in an organisation, often her or his own, while fulfilling her or his normal working role.

pragmatism A position that argues that the most important determinant of the research philosophy adopted is the research question, arguing that it is possible to work within both positivist and interpretivist positions. It applies a practical approach, integrating different perspectives to help collect and interpret data. *See also* interpretivism, positivism.

pre-coding The process of incorporating coding schemes in questions prior to a questionnaire's administration.

predictive validity *see* criterion-related validity.

preliminary inquiry The process by which a research idea is refined in order to turn it into a research project. This may be simply a review of the relevant literature

preliminary search This way of searching the literature may be a useful way of generating research ideas. It may be based, for example, on lecture notes or course textbooks.

pre-set codes Codes established prior to data collection and often included as part of the data collection form.

pre-survey contact Contact made with a respondent to advise them of a forthcoming survey in which she or he will be asked to take part.

pre-test Baseline measurement for the dependent variable in an experiment. *See also* post-test.

primary data Data collected specifically for the research project being undertaken.

primary literature The first occurrence of a piece of work, including published sources such as government white papers and planning documents and unpublished manuscript sources such as letters, memos and committee minutes.

primary observation Observation where the researcher notes what happened or what was said at the time. This is often done by keeping a research diary.

privacy Primary ethical concern relating to the rights of individuals not to participate in research and to their treatment where they agree to participate. *See also* research ethics, informed consent.

probability sampling Selection of sampling techniques in which the chance, or probability, of each case being selected from the population is known and is not zero.

probing questions Questions used to explore further responses that are of significance to the research topic.

professional journal Journal produced by a professional organisation for its members, often containing articles of a practical nature related to professional needs. Articles in professional journals are usually not refereed.

project report The term used in this book to refer generally to dissertations, theses and management reports. *See also* dissertation, management report, thesis.

pure research *see* basic research.

purposive sampling Non-probability sampling procedure in which the judgement of the researcher is used to select the cases that make up the sample. This can be done on the basis of extreme cases, heterogeneity (maximum variation), homogeneity (maximum similarity), critical cases, theoretical cases or typical cases.

Q

qualitative data Non-numerical data or data that have not been quantified.

qualitative interview Collective term for semi-structured and unstructured interviews aimed at generating qualitative data.

qualitise Conversion of quantitative data into narrative that can be analysed qualitatively.

quantifiable data *see* numerical data.

quantitative data Numerical data or data that have been quantified.

quantitise Conversion of qualitative data into numerical codes that can be analysed statistically.

quantity question Closed question in which the respondent's answer is recorded as a number giving the amount.

quartile one of four sections when data are ranked and divided into four groups of equal size. *See also* lower quartile, upper quartile.

quasi-experiment Experimental design using an experimental group and a control group but where experimental participants cannot be assigned randomly to each group. *See also* matched pair analysis.

questionnaire General term including all data collection techniques in which each person is asked to respond to the same set of questions in a predetermined order. *See also* delivery and collection questionnaire, interviewer-administered questionnaire, online questionnaire, postal questionnaire, self-administered questionnaire.

quota sampling Non-probability sampling procedure that ensures that the sample represents certain characteristics of the population chosen by the researcher.

R

radical change A perspective which relates to a judgement about the way organisational affairs should be conducted and suggests ways in which these affairs may be conducted in order to make fundamental changes to the normal order of things.

radical humanist paradigm A position concerned with changing the status quo, of existing social patterns.

radical structuralist paradigm A position concerned with achieving fundamental change based upon an analysis of underlying structures that cannot be easily observed, for example organisational phenomena as power relationships and patterns of conflict.

random sampling *see* simple random sampling.

range The difference between the highest and the lowest values for a variable.

ranked data Data whose values cannot be measured numerically but which can be placed in a definite order (rank).

ranking question Closed question in which the respondent is offered a list of items and instructed to place them in rank order.

rating question Closed question in which a scaling device is used to record the respondent's response. *See also* Likert-type rating question, numeric rating question, semantic differential rating question.

ratio data Numerical data for which both the difference or 'interval' and relative difference between any two data values for a particular variable can be stated. *See also* numerical data.

rational thinking technique One of a number of techniques for generating and refining research ideas based on a systematic approach such as searching the literature or examining past projects.

raw data Data for which little, if any, data processing has taken place.

reactivity Reaction by research participants to any research intervention that affects data reliability. *See also* habituation, observer effect.

realism The epistemological position that objects exist independently of our knowledge of their existence. *See also* critical realism, direct realism.

realist ethnography Ethnographic strategy stressing objectivity, factual reporting and identifying 'true' meanings. *See also* ethnography, critical ethnography, interpretive ethnography.

re-coding The process of grouping or combining a variable's codes to form a new variable, usually with less detailed categories.

reductionism The idea that problems as a whole are better understood if they are reduced to the simplest possible elements.

refereed academic journal Journal in which the articles have been evaluated by academic peers prior to publication to assess their quality and suitability. Not all academic journals are refereed.

references, list of Bibliographic details of all items referred to directly in the text. The university will specify the format required.

reflective diary Diary in which the researcher notes down what has happened and lessons learnt during the research process. *See also* research notebook.

reflexivity Self examination and evaluation of your attitudes and beliefs, reactions to data and findings, and interactions with those who take part in the research to overcome barriers to interpretation and gain greater insights.

regression analysis The process of calculating a regression coefficient and regression equation using one independent variable and one dependent variable. For data collected from a sample, there is also a need to calculate the probability of the regression coefficient having occurred by chance alone. *See also* multiple regression analysis, regression coefficient, regression equation.

regression coefficient Number between 0 and +1 that enables the strength of the relationship between anumerical dependent variable and a numerical independent variable to be assessed. The coefficient represents the proportion of the variation in the dependent variable that can be explained statistically by the independent variable. A value of 1 means that all the variation in the dependent variable can be explained statistically by the independent variable. A value of 0 means that none of the variation in the dependent variable can be explained by the independent variable. *See also* regression analysis.

regression equation Equation used to predict the values of a dependent variable given the values of one or more independent variables. The associated regression coefficient provides an indication of how good a predictor the regression equation is likely to be. *See* regression coefficient.

regulatory perspective A perspective that seeks to explain the way in which organisational affairs are regulated and offer suggestions as to how they may be improved within the framework of the way things are done at present.

relevance tree Technique for generating research topics that starts with a broad concept from which further (usually more specific) topics are generated. Each of these topics forms a separate branch, from which further sub-branches that are more detailed can be generated.

reliability The extent to which data collection technique or techniques will yield consistent findings, similar observations would be made or conclusions reached by other researchers or there is transparency in how sense was made from the raw data.

repeated measures *see* within-subjects design.

representative sample Sample that represents exactly the population from which it is drawn.

representative sampling *see* probability sampling.

research The systematic collection and interpretation of information with a clear purpose, to find things out. *See also* applied research, basic research.

research approach General term for inductive, deductive or abductive research approach. *See also* abductive approach, deductive approach, inductive approach.

research design Framework for the collection and analysis of data to answer research question and meet research objectives providing reasoned justification for choice of data sources, collection methods and analysis techniques.

research ethics The standards of the researcher's behaviour in relation to the rights of those who become the subject of a research project, or who are affected by it. *See also* code of ethics, privacy, research ethics committee.

research ethics committee Learned committee established to produce a code of research ethics, examine and approve or veto research proposals and advise in relation to the ethical dilemmas facing researchers during the conduct and reporting of research projects. *See also* code of ethics.

research idea Initial idea that may be worked up into a research project.

research interview Purposeful conversation between two or more people requiring the interviewer to establish rapport, to ask concise and unambiguous questions and to listen attentively.

research notebook Notebook in which the researcher records chronologically aspects of their research project such as useful articles they have read, notes of discussions with their project supervisor etc. and their emergent thoughts about all aspects of their research. Can be used as an analytical aid. Can incorporate a reflective diary. *See also* reflective diary; self memo.

research objectives Clear, specific statements that identify what the researcher wishes to accomplish as a result of doing the research.

research philosophy Overarching term relating to the development of knowledge and the nature of that knowledge in relation to research.

research population Set of cases or group members that you are researching.

research proposal Structured plan of a research project, occasionally referred to as a protocol or outline.

research question The key question that the research process will address, or one of the key questions that it will address. The research question is generally the precursor of research objectives.

research strategy General plan of how the researcher will go about answering the research question(s).

respondent The person who answers the questions usually on a questionnaire. *See also* participant.

response bias *see* interviewee bias.

response rate The total number of responses divided by the total number in the sample after ineligible respondents have been excluded. *See* ineligible respondent. *See also* active response rate, break off, complete refusal, complete response, partial response.

review article Article, normally published in a refereed academic journal, that contains both a considered review of the state of knowledge in a given topic area and pointers towards areas where further research needs to be undertaken. *See also* refereed academic journal.

review question Specific question you ask of the material you are reading, which is linked either directly or indirectly to your research question. *See also* research question.

S

sample Sub-group or part of a larger population.

sampling fraction The proportion of the total population selected for a probability sample.

sampling frame The complete list of all the cases in the population, from which a probability sample is drawn.

saturation *see* data saturation.

scale Measure of a concept, such as customer loyalty or organisational commitment, created by combining scores to a number of rating questions.

scale item Rating question used in combination with other rating questions to create a scale. *See* rating question, scale.

scale question *see* rating question.

scatter graph Diagram for showing the relationship between two numerical or ranked data variables.

scatter plot *see* scatter graph.

scientific research Research that involves the systematic observation of and experiment with phenomena.

scoping study Preliminary exploratory study undertaken as part of Systematic Review to establish whether Systematic Reviews have already been published and determine the focus of the literature search. *See also:* Systematic Review.

search engine Automated software that searches an index of documents on the Internet using key words and Boolean logic.

search string Combination of key words or search terms used in searching online databases.

search term Basic terms that describes your research question(s) and objectives, and is be used to search the tertiary literature.

secondary data Data that were originally collected for some other purpose. They can be can be further analysed to provide additional or different knowledge, interpretations or conclusions. *See also* documentary secondary data, multiple source secondary data, survey-based secondary data.

secondary literature Subsequent publication of primary literature such as books and journals.

secondary observation Statement made by an observer of what happened or was said. By necessity this involves that observer's interpretations.

selective coding The process of integrating categories to produce theory in grounded theory.

self-coded question Question each respondent codes her or himself as part of the process of recording their answer.

self-completed questionnaire Data collection technique in which each respondent reads and answers the same set of questions in a predetermined order without an interviewer being present.

self memo Way of recording own ideas about research as they occur, which may then be used as an analytical aid. *See also* research notebook.

self-selection sampling Non-probability sampling procedure in which the case, usually an individual, is allowed to identify their desire to be part of the sample.

semantic differential rating question Rating question that allows the respondent to indicate his or her attitude to a concept defined by opposite adjectives or phrases.

semi-structured interview Wide-ranging category of interview in which the interviewer commences with a set of interview themes but is prepared to vary the order in which questions are asked and to ask new questions in the context of the research situation.

sensitive personal data Category of data, defined in law, that refers to certain specified characteristics or beliefs relating to identified or identifiable persons.

sensitivity Level of concern on the part of a potential host organisation, informant, participant or respondent about the nature of a research project and use of data that will affect willingness to cooperate.

sequential explanatory design Mixed methods research design where initial phase of quantitative data collection is followed by second phase of explanatory qualitative data collection. *See also* sequential mixed methods research.

sequential exploratory design Mixed methods research design where initial phase of exploratory qualitative data collection is followed by second phase of quantitative data collection. *See also* sequential mixed methods research.

sequential mixed methods research Research using both quantitative and qualitative methods that are conducted in more than one phase of data collection and analysis. *See also* double-phase research design, multi-phase research design, sequential explanatory design, sequential exploratory design.

sequential multi-phase design Mixed methods research design involving multiple phases of data collection and analysis.

serial correlation *see* autocorrelation.

shadowing Process that the researcher would follow in order to gain a better understanding of the research context. This might involve following employees who are likely to be important in the research.

Shapiro-Wilk test Statistical test to determine the probability (likelihood) that an observed set of values for each category of a variable differs from a specified distribution.

significance testing Testing the probability of a pattern such as a relationship between two variables occurring by chance alone if the null hypothesis were true.

simple random sampling Probability sampling procedure that ensures each case in the population has an equal chance of being included in the sample.

single-phase research design Research involving one phase of data collection and analysis. *See also* concurrent mixed methods research. *See also* concurrent mixed methods research.

snowball sampling Non-probability sampling procedure in which subsequent respondents are obtained from information provided by initial respondents.

social constructionism Research philosophy that views the social world as being socially constructed.

social norm The type of behaviour that a person ought to adopt in a particular situation.

socially desirable response Answer given by a respondent due to her or his desire, either conscious or unconscious, to gain prestige or appear in a different social role.

source questionnaire The questionnaire that is to be translated from another language when translating a questionnaire.

Spearman's rank correlation coefficient Statistical test that assesses the strength of the relationship between two ranked data variables. For data collected from a sample, there is also a need to calculate the probability of the correlation coefficient having occurred by chance alone.

split infinitive Phrase consisting of an infinitive with an adverb inserted between 'to' and the verb: for example, 'to readily agree'.

stacked bar chart Diagram for comparing totals and subtotals for all types of data variable.

standard deviation Statistic that describes the extent of spread of data values around the mean for a variable containing numerical data.

statistical inference The process of coming to conclusions about the population on the basis of data describing a sample drawn from that population.

statistical significance The likelihood of the pattern that is observed (or one more extreme) occurring by chance alone, if there really was no difference in the population from that which the sample was drawn.

storyline The way in which the reader is led through the research project to the main conclusion or the answer to the research question. The storyline is, in effect, a clear theme that runs through the whole of the project report to convey a coherent and consistent message.

stratified random sampling Probability sampling procedure in which the population is divided into two or more relevant strata and a random sample (systematic or simple) is drawn from each of the strata.

structured interview Data collection technique in which an interviewer physically meets the respondent, reads them the same set of questions in a predetermined order, and records his or her response to each.

structured methodology Data collection methods that are easily replicated (such as the use of an observation schedule or questionnaire) to ensure high reliability.

structured observation Observation method using a high level of predetermined structure, often used to quantify observed behaviours. *See also* participant observation.

subject directory Hierarchically organised index categorised into broad topics, which, as it has been compiled by people, is likely to have its content partly censored and evaluated.

subject or participant bias Bias that may occur when research subjects are giving inaccurate responses in order to distort the results of the research.

subjectivism An ontological position that asserts that entities are created from the perceptions and consequent actions of those social actors responsible for their creation. *See also* ontology, objectivism.

sufficiency [of access] Being able to negotiate adequate access to conduct research.

survey Research strategy that involves the structured collection of data from a sizeable population. Although the term 'survey' is often used to describe the collection of data using questionnaires, it includes other techniques such as structured observation and structured interviews.

survey-based secondary data Data collected by surveys, such as by questionnaire, which have already been analysed for their original purpose.

symbolic interactionism Social process through which the individual derives a sense of identity from interaction and communication with others. Through this process of interaction and communication the individual responds to others and adjusts his or her understandings and behaviour as a shared sense of order and reality is 'negotiated' with others.

symmetric distribution Description of the distribution of data for a variable in which the data are distributed equally either side of the highest frequency.

symmetry of potential outcomes Situation in which the results of the research will be of similar value whatever they are.

synchronous Undertaken in real time, occurring at the same time.

synthesis Process of arranging and assembling various elements so as to make a new statement, or conclusion.

systematic random sampling Probability sampling procedure in which the initial sampling point is selected at random, and then the cases are selected at regular intervals.

Systematic Review A process for reviewing the literature using a comprehensive pre-planned strategy to locate existing literature, evaluate the contribution, analyse and synthesise the findings and report the evidence to allow conclusions to be reached about what is known and, also, what is not known.

systematic sampling *see* systematic random sampling.

T

table Technique for summarising data from one or more variables so that specific values can be read. *See also* contingency table, frequency distribution.

tailored design method Approach to designing questionnaires specifying precisely how to construct and use them; previously referred to as the 'total design method'.

target questionnaire The translated questionnaire when translating from a source questionnaire.

teleological view View that the ends served by research justify the means. Consequently, the benefits of research findings are weighed against the costs of acting unethically.

telephone questionnaire Data collection technique in which an interviewer contacts the respondent and administers the questionnaire using a telephone. The interviewer reads the same set of questions to the respondent in a predetermined order and records his or her responses.

template analysis Analysis of qualitative data that involves creating and developing a hierarchical template of data codes or categories representing themes revealed in the data collected and the relationships between these.

tense The form taken by the verb to indicate the time of the action (i.e. past, present or future).

tertiary literature source Source designed to help locate primary and secondary literature, such as an index, abstract, encyclopaedia or bibliography.

theoretical replication Realisation or replication of predicted theoretical outcomes in selected case studies in a case study strategy. *See also* case study, literal replication.

theoretical sampling A purposive sampling method particularly associated with Grounded Theory which focuses on the needs of the emerging theory and the evolving story line, participants being chosen purposively to inform this.

theoretical saturation Procedure used in Grounded Theory Method and reached when data collection ceases to reveal new data that are relevant to a category, where categories have become well developed and understood and relationships between categories have been verified. *See also* Grounded Theory Method.

theory Formulation regarding the cause and effect relationships between two or more variables, which may or may not have been tested.

thesis The usual name for research project reports undertaken for Master of Philosophy (MPhil) and Doctor of Philosophy (PhD) degrees, written for an academic audience.

time error Error, usually associated with structured observations, where the time at which the observation is being conducted provides data that are untypical of the time period in which the event(s) being studied would normally occur.

time series Set of numerical data values recorded for a single variable over time usually at regular intervals. *See also* moving average.

total response rate The total number of responses divided by the total number in the sample after ineligible respondents have been excluded. *See* ineligible respondent. *See also* active response rate, break off, complete response, complete refusal, partial response.

trade journal Journal produced by a trade organisation for its members, often containing articles of a practical nature related to the trade's needs. Articles in trade journals are usually not refereed.

traditional access Use of face-to-face interactions, correspondence for postal questionnaires, 'phone conversations or visits to data archives to conduct research.

transcription The written record of what a participant (or respondent) said in response to a question, or what participants (or respondents) said to one another in conversation, in their own words.

transcript summary Type of summary produced following the transcription of an interview or observation and used as an analytical aid. *See also* document summary; interim summary.

triangulation The use of two or more independent sources of data or data-collection methods within one study in order to help ensure that the data are telling you what you think they are telling you.

***t*-test** *see* independent groups *t*-test, paired *t*-test.

Type I error Error made by wrongly coming to the decision that something is true when in reality it is not.

Type II error Error made by wrongly coming to the decision that something is not true when in reality it is.

type of access Way used to gaining access to conduct research. *See also* Internet-mediated access, intranet-mediated access, hybrid access, traditional access.

typical case sampling A purposive sampling method which focuses on selecting those cases on the basis that they are typical or illustrative. *See also* purposive sampling.

U

uninformed response Tendency for a respondent to deliberately guess where they have sufficient knowledge or experience to answer a question.

unitising data The process of attaching relevant 'bits' or 'chunks' of your data to the appropriate category or categories that you have devised.

unit of data A number of words, a line of a transcript, a sentence, a number of sentences, a complete paragraph, or some other chunk of textual data that fits the category.

unreachable respondent Respondent selected for a sample who cannot be located or who cannot be contacted.

unstructured interview Loosely structured and informally conducted interview that may commence with one or more themes to explore with participants but without a predetermined list of questions to work through. *See also* informant interview.

upper quartile The value above which a quarter of the data values lie when the data values for a variable have been ranked.

URL Uniform resource locator specifying where a known resource can be found.

V

validity (1) The extent to which data collection method or methods accurately measure what they were intended to measure. (2) The extent to which research findings are really about what they profess to be about. *See also* construct validity, criterion related validity, ecological validity, face validity, internal validity, measurement validity, predictive validity.

variable Individual element or attribute upon which data have been collected.

variance Statistic that measures the spread of data values; a measure of dispersion. The smaller the variance, the closer individual data values are to the mean. The value of the variance is the square of the standard deviation. *See also* dispersion measures, standard deviation.

variance inflation factor (VIF) Statistic used to measure collinearity *see* collinearity.

VIF *see* variance inflation factor.

virtual access The initial level of gaining access to online communities to conduct research. *See also* cognitive access, continuing access, gatekeeper.

visual aid Item such as an overhead projector slide, whiteboard, video recording or handout that is designed to enhance professional presentation and the learning of the audience.

W

web based questionnaire *see* Internet-mediated questionnaire

web log *see* blog.

weighting The process by which data values are adjusted to reflect differences in the proportion of the population that each case represents.

within-subjects design Experimental design using only a single group where every participant is exposed to the planned intervention or series of interventions. *See also* experiment, between-subjects design.

Index

Page numbers in bold refer to glossary entries

50th percentiles *see* medians

A

abduction 144, 145, 147–8, 149, 186, **665**
abstracts 601–3, **665**
  literature sources 98, 100, 102
  project report 601–3
  utility of articles, assessing using 106
academic journals 84, 86
acceptable knowledge 132–3
access 14, 17, 208–10, **665**
  difficult or costly for secondary data 320
  email 214–15
  ethics 237–41
  Internet-mediated, issues associated with gaining 214–16, 217
  levels of 210, **674**
  participant observers 347
  strategies to gain access 216–26
  sufficiency 212–13, **682**
  traditional, issues associated with gaining 210–14, 215–16
  types of 210, **683**
action research 173, 183–5, **665**
active response rates 268, **665**
active voice 617, **665**
actual sample size 269–70
ad hoc surveys 307, 313, **665**
adjusted minimum sample size 660
advertising 357–8, 573
aggregations 310, 320
alpha coefficient (Cronbach's alpha) 430, **665**
alternative form test for reliability 430–1
alternative hypotheses 174, 561, 579, **665**
ambiguity about causal direction 193
American Psychological Association (APA) style 111, 608, 656, 657
analysis 619, **665**
analysis of data *see* data
analysis of variance (ANOVA) 509, 519, 520, **665**
analysis stage, ethics 245–7
Analytic Induction 351, 574–5, **665**
annotating 74–5
anonymity 223, 231, 234, 241–2, 245, 248–9, 396, 406, 618, **665**
ANOVA (analysis of variance) 509, 519, 520, **665**
answerability 44
APA *see* American Psychological Association
appendices 609, **665**
application 619, **665**
applied research 12, **665**
appropriateness 30, 386–7, 388
archival research 173, 178–9, **665**
area-based data sets 314
assessment criteria 619–20
assessors' requirements, meeting 51–2
associated variables 514–17
asynchronous electronic interviews 405–6, **665**
attribute variables 425, 426, **665**
audio CDs and downloads, referencing Harvard style 654
audio-recordings
  interviews 396–8, 400
    group 402
  transcriptions 400, 550–2
authenticity criteria 194
author-date systems 644–56
authority, critique of 77
autocorrelation 529, **666**
availability sampling *see* convenience sampling
axial coding 186, 568, 571, **666**
axiology 137–9, 140, **666**

B

back-translation 442
background to research 53–4
bank lending 89
bar charts 488, 489, 490–1, 494, 496, **666**
  see also multiple bar charts; percentage component bar charts; stacked bar charts
base periods 527, **666**
basic research 12, **666**
behaviour
  researchers 393
  variables 425, 426, **684**
beneficence 230, **666**
benefits 232
between-subjects design 176, **666**
bias 127, 155
  interviews 381, 382–3, 389
  measurement bias 329
  non-response 267
  observer bias 352
  participant bias 192
  researcher bias 192
bibliographic details 110–11, **666**
bibliographies 110, **666**
  abbreviations 658
  referencing in 656, 657
Big Mac index 473
blogs 215, 233, 341, 350, **666**
  referencing Harvard style 651
bookmarking 105
books 85, 88
  referencing Harvard style 645–6
bookshops 101
Boolean logic 100, **666**
boundaryless careers 608
box plots 489, 495–7, 502, **666**
brands 253–5
brainstorming 36–7, 96, **666**
break-off 267, **666**
brochures, referencing Harvard style 651

brokers 215
 see also gatekeepers
browsing 101–2
bulletin boards 215, 233
 referencing Harvard style 652
business schools 6–7

C

capability 28, 30
CAPI (computer-aided personal interviewing) 422–3, 477, **687**
CAQDAS (computer aided qualitative data analysis software) 18, 546, 551–3, 555, 558, 563, 566, 573, 581–3, **666**
carbon footprints 535–40
careers 202–3
 boundaryless 608
case studies 173, 179–81, 260, **666**
cases 259–60, **666**
 choice, Grounded Theory 568–9
 data collection 478–82
  relationships between cases 502
  weighting cases 486–7
 negative 562, **676**
catalogues 316
categorical data 475, 476, 483–5, 489, 504, 509, **666**
categorising data 557–8, 560, **666**
category questions 434, **666**
CATI *see* computer-aided telephone interviewing
causal relationships 193, 523, **666**
causality 45, **666**
CD-ROMS, referencing Harvard style 651
censuses 258, 307, 310–12, 433, **666**
central limit theorem 265–6, **666**
central tendency measures 503–6, **666**
CEO (chief executive officers) 479
chapters in books, referencing Harvard style 646–7
chat rooms 233, 405, 406, **666**
check questions 431
checking data for errors 486
chi square tests 509, 514–17, **666**
chief executive officers (CEO) 479
children's brand choices 253–5
clarity 614–15
classic experiments 175–6, **667**
closed questions 392, 432, **667**
cluster sampling 261, 270–2, 278–80, **667**
clustering method 598
co-creation 63–6
codebooks 483–5, **667**
codes of ethics 228–9, 230, **667**
coding 185–6, 558, **667**
 axial 186, 568, 571, **666**
 data 443–4, 480–5
 focused 186, 568, 569–71, **671**
 initial 186, 568, 569, 571
 open 186, 568, 569, 570, **676**
 pre-coding 443, **678**
 question responses 443–4
 schedules 358–61
 selective 186, 568, 572, **681**
 Template Analysis 572–3
coefficient of determination *see* regression coefficient
coefficient of multiple determination *see* multiple regression coefficient
coefficient of variation 504, 507, **667**
cognitive access 211, 215, 216, 353, **667**
coherence 51, 159–61
cohort studies 314, **667**
collaborative innovation networks 412
collection of data *see* data
collinearity 524–5, **667**
comparative data 318
comparative proportional pie charts 489, 494, 501, **667**
comparing and contrasting 74
comparisons, constant *see* constant comparisons
compiled data 307, **667**
complementarity reason for using mixed methods design 169
complete observer roles 344–5, **667**
complete participant roles 344, 346, **667**
complete refusal 267, **667**
complete response 267, **667**
complex methodological choices 165
computer-aided personal interviewing (CAPI) 422–3, 477, **667**
computer aided qualitative data analysis software *see* CAQDAS
computer-aided telephone interviewing (CATI) 273, 422–3, 477, **667**
concept-driven data categories 558
conclusions 607–8, **667**
concurrent embedded design 168, **667**
concurrent mixed methods research 167, **667**
concurrent mixing methodological choices 165
conference papers, referencing Harvard style 653
concurrent triangulation design 167, **667**
conference proceedings 85, 90
confidence reason for using mixed methods design 169
confidentiality 223, 231, 234, 241–2, 245, 249, **667**
confounding variables 174–5, **667**
conjunctions 499–501
consent 237–8
 forms 239–40, **667**
 inferred 238, **672**
 informed *see* informed consent
 questionnaires 455
constant comparisons 186, 569, 571, **667**
construct validity 193, 430, **668**
construction industry statistics 431
consultancy reports 609, 613–14, **668**
contacts, personal 218–21, 378–9
content
 project reports 610–14
 validity 429, **684**
contextual data 318, 348, 395–6, 553, **668**
contingency tables 489, 498, **668**
continuing access 211, **668**
continuous and regular surveys 307, 310–13
continuous data 476, 479, 489, 504, 509, **668**
control groups 175, **668**
control variables 174–5, **668**
controlled index languages 100, **668**
controls to allow the testing of hypotheses **668**
convenience sampling 261, 282, 284, 291, **668**
convergence 93
co-production 63–6
correlation 521, **668**
correlation coefficients 509, 521–2, **668**
costs and benefits analysis 321, 329–31
costs, interviewing issues 398
course materials, referencing Harvard style 654–5
coverage 323, **668**
covering letters 446, 449, **668**
covert observation 343
covert research 243, **668**
Cramer's V 509, 515–16, 517, **668**
creative thinking technique 30–1, 34–7, **668**
credibility 194
 interviews and 385
 researchers 222, 225–6
criterion-related validity 429–30, **668**
critical case sampling 261, 282, 284, 288–9, 290, **668**

critical discourse analysis 577–8
critical ethnography 182, **668**
critical friends 600
critical incidence technique 390–1, **668**
critical incidents 391, **668**
critical realism 136–7, **668**
critical reviews of literature *see* literature: reviews
Cronbach's alpha 430, **668**
crop science 138–9
cross-cultural research 343
cross-posting 454, **669**
cross-sectional research 190, **669**
cross-tabulation 489, 498, **669**
culture
  differences, interviews 384–5
  organisational 132

D

data 46, **669**
  analysis 14, 18, 232, 234
    ethics 236, 245–7
    observation 351, 361
    qualitative *see* qualitative data
    quantitative *see* quantitative data
    questionnaires 422–3
    software 422–3, 473–4
  archive catalogues 316
  categorising data 557–8, 560, **666**
  checking for errors 486
  cleaning 550
  clouds 565
  coding 443–4, 480–5
  collection 14, 17–18
    email use during 242
    ethics and 236, 241–4
    interactive nature of data analysis and 562
    measurement bias 329
    observation 348–50, 358–61
    philosophies 140
    questionnaires 423–8
  confidentiality 231, 234
  display and analysis 564–6, 572, **665**
  harvesting 233
  management compliance 232, 235
  matrices 478–82, 564, **665**
  non-standardised 546
  primary *see* primary data
  processing 236, 247–9
  protection 247–9
  qualitative *see* qualitative data
  quality
    interviews and 380–4
    lack of control over 320
  quantitative *see* quantitative data
  reduction 564, **680**
  requirements table 425–8
  research proposals and 54–5
  sampling 551, **681**
  saturation 283, **681**
  secondary *see* secondary data
  storage 236, 247–9
  types 475–7, 478
  use 144
data-driven data categories 558
Data Protection Act 1998: 247–8
databases 98–100, 102
debriefing 243, **669**
deception 233, 238, 241, **669**
deciles 504, 506, **669**
deductive approach 48, **669**
  abductive approach and 144–5
  characteristics 145–6
  critical reviews 73–4
  inductive approach and 144–5, 146–7, 148–9, 153, 155
  premises 143–4
  qualitative analysis 548–9, 578–81
  sequential steps 145
definitions, secondary data and 320, 321
degrees of freedom 510
deliberate distortion 329, **669**
delivery and collection questionnaires 419–20, 421, 457, **669**
Delphi technique 37, 38, **669**
deontological view 227, **669**
dependability 194
dependent variables (DV) 174–6, 424, 502, 579, **669**
descriptive data 475, 476, 479, 489, 504, 509, **669**
descriptive observation 348, **669**
descriptive research 171, 172, 377, 419, **669**
descriptive statistics 502–8, **669**
descripto-explanatory studies 171, **669**
design
  questionnaires 428–52
  research *see* research design
determination, coefficient of *see* regression coefficient
deviant sampling *see* extreme case sampling
diagrams 46, 487, 488, 612
  online, referencing Harvard style 652–3
  see also bar charts; box plots; histograms; line graphs; pictograms; pie charts; scatter graphs/plots
diaries
  electronic 217
  reflective 13–15, 555–6, **669**
  video 349–50
dichotomous data 475, 476, **669**
dictionaries 92–3
  referencing Harvard style 647
differences
  cultural, interviews 384–5
  qualitative and quantitative data, between 546–7
  testing for 509, 512–20
difficult interviewees 394, 395
digital object identifiers (DOI) 644, **669**
direct realism 136–7, **669**
direct translation 442
disability guidelines 663–4
discourse analysis 577–8, **669**
discoveries, unforeseen 318
discrete data 476–7, 479, 489, 504, 509, **669**
discriminatory language 618
discursive practice 578
discussion groups, Internet 214
discussion lists, referencing Harvard style 652
discussions 32, 92, 605–6, **669**
dispersion measures 504, 506–8, **670**
dissertations 32, **670**
distortion, deliberate 329, **670**
distribution of values 495–8, 501–2
distribution systems 535–40
divergence 93
diversity reason for using mixed methods design 169
document summaries 554, **670**
documentary secondary data 307, 308–9, **670**
DOI (digital object identifiers) 644, **670**
dominant chief executive officers 479
double phase methodological choices 165
double-phase research design 167
Dow Jones Industrial Average 528
drafts of reports 618–19
Durbin–Watson statistic 529, **670**
DV *see* dependent variables
DVDs, referencing Harvard style 654
dynamic capabilities 404

E

ecological validity 352, **670**
EDA (exploratory data analysis) 487, **670**
effect size index 513, **670**
electronic data gathering 305
electronic diaries 217

electronic interviews *see* interviews
electronic questionnaires 419–20, 446, 454–5, **670**
electronic textual data 553
elements 258, 259, **670**
emails
  access 214–15
  data collection, use during 242
  delivery of questionnaires 454–5
  interviews 214, 405, 407–8, **670**
  lists 215, 233
  referencing Harvard style 652
  requesting access 221–2
embedded mixed methods research 168, **670**
emotional labour 204–5, 337–8, 589–91
encyclopaedias 92–3
environmental impacts of business activities 535–40
environmentally friendly office spaces 587–9
epistemology 132–4, 140, **670**
errors
  checking for 486
  grammatical 616, 617, **671**
  informants 361–2
  observers 352
  participants 192
  researchers 192
  time 362, **683**
  Type I 513–14
  Type II 513–14
ethical clearance 52
ethics 14, 17, 208–10, **670**
  access gaining stage 237–41
  analysis stage 236, 245–7
  checklist 246–7
  codes of 228–90, 230, **667**
  complete participant roles and 344
  data collection stage 236, 241–4
  defining research ethics 226–30
  general categories of 230–5
  Internet issues 232–5
  participant observation 344, 348
  principles for recognition and overcoming or minimising 230–5
  reporting stage 245–7
  research design 191, 237–41
  at specific stages of research process 236–47
ethnicity guidelines 662–3
ethnography 130, 155, 173, 181–2, 341, **670**
European Union (EU)
  data protection 247
evaluation 619, **670**
  literature 107–8
  secondary data sources 321–31
evidence 22–3
  see also literature: reviews
existing contacts 219–20, **670**
experiential data 348, **670**
experiential meanings 442, **670**
experimental group 175, **670**
experiments 173, 174–6, 214, **670**
expert systems **670**
explanation building 580–1, **670**
explanatory research 172, 377, 419, 580, **670**
exploratory data analysis (EDA) 487, **670**
exploratory studies 171, 172, 377, 419, 580, **670**
extended text 565
extension questions 393
external researchers 195–6, 213–14, **671**
external validity 176, 194, **671**
  see also generalisability
extreme case sampling 261, 282, 284, 287, **671**

F

F-tests 525, 527
face-to-face interviews 375
face validity 429–30, 451, **671**
facilitation reason for using mixed methods design 169
facilitators 403
false assumptions 194–5
familiarity 217
farm shops 535–6, 538–9
fast food retailers 356–7
feasibility 52, 212–13, **671**
feelings, researchers 134
films, referencing Harvard style 653–4
filter questions 444, **671**
findings, reporting *see* project reports
flash-mobs 412–13
focus groups 375, 400–2, 403, **671**
focus reason for using mixed methods design 169
focused coding 186, 568, 569–71, **671**
focused interviews 374, 375, **671**
focused observations 349, **671**
follow-ups 392, 454, 457, **671**
food
  crop science 138–9
  farm shops 535–6, 538–9
  fast food retailers 356–7
food miles 535–40
footnotes (Vancouver) system 111, 608, 656–7
forced-choice questions *see* closed questions
forecasting 527–9
forums *see* Internet: forums
freedom, degrees of 510
Freedom of Information Act 2005 318
frequency distributions 488, 489, **671**
frequency polygons 489, 493
FTSE 100 index 527, 528
full text online databases **98**
full-text searches 100
fully integrated methodological choices 165
fully integrated mixed methods research 166–7, **671**
functionalist paradigm 141–2, 155, **671**
fundamental research *see* basic research

G

Gantt charts 56–9, **671**
gatekeepers 210–11, 317, **671**
  see also brokers
gender 617–18, 662
general focus research questions 43, **671**
general search engines 103, 104, 317
generalisability 144, 169, 194, 195, 262–5, 382, 383–4, **671**
  see also external validity
generalisations 144, 146, **671**
generic approaches to qualitative data analysis 556–66
goal setting 597
Goldilocks test 42, **671**
Google 93
government publications 90, 310, 312
  referencing Harvard style 648–9
government statistics 317, 319–20
government websites 316
graduate recruitment 263
grammar 442, 616–18
grammatical errors 616, 617, **671**
grand theories 49–50
graphics in project reports 612
graphs *see* line graphs; multiple line graphs; scatter graphs
green jobs 606
grey literature *see* primary literature
Grounded Theory 173, 185–7, 386, 556, 565, 567–72, 574, **671**
group interviews 14, 18, 375, 400–3, **672**

H

habituation 243, 353–4, **672**
handbooks 92–3

haphazard sampling 261, 284, 290–1, **672**
happiness 177–8
harm
  avoidance of 230, 231
  causing 233
Harvard system 111, 608, 644–56, 657
harvesting 233
heterogeneous sampling 261, 282, 284, 287–8, **672**
heteroscedasticity 524, **672**
highest and lowest values 488–93, 499
Hippocratic Oath 209
histograms 489, 490–2, **672**
home pages 103
homogeneous sampling 261, 282, 284, 288, **672**
homoscedasticity 524, **672**
hybrid access 210, 215, **672**
hyperlinks 215
hypotheses 46, 135, 145, 174, **672**
  alternative 174
  generation 580
  null 174
  testing 508, 513, 560–1, 571
    see also significance testing

I

Ibid. 658
ideas
  notebooks of 34, **676**
  see also research ideas
idiomatic meanings 442, **672**
immersive market research 547
implied consent 238
in-depth interviews *see* interviews
'in vivo' codes 557–8, 565, 569, **673**
incremental access 211, 225
independent groups t-tests 509, 517, 520, **672**
independent measures 176, **672**
independent variables (IV) 174–5, 424, 502, 579, **672**
index numbers 504, 507–8, 509, 525–7, **672**
indexes 98, 316
individual workplace performance 119–23
inductive approach 48, **672**
  abductive approach and 144–5
  critical reviews 74
  deductive approach and 144–5, 146–7, 148–9, 153, 155
  premises 143–4
  qualitative analysis 548, 549, 566–78
ineligible respondents 268, **672**
inference, statistical 266, **672**
informants 340, **672**
  error 361–2, **672**
  interviews 375, **672**
  verification 352–3, **672**
information
  gateways 104, 311–12, 317
  provision to interviewees 385–6
  public 379
  sources, students' use 438
informed consent 231, 234, 238, 241, **672**
initial coding 186, 568, 569, 571
initial samples 568, **672**
initiation reason for using mixed methods design 169
insider researchers 346–7
instant messaging 214, 215, 233, 406
instrumentation 193
integers 477, **672**
integration of ideas 38–40
integrity of researchers 231
interconnectivity 44
interests of researchers 31
interim summaries 553–4, **672**
inter-library loans 105, **672**
internal consistency 430
internal researchers 196, 214, 243, **673**
internal validity 176, 193, 428, 429, **673**
Internet 83
  access, issues associated with gaining 214–16, 217
  bibliographic details 110
  data collection, use during 242
  ethics 228, 229, 232–5
  forums 405, 406–7, **673**
  information gateways 104, 311–12, 317
  interviews 214, 375, 404, 405–8
  netiquette 235, 454, **676**
  questionnaires 214, 217, 419–20, 421, 446, 447, 454–5, **673**
  referencing Harvard style 651
  research ethics and 232–5, 242
  searching 103–5, 109–10
  secondary data 311–12, 317, 325
  see also entries beginning with online *and* web
interpretation questions 393
interpretation reason for using mixed methods design 169
interpretive ethnography 182, **673**
interpretive paradigm 141, 142–3, **673**
interpretivism 137, 140, 155, **673**
inter-quartile range 504, 506, **673**
interval data 475, 476, **673**
intervening variables 561
interviewee bias 381, 382–3, **673**
interviewer-administered questionnaires 420, **673**
interviewer bias 381, 382–3, **673**
interviews 372–4, **673**
  data quality issues 380–4
  electronic 375, 404, 405–8, **670**
  email *see* emails
  ethics 242
  focus groups *see* focus groups
  focused 374, 375, **671**
  group *see* group interviews
  guides 386
  in-depth 14, 18, 374, 375, 377
    checklists 387, 397
    conducting 388–98
    data quality issues 380–4
    management of 399
    occasions for use 378–80
    opening comments 389, 390
    preparation for 384–7
    questions 389–93
    researchers' appearance 388
    scheduling 399
  Internet *see* Internet
  journalism 373
  links to the purpose of research and research strategy 376–7
  logistical issues 398–400
  non-directive 374, 375
  non-standardised 375
  preparation for 384–7
  resource issues 398–400
  schedules *see* structured *below*
  semi-structured 14, 18, 374–5, 377, 413, **681**
    checklists 387, 397
    conducting 388–98
    data quality issues 380–4
    management of 399
    occasions for use 378–80
    opening comments 389, 390
    preparation for 384–7
    questions 389–93
    researchers' appearance 388
    scheduling 399
  structured 374, 375, 377, 420, 421, 458, **682**
  telephone 375, 404–5
  themes 385–6
  transcribing 550–2
  types of 374–5
  unstructured 374, **684**
    see also in-depth *above*
  word processing notes of 598
intranet-mediated access 210, **673**

intranet-mediated interviews 375, 404, 405–8
intranet-mediated questionnaires 419–20, 421, 446, 454–5, **673**
introductions 603, **673**
introductory chapters 603
introductory letters 222, **673**
intrusive research methods 212, **673**
investigative questions 425, 427–8, **673**
IV *see* independent variables

J

jargon 615
journals 84, 86, **673**
  articles, referencing Harvard style 649–50
journalism 373
judgemental sampling *see* purposive sampling

K

Kendall's rank correlation coefficient (Kendall's tau) 509, 521, **673**
key words 566, **673**
knowledge
  acceptable 132–3
  creation 8–9
  level of 384–5
Kolmogorov–Smirnov test 509, 510–11, 517, 518, **673**
kurtosis 495, **674**

L

labelling categories 558
language
  discourse analysis 577–8
  non-discriminatory 618, 662–4
  report writing 615
  suitability 224
  translating questions 442–3
law of large numbers 266, **674**
layout
  quantitative data 477–82
  questionnaires 444–6, 447–8
leading questions 393
lean supply chains 535–40
learning cycle 13
learning, organisational 153–5
letters
  covering 446, 449, **668**
  introductory 222, **673**
  referencing Harvard style 652
lexical meanings 442, **674**
libraries 105–7, 316–17
Likert-style rating scales 436, **674**
limited character blogs 215
line graphs 489, 493, 494, **674**
  see also multiple line graphs
linearity 524, **674**
link terms 100
linked web pages 215
list questions 433–4, **674**
listening skills 393
lists
  email 215, 233
  of names, addresses and email addresses 262–5
literal replication 180–1, **674**
literature
  abstracts as sources 98, 100, 102
  deductive approach impact on 580
  critical reviews *see* reviews *below*
  exploring relevance using 34–6
  grey *see* primary *below*
  primary 82–5, 89–90, **678**
  quotations from 616
  relevance exploring using 34–6
  relevance of 107–8
  reports as sources 85, 90
  reviews 14, 17, 70–3, **668**
    content 76–7
    evaluating literature 107–8
    literature search *see* searches *below*
    literature sources 82–90
    obtaining literature 105–7
    plagiarism 113–15
    project reports, positioning in 603–4
    purpose of 73–4
    reading, adopting critical perspective in 74–5
    recording literature 108–11
    research questions, chapters informing 604
    structure 77–82
    systematic reviews 112–13, 119–23
    writing 596
  scanning 101–2
  searches 32–3
    conducting 97–105
    planning 90–7
  secondary 82–9, **681**
  sources 82–90
    tertiary *see* tertiary literature sources
  sufficiency 108
  tertiary sources *see* tertiary literature sources
  value of 107–8
Loc. cit. 658
locations
  interviews 386–7, 401
  for writing 597
logic 144
logic leaps 194–5
logical reasoning 45, **674**
logical sequences 575
logistical issues of interviewing 398–400
London Olympics 5
long-term trends 529, **674**
longitudinal secondary data 307, 314, 327–8
longitudinal studies 190–1, 318, 404, **674**
lower quartile 506, **674**
lowest and highest values 488–93, 499
lurking 233

M

magazine articles, referencing Harvard style 650
mail questionnaires *see* postal questionnaires
management reports 609, 613–14, **674**
Mann–Whitney *U* tests 509, 520, **674**
market research 547
marketing 189
matched pair analysis 175, **674**
matrices
  data display 478–2, 564
  project report conclusions 607
matrix questions 440, **674**
maturation 193
mature markets 366–8
maximum variation sampling *see* heterogeneous sampling
means 504–6, **674**
measurability 44
measurement bias 329
measurement validity 322–3, 429, **674**
media
  releases, referencing Harvard style 651
  scanning 33–4
  trust of 376
medians 504, 505, **674**
mediating variables (MV) 174, 424, **674**
memos to self 554–5, **674**
metasearch engines 103–4
method 3–4, 54–5, 57, **674**
methodological choices 165
methodology 3–4, 604, 605, **674**
middle-range theories 49–50
mind maps 36, 394, 607
mindcam technique 350

minimal interaction 353, **674**
minimum sample size 265–7
missing data, coding 485
mistrust 233
mixed methods 165, **674**
mixed methods research 165–70, 217, **675**
mixed model research 165, **675**
mixed translation techniques 442
modal groups 504, **675**
Mode 1 knowledge creation 8, **675**
Mode 2 knowledge creation 8–9, **675**
Mode 3 knowledge creation 9, **675**
moderating variables 174, 424, **675**
moderators 403, 406, **675**
modes 503–4, 505, **675**
mono method 164–5, **675**
mortality (withdrawing from studies) 193
moving averages 509, 527–9, **675**
multicollinearity 524, **675**
multi-method qualitative studies 165, **675**
multi-method quantitative studies 165, **675**
multi-method research 165
multi-phase research design 167, **675**
multiple bar charts 489, 498, 499, **675**
multiple determination, coefficient of *see* multiple regression coefficient
multiple-dichotomy coding method 481, 482, **675**
multiple line graphs 489, 499–500, **675**
multiple methods 148–9, 164–70, 377, **675**
multiple phase methodological choices 165
multiple regression analysis 523, 526–7, **675**
multiple regression coefficient 509, 523, **675**
multiple reports for multiple audiences 612–13
multiple-response coding method 480–2, **675**
multiple-source secondary data 307, 313–14, 327–8, **675**
multi-stage sampling 261, 270–2, 279–80, **675**
MV (mediating variables) 174, 424, **674**

N

narrative accounts 348, **675**
Narrative Analysis 575–7, **676**
Narrative Inquiries 173, 187–90, 575, **676**
narratives 188, **675**
narrowing down, working up and 38–40
National Health Service (NHS) 229, 230
national income accounts 177–8
naturalism 181, **676**
negative cases 562, **676**
negative correlation 521, **676**
negative skew 495, **676**
netiquette 235, 454, **676**
netnography 341
networks 564–5
new contacts 220–2, **676**
newspapers 85, 88–9
  referencing Harvard style 650
NHS 229, 230
nominal data *see* descriptive data
non-directive interviews 374, 375
non-discriminatory language 618, 662–4
non-maleficence 230, 231, **676**
non-parametric statistics 508, **676**
non-probability sampling 261, 262, 271, 281–91, 298–9, 580, **676**
non-random sampling *see* non-probability sampling
non-refereed academic journals 84, 86
non-response 267–8, 485, **676**
non-response bias 267
non-standardised data 546
non-standardised interviews *see* interviews: semi-structured
non-text materials 307, 308–9
normal distribution 495, **676**
normality testing 509, 510–12
note making 108–10, 348, 394–8, 402
notebooks
  of ideas 34, **676**
  research 13–15, 555, **680**
null hypotheses 174, 513, **676**
numeric rating scales 438, **676**
numeric referencing systems 656–7
numerical data 475, 476, 482, 489, 504, 509, 517–20, **676**

O

objectivism 131, 141, **676**
objectivity **676**
  critique of 77
  researchers 231, 241
observation 14, 18, **676**
  ethics and 242–3
  participant 340–1, 342–55, **676**
  structured 340–1, 355–62, **682**
observer-as-participant roles 344, 345, 346, 353, **676**
observer bias 352, **676**
observer effect 353–4, **676**
observer error 352, **676**
office spaces 587–9
Olympic Games, London 5
one-stage cluster sampling *see* cluster sampling
one-to-many interviews 375
one-to-one interviews 375
one-way analysis of variance 520, **676**
online advertising 357–8
online catalogues 316
online communities 215, 406–7
online databases 98–100, 102
online diagrams, referencing Harvard style 652–3
online images, referencing Harvard style 652
online indexes 316
online news 376
online public access catalogues (OPAC) 98–9
online questionnaires 419–20, 421, 443–4, 446, 447, 454–5, 464–6, **676**
online shopping 297–9
online teaching materials, referencing Harvard style 654–5
online video diaries 341
ontology 130–1, 140, **676**
Op. cit. 658
OPAC (online public access catalogues) 98–9
open coding 186, 568, 569, 570, **676**
open questions 391, 432–3, **677**
opening comments, interviews 389, 390
operationalisation 44, 146, **677**
opinion variables 425, 426, **677**
optical mark readers 423, **677**
oral presentations *see* presentations
ordinal data *see* ranked data
organisation-provided topics 40
organisational access 347
organisational behaviour 33
organisational benefits 223–4, 232
organisational concerns 223
organisational culture 132
organisational documentation 304–6, 308, 385
organisational learning 153–5
outcomes, potential, symmetry of 29
outliers 495–7
outline structures 598
overall suitability 322–3
overt observation 343

P

paired t-tests 509, 518–19, **677**
paradigms, research 140–3, **677**
parallel translation 442
parameters of literature search 91
parametric statistics 508, **677**
partial response 267, **677**
partially integrated methodological choices 165
partially integrated mixed methods research 166–7, **677**
participant-as-observer roles 344, 345, 346, **677**
participant bias 192, **677**
participant error 192
participant information sheets 238, 239, **677**
participant observation 340–1, 342–55, **677**
participant researchers 214, 243, **677**
participants **677**
  difficult interviewees 394, 395
participation 184, 231
participation bias 381, **677**
passive analysis 233
passive voice 616–17, **677**
past events 193
past project titles 32
past tense 616–17
patterns
  matching 579-81, **677**
  recognising 565
Pearson's product moment correlation coefficient (PMCC) 509, 521–2, **677**
peer reviewed academic journals *see* refereed academic journals
percentage component bar charts 489, 499, **677**
percentiles 504, 506, **677**
permanence of data 318–19
personal contacts 218–21, 378–9
personal data 247–9, **677**
personal entry 212, **677**
personal pronouns 617, **677**
phenomenology 137, **677**
Phi 509, 516, 517, **677**
physical access 210–11, 216, **677**
pictograms 489, 492–3, **677**
pie charts 489, 494, 495, 496–7, **677**
  see also comparative proportional pie charts
pilot testing 451–2, **677**
plagiarism 113–15, **678**
planning
  literature searches 90–7
  project reports 620–3
  writing 598
PMCC (Pearson's product moment correlation coefficient) 509, 521–2, **677**
populations 259, 260, **678**
positive correlation 521, **678**
positive skew 495, **678**
positivism 134–5, 140, 154–5, **678**
Post-it notes 3
post-tests 175–6, **678**
postal questionnaires 419–20, 421, 447, 453, 456–7, **678**
poster presentations 18
potential outcomes, symmetry of 29, **678**
power, cross-cultural integration 343
PowerPoint 612–3, **678**
PR (public relations) 379
practitioner-researchers 196, 243, **678**
pragmatism 130, 140, **678**
precise suitability of secondary data 322, 323–9
pre-coding 443, **678**
preconceived ideas avoidance 52
prediction of values 509, 524–5
predictive validity 429–30, **678**
Preferred Reporting Items for Systematic Reviews and Meta Analyses (PRISMA) 113
preliminary inquiries 37–8, 39, **678**
preliminary searches 33, **678**
present tense 617
presentations 14
  oral 18, 620–4
  poster 18
  project reports 620–4, 627–30
pre-set codes 483, **678**
press agencies 379
press releases, referencing Harvard style 651
pre-survey contact 219–21, 454, **678**
pre-tests 175–6, **678**
previewing 74
  project report chapters 612
primary data 304, 306, **678**
  see also interviews; observation; questionnaires
primary literature 82–5, 89–90, **678**
primary observations 348, **678**
PRISMA (Preferred Reporting Items for Systematic Reviews and Meta Analyses) 113
privacy 231, 233, 247, 249, **678**
probabilities 512
probability sampling 261, 262, 282, **678**
  sample size 265–70
  sampling frame 262–5
  techniques 270–81
probing questions 392, **678**
problem solving reason for using mixed methods design 169
professional journals 84, 86, **678**
progress summaries 553–4
project reports 14, 18, 594–6, **678**
  abstracts 601–3
  appendices 609
  assessment criteria 619–20
  conclusions chapters 607–8
  content organisation 610–14
  discussions 605–6
  dividing the work 611–12
  ethics 236, 245–7
  of findings 232, 234
  findings chapters 604–5
  introductory chapters 603
  length 610
  literature reviews positioning 603–4
  methodology chapters 604, 605
  multiple reports for multiple audiences 612–13
  presentations 620–4, 627–30
  previewing chapters 612
  recommendations 609
  references 608–9
  structuring 600–10
  summarising chapters 612
  titles 610
  writing styles 614–19
prompt cards 435
proportions
  comparison of 489, 499, 501
  showing 489
proposing type questions 393
propositions
  development and verification 562
  testable 560–2, 579
  testing 580
public information 379
public relations (PR) 379
publishers' web pages 98, 101
pure research *see* basic research
purpose
  data presentation and 320
  literature reviews 73–4
  questionnaires, explaining 446–51
  research
    clear account of, providing 222
    disadvantages of secondary data 319–20
    interviews and 376–7, 378
    participant observer roles and 345–6
purposive sampling 261, 282, 284, 287–9, **678**

Q

qualitative data 544–6, **678**
analysis 14, 18
aids 553–6
CAQDAS use 581–3
deductively-based 548–9, 578–81
generic approaches 556–66
inductively-based 548, 549, 566–78
preparation of data for analysis 550–3
meaning 546–8
quantitative data and, differences between 546–7
quantitisation of 166, 563–4, **679**
reporting results 563
qualitative interviews 377, 400, 404, **679**
qualitative research
design 161, 163–4
Internet 214
quality
data *see* data
research design 191–5
quantifiable data *see* numerical data
quantitative data 472, **679**
analysis 14, 18, 472–5
checking for errors 486
coding 480–5
data layout 477–82
descriptive statistics 502–8
entering data 485–6
examining relationships, differences and trends using statistics 508–29
exploring and presenting data 487–502
inputting data 485–6
qualitisation of 166, **679**
preparing data 477–85
significance testing 508–29
weighting 486–7
qualitative data and, differences between 546–7
types of 162, 475–7, 478
quantitative research
design 161–3
Internet 214
quantity questions 440, **679**
quartiles 506, **679**
quasi-experiments 175, **679**
questionnaires 14, 18, 416–19, **679**
choice of 420–3
closing 451
consent 455
constructing 444–6
deciding on data to be collected 423–8
delivery and collection 452–8
design 428–52
ethics 245
Internet *see* Internet
introducing 446–50
layout 444–6, 447–8
occasions of use 419
overview 419–23
pilot testing 451–2
purpose, explaining 446–51
reliability 430–1
types of 419–20
validity 428–31, 451–2
questions
coding 443–4
designing for questionnaires 431–43
in-depth interviews 379, 389–93
order and flow in questionnaires 444, 445
semi-structured interviews 379, 389–93
sensitive 391
translating questions into other languages 442–3
wording 440–1
quota sampling 261, 282, 284–7, **679**
quotations from literature 616

R

radical change 141, **679**
radical humanist paradigm 141, 143, **679**
radical structuralist paradigm 141, 143, **679**
radio programmes, referencing Harvard style 653
random digit dialling 273, 274
random number tables 273
random sampling 261, **679**
numbers 661
see also simple random sampling; stratified random sampling; systematic random sampling
ranges 504, 506, **679**
rank correlation coefficients 509, 521–2
ranked data 475, 476, 489, 504, 509, 517, **679**
ranking questions 434–6, **679**
rating questions 436–9, 445
ratio data 475–6, **679**
rational thinking technique 30–4, **679**
raw data 307, **679**
reactivity 243, **679**
reading, critical 74–5
realism 136–7, 140, **679**
realist ethnography 182, **679**
reasoning
backwards 611
logical 45, **674**
recent events 193
re-coding 482, **679**
recommendations 609
recorded materials 349
recording
interviews 394–8, 394–8, 402
literature 108–11
participant observation data 348
reductionism 146, **679**
refereed academic journals 84, 86, **679**
reference books, referencing Harvard style 647
references 46, 58, 59, 110, 608–9, 656, **679**
referencing styles 110–11, 608–9, 644–58
reflective diaries 13–15, 555–6, **679**
see also research notebooks
reflective questions 393
reflexivity 346, **679**
regression analysis 509, 523, 526–7, **679**
regression coefficient 509, 523, 525, **680**
regression equation 509, 524, **680**
regular surveys 307, 310–13
regulatory perspective 141, **680**
relationships 565
causal 193, 523
recognising 560, 565
significant, testing for 512–20
strength of 509, 521–3
relevance 44
gap 8–10
exploring using literature 34–6
of literature 107–8
trees 36, 96–7, **680**
reliability 192–3, **680**
interviews 381, 382
participant observation issues 352–5
questionnaires 430–1
secondary data 323–9
structured observation issues 361–2
repeated measures **680**; *see also* within-subjects design
reports
ethics and 245–7
of findings *see* project reports
literature sources 85, 90
project reports *see* project reports
purpose and data presentation 320
qualitative data results 563
referencing Harvard style 647–8
see also consultancy reports; management reports
representation 181

representative samples 267, **680**
representative sampling *see* probability sampling
representativeness of samples 280–1, 518
research **680**
business and management research 6–12
nature of 4–6
process 12–13, 14
research approaches 14, 17, 143–9, **680**
multiple methods research design 164
qualitative research design 163
quantitative research design 162
research design 14, 17, 158–9, **680**
choice and coherence 159–61
concurrent embedded 168
concurrent triangulation 167
double-phase 167
ethics 191, 237–41
mixed methods 166–70
multi-phase 167
multiple methods 164–70
nature of 170–2
qualitative methods 161, 163–4
quality 191–5
quantitative methods 161–3
requirements and questionnaires 423–5
researchers' roles 195–6
sequential explanatory 167
sequential exploratory 167
single-phase 167
strategies *see* research strategies
time frames 190–1
research ethics *see* ethics
research ethics committees 229–30, **680**
research gaps 93
research ideas 30, **680**
generating 30–7
refining 37–40
turning into research projects 40–50
research interviews *see* interviews
research notebooks 13–15, 555, **680**
see also reflective diaries
research objectives 56–7, **680**
deductive approach impact on 580
in research proposals 54
writing 42, 43
importance of theory in 44–50
research 'onion' 128–9, 160
research paradigms 140–3
research philosophies 14, 17, 153–5, **680**
diagnosing 151
multiple methods research design 164
qualitative research design 163
quantitative research design 162
understanding 126–43
research population 195, **681**
research proposals 50, **680**
need for 50–2
structure 52–9
worked example 55–8
research questions 129, **681**
deductive approach impact on 580
literature review chapters informing 604
in research proposals 54
writing 40–3
importance of theory in 44–50
research strategies **680**
action research 173, 183–5
archival research 173, 178–9
case studies 173, 179–81
choice 173–90
ethnography 173, 181–2
experiments 173, 174–6
grounded theory 173, 185–7
interview links to 376–7
multiple methods research design 168–70
narrative inquiries 173, 187–90
qualitative research design 163–4
quantitative research design 163
surveys 173, 176–8
research topics 14, 17, 26–8
good, attributes of 28–30
research ideas, generating and refining 30–50
research proposals, writing 50–9
turning ideas into research projects 40–50
researcher bias 192
researcher error 192
researchers
appearance at interviews 388
behaviour 393
credibility 222, 225–6
insiders 346–7
integrity 231
interests 31
objectivity 231, 241
participant observation roles 343–8
personal preferences 34
personal safety 244, 244
preferred style 148–9
roles 195–6
safety 232, 235
status 346–7
strengths 31
values 137–40
resource stocks 528
resources 57–8, 59, 223
interviewing issues 398–400
'resources' researchers 134
respect
lacking 233
for others 231
respondents 268, 374, **680**
response bias 381, 382, **680**
response rates 267–70, **680**
restarting writing sessions 600
re-storying narratives 575–7
review articles 32, **680**
review questions 765, **680**
reviews of literature *see* literature
rhetoric, critique of 77
risk evaluation 230–1
rock 'n' roll 133
Russian doll principle 43

S

S&P 500: 528
safety of researchers 232, 235
samples 258–60, **681**
initial 568
representativeness 280–1, 518
size
minimum, calculation 659–70
non-probability sampling 283
probability sampling 265–70
statistical significance determined by 513
sampling 14, 17, 258–60
deductive approach impact on 580
fractions 275–6, **681**
frames 262–5, **681**
need for 260–1
non-probability *see* non-probability sampling
overview of techniques 261–2
probability *see* probability sampling
theoretical *see* theoretical sampling
saturation
data 283, **669**
theoretical 186, 569, **683**
scale items 439, **681**
scale questions *see* rating questions
scales 436, 439, **681**
scanned documents 553
scanning literature 101–2
scatter graphs/plots 489, 500, 502, **681**
scheduling in-depth and semi-structured interviews 399
scientific evidence 22–3
see also literature: reviews
scientific research 145, **681**

scoping studies 112, **681**
search engines 103–4, 215, 317, **681**
search strings 100, **681**
search terms 91–2, 96, 99, **681**
search tools 104, 103–5
secondary data 14, 18, 304–7, **681**
  advantages 317–19
  disadvantages 319–21
  ethics 246
  evaluating sources of 321–31
  likely availability 315–16
  locating 314–17
  pitfalls 319
  types of and uses in research 307–14
secondary literature 82–9, **681**
secondary observations 348, **681**
selective coding 186, 568, 572, **681**
self-administered questionnaires 419–20, 450, **681**
self-coded questions 440, **681**
self-employment 464–6
self-memos 554–5, **681**
self-selection sampling 261, 282, 284, 289–90, **681**
self-service technology 63–6
semantic differential rating questions 438, **681**
semi-structured interviews *see* interviews
sensitive personal data 248–9, **681**
sensitive questions 391
sensitivity 223, **681**
sentences 615
sequential explanatory research design 167, **681**
sequential exploratory research design 167, **681**
sequential mixed methods research 167, **681**
sequential mixing methodological choices 165
sequential multi-phase design 167, **681**
serial correlation 529, **681**
service quality 356–7
shadowing 38, **681**
Shapiro–Wilk tests 509, 510–11, **682**
significance testing 508–29, **682**
silence during questioning 393
simple methodological choices 165
simple random sampling 261, 270–2, 273–4, **682**
simplicity 614–15
single phase methodological choices 165
single-phase research design 167, **682**
skew 495, 528
snap shot secondary data 307
snowball sampling 261, 282, 284, 289, 290, 413, **682**
social constructionism 132, 546, **682**
social networking 324, 376, 406
social norms 227, **682**
social practice 578
social theory 141–3
socially desirable responses 420–2, **682**
source questionnaires 443, **682**
Spearman's rank correlation coefficient (Spearman's rho) 509, 521, **682**
specialised search engines 104
specific questions 392
specific values 488, 498
specifications 50–1
specificity 44
spelling 616
split infinitives 616, **682**
stacked bar charts 489, 501, 502, **682**
staff research interests 31–2
standard deviation 504, 506–7, **682**
standardised interviews 375
statistical inference 266, **682**
statistical significance 508, 513, **682**
  see also significance testing
statistics
  descriptive 502–8
  government 317, 319–20
  significance testing 508–29
status, researchers 346–7
storylines 601, 610–11, **682**
stratified random sampling 261, 270–2, 276–8, **682**
strengths of researchers 31
structured interviews *see* interviews
structured methodology 145, **682**
structured observation 340–1, 355–62, **682**
subject bias **682**
subject directories 104, 105, **682**
subjectivism 131–2, 141, 142, 155, **682**
substantive theories 50
sufficiency
  of access 212–13, **682**
  of literature 108
suitability
  recorded materials 349
  researchers for participant observation 347
  secondary data 321–9
summarising
  effective reading 74
  project report chapters 612
supermarkets 297–9, 537–9
supplementary information 111
supply chains 535–40
survey-based secondary data 307, 310–13, **682**
surveys 173, 176–8, **682**
swarms 412
symbolic interactionism 137, 342–3, **682**
symmetric distribution 495, **682**
symmetry of potential outcomes 29, **682**
synchronicity 405–6, **682**
syntax 442
synthesis 619, **683**
systematic random sampling 261, 270–2, 275–6, **683**
systematic reviews 112–13, 119–23, **683**
systematic sampling *see* systematic random sampling

T

t-tests 509, 517–20, 525, 527, **683**
tables 487, 488, 497, **683**
  contingency tables 489, 498
  data requirements tables 425–8
  frequency distribution 488, 489
  in project reports 612
  random sampling numbers 661
tactics 161
tailored design method 417, **683**
target questionnaires 443, **683**
teleological view 227–8, **683**
telephone interviews 375, 404–5
telephone questionnaires 420, 421, 445, 458, **683**
television programmes, referencing Harvard style 653
Template Analysis 572–4, **683**
temporal sequences 575
tenses 616–17, **683**
terminology in interviews 390
tertiary literature sources 82–3, 87–8, 98–100, 316, **683**
test re-test estimates of reliability 430
testable propositions 560–2, 579
testing 193
text
  critical discourse analysis 578
  data 307, 308–9
  referencing in 644–55, 656–7
theoretical replication 180–1, **683**
theoretical sampling 186, 261, 282, 284, 289, 569, **683**
theoretical saturation 186, 569, **683**
theory 44, **683**
  definition 45
  development 47–9
  importance 46–7
  research approaches 144
  in terms of relationships between variables 424
  types of theoretical contribution 49–50

theory dependent decisions **683**
thesauruses 92–3
theses 32, 85, 90, **683**
time
errors 362, **683**
frames, research design 190–1
gaining access 218–19, 223
interviews and 379–80, 398–9
participant observer role and 347
series 509, 527–9, **683**
timescale and research proposal 55–9, 57
for writing 596–7
timing of writing 597
titles 53, 57, 610
topics for research *see* research topics
total response rates **268**
totals, comparisons of 501
trade journals 84, 86, **683**
tradition, critique of 77
traditional access 210–14, 215–16, **683**
transcript summaries 554, **683**
transcription 550–2, **683**
transferability 194
translation of questionnaires 442–3
transparency 44
trends
comparing 489, 499–501
examining 509, 525–9
showing 489, 494
triangulation 179, **683**
reason for using mixed methods design 169
trust
in interviews 391
repair 335–7
tweets 215
Type I errors 513–14, **683**
Type II errors 513–14, **683**
typical case sampling 261, 282, 284, 289, **684**

U

understanding, testing 394
unforeseen discoveries 318
uniform resource locators (URL) 110, **684**
uninformed responses 420, **684**
unitising data 558, **684**
units of data 558, 559, **684**
university fees 315
unmeasured variables 323
unobtrusiveness 318
unreachable respondents 268, **684**
unstructured interviews *see* interviews
unsuitability 322
upper quartile 506, **684**
URL (uniform resource locators) 110, **684**

V

validity 193, **684**
external *see* external validity
internal *see* internal validity
interviews 384
observation issues 352–5, 361–2
participant observation issues 352–4
questionnaires 428–31, 451–2
secondary data 323–9
structured observation issues 361–2
value of literature 107–8
values 137–40, 501–2
Vancouver system 111, 608, 656–7
variables 46, **684**
comparing 498–502
confounding 174–5
control 174–5
dependent *see* dependent variables
independent *see* independent variables
individual, exploring and presenting 488–98
interdependence between 489, 498
intervening 561
mediating (MV) 174, 424, **674**
moderating 174, 424, **675**
predicting value from one or more other variables 524–5
questionnaires and data collection 424–5
relationships between 424, 509
types of 174, 425
variance 504, 519–20, **684**
variance inflation factor (VIF) 525–9, **684**
variation, coefficient of 504, 507, **684**
video cameras 350
video-conferencing 406
video diaries 349–50
video downloads, referencing Harvard style 654
videography 341
VIF (variance inflation factor) 525–9, **684**
virtual access **215**
visual aids 623–4, **684**
Voiceover Internet Protocol (VoIP) 405, 406
voluntary participation 231, 233
volunteer sampling 261, 284, 289–90

W

web based questionnaires *see* Internet: questionnaires
web conferencing 406
web forums, referencing Harvard style 652
web logs *see* blogs
web pages 98, 101, 233
webcams 214, 215
websites, referencing Harvard style 651
weighting 486–7, **684**
Wikipedia 93–5
Wikis 407
referencing Harvard style 651
wines 288
withdrawal from participation 231, 233
withdrawal from studies (mortality) 193
within-subjects design 176, **684**
word processing 597–9
words
key 566
meanings 546
working up and narrowing down 38–40
writing 594–6
completing sessions 599–600
getting started 596–600
goals 597
literature reviews 596
location 597
outline structures 599
planning 599
project reports *see* project reports
reading by friends 600
research proposals 50–9
restarting sessions 600
styles 614–19
time for 596–7
timing of 597
word processing 597–9